# The Java™ Developer's C

## Second Edition

# The Java™ Developer's Guide to Eclipse

## Second Edition

**Jim D'Anjou**

**Scott Fairbrother**

**Dan Kehn**

**John Kellerman**

**Pat McCarthy**

♦♦ Addison-Wesley

*Boston*

The publisher offers discounts on this book when ordered in quantity for bulk purchases and special sales. For more information, please contact:

U.S. Corporate and Government Sales
(800) 382-3419
corpsales@pearsontechgroup.com

For sales outside of the U.S., please contact:

International Sales
international@pearsoned.com

Visit Addison-Wesley on the Web: www.awprofessional.com

*Library of Congress Cataloging-in-Publication Data*
The Java developer's guide to Eclipse / Jim D'Anjou ... [et al.]. — 2nd ed.
    p.  cm.
  Rev. ed. of: The Java developer's guide to Eclipse / Sherry Shavor ... et al. 2003.
  Includes bibliographical references and index.
    ISBN 0-321-30502-7 (alk. paper)
    1. Computer software—Development.   2. Java (Computer program language)   I. D'Anjou, Jim, 1949–  II. Title.

QA76.76.D47J39 2004
005.1—dc22
    2004017885

ISBN 0-321-30502-7
Text printed on recycled paper
4 5 6 7 8 9 10—CRS—08070605
Fourth printing, April 2005

# Contents

# Foreword

Eclipse is a game-changing industry phenomenon. Launched in open source in the fall of 2001, Eclipse has come a long way from its roots as an internal project at IBM's OTI subsidiary—designed originally as a way for IBM to integrate its desktop tools onto a common software base. In 2004 the first ever EclipseCON conference in Anaheim, California, was an overwhelming success, and the Eclipse Foundation was launched that year as the independent entity overseeing the future evolution of the technology in open source. Eclipse truly has taken flight on its own wings.

Why has Eclipse had such an impact on the tools industry? The answer is because it's great technology, it's open source, it has phenomenal support from a worldwide community of developers, and a whole lot of important industry players are using it to build great products.

The Eclipse vision is different—it's a "platform-centric" rather than "tool-centric" way of thinking. The bare-bones Eclipse Platform is essentially a "Universal IDE"—an IDE for anything and nothing in particular, all at the same time. When you want to build a new tool for Eclipse, you think about how you "teach" the Eclipse Platform about your problem, rather than about how you can bolt a monolithic "tool" on top of it. And the way you teach Eclipse about your problem is by writing tool plug-ins that hook into well-defined plug-in points. The result is that rather than see a new "tool" added to Eclipse, users instead see new capabilities that the Eclipse Platform is now able to perform. Different people, different teams, different organizations can build different tools at different times, yet when they are assembled into the Eclipse Platform on the user's desktop they behave—if it's done right—as if they were designed to provide a single integrated experience.

The best tools integrate so seamlessly you can't tell where one tool starts and another ends. Of course, it's possible to get this wrong and build tools that *don't* fit well with Eclipse and don't work well with other Eclipse-based tools! To get this right you need to understand how your tool should extend Eclipse to solve your particular problem—how your tool should "plug in" to the integration points defined by Eclipse. You also need to decide when to invent something new and when you should just extend or enhance existing function. That's why this book is such an indispensable reference, not only for tool builders and rich client application developers but also for anyone customizing or extending the Eclipse environment.

Last time I checked, the first edition of this book had an *average* rating of five stars at Amazon.com—not at all surprising given the book's heritage. Fully updated and revised for Eclipse 3.0, this book was written by members of the IBM Eclipse Jumpstart team from their experience teaching courses, and it is the definitive Eclipse reference. Not only do they set out to show you how to *use* Eclipse proficiently, they then transition nicely into a comprehensive, authoritative guide to extending the environment yourself and building your own Eclipse-based tools. The examples and exercises included have been proven in real-life situations and will get you up and running quickly.

The idea of Eclipse has captured the imagination of developers from all corners of the globe—it has caught on beyond anyone's wildest dreams. But the real value of Eclipse comes not from Eclipse itself, but from what people do with it and how they extend it. It's limited only by your imagination!

*—Dave Thomson*
*Eclipse Project Program Director, IBM*

# Preface

## Origin of the Book

Starting in late 1999, the authors formed the core of a group within IBM called the Eclipse Jumpstart team. The team was created to share knowledge of what would become Eclipse technology throughout IBM and with its business partners—that is, to "jumpstart" the IBM and IBM partner development community on Eclipse. Part of this effort included the creation of a set of presentations, lecture materials, and accompanying exercises. Over the ensuing months, as the Eclipse technology matured, the presentations and exercises matured as well. As the Eclipse community grew to include various companies and academic institutions, requests for this information also grew. After every class we taught, we revised and improved the materials. When our schedules could not keep pace with the demand, we adapted the materials and made them available for use in a self-study mode. This was the genesis of this book. You can think of each chapter in the book as a classroom lesson. The exercises and examples reinforce the concepts of the chapters and provide you with practice using or extending aspects of Eclipse.

## The Second Edition

Late 2003 found most of the original authors still actively engaged in Eclipse. We have been unexpectedly and very pleasantly surprised with the public acceptance of the first edition. The public and private commentary on the first edition was very positive. In July 2004 the first edition received an Editors' Choice Award from the *Java Developers Journal*. The authors express their sincerest thanks and appreciation to our many readers. With the first edition barely six months old, we realized that Eclipse 3.0 would be very special and has the potential to take Eclipse to new heights. It will reach a much larger developer community and potentially millions of users now that Eclipse is not limited to integrated development environments (IDEs) but can host any kind of client application. The authors remain passionate about this technology and the opportunities it offers for innovative tools and applications. We decided to create a second edition earlier than planned. Our objectives for the second edition were to upgrade the book to Eclipse 3.0, improve it based on reader feedback, and add a select number of new topics. This edition is nearing the limit in sheer weight and volume that anyone should have to carry. We hope it continues to serve you and the Eclipse community well.

### What's New in the Second Edition

- All chapters, exercises, and examples from the first edition are updated for Eclipse 3.0.
- The Guide to Reading This Book section has been added. This topic provides a plan to help readers who are new to Eclipse get the most from this comprehensive book.
- There are seven new chapters and three new exercises. There is a special focus on the new rich client support. The book was restructured to acknowledge this significant new feature. A chapter is devoted to the rich client topic along with two detailed exercises. One of the exercises demonstrates the new Eclipse runtime support for dynamic plug-ins.
- For readers who use Eclipse as their Java development environment, a new exercise is included in which you develop a simple Web commerce site using a Java servlet application running on an Apache Tomcat server.
- There is an entirely new introduction to extending Eclipse. A comprehensive chapter devoted to JFace viewers was added and the chapter on views has been expanded. The chapter on concurrency will show you how to create a more responsive user interface by delegating work for processing behind the scenes. You can better manage a rich or complex user interface after reading the chapter on Eclipse capabilities. A chapter devoted to plug-in performance tuning will help you avoid common development pitfalls. A new chapter on internationalization and accessibility will help you develop products that reach wider markets. The chapter on Java Swing interoperability covers Eclipse's improved support for Swing.
- The book's organization has been restructured, reflecting both the size of the book and the breadth of Eclipse functionality. The book is divided into six parts. Part I is devoted to Eclipse users, and Parts II

through V are for developers extending Eclipse. Part VI includes detailed exercises for both using and extending Eclipse.
- The CD-ROM has been restructured for easier access and loading. There are many new examples. All of the example documentation has been packaged into its own help book that can be installed alongside the other books in the Eclipse online help.

Final screenshots in this book were created just as Eclipse 3.0 was about to ship. There may be minor discrepancies between the images in this book and the final version of Eclipse.

## Goals

We have several goals in bringing this book to you.

- Provide information for those new to Eclipse.

  A new user can leverage this book as a tutorial and a later as a reference. We do not assume prior Eclipse knowledge.

- Explore the capabilities of Eclipse.

  The book covers both using Eclipse as your development environment and extending Eclipse. The chapters in Part I start with Eclipse as a general development environment and then progress to developing and debugging Java, as well as more advanced usage topics, for example, using Eclipse in a team environment. The chapters on extending Eclipse in Parts II through V cover the most frequently used classes in the Eclipse framework. References to design patterns, where applicable, illustrate the architectural relationships among the classes. The intent is not to replace the Javadoc that is included with Eclipse but to complement the documentation by focusing on how to bring a set of classes together to complete a task.

- Provide exercises and working examples that are simple and focused on the chapter topic.

  The exercises and examples augment the chapter topics and illustrate key points. The chapter text concentrates on the concepts and outlines the basic steps to accomplish a task while providing small sections of code or screen captures to illustrate the point. The exercises provide detailed coding instructions and screen captures to apply the concepts described in the chapter. The CD-ROM that comes with this book contains solutions to the step-by-step exercises as well as additional working examples to supplement chapters in the book.

- Provide comprehensive coverage of Eclipse that is usable at any level of experience.

  The fundamentals of Eclipse are covered, providing a foundation. From there you are free to roam among the many additional topics based on your needs and interests.

- Promote the Eclipse community.

  This book provides you with the basic knowledge of Eclipse so that you can become an active participant and help grow the Eclipse open source community.

Although the term "Eclipse" conveys the image of a solar event causing darkness, the intent of this book is to shed light, add clarity, and focus on a powerful new platform. Whether you are new to Eclipse or one of the early adopters, we welcome you to the Eclipse community.

## Intended Audience and Prerequisites

The audience for this book includes Java programmers who plan to use Eclipse as their development environment, those who will use Eclipse-based offerings, advanced users who want to customize Eclipse further, tool providers who seek to develop tools that will integrate with Eclipse, and application developers who want to use Eclipse as the framework for their client applications. Prior experience with Eclipse is not necessary; however, this book assumes that you are familiar with the Java programming language. While it describes how to use the Java Development Tools provided by Eclipse, it does not teach the syntax and semantics of the Java programming language.

## How the Book Is Organized

This comprehensive book can help you learn to use and extend Eclipse. After you have mastered the basics, you will likely use this book as a reference. To help you learn Eclipse, you should start with the Guide to Reading This Book section. It breaks down this formidable text into manageable chunks that you can read in a sequence better suited for learning.

The book is divided into six parts. Part I, Using Eclipse, applies to those using Eclipse as their development environment. The book begins by covering the basic navigation and terminology of Eclipse. You will learn about the Java development environment, including secrets to becoming a power user. Using Eclipse in a team programming environment is explained. You will learn how to use the flexibility of Eclipse to maximize your productivity and fit your own personal style. Students who are studying the Java programming language may find using Eclipse, instead of simply a command line environment, a much more productive and exciting way to learn the richness and power of the language. Instructors may discover how using Eclipse in the classroom will accelerate the student's mastery of the language and be a productive tool to use in research.

Part II, Fundamentals of Extending Eclipse, focuses on the important elements of extending Eclipse independent of whether you are extending Eclipse to develop tools or creating a client application. It covers the architecture of Eclipse, how to develop plug-ins, the creation of client applications using the rich client support, how to make your plug-ins extensible to others, and packaging and deployment.

Part III, Extending the Eclipse Workbench, covers the most commonly required topics to extend Eclipse functionality. Using the Eclipse architecture as a base, Part III covers the frameworks needed to extend the Eclipse user interface. It covers basic graphical user interface (GUI) development using the Standard Widget Toolkit (SWT), dialogs and wizards, menus, viewers, views, editors, perspectives, and online documentation.

Part IV, Extending the Eclipse IDE, focuses on those services that apply when extending Eclipse as an IDE. This is in contrast to Part II, which covers services that apply to both IDE-based and non-IDE-based applications. Part IV includes topics like accessing the workspace and extending the Java Development Tools.

Part V, Extensibility Special Topics, rounds out your knowledge of Eclipse by covering a variety of topics that you may not need right away or that are specialized to specific situations. Chapters covering serviceability, Swing interoperability, concurrency, capabilities, performance tuning, OLE and ActiveX support (Windows), and internationalization are among the topics in Part V.

Learning in a programming environment without actually writing code is difficult. Part VI, Exercises, contains a series of detailed exercises to reinforce the concepts presented in the book. Part VI depends on the files included on the CD-ROM. The CD-ROM contains solutions to all of the exercises and contains many code samples augmenting the material in the chapters. The exercises do not depend on one another, so you can perform them in any order.

Many chapters contain a reference to the book *Official Eclipse 3.0 FAQs* by John Arthorne and Chris Laffra (Boston, MA: Addison-Wesley, 2004). We recommend it as a complementary addition to this book. Specific frequently asked questions (FAQs) that augment the chapter content are cited in the chapter references and on the CD-ROM. See also http://eclipsefaq.org.

## Coding Conventions

XML and Java code in this book is set in Lucida Sans Typewriter typeface. To highlight a section of the code under discussion, the code will be **bold**. Specific filenames are also set in Lucida Sans Typewriter.

References in the book that describe the user interface, such as a series of menu selections, are set in **Gills Sans bold**. For example, **File > New > Project** indicates that the first menu choice selected is **File** followed by the menu choice **New** and then **Project**. Often menu choices have a corresponding toolbar icon. Icons used in Eclipse, such as those found on the toolbar or those used with editors and views, are inline next to the appropriate text.

Double-click on a Java source file 🗾, class ⓒ, or interface ⓘ, or select one of these in a view and press **F3** or **Enter**.

## CD-ROM

The CD-ROM included with this book contains the following

- Eclipse SDK version 3.0
- Eclipse 3.0 example plug-ins
- Chapter examples
- Exercise template files and solutions
- The documentation for the examples and exercises (contained in an Eclipse Help plug-in; see Figure P.1)
- A readme.html file with installation instructions

To complete the exercises, you must install Eclipse SDK version 3.0. The Eclipse SDK requires that you install a Java Runtime Environment (JRE) version 1.4 or higher. You can download a JRE (or JDK) from http://www.ibm.com/developerworks/java/jdk or http://java.sun.com. Unless stated otherwise, the examples and exercises on the CD-ROM were tested on Windows XP. Because the examples are written in the Java programming language, you can use them on other operating systems as well, as long as the code or instructions do not depend on Windows-specific function. See the file readme.html on the CD-ROM for more information.

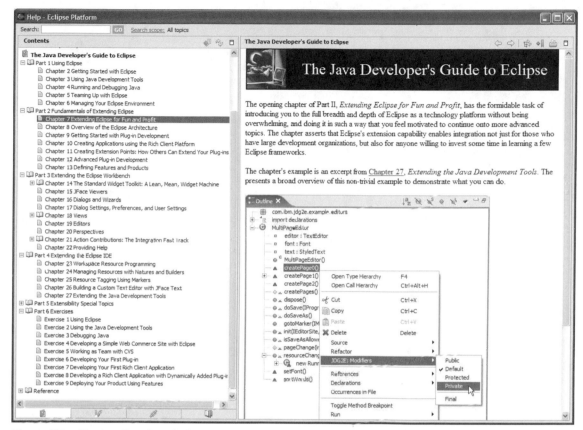

**Figure P.1** The Java Developer's Guide to Eclipse Online Infocenter Integrated with the Eclipse Help System

## Where to Find Further Information

Additional information, including any errata, will be made available at http://www.awprofessional.com/title/0321305027. You can report problems or errors found in the book or the CD-ROM to the authors at JDG2E@yahoogroups.com. Suggestions for improvement or other feedback are also very welcome.

# Guide to Reading This Book

This book is intended for everyone who is interested in Eclipse. You could read this book sequentially from cover to cover, but that's a formidable undertaking for many. This guide offers recommended reading and exercise sequences, broken down into manageable chunks that incrementally improve your knowledge and skills. There are two tracks: **Using Eclipse** and **Extending Eclipse**. If you are new to Eclipse, you probably want to start in the Using Eclipse track. If you are an experienced Eclipse user, you might skip the first couple chapters of this track and selectively read other chapters to enhance your knowledge. After your basic skills are in place, you're ready to start learning about making your own enhancements to Eclipse. Even if you originally hadn't considered that possibility, we suspect that, after a few days of using Eclipse and seeing what it's capable of, the thought of extending it yourself will pique your interest enough to want to explore it some through the Extending Eclipse track. Though obvious by its title, we recommend that all readers start with Chapter 1, Read Me First.

## Track 1: Using Eclipse

This track is all about learning how to use Eclipse, the user interface, and the Java Development Tools included with it. If you have never used Eclipse before, start here.

### Getting Started

Once complete, you will be comfortable with the Eclipse platform and the basics of Java development.

- Chapter 2, Getting Started with Eclipse, and Exercise 1, Using Eclipse
- Chapter 3 and Exercise 2, both titled Using Java Development Tools

### Becoming Proficient

With the fundamentals behind you, learn more about the Java tools, including debugging, and practice with an exercise involving the creation of a Java servlet.

- Chapter 4 and Exercise 3, both titled Running and Debugging Java
- Exercise 4, Developing a Simple Web Commerce Application with Eclipse

### Mastery

These optional chapters help complete your understanding of using Eclipse.

- If you use CVS: Chapter 5, Teaming Up with Eclipse, and Exercise 5, Working as a Team with CVS
- To become a power user: Chapter 6, Managing Your Eclipse Environment

## Track 2: Extending Eclipse

Eclipse makes it a lot easier to write, debug, and share code with your colleagues—but it doesn't have to stop there. You can also customize Eclipse to meet your own needs or even develop client applications based on Eclipse. The entry threshold to introducing enhancements to Eclipse is surprisingly low, often starting with simply a new menu choice or a new view that you implement to make your work more productive. Part II begins by establishing the fundamentals of extending Eclipse that will serve as the launch point for the rest of your studies. Once you've mastered these basics, you can jump to those areas specific to your interests and needs.

### Just Curious

Start here if you want to know more but are not yet committed to extending Eclipse. Only basic programming experience is necessary.

- Chapter 7, Extending Eclipse for Fun and Profit
- Chapter 8, Overview of the Eclipse Architecture

### Getting Started

Learn the basics of extending Eclipse, create your first plug-in, and optionally create your own Eclipse application.

- Chapter 7, Extending Eclipse for Fun and Profit
- Chapter 8, Overview of the Eclipse Architecture

- Chapter 9, Getting Started: Plug-in Development, and Exercise 6, Developing Your First Plug-in
- Chapter 10, Creating Applications Using the Rich Client Platform (which will deepen your architectural understanding of the platform even if you are not planning to use Eclipse this way), and Exercise 7, Developing Your First Rich Client Application

## The Prerequisites

These topics lay the groundwork for the next big chunk of learning.

- Chapter 11, Creating Extension Points: How Others Can Extend Your Plug-ins
- To learn more about contributing to menus and toolbars: Chapter 21, Action Contributions: The Integration Fast Track (some knowledge of views, editors, and perspectives is helpful, so return to Chapter 21 after you have learned about views and editors in Chapters 18 and 19)
- Chapter 14, The Standard Widget Toolkit: A Lean, Mean Widget Machine
- If you are creating plug-ins for the Eclipse IDE: Chapter 23, Workspace Resource Programming

## Contributing to the User Interface

For many developers this is a primary objective. Take your time here. Pick the topics you need first and come back to others. In some cases, especially the longer chapters, consider reading enough of a chapter to feel comfortable and follow up later with a more comprehensive reading. Most importantly, examine and run the examples on the CD-ROM. You will need to understand the basics of JFace Viewers (see Chapter 15) to create a view or an editor.

- Chapter 15, JFace Viewers
- Chapter 16, Dialogs and Wizards
- Chapter 18, Views
- Chapter 19, Editors
  If you have a special interest in text editors, see Chapter 26, Building a Custom Text Editor with JFace Text
- Chapter 20, Perspectives
- Chapter 21, Action Contributions: The Integration Fast Track

## Becoming Proficient

Now you should feel very comfortable extending Eclipse. You have probably written a few plug-ins on your own and are ready to chart your own course. Here are some suggestions.

*Putting together the last few parts of the puzzle*:

- Chapter 12, Advanced Plug-in Development
- Chapter 17, Dialog Settings, Preferences, and User Settings
- Chapter 24, Managing Resources with Natures and Builders
- Chapter 25, Resource Tagging Using Markers
- Exercise 8, Developing a Rich Client Application with Dynamically Added Plug-ins

*Improving your plug-ins' fit and finish*:

- Chapter 22, Providing Help
- Chapter 13, Defining Features and Products, and Exercise 9, Deploying Your Product Using Features
- Chapter 29, Implementing Responsiveness and Concurrency Using Jobs
- Chapter 30, Using Capabilities to Manage Too Much of a Good Thing

*Dealing with problems that invariably occur*:

- Chapter 28, Serviceability
- Chapter 32, Performance Tuning

Selectively evaluate the remaining chapters in Parts IV and V based on your needs and interests. Good luck!

# Acknowledgments

The authors would like to express their gratitude to all of those who have graciously given us their support and encouragement and shared their wisdom.

Most importantly, to our first edition readers who made that edition a success. We hope that you find comparable value in this edition.

To the entire Eclipse development team who gave us Eclipse 3.0, a version with exciting possibilities that thoroughly justified a new edition to this book.

To our reviewers who helped improve the quality of the book. A special thanks to Jeff Mitchell for his extensive review and testing of this edition, to Kevin Haaland, whose timely suggestions helped shape Chapter 10, and to John Arthorne for his technical assistance and collaboration.

To all those who worked so hard to help produce the book: Ann Sellers, Tyrell Albaugh, John Fuller, Julie Nahil, Kim Arney Mulcahy, Chrysta Meadowbrooke, Rebecca Greenberg, Joe Fatton, Jack Lewis, and Ebony Haight.

To the management team at IBM for their interest and support.

To the IBM Rational/WebSphere ISV Enablement team for their help in testing the exercises: Eric Chaland, Terry Chan, Robert Ciskowski, Sandy Minocha, and Lorna Reyes.

Jim thanks his loving wife, Maya, and children, Christopher and Lisa, for their patience and support. Again!

Scott would like to thank his wife, Melanie, and children, Ashley and Kelly, for putting up with a real pain in the neck.

Dan would like to thank his wife, Laura, for her love, patience, and support while working on this book, and his three sons, Nico, Matthew, and

Nathan, for both driving him crazy and keeping him sane during those rare writing breaks.

John would like to thank his wife, Kristin, and his sons, Ben and Peter, for their patience and support.

Pat would like to thank his wife, Chris, for her gift of the time spent working on this book, his children, Brendan and Caitlin, for the smiles and questions such as "Are you done yet?" and his parents, Pat Sr. and Sandy, along with the whole McCarthy clan, who thought the book was a pretty cool thing at the last family reunion.

# About the Authors

**Jim D'Anjou** is a Senior Software Engineer and a certified IT Specialist located at the IBM Silicon Valley Lab in San Jose, California. He has a degree in computer science from the University of California at Berkeley. Jim has over 25 years of industry experience at IBM and elsewhere. He has held a variety of technical and management positions developing products for relational databases, database tools, application repositories, and application development tools. He holds two U.S. patents for work in software process automation. In March 2001 he joined the Eclipse Jumpstart team and serves as an instructor and industry consultant.

**Scott Fairbrother** is an Advisory Software Engineer at IBM in Research Triangle Park, North Carolina. Scott is a software developer with over 20 years of experience. He has developed object-oriented application frameworks for business process management. He has written specifications for IBM middleware on Windows 2000 and has also written about Microsoft Visual Studio .NET. Most recently, Scott joined the Eclipse Jumpstart team in February 2001. Scott is an Eclipse instructor and continues to consult with IBM and ISVs to help create commercial offerings based on Eclipse.

**Dan Kehn** is a Senior Software Engineer at IBM in Research Triangle Park, North Carolina. His interest in object-oriented programming goes back to 1985, long before it enjoyed the acceptance it has today. He has a broad range of software experience, having worked on development tools like VisualAge for Smalltalk, operating system performance and memory analysis, and user interface design. Dan worked as a consultant for object-oriented development projects throughout the United States as well as for four years in Europe. His recent interests include object-oriented analysis/design, application development tools, and Web programming with the WebSphere Application Server.

He is currently concentrating on performance analysis and tuning of IBM Eclipse-based products.

**John Kellerman** joined IBM in 1984 with a computer science degree from Purdue University. He has since completed graduate degrees in computer engineering at North Carolina State and business administration at the University of North Carolina at Chapel Hill. He has spent the majority of his 20 years at IBM in the development and management of application development tool products, including ISPF/PDF, VisualAge Smalltalk, VisualAge Generator, and Eclipse. John was a founding member of the Eclipse Project, which got under way in late 1999. He is currently IBM Product Manager of Eclipse. His responsibilities include working closely on behalf of IBM with eclipse.org, the Eclipse Foundation, and the member companies to help grow the Eclipse community of contributors and commercial offerings.

**Pat McCarthy,** a Senior Software Engineer at IBM, is a specialist in the use and management of development technologies on a variety of runtime platforms. Pat's IBM career has included hands-on development of business application systems in Poughkeepsie, New York, and 12 years of project management for the development of IBM Redbooks and education offerings in San Jose, California. He has spent the last several years in Raleigh, North Carolina, focused on supporting the use of Eclipse technology in IBM application development products. Pat has a B.S. from Indiana University of Pennsylvania and an M.S. from Marist College. He is the coauthor of more than 20 IBM Redbooks.

# CHAPTER 1

## *Read Me First*

In November 2001, IBM and seven other companies launched Eclipse as an open source project. It was a bold move by IBM to donate a $40 million development effort to the international software community, a move that would be tested by the best and brightest in the industry. Community acceptance was not assured. Would there even be an Eclipse community after the first year? Since that launch, Eclipse has far exceeded all the expectations of its founders and those initial prophets of its success. Eclipse has become one of the hottest technologies in all of software. Tens of millions of downloads later, Eclipse has established itself as a software *tour de force*. From its beginnings as an integration platform to serve the domain of software development tools, it has evolved to a platform that can host any desktop-centric application. Eclipse.org sponsors several major projects that run on top of the Eclipse Platform and numerous open source tools and technology subprojects on its open source site (http://www.eclipse.org). It has a very large following in the commercial, open source, and academic software communities. Hundreds of software components and products are built on Eclipse. Universities use Eclipse to teach Java and to provide a platform base for their research. Eclipse has even reached high schools. To appreciate its impact, go to the Eclipse Community page at eclipse.org (see References at the end of this chapter). The excitement and interest over Eclipse continues to build. From the original eight companies the Eclipse organization has grown immensely and is now organized as a nonprofit corporation known as the Eclipse Foundation.

1

Whether you are new to Eclipse or just want to know more about it, this book will help you. If you are not yet excited about the capabilities and opportunities that Eclipse provides, we believe you will be after reading this book and using the Eclipse Platform. This book is intended for anyone who wants to use Eclipse as their Java integrated development environment (IDE) and for those who want to add function to Eclipse using its pluggable architecture. In either case, no prior knowledge of Eclipse is required; this book will be your guide.

So why all the excitement about Eclipse? For starters, it is free and it is freely redistributable; after all, it's an open source project. It provides an excellent Java development environment that offers a high degree of productivity and flexibility. But it's more than that, much more. Eclipse is an open source integration platform for development tools and general-purpose applications. When Eclipse was developed, its top priority was to provide a platform that supported the integration of development tools. Providing a platform that addressed tool integration in a first-class way was so important that, arguably, one might suggest that integration formed the second and third priorities as well. It originated as a platform to host development tools and is evolving to a platform than can host any kind of client application on the operating systems where it runs. Why is all this important? What problems was Eclipse designed to solve? Let's examine those questions next.

## Eclipse as a Host for Application Development Tools

The 1990s saw phenomenal growth in Internet use, both private and commercial. This had a profound effect on the kinds of applications companies developed and the size and skills of the teams that developed them. Applications evolved from standalone, batch, or large client applications consisting of relatively few programming artifacts or files and, more importantly, relatively few types of artifacts. They evolved, and are continuing to evolve, into the Internet applications we see today that are comprised of hundreds of files of many different types: Java, Perl, HTML, rich media, digital audio and video, servlets, Web services, and Enterprise JavaBeans (EJBs).

With each different type of programming artifact, there came a need for a new editor or tool to create and maintain it. For example, tools arose to edit and create Web pages as HTML files. To process the logic for the Web pages, the developer wrote Java source code with Java editors. Unfortunately, as different companies brought these diverse tools to market, programmers quickly learned that the tools did not work well together. To complicate matters, programmers needed to manage the assortment of deliverables in multiple repositories. Yet each tool and repository worked as an island of its own. Often the programmer had to resort to manual methods of moving files from one tool to another, performing endless export/import cycles—a very unproductive way to work.

Another challenge that continues to face developers is overcoming the learning curve of a new tool. There is often a lack of consistency in the way tool user interfaces present similar functions. For example, defining user preferences in one tool can vary drastically from how you define preferences in another tool. Software navigations patterns differ. (Is Search under the File menu, the Edit menu, or the Tools menu this time?) A consistent user interface would help developers become proficient more quickly.

In addition to the explosive Internet growth that preceded the Eclipse announcement, another sweeping change occurred. The open source movement took off and gained credibility and acceptance in not just the academic world but also the commercial world. The rising popularity of the Linux operating system, the Mozilla browser, the Emacs editor, the Perl scripting language, and the Apache Web server are a few examples of the activity in the open source community. Freely available and redistributable source code contributed to and run by a community of developers changed the software development process. Companies became willing to use and to contribute to open source software. They were attracted to the ability to change code, customize it, and avoid being locked into a proprietary environment.

These mini-revolutions in software led to very clear requirements for programmers. Programmers needed a robust set of application development tools that worked together in an integrated and productive environment. This environment needed to be open and extensible, as most development shops purchased tools from more than one vendor and often had their own homegrown tools. The real goal was an environment that made it easy to integrate tools.

Eclipse fulfills this requirement through an architecture designed from the ground up to host a variety of tools on a single platform. The architects of Eclipse had considerable experience with developing IDEs. They understood the issues previously described. They set out to address the common requirements that every IDE must deal with by providing reusable frameworks that could be utilized by any tool. They built a framework for a consistent user interface and another for organizing and accessing programming artifacts from the file system. They built frameworks for editors, builders, debuggers, team programming, and much more. Most importantly, they defined an architecture for integrating code as pluggable units of functionality. In this book you can learn about all the most important frameworks. Chapter 8, Overview of the Eclipse Architecture, is a good place to get more detail.

Eclipse can run on a variety of different operating systems and is language and technology neutral. It welcomes tools for building applications in Java, C, C++, HTML, and so on. Design tools like modeling tools, as with any other development tool, can integrate with Eclipse as well.

## Beyond Tools: Eclipse as a Host for Client Applications

Though the initial development of Eclipse was clearly motivated by the issues of tool integration just described, it has evolved to become a platform that can host other kinds of applications serving a wide variety of end users. Early Eclipse developers and contributors recognized that the Eclipse technology base could apply to applications beyond the spectrum of development tools. In addition, the facility with which Eclipse welcomed the integration of new functionality was also useful beyond the originally conceived confines of IDEs. So one of the central themes of Eclipse 3.0 was the extraction of this general-purpose client platform from its IDE origins, becoming what is now referred to as the Rich Client Platform or, simply, RCP. Consider the RCP as an integration platform with the same raw function as the Eclipse Platform, but one with a smaller overall footprint and a more flexible user interface.

With some restructuring and inclusion of a more flexible runtime that can dynamically add and remove functionality, Eclipse can be applied to a wide variety of desktop applications. This opens the door to finally achieving pervasive desktop applications written in Java. Extensible, manageable applications based on Eclipse's pluggable architecture can be targeted to serve hundreds of thousands of desktop users. The footprint of Eclipse in a rich client configuration is small enough that it is not unrealistic to think about Eclipse applications on devices smaller than a personal computer. The rich client will expand the horizons of Eclipse well beyond its original charter as an IDE platform. Chapter 10, Creating Applications Using the Rich Client Platform, discusses the considerations for using Eclipse as a general application framework.

## What Is Eclipse?

The Eclipse Platform is primarily an integration platform for tools and other kinds of client applications. It is also a Java development environment and an open source community.

## Integration Platform for Tools and Applications

As an IDE, Eclipse is a platform for tool integration. You can think of it as a home where tools can coexist happily. It makes your modeling, design, programming, and testing tools all come together to get the job done in a more efficient, productive fashion. Eclipse provides a common way for all members of a team to work together to create, manipulate, and manage sets of software artifacts. Team members have access to each other's work products managed in one of the numerous Source Code Management (SCM) systems that integrate with Eclipse through its repository neutral interface. Say goodbye to import and export and the resulting miscommunications. Eclipse-based tools work together in a consistent and cohesive fashion.

Eclipse accomplishes this by providing an architecture and a set of Java frameworks that make writing integrated tools easier. You can use Eclipse to integrate the myriad of existing tools you use to do your job, and as you gain experience, you can use Eclipse to build additional tools. The frameworks also provide a consistent way for tools to contribute to the user interface, package and deploy new functions, and offer online help. You can use the power and extensibility of the Java Development Tools (JDT) that comes with Eclipse to create new Java tools. The extensive Java model and set of application programming interfaces (APIs) to access the Java model that are part of the JDT are a competitive advantage in Eclipse.

Eclipse provides support for groups of developers through integration with SCM repositories. Eclipse has embedded support for Concurrent Versions System (CVS), a popular and widely used open source SCM repository (see http://www.cvshome.org). This support allows you to share code, create versions of your code, develop parallel code streams (called branches), merge changes, compare sets of changes, and so on. A key benefit to working with Eclipse is that you can work with multiple and different repositories. You can have some of your files stored in one repository and other files in another, and both repositories are easily accessible through the Eclipse user interface. See Chapter 5, Teaming Up with Eclipse.

Eclipse includes several facilities that assist the user. The Help system provides an integrated web of online documentation, which can come from multiple suppliers. You can add your own online documentation without any programming required. The Help system can run standalone on the client or as a Web-based Help system. See Chapter 22, Providing Help, for more information. The Eclipse user interface provides both context-sensitive help and hover help. For those processes requiring a more involved sequence of steps and explanation, Eclipse provides a framework called cheat sheets that explains and assists the user with the task at hand.

## Platforms Supported

Eclipse is supported on a wide variety of platforms, reflecting the desire to make Eclipse available on the most widely used operating systems. These include Windows, Linux, Apple Mac OS, and most major UNIX systems.

## Methodologies Supported

Eclipse is methodology independent. If your team works in a traditional waterfall process—where you design the system, write the code, and then test—you can use the platform with your tools and progress through the phases of development. If you prefer to use a methodology similar to extreme programming, where you frequently iterate through your code and testing, you will enjoy the tight integration provided by the Java tools, the debugging environment, and the platform.

## Internationalization

Eclipse is internationalized. There are translations for the user interface strings and online documentation in German, Italian, Spanish, Portuguese, French, Japanese, Korean, Chinese (Simplified), and Chinese (Traditional). On Windows and Linux there is support for users to work in other language structures, including bidirectional ones like Arabic and Hebrew and complex scripts like Thai and Indic (language translations are not provided). Eclipse makes it easier to build tools and applications that are internationalized. For example, the JDT provides functionality to help externalize strings to make them easier to translate. This lowers the barriers of entry to the international market. See Chapter 31, Internationalization and Accessibility, for more information.

## Accessibility

Eclipse is not just open—it is also accessible. Eclipse operates so that people with disabilities can still productively use all the functions provided. On Windows, Eclipse uses Microsoft Active Accessibility (MSAA) APIs to make the user interface accessible to assistive technology. There are keyboard alternatives to the mouse for all menu bar and toolbar actions. Eclipse works with screen-reader software to have audio services describe the contents of the screen. In addition, voice recognition software can be used to enter information and navigate the system. Eclipse preferences allow for further customization by letting you specify font and color settings that suit your needs. See Chapter 31 for more information.

### *Java Development Environment*

Eclipse is a superlative Java development environment. Whether you are new to Java or are an experienced Java programmer, you can use Eclipse to develop Java efficiently. The philosophy behind the JDT in Eclipse is to make you as productive as possible by automating mundane and time-consuming operations and by providing advanced tools to help you generate, edit, and navigate your Java code. It includes a first-class editor, a debugger, and a variety of refactoring operations to help you effortlessly improve your code. See Chapters 3 and 4 to learn how to use the JDT.

The Java environment contains integrated support for Apache Ant, a Java-based build tool that uses XML files to specify what needs building. Eclipse also supports unit testing with integrated JUnit support. Wizards generate test cases, and the test cases are executed and the source code debugged within an IDE.

### *Open Source Community*

Who is this community and how can you be a part of it? Eclipse.org is a collection of technical professionals united by a common interest in using and contributing to a platform that serves software developers and end users. Through collaboration, corporate professionals, researchers, members of academia, and individual developers who build on Eclipse can further the goal of producing interoperable products and offerings. Figure 1.1 shows the home page of the Eclipse Web site.

The Eclipse Consortium has evolved from its origins as a loosely coupled group of companies to a formal structure organized as a nonprofit corporation known as the Eclipse Foundation, with bylaws and a formal membership structure. The Board of Directors is drawn from four classes of membership: strategic developers, strategic consumers, add-in providers, and committers. Each member class has different membership requirements described in the membership agreement. The most strategic classes require significant commitment to Eclipse, including financial and/or personnel resources. The intent is to allow for a diverse set of members from commercial, academic, and standards organizations. An Executive Director provides overall management leadership of the foundation.

Eclipse is much bigger than its formal structure because it encompasses a very large community of technical professionals who are enthusiastic and committed to the success of Eclipse. If you want to get started, the place to go is the download section at http://www.eclipse.org/downloads/index.php. You will

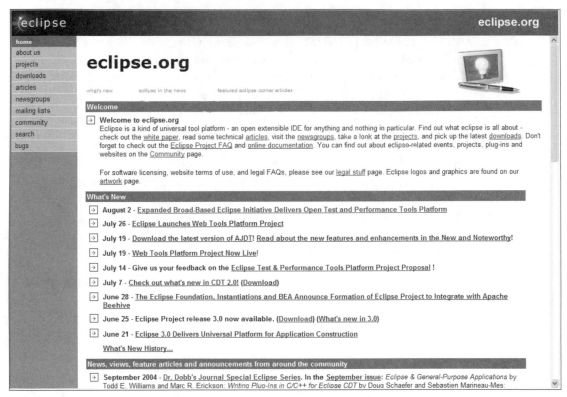

**Figure 1.1**    Eclipse.org Web Site

see different kinds of builds that you can download. If you are simply looking for a development environment to adopt, you should download one of the release builds. A **release build** is a stable, tested build declared as a major release by the development team (e.g., 3.0) and does not contain code that is still a "work in progress." This book is based on the Eclipse 3.0 release.

To learn more about Eclipse beyond what is contained in this book, we encourage you to read the excellent assortment of technical articles on eclipse.org. These articles are authored by the Eclipse developers and by Eclipse users with substantial expertise. They are straightforward, well-written articles with additional code samples.

## The Goals of the Eclipse Foundation

Up to this point, we have discussed the core of Eclipse, the platform, and the JDT. Together they form a software integration framework that supports a rich variety of technologies and applications. The larger goal of the Eclipse Foundation, as stated in the bylaws, is to advance the creation, evolution, promotion, and support of the Eclipse Platform and to cultivate both an open source community and an ecosystem of complementary products, capabilities, and services. On eclipse.org these efforts are managed as projects and subprojects. Eclipse itself is known at the Eclipse Project. The JDT is a subproject of the Eclipse Project. There are additional projects as well. At the time of this book's publication, there were three other projects: the Eclipse Tools Project, the Eclipse Technology Project, and the Eclipse Web Tools Platform Project. Each of these projects has the mission to add significant value to the Eclipse Platform and the software community.

The Eclipse Tools Project encourages best-of-breed tools with the goal that they will become widely used like Eclipse. It contains several subprojects that have funded development efforts, well-defined organizations, and formal development schedules. These are tools you should consider for your own use. Some are standalone tools like the C/C++ IDE, and others are frameworks that serve as infrastructure for other tools. The Graphical Editing Framework (GEF) is available for building graphical editors, and the Eclipse Modeling Framework (EMF) can be used for hosting application models of all sorts. Hyades focuses on automated software quality (ASQ) tooling. GEF, EMF, and Hyades are used extensively in Eclipse-based products from IBM and others. The newer subprojects, Visual Editor (VE) and the UML2, will offer frameworks for visual builders and modeling tools based on the Unified Modeling Language (UML).

The Eclipse Web Tools Platform Project, as the name suggests, intends to focus on Web tools. Its mission as stated on the project Web site "...is to build a generic, extensible and standards-based tool platform upon which software providers can create specialized, differentiated offerings for J2EE and Web-centric application development" (see http://www.eclipse.org/webtools/index.html). The Eclipse Technology Project serves as a host for projects representing research efforts, technology exploration, and education. The goal is to nurture these efforts under the Eclipse umbrella with the hope that many of them will flourish. The projects aren't required to have the same organizational and funding infrastructure, nor any assurance that they will become mature technologies. Most are quite interesting, and it is worthwhile to see what might interest you there.

## *Participating in the Community as a User and a Contributor*

Do you have a question? Use the newsgroups to ask questions. Over time, you will find that you can help answer some of the questions. The newsgroups are quite active. If you don't have time to read them every day, use the search facility provided to search for your answer before posting a question.

Discussion of code that is under development for a future release occurs on a mailing list for those developing the Eclipse code. General use questions should be addressed to the newsgroups. If you are an Eclipse committer, contributing fixes, suggesting improvements, or experiencing problems with pre-release code, you should participate in the appropriate mailing list. The mailing lists are organized based on the structure of the Eclipse code. You can subscribe to a particular mailing list; for instance, if you are interested in the development of the user interface, you can subscribe to the platform-ui-dev mailing list. Another alternative is to read the archive. You can contribute to the design of a user interface enhancement or get an early insight to some upcoming function.

If you find something is not working correctly or want to request a new function, you should go to the bugs section. Using Bugzilla, you can open a defect report or a feature request. First search the bug database to be sure that you do not enter a duplicate report, and as a good community participant be prepared to possibly test the resulting fix.

As your competency with Eclipse improves, you may be interested in contributing to Eclipse more directly. Opening bugs might evolve to contributing fixes or ultimately becoming a committer on some component of Eclipse or one of the other projects it sponsors. There are various stages to becoming a committer, and you have to earn that right from existing committers. As a successful open source technology, Eclipse will evolve and thrive from the contributions (big or small) it receives from the diverse community that supports it.

## The Eclipse License

How is Eclipse licensed? Eclipse is offered under the Common Public License (CPL), a license compliant with the Open Source Initiative (OSI). The CPL permits effective commercial use of the software under license and provides royalty-free source code and worldwide redistribution rights. Yes, you can really redistribute the code free. This licensing provides the ultimate flexibility and control over the use of the open source software. For more information about the license, you can find the license text and frequently asked questions (FAQs) on the Eclipse "legal stuff" page at http://www.eclipse.org/legal/main.html.

Note that some of the components in an Eclipse release are not actually part of Eclipse and are not governed by the CPL; they are governed by other license agreements. Eclipse downloads include this code for your convenience. You can see these other license agreements from the Eclipse About dialog by selecting **Help > About Eclipse Platform**.

## Getting and Installing Eclipse

Eclipse 3.0 is included on the CD-ROM that accompanies this book. If you download Eclipse instead of using the version provided on the CD-ROM, you will want to get the Eclipse 3.0 driver from the downloads page (or one of its mirror sites) because that is the version used as the base for the examples and exercises in this book. Select the appropriate **Windows Eclipse SDK** download for your system. The SDK download includes all of Eclipse and the Eclipse source code. If you're going to be building tools or extensions to Eclipse, you might also want to download the **Example Plug-Ins**.

Installing Eclipse is easy. Simply unzip the driver with pathnames to a folder or directory of your choice. If you've downloaded the examples, do the same for these. Based on the pathnames for the examples, they will be unzipped to the right location. Eclipse requires a Java Runtime Environment (JRE) to be installed on your computer at level 1.4.1 or higher. The eclipse.org download site, http://www.eclipse.org/downloads/index.php, lists a table of available JREs from IBM and Sun. See Chapter 6, Managing Your Eclipse Environment, for additional hints and tips.

## Chapter Summary

Eclipse is several things: a platform for IDEs and general-purpose applications, a Java development environment, and a community. For the Java developer, Eclipse is not just a set of excellent Java tools but also a base in which you can integrate tools from other vendors and open source providers. You can acquire your preferred development tools and favorite source code repository and integrate them with your development environment. It is all about choices: applications, tools, programming language, and operating system. Eclipse does not lock you into a proprietary solution but instead opens you to the possibilities available in a global community. In the References section at the end of this chapter there is a link to a clearinghouse of Eclipse-based applications.

With the projects hosted on eclipse.org, extending Eclipse, building tools, and creating applications is quicker and easier, and it allows for a more consistent user interface and behavior. This in turn gives the end user a more productive and integrated environment.

Whereas extending Eclipse was previously the domain of tool builders, it is now equally valuable to any application developer who needs a framework for hosting client applications. We hope you will come to share our enthusiasm and passion for this technology. Welcome to the community of Eclipse!

The remainder of this book will help you become knowledgeable on how to use and extend Eclipse. Part I teaches you how to use Eclipse, develop and debug Java applications, and use CVS; Parts II through V help you learn to extend Eclipse through the development of plug-ins; and Part VI contains a variety of helpful exercises. This book is substantial in size and content. It is intended to be both a learning text and a reference guide. The authors anticipate that few will read it cover to cover. To help you navigate, examine the Guide to Reading This Book section and the introductions at the beginning of each part of the book. These introductions will help you determine which topics or exercises might be best to examine first and which are worth a follow-up visit.

## References

Arthorne, John, and Chris Laffra. 2004. *Official Eclipse 3.0 FAQs*. Boston, MA: Addison-Wesley. http://eclipsefaq.org. (See Chapter 1.)

Budinsky, Frank et al. 2003. Eclipse Modeling Framework. Boston, MA: Addison-Wesley.

The Eclipse Community page, a comprehensive list of Eclipse activities, resources, and commercial and noncommercial applications of Eclipse. http://www.eclipse.org/community/index.html.

The Eclipse organization description in the "about us" page. http://www.eclipse.org.

The Eclipse Platform Technical Overview. http://www.eclipse.org/whitepapers/eclipse-overview.pdf.

The Eclipse Series books published by Addison-Wesley. http://www.awprofessional.com/series/series.asp?st=44100.

# PART I

## *Using Eclipse*

The objective of the first part of this book is to reach out to the Java developer community and to teach the use of Eclipse and its Java development environment.

- Chapter 2, Getting Started with Eclipse, is where you will learn the basics of using Eclipse. At the end of this chapter, you should have a sound, comprehensive knowledge of general Eclipse use that can be applied to all Eclipse-based offerings.
- Chapter 3, Using Java Development Tools, and Chapter 4, Running and Debugging Java, are dedicated to the Java programmer, covering the ins and outs of coding, running, and debugging Java. You'll become a skilled Eclipse Java programmer, as the chapters share many helpful preference settings and productivity tips. Chapter 3 not only covers the basics of Java programming in Eclipse but also describes advanced Java development features such as programming with multiple JDKs. Chapter 4 focuses on the areas of running and debugging Java code, including remote debugging.
- Chapter 5, Teaming Up with Eclipse, introduces team programming using CVS.
- Chapter 6, Managing Your Eclipse Environment, discusses some advanced installation options and how you can add new tools, upgrade existing features, and apply service corrections to Eclipse.

To help you learn about Eclipse through hands-on experience, Part VI of this book includes practical exercises associated with these chapters. The exercises require the files on the CD-ROM included with this book. As you study Part I, you'll find it helpful to work through these exercises and browse the solutions on the CD-ROM. The CD-ROM also includes documentation for the examples and exercises, both of which are integrated with the Eclipse Help system. See the `readme.html` file for installation instructions.

# CHAPTER 2

## *Getting Started with Eclipse*

Let's jump right into using Eclipse. It's easy! While its original goals were as a technology for programmers, we're seeing Eclipse being used beyond the programming community. Much of the user interface design and concepts provide a productive, simple-to-use work environment for professionals, students, and general computer users not engaged in application development activities. As a technology used by a large and growing number of computer application providers, Eclipse provides a common way to do many activities that are shared by most computer applications—activities such as getting help, using wizards to perform tasks comprising a number of steps, creating and managing your files, searching the files you are working on, marking locations in your files, and customizing settings for tools you are using. This means skills you develop using Eclipse, or an offering based on it, are valuable and transferable to other work, tools, roles, and jobs using these kinds of tools.

In this chapter we'll look at how you use Eclipse to do your work. We'll get you started quickly by showing you how to create projects, populate the projects with files, and work with those files. We'll then go into more detail: an overview of the user interface, the set of **actions** (menu commands or choices) available to you, tasks and bookmarks for marking files, **preferences** (settings), and sources of help. Next, we'll cover working with **resources** (projects, files, and folders) and managing your work, as well as important aspects of some of the views and perspectives in more detail. We'll close with a discussion on customizing your environment.

The content we present in this chapter, and the next four after this one, is a mixture of conceptual and mechanical material. Given these chapters are designed to help you learn how to use Eclipse, they need to explain concepts as well as give you specific instructions for doing things in Eclipse. If you have used Eclipse before, or a product or offering based on Eclipse, you may be familiar with some or even a lot of the content in this chapter. We encourage you to scan it anyway. We'll throw down the gauntlet and claim that even if you're an experienced Eclipse user, you'll find useful hints, tips, and other stuff you didn't know. In Part VI, we have assembled a number of exercises designed to walk you through and reinforce many of the things we present here. We encourage you to take a look at these.

## Your First Steps

In Chapter 1 we told you where to go to get Eclipse (from the CD-ROM or the Web site). We're going to assume you have installed (unzipped) it on your computer. Starting Eclipse is simple: Go to the folder in which you installed it and run `eclipse.exe`. Yes, the executable accepts parameters, but to get started you don't have to worry about these. We'll get to some important parameters later in this chapter. For a more detailed explanation of the command line parameters, see Running Eclipse in the Tasks section of the *Workbench User Guide*. The *Workbench User Guide* is one of five online books that come with Eclipse. To see them, select **Help > Help Contents**.

When you start Eclipse, you'll see a prompt asking which workspace you want to use for this Eclipse session. We'll get to workspaces in Your Workspace, a subsection later in this chapter. For now, take the default that Eclipse presents.

When Eclipse first starts, you will see the welcome page. This is a collection of information designed to be helpful in getting you started or as reference material. Peruse the links if you like. When you are ready to continue, select the **Go to the workbench** link indicated by the graphic in Figure 2.1. If you want to get back to the welcome page, select **Help > Welcome** from the menu bar.

**Figure 2.1**   Go to the workbench Link

## Oops!

If you see the error message illustrated in Figure 2.2 when you start Eclipse, it means Eclipse can't find a JRE to use. If you see this message, refer to Getting and Installing Eclipse in Chapter 1, where we discuss getting and installing a JRE.

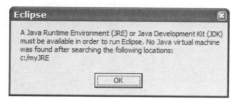

**Figure 2.2** No JRE Dialog

## Creating Your First Project

Let's get you started quickly with a simple hands-on exercise. We are going to create a project, populate it with some files on your computer, and then work with those files. Follow these steps to create a project.

1. From the menu, select **File > New > Project…**.

   You will see the New Project wizard.

2. Select **Project** in the **Simple** category (see Figure 2.3), and then select **Next**.

3. For **Project name**, enter My First Eclipse Project.

4. Select **Finish**.

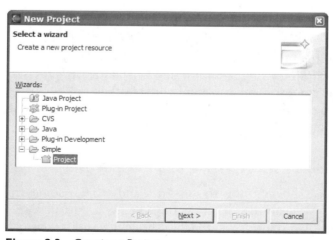

**Figure 2.3** Creating a Project

Great! You have defined your first project. You can see this in the Navigator view (the upper left pane). If you expand the project in the view, you'll see that it contains one file, `.project`. This is a file used to keep track of information about your project. You don't need to understand its contents at this point. Certainly don't mess with it.

Projects contain files and folders. Folders contain files and other folders. To add a folder, right-click a project in the Navigator view, select **New > Folder** from the context menu, and enter the name of the folder.

---

**NOTE**   Eclipse uses icons, or toolbar buttons, to identify objects. When we refer to a command or object, we may include the icon immediately following it to aid in your understanding (e.g., the **Forward** ⇨ and **Back** ⇦ buttons).

---

To see the context menu for an item, right-click on the item. When we say "right-click" we mean use mouse button 2. This assumes, of course, you're not using a mouse configured for left-handed use. If you are, "right-click" means use the mouse button on the left.

To add a file, select a project or folder, select **New > File** from the context menu, and then give the file a name. A text file is created and opened in the text editor and you see the file show up in the Navigator view. Enter some text and save the file by selecting **Save** from the context menu of the editor.

It's also easy to copy existing files to projects. In the Navigator view, select the project or folder you want to put the files in and then select **Import...** from the context menu. Select to import from the **File system** and then use the File System Import wizard to browse your computer files and select those you want to add to your project.

You can also drag files from Windows Explorer to a project or folder in the Navigator view to add these files to the project or folder. This copies the files into the project; they also continue to exist where they originated.

To work on a file, select it in the Navigator view and then select **Open** from the context menu, or simply double-click on the file. Try this for different types of files. Observe that Eclipse uses file type associations defined to your computer.

### The Eclipse Look: Editors, Views, and Perspectives

Let's take a moment now to step back and provide some explanation on the user interface you're working with. When you start Eclipse, you will see a window divided into several panes showing various views of the resources (projects, folders, and files) you're working with.

**Editors** allow you to create and change resources and are associated with a specific resource type. The focus of your attention will be working in an editor. When you start Eclipse for the first time, you will see an editor open on the welcome page. The welcome page contains introductory information and links to learn more about Eclipse.

The other panes around the editor are views. A **view** presents a way to navigate through resources or other information in Eclipse. Even though they are called "views," you can use them to make changes to resources. For example, you can rename files in the Navigator view and perform various Java refactoring in the Java views. The Outline view shows the structure of the contents of the file being edited. The Properties view displays the properties of the file, such as the size and date it was last modified. Views can be resized, stacked, tiled, torn off, and placed on the fast view bar.

A **perspective** in Eclipse defines a set of editors and views arranged in an initial layout for a particular role or task. For example, the Debug perspective is designed for the task of debugging source code. The initial layout of the Resource perspective lists folders and files in the Navigator view and contains an editor area and supporting views such as the Outline and Tasks views. Eclipse can have one or more perspectives open at a time, though only one is visible. Perspectives also can be designed with a predefined set of functions available through the menu bar and toolbar that you can perform while in the perspective. Eclipse has the following perspectives:

- Resource
- Java
- Java Browsing
- Java Type Hierarchy
- CVS Repository Exploring
- Debug
- Team Synchronizing
- Plug-in Development

Eclipse provides many different editors and views. Throughout this book, you'll explore the variety of supplied perspectives and their editors and views. You will also learn how to extend Eclipse to build your own perspectives, views, and editors.

In an effort to provide a good overall user experience, and especially a good "out of the box" experience, Eclipse provides for the progressive disclosure of aspects of the user interface. The goal is to reveal the function presented in a way so as not to overwhelm you. Function is progressively introduced based on the activities or tasks you are doing. These activities includes things like using wizards, perspectives, and preferences. Eclipse calls these **capabilities**. In Eclipse itself, you will not see too much of this; just about all functions are enabled. We're mentioning this now because, as you use other Eclipse-based offerings that build on Eclipse, you will most likely see more of this progressive disclosure. For more information, see the Progressive Disclosure subsection later in this chapter.

## Overview of the User Interface

Let's spend a little time on the layout of the user interface. This is the default perspective and the first one you'll see when you start Eclipse. Figure 2.4 shows the Resource perspective with some slight modifications. We made the modifications to better explain the layout.

The Eclipse user interface is presented as an adjustable multipaned window comprising the following items.

- All user interface actions are available from **menu bar** items.
- The **toolbar** is a set of icons that represent shortcuts to some Eclipse actions that also appear as menu items.
- **Editors** appear in the middle pane with tabs for navigation. In Figure 2.4, several files are open for editing. One is visible in front. The other editors are represented by the ">>" mark with "2" as a subscript. You can resize the editor pane by grabbing and moving one of the interior edges of the pane.
- Each perspective defines **views** it includes and their initial placement. The Resource perspective includes the Navigator view for navigating through and operating on resources, the Outline view for navigating within a resource that supports an outline view (such as Java source code), and the Tasks view for listing things to do. To better illustrate user interface organization, we've added and moved some views in the Resource perspective as shown in Figure 2.4. The Outline and Console views and one other are stacked behind the Navigator view. As with the editors, this is indicated by the ">>" annotation with a "1" subscript. When there's room for view tabs, they all appear horizontally as you see with the Tasks, Bookmarks, and Problems views.
- A **tear-off view** is a view you remove from the main Eclipse window to have float freely. We've done this with the Properties view.
- Open perspectives are shown to the right of the toolbar on the **perspective bar**. To switch to another perspective, select it on the perspective bar.
- The **fast view bar** holds icons for the views you have made into fast views. Briefly, as we'll get to these more in the Views subsection a bit

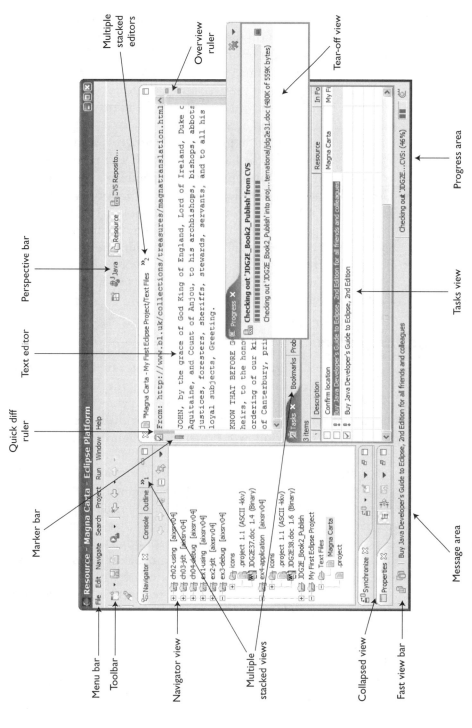

**Figure 2.4** Resource Perspective

Menu bar

Toolbar

Navigator view

Multiple stacked views

Collapsed view

Fast view bar

Quick diff ruler

Marker bar

Perspective bar

Text editor

Multiple stacked editors

Overview ruler

Tear-off view

Tasks view

Progress area

Message area

21

later, a fast view is created when you take a view off the main window and save it as an icon on the fast view bar. By default, the location of the fast view bar is the bottom border of the main window.

- Just to the right of the fast view bar is the **message area**. Information is displayed here based on the active view or editor and your current selection. For example, you can select a file in the Navigator view and see its path information here.

- On the right of the bottom margin is the **progress area**. When you have operations running in the background, such as a repository operation or a search, status information on the operation appears here.

- The **marker bar** and **overview ruler** display annotations in the file being edited. Annotations might include bookmarks, tasks, compiler errors, breakpoints, and search results. The specific annotations that appear on the marker bar and overview ruler can be editor specific.

- The **quick diff ruler** displays color coding to provide a quick and simple reference for understanding what lines you've added, deleted, and changed in the file you're editing.

## Introducing Preferences

Before we go too much further, we need to introduce preferences. **Preferences** allow you to change the appearance and behavior of everything from fonts and colors to settings for opening new views and perspectives and file type associations for using other computer programs with Eclipse. View your preferences by selecting **Window > Preferences**. Figure 2.5 shows the Preferences dialog.

Recall that we talked about progressive disclosure and capabilities. This progressive disclosure dictates how some things show up in the user interface, including preferences. So based on what you've done and what you're doing, what you see as your preferences may differ from what's shown in Figure 2.5.

You can share your preference settings with others, which is a feature very helpful for working as a member of a team. Select **Export...** to save your preference settings to a file or **Import...** to configure with settings from a file. For more information on sharing preference settings between workspaces and/or team members, please see the Coordinating Preferences section in Chapter 6, Managing Your Eclipse Environment.

One of the neat things about other tools or offerings built on Eclipse is that their preferences will appear in the Preferences dialog as well. You have one place to go to manage preferences for everything you have installed and configured to run with Eclipse.

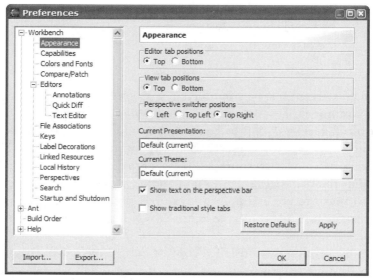

**Figure 2.5**    Preferences Dialog

We wanted to present preferences early in this discussion because there are preferences for almost any appearance or behavior you might want to customize. Throughout the rest of the book, unless otherwise stated, when we describe behavior we are referring to the default preference settings. In addition, as we discuss topics, we'll often refer to the preference settings applicable to the subject matter and ones in which you might be interested. For example, when we refer to **Workbench > Editors** preferences, you access these preferences by selecting **Window > Preferences** and then **Editors** under **Workbench**. We won't cover all the preferences—that's best left to the documentation. If we don't hit a preference you're interested in, refer to Preferences in the Reference section of the *Workbench User Guide*.

## Basic Eclipse Use

The designers of Eclipse went to great lengths to ensure that Eclipse looked and felt to you like other programs running on your computer and behaved as the operating system expected it to. On Windows systems, Eclipse looks and feels like other Windows programs. On other operating systems, Eclipse looks and feels like programs designed for those operating systems. It works well with other applications running on your computer and permits things like dragging and dropping between programs. This means that what you know about manipulating the user interfaces of computer programs in general applies to Eclipse as well.

## Working in Eclipse

All resources must be contained in a project, with one exception we'll get to in a moment. That exception is using **File > Open External File…**. Within a project, resources can be contained in folders, and folders can be nested in other folders. Projects serve as an organizational construct because they can contain other resources. Projects are also used to keep information about the resources they contain and how they are built, such as repository information. For example, a Java project contains Java files. Editing and saving a Java file results in Eclipse invoking the Java compiler associated with the project.

By default, each installed copy of Eclipse has a workspace for storing your projects, their resources, and information about them. Your default workspace location is on your local file system under your Eclipse directory in a subdirectory called workspace. The file system does not need to be local. Eclipse allows projects to be located anywhere in the file system, including remote file systems and distributed file systems such as Andrew File System (AFS). Your workspace is file based, so it can integrate easier with a broad range of source code repositories and other tools.

Eclipse keeps a local change history of your Eclipse resources in your workspace. Each time you edit and save a resource, Eclipse makes a note of the changes you made. You can use this information to compare the current state of a resource with past states to undo and redo changes or to replace a resource with an earlier copy.

When you start Eclipse you'll see a dialog prompting you for which workspace you want to use. There's no magic to the list of workspaces; it's simply a remembered list of workspaces you previously selected from this dialog. If you have several workspaces, you can switch between them by selecting **File > Switch Workspace…**. You'll be prompted, with the same dialog, to select another workspace. Eclipse will switch to the workspace you selected. In the Running Multiple Eclipse Windows and Workspaces subsection later in this chapter, you'll see how to have multiple Eclipse sessions running at the same time. Switching between workspaces is quicker than opening an Eclipse session on another workspace. Though, depending on what you're working on, your work habits, and your computer's resources, you'll need to decide if it's more efficient to switch between workspaces or to open multiple Eclipse sessions on the different workspaces you are using.

## Understanding the User Interface

You drive Eclipse through user interface actions on the menu bar, toolbar, editor and view toolbars, and context menus. Many of these actions and their behaviors are configurable with your preference settings. The user interface actions that are visible depend on what tools or Eclipse-based offerings you have installed and configured to run on Eclipse and your current perspective. The enabled user interface actions, that is, those you can select, depend on the active view and your selection in that view. All actions are available from the menus. Selected actions are available on the toolbars. You also have a large number of keyboard shortcuts defined. Some shortcuts are global; some are specific to a given activity. Select **Window > Navigation** to see a summary of some general shortcuts. To define your own keyboard shortcuts, use your **Workbench > Keys** preferences.

The toolbar (see Figure 2.4 earlier in the chapter) is comprised of groups of buttons. You can reconfigure the toolbar by dragging the group dividers to expand or compress a group of buttons or to move a group to a new line. By default, the perspective bar is to the right of the toolbar. You can move the divider between the toolbar and the perspective bar by dragging it. You can change the location of the perspective bar with your **Perspective switcher positions** setting in your **Workbench > Appearance** preferences. Or right-click on the perspective bar and select one of the **Dock on** options. You can also change the location of the fast view bar from its default on the left of the bottom border. Right-click on it and select one of the **Dock on** options.

Eclipse 3.0 introduced a new look to its user interface. If you are more comfortable with the previous presentation, you can change to it by editing your **Workbench > Appearance** preferences. Set **Current Presentation** to **R21Presentation**.

### Navigating Resources

The Navigator view (see Figure 2.6) is the workhorse of the Resource perspective. Use it to manage your projects, files, and folders; to invoke editors to work with the files; and to perform other actions such as importing and exporting files.

Earlier we saw how to import files by dragging them from Windows Explorer and dropping them in the Navigator view. You can also move files and folders between projects and folders in Eclipse by dragging and dropping them or by using **Copy** and **Paste**.

As your work grows and the number of entries in the Navigator view increases, you can navigate into a project or folder by selecting **Go Into** from

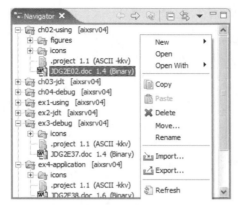

**Figure 2.6**   Navigator View

the context menu. This replaces the contents of the view with the contents of
the selected project or folder. **Up** ![icon] replaces the contents of the view with
the contents of the folder or project containing the current contents. **Forward**
⇨ and **Back** ⇦ work as they would in a Web browser. Select **Filters...** ![icon]
from the pull-down menu ▼ on the Navigator view title bar to restrict the
files that appear.

## Using Editors

Files are associated with editors by their file type (extension). When you
change the contents of a file in an editor, the file is marked as changed by an
asterisk (*) in front of the file name on the editor tab. Maximize an editor to
occupy the entire window by double-clicking on the editor tab. Double-click
on it again to return it to the original size.

When you select a file to edit, the editor is chosen based on the following
priority.

1. The last editor used, if the file has been edited.
2. The default editor defined for the selected file type. (You'll see how to
   do this later in this chapter in the section Using Other Computer Programs with Eclipse.)
3. A computer program defined to your operating system for the selected
   file type.
4. The Eclipse text editor.

This protocol is also used to select an editor for new files you create.
Override this behavior by selecting a file and then selecting **Open With** from

the context menu to see a list of editors defined for the selected file type.
**Open With > Default Editor** uses the default editor for this file type as
defined in your **Workbench > File Associations** preferences. **Open With >
System Editor** uses the associated editor or application defined by the operating system outside of Eclipse. **Open With > In-Place Editor** opens the operating system–defined editor for this file type in the editor area.

   **Link with Editor** 🖹 causes the file you are editing to be selected in the
Navigator view. This means that as you select resources in the view, editors
on those resources (if open) are shown. As you switch between editors, the
file you are currently editing is selected in the Navigator view. The default
action to open a file for editing is to double-click on it. Change this with
**Workbench** preferences to open a file by single-clicking on it, hovering over
it, and/or using arrow keys.

   Eclipse allows you to use its editors to edit files that are outside your
workspace. To do so, select **File > Open External File….** Note, however, that
there are some limitations with this approach. Normally, files you work on
are contained in projects. And the project definitions themselves contain
information about their resources. For example, for Java, projects contain
information about JREs and build paths. Editing a project outside your
workspace, and outside a project definition, means Eclipse does not have this
additional information.

   As the number of files you edit increases and you quickly move between
files, editing one and then another, managing your editor sessions can
become more challenging. There are several things you can do. Keyboard
shortcuts allow you to quickly select from your open editors. Select **Ctrl+F6**
or **Ctrl+Shift+F6** to select the next and previous editors, respectively. Select
**Ctrl+E** to display a list of editor sessions. Begin typing the name of the file
you want to see, and the list is narrowed (see Figure 2.7). If multiple editor
tabs becomes bothersome, deselect **Show multiple editor tabs** in your **Workbench > Editors** preferences. This causes the tabs for the nonactive editor sessions to be represented by ">>" and a numerical subscript. The subscript
indicates the number of nonactive editor sessions (see Figure 2.7).

   You can get back to the last file you were editing by selecting **Last Edit
Location** 🖹. You can also use **Forward** ⇨ and **Back** ⇦ and their associated
pull-down menus to navigate through the files and locations in those files you
were editing.

   **Workbench > Editors** preferences provide several other notable settings.
You can customize the number of recently opened files listed under **File** on
the menu. You can also choose to recycle a fixed number of editor sessions.
To do this, select **Close editors automatically** and then specify the maximum

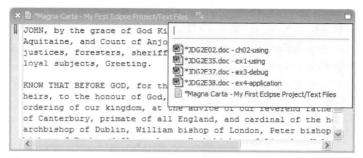

**Figure 2.7**   Switching between Editor Sessions

number of editors kept open with **Number of opened editors before closing**. For example, if you do this and specify five editors, when you have five editors open and you select another file to edit, the editor of the oldest file will be closed before another is opened. This is useful if you tend to end up with a lot of open editors and find it cumbersome navigating through them. If reducing startup time is a premium for you, consider enabling **Close all editors on exit**. Eclipse closes all open editors when you exit and asks if you want to save unsaved changes. Then, the next time you start Eclipse, it will start quicker because it will not have to open the editor sessions you had open when you exited.

On Windows operating systems, Eclipse supports Object Linking and Embedding (OLE) document editors, for example, for Lotus spreadsheet *.123 or Microsoft word processing *.doc files. When you select a file for editing that has associated an OLE document editor defined by your operating system but not Eclipse, the editor opens in the editor pane (see Figure 2.8). The OLE document editor adds its menu items to the Eclipse menu and replaces the Eclipse **Help** menu. It does not make changes to the **File** and **Window** menus. If you need to access Eclipse **Help** menu items, switch the focus from the OLE document editor to another Eclipse editor or view. If you would rather open OLE document editors in new windows and not within the editor pane, you'll need to change your **Workbench > File Associations** preferences. You'll see how to do this in Using Other Computer Programs with Eclipse later in this chapter. When you edit a file in the editor pane with an OLE document editor, the file is automatically marked as modified.

## Views

All views share the same user interface organization (see Figure 2.9). At the top, on the left, is a tab with the view icon (e.g., ⊞ for the Outline view) and

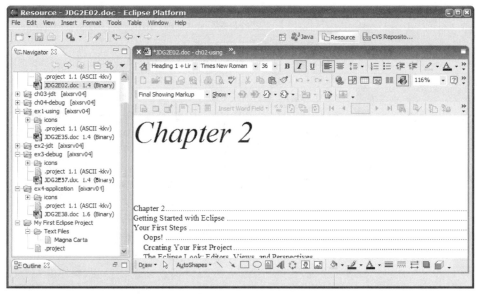

**Figure 2.8**　OLE Document Editor in Eclipse

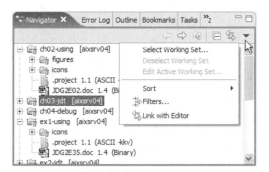

**Figure 2.9**　View User Interface Organization

title and a **Close** button ⊠. To the right of the tab and below may be one or more view-specific toolbar buttons. Some views also have a pull-down menu button ▼ with more view-specific actions. On the right are buttons for minimizing ▭, maximizing ☐, and restoring ⯬ the view. Reopen a closed view or open another view by selecting **Window > Show View**. On some views the actions on the pull-down menu are also available from the view context menu. On others, the pull-down menu is the only place an action is available.

As with editors, there are keyboard shortcuts for navigating through open views. Select **Ctrl+F7** or **Ctrl+Shift+F7** to select the next and previous views, respectively, from a list.

Views can be resized, moved, and stacked. This is useful for organizing the user interface according to your tastes or to optimize use of screen real estate. To resize a view, simply drag one of its borders. To move a view, drag it by its title bar. When you are moving a view, the cursor provides feedback on where it can be dropped. For example, a left-pointing arrow ◀ means dropping the view here will position it to the left of the view under the cursor, and a folder icon 🗐 means dropping it here will cause it to be stacked on top of the view under the cursor. You will also see an outline of where the view will be positioned if you drop it (see Figure 2.10).

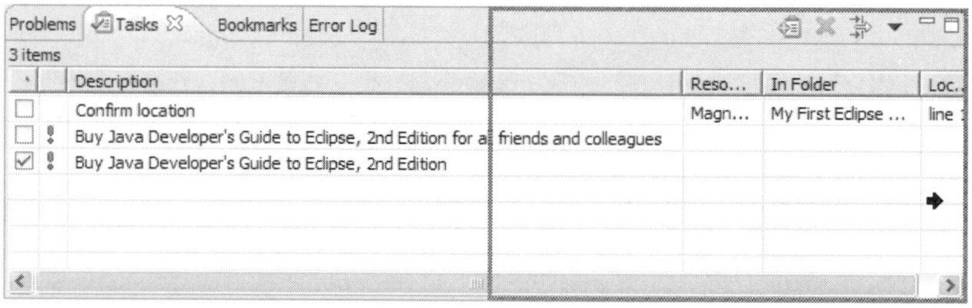

**Figure 2.10**   Moving a View

This ability to resize, move, stack, and reposition views affords a great deal of flexibility in customizing Eclipse's layout and organizing it to your tastes and needs. For example, as shown in Figure 2.4 with the Navigator, Synchronize, and Properties views, you can line up views and use the **Restore** 🗗 and **Minimize** ▭ actions to selectively expand and collapse the views. You can also stack views, as shown in Figure 2.9. Click on **>>** to see the other stacked views.

You can "tear off" a view and leave it as a separate window from your main Eclipse one. To do so, grab a view by its title bar and drag it outside the Eclipse window. To return it, simply drag it back onto the main Eclipse window.

Perhaps the ultimate in screen real estate savings come with making a view into a fast view. In a nutshell, a fast view is a view reduced to and represented by an icon on the the fast view bar. By default, and as shown earlier in Figure 2.4, this is on the bottom border of the Eclipse window. To make a view a fast view, either drag it onto the fast view bar, or right-click on the view title bar and then select **Fast View**. To display a fast view, select the icon on the fast view bar. The view slides out to become visible. Select the icon again to hide the view. To restore a view in the fast view bar to where it was in the user interface, right-click on the fast view icon on the fast view bar and then deselect **Fast View**. Alternatively, simply drag the fast view icon from the fast view bar and place the view in the Eclipse window.

You can relocate the fast view bar to the left, right, or bottom border of the Eclipse window by selecting one of the **Dock On** options from the fast view bar context menu. As fast views become visible, you can also toggle their orientation between horizontal and vertical. Do this by right-clicking on the fast view icon and then selecting one of the **Orientation** options. This makes horizontally oriented views like Bookmarks and Problems work better as fast views. Each fast view has its own setting, so you can have some orient horizontally and some orient vertically.

### Perspectives

Recall that perspectives contain, among other things, an organization of views and editors. Up to this point, we've been working in the Resource perspective. If you've moved around and resized views and want to return the perspective to its default configuration, select **Window > Reset Perspective**. To open another perspective, for example, the Java perspective, select **Window > Open Perspective** and then the perspective. Your open perspectives, by default, are shown to the right of the toolbar. You can change this with your **Workbench > Appearance** preferences. If you tend to have a lot of perspectives open and you want to see all the perspective icons, do one or more of the following.

- Drag the divider between the toolbar and the perspective bar to the left to create more room for the perspective icons.
- Drag parts of the toolbar to create a second line of toolbar icons. This will give you another line for perspective icons as well.
- Right-click on the perspective bar and deselect **Show Text** from the context menu. This will reduce the size of the icons.

### *Tasks, Bookmarks, and Problems*

Tasks, bookmarks, and problems are tracking mechanisms that may associate information with resources in your projects. Because Eclipse manages them with the resources they reference, they are an efficient way to communicate additional information and work about a project's resources among team members. Tasks, bookmarks, and problems each have their own view.

In addition, tasks, bookmarks, and problems appear in the editor of their associated resource. You can see this in Figure 2.4 earlier in the chapter. If you have a large number of tasks, bookmarks, or problems, you can filter those that appear in their respective view by selecting **Filters...** ⇶. For example, you can restrict the tasks or problems shown based on your selection in the Navigator view and several other criteria. To sort, click on any of the column headings. To navigate to the associated resource, double-click on the task, bookmark, or problem. The associated resource is opened in an editor and the associated line selected.

**Tasks** ☑ are textual reminders. They have a completion status and priority. Tasks may or may not be associated to a specific resource. You define new tasks from the context menu of the Tasks view by right-clicking on the marker bar of an editor and selecting **Add task....** The Java editor allows you to define tasks through the use of task tags in your source code. You'll see this in Overview of the Java Editor in Chapter 3, Using Java Development Tools.

**Bookmarks** ▯ are similar to tasks with the exception that bookmarks *must* be associated with a file and they do not have a completion status or priority. You define new bookmarks from the marker bar of an editor from the context menu, or in the Navigator view by selecting a resource and then selecting **Add Bookmark...** from the context menu.

**Problems** ▣ are, as you'd expect, warnings and errors Eclipse detects as you work. Java build and classpath errors are shown here. Errors you encounter importing resources appear here. You don't unilaterally create a problem, at least in the context of our discussion here <grin>; Eclipse does this for you.

## Background Processing

Eclipse provides the ability for work to be done in the background so that you are not prevented from doing other work. For example, Eclipse enables CVS repository actions such as **Check Out**, **Commit**, and **Update** (we'll see these in Chapter 5, Teaming Up with Eclipse) to be performed in the background. When you perform an action that's been enabled for background processing, you'll see a prompt like that shown in Figure 2.11. You can do nothing and allow the operation to complete, or select **Cancel** to stop the operation and return to your work. Or, you can select **Run in Background** to relegate the operation to background processing. This allows you to continue your work while the operation completes. If you want all operations enabled for background processing to run in the background without prompting, select **Always run in background** in your **Workbench** preferences.

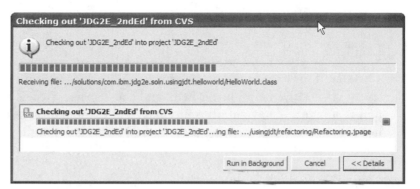

**Figure 2.11**    Background Processing Prompt

When background processing is under way, you'll see status information in the progress area on the right side of the bottom border of the Eclipse window (see Figure 2.12).

**Figure 2.12**    Background Processing Status

Click on the Progress view proxy button 🕐 to open the Progress view (see Figure 2.13). To stop a background operation, click on the stop button ■ for the operation in the Progress view. The Progress view proxy button indicates the operation had results 🕐 or resulted in an error 🕐. Click on the respective proxy button to see the details.

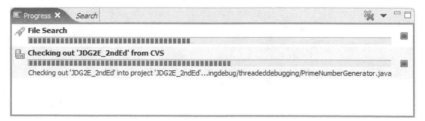

**Figure 2.13**    Progress View

When background processing is under way for a view, the view's name on its tab changes to *italic*. When a view has been updated due to completed background processing, the view name changes to **bold**.

### *When You Need a Little Assistance*

A wealth of information about how to use and extend Eclipse is available through integrated and cross-linked online content and the search capability. There are four basic types of assistance: online documentation, infopops (context-sensitive help), hover help, and cheat sheets. Access to online content is simple and navigation is intuitive. The combination of online content, links, and navigation makes it easy to find information and get answers to your questions.

### Online Documentation

To view all online documentation, select **Help > Help Contents**. If this is the first time you've requested help, you will see a slight delay as the engine for the Help system starts up and initializes. Figure 2.14 shows the first Help window.

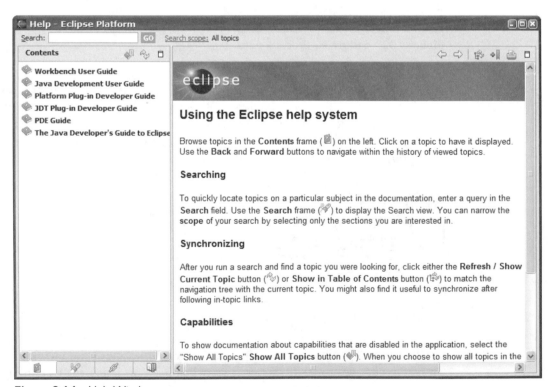

**Figure 2.14**    Help Window

The Navigation pane is on the left and the Contents pane is on the right. The Navigation pane has four pages: Contents, Search Results, Links, and Bookmarks. The Contents *page* (not to be confused with the Contents *pane* on the right) lists the available online content you have, organized by books.

Navigating online documentation is straightforward. You expand entries on the Contents page to drill down to "leaf" topics and select these to view the information in the Contents pane. Use the **Forward** ⇨ and **Back** ⇦ buttons to display and redisplay pages. These work like browser forward and back buttons. **Show in Table of Contents** ⌗ synchronizes the Contents page of the Navigation pane with the topic that is currently displayed in the Contents pane on the right. This is especially useful if you get to a piece of information from a search or infopop and need to navigate back to where it is located in a book. Save the location of a document you find interesting with **Bookmark Document** ▯ and navigate back later by selecting the bookmark on the Bookmarks pane in the Navigation pane. **Print Page** 🖶 is the same as the browser **Print** action and prints what is currently shown in the Contents or Navigation pane. The online documentation contains a large number of cross-links. Be aware that printing with links can result in voluminous output.

Eclipse provides five online books. The *Workbench User Guide* is for all users and explains how to use Eclipse. The *Java Development User Guide* is for all Java developers and explains how to use Eclipse to write and debug Java code. The remaining three online books, *Platform Plug-In Developer Guide*, *JDT Plug-In Developer Guide*, and *PDE Guide*, are for those who want to extend and/or build offerings based on Eclipse (discussed extensively later in the book in Parts II through V). If you are working with or have integrated other Eclipse-based offerings, you may see additional book entries. This is another example of how Eclipse provides a common mechanism for other providers to integrate their offerings. If you're interested, it's simple to add your own content and have it appear in the Help system. Writing Java code is not required, only some XML and your content, perhaps HTML. We'll get to this in Chapter 22, Providing Help.

Each of the online documentation books is organized into three sections: concepts, tasks, and reference. Some of the books also include a getting started section. The concepts sections provide general overview information on capability, user interface organization, and navigation. The tasks sections go into more detail to provide specific instructions on how to accomplish things, for example, how to create a project or how to move a view. Finally, the reference sections provide additional detail on specific user interface actions and preference settings.

## Infopops

To view online content for a specific item in the user interface, shift focus
to the item and press **F1**. You will see an **infopop**, a small modal window,
with a list of topics related to the selected user interface item (see Figure 2.15).
You may need to shift focus by using the arrow keys or mnemonics to
select an item without actually performing the action. Select one of the
topics in the infopop to see the related information displayed in the
online documentation.

**Figure 2.15**   Infopop Help

    The Links page in the Navigation pane shows the links that appeared in
the infopop you used to access the current information. The Links page
allows you to go to the other help topics identified on the infopop without
having to press **F1** again.

## Hover Help

To quickly see information about an icon (on a toolbar, on a title bar, or in
the view fast view bar), or to see a long entry that is not completely displayed
(such as a file name or task), hover over the icon or name and a short description, called **hover help**, will display.

## Cheat Sheets

Sometimes when you ask to see information on a topic, especially when the
information needs to be presented as a nontrivial sequence of steps, Eclipse
will display the information in the form of a **cheat sheet**. Unlike the other
types of assist information, cheat sheets show up in their own view, which
you can then position and manage like any other view. Figure 2.16 shows a
cheat sheet for creating a simple Java application. From the Eclipse welcome
page, if you select **Tutorials**, the tutorials listed are implemented as cheat
sheets.

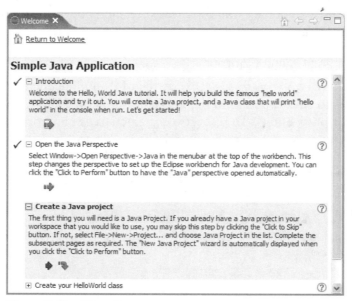

**Figure 2.16**   Cheat Sheet

Using cheat sheets is easy. As you work through each of a cheat sheet's steps, you will use one or more of the buttons listed in Table 2.1 to navigate the cheat sheet.

**Table 2.1**   Cheat Sheet Actions

| Icon | Description |
| --- | --- |
| ☑ | Indicate that you have completed the step. |
| | Reset status for all cheat sheet steps. |
| | Restart this step. |
| | Skip this step and go on to the next. |
| | Start a cheat sheet. |
| | Perform the step. This usually causes Eclipse to invoke some action. |

Status for each step is indicated by an icon. No icon means the step has not been completed, ✓ means the step is complete, and ↲ means you skipped the step.

To see all of the available cheat sheets, first open the Cheat Sheet view. Then use the view pull-down menu ▼.

## Searching Online Content

There are two ways to specify a search of the online documentation. One way is to enter a phrase in the **Search** field on the Help window and select **Go** (or press **Enter**). To restrict your search to a subset of the topics, click on **Search Scope**. You can also search the online documentation from the main Eclipse window by selecting **Search** 🔍 or by pressing **Ctrl+H** and then selecting the **Help Search** tab (see Figure 2.17).

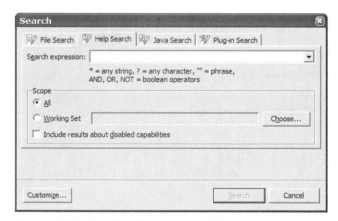

**Figure 2.17**    Searching Help from the Eclipse Window

Search expressions are based on a few relatively simple rules and can themselves be simple or complex. Search expressions are not case sensitive. They support the Boolean operators AND, OR, and NOT; asterisk (*) and question mark (?) wildcards; and double quotes (" ") for expressions of multiple words. The following are examples of different search expressions entered in the **Search** field in the Help window. For a complete description of search expression rules, refer to Using the Help System in the Tasks section of the *Workbench User Guide*.

keyboard shortcuts: This search returns all entries with "keyboard" or "shortcuts" or both. You would enter this search term for information on keyboard equivalents for user interface commands. If you wanted to find instances that contain both words, you would specify keyboard and shortcuts.

"keyboard shortcuts": This returns all entries with the phrase "keyboard shortcuts." This narrows the search by specifying a phrase.

"keyboard shortcuts" not bindings: This returns the previous set of matches minus those with the word "bindings." This narrows the search further by eliminating matches having to do with changing editor key bindings.

"keyboard shortcuts" or ctrl*: This returns all entries with the phrase "keyboard shortcuts" or a word beginning with the characters "ctrl" (not case sensitive), or both. The or operator is optional; if not specified, it is inferred.

Recall that earlier we introduced the concept of progressive disclosure in Eclipse in the form of capabilities. Normally, when a capability is disabled, or not shown, the documentation associated with it is also not shown. When you search from the Search dialog, you can include this hidden documentation by enabling **Include results about disabled capabilities**.

The help system comes with language analyzers for German and English. The language analyzers codify certain language characteristics to enable more powerful searches. This allows the search to ignore "stop" words, for example, in English words like "and," "or," and "the," and to match through word stemming, for example, "code" would match "codes," "coding," and "coded."

The results of your search appear on the Search Results page in the Navigation pane on the left (see Figure 2.18).

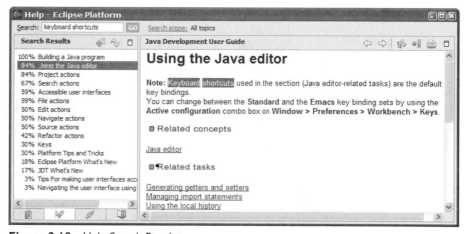

**Figure 2.18**  Help Search Results

The results are ranked based on an algorithm that considers the number of hits, the length of the file with the hits, and whether or not there are hits in the title. Ranking is shown as a percentage. The hits to your search terms are highlighted in the Contents pane, as shown in Figure 2.18.

## Resource Management

Eclipse provides a great deal of capability for operating on your resources. Recall, these are your projects, folders, and files. Eclipse makes it simple and efficient to manage, search, compare, and replace them with previous versions. All resources you have defined are kept on your computer's file system. This makes it very easy to move files into and out of Eclipse and to use Eclipse with other computer programs.

### Your Workspace

Resources you're working on are kept in your workspace. By default, on Windows operating systems this is in the folder `workspace` in your main Eclipse folder. As you saw earlier, you have the option to change this when you start Eclipse.

Take a moment to browse your `workspace` folder to understand its contents. You'll see a folder structure similar to your project structure. Information about your workspace is kept in the `.metadata` folder. You don't want to touch this. Observe the `.project` files in each of the projects. This is where information specific to each project is kept, for example, references to other projects. You'll see in the Running Multiple Eclipse Windows and Workspaces subsection later in this chapter that you can have multiple Eclipse workspaces for a single Eclipse installation. This is a useful technique, for example, for partitioning your work. You'll also see in a moment that you can create a project with an alternate location that is not in your workspace folder. While not in the default workspace location, the project is still considered part of your workspace. This means your workspace can be physically distributed.

The Properties view displays information about the resource selected in the Navigator view. For more detailed information about a resource's properties, select a resource in the Navigator view and then select **Properties** from the context menu to see the Properties dialog (see Figure 2.19). For example, if you've lost track of where a resource is actually located on your file system, this is how you can find it.

Because resources in your workspace exist as files on your file system, you may at some point manipulate the files in your workspace outside of Eclipse, whether from a command line prompt, with a file system navigator,

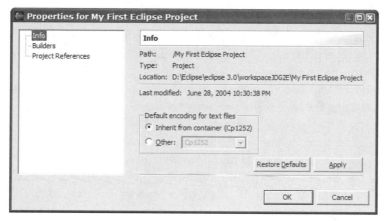

**Figure 2.19**   Properties Dialog

or with a computer program not integrated with Eclipse. Thus, you can make changes to resources Eclipse is managing without its knowledge. This means that the information Eclipse keeps in your workspace about its files can be out of sync with what is on your file system. Some Eclipse operations need your workspace information to be in sync with your file system, for example, moving and copying files. If it is not and you attempt one of these operations, you will see an error message like the one in Figure 2.20.

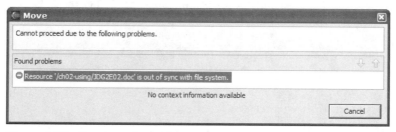

**Figure 2.20**   Resource Out of Sync Error

Should you get this kind of error, or if you know you have made changes to resources in your workspace that Eclipse is not aware of, you need to refresh your workspace. To do this, select one or more resources in the Navigator view and then select **Refresh** from the context menu. Alternatively, you can set one of your auto refresh preferences to have Eclipse do this automatically for you. Select **Refresh Workspace automatically** from your **Workbench** preferences. Or select **Refresh workspace on startup** in your **Workbench > Startup and Shutdown** preferences.

## Local History

One type of information Eclipse maintains is previous versions of the resources in your workspace. This is called your **local history**. This information allows you to compare and replace resources with previous versions of them and to recover files you've deleted. Your **Workbench > Local History** preference settings specify how many previous versions of files are maintained. These settings are pretty much self-explanatory. If you have disk space to spare, you might choose to keep more local history information; if you're constrained, change these settings to minimize your disk space requirements.

Local history capability occupies a middle ground between what you get with **Edit > Undo** and **Redo** within an editor session and what you get with code management through a repository. Editors let you undo changes but only within an edit session. SCM repositories keep only changes that you have explicitly committed. Local history keeps editions of the files you save between editor sessions and without any SCM system.

## Comparing and Replacing Resources

An extremely useful function is the ability to compare and replace or merge resources with previous versions of the resources or with each other. This is done based on local history information in your workspace. To compare a file, select a file in the Navigator view and then select **Compare With > Local History...** from the context menu. A comparison of the file with previous versions is shown in the Compare dialog (see Figure 2.21).

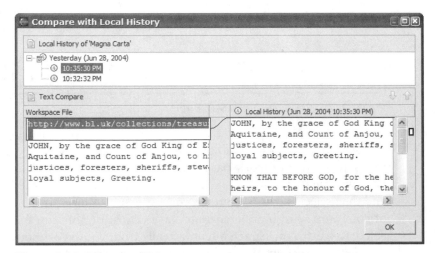

**Figure 2.21**   Compare Dialog

The file's current contents are on the left in the Compare dialog. On the right is the selected version from the file's local history. Navigating in this dialog is straightforward. Use **Select Next Change** ⇩ and **Select Previous Change** ⇧ to scroll through the changes. On the far right is an overview ruler. The length of the ruler represents the total length of the file. Changes are marked by rectangles. This is useful for seeing the total number of changes. Go to any change by selecting the rectangle on the overview ruler.

You can select two projects or two folders or two files and use **Compare With > Each Other** from the context menu in the Navigator view to compare their contents. Figure 2.22 shows the sample output of comparing two projects.

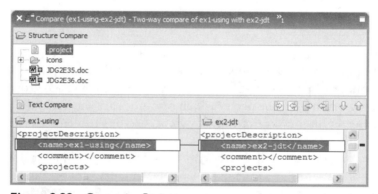

**Figure 2.22**   Comparing Projects

The small **+** and **–** signs in the top pane indicate whether the file (or folder if you compared projects) was added or deleted. For changed files, double-click on the file to see the changes in the bottom pane. In addition to the change navigation buttons, **Select Next Change** ⇩ and **Select Previous Change** ⇧, there are buttons to process changes between the different editions of the changed file: **Copy All Non-Conflicting Changes from Right to Left**, **Copy All from Left to Right**, **Copy Current Change from Right to Left**, and **Copy Current Change from Left to Right**.

Replacing a file with a previous version is similar to the way you do a comparison. Select a file in the Navigator view and then select **Replace With > Local History...** from the context menu. The Replace from Local History dialog is almost identical to the Compare dialog, with the addition of a **Replace** button. Select this to have the current contents of the file (in the left pane) replaced with the selected version from local history (in the right pane).

### Recovering Deleted Files

Local history information is kept for a file even if you delete the file from a project. This allows you to recover files you've deleted from projects or folders. To recover a deleted file, from the Navigator view, select the project or folder that contained it and then select **Restore From Local History...** from the context menu. You will see a list of files you have deleted from the project or folder and their editions. Select the file and edition you want to recover and then select **Restore**.

Eclipse is designed so that it can be run integrated with an SCM repository. We'll get to this in more detail in Chapter 5, Teaming Up with Eclipse. Many of the operations we've just seen can also be performed through the repository, for example, recovering deleted files.

### Working Sets

**Working sets** are defined collections of projects, folders, and/or files in your workspace. Working sets are especially useful as a filtering mechanism as the number of projects and/or resources in your workspace grows. For example, use working sets to specify which resources are shown in the Navigator view. You can filter tasks in the Tasks view and the Problems view by working sets.

There is no general-purpose wizard for creating working sets. Rather, you create, edit, and delete working sets from prompts or dialogs that take a working set as an input. For example, to create a working set to filter the resources shown in the Navigator view, select **Select Working Set...** from the Navigator view pull-down menu ▾ and select to create a new **Resource** working set. Select the files you want in this working set, save it, and set it as the Navigator view working set. You'll see only the resources defined in the working set shown in the view. Note your working sets show up in the Navigator pull-down menu for quick access.

Working set definitions are global. This means you can use the working set you defined to filter the contents of the Navigator view to filter which tasks are displayed in the Tasks view or which resources are searched as part of a search.

### Searching

Eclipse provides a powerful search capability for resources in your workspace. Select **Search** from the menu bar, use **Search** 🔍, or press **Ctrl+H** to display the Search dialog (see Figure 2.23). There are four kinds of searches: File, Help, Java, and Plug-in. We discussed a Help search earlier in this chapter in the section When You Need a Little Assistance. We'll cover searching

PART I

Java in Searching in Chapter 3, Using Java Development Tools. Let's take a look now at a File search.

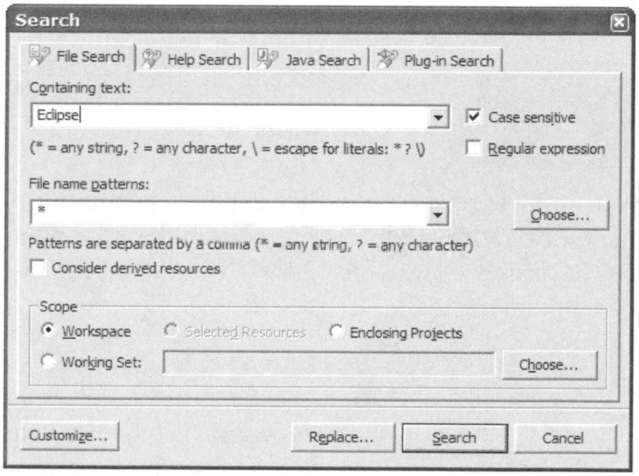

**Figure 2.23**    Search Dialog

On the File Search page, you specify a text string, pattern, or regular expression to search for and/or a file name or pattern. If you use only **Containing text**, the search is for the text in all files in the specified scope. If you use only **File name patterns**, the search is for all files whose names match the pattern in the specified scope. If you use both **Containing text** and **File name patterns**, the search is for the text only in files whose names match the pattern in **File name patterns**. The **Case sensitive** option applies only to the **Containing text** field, not the **File name patterns** field. Identify a regular expression by using the **Regular expression** check box.

Select **Search** to execute the search and view the results in the Search view. Select **Replace…** to do the same and in addition display the Replace dialog for selectively replacing the matching text, pattern, or expression.

Results from searches are shown in the Search view (see Figure 2.24). Double-click on an entry to open the file in an editor and select the match. Navigate through the matches and see the matches in editors by selecting **Show Next Match** ⇩ (or by pressing **Ctrl+.**) and **Show Previous Match** ⇧ (or by pressing **Ctrl+,**). The Search pull-down menu 🔍 ▼ on the Search view title bar shows a list of results from previous searches. Select one of these to see the results without having to execute the search again.

One final word on searching online documentation. When you search using the Search dialog from the main window rather than from the Help

**Figure 2.24**   Search Results

window, your results are shown in the Search view and not on the Search Results page of the Help window. This is useful because your search results are saved in the Search view, which allows you to cull the results to remove entries you're not interested in.

## More on Projects

When you create a project, its default location is the folder workspace in your main Eclipse folder. You can override the location of a project to specify another destination on your file system by deselecting **Use default** for **Project contents** and specifying a destination (see Figure 2.25). Even though the location of your project (and eventually its contents) is not in the default location, it is still part of your workspace and managed by Eclipse. There are several reasons you might want to do this. You may want to locate your work for a particularly important project on a server that is backed up regularly. Or, if you want to work directly on a Web site, set your project location to point to the correct place on the Web server to edit the Web site directly (this takes permission and a little courage). When you create a project and specify a location that contains folders and/or files, the existing folders and/or files become part of the new project.

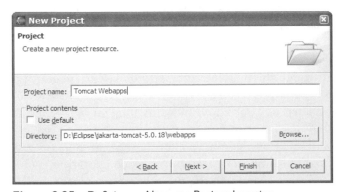

**Figure 2.25**   Defining an Alternate Project Location

The most common organization of a project is that it physically contains all of its resources. Eclipse, however, provides you with more flexibility. Top-level folders and files, that is, folders and files directly contained by a project, can exist outside a project. These are called **linked resources**. To enable this capability, set **Enable linked resources** in your **Workbench > Linked Resources** preferences. Create linked resources from the New Folder wizard by selecting **Advanced** and then selecting a destination folder for the file. Linked resources are just pointers to destination folders and files. The name by which Eclipse knows the file or folder does not need to match the physical resource it is linked to. The files are not physically copied. Linked resources are logical extensions of your workspace. This is a much easier way to man age collections of files that have to exist apart from one another without having to resort to a lot of copying.

Take care when you clean up your work. If you delete a linked file or folder, only the link is deleted—the folder and files they point to are not. However, if you open a linked folder and delete files or folders it contains, you are deleting them from the file system.

When you select to delete a project, you'll see the prompt asking if you want to delete the contents of the project, in addition to the project definition. The default is to delete a project definition, that is, information about the project, but not its resources. They remain in their current organization on your file system. Selecting the option **Also delete contents under <*path*>** will do just that. So take care. Ensure that you don't need the resources or that the resources have been backed up or copied to an alternate location. If you create a project and specify an alternate location, that location has existing files that are defined to the project, and if you then select to delete the project and its contents, the files at this alternate location will also be deleted. If you delete a project *but not its contents*, you can restore the project by simply creating the project again using the same name and specifying the same location. As mentioned earlier, when you delete a linked file or folder, only the link is deleted. The file or folder and files are left in their current state.

In addition to location, projects have two other properties: **Builders** and **Project References**. We'll get to **Builders** later in this chapter in the Customizing Eclipse section. **Project References** are a way to keep track of projects that refer to other projects. This property is set so that when the resources in a project change, Eclipse can process other projects that refer to the changed project. Generally speaking, Eclipse tools manage this property for their own use. Changing it may or may not have an impact on the tools; it's up to the tool. For example, if you are using the Eclipse Java tools, changing this property for Java projects has no impact. The Eclipse Java tools manage this property for their use and ignore your changes.

Eclipse also provides the ability for projects to have properties that override Eclipse preferences. This depends on the kind of projects. "Simple" projects do not do this. Eclipse Java projects do permit you to specify **Task Tags** and **Java Compiler** properties. These specifications take precedence over the general Eclipse preferences for this project.

When you use Eclipse with an integrated repository, each project is associated with a repository. These can be the same repository, different installations of the same type of repository, or different types of repositories. A given project can be associated with, at most, only one repository. We'll see how to do this in more detail in Chapter 5, Teaming Up with Eclipse.

## Importing and Exporting Resources

The best way to move collections of resources en masse to and from your workspace is to use its import and export facilities. We saw a simple example of importing files earlier in Creating Your First Project. Let's look at this in more detail. To import resources, select **File > Import...** or **Import...** from the Navigator view context menu.

You can import from a variety of destinations. Our discussion here focuses on importing from existing projects, the file system, and ZIP files. We'll get to checking out projects from CVS and using team project sets in Chapter 5. External features and external plug-ins and fragments are for managing development of Eclipse plug-ins and Eclipse-based offerings. We'll get to this in Chapter 9. Importing an existing project allows you to browse your file system for a project and import it as it is currently defined. This results in a new project to be created in your workspace based on what you're importing. Valid projects contain a .project file. When you import an existing project, it is not moved on your file system. It is left in its original location. When importing an existing project into your workspace, take care if you delete the project in your workspace. If you select to delete the project contents also, when prompted, the files in the original location will be deleted.

You cannot import Eclipse Release 1.0 projects to Eclipse 2.0, 3.0, or later this way. Eclipse will not recognize 1.0 projects as valid projects. This is because 1.0 projects do not have .project files. If you need to import a 1.0 project, define a similarly named project in your Eclipse 2.0 or 3.0 workspace, select the project in the Navigator view, select **File > Import** and then the **File System** option, and then browse your file system and select the Eclipse 1.0 project you want to import.

When you're importing from the file system, you import files into an existing project definition. Importing from the file system and a ZIP file

(*.zip and *.jar files) is similar. The contents of the ZIP file are treated as an extension to your file system. When you select to import from the file system or a ZIP file, you must specify a destination project or folder.

The Import wizard provides a nice facility for selecting which files you want to import (see Figure 2.26). From the list of folders on the left, select a folder to select all of its contents. Or, select files (on the right) individually from the list of files. If you have a large number of files, you can select **Filter Types...** to filter the files you see. For example, you might select to see only .html and .jsp files and then use **Select All**.

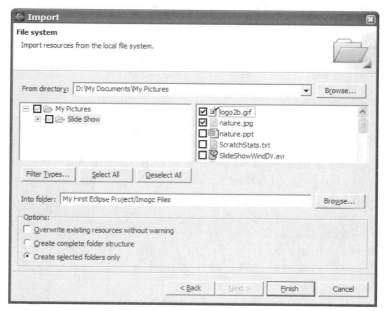

**Figure 2.26**    Importing from the File System with the Import Wizard

The check box and radio button options specify how to create the folder structure of what is imported.

- **Overwrite existing resources without warning**. If you attempt to import a file to a destination with an existing file of the same name, selecting this option will cause the file to be overwritten with no notification. If you do not select this option, you will first see a prompt.
- **Create complete folder structure**. Selecting this causes all the folders under the root you have selected in the left pane in the Import dialog

to be created, regardless of whether or not they have resources to import.

- **Create selected folders only.** Selecting this causes only those folders needed to hold the resources selected for import to be created.

Exporting resources takes resources and puts them in one of several formats that can be shared. Like importing, exporting supports several file formats. Given the resources are already on the file system, you might wonder why you need to export resources. There are two reasons. First, it's easier to export than it is to scan your file system for the resources you want to export; recall they might not be in the default location. Second, the Export wizard, like the Import wizard, makes it easy to select groups of resources by project, folder, or type through the use of a filter. We'll get to importing and exporting Java Archive (JAR) files and Javadoc in Chapter 3, Using Java Development Tools.

## Moving Resources

We've discussed creating and deleting projects, folders, and files. You may also find you need to move files and folders between projects and other folders. To move a file or folder or a group of them, from the Navigator view select the source resources and select **Cut** or **Copy** from the context menu. Select the target project or folder in the Navigator view and select **Paste** from its context menu. Drag and drop works quite nicely as well. If the resources you're moving are being managed in Eclipse by a repository, depending on how the provider integrated the repository, the integration may place restrictions on how you can move resources around. You should consult your repository's documentation.

As your use of Eclipse increases, you will encounter additional types of projects. For example, Eclipse includes a Java project definition. Other Eclipse-based tools define Web projects. Moving resources between projects of different types is possible, but you need to be aware of the effects. Different types of projects maintain different kinds of information about the resources they contain. Moving resources between different types of projects can cause some of this information to be lost. For example, if you move resources from a Java project to a simple, or "regular," project, information specific to Java projects is discarded.

Moving projects means moving them between workspaces. One way to do this is to import an existing project definition from one workspace to another. Recall that the files making up the project do not move. This is the easiest way, but it means your work will not be moved to the new location. If you want the project you are moving to be physically located in the new workspace, first copy the folder representing the project and its contents from their location in the original workspace to the workspace folder for the destination workspace. Then select to import an existing project and select the folder representing the project in the workspace folder of the destination workspace (the one you're importing into).

When dealing with large projects on a large scale, the best way to share projects is through an SCM repository. We'll get to this in Chapter 5.

## Text Editor

The Eclipse text editor is a standard editor for text-based files (see Figure 2.27). While not especially flashy, it serves a valuable purpose. Editors (programs) are associated with files by file type. Eclipse maintains this association in addition to what is maintained by most operating systems. In the absence of any program associated with a file type, either by Eclipse or by the operating system, the text editor is used. This is useful, for example, when examining .project files and Java .classpath files. Many of the capabilities we'll discuss next for the text editor are available more broadly in other Eclipse editors, such as the Java editor. These include incremental find (see below), quick diff, and the overview and vertical rulers.

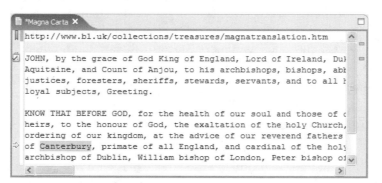

**Figure 2.27** Text Editor

The text editor has standard capabilities, including an unlimited **Undo** (**Ctrl+Z**) and **Redo** (**Ctrl+Y**). Select **Edit** from the menu bar to see all of the text editor's keyboard shortcuts. Press **Ctrl+F** to see the Find/Replace dialog. **Edit > Find Next** and **Find > Previous**, or **Ctrl+K** and **Ctrl+Shift+K**, respectively, find the next and previous occurrences of the last string you searched for. One notable capability is **incremental find**. To use this, select **Edit >**

**Incremental Find Next** or press **Ctrl+J**. In the message area, you'll see a prompt. Begin typing a string; you'll see the string in the message area and the first match selected in the editor. Press **Ctrl+J** to find the next occurrence or **Ctrl+Shift+J** to find the next previous occurrence.

The left margin of the editor is the marker bar. The right margin is the overview ruler. On these appear things like tasks, bookmarks, and search results (see Figure 2.27). The key feature of the overview ruler is that the length of the ruler you see represents the complete file being edited. This provides a convenient way to jump to annotated parts of the file without excessive scrolling. How these various annotations appear is defined by your **Workbench > Editors > Annotations** preferences.

### Quick Diff—Real-Time Change Notification

The Eclipse text and Java editors provide a "quick diff" capability to enable you to quickly identify the differences between the version of the file you're editing and the reference version of the file (either the latest in your repository if you're using one, or the version on disk). The mechanism is a thin ruler on the left margin of the editors, just inside the marker bar. New lines are marked in gray-blue, changed lines in lilac, deleted lines as a dark bar. In Figure 2.27, you can see markings on the quick diff ruler indicating changes. Hover over the color indicator to see the lines as they are in the reference version of the file. You can back out any of the changes by right-clicking on the change indicator on the quick diff ruler and then selecting an entry from the context menu, such as **Revert Block** or **Revert Line**. Quick diff preferences are located with your **Workbench > Editor > Quick Diff** preferences. This includes the file version used as the baseline for the quick diff.

### File Encoding

Prior to Eclipse 3.0, file encoding (e.g., ASCII or UTF-8) was a global preference, making it very difficult to manage files with different encodings. This setting is now file specific. You can set a file's encoding while you are editing the file by selecting **Edit > Encoding** and then selecting the encoding. To enable the encoding selections, you first must save any changes you made to the file.

### Printing

Eclipse has basic printing support that's available from the toolbar or by selecting **File > Print…**. This is an invocation of the operating system's print function with the file in the active editor.

# Customizing Eclipse

As a general-purpose development environment for both programming and nonprogramming tasks, the Eclipse designers recognized the need for comprehensive customization as Eclipse users have different skills, different levels of ability, and very different tasks to perform. To provide a common environment in which a variety of people could work requires that most aspects of the environment be customizable. We've already seen some of this capability in preferences and the ability to add, remove, and move views. There's more. In this section, we'll look at additional ways you can customize Eclipse to meet your needs and work habits.

## Perspectives

Previously, we saw how to add and delete views, resize them, and move them around. In effect, you were modifying an instance of the Resource perspective. Configurations of open perspectives are remembered so that when you close and restart Eclipse, it restores the perspectives as they had been. These changes, though, are temporary in that they apply only to the open instance of a perspective. If you close a perspective you've changed and open it again, you will see its original configuration.

You can create your own perspective customized for the way you work. Change the perspective you're working in by adding views you need and organizing the views the way you like them. Then select **Window > Save Perspective As...** and give it a name. Now when you select **Window > Open Perspective**, your customized perspective appears on the list. **Window > Reset Perspective** restores a perspective to its original configuration.

You can customize other things in addition to which views your customized perspective has and their configuration. To do this, select **Window > Customize Perspective...**, which opens the Customize Perspective dialog (see Figure 2.28).

The Customize Perspective dialog has two pages. On the Shortcuts page, which you can see in Figure 2.28, you specify which items you want to appear on the **File > New**, **Window > Open Perspective**, and **Window > Show View** submenus. Selecting an entry in one of these first three categories causes the entry to show up in the short list; that is, the user can find the entry without having to first select **Other...**. Select the submenu from the pull-down on the left and then in the right pane, check the shortcuts you want to appear on the selected submenu. On the **Commands** page, shown in Figure 2.29, you specify the items you want to appear on the menu bar and the toolbar. The items are organized by groups in the left pane. Select a group

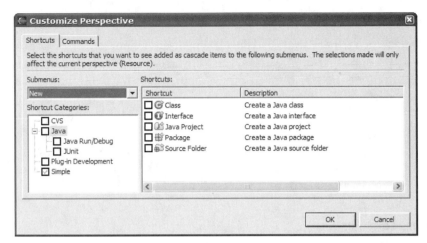

**Figure 2.28**   Customize Perspective Dialog

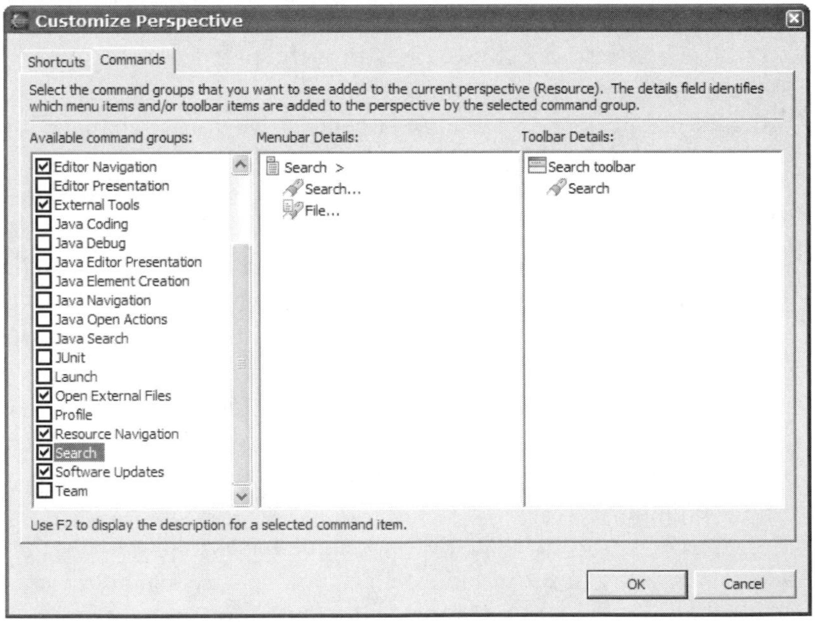

**Figure 2.29**   Customizing Perspective Commands

to see the menu bar items (middle pane) and toolbar items (right pane) that would be added. Add them by checking the group in the left pane. To make these changes permanent so that they'll apply every time you open a new instance of the perspective, save the changes by selecting **Window > Save Perspective As...**.

When you create a new project, the default Eclipse behavior is to open a new instance of the default perspective for the project. Your **Workbench > Perspectives** preferences allow you to change this as well as other settings for opening and switching perspectives. Changing your default perspective is especially useful if you've created your own customized perspective. To do so, select your perspective from the list and then select **Make Default**.

### Progressive Disclosure

With the increasing adoption of Eclipse and the growth in number and function of Eclipse-based offerings, integrating a number of functionally rich offerings in one Eclipse installation can make the user interface very busy and potentially confusing. There can be simply too much to efficiently navigate. Eclipse provides a mechanism for this that enables a progressive disclosure of function (manifested through, e.g., menu entries, toolbar buttons, New wizard entries). In the base Eclipse SDK, this progressive disclosure is limited because all the function provided is pretty fundamental. You can customize progressive disclosure through your **Workbench > Capabilities** preferences. As you work with other Eclipse-based offerings, you will see more of this progressive disclosure. For example, you might create a certain type of project, and in doing so, you cause additional function to be disclosed specific to that project.

### Running Multiple Eclipse Windows and Workspaces

You can open a new window by selecting **Window > New Window**. Eclipse can open a new window for you when you open a new perspective. Set this in your **Workbench > Perspectives** preferences. In each of these cases, both windows use the same workspace. Activity in one is reflected in the other. For example, if you create a new resource in one window, you will see it appear in the other. If you have editors open in both windows on the same file, changes in one window will be reflected in the other. Filtering, however, is specific to a window. This means you can have multiple windows open on the same workspace and have different filters defined to have different resources appear in the windows. For example, you can define working sets to partition the different projects you're working on, open multiple Eclipse windows, and then use a different working set filter for each window.

Eclipse can run concurrently on different workspaces. You may choose multiple workspaces simply to make it easier to manipulate the resources in your workspace or to keep your work on different projects separate (perhaps for different customers or for different versions of the same project). In addition to personal preferences, there are performance considerations as the number of resources in your workspace grows. We'll get to this in the Performance subsection later in this chapter.

When you start Eclipse, you see a dialog prompting you for the workspace you want to use with this Eclipse session (see Figure 2.30). The default workspace location is folder workspace under the main Eclipse folder. Select the default or select **Browse...** to browse for another workspace folder or create a new one. What shows up on the drop-down list is simply a list of previous selections from this dialog. Only one Eclipse instance can be running on a workspace at any one time.

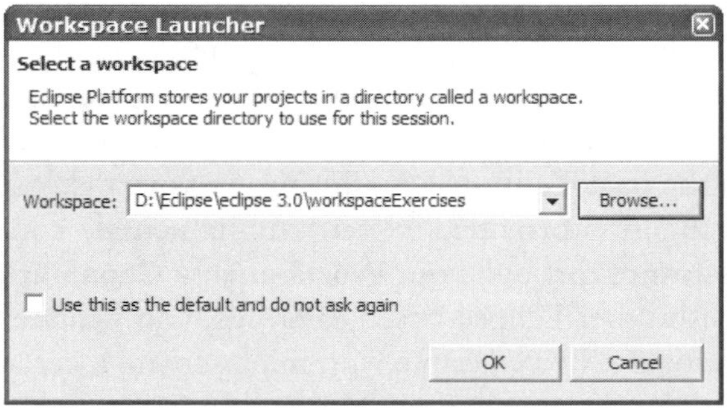

**Workspace Launcher**

**Select a workspace**

Eclipse Platform stores your projects in a directory called a workspace.
Select the workspace directory to use for this session.

Workspace: D:\Eclipse\eclipse 3.0\workspaceExercises     Browse...

☐ Use this as the default and do not ask again

OK     Cancel

**Figure 2.30**   Workspace Launcher Dialog

By default, the prompt will remember the last five workspaces used. This can be tweaked if you search a bit. The data is kept in the following file:

```
\configuration\org.eclipse.ui.ide\recentWorkspaces.xml
```

This number of remembered workspaces is specified by the following line. If you need more workspaces remembered, increase the value.

```
<recentWorkspaces maxLength="5">
```

There is also a command line parameter that specifies the workspace to be used, the -data command line parameter. Specify it with the workspace location. The location can be absolute or relative to the main Eclipse folder. When you use the –data parameter, the Workspace Launcher dialog does not appear. If you have multiple Eclipse instances running on different workspaces, to make it easy to tell which workspace a window refers to, use the –showlocation parameter (see Figure 2.31).

For example, to start a workspace in folder workspaceExercises, open a command prompt and enter the following command.

```
eclipse -data workspaceExercises -showlocation
```

**Figure 2.31**    Showing the Workspace Location

If no workspace exists at the location, one is created. In this case, the workspace location will be in folder workspaceExercises under the main Eclipse folder. Given the default workspace location is the folder workspace, if you prefix all your workspace names with workspace, the folders will be listed together under the main Eclipse folder. If you did not use –showlocation when you started Eclipse, you can determine the location of a workspace by selecting **Properties** from the context menu on a resource and reading the **Info page** content. The physical location on the file system is included on the Info page.

When you use multiple workspaces, the information Eclipse maintains about its configuration, the resources you have defined, and your preferences are specific to each workspace. Changes in one workspace are not reflected in others. If you have preference settings you like, you can export them from one workspace and then import them into others. You might also consider the following options for improved management and access.

- Create multiple shortcuts for eclipse.exe with different customized parameters.
- Create a folder with shortcuts to your different workspaces. If your projects are physically located in the workspace, you will find them faster and can use the shortcut to search the full workspace/project file system tree.
- Consider adding all workspaces to the same higher-level directory. If you need to back them up they are easy to find this way.

### *Changing Keyboard Shortcuts*

Eclipse provides a great deal of flexibility in keyboard shortcuts, including a configuration or Emacs. These are your **Workbench > Keys** preferences. You can define your own configuration or add a shortcut or two to the default Eclipse configuration (see Figure 2.32).

To define your own keyboard shortcut, first select an action to associate with a shortcut. Select a **Category** and then an action (under **Name**), in the **Command** section. Tab to the **Key Sequence** section. Press a key sequence, for example, **Alt+Shift** plus some character. Watch as the **Key Sequence Name** field reflects your choice. If there is an existing assignment for the key

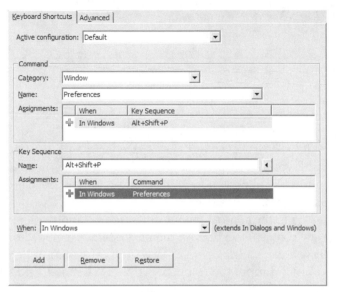

**Figure 2.32**   Keyboard Shortcut Preferences

sequence, you'll see it show up in **Key Sequence Assignments**. Select **Add** to define your shortcut. In Figure 2.32, you can see a new shortcut that associates **Alt+Shift+P** with **Window > Preferences**. By default, your definitions will be global. If you want to restrict your shortcuts to specific activities, for example, debugging, use the **When:** field.

### Customizing Your JRE

When you start Eclipse, it first looks for a Java JRE in the folder JRE in the main Eclipse folder. If it does not find a JRE there, then it looks for one known to your operating system. This search policy allows you to associate different JREs with different Eclipse installations, something that may be required by different Eclipse-based offerings. If Eclipse cannot find a JRE, you will see the error message shown earlier in Figure 2.2.

If you have a JRE installed in your system, you can direct Eclipse to it with the –vm parameter. When you do this, the JRE search is bypassed. For example, on a Windows system, you could enter:

```
eclipse -vm E:\Java\IBM\Java142\jre\bin\javaw.exe
```

To specify the JRE and open a Java console to see any directed output, use java.exe instead of javaw.exe.

```
eclipse -vm E:\Java\IBM\Java142\jre\bin\java.exe
```

You can pass parameters to the Java Virtual Machine (JVM) in your JRE by invoking `eclipse.exe` with the -vmargs parameter. The JVM arguments, but not the –vmargs parameter itself, are passed directly to the JVM. If you use the –vmargs parameter, make it the last parameter you specify. Any parameters that follow are passed to the JVM and are not processed by Eclipse when it starts up.

## Using Other Computer Programs with Eclipse

One of the key design points of Eclipse was to provide for integration with other computer programs. This is why the files you have defined in your projects are maintained on the file system, in a form that can be used by other computer programs. While programs built on Eclipse provide the tightest and most seamless integration, you can use just about any computer program with Eclipse. There are two ways to do this: You can associate a program with a file type as an editor, or you can define a program as an external tool or a builder.

### File Type Associations

Eclipse associates editors with file types. You can add, delete, and modify these associations to change the editors invoked when you open files, for example, from the Navigator view. Note that doing this affects only Eclipse file type associations, not the file type associations your operating system manages. You do this with your **Workbench > File Associations** preferences. Figure 2.33 shows the default file associations with one added, associating WinZip with file extension *.zip, a very useful new association.

The defined file types appear in the upper pane. Select one of these to see the editors and other programs defined for it in the bottom pane. The definitions here show up on the list of editors when you select **Open With** from the context menu in the Navigator view.

You can add a program to a file type and then define new file types and associate programs with them. To add a program to an existing file type, select the file type and then select **Add...** for **Associated editors**. This displays the Editor Selection dialog. Select from the list of Eclipse editors or other programs defined on your computer.

To associate a program with a file type not defined, first define the file type by selecting **Add...** for **File types** and entering a file type, for example, *.jar. Then add the editor association. Some file compression programs, for example, WinZip, work on JAR files. Define a file type for *.jar files and associate a program with the file type to make it easy to view their contents.

**Figure 2.33**   File Association Preferences

Recall that when you open a file with an editor, Eclipse remembers the last editor you used when working on that file. When you define a new program for a file type and you have previously edited files of this type, the previous editors will be used and not the new program you defined. To use the new editor, edit the file with **Open With** and select the editor. Eclipse will then remember this choice.

As we saw earlier, if a file you select to edit does not have an associated editor, your operating system associations are used. You may still want to add these operating system program associations to Eclipse for two reasons. First, doing so causes the program to appear on the **Open With** list. Second, doing so causes programs that are OLE document editors to be opened in their own window and not in the editor pane. When a file is opened with an OLE document editor in the editor pane, it always marks the file as having been changed. When you define the same program to the file type as an associated editor and you edit it, the file is not marked as changed.

When you use a program defined as an editor through a file association and you change and save the file, you still need to refresh this file in your workspace. You also need to do this if you use the program to create a new file in your workspace, for example, with **Save As....** Recall that you can do this automatically by enabling **Refresh workspace on startup** in your **Work-**

bench > **Startup and Shutdown** preferences or with **Refresh Workspace automatically** in your **Workbench** preferences. Or, you can refresh manually by selecting one or more resources in the Navigator view and then **Refresh** from the context menu.

## External Tools

**External tools** are computer programs that are not specifically designed to be used with Eclipse but that you define to invoke from Eclipse. External tools have some nice features. You can pass information from your workspace, have the tool output sent to the Console view, and most importantly, have your workspace refreshed when the program completes. There are many reasons you might want to define a program as an external tool. For example, you could use an external tool as a simple publishing mechanism to move files from your workspace to a Web server, or you could use an external tool to periodically back up files in your workspace. You can run Ant scripts as external tools. You run external tools from the **External Tools** pull-down menu 🔧 ▾.

To add, edit, or remove external tools definitions, select **External Tools...** from the **External Tools** pull-down menu. This displays the External Tools dialog. To create a new external tool configuration, on the left pane select **Program** and then select **New**. You're presented with several pages to specify the configuration (see Figure 2.34).

The **Main** and **Refresh** pages on the External Tools dialog are pretty much self-explanatory. You specify a name for the external tool configuration, the location of the tool (or application), its working directory, and any arguments. For **Location** and **Working Directory**, select **Variables...** to use variable values instead of direct references. The variable values include ones you have defined in your **Run/Debug > String Substitution** preferences. To pass workspace values like project and resource name and location, select **Variables...** for **Arguments**. You can select to have your workspace or parts of it refreshed when the tool finishes. You need to specify a refresh option only if your program adds, deletes, or changes resources in your workspace. The **Environment** page presents a structured way to set and append to environment variables. On the **Common** page, you can select to have your external tool configuration saved in a project in your workspace so it can be shared. Also on the **Common** page is an option to launch the program in the background. If your program is going to take a nontrivial amount of time to complete, we recommend you run it in the background so you can continue working while the external tool completes.

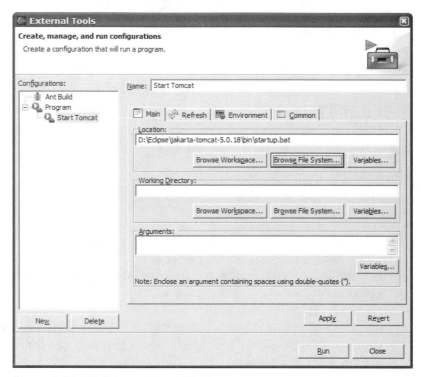

**Figure 2.34**   Defining an External Tool

## Builders

A **builder** is a program that runs when a resource changes. Builders provide a simple way for you to process resource changes in your workspace. For example, you might want to define a builder to collect statistics on the files in your projects. In Java projects, builders are used to compile Java source code. Resources in your workspace can change for a number of reasons. Files change when you edit them in an editor and save the changes. Resources change when you create or import them and when you delete them. Resources can also change when your workspace is refreshed.

You define builders for a specific project. That is, the builders for a given project—and only that project—are run when resources in only that project change. To define a builder for a project, select the project in the Navigator view, select **Properties...** from the context menu, and then select **Builders**. On the Builders page, select **New...** to create a new builder. This next dialog can be misleading. Don't type anything. Just select **Program** and then **OK**.

Defining builders is similar to configuring external tools, with a couple of exceptions (see Figure 2.35).

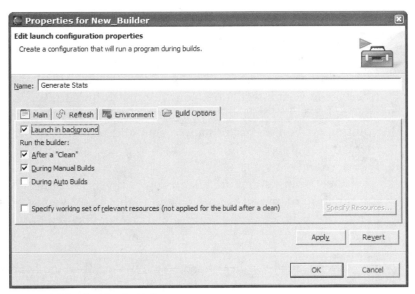

**Figure 2.35**   Builder Build Options

On the **Build Options** page, the **Run the builder** options specify two things: when the builder should run, and how it should build. When the builder runs is determined by this setting and whether or not you have the **Project > Build Automatically** menu item enabled. Starting at the bottom of the list of **Run the builder** options, **During Auto Builds** means you have **Build Automatically** enabled and Eclipse performs a build based on some explicit or implicit resource change. This can include saving a file, moving a file or folder, and importing resources. **During Manual Builds** means you have **Build Automatically** disabled and you explicitly perform a build by selecting **Project > Build All**, **Build Project**, or **Build Working Set**. In all of these cases, Eclipse builds what it needs to based on the resource changes and the results of previous builds. **Project > Clean...** discards all previous build results and builds the selected projects from scratch. So, **After a "Clean"** means this builder will run only after one of the **Clean** operations is selected. The option at the bottom of the **Build Options** page allows you to specify a set of resources, any one of which, when changed, will cause the builder to run. Finally, depending on how long the builder takes to run and how many times it will be run when your resources change, you should consider running the builder in the background by selecting **Launch in background**.

### Performance

As your use of Eclipse grows and the number of projects and their contents and interdependencies grow, or as you configure additional Eclipse-based offerings in your installation, your resource requirements, as you would expect, grow. Depending on your computer's resources, you may reach a point where you see performance begin to deteriorate. Should this happen, there are a number of things you can do to improve performance and/or reduce resource requirements.

When Eclipse starts up, it starts up as it was last shut down. Startup cost is a function of several factors related to the size of your workspace and the number of Eclipse-based offerings you have configured. You have several options for improving startup performance.

- Reduce the number of projects you have open in your workspace. You can close a project by selecting it in the Navigator view and then selecting **Close** from the context menu. Information for the project will not be loaded when Eclipse starts up. The project definition and resources remain.
- If you have selected to have your workspace refreshed on startup, disable this option in your **Workbench** preferences.
- You can partition your projects among multiple workspaces and then run multiple Eclipse workspaces with the –data and –showlocation parameters.
- If you have configured a number of Eclipse-based offerings and your work habits permit it, run multiple workspaces and configure each workspace to run a subset of the offerings. For more information on this, refer to the Chapter 6 section Update Manager—An Introduction.

## Exercise Summary

In Part VI you'll find Exercise 1, which has step-by-step instructions to illustrate much of what we've just discussed. No coding is required. The objective is to reinforce the material covered in this chapter through hands-on work. The exercise is broken down into a number of sections, each demonstrating different concepts.

1. Your First Eclipse Project

   You'll create projects, folders, and files and import files into a project.

2. Editors and Views

   You'll see how to manipulate editors and views, including moving, resizing, and stacking them. You'll reorganize the toolbar and see how to use tasks and bookmarks.

3. Working with Resources

   You'll go into more detail on working with resources, including comparing and replacing them and recovering resources you've deleted. You'll create a project outside the default workspace location.

4. Perspectives

   You'll learn how to change perspectives and customize your own.

5. Using Multiple Eclipse Windows and Workspaces

   You'll see how to run multiple Eclipse windows on the same workspace and on different workspaces.

6. Getting Assistance

   In the final section of the exercise, you'll look at using the Help system to access online information, including searching.

## Chapter Summary

This chapter provided an introduction to using Eclipse as a general-purpose development environment. It described the organization of the user interface and how to manipulate it, including resizing views and editors, stacking them, creating shortcuts, and customizing perspectives. It discussed how to run multiple windows on the same workspace and on different workspaces, and how preferences affect almost all aspects of Eclipse behavior. It covered how to create, edit, import, export, and otherwise manage resources. The chapter explained how to compare and replace resources, projects, and folders; how to recover deleted resources; and how to search your workspace and use the Help system. It described how to use other computer programs as editors and external tools, and factors that affect the performance of Eclipse.

## Reference

Arthorne, John, and Chris Laffra. 2004. *Official Eclipse 3.0 FAQs*. Boston, MA, Addison-Wesley. http://eclipsefaq.org. (See Chapter 2 and FAQs 40–43, 297, 298.)

# CHAPTER 3

## *Using Java Development Tools*

Eclipse provides a first-class set of Java Development Tools (JDT) for developing, running, and debugging Java code. These tools include perspectives, project definitions, editors, views, wizards, refactoring tools, a Java compiler, a scrapbook for evaluating expressions, search tools, and many others that make writing Java code quick, fun, and productive.

The JDT views and editors provide an efficient and effective way to quickly and intuitively navigate through your source code, view Javadoc, and even view Java class files. The editors support syntax highlighting, code assist, error cluing and correction, state-of-the-art refactoring, type-ahead assistance, and code generation, among a host of other capabilities. The Eclipse compiler is an incremental compiler; it compiles only what it must based on your changes. It can be configured with different JREs. You can develop code with one JRE and debug with another. You might want to do this, for example, if you need to support multiple JREs at runtime. In the spirit of rapid, iterative development, JDT allows you to run and debug incomplete code and code with compile errors.

The editors are more than source code editors. They build and maintain indexed information about your code, enabling you to quickly search for references to classes, methods, and packages. The incremental compiler is constantly running in the background and will discretely alert you to potential errors in your code before you save it. In many cases the JDT will propose several solutions to the problems it detects, such as adding an `import` statement that was omitted, suggesting typographical corrections, or even creating a new class or interface. This allows you to focus on your code and not be distracted by compiler demands.

In the following sections we look in more detail at the capabilities and use of the Java tools. We start with an overview of the JDT user interface and the fundamental skills you'll need for creating and navigating Java resources, that is, Java projects, input and output folders, and source code files. We then look in much more detail at JDT capabilities for coding Java: writing, searching, refactoring, and generating code. In the final sections of this chapter we peel the onion a bit more and get into further detail on working with Java resources (including more advanced Java project properties, resource local histories, and imported Java resources), tuning the performance of JDT, and using specific functions in the JDT views and perspectives that are useful but not immediately obvious.

In Part VI, we have assembled a number of exercises designed to help you perform many of these tasks and reinforce what we present. Exercise 4, Developing a Simple Web Commerce Application with Eclipse, brings together a number of the concepts and tasks you'll see in this chapter and the next in a robust example. We encourage you to take a look at these exercises.

## Getting Started with JDT

To get things going, we start with a quick overview of the JDT user interface. Then we cover the fundamentals, like opening a class and navigating to a method or field. We also provide an introduction to running a Java program. (You'll see much more on running Java programs in the next chapter.) We also discuss how to search Java code.

### Overview of the JDT User Interface

The Java perspective is the default perspective for Java development and the one opened when you create a new Java project (see Figure 3.1).

The left pane contains the Package Explorer view and the Hierarchy view (hidden behind the Package Explorer view in Figure 3.1). The Package Explorer view does for the Java perspective what the Navigator view does for the Resource perspective. Use the Package Explorer view to navigate in your Java projects, perform operations on resources, open files for editing, and run your programs. The middle pane contains open editors, Java and otherwise. An editor tab with an asterisk (*) in front of the file name means that the file has unsaved changes. The active editor is the one on top. In Figure 3.1, file `PrimeNumberGenerator.java` is open in the Java editor. The right pane is the

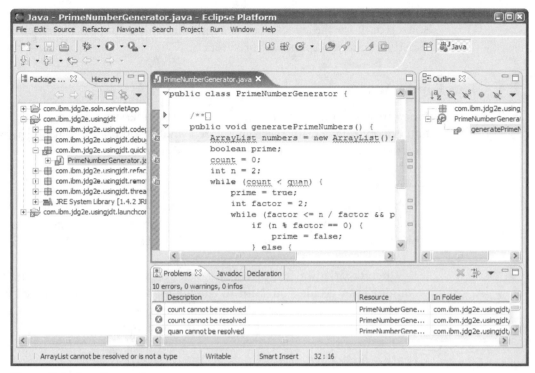

**Figure 3.1** Java Perspective

Outline view, which presents a structured, hierarchical view of the contents of the active editor. On the bottom right is the Problems view, which shows code errors. Stacked behind it are the Javadoc and Declaration views. We'll get to these shortly. As you navigate in the user interface, selecting Java files for editing and modifying Java elements, all the views and the editor stay synchronized with your actions.

The Java views display Java elements with icons to help you readily identify the element type and visibility, such as ⊞ for packages and ● for public methods. To provide further information, some of these icons are decorated with overlays, such as ● to indicate a class has a `main` method or ▲ to indicate a method overrides a method in a superclass. For a complete list of the JDT icons and decorations, refer to the "Icons" topic in the "Reference" section in the *Java Development User Guide*.

You have two options for how code appears in the editor as you navigate in the user interface. **Show Selected Element Only** ▦ on the toolbar controls this. The default is to show the contents of the entire file. If you prefer to focus on smaller portions of code, toggling this option will show the source only for the selected class, method, field, or import statement. This is mostly a matter of personal preference.

## The Fundamentals

Here are the fundamental tasks you need to understand to create and navigate through Java resources. These are available on the toolbar and as wizard shortcuts when you are in one of the Java perspectives.

### Creating a Java Project

All Java elements must exist in a Java project for the JDT to correctly recognize them as Java elements. To create a Java project, select **File > New > Project... > Java Project** from the menu or select **New Java Project** from the toolbar.

When creating Java projects and other elements, if you get the names wrong or later decide you want to change them, the JDT refactoring capabilities make it easy to rename elements and update references to them. (Refactoring is discussed in more detail later in this chapter.)

### Creating a Package

Java types, that is, classes and interfaces, must exist in a package. If you do not create one, a default package will be created for you when you create a class. To create a package, select the containing project and select **File > New > Package** from the menu or select **New Java Package** from the toolbar.

### Creating a Type

To create a type, select the containing project or package. Then you have two choices: (1) select **File > New > Class** or **File > New > Interface** from the menu, or (2) select **New Java Class** or **New Java Interface** from the toolbar.

### Opening a Type

To open a Java class or interface for editing, do one of the following.

- Double-click on a Java element, such as a source file, class, or method. Or select one of these in a view and press **F3** or **Enter**.
- From the editor, select the name of a class or interface in the source code (or simply position the insertion cursor in the name), and then select **Open Declaration** from the context menu or press **F3**.

- Select **Ctrl+Shift+T** and enter the name of a class or interface in the **Open Type** dialog.
- In the editor, press and hold the **Ctrl** key, and the names of Java classes and interfaces become hyperlinks you can click on to open the definition.

### Opening a Method or Field

To open a method or field definition for editing, do one of the following.

- Double-click on a method or field, or select a method and press **F3** or **Enter** to see its definition. You can do this from any Java view.
- From the editor, select the name of a method or field in the source code (or simply position the insertion cursor in the name), and then select **Open Declaration** from the context menu or press **F3** to see its definition.
- In the editor, press and hold the **Ctrl** key, and the names of Java methods and fields become hyperlinks you can click on to open the definition.

### Viewing Supertypes and Subtypes

To view the supertypes or subtypes for a class or interface in the Hierarchy view, do one of the following.

- Select a Java element, such as a Java source file, class, method, or field. Then from within a Java view or the editor, select **Open Type Hierarchy** from the context menu or press **F4**.
- Select **Ctrl+Shift+H** and enter the name of a class or interface in the **Open Type in Hierarchy** dialog.
- Drag a type from one of the views and drop it in the Hierarchy view.
- Select a type in the editor and then press **Ctrl+T**.

### Viewing Called Methods or Calling Methods

To view all the methods called by a given method, or all the methods that call a given method, do one of the following.

- Select a method, and then select **Open Call Hierarchy** from the context menu or press **Ctrl+Alt+H**. You can do this from any Java view.
- From the editor, select the name of a Java element in the source code (or simply position the insertion cursor in the name), and then select **Open Call Hierarchy** from the context menu or press **Ctrl+Alt+H**.
- Drag a type from one of the views and drop it in the Call Hierarchy view.

### Navigating to a Type, Method, or Field

Ensure **Link with Editor** 🔄 is enabled in your Java views, either on the toolbar or from an entry on the pull-down menu. Select a class, interface, method, or field definition in one of the views. The editor and open views scroll to your selection. If you select an element and you do not see it in an editor, it means the file containing the definition is not open. This also works in reverse: You can activate a specific editor, and the Java element will be selected in the Package Explorer view.

### Locating Elements in Projects

Opening an editor on a class with **F3** shows its source but doesn't update the Package Explorer view to show which package the class is located in. To see where a class is located in the Package Explorer view, select a Java element in the editor (or position the insertion cursor in the element name), and then select **Show in Package Explorer** from the context menu. The Package Explorer view scrolls to the selected element. Note that this works only for elements defined in the file you are currently editing.

### Running a Java Program

To run a Java program, select a class with a main method, and then select **Run > Run As > Java Application** from the menu. Output is shown in the Console view.

## *Using the JDT Views*

Like the Navigator view in the Resource perspective, the Package Explorer view in the Java perspective is the workhorse for managing your Java code. This view can fill up, and its presentation can get busy. We have two suggestions. First, consider using one or more filters to limit what appears in the view. To add filters, select **Filters...** 🔧 from the Package Explorer view pull-down menu ▼. A common choice is to select the **Referenced libraries** option. Doing this hides any libraries defined for the project, for example, the JRE libraries. Second, deselect **Link with Editor** 🔄. This prevents a lot of scrolling in the Package Explorer view.

We've mentioned the Outline, Hierarchy, and Call Hierarchy views previously. In addition to these views, you will find two others very useful, the Declaration and Javadoc views. They are part of the Java perspective. In the Java editor, if you position the cursor on a variable or method, both the Declaration and Javadoc views show information for the selected Java element. The Declaration view displays the source code, while the Javadoc view shows any associated Javadoc. This eliminates the need to chase off after the definition. This also works for view selections; when you are navigating through elements in any of the Java views, the Declaration and Javadoc views show content for the element you have selected—no need to open an editor to take a quick look at the code.

**Source > Sort Members** allows you to organize the order in which initializers, fields, and methods appear in Java views. The order is specified in your **Java > Appearance > Members Sort Order** preferences.

We saw in Chapter 2, Getting Started with Eclipse, how to compare files or different versions of the same file. Some of the same compare and replace operations are available on individual Java elements through the Java views. We'll talk about this more in Local History for Java Elements later in the current chapter.

Eclipse includes a class file editor—a viewer, really, because you can't change the contents of the class file—to allow you a limited view into a class file for which you do not have source. From one of the views, for example, the Navigator view, simply open a class file for editing.

## Searching

There are two types of searches: a general Eclipse file search for text strings, and a Java-specific search of your workspace for Java element references. The search capability uses an index of the Java code in your workspace that is kept up-to-date in the background, independent of Java builds. This means that you don't have to have your auto-build preference selected or save your modifications in order to do a search.

### Searching a File

To search the file in the active editor for any text, select **Edit > Find/Replace**, or press **Ctrl+F**. Specify the string for which you are searching or a regular expression. Eclipse also has an "incremental find" feature that provides a keystroke-efficient way to do this. Select **Edit > Incremental Find Next** from the menu or press **Ctrl+J** and note the prompt in the message area to the left on the bottom margin. Start typing the text you're searching for. The message area displays that text, and the first match is selected in the editor. Press **Ctrl+J** to find the next occurrence or **Ctrl+Shift+J** to find the previous one.

### Searching Your Workspace

Select **Search** 🔍 or press **Ctrl+H** and then select the **Java** page to search your entire workspace, or a subset of it, for references to Java elements. This searches both Java source code and Javadoc. There are three aspects to a Java search: what kind of reference, what kind of Java element, and within what scope. You can specify these by using **Limit To**, **Search For**, and **Scope**, respectively, in the Search dialog, as shown in Figure 3.2. To restrict a search, you can either select one or more Java elements in one of the Java views and then select **Search**, or you can define a working set and then specify that working set under **Scope**. (For more information on working sets, refer to the Working Sets section in Chapter 2, Getting Started with Eclipse.) For example, if you want to search for methods returning void in your projects, select **Search**, specify the **Search string** as * void, select **Search For Method** and **Limit To Declarations**, select **Workspace**, and then select the **Search** button (or press **Enter**).

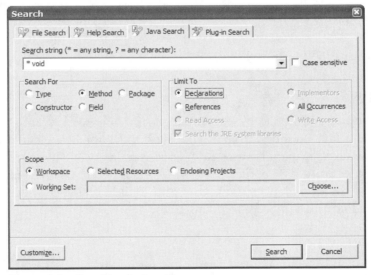

**Figure 3.2**   Searching for Java Elements

Java search results are shown in the Search view (see Figure 3.3). Matches are indicated in the editor with entries on the marker bar. You can filter the search results by selecting one of the available filters from the Search view pull-down menu ▼. For example, you can filter out Javadoc comments, read accesses, and write accesses this way. Navigate to matches from the Search view by double-clicking an entry or by selecting **Show Next Match** ⇩ and **Show Previous Match** ⇧ from the Search view toolbar. You can also use **Next Annotation** ⤓ or **Ctrl+.** and **Previous Annotation** ⤒ or **Ctrl+,** from

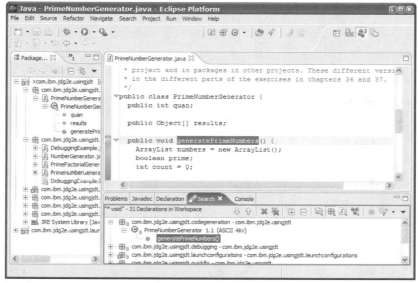

**Figure 3.3** Search View

the Eclipse toolbar to navigate matches within the active editor. First select to use the annotation navigation buttons to match **Search Results** with the pull-down menu on either of the buttons.

In all of the JDT views, including the Search view and the editor, you can select a Java element or search result entry and then search on that element from the context menu by selecting one of the **References** or **Declarations** submenu choices. This ability to successively search for Java elements from the views, especially the Type Hierarchy and Search views, provides a simple, efficient way to explore and understand Java code.

## Writing Java Code

Now that you've seen how to create and navigate Java resources, let's get to what we get paid for, writing Java. The Java editor provides a wealth of functions to help you write Java code more efficiently with greater productivity and, quite frankly, more fun. Among the capabilities provided by the Java editor are code assist for Java expression completion, code generation, real-time error detection, quick fix remedies for coding errors, Javadoc generation, and the ability to work with different JREs.

## Overview of the Java Editor

The organization of the Java editor pane is straightforward and similar to other editors (see Figure 3.4).

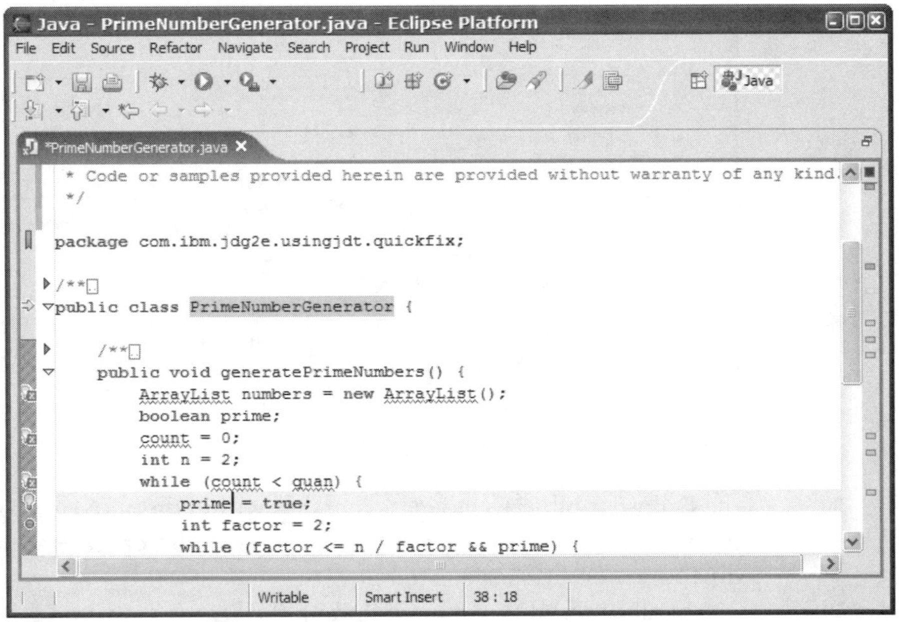

**Figure 3.4**    Java Editor

On the left border is the **marker bar**, which shows tasks 🗒, bookmarks 🔖, compiler errors ⊗, quick fixes 🔧, quick assists 💡, and overridden methods ▲. The marker bar also is shaded to indicate the scope in the file of the type, field, or method you're editing. In Figure 3.4, the `generatePrime-Numbers` method is being edited. Just inside this is the **quick diff ruler** that indicates, through shading, changes to the file you are editing. (We discussed this in Chapter 2, Getting Started with Eclipse, in the section Quick Diff—Real-Time Change Notification.) To the right of the quick diff ruler is a ruler that shows markers for sections of code that can be folded or expanded to allow more efficient viewing. Click on an icon to expand or fold a section of code. Hover over an icon indicating a folded section of code to see a pop-up with the code (see Figure 3.5). Settings for enabling folding and what gets folded are available in your **Java > Editor** preferences on the **Folding** page.

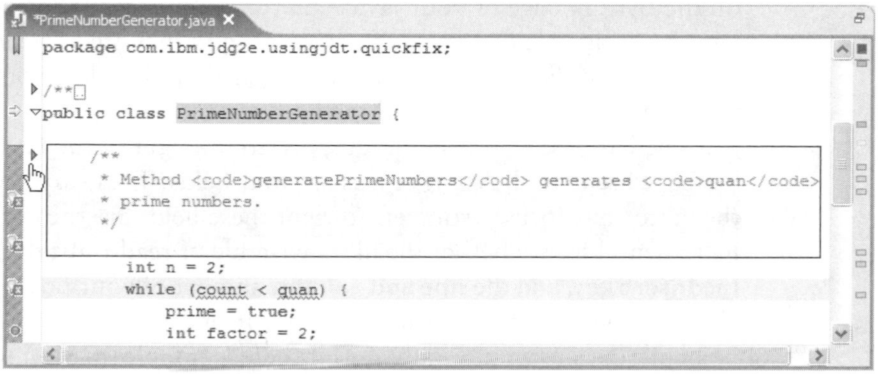

**Figure 3.5**   Viewing Folded Code

The right margin is the **overview ruler**, which includes color-coded marks that indicate where errors, warnings, bookmarks, tasks, and search match annotations are located in the file. This navigation aid helps you quickly scroll to annotations that are currently not visible. Simply click on one of the marks. At the top of the overview ruler, a red rectangle appears if errors are present in the file. A yellow rectangle indicates warnings. Hover over this to get a count of the errors or warnings in the file.

You can configure the annotations that appear on the marker bar and the overview ruler with your **Workbench > Editors > Annotations** preferences. If there are multiple annotations for a line, so that they overlay each other, hover over the group to see all of them shown next to each other. Navigate through the annotations with **Next Annotation** (**Ctrl+.**) or **Previous Annotation** (**Ctrl+,**). Use the toolbar drop-down menu to specify which annotations you navigate to.

The editor is, as you would expect, completely integrated. This means Java views, such as Type Hierarchy, Outline, and Declaration, update in real time as you type in the editor. Just as you can with a view, double-click on the editor title bar to maximize the editor. The editor allows a great deal of customization. There are many preferences you can use to customize behavior. Be sure to look at these. For example, you can configure which rulers are shown, how annotations (errors, tasks, search occurrences) appear in the code and on the rulers, and how your code should be formatted. The behavior of the editor, for the most part, is specified in your **Java > Editor** preferences. **Workbench > Editors** also has some general editor preferences. You can set fonts in **Workbench > Colors and Fonts**. The JDT provides a more advanced set of color highlighting, which is not enabled by default. Enable it on the **Syntax** page of your **Java > Editor** preferences. The advanced highlighting adds specific settings for abstract and inherited method invocations, constants and fields, local variable references and declarations, parameter variables, and static fields and method invocations.

The left of the bottom margin, just to the right of the **fast view bar**, is the **message area**. To the right of this are four fields. These are shown only when the editor has focus. From left to right these fields are the current target of incremental find, whether the file is writable or read-only, the toggle status of the **Insert** key, and the line and column number of your position in the editor. The message area and the area for the current target of incremental find will be blank (as shown in Figure 3.4) if there is no information to display. The right of the bottom margin is the **progress area**, for information about background processing. (See Overview of the User Interface in Chapter 2 for more information on the fast view bar, the message area, and the progress area.)

The editor provides virtually unlimited undo/redo capability through **Edit > Undo** and **Edit > Redo**, or **Ctrl+Z** and **Ctrl+Y**, respectively. You can see other keyboard shortcuts by examining the menu items on the menu bars. If there are keyboard shortcuts, they are listed with the menu item. Recall that you can define your own keyboard shortcuts with your **Workbench > Keys** preferences. Format your code by selecting **Source > Format** or by pressing **Ctrl+Shift+F**. You can also select a Java project, source folder, or package and select **Source > Format** to format all the contained Java source files. JDT provides multiple formatting options and the ability for you to customize your own formatter. Refer to your **Java > Code Style > Code Formatter** preferences.

The Java editor provides a good deal of information through hover help. This works for all types of annotations in the editor and on the marker bar and overview ruler. Hover over a Java element and you'll see its Javadoc. If there is more Javadoc than fits in the pop-up window, press **F2** to anchor the pop-up and then scroll. Press **Ctrl** and hover, and you'll see the element's source. When you have **Ctrl** pressed, the element source changes to a hyperlink that you can click on to open the element in an editor. Figure 3.6 shows both the hyperlink display, mouse indication of the link, and the source hover help. Position your cursor in the parameters for a method invocation to see parameter hints. If there are multiple parameters, the editor will highlight the type of the parameter you are editing.

Select a method, type, or package reference and then press **Ctrl+T**. You'll see a quick type hierarchy view in a pop-up. For types, this is a type hierarchy. For methods, this is a hierarchy of all implementers. Successively press-

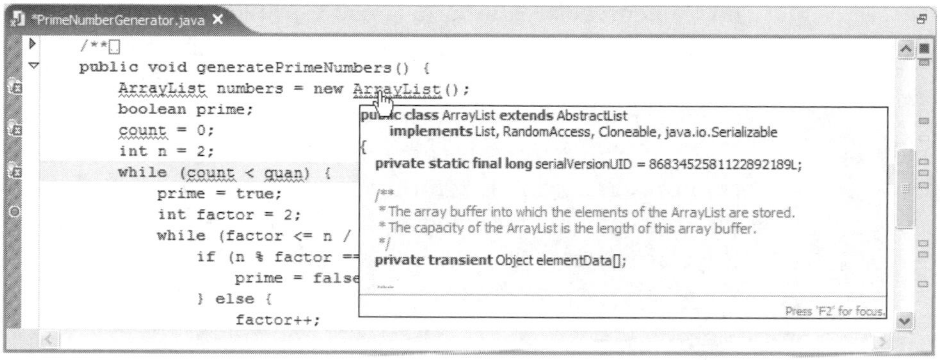

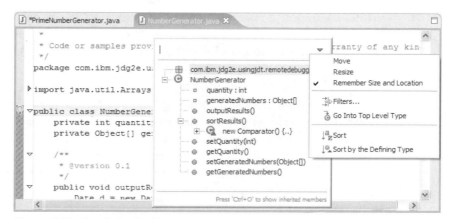

**Figure 3.6**   Hovering for Element Source

ing **Ctrl+T** toggles between subtype and supertype hierarchies. Select **Ctrl+O** to see a quick outline view in a pop-up. Successively pressing **Ctrl+O** toggles the display of inherited members. Figure 3.7 shows a quick outline view. In these pop-ups, you can navigate through the entries, select one, and press **Enter** to open it in the editor. At the top of the view, begin typing, and only those elements matching the string you typed are shown. One advantage of using these pop-ups to view hierarchies and outlines is that you do not need to keep the respective views open, and hence you can free up real estate in your Eclipse window. Or you can work for a while with the editor in full-screen mode and use the outline pop-up to navigate as required. Try it—this can be very effective depending on the task at hand.

**Figure 3.7**   Quick Outline View

When you're editing Java code, you'll often find it useful to quickly see all occurrences of references to a field, constant, method, type, local variable, or exception. Position the insertion cursor on one of these items in the Java file you're editing to see other references to the same item highlighted (see Figure 3.8). Enable this capability by toggling **Mark Occurrences** 🔍. Position the cursor on the return type of a method to see all the method exit points highlighted. Likewise, position the cursor on an exception to see all the places where that exception is thrown highlighted.

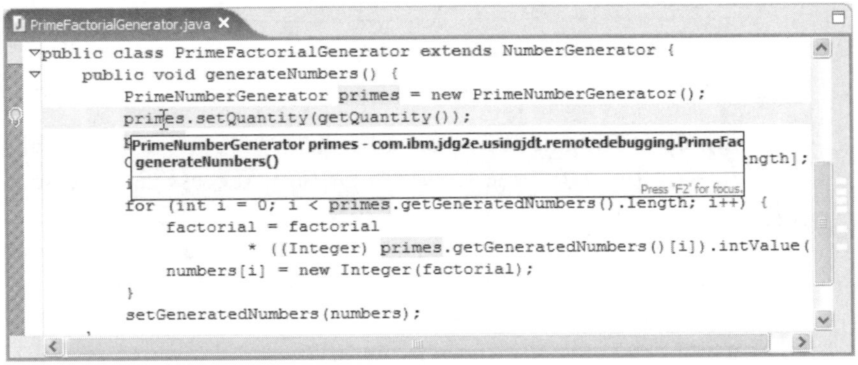

**Figure 3.8**   Viewing All Occurrences of a Java Item

To see the full Javadoc for an element, select the element in the editor or one of the views and press **Shift+F2**. In order to see Javadoc for your JRE, be sure to set the **Javadoc URL** for your JRE in your **Java > Installed JREs** preferences. To associate Javadoc with a JAR file, select the JAR file on the **Libraries** page of the **Java Build Path** properties on a project. Expand the entry, select **Javadoc location**, and then select **Edit…**. To see full Javadoc in a browser for your code, set the **Javadoc Location** property for your projects. We'll get to generating Javadoc for your Java projects later in this chapter.

Comment and uncomment a line or block of code quickly with **Source > Toggle Comment, Add Block Comment**, and **Remove Block Comment**. The keyboard shortcuts are **Ctrl+/, Ctrl+Shift+/,** and **Ctrl+Shift+\**, respectively. Move the current line, or multiple lines when they have been selected, up or down in the editor with **Alt+Up Arrow** or **Alt+Down Arrow**.

Many of the code generation, block comment, and refactoring operations require a valid Java expression to be selected (we'll discuss refactoring in a moment). Finding a complete logical expression can be at times difficult and/or tedious. Eclipse makes this easy. Place the cursor anywhere in your code, press **Alt+Shift,** and then press an arrow key (**Up**, **Right**, **Left**, and **Down**) to select logical expressions. These are the shortcuts for **Edit > Expand Selection To**, with the options **Enclosing Element**, **Next Element**, **Previous Element**, and **Restore Last Selection**, respectively.

If you attempt to add an import statement and the type or package you want to import does not appear in the dialog, it means you need to add the declaration to your project's **Java Build Path** properties. We'll see how to do this later in this chapter in the Java Projects section.

We saw in Chapter 2, Getting Started with Eclipse, how you can compare different files or different versions of the same file. We'll see in Local History for Java Elements, later in the current chapter, how JDT adds to this for individual Java elements. These are versions of a file that you have saved.

The quick diff ruler indicates changes you've made to the file in your current editing session. This is a lighter-weight, real-time comparison that doesn't rely just on what's in a code repository. It can compare edits that have not been saved yet with those already on disk or those in a code repository. If you don't see this bar, be sure you've enabled it with your **Workbench > Editors > Quick Diff** preferences. Color coding indicates whether the lines are new, changed, or deleted. Hover over an entry on the quick diff ruler to see what has changed. Use the context menu from the quick diff ruler to revert one of more of the changes. In the preferences, you can select to have the reference for the changes be the current file in your workspace or the latest edition in a CVS repository. (We'll discuss using CVS in Chapter 5, Teaming Up with Eclipse.) You can then configure the **Next Annotation** 🔽 and **Previous Annotation** 🔼 buttons to navigate to the quick diff changes in your file.

In Chapter 2, we presented tasks and bookmarks and how you could use them to mark files and track work. Your Java source is stored in files, so obviously tasks and bookmarks work as we described on your Java files. You can also embed tasks in Java comments through special tags. The default tags configured are TODO, FIXME, and XXX; these are common terms or identifiers used in open source projects. You can customize these tags, create your own tags, and assign priorities in your **Java > Task Tags** preferences. These task tags have many applications. For example, you could define tags of JOHN or DENISE for team members to record tasks, for example, //JOHN -- check this, and //DENISE -- need doc here.

## Typing Assistance

As you begin to edit Java source, you will notice that the JDT automatically completes some kinds of typing for you. For example, by default, JDT will close parentheses and braces and put closing quotes on strings. When this occurs, use the **Tab** key to skip past the inserted text to continue typing. The visual clue that you can do this is the green vertical line that indicates where the cursor will jump if you press the **Tab** key. Modify the settings for the kind of assistance you get in your **Java > Editor** preferences on the **Typing** page.

JDT enables you to quickly find a matching brace or parenthesis. Simply position the insertion cursor right after a brace or parenthesis, and its mate will be marked by an enclosing rectangle (see Figure 3.9). To adjust the color of the matching braces indicator, as well as many other things, edit your **Appearance color options** section on the **Appearance** page of the **Java > Editor** preferences.

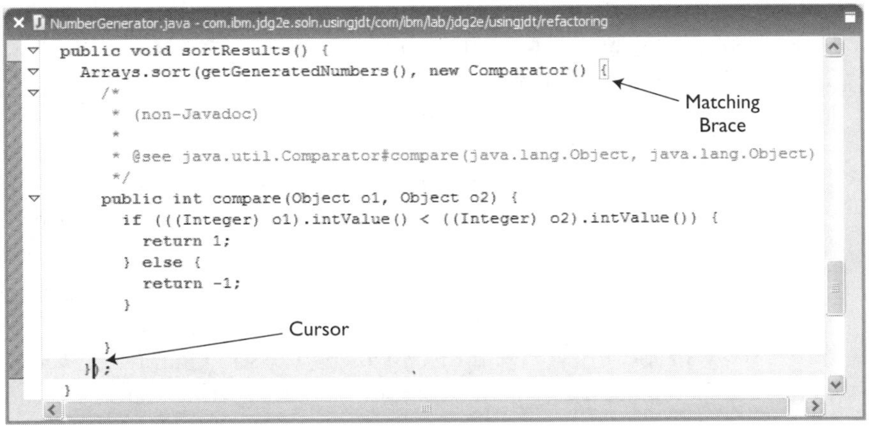

**Figure 3.9**   Matching Braces and Parentheses

**Quick assist** is a kind of typing assistance that anticipates your needs based on your editing context and location. As you navigate through your editing session, if the JDT has a proposed quick assist, you'll see a marker 💡 on the marker bar. You need to enable this in your **Java > Editor** preferences on the **Appearance** page. Select **Light bulb for quick assists**. Click on the marker or press **Ctrl+1** and you'll see a pop-up with possible assists. Scroll through the proposed assists in the first pane. The corresponding change will display in the second pane (see Figure 3.10). To accept a suggestion, select it and press **Enter**.

The JDT includes a framework for spell-checking your code comments. There are some convenient exclusions, for example, for Internet addresses and words in all caps. Spell-checking is not enabled by default, and you need to configure it with a dictionary. To enable and configure this, edit your **Java > Editor > Spelling** preferences. The preferences are more or less self-

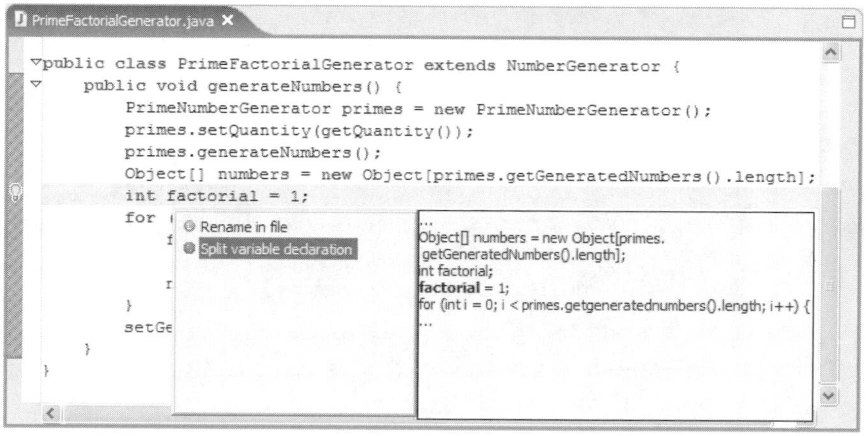

**Figure 3.10** Quick Assist Suggestions

explanatory. The dictionary Eclipse needs is simply a flat text file with a list of words. There are several online sources for word lists. Check out http://wordlist.sourceforge.net/.

In the next two sections, we'll see additional assistance the JDT provides for editing Java code—code assist and code generation—including the use of user-customizable templates.

## Code Assist

As you edit Java code, you can press **Ctrl+Space** to see phrases that complete what you were typing. This is done based on an ongoing analysis of your Java code as you edit it. You can do this for both Java source and Javadoc. For example, to quickly enter a reference to class `ArrayIndexOutOfBounds-Exception`, type `arr`, press **Ctrl+Space**, continue typing `ayi` to narrow the list to that class, and press **Enter**. The complete reference is inserted. **Code assist** can also be activated automatically by setting this preference on the **Code Assist** page of the **Java > Editor** preferences. Automatic invocation works based on a character activation trigger and a delay. The default activation trigger for Java is the period (.), and for Javadoc it's the "at" sign (@). If you type the activation trigger character as you are entering Java source or Javadoc and then pause, code assist will display suggestions (see Figure 3.11).

The code assist pop-up lists matching code generation templates 📄 (we'll get to these shortly) and Java references on the left along with their respective icons (class, interface, and method); on the right is the proposed code for the

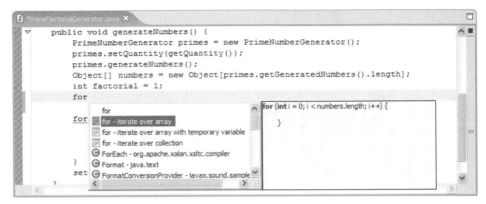

**Figure 3.11**   Code Assist Suggestions

selected item. These suggestions come from two places: Java references based on an analysis of your code and your defined code templates. Code templates match what you are typing by template name. Pressing **Enter** inserts the selected proposal.

In some cases, you can save typing if you have an idea what you want next or what the suggestion should be. Keep typing with the code assist prompt displayed, and you will see the list narrowed to match your typing. At any point, select an entry and press **Enter**. Or continue typing and when no suggestions apply, the code assist prompt will disappear. This is useful when you have automatic code assist enabled because you can choose to ignore prompts that come up by simply continuing to type what you had been typing.

To reduce the entries that appear as code assist suggestions, consider setting a **type filter**. This is a preference setting, **Java > Type Filters**, that restricts what appears in the Open Type dialog, quick assist suggestions, and quick fix suggestions. For example, if you don't want to see the Abstract Widget Set (AWT) classes, set a type filter for java.awt.*.

You can use code assist in a variety of situations, including stubs, for loops, public methods, and try/catch expressions. Take a look at the templates in your **Java > Editor** preferences on the **Templates** page to see what's available. In addition, code assist works for the following.

- *Overriding inherited methods.* Position the insertion cursor within a class definition, but outside any method, and activate code assist. You'll see a list of methods this class can override or must define based on an interface implementation.

- *Import statements*. Type `import` and begin typing the name of a package or type, and then activate code assist to see a list of types and packages.
- *Variable references*. Begin to type the name of a variable or field in an expression, and then activate code assist. It provides a list of possible references, including variables within the scope of the expression.
- *Getters and setters*. Activate code assist within the body of a type, and code assist will suggest getter and setter methods for fields lacking them.
- *Default constructors*. Code assist can present a suggestion for a default constructor for a class.
- *Anonymous inner classes*. Activate code assist within the body of an anonymous inner class and it will present a list of methods to define.
- *Javadoc*. Activate code assist in Javadoc. You can add Javadoc HTML tags and keywords. What's slick about this is that code assist can make smart suggestions based on an understanding of your code. For example, typing `@param` and then activating code assist will display a list of method argument names. Typing `@exception` and then activating code assist will display a list of exceptions a method throws.

When the JDT inserts a code stub from a template, if there were variables to substitute, the JDT makes suggestions based on the template, your Java source, and where in your Java source you are inserting the template. For example, if you use a template to insert a `for` statement to iterate over an array, and your method has an array as a local variable or parameter, the JDT will suggest this local variable or parameter is the array to use and substitute its name for the template variable.

Some assists, when they are inserted in your code, are enabled for further editing. This special editing mode is indicated with outlining and shading. For example, in Figure 3.12, a `for` loop was inserted. Values you can edit (in this case, the first `i` and `numbers`) have a border around them. Multiple instances (in this case, the additional `i`'s) are shaded. When you change one of the multiple instances, all change. There is a placeholder, a vertical line, for the body of the `for` loop. This notation makes it easy to edit the insertion and continue coding. Tab through the editable values, changing those you want, end at the insertion point for the `for` loop body, and continue your coding there. Very efficient. If you want to bypass this selective editing assistance, press **Esc** and you'll be able to edit the entire inserted expression.

Some JDT dialog entry fields are enabled for code assist. The enabled entry fields are indicated by a small light bulb annotation near the field on

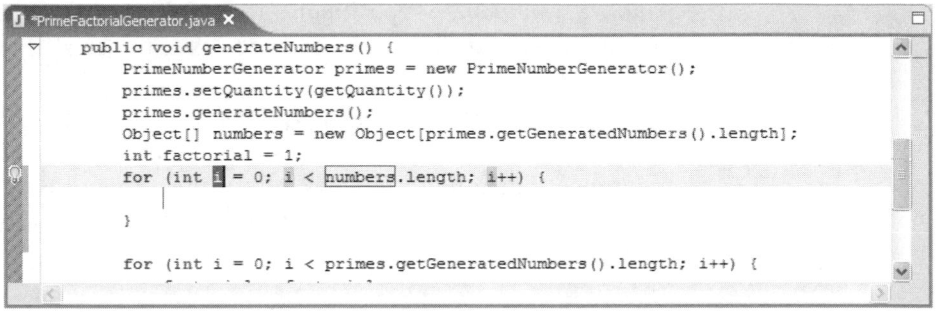

**Figure 3.12**   Code Assist

the dialog. This light bulb will not appear until you tab to the field. Position the cursor in the entry field, optionally begin typing, and press **Ctrl+Space**. In Figure 3.13, we are using code assist while creating a new Java class to help identify its package.

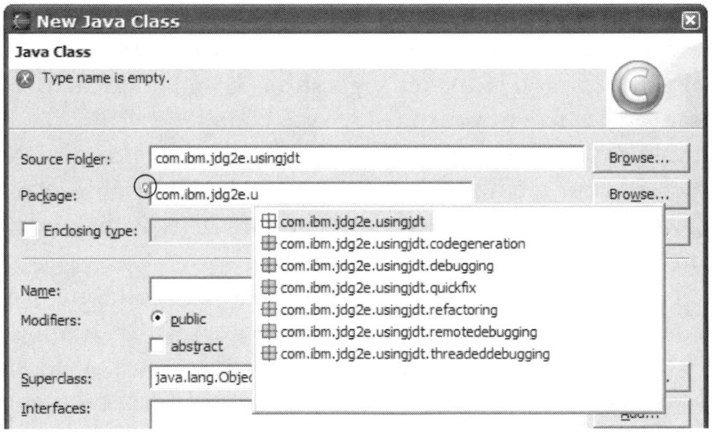

**Figure 3.13**   Code Assist in a Dialog

## Code Generation

In addition to code assist, the JDT provides other code generation capabilities. These are options available under the **Source** menu item, from the editor's context menu, or by pressing **Alt+Shift+S**. Earlier in the Overview of the Java Editor section, we showed how to generate comments and to uncomment code. This is a kind of code generation. In addition, you can generate the following types of code.

- *Import statements.* To clean up unresolved references, select **Source > Organize Imports** to add import statements and remove unneeded ones. You can also select an unresolved reference and use **Source > Add Import** to add an import statement for that reference only. The keyboard equivalents are **Ctrl+Shift+O** and **Ctrl+Shift+M**, respectively.

- *Method stubs.* Select **Source > Override/Implement Methods...** to see a list of methods to override. Select one or more to have stubs generated.

- *Getters and setters.* A quick way to create getter and setter methods is to select a field and then select **Source > Generate Getters and Setters....**

- *Delegate methods.* You can generate delegate methods for fields from the editor or any of the Java views. Delegate methods are a form of shortcut for other classes accessing fields in this class. For example, let's say you have a class Foo with a field list of type ArrayList. Further, you know most classes accessing this field are going to be inquiring about its size. Rather than have another class code aFoo.getList().size(), you could generate a delegate size method for your class for field list. To get the size of list, you would instead code aFoo.size(). Eclipse makes it easy to generate these shortcuts. From a Java view, select a type or a field, or within the editor position your cursor in the body of a type with fields, and then select **Source > Generate Delegate Methods....**

- *Try/catch statements.* If you select an expression and then **Source > Surround with try/catch block**, the code is analyzed to see if any exceptions are thrown within the scope of the selection, and try/catch blocks are inserted for each. This works well with the **Alt+Shift+Up** and **Alt+Shift+Down** expression selection actions to accurately select the code to which you want to apply try/catch blocks.

- *Javadoc comments.* You can generate Javadoc comments for classes and methods with **Source > Add Javadoc Comment**. The Javadoc is generated based on template definitions in your **Java > Templates** preferences.

- *Constructors from fields.* Create a constructor for any combination of fields by selecting **Source > Generate Constructor Using Fields....** Select the fields you want the constructor to accept as input.

- *Superclass constructors.* When you create a class, you have the option to generate constructors from its superclass. If you elect not to do this, you can come back later and add the superclass constructors with **Source > Add Constructor from Superclass....**

You can view and modify the specifications for the code and commentary the JDT generates. Customizing these preferences is useful, for example, to include a common copyright statement for all your source files. We'll see how to edit these later in this chapter in the section Using Code Templates.

## Navigating Java Errors and Warnings

The JDT can flag many different kinds of errors and warnings, including syntax errors, build path errors, unnecessary type checks, indirect access to static members, and superfluous semicolons. Errors and warnings show up in several ways (see Figure 3.14).

Errors are shown as entries in the Problems view, as markers on the marker bar, as label decorations in the views, as error clues (red underlining) in the source, and as small red and yellow rectangles on the overview ruler on the right border. A quick fix icon is displayed for errors for which the JDT can suggest a solution. We'll get to quick fix in the next section.

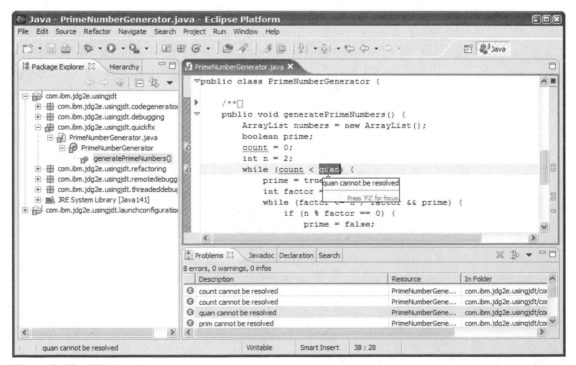

**Figure 3.14**   JDT Error Indicators

Hovering over an error indicator in the marker bar or overview ruler displays the error message. You can do the same by hovering over error text, underlined in red, within the editor. When you do this, if you want to copy the error message, press **F2** to put the focus on the pop-up, select the error message text, and then use **Ctrl+C** to copy it. Click on an error indicator in the overview ruler to cause the code in error to scroll into view and the error to be selected. Recall that because errors are annotations, you can use **Next Annotation** ⬇ (**Ctrl+.**) or **Previous Annotation** ⬆ (**Ctrl+,**) to scroll through and select errors. When you do so, the error message is displayed in the message area.

In the Problems view, double-click on an entry to go to the line in the file with the error. If the file is not open, it is opened in an editor. If the error is in the file you're currently editing, click on an entry in the Problems view to scroll the file, and select the error. If the error message is truncated in the Problems view because of the width of the column, hover over it to display the full message, or select the error to see the full text of the error in the message area.

### Fixing Java Errors with Quick Fix

For errors that have suggested corrections, you will see a quick fix icon on the marker bar 💡. You can use quick fix to correct a wide variety of problems, from spelling errors and missing import statements to declaring local variables and classes and externalizing strings. Quick fix also works on build path errors such as unresolved import statements. Click on the icon to see a list of possible solutions. You can also position the cursor within the red underlined text and then press **Ctrl+1** to display a pop-up with a list of suggestions. Select an item in the pop-up to see the proposed fix or a description. Press **Enter** to make the correction. As we described earlier in the Code Assist section, text in the inserted code is marked for quick customization. Use the **Tab** key to quickly cycle through these. This display, selection, and editing works as it does for code assist.

### Refactoring

**Refactoring** refers to a class of operations you use to reorganize and make other global changes to your code. This includes changes to Javadoc, string literals, launch configurations, and XML files that define plug-ins, called **manifest files**. We'll get to launch configurations in Chapter 4, Running and Debugging Java, and plug-in manifest files in Chapter 7, Extending Eclipse for Fun and Profit. You may need to refactor code in response to API changes, to improve maintainability, or to make naming more consistent.

To refactor your code, select a Java element in one of the views, position the insertion cursor in an element reference in the editor, or select an element or an expression in the editor. Then select **Refactor** from the menu bar or the Java editor or view context menu, or press **Alt+Shift+T**. You will see a menu with a list of possible refactorings. What appears on this list depends on your code and what you have selected. Some of the refactoring operations require a valid expression to be selected. The **Expand Selection To** menu choices and **Alt+Shift** keyboard shortcuts we discussed earlier in the Overview of the Java Editor section make this easy.

The JDT refactoring capabilities include the following.

- **Move**
  You can move Java elements and, optionally, modify references to the element being moved. This can be used for fields, methods, classes, interfaces, packages, source files, and folders.

- **Rename**
  You can rename Java elements and, optionally, modify references to the element being renamed. This can be used for fields, variables, methods, method parameters, classes, interfaces, packages, source files, and folders.

- **Pull Up**
  This moves a field or method from a class to its superclass, if possible. For example, you can't pull a method up into a class you can't modify.

- **Push Down**
  This moves a field or method to a class's subclass.

- **Extract Method**
  This creates a method from a selected code fragment, complete with parameters based on variables used in the fragment. The JDT looks for other instances of the code fragment and offers to replace them with the method invocation.

- **Change Method Signature**
  This lets you change parameter names, order, and type; exceptions thrown; and access modifiers. You can also update all references to the method being modified.

- **Extract Interface**
  Use this to create an interface based on a class definition.

- **Generalize Type**
  Select a variable, parameter, field, or method return type. This displays a view up the type hierarchy to allow you to quickly change the type of the selected element.

- **Use Supertype**
  Select a field. This replaces references to a type with references to one of its supertypes, if possible, based on use in your code.

- **Extract Local Variable**
  This creates a new variable from the selected expression and replaces all occurrences of the expression with a reference to the variable within the scope of the enclosing method.

- **Extract Constant**
  Select a literal, such as an integer or a string. This creates a static final variable and replaces all occurrences of the literal.

- **Inline**
  This does the opposite of the **Extract** actions. You can use it for method declarations, invocations, static final fields, and local variables. For example, for a method invocation, the method source is inserted inline where the method invocation had been.

- **Convert Local Variable to Field**
  This does just what it says. Start by selecting a local variable in a method.

- **Introduce Parameter**
  Within the body of a method, select a valid expression that returns something other than void. **Introduce Parameter** adds a parameter of the same type as the selected expression to the method, replaces the selected expression with the parameter, and updates invocations to the modified method. Note that you still need to update the changed method invocations to add the parameter—there's no magic here.

- **Introduce Factory**
  This marks a static constructor private and replaces it with a static factory method. Calls to the constructor are replaced with calls to the factory method.

- **Encapsulate Field**
  This goes one step beyond what **Source > Generate Getters and Setters...** does. It both generates getters and setters for a field and replaces direct references to the field with getter and setter invocations.

You can refactor by dragging and dropping Java elements in the Java views, for example, dragging a type from one package to another in the Package Explorer view, or dragging a type onto another class to create a nested type.

When you request a refactoring operation, a dialog appears (see Figure 3.15). The first page displays the minimum information needed to complete the operation. Typically this is a new name or destination and options, for example, to update references to the changed element. Specify this information and select to perform the refactoring, or select **Preview** to see what code changes would result.

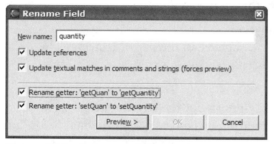

**Figure 3.15**    Refactoring Wizard

If you select to preview the proposed code changes, you'll see a side-by-side comparison (see Figure 3.16), which shows each of the changes and a before-and-after view of the code. Select the changes you want to apply by checking entries in the top pane. Navigate quickly through changes by clicking on the change entries (rectangles) on the overview ruler to the right.

To undo or redo a refactoring operation, use **Refactor > Undo** or **Refactor > Redo**, respectively. These operations are different from **Edit > Undo** and **Edit > Redo**. The refactoring undo is aware of all of the changes made across all projects; the edit undo is aware of only the changes made as a result of the refactoring operation in the active editor. When you drag and drop elements in the views to affect refactoring, the **Refactor > Undo** and **Refactor > Redo** actions are not available.

### Using Code Templates

**Templates** are outlines, or skeletons, for common Java code or Javadoc patterns. Templates allow you to quickly insert and edit code expressions with a minimum number of keystrokes. They help ensure more consistent code. Templates can contain Java or Javadoc source, variables that are substituted when

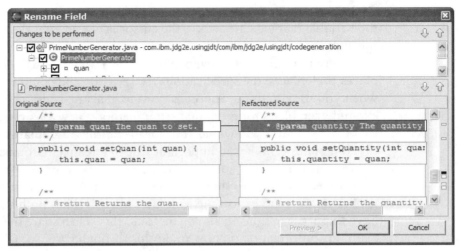

**Figure 3.16** Previewing Refactoring Changes

the template is inserted in the Java code, and a specification of where the cursor should be positioned when you've finished editing the inserted code.

It's easy to create your own templates or to modify those provided. For instance, you might add your own template with a try/catch block to invoke a special error handling routine. Or you might choose to generate a comment with the user's name and date, or add a task tag to create a task to record additional work. You create templates in your **Java > Editor > Templates** preferences. Select a template to preview it in the bottom pane. Disabling a template will cause it not to appear as a suggestion in the code assist prompt. You create and edit templates in the Edit Template dialog, shown in Figure 3.17. To insert a variable, use the **Insert Variable...** button on the dialog, or press

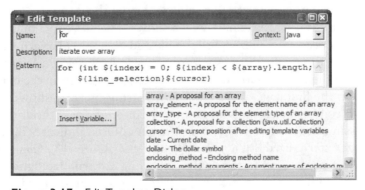

**Figure 3.17** Edit Template Dialog

**Ctrl+Space** in the **Pattern** field to see a list of possible variables. `${cursor}` is the variable that indicates where the cursor is placed after the user has tabbed through the variable fields.

There is another set of templates in your **Java > Code Style > Code Templates** preferences: the specifications for the code and comments inserted when you use one of the **Source** actions to generate code. These include, for example, templates for getter and setter methods, new Java files, and methods. Customize these as you would your **Java > Editor > Templates** preferences.

Templates can play an important role in a team environment to help ensure consistency and adherence to coding conventions and standards. This means you may need to share your templates among team members. One way to do this is to export the templates to XML files. Both sets of templates have **Export...** options to allow you to do this. Then share them among your team. For information on how to do this through CVS, see Chapter 5, Teaming Up with Eclipse. You can also alter the default preference settings for Eclipse. For this, refer to Chapter 6, Managing Your Eclipse Environment.

### Externalizing Strings

The JDT allows you to externalize strings in your Java code, that is, to remove string literals from your Java code to separate files and replace them with references. This is most often done in order to have the strings translated into other languages. The Externalize Strings wizard scans your code for string literals and allows you to indicate which string literals are to be externalized and which are not. The JDT also provides support for finding unused and improperly used references to externalized strings. You can use a preference setting to flag strings that have not been externalized as compile errors or warnings. This is on the **Advanced** page of the **Java > Compiler** preferences.

To begin the process, select a project, package, or folder, and then select **Source > Find Strings to Externalize...** from the menu to display the Find Strings to Externalize dialog, which shows Java files containing strings that have not been externalized. Select a file and then select **Externalize Strings...** to go to the Externalize Strings wizard. Alternatively, select a Java project or package and then select **Source > Externalize Strings...** from the context menu.

On the first page of the Externalize Strings wizard, shown in Figure 3.18, you specify which strings are to be externalized (for translation) and keys for accessing the strings. The icon in the left column indicates the status of the string: externalized ☑, ignored ☒, and internalized 🔁. Change the status by clicking on the icon to toggle it or by using **Externalize**, **Ignore**, or **Internalize**. If you have your preferences set to flag nonexternalized strings as errors or warnings, and you select **Externalize** or **Ignore** for the string, it will no longer be flagged as an error or warning. If you select **Internalize**, the error or warning will remain. You can specify a prefix that will be added to the key (when your code is modified, not in the dialog). You can also edit the key to specify a different value by selecting the entry and then clicking on the key.

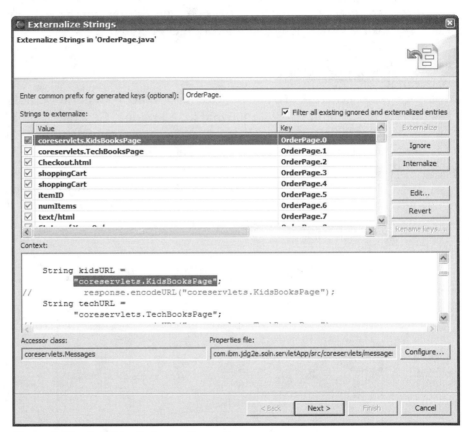

**Figure 3.18** Specifying Strings to Externalize

Even if you do not intend to translate a string, it still may be useful to externalize it. For example, if you reference the same string value in several places in your code, perhaps a user interface element, externalize it to get it declared once. Then changing it in the future will be easier.

The JDT generates and adds to your project an accessor class, a method, and a properties file. To change the defaults Eclipse provides, or to specify you're using an alternative implementation, select **Configure...**.

The final page of the wizard is a before-and-after view of your code, similar to the before-and-after view when refactoring. In fact, here you are doing a sort of refactoring. In the top pane, you select to apply or not apply changes for each of the proposed modifications and select **Finish** when ready to make the changes to your code. This replaces the selected strings with references based on the accessor class, generates the accessor class, and creates the file containing the strings. To undo string externalizations, select **Refactor > Undo**. This also removes the generated accessor class.

## Generating Javadoc

You generate Javadoc by selecting **Project > Generate Javadoc...** or by exporting it with **File > Export... > Javadoc**. Generating Javadoc requires that the JDT know where to find javadoc.exe, the program that actually performs the Javadoc generation. The javadoc.exe program is not shipped as part of Eclipse; it comes with a JDK distribution. For example, in Sun's 1.4.2 JDK, javadoc.exe is located in the bin folder under the main installation folder. If this is not set, do so by selecting **Configure...** from the Generate Javadoc wizard (see Figure 3.19).

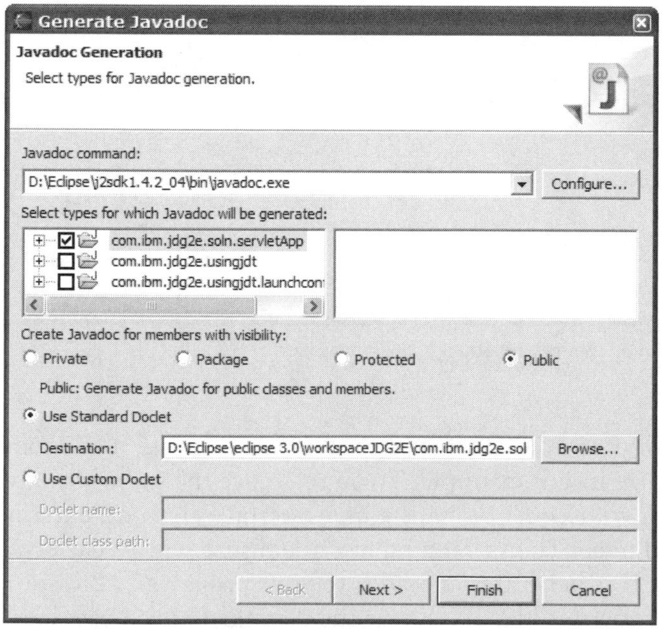

**Figure 3.19**   Generating Javadoc

You have a number of options for generating Javadoc for one or more of your Java projects. Figure 3.19 shows the first page of options. Select **Finish** to generate the Javadoc or **Next** for more options.

For the visibility settings, **Private** generates Javadoc for all members; **Package** for all default, protected, and public members; **Protected** for all protected and public members; and **Public** for only public members. For more information on all the Javadoc generation options, refer to the "Preferences" topic in the "Reference" section of the *Java Development User Guide*.

The second page of the wizard allows you to specify Javadoc for references to external libraries or other Eclipse projects you select. This is very useful. To do so, the Javadoc location for the library or project must be specified. If it is not, when you select a library or project, you will see a "not configured" warning message at the top of the wizard. Use the **Configure...** button on this page, or go to your library definition or project properties, to define the Javadoc location.

The third page allows you to save your Generate Javadoc wizard settings as an Ant script, among other options. This is also useful. You can then manage this script as part of your project and add it to the Ant view or define it as a builder on the project.

When you generate the Javadoc, you will see a prompt asking whether you want to update the **Javadoc Location** properties of the projects you are generating Javadoc for. You should select to do so. This enables you to browse the generated Javadoc in an external browser. It also allows you to generate Javadoc references to this project from other projects. Output from the Javadoc generation shows up in the Console view. You should review this to ensure there were no errors.

### Writing Java for Alternative JREs

Eclipse uses a JRE for two purposes: as a way to run Eclipse itself and as a target execution environment for your Java code. This target execution JRE can be the same one used to run Eclipse or an alternative one. If you want to develop Java code that uses a different JRE as a target from the one that runs Eclipse, you need to configure Eclipse to define an additional JRE and the associated JDK compliance preferences. You can make this configuration change global or specific to a project.

In either case, first you need to specify the JRE you want to use as your target environment. Do this with your **Java > Installed JREs** preferences (see Figure 3.20). Set the **Javadoc URL** field in order to enable browsing of the JRE Javadoc. If you anticipate debugging into the JRE classes, associate source code with the JRE system library files by selecting **Attach Source....** Normally, Javadoc and JRE source are not included with JRE distributions; rather, you need to get a corresponding JDK distribution.

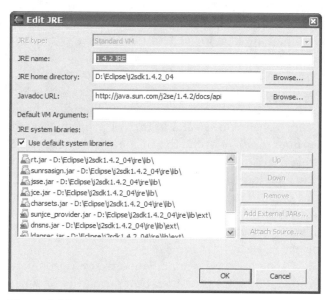

**Figure 3.20**   Setting Installed JRE Preferences

If you want to make this JRE the global default, set the default JRE in the preference (with the associated check box) to be the one you just installed. This specifies the JRE used as your development target. It does not affect the JRE used to run Eclipse. You'll see in Chapter 4, Running and Debugging Java, how to pass parameters to the JVM when you run or debug your programs. If you use some common JVM parameters, specify them here in **Default VM Arguments** so you don't have to specify them for each project. To specify project-specific JVM parameters, you will use a launch configuration. We'll get to that in Chapter 4.

Second, set your **Compiler compliance level** setting, on the **Compliance and Classfiles** page of the **Java > Compiler** preferences, depending on what your code requires.

If you do not want to make this JRE the global default but rather want to use it in a specific project, you can do this through the project's properties. Once you've defined the JRE in your **Java > Installed JREs** preferences, open the properties for the project by selecting the project in the Package Explorer view and then selecting **Properties** from the context menu. On the **Libraries** page of the **Java Build Path** properties, select **Add Library…**. In the Add Library wizard, select to add a **JRE System Library**. On the next page of the wizard, under **Alternate JRE**, select the JRE you just installed. Back on the **Libraries** page, remove the default JRE entry. Switch to the **Java Compiler** properties, and select **Use project settings**. Adjust these preferences, which are now project specific, as appropriate. Verify the **Compliance and Classfiles** preferences.

### Developing for J2SE 1.5

At the time of this writing, J2SE 1.5 was still under development, and the Eclipse JDT team was in the midst of implementing J2SE 1.5 support in Eclipse, code name Cheetah. Instructions on using the interim work on Eclipse 3.0 drivers are available on the Development Resources page of the JDT Core component, JDT subproject. To use the early support, you need to install it from an Eclipse update site. The Cheetah instructions include a pointer to the update site. For more information on installing from update sites, refer to Installing a Feature from an Update Site in Chapter 6, Managing Your Eclipse Environment. This early support shows up first in the compiler and manifests itself in some J2SE 1.5-specific preferences. As the core work stabilizes, you can expect to see enhancements begin to show up in the JDT user interface.

## *Compiling Your Code*

By default, whenever you create, rename, delete, or edit and save a Java element, the JDT compiles (or "builds" in Eclipse terms) the changed element and all other elements impacted by this change. The resulting `*.class` files are put in the project's output folder(s). The output folders can be different folders from the source folders or the same folders. By default, they are the same. We'll see in Java Projects later in this chapter how you can organize your projects into separate source and output folders. When you have this organization and build your project, other non-Java files in your source folder(s) are copied to the output folder(s), subject to inclusion and exclusion patterns.

The JDT is a complete development environment. All it requires is a JRE, not a JDK. This means Eclipse comes with its own Java compiler. It does not use `javac`. If you want to compile the code you develop in Eclipse with `javac`, you can do so through Ant build scripts. We'll get to those in a moment. The JDT provides a great deal of flexibility in allowing you to customize this build process through Java project properties and **Java > Compiler** preferences. In these preferences, set global settings for how you want various kinds of errors to be handled, how you want your class files to be generated, and how build path errors (such as circular dependencies) should be handled.

In your project properties, you define the inclusion and exclusion patterns for which files in your source folders get processed during builds. The goal here is to provide a mechanism so that only the files needed by your application at runtime are copied to the output folder(s). It allows greater flexibility in how you organize to develop your application. Your project properties include settings for defining additional builders (compilers), overriding the global compiler preferences with project-specific ones, a more general mechanism for excluding files and folders in the source folder from being built, and build path customization. We'll see this in more detail in Working with Java Elements later in this chapter.

## Eclipse Ant Integration

Ant is a Java-based make-like utility offered by the Apache Software Foundation that you can use to drive your build process. For more information on Ant, see http://ant.apache.org/. Ant runs on any Java 1.1 system or later, which makes it largely portable. As a Java-based open source project, it's easy for people to improve and add to Ant. We'll see an example of this in Exercise 4, Developing a Simple Web Commerce Application with Eclipse, with some specific Ant tasks the Tomcat folks created and delivered with Tomcat.

### A Quick Ant Primer

Ant scripts (i.e., build files) are XML files that specify tasks and their dependent tasks. Ant itself is command line driven. However, Eclipse comes with Ant built in and with some pretty slick integration. You may be thinking, "Eclipse compiles Java code, so why do I need another build utility?" The simple answer is that compiling is only one step in a build process that can often get quite complicated when you factor in automated testing, statistics generation, JAR creation, and deployment.

The basic Ant constructs are projects, properties, targets, and tasks. A **project** is a top-level construct, one per build file. Projects contain properties and targets. **Properties** are name/value pairs that you specify inside or outside a build file. For example:

```
<property name="output.home" value="bin"/>
```

You can then reference the property with ${output.home}. Ant comes with some predefined properties, such as ${basedir} for the directory in which the

Ant script is running. Eclipse also adds some properties, such as
${eclipse.home}. These are located on the **Properties** page of your **Ant >
Runtime** preferences. Don't confuse these with Eclipse properties on
resources. Ant properties are different and apply to Ant only.

**Targets** are the units of work that make up projects. Targets are comprised of sequences of tasks, and they depend on other targets. **Tasks** are the
commands executed inside targets. They do the work. Examples of tasks are
<javac> to compile and <copy> to copy files.

### Using Ant in Eclipse

Ant integration in Eclipse shows up in several ways. Eclipse has an Ant script
editor, including code assist (**Ctrl+Space**) and formatting (**Ctrl+Shift+F**).
When you're using the Ant script editor, the Outline view shows an outline of
the script you're editing, broken down into properties, targets, and tasks. Ant
build scripts in Eclipse are called, by default, build.xml. The Ant editor is
associated with this file name.

There are two basic ways to run Ant scripts (i.e., to execute Ant targets)
in Eclipse. You can do this through the Ant view, or you can define Ant
builders. To run Ant targets from the Ant view, you need to add the Ant
script, for example, build.xml, to the view (see Figure 3.21).

**Figure 3.21**　Ant View

You can do this by dragging and dropping the file onto the view or by
using one of the **Add Buildfiles** buttons, ⬕ or 🚀, on the toolbar. Then
double-click on a target to invoke it. Output is shown in the console view.
Selected sections of the output are enabled as links, including specific tasks
and error messages (see Figure 3.22). Select a link to go to the task in the
build script or the failing statement.

**Figure 3.22**   Ant Script Output

This is a great way to execute Ant scripts, but it is manual. There is a way to automate this. As you saw in Chapter 2, Getting Started with Eclipse, Eclipse projects have builders. Eclipse allows you to define Ant targets as builders. Do this by opening the properties for a project and editing the **Builders** properties (these are Eclipse properties now, not Ant properties); you want to create a new **Ant Build**. You then select an Ant script and one or more targets in that script.

There are **Ant** preferences you can use to define your Ant runtime, Ant properties, and Eclipse Ant tasks. These are your **Ant > Runtime** preferences. The **Classpath** page lists JAR files that make up the Ant runtime. If you define your own Ant tasks or need to reference Ant tasks in other JAR files, you need to list them here, under **Ant Home Entries**. The **Tasks** page lists the tasks Eclipse defines for your, and its, use. The **Properties** page lists the Ant properties Eclipse defines. You can add your own here. Consider defining properties here if they are global to your Eclipse environment.

## Working with Java Elements

In the Fundamentals section earlier in this chapter, we presented an overview of how to create different kinds of Java elements. In this section we'll go into more depth on Java projects, the creation and import of Java elements, and details on local history for Java elements.

### Folders

There are three types of folders in Java projects: source folders ⏚, output folders ⏚, and other nonsource folders ⏚. This is an important distinction because it affects how builds are performed. When you create a source folder, the JDT adds the source folder to the project's build path. Nonsource folders are not added to the project's build path. If you create a folder and later want to make it a source folder, do so from the Java Project Properties dialog, **Java Build Path** properties, on the **Source** page. When in doubt, check the project's .classpath file. It is the persistent representation of the properties shown on the project's build settings pages. Source and output folders can exist only in Java projects.

If you create a Java project and select to have your Java source and output files in the same folder, and then decide later to create a source folder, this forces the JDT to change the organization of the project to have separate source and output folders. If you already have Java files in the project, you will have to move these manually to a source folder. It may be easier to create a new project with the folder and package organization you desire and then use the refactoring actions to move the Java elements.

Folders do not have to physically reside in your workspace or within the containing project. You can have linked folders as source and output folders. For example, you might create one or more remote output folders and use the JDT build process to do a simple deploy of your binaries and other output resources. For more information on linked folders, see More on Projects in Chapter 2, Getting Started with Eclipse.

## Java Projects

The JDT projects permit you to override certain global Eclipse preferences with settings specific to a project. These include the target JRE and preferences for warnings and errors, JCK (Java Constraint Kit) compliance, and class file generation. To set project-specific preferences, open the properties for a project by right-clicking on the project and selecting **Properties** from the context menu. Select **Java Compiler** properties, and then select **Use project settings**. The preference pages are enabled so you can set these project-specific preferences.

Within a Java project, there are two basic ways to organize your code. For small projects, you may choose to have everything in the same package or folder: *.java source files, *.class output files, and other files required by your program. With this organization, when you save a .java file and the file and project are built (compiled), the resulting .class files are put with source files in the same folder.

For projects that have lots of modules, you may choose to organize your *.java source and *.class output files in separate folders in a project. In this case, each project has one or more source folders and one or more output folders. The build process takes inputs from one or more source folders, or folders under them, builds them if necessary, and puts the results in the respective output folders. This approach allows you to organize and subdivide your Java packages, while the output folders contain all runtime resources.

Two preference settings allow you to customize this source code organization and build processing. **Java > Build Path** preferences allow you to specify the default organization for when you create new Java projects. You can override this in the New Project wizard when you create a new Java project. If you have already created a project, you can change this organization on the **Source** page of the project's **Java Build Path** properties. You can also change the policy for which files do *not* get copied to the output folder when a project is built. This is the **Filtered Resources** preference on the **Build Path** page of the **Java > Compiler** preferences. You can also selectively include and/or exclude files and folders from the build process with a project's **Java Build Path** property, on the **Source** page. Expand a source folder entry and edit the **Included:** and/or **Excluded:** entries. If you specify both an inclusion pattern and an exclusion pattern and there is a conflict, the exclusion pattern takes precedence.

When you organize your code into separate source and output folders, by default, there is one output folder per project. You can configure multiple output folders in a project, one per source folder. On the **Source** page of the **Java Build Path** project properties, select **Allow output folders for source folders**. Then expand each source folder and edit the **Output folder** definition for the selected source folder (see Figure 3.23). This is useful, for example, to separate Java source from, say, HTML and image files in your project. When your project is built, your Java class files are put in one folder, HTML in another, and image files in a third.

## Builders

The **Builders** Java project property defines the builders (compilers or other programs) that get run when resources change. With Eclipse it is easy to add Ant builders as well as other programs. For more information on builders, see Chapter 2, Getting Started with Eclipse.

## Java Build Path

A project's build path serves two purposes: It specifies the search sequence for Java references in the code in the project, and it defines the initial runtime classpath for the code. When you first create a project, its build path is set to

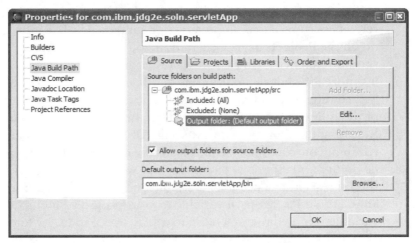

**Figure 3.23**   Defining an Output Folder for a Source Folder

contain the project itself and the default JRE. The default JRE is defined in your **Java > Installed JREs** preferences. At runtime, you can modify a project's classpath, which is generated from its build path information, by defining a launch configuration (see Chapter 4, Running and Debugging Java). This is useful, for example, if you need to test different runtime environments without modifying your build.

Build path errors show up with other errors in the Problems view. If you have trouble diagnosing build path errors, open the properties on the project and check the **Java Build Path** pages. The icons for the entries indicate whether they cannot be found. For example, a JAR file is represented by 🗄. A JAR file that cannot be found is represented by 🗄. Preferences for how to handle build path errors are located on the **Build Path** page of your **Java > Compiler** preferences.

Use **Add Folder...** on the project's properties **Source** page to add source folders (see Figure 3.23). You can reference an existing folder or create a new one. The **Projects** page allows you to add other Java projects to the build path of the new project. You need to do this if you are going to make references from the project you are creating to Java declarations in other projects in your workspace.

The **Libraries** page allows you to add other Java libraries to the project build path in order to reference their declarations. For example, if you wanted to develop a Java servlet, you would need to get a J2EE (Java 2 Platform, Enterprise Edition) runtime, extract a JAR file that contained the servlet definitions, and add that JAR file to the project's build path. Select **Add**

**Jars...** to add JAR or `*.zip` files from other projects, as opposed to adding references to resources in projects not contained in JAR or `*.zip` files, as you do on the **Projects** page. Generally, if you have the resources in a project, you should reference them that way, not within the JAR. This is simply because it's more efficient to modify code in a Java project than code in a JAR file.

To reference a library not defined in a project in your workspace, use one of the following: **Add External JARs...**, **Add Variable...**, or **Add Library....** Referring to a library as an external JAR is a direct reference to a JAR or `*.zip` file on your file system. This is the quick and easy approach. For more flexibility and especially to enable your work to be more easily shared, you should use either a classpath variable or a user-defined library. Use **Add Variable...** to add a classpath variable to your project's build path. A **classpath variable** is an indirect reference to a JAR or `*.zip` file or folder. To define a classpath variable, use your **Java > Build Path > Classpath Variables** preferences. A **user-defined library** is another indirect reference. A user-defined library allows you to refer indirectly to a series of JAR or `*.zip` files. Do this through your **Java > Build Path > User Libraries** preferences. With an indirect reference, if the location of the target changes, you only have to update the classpath variable or user library definition, not each project. Both classpath variables and user libraries are indirect references.

The advantage of classpath variables is that you can define a single reference to a folder and its contents. However, to reference a library in the folder, you need to select the library file when you add the classpath variable to the project's build path. The advantage of user-defined libraries is that you can define one reference to multiple individual library files, not necessarily in the same folder. User-defined libraries are also easier to share. They can be saved individually as XML files. Classpath variables can only be shared as part of all your exported preferences.

Regardless of whether you refer to a library directly or use a classpath variable or a user-defined library, be sure to set the Javadoc and source location attributes. This will allow you to browse the Javadoc for the library and step into methods in the library while debugging, respectively. For classpath variables, set these attributes in your projects' **Java Build Path** properties on the **Libraries** page. For user-defined libraries, set these attributes when you define the library in your **Java > Build Path > User Libraries** preferences. This illustrates another advantage of user-defined libraries: You specify the associated source code and Javadoc once. With classpath variables, you associate source and Javadoc with each project that references the classpath variable. One final note: While Eclipse supports file-specific encoding, source code read from archives is read using the workspace default encoding.

The **Order and Export** page serves two purposes. First, it allows you to change the order of references to entries in your project's build path. This order becomes important if you have the same declarations in multiple build path entries. Second, by selecting an entry for export, other projects that reference this project will implicitly inherit these exported entries. This means that others can reuse the selected project's referenced libraries without needing to respecify them, reducing the explicit dependencies should the organization of the code later change.

### Project References

**Project references** indicate other projects a given project refers to and dictate how projects in your workspace are built. This property is set based on the projects you include on the **Projects** page of a project's **Java Build Path** properties. For example, if you specify in project A's **Java Build Path** properties that it refers to project B, project A's **Project References** properties are updated. Then, whenever project B is built, project A is (re)built as well, because A referenced B. You affected this when you set the **Java Build Path** properties for project A. You do *not* affect this if you simply set project A's **Project References** properties to refer to project B. Doing so will *not* cause A to be (re)built when B is built. The bottom line is that project references for Java projects are managed by the JDT. You can examine them, but making changes will have no impact.

## Classes and Interfaces

When creating a new class or interface, there are several options worth noting. In the New Java Class wizard, **Enclosing Type**, used for nested classes, specifies the class that will contain the class you are creating. As you type the **Name** of the class, watch the message at the top of the wizard page—it will flag invalid class names. If you elect to not generate stubs for superclass constructors or inherited methods, you can later generate the code from the editor by selecting **Source** from the context menu or by using code assist and a code template. If you do not select to have **Inherited abstract methods** generated when you created the class, you will see errors in the Problems view indicating the methods you still need to create. Once the class is created, you can generate stubs for these by selecting the class in one of the Java views and then selecting **Source > Override/Implement Methods...** from the context menu.

## Importing Java Elements

In the Resource Management section in Chapter 2, Getting Started with Eclipse, we discussed importing resources with the Import wizard. Recall that you invoke the Import wizard by selecting **Import...** from the Navigator or Package Explorer context menu or by selecting **File > Import....** With Java projects and Java elements, it is generally easier to deal with projects than individual Java elements because Java projects contain build path and builder information. Note that a Java project import creates a pointer to the project in its original location; if you delete the project from your workspace and say yes to the delete from file system prompt, you have deleted the project for good. Some import wizards copy the target into the workspace; the Java project Import wizard does not.

## Local History for Java Elements

The Resource Management section in Chapter 2 also described how you could compare and replace or merge a file with another edition of it from local history, compare two files, compare two projects, and recover files deleted from a project. In addition to this, with the JDT you can compare and replace individual elements, including methods and fields. You can select an element in one of the Java views and then select **Compare With**, **Replace With**, or **Restore from Local History...** from the context menu. Figure 3.24 shows comparing a single method, generatePrimeNumbers, with a previous edition.

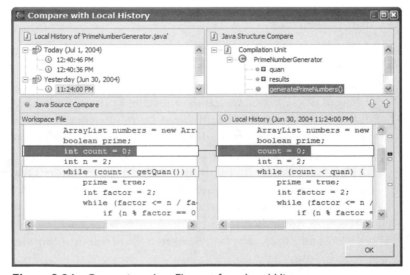

**Figure 3.24**   Comparing a Java Element from Local History

When you compare Java elements, you can select an element in the **Java Structure Compare** pane to see only its differences. You can restore a deleted method or field by selecting a type in one of the JDT views and then selecting **Restore from Local History...** from the context menu.

## Tuning the Performance of the JDT

In the Customizing Eclipse section in Chapter 2, Getting Started with Eclipse, we discussed a number of factors that affect the performance of Eclipse, including startup time and memory usage. These factors include the number of installed tools; how many views, editors, and projects are open; and the number of resources they contained. In addition to these, several other factors can affect the performance of the JDT. These relate to the amount of real-time processing JDT does to analyze and build code you're editing. If the performance of JDT degrades, there are several things you can do.

- Reduce the amount of Java code in your workspace. Do this by partitioning code into multiple workspaces and/or closing projects you're not currently working on. You can also move code to JAR files and define these as user libraries.
- Under **Workbench** preferences, deselect **Build automatically**. If you do this, you will need to perform builds manually by selecting **Project > Build Project** or **Build All** (**Ctrl+B**) from the menu.
- If you are defining your own builder(s), consider defining a working set of relevant resources that will cause the builder to run. This is on the **Build Options** page of the builder's properties.
- Under **Java > Editor** preferences, on the **Code Assist** page, deselect **Enable auto activation**. On the **Mark Occurrences** page, deselect **Mark occurrences in file**.
- Turn off quick assist and code folding. Under your **Java > Editor** preferences are, respectively, **Light bulb for quick assists** on the **Appearance** page and **Enable folding when opening a new editor** on the **Folding** page.
- Turn off quick diff. This is your **Workbench > Editors > Quick Diff** preference.
- On the **Typing** page of your **Java > Editors** preferences, disable **Analyze annotations while typing**. This means, for example, that you will not get real-time error cluing and annotations in the editor. You'll need to save the file you're editing to have the annotations updated, including any errors flagged.

## More on the JDT Views and Preferences

We'll end this chapter with a little more detail on some of the views and perspectives that comprise the JDT and some cool stuff that may not be immediately obvious.

### Filtering View Contents

The JDT views allow you to filter the elements that are displayed. You can select to hide static members ⬟ˢ, fields ⬟, nonpublic members ●, and local types ⬟ᴸ. These filtering criteria are useful if your workspace contains a significant amount of code, and navigating (especially in the Package Explorer view) becomes cumbersome. From the pull-down menu ▼ on the title bar, several of the views allow you to specify filters and/or working sets.

### Package Explorer View

If the package names in the Package Explorer view are long and/or you have sized the width of the view small enough that you often find yourself scrolling the view horizontally to find the right package, you can abbreviate the package names in the view. In your **Java > Appearance** preferences, select **Compress all package name segments, except the final segment**, and enter a pattern to represent the compression scheme. The pattern is a number followed by one or more optional characters specifying how each segment of the package name is to be compressed. The pattern number specifies how many characters of the name segment to include, and the pattern characters become the segment separators. The compression is applied to all package name segments, except the last one. For example, for the package name `org.eclipse.jface`:

"`1.`" causes it to be compressed to `o.e.jface`,
"`0.`" results in `jface`, and
"`2.`" results in `or.ec.jface`.

If you have compressed names, you can quickly determine the full name of a resource by selecting it in the Package Explorer view. The full name is displayed in the message area.

In addition to filters, you can use **Go Into** from the context menu to focus the contents on the selected element, thereby reducing the content in the view. If you do this often, select **Go into the selected element** in your **Java** preferences to make this the double-click default, instead of expanding the element in the view.

Finally, if you work with JAR files in your projects, in your **Workbench > File Associations** preferences, add a file compression program that understands \*.jar files to make it easy to view their contents.

## Hierarchy View

The Hierarchy view is an exceptionally useful one, especially for exploring Java code (see Figure 3.25). There are three presentations available from the toolbar: the **type hierarchy**, the **supertype hierarchy**, and the **subtype hierarchy**. These three presentations revolve around a focal point type in the view, indicated by the label decoration ▶. This is the type on which you opened the view. Change this with **Focus On...** from the context menu. For classes, the type presentation shows a single slice of the class hierarchy from **Object** through to all of the subclasses in a class. For interfaces, it shows all classes that implement the interface and their subtypes. The supertype presentation shows classes that are extended and interfaces that are implemented. The subtype presentation shows a class and its subclasses or an interface and the classes that implement it.

**Figure 3.25**   Hierarchy View

**Lock View and Show Members in Hierarchy** locks the contents of the bottom pane and prevents it from changing as you select elements in the top pane. With this and **Show All Inherited Members**, it's easy to get a handle on where fields are defined and what classes and interfaces implement which methods.

You can drag any Java element from one of the Java views and drop it on the empty area of the Hierarchy view to open it there. Do not drop an element on an existing element in the view; that may be interpreted as a refactoring move request.

The Hierarchy view also maintains a list of the elements you have opened. Rather than opening an element again, you can select **Previous Type Hierarchies** to see a list of those available. Change the orientation of the view from vertical to horizontal by selecting **Layout > Horizontal View Orientation** from the pull-down menu ▼ on the Hierarchy view toolbar.

One last Hierarchy view tidbit: You can use a package, a source folder, or even a project as input to the Hierarchy view by dragging it to the view or using the pop-up menu option. The end result is an overview of all the types contained in or implemented by the input, which can sometimes be useful when naming patterns alone are not sufficient to organize your code.

## Call Hierarchy View

The Call Hierarchy view is a useful one that shows all invocations of a given method or all methods invoked by a given method (see Figure 3.26). This view does not appear by default on the **Window > Show View** list. You need to select **Window > Show View > Other…** and then select it from the **Java** category. The Call Hierarchy view behaves a lot like the Hierarchy view. One of the methods listed in the view has the focus. This is the method for which callers or callees are shown. Change this method by selecting another method and then **Focus On** from the context menu. The pull-down menu ▼ allows you to switch between caller and callee views, to orient vertically or horizontally, and to set the scope of the search for callers and callees.

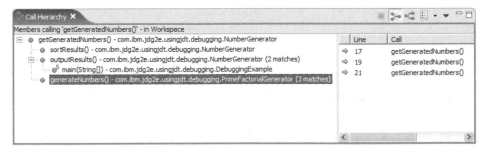

**Figure 3.26**   Call Hierarchy View

## Outline View

The Outline view provides a filtering mechanism you might use to reduce unnecessary content in the view. Select **Filters…** from the view's drop-down menu. You can define name pattern filters or select from predefined filters that can suppress import and package declarations.

## Problems View

If you end up with a lot of errors and warnings, say, after you've imported a chunk of code, the errors can be easier to digest if you filter them. Select **Filter...** on the title bar and then select **On selected resource only**, **On selected resource and its children**, or even **On any resource in same project**.

## Search View

In addition to displaying the results of a search, you can use the Search view to quickly navigate through Java references and declarations. Once you have a set of search results, select a declaration, reference, and implementer, then select **References** or **Declarations** from the context menu to execute another search. The view also maintains a history of your search results. Rather than executing a search again, select **Show Previous Searches** and then select from the list.

## Java Type Hierarchy Perspective

The Java Type Hierarchy perspective is a perspective optimized for use with the Hierarchy view (see Figure 3.27). When you select **Open Type Hierarchy**, the JDT replaces the contents of the Hierarchy view if it is open or opens a new one in the current perspective. Preferences provide a useful alternative to this default behavior. In the **Java** preferences, select **Open a New Type Hierarchy Perspective**. This causes the Java Type Hierarchy perspective to open in a new window.

## Java Browsing Perspective

The Java Browsing perspective, shown in Figure 3.28, provides a slightly more structured approach to navigating through Java resources than the Java perspective. In addition to an editor pane, it contains Projects, Packages, Types, and Members views. The organization of this view will be familiar to users of VisualAge for Java. In fact, it's intended to mimic the VisualAge for Java user interface.

The navigation model is to select an element (by single-clicking it) in a pane to see its contents in the next pane. **Open** and **Open Type Hierarchy**

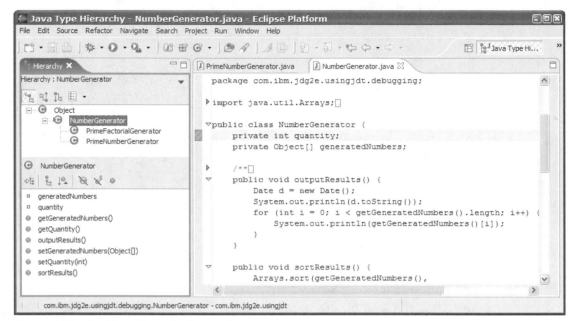

**Figure 3.27**    Java Type Hierarchy Perspective

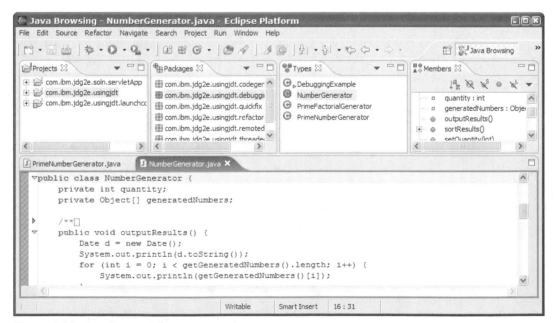

**Figure 3.28**    Java Browsing Perspective

actions are available from all the views and the editor. You can specify different filters for the contents of each of the views. The default orientation of the Java Browsing perspective is shown in Figure 3.28. You can also orient the views vertically on the left with the editor on the right by changing your **Java > Appearance** preferences to **Stack views vertically in the Java Browsing perspective**.

## Exercise Summary

Exercise 2, Using the Java Development Tools (found in Part VI), accompanies this chapter. The exercise is broken down into a number of parts, each demonstrating different concepts and building on the previous part.

1. Hello World

   You'll create the ubiquitous "Hello World" program, and you will see how to run it, including how to use a scrapbook page.

2. Quick Fix

   You'll use the JDT's quick fix capabilities to fix a series of errors in a Java program.

3. Code Generation

   You'll see how to significantly improve your productivity by generating Java code to complete expressions, including the use of code templates.

4. Refactoring

   In this part, you'll really start to see the power of the JDT when using refactoring to clean up, reorganize, and extend a program.

In addition, Exercise 4, Developing a Simple Web Commerce Application with Eclipse, provides a more robust programming example, developing, deploying, and debugging a servlet application in Apache's Tomcat. This exercise brings together a number of individual concepts presented in Part I.

## Chapter Summary

This chapter provided a comprehensive overview of using the JDT to explore, write, and run Java. We described how to create different kinds of Java elements, how to navigate and search them with the different views, and how to write Java code using code assist, code generation, and refactoring. We covered how different kinds of errors are marked and how to fix errors with quick fix. We also discussed how to set Javadoc locations and view Javadoc. Next we looked in some detail at Java projects and their properties, how these properties impact your projects, and how to use different JREs and reference declarations in other projects and JAR files. The chapter also described editing code templates used in code generation and externalizing strings.

## Reference

Arthorne, John, and Chris Laffra. 2004. *Official Eclipse 3.0 FAQs*. Boston, MA, Addison-Wesley. http://eclipsefaq.org. (See Chapter 3 and FAQs 313, 315–318.)

# CHAPTER 4

## *Running and Debugging Java*

In the previous chapter, we discussed writing Java code. Perhaps you've tried this with our exercises or some of your own code. You'll probably want to try running your code and, if you're like us, you may *occasionally* find that your code is not quite working as expected.

The set of Eclipse Java Development Tools (JDT) provides a flexible and customizable environment for running and debugging the Java code you develop. What sets the JDT and, more specifically, its debugging capabilities apart is the degree of control you have over the development and testing of your applications—control that lets you specify the JRE you test on; determine how problems are classified; provide information, warnings, and errors; deploy and debug with compiler and build path errors; and filter the classes and packages you step through in the debugger. And much of this control is specific to each project.

The Java debugger allows you to detect and correct errors in your code as your code executes. It can debug your code locally or remotely. You can control the execution of your code with varying degrees of refinement, set simple and conditional breakpoints, and examine and change variable values. The JDT provides support for **hot code replace**, a feature that allows you to replace class definitions once execution has started, provided your JVM implements the appropriate support. This is valuable because it means you can change your code while it is executing to fix errors without having to restart and attempt to recreate the same conditions.

In this chapter, we start by looking at how you run the Java code you're developing. Eclipse provides several ways to do this. We introduce launch configurations as a mechanism used by the JDT to allow you to control the environment in which you run your code. Then we get into the heart of this chapter, debugging. We start with the basics, like setting breakpoints and controlling program execution, and then go into more detail on debugging Java with the JDT.

In Part VI, we have assembled a number of exercises designed to walk you through doing many of the things we present here and to reinforce what we present. Exercise 4, Developing a Simple Web Commerce Application with Eclipse, will bring together a number of the concepts and tasks you'll see in this chapter in a robust example. We encourage you to take a look at these exercises.

# Running Java Code

There are two basic ways to run code in your Java projects: You can run (launch) a Java program with one of the **Run** ⃝ or **Debug** 🔆 commands, or you can evaluate (execute) a Java expression in a scrapbook page. You can run code even if it still has compiler errors. The JDT doesn't force you to correct all your source code errors in order to begin testing. For example, if you have some unresolved errors in your code due to references to classes you haven't finished yet, you can still launch the debugger. If the code path avoids the methods that have errors, no problem. Even if a method with an error is called, the debugger will automatically stop there and, using hot code replace, give you the opportunity to continue execution. If the scope of an error is at the class level, for example, a problem with a static declaration, you can run code in other classes but not the one with the error. This flexibility puts you in control of the environment instead of the compiler dictating when something must be corrected.

## Using the Run and Debug Commands

Java programs, that is, classes with `main` methods, are identified with the **Run** label decoration 📭. To run a Java program, select a class or a Java element containing a class, and select **Run** from the menu bar, the **Run** pull-down menu ⃝ ▾, or **Run** from the Package Explorer view's context menu, and then select **Run As > Java Application**. To debug your program, select **Debug** from the menu bar, the **Debug** pull-down menu 🔆 ▾, or **Debug** from the Package Explorer view's context menu, and then select **Debug As > Java Application**. The **Run** and **Debug** commands are also available from the Navigator context menu for `main` methods. The JDT executes the `main` method and sends output to the Console view. If you have previously run or debugged Java programs, you will have entries under **Run > Run History** and/or **Debug > Debug History**. Select from these to rerun or debug programs. Select **Run** or **Debug** from the toolbar, or press **Ctrl+F11** or **F11**, respectively, to rerun or debug the last program you ran or debugged.

The **Run** command executes your program in the current perspective. The **Debug** command does the same thing but asks if you want to switch to the Debug perspective if you have breakpoints defined. If you decline to switch to the Debug perspective, you debug your program from the current perspective. You can configure whether or not you are asked to switch to the Debug perspective in your **Run/Debug > Launching** preferences.

When you run a Java program, the **Run** and **Debug** commands provide several choices. We're going to focus on Java applications here. Running as a **Runtime Workbench** is for testing your extensions to Eclipse. We'll get to that in Chapter 7, Extending Eclipse for Fun and Profit. Running as a **JUnit Test** is beyond the scope of this book. Testing with JUnit is covered very well in the online documentation that comes with Eclipse, so we will not labor over details about it here. For more information on this, refer to "Writing and running JUnit tests" in the "Getting started" section of the *Java Development User Guide*.

To run a Java program, the JDT needs two things: a main method and a launch configuration. If a unique class with a main method can be determined from the current selection, its main method will be run. For example, if the Java editor is active on a class with a main method, its main method will be run. If you have a project selected in the Package Explorer view and there are multiple classes in that project with main methods, you will be prompted to select one. We'll get to launch configurations in the next section. If you don't specify a launch configuration when you run or debug a program, the JDT will create a default one for you. This is what happens when you use **Run As > Java Application** or **Debug As > Java Application**.

If the program encounters a runtime error, the exception information goes to the Console view and is displayed using the defined error text color to distinguish it from other output types. Color-coding for output text in the Console view is defined in your **Console** preferences under **Run/Debug**.

## Managing Launch Configurations

**Launch configurations** define information for running Java programs. With launch configurations you can specify input parameters, JVM arguments, environment variables, source location for your code, and set the runtime classpath and JRE. To define a launch configuration, select the **Run** pull-down menu ▶ ▼ and then **Run...** or select the **Debug** pull-down menu ☼ ▼ and then **Debug...**. In the Run launch configurations dialog (see Figure 4.1), select **Java Application** for **Configurations** and then select **New**. If you have previously run Java programs with the **Run** or **Debug** commands, you will see the default launch configurations that were created for you. You have one set of launch configurations. Whether you execute the **Run** or **Debug** command, you are selecting from the same set of launch configurations.

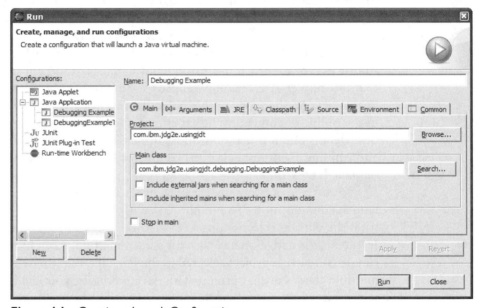

**Figure 4.1**    Creating a Launch Configuration

On the **Main** page, **Project** is optional. If you specify it, its build path is used to set the classpath, source lookup, and JRE. Use **Search...** to search a project's build path for Java programs. If a valid project is specified, the build path of that project is searched for classes with main methods matching the search pattern (you can use wild cards) in **Main class**. If a project is not specified, the build paths of all the projects in your workspace are searched for classes with main methods matching the search pattern. When you use the **Debug** command, **Stop in main** causes execution to suspend on the first statement in the main method. You don't have to first set a breakpoint. This option has no impact when you use the **Run** command.

On the **Arguments** page, you can set the input parameters for the Java program and any JVM parameters. The Java program parameters are strings separated by spaces. For more information on JVM arguments, see "Running Eclipse" in the "Tasks" section of the *Workbench User Guide*. On the **JRE** page, you set the JRE used to execute the Java program. Use this to override the JRE defined in the build path properties of the project containing the program.

The **Classpath** and **Environment** pages are pretty straightforward. The classpath is set based on the build path information from the project specified on the **Main** page. You can add additional projects or libraries on the **Classpath** page. Select **Advanced...** to add a user library.

On the **Source** page, you specify the location of the Java source being debugged, so that it can be presented in the Debug perspective. To add projects and/or JARs containing the source, select **Add....** You need to do this if you do not have a project specified on the **Main** page. You may also want to do this for libraries you reference. If you do not do this, when you attempt to step into a method for which you don't have source, the debugger will prompt you for the location of the source.

On the **Common** page, you specify information about how to save the launch configuration. By default, launch configurations are saved as metadata in your workspace. If you select **Shared**, you specify a Java project that will be used to save the launch configuration as a .launch file. In this way, it's easy to not only keep and manage launch configurations with the code they run but also share them with others accessing the project; this is especially important for teams. You can indicate which favorites list displays the launch configuration, the **Run** ◐ or the **Debug** ⚙ toolbar pull-down menus. You can also add launch configurations to the **Run** and **Debug** favorites menus by selecting **Organize Favorites...** and **Add...** from the **Run** and **Debug** pull-down menus.

### Evaluating Expressions in Scrapbook Pages

Java scrapbook pages (*.jpage files) allow you to edit and evaluate Java code expressions and display or inspect the results. They are a quick and easy way to test code and experiment with Java code expressions. You can evaluate an expression that's a partial statement, a full statement, or a series of statements. To create a scrapbook page, select **File > New > Other...**, then **Java > Java Run/Debug**, and finally **Scrapbook Page**. Scrapbook pages can be located in Java projects, folders, source folders, and packages.

Enter an expression in the scrapbook page. This could be something simple, like System.out.println("Hello World"), or an invocation of your

PART I

Java code, for example, its main method. Content assist (**Ctrl+Space**) is available in scrapbook pages. Select the expression and then select **Display** 🗾 from the toolbar or the context menu or press **Ctrl+Shift+D**. The JDT evaluates the expression, sends output to the Console view, and displays the toString value returned by the expression you selected in the scrapbook page. Select **Inspect** 🔍 or press **Ctrl+Shift+I** to display the results in a similar pop-up window. Press **Ctrl+Shift+I** again to save the results in the Expressions view. (We'll discuss the Expressions view in more detail in the Evaluating Expressions section.) **Evaluate** 🗾 or **Ctrl+U** simply runs the code and sends the output to the Console view.

There are a couple of properties worth noting on the **Scrapbook Runtime** page of the scrapbook properties. To edit these, select the scrapbook page in the Package Explorer view and then select **Properties** from the context menu or press **Alt+Enter. Working directory** by default is the Java project in your workspace containing the scrapbook page. This is for relative file references. You can also change the JRE used for the scrapbook page and pass arguments to the JVM.

Scrapbook pages get their classpath from the containing project's build path. If in a scrapbook page you want to reference a Java element that is not on the build path of the containing Java project, you need to add it to the Java project's build path. Scrapbook pages also allow you to specify import statements. Do this by selecting **Set Imports...** from the context menu of a scrapbook page or **Set the Import Declarations for Running Code** ⬆≡ from the toolbar. You need to set import statements for references to Java declarations in your projects. This is a common oversight. If the type or package you are attempting to import is not listed in the Add dialog, it means you need to add it to the build path of the project containing the scrapbook page. If you are referencing an element that has multiple declarations, you will need to add an import statement to uniquely identify the element.

To assure the code you are executing does not corrupt the Eclipse development environment or another program execution, evaluated expressions are executed in a separate JVM, in a separate process. The JVM is started the first time you evaluate an expression in a scrapbook page after it is created or opened. The JVM for a scrapbook page runs until the page is closed or explicitly stopped with **Stop the Evaluation** ■ from the context menu or the toolbar. You can leave the JVM associated with your scrapbook page running and return to it later if you want to try a test; of course it will still have in-memory state from your previous evaluations. When a scrapbook page is in the process of evaluating, the run label decoration id is displayed 🗾. If the expression you're evaluating results in a loop or a hang, select **Stop the Eval-**

**uation**. In some cases this may not stop execution. If it doesn't stop, simply close the scrapbook page and then reopen it.

In the next section, we're going to get into debugging. You'll see that some debugging function is not available if you start your program from a scrapbook page. For example, you cannot evaluate expressions with **Display** and **Inspect**.

## Debugging

The JDT debugging capability comprises the Debug perspective, several views, and enhancements to the Java editor to allow you to find and fix runtime errors in your programs. You control the execution of your Java program by setting breakpoints and watchpoints, examining and changing the contents of fields and variables, stepping through the execution of your programs, and suspending and resuming threads. Figure 4.2 shows the default configuration of the Debug perspective as it appears when you first start a debugging session.

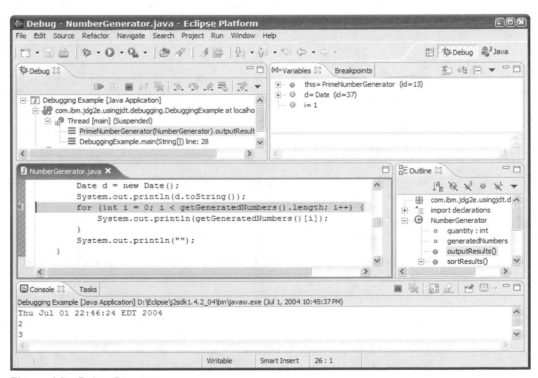

**Figure 4.2** Debug Perspective

In the Debug view in the upper left portion of the perspective are entries for the programs you're debugging. The display in Figure 4.2 shows that an instance of `DebuggingExample` has been launched. The current stack frame ☰, where execution is suspended, is selected. You can think of a stack frame as a method invocation. When one method invokes another, a stack frame is added to the top of the stack. When the method returns, that stack frame is removed from the top of the stack. This means you can traverse the series of method invocations that resulted in your program's current state by examining the series of stack frames.

The Variables view, in the upper right, shows the values of local variables. Stacked behind this is the Breakpoints view, which contains breakpoints for controlling program execution. The code for the current stack frame is in the editor in the middle on the left. The line that is about to be executed (the instruction pointer) in the current stack frame is selected and indicated with a solid arrow ➡. You may also see a hollow arrow ⇨. This is an instruction pointer for another stack frame referencing this code. The contents in the Outline view (in the middle on the right) correspond to the source in the editor. On the bottom, the Console view shows the output from the program. Breakpoints show up on the editor marker bar, ⬤, and by default they also show on the overview ruler as small blue rectangles and, of course, in the Breakpoints view.

## The Fundamentals

When you debug Java, your fundamental activities are the following.

- Step through the execution of your program with actions in the Debug view.
- Follow the source in the editor as it executes.
- Manage your breakpoints from the editor and the Breakpoints view.
- Examine variable values in the Variables view.
- Evaluate expressions and view the results.
- Follow the output of your program in the Console view.

Getting started with debugging is simple. You set a breakpoint in your code, start a debugging session, control execution of your code, and examine the state of your program as it runs. The following sections describe these steps.

### Setting a Breakpoint

The simplest way to set a breakpoint is to double-click in the editor's marker bar on the line where you want the breakpoint defined. You can also position the insertion cursor in a line and then press **Ctrl+Shift+B**. Press **Ctrl+Shift+B** again to remove the breakpoint. Another simple solution is to select **Stop on Main** on the **Main** page of your launch configuration.

## Starting a Debugging Session

To start a debugging session, select a Java program or a Java element containing the `main` method you want to debug, and select **Debug ☼ ▼ > Debug As... > Java Application** from the menu or the toolbar. The behavior here is the same as the respective **Run** actions to run a Java program. The JDT executes the Java program and suspends execution prior to the line with a breakpoint you defined. If you start execution with one of the **Run** actions, even if you have breakpoints defined, you will not be switched to the Debug perspective.

## Controlling Program Execution

You control program execution from the Debug view with the following actions.

- **Step Over** ⟳ or **F6** executes a statement and suspends execution on the statement after that.
- **Step Into** ⟱ or **F5**, for method invocations, creates a new stack frame, invokes the method in the statement, and suspends execution on the first statement in the method. For other statements, like assignments and conditions, the effect is the same as **Step Over**.
- **Step Return** ⟰ or **F7** resumes execution to the end of the current method and suspends execution on the statement after the method invocation or until another breakpoint is encountered.
- **Resume** ⫘ or **F8** causes execution to continue until the program ends or another breakpoint is encountered.
- **Terminate** ■ stops the current execution without executing any more statements.

## Examining an Executing Program

When your program's execution is suspended in the debugger, you can examine its execution state in the following ways.

- **Manipulating values**—examine values in the Variables and Expressions views. Change a value by double-clicking it or editing it in the detail pane. If you edit a value in the detail pane, you need to save the change with **Ctrl+S** to have it take effect.
- **Viewing field values**—see the value of a field by hovering over it in the editor.

- **Viewing method invocations**—see the series of method invocations that led to the current stack frame by selecting previous stack frames in the Debug view.
- **Evaluating expressions**—select an expression in the editor, the Display view, or in the detail pane of the Expressions or Variables view, and then select **Display** [ⅉ] or **Ctrl+Shift+D** to display results of evaluating the expression. Select **Inspect** 🔍 or **Ctrl+Shift+I** to inspect the results of evaluating the expression.
- **Viewing program output**—see program output in the Console view as you step through your program's execution.

Values of variables and fields presented in many of the views are results returned by toString. If that is not enough, you can customize what's shown in the debugging views by defining a **detail formatter**. Do this by setting your **Java > Debug > Detail Formatters** preferences or by selecting a nonprimitive variable in the Variables view and then selecting **New Detail Formatter...** or **Edit Detail Formatter...** from the context menu. In the Detail Formatter dialog, enter a code expression to replace toString for the variable.

## Evaluating Expressions

The Variables and Expressions views have detail panes that appear in the bottom half and right half of the views, respectively, so you can edit values (see Figure 4.3). In these detail panes, in the Display view, and in the Java Editor, you can edit a code expression, including using content assist, and evaluate it by selecting **Inspect** (**Ctrl+Shift+I**) or **Display** (**Ctrl+Shift+D**) from the context menu. The results will appear in a pop-up. If you need to keep the results of the operation, press **Ctrl+Shift+I** or **Ctrl+Shift+D** again and the information in the pop-up will be saved in the Expressions view or Display view, respectively. When you use **Inspect**, you get a hierarchical representation of the results, similar to what you see in the Variables view, that you can edit. When you use **Display**, you get the toString value of the result of evaluating the expression.

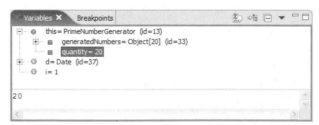

**Figure 4.3**   Detail Pane in the Variables View

When you evaluate an expression, it is done in the context of the current (selected) stack frame, so you must have a stack frame selected to evaluate an expression. You cannot evaluate expressions if you have manually suspended execution. The expression must be complete and valid. Recall the keyboard shortcuts for selecting expressions we discussed in Chapter 3, Using Java Development Tools: **Alt+Shift+Up**, **Alt+Shift+Down**, **Alt+Shift+Left**, and **Alt+Shift+Right**. Finally, some expressions, for example, variable declarations, cannot be evaluated.

### Changing Variable and Field Values

To change values in the Variables and Expressions views, double-click on a value and enter a new one. You can also simply edit the value in the detail pane and then select **Assign Value** from the context menu, or press **Ctrl+S**. Code assist is available in the detail pane. As you step through program execution and values change, the Variables view notes this by changing the color of its entries.

Changing values in the Variables and Expressions views changes them in the context of the current stack frame. If you use **Inspect** to evaluate an expression and that expression returns an object reference, that reference points to objects in the current stack frame. At this point, changing the value of an object shown by reference in the Expressions view changes the value in the current stack frame, thus impacting the execution of your program. This illustrates one of the reasons you might choose **Inspect** over **Display**. With **Inspect**, a reference to the result is added to the Expressions view. This is useful if you want to probe into complex types, refer back to the same result multiple times during an execution, or get in and modify values.

### Debugging with the Java Editor

The Java editor shows the code for the stack frame selected in the Debug view. This is the same Java editor that appears in the Java perspectives. Content assist, code generation, and refactoring work the same as in the Java perspectives.

If you attempt to **Step Into** a method for which the debugger does not have a source, you'll see the class file in the class file editor (see Figure 4.4). At this point, if you have the source, you can attach it. (We'll get to this in the section Associating a Source with Your Programs later in this chapter.) If not, select the previous stack frame (the one that invoked the method having no source) and then select **Step Over** 🔄 or **Drop to Frame** 🔽.

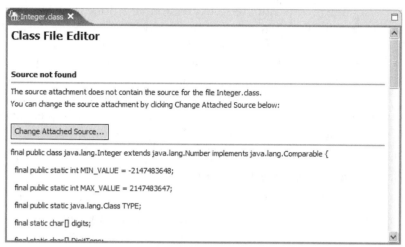

**Figure 4.4**   Class File Editor—Source Not Found

From the editor's context menu, select a line and then select **Run to Line** or **Ctrl+R** to have execution resume and then suspend on the selected line or at the next breakpoint encountered. If you want **Run to Line** to really run to the selected line regardless of any other breakpoints, enable this on your **Run/ Debug** preferences. **Step into Selection**, from the editor's context menu, provides a simple way to step into a single method invocation from among several on a single line of code. Simply select the method and **Step into Selection** from the editor's context menu. This is neat because you do not have to first set a breakpoint.

In Chapter 3, we showed how you can hover over a Java element to see its Javadoc in a pop-up. And you can press **Ctrl** while hovering in the editor to see the source for a Java element. When you navigate while pressing **Ctrl**, you'll notice Java elements in the source code turn to hyperlinks. Click on the link to go to the definition for the element. This is a convenient way to navigate through code while you're debugging.

If you're in the Debug perspective and you switch to the Java perspective to edit another file, when you switch back to the Debug perspective, the editor will still show the last file you were editing, not the one you were debugging. At this point, select the file you were debugging (if you recall) or select a stack frame entry in the Debug view to get back to where you were in your debugging session. You can also use the **Back** navigation button ⇦.

## *Manipulating the Programs You're Debugging*

The Debug view shows the programs you're currently debugging (and maybe others you were debugging that have terminated depending on your preference settings) and their associated processes and threads (see Figure 4.5).

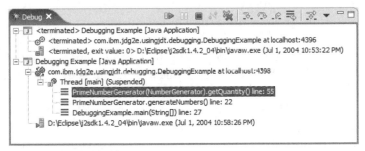

**Figure 4.5** Debug View

You will see a launch configuration entry for each program you are debugging, for example, a Java application ☐ or a remote Java application ☐. Each of these has a debug target 📦. A **debug target** is a running instance of a JVM executing code. Debug targets have properties that are useful for understanding the context in which the code is executing, such as the main method being executed, Java command line and JVM parameters, and classpath information. To see this information, select a debug target in the Debug view and then select **Properties** from the context menu (see Figure 4.6).

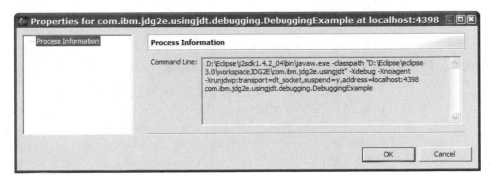

**Figure 4.6** Debug Target Properties

Your initial focus will usually be on the main thread 🔧 and the stack frame(s) ☰ under it. This is the thread of execution you're debugging and seeing in the editor. Stack frames appear with the most recent method invocation at the top of the list. Select the stack frames in this view to see the method invocations that led to the current state of execution. You can reset your program's execution to a previous stack frame. Select the stack frame in the Debug view and then select **Drop to Frame** ⭳. This is useful for "going back in time" to an earlier state in your program's execution without having to start from the very beginning.

A number of useful options in the Debug view are available from the toolbar and/or context menu. While a program is executing, you can manually suspend it with **Suspend** ⏸. The current stack frame is displayed, and the line that was executing is selected. This is useful if, for example, your program appears to be hung and you want to find out where it is looping. When you terminate a program or it finishes execution, it remains in the Debug view. This allows you to view the output of terminated programs in the Console view. By default, terminated launches are removed when a new one is created. If you want to keep your older, terminated launches around, change this setting in your **Run/Debug > Launch** preferences. If the list becomes cluttered, clean it up with **Remove All Terminated Launches** 🗑.

If you don't want to be bothered with the "Source not found" message if you inadvertently use **Step Into** while invoking a method for which you don't have the source code, or if you simply want to bypass system or other libraries to better focus your debugging, define step filters for packages or types and use **Step with Filters** ⏩. This causes **Step Into** to bypass method invocations matching the packages and types defined in your step filter preferences. Define step filters in your **Java > Debug > Step Filtering** preferences. You can also select **Filter Type** or **Filter Package** from the Debug view's context menu.

### Program Output in the Console View

The Console view provides for multiple console instances, one per debug session. As you select between the different debug sessions in the Debug View, the console instance shown in the Console view changes to match. Within each console view, Java elements in error output from exceptions are enabled for navigation (see Figure 4.7). Click on an exception and you'll see a dialog to allow you to define a Java exception breakpoint on the exception. Click on the name of a type and you'll see the type opened in the editor.

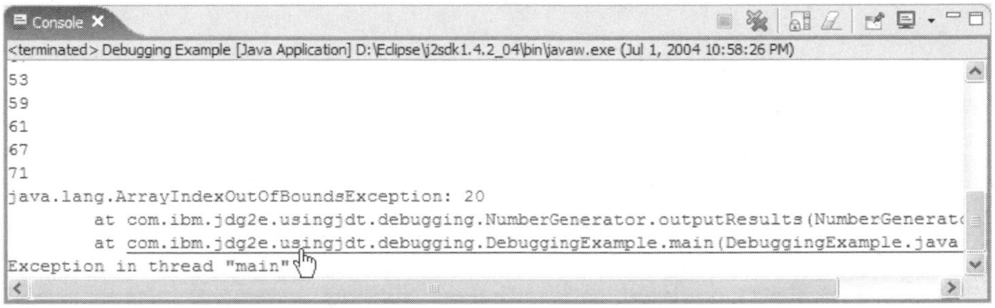

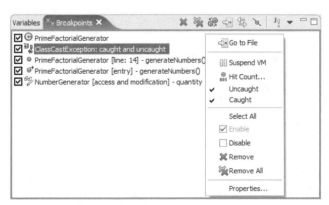

*Figure 4.7*    Opening a Type from the Console View

## More on Breakpoints

The JDT provides several kinds of breakpoints: line breakpoints, method breakpoints, watchpoints (field breakpoints), Java exception breakpoints, and class load breakpoints. Some of these can have conditions under which they become enabled, or active. The Breakpoints view (see Figure 4.8) shows all line breakpoints, exception breakpoints, watchpoints, method breakpoints, and class load breakpoints defined in your workspace. Double-click on a breakpoint or select **Go to File for Breakpoint** to go to the line on which it is defined. Check and uncheck breakpoints to quickly enable and disable them, without removing their definitions. You can disable all breakpoints in your workspace with **Skip All Breakpoints** . When you see breakpoint icons decorated with a small check mark, it means that that class has been loaded.

Table 4.1 shows the icons and the types of breakpoints they indicate.

*Figure 4.8*    Breakpoints View

**Table 4.1**   Breakpoint Icons

| Icon | Description |
|------|-------------|
| ● | Line breakpoint (enabled) |
| ○ | Line breakpoint (disabled) |
| 🔍 | Field access watchpoint |
| ✏ | Field modification watchpoint |
| 🔍✏ | Field access and modification watchpoint |
| J! | Java exception breakpoint (with a yellow exclamation mark) |
| J! | Java runtime exception breakpoint (with a red exclamation mark) |
| J! | Java exception breakpoint (disabled) (with a gray exclamation mark) |
| Ⓒ | Class load breakpoint |
| ✔ | Breakpoint decoration indicating the class is loaded |
| → | Decoration indicating an entry method breakpoint |
| ← | Decoration indicating an exit method breakpoint |
| ∓ | Decoration indicating a caught Java exception breakpoint |
| † | Decoration indicating an uncaught Java exception breakpoint |
| ⌐⌐ | Decoration indicating a scoped Java exception breakpoint |

Select a breakpoint and then select **Properties** from the context menu to set the properties for a breakpoint, including hit counts and conditions. See Figure 4.9 for properties on a line breakpoint. The breakpoint properties dialog will differ depending on the kind of breakpoint. When a hit count of *n* is defined on a breakpoint, the breakpoint suspends execution the *n*th time it is hit. At this point, the breakpoint becomes disabled. A **condition** is an expression that is evaluated in the context of the current stack frame. Execution suspends when the condition evaluates to true or the value of the expression changes, depending on the option you select in the breakpoint properties. Hit counts and conditions are useful for selectively suspending

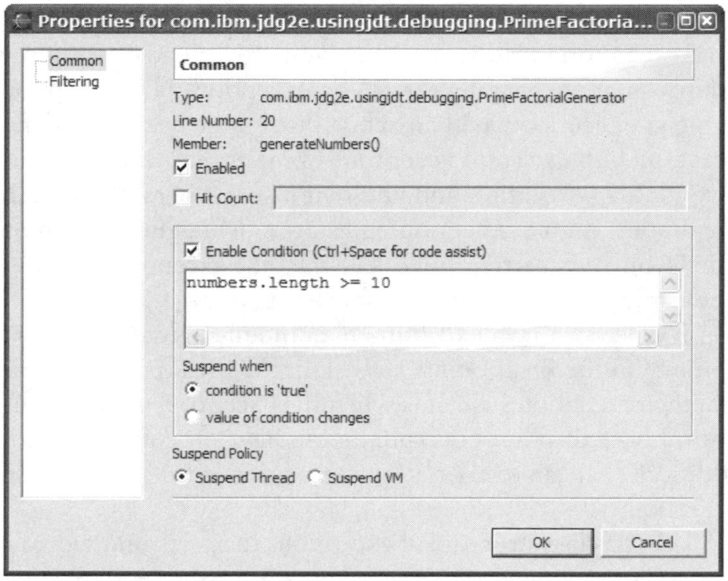

**Figure 4.9** Breakpoint Properties

execution on code that gets executed a lot, for example, an add method. Breakpoints can be restricted to one or more threads. Do this on the **Filtering** page. The **Suspend VM** option does just that—it suspends all processes and threads when the breakpoint is hit. This is useful for getting a handle on the execution state of the entire program when the breakpoint is encountered. Hover over a breakpoint on the editor marker bar to see information about its hit count and condition.

You can define breakpoints in JAR files outside your workspace. To define a line breakpoint, you need source defined for the external JAR file. You do not need source for the code in the JAR file to define class load breakpoints, method breakpoints, watchpoints, and Java exception breakpoints. The simplest way to do this is from the editor: select to open the declaration on some Java element defined in the external JAR file by using **F3** or **Ctrl+T** and selecting from the Type Hierarchy pop-up. You won't see source in the editor, but you will see the elements in the Outline view. Or you can expand the JAR file in the Package Explorer view to see its methods. When you define breakpoints on classes for which you do not have a source, ensure the Breakpoints view is visible because a new entry in the Breakpoints view is the only indication the breakpoint was defined.

## Java Exception Breakpoints

**Java exception breakpoints** allow you to suspend execution when the program you are debugging throws an exception. Java exception breakpoints suspend execution when any code throws the exception defined in the breakpoint, including classes in runtime libraries (e.g., the JRE). If your program is throwing an exception and you're not sure where it's originating, define a breakpoint on the exception and start a debugging session on the program. The Debug perspective will open when the exception is thrown, allowing you to examine the execution state at that point.

To specify a Java exception breakpoint, select **Add Java Exception Breakpoint** ᴶ in the Breakpoints view. Edit the breakpoint's properties to specify whether execution suspends when the exception is caught, not caught, or both. Java exception breakpoints can have hit counts but not conditions. In addition, you can restrict a Java exception breakpoint to a set of classes and/ or packages.

Use the class structure of exceptions to specify individual breakpoints that suspend execution when any of their subclass exceptions are thrown. For example, to suspend execution on any I/O exception, set an exception breakpoint on `java.io.IOException`. When you define more general exception breakpoints, you may want to restrict them only to uncaught exceptions.

The following Java exception breakpoints are generally useful. Define them and leave them in your workspace. Enable and disable them, or restrict them to selected packages, as may be required.

```
java.lang.NullPointerException
java.lang.ArrayIndexOutOfBoundsException
java.lang.ClassCastException
```

## Method Breakpoints

A **method breakpoint** suspends execution on entry to and/or exit from a method. This includes methods in classes for which you don't have a source, for example, in external libraries. Select a method in one of the Java views, such as the Outline view or Package Explorer view, and then select **Toggle Method Breakpoint** from the context menu. Edit its properties to specify when the breakpoint suspends execution: on entry, exit, or both. Like other types of breakpoints, method breakpoints can have hit counts and conditions.

## Watchpoints

A **watchpoint** (or field breakpoint) suspends execution on the line of code that is about to access the field on which the watchpoint is defined. When you want to observe how a field is accessed, it's often easier to use a watchpoint on the field than it is to try to set breakpoints on all the lines that might access the field. To define a watchpoint, select a field in one of the Java views and then select **Toggle Watchpoint** from the context menu. Edit the breakpoint's properties to specify when the watchpoint should suspend execution: on access, modification, or both. Watchpoints can also have hit counts and conditions.

### Class Load Breakpoints

A **class load breakpoint** suspends execution the first time a class is loaded. This is useful to understand when your classes or other system classes are being loaded or when you need to debug class loading behavior from custom class loaders. To set a class load breakpoint, select a class in one of the Java views, and then select **Toggle Class Load Breakpoint** from the context menu.

## *Associating a Source with Your Programs*

As you are stepping through code in a debugging session, you may see a message indicating source cannot be found for a method along with the class file shown in the class file editor. If you want to define source code for the method and class, the simplest thing to do at this point is use the **Attach Source...** button to specify the location of the source, assuming, of course, you have it. When you use **Attach Source...**, you are editing the source specification for the respective library. For example, for JREs, this is your **Java > Installed JREs** preferences. For JAR files you added to your project's build path, this is the **Libraries** page of the project's **Java Build Path** properties.

## *Hot Code Replace*

**Hot code replace** is a powerful tool that enables you to change the code that is currently running in your debug session to quickly try fixes and/or alternative code, without having to restart your program and reproduce the state you were debugging. Even if you intend to deploy on a JRE that does not support hot code replacement, developing on one prior to final testing can be more productive.

To use hot code replace, you need to debug your program with a JVM that supports it. To install a JRE (and associated JVM), do so with your **Java > Installed JREs** preferences. Set this to be the default JRE. Alternatively, create a launch configuration for your program, and on the **JRE** page specify a JRE that supports hot code replace.

Once you're configured for hot code replace, simply set a breakpoint in your code and start a debugging session. When you stop at a breakpoint, change the code in the editor and save it. The changed class is compiled, the stack frame replaced, and debugging resumes. If you do not have auto-build enabled in your preferences, you'll need to do a manual build by selecting one of the **Project > Build** commands.

If you get an error when attempting hot code replace, one or more of your stack frames may be obsolete or invalid. You'll know this because you'll get a pop-up to this effect. Bypass these stack frames by selecting the most recent (top-most in the Debug view) valid stack frame and stepping over the selected line (method invocation). Or select a previous stack frame in the Debug view and then select **Drop to Frame** 🖐.

There are some limitations with hot code replace worth noting. You can't change the shape of a class, for example, by adding or deleting methods or fields. Also, changing variable references in an inner class can cause the compiler to generate synthetic methods in the outer class, changing its shape. You need to use the `*.class` files that the Java compiler creates; using those generated by `javac` is not supported. Some JVMs can't replace the bottom (`main` method) stack frame if you change it or stack frames above a native method. In this case, you'll need to step into a method first before you can change code and have the JVM replace the stack frame. There are limitations on the kinds of code changes you can make, for example, changes in and around `try/catch` blocks. Some JVMs may require command line parameters; refer to the documentation for the JVM. If you're having difficulty getting hot code replace to work, do the following.

- Ensure the JVM you're using supports hot code replace.
- Use the `showversion` JVM command line parameter to verify the JVM running in the debugging session is the correct one.
- Try a simple change (not in the `main` method), like changing a string literal or value of an `int`.

## Remote Debugging

The Java debugger allows you to debug programs remotely, including using hot code replace with JVMs that support it. Remote programs include those running on your local machine outside of Eclipse and programs on another machine, either standalone or in a server environment. One of the most common uses for this is to debug Java running outside of Eclipse in an application server, for example, servlets or EJBs. It also works for "standalone" Java programs and for Java applets.

Debugging a remote program is similar to debugging a local one, except that the remote program must be launched first with certain JVM parameters, and you need to specify a Remote Java Application launch configuration. When you launch your remote program with the parameters specified below, it starts and then suspends, waiting for a connection from a debugger. The launch configuration contains information for the JDT debugger to connect to the JVM running the remote program and initiate a debugging session. The debugger gets the source for the code being debugged from your workspace.

To debug a program remotely, you need to start the remote program with the following JVM command line parameters (which should appear together on one line). How you specify these depends on what you're remotely debugging. If it's a standalone Java application, these parameters go on the command line with the program invocation. For servlets, the answer is specific to the application server. For Tomcat 5.0 from the Apache Software Foundation, for example, you set these in the CATALINA_OPTS environment variable. For applets, use the Java console for the browser Java plug-in. There should be a field for JVM parameters.

```
-Xdebug -Xnoagent
  -Xrunjdwp:transport=dt_socket,server=y,suspend=y,address=8000
  -Djava.compiler=NONE
```

The -Xdebug parameter enables debugging, -Xnoagent disables support for oldjdb (old Java debugger), -Xrunjdwp: specifies Java Debug Wire Protocol (JDWP) options for the connection, and 8000 is the port the debugger will use to communicate with the JVM. Remember this because you'll need to specify it in your launch configuration. The server=y parameter tells the remote JVM not to attempt to connect to the debugger after the JVM starts but rather to wait for an inbound connection. The suspend=y parameter causes the JVM to start but suspend execution before the main method is loaded and then wait until a connection is received from the debugger. The –Djava.compiler=NONE parameter disables the Just in Time (JIT) compiler.

To define a Remote Java Application launch configuration, select **Debug > Debug...** to see the Launch Configurations dialog. Select **Remote Java Application** as the type of launch configuration and then select **New**. On the **Connect** page, **Project** specifies the Java project containing the source for the remote program you are debugging. In **Connection Properties**, specify the same port number that you used in the JDWP options (address=8000) to launch the remote Java program. For programs running on the same machine, use localhost for **Host**. Specifying **Allow termination of remote VM** allows you to terminate the remote program from the debugging session.

When you have your JVM command line parameters set and your launch configuration defined, first start the remote Java program (with the command line parameters) and then start a debugging session using the launch configuration. A debugging session starts on the remote program. At this point, continue debugging as if you were debugging a local program.

If you are unable to get a remote debugging session started, try the following.

- Run your program without the additional JVM command line parameters to ensure the program will run correctly without having the JVM attempt to configure for remote debugging.
- Check communication between the machines. Ping the remote machine from the local machine using the hostname or IP address you specified in the launch configuration.
- Ensure the port numbers in the launch configuration and in your JVM command line parameters match.
- Ensure that the .dll files the JVM requires (e.g., jdwp.dll and dt_socket.dll) on the remote machine are on the search path, for example, in the PATH variable. Ensure the .dll files that the JVM is finding are the correct ones, for example, if there are multiple JREs in the search path of the remote machine.

If all else fails, search the Eclipse newsgroup archives for others who have had difficulty getting remote debugging working and then get on the newsgroup; the community is a helpful one.

## Exercise Summary

Exercise 3, Running and Debugging Java, reinforces much of the material presented in this chapter. The exercise is broken down into a number of sections, each demonstrating different debugging concepts.

1. Launch Configurations

   In this first section, you'll see how to run Java programs using launch configurations. This includes passing program arguments, passing JVM parameters, and referring to classes in a runtime library (JAR file).

2. Debugging

   In this section, you'll debug a Java program, use breakpoints, examine program execution, and see how to control program execution.

3. Debugging II

   This section starts where the previous one left off. You'll see more kinds of breakpoints, view and change variable values, use launch configurations to start a debugging session, and refer to classes in a runtime library.

4. Debugging Threads

In this section, you'll debug a multithreaded program and see watch-points and method breakpoints on a class in a JAR file for which you do not have the source.

5. Remote Debugging

In the final section of the exercise, you'll see how to debug a program running outside of Eclipse.

Exercise 4, Developing a Simple Web Commerce Application with Eclipse, provides a more robust programming example, developing, deploying, and debugging a servlet application in Apache's Tomcat. This exercise brings together a number of individual concepts presented in Part I.

## Chapter Summary

The JDT provides a wide range of capabilities for developing, testing, running, and debugging your Java code. This chapter first explored mechanisms available to run Java code and to manage runtime environments with launch configurations. We then looked at debugging using the JDT. This chapter described the different kinds of breakpoints and how to define them, enable and disable them, and set their properties, including hit counts and conditions. Next we discussed how to control program execution through the debugger step commands and how to examine and change variable and field values. The topic of launch configurations reappeared, and we covered how to use them to start debugging sessions, including ones on remote programs. Finally, we outlined how to debug a program remotely, including the command line parameters required.

## Reference

Arthorne, John, and Chris Laffra. 2004. *Official Eclipse 3.0 FAQs*. Boston, MA, Addison-Wesley. http://eclipsefaq.org. (See Chapter 3 and FAQs 313, 317, 318.)

# CHAPTER 5

## *Teaming Up with Eclipse*

If any lesson has become abundantly clear in software development, it is this: No one is an island. The reach and scope of software development has encompassed multiple disciplines that can no longer treat each other at arm's length. The days of finishing your work and then "tossing it over the wall" to the next group in the software cycle are over, over, over. Eclipse recognizes this reality and supports integration with repository providers within its IDE. Collaborators can easily share their portions of an application in a single, version-controlled location. Since Eclipse has a common IDE infrastructure, everyone has a common view, as well as additional integrated tools of choice, for how they interact with others. In the ultra-fast pace of today's software environment, rarely is one person confined to a single role. While some large organizations may have the luxury of mammoth development groups separated by base technology or core discipline, most organizations must have the flexibility to move skilled personnel from project to project, without the overhead of adapting to the local toolset of each group. The team repository, coupled with Eclipse as your tool integration platform, becomes the lingua franca of these roaming professionals.

Naturally, repositories offer asset protection for both the organization and the individual. Your work, as well as the collective work of your team, when placed in a repository, provides safe storage. However, it does more—the repository becomes the collective intellectual knowledge of the team as it applies to a particular problem domain. It is a source of learning, as the techniques used by some become the inspiration for others. Depending on your provider, your repository may allow you to track defects and features, manage workflow, and provide a robust development process. Repositories are no longer limited to "programmers" to store their "source code"; content of all types make up today's software application, involving Web pages, documentation, database descriptions, and code, of course. A variety of professionals have a need for these repositories.

With this in mind, a fundamental objective of Eclipse is to provide first-class support for team programming. Since Eclipse is an extensible platform, it offers, through its architecture, the capability for any provider to enable their repository to it. A repository provider, using the integration mechanisms of Eclipse, can make their repository directly accessible to users. A number of commercial and noncommercial providers have integrated their repositories with Eclipse.

Eclipse comes configured with direct support for a specific repository called Concurrent Versions System (CVS). CVS is a widely used, open source repository. You do not need to install anything to use Eclipse with CVS; support is built in. Just connect to a CVS server and you are all set. The Eclipse team uses CVS for its own development. In fact, the authoring team for this book managed development of all the chapters, exercises, examples, and associated graphics files using Eclipse and CVS.

In this chapter we cover team support and, specifically, support for CVS repositories. Exercise 5, Working as a Team with CVS, shows you how to use CVS with Eclipse. You can perform the exercise steps or simply read it for understanding. The exercise is essential to gain a full understanding of support for CVS.

You may wish to complement your reading of this chapter with information in the *Workbench User Guide* in the online help. Refer to "Working in the team environment with CVS" in the "Tasks" section. Speaking of help, check out the cheat sheets available for CVS under the action **Help > Cheat Sheets... > CVS Tasks** (cheat sheets are discussed in Chapter 2, Getting Started with Eclipse).

## Eclipse Support for CVS

Before we get into the details of team programming support, let's take a brief look at what is available "out of the box." You get a complete and easy-to-use interface to CVS. If you are already a CVS user, you can set those complex, hard-to-remember commands syntax aside. If you are new to CVS, you are in luck. Assuming you have access to a CVS repository, you should be able to complete a connection and, within minutes, check out projects into your workspace or share your projects with others. Eclipse offers many benefits and features for the new or experienced CVS user.

- The views and editors that help you with your code management needs are found in one place, the CVS Repository Exploring perspective. It contains a view of the contents of one or more repositories, an editor area to examine files in CVS, and a view of the change history of any file.
- Do you want to see what's out there? Using the CVS Repositories view, you can connect to a repository using a simple dialog, explore the repository contents, and check out one or more projects of interest.
- Other views provide visual "clues" about the state of your work as it relates to the repository. The use of icon decorators and textual information in the Navigator and Package Explorer views shows which projects are under CVS control and which files have been modified and are no longer in sync with the CVS repository.
- You have ready access to CVS from your workspace. The **Team** context menu is available from projects, folders, and files. It allows you to put new projects under CVS control, refresh or **update** your workspace with the latest contents in CVS, share or **commit** your changes to the repository, and version projects that have reached important milestones.
- Are you ready to share your changes? The Team Synchronizing perspective is a very powerful tool that allows you to see differences between your local files and CVS before committing changes to the repository. Conflicts are identified automatically, and assistance is available to help you merge your changes. The synchronization support is also available for other repository providers to use.
- Do you have a complicated change and need a little privacy while you work through it? **Branching** and **merging** allow for independent parallel development.
- Did you have a long weekend and forgot where you left off on Friday? Using the **Compare With** menu action you can compare workspace resource contents with the repository.
- Do you want to abandon some local changes you decided were incorrect? The **Replace With** action allows you to replace your workspace project, or any previous instance, with the latest CVS contents.

- Are you scratching your head trying to figure out what has gone wrong with some code that was working the last time you looked at it? The CVS Annotate view will tell you who changed the code and what the change was.
- Were you a good team member and fixed someone else's code but you would rather not update his or her code permanently? Use Eclipse to create a patch and send it to your grateful colleague.

These features sound useful and easy . . . and they are! Later, we will explore these capabilities in detail, as well as examine some working scenarios. However, before we go there, let's look at Eclipse team support a little more thoroughly.

## General Team Support by Eclipse

It is important, as a general-purpose IDE, that Eclipse work with the widest possible range of technologies and user audiences. This means that software artifacts in Eclipse are best managed in the local file system. Eclipse then has to be able to connect and store the resources in whatever repository the user chooses.

Repository providers are free to integrate their repository as they see fit and take full advantage of the features of their technology. Eclipse offers some areas of consistency in the user interface and provides mechanisms to help the repository provider manage resources between a user's workspace and the repository. The "Team Repository Providers" section of the Eclipse Community Projects and Plug-ins page on eclipse.org (http://www.eclipse.org/community/plugins.html) lists a large number of available repository access plug-ins. Many commercial repository suppliers provide support for Eclipse, and there are some open source contributions as well. Each provider's implementation will differ significantly, since each focuses on the features appropriate to their own repository.

Information on how to integrate a repository with Eclipse can be found in the online help. The *Platform Plug-in Developer Guide* has an entire section devoted to the topic of team support.

### Common Principles of Eclipse Team Support

Before we discuss how to use a specific repository like CVS, let's briefly cover the principles of Eclipse team support that are common to any integrated repository.

Here are the fundamental principles of team support.

- A workspace may be connected to one or more instances of any type of repository. For example, you might have project A managed by CVS, project B managed by Rational ClearCase, and project C managed by PVCS from Serena.
- Only one repository instance can be associated with a project. That is, you can't have some files in a project managed by one repository and other files managed by another. If you require this, place the files into separate projects.
- Eclipse should be able to operate disconnected from the repositories that are managing your projects. The intent is that after you check out your code from the repository, you should be able to work independently and without the need to maintain an active repository connection. You should only need to connect to the repository to receive updates from others or commit changes you have made. However, it is up to the specific repository provider to support this.
- Linked resources in a project have to be explicitly supported by a repository provider. Most providers, including Eclipse's CVS, do not provide this support.

### Configuring Team Support

Repository providers implement their support in a way that best suits their users and their technology. Eclipse maintains a category of pages in the Preferences dialog labeled **Team**. CVS and other repository providers define their preference pages under the **Team** category.

The preference pages **File Content** and **Ignored Resources** are part of the team support, but they work only if a repository supports those pages. CVS does support them.

Eclipse provides a common context menu for projects, folders, and files. Not surprisingly, the menu is labeled **Team**. CVS and other repository providers define their context menu actions under this menu. If you have a workspace with more than one repository associated with it, then for any particular project, you will see only the actions for the repository associated with that project.

To get started, select a project in the Navigator view, and then select **Team > Share Project....** This action, available to any project not under repository management, is how you place a project under control of a specific repository. A wizard is displayed that allows you to associate the project with a previously defined repository, or you may define a new repository connection. The repository provider may add pages in the wizard to complete the sharing task.

## An Overview of CVS for the Novice

If you are already familiar with CVS, you may want to skip this section. Otherwise, let's spend a little time to get you comfortable with the fundamentals of CVS and learn some of the lingo.

CVS is an open source project. It dates back to 1986 as a simple set of UNIX shell scripts provided by Dick Grune. It evolved significantly in 1989, when Brian Berliner designed and coded CVS. It has evolved over time with contributions from many others. It is available on several platforms including Windows, UNIX, and Linux. For more information on CVS, go to http://www.cvshome.org.

Like any software management repository, CVS records a history of changes to the files it manages. The files it is managing are available to other members of your team. There are more sophisticated repositories than CVS, but for modest-sized teams with clear definitions of code ownership, it can be quite effective. CVS does not have features like defect or feature tracking, build capabilities, or support for development processes that other repositories might offer.

Eclipse maintains an index of CVS information and a frequently asked questions (FAQ) list (see the references at the end of the chapter).

### Some Key CVS Design Principles

Your project is known to CVS as a **module**. A module appears as a directory in CVS, much like a project in your workspace. This is sometimes referred to as a **physical module**. CVS also has a notion of a **logical** or **virtual module**, which is a collection of related resources defined in the CVS special file called modules. Eclipse supports both logical and physical modules.

CVS uses a traditional command interface, and Eclipse communicates with CVS using this interface. Retrieving a file from a CVS repository requires use of a command called **checkout**. Changes are put back into CVS using the **commit** command. If you want to refresh the local copy of your code with any changes that exist in CVS since the last time you checked it out, you would use the **update** command. Fortunately, Eclipse provides a GUI interface to CVS so you don't have to deal directly with these commands. You will see these terms in the Eclipse user interface for CVS. If you are interested, there is a preference setting that allows you to see the actual CVS commands executed for any given Eclipse action that communicates with CVS (**Team > CVS > Console** page). If you are comfortable with CVS commands, you can execute them directly against workspace projects in a command line environment (see the online help for more information). Be sure to refresh your workspace afterward or use the Eclipse automatic refresh support.

The CVS repository uses what is known as an **optimistic locking model**, which means that when you check out a file, it is not locked in the repository. Others with CVS access can also check out the same file and make changes. You manage collisions when you put the files back. Many repositories use a **pessimistic locking model**. In the pessimistic model, when a file is checked out, it is locked. This prevents others from updating it until it is checked in. Eclipse permits integration with repositories using either type of model. CVS works well in an environment where collisions are rare. From time to time conflicts can occur. As you will learn, Eclipse and CVS assist you in resolving these situations.

### Revisions: Nothing Ever Goes Away

Since CVS keeps track of file changes, each change must be identified. CVS does this by applying a revision number to each file it is managing. Each time a file is modified and committed to CVS, it receives a new revision number. The first time a file is committed, its revision number is 1.1. The next time, it gets a revision number of 1.2, then 1.3, and so on. Revision numbers can get longer and a bit more complicated. We will cover that a little later in this chapter.

Revision numbers are displayed in the CVS Resource History view, the Navigator view, and other views displaying workspace resources. You can always access previous revisions of a file. CVS also allows you to identify resources of interest with a textual label called a **tag**. This is sometimes an easier way to access older instances of resources. We will cover tags in more detail when we discuss versioning.

### Updating: Keeping Up with the Team

**Updating** allows your CVS managed projects to receive any changes made by your colleagues, thus keeping your workspace up-to-date with the latest in the repository. An update does not overwrite your files. Instead, it automatically merges differences between your local file and the latest file instance in CVS (except for binary files). If there are conflicts, the merge will complete, but the conflicting lines of text will be replaced with a special CVS markup text identifying the conflicts (which could introduce undesirable errors). Eclipse offers alternative synchronization mechanisms to minimize unexpected conflicts. If code ownership is well defined among your colleagues, conflicts will be rare, and a CVS update is more like a catch-up operation.

Eclipse provides support for CVS update operations through its **Team > Update...** and **Team > Synchronize with Repository...** actions, available for any workspace resource. We will explore these in detail. There is an informative description of how conflicts are handled in the *Workbench User Guide* under the topic "Working in the Team Environment with CVS" titled "Updating."

### Committing: Your Turn to Share

**Commit** is the reverse of an update. An update is a pull from the repository, and a commit is a push. When you perform a CVS commit, you are pushing your changes to the CVS repository and sharing them with your team. This results in a new revision number for the files you modified. Of course, a commit is a serious operation, and you want to be confident of your changes before committing. If there are conflicts because someone committed a change ahead of you, the commit operation will fail. *You should always resynchronize with CVS before committing your changes to minimize the possibility of a conflict.*

### Versioning: Capturing the Moment

CVS provides a mechanism that allows you to tag a specific revision of a file with a text label. This label becomes a symbolic name that can be used to refer to the specific revision. Tagging individual files is usually not terribly useful. Normally, you want to tag a set of files that represents a completed piece of work. In CVS terms, you tag a module (which corresponds to an Eclipse project) when a significant milestone has been reached. All the latest revisions of the files in the module are tagged with the same symbolic name. You can think of this set of tagged files as a **version**. It is important to understand that a project's files, with the same assigned tag, may have different revision numbers. For any particular external change (like a bug or a functional enhancement), some files may change a lot, some may change a little, and some do not change at all. When you version a project, you are tagging the **latest revision level** of each file in the project. Versions are not intended to be changed; they represent a static snapshot of your project after some milestone. While you can check out a versioned project into your workspace, you cannot commit changes to it. However, you can create a branch from a version and make changes from there. We cover branches in the next topic.

CVS reserves a tag name called **HEAD**. You will see **HEAD** in the Eclipse user interface. It represents the main development branch (or trunk) of the repository.

Tagging by date is also possible. This allows you to take a snapshot of the repository for a particular date (and, optionally, time). You can use date tags to compare, check out, merge, or simply browse a CVS repository. As with other tags, the date tag is just a reflection of the revision numbers of the repository contents at the time the tag was created.

### Branching and Merging: Support for Parallel Development

A **branch** represents a fork in the development process. It allows you to make changes to your project independent of the main development stream called **HEAD**. You might do this for several reasons.

- You are working on a bug in a completed release of your product while development is going on for the next release, and you don't want to mix the correction with the current development code.
- You want to create a maintenance branch separate from a major functional release that is going on concurrently. All maintenance will be performed in this branch and later merged to the next major functional release. You have a big development change that won't be ready for a while. You want to complete it independently of the main line of development to avoid causing problems with the shared base code. You will merge your change after it is completed.

In CVS, a branch is identified by using a branch tag that splits the latest revision levels of a set of files. In Eclipse terms, this means that resources in a CVS managed project in your workspace are tagged with the branch name. You can then make your changes and check them in to CVS, independent of other changes that may be going on in that project.

It is possible to have more than one branch on a file or project at the same time. A branch can even spawn another branch. **HEAD** is, essentially, the main branch.

After you have completed the code in your branch, you may want to merge it with the main trunk. We'll cover how to merge using Eclipse shortly. The effect of a **merge** is to bring the changes you made in your branch back to the development stream in which the branch started. For example, after you have fixed and tested a bug, you may want to merge it back into the base code. Merging may involve resolving conflicts because the files you are working on may be undergoing changes by others. Eclipse provides assistance in helping resolve conflicts. Eclipse CVS support offers a cheat sheet for this process that is available from the Cheat Sheet Selection dialog under Help.

### What Happens to Revision Numbers When Branching and Merging

In order to keep track of changes in a branch, the revision number is expanded to incorporate the branch. If a file in the main branch, **HEAD**, is at revision level 1.3 when a branch is created, its revision number becomes 1.3.2.1. The ordinal 2 defines the branch, and the final ordinal 1 indicates the revision within the branch. When the branch instance of the file is committed to CVS, it becomes 1.3.2.2, then 1.3.2.3, and so on. Branching off the existing branch adds two more ordinals to the end of the revision number reflecting the new branch and its revision. Consequently, a revision number might become quite lengthy. Recall that we branched at revision 1.3, thus creating revision 1.3.2.1. When we complete our merge, the latest revision number will be 1.4, just where we left off when we started our branch (unless, of course, there were other changes committed between the start of our branch and our merge). Fortunately, branches are tagged with names that make it unnecessary for you to remember all of this.

### Managing Binary Files Using CVS

Though CVS provides considerable assistance with character-based (ASCII) files, it has only basic support for binary files. You can store binary files in CVS and manage them as revisions, but that is about all. Binary files need to be identified as such. A list of files by type, either ASCII or binary, is contained in the **Team > File Content** preference page.

CVS will detect conflicts in binary files using simple file time stamps. In a CVS update operation, if a conflict is detected on a binary file, the repository instance replaces your local instance. In addition, a copy of the local file instance is added to your project. The file name is prefixed with the characters .# (a period followed by a pound sign) and suffixed with the revision number. You must use other techniques to handle the conflict.

## The CVS User Interface in Eclipse

Now that you have a basic understanding of CVS, we'll discuss how Eclipse supports you as a CVS user. To do this, let's look at the user interface in some detail. Before starting, it is worth noting that, like many operations in

Eclipse, most of the CVS repository access operations run in the background and don't block you from doing other work. Potentially long-running operations like checkout, commit, and synchronization will run without interfering with other tasks you want to perform. Here is a short list of the most common tasks you will perform with CVS through the Eclipse user interface. You will get experience with all of them in Exercise 5.

- Define a connection to a CVS repository.
- Browse a CVS repository.
- Define a new workspace project to CVS.
- Check out an existing project from CVS.
- Commit changes in your workspace to CVS.
- Update your workspace project with the lastest updates in CVS.
- Version your project at appropriate milestones.
- Compare or replace workspace resources with repository resources.

### The CVS Repository Exploring Perspective: Your Repository Home Page

The CVS Repository Exploring perspective, shown in Figure 5.1, is your home base for working with CVS. It contains the CVS Repositories view, the CVS Resource History view, and an editor area. The CVS Repositories view displays the CVS repositories known to your workspace. The CVS Resource History view shows the history of changes to any given file under CVS control. Establishing a connection to a CVS server can be performed from here.

### The CVS Repositories View

The CVS Repositories view serves as a repository browser. In it you can select projects that exist in the repository and check out these projects to your workspace. It occupies the left pane of the CVS Repository Exploring perspective, as shown in Figure 5.1. Use the context menu **New > Repository Location...** or select **Add CVS Repository** to define a CVS repository location in your workspace. Eclipse supports all the various CVS connection types (see Figure 5.2). You can have more than one CVS repository defined in this view. As you browse in the repository, you can see the contents of the repository, including projects in **HEAD**, in branches, in versions, and at specific points in time. You can drill all the way down to specific files by expanding the tree or using the toolbar actions **Go Into** ⇨ and **Back** ⇦. There is a **Refresh View** action on the toolbar; you will probably want to refresh the view before doing anything significant, as it is not automatically kept current with changes in the repository.

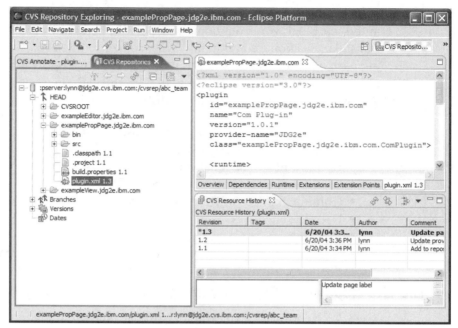

**Figure 5.1**    CVS Repository Exploring Perspective

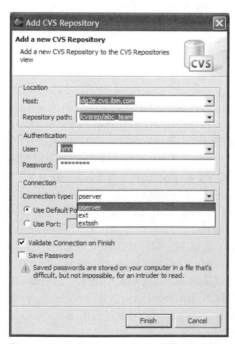

**Figure 5.2**    Defining a New CVS Repository Location to a Workspace

As a convenience, if you open the CVS Repositories view from the Resource perspective, it will appear as a tabbed view alongside the Navigator view.

One of the most common tasks in this view is to check out a project from the repository to your workspace. To do this, select a project under **Branches**, **HEAD**, or **Versions** and select the context menu **Check Out**.

The first time you expand the **Branches** element of the view, you won't see anything. The context menu action, **Refresh Branches...**, presents a dialog (see Figure 5.3) in which you can request that branch tags be retrieved from CVS for one or more repository projects. A CVS repository could contain a large number of branches. You are probably interested in just a few of them. This dialog allows you to retrieve branch tag information for just the projects you want. Table 5.1 provides a reference list of all the context menu actions available in the CVS Repositories view. Some actions depend on what

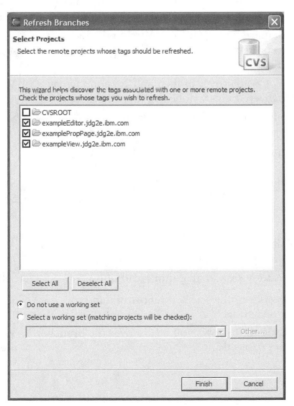

**Figure 5.3**   Refresh Branches Dialog

ailable in the CVS Repositories View

| | Description | Available from This Context |
|---|---|---|
| Ad..<br>List... | Adds a project (but not its content) to a new or existing branch. This is not the normal process for working in a branch. Instead use the **Team > Branch** action. This action might be useful for new projects that will be developed exclusively in a branch. | Selected project |
| Check Out | Copies the selection from the repository to your workspace. A folder may be checked out and its identity with its project is maintained. This can be useful when working with large projects with self-contained portions. | Selected project or project folder under **Branches**, **HEAD**, or **Versions** |
| Check Out As... | Copies the selection from the repository to your workspace under another name. The project retains its original identity in CVS when committing changes. This could be useful when you need to have more than one instance of the same project in your workspace at the same time. | Selected project or project folder under **Branches**, **HEAD**, or **Versions** |
| Compare | Displays the Compare view when two repository files are selected. | Two resources selected |
| Compare With... | Opens the Compare with Branch or Version dialog and allows you to compare the selected resource with a resource in **HEAD**, a branch, or version. | Selected resource |
| Configure Branches and Versions... | Presents a dialog to discover branch and version tags on resources. Discovered tags will be displayed in the view. | Various |
| Copy to Clipboard | Copies the connection string to the Clipboard. Example: `:pserver:anonymous@dev.eclipse.org:/home/eclipse` | Selected repository |
| Discard location | Removes a repository location definition from the view. | Selected repository |
| New > Date Tag... | Presents a dialog to create a new date tag. | Selected repository Selected **Dates** in repository tree view |
| New > Repository Location... | Presents a dialog to define a new CVS repository location. A toolbar icon is also available. | Any |
| Open | Opens the latest revision in an editor (read only). | Selected file |
| Properties | Displays properties of the selected repository and connection information. | Selected repository |
| Refresh Branches... | Displays a dialog that allows you to discover the branches for one or more projects. | Selected **Branches** in the repository tree view, a repository location selected, or no selection |

**Table 5.1**   Actions Available in the CVS Repositories View (*continued*)

| Action | Description | Available from This Context |
| --- | --- | --- |
| **Refresh View** | Refreshes the view with current repository information. | Various |
| **Remove** | Removes the date tag from the view. | Selected date tag |
| **Show Annotation** | Displays the CVS Annotate view for the selected file. | Selected file |
| **Show In Resource History** | Presents the file's revision history in the CVS Resource History view. | Selected file |
| **Tag As Version...** | Applies a version tag to the selected resource and its children. | Selected resource |
| **Tag With Existing...** | Applies an existing repository version or branch tag to the selected resources. This is a specialized operation. See the online help topic "Moving Version Tags" for more information on when this might apply. | Selected resource |

you have selected, as specified in the third column. The actions you will probably use initially are **New > Repository Location...**, **Check Out...**, **Compare With...**, and **Show in Resource History**. You are not expected to understand these yet; this is only a reference.

## The CVS Annotate View

The CVS Annotate view, which shares the same space as the CVS Repositories view in the perspective, is used to identify the new and changed lines in a file during each revision. It also indicates who made the change. Now you know who to see (or blame?) for those inexplicable updates! For any selected revision the new lines are highlighted in the editor (see Figure 5.4). This view is opened from the **Show Annotation** action available from the **Team** menu, CVS Repositories view, and CVS Resource History view. A convenient way to use this function is to select **Team > Show Annotation** from a file in the Navigator or Package Explorer views. The CVS Repository Exploring perspective is opened with the CVS Annotate view, the latest file revision in the editor, and the CVS Resource History view. A selection in the CVS Annotate view will reposition the editor to the updated lines of code, and the appropriate revision will be highlighted in the CVS Resource History view. Conversely, a selected line in the editor will highlight the change appropriately in those views. Now you can easily review the detailed change history of any text file.

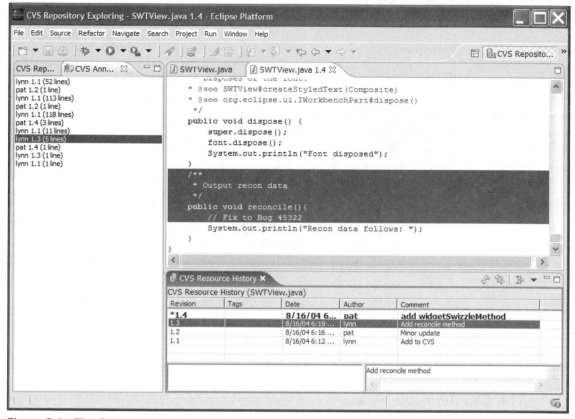

**Figure 5.4**    The CVS Annotate View in the CVS Repository Exploring Perspective

### The CVS Resource History View

The CVS Resource History view provides details on every revision for a specific file (see Figure 5.5). This view is part of the CVS Repository Exploring perspective. Select a file and then select **Show in Resource History** from the context menu of the CVS Repositories view to see its revision history. It is also available from the **Team** context menu item on projects under CVS control. You can drag a file in your workspace that is under CVS control and drop it on this view as a quick way to see its history.

For any selected revision, the branch and version tags associated with the revision, along with the comment provided when the revision was committed to the repository, are displayed at the bottom of the view (see Figure 5.5). The Tag Viewer and Comment Viewer can be hidden using actions available from the view's pull-down menu.

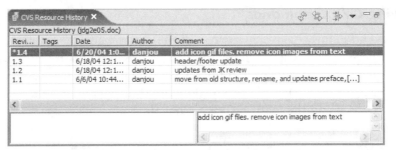

**Figure 5.5**   CVS Resource History View

Since a file might have a long history, you can filter this view using the **Filter History** action ⇥ available from the view's toolbar. You can filter the history by author, comment values, and date ranges. The **Link with Editor** toolbar action ⇗ will keep the view in sync with the current active editor (only for files under CVS control).

Actions on a selected revision in the CVS Repository History view vary depending on whether or not that resource has already been copied to your workspace. They are listed in Table 5.2.

**Table 5.2**   Actions Available in the CVS Resource History View

| Action | Description |
| --- | --- |
| **Compare** | Compares two selected revisions with each other. |
| **Get Contents** | Replaces the contents of the local working copy of the resource with the contents of the selected revision. |
| **Get Sticky Revision** | Reverts the local working copy of the resource to a previous revision. The local copy retains the same revision tag as the repository revision. Do this only if you are very familiar with CVS. A consequence of this action is that you cannot commit any further changes unless the "sticky revision" tag is removed (using CVS directly via commands). You can replace this revision using **Replace With > Latest from Repository**. In general, you are probably not interested in "sticky tags" unless you are a sophisticated CVS user. |
| **Open** | Opens the selected revision in an editor. No changes are permitted. |
| **Refresh View** | Updates the view with the CVS repository contents. |
| **Show Annotation** | Switches to the CVS Repository Exploring perspective and places the focus on the CVS Annotate view, showing the annotations for the selected file. |
| **Tag with Existing...** | Applies an existing repository version or branch tag to the selected resources. This is a specialized operation. See the online help topic "Moving Version Tags" for more information on when this might apply. |

### Viewing CVS Commands

The Eclipse Console view can display all the commands and responses between CVS and Eclipse; this can be useful if you are experiencing problems. It also shows all of the CVS commands issued for any Eclipse CVS action by the user. You can configure the appearance and behavior of the console on the **Team > CVS > Console** preference page.

### How CVS Managed Projects Appear in Your Workspace

Figure 5.6 shows a project in the Package Explorer view that is under CVS control. This is evident by the label decorations on the icons and additional informational text. This information displays only if you have the preference **Workbench > Label Decorations** enabled for CVS. Each resource under version control has a tiny disk label decoration ▯ on its resource icon. Files that have been added to a project but not known to CVS have a tiny **?** decorator in the icon. Adjacent to the project is the name of the CVS repository server in brackets. If the project is being worked on as part of a branch, the branch name is included. The text decorator **>** indicates that a local resource is an outgoing change, meaning it has been modified locally and is not current with CVS. Parent folders up through the project will also display this character. Beside each resource in parentheses is text indicating the file format, either some form of ASCII text or binary. Recall that concurrent changes between a CVS file instance and the local file instance can be merged for ASCII files. Binary files can only be replaced.

**Figure 5.6**   Project Under CVS Control with Label Decorations Enabled

You can modify the presentation and the rules for CVS label decorations in the preference page **Team > CVS > Label Decorations**.

## CVS Actions Available from the Team Menu

The **Team** menu, available from the context menu of any workspace resource, has several CVS actions associated with it. We will summarize the most common actions you will use to maintain your work with CVS. The specific menu contents vary depending on whether or not the selection is a project. A project will have a **Share Project...** action only if CVS or any other repository is not managing the project. Table 5.3 provides a reference list of all the CVS team actions. Some of the actions are probably unfamiliar and are discussed later in this chapter. The most common actions you will use in everyday situations are **Share Project...**, **Synchronize with Repository...**, **Update...**, and **Commit...**. The **Share Project** action is a comprehensive wizard that allows you to put a project into CVS. Every step along the way from defining a CVS repository connection to committing the project resources is incorporated in this wizard.

**Table 5.3**   Team Menu Actions for CVS

| Action | Description |
| --- | --- |
| **Add to .cvsignore...** | Excludes project files that should not be managed by CVS. They will never appear in the Synchronization view or get committed. CVS maintains a .cvsignore file in your project that identifies these file instances. This file does not initially exist; it will be created the first time this action is performed. You must add the .cvsignore file to version control and maintain it in CVS. |
| **Add to Version Control** | Makes a file known to CVS. It is typically used when a new file is created in the project. If you don't explicitly add a resource to version control, you will be prompted when you perform a commit. |
| **Apply Patch...** | Applies a patch from the patch file created using the **Create Patch** action. |
| **Branch...** | Creates a branch so that the project (or selected resource) can be modified independently of other development. |
| **Change ASCII/Binary Property...** | Displays the Set Keyword Substitution wizard, which allows you to choose the desired CVS keyword substitution mode for the selected files. This defines how CVS interprets a file as either ASCII or binary. |
| **Commit...** | Updates the CVS repository with your local changes, if there are no conflicts. You will be prompted to include a comment. When selected from a project or folder, all the modified resources in the project or folder will be committed to CVS. A **Commit** action will fail if the file in CVS supercedes the file in your workspace. |

*continues*

**Table 5.3**  Team Menu Actions for CVS (*continued*)

| Action | Description |
|---|---|
| **Create Patch...** | Creates a patch file of differences between the local resources and CVS. The patch file can be shared with others. This allows work to be shared outside the repository. |
| **Disconnect...** | Removes all the CVS connection information from the selected workspace project. |
| **Edit** | Applies only to files in projects that have Watch/Edit enabled (from the project's CVS property page or as a CVS preference). This informs the CVS server that you are updating this file. If one or more other users are editing this file, you will be prompted to continue or not. You can override this prompt and modify the file, but you will probably encounter conflicts when you attempt to commit your changes. If you simply open the file for editing, the file will open. As soon as you attempt to modify it, you will receive the same prompt. If you are opening an external editor, you need to do this first to remove the read-only state of the file, followed by opening the file with the external editor. This operation will be discussed later. |
| **Merge...** | Merges changes in a specific branch back to the code base prior to the branch. |
| **Restore from Repository...** | Displays a list of deleted files if they exist for this project and allows you to restore them to your workspace. This topic is discussed in detail later in the chapter. |
| **Share Project...** | Is available only from a project and is visible only on projects that are not under repository management. It displays a wizard that completes the task of associating the project with an available repository and committing the project's resources. This action is also used by other repository providers. |
| **Show Annotation** | Switches to the CVS Repository Exploring perspective and places the focus on the CVS Annotate view, showing the annotations for the selected file. |
| **Show Editors** | Applies to folders and files in projects that have Watch/Edit enabled (from the project's CVS property page or as a CVS preference). The CVS Editors view will open. This view will identify other users who are editing the file or contents of the folder. Only those users who have Watch/Edit enabled on that project will be visible in this view. |
| **Show in Repository History** | Displays the CVS Repository History view for the selected resource. |
| **Synchronize with Repository...** | Compares the selected resources to the CVS repository and switches to the Team Synchronizing perspective. Any differences are shown in the Synchronize view. For a project or folder, all subordinate resources are also compared with CVS. The Synchronize view will display all resources that have differences with CVS. This is the safest way to work with CVS as you can examine each change, compare with the repository instance, and resolve conflicts. |

**Table 5.3** Team Menu Actions for CVS (*continued*)

| Action | Description |
|---|---|
| **Tag as Version...** | Adds a version tag to the selected project, folder, or file and all the CVS instances of all child file resources. Individual resources may be versioned. Versioning can also be done from the CVS Repositories view. |
| **Unedit** | Applies only to files in projects that have Watch/Edit enabled (from the project's CVS property page or as a CVS preference). This action removes you from the list of users actively editing a file. When you perform this action, you are removed from the active editors list and any changes you made will be backed out. The file will revert to the contents before you performed any updates. This action happens implicitly when you commit a file to CVS since your workspace copy is now identical to the server copy. This operation will be discussed later in the chapter. |
| **Update...** | Updates the local resources with any newer changes in CVS. Updates in CVS will be merged with the local resources (except for binary files). It is recommended that you perform **Update...** before **Commit....** Your commit will fail if others have committed changes since your last update. The action **Synchronize with Repository...** is recommended over **Update....** |

## The Team Synchronizing Perspective and the Synchronize Wizard

This is your home base for synchronizing your workspace with CVS (other repository providers can integrate to this perspective). You are prompted to switch to it when you select **Team > Synchronize with Repository....** The Team Synchronizing perspective consists of the Synchronize view and an editors area showing all open editors. Figure 5.7 shows an example. The view allows you to observe and act on differences between your local project and the CVS copy of your project. This view is available to other repository providers who wish to use it. Opening a file opens an appropriate compare editor (Text, Java, XML, or Image) showing the differences between your workspace file and the latest in CVS. This comparison allows you to view and finalize a file's content before committing it to CVS.

A set of buttons on the view's toolbar allows the synchronization information to be filtered by **Incoming Mode** ▣ (updates from CVS), **Outgoing Mode** ▣ (commits to CVS), **Incoming and Outgoing Mode** ▦, and **Conflicts Mode** ◆. You might use **Incoming Mode** just to see what others have been doing. If you are a one-person team, **Outgoing Mode** may be all that is of interest. To receive all incoming changes, you can use the **Update All Incoming Changes...** toolbar button ▦, and to commit all your changes, use the

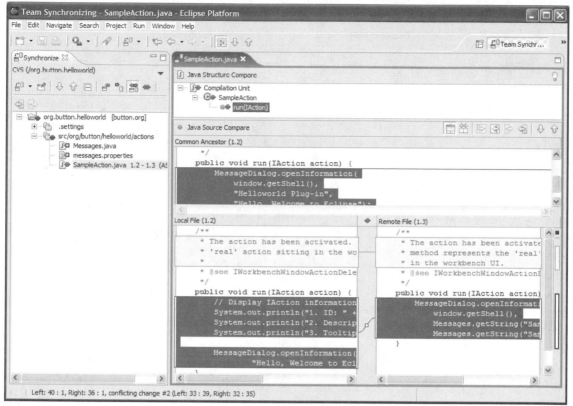

**Figure 5.7**   Team Synchronizing Perspective Showing Incoming Changes and a Three-Way Compare of the Conflicting Outgoing File

**Commit All Outgoing Changes...** button ⊟. The **Pin Current Synchronization** toolbar action ⊡ allows you to refer to a set of resources used in a previous synchronization. The view's menu allows you to filter the content by a working set. You can adjust the comparison criteria and, using the **Layout** menu, switch the view between **Tree**, **Compressed Folders**, and **Commit Sets. Commit Sets** allows you to see repository changes grouped by committer, comment, and commit date. This can be very helpful in determining more detail about an incoming set of changes. The view has its own preferences dialog available from the view's menu. Also available in the view's menu is the **Schedule...** action. This allows you to perform automatic repository synchronizations on a repeating schedule that you choose.

### The Synchronize Wizard

This wizard appears when you select the **Synchronize...** action 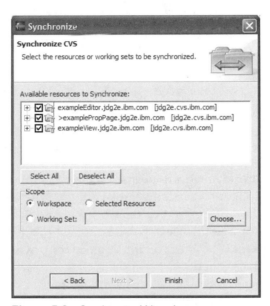 from the Workbench toolbar pull-down menu or the Synchronize view toolbar pull-down menu. It allows you to choose projects to synchronize with CVS (and other repository providers that are enabled to use Eclipse team synchronization support). As shown in Figure 5.8, you can synchronize the workspace, selected resources, or a working set. When it finishes, you are returned to the Team Synchronizing perspective.

**Figure 5.8**   Synchronize Wizard

## *Handling Concurrent Updates to the Same File*

Let's discuss a suggested protocol for making changes. When working with resources in your workspace, you are working independently from the CVS repository. Since changes could occur in the repository without your knowledge, it is very important that you never commit any changes without checking to see if there are updates in the repository that supercede your changes. The **Team > Update...** action will update the local copy of your project with any changes in the repository that supercede your changes. For text files (including Java classes), it will automatically merge any changes, even those that might be in conflict, from the repository to your workspace. When conflicts are encountered, the merge will identify them in the file with special CVS markup text to help identify the conflicting lines. The markup text is not compatible with any type of file and could result in compile errors, for example.

**Update...** is a powerful action and should be exercised with care. In the following example, Pat and Lynn updated a simple text file. Without knowing it, they both updated the lines starting with "B" and "C." The markup text identifies the conflicting lines and the revision number (1.2) that introduced the conflict. A complex Java file with multiple conflicts might be much more difficult to resolve.

```
A is for apple
<<<<<<< sample.txt
B is for bird          (updated by Pat)
C is for crow          (updated by Pat)
=======
B is for bobcat        (updated by Lynn)
C is for cow           (updated by Lynn)
>>>>>>> 1.2
D is for dog
E is for excellent
F is for farm
G is for goat...
```

The **Team > Synchronize with Repository...** action supports updating also, but it does not do it automatically. It displays the Synchronize view and lists those resources that differ between the workspace copy and the latest revision in the repository. In this view, you can inspect the differences and decide what action to take. It gives you much more control and is recommended over the **Update...** action.

Let's summarize the basic rule: Before modifying files in your workspace, you should always *update* resources in your workspace with any changes that have occurred in the repository. To be safe, do this using the **Team > Synchronize with Repository...** action. In the Synchronize view, you can perform updates, commit changes, and reconcile conflicts.

### Avoiding Concurrent Updates to the Same File by Using CVS Watch/Edit

You and your teammates can avoid conflicts during commits altogether if you agree to use the CVS Watch/Edit support built into Eclipse. It allows your team to better understand who is currently updating files in any particular project. In contrast, the CVS Annotate view, discussed earlier, shows you previous changes and who made them. Watch/Edit support is enabled at the project level. This occurs automatically when the project is checked out if this preference is set on the **Team > CVS > Watch/Edit** page. You can also enable it on an existing CVS managed project by using the project's CVS properties. When Watch/Edit is enabled, the files in the project are read-only. When you open a file in an editor and attempt to make a change, the CVS server is interrogated. If others are editing the same file, you are notified with a dialog that identifies the other parties editing this file (see Figure 5.9). You may continue editing, but you may have a conflict to manage during commit. A check mark decorator ⧉ is added to files when they are modified.

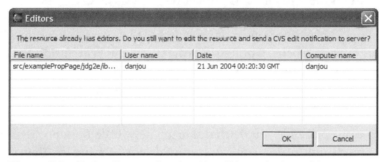

**Figure 5.9**    Dialog Showing Another User Editing the Same File

The **Team > Show Editors** action at the project, folder, and file level will open the CVS Editors view, listing all resources that are being updated by others (see Figure 5.10). This action is available from any project or its resources regardless of whether it is under Watch/Edit control. However, it will only identify resources in projects in which Watch/Edit is enabled.

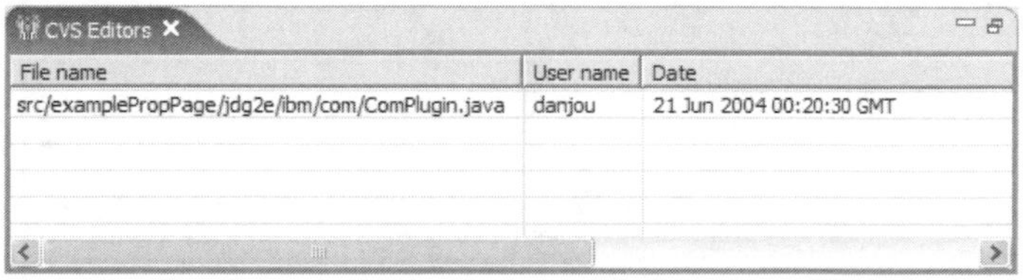

**Figure 5.10**    CVS Editors View Listing Which Users Are Updating the Files in a Folder

You can use the **Team > Edit** action to explicitly inform the CVS server that you intend to update a file. The **Team > Unedit** action informs CVS that you no longer wish to edit the file. Any changes you made are backed out. See Table 5.3 for information on these actions. A commit to CVS implicitly removes resources from the Watch/Edit list.

This Watch/Edit capability can be a very useful tool, but there are some rules and considerations. First, for this to be effective, everyone on the team has to enable Watch/Edit on projects where potential conflict exists. Second, you have to be connected to your CVS server. If you are disconnected and want to update a file, you will have to explicitly remove the read-only status for the file (available from the file's property page). Of course, the support is now compromised because no one knows of the update, and the potential for conflict during commit exists. If you delete a project and there are open Watch/Edit references to project resources, the CVS server is not informed and will continue to report that you are editing these resources. If your team plans to use this support, it is advisable that everyone set the CVS Watch/Edit preference labeled **Configure projects to use Watch/Edit on checkout**.

### Restoring Deleted Files

Occasionally, you may delete a file, commit the change to CVS, and later need to restore the file you deleted. Fortunately, CVS does not remove deleted files from its repository. You can restore deletions using the **Team > Restore from Repository...** action. If deleted resources exist, you see a dialog from which you can select a particular revision to restore (see Figure 5.11). The latest revision is a reference to the deleted file because a file delete is a CVS revision.

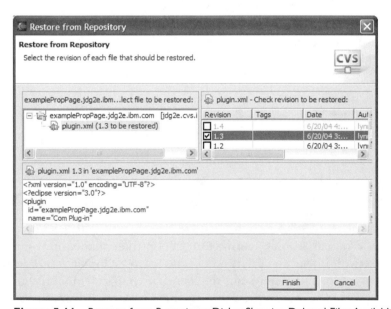

**Figure 5.11**   Restore from Repository Dialog Showing Deleted Files Available for Restoration

When a file is restored to your workspace, it is considered a new file that must be added to version control before or during commit.

## Other CVS User Interface Elements

### Checkout Wizard

Available in the New wizards dialog is the Checkout Projects from CVS wizard. Usually you will check out projects using the CVS Repositories view, but some CVS repositories do not allow browsing. This wizard can be helpful in that situation, but you have to know the name of the project in advance.

### CVS Cheat Sheets

The Cheat Sheet Selection dialog is available by selecting **Help > Cheat Sheets....** For CVS tasks, a cheat sheet exists to assist with branching and merging.

## Special Situations and How to Handle Them

Here are some common situations that you might encounter, day to day or over the life cycle of your development effort, and some proposals on how you might handle them using Eclipse. Some situations may require you to work natively with CVS, but more often than not Eclipse can handle them.

### Renaming, Moving, and Deleting Project Resources

- *Avoid renaming a project under CVS control.* If you do, the change is local to your workspace only. The original name remains in CVS. If you must rename a project, it is better to disassociate it from CVS using the **Team > Disconnect...** action and then rename it. This is effectively a new project. You must define it to CVS just as with any new project.
- Renaming a folder results in a new folder in CVS. Fortunately, the folder contents are moved to the new folder. If you enable the CVS preference **Prune empty directories**, the old folders will not appear in your workspace upon checkout.
- When resources are deleted in your workspace, they will be deleted in CVS when the next commit occurs. Keep in mind that folders are never deleted in CVS. The CVS preference **Prune empty directories** will hide them from view. This preference is enabled by default.
- For changes that might span projects, make sure that all projects in your workspace are up-to-date with the repository before making this

global change. Refactoring Java classes is an operation that can result in widespread changes across your workspace. Moving resources between projects can also have this effect.

- Moving resources between projects, from a CVS perspective, is a resource delete from the source project and an addition to the target project. The resources in the target project must be added to version control. Renaming a resource has the same affect.

- When you perform CVS actions like synchronizing after a file change, we recommend that you synchronize at the project level, even though your change may involve only a single file. For example, if you rename a file, which is a CVS delete and add, synchronizing at the file level will only detect the addition and not the deletion. Synchronizing at the project level will handle both.

- When making application-wide changes, keep your team informed to avoid unnecessary conflicts. Commit your changes as soon as possible. Resolving conflicts can be tedious and potentially problematic.

### Backing Out a Change: Using Replace and Compare

From time to time, we all wish we could just start over. That may not be easy in life, but with Eclipse and CVS it is a little easier. Depending on what you want to do, you have several choices. In earlier chapters you saw how to use the context menu operations **Replace With** and **Compare With** to replace and compare resources with information from your workspace local history. With CVS, you have additional choices. If you were in the middle of an incomplete change and had stepped away from it for a while, **Compare With** can be quite helpful to remind you of your work in progress. When you use these operations, you replace or compare a resource with the latest from the **HEAD** stream, another branch or version, or a specific revision (files only).

### Setting Up Branches for Maintenance and New Release Development

Your team has delivered your application and is ready to start working on the next release. You would like to have all subsequent development occur in a special branch assigned to that release while allowing service of the prior release. Here is a way you can do that within Eclipse.

- Select all the projects in the branch (or **HEAD**) comprising your recently finished release. Use the context menu **Branch...** on the selected projects and enter the new branch name of the new release. All the projects and their contents will be tagged with the next release branch name. The projects will be listed in the CVS Repositories view under that branch name. When they are checked out from that branch into your workspace, subsequent work will be applied to that branch.

- You can repeat this process to create a separate maintenance branch that is independent of the new release branch.
- To assist in forward-fitting changes from the maintenance branch to the new release branch, from your workspace you can use the action **Compare With > Another Branch or Version...** to identify the differences. From the Compare view, you can manually merge the changes from the maintenance branch to the new release branch.

## Additional Features

Here are a few more useful features that will help make you more productive using CVS and Eclipse.

### Quick Diff Editor Support for CVS

In Chapter 2, Getting Started with Eclipse, you learned that the quick diff support in the editor can annotate additions and changes to a file. If you set the **Workbench > Editor > Quick Diff** preference page to use the setting **Latest CVS Revision**, the file annotations will be against the latest revision in CVS. Annotations will be removed when you commit your changes to CVS or replace the file with a CVS revision.

### Patches: Sharing Changes Quickly and Easily

A **patch** is a file that contains differences between the repository instance of a resource and the workspace instance of that resource. A patch can represent the difference in a single file or an entire project. Patches allow you to share a change without committing it to CVS. This could be useful for a number of reasons.

- You don't have the authority to commit resources to CVS, so you need to send the patch file to someone with authority who can do this for you.
- You need to prepare an emergency fix or a temporary workaround to a problem.
- Before you commit a significant change to CVS, you want to have someone verify your change. In this case, you might send them the patch file for testing purposes.

A patch file is created using the context menu **Team > Create Patch...**. This invokes the Create Patch wizard, which guides you through the task. A patch is applied using the **Team > Apply Patch...** action, which invokes the Apply Patch wizard. A good description of these operations is available in the *Workbench User Guide* in the section "Working with patches."

### Project Sets: Getting That New Workspace Up to Speed

Team support provides a capability to encapsulate the version control information for one or more projects in your workspace. This is called a **project set**. The purpose of a project set is to prime a workspace with all the required projects from a repository that are needed to perform some task. Perhaps building your application requires several projects with interdependencies. Determining which projects are required and manually populating your workspace with the correct projects from a repository can be tedious and error prone. Project sets are a functional element of Eclipse, and repository providers can choose to support this function or not (many do). CVS supports project sets. A project set might encapsulate projects managed by different repositories.

The project set information is contained in a file that you create with **File > Export > Team Project Set** and apply with **File > Import > Team Project Set**. Use the Export wizard to define which projects to include in the project set. The resulting file can be sent to someone to import or maintained in CVS for general use. You might maintain several project set files for snapshots of an application taken at key points in its development life cycle.

During import, all the projects defined in the project set file are automatically checked out from CVS into your workspace. It may be prudent to turn off the automatic build preference setting during import (see the first **Workbench** preference page item, **Build Automatically**). This will speed up the process by avoiding compilations and builds during the import process. Remember to turn the preference back on afterward.

### Disconnecting or Reassigning a CVS Project

You can disconnect a project from CVS using the **Team > Disconnect...** operation. The dialog asks you to decide whether the CVS metadata for the project should be kept or not. If you choose to keep the metadata, the project can be reconnected to the same CVS repository using the **Team > Share Project...** action. If you delete the CVS metadata, you can share the project with a different repository.

Alternatively, if you want to reassign your project to another CVS repository, open the **CVS** property page for the project and select the **Change Sharing...** button. This is the logical equivalent of using the **Disconnect...** and **Share Project...** actions.

## Exercise Summary

Now that you have a general idea of what CVS is and what Eclipse support is available, let's take it for a road test. In Exercise 5, Working as a Team with CVS, you will examine a series of progressively more sophisticated scenarios to learn how you can use Eclipse and CVS in everyday situations. This exercise is highly recommended if you are going to be using CVS regularly. Here is what you'll learn.

1. Getting Started

   You will define access to a CVS repository and explore its contents using the CVS Repository Exploring perspective. You'll place a new project under CVS control, check its contents into the CVS repository, and version it.

2. Updating, Committing, and Resolving Conflicts

   You will update your project and commit the changes to CVS. Then, to make it more interesting, a colleague will make changes to the project while you are also making changes. You'll use Eclipse CVS support to help resolve the resulting conflict.

3. Branching and Merging

   In this scenario, you will avoid any conflicts with the main development trunk by making changes in a branch and then merging them back.

## Chapter Summary

By now, you should realize that team support was a priority in Eclipse. This chapter showed that Eclipse provides a foundation for team programming that allows repositories from various providers to be tightly integrated with the Workbench. Repositories help you share your work with colleagues. Many commercial repository providers have enabled their products for Eclipse.

CVS is an open source repository that is supported by Eclipse and uses the same integration mechanisms available to other repository providers. CVS allows resources to be centrally managed yet be accessible to anyone who is authorized. In CVS, resources are never locked. Resources can be checked out, changed, and committed back to the repository. Conflicts are detected automatically, and the Synchronize view helps you resolve these conflicts. Resources can be versioned for future reference. Changes to the same resources can be made in parallel with other changes using a branch. Later these parallel changes can be merged together.

## References

The CVS home site is http://www.cvshome.org.

The eclipse.org site maintains CVS information and links to recommended CVS sites at http://dev.eclipse.org/viewcvs.

The Eclipse team maintains useful information at its project site on eclipse.org. Navigate to **Projects > The Eclipse Project > Platform > Team > Development Resources**. The **Eclipse CVS FAQ** link on this page specializes in CVS.

To learn more about the team environment, refer to the topic "Working in the Team Environment" in the "Tasks" and "Reference" sections of the Eclipse online help book *Workbench User Guide*.

The "Team Repository Providers" section of the Eclipse "Projects and Plug-ins" page under the "Community" heading on eclipse.org lists several available repository access plug-ins.

Two other resources are particularly helpful.

Arthorne, John, and Chris Laffra. 2004. *Official Eclipse 3.0 FAQs*. Boston, MA: Addison-Wesley. http://eclipsefaq.org. (See FAQs 65, 67, 79, 299, 310, 312.)

Glezen, Paul. July 2003. Branching with Eclipse and CVS. http://www.eclipse.org.

# CHAPTER 6

## *Managing Your Eclipse Environment*

Whether you are using Eclipse or an Eclipse-based product, you really should know how to manage your environment. By developing Eclipse environment management skills you can feel comfortable doing the following:

- Adding and removing features
- Controlling the state of a feature (enabled/disabled)
- Sharing preferences between workspaces
- Defining your own customized default preferences
- Defining alternative configurations
- Managing a shared configuration

This list could go on—the more you know, the more you can do to change how Eclipse works without actually writing a plug-in (but we cover that too, of course). Heck, tired of the Eclipse splash image, want to put your own company or organization identity on your IDE? Not a problem; you can change the configuration so it shows your favorite bitmap instead.

To fully control and customize Eclipse you need to have a solid understanding of the structure of an Eclipse installation and how you can manage the ability of Eclipse to dynamically extend and self-service the installed features. This understanding will help you be more aware of how Eclipse works and how you can better configure new functions as part of your installation.

**NOTE** Features are the management unit of function in Eclipse. They are visible in the About Eclipse Platform dialogs and the Product Configuration dialog. Features are defined by plug-in developers to organize plug-ins. They are discussed more in Part II, Fundamentals of Extending Eclipse.

This chapter discusses the control points that allow you to manage and modify your Eclipse environment and suggests best practices for common scenarios. But the first thing we do is discuss what you have on disk so you know where to find the customizable bits of Eclipse (or an Eclipse-based product).

## An Overview of Your Eclipse Installation

Eclipse, as well as any product that builds on Eclipse, has a standard structure. Understanding this structure and some basic behaviors is the starting point for effective management of the configuration.

### Eclipse Directory Content

Figure 6.1 shows the directory structure after you first install Eclipse, by unzipping the appropriate eclipse.org download, and before it has been started.

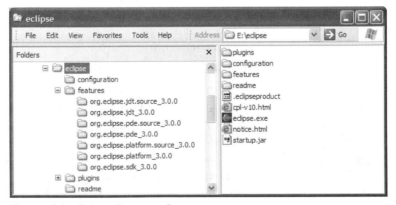

**Figure 6.1**    Eclipse Directory Structure

Table 6.1 lists the important directories and files included in an Eclipse SDK installation.

**Table 6.1**   Directories and Files in an Eclipse Installation

| Directory or File | Description |
| --- | --- |
| configuration directory | The default location for the active configuration. Preloaded with the config.ini file that defines the active product configuration for the installation. |
| features directory | A directory that contains a subdirectory for each feature included in the installation. Each feature references one or more plug-ins. (The features directories for an Eclipse platform SDK install are shown in Figure 6.1.) |
| plugins directory | A directory that contains a subdirectory for each plug-in included in the installation. |
| readme directory | A directory that contains a readme_eclipse.html file (have you read yours yet?). |
| .eclipseproduct | A file that identifies this as a directory that contains an Eclipse-based product (the Eclipse SDK in this example). |
| cpl-v10.html | The Common Public License for Eclipse. |
| eclipse.exe | An executable file used to launch Eclipse. |
| notice.html | The eclipse.org Software User Agreement. |
| startup.jar | Java runtime code used to help launch Eclipse. |

> **NOTE**  If you are using a product built on Eclipse, it may include a JRE subdirectory. The JRE subdirectory, when provided, contains the default Java runtime environment for Eclipse.

If a workspace directory exists, this is because you previously started Eclipse without using the -data parameter to control where workspace data is located. We point out in Running Multiple Eclipse Windows and Workspaces in Chapter 2, Getting Started with Eclipse, that allowing this to happen is not a user best practice.

You may want to review the .html files in the Eclipse install root directory; they are the license for the software you have installed, and they might be supplemented by other license agreements if you are using an Eclipse-based product. Do not delete the .eclipseproduct file because some installation routines look for it when trying to locate Eclipse or Eclipse-based product installations in order to install additional features as an extension to your Eclipse installation. Other Eclipse-based products may define their own schemes to supplement the role of the .eclipseproduct marker file.

The features and plugins directories are important if you intend to add function to your current installation. The quick and dirty way to add additional function to Eclipse is by copying the contents of the provided features and `plugins` subdirectories to the same directories in your Eclipse installation. Of course we do not recommend this approach—why clutter up your Eclipse installation when all you have to do is create your own install site? (See Adding and Removing Install Sites later in this chapter.) To Eclipse, an install site is an `eclipse` directory that contains `features` and `plugins` directories.

The Eclipse environment is controlled by the configuration, so we'll start there and work down as we point out some details about what is going on inside your Eclipse installation.

### Eclipse Platform Configuration

By default, Eclipse uses a single configuration for a given installation. The configuration information is saved in the `platform.xml` file found in the `\configuration\org.eclipse.update` directory. The primary content in the configuration is a list of install sites. An **install site** is a location on the file system where an `eclipse` directory tree, with `features` and `plugins` directories, can be found. The configuration identifies what install sites are accessible, lists the features that exist in each site, and determines what features are available and active when Eclipse is started. This information is managed by the Eclipse Update Manager. We'll discuss the Update Manager in more detail a bit later. For now just think of it as the portion of Eclipse that manages the configuration by adding new install sites and by supporting direct disable and enable requests on features that are part of the current configuration.

The following example shows the default configuration content for an Eclipse installation; bold text highlights the install site information.

```
<?xml version="1.0" encoding="UTF-8"?>
<config date="Wed May 05 14:18:21 EDT 2004"
  transient="false" version="3.0">
  <site enabled="true" policy="USER-EXCLUDE" updateable="true"
  url="platform:/base/">
    <feature application="org.eclipse.ui.ide.workbench"
      id="org.eclipse.platform" primary="true"
      url="features/org.eclipse.platform_3.0.0/"
        version="3.0.0"/>
    <feature id="org.eclipse.platform.source"
      url="features/org.eclipse.platform.source_3.0.0/"
        version="3.0.0"/>
    <feature id="org.eclipse.jdt"
      url="features/org.eclipse.jdt_3.0.0/" version="3.0.0"/>
    <feature id="org.eclipse.jdt.source"
      url="features/org.eclipse.jdt.source_3.0.0/"
        version="3.0.0"/>
    <feature id="org.eclipse.pde"
      url="features/org.eclipse.pde_3.0.0/" version="3.0.0"/>
```

```
    <feature id="org.eclipse.sdk"
      url="features/org.eclipse.sdk_3.0.0/" version="3.0.0"/>
  </site>
</config>
```

The `platform:/base/` site is a reference to the `eclipse` directory structure from which the `eclipse.exe` was started.

The default configuration is used when Eclipse is launched and applies to any workspace that might be accessed. The `-configuration` startup parameter can be used to identify an alternate configuration.

We will discuss alternative sites, which have a specific file system location, and scenarios for the use of an alternative configuration in Managing Your Configuration later in this chapter.

## The *features* Directory

Eclipse looks in the `features` directory for directories that contain a file named `feature.xml`; without a `feature.xml` file, the directory is ignored. If found, the `feature.xml` file is processed as part of the install site.

Features are the management unit for function in Eclipse. Features are used to organize and structure plug-ins and other features. As a user of Eclipse, all you need is a general understanding of what a feature is and what it can do for you. A feature can be one or more of the following.

- An installable unit of function.
  Depending on their definitions, installed features can often be directly disabled or enabled.

- A packaging construct.
  Plug-ins add function to Eclipse. Features organize plug-ins so that they can be installed and managed by the Update Manager.

- A logical container for plug-ins.
  A feature identifies the plug-ins, at a specific version level, that are part of the feature. This allows the Update Manager to manage plug-ins by managing the features that contain the plug-ins.

- Capable of nesting other related features.
  This technique is used to manage the source of service for a set of features.

- Installed and managed using the Update Manager.
  Plug-ins can be copied to the install directory, but they are unmanaged. Features, regardless of how they are added to your configuration, are managed by Update Manager.

Features are in directories below the `eclipse\features` directory. The expected directory name is the feature id appended with the feature version.

### The plugins Directory

The `plugins` directory contains a directory for each plug-in. The expected directory name is the plug-in id appended with the plug-in version. **Plug-ins** provide the function that exists in your Eclipse configuration. This includes Eclipse itself (everything is a plug-in) and any other plug-ins that have been added to extend Eclipse.

Eclipse itself, and any additional code packaged with it, must exist as a set of plug-ins that can be found and loaded at startup. By default Eclipse looks only for plug-ins in the `plugins` directory of the Eclipse installation, but as you will see, the configuration can be extended to include plug-ins from other sites as well.

## Understanding the Runtime Configuration

Imagine that you are running Eclipse and using some cool tool or just playing some cool game (anything can be a plug-in), and somebody asks you, "What is that?" Or your Eclipse or Eclipse-based product install is not quite right and your support team or local Eclipse guru says, "Tell me what you have installed." How do you answer them? Not a problem—once you know where to look, Eclipse itself will tell you.

Features are defined by plug-in developers to package their plug-ins for effective integration with Eclipse. The Eclipse user interface provides several ways to identify the features that are active in the current configuration. The Eclipse Platform provides a snapshot of the entire configuration through the About dialog. You can also use the Update Manager to identify the enabled and disabled features in your configuration. As you read about plug-in development, you will learn that a plug-in that is not referenced by a feature is unmanaged. The plug-in developer should not share plug-ins without a feature; as a consumer of plug-ins you should demand that they be packaged using features. The Update Manager can only manage features; you have to work with unmanaged plug-ins by copying directories.

### Feature Details in the User Interface

There are four About dialogs: About Eclipse Platform, About Eclipse Platform Features, Feature Plug-ins, and About Eclipse Platform Plug-ins. You might not use these dialogs on a daily basis, but they are a source of information you may need as an Eclipse user. We will not show you all of the dialogs here but instead describe their role and content.

Select **Help > About Eclipse Platform** to open the About Eclipse Platform dialog (see Figure 6.2).

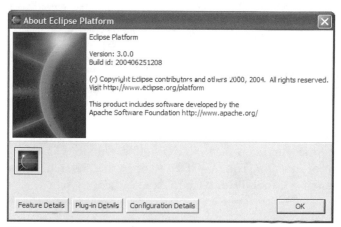

**Figure 6.2**　About Eclipse Platform Dialog

The About Eclipse Platform dialog exposes the product- and feature-branding content provided as part of the features in the active configuration. In our scenario where we have only Eclipse installed, this branding is only for Eclipse. If you had other features configured that included branding content, you would see additional icons above the buttons, next to the Eclipse icon. If you were using an Eclipse-based product, its product-branding content would be shown along with unique feature-branding content for all the configured features (this would be shown as additional icons in Figure 6.2). Buttons on the About Eclipse Platform dialog open the other three dialogs. You can use **Feature Details** to see a list of branded features and from there see a list of plug-ins for a specific feature. Using **Plug-in Details** opens a list of active plug-ins.

An alternative to the branding dialogs is the information presented by the Update Manager's Product Configuration dialog. This dialog displays all enabled features and, if requested, even the disabled ones. Open this dialog by using the **Help > Software Updates > Manage Configuration...** menu option (see Figure 6.3).

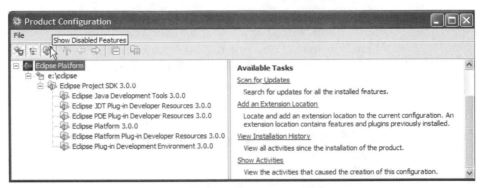

**Figure 6.3**   Product Configuration Dialog

**NOTE**   The option to show the Product Configuration dialog may be hidden; Eclipse-based products may choose to hide certain capabilities as part of the initial presentation of function. You may have to open the Preferences dialog and use the **Workbench > Capabilities** page to expose this capability.

We will return to the Product Configuration dialog soon; not only does it display the current configuration, but it is one of the ways you can make configuration changes.

### Configuration Details

You will want to be familiar with the **Configuration Details** option in the About Eclipse Platform dialog. It provides useful details about your current configuration.

Selecting **Configuration Details** opens a dialog that displays the current set of configuration information, such as loaded plug-ins, the JRE version, and so on. It is a very detailed, somewhat free-form listing. Each section has a descriptive heading; the contents are self explanatory.

This is useful information if you are trying to solve a problem with your Eclipse installation. If you are using an Eclipse-based product, the support team may ask you for a copy of the information shown in this dialog.

### Coordinating Preferences

As soon as you use a second workspace, you have preference troubles. Let's say that you like to keep things neat and clean. Abstract that into a scenario where you think there is only one set of preference settings that make sense. Given that most preference settings are specific to the workspace in use, you are faced with a need to make multiple visits to the Preferences dialog to coordinate updates to preference settings across workspaces.

**NOTE**    The concept of workspace-specific preference settings will change over time for some tools, Eclipse included. The Eclipse Platform stores preferences, but the Eclipse API has evolved to allow tools to use a more sophisticated approach. Now termed **user settings**, these preference values can be stored with a scope that makes them unique and consistent for the configuration, the workspace, or a project in the workspace. When tools adjust to use this new capability, some preferences may no longer be workspace specific; this will be a good thing if you are tired of managing preference settings for multiple workspaces. The user settings APIs are discussed further in Chapter 16, Dialogs and Wizards.

There is a better way to manage preferences. Two approaches are discussed in the following sections; each has a place in your bag of Eclipse-user strategies. Use one or both—it is your call. The skills required to perform the synchronization approach are used to find content for the alternative defaults technique.

### Synchronizing Preference Settings

Eclipse has a wealth of preference pages and settings that allow you to personalize the look and behavior of the environment. In rough numbers, how many preference pages do you think there are? How many preference settings? These are not static values because pages and settings tend to come and go, but at this moment in time (using the GA version of Eclipse 3.0), there are 74 pages. Most pages have at least 5 settings, but some have more; the Java compiler page has at least 45. A rough guess gives you a value between 350 and 500 total settings, but that may be low. That rough guess does not count the values stored as preferences that are not shown on preference pages. For example, when the Outline view is supporting the Java source editor, it has a pull-down toggle option of **Go Into Top Level Type**; this choice is stored as a preference setting.

Now let's assume you visited 10% of the pages and changed 10% of the options; that would mean you had customized at least 35 settings. Now open a new workspace and do that again. Can you? Of course you can, if you let Eclipse do most of the work. Have you ever noticed the **Import** and **Export** buttons on the lower left corner of the Preferences dialog? If you export your preference page settings from one workspace, you can then import them to another, appropriately setting 35 (or more) of your favorite preferences in your new workspace.

Take that a step further and you can share that file with your teammates; that way everyone starts at the same point. From there they can make the changes they want to improve on your definition of perfection.

---

**NOTE**  The technique for team-specific settings can be refined in some areas. The **Java > Code Style > Code Formatter** preference page lets you define formatting rules that are stored as a preference and also supports direct import/export of just this definition in XML format. This allows for a more granular definition of the rules for a team.

---

## Defining New Preference Defaults

Each plug-in that defines preference settings can define default values for these settings. You have the right to change the default preference values for any plug-in. This right was designed for Eclipse-based products so they can define defaults that work best for their product. But you as a user of Eclipse, or any Eclipse-based product, can replace or adjust these defaults to suit your needs. This represents another chance to make Eclipse perfect—for you. To implement a customized set of default preferences you can use either of the following techniques.

- Identify your own customization file. You can use the invocation parameter `-plugincustomization` to identify a set of alternative defaults for selected preference keys.
- Modify an existing customization file. You can find the active product's `plugin_customization.ini` file and customize it to meet your needs.

First you need to be aware of your current environment. Eclipse or an Eclipse-based product could be using the `plugin_customization.ini` file to supply alternative preference defaults. This file is part of the product's branding content, which is used to personalize the configuration when a product builds on the Eclipse Platform. You may not want to override their defaults, or at least be aware that this is what you are going to do.

The invocation parameter will override any existing product-level customization, so you might want to blend the approaches by using the parame-

PART I

ter to identify a copy of the product's customization file, which you used as a base for your own modifications and additions.

To find the product's customization file and create a set of your own preference defaults that will be used at runtime, follow these steps.

1. Find the \configuration\config.ini file, open it, and find the id for the active product (eclipse.product=). For Eclipse the entry will be eclipse.product=org.eclipse.platform.ide. Note that the active product could also be defined using an invocation parameter.

2. Find the branding plug-in for the product. The product value is the concatenation of a plug-in id and an extension id from that plug-in. Look in the \plugins directory for a plug-in with an id similar to the product id and see if you can find a file named plugin_customization.ini.

   Features can also have a branding plug-in. For Eclipse and many Eclipse-based products the ids are the same, but the feature.xml file for the product's feature could be identifying an alternate branding plug-in using the plugin="another.plugin.id.value" attribute for the <feature> element.

3. Copy the plugin_customization.ini file to a private location, maybe even your eclipse root directory.

4. Add or modify the plugin_customization.ini file content to suit your needs.

5. Invoke Eclipse with the appropriate parameter to have your file used at runtime:

```
eclipse -pluginCustomization file_reference
```

Step 4 in this list is the kicker. How do you find the magic values to add the customization file? With practice and patience, of course. The key is to start with a clean workspace and find just a few at a time. Use a new workspace, change one or two preference settings, and then export the preferences as discussed earlier in the Synchronizing Preference Settings section. Then open the file and review the keys used for each entry. They are somewhat meaningful, and through the key name and possibly the value you will find those you want to make part of your standard set of choices. Here is one of my favorites:

```
/instance/org.eclipse.ui.workbench/
   SHOW_TEXT_ON_PERSPECTIVE_BAR=false
```

It may surprise you to learn that not all values kept as preferences are controlled from the preference page. This value customizes the Outline view display when a Java source editor is contributing the outline content:

```
/instance/org.eclipse.jdt.ui/
   GoIntoTopLevelTypeAction.isChecked=true
```

So, as you can tell, we do not have a magic bullet for finding all the interesting preference settings for which you want to define new defaults. The alternative to this technique is to load and search the Eclipse source, or write code to capture the API calls that get and set preference values. But if you find just five or ten settings that you know you change every time you open a new workspace, you may consider this time well spent. If you are coordinating the work of a team, you might leverage this approach by sharing the new version of the `plugin_customization.ini` file so that everyone can start with the same rules.

**NOTE** The process of finding preference settings for use in a customized launch of the Eclipse Platform was detailed in an article on the IBM developerWorks site. The article was written for Eclipse 2.1, but the more detailed review of the strategy may prove helpful here. You can find the article "Put Eclipse features to work for you" at http://www-106.ibm.com/developerworks/opensource/library/os-ecfeat/.

## Understanding Configuration Management Fundamentals

You can use Eclipse as it comes out of the box (ZIP file), but odds are that you will want to add something to your Eclipse environment. The real beauty of Eclipse is that you can adjust it to get a custom fit for your needs, either by finding plug-ins on the Web or by writing your own and then adding them to the Eclipse base.

Finding plug-ins you want to add is easy; the hard part can be adding them to your configuration effectively. We will not tell you to take the easy "dump and run" approach, copying the features and plug-ins into the directory tree of your current Eclipse install; you can do better.

Say you are given five minutes to remove your current Eclipse install and replace it with a new Eclipse-based product or a new version of Eclipse itself. Do you really want to find and copy all the features and plug-ins you have added before deleting the Eclipse directory tree? What if you have multiple Eclipse instances, some pure Eclipse, others Eclipse-based products, and you want the same plug-ins configured as part of every instance? Are you really going to copy the plug-ins to each and every `eclipse` directory tree? What if you added some fabulously expensive plug-ins to your Eclipse-based product and then when servicing the product you realize the service routine's version of an update is a delete of the old version and a fresh install of a new version? Odds are your plug-ins are history. Products rightfully view their `eclipse` directory tree as their property, not a dumping ground for your extras. There is a better way to manage your configuration.

Before we can get into those details, we need a quick primer on the Update Manager, the tool you use to manage your Eclipse configuration.

## Update Manager—An Introduction

The Update Manager controls your Eclipse configuration. The Update Manager creates this configuration and manages changes that occur to it either through your use of the Update Manager or through file system manipulation.

The Update Manager is involved when Eclipse starts up so it can build the configuration if missing and read the active configuration to pass startup information to the Eclipse launcher. In the next several sections we will cover how you can use the Update Manager to accomplish the following tasks:

- Enable and disable features in the current configuration
- Add new sites to the current configuration
- Remove sites from the current configuration
- Access update sites to download and install new features or maintain existing features
- List the sites and features currently included in the configuration
- Back out service updates if they are not working to your satisfaction

If you are using an Eclipse-based product, you may be directed to use the Update Manager to install new features or download service to existing features. If you are adding additional features to your Eclipse installation, you should use the Update Manager to add them, but use a new install site unless directed otherwise; remember, we do not approve of the "dump and run" approach to configuration management.

Using the Update Manager is a learned skill, but one worth investing the required time.

**NOTE** In this chapter, we're going to talk about using packaged updates someone else has prepared. If you're interested in the process of feature definition and packaging updates for delivery by the Update Manager, see Chapter 13, Defining Features and Products, for a discussion of this plug-in development topic

## Configuration Basics

At runtime, the functions available in Eclipse are provided by a set of configured features, either as part of the base Eclipse installation or as later additions. They might exist in the installation directory for Eclipse or be located somewhere else on the file system. The Update Manager creates the initial configuration of features and allows the user to add to and modify this configuration.

A **configuration** is a list of install sites and the features found in each of these install sites. An **install site** is a location that contains features and plugins that can be included in the configuration. The Update Manager processes the content of the features and plugins directories of the install site; if the content is valid, it can be included in the configuration.

The eclipse\configuration directory is the default location for the Eclipse Platform configuration. The configuration details are kept in a file named platform.xml, which can be found in the configuration's \org.eclipse.update directory. Here is the platform.xml content if the Eclipse SDK is all you have installed.

```
<?xml version="1.0" encoding="UTF-8"?>
<config date="Sat May 08 22:38:14 EDT 2004"
    transient="false" version="3.0">
  <site enabled="true" policy="USER-EXCLUDE" updateable="true"
    url="platform:/base/">
    <feature application="org.eclipse.ui.ide.workbench"
        id="org.eclipse.platform" primary="true"
        url="features/org.eclipse.platform_3.0.0/"
            version="3.0.0">
      <root>platform:/base/plugins/org.eclipse.platform_3.0.0/</root>
    </feature>
    <feature id="org.eclipse.platform.source"
        url="features/org.eclipse.platform.source_3.0.0/"
        version="3.0.0"/>
     <feature id="org.eclipse.jdt"
        url="features/org.eclipse.jdt_3.0.0/" version="3.0.0"/>
     <feature id="org.eclipse.jdt.source"
        url="features/org.eclipse.jdt.source_3.0.0/"
            version="3.0.0"/>
     <feature id="org.eclipse.pde"
        url="features/org.eclipse.pde_3.0.0/" version="3.0.0"/>
     <feature id="org.eclipse.sdk"
        url="features/org.eclipse.sdk_3.0.0/" version="3.0.0"/>
  </site>
</config>
```

This platform.xml content shows one site (platform:/base/); the features found at the site are listed too.

## Install Site Types

There are two types of install sites: the platform base and any other site that might be added to the configuration. It does not matter how the site is discovered or which technique was used to add the site; all sites are treated pretty much the same.

The base site is where Eclipse itself is installed. By convention, this is a directory named `eclipse`, with `features` and `plugins` subdirectories that contain the components included as part of the base install (see An Overview of Your Eclipse Installation earlier in this chapter). This site is discovered when Eclipse is started. The discovery is based on the location of the `eclipse.exe` file launched and the `features` and `plugins` subdirectories found in the file system.

Other sites can exist in the configuration. Sites can be added by using the Update Manager's user interface or command API. Sites can also be discovered through the use of a link file. The use of Update Manager to add sites is discussed in detail in the upcoming Adding and Removing Install Sites section.

If a `links` directory exists in the eclipse install directory, files in the `links` directory are searched for entries that identify the location of a valid install site, that is, one that contains an `eclipse` directory with `features` and `plugins` subdirectories inside. Here is an example of what you might find in a link file:

```
path=E:/Eclipse-3.0/examples
```

If the location is found and valid, the site is automatically added to the configuration. You can use this technique yourself, or you may be using an Eclipse-based product that uses this technique. Just keep in mind that this technique is a carryover from older versions of Eclipse and may not be supported forever.

### Update Manager Command API

The Update Manager user interface options found in the **Help > Software Updates** menu are not hard to figure out. What is new, and possibly more interesting, is the Update Manager command API.

The command API is a set of Update Manager operations that can be requested by running a specific Eclipse application with the required command API parameters. Using the command API you can do the following:

- Add and remove install sites
- List install sites and the features they contain
- Enable and disable features
- Install new features or service existing features using an update site
- Uninstall features that have been installed from an update site

We will not replicate the command API documentation here, but we show how many of these commands can be used to control the install sites and features included in an Eclipse configuration.

## Interacting with the Update Manager

The Update Manager user interface and command API can be used to add new install sites, manage features, and interact with update sites. The choice between using the user interface or the command API may depend more on who is making the changes (a user or the install routine). The user interface and command API offer equivalent function, but the feedback and discovery options provided by the user interface are superior.

Install sites are the basic building block in a configuration. The base or root install site is always there, but others may be added or removed as required. You may create install sites to isolate features, or different software providers may create install sites as they integrate their offerings on a common installation. An install site is a single location on the file system, but the same location could be included in multiple configurations in multiple Eclipse or Eclipse-based product installations.

The smallest unit on which the Update Manager operates is a feature. A feature that is added to an existing configuration can contain new plug-ins, updates to existing plug-ins, or both.

### Adding and Removing Install Sites

Install sites can be added by using either the Product Configuration dialog or the Update Manager command API. An install site is an `eclipse` directory that contains an `.eclipseextension` marker file. In this directory are the `/features` and `/plugins` subdirectories.

To add an install site by using the Product Configuration dialog, select **Help > Software Updates > Manage Configuration...** to open the dialog. When the configuration root or an existing site is selected, the **Add an Extension Location** option is visible. When using this option you have to find a file system location that contains a valid Eclipse install site.

By using the Update Manager command API you can add an install site and then remove it later. Issue the following commands to add and then remove an install site.

```
java.exe -cp startup.jar org.eclipse.core.launcher.Main
   -data tempwork
   -application org.eclipse.update.core.standaloneUpdate
   -command addSite -from E:\Eclipse-3.0\Install-Extras\Tools
```

```
java.exe -cp startup.jar org.eclipse.core.launcher.Main
  -data tempwork
  -application org.eclipse.update.core.standaloneUpdate
  -command removeSite -to E:\Eclipse-3.0\Install-Extras\Tools
```

This is the approach you should use if you have a set of plug-ins you would like to add to your Eclipse installation.

### Disabling and Enabling Features

You can select features in the Product Configuration dialog. Depending on the current state of the feature, you will be able to start a **Disable** or **Enable** request. You will need to select the **Show Disabled Features** toolbar filter to see disabled features you wish to enable.

The state of a feature can be modified by using the Update Manager command API. Use these commands to disable or enable a feature that existed in the identified install site.

```
java.exe -cp startup.jar org.eclipse.core.launcher.Main

  -data tempwork
  -application org.eclipse.update.core.standaloneUpdate
  -command disable -featureId com.ibm.jdg2e.tools -version 3.0.0
  -to E:\Eclipse-3.0\ConfigTest\fromUpdateSite
```

```
java.exe -cp startup.jar org.eclipse.core.launcher.Main
  -data tempwork
  -application org.eclipse.update.core.standaloneUpdate
  -command enable -featureId com.ibm.jdg2e.tools -version 3.0.0
  -to E:\Eclipse-3.0\Install-Extras\Tools
```

### Installing a Feature from an Update Site

You can use the Install wizard of the Update Manager to find and install new features. Open this wizard by selecting **Help > Software Updates > Find and Install…**. To find features you may want to install, choose the **Search for new features to install** option. This will take you to a list of update sites you can search for features.

This list might be empty at first. In that case you might add a site based on an http: or file: URL you have been given. Entries may exist if you added them previously, or they may have been added by features you have installed. Features can also define **discovery sites** to identify locations you might browse for new features.

You can browse update sites for available features, select a set of features, and then request that the Update Manager download and install them to local install sites.

The process of installing a feature from an update site can also be performed by using the Update Manager command API. Use the following commands to install a specific feature from an update site to an identified install site.

```
java.exe -cp startup.jar org.eclipse.core.launcher.Main
   -data tempwork
   -application org.eclipse.update.core.standaloneUpdate
   -command install -featureId com.ibm.jdg2e.tools -version 3.0.0
   -from http://jumpstart.raleigh.ibm.com/UpdateSite
   -to E:\Eclipse-3.0\ConfigTest\fromUpdateSite
```

If a target install site is not specified, the feature is added to the Eclipse base site. Features can also identify another feature in their definitions to request that they be installed in the same site as that feature, if that feature exists in the current configuration. This linkage is defined when the feature to be installed from an update site includes the `colocation-affinity` attribute.

### Applying Service to Features

Features can be defined so that they know where to look for service. The process of finding and applying the service can be performed with either the Install wizard or the Update Manager command API.

To use the Install wizard, all you do is choose the **Search for updates to currently installed features** option. The Update Manager will check the update sites known to the configured features for versions that might be appropriate to install as part of the current configuration.

To use the Update Manager command API, define a request to update any features, or just a specific feature, as follows.

```
java.exe -cp startup.jar org.eclipse.core.launcher.Main
   -data tempwork
   -application org.eclipse.update.core.standaloneUpdate
   -command disable -featureId com.ibm.jdg2e.tools -version 3.0.0
   -to E:\Eclipse-3.0\ConfigTest\fromUpdateSite
```

```
java.exe -cp startup.jar org.eclipse.core.launcher.Main
   -data tempwork
   -application org.eclipse.update.core.standaloneUpdate
   -command enable -featureId com.ibm.jdg2e.tools -version 3.0.0
   -to E:\Eclipse-3.0\Install-Extras\Tools
```

### Next Steps

If you want to practice the skill of using the Update Manager to perform configuration management, you can use the materials provided on the CD-ROM.

These are arranged in a fashion that will either let you copy a directory structure to your machine and then add the code as an extension or allow you to use the CD-ROM directly as an update site to download and configure the features as part of your Eclipse or Eclipse-based product. If you are going to be an active plug-in developer, you can learn more about this by reading Chapter 13, Defining Features and Products. You could even take on the role of a feature developer in Exercise 9, Deploying Your Product Using Features. This exercise includes the use of the Update Manager to add extensions and install features from an update site.

## Managing Your Configuration

Configurations are discovered, created, and modified by the Update Manager as part of Eclipse startup and shutdown processes. If you understand how Eclipse implements configuration processing, you will be better able to manage your own configuration.

### Understanding Default Configuration Processing

The default configuration processing supported by Eclipse does what you need, at least for most scenarios. You start Eclipse, it finds the `configuration\config.ini` file to get things rolling, and a configuration is created that includes the platform base site and any install sites defined using a link file in the `eclipse\links` directory. Given an Eclipse install, with a link file that points to the Eclipse plug-in examples, here is the default configuration created.

```
<?xml version="1.0" encoding="UTF-8"?>
<!--Created on Sat Jun 26 16:17:52 EDT 2004-->
<config date="1088281072284" transient="false" version="3.0">
  <site enabled="true"
    linkfile=
      "e:/Eclipse-3.0/Install_Test/eclipse/links/examples.link"
    policy="USER-EXCLUDE" updateable="true"
    url="file:/E:/Eclipse-3.0/Install_Test/examples/eclipse/">
    <feature id="org.eclipse.sdk.examples"
      url="features/org.eclipse.sdk.examples_3.0.0/"
        version="3.0.0"/>
  </site>
  <site enabled="true" policy="USER-EXCLUDE"
    updateable="true" url="platform:/base/">
    <feature application="org.eclipse.ui.ide.workbench"
      id="org.eclipse.platform" primary="true"
      url="features/org.eclipse.platform_3.0.0/"
        version="3.0.0"/>
```

```
        <feature id="org.eclipse.platform.source"
          url="features/org.eclipse.platform.source_3.0.0/"
          version="3.0.0"/>
        <feature id="org.eclipse.jdt"
          url="features/org.eclipse.jdt_3.0.0/" version="3.0.0"/>
        <feature id="org.eclipse.jdt.source"
          url="features/org.eclipse.jdt.source_3.0.0/"
            version="3.0.0"/>
        <feature id="org.eclipse.pde"
          url="features/org.eclipse.pde_3.0.0/" version="3.0.0"/>
        <feature id="org.eclipse.sdk"
          url="features/org.eclipse.sdk_3.0.0/" version="3.0.0"/>
        <feature id="org.eclipse.pde.source"
          url="features/org.eclipse.pde.source_3.0.0/"
            version="3.0.0"/>
    </site>
  </config>
```

This configuration is managed using the Update Manager user interface or command API. Configuration changes are under the direct control of the install owner; in this instance this is assumed to be a single person. New install sites can be added, features can be disabled and enabled, and service can be applied. There are no restrictions beyond the standard Update Manager processing; you are not permitted to disable a site or feature that would invalidate the configuration. This is essentially the way most users of Eclipse or an Eclipse-based product work.

It is possible to clean a configuration to return it back to the start point. To do this you should delete everything in the configuration directory except the config.ini file. This will not harm existing workspaces. If you do not want to lose your list of last used workspaces, then do *not* delete the org.eclipse.ui.ide directory. Make a copy of the org.eclipse.update\platform.xml file first if you want to be sure you can return to the existing configuration.

## Using an Alternative Configuration

It is not hard to use an alternative configuration; you simply start Eclipse using the -configuration parameter. This creates a new configuration in the specified location. The configuration you create might be based on a shared configuration or could be an independent configuration, which depends on the current state of your Eclipse installation.

If there is no default configuration when you use the -configuration parameter to create an alternative, you have essentially created a configuration that looks and behaves like the default configuration discussed in the previous section; it is just physically written to a new location.

If a default configuration exists, things work differently. Your alternative configuration is based on the default configuration if the default configuration exists when the alternative is first created. You can tell that this has happened if you peek at the platform.xml file. This alternative configuration is created when Eclipse is invoked using this parameter after the default configuration was in place:

```
eclipse -configuration e:\altSharedConfig
```

Compare the following altSharedConfig\platform.xml content with the default configuration shown previously (this assumes Eclipse was installed at e:\Eclipse-3.0\Install_Test\eclipse).

```
<?xml version="1.0" encoding="UTF-8"?>
<!--Created on Sat Jun 26 16:28:32 EDT 2004-->
<config date="1088281712284"
    shared_ur=
      "file:/e:/Eclipse-3.0/Install_Test/eclipse/configuration
        /org.eclipse.update/platform.xml" transient="false"
          version="3.0"/>
```

The alternative configuration references the default configuration as a shared configuration. If you ask the alternative configuration for a list of features, you will see this list.

```
e:\eclipse-3.0\jre\bin\java.exe -cp startup.jar
    org.eclipse.core.launcher.Main -data tempwork
    -application org.eclipse.update.core.standaloneUpdate
    -configuration e:\altSharedConfig -command listFeatures

Site: file:/E:/Eclipse-3.0/Install_Test/examples/eclipse/
  Feature: org.eclipse.sdk.examples 3.0.0  enabled
Site: file:/e:/Eclipse-3.0/Install_Test/eclipse/
  Feature: org.eclipse.jdt.source 3.0.0  enabled
  Feature: org.eclipse.platform 3.0.0  enabled
  Feature: org.eclipse.jdt 3.0.0  enabled
  Feature: org.eclipse.pde 3.0.0  enabled
  Feature: org.eclipse.pde.source 3.0.0  enabled
  Feature: org.eclipse.platform.source 3.0.0  enabled
  Feature: org.eclipse.sdk 3.0.0  enabled
Command completed successfully.
```

So, what you actually have configured are the install sites in the default configuration with their respective features. More important is what you can now do to manage those shared install sites: not much. That is, by using your alternative configuration you can add new sites and change the state of features in sites you have added, but you cannot disable, enable, service, or otherwise manipulate the content obtained from the shared configuration. And, in reverse, neither can you stop changes that occur to the shared default configuration from becoming part of your configuration the next time you start Eclipse. This in fact may be your goal; it starts to sound like you can push features from a shared configuration to the alternative configuration. What this is good for depends on your goals. Here are some examples.

- Use the default configuration as a base. You can keep this base clean and make additions only in alternative configurations based on the shared configuration
- Never establish a default configuration. You can then create any number of alternative configurations that allow for full control of install sites, features, and the application of service.
- Share a read-only instance of an Eclipse installation for use by others. They will always create an alternative configuration but will be forced to accept the sites and features you include in the shared configuration. This includes adding new features and applying maintenance. With this approach you can push code to the general user community.

As you can see, there are numerous strategies for managing your configuration. And of course if you accept the defaults, the configuration created for you works just fine. The important part is realizing how Eclipse reacts to the existence of a default configuration when you use the `-configuration` parameter to identify an alternative configuration. If you manage your install appropriately, you can essentially have a mandatory default configuration that is managed at a central location. This could apply to a single system or an Eclipse install used from a shared file system resource.

### Forcing a One-to-One Workspace–Configuration Relationship

If you are familiar with Eclipse 2.x, you know that each workspace kept its own configuration of install sites, features, and enablement information. This was viewed as a problem on occasion. One common reason was that you could add new code using the Update Manager with a unique install site (best practice), but when you started Eclipse with a different workspace it could not see the newly installed code. For this and other reasons the configuration is now managed outside a workspace so that it spans multiple workspaces.

This changes the default scenario but does not prevent you from achieving results similar to the previous way of working, if desired. Let's assume your goal is to have unique configurations for each workspace; essentially, a return to the *old* way. You can do this with a simple strategy. Make sure there is no default configuration; if one exists, you can clean it out by deleting everything in the `configuration` directory but the `config.ini` file. (If you are the cautious type, make a backup first.) Start Eclipse using both the `-data` and `-configuration` parameters, and have each identify a unique location for the workspace and associated configuration. The following invocations of Eclipse would result in not only a unique configuration for each workspace but also an organized approach to managing that content on the file system.

```
eclipse -data d:\ws\javaWork -configuration d:\ws\javaWork
eclipse -data d:\ws\pluginWork -configuration d:\ws\pluginWork
```

This would result in the file system organization shown in Figure 6.4.

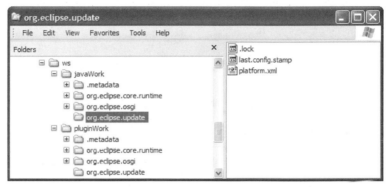

**Figure 6.4**    Strategy for Linking Workspace and Configuration

To have total freedom of management when using these unique configurations, you should make sure that you do not have a default configuration.

## Chapter Summary

This chapter discussed the Eclipse installation structure and reviewed strategies for managing your Eclipse environment. These strategies covered the management of preferences and workspaces, as well as the installation configuration. The capabilities of the Update Manager, using its user interface or command API, were also reviewed.

You should now be able to make changes in how you use your Eclipse or Eclipse-based product that will improve your control of the environment. Just keep in mind that you will need to experiment a bit to both become comfortable with the new approach and feel capable of correcting

any problems that might occur later. It is often wise to have two installations of Eclipse itself; use one to practice strategies for managing the environment and the other to do your day-to-day work. Apply your strategies
to production when you are comfortable with their behavior.

## Reference

Arthorne, John, and Chris Laffra. 2004. *Official Eclipse 3.0 FAQs*. Boston,
  MA: Addison-Wesley. http://eclipsefaq.org. (See FAQs 30–32, 34, 111.)

# PART II

## *Fundamentals of Extending Eclipse*

Having finished Part I, Using Eclipse, you now have an appreciation of what Eclipse offers you in general and specifically as a Java programmer. The goal of Part II is to show you how to make Eclipse your own by explaining the fundamentals of enhancing and extending it with your own ideas. As you will soon learn, Eclipse is more than just an integrated development environment; it is also a platform from which you can create feature-rich applications and tools. Whether it is your goal to create an application or enhance the Eclipse IDE, you'll start with Part II. After you've mastered these base concepts that apply regardless of whether you're building a general application or a tool, Part III, Extending the Eclipse Workbench, teaches you how to use your plug-in development skills to extend the Eclipse user interface.

- Chapter 7, Extending Eclipse for Fun and Profit, is an introductory chapter to help you understand and appreciate what extending Eclipse is all about. Even if you are just curious about what it takes to extend Eclipse, this chapter is the place to start. It may be easier than you think.
- Chapter 8, Overview of the Eclipse Architecture, as the title suggests, provides you with a foundation on Eclipse and its extensibility framework.

- Chapter 9, Getting Started: Plug-in Development, explains how to create a plug-in and the Eclipse tools available to support development and testing of plug-ins.
- Chapter 10, Creating Applications Using the Rich Client Platform, explains the fundamentals required to create a rich client application using Eclipse. This chapter revisits some of the points covered in Chapter 8, so if you're really anxious to learn about the Rich Client Platform, you could skip the previous two chapters and then return afterward to deepen your understanding.
- Chapter 11, Creating Extension Points: How Others Can Extend Your Plug-ins, explains how your plug-ins can be of service to others. It's not hard and is an important item to have in your personal Eclipse toolkit.
- Chapter 12, Advanced Plug-in Development, rounds out the topic of extending Eclipse.
- Chapter 13, Defining Features and Products, teaches you how to package and share your plug-ins.

Remember that this book comes with a CD-ROM that contains working examples that demonstrate the concepts presented in the book. Many chapters refer to contents on the CD-ROM as part of their explanations, extracting bits of code to reinforce your understanding. These examples are well documented with both Javadoc and inline comments. The CD-ROM also includes documentation for the examples and exercises, both of which are integrated with the Eclipse Help system. See the `readme.html` file for installation instructions.

# CHAPTER 7

## *Extending Eclipse for Fun and Profit*

The book you hold in your hands is sizable, one might even say imposing. We like to think of it as "impressively comprehensive," yet we appreciate how it may appear daunting as you turn to the first chapter that leads you into this next part. Still, we didn't want to abandon a winning formula that brought the first edition to the Java bestsellers lists for amazon.com, Barnes & Noble, and JavaOne in 2003 and 2004. Instead, we've restructured this unabashedly large book to make it more approachable as both a learning guide and reference.

This opening chapter of Part II has the formidable task of introducing you to the full breadth and depth of Eclipse as a technology platform without being overwhelming, and doing it in such a way that you feel motivated to continue onto more advanced topics. This eliminates any simple "Hello, World" introduction, since that surely won't inspire your imagination of the possibilities Eclipse offers. Instead, we'll present a useful example of how you might extend Eclipse's Java development tools—without writing much code at all. Along the way, we'll play a little loose with details and focus mostly on concepts. Rest assured that after this brief respite, the subsequent chapters will resume a more methodic approach to solving general Eclipse programming problems.

### Excited About Extending Eclipse? You Should Be!

Eclipse has received much fanfare and accolades because of its powerful Java development environment. That—coupled with the team environment and other base capabilities—makes Eclipse a compelling integrated development environment, which is great news for Java developers. Moreover, Eclipse is an open source project. But what makes Eclipse truly exciting are the extension possibilities that it offers you.

A number of open source and commercially available products based on Eclipse show the practical implications of this way of delivering integrated products. Check out the "Community Projects and Plug-ins" page on eclipse.org. You'll see over one hundred projects that demonstrate the impact that Eclipse has already had by lowering development costs and reducing their users' learning curve because of their similar user interfaces and behavioral consistency. Sure, the value of this is self-evident for large software houses, but what's in it for the "little guy?"

That's where the extensibility story of Eclipse gets interesting. Not just integration for those who have large development organizations, but also for anyone willing to invest some time in learning a few Eclipse frameworks. "Oh no," you may be thinking, "not more frameworks. I don't have the time to learn more frameworks." Don't worry; it will be quick and easy. And before that little voice in your head has time to say it, no, we'll keep this chapter's promise of not boring you with a trivial extension of Eclipse. You'll see practical value and a clear demonstration of how you can enhance your use of Eclipse's Java development environment. These same techniques can be applied more generally to enhancing Eclipse to integrate your own homegrown tools and applications. You may even be a little surprised to see that it often takes only a few dozen lines of code to do some amazing things.

This chapter will show you what is possible and where to start, and will give you a firm appreciation for what's involved in getting there. Though extending Eclipse is an advanced topic, you can start with only a passing knowledge of how to use Eclipse's Java development environment.

## An Easy and Practical Example

Many Java developers don't worry too much about categorizing method visibility as default (package), private, public, or protected when initially writing code. As they create methods, they often make them all public. Only after they've finalized the organization of packages and finished refactoring methods—whether by extracting new methods from existing code by pulling up or pushing down methods in the hierarchy, or by moving them to another class entirely—do they go back and review method visibility. That's reasonable, since they may not know the final class shapes and have only a little practical usage of the code, so they don't want to declare what their "clients" might need. In other words, before sharing a new framework, you must decide what is implementation detail and what is necessary for others to use.

It would be handy if you could merely select methods in the Outline view, Hierarchy view, or wherever you see methods—and with a click of a menu choice, set one or more methods to the desired visibility. Figure 7.1 shows such an extension to Eclipse's Java development environment in the context of the Java editor's Outline view.

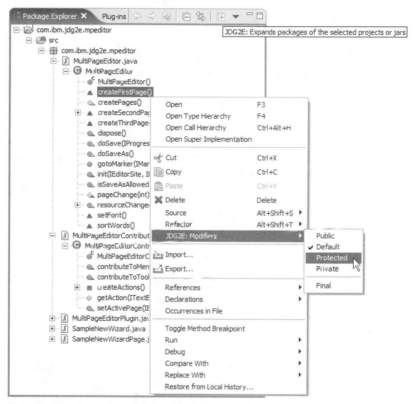

**Figure 7.1**    Extension of a Member's Context Menu

This is subtle, from a user's perspective, because of the natural way this was introduced into the user interface. There is no inkling that these new menu choices weren't part of Eclipse's original Java Development Tools (JDT). In fact, that's why the menu cascade is prefixed with the abbreviation of this book's title, "JDG2E"—so you can tell it's our extension! What's more, the developer doesn't have to remember that these choices are only available in a particular view or editor because they will be shown anywhere a method is shown. This is the power of Eclipse's extensibility. If you look carefully at Figure 7.1, you may also notice another addition to the Package Explorer (⊞). This "smart expand all" is the converse of the collapse all on the Package Explorer's toolbar. It's also available in the com.ibm.jdg2e.jdt project and we'll return to it later in Chapter 27, Extending the Java Development Tools. For now, we'll focus on the workings behind the **JDG2E: Modifiers** extension to Java members.

## A Brief Tour of "Hello, World"

"Hey, wait a minute, you promised no 'Hello, World'!" True, but we do need to cover a little about Eclipse's underpinnings before getting to the really interesting stuff. So if you have never written your own extension to Eclipse, please join us in a quick tour of the Eclipse architecture and plug-in development environment. Otherwise, skip to the next section. On with the tour!

In essence, Eclipse is a collection of loosely bound yet interconnected pieces of code. How these pieces of code are "discovered" and how they discover and extend each other captures the fundamental principles of the Eclipse architecture. These functional units are called **plug-ins**. The Platform Runtime, shown in Figure 7.2, is responsible for finding the declarations of these plug-

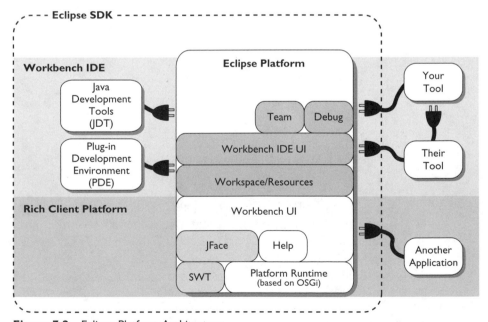

**Figure 7.2**   Eclipse Platform Architecture

ins, called a **plug-in manifest,** in a file named `plugin.xml`. Each plug-in is located in its own subdirectory below a common directory of Eclipse's installation directory named `plugins` (specifically, `<inst_dir>\eclipse\plugins`).

During startup these files are used to build a global registry, called the **extension registry.** A plug-in refers to this registry to determine what other plug-ins wish to take advantage of its services. A plug-in that wants to allow others to extend it will declare an **extension point.** This is a sort of "power strip" one plug-in provides that others can take advantage of by declaring an **extension** to it.

Returning to our example, the mission is to decide where to "plug into" Eclipse by finding the appropriate extension point offering the services we require. Fortunately, once you have used Eclipse as an IDE for a while, you know a surprising amount about what is available, perhaps without realizing it. This is because what you see in the Eclipse user interface and what is modeled by the classes that make up the Eclipse plug-ins often correspond nearly one-for-one to each other. Figure 7.3 makes this point clearer where the different views, that is, different levels of abstraction, are shown.

Here we see a progression of user interfaces showing the same files presented in a different manner, starting from the lowest common denominator on the right, the file system contents shown by a `dir` command in a Command Prompt window, continuing to a highly specialized view, that of the JDT's Package Explorer on the left. That is, the file `MultiPageEditor.java` is the same source in all three views, but its presentation is quite different and the available actions are different too. From a user interface perspective, all these views are visualizing a representation of the same "model," namely some files. As Eclipse users, we naturally expect views to present us different ways of looking at the same thing simultaneously, ways that adapt to the work we are doing. Recognizing how the Eclipse user interface reflects its underlying model and how its models build upon each other gives us an important clue about how we can find the best place to plug in our extension. The Navigator view in Figure 7.3 shows instances of `IFile` and the Package Explorer view shows instances of `ICompilationUnit`. As you can see, the names of these model classes and many like them correspond with what is shown in the user interface; therefore, you already have an intuitive appreciation for what's available programmatically.

That is the first half of our tour. The second half is a look at developing the solution. Rather than present the solution and explain it piece-by-piece, wouldn't it be more interesting to discover some of it? Let's start with some questions related to the problem at hand: Extending the JDT with our own method visibility refactoring capability.

Files modeled as instances of `java.io.File`

Files modeled as instances of `org.eclipse.resources.core.IFile`

Files modeled as instances of `org.eclipse.jdt.core.ICompilationUnit`

**Figure 7.3**    Views and Their Models

# Asking the Right Question Is More Important Than Knowing the Answer

Our quest begins with some general questions.

- How and where will the extension be shown in the user interface?
- How do you extend the user interface in general?
- How does an extension to the user interface know about events like a user's selection?

Once you have a good handle on the basic Eclipse landscape, we'll turn to some questions more specific to the solution we want to develop.

- How do you extend the user interface of specific objects of the JDT, like members shown in the Outline view? Do you extend the view(s) or their underlying model?
- What is the relationship between objects shown in the Package Explorer and the same objects shown in other views like the Outline view? Does your extension need to be aware of any differences between them?
- How do you change the JDT model programmatically?
- How do you analyze Java source code to apply modifications?

And of course, the final big question:

- Where to go from here?

## How and Where the Extension Is Shown in the User Interface

As you recall, we decided to show context menu choices for one or more selected methods that allow us to change their visibility with a single action. We prefer that they be available wherever the methods can be displayed, such as the Hierarchy view and Package Explorer. This leads to our next question.

## How to Extend the User Interface in General

Learning by example is more fun, and this is where the Plug-in Project wizard can give you a hand. It provides sample code that you can modify to meet your needs. You answer just a few of its questions and the wizard will automatically launch the specialized perspective for plug-in development, known as the **Plug-in Development Environment** (PDE), ready for testing. This wizard includes a number of examples that will get you started. In fact, your old friend "Hello, World" is there. Just for old time's sake, let's generate it, look at the result to verify that the environment is set up correctly, and then modify it to help answer the current question and lead to the next question: *How does an extension to the user interface know about events like selection?* That will be important, since you want to apply your newly introduced menu choices to the currently selected method(s).

Note that these instructions assume that you're starting from a fresh Eclipse installation. If you have modified the environment or changed preferences, things may not work precisely as described below. You might consider starting Eclipse with a fresh workspace by selecting another one on startup (see Running Multiple Eclipse Windows and Workspaces in Chapter 2 if you need a reminder of how to do this).

Begin by creating a plug-in project using the New Plug-in Project wizard.

1. Select **File > New > Project**.
2. In the New Project dialog, select **Plug-in Development > Plug-in Project** in the list of wizards and then select **Next**.
3. Name the project com.ibm.jdg2e.helloworld. The wizard will create a plug-in identifier based on this name, so it must be unique in the system (by convention, the project name and the plug-in identifier are the same). The proposed default workspace location shown under **Project contents** is fine; select **Next**.
4. The next page, shown in Figure 7.4, proposes a plug-in name and plug-in class name. These are based on the last word of the plug-in project, com.ibm.jdg2e.**helloworld**. This example doesn't need a plug-in class because we are accepting the default implementation for controlling the plug-in life cycle, so deselect its code generation option, as shown in Figure 7.4, and select **Next** (not **Finish**; you have two more pages to go).
5. The next page allows you to choose a code template. Select the **Create a plug-in using one of the templates** check box, select **Hello, World**, and then select **Next**. The following page, shown in Figure 7.5, is where you can specify parameters that are unique to the "Hello, World" example, such as the message that will be displayed.
6. To simplify the resulting code, change the target package name for the action from com.ibm.jdg2e.helloworld.**actions** to com.ibm.jdg2e.**helloworld**, the same name as the project. While you might choose to have separate packages for grouping related classes in a real world plug-in, in this case there will be only one class, so there's no need. It also adheres to the convention that the "main" package is named the same as the project.

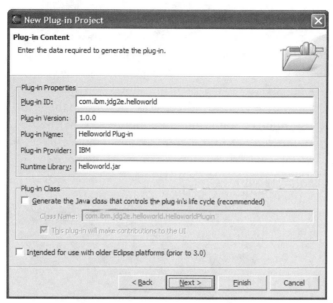

**Figure 7.4**   Plug-in Content

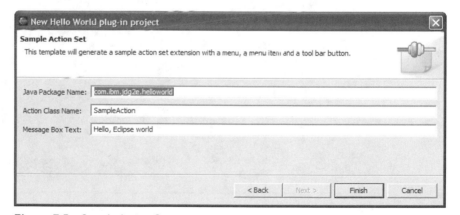

**Figure 7.5**   Sample Action Set

7. Now select **Finish**.
8. If this is a fresh workspace, you may see the information message "This kind of project is associated with the Plug-in Development Perspective. Do you want to switch to this perspective now?" Select **Yes** to switch as the message suggests.

To verify that everything is set up correctly, let's test your new plug-in.

1. Select **Run > Run As > Run-Time Workbench**. This will launch a second instance of Eclipse that will include your plug-in. This new instance will create a new workspace directory named `runtime-workbench-workspace`, so don't worry—whatever testing you do with that instance will not affect your development setup.
2. You should see something like Figure 7.6, with a new pull-down menu labeled **Sample Menu** having a single choice, **Sample Action**. Selecting it will show the information message below.

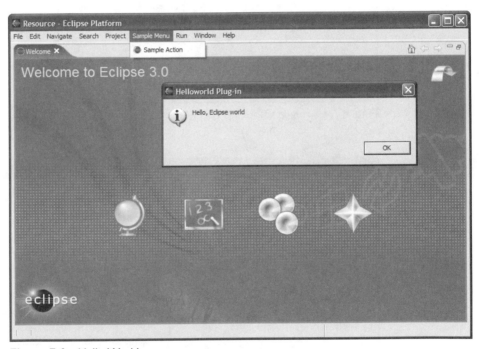

**Figure 7.6**    Hello, World

3. Close the runtime workbench and return to the PDE.
4. Let's take a quick glance at the plug-in manifest file, `plugin.xml`. Double-click it to open it in the Plug-in Manifest editor. This editor presents several wizard-like pages and a "raw" source page. Turn to it by selecting the **plugin.xml** tab. You'll see something like what's shown on the next page; we're interested in the text highlighted in bold.

```
<extension point="org.eclipse.ui.actionSets">
  <actionSet
     label="Sample Action Set"
     visible="true"
     id="com.ibm.jdg2e.helloworld.actionSet">
    <menu
       label="Sample &Menu"
       id="sampleMenu">
    <separator
      name="sampleGroup">
    </separator>
    </menu>
    <action
      label="&Sample Action"
      icon="icons/sample.gif"
      class="com.ibm.jdg2e.helloworld.SampleAction"
      tooltip="Hello, Eclipse world"
      menubarPath="sampleMenu/sampleGroup"
      toolbarPath="sampleGroup"
      id="com.ibm.jdg2e.helloworld.SampleAction">
    </action>
  </actionSet>
</extension>
```

It isn't necessary to study this too closely. The purpose of the second half of this tour is only to familiarize you with some of the basic mechanisms whereby you can introduce your extensions to the JDT. Here you see a sample of one such technique to add menus and menu choices to Eclipse as an action set. It begins with an extension, declared with the `<extension point="org.eclipse.ui.actionSets">` tag. The Eclipse user interface plug-in defines this extension point, `org.eclipse.ui.actionSets`, and several others like it where other plug-ins can contribute to the various user interface elements.

We still haven't answered how we can add menu choices to the context menu of Java methods. A simple modification can give you some hints. Begin by opening the class that displays the "Hello, World" message, `SampleAction`, and note its `run` method. It isn't particularly interesting; however, you also see another method, `selectionChanged`. Aha! The answer to the next question awaits.

## How an Extension to the User Interface Knows About Events Like Selection

Contributed actions, like our contributed menu pull-down choice, are notified when the selection changes. Let's modify this method to tell a bit more about the selection. First, if you haven't already closed the runtime instance of the Workbench, do so now (this won't be necessary if Eclipse is running the debugger under a JRE that supports hot code replace; in that case you can modify the code directly without restarting and see the result immediately). Add the code below to the selectionChanged method.

```
public void selectionChanged
    (IAction action, ISelection selection) {
  System.out.println("==========> selectionChanged");
  System.out.println(selection);
}
```

With this debug code, you'll see what is selected and learn a little more about what makes Eclipse tick. Save the method and relaunch the runtime Workbench.

**IMPORTANT**   Eclipse has a deferred load strategy to avoid activating plug-ins until the user does something that requires its code. So you must *first* select the **Sample Action** menu choice to load your plug-in before your selectionChanged method will be called.

To test your code, begin by creating a few projects, folders, and text files in your runtime Workbench. Now select different things like text in an editor, files in the Navigator, and, of course, members in the Outline view (recall that you'll need to create a Java project and an example Java class to do this, since the runtime instance uses a different workspace). The output below shows some sample messages that are similar to what you will see in the Console of the *development* instance of Eclipse.

```
==========> selectionChanged
[ColorManager.java [in com.ibm.jdg2e.test
    [in src [in com.ibm.jdg2e.test]]]
    package com.ibm.jdg2e.test
    import java.util.HashMap
 //  ...lines omitted...
==========> selectionChanged
<empty selection>
==========> selectionChanged
org.eclipse.jface.text.TextSelection@9fca283
==========> selectionChanged
[Color getColor(RGB) [in ColorManager [in [Working copy]
    ColorManager.java [in com.ibm.jdg2e.test
    [in src [in com.ibm.jdg2e.test]]]]]]
```

Well, that isn't as enlightening as you'd hoped. Clearly the selection isn't something as primitive as an instance of String, but it isn't evident what classes are involved either, because these classes have clearly overridden their default toString method. We're not yet at the point where you can appreciate what information they are showing without a little more investigation. Returning to the selectionChanged method, browse the hierarchy of the interface of the selection parameter, ISelection. Its hierarchy reveals the general-purpose subtype interfaces, IStructuredSelection (for lists) and ITextSelection.

---

**NOTE** You must import an additional plug-in that wasn't originally specified in the list of "Hello, World" required plug-ins so ITextSelection shown in the code below is visible to your plug-in. Add it now by inserting the following to the plugin.xml file, beneath the other import statements: <import plugin="org .eclipse.jface.text"/>

---

We'll make the selectionChanged method a bit smarter by outputting the class that's selected. The modified selectionChanged method is shown below.

```
public void selectionChanged
    (IAction action, ISelection selection) {
  System.out.println("==========> selectionChanged");
  if (selection != null) {
    if (selection instanceof IStructuredSelection) {
      IStructuredSelection ss = (IStructuredSelection) selection;
      if (ss.isEmpty())
        System.out.println("<empty selection>");
      else
        System.out.println("First selected element is " +
          ss.getFirstElement().getClass());
    } else if (selection instanceof ITextSelection) {
      ITextSelection ts = (ITextSelection) selection;
      System.out.println(
          "Selected text is <" + ts.getText() + ">");
    }
  } else {
    System.out.println("<empty selection>");
  }
}
```

Relaunch the Workbench and you'll see different messages in the console, depending if the selection is empty, from a list (IStructuredSelection), or an entry field (ITextSelection). Again, remember to close the runtime instance, relaunch, and select the **Sample Action** menu choice to load your plug-in. Now when you select various elements of the user interface it is far more revealing. The sample output shown on the next page is similar to what you'll see, depending on what your workspace contains and what you select. The interspersed annotations in bold explain what user action preceded the output.

```
     select a method in the Outline view
==========> selectionChanged
First selected element is class
    org.eclipse.jdt.internal.core.SourceMethod
==========> selectionChanged
<selection is empty>
     activated the Java editor
==========> selectionChanged
Selected text is <getResourceBundle>
     selected method, class, and
     package in the Package Explorer
==========> selectionChanged
First selected element is class
    org.eclipse.jdt.internal.core.SourceMethod
==========> selectionChanged
First selected element is class
    org.eclipse.jdt.internal.core.SourceType
==========> selectionChanged
First selected element is class
    org.eclipse.jdt.internal.core.PackageFragment
     activated the Navigator view, selected some files,
     folders, and projects
==========> selectionChanged
First selected element is class
    org.eclipse.core.internal.resources.File
==========> selectionChanged
First selected element is class
    org.eclipse.core.internal.resources.Project
==========> selectionChanged
First selected element is class
    org.eclipse.core.internal.resources.Folder
     reactivated the Package Explorer,
     selected some classes and methods in
     JARs of reference libraries
==========> selectionChanged
First selected element is class
    org.eclipse.jdt.internal.core.JarPackageFragment
==========> selectionChanged
First selected element is class
    org.eclipse.jdt.internal.core.ClassFile
==========> selectionChanged
First selected element is class
    org.eclipse.jdt.internal.core.BinaryMethod
```

Specifically, you can confirm that what you see in the user interface corresponds one-for-one with model classes of the JDT. Why you're seeing what appears to be models as selections and not lower-level primitives like strings and images is thanks to another Eclipse framework, called **JFace**. As you'll see in Chapter 15, JFace Viewers, this framework maps between primitives like strings that the widgets close to the operating system expect and the higher-level model objects with which your code prefers to work. This chapter only peripherally touchs on this topic, since our stated goal is extending the JDT. Later chapters covering topics like JFace viewers, views, editors, and JFace Text will broaden your understanding of the JFace framework. This chapter will only cover what's necessary to understand the implementation of our JDT extension.

Returning to the output, two particular selection results draw our attention: those corresponding to the selection of Java members in the user interface. They are repeated below.

```
==========> selectionChanged
First selected element is class
   org.eclipse.jdt.internal.core.SourceMethod
==========> selectionChanged
First selected element is class
   org.eclipse.jdt.internal.core.BinaryMethod
```

The `internal` in the middle of the package name for these classes is a little disquieting. However, as you'll often find, Eclipse will have a public interface that corresponds to the (internal) implementation class, as is the case here. A quick class lookup reveals that these classes all implement a common set of interfaces that look promising, namely `ISourceReference`, `IJavaElement`, and especially `IMember`. Finally! Now you have what you had hoped to extend, leading to the answer to the next question.

## How to Extend Objects Like Those Shown in the Outline View

Our simple "Hello, World" example showed that adding a menu choice requires just a few lines of XML in the plug-in manifest file (`<extension point="org.eclipse.ui.actionSet">`) and a class that handles the actual action (`com.ibm.jdg2e.helloworld.SampleAction`). Adding actions to views' pull-down menus, the common editors' toolbars, and pop-up menus is nearly as straightforward. Contributed pop-up menus come in two flavors: Those that are associated with just the view and not selected objects (that is, the default pop-up menu that views display when you right-click on their "whitespace"), and the more common variety, choices that apply to the selected object(s). In this case, we want to target only specific selected objects, so we'll contribute what's called an **action object contribution** to their pop-up menus by defining an extension in the plug-in manifest (some of the identifiers are shortened to format better; they are denoted by "..."), as shown below.

```
<extension point="org.eclipse.ui.popupMenus">
   <objectContribution
       objectClass="org.eclipse.jdt.core.IMember"
       id="...imember">
```

```
<menu
    label="JDG2E: Modifiers"
    path="group.reorganize"
    id="...imember.modifiers">
  <separator name="group1"/>
  <separator name="group2"/>
</menu>

<action
  label="Private"
  menubarPath="...imember.modifiers/group1"
  class="...jdt.extras.MakeIMemberPrivateAction"
  id="...imember.makeprivate">
</action>

<action
  label="Protected"
  menubarPath="...imember.modifiers/group1"
  class="...jdt.extras.MakeIMemberProtectedAction"
  id="...imember.makeprotected">
</action>

//    ...all menu choices not shown...

</objectContribution>
</extension>
```

The extension point is named org.eclipse.ui.popupMenus, and as the name suggests, it defines contributions to pop-up menus appearing in Eclipse. This particular example will contribute only to specific selected objects, those implementing the IMember interface (recall that as defined in the Java language specification, members include both methods and fields). Our investigation has paid off; we have the answer to the current question and we're almost ready to move to the next question.

Before doing so, note at this point that the pattern used for the simple "Hello, World" action example will repeat itself for other menu action contributions. That is, the class named in the class attribute will be notified of selection changes (by its selectionChanged method) and will be notified when the user selects the menu choice (by its run method). The user interface portion of the tour is almost over; the harder part, effecting the desired change, lies ahead. There is only an observation or two to make before continuing, as stated in the next question.

## The Relationship Between the Same Objects Shown in Different Views

You may have noticed that when you selected methods in the Outline and Hierarchy views, the class of the selected object was not always the same. For example, if you expanded the contents of a library (JAR file) in the Package Explorer, then selected a class or method, it was also not the same class as a similar selection in the Java editor's Outline view. What's up with that?

Here you are observing the difference between those parts of the JDT's Java model that are "editable" versus those that are always read-only. Both parts of the Java model will implement a common interface, like IMember, but have different implementation classes that understand the underlying restrictions. As another example, there is an implementation class representing a Java compilation unit derived from a .class file in a JAR file shown in the Package Explorer and another class representing a compilation unit derived directly from a .java file. The latter implementation will allow modifications where the former cannot, yet a shared portion of their API is represented by the interface ICompilationUnit. This interface and others from the JDT model are shown in Figure 7.7 along with their corresponding visual representation.

Subsequently, our contributed action that will modify Java members has to be aware of the context in which it is invoked. That is, it will have to recognize that some selected members are modifiable (those in the Java editor's Outline view) while others are not (members from .class file stored in a JAR file and shown in the Package Explorer). Keeping this in mind, let's continue on to the next question.

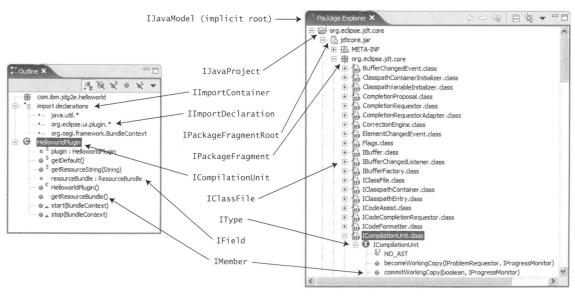

**Figure 7.7** JDT Model

## How to Change the JDT Model Programmatically

If you explored a bit during the prior tour, you may have noticed that
IMember, IJavaElement, and what appears to be the majority of the interfaces implemented by the selected Java-related items our action saw have
no setXXX methods. So how do you modify them?

You'll find it is surprisingly easy, yet perhaps not immediately obvious.
The JDT's Java model is in most practical respects "read only." With the integrated cooperation of the Java compiler, changes to the underlying Java
source of a given element are synchronized with the rest of the Java model. In
effect, all you have to do is update the Java source, and the rest of the necessary model changes are propagated to whoever is dependent on them.

That's a relief! This point is why the Java model is key to plug-in integration: It provides a common shared in-memory model of the entire Java
environment, its scope beginning from a project and continuing to all its
referenced libraries, all without you having to worry about manipulating
.java files, .class files, and .jar files in the file system. You can focus on
the high-level model and let the JDT deal with many of those messy details.

Not yet convinced it is that easy? The listing below contains the diminu-
tive snippet of code that is at the heart of this solution, extracted from the
contributed action's run method and simplified slightly for readability.

```
public void run(IAction action) {
  IMember member = (IMember)
      ((IStructuredSelection) currentSelection).
      getFirstElement();
  ICompilationUnit cu = member.getCompilationUnit();
  cu.becomeWorkingCopy(...);
  IBuffer buffer = cu.getBuffer();
  buffer.replace(...); // update member's source code
  cu.reconcile(...);
  cu.commitWorkingCopy(...);
  cu.discardWorkingCopy();
}
```

Seems a bit anticlimactic, doesn't it? Your contributed action is given the
selected member. You ask it for its parent container (the model of the Java
.class or .java file, collectively referred to as a **compilation unit** in JDT parlance) because that's who manages the underlying source. Next, update the
source code returned using a buffer. The IBuffer interface is similar to
StringBuffer, the principal difference being that changing the buffer associated with a compilation unit updates the corresponding elements of the Java
model. The call to reconcile tells the JDT to notify other interested parties
like the Package Explorer view that your model updates are ready for public
consumption.

You no doubt noticed the ellipsis in the code "buffer.replace(...)" shown above. That's where you have to analyze the source code itself to apply your modifications, which in this case will modify the method visibility from its current value to public, private, or protected. Again, the JDT comes to your aid and helps you finish the task. We'll not dwell on those details just yet, saving them instead for later in Chapter 27, Extending the Java Development Tools. You'll find the source code on the CD-ROM in the com.ibm.jdg2e.jdt project, if you want to peek ahead.

Leaving the implementation details aside for a moment, we hope you've gained an appreciation that you can introduce other worthwhile extensions to Eclipse using a similar discovery-oriented approach presented here. This isn't to suggest that you won't have lots of guidance—the weight of this book alone confirms there's a lot to learn! We encourage you to approach the task of learning about extending Eclipse by combining your experience from the user's point of view and the concepts and exercises of this book.

We covered quite a few new terms. Before closing, let's pause for just a moment and briefly review them as a reminder to you.

- Plug-in: a structured bundle of code
- Plug-in manifest: a formal declaration of a plug-in specified in a file named plugin.xml
- Extension points: a portion of the plug-in manifest defining where others can contribute
- Extensions: a contribution to a plug-in's extension point
- Action contributions: one of the Workbench extension points where the contributor defines a new action; actions can appear in several places within the Workbench user interface, such as our example, in an object's context menu

If some of the ideas presented in this chapter aren't yet solidified in your mind, don't worry. The next chapter will return to the terms and concepts underlying Eclipse, and in doing so, cover them more thoroughly and using more developed examples to assure your firm understanding.

## Where to Go from Here?

The stated goal of this chapter was to give you a nontrivial extension to Eclipse's Java development tools that enhances your productivity and paves the way for further study. In all honesty, more than once we skipped over some details for reasons of brevity. Nonetheless, we hope that you got a good taste of what's possible and you're convinced that it isn't all too difficult.

What we've covered in this chapter will be covered in more detail starting with Chapter 8, Overview of the Eclipse Architecture. Chapter 21, Action Contributions: The Integration Fast Track, and more specifically in Chapter 27, Extending the Java Development Tools, will reprise their respective topics that we briefly introduced here. Like this chapter, they include a documented working example that reinforces what you've learned, much in the same style as what you've seen here (though perhaps not covered at such a breakneck pace!).

As a final reminder, note this chapter only covered one aspect of Eclipse plug-in development, namely extending the Eclipse IDE itself. There is an exciting and much broader aspect to Eclipse development, one to which this book dedicates the remainder of Part II. We'll pick up this theme in the next chapter, and then really address the subject in earnest starting with Chapter 10, Creating Applications Using the Rich Client Platform. After you've understood the concepts presented in these early chapters, you may choose to skip around to specific topics that apply to the task before you. The Guide to Reading This Book suggests pathways you might consider based on your experience and interests. The close of each chapter will summarize what you've learned, and if there are additional pathways to other chapters to consider, the closing will give recommendations of the directions in which you might choose to continue.

# CHAPTER 8

## *Overview of the Eclipse Architecture*

Eclipse provides a common Workbench for organizing a developer's tasks and working with others via a common repository. It also includes a full-function integrated development environment (IDE) for Java. Given these capabilities alone, Eclipse compares favorably with commercial Java IDEs that are available on the market.

However, the Eclipse project is about more than delivering a good Java IDE. While it is true that the Eclipse SDK configuration includes Java technology support, the project's broader goal is to deliver a general-purpose application and tool-integration platform. In order to fulfill this goal, it must be capable of integrating new functionality from different independent software vendors (ISVs) while preserving the appearance of a single cohesive environment.

What does all this mean to you in practical terms? It means that your product can integrate with other tools and applications, where "integration" is not just a polite euphemism for exporting and importing files. With Eclipse, a common user interface goes beyond the similar appearance of buttons and dialogs—it means common user interactions. It also means that your users can focus on their work and not on managing an array of disparate tools.

And the best part? As you learned in the previous chapter, it isn't difficult. Eclipse includes comprehensive frameworks that provide reusable user interface components, so you can concentrate on the last 20% of your code that is the real jewel of your product. In the end, Eclipse gives its users the freedom to choose the right tool for the task without later being punished by incompatibility problems among applications. You are freed from having to write the same code that's been written many times before. Instead, you can reuse the Eclipse Platform and its associated development tools to focus on your product's innovation, not on maintaining its latest renovation.

What makes this all possible is the fact that Eclipse was designed from the very beginning with extensibility and integration in mind. It started when Eclipse developers studied the common patterns in many IDEs. They abstracted these "IDE patterns," aiming to deliver tools with simpler and more consistent implementations. Starting in version 3.0, Eclipse grew beyond its origin as a universal tools platform and embraced general application development as well. Whether an IDE or an application platform, Eclipse developers recognized that to make extensibility a meaningful goal, it must be readily understood that architected component integration from disparate sources must be their top priority. Simply stated, integration is everything to Eclipse's success. The Java development environment you see today was built on the Eclipse Platform as a test of the viability of its architecture and a demonstration of how one integrates tools on an equal footing as peers. Starting with this chapter, you will learn the ins-and-outs of how to extend Eclipse exactly as it itself does.

## That Was Then, This Is Now

Before we begin, a little history is necessary. Eclipse was initially designed exclusively as an extensible integrated development environment for programmers. As the product matured, more and more developers recognized that Eclipse could be useful beyond its origins. First attempts at reusing Eclipse's functionality began with its Java-based widget framework, the Standard Widget Toolkit, and culminated in the creation of a separate download specifically for GUI developers searching for an alternative to AWT/Swing. Later ad hoc efforts focused on "stripping away" portions of Eclipse's workspace-centric IDE framework to exploit the general-purpose rich client application framework that is the core of the Eclipse Workbench. These efforts proved to be awkward and fragile. Clearly restructuring of Eclipse into separate layers of rich client capabilities and specialized IDE functionality was necessary. Thus, the idea of the "Rich Client Platform" was born; it was a major theme of the version 3.0 release and generated lots of excitement in the Eclipse community and beyond.

The separation of "Eclipse the IDE" and "Eclipse the rich client" began with identifying what components belonged in which camp (where it is necessary to make a distinction between these two, we will hereafter referred to them as an **application** and **Workbench IDE**, respectively). It was clear enough that the idea of plug-ins applies to both, as do most of the user interface components. Those components that relied on the presence of IDE-centric artifacts, like the workspace and its project structure, were moved into new plug-ins specifically for IDE functionality. The most noteworthy examples of this separation are the plug-in `org.eclipse.ui`, which defines the base for developing the user interface of an Eclipse application, and the base IDE user interface plug-in, having the identifier `org.eclipse.ui.ide`. This plug-in includes many of the views and editors you'll recognize from Part I, such as the Tasks, Bookmarks, and Navigator view, all of which rely on the workspace as their model.

By default, an application will inherit the appearance you recognize from using Eclipse as an IDE, specifically, the notion of user task organization centered on perspectives, views, and editors. If you wish to create an application based on Eclipse, you have the choice of revealing the IDE-flavored appearance of a perspective-centric organization to the user or not. An Eclipse application also takes responsibility for much of the main window's appearance, allowing you to configure it to your liking by providing things like an alternative menu layout or controlling whether a view is moveable or closeable.

All of the concepts that you will learn in Part II apply to an Eclipse application and an Eclipse IDE. Because much of your experience with Eclipse may be as an IDE user, many of the examples you'll see in this chapter and those that follow will show something in the development environment, but keep in mind that the concepts and code development steps illustrated in these examples apply to both IDE and rich client applications. Part III, in contrast, will focus on those areas that apply to Eclipse as an IDE.

## Architectural Top Priorities: Extensibility and Integration

The prior chapter was a whirlwind tour of the Eclipse architecture. Now let's pause for a moment and cover it at a more leisurely pace. The architecture begins with Eclipse's central mechanism for defining new functionality, called a **plug-in**, which is the smallest unit of function that Eclipse recognizes. The Eclipse architecture does not specify a minimum or maximum size of a plug-in. However, to give you an idea of the range in size, Eclipse's Java development environment, the JDT, is one of the largest components and it defines around ten plug-ins.

Of course, most tools are not composed of so many plug-ins. Many plug-ins are rather small. As you'll discover, Eclipse allows for a very low "entry threshold" when introducing new capabilities to the platform. Do you love Eclipse's development environment, but wish there were "just one little improvement" to make you more productive? No problem—just add it. This part of the book is going to show you just how simple it is.

A plug-in introduces new capabilities using a contribution mechanism called **extension points**. These extension points represent an architected means of publicly declaring a plug-in's extensibility, either for your own reuse or use by other plug-ins that will extend your plug-in's capabilities. Plug-in developers must carefully consider where in their product they would expect (or hope) that other products would want to introduce enhancements. For the Eclipse Workbench user interface, for example, this means allowing other plug-ins to contribute a new editor for a given file type, a new view such as the Outline view to complement an existing editor, or something as minor as a new menu choice in an object's pop-up menu.

Figure 8.1 shows several simple extensions of Eclipse's standard Java development environment from the example associated with Chapter 27, Extending the Java Development Tools.

In this figure you can see one of the most common forms of extensions: extensions to the user interface. In this case, a plug-in has contributed a button to the main toolbar and a new view. Selecting the newly contributed **Add Trace Statements** toolbar button (  ) adds System.out.println statements to the beginning of each method to aid debugging. The new view to the right of the editor, **Java Metrics**, displays some basic code metrics for the selected Java source file.

In the most basic terms, an extension point defines where another plug-in can contribute what is called an **extension**. Let's look a little closer at this

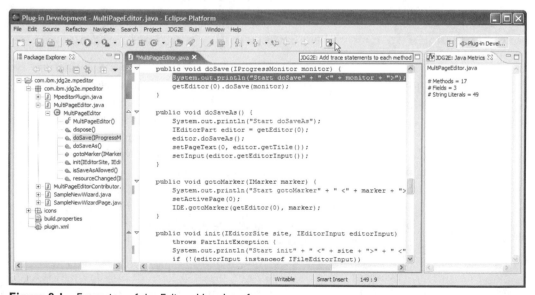

**Figure 8.1**   Extension of the Eclipse User Interface

relationship between extension points and extensions by considering the workings behind the example displayed in Figure 8.1. Figure 8.2 shows how a plug-in contributes a button to the editor's toolbar.

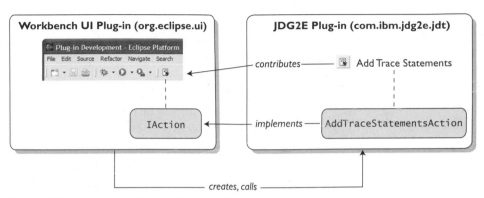

**Figure 8.2**   Connecting Classes Between Plug-ins

For this initial discussion, let's not worry about the precise syntax for defining a plug-in or specifying an extension or an extension point.

The Workbench user interface plug-in ("Workbench" for short) defines the base user interface of Eclipse. It creates the main window and coordinates the creation of initial menu pull-downs like **File, Edit, Window,** and **Help,** and their initial menu choices. The majority of the user interface elements, however, are defined by extensions. This includes our particular case, contributions to the editor toolbar.

When the Workbench constructs this toolbar, it first coordinates the addition of "required" toolbar buttons with the help of an "advisor." We'll return to the Workbench advisor in more detail in Chapter 10. For the moment, you only need to remember that it helps the Workbench set up the visual components that are not added by contribution (e.g., the Workbench IDE's Save button). The Workbench then checks to see if other plug-ins want to contribute to the toolbar. It looks in a registry of extensions (or **contributions** as they are often called) under its named extension point. For now, we'll call it the "Editor toolbar" extension point. All extension points define the information they need from contributors in order to handle their contribution. In the case of the Editor toolbar extension point, the Workbench requires the image to be displayed in the button, tooltip text, and most importantly, the name of the Java class that will handle the user's request. Given this information, the Workbench creates the button.

This is where the notion of extension points gets interesting. Once the user selects the button, what must the Workbench do? When you contribute an extension to this extension point, you provide the name of a class in your plug-in that the Workbench will instantiate to handle the user's request. Of course, there has to be some agreement on how the Workbench will communicate with this "executable extension." Therefore, the extension point includes, as part of its definition, an expected interface that the contributor must implement. In this particular case, the Workbench defines the expected interface, a subtype of IAction, and the contributing plug-in shown in Figure 8.2, com.ibm.jdg2e.jdt, provides a class named AddTraceStatements-Action that implements the required interface.

Those are the basics of how extensions use extension points to contribute to the Workbench user interface and how they work together. But remember, a plug-in's extensions are not limited to user interface contributions. In fact, with the exception of a core runtime, all of Eclipse is implemented by plug-ins using these mechanisms.

The details of a plug-in, including the extensions it uses and the extension points it defines, are specified in the **plug-in manifest** file. The manifest also includes the declarations of the code that provides the plug-in's functionality and the plug-in's dependencies on other plug-ins.

At this point you already have enough information to create your first plug-in from scratch, the venerable "Hello, World," as was shown in Figure 7.6 in the previous chapter. If you are interested in trying this, turn to the exercise in Exercise 6, Developing Your First Plug-in. This exercise offers two approaches: The "five minutes and you're done" approach using the plug-in code generator, and the step-by-step approach that explains the process as you go along.

The choice to begin the exercise now or after reading this chapter and the next chapter is your personal preference. If you prefer to know a bit more about Eclipse and develop a deeper understanding of the programming elements that you'll create as part of extending Eclipse, read on. If you choose this approach, you may have a better appreciation of what is going on during the exercise. On the other hand, if you are anxious to see some real code, go ahead and do the exercise, then come back here when you're finished.

## Eclipse the IDE Platform and Rich Client Application

Up to this point, we have mostly discussed Eclipse as you know it from Part I, specifically Eclipse's Workbench as an integrated Java development environment. This is a great demonstration of what you can accomplish with

Eclipse as a software developer, but the picture it may suggest is incomplete. As was mentioned earlier, Eclipse is a reusable and extensible framework for creating IDE-oriented tools. In addition, it is a framework for creating general applications conforming to the native look and feel for which Eclipse is well known.

Eclipse has a layered architecture, one that allows you to reuse parts of it for different purposes. Those wishing to extend the development environment, such as the Java Development Tools, will look to the model, views, and editors that are part of that component, as was discussed in the prior chapter. Implicit in this choice is the acceptance of an existing user interface design. However, as you will see, the behaviors of "Eclipse the IDE" and "Eclipse the application" are not intrinsically coupled, thanks to its layered architecture.

Thus your plans for extending Eclipse begins first with deciding not just where your extensions will appear in the user interface, but also at what layer in the architecture. That choice is driven by what you wish to accomplish with Eclipse. Do you want to leverage its component-based plug-in architecture for a non-UI service application? Or its portable graphics framework and higher-level user interaction framework? Or its Workbench with its perspectives, editors, and views for organizing your own application's tasks? Or maybe extend the Java development tools for "fun and profit"? This chapter will help guide your decision.

The development of the third major release of Eclipse presented itself as the ideal opportunity to reflect on what worked well in the first two releases and what needed additional attention, culminating in the refactoring of the base components, as was shown in Figure 7.2, into the Rich Client Platform, Workbench IDE, and of course the sum of all, the Eclipse SDK itself.

We'll return to this theme many times because it defines the overall structure of the book. In the next few sections we'll look at what other problems the architecture addresses and the components that fit within it. Often the examples presented will be IDE-centric because they are more familiar; however, keep in mind that the notion they introduce will very often also apply more generally to non-IDE Eclipse applications.

## The Eclipse Platform Runtime

All Eclipse functionality is supplied by plug-ins. The **Eclipse Platform Runtime,** which is responsible for managing them, handles the Eclipse startup, discovering the locally installed plug-ins, reading their manifests, and matching extensions and extension points. The resulting in-memory registry is available to all plug-ins.

Eclipse version 3.0 introduced a replacement of the homegrown Platform Runtime that handled plug-in management through the first two major releases. The new Platform Runtime is based on the OSGi component-based runtime. One of the features this allows is the ability to load plug-ins dynamically, while before it was necessary to restart Eclipse for the new plug-ins and extensions to be recognized. Plug-ins declare their interface in the OSGi and the Eclipse frameworks in a similar fashion. In the case of OSGi, their declarations are called **bundle manifests** (`manifest.mf`); in earlier versions these were called **plug-in manifests** (`plugin.xml`) The two manifest formats have a lot in common, but there are differences in syntax. To simplify migration to version 3.0 and support continuing development, the Eclipse Platform Runtime accepts either means of plug-in/bundle declaration, and version 2.x plug-ins are binary compatible. If the Platform Runtime finds a `plugin.xml` declaration and no `manifest.mf` declaration, it generates the latter using the `<plugin>`, `<runtime>`, and `<requires>` section of the plug-in manifest and stores the result in `<inst_dir>\configuration\org.eclipse.osgi\manifests`. When testing the Runtime Workbench in the Plug-in Development Environment, a separate area is used to store these generated files. In the majority of cases, this "under the covers" generation is entirely transparent to you as an Eclipse plug-in developer.

The term "plug-in" is heavily engrained in Eclipse; the number of references to it in the source code, Javadoc, and external publications is staggering. The Eclipse developers decided early on that it would not be a worthwhile use of their time and talents to correct every class, method, and scrap of documentation in an effort to expunge the term. This book will follow suit and only use the term **bundles** where it is necessary to clarify specific references to the capabilities provided by OSGi.

We'll return to how you can take advantage of this new runtime capability in Chapter 11 and Exercise 8. Until then, remember that nearly all of the example declaration extracts will use the traditional plug-in manifest syntax of the `plugin.xml` file.

The **Rich Client Platform**, depicted in Figure 7.2 above the Platform Runtime, is the common base of plug-ins that wish to present a graphical user interface. You'll recognize other plug-ins shown in this figure, like the Workbench and the JDT, by the editors, views, perspectives, and actions that they contribute to the Eclipse user interface. The functionality provided by these plug-ins was the focus of Part I, that is, Eclipse as an IDE from the user's point of view. The following sections of this chapter look at Eclipse from a plug-in developer's point of view, introducing the underlying frameworks of the platform that you'll need to learn about to extend Eclipse.

## User Interface Frameworks

A considerable amount of Eclipse is user interface code, centered in the three framework sets shown in Figure 8.3.

Starting from the bottom up, the frameworks are:

- Standard Widget Toolkit (SWT)—A generic, portable, low-level graphics and widget set built upon the native controls provided by the operating system.
- JFace—A model-based UI framework for common UI tasks.
- Workbench—The editors, views, and perspectives that make up the UI personality of Eclipse.

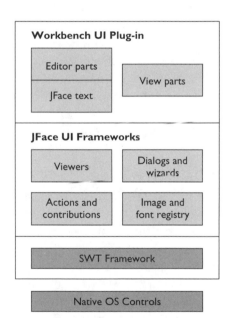

**Figure 8.3**   Eclipse User Interface Frameworks

### Standard Widget Toolkit

The SWT is a generic graphics and GUI widget set. It defines a set of widgets, such as buttons, lists, text, menus, and tree lists, which are based on native widgets when possible. If a particular widget is not available in the native window system, SWT provides an emulated equivalent.

PART II

SWT is contained in a plug-in, but this is principally to allow other plug-ins easy access to its functionality. In fact, SWT has no dependency on the Platform Runtime at all. Eclipse uses it to help create the Workbench user interface, but it works equally well as the user interface framework of any client application.

At this point you may be wondering why Eclipse doesn't use Swing and AWT. Early in the project, the Eclipse developers concluded that it was hard to produce professional-looking shrinkwrapped products with them. The team also had considerable experience in producing fast, portable widget sets. Eclipse's tight integration with the native windows system (e.g., support for OLE and ActiveX) and native look and feel are a result of this decision. You will learn more about SWT in Chapters 14 and 34.

## JFace User Interface Framework

The SWT designers want to keep their framework lean and close to the capabilities of the native windows system; this makes it easier to maintain and to port to a new environment. The JFace designers want to reduce the tedium of creating a user interface and enhance the capabilities of the widgets coming from SWT. The JFace UI fulfills these goals by providing the several frameworks described in the following sections.

### Why Use JFace Viewers Instead of Directly Using a Widget from SWT?

JFace was designed to complement SWT. To appreciate why you might choose to use one versus the other, consider this example that uses one of JFace's frameworks, the viewer framework.

Imagine that your application wants to display part of your model, for example, a list of "person" objects. If your user interface code were written directly to SWT, it would obviously have to conform to its APIs, which expect primitive types like String, int, and boolean. This choice is intentional, since SWT is designed to be a thin, portable layer on top of the window system's native widgets. However, this requires that your code must first convert your list of person objects into an array of strings, and then give that array to SWT's list widget for display.

If you were to write your user interface code directly to JFace, the approach is different. Rather than a widget that expects primitive types like strings, you work with what is called a **viewer**. A viewer is a model-based analogue of an SWT widget. Back to the example: You would provide the list viewer with your list of person objects. Of course, it has no idea what the structure of this list is or what its interface might be; for all it knows, the "list" could in fact be a database table. The viewer collaborates with a set of "helper" classes that you provide to be able to display the data contained in a model. This model-based approach to creating a user interface results in code that requires less time to write, is easier to understand, is more reusable, and has more centralized model-view interactions.

Many widgets have a corresponding viewer, but not all do. For example, text fields, lists, and tables have a corresponding viewer in JFace. Buttons, being quite straightforward, do not. In those cases, you'll go directly to the SWT API. You'll learn about what these two frameworks can do in Chapter 14, The Standard Widget Toolkit: A Lean, Mean, Widget Machine and Chapter 15, JFace Viewers.

### The Role JFace Actions and Contributions Play in Extending the Eclipse UI

Again, JFace's goal is to reduce redundant code and enhance the capabilities of the widgets that SWT provides. The Actions framework reduces redundancy by recognizing that many actions of a user interface are semantically the same, although their appearance is different. For example, a menu choice on a pull-down menu, a menu choice on a pop-up menu, a push button, and a toolbar button are semantically equivalent from the programmer's perspective. Why represent them as four different classes?

SWT doesn't have the luxury of treating these all the same, because there are real differences in the implementation of the native window system. JFace, in contrast, can create an abstraction of them called an **action**. Then the programmer can focus on providing an action and let the rest of the framework worry about rendering it appropriately in the context in which it ultimately appears. If you chose to do Exercise 6, you already have a taste of what this brings you. The "Hello, World" action that you defined appeared as a menu choice in a pull-down menu, but with a minor change to your extension of the Workbench user interface, it could appear as a toolbar button, while your code is unchanged.

Taking this a step further, JFace defines the notion of a "contribution-based" user interface. This brings us back to our first discussion of how to extend a user interface, specifically the contribution of new actions to an existing user interface. This chapter opened with an example that showed contributions to the Java editor toolbar. This relied on the JFace contribution framework. We'll cover in detail how you can make your own action contributions in Chapter 21.

### The Role JFace Wizards and Dialogs Play in Defining Eclipse's User Interaction

Until this point, we have focused on relatively small elements of the user interface, such as buttons, menu choices, lists, and tables. However, to assure a reasonable level of look and feel consistency, Eclipse must deliver frameworks that prescribe higher levels of user interaction. You have seen and experienced this already: The Preferences dialog displayed from the **Window > Preferences** menu choice and resource creation wizards available from the **File > New** menu choice were built with these frameworks.

You could think of these frameworks and those that will follow as a transition from a user *interface* framework to a user *interaction* framework. The interest lies not just in helping the programmer be more productive, but also in assuring a more consistent interaction with the user.

Figure 8.4 is the wizard dialog that leads the programmer through the steps of creating a new plug-in project.

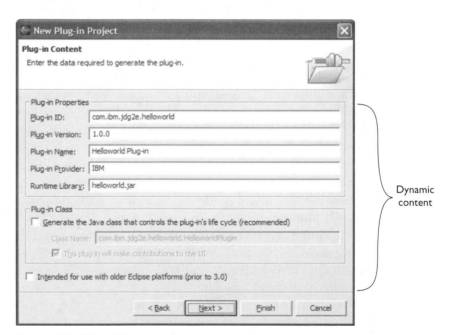

**Figure 8.4**   Wizard Framework

The Wizard framework handles page-to-page navigation, creation and update of common dialog elements like the information/error message area, dialog title and wizard title, wizard icon, and so on.

You, the plug-in developer, create the dynamic content in the center of this dialog. You spend your time adding your tool logic while the framework's page and wizard classes handle common behavior. Generally, you will subclass them and override only those methods that interest you. For example, you might override the wizard's `performFinish` method, which is called when the **Finish** button is selected. Other methods that you override or invoke help the framework synchronize the wizard state with the user interface. For example, based on the pages you have added and the user's progression through them, the wizard automatically handles the enablement of the **Back** and **Next** button.

The Workbench Preferences dialog, available from the **Window > Preferences** menu choice, works in a similar fashion. The user navigates the available preference pages using the tree to the left of the Preferences dialog area, and again your plug-in can contribute preference pages, providing the dynamic content. The Preferences framework will handle instantiating and activating the requested page. In addition to helping manage portions of the user interface, both of these frameworks include classes that help manage persistent values. The Preference **Import...** and **Export...** buttons rely on plug-ins using this framework to allow users to share preferences. When your tool adds preferences with this framework, this will work for your tools, too. You'll learn about managing preferences and creating dialogs and wizards in Chapter 16, Dialogs and Wizards; the generalized support for storing user- and tool-defined values is discussed in Chapter 17, Dialog Settings, Preferences, and User Settings.

## Building a Custom Text Editor with JFace Text

The JFace Text framework offers a high-function editor with extensible capabilities and assistance aids for creating, displaying, and editing text documents. This text infrastructure builds on the SWT-styled text widget and provides a document model of text rather than a simple string. The framework dictates the overall structure, key responsibilities, and relationships of the JFace Text classes. Your development effort to build a specific editor is principally an exercise in customization, allowing you to apply domain-specific syntax coloring, reformatting, and completion aids. Your users benefit from an integrated text editor having common core behaviors, thereby saving them from having to relearn the differences among disparate text editing environments. Chapter 26 will walk you though all the steps of building your own custom text editor with JFace Text.

## Image and Font Registries

This framework helps reduce the work of managing the creation and disposal of images and fonts. SWT is close to the native window system, and it lives by the rules that the window system imposes. One of those rules is, "If you create it, you dispose of it." This framework facilitates the sharing of common fonts and images by providing a global registry and simplifying the life cycle management of these resources.

## Workbench Frameworks

You may have noted that the previous section mentioned little that is visually or behaviorally unique to Eclipse. That's because those frameworks are principally concerned with the construction of a user interface from widgets like buttons and listboxes, and to some extent, defining the building blocks of larger user interaction behaviors through predefined dialog and wizard templates. This section introduces the next layer in the Eclipse user interface, that of the Workbench.

### Storing Persistent Values

The Workbench includes several options that enable plug-ins to define and store values in a consistent and coordinated fashion. This includes APIs for dialog settings, preferences, and user settings. These APIs are general purpose, but are commonly used for specific tasks.

User interface-oriented plug-ins inherit support for dialog settings and stored preference values; nonuser interface plug-ins inherit an alternative but compatible preferences API. Plug-ins use preferences to save the user's personalization of the Eclipse environment. Dialog settings are often used to record previously entered values, such as an export wizard's drop-down list of target directories. Users generally enter their choices on preference pages, but that's not the only way Eclipse extensions store user options as keyed preferences. For example, the last setting of the **Go Into Top Level Type** option of the Java editor's Outline view is implicitly recorded as a preference.

Any plug-in can record stored values using the general-purpose user settings API. These settings can be associated with a different scope, such as the entire Eclipse configuration, a specific workspace, or a project. The options for storing persistent values are discussed in Chapter 17, Dialog Settings, Preferences, and User Settings.

### Creating Applications with the Rich Client Platform

The Workbench is the "UI personality" of the Eclipse Platform. It defines the actions, editors, views, and perspectives that make up the environment that you know as Eclipse. The Workbench manages, among other things, the navigation, layout, and activation of windows, views, editors, and perspectives. From a user's viewpoint, the Workbench user interface and Eclipse are the same thing, so this book will generally refer to them synonymously as simply "Eclipse."

Views and editors in the Eclipse user interface correspond to the two types of Workbench part classes: view parts and editor parts. They define the basic appearance and behavior of these user interface components. For example, views distinguish themselves in several ways.

- They have their own local menu and toolbar.
- They can be stacked or placed just about anywhere in the Workbench client area, except the editor area. They can be "torn off" to create a separate window.
- They generally work in concert with an editor or show information related to the current selection.
- The Workbench only allows one view of a given type to be displayed in the same perspective.

Editors have different characteristics.

- They have no local menu or toolbar; all editors share a common window menu and toolbar area.
- They can be stacked and tiled, but only in the editor area.
- Each editor manipulates a unique input, typically a file.
- More than one editor of a given type can be displayed in the same perspective.

Practically all the editors that you have seen up to this point have been text editors, but there are other kinds in Eclipse. For example, you will see that a specialized perspective, called the Plug-in Development Environment (PDE), has several multipage editors where one page is a "raw" text editor's view of the file and the other pages are form-like pages.

In the final analysis, the overriding characteristic of the Eclipse user interface is its ability to support a user in a wide variety of tasks. The Eclipse user interface guidelines document defines many other characteristics of the Workbench user interface. If you want to create a user interface that looks and behaves similarly to other Eclipse-based products, you should read these guidelines. They are available on the eclipse.org Web site in the Articles section. However, Eclipse is not just a pretty face. It also provides base frameworks that solve sticky application problems, as is evidenced by the Concurrency framework described in the next section.

## Remaining Responsive to the User Using the Concurrency Framework

Responsiveness should be one of the key goals of any user interface. And while the Eclipse platform has always been viewed as a well-designed user interface, it got significantly better with Eclipse 3.0. Prior to this version, all you could do was watch a progress dialog during long-running operations such as builds and CVS checkouts. Now it's different; very few tasks actually make you wait for their completion.

These improvements are made possible by the addition of support for background processing, called **jobs**, to the Eclipse platform. A job is a unit of work that can be defined and then passed to the platform for execution.

Using jobs, your tool can run multiple background operations concurrently, or schedule work that is queued to run on the thread that manages the user interface. In short, jobs can completely change the way your tool performs work and interacts with the user. You should consider incorporating the use of jobs in your tool to help provide a very responsive user interface. This is discussed in Chapter 29, Implementing Responsiveness and Concurrency Using Jobs.

## Managing the User Interface Through Capabilities

Creating functionally rich applications can be tricky. If an application has too much functionality, new users may be lost in a sea of choices. If an application doesn't have enough choices, power users will look elsewhere for products that are more capable. How do you balance the conflicting needs of these two very important groups?

Eclipse addresses this issue through a facility called **capabilities**, which serves as a filter on what is exposed in the user interface (you can enable and disable them in the Workbench preferences). For example, Team and CVS support are capabilities. If these capabilities are enabled, then the Team component with its perspectives, wizards, views, and actions are visible to the user; otherwise, they are not. Capabilities can be used to filter what functionality is visible. Based on usage, additional capabilities exposing more functions can be enabled automatically. This is discussed in Chapter 30, Using Capabilities to Manage Too Much of a Good Thing.

## Extending the Workbench Integrated Development Environment

After reading how you can have fun extending Eclipse in the prior chapter, you have a good idea of the basic steps of enhancing the IDE. It begins when you recognize how you can enhance Eclipse, visualizing where those improvements might show up in the user interface, and then learning about the underlying models supporting what you see on the display, as was the case in our extension of the JDT. Part III will show you how you can extend them and often presents step-by-step examples. For now, we'll briefly introduce you to these IDE-specific frameworks; turn to the associated chapter when you want to learn more.

## Resources and Workspace API

As you learned in Part I, Eclipse operates on files in the user's workspace, organized in one or more top-level projects. These projects map to directories in the file system. The plug-in developer collectively refers to these three entities (files, folders, and projects) as **resources**.

Resources are more than a thin wrapper of the file system; they add key behaviors that are necessary to support a multifaceted user interface. This starts with the ability to monitor changes in resources. Views like the Navigator listen to these notifications to present an accurate representation of the workspace contents in real time. However, these resource notifications can help to do more than synchronize different elements of the user interface. They can also be used to coordinate other activities, such as the transformation of changed resources from one form to another. Assuming that you have the **Build automatically** option in the Workbench Preferences dialog checked, you have already seen this in action; each time you saved your Java source code, the Workbench automatically invoked the Java compiler to create your .class files. These specialized resource listeners are called **builders** and are available to any tool that has a "build" requirement.

The Resources and Workspace API provides other capabilities that you've seen as part of the user interface. For example, the local history of changed or deleted files is made possible by the Workspace API. These APIs include methods for basic file system manipulation, such as reading, writing, creation, and deletion. These same methods also capture the file data in its current state before a modification is written to disk. It manages these copies in a separate area of the workspace, so the user can recover them with menu options like **Replace with > Local History**.

The bookmarks, error markers, and task items are also defined in the Resources plug-in. You'll look in detail at all of these and much more in Chapters 23, 24, and 25.

## Additional Eclipse IDE APIs

You no doubt have noticed this is a large book. We carefully chose each topic that we felt would be interesting to our readers. This of course means that there are areas of extending Eclipse that we'll only mention in passing, deferring to the well-written online documentation that accompanies the product as well as articles available at eclipse.org. These areas include the extension capabilities associated with Team, Search and Compare, Program and Debug Launch, JUnit, and Ant support, all of which are specialized topics that are well treated in the online documentation.

## Chapter Summary

It is no longer practical for vendors to produce the base application and IDE infrastructure upon which to deliver their product-specific functionality. Not only is it a wasteful use of programmer time, but it also has led to islands of tools and applications that are disjointed and inconsistent. This chapter introduced the Eclipse architecture and the underlying frameworks that make the developer more productive and the resulting product more consistent. Adding new capability to Eclipse, without sacrificing the user's impression of a single environment, involves learning how to program with these frameworks.

One of the major themes of Eclipse 3.0 is the refactoring of its frameworks and plug-ins. Part III will focus on how you can create an Eclipse-based application. Keep in mind when reading these chapters that everything you learn would apply equally to your efforts, if you choose, to extend the Eclipse IDE. The next chapter will help guide you on which architecture layer will serve your needs best and what steps are next.

## References

Arthorne, John, and Chris Laffra. 2004. *Official Eclipse 3.0 FAQs*. Boston, MA: Addison-Wesley. http://www.eclipsefaq.org. (See FAQs 13, 73, 115, 134, 149, 244.)

Eclipse project slide presentation. http://www.eclipse.org.

Edgar, Nick, Kevin Haaland, Jin Li, and Kimberley Peter. February 2004. Eclipse user interface guidelines. http://www.eclipse.org.

# ⟨ 9

## d: Plug-in Development

uced the notion of plug-ins, extension points, and
hree define the "bricks and mortar" that make up
an to you as a programmer in practical terms? In
you have to create and what code do you have to
tuff recognized and integrated into Eclipse?

It all starts ............. -in manifest file. In this file you declare where
you'll accept contributions from others and where you'll contribute to others,
whether that is the Eclipse Platform itself or other Eclipse-based tools with
which you want to integrate. Before getting to the details of specifying a manifest, let's consider what the platform does with them to get Eclipse going.

When Eclipse starts up, one of the first things the Platform Runtime does
is discover what plug-ins are available. It looks in the subdirectories of the
<inst_dir>\eclipse\plugins directory for files named plugin.xml, the plug-
in manifest we've been talking about. It parses each file, looking for dependencies, what code makes up the plug-in, and, of course, the extensions that
the plug-in makes and the extension points that it defines. You can see this
stored information in the **Plug-in Registry** view, keyed by the plug-in identifier, which we'll discuss later in this chapter in the section PDE Views and
Editors. After the plug-in manifests are processed, the Platform Runtime
turns the rest of the responsibility for bootstrapping the environment over to
a specific plug-in, called an **application plug-in**. The Eclipse Platform IDE
application plug-in opens the main window, builds the initial toolbars and
menus, and otherwise prepares the platform for business.

PART II

---

**NOTE**  The Eclipse SDK default application is `org.eclipse.ui.ide.workbench`. This is defined as part of the `org.eclipse.ui.ide` plug-in. Applications are defined using the `org.eclipse.runtime.applications` extension point. This is discussed further in Chapter 10, Creating Applications Using the Rich Client Platform.

---

In general, you'll simply define your plug-in manifest, write some code, and hope to arrive home early for dinner. The purpose of this chapter is to learn more about plug-ins in general, understand their common steps of development, and then branch out to more specific topics in subsequent chapters. Since Eclipse plug-in development starts with design-integration considerations, we'll start there, then drill down to the implementation details. Finally, we'll finish with a quick tour of the Plug-in Development Environment (PDE).

## Getting Started with Plug-ins

Building a tool with Eclipse is different. You don't start with a blank screen and start writing code. Instead, you start with a robust platform and look at where you want to extend and integrate additional function. Given this distinction, the following points are worth considering in your development process.

1.  Describe your user scenarios.

    The first step is to walk through user scenarios of your integrated function to determine the best flow from the user's point of view. Consider the full spectrum of Eclipse's base capabilities with which users would expect your product to interact, such as its views, editors, and perspectives; for example, if you are extending the IDE, include scenarios that exploit Eclipse's team programming environment. As you'll learn in the next chapter, there are additional considerations, like should you have a menu bar or toolbar and what options they will contain. You should also think about what standard menu options and dialogs you might reuse from the Eclipse base. Again, these considerations are the focus when you're writing your own Eclipse application as opposed to extending the Eclipse IDE application.

2.  Look for Eclipse integration points.

    All extensions are added to Eclipse via a plug-in. In most cases, you use an extension point provided by the Eclipse Platform. Once you know what user scenario you are implementing, you will be able to derive the set of applicable extension points to use. This chapter serves as a guide in finding those extension points.

3. Separate your UI from your model.

   In most cases, your plug-in will have visual and nonvisual aspects that you might choose to separate into different plug-ins. Eclipse itself follows this design pattern. You will note that the user interface plug-ins include `ui` in their plug-in ids, for example, the Workbench plug-in, `org.eclipse.ui`, and the Java Development Tools UI plug-in, `org.eclipse.jdt.ui`. The plug-ins containing the model often include `core` in their identifier, such as `org.eclipse.core.runtime`. There is certainly no requirement that you have to separate plug-ins for your model and user interface components, but you will find that it may result in a cleaner implementation and potentially decrease the platform startup time since fewer plug-ins may need to be initially loaded, and those that are loaded will be smaller. It also leaves open the possibilities that the non-UI portion of your tool could be used outside the Workbench (e.g., as part of an Apache Ant build script or as part of a UI-less Eclipse application). So start by considering what your plug-in might look like and how it might integrate with the existing Eclipse user interface. This is largely a question of whether you're simply augmenting existing elements of the user interface or defining your own. You should also consider whether you are using a model supplied by Eclipse, such as the model underlying the workspace and its Resource API described in Chapter 23, or if you are creating your own model. If you are providing additional Java development functionality, then you may want to tap into the powerful Java model provided by the JDT. In either case, our recommendation is to separate the user interface from the model.

4. Separate distinct functional groups of your tool into separate plug-ins.

   Since Eclipse is an integration platform that brings together many different tools into a single environment, it is especially important that distinct parts of your tools can be loaded separately to reduce their contribution to Eclipse's performance and memory burden. Chapter 32 offers other ways that you can improve the performance of your Eclipse-based product.

## Integration Scenarios

The following scenarios are just a few examples of how you can extend Eclipse. It is not intended to be an exhaustive list.

## Delivering User Documentation

A very simple integration scenario is to integrate your own documentation with the Eclipse documentation. This scenario is useful to integrate privately produced documentation, such as a FAQs document, team coding standards, or your own tool documentation. The documentation content can be in an HTML or a PDF file. All you need to do is write the XML to integrate the documentation in the Eclipse Help system. No Java code is required. To learn more about integrating help documentation, see Chapter 22, Providing Help.

## Adding Small Functional Enhancements

Another simple integration scenario involves introducing an incremental improvement that is self-contained. The JDT enhancements presented in Chapter 7 that enabled you to change the visibility of the selected members in the Outline or Package Explorer with a simple menu choice is such an example. You can contribute an action to the existing Workbench menu bar or toolbar, views, or editors that, when selected, will invoke your function. Chapter 21, Action Contributions: The Integration Fast Track, will discuss contributing actions of varying types and scope to the Workbench. This same approach works well if you're planning to use Eclipse as a basis for your desktop applications. That is, your development team can create an application foundation specific to your domain, and then the remaining functionality you need is added by small functional enhancements to that base, just as IDE tool developers build from the Eclipse IDE workbench.

## Supporting New Resource Types

In a more complex scenario when extending the Eclipse IDE, you might be interested in adding support for a new resource type. For instance, suppose you want to add support for your own proprietary programming language or integrate an application development tool that supports a specific type of file.

The first step would be to identify your resources. You should list the types of files you will support. For each resource, you will want to explore its life cycle: creating the resource, modifying it, and saving it on disk or in a repository. For example, your design should support an easy process to create the resource. You might also be interested in importing and exporting the contents. The wizard framework allows you to develop a creation wizard, accessible from the **File > New** menu choice, for the resource, as well as import and export wizards. Chapter 16 discusses the wizard framework.

The next step would be to investigate what should happen when the resource is selected and what actions would be appropriate for this type of resource. Contributed actions would appear on the context menu upon selection of the resource in the Navigator view. You may require a specialized editor for the resource. If the resource is text-oriented and lends itself to assisted text entry, Eclipse provides a configurable text editor with capabilities like content assist and color highlighting. In this case, you would need to build functional add-ons to configure the editor. Chapter 26 provides insight into building customized JFace Text editors. If not, a simple text editor might be sufficient. If the resource would best be edited by a specialized nontext editor (e.g., a graphical editor), turn to the basics of editors in Chapter 19. You should decide if your editor accepts bookmarks or other specialized markers (see Chapter 25).

To adequately present and navigate the resource, what complementary views are required? If the resource contains structured data, the Outline view might be useful content when your editor is active (see Chapter 19). You can use the Properties view to display properties for an object from your model when it is selected in a view (see the section Properties View Basics in Chapter 18).

Are the Eclipse-supplied views sufficient? If not, you may decide to create custom views. As you design the views that you will use, you should specify the communication and notification requirements that will be required. For instance, if the user changes the resource with an editor that affects the data shown in the view(s), you will need to write the code to notify them about the changes. For each custom view, you should build any actions that are view-specific, including sort and filter behavior if there is a large amount of data that could be displayed. View development is discussed in Chapter 18.

We strongly recommend that you run through some user scenarios to make sure your editor and views will work well together. Walking through the scenarios will drive the requirements for notification, event handlers, and the appropriate set of editor and view actions.

While modifying your resources, you might want to allow users to customize the behavior of your editor and view to their preferences. Integrating your own preference page into Eclipse is described in Chapter 16.

In some cases, files are not created by manually editing them, but are derived by running a program that builds the file when a dependent file is saved or when a build of a dependent file is explicitly requested. The common role of a builder in Eclipse is to take a resource of one type and build a new resource. For example, the Java builder builds class files from Java source files. Builders can also be used to monitor resource changes to analyze the change resource(s) and report problems, if any.

Your design may also need special resource handling, such as notifications when the resources are changed, which enables you to coordinate the

PART II

synchronization of multiple views of a resource. In addition, your users can benefit from the convenience of menu choices like **Replace with > Local History** when your plug-in uses the workspace API to persist your data. Resource notifications and the workspace API are covered in Chapter 23, and creating a builder is described in Chapter 24.

The last aspect to a resource life cycle is the persistence and management of the resource. Your design should consider how the resource should be saved. If the resource requires change management, your users can benefit from Eclipse's integrated repository support.

## Creating Rich Client Platform Applications

In this scenario you're not implementing an enhancement to the Eclipse IDE, but rather delivering a desktop application. There are few assumptions about what composes such an Eclipse-based application, so the initial user interface design considerations are very much like any other application development you've done in the past, with the added benefit that you leverage the reusable frameworks and inherent extensibility of Eclipse. All of what you'll learn in Part II applies to creating RCP applications. The following chapter and exercises address the issues specific to RCP.

- Chapter 10, Creating Applications Using the Rich Client Platform
- Exercise 7, Developing Your First Rich Client Application
- Exercise 8, Developing a Rich Client Application with Dynamically Added Plug-ins

Chapter 10 presents the concepts and the two exercises will further solidify the ideas and necessary mechanics behind creating RCP applications.

## Supporting Contributions from Others

In all these scenarios, you will first look to what reusable code Eclipse provides and how it addresses your application development needs. However, you should also consider how you could make your code extensible to others. This involves the creation of new extension points, which is described in Chapter 11. In addition, supporting others' contributions also means that your views, editors, and data model need to be open and extensible.

## *Distributing Your Plug-in*

Once you have integrated your tool with Eclipse, you need to distribute it to your users. At design time, you will want to decide whether you will require your users to have Eclipse already installed before installing your tool, or if you will package Eclipse along with your installation medium. You will also want to design the look you want to present to your users in terms of branding—that is, what type of splash screen, license, and initial perspective should appear when your tool starts? Packaging your plug-ins for distribution is described in Chapter 13, Defining Features and Products.

## Getting Started with Extensions and Extension Points

Extension points define where other plug-ins may contribute functionality to a plug-in. As just discussed, discovering the appropriate extension points to use is an important part of extending Eclipse. In a sense, the extensions and extension points of a plug-in manifest file detail the interconnections among plug-ins.

The similarity of these terms merits a few words of further explanation. They correspond to two plug-in manifest tags having similar names, `<extension-point>` and `<extension>`. The first *defines* a new extension point; the second *contributes to* an already-defined extension point. In plug-in developer parlance, when you use an extension point, you "extend" it. This chapter and those that follow will focus on contributing to already-defined extension points using the `<extension>` tag. Chapter 11, Creating Extension Points: How Others Can Extend Your Plug-ins, will focus on usage of the `<extension-point>` tag.

Each extension point has an identifier, specified using the Java package naming convention. Over the course of this book, you'll learn about the majority of the extension points defined by Eclipse. Table 9.1 summarizes what you can contribute and where you'll recognize it from the Eclipse user interface, the associated extension point, and the chapter that describes how to use it.

The last column lists the chapter(s) where the extension points in the middle column are first introduced. You may notice that this table doesn't have entries for every chapter. This is because Eclipse isn't exclusively about extensions points. There are other useful frameworks that you'll need to know about, too. For example, the Standard Widget Toolkit and JFace are user interface frameworks, not plug-ins, but you may decide to use them in your plug-in implementation. The advanced topics in later chapters will go beyond the general use of extensions, for instance, introducing how other Eclipse plug-ins, like the JDT, can be extended.

As a part of learning to contribute to a given extension, you'll need to know something about its supporting framework. For example, contributing a wizard to the **File > New** menu choice requires that you understand more than the parameters of its extension point. You will also need to learn about

**Table 9.1**   Contributing to the Eclipse Platform Extension Points

| Purpose | Extension Points | Covered in |
|---|---|---|
| Add additional textual or iconic decorations to object labels. | org.eclipse.ui.decorators | Chapter 15 |
| Define new views for the **Window > Show View** menu choice. | org.eclipse.ui.views | Chapters 15 and 18 |
| Contribute a New wizard to the standard **Export...** and **Import...** menu choices. | org.eclipse.ui.exportWizards<br>org.eclipse.ui.importWizards | Chapter 16 |
| Contribute a New wizard to the standard **File > New** menu choice. | org.eclipse.ui.newWizards | |
| Contribute a preference page to the **Window > Preferences** dialog. | org.eclipse.ui.preferencePages | |
| Contribute pages to an object's Properties dialog. | org.eclipse.ui.propertyPages | |
| Define new editors on resources; this is shown as a choice on its **Open With** menu cascade. | org.eclipse.ui.editors | Chapters 19 and 26 |
| Define new perspectives for the **Window > Open Perspective** menu choice. Add new perspective shortcuts, view shortcuts, and actions sets to an existing perspective. | org.eclipse.ui.perspectives<br>org.eclipse.ui.perspectiveExtensions | Chapter 20 |
| Contribute actions to the Workbench window menu bar or toolbar. | org.eclipse.ui.actionSets | Chapter 21 |
| Contribute actions to the Workbench window menu bar or toolbar if the specified view/editor is opened in the perspective. | org.eclipse.ui.actionSetPartAssociations | |
| Contribute actions to an editor's toolbar or menu choices. | org.eclipse.ui.editorActions | |
| Contribute actions to an editor, view, or object's context menu. | org.eclipse.ui.popupMenus | |
| Contribute to a view's toolbar or pull-down menu. | org.eclipse.ui.viewActions | |
| Define online help available from the **Help > Help Contents** choice. | org.eclipse.ui.help<br>org.eclispe.help.contentProducer | Chapter 22 |
| Define additional filters for the Navigator view's **Filter...** menu choice. | org.eclipse.ui.ide.resourceFilters | Chapter 23 |
| Define your own incremental build processing (**Project > Rebuild Project**) for existing resource types or your own resources. Enhance project capabilities. | org.eclipse.core.resources.builders<br>org.eclipse.core.resources.natures | Chapter 24 |

**Table 9.1**   Contributing to the Eclipse Platform Extension Points (*continued*)

| Purpose | Extension Points | Covered in |
|---|---|---|
| Tag a resource with some user information. Markers can be displayed in views or editors, such as the Tasks view, vertical ruler of text editors, and as label decorations in the Outline view. | `org.eclipse.core.resources.markers` | Chapter 25 |
| The built-in text editor, JFace Text, offers an extensible and reusable text editor to ensure the user a consistent editing experience. You can customize it to your editing needs for unique text annotations in rulers, additional information such as line numbers, syntax highlighting, and content assist, to name only a few of the possibilities. | `org.eclipse.core.filebuffers.`<br>   `documentSetup`<br>`org.eclipse.ui.editors.templates` | Chapter 26 |
| Help reduce the number of available options presented to the user based on their activities. Externally this is referred to as capabilities. | `org.eclipse.ui.activities` | Chapter 30 |

the framework behind it that creates the wizard dialog, its pages, how it handles page-to-page navigation, and so on. This will be covered in Chapter 16. Similarly, other chapters will present the extension points related to the area of Eclipse you wish to contribute to or enhance.

Now that you have a better appreciation of what you will find in a plug-in manifest, let's return to the basics of creating one. All extensions and extension points are specified in XML in a plug-in's manifest file. The content of the <extension> element is declared using the ANY rule. This means that any well-formed XML can be specified within the extension configuration section (between the <extension> and </extension> tags). Subsequently, you need to enter these tags and attributes carefully, since there is limited development-time checking for those that are entered manually. Don't worry, though; Eclipse defines a perspective that offers specialized editors and wizards to help you, called the **Plug-in Development Environment** (PDE). The PDE can lead you through the extension creation process in several ways. First, the New Extension wizard can use a template that presents one or more extension-specific wizard pages to request the necessary parameters, as shown in Figure 9.1.

PART II

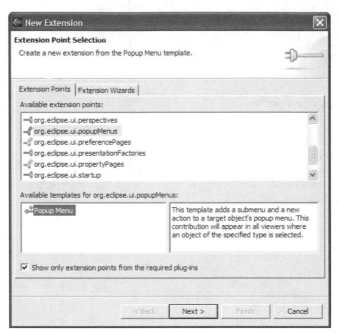

**Figure 9.1**    New Extension Templates and Extension Wizards

Alternatively, you can fill in the extension parameters using the Extension Details fields of the Manifest Editor's Extensions page. It ensures that you create a valid extension based on a schema definition of the expected child tags and attributes.

We will cover more about the PDE in this chapter. As you will discover, Eclipse provides considerable help to those who want to extend the Eclipse environment, including specialized editors, views, and wizards as already mentioned, plus support for runtime testing.

## Basic Steps of Implementing a Plug-in

The following are the common steps to developing any plug-in.

1. Decide how your plug-in will be integrated with the platform, and find the respective extension point(s); these are the extension points to which you will contribute.

   As you learned in the previous chapter, the Eclipse API is divided into two layers, one containing IDE components and another containing more general rich client application components. Roughly speaking, these components are further divided into user interface (e.g., Workbench) and non-UI (e.g., Workspace).

2. Determine the requirements of the extension points.

   Each extension point requires you to provide information specific to it. The online documentation and generated Javadoc is a great resource to help you understand the required information (as well as, of course, the chapters of this book and the examples on the CD-ROM).

3. Declare your plug-in manifest.

   The PDE's Plug-in Manifest Editor will help you correctly compose your plug-in's manifest file.

4. Implement the function for your extensions.

   Many extension points require that you write some code to complete their functionality. The extension point author will typically provide either an interface class that defines the expected methods that your class must implement, or an abstract superclass that you can extend.

5. Define your plug-in class (optional).

   A plug-in represents a bundling of some well-defined functionality that extends Eclipse. A **plug-in class,** however, is the singleton class associated with each plug-in. You can define your own plug-in class in order to be notified of key life cycle events or as a reference to resources required by other extensions within the plug-in. We see this pattern in Eclipse itself. For example:

   ```
   IWorkspace workspace = ResourcesPlugin.getWorkspace();
   IWorkbench workbench = PlatformUI.getWorkbench();
   ```

   These methods return the workspace or Workbench instance from their respective plug-ins.

6. Install your plug-in.

   The section Installing Your Plug-in later in this chapter provides a brief overview of the installation options. Chapter 13, Defining Features and Products, covers them in detail.

With all this talk of plug-ins, extensions, and extension points, you may be anxious to see just what a plug-in manifest file looks like. The following example is an extract of one of the plug-in manifests of the SDK's plug-in examples download, which brings together many of the tags that we have discussed.

```
<?xml version="1.0" encoding="UTF-8"?>
<?eclipse version="3.0"?>
```

```
<plugin
    id="org.eclipse.ui.examples.javaeditor"
    name="%pluginName"
    version="3.0.0"
    provider-name="%providerName"
    class=
      "org.eclipse.ui.examples.           (one line)
      javaeditor.JavaEditorExamplePlugin">

    <runtime>
       <library name="javaeditorexample.jar">
          <export name="*"/>
       </library>
    </runtime>

    <requires>
     <import plugin="org.eclipse.core.runtime"/>
     <import plugin="org.eclipse.ui"/>
     <import plugin="org.eclipse.core.filebuffers"/>
     <import plugin="org.eclipse.jface.text"/>
     <import plugin="org.eclipse.ui.workbench.texteditor"/>
     <import plugin="org.eclipse.ui.editors"/>
     <import plugin="org.eclipse.ui.views"/>
    </requires>

    <extension
        point="org.eclipse.ui.editors">
        <editor
          name="%javaEditorName"
          icon="icons/obj16/java.gif"
          extensions="%javaFileExtensions"
          contributorClass=
            "org.eclipse.ui.examples.            (one line)
            javaeditor.JavaActionContributor"
          class="org.eclipse.ui.examples.javaeditor.JavaEditor"
          id="org.eclipse.ui.JavaEditor">
        </editor>
    </extension>
</plugin>
```

There's not a lot to it, is there? This plug-in defines the sample Java editor that is part of Eclipse's SDK Examples Plug-in download. The editor itself is defined in the class org.eclipse.ui.examples.javaeditor.JavaEditor, and packaged in the JAR file javaeditorexample.jar.

At this point, the particular parameters of this example are not important, just the general structure. The examples in subsequent chapters will cover the various extension points, their child tags, and attributes in detail. Now let's look at the tags that are common to all plug-ins.

### Declaring Your Plug-in Manifest

A plug-in manifest is specified in XML and must have the name `plugin.xml`.
A plug-in is typically composed of several files. At a minimum, it must
include the `plugin.xml` manifest file. In addition, most plug-ins include executable code written in Java, and whatever other resources that the plug-in
requires to perform its function, such as image, properties, and HTML files.

A plug-in manifest file is divided into sections, beginning with the `<plugin>`
element.

```
<plugin
    id="com.ibm.jdg2e.helloworld"
    name="Hello, World"
    version="3.0.0"
    vendor="The Java Developer&apos;s Guide to Eclipse"
    class="com.ibm.jdg2e.helloworld.HelloWorldPlugin">
```

The attributes shown in **bold** are required. The `id` attribute, like most `id`
parameters in the manifest file, is specified using the Java package naming
convention to avoid namespace collisions. It defines a programmatic reference to the plug-in itself. The `name` attribute is the label shown in the Plug-in
Registry view and similar dialogs. The optional `class` attribute specifies the
class that will be notified of life cycle events like startup and shutdown once
your plug-in is activated.

The `<requires>` section defines your dependent plug-ins. The Platform
Runtime uses this information to determine what JAR files your plug-in
needs access to.

```
<requires>
  <import
    plugin='org.eclipse.ui'
    version='3.0.0'
    match='compatible'
    optional='false'
    export='false'/>
</requires>
```

The `version` and `match` attributes specify the desired plug-in version and
matching algorithm to employ. While these attributes are not required, they
nonetheless merit special attention. The `version` attribute is generally specified as three numbers ("`3.0.0`" in the example above) in the format
`major.minor.service` where:

`major` defines the level of compatibility among releases. A larger value of
`major` implies there are elements of the release that are incompatible
with the prior release.

minor signifies the variation of the major release that is acceptable if
   match='compatible'.

service is the update of a specific major.minor release that is accepted if
   match='equivalent'.

While infrequently used, a fourth number can also be specified in the format major.minor.service.qualifier where:

qualifier indicates the source code control version of the same component. For the purposes of version matching, the qualifier is ignored in
   all cases except where match='perfect'.

The attribute match='greaterOrEqual' is specified when a more recent
plug-in version is acceptable. In some cases, the version attribute is omitted,
since plug-in versions are generally upward-compatible. The version and
match attributes allow for the specification and enforcement of dependencies
between plug-ins.

To illustrate this point, consider the case where version='1.0.0' is specified and the match attribute of the <import> tag has the values shown in
Table 9.2.

**Table 9.2**    Results of Different Values of the <import> Tag's match Attribute

| **Installed Versions** | 'greaterOrEqual' | 'compatible' | 'equivalent' | 'perfect' |
|---|---|---|---|---|
| 1.0.0 | Accepted | Accepted | Accepted | Accepted |
| 1.0.1 | Accepted | Accepted | Accepted | Rejected |
| 1.1.0 | Accepted | Accepted | Rejected | Rejected |
| 1.2.2 | Accepted | Accepted | Rejected | Rejected |
| 2.0.0 | Accepted | Rejected | Rejected | Rejected |

As you move to the right of the table, the rules are more restrictive, and
thus the risk of your plug-in not loading increase. By adhering to those APIs
defined in early versions of your dependent plug-ins, you may increase the
likelihood that the version (or a compatible version) is available.

Multiple versions of a plug-in can be installed at the same time. This is
supported and expected. However, this brings up the next possibility: What if
several plug-ins depend on different versions of the same plug-in? Only one
version of a plug-in can be loaded, so the Eclipse runtime will choose the
most recent compatible version available and match against that.

**NOTE** The version matching rules in Table 9.2 are about compatibility, not enhanced functionality. Your marketing experts may insist the follow-on release to your version 1.0 product should be 2.0. However, from a programmatic perspective, it may be 1.1.0, if it is 100% API compatible with version 1.0.x. Version numbers for branding your functionality as "new and improved" are defined in features, a topic we'll return to in Chapter 13.

The `optional` attribute specifies whether the import dependency will be strictly enforced. The default is `false`, that is, plug-ins listed in the `<import>` clause(s) must be available for your plug-in to load. Setting this attribute to `true` allows for a required plug-in to be absent and yet not prevent your plug-in from loading. You can use this attribute in combination with your menu action contributions to allow for choices that appear only if a plug-in is available. As an example, JDT uses this approach to contribute debugger-related menu choices to the user interface only when the debug environment is available. These examples will be more fully explored as part of Chapter 21, Action Contributions: The Integration Fast Track.

The `<runtime>` clause specifies one or more libraries (JAR files) that define the plug-in runtime code.

```
<runtime>
  <library name="runtime.jar">
    <export name="*"/>
  </library>
</runtime>
```

You're familiar with how the Java visibility modifiers (`public`, `private`, `protected`, and so on) affect access to your classes. The `export` clause further refines what packages or classes are visible to others outside of the plug-in itself. This lets you define classes that are public to your plug-in but not visible to other plug-ins. The `name="*"` attribute indicates that all public classes defined in the plug-in class libraries are visible. You can refine this by specifying package names using the same format accepted by the Java `import` statement or fully qualified class names. A best practice is to minimize your exports. Otherwise, you risk a tighter coupling between plug-ins and reduced flexibility, especially of required plug-ins. In general, you should only need to export required plug-ins or libraries that contribute to the public interface of a plug-in. However, keep in mind that the `export` clause is enforced at runtime but not by the Plug-in Development Environment. That means that your code can compile correctly despite having a reference to a class in another plug-in that isn't visible because there's no corresponding `export` clause, resulting in a ClassNotFoundException at runtime. You will have to weigh the advantage of avoiding inadvertent references to public but non-API classes versus the risk that an errant reference will go undetected until runtime. Eclipse itself follows the convention that everything is exported, allowing you to reference its internal classes, under the assumption that you accept the risks. Eclipse's implementation classes are in packages that include internal in their name. It is prudent to search your code for references to import statements that include "internal" to verify you have not inadvertently referred to one of Eclipse's implementation classes.

The <library> tag accepts subdirectory paths relative to the plug-in installation directory. You might use this, for example, if you want to specify the locations of those resources for which the class loader will search (e.g., *.properties files).

```
<runtime>
  <library name="translations/"/>
</runtime>
```

This tells the class loader to add the translations subdirectory of the plug-in's installation directory to its search.

### Defining Your Plug-in Class

Optionally, a plug-in can define a class, called the **plug-in class**, by specifying the class attribute on the <plugin> tag. Your plug-in class will extend either Plugin or its subclass, AbstractUIPlugin. Your plug-in class is notified of Workbench life cycle events via the start and stop methods. The Plugin class defines useful methods, such as the following.

getStateLocation returns a file directory where a plug-in can write persistent data (the plugins directory and its subdirectories are considered read-only).

openStream returns an input stream for a file that is relative to the plug-in install directory.

getPluginPreferences returns a plug-in specific preference store (a keyed persistent table of basic values like string, integer, Boolean, and float). See Chapter 17, Dialog Settings, Preferences, and User Settings, for more information on using the preferences support.

The AbstractUIPlugin class adds a few other methods that are helpful to user interface plug-ins.

getImageRegistry returns a registry of shared images.

getDialogSettings returns a table of persistence dialog settings for the various wizards and dialogs. Dialog settings are generally used to help save the user reentering information, for example, showing the last ten search entries in a combo box.

getWorkbench is a convenient method that returns the current IWorkbench instance. The Workbench is the root object of the Eclipse user interface. From it, you can query all active windows showing the Workbench content, register for window events, and so on.

Your code should treat the plug-in's subdirectory as read-only at runtime in order to ensure that a plug-in will work in a given platform configuration (e.g., on the Linux platform where Eclipse and its plug-ins may be installed on a common read-only server directory and the read-write workspace is created in each user's home directory).

If a plug-in needs to write state data, it should use the platform API to get its working path. Plug-ins use a working directory under the workspace's .metadata\.plugins subdirectory to read and write their plug-in-specific files. The Plugin.getStateLocation method returns the plug-in's .metadata subdirectory. For example, a plug-in having the id com.ibm.jdg2e.example and the plug-in class ExamplePlugin implementing the singleton method getDefault might code a method to return a read-write instance of java.io.File.

```
private File getStateFile() {
  IPath path = ExamplePlugin.getDefault().getStateLocation();
  path = path.append("state.dat");
  return path.toFile();
}
```

In this example, calling this method would return a File instance located in <inst_dir>\eclipse\workspace\.metadata\.plugins\com.ibm.jdg2e .example\state.dat.

Similarly, there are methods in the Plugin class to get the plug-in's install location. For example, ExamplePlugin.getDefault().getBundle().get-Entry("/"). Platform.getBundle("*pluginId*").getEntry("/") retrieves the location of any installed plug-in. Opening an input stream for a file located off the plug-in installation directory is as easy as calling ExamplePlugin .getDefault().openStream(new Path("*config.ini*")). You might use this method for retrieving configuration files that were installed in your plug-in's directory.

All classes in the JAR files specified in the <library> tag of a plug-in's manifest file have visibility to the plug-in class. Therefore, the plug-in class represents an ideal location for methods that would be generally useful to those classes that make up the plug-in as a whole. Other plug-ins that import your plug-in can have access to such methods, too. The ResourcesPlugin .getWorkspace() method is a good example of a useful method that is available to any plug-in that imports the Resources plug-in.

When a plug-in is first activated, the plug-in class loader verifies that the associated plug-in class, if defined, has been loaded and initialized. As a convenience, the PDE plug-in code generator defines a static `getDefault` method that returns the singleton instance of the plug-in class.

## Installing Your Plug-in

Chapter 6, Managing Your Eclipse Environment, introduced you to the Update Manager. If you choose, you can have the Update Manager handle the installation of your plug-in. This requires that you define a feature to represent it. This is the preferred method for ultimately delivering your plug-in. However, for test and development purposes, many plug-in developers use the alternative presented in the next subsection.

### Installing Your Plug-in Without the Update Manager

To test and install your plug-in without the Update Manager, you will need to understand the basics of the Eclipse installation directory structure.

Eclipse has a reserved subdirectory off the root install directory, called `plugins`, that contains one subdirectory per plug-in. By convention, the subdirectories have the same name as the plug-in id. An additional convention for deployed plug-ins includes adding the version number as a suffix, for example, `org.eclipse.core.runtime_3.0.0`. Each subdirectory will contain a plug-in manifest file, `plugin.xml`. There is no enforcement of the subdirectory naming conventions—you are free to call your plug-in install directory anything you like, but we strongly advise you to follow the above conventions to avoid potential namespace collisions. All plug-in resources, including JAR, HTML, image, and properties files, must be stored in or be relative to the plug-in's installation directory. This ensures that each plug-in is location-independent and simplifies plug-in installation and updates.

For initial testing, you will use the PDE to manage and test your plug-ins. The PDE allows you to select the list of external plug-ins that you want to test using the PDE's **Target Platform** preferences page (**Window > Preferences > Plug-In Development > Target Platform**). Once you are ready to test, you will select either the **Run > Run As > Run-time Workbench** or **Debug > Debug As > Run-time Workbench** menu choice to launch a second instance of Eclipse using the plug-ins you specified. This is the approach that you will learn in Exercise 6, Developing Your First Plug-in, and follow for the rest of this book.

For testing your plug-in outside of the PDE, you may choose to install a second copy of Eclipse, separate from your development installation. This will represent your final deployment configuration more accurately than the PDE-managed testing. Once you are ready to test, you'll copy your plug-in manifest file, its packaged JAR file, and its required resources to a new subdirectory off the plugins directory using the PDE's **Export > Deployable Plug-ins and Fragments** option, then start your test installation of Eclipse.

### Delivering Your Plug-in as an Update Manager Feature

Features allow for the organization of plug-ins so they can be managed by Eclipse. You have already seen the Update Manager in Part I of this book. Plug-ins added directly to the plugins directory, as described in the prior section, are recognized by the Platform Runtime, but the Update Manager treats them as "unmanaged plug-ins" and ignores them.

A feature is defined with the same approach as a plug-in, that is, by defining a feature manifest file (feature.xml), which exists in a directory with the same name as the feature id. Feature directories exist in the Eclipse platform in a subdirectory named features.

Chapter 13 and Exercise 9 will cover creating features, describing the necessary steps so the Update Manager can find, install, and apply service updates to your feature.

## Using the Plug-in Development Environment

Eclipse is based on a plug-in architecture and was conceived with the expectation that developers would use Eclipse itself to build extensions to Eclipse. To help plug-in developers create and maintain the necessary programming artifacts, and help manage the somewhat recursive nature of using a development tool to develop the tool itself, Eclipse includes an environment designed specifically for this purpose, namely the PDE.

What follows is a brief overview of the PDE. Exercise 6, Developing Your First Plug-in, will walk you though the PDE and demonstrate how it helps you create, test, and debug your plug-ins.

### PDE Views and Editors

You've already become familiar with Eclipse's Java Development Tools in Part I. The PDE includes all the capabilities of the JDT plus several new PDE-specific views and editors. Figure 9.2 shows the PDE as it initially opens on a plug-in project.

You may have noticed that when creating a project, you must choose a project type, such as Simple, Java, or Plug-in. The New Project wizard creates the project directory and the required folders for the particular project type (e.g., bin and src in the case of a plug-in project). A project can define specific behaviors that are appropriate for the types of resources that it contains, such as the incremental compilation of Java source files. When you

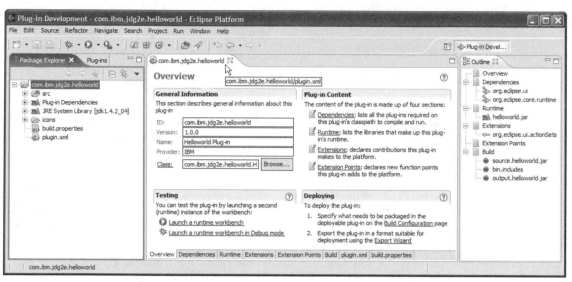

**Figure 9.2**    Plug-in Development Environment

create a plug-in project, the PDE perspective opens automatically, and it opens the plug-in's manifest file, plugin.xml, in its associated editor, the Plug-in Manifest Editor. Figure 9.2 shows its **Overview** page.

Each page in the Plug-in Manifest Editor shows the content of a section of the plugin.xml and build.properties files for the plug-in project in a clear and easy-to-understand format, as described in Table 9.3.

**Table 9.3**    Contents of Pages in the Plug-in Manifest Editor

| Page | Contents |
| --- | --- |
| **Overview** | A summary of the plug-in manifest and reminders of related errors or information messages under "Alerts and Action Items" |
| **Dependencies** | The <requires> clause |
| **Runtime** | The <runtime> clause |
| **Extensions** | The list of <extension> clauses |
| **Extension Points** | The list of <extension-points> clauses |
| **Build** | The list of plug-in runtime information, source, and binary build information represented in the plug-in's build.properties file |
| **plugin.xml** | Formatted plugin.xml content, ready for direct editing |
| **build.properties** | Formatted build.properties content, ready for direct editing |

You can use these pages to modify sections of the associated plugin.xml and build.properties file, or turn to the **plugin.xml** or **build.properties** pages respectively to update the source directly. The source content of these files is automatically updated, so switching pages within the PDE always shows the current content.

The PDE provides two runtime views, the Plug-in Registry and Error Log, which may help you in debugging your plug-in, as shown in Figure 9.3.

The Plug-in Registry view shows the content of plug-in manifest files, sorted by plug-in identifier, that were read during startup. When a plug-in is started, the Plug-in Registry view adds a triangular "play button" decoration (▶) to the plug-in entry. Chapter 28, Serviceability, shows how your plug-in can add to the error log and other techniques, like tracing, for enhancing the troubleshooting of your plug-in.

A third PDE view, Plug-ins, is part of the development environment, as shown in Figure 9.4.

This view provides menu options that help you import the code of external plug-ins into your current workspace so you can modify them. You'll learn how to use these menu options in Exercise 6. The final PDE view that we'll point out this chapter isn't part of the Plug-in Development perspective's layout, so you will have to open it explicitly using the **Window > Show View > Other...> PDE > Plug-in Dependencies** menu choice, and is shown in Figure 9.5.

This view is especially handy when you need a reminder of what plug-ins your plug-in uses belonging to the RCP or IDE layers of the Eclipse architecture, since it lists your plug-in's dependents and all their dependents, not just those listed in your plug-in's <import> clause(s).

### Managing the Runtime and Development Environments

Since Eclipse is used to build Eclipse plug-ins, it is easier to manage these two environments separately. We'll refer to the first as the **development** (or **host**)

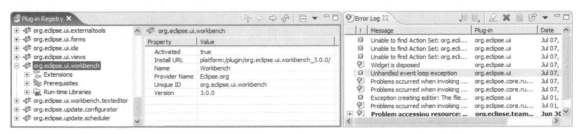

**Figure 9.3** PDE Plug-in Registry and Error Log Views

**Figure 9.4**    PDE Plug-ins View

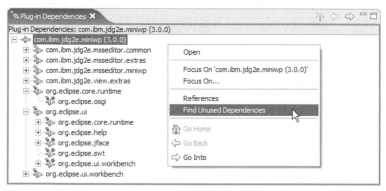

**Figure 9.5**    Plug-in Dependencies View

**environment,** that is, the instance that you initially launched. We'll refer to the second as the **runtime** (or **target**) **environment;** it's the instance that the development environment launches to test your plug-ins.

Eclipse must know which plug-ins belong to the development environment and which will belong to the runtime environment. The definition of plug-ins that belong to the development environment is easy: They are all the plug-ins that are located beneath the `plugins` directory. Defining those that are part of the runtime environment offers a few choices. By default, it includes all plug-ins in open projects in the workspace in addition to those specified in the PDE's **Target Platform** preferences page. You can use this list to selectively make "external" plug-ins (those not in your workspace) visible in the runtime instance, as shown in Figure 9.6. These plug-ins may be the same as your development environment, or if you choose, refer to another Eclipse installation using the **Location** entry field. Changing the location allows you, for example, to use one version of Eclipse for development purposes and another for runtime testing.

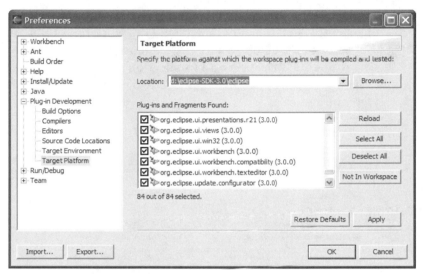

**Figure 9.6**   PDE Target Platform Preferences

In order to test, the plug-ins that your plug-in manifest specifies in its <requires> clause must be available to the runtime environment either through this page or by importing them into your workspace. Typically, you will import some of the Eclipse plug-ins into your workspace to more conveniently reference or modify the source. In this case, you can select **Not In Workspace** to specify that the runtime environment is composed of all plug-ins that are in the plugins directory beneath the directory specified in the **Location** entry field but are not already in your workspace. This choice may include more plug-ins in your test environment than your plug-in actually needs, such as those belonging to Eclipse's development environments, the JDT and PDE. Therefore, in general, you'll use a launch configuration (available from the **Run** pull-down menu in the PDE perspective) to specify what plug-ins should be included in the runtime environment. The remaining details of how to configure the PDE environment before importing the examples are covered in the exercises.

## Creating and Running a Plug-in

Creating your first plug-in is quite easy, especially since the PDE provides plug-in code generation wizards as part of creating a plug-in project, as we discussed in Chapter 7. In Exercise 6, you will have the choice of creating the "Hello, World" plug-in using the code generation wizard, or doing it manually step-by-step to better understand the workings of plug-ins and the PDE. The steps this will follow are very similar to that proposed by the **Help > Cheat Sheets > Hello, World Application** selection, as shown in Figure 9.7, except we'll provide more detail and review what you've learned as you complete the exercise.

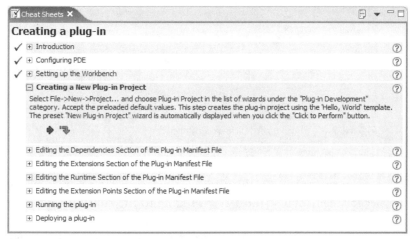

**Figure 9.7**   Hello, World Plug-in Cheat Sheet

Once you have a plug-in written, the next step is to run and, if necessary, debug it. When you select **Run** in the PDE, a runtime instance of Eclipse is launched. This instance of Eclipse will include the plug-ins in your workspace and those you specified on the **Target Environment** page of the Plug-in Development Preferences dialog. To simply execute your plug-ins, select **Run > Run As > Run-time Workbench**, or to invoke the debugger select **Run > Debug As > Run-time Workbench**. Alternatively, for more complex

PART II

launches, you can create custom launch configurations by selecting **Run > Run...** or **Run > Debug...** to open the Launch Configurations dialog, as shown in Figure 9.8.

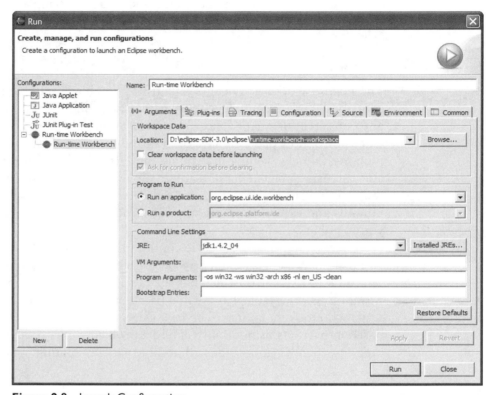

**Figure 9.8** Launch Configuration

A good strategy here is to define launch configurations that meet specific testing needs. By default, the test workspace of a newly created launch configuration is called runtime-workspace. However, you may want to specify a separate workspace for each launch configuration (look in the **Location** field in Figure 9.8) to help keep your test scenarios' data separate.

A launch configuration enables you to manage the startup environment of your runtime instance on a per-case basis rather than platform-wide. The exercises will show you more about launch configurations and Chapter 28, Serviceability, will specifically cover enabling your own plug-ins options on the **Tracing** page.

## Exercise Summary

If you haven't already done Exercise 6, Developing Your First Plug-in, you should definitely do so now. It will lead you through the creation of a simple "Hello, World" plug-in, pointing out the features of the PDE as you go along. This exercise doesn't have an associated code template, so you're ready to go.

## Chapter Summary

The Eclipse Workbench defines a platform capable of integrating functions contributed by different developers while preserving a seamless user interface and consistent user experience. This integration occurs via plug-ins and their extensions. Now that you have been introduced to the starting point of all plug-ins, namely the plug-in manifest, and its principal elements, extensions, and extension points, you're ready to move onto using those that make up the Eclipse Platform. The remaining chapters of this book will focus on these plug-ins and extension points, and their underlying frameworks to enable you to enhance Eclipse.

One recommendation before continuing to the next chapter: Whether you feel the need to do Exercise 6 or not, you should bookmark the page for Section 8 in Exercise 6, which has the table Common Errors and Possible Resolutions. This table was created based on the findings of hundreds of students who took the course "The Java Developer's Guide to Eclipse," which is based in part on this book. If you find a problem while coding your first few plug-ins, there's a good chance that table has the solution.

## References

Arthorne, John, and Chris Laffra. 2004. *Official Eclipse 3.0 FAQs*. Boston, MA: Addison-Wesley. http://www.eclipsefaq.org/. (See FAQs 27, 72, 79.)

Eclipse platform technical overview. February 2003. http://eclipse.org/whitepapers/eclipse-overview.pdf.

# CHAPTER 10

## *Creating Applications Using the Rich Client Platform*

This chapter will help you understand how to implement your own applications using Eclipse. As part of this, we'll discuss the reusable frameworks in Eclipse, how they relate to one another, and scenarios for building on the common configurations of Eclipse technology. Since we expect many readers who want to learn right away about the Rich Client Platform (RCP) will come directly to this chapter, we'll briefly revisit some of the topics covered in Chapter 8, Overview of the Eclipse Architecture, reframed in an RCP-centric viewpoint. If you are reading straight through from the beginning of Part II, we ask for your patience during this review; we believe it will be worth your time.

It's easier to understand where you're going if you start from a familiar place and then move towards the destination. Therefore, the opening sections of this chapter will relate what you recognize in Eclipse's user interface to its underlying architecture. We'll also present a survey of the kind of applications you might develop using Eclipse. The chapter closes with a review of the steps involved in creating your own Eclipse-based application, after which you can jump right to Exercise 7, Developing Your First Rich Client Application.

**Reminder**: We recommend that you complete Exercise 6, Developing Your First Plug-in, before reading this chapter; you need to have a good understanding of how plug-ins can be used to extend the Eclipse SDK before embarking on rich client application development.

# Reasons Applications Are Being Built on the RCP

The Eclipse Platform allows you to integrate multiple components in a consistent user interface. You begin with the Eclipse base components, and then based on your needs, you purchase or develop additional components. The advantages of using an Eclipse-based integration approach touch on different parts of your business. Let's consider them in turn.

## Advantages for the Enterprise

As we discussed earlier, Eclipse provides an application infrastructure so you can focus on your enterprise's core competency and business value. Below are some of the issues Eclipse addresses.

- Eclipse's ability to integrate disparate tools and applications saves development costs. In addition, its common interface reduces the cost of end user training.
- Eclipse uses open standards. For example, Eclipse's plug-in model is based on the OSGi runtime. The reliance on open standards leverages existing work while not binding the platform to a propriety design, thus reducing development and maintenance costs. It also opens the future for later advancements both within and beyond the Eclipse community's efforts, such as OSGi Alliance's definitions of a standard mechanism for plug-in signing and a common platform security model for user authentication.
- Plug-ins can be deployed and the desktop configuration updated from a centralized server using the Eclipse Update Manager, thereby reducing maintenance costs. The standard use of the Update Manager is on demand, but the infrastructure it provides can serve as the basis for a variety of other use cases, such as silent install or scheduled user-approved install. The installation of plug-ins can be managed locally by the user using standard filed-based copy techniques (e.g., InstallShield). However, Eclipse provides and encourages the managed deployment of plug-ins and updates to the Workbench configuration directly from a centralized server using the Eclipse Update Manager component. No more searching for lost CD-ROMs!
- Eclipse provides a set of common serviceability tools for problem determination.
- Eclipse is a stable and well-funded project.
- Eclipse 3.0 has a critical mass of adopters, and books and training are readily available, so an enterprise benefits from a growing pool of

developers skilled on the platform. University students are using Eclipse in the classroom and for projects. This reduces training costs and increases synergy among development teams.

## Advantages for Software Developers

Eclipse began as an IDE, and its popularity among developers has exploded. The implementation of Eclipse itself intrigued developers as much as the tool itself. The following are a few of the top reasons why.

- Applications are built as self-contained plug-ins. A developer concentrates on value-added function and does not reinvent the general-function code base.
- Plug-ins can be installed side-by-side without conflicts.
- The code base is public and source code is available.
- Eclipse supports all major desktop platforms.

## Advantages for Users

No means of saving development costs will be popular unless it benefits end users. These are some of the issues Eclipse addresses that interest them.

- Eclipse is a Java framework that leverages the operating system's native windowing system. Eclipse's SWT provides an easy-to-program Java-based framework for the programmer and a familiar, native look and feel for the user.
- You can reuse existing application code with which the user is already familiar. The Eclipse GUI interoperates with Swing, OLE documents, and ActiveX controls on Windows. SWT includes a Web browser control for hosting Web-based applications. This reuse of native applications and widgets benefits the user and the developer alike; users like the familiarity of the user interface and developers have less code to write.
- The Workbench reconfigures the plug-in contributions without restarting the platform. The dynamic plug-in support enables adding new perspectives, views, editors, and action contributions. Users can install and begin working with new extensions to their Workbench environment immediately.

Many of the advantages listed above are new to version 3.0, and their introduction required refactoring of the previous version's architecture. The next section returns to these decisions and how they affect your reuse of the Eclipse Platform.

## Eclipse Architecture, Revisited

Eclipse is a layered architecture with frameworks that can be reused depending on what sort of application or tool-related task you wish to support. As a general statement, the frameworks comprising this layered architecture can be divided into three groups: Platform Runtime, Rich Client Platform, and the Workbench IDE. You are probably most familiar with the user interface provided by the Workbench IDE, shown in Figure 10.1, since that's what you see when you installed and started the Eclipse SDK.

The Eclipse SDK includes tools you need for Java and plug-in development, team programming, and more. Most of what you see in the SDK was added by plug-ins defining extensions to the base Workbench IDE. To make this point clearer, Figure 10.2 shows the Eclipse Workbench that you would see if you downloaded just the Eclipse Platform Runtime binaries. This download is for those who wish to extend the Eclipse Workbench IDE but don't need the Java or plug-in development environment.

The Eclipse Platform has some characteristics of a programmer's tool, with its Resource perspective and notion of a workspace containing projects, folders, and files. It also includes the default text editor and several basic

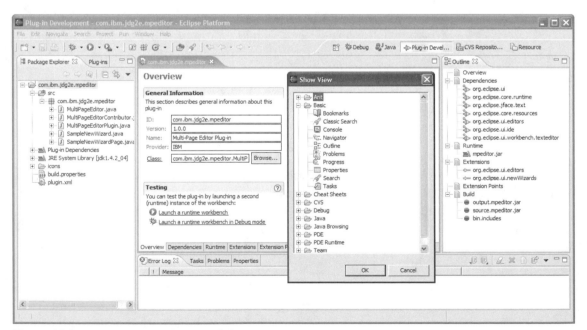

**Figure 10.1**    Eclipse IDE Workbench (SDK)

**Figure 10.2**   Eclipse IDE Workbench (Platform Runtime)

views like the Navigator, Tasks, and Bookmarks. The fact that these views and editors are workspace-oriented is important; this distinguishes the components belonging to the Workbench IDE layer from those belonging to its foundation, the Rich Client Platform. We'll return to this point shortly.

If you compare the Eclipse Platform shown in Figure 10.2 with the Eclipse SDK shown in Figure 10.1, you see many visual elements in common. From the user's point of view, the contribution of new views, toolbars, menu choices, and perspectives and the functionality they bring is what distinguishes the Eclipse SDK from the Eclipse Platform downloads. They both have similar title bars, tool bars, menu bar pull-downs, and menu choices like **Window > Show View**. This shared IDE appearance is because they both rely on the same component responsible for selecting these top-level elements. Those who create extensions to the Eclipse IDE define plug-ins and extensions to contribute to the user interface with this in mind, knowing that their contributions will always add to the existing Workbench IDE, never subtract.

In contrast, those who create an application based on the Rich Client Platform have more control over what the overall appearance of the Workbench will be. They may choose a presentation that doesn't look very much like a Workbench at all, as shown in the example associated with this book, the Mini-Workplace in Figure 10.7 on page 281.

If you were to create a minimal "Hello, World" equivalent RCP application, it would only have to contain a default perspective. Top-level elements like the menu bar, toolbar, status line, and even the window title text and image are optional. Our example Mini-Workplace implements a class that mediates the decisions of whether there will be a menu bar, what will be its initial pull-down menu choices, and so on. The exercise associated with this chapter leads you through the steps of creating the infrastructure that brings the pieces of an RCP application together.

What makes the Mini-Workplace interesting is more than its neat appearance. As you learned in Chapter 7, Extending Eclipse for Fun and Profit, the interest lies in Eclipse's architected ability to welcome extensions and embrace integration with other application functionality. Eclipse as an integrated development environment has amply demonstrated this ability through its own SDK, and this is further demonstrated by other commercial and noncommercial programmer tools based upon Eclipse. The breadth of the tools available for the Eclipse programmer is only the beginning of the Eclipse story. In other words, Eclipse is an application integration platform first. It just happens to be that Eclipse's IDE persona as the SDK is widely known, but keep in mind that the extensibility it demonstrates applies to both tool developers and the more general application program developers.

Figure 10.3 shows the Eclipse framework layers that correspond to the user interfaces shown in Figures 10.1, 10.2, and 10.7.

Relating Figure 10.3 to the three other figures, the Mini-Workbench shown in Figure 10.7 represents an example of the base Rich Client Platform and the Eclipse Platform, as shown in Figure 10.2; and the dashed box encircles the complete Eclipse SDK, as shown in Figure 10.1. Keep your finger on this page because we'll refer to Figure 10.3 several times in this chapter.

## Eclipse Application Types

When you create your own Eclipse application, you are free to choose the top-level elements in the Workbench. This is unlike prior releases of Eclipse, where the supported choices of how to reuse Eclipse were at two extremes because "IDE-ness" pervaded the Workbench framework, leaving you the choice of (a) extending the Eclipse IDE, or (b) building your plug-in upon only the Eclipse Platform Runtime and ignoring the Eclipse Workbench frameworks entirely.

The first option was the major focus of the first edition of this book. What was hard before version 2.1 was writing something in-between without

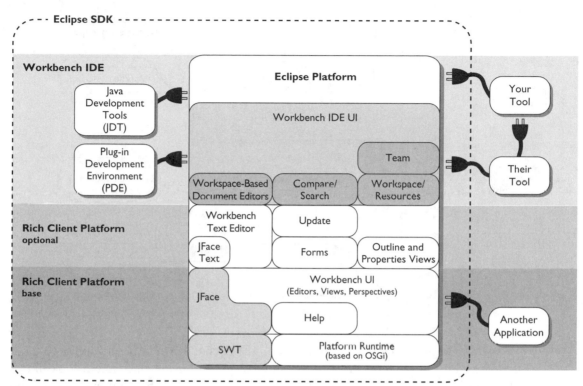

**Figure 10.3** Eclipse Architecture

having to do all the work yourself. If you wanted less than the full Eclipse IDE, you could copy and hack at the code to trim the parts you did not need, but the china shop rule "you break it, you bought it" applied; that is, you could no longer open up a bug report when things did not work. The Rich Client Platform framework was refactored from the IDE to fix this problem and encourage the use of Eclipse for a new world of application types. The three general types of applications you can create using Eclipse are shown in Figure 10.4. These correspond to the layers of the Eclipse architecture presented in Figure 10.3.

A Platform Runtime (non-GUI) application simply runs code until complete without displaying a user interface. The Platform Runtime offers the benefit of the deferred load strategy and extensibility of the Eclipse plug-in architecture. Eclipse's infocenter, which relies on the Tomcat server plug-in, is an example of an application based on this platform.

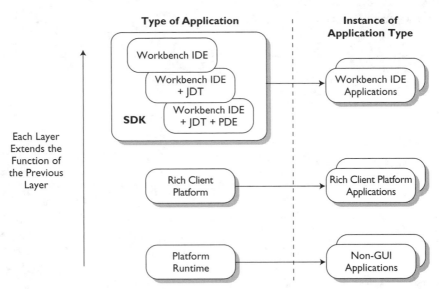

**Figure 10.4**   Eclipse General Application Types

A desktop application builds on the Rich Client Platform framework, and there are fewer limitations on what your user interface might look like compared to the IDE. The IBM Lotus Workplace, as shown in Figure 10.5, is an example of an application based on the RCP.

An enhancement to the Eclipse IDE was described in Chapter 7, Extending Eclipse for Fun and Profit. In that example, you accepted the look and feel and style of user interface interaction available in Eclipse itself, in addition to its workspace and other IDE components.

## How Eclipse Gets Going

To appreciate more fully how the application types described in the previous section work, it is worth understanding a little about how the Platform Runtime "bootstraps" Eclipse. It is at this point that some key decisions are made about how the rest of the application will operate.

When you start `eclipse.exe` from an Eclipse Platform or SDK download, you are actually starting the Platform Runtime. The Platform Runtime gets the "engine" started and then looks for the identified contribution to the `org.eclipse.core.runtime.applications` extension point. The application to run is identified using the `-application` command line parameter. After the Platform Runtime has interpreted all the plug-in manifests, it looks to

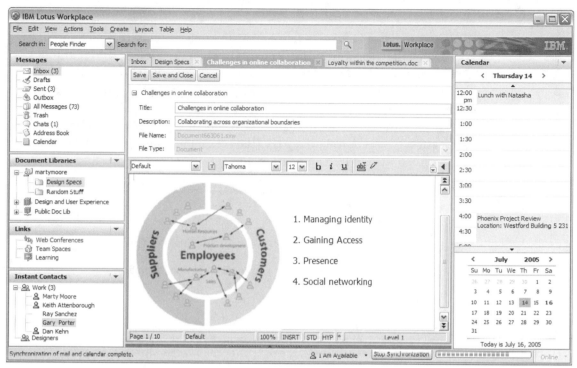

**Figure 10.5**   Lotus Workplace

this extension point for the name of the class that is responsible for directing what happens next.

If you are writing an extension to the Eclipse IDE, the application that gets started is provided by the org.eclipse.ui.ide plug-in, so your plug-in only has its own startup to worry about, not the platform's. Your plug-in is composed of extension definitions to the Workbench IDE and the code associated with these extensions. However, if you want to build your own Eclipse-based application, which may look only reminiscent of the Workbench user interface or even have no user interface at all, you contribute your own application extension and ask that the Eclipse executable select your application at startup. The next section begins with showing the code behind a simple non-GUI "Hello, World" application based on Eclipse plug-ins, and then later we'll return to the code of an equivalent application based on RCP. After learning the concepts behind the RCP and seeing the code for these simple examples, you'll be ready to launch into the two RCP exercises in Part VI.

### Defining an Eclipse Application

Writing your own Eclipse "Hello, World" application is very simple: First you define an extension to the `org.eclipse.core.runtime.applications` extension point that specifies a class implementing the `IPlatformRunnable` interface in the `class` attribute, then launch Eclipse with your application id specified in the `-application` command line parameter to `eclipse.exe`. It is so easy we can show you all the relevant bits of typing for a simple non-GUI application on less than half a page (the plug-in manifest content, application class, and command line invocation are shown below).

```
<plugin id="com.ibm.jdg2e.hello" ...>
  // ...lines omitted...
  <extension
      id="HelloWorld"
      point="org.eclipse.core.runtime.applications">
    <application>
      <run class="com.ibm.jdg2e.hello.Application"/>
    </application>
  </extension>
</plugin>

public class Application implements IPlatformRunnable {
  public Object run(Object args) throws Exception {
    System.out.println("That is all it takes!");
    return IPlatformRunnable.EXIT_OK;
  }
}

java -cp startup.jar org.eclipse.core.launcher.Main -consoleLog
    -application com.ibm.jdg2e.hello.HelloWorld
```

That is all it takes—if all you want to do is write a message to the console. What you see above is the simplest form of a non-GUI application.

---

**NOTE**  The `-application` parameter is not a class name; it is a concatenation of the plug-in id (`com.ibm.jdg2e.hello`) that defined the extension to the `org.eclipse.core.runtime.applications` extension point and that extension's `id` attribute (`"HelloWorld"`).

---

As was mentioned earlier, those who extend the Eclipse Platform don't need to worry about specifying a startup application since it's already provided. What if you want to reuse some Eclipse functionality but you're not writing a programmer's tool? The answer is to start with the Rich Client Platform as the base of your desktop application, configure it appropriately, and then decide what function found in the optional RCP components (and above) might be helpful.

We will describe some of these components in the next section, beginning with a review of the function available in Eclipse, and how it might be reused; then we will get into the details on how to create an application based on the RCP.

## Opportunities for Reuse of Eclipse

In its first release, Eclipse was seen as a tools integration platform, period. Today Eclipse's domain has expanded so that you can use the Eclipse platform to address a wider range of application development problems. To help you better appreciate these areas of interest, let's cover a few definitions to give us a common nomenclature to approach the task of reusing Eclipse's rich capabilities. These aren't rigid categories; they are ways of describing the typical applications you might create using a subset of Eclipse's frameworks. Then the next section will cover how each category of framework reuse represents a richer exploitation of the Eclipse Platform.

### Non-UI Plug-in Components

This category corresponds to the Platform Runtime component shown in Figure 10.3.

Recall that one of the fundamental goals of Eclipse is to support extensibility and scalability. Its capability to act as an integration platform is grounded in the Platform Runtime's definition of the building blocks that make this possible, namely plug-ins, extension points, and extensions. While much of this book focuses on the components of the Eclipse Workbench that rely on the Platform Runtime, there is value in exploiting the runtime component outside of a user interface-oriented application.

One of the best-known examples of a non-GUI application is the Help system, which is based on the Tomcat Web application server. The Help system allows an Eclipse application to deliver its online help either locally through the **Help > Help Content** menu choice, or remotely in a Web browser via Eclipse's standalone Help system known as the **infocenter**. In an infocenter configuration, the Eclipse Platform is running help as a non-GUI application. The online documentation on the eclipse.org Web site is provided this way. Users accessing online help in this manner will have all the features of Eclipse's local Help system except for infopops (field-specific pop-up help) and active help (clickable actions in the online help, which often demonstrate how to accomplish the task described in the online help).

The Help system takes advantage of Eclipse's deferred load strategy and extensibility. If you are writing similar server applications, you may be interested in using plug-ins to organize and design your product's extensibility. Chapter 11, Creating Extension Points: How Others can Extend Your Plug-ins, and Chapter 12, Advanced Plug-in Development, will broaden the discussion of plug-ins that was introduced in the first chapters of Part II.

## SWT Graphic User Interface

This category corresponds to the SWT and JFace components shown in Figure 10.3.

The Eclipse Workbench, presented to the user as either an IDE or a more general application, defines higher-level user interface constructs like perspectives, editors, views, properties and preferences dialogs, and so on. Together these constructs make up Eclipse's "user interface personality." As discussed in the previous chapter, the basis of the Workbench user interface framework is SWT and JFace. SWT was designed as a small, native, multiplatform set of widgets for Java; JFace was designed as a model-based framework on top of SWT to further simplify and enhance the productivity of those writing user interfaces in Java.

If your application doesn't lend itself to a user interface design based on the views, editors, and perspective decomposition that characterizes Eclipse, you can choose to develop graphical applications directly using SWT and without anything to do with plug-ins. The SWT framework provides a fast, easy-to-learn means of creating your user interface from a reasonably small set of widgets. SWT's simplicity is why many developers originally referred to it as the *Simple* Widget Toolkit. While the SWT framework retains this moniker in spirit, its abbreviation was later reaffirmed as the *Standard* Widget Toolkit to reflect its wider mission.

In addition to its easy-to-learn programming interface, SWT addresses a concern that Java developers have faced for many years—delivering applications that are fast and maintain high fidelity to the native platform's user interface. This is SWT's prime objective and one of the principle reasons for Eclipse's widespread popularity. The focus of this book is plug-in development for extending the Eclipse IDE and delivering plug-in based desktop applications. As part of that, Chapter 14, introduces you to SWT, and several other chapters describe its companion framework, JFace. However, if you are especially interested in Eclipse's SWT and JFace, you may want to supplement your learning with other books that focus exclusively on the subject.

As Chapter 14's title suggests, SWT is about delivering a thin, efficient graphical library. JFace, in combination with the rest of Eclipse, turns the focus to delivering an extensible integration platform by way of a contributions-based approach to user interface development. We covered this notion briefly in the last chapter; plug-ins provide extensibility by defining and then contributing to extension points while the JFace framework provides extensibility by allowing the contribution of user interface elements like actions to existing applications. You'll see many references to JFace interfaces in Eclipse's user interface plug-ins, but not the other way around, underscoring the fact that the purpose of JFace is to raise the level of abstraction and thereby enhance the productivity of the Eclipse UI developer. If your application has no need for the flexibility that plug-ins offer, you might consider two alternatives:

- Use SWT alone as a graphics layer that works with a level of abstraction near to the operating system (i.e., dealing with strings, images, displays, and so on), or
- Use SWT and JFace together to add an additional model-based abstraction that simplifies your user interface code by allowing you to specify widget inputs in terms closer to your application model (e.g., objects like customers and invoices instead of arrays of strings).

Using SWT and JFace separate from the rest of the Eclipse plug-in environment isn't a common case; while investigating this possibility we found that some references to classes in the Platform Runtime had worked their way into the JFace code, creating a dependency. It turns out this dependency is benign since the references are to innocuous classes, and you can build a pure SWT/JFace application if you choose. This book doesn't specifically address this category, but rather focuses on SWT and JFace in the context of creating and extending desktop applications and tools based on plug-ins.

## Contribution-Based Workbench User Interface

This category corresponds to the base and optional Rich Client Platform layers shown in Figure 10.3.

You probably noticed that the word "contributions" appeared frequently in the past three chapters. The first inkling of its importance starts in the JFace user interface framework. JFace views and editors accept action contributions, as do JFace toolbars, status lines…. Starting to see a pattern? This contribution-based capability is broadened by the plug-in architecture, once again a contribution-based capability of composing an application from loosely coupled parts.

JFace is contribution-based, plug-ins are contribution-based, so the next natural step? Of course, a contribution-based Workbench! This is the essential definition of Eclipse's Rich Client Platform—a framework of reusable components, many of them delivering their functionality as extension points.

> Figure 10.7 (shown on page 281) depicts an example of a "Generic Workbench" based on Eclipse, the Mini-Workplace. Since it appears so prominently in Eclipse's APIs, it's easy to overestimate the importance of the term "Workbench." Much of this word choice is historical, owing to the fact that Eclipse evolved beyond the confines of an IDE to encompass desktop applications as a group. Yet the word remains. Try not to be distracted by the term—when you see "Workbench" in this book or Eclipse's documentation, keep in mind that in most contexts, it means "application" too.
>
> There are, however, some aspects where the IDE-ness of Eclipse becomes more noticeable—not just to you as an Eclipse plug-in developer reading programmer documentation making references to terms like Workbench, but potentially to your users as well. As you'll see in the next category, this is the most distinct dividing line between "Eclipse the application" and "Eclipse the IDE," and it begins with the introduction of the workspace.

In essence, this category represents two subcategories: those who wish to invite contributions (from their customers or third parties) and those who want to package their products grouped by features (e.g., entry level, midrange, and full function) in order to sell additional features appealing to different needs and potentially having different pricing.

Most of Eclipse is defined in terms of contributions to extension points. Part II is dedicated to explaining and demonstrating how to contribute to the extension points defined in the Workbench and reuse the frameworks associated with these extensions.

## IDE Extensions

This category corresponds to the Workbench IDE UI layer shown in Figure 10.3. Those familiar with the first edition of this book and Eclipse 2.1 will recognize this category immediately. There are two typical use cases. One use, like the Eclipse IDE creators, focuses on creating a base framework that others can build upon that is domain-specific. The second use focuses on enhancing the base created by the first group of developers as part of a company-wide strategy of building their own tool integration platform. Much of what got the Eclipse bandwagon rolling was the introduction of an IDE development foundation that addressed many of the fundamental needs of tools providers, freeing them up to deliver value-add capability specific to their interests instead of common functionality. As the popularity of Eclipse rose, its early adopters of the technology evolved from exploiting the base capability to contributing back to it. Depending on the situation, you may be in either group—leveraging existing capabilities or contributing new ones for others to leverage—at any given point in time. Eclipse users also benefited since this naturally led to greater compatibility and similarity between products, saving them learning time and avoiding interoperability problems that are so common to independently developed products.

While perhaps not a common case, you can imagine applications that might want to use the workspace component but won't appear to be IDE-based from the user's perspective. That is, an application that needs to manage a set of file-based artifacts that may or may not be visible to the user. If these resources are shown to the user, they might be presented in a specialized view, like the JDT's Package Explorer, which shows a more natural presentation of Java source code and downplays its file-based nature.

The advantage of this approach is that it leverages the portable resource management component and its features like change notification, local history, and so on. From the user's point of view through custom navigators it seems more natural, and the underlying implementation masks the fact that the local file system artifacts may well be stored in a single "product" project.

All of what you'll learn in Part II and Part III about developing Eclipse-based applications applies equally well to Eclipse IDE extensions. Part IV covers the IDE-specific extension points and frameworks of Eclipse. For example, Chapter 27, Extending the Java Development Tools, will pick up where Chapter 7 left off, showing you how to enhance Eclipse's Java source editor, add your own code refactoring, and more.

## Implementing Your Own Workbench

There are only a few assumptions about what composes an Eclipse-based application. Creating the minimal application yields a minimal main window, as shown in Figure 10.6.

Generally, this book doesn't show entire code extracts. However, in this case it's worth showing all the code for the equivalent of RCP's "Hello,

**Figure 10.6**   Starting Point for the Generic Workbench

World" if only to etch firmly in your mind the skeletal code common to all RCP applications. The application code is shown below. (Note that package and import statements are omitted. Furthermore, this code uses two inner classes for brevity; realistically, these classes would not be so trivial and thus would justify their own source files.)

```
public class HelloRCPApplicationRunnable implements
    IPlatformRunnable {
  public class HelloRCPWorkbenchAdvisor
      extends WorkbenchAdvisor {
    public String getInitialWindowPerspectiveId() {
      return "com.ibm.jdg2e.helloworld.rcp";
    }
  }
  public class HelloRCPPerspectiveFactory
      implements IPerspectiveFactory {
    public void createInitialLayout(IPageLayout layout) {
    }
  }
  public Object run(Object args) throws Exception {
    WorkbenchAdvisor advisor = new HelloRCPWorkbenchAdvisor();
    Display display = PlatformUI.createDisplay();
    int rc = PlatformUI.createAndRunWorkbench
      (display, advisor);
    return (rc == PlatformUI.RETURN_RESTART ?
      IPlatformRunnable.EXIT_RESTART :
      IPlatformRunnable.EXIT_OK);
  }
}
```

This is essentially equivalent to the main method of a Java application, and it introduces the minimal set of players in an RCP application, namely the IPlatformRunnable, WorkbenchAdvisor, and IPerspectiveFactory. The runnable's createAndRunWorkbench method gathers all the contributions and parameterization for the Workbench and then starts the user interface loop. It exits when the user has closed the Workbench.

For the sake of completeness, the entire plug-in manifest, `plugin.xml`, is shown below. Don't worry about studying it too closely now, you'll see it again in Exercise 7, Developing Your First Rich Client Application.

```xml
<?xml version="1.0" encoding="UTF-8"?>
<?eclipse version="3.0"?>
<plugin
    id="com.ibm.jdg2e.helloworld.rcp"
    name="JDG2E: Hello, RCP"
    version="1.0.0"
    provider-name="The Java Developer&apos;s Guide to Eclipse">

  <requires>
    <import plugin-"org.cclipse.core.runtime"/>
    <import plugin="org.eclipse.ui"/>
    <import plugin="org.eclipse.ui.workbench"/>
  </requires>

  <runtime>
    <library name="rcp.jar"/>
  </runtime>

  <extension
      id="application"
      point="org.eclipse.core.runtime.applications">
    <application>
      <run class=
        "com.ibm.jdg2e.helloworld.rcp.HelloRCPApplicationRunnable"/>
    </application>
  </extension>

  <extension point="org.eclipse.ui.perspectives">
    <perspective
        name="Hello, RCP"
        class=
          "com.ibm.jdg2e.helloworld.rcp.HelloRCPPerspectiveFactory"
        id="com.ibm.jdg2e.helloworld.rcp">
    </perspective>
  </extension>
</plugin>
```

When implementing an extension to the Workbench IDE, many decisions about the main window's general appearance and the how and where your enhancements will be introduced are already made. This is the domain of programmer tools, and this creates a certain style of presentation consistent with other tools that are already present in your IDE.

While it probably has already occurred to you, it's worth explicitly stating: Creating an Eclipse extension means adding functionality, not subtracting it. However, once you go down the path of using Eclipse's Rich Client

Platform, often referred to as the **Generic Workbench**, you can pick and choose among options instead of simply adding your own contributions to a collection of existing tools. Some of these options, like what the menu bar and toolbar will initially contain, are almost implementation details. Other decisions about the user interface are a direct reflection of your application's domain, for example:

- Where does the data represented in your application come from?
- Does your application have several distinct activities that lend themselves to a set of perspectives, editors, and views? Or does a single perspective with a fixed collection of editors and views suffice?

The minimum Workbench application includes all the components in the base Rich Client Platform. This includes the core runtime and the skeletal Eclipse user interface. The next layer above contains the plug-ins that are not dependent on the workspace and the Resource API. Your first task is mapping the needs of your application to what Eclipse provides. For example, the following are some scenarios that might represent ways to reuse this potential.

- **Skinny client**
  A single-perspective application where there's no need to expose the idea of perspectives.

- **Complex client**
  An application encompassing a set of related tasks that lend themselves to structuring into two or more perspectives, or multiple top-level windows.

- **Client with strong reuse**
  A complex application that includes some optional components, such as text editors, properties views, or preferences dialogs.

- **Clients that are an IDE except in name**
  As mentioned earlier, although your users may not think of your application as workspace-oriented, you might find it beneficial to reuse it. Your implementation might reuse the workspace while presenting it in a fashion appropriate to your users. This approach can leverage capabilities like the workspace's local file history without explicitly exposing the idea of the workspace to the user.

Once you have made these design decisions, you turn to the implementation details. The next section will introduce the steps for implementing your Workbench, and the chapter's associated exercise will walk you through them in detail.

## What You Can Configure in the Workbench

The first and most visible example is your selection of the main window's appearance. As an IDE contributor, you have little say in things like what the title of the window will be, what menu options will always be shown, if the status line will be present or not, and so on. This is different with the generic Workbench. You start without a default menu, default toolbar, shortcut bar, status line—literally an empty window—and then select among all these options as suits your needs.

Figure 10.7 shows some of the choices you'll make. This application is in the project com.ibm.jdg2e.miniwp on the book's CD-ROM. It is our beefed-up version of "Hello, World" for those creating generic Workbench applications.

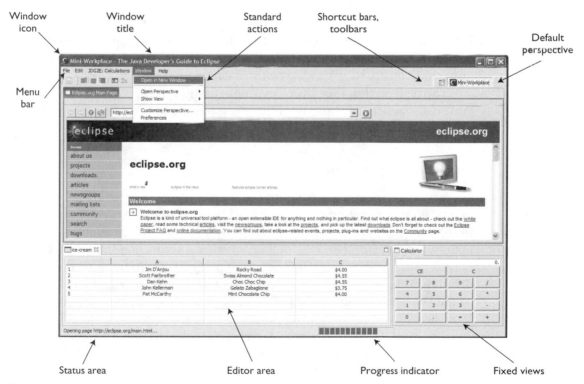

**Figure 10.7**   Customizing the Workbench Appearance

The call outs in Figure 10.7 indicate some of the parts of the UI that you can configure. The first exercise associated with this chapter will walk you through the specification of the window title, window icon, menu bar, toolbar, shortcut bars, and status line.

Eclipse defines a framework that handles the coordination of the Workbench's creation. To introduce your input into these decisions, you define a few classes whose instances will be consulted during the Eclipse Workbench's startup processing. We'll cover these steps briefly in the next sections.

### Getting Your Application Up and Running

When you're writing an extension to the Eclipse Platform, the application started is implemented as part of the IDE UI plug-in, `org.eclipse.ui.ide`. Once you decide to create your own Workbench implementation, you must take over that responsibility in your application plug-in. Before initializing the rest of the Workbench, your application plug-in can do whatever is necessary to get your program going. For example, this might include logging in or authentication of access rights; whatever you would prefer to have done before opening the main window. One that is done, your application will certainly include the boilerplate Eclipse startup code for RCP applications, similar to the "Hello, RCP" code presented earlier.

The next section introduces the configuration of the Workbench with your own implementation of the class responsible for deciding the main window's appearance, a subclass of the `WorkbenchAdvisor` class.

### Configuring Your Application

To decouple the inner workings of the Workbench from your own implementation, your application provides a **Workbench advisor** that determines things like what perspective is initially displayed, the initial content of the main window menu bar and toolbar, whether a status line should be displayed, and so forth. Your implementation only needs to focus on the task of defining and configuring these elements. Once you've provided your advisor to the Workbench during the launch code shown in the prior section, the Workbench will call it at the appropriate time as needed.

The `WorkbenchAdvisor` is an abstract class that provides default implementations for all methods except one: `getInitialWindowPerspectiveId`. You must define at least one perspective, even if it's an empty one, and return its identifier in this method. Keep in mind that you're not required to provide more than one perspective if that doesn't fit your user interface design. That is, if the decomposition of your user interface doesn't lend itself to this notion of the Eclipse user interface personality (for example, because your application has only a few views and editors, and thus doesn't need a perspective's higher-level organization), you can define just one perspective and lay out your views and editors within it. In this case, you can create an application that ignores the notion of Eclipse perspectives and your users will be none the wiser.

More specifically, since your Workbench advisor controls the content of the main menu bar, you may choose not to provide menu choices like **Window > Open Perspective** or even **Window > Open View**. This makes perfect sense, for example, in the case where your application has a fixed number of views and editors that are presented in a single page, similar to the default perspective of our example Mini-Workplace.

The exercise shows you how to create a Workbench having a single perspective. You can treat the code you develop as part of this exercise as a template for other Eclipse-based applications. When you see the need for more perspectives, turn to Chapter 20 for more information on how to define things like the default view layout and placement, shortcuts to related perspectives, and shortcuts to associated creation wizards.

Much of the configuration you may choose to do must be done at a specific time in the Workbench creation life cycle. You can't create a menu bar before the window exists, right? Therefore, your `WorkbenchAdvisor` subclass will override methods that correspond to these various life-cycle events:

- Before the *first* Workbench window opens
- Before each Workbench window opens
- After each Workbench window is opened
- Before each Workbench window is closed
- After each Workbench window is closed
- As the Workbench shuts down
- Before the Workbench closes

Exercise 7 includes many of the methods you'll want to override that correspond to these lifecycle events.

## Enabling UI Contributions from Other Plug-ins

Plug-ins that contribute to the user interface sometimes must be aware of assumptions about the requirements of those extensions, not all of which are specifically stated in the extension definition. For example, a plug-in that wants to contribute a view that will appear under "Basic" in the **Window > Show View** menu choice must know the identifier of that category. Plug-ins that contribute to a toolbar or menu bar must know the identifier where their contribution should appear.

In the case of the IDE, the internal class `IDEWorkbenchAdvisor` is responsible for providing the details necessary to create the menu bar, toolbars, and other visual elements of the Workbench window. For the benefit of those who want to extend the Workbench user interface, the Workbench advisor uses predefined public constants for well-known contribution locations. For example, the IDE Workbench advisor specifies `IWorkbenchActionConstants` `.M_FILE_START` as the id of the group of menu choices at the beginning of the File menu, or more generally, `IWorkbenchActionConstants.MB_ADDITIONS` for the location where new top-level menus should be inserted in a toolbar, pull-down menu, or pop-up menu.

If you want to reuse a component that exists in the Workbench IDE layer in your RCP application, you need to be aware of what contributions it makes and where. For example, the IDE editors plug-in (`org.eclipse.ui.editors`), which defines the default text editor for resource files in the workspace, assumes there is an **Edit** pull-down menu and that it contains specific insertion points for the editor plug-in's menu extensions. This, of course, isn't your responsibility if you are writing an extension to the IDE Workbench since the `IDEWorkbenchAdvisor` handles it, but once you decide to provide your own Workbench Advisor and your own main window layout, you must be aware of the assumptions of other components you hope to reuse.

To make this easier, the Workbench defines `IWorkbenchActionConstants` to declare standard insertion points and the class `ActionFactory` to create instances of the standard actions. For example, the code `ActionFactory` `.OPEN_NEW_WINDOW.create(window)` creates the action associated with the **Window > New Window** menu choice, and `ContributionItemFactory` `.VIEWS_SHORTLIST.create(window)` creates the menu associated with the **Window > Show View** menu cascade. The exercises associated with this chapter will discuss more examples of how to enable standard actions and dialogs.

## Exercise Summary

To see how to construct our modest "Hello, World" example, turn to Exercise 7, Developing Your First Rich Client Application. For a more advanced example, see Exercise 8, Developing a Rich Client Application with Dynamically Added Plug-ins.

After you complete Exercise 7, you may want to explore the implementation of the Mini-Workplace shown in Figure 10.7. This sample code is defined in several related projects.

- `com.ibm.jdg2e.miniwp` contains the common classes for all RCP applications: a Workbench advisor, a perspective factory, and an application runnable.
- `com.ibm.jdg2e.view.extras` adds a little flair by contributing a working calculator and Web browser to the Mini-Workplace.
- `com.ibm.jdg2e.msseditor.*` is a collection of several plug-ins that define a "mini-spreadsheet" and demonstrate how to integrate an editor into an RCP application. Chapter 19 discusses how to create editors destined for RCP and IDE applications; at this point in your study, you may want to simply consider these plug-ins reusable "black box" components and revisit their implemention details after you have read Chapter 19.

The example is a simple but functionally complete RCP application. You will find more documentation and instructions on how to install and launch the Mini-Workplace on the book's CD-ROM.

## Chapter Summary

It's a lot more fun and satisfying to spend your time writing code that adds value specific to your domain than rewriting infrastructure that's been done a thousand times over. That's why developers choose to build on the Eclipse platform—so they can construct their application in layers (many of which are free), focus on the function and not building a framework to host their function, and as an added bonus, potentially make their tool open for extension by others.

Eclipse has already succeeded in bringing one of the best tool integration platforms to the market. The long-awaited goal of "Java on the desktop" is only steps away. The authors of this book have every reason to expect that the future's best office applications will be based on Eclipse.

## References

Arthorne, John, and Chris Laffra. 2004. *Official Eclipse 3.0 FAQs*. Boston, MA: Addison-Wesley. http://www.eclipsefaq.org. (See FAQs 199, 246, 247, 249.)

Eclipse Rich Client Platform FAQ, http://dev.eclipse.org/viewcvs/index.cgi/%7Echeckout%7E/platform-ui-home/rcp/faq.html

# CHAPTER 11

*Creating Extension Points:
How Others Can Extend Your Plug-ins*

You've spent a lot of time learning how to contribute to existing extension points. Now we're going to look into how to define extension points that others can use—including your own Eclipse-based product.

Except for a small runtime core, nearly all of Eclipse is bound together using extensions. This late-binding strategy dovetails nicely with the ultimate Eclipse goal of creating a flexible, extensible platform. To continue to support the Eclipse spirit of extensibility, it behooves you to structure your product with this in mind. Will you have user interface capabilities beyond what is defined by the Workbench plug-in extension points, unique to your plug-in, that you wish to share? Extensibility should also include model-oriented extension points. What sort of logic are you writing that others may want to build upon? These consumers are not necessarily external to your product; you may choose to use extension points as a way of integrating your own components. Of course, this is the way that Eclipse itself was created.

By the way, this chapter could be summarized in one sentence: To create an extension point, define an `<extension-point>` tag in your `plugin.xml` file, then at runtime, process the extensions contributed via `<extension>` tags that specified your extension point id. That's a long sentence, but it is all there.

This chapter and its associated sample code present recommended steps to enable others to extend your plug-in using extension points that you've defined. You can let your imagination go wild, since we're now considering what you might provide to others, not just what already exists in Eclipse.

## Relationship Between Extension Points and Extensions

In the most basic terms, an extension point defines where an extension can contribute to a plug-in. Let's look a little closer at this relationship by considering an example: an action contribution to an object's pop-up menu. This should look familiar, since we looked at a similar example in Chapter 8. This time we'll add more detail, since you now understand much more about the underlying implementation issues.

The following is a plug-in manifest extract showing the XML for specifying an action that will be contributed to an object's pop-up menu.

```
<plugin
  id="com.ibm.jdg2e.example.myaction"
  name="MyAction"
  version="3.0.0">

 <extension point="org.eclipse.ui.popupMenus">
    <objectContribution
        objectClass="org.eclipse.core.resources.IFile"
        id="com.ibm.jdg2e.example">
      <action
        label="My Object Action"
        class="com.ibm.jdg2e.example.MyObjectAction"
        menubarPath="additions"
        id="com.ibm.jdg2e.example.myobjectaction">
      </action>
    </objectContribution>
 </extension>
```

Let's look at how this specification "connects" code from the two plug-ins, Workbench and MyAction. This connection is depicted in Figure 11.1.

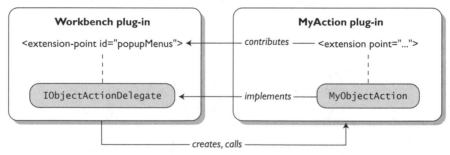

**Figure 11.1**    Connecting Classes Between Plug-ins

You have already seen how the MyAction plug-in specifies the contribution to the Workbench extension point, org.eclipse.ui.popupMenus.

Here is how the Workbench plug-in specifies the definition of this extension point.

```
<extension-point
   id='org.eclipse.ui.popupMenus'>
</extension-point>
```

Not much, is it? That is all the information that the Platform Runtime requires to recognize a plug-in's extension point. You have seen many times that contributing to an extension point requires much more information, specified as **tag attributes** or **child tags**. The Workbench plug-in's pop-up menu extension point is no different. It requires attributes that define, for example, the desired label, location, tooltip text, and most importantly, a class to perform the action when the user selects the menu choice. In this particular case, that class must implement IObjectActionDelegate.

The MyAction plug-in provides this information via the <extension> tag in its plug-in manifest file. During the startup of Eclipse, this information is recorded in a global extension registry that the Workbench plug-in will read to add menu choice contributions, if any, before displaying a pop-up menu. Because the attributes already contain enough information to create a menu choice, there is no immediate need to create an instance of MyObjectAction; the Workbench plug-in can wait until the menu choice is actually selected to avoid loading the MyAction plug-in unnecessarily. However, when the action is selected, the Workbench plug-in knows to create an instance of MyObjectAction and call the appropriate methods defined in the IObject-ActionDelegate interface.

## Viewing the Official List of Enabled Plug-ins, Extensions, and Extension Points

As part of creating a new extension point that others can use, you'll have to process the Platform Runtime's extension registry. You probably have already used the Plug-in Registry view, shown in Figure 11.2, to help you debug your plug-ins. It is particularly handy when you wish to look at the extensions to your own extension points without adding debug System.out.println calls to your code. You can open it by selecting **Window > Show View > Other... > PDE Run-time > Plug-in Registry**.

The Plug-in Registry view displays its contents in a tree format. The top-level nodes are the enabled plug-ins (corresponding to the <plugin> tag of the manifest files) that were discovered at startup. The Plug-in Registry view shows all the extensions that a given plug-in contributes to other plug-ins (corresponding to its <extension> tag[s]) and extensions that it accepts from

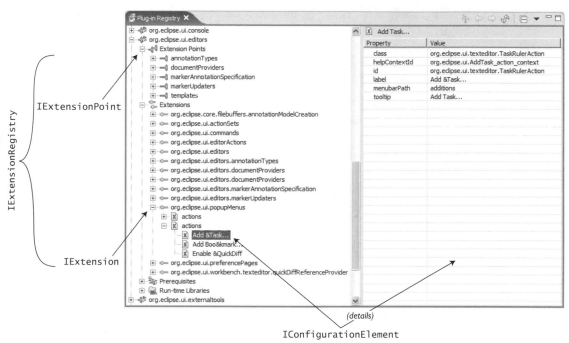

**Figure 11.2**   Plug-in Registry View

other plug-ins (corresponding to its `<extension-point>` tag[s]) under each plug-in in the list. We'll return to the interfaces behind this view in the section Processing the Registry Entries for Your Extension Points later in this chapter.

## How to Define Extension Points

Here are the steps for defining extension points for all plug-ins. The following sections describe these steps in detail.

1. Choose the existing code you want to enable others to extend or configure.
2. Declare the existence of the new extension point.
3. Define an interface or abstract class for expected behavior of contributed classes.
4. Process the registry entries for your extension point.
5. Invoke the appropriate methods of the extension's contributed class per the previously defined interface contract.

### Choosing the Existing Code You Want to Enable Others to Extend or Configure

Eclipse does not prescribe how you should determine what areas of your existing code merit extensibility via extension points. However, Eclipse does provide a good model of how you might consider doing so. In this spirit, let's distill some of the salient characteristics of the different Eclipse extension points.

Extension points are used to:

- Create new functionality (e.g., create a new action set, view, or editor), or augment the functionality of an existing plug-in (e.g., contribute a menu choice to an existing editor or view)
- Define data-only configuration extensions (e.g., help contributions)

Extension points that require one or more attributes referencing a class fall into the first category. The following excerpt from the `org.eclipse.ui.ide` plug-in defines a new view, ResourceNavigator, available from the **Window > Show View > Navigator** menu choice in the Eclipse IDE.

```
<extension point="org.eclipse.ui.views">
  <view
    name="Navigator"
    icon="icons/full/eview16/filenav_nav.gif"
    category="org.eclipse.ui"
    class="org.eclipse.ui.views.navigator.ResourceNavigator"
    id="org.eclipse.ui.views.ResourceNavigator">
  </view>
</extension>
```

The majority of Eclipse extension points are of this type; that is, they reference a class that adds the fine-grain behavior that completes the desired functionality of the extension point. The tag attribute might be called `class` or `run`, but ultimately the goal is the same: to provide code that adds the desired runtime behavior, since the behavior cannot be fully expressed as a static XML definition.

The second general type of extension points are those that include only configuration data. The following excerpt from the `org.eclipse.ui.ide` plug-in defines a group of commands and keybindings associated with Workbench actions.

```
<extension point="org.eclipse.ui.commands">
  <category
    name="Project"
    description="%category.project.description"
    id="org.eclipse.ui.category.project">
  </category>
```

PART II

```
// ...lines omitted...
<command
  name="Go to Resource"
  description="%command.goToResource.description"
  categoryId="org.eclipse.ui.category.navigate"
  id="org.eclipse.ui.navigate.goToResource">
</command>
// ...lines omitted...
<keyBinding
  commandId="org.eclipse.ui.navigate.openResource"
  keySequence="Ctrl+Shift+R"
  keyConfigurationId=
      "org.eclipse.ui.defaultAcceleratorConfiguration">
</keyBinding>
// ...lines omitted...
</extension>
```

In this example, the extension point provider has enough information with static data alone. Although configuration data-only extension points are not the majority, there are a few of them in Eclipse, most notable among them being those associated with help, which you'll learn about in Chapter 22, and capabilities, which is covered in Chapter 30. You may be familiar with these extension points, their usage, and tag attributes, but if not, don't worry. The interest in this chapter doesn't lie in the details of a particular extension point, but instead in their general characteristics as a way of better understanding how you might design your own. That being understood, here is a sample list of data-only extension points.

- org.eclipse.ui.commmands
- org.eclipse.ui.editors (when the command attribute is specified instead of class or launcher)
- org.eclipse.ui.ide.markerHelp
- org.eclipse.ui.ide.projectNatureImages

Sometimes these two categories of extension points are combined:

```
<extension point="org.eclipse.core.resources.builders"
    id="mybuilder"
    name="My Builder">
  <builder hasNature="false">
    <run class="com.ibm.jdg2e.example.MyBuilder">
      <parameter name="compatibilityMode" value="true"/>
    </run>
  </builder>
</extension>
```

Here the extension point provider requires executable code and allows for optional configuration data that will be passed to the instance of the class specified in the <run> tag after its instantiation. Ultimately, it is your decision what can or must be specified by consumers of your extension point. The discussion above is only to give you an idea of how your extension points might be architected. Eclipse itself doesn't impose any particular style, although it does encourage extension point definitions that defer plug-in loading. We'll return to this point again before ending this chapter.

As you've seen, extension points can be used to configure a plug-in, but you might also consider whether another technique might better serve your needs, such as using configuration files, preferences, or command line parameters. Extension points are perhaps the best solution in those cases where runtime classes are required to provide specific behaviors that complete the plug-in's functionality, and you anticipate multiple consumers of your extension point. If you only expect one consumer of your extension point, it might be a candidate for a preferences or INI file configuration.

Again, the best model you may find for how to design your extension points is probably the Eclipse Platform itself.

### Declaring the Existence of the Extension Point

The next step is declaring an extension point. It is quite easy—there are just three parameters for the `<extension-point>` tag, of which only two are required.

```
<extension-point
  id="toolAction"
  name="JDG2E: Tool actions"
  schema="schema/toolAction.exsd"/>
```

There are no child tags. The `<extension-point>` element has the following attributes.

- `id` is a simple id token, unique within this plug-in. The token cannot contain a period or whitespace.
- `name` is the user-displayable (translatable) name for the extension point.
- `schema` is the schema specification for this extension point.

The functions of the `id` and `name` attributes are obvious. The `schema` attribute references a schema definition file that the PDE will use to help developers who wish to create a new extension of an extension point. With an extension schema definition, the PDE can ensure that the developer correctly specifies the new extension by only prompting for appropriate tag attribute values and valid child tags. The `schema` attribute names a file relative to the plug-in installation location named *your_extension_point_id*.exsd.

While an extension schema is used at development time to help guide the developer, it is not used at runtime. You defined the extension point, and therefore your plug-in's extension processing code must validate the tags at runtime.

Note that when another plug-in contributes to your extension point, the contributing plug-in refers to the extension point by your plug-in id (italics below) + extension point id (underlined below).

```
<extension point="com.ibm.jdg2e.extensionpoint.toolAction">
  <tool
    label="JDG2E: New Command 1"
    action=
      "com.ibm.jdg2e.extensionpoint.test.        //(one line)
      ContributedTestToolAction">
  </tool>
</extension>
```

Here you see that the consumer of the toolAction extension point specifies the defining plug-in id, com.ibm.jdg2e.extensionpoint, plus the extension point id, toolAction, separated by a period.

## Defining an Interface for Expected Behavior

As mentioned in the first step, there are cases where an extension point only passes configuration information to a plug-in. That is, it does not specify any attributes referencing classes to instantiate at runtime. More likely, you'll find that an extension point needs the help of executable code to complete its task. Let's consider as an example a tag that you are very familiar with at this point, <action>, used for defining menu choices in an action set.

```
<extension point="org.eclipse.ui.actionSets">
  <actionSet
      label="JDG2E: JDT Actions"
      visible="false"
      id="com.ibm.jdg2e.jdt.actionSet">
    <menu
        id="com.ibm.jdg2e"
        label="JDG2E">
      <separator
        name="jdt">
      </separator>
    </menu>
    <action
      label="Run Hello JDT AST"
      class="com.ibm.jdg2e.jdt.HelloASTAction"
      tooltip="JDG2E: Execute the Hello AST example"
      menubarPath="com.ibm.jdg2e/jdt"
      id="com.ibm.jdg2e.jdt.runHelloAST">
    </action>
  </actionSet>
</extension>
```

Here you see that the `<action>` tag has static attributes for those initial values that are needed to render the desired menu choice (`label`, `tooltip`, and `menubarPath`). The executable code that actually handles the user action, `HelloASTAction`, isn't loaded until the user chooses the menu choice.

In fact, this explains the origins of the interface's name that the executable code identified by the `class` attribute must implement in this case: `IWorkbenchWindowActionDelegate`. As the name suggests, the Workbench initially creates an instance of `ActionContributionItem` to represent the `<action>` menu choice, and then instantiates and delegates to the target action, an implementer of `IWorkbenchWindowActionDelegate`, once the user actually makes the selection.

This deferred reference to the target action is an example of how the plug-in architecture enables a faster Workbench startup, since the Workbench only loads code when needed. This is accomplished by defining only a few APIs that are capable of loading (activating) a plug-in. The majority of the other APIs referencing plug-in attributes do so only indirectly via a registry, not references to plug-in instances themselves.

This leads us to an important consideration when creating extension points: They should be defined, to the extent possible, such that the processing of the extension point definition itself is deferred until needed. The same is true for any class(es) specified as tag attributes. The `<action>` tag accomplishes these goals using the following two techniques.

- Including necessary static information in the extension data such that the user interface can be presented without loading the plug-in containing the action.
- Providing a proxy menu choice that instantiates and delegates to the target action—when and if the proxy menu choice is selected.

Returning to our example, note that the class specified in the `class` attribute must implement the interface expected by the extension point definition, `IWorkbenchWindowActionDelegate`. The interface is specified as part of the extension point schema definition (`actionSets.exsd` file), so the developer has a clear specification of the expected implementation. Given a class implementing the desired interface, the extension point implementer can instantiate an instance and interact with it using the previously agreed-upon methods, such as `selectionChanged` and `run`.

Thus, the interface is the contract between the creator and the contributor to an extension point. The extension point creator may also choose to create an abstract class from which others can extend. Obviously, the extension point documentation must define the semantics of the interface, that is, in what context it will be invoked, what the expected interaction sequence is, and so on.

Before moving on, you should note the relationship between the interface that you define for others to implement and the <export> tag in your plugin .xml file. Those interfaces that you expect developers to use as part of their extensions to your new extension point must be exported. For example, you have seen that HelloASTAction specified in the <action class="..."> tag must implement the IWorkbenchWindowActionDelegate interface. For the extender of the <action> tag to "see" this interface, it must be exported *from* the plug-in defining the extension point using the <library>/<export> tags and imported *into* the plug-in extending the extension point using the <import> tag. Here is an extract of the Workbench plugin.xml file that exports the IWorkbenchWindowActionDelegate class from the workbench.jar file so it is visible to plug-ins that import this plug-in.

```
<plugin id="org.eclipse.ui.workbench" ...>
  <runtime>
   // ...lines omitted...
    <library name="workbench.jar">
       <export name="*"/>
    </library>
  </runtime>

  <requires>
    <import plugin="org.eclipse.core.runtime"/>
    <import plugin="org.eclipse.help"/>
    <import plugin="org.eclipse.jface"/>
    <import plugin="org.eclipse.swt"/>
    <import plugin="org.eclipse.core.expressions"/>
   </requires>
  // ...lines omitted...
</plugin>
```

This tells the plug-in class loader which portions of a plug-in's JAR file are available to other plug-ins. As shown above, some plug-in developers specify <export name="*">, meaning all public classes. However, if you prefer to be more prudent, you can limit the classes available outside your plug-in to only those that are necessary to implement an extension of your extension point. So instead of specifying "*" (all), specify a specific package or class name(s) as name attributes using the same syntax as is allowed for the Java import statement.

To restate this another way, the standard class loader assumes that if the public keyword is specified on a class or method, it is available to anyone. However, there are cases where "public" doesn't necessarily mean "API." To use C++ terminology, they could be "friend" classes or methods. The plug-in class loader uses the <export> tag to offer a finer grain of visibility control. Listing classes, interfaces, or packages in the export tag's name attribute allows others access to your public classes and methods, while omitting them will deny access to those outside your plug-in.

You can choose to hide public but non-API code with the <export> tag. However, be aware that there is no way to create "private" extension points for intra-tool use; once you have defined a new extension point and its required public interface classes, the platform makes no distinction between an extension from your plug-in or any other.

## Processing the Registry Entries for Your Extension Points

As an extension point creator, you are responsible for dealing with everyone who extends it once your plug-in is loaded. All the information specified by those plug-ins that declared an extension to your plug-in's extension point, including all their attributes and child tags, is stored in the extensions registry. Figure 11.2 shows the Plug-in Registry view annotated with the names of the interfaces that are responsible for providing the displayed data, most of which correspond to tags from the plug-in manifest.

Your plug-in extension code will probably only deal with the Platform class and the IExtensionsRegistry, IExtension, IExtensionPoint, and IConfigurationElement interfaces. However, it helps to be aware of with what they are associated and where they are displayed when you need to debug them.

The first choice is to decide when to read the extensions registry and process those entries that apply to the extension points defined in your plug-in. This processing is largely mechanical because there are only minor variations from one plug-in's implementation to another. It is, nonetheless, a noteworthy step, since your implementation decisions can affect the overall performance of Eclipse, especially the startup time.

Some plug-ins process all their extension point entries when their plug-in class is loaded by overriding the start method. However, we highly recommend that plug-ins wait until they actually need the extension point entries and only process those specifically required by the code at that moment. If you recall from Exercise 6, the "Hello, World" sample action wasn't loaded until the menu choice was actually selected; this is an example of the Workbench deferring the instantiation of the target action until needed and therefore delaying the loading of the target action's plug-in.

The basic structure of the extension point processing code will look similar to the following, where the elements in *italics* are changed to your extension-specific values.

```
IExtensionRegistry er = Platform.getExtensionRegistry();
IExtensionPoint ep = er.getExtensionPoint
        (myPluginId, myExtensionPointId);
IExtension[] extensions = ep.getExtensions();
List myProxies = new ArrayList();
for (int i = 0; i < extensions.length; i++) {
  IConfigurationElement[] ces =
      extensions[i].getConfigurationElements();
  for (int j = 0; j < ces.length; j++)
    myProxies.add(new MyExtensionPointProxyAction(ces[j]));
}
```

The example continues with the skeletal version of the proxy that will represent the class specified in the extension until its creation in response to some triggering event (e.g., in this case, by calling run to handle the user selection).

```
public class MyExtensionPointProxyAction {
    implements IMyExtensionPointAction {
  IConfigurationElement ce;
  IMyExtensionPointAction action;
  public MyExtensionPointProxyAction(IConfigurationElement ce) {
    this.ce = ce;
    // Initialize other fields from
    // the configuration element attributes (not shown)
  }
  public void run() {
    if (action == null)
      action = (IMyExtensionPointAction)
          ce.createExecutableExtension("class");
    action.run();
  }
}
```

This code reads and processes all plug-ins that contribute to your extension point, as defined by your plug-in id and extension point name. Don't bother studying this too closely now; you'll see similar code in an example associated with this chapter.

### Invoking the Appropriate Methods Per the Previously Defined Interface Contract

Returning to the sample code, the sample proxy class, MyExtensionPoint-ProxyAction, merits extra attention. This is where the connection between the contributor's code defining an extension's runtime capabilities and the extension point processor is made. That is, this is where the extension point proces-

sor code of the Workbench plug-in instantiates the class specified in the
`<action>` tag, and then invokes the appropriate methods when it is time to perform the required operation. This comes back to the question that was implied
in the first step: Will your new extension point be principally for configuring
your plug-in, or will it require code written by those who extend your extension point? The example's `IMyExtensionPointAction` interface addresses this
question by defining a class that will be instantiated based on the value of the
tag attribute, `class`. The attribute value must specify a fully qualified class
name, for example, `com.ibm.jdg2e.example.MyExtensionPointAction`.

As mentioned earlier in this chapter, the Workbench code that processes
pop-up menu contributions to the `org.eclipse.ui.popupMenus` extension
point was responsible for creating an instance of the class specified in the
`<action>` tag. It said nothing about how that class was instantiated. Now we
are ready to fill in the details.

To create an instance of the class specified in a particular plug-in's extension, a plug-in's processing code will invoke the `createExecutableExtension`
method defined in the `IConfigurationElement` interface. Why couldn't it simply call the constructor of the class specified in the `class` attribute? Remember that the contributor to your extension point generally isn't specified in
the same plug-in that defined the extension point, nor is it necessarily listed
among the `<requires>` clauses of that plug-in's manifest. In other words, the
contributor's class libraries are not visible to the plug-in defining the extension point. The `createExecutableExtension` method solves this problem by
calling the contributor's plug-in class loader to activate, if necessary, the
plug-in containing the target class and then creates an instance using its zero-
argument constructor.

This is where, for example, a method like `IObjectAction.run()` would
be invoked per the interface contract. This is the grand finale of this chapter:
the explanation of how an extension point, in effect, loads and then invokes
its extenders.

The `createExecutableExtension` method does more than activate plug-
ins and create instances. It will also check if the target class implements
`IExecutableExtension`. If so, its `setInitializationData` method will be
invoked, passing the current configuration element and name of the tag
attribute. In other words, implementers of the `IExecutableExtension` interface can process arguments from their XML specification after their instantiation. This technique is also a way of simplifying your tag processing code.
Instead of writing centralized extension processor code to handle *all* possible
tags, child tags, and their attributes, it may choose to handle only the processing of the top-level tags, expecting that one of the required attributes of

the top-level tag will implement IExecutableExtension and process the remaining attributes and child tags.

Your extension processing does not have to worry about parsing XML. The Platform Runtime parses the plug-in manifest files to build the extension registry. Nevertheless, don't forget that the content of the registry is derived from *syntactically* correct XML in the plugin.xml files, but not necessarily *semantically* correct XML. Your processing code must validate the attributes and child tags. If you find any anomalies, at a minimum you should log them in the plug-in log as described in Chapter 28, Serviceability.

## Handling Dynamic Plug-ins

Prior to version 3.0, all extensions from all defined plug-ins were read at startup and never changed thereafter. Now that Eclipse supports dynamic plug-ins, those declaring extension points need to handle this case using extension registry change listeners. These listeners are notified when extensions or extension points are removed or added, for example, when the Update Manager installs a new feature, as shown in Figure 11.3.

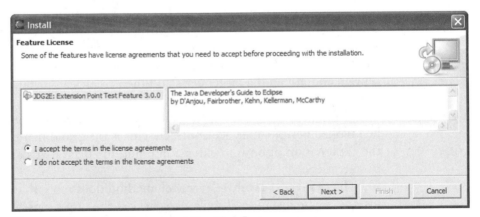

**Figure 11.3**   Update Manager Installs a New Feature

In this case, the extension registry will be updated with new extensions and extension points defined by the plug-ins that the newly installed feature references. For example, one listener is the Workbench UI plug-in, and it responds by updating the extension points it defines related to contributed menus, action sets, views, and editors.

Your own code should respond similarly for the extension points that you define. The following is a code extract that registers for these changes:

```
Platform.getExtensionRegistry().addRegistryChangeListener(
    new IRegistryChangeListener() {
        public void registryChanged(IRegistryChangeEvent event) {
            // Respond to the removal or
            // addition of extensions and/or extension points
        }
    });
```

If your class defines extension points, you should look to see if there are changes to the list of extensions that your class processed earlier. A simple way of handling this case is to clear all the references to your earlier extensions and reprocess them as if it were the first time. If that is too costly, your code can examine the `IRegistryChangeEvent` parameter to retrieve which `IExtension` and `IExtensionPoint` entries were added or removed and update your local cache appropriately. Be aware that this notification is from a non-UI thread; if your code needs to update a control in the Workbench window, use the `Display.syncExec` or `Display.asyncExec` method to run your code on the UI thread to avoid the SWT exception "Invalid thread access."

Registering as an extension registry listener will make your class aware of plug-ins that are added or removed dynamically, but you should also handle the case where your own plug-in is unloaded by overriding the `Plugin.shutdown` method and removing whatever references your extension point processing may have created.

## How to Enable the Schema-Based New Extension Wizard

The Plug-in Manifest Editor of the PDE includes an **Extension** page where you can add extensions to existing extension points. Selecting **Add...** from this page displays the New Extension wizard (shown earlier in Figure 9.1 and used in Exercise 6).

The New Extension wizard includes a choice for invoking a generic wizard for adding extensions based on their extension point schema definition (the *your_extension_point_id*.exsd files located in the plug-in's directory). The PDE also includes an editor for creating and modifying such a schema. This helps the developer wishing to contribute to your extension point avoid creating invalid XML by following the wizard's prompts for attributes, pop-up menus for appropriate child tags, and so on.

The Schema editor can optionally generate documentation in the plug-in's doc subdirectory for the extension point. It includes the Document Type

Definitions (DTD) in documentation format, element and attribute definitions, usage, and examples.

### Why Define a Schema?

Extensions cannot be arbitrarily created. They are declared using a clear specification defined by an extension point, but until now we haven't discussed how to create a specification capable of validating that extensions will conform to the extension point's expectations.

Whether specified programmatically via a schema or implicitly via reference documentation, each extension point defines attributes and expected values that must be declared by an extension. In the most rudimentary form, an extension point declaration is very simple. It defines the id and name of the extension point.

Reference documentation is useful, but it does not enable any programmatic help for validating the specification of an extension. For this reason, the PDE introduces an extension point schema that describes extension points in a format appropriate for automated processing, in addition to a specialized editor. The new schemas have the same name as the extension point id with an .exsd file extension. By default, the PDE will generate them in the schema subdirectory of your plug-in's directory.

When a new extension point is created in the PDE, the initial schema file will also be created and the schema editor will be opened for editing. The PDE schema editor is conceptually the same as the Plug-in Manifest Editor. It has two form pages and one source page. Since the XML schema is verbose and can be hard to read in its source form, it is especially helpful for most editing. The source page, which has the same name as the file itself, is useful for reading the resulting XML tags.

### Schema Editor

Figure 11.4 shows the **Definition** page of the extension point schema editor. The list on the left includes all the elements defined by the DTD. You should start there when creating a new extension point. The tree list on the right is where you define the relationships between the elements on the left. Obviously, you must define those elements before you can define their relationships.

Note that it helps to be familiar with DTD terminology (sequence, group, etc.) to understand the **Element Grammar** tree list on the right.

PART II

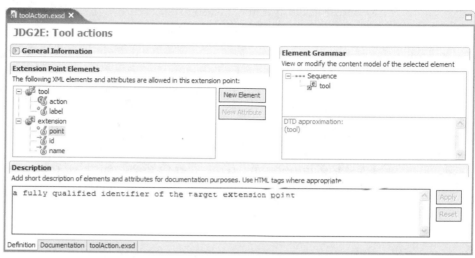

**Figure 11.4** Extension Point Schema Editor—Definition Page

See the Resources section of http://www.xml.org for XML basics, FAQs, and articles.

## Example Summary

The example for this chapter, defined in project `com.ibm.jdg2e`
`.extensionpoint` on the CD-ROM, implements a menu choice similar
to **Run > External Tools** in the Workbench by defining a new extension
point, `com.ibm.jdg2e.extensionpoint.toolAction`. That is, it adds a general toolbar pull-down to gather common tool commands, whether they
are to invoke external tools or internal commands. The "tool actions"
plug-in responds to notifications about a newly activated plug-in by updating its list of available actions, if necessary. A second plug-in, defined in
project `com.ibm.jdg2e.extensionpoint.test`, demonstrates how to use the
newly defined extension point. These two plug-ins provide a model of
defining your own extension points and then contributing to them.

## Chapter Summary

Extension points and their extensions are the glue that holds Eclipse together,
and they represent the bulk of the content of the plug-ins manifest file, which

defines the Eclipse integration architecture. When defining your own extension points, keep the following in mind.

- Top-level tags define integration points, while executable attributes implement specific behavior.
- Design your extension points in such a way as to facilitate late binding of code.
- Respond to changes in the extension registry to address dynamically loaded plug-ins.

Most importantly, remember to document how others can extend your product!

## References

Arthorne, John, and Chris Laffra. 2004. *Official Eclipse 3.0 FAQs*. Boston, MA: Addison-Wesley. http://www.eclipsefaq.org. (See FAQs 88, 100, 114, 117.)

Object Technology International, Inc. March 2003. Eclipse platform technical overview. http://www.eclipse.org.

XML Basics page in the Resources section of http://www.xml.org.

# CHAPTER 12

## *Advanced Plug-in Development*

The previous chapters in Part II laid the groundwork for this "advanced" discussion. This chapter introduces a collection of general topics that will give you a deeper insight into the plug-in architecture and plug-in development.

## Migrating Your Plug-ins from Eclipse 2.1

The *Platform Plug-in Developer Guide* in the Eclipse SDK's online help includes a migration guide. However, you may find the following hints that we used while migrating our own code from version 2.1 useful.

- Begin by migrating the `plugin.xml` file using the **PDE Tools > Migrate to 3.0...** choice. This will map extension point identifiers that have changed and adjust your plug-in's `import` statements.
- The PDE migration choice will insert an import statement for the version 2.1 compatibility plug-in, `<import plugin= "org.eclipse.core .runtime.compatibility"/>`. This plug-in includes APIs that have been deprecated in the Platform Runtime, such as `IPluginDescriptor`, so version 3.0 would be binary compatible with plug-ins written to the 2.1 APIs.

The rest of the hints assume that you prefer to eliminate your plug-in's reliance on the compatibility plug-in.

- Begin by removing this import statement. Verify that the `<import plugin= "org.eclipse.core.runtime"/>` is specified (it was implicit in the previous version).

- If your plug-in defines a plug-in class, remove the parameter IPluginDescriptor from its constructor (i.e., the new runtime uses a zero-parameter constructor).

- Change the plug-in class startup method to start(BundleContext) and shutdown to stop(BundleContext). Change these methods' throws CoreException clause to throws Exception. Remember to call super *after* your processing.

- The org.eclipse.ui.startup extension point now includes a child tag <startup>, which expects an implementer of IEarlyStartup in its class attribute. Do not specify your plug-in class for this attribute (otherwise the Workbench UI plug-in will attempt to create an instance using its zero-parameter constructor, which is not allowed since only the Platform Runtime can instantiate plug-ins/bundles). If the <startup> child tag is omitted, the plug-in's earlyStartup method will be called.

- Change references to YourPlugin.getDefault().getDescriptor .getIndentifier() to YourPlugin.getBundle().getSymbolicName(). Note that if your plug-in has no need for a plug-in class, you can retrieve the plug-in's bundle with Platform.getBundle("*plugin-id*").

- (Optional) If your plug-in calls ImageDescriptor.createFromURL, you may want to change it to use the new method defined in your super-class, AbstractUIPlugin.imageDescriptorFromPlugin. Be aware, however, that the latter method returns null instead of a red image if the image isn't found.

- There are two interfaces named IPlatformRunnable, one in the org.eclipse.core.boot plug-in and the other in org.eclipse.core .runtime. The latter is the newer interface. If you have references to IPlatformRunnable, verify that the import statement specifies org.eclipse.core.<u>runtime</u>.IPlatformRunnable.

- The IPluginRegistry interface is deprecated. Change references to Platform.getPluginRegistry to Platform.getExtensionRegistry. All other extension-related APIs are unchanged. References to IPluginDescriptor will have to be treated separately (see the Javadoc for deprecation instructions).

- The migration tool tends to overestimate the required plug-ins. Open your plugin.xml file and turn to the **Dependencies** page of the Manifest Editor, and then select the **Find unused dependencies** choice. It will scan your code and prompt you with a list of plug-in imports that can be removed.

- In general, the Javadoc associated with the deprecation warnings instructs you how to correct or avoid using the deprecated API.

These are only the most general steps. For the definitive word on migrating, see the online *Migration Guide*.

## Plug-in Class Loader

The Eclipse runtime defines its own Java class loader, called `PluginClass-Loader`. It uses the `<requires>` and `<runtime>` clauses to simplify classpath management. The `<runtime>` clause defines the JAR files or paths that compose the target plug-in executable code and resource locations. The `<requires>` clause defines the other plug-ins that are necessary to load the target plug-in. Note that the `<requires>` clause defines dependencies by plug-in id and not JAR files. One benefit of this approach is that you are free to deliver your code as a single JAR file in one release, then later decide to split it into several JAR files in a subsequent release, without the risk of breaking dependent plug-ins. You can also choose to export only a portion of your runtime code, using multiple JARs or specific export definitions in the `<runtime>` clause to control the access other plug-ins have to your code. This is possible because the dependency is expressed in terms of the plug-in identifier and not the specific JAR file(s).

Typically, a plug-in contributes extensions implemented by classes in its JAR file. However, it is reasonable for a plug-in to contribute only a JAR file containing common classes that other plug-ins will depend on. By listing such a plug-in in their `<requires>` clause, Eclipse will ensure that its library is present before loading the dependent plug-in, thereby avoiding a potential "class not found" runtime error and also simplifying the sharing of a common JAR file.

## Runtime Discovery and Delayed Loading

One of the key design points of the plug-in architecture is to enable dynamic discovery of functional extensions to Eclipse. This allows many tools and applications to integrate seamlessly into a single environment. But what about the cost of loading all these extensions?

Indeed, that was a concern of the Eclipse architects. Other products in the past that allowed unlimited executable extensions suffered from slow

PART II

startup times. To avoid this cost while retaining flexibility, the extensions defined in the manifest files include enough information in a static nonexecutable form to postpone loading code. For example, you will see that user interface extension points require enough information to render the initial user interface element (e.g., the icon and tooltip text of a contributed toolbar button) so the platform can defer loading the plug-in code until the user actually chooses a menu option, selects a toolbar button, opens a preferences page, or starts a creation wizard. The initial cost of a plug-in is only the parsing of its manifest.

There are, however, means by which this benefit could be unwittingly defeated. Eclipse stores a list of all the open projects, perspectives, views, and editors when Eclipse closes so they can be restored during the next startup. Closing a project recovers memory and helps performance, since closing a project automatically closes all editors and views associated with its resources, and closed projects are not included in searches, builds, and so on. If the user has many plug-ins activated because of open views and editors, the next startup will be slower if all the associated plug-ins must be loaded to render the user interface. Recognizing this common and potentially costly occurrence, the Workbench addresses the problem by rendering the topmost editor or view in a given tabbed notebook while only restoring the others as references. The plug-ins associated with the others are loaded as the user turns to the particular notebook tab.

Plug-ins can also be used to separate clearly delineated functionality. For example, the JDT plug-ins separate the development and debug environments, so the user doesn't pay the startup time for loading the debug environment until it is actually needed. Inadvertently combining the model and user interface code into a single plug-in will limit the reusability of the model code in a non-UI environment, and increase the minimum footprint in which it can be deployed. Keeping them separate will also simplify the development of the model project code by disallowing references to UI code.

You might be wondering: If a user interface extension in the manifest file has enough parameters (tag attributes) to render the initial user interface, then when is the plug-in code actually loaded and for what reason? Invariably, an extension point defines among its attributes at least one class that handles the user's request. This class will be instantiated when the plug-in is activated; plug-in activation occurs because one of the plug-in's extensions is being processed. As you'll see in Chapter 32, Performance Tuning, detecting unnecessary early extension point processing is an important first step to improving application startup time.

## Forcing Early Plug-in Activation

The Eclipse architecture helps ensure that plug-ins are only loaded (activated) when needed. However, the extension point `org.eclipse.ui.startup` forces the Workbench to activate a plug-in as soon as the Workbench window opens. It is as simple as adding an extension to your plug-in manifest file and implementing the `IStartup` interface in a class in your plug-in. This example is from the Performance Monitor, which you'll learn about in Chapter 32.

```
<extension point="org.eclipse.ui.startup">
  <startup
      class="org.eclipse.perfmsr.ui.EarlyStartup"/>
</extension>
```

The Performance Monitor defines this extension because it needs to capture startup performance metrics. It defines the class `EarlyStartup`, which in turn calls the plug-in class instance to do the actual work.

```
public class EarlyStartup implements IStartup
  public void earlyStartup() {
    PerfMsrUIPlugin.getDefault().captureStartupInfo();
  }
}
```

---

**NOTE**   Do not specify your plug-in class for this attribute. Otherwise, the Workbench UI plug-in will attempt to create an instance using its zero-parameter constructor, which is not allowed since only the Platform Runtime can instantiate plug-ins or bundles.

---

There are legitimate uses of the `org.eclipse.ui.startup` extension point; for example, when your plug-in's contributed actions must perform runtime tests that cannot be expressed statically as XML, even using action filters. However, remember that this extension point circumvents the deferred loading strategy and therefore should be used only when truly necessary. To put this more bluntly, if everyone uses the `org.eclipse.ui.startup` extension point, Eclipse's fast-start architecture will be defeated.

The user can disable any extensions of `org.eclipse.ui.startup` using the **Preferences > Workbench > Startup** page. This option gives the user control over those plug-ins that they want to be loaded at startup time. If your plug-in uses this extension point, add to the previously mentioned caveats the possibility that your request may not be honored if the user deselects your plug-in's startup extension; you should code your plug-in accordingly

PART II

(e.g., by including lazy initialization). That is, don't assume that your plug-in is loaded at startup and the earlyStartup method of the startup class is called simply because it contributed to this extension point.

## Plug-in Granularity

Plug-ins are intended to be reusable, extensible units of code. Using the existing Eclipse plug-ins as a guide, you'll find that they typically represent a fully functional component, often from the end user's perspective. A plug-in invariably spans several Java packages. Components that have a user interface are typically divided into two plug-ins at a minimum, which separate the model and its user interface.

Plug-ins should be defined within the context of a specific set of tools, rather than defining a plug-in for each JAR file for reuse purposes. Plug-ins should not reflect development organizations; for example, don't define one plug-in per development team, but rather how they will be installed as features and used at runtime.

## Plug-in Fragments

A **plug-in fragment** is used to provide additional functionality to an existing plug-in after it has been installed. When the platform finds a fragment and its target plug-in during startup, the fragment's extension and extension point declarations are merged with the target plug-in. That is, it is as if the fragment's manifest file was concatenated to the target plug-in's manifest file. If you display the Plug-in Registry view, you will see the contributions made by a fragment as if they were defined by the original plug-in.

You can think of a fragment as a "reduced functionality" plug-in. In practical terms, there is only one difference between a plug-in manifest (plugin.xml) and a fragment manifest (fragment.xml): The latter inherits the declared dependencies of its target plug-in; that is, it cannot declare additional dependencies via the <imports> tag. The fragment declares its target plug-in with the plugin-id and plugin-version attributes of its <fragment> tag.

```
<?xml version="1.0" encoding="UTF-8"?>
<?eclipse version="3.0"?>
<fragment
    id="org.eclipse.core.resources.win32"
    name="Core Resource Management Win32 Fragment"
    version="3.0"
    provider-name="Eclipse.org"
```

```
        plugin-id="org.eclipse.core.resources"
        plugin-version="3.0">

    <runtime>
      <library name="resources-win32.jar">
        <export name="*"/>
      </library>
    </runtime>
    //...lines omitted...
  </fragment>
```

Fragments are stored in subdirectories within the plugins directory. The same class loader as the base plug-in loads them, so they have full visibility to the base plug-in classes. In the example above, the JAR file resources-win32.jar is added to the target plug-in's class loader path. The fragment could also declare additional extensions or extension points.

## Fragments as Language Packs

Plug-in fragments are used to distribute Eclipse-translated information including HTML, XML, properties, and GIF files. The Eclipse translations are packaged in fragment JAR files and are added to existing Eclipse installations without changing or modifying any of the original runtime elements. This leads to the notion of a "language pack."

Eclipse merges plug-in fragments in a way that the runtime elements in the fragment augment the original targeted plug-in. The target plug-in is not removed or modified in any way. Since the fragment's resources are located by the class loader, the plug-in developer doesn't need to know whether resources are loaded from the plug-in's subdirectory or one of its fragments' subdirectories. Chapter 31, Internationalization and Accessibility, covers this usage in detail.

## Fragments as Platform-Specific Content

Some plug-ins have operating system-specific contents, for example, the Standard Widget Toolkit plug-in and the Core Resources Management (i.e., workspace) plug-in, as was shown in the previous fragment manifest excerpt. The SWT base plug-in provides the platform-independent code, and then it is "completed" by a platform-specific fragment, for example org.eclipse.swt.win32 on the Windows platform and org.eclipse.swt.linux on the Linux platform.

Note that fragments are not the sole means of defining platform-specific content. Eclipse defines a number of substitution variables that can be referenced in the name attribute of the `<library>` tag. Again, the SWT uses this technique to declare its platform-specific library, as shown in this extract of its `plugin.xml` file.

```
<plugin id="org.eclipse.swt" ... >
  <runtime>
    <library name="$ws$/swt.jar">
      <export name="*"/>
    </library>
  </runtime>
</plugin>
```

The `$ws$` variable is substituted with the appropriate window system platform designation (win32, gtk, carbon, etc.) using the `Platform.getWS` API. These replacement variables used in library names can be displayed or changed for test purposes on the **Window > Preferences > Plug-in Development > Target Environment** page.

## Chapter Summary

This chapter introduced a few advanced topics that you should be aware of to make better plug-in design decisions. Having reached this point in Part II, you should be well-positioned to branch out in independent study that aligns with your personal interests; if you haven't read it already, The Guide to Reading This Book suggests pathways you might consider.

## References

Arthorne, John, and Chris Laffra. 2004. *Official Eclipse 3.0 FAQs*. Boston, MA: Addison-Wesley. http://www.eclipsefaq.org. (See FAQs 71, 80, 104, 107, 114.)

Azad Bolour. July 2003. Notes on the Eclipse Plug-in Architecture. http://www.eclipse.org.

# CHAPTER 13

## *Defining Features and Products*

This chapter discusses the definition of features and products, which are instrumental in the delivery, packaging, and branding of the plug-ins you wish to add to the Eclipse Platform.

Features are the management unit for plug-ins. They can be used to define structure and installation prerequisites and to optionally identify update sites for delivery of service. Features can also be used to help drive the PDE build and packaging process.

A runtime product is defined in Eclipse to contribute product branding and identify the application that should be started. This is a required step if you want to create your own branded identity as part of adding your features to Eclipse.

---

**NOTE** Many of the concepts in this chapter require that you understand the role and capabilities provided by the Update Manager. To prepare, you might want to read the appropriate sections of Chapter 6, Managing Your Eclipse Environment.

---

## Features

The feature definition as a way of providing support for developed plug-ins was introduced in Chapter 9, Getting Started: Plug-in Development. Now it is time to get into the details. The role of features in Eclipse, including how they support configuration management, feature branding, installation, and delivery of service, are covered in this chapter. This knowledge will help you define features that support the use of your plug-ins in an Eclipse environment.

## Feature Concepts

Feature definitions provide support for plug-in management. Plug-ins can be directly added to Eclipse, but plug-ins that are not referenced by a feature cannot be managed by the Update Manager. The Update Manager is part of the Workbench and can interact with features and through the feature their referenced plug-ins.

Features can also be branded. This allows you to identify the source of features in the Workbench About [product] dialogs (where [product] is the name of the active product). You should add appropriate branding content to your feature definitions to provide end user awareness of your function.

The Update Manager controls the configuration of an Eclipse-based product and the delivery of both new features and service to existing features. You can use the Update Manager user interface or command API to add function to an existing Eclipse installation and delivery service to its installed features.

### Creating Structure with Features

Features identify prerequisites, support the organization and management of plug-ins, and can include other features to provide structure (see Figure 13.1).

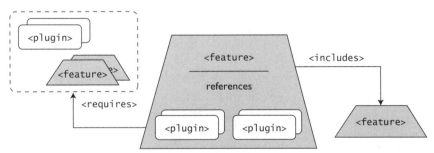

**Figure 13.1**   Feature Content, Prerequisites, and Structure

Feature types are an indication of their position in a nested feature hierarchy. A feature can be a **root feature** or an **included feature**. Root features are those that are not included by another feature. You can choose to have just one root feature, one root feature that includes other features, or multiple root features. The available Update Manager processing options can vary by feature type. The decision to define a feature structure or tree is based on two objectives.

1. To ensure the features are installed and configured as a set
2. To control how service is delivered for any included features

Features should package related sets of plug-ins. If only one feature is used, and this feature includes a large number of plug-ins, this can create an environment that might be harder to manage. A more granular approach provides flexibility for the delivery of service and reuse of the function provided by a feature in other configurations. Some of this flexibility is also for the user, who could disable a feature or two and leave others active, allowing the user to control the availability of feature function at runtime.

You have the flexibility to create almost any structure you want. Choose the simplest organization that meets your objectives. If you have a highly structured configuration, with multiple levels of included features, you may want to restrict feature branding to major nodes in your feature tree. This can simplify the user's view of your function.

## Root Features

Root features have two important properties: They can define the active update site for themselves and the features they include, and they can be enabled and disabled using the Product Configuration dialog. (Note that included features defined as optional can also be disabled and enabled using this dialog.)

Feature definitions can contain URLs for update site locations. The Update Manager uses this information to check for updates to the feature that might be available. While all features might include this update site location information, by default the Update Manager uses only the update site definition provided by root features. In other words, root features own the right to define where updates to the included features can be found. If you include other features, your feature is responsible for either providing service for the features you include or delegating that right to the included feature using the search_location attribute. The use of the Update Manager is discussed further in Servicing Your Features later in this chapter.

## Included Features

When a feature is included, this means two things: It is disabled if its parent is disabled, and by default its service updates are obtained from the update site identified by the root feature under which it exists. An included feature can also be directly disabled and enabled if it is defined as optional by the parent feature.

For example, in the Eclipse SDK, all features are included under one root, the Eclipse Project SDK 3.0.0 feature. All other features are included features; none of these are defined as optional. However, as an experiment, if you were to modify the included feature entries in the org.eclipse.sdk feature definition to add optional="true", you would be able to use the Product Configuration dialog to disable the optional features. Note that even if you define the org.eclipse.platform feature as optional, the Update Manager will not disable this feature. Any disable request that will result in an invalid configuration will not be processed.

## Feature Definition

A feature definition is easier to understand if you consider it as having three sections.

1. A base feature manifest with definitions for the feature attributes, description, and license
2. URL definitions for update and discovery sites
3. Structural entries for prerequisite definitions, included feature content, and managed plug-ins

These sections are not necessarily listed in this order in a feature.xml file, but we will look at them in this fashion as this is a more natural progression. The following sections discuss feature definition and details for defining required features and feature types. Details about choosing the right prerequisite matching rules are also provided later in Version-Matching Rules for Prerequisites. The use of update and discovery sites is discussed later in Servicing Your Features.

### Feature Manifest

A feature is defined with the same approach as a plug-in. There is a feature manifest file (feature.xml), which exists in a subdirectory in eclipse\features. The expected subdirectory naming pattern is featureID_versionID. All feature manifest files begin with a set of attributes defined as part of the <feature> tag.

```
<?xml version="1.0" encoding="UTF-8"?>
<feature
      id="com.example.feature"
      version="3.0.0"
      label="An Example Feature Definition"
      provider-name="IBM">
...
</feature>
```

The id and version attributes are required. The id attribute follows Java package naming conventions to avoid namespace collisions. It is the unique identifier for a feature, but it can be the same as a plug-in id.

Optional attributes, such as os, arch, ws, and nl, are available to identify the supported operating system, machine architecture, windowing system, and national-language locale, respectively. When these attributes are defined, the Update Manager's Install wizard can filter out features that do not support the current environment.

The feature manifest definition can also identify a license and description.

```
<description>descriptive text</description>
<license url="licenseURL">%license</license>
```

The URL for the license can be as simple as an HTML file in the feature's directory. If the URL identified for the license is provided, the user can open it from the About [product] Features dialog.

> **NOTE** A license definition is required if you package your feature for delivery and installation using the Update Manger. The Update Manager Install wizard has a **Feature License** page. If a license is not specified, it cannot be accepted; without a license to accept, the feature cannot be installed. Of course, your license text could simply be "no license."

Use a feature.properties file for any values in the feature.xml file that may need to be translated. The use of a key in the feature definition that will be resolved using the feature.properties file is shown in the <license> tag above.

## Structural Elements

An important role of a feature definition is the identification of prerequisites, structure, and content for a related set of function. This gives a feature structure.

- Prerequisites are identified using the <requires> tag.
- Included features are defined using <includes> tags.
- Managed plug-in content is identified using the <plugin> tag.

The following snippet from a feature.xml file contains entries for prerequisites, structure, and plug-in content.

```
<requires>
   <import feature="com.funco.core" version="1.0.0"
     match="compatible" />
   <import plugin="com.funco.foundation"/>
</requires>
```

```
<includes id="com.funco.base" version="1.0.0"/>
<includes id="com.funco.extras" version="1.0.0"
  optional="true"/>

<plugin id="com.funco.tool.ui.dialogs" version="1.0.0"/>
<plugin id="com.funco.tool.ui.views" version="1.0.0"/>
```

## Prerequisites

The `<requires>` tag syntax is identical to the syntax used in a `plugin.xml` file, but the role of the entry is different. The list of features and/or plug-ins in the feature definition `<requires>` tag is used by the Update Manager during configuration processing. If the required components are not available, the feature cannot be added or enabled as part of the current configuration. The list of required plug-ins in a plug-in definition is used to define the content available to the plug-in's class loader.

The Update Manager will not allow your feature to be installed if its required plug-ins and features are not available, but the plug-ins required by a plug-in are not checked at this stage. Later, when you actually start Eclipse, your plug-in will not be included in the runtime environment if the plug-ins required by your plug-in are not available. See the upcoming Version-Matching Rules for Prerequisites subsection for additional detail on matching options.

**NOTE** When you use the feature manifest editor and add plug-ins to the feature using the **Content** page, all plug-ins required by the newly referenced plug-in are identified as prerequisites for the feature. You will see this firsthand in Exercise 9, Deploying Your Product Using Features. There is no requirement that the `<requires>` tag defined in a feature be the union of the `<requires>` tags defined in the referenced plug-ins. This is one of the scenarios for when to identify a feature instead; you require the feature and assume that its plug-ins will be available. This simplifies the definition of the `<requires>` tag for a feature.

## Included Features

The `<includes>` tag identifies a feature by its id and version. If desired, an included feature can be defined as optional (`<includes ... optional="true"/>`). There is no error if the identified feature does not exist, but if it does exist, it will be nested as part of the parent feature. An optionally included feature can also be directly disabled or enabled by the user when using the Update Manager. This flexibility extends to the Update Manager's Install wizard; if you are attempting to add a feature that optionally includes another feature, you can choose to not install the optional feature.

## Managed Plug-ins

The `<plugin>` tag identifies a plug-in managed by the feature. Plug-ins are identified by their id and version. These values must exactly match the values in the target plug-in. Version matching is exact in that the reference can point to only one instance of a plug-in.

A single plug-in could be managed by more than one feature. The plug-in will stay in the configuration as long as at least one feature that references the plug-in is active.

## Version-Matching Rules for Prerequisites

When the version of a required feature or plug-in is specified, you have the option of defining the matching rule used to determine whether the available version is acceptable. Matching rules can be specified for import entries in the `<requires>` tag, as shown below. The possible values are `compatible`, `equivalent`, `perfect`, and `greaterOrEqual`; the default value is `compatible`.

```
<requires>
    <import plugin="q.r.s" version="2.6.1" match="perfect"/>
    <import feature="a.b.c" version="3.0.0" match="equivalent"/>
</requires>
```

Your feature can be configured only if acceptable versions of the prerequisite features and plug-ins exist. Whether the versions are acceptable is determined by the specified version, the available version, and the matching rule. The section Declaring Your Plug-in Manifest in Chapter 9, Getting Started: Plug-in Development, describes the acceptability of different versions based on the specified match value. See Table 9.2 for details.

If strict (`perfect`) version-matching rules are used, your feature may block even minor service updates. If loose (`greaterOrEqual`) or default version-matching rules are used, you may find that the versions of the plug-ins that were loaded by name do not actually support your plug-in's use of their functions.

If there is an inconsistency between the feature and one or more plug-in definitions, the Update Manager might allow the configuration of a feature update that brings in new plug-in versions when one or more of these plug-ins fail at the next startup. This would be because the plug-in's matching criteria was more restrictive than that of the feature, or the feature `<requires>` tag was not complete with respect to the referenced plug-ins. Choose your match values carefully and make sure that the feature `<requires>` tag will ensure that the requirements of your referenced plug-ins are met.

The point of defining prerequisites is to ensure your feature will work once configured. If you expect all service changes to required plug-ins to maintain a consistent API and be acceptable to your code, you can choose the match=compatible option. If you only want to accept maintenance updates but not minor version updates, choose the match=equivalent option. Your match value choice may depend on the source of the plug-ins you require; they may be from eclipse.org or from other providers. Your ability to get early copies and test API compatibility may determine whether you choose a tight (equivalent) or loose (compatible) matching strategy.

**NOTE**  In previous versions of Eclipse, the <includes> tag supported the match attribute. This identified that an included feature might have alternative versions and indicated the rule for when these versions were acceptable. Since Eclipse 3.0, a specific version of the feature must be included; the match attribute is not supported. If the feature must be serviced, which will result in a change to the version id, a feature patch is used. A feature patch can replace the existing version while still being viewed as the target of the <includes> tag in the parent feature. See Servicing Your Features later in this chapter for more detail.

You should also be aware that the feature manifest editor is flexible enough to support the definition of features that meet the needs of Eclipse 2.x and 3.0. This means that while it may allow you to use the match attribute as part of an <includes> tag, this attribute is not used in an Eclipse 3.0 environment.

## Feature Branding

All features have the option of providing their own branding content, although branding content is not required. Any feature-branding information provided is used by Eclipse to create content in the About dialogs.

Feature-branding content is defined in a plug-in associated with the feature. The branding content is defined in control files processed by Eclipse when the plug-in is known to provide branding for a specific feature.

### Feature Branding in the User Interface

There are four About dialogs: About [product], About [product] Features, Feature Plug-ins, and About [product] Plug-ins. The first three of these dialogs only display the features available in the active configuration that have feature branding. You can always use the Product Configuration dialog to see all features known to the installation.

The About [product] dialog exposes icons for each family of features in the active configuration. The family is typically defined as the provider, but individual technology layers from a single provider may be branded separately. Eclipse will attempt to display only unique feature family images in the About [product] dialog. The logic for this is based on file name and image content. You will see at least one feature image if you open the About Eclipse Platform dialog. See Product Branding in the User Interface for additional information on the product content in this dialog.

Selecting the **Feature Details** button in the About [product] dialog opens the About [product] Features dialog. Note that the feature images in the About [product] dialog are also buttons; they lead to an About [product] Features dialog that includes only the matching feature content. The About [product] Features dialog contains the following information:

- A list of the branded features that are active in the current configuration
- Feature-branding content (image and text) for the selected feature

The image and text feature-branding content is provided by the plug-in. The image shown is the same image seen in the About [product] dialog.

### Providing Branding Content for a Feature in a Plug-in

By default, feature-branding information is contained in a plug-in that has the same id as its feature. The `plugin="id.of.branding.plugin"` attribute in the `<feature>` tag can be used to identify an alternative branding plug-in. A branding plug-in contains additional files that identify the branding content for the feature. This plug-in could also be contributing other function as part of the feature. Individual plug-ins can also provide a short description in an `about.html` file. This file can be opened from the About [product] Plug-ins dialog. All of these files are described in Table 13.1.

**Table 13.1**   Plug-in Files Included to Provide Branding Content

| File | Location | Description |
| --- | --- | --- |
| `about.html` | Any plug-in directory | Plug-in information that can be displayed by user. Displayed using the **More Info** button on the About [product] Plug-ins dialog. This file should exist in the directory of every plug-in. |
| `about.ini` | | Control file for feature branding. |
| `about.properties` | Branding plug-in directory | Substitution values for `about.ini` defined keys. Good for translation. |
| `about.mappings` | | Text substitution values for `about.ini` and `about.properties` files. |
| `feature.gif` | | Image in About dialogs. |

The about.ini file identifies the branding content; the keyed values in the file are described in the IBundleGroupConstants interface. Other files identified in the about.ini file are also included as part of the branding content in the plug-in. The most common values are aboutText and featureImage. The aboutText key defines the text in the dialog, and the featureImage key identifies the graphic used on both the About [product] and About [product] Features dialogs. Figure 13.2 shows the customized content displayed in the About [product] Features dialog.

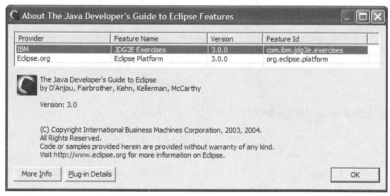

**Figure 13.2**    Custom Feature Branding in the About Eclipse Platform Features Dialog

Every feature in the Eclipse SDK includes feature-branding content. You can review these definitions and use them as a model for your own. Exercise 9, Deploying Your Product Using Features, provides a template and guides you through the process of building a branded feature.

## Installing Features

The first step in the installation process is the definition and preparation of an installable feature. An installable feature is a feature and its managed plug-ins with all the JAR files and other files required at runtime. Given an installable feature, you can add your function to Eclipse or an Eclipse-based product as a product extension or as a feature installed by the Update Manager.

In addition to installing your feature, you may also want to contribute to the introduction content integrated into the Eclipse environment. See Defining Product Introduction Content later in this chapter for a description of this process.

The techniques available for building, installing, and servicing features are outlined in the following subsections. You may also wish to develop skills in this area. See Exercise Summary at the end of this chapter for a description of what you can learn using Exercise 9, Deploying Your Product Using Features.

### Building and Installing Product Extensions

When a product extension is installed, your features are configured as part of a previously installed Eclipse-based product. The product extension approach is typically accompanied by a formal installation routine (`setup.exe`) that will find the target product, create an install site for the extension, and make the product aware of the extension. The Eclipse-based product installations to be extended can be identified by the user, or your installation procedure can scan for the `.eclipseproduct` marker file that identifies existing Eclipse-based product installation(s).

You can use a formal installation routine to install a product extension on a workstation where an Eclipse-based product is already installed. The routine can find other Eclipse-based products to extend and can guide the user through the process. The installation routine should automatically update the product configuration to identify the install site for the new extension. You can download an example of an extension installation routine from eclipse.org (see the References section at the end of this chapter for location information).

Your extension's install site is a separate location on the file system. This location includes the standard `eclipse` directory tree structure (`eclipse\features` and `eclipse\plugins` directory set).

---

**NOTE** It is considered bad form to add your features and plug-ins to an existing product's `eclipse\features` and `eclipse\plugins` directory structure. If that product needs to be uninstalled, it might not know how to handle your content, or more likely, it might delete your content. You should guide your users to create a new install site when using the Update Manager, or use an extension installation technique to install your function in your own target installation directory.

---

By convention, an extension installation directory is identified by a marker file in the target directory (`.eclipseextension`). The marker file contains the following information about the installation.

```
name=Extension_Name
id=product.branding.feature.id
version=1.0.0
```

PART II

The extension marker file must be created by your extension installation logic. The file is required by the Update Manager; if missing, the site will not be processed.

If the product extension exists on the file system as described, the user can actually add it to the product configuration using the Product Configuration dialog. This dialog can be used to locate the extension and add it to the configuration as long as the required .eclipseextension file exists. This process is discussed in Adding and Removing Install Sites in Chapter 6, Managing Your Eclipse Environment.

**NOTE** You can use a link file in the product's installation directory (eclipse\links\your.feature.id.link) to instruct Eclipse to look for additional features and plug-ins at another location (your installation site). The link file contains a path=*file* URL entry for where your extension code is installed, for example:

    path=e:\\YourExtension_Install_Dir

or

    path=e:/YourExtension_Install_Dir

The features and plug-in directories would be found in a directory named like this:

    E:\YourExtension\eclipse\...

While Eclipse still supports the use of a links directory and a link file to add extensions to an Eclipse-based product, the more appropriate technique is to add a site to the configuration. This can be done using the Product Configuration dialog or the addSite command. These alternatives are discussed in Adding and Removing Install Sites in Chapter 6.

## Using Update Manager to Deliver Features

The Update Manager is a layer of function in Eclipse that can manage features and install sites as well as access update sites. Update sites are URLs that contain a site.xml file, which describes features that can be downloaded for installation by the Update Manager.

When the Update Manager is used to install your feature, the user is typically in charge. The user selects the menu option **Help > Software Updates > Find and Install...** to find your update site. The update site can be used to download and install your features. This update site could be a Web or file URL. Technically you could build your update site and ship it on a CD-ROM. The Update Manager would still be able to perform the initial install.

There is even a command API that allows you to use a command to request that the Update Manager download and install your feature (find the "Running update manager from command line" topic in the *Platform Plug-in Developer Guide* or search for the entry standaloneUpdate).

A feature installed this way can actually be removed from the system by performing an **Uninstall** using the Product Configuration dialog or Update Manager command API. Features that exist as part of a product or product extension may be disabled but not uninstalled using this approach. The Update Manager also supports an undo function. After updates have been made, the configuration can be changed to return to an older version; this **Revert to Previous** option is supported by the Update Manager using the Product Configuration dialog.

What you are not able to do is control the install site location. The default is the eclipse directory tree for the product, which is bad form. Features can be defined to force the choice of a specific install site during an Update Manager installation using the colocation-affinity attribute. If the feature id identified in the colocation-affinity attribute exists in the current configuration, the new feature must be installed in the same install site location. A new feature that includes an existing feature is also forced to use the same install site location. If you are unable to use the colocation-affinity attribute to control install site selection, your supporting documentation should request that the user create a new install site location using the Install wizard.

The Update Manager is a high-function technique that allows for rapid distribution and installation of your code. The same technique used to install code is used to service code, so while you may not choose to install your code with the Update Manager, you will probably want to consider providing service using this approach.

## Servicing Your Features

Choosing the Update Manager as the technique used for service delivery allows for automated delivery and installation of updates. The active update sites identified by the installed features can be searched and any updates found prepared for installation using the Update Manager Install wizard. See Chapter 6, Managing Your Eclipse Environment, for additional detail on this process.

Your feature.xml file definition can identify an update site, as well as discovery sites. The Update Manager will search an update site for new versions of existing features; both an update site and a discovery site can be browsed for additional features that can be installed. Update and discovery sites are defined in a `feature.xml` file such as the following.

```
<url>
    <update url="http://www.company.com/updatesite"
        label="YourTool Update Site" />
    <discovery url="http://www.company.com/newcode"
        label="YourTool Add-ons Site" />
</url>
```

An update site must be defined in the feature to be installed if you want to use the Update Manager to automatically find updates at a later date. All you need to start is a URL; the install site does not need to exist until you have update content to share.

You can control the search using the Install wizard (**Help > Software Updates > Find and Install...**). The search process can be automated to service existing features if you set the appropriate preference value (**Preferences > Install/Update > Automatic Updates**).

By default, only the update site identified in a root feature is processed. Update sites identified by included features are not used during service processing unless authorized by the parent feature. A root feature owns the right to manage delivery of service for its included features. When a feature is included in another feature, the `search_location` attribute in the `<includes>` tag can be used to define where the included feature can obtain service updates. The acceptable values are `root`, `self`, and `both`; `root` is the default.

---

**NOTE**  If you are building a product based on Eclipse, you should consider having one of your features include the Eclipse features. This allows the content on your update site to synchronize the delivery timing of your product updates and Eclipse updates. If you do not do this, updates to Eclipse could be delivered directly to your product platform. This could happen as all Eclipse features identify an update site in their feature definition. If your user asks the Update Manager to search for service, the Eclipse update site will be searched unless you have a feature that includes the Eclipse features.

---

Features can be serviced by either providing a new version of the feature on the update site or providing a patch to an existing feature. The proper choice depends on your goal. When a new version is provided, it replaces the existing version. If necessary, the new version can reference new versions of a plug-in, remove plug-ins, and add new plug-ins. The older version still exists but is no longer active. If the feature being modified is included by another feature, that parent feature must also be updated if you are not providing a patch.

When a patch is provided, it logically replaces the existing feature version. A patch can replace current versions of existing plug-ins or add a new plug-in; a plug-in in the original feature may not be removed. Using a patch you can modify a feature included by another feature without having to update the parent feature to change the version reference on the include statement.

## Defining an Update Site

An update site is a file: or http: URL that is accessible by Eclipse. In the root directory identified by the URL, there should be a `site.xml` file. This file identifies features that can be installed. The `site.xml` file structure and content is straightforward.

```xml
<?xml version="1.0" encoding="UTF-8" ?>
<site>
  <description url="info/siteInfo.html"/>

  <feature url="features/com.ibm.jdg2e.tools_3.0.0.jar">
    <category name="TOOLS"/>
  </feature>
  <feature url="features/com.ibm.jdg2e.demos._3.0.0.jar">
    <category name="TOOLS"/>
  </feature>
  <category-def label="Category Label for Organization"
    name="TOOLS">
    <description>Category description text </description>
  </category-def>
</site>
```

The features and their associated plug-ins are packaged in install JAR files for download and installation by the Update Manager. Unless signed, the install JAR file is the equivalent of a ZIP file of the feature or plug-in directory content. These feature and plug-in install JAR files are downloaded and installed to either an existing Eclipse product installation directory or a new install site. By using a new install site as an alternative to the product installation directory, the features and plug-ins being installed will not be mingled with other features and plug-ins known to the current configuration. More importantly, these features and plug-ins will not be deleted if the user decides to uninstall the product.

If you have data beyond what is normally kept in a plug-in or feature, or processing that the default Update Manager approach does not support, you may need to either use a formalized install program or implement a private install handler. A feature definition can specify an `install-handler` attribute to identify code that will implement customized install processing. You can build an install handler using the `org.eclipse.update.installHandlers` extension point. Your code must implement the `IInstallHandler` interface. See the *Platform Plug-in Developer Guide* for details.

A series of steps are required to prepare your installable features for installation using the Update Manager. The same process is used for features that will be installed for the first time or service that is being provided for features that already exist. The definition of the site and creation of the required content can be done in an automated fashion using the PDE. Exercise 9, Deploying Your Product Using Features, guides you through this entire process. The use of the Install wizard to find and install features is also discussed in Installing a Feature from an Update Site in Chapter 6, Managing Your Eclipse Environment.

## Products

This section discusses the creation of a runtime product definition, how product branding is defined, and how to configure the Eclipse environment to use your product definition.

An Eclipse runtime product definition controls the behavior of the Eclipse environment. When you start Eclipse, the `org.eclipse.plat-form.ide` product takes control. Products are defined using an extension; this includes the product brand identity and the id of the Eclipse application that will get control.

### Creating a Product Definition

By defining your own product you can customize the product branding or identity associated with a specific Eclipse configuration. This identity will still start the `org.eclipse.ui.ide.workbench` application, which will start the Workbench.

#### Product Extension

The `org.eclipse.core.runtime.products` extension point is used to define a runtime product. You need to define a product only when you will be starting the Eclipse Platform with your product identity in charge. You do not need a product if all you will do is add features to an existing Eclipse or Eclipse-based product instance.

The extension can be part of any plug-in, but there is a natural relationship between a product definition and associated product and feature branding. You might consider defining a product in the plug-in used to define feature branding.

A product definition is very straightforward; there is no Java code to write. You simply identify the application that should be run, product name, and description. Product branding is also included by setting values for the appropriate attributes. The product-branding attributes are defined and described in the `IProductConstants` interface. Here is an example of a product definition with the associated branding.

```
<extension id="demo" point="org.eclipse.core.runtime.products">
  <product application="org.eclipse.ui.ide.workbench"
      name="%productName" description="%productBlurb">
    <property name="windowImages"
        value="icons/jdg2eProd.gif,icons/jdg2eFeat.gif"/>
    <property name="aboutImage" value="icons/jdg2eAbout.gif"/>
    <property name="aboutText" value="%productBlurb"/>
    <property name="appName" value="JDG2E"/>
    <property name="preferenceCustomization"
        value="plugin_customization.ini"/>
  </product>
</extension>
```

The *%key* values are replaced by content from the `plugin.properties` file. The other references are to files found in the plug-in directory.

## Product Branding in the User Interface

Product-branding information is used by Eclipse to control the name of the active program, provide the splash and icon graphics used to represent it, and create content in the About [product] dialog. Table 13.2 describes the attributes that can be used to control product branding as defined in the `IProduct-Constants` interface and information on how the splash image is defined.

**Table 13.2** Product-Branding Definitions

| Attribute Name | Location | Description |
| --- | --- | --- |
| appName | Product extension | Used to initialize the SWT Display (SWT Application). |
| aboutText | | The text shown in the About [product] dialog. |
| aboutImage | | The image shown in the About [product] dialog. |
| preferenceCustomization | | The name of the properties file used to override default preference values. |
| windowImage | | The 16 × 16 icon to be used for the Workbench window. |
| windowImages | | A list of images that can be used for the Workbench window icon (16 × 16, 32 × 32). |
| osgi.splashPath | config.ini | The directory location for `splash.bmp` file. |

The welcomePage entry is not listed in the table; instead, you should use the product introduction technique for attaching additional user content to your product definition. You see these definitions in action every time you start Eclipse or open the About [product] dialog. The product extension for Eclipse can be found in the org.eclipse.platform plug-in.

### Identifying the Active Product at Runtime

The product used at runtime can be identified in the config.ini file or by using the -product startup parameter. The config.ini file found in the \configuration directory is used by default when Eclipse is started. The product is identified by id; this id is the concatenation of the id of the plug-in and the product extension id.

Other runtime parameters can be used to adjust the invocation of Eclipse. You could even override the application that is run for a given product. These runtime parameters are documented in the *Platform Plug-in Developer Guide*.

## Defining Product Introduction Content

The platform supports the notion of a product introduction. This allows a product, and potentially other contributed product extensions, to use a specialized view in Eclipse to deliver information about new functions, documentation, guided exercises, and other tidbits of helpful content.

A brief description of this function follows. The extension point descriptions and the "Intro support" topic in the *Platform Plug-in Developer Guide* should be consulted for details. You can see the existing product introduction for Eclipse using the **Help > Welcome** menu option. You can find the extension definitions and implementation in the plug-ins that are part of the Eclipse SDK.

### Introduction Part

The existence of product introduction support is defined and implemented using the org.eclipse.ui.intro extension point. Contributions to this extension point are used to define an introduction part shown when a product first starts. Eclipse provides a customizable implementation of this part (CustomizableIntroPart), which can be configured to support your product. This makes the process much easier.

### Defining a Product Introduction Configuration

The Eclipse implementation of an introduction part is configured with content using the org.eclipse.ui.intro.config extension point. A product can contribute to this extension point to add content. The content is described in the XML file identified in the extension. The CustomizableIntroPart defines the syntax of this XML file, which is used to define pages in the introduction. The pages defined can link to other pages, help content, or processing contributed by plug-ins in the Eclipse Platform.

### Adding Content to an Existing Product Introduction

Extensions to products can participate in an existing product introduction scheme. The extension point org.eclipse.ui.intro.configExtension is used to add additional content. The extension identifies the introduction configuration that will be extended and identifies an XML file that contains the introduction content. This content can target anchor points defined in the product introduction.

## Building Your Own Product on the Eclipse Platform

When you build a product on the Eclipse Platform, you add your features and plug-ins to the standard directory structure (eclipse\features and eclipse\plugins), adjusting the runtime configuration to identify your product. That's all it takes.

The config.ini file customization identifies your product extension id as the product to be started (eclipse.product entry) and the location of your splash image (osgi.splashPath) entry. Once the file is customized, you can validate that the modified configuration launches and uses your product branding using the eclipse.exe file to start the user interface. Once the launch has been validated, you can reset the install by deleting the workspace directory and all but the config.ini file in the configuration directory.

By convention, an Eclipse-based product installation includes a customized .eclipseproduct marker file in the eclipse directory. This file contains the following information about the installation.

```
name=Product name
id=product.feature.id
version=1.0.0
```

Other product extension installers can attempt to use this marker file to find your Eclipse-based product in order to extend it with their offering(s). You should ensure your product includes this file in the eclipse directory with content that reflects your product.

The eclipse directory structure, now configured with your features, plug-ins, and customized configuration, can be packaged to support installation by your customer. This package can be directly installed and independently started as long as a JRE is available.

A formal installation routine is the standard technique for adding a product to a user's workstation. An example of a product installation routine created using InstallShield technology can be downloaded from eclipse.org at this location: http://dev.eclipse.org/viewcvs/index.cgi/%7Echeckout%7E/platform-update-home/dev.html.

## Exercise Summary

There are many steps required to define features and prepare both features and the plug-ins they manage for installation. The PDE provides support, with some automation, for many of these steps. This automation provided by the PDE is available for each project type: plug-in, feature, and site. For plug-in and feature projects, the automation process is supported using the actions on the plug-in and feature manifest files; these **Create Ant Build File** actions would read the manifest and the associated build.properties file and generate a build.xml file. For a site project, the automation is provided using either an action on the site.xml file or buttons in the site.xml editor.

In addition, specialized export wizards provided by the PDE can export runtime versions of a plug-in or a feature and its referenced plug-ins.

The export wizard technique is used in Exercise 6, Developing Your First Plug-in. The Ant-based approach to feature and plug-in packaging is included as part of Exercise 9, Deploying Your Product Using Features. Exercise 9 will help you learn how to:

- Use the PDE to prepare installable features
- Install these features as an extension to Eclipse
- Configure Eclipse so that it starts as your branded product
- Service the installed features using an update site

## Chapter Summary

The Eclipse Platform is extensible by developing plug-ins. This process is not complete until these plug-ins are configured as part of an Eclipse Platform using features. Features are the method used to package plug-ins so they can be added to and managed as part of an Eclipse configuration. Features are instrumental in the process of building a product or an extension to a product based on Eclipse; they also support delivery and configuration of features using the Update Manager.

Features can also provide branding content, which gives your feature the ability to identify itself as part of an Eclipse configuration. Feature branding allows features installed in Eclipse to describe themselves to the user.

Products are a configuration element in Eclipse. A product is defined to identify both the Eclipse runtime application that should be started and the product branding that should be used. Product branding is the splash, name, and other image and descriptive content associated to the running Eclipse instance.

This chapter also discussed the use of the Update Manager to install and service features. What you have to decide is how to use this function effectively. If you have built and offered a product to your users, they will want to obtain updates. You will want to deliver those updates and make sure their runtime platform continues to function. You can do this with the function provided by the Update Manager, a formal install routine, or a mix of both techniques.

## References

You should now be prepared to read the various documentation topics that discuss features, install, extensions, and the Update Manager in the *Platform Plug-in Developer Guide* and on the eclipse.org site.

Review the Development Resources page for the Update Component at http://dev.eclipse.org/viewcvs/index.cgi/%7Echeckout%7E/platform-update-home/dev.html. An example of an extension installation routine can also be downloaded from this page.

Arthorne, John, and Chris Laffra. 2004. *Official Eclipse 3.0 FAQs.* Boston, MA: Addison-Wesley. http://eclipsefaq.org. (See FAQs 89, 92, 250, 251, 259.)

PART II

# PART III

## Extending the Eclipse Workbench

In Part II you developed an understanding of what extending Eclipse is all about. Presumably, you have tried your hand at creating a plug-in either using the templates provided by the PDE or by performing Exercise 6, Developing Your First Plug-in, or Exercise 7, Developing Your First Rich Client Application. Part III explains how to extend the Eclipse user interface, regardless of whether your target is the IDE Workbench or a rich client application. Perspectives, views, editors, dialogs, help, and contributions to menus and toolbars—everything you need to know to about the Eclipse user interface is covered here.

- Chapter 14, The Standard Widget Toolkit: A Lean, Mean Widget Machine, explains how to use the Eclipse GUI framework. Constructing basic user interface controls like buttons and input fields is covered.
- Chapter 15, JFace Viewers, helps you use a higher-level GUI framework to present your data. It applies to dialogs and is fundamental to views and editors.
- Chapter 16, Dialogs and Wizards, as the title suggests, offers a comprehensive discussion of the Eclipse dialog and wizard framework.
- Chapter 17, Dialog Settings, Preferences, and User Settings, focuses on how you manage all the Workbench information you collect from users.

335

- Chapter 18, Views, Chapter 19, Editors, and Chapter 20, Perspectives, show you how to create these basic Workbench parts.
- Chapter 21, Action Contributions: The Integration Fast Track, is all about contributing to menus and toolbars. You might end up here earlier, though some understanding of JFace viewers, views, and editors is helpful.
- Chapter 22, Providing Help, explains how to contribute to Eclipse help and create context-sensitive help.

Many chapters refer to the working examples on the CD-ROM as part of their explanations, using code to reinforce your understanding of the concepts. The readme.html file on the CD-ROM provides instructions on how to install these examples. The CD-ROM also contains a short overview of each example that explains the objective and basic structure of the project. Documentation included on the CD-ROM covers the examples and exercises, both of which are integrated with the Eclipse Help system.

# CHAPTER 14

## *The Standard Widget Toolkit: A Lean, Mean Widget Machine*

Key priorities in the design of Eclipse were performance, robustness, and fidelity to the user's operating system. To be competitive with other client applications, it was important that the Eclipse platform look and feel like a native application. The user interface needed to be lightweight but rich enough to meet the demands of a sophisticated application. Eclipse is written entirely in Java (well, almost, as you will learn in a moment). How could this be done with available technology? The answer was to provide a Java API to the user interface supplied by the host operating system. This would allow Eclipse, a Java application, to look, behave, and perform like a native application on whatever operating system it is running. This portable API is called the **Standard Widget Toolkit** (SWT). It uses the Java Native Interface (JNI) package to provide a Java API to the underlying operating system user interface. An SWT implementation of a native control is, for the most part, a one-to-one mapping between the SWT widget and its equivalent native control in the host operating system. There is much more to SWT than that, but this is the critical architectural element.

SWT lies at the bottom of the overall UI framework, just above the native operating system controls. All higher-level UI frameworks, like JFace, use SWT to host themselves within Eclipse. SWT must be ported to each target operating system, but once that is done the rest of the user interface just works.

SWT has been ported to a variety of windowing and operating system environments, including Windows, a variety of Linux and UNIX platforms, QNX

Photon, and Apple Mac OS. Generally, SWT is functionally equivalent at the API level across all implementations. There may be minor behavioral variations, typically due to the underlying platform. SWT on Windows has one significant exception: There is additional support for OLE and ActiveX, which is unique to the Windows platform. OLE and ActiveX are covered in Chapter 34.

So what does SWT mean to you as a plug-in developer? How much of SWT do you need to know to get your job done? The answer varies, but it could be surprisingly little. Typically, SWT controls like buttons, labels, text fields, check boxes, and the like are used to gather and present data to the user. They show up most frequently in dialogs like wizards, property pages, and preference pages. Knowing a handful of SWT widgets that you can lay out attractively will carry you a long way. In subsequent chapters, you will learn about the rest of the UI framework that will take you the rest of the way. SWT has a rich set of functions (there are over a dozen Java packages), and one could write a treatise on SWT. In fact, SWT and JFace are quite mature, having existed inside IBM well before Eclipse was developed.

This chapter is an introduction to SWT. By the end of this chapter you will have a basic, working knowledge of SWT that provides a foundation for understanding and using the rest of the Eclipse UI framework. We will assume that, as a Java developer, you have some experience with Java GUIs like the Abstract Window Toolkit (AWT) or Swing. You will find that from an API perspective, SWT has enough similarities that you will soon feel quite comfortable with it.

## The Basic Structure of an SWT Application

Eclipse is an SWT application in the same way that other Java client applications might be called AWT or Swing applications. SWT is packaged within Eclipse for its own use and is also available as a separate download if you wish to use it in other Java applications. All SWT applications have a common structure. If you were to write a native SWT application, you would use this same structure. Creating plug-ins in Eclipse does not require that you use this, but it is useful to know and not terribly difficult to understand. Let's examine it a little further. An SWT application can be started using two classes: Display and Shell. A Shell class represents a window in the underlying operating system. The Display class connects SWT to the GUI system of the operating system. It handles such things as events and manages communication between the UI thread and other threads. If you are familiar with windowing systems like Motif, these class names might sound a bit familiar.

A simple SWT application with a window containing a single button might look like Figure 14.1.

**Figure 14.1** Simple SWT Shell and Button

Here is the code for this SWT application.

```
public class SWTShell {
  public static void main(String [] args) {
    Display display = new Display();
    Shell shell = new Shell(display);
    shell.setLayout(new RowLayout());
    Button b = new Button(shell, SWT.PUSH);
    b.setText("Click Me");
    shell.setSize(200, 200);
    shell.open();
    while (!shell.isDisposed()) {
      if (!display.readAndDispatch()) {
        display.sleep(); }
    }
    display.dispose();
  }
}
```

How do you do this? First, you create `Display` and `Shell` objects. The `Shell` is linked to the `Display` in the constructor of `shell`. The layout manager, `RowLayout`, will be discussed later, along with handling a button click event. A button was created, hosted by the `shell` (our window) using the class `Button`. The button label is assigned. The `shell`, which represents the window, has been sized at 200 by 200 pixels. Finally, you set up an event dispatching loop in the `while` statement. This loop will react to events if they exist; otherwise, the `Display` will remain idle. The purpose is to avoid polling, so the UI thread can remain idle without needlessly consuming resources.

When Eclipse starts up as an SWT application, it does the same thing. The main Workbench window is a `Shell`. It is a top-level window. Top-level windows can be moved and resized, and they are always associated with a `Display`. Secondary windows, or child windows, are typically transient and often represent dialogs. They are linked to a parent window, which eventually is linked to a top-level window.

Sometimes a UI item needs to access the shell that represents the active Workbench window. There are numerous `getShell` methods that return a `Shell` object in the context of whatever UI object you are working in. If none of those are appropriate, here is a convenient static method for getting the `Shell` of the active Workbench window. In this example, it is the parent of an error message dialog. Similarly, the static method `Display.getCurrent` returns the Workbench `Display` object (where the UI thread is running).

```
Shell workbenchShell =
  PlatformUI.
    getWorkbench(). // IWorkbench
    getActiveWorkbenchWindow(). //IWorkbenchWindow
    getShell();
MessageDialog.
  openError(workbenchShell,"Error","File not found.");
```

Until now, the terms "widget" and "control" have been used interchangeably. A **widget** is an abstract object representing all UI objects and is represented by the `Widget` class (see Figure 14.4 in the next section). A **control**, represented by the `Control` class, is an object that maps directly to an object in the platform windowing system. A **button** is a control. In SWT terms, a menu is a widget but not a control. In this book, these terms are often used interchangeably.

## Common SWT Widgets

SWT has over 40 widgets. They consist of widgets that map to the underlying operating system and custom widgets that provide Eclipse's common look and feel. They are defined in the packages `org.eclipse.swt.widgets` and `org.eclipse.swt.custom`. All the common controls like labels, text, rich (or styled) text, buttons, list boxes, combo boxes, groups, progress bars, sliders, tables, and trees are present. The easiest way to get a feel for what SWT offers is to open the SWT Controls and SWT Custom Controls views. The examples shown there are among the SWT example plug-ins. If you have already installed the Eclipse example plug-ins (available from the downloads page at eclipse.org), you can run these examples by opening them from **Window > Show View > Other... > SWT Examples**. Figures 14.2 and 14.3 show the SWT Controls and SWT Custom Controls views, respectively, when fully expanded in Eclipse. You can browse the various tabs to see what is available. Another interesting example is the SWT Browser view, which demonstrates the SWT HTML Browser control.

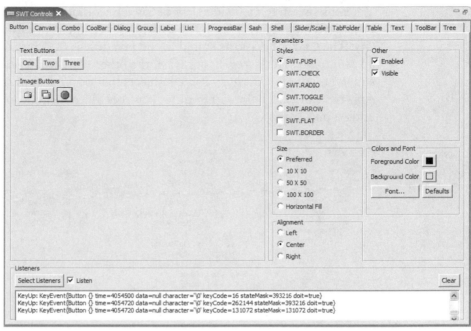

**Figure 14.2** SWT Controls Example

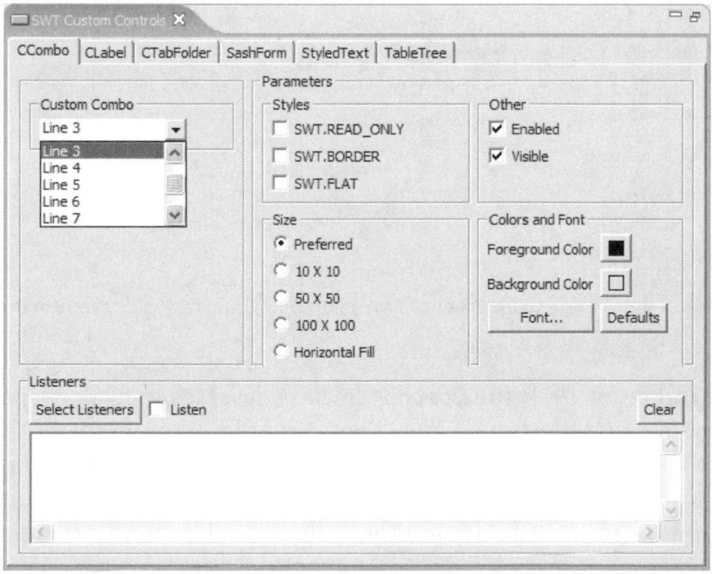

**Figure 14.3** SWT Custom Controls Example

Let's switch to an inside view of SWT by looking at how SWT classes are organized (see Figure 14.4). The `Widget` class is the root of the class hierarchy. The `Control` class, as stated in the Javadoc, is the abstract superclass of all *windowed* UI classes. In contrast, the other key class, `Item`, is the abstract superclass of all *nonwindowed* UI objects that occur within specific controls. An `Item` can exist only within other controls like a menu, toolbar, table, tree, and so on.

**Figure 14.4**    SWT Component Class Hierarchy (courtesy of Steve Northover, IBM)

In Figure 14.4, the `Composite` class deserves special attention. A `Composite` is a container-type widget that can hold other widgets. You will encounter this control frequently when creating views, editors, and dialogs. Eclipse creates the top-level components like the shell, title bar, menu bar, and navigation buttons for you and then calls your code to fill in the client area, represented by an instance of `Composite`. You can also create a `Composite` for use as a widget container. We will discuss a possible use later in the section Summary of Layout Managers.

The best way to learn how to code and use all the features of SWT is by looking at examples. Fortunately, there is an excellent source of SWT code snippets available at the SWT subproject page on eclipse.org. There are nearly 150 short examples of SWT usage posted. The directions to this Web page are described among the references at the end of this chapter. Better yet, all of the SWT snippets at the time this book was completed have been included on the CD-ROM along with a snippet launcher application. (See the Example Summary section at the end of this chapter.) This allows you to explore these examples more easily.

## Refining a Widget's Appearance Using Style Bits

Evident on almost every page of the SWT Controls and Custom Controls examples is a group labeled "Styles," which contains a set of check boxes or radio buttons with values like SWT.PUSH, SWT.CHECK, and so on. What do these mean? Well, if you played with them, you noticed that they changed the presentation of the control. When selecting SWT.PUSH on a button, a normal push button is displayed. Selecting SWT.CHECK changes the button to a check box. These are called **style bits**. They are passed in the control's constructor as an integer to define the appearance and behavior of the control. These style bits can be logically aggregated using a bitwise OR of all the style bits that you want to apply (assuming they are not mutually exclusive, of course). The Javadoc for each widget identifies the available style bits. The Eclipse SWT reference documentation, available as online help in the *Platform Plug-in Developer Guide*, *Programmer's Guide*, and *Standard Widget Toolkit*, contains a handy table of styles available for each control. The SWT class in the API reference has a list of static final constants that are available to specify each style bit.

If you are familiar with Swing, you will note that where Swing uses unique classes for the different types of controls, SWT uses style bits to define the minor appearance or behavior variations of the same base control. For example, a list box can have a horizontal scroll bar, a vertical scroll bar, or both. To define a list box with both, you would use the style bits SWT.H_SCROLL and SWT.V_SCROLL in the constructor as follows.

```
List myList = new List(parent, SWT.H_SCROLL|SWT.V_SCROLL);
```

Another common element in the constructor of a widget, like this List object, is the parent argument. All widgets are created in the context of a parent widget. This concept is fundamental to the SWT architecture and is vital to providing an efficient GUI library.

PART III

## Responding to Events

All GUI systems support event-triggering mechanisms in response to user interactions from a mouse, keyboard, or other device. SWT provides event handling in the package `org.eclipse.swt.events`. Event handling in SWT follows a pattern similar to AWT and Swing. There are **listeners** that register interest in specific events. When those events occur, you are notified, an event object is passed to your application, and your code can respond appropriately. Figure 14.5 lists all the SWT event and listener classes.

**Figure 14.5**    SWT Events and Event Listeners (courtesy of Steve Northover, IBM)

Here is an example using an adapter that should look familiar to a Java GUI programmer.

```
StyledText sText =
  new StyledText(parent,SWT.SINGLE|SWT.BORDER);
sText.addMouseListener
  (new MouseAdapter(){
```

```
    public void mouseDoubleClick(MouseEvent e) {
      System.out.println("Mouse double-click received.");
    }
  });
```

As you can see in this trivial example, we have registered an interest in mouse events through the addMouseListener method. The inner class, Mouse-Adapter, has a method, mouseDoubleClick, which allows you to process mouse events. Note that the MouseAdapter class is a member of the SWT events package, even though it looks and behaves in a remarkably similar way to a class by the same name in AWT. Using the wrong one will cause you some grief!

More generally, there are different listener interfaces for various types of events. The interface classes in the org.eclipse.swt.events package consist entirely of various types of listeners. The basic pattern is to add a listener to a widget of interest and then respond to the event passed to you. With this pattern in mind, let's revisit the simple SWT application involving a button. You want to respond to a button click. Looking at the Javadoc for the Button class, you see that the addSelectionListener method, which passes a Selection-Listener object, will do the job. The SelectionListener interface has two methods— widgetSelected and widgetDefaultSelected—that you must implement. They pass along a SelectionEvent object. For some listeners there are adapter classes that implement the listener's interface. You extend the adapter class and override only those events you are interested in (this should sound very similar to Java AWT). For SelectionListener there is an adapter class called SelectionAdapter. Using this shorthand approach, you only need to override the widgetSelected method, which is what you are interested in.

With all this newfound knowledge, your simple SWT application handles a button selection event as follows.

```
public static void main (String [] args) {
  Display display = new Display();
  Shell shell = new Shell(display);
  shell.setLayout(new RowLayout());
  Button b = new Button(shell, SWT.PUSH);
  b.setText("Click Me");
  b.addSelectionListener(new SelectionAdapter() {
    public void widgetSelected(SelectionEvent e) {
      MessageDialog.openInformation
        (shell,"SWT", "Button selected.");
    }
  });
  shell.setSize(200, 200);
  shell.open();
```

```
while(!shell.isDisposed()) {
  if(!display.readAndDispatch()) {
    display.sleep();}
}
display.dispose();
}
```

The Javadoc for the package `org.eclipse.swt.events` specifies the events that apply for each control. Here are some event listener interfaces you are likely to use.

- `ControlListener`—for events involving movement or resizing.
- `DisposeListener`—for events generated when a widget is disposed. This is discussed later in the section Widgets Have Special Disposal Requirements.
- `FocusListener`—for events involving gain or loss of focus.
- `KeyListener`—for events involving keystrokes.
- `ModifyListener`—for events involving text modification. This is often used to trigger validation of user input in a dialog. See also the `VerifyListener` class, which informs you when text is about to be modified.
- `MouseListener, MouseMoveListener, MouseTrackListener`—for mouse events.
- `SelectionListener`—for events involving widget selection.

In summary, the pattern of event handling in SWT is not significantly different from what you are probably already familiar with in Java AWT.

## How to Arrange SWT Widgets Using Layout Managers

**Layout managers** in SWT, as in Java AWT, define how your controls will be arranged in windows and dialogs. With a basic knowledge of layouts, the basic controls, and event handling, you have a reasonable working knowledge of SWT that allows you to handle many of your plug-in's requirements.

Before we dive into layout managers, let's talk about SWT GUI builders. A GUI builder allows you to lay out your widgets by dragging them from a palette of widgets onto a target window. They are quite popular, and most IDEs offer them for the UI technology they support. Eclipse does not provide a GUI builder for SWT, but some independent providers are producing and marketing them. The Visual Editor Project under the Eclipse Tools Project on eclipse.org has the charter of providing a GUI builder framework. One of the framework reference implementations is an SWT GUI builder. You might want to check it out.

Now, let's return to layout managers. There are five layout manager classes in SWT. Let's take a quick look at each one. Later, we will explore them in some detail.

- `FillLayout`

  In a `FillLayout`, controls are positioned in a single row or column, and each control is of equal size. This layout has limited use. Typically, it is used when a widget has a single child widget that fills the entire space (e.g., `Group`). A simple toolbar, which contains a vertical or horizontal set of icons, could be constructed using a fill layout. A stack of check boxes in a group might be another application (see Figure 14.6).

**Figure 14.6**   Simple Fill Layout

- `RowLayout`

  In a `RowLayout`, controls are laid out in one or more rows or columns. Unlike `FillLayout`, a variety of margin and spacing options are available. The size of the individual controls can be defined. You might use a row layout for a simple list of buttons (see Figure 14.7).

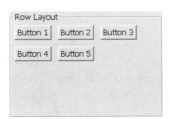

**Figure 14.7**   Simple Row Layout

- `GridLayout`

  `GridLayout` is the commonly used layout manager. Controls are laid out in a grid defined by some number of columns. A variety of configuration fields exist. Individual configuration attributes can be defined for each control in the layout (see Figure 14.8).

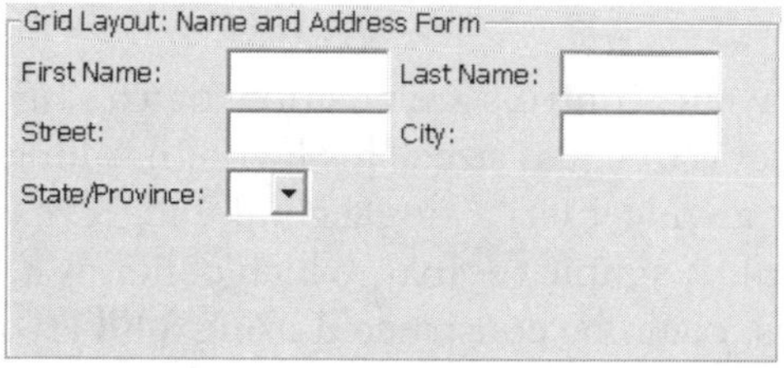

**Figure 14.8**  Grid Layout

- FormLayout

  The newest layout, FormLayout, allows for very precise individual positioning of controls. The sides of a control can be positioned relative to the parent or a peer control. Precise positioning at the pixel level can be applied. See Figure 14.9 for an example of the layout.

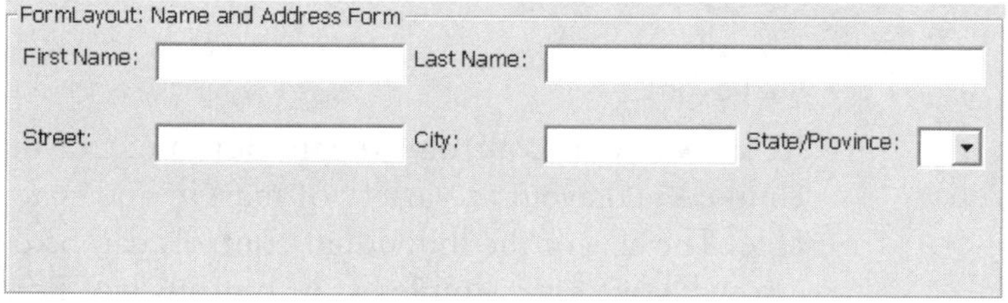

**Figure 14.9**  Form Layout

- StackLayout

  The last layout class we will discuss is StackLayout. It allows you to stack a set of widgets together and reveal only one at a time. You decide which widget in the set to reveal, frequently based on a user selection in another widget. It serves the same purpose as the Java AWT CardLayout class. In Figure 14.10, we have stacked all the previous layout manager examples along with a selection list to switch between examples.

  The strategy behind all these layout managers is that you use them to organize or lay out your controls independent of the size of the individual

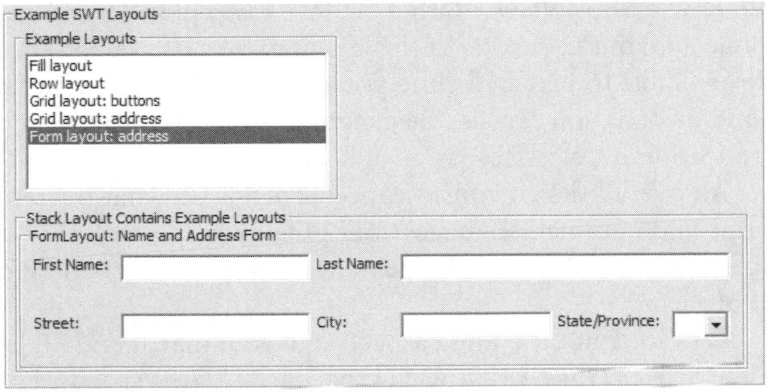

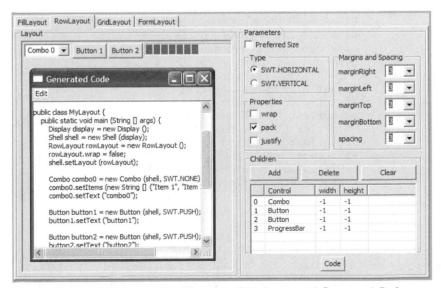

**Figure 14.10** Stack Layout

controls. You will learn that SWT has separate layout data classes where you specify the exact size of a control and other attributes that define its physical appearance within the chosen layout.

Each layout manager will be covered in some detail. The important ones to understand are GridLayout and FormLayout. If you have installed the Eclipse example plug-ins, you may find it useful to have the SWT Layouts example open (see Figure 14.11). It is available as a view. Launch it from

**Figure 14.11** SWT Layouts Tool Showing a Row Layout and Generated Code

PART III

**Window > Show View > Other > SWT Examples > SWT Layouts**. You can define a layout using one of the layout managers. Various layout attributes are available to play with, and you can immediately see the results. Using the **Code** button, you can see the generated code. You can even copy it to your application if you wish.

An overall design consideration depends on what operating system platforms and national languages your plug-in supports. Either of these design parameters may affect the appearance of your layouts and require you to test all of them.

Let's look at the coding aspects of layout managers. All layout classes are in the `org.eclipse.swt.layouts` package. All the specific layout classes extend `Layout`. A `Layout` object is assigned to a parent control using its `setLayout` method.

## Fill Layout

A fill layout is very easy to code because there is not much to it. The only attribute is orientation: horizontal or vertical. The following code produces the set of check boxes contained in a group as seen in Figure 14.6. You have no control over the size of the controls—they will occupy equal-size portions of the parent control.

```
Group myGroup = new Group(parent, SWT.NONE);
myGroup.setText("Fill Layout");
Button b1, b2, b3, b4, b5;
b1 = new Button(myGroup, SWT.CHECK);
b2 = new Button(myGroup, SWT.CHECK);
b3 = new Button(myGroup, SWT.CHECK);
b4 = new Button(myGroup, SWT.CHECK);
b5 = new Button(myGroup, SWT.CHECK);
b1.setText("Check box 1");
b2.setText("Check box 2");
b3.setText("Check box 3");
b4.setText("Check box 4");
b5.setText("Check box 5");
FillLayout myFillLayout = new FillLayout();
myFillLayout.type = SWT.VERTICAL;
myGroup.setLayout(myFillLayout);
```

## Row Layout

A row layout is also very straightforward to code. Compared with `Fill-Layout`, you have more flexibility with the final appearance. Like `FillLayout`, the orientation can be set to horizontal or vertical using the `type` attribute with a value of `SWT.VERTICAL` or `SWT.HORIZONTAL`. You can define margins by using the following attributes: `marginRight`, `marginLeft`, `marginTop`, and `marginBottom`. Values are specified in pixels. Spacing between controls is specified in pixels by using the `spacing` attribute. The placement of controls is handled by the `wrap`, `justify`, and `pack` Boolean attributes. The `wrap` attribute permits a control to flow to the next row if there is insufficient space. The default is `true`. Controls are left-justified because the default value for `justify` is `false`. When `justify` is `true`, controls are evenly distributed across the available space, and as its parent container is resized, the spacing between controls grows or shrinks according to the available space. If `pack` is `false`, controls are forced to be of equal size; otherwise they are displayed using their actual size. The default is `true`.

A complementary class named `RowData` allows you to define the height and width of an individual widget in the layout. It is assigned to a specific widget using the `setLayoutData` method. The following code assigns the size of the button to 100 by 50 pixels. `RowData` along with `GridData` and `FormData` (discussed soon) are among the layout data classes described earlier that separate the layout strategy from the exact details of how the controls appear.

```
Button button = new Button (shell, SWT.PUSH);
button.setText ("Click Me");
RowData data = new RowData (100, 50);
button.setLayoutData (data);
```

The following code produces the row layout shown in Figure 14.7. It specifies margin widths of five pixels and spacing between the buttons of ten pixels. The five buttons span two rows. This is because `wrap=true` and the container was sized so that the last two buttons wrapped to the next row.

```
Group myGroup = new Group(parent, SWT.NONE);
myGroup.setText("Row Layout");
Button b1, b2, b3, b4, b5;
 ... Omitted some button construction code ...
RowLayout rowLayout = new RowLayout();
rowLayout.wrap = true;
rowLayout.pack = false;
rowLayout.justify = true;
rowLayout.marginLeft = 5;
rowLayout.marginTop = 5;
rowLayout.marginRight = 5;
rowLayout.marginBottom = 5;
rowLayout.spacing = 10;
myGroup.setLayout(rowLayout);
```

`RowLayout`, like `FillLayout`, is used in specialized situations. `RowLayout` has more applications because you have more flexibility in the layout. A row layout works best when laying out a set of identical controls. The buttons on a calculator might be an interesting application of `RowLayout`.

You might want to play with the SWT Layouts example now and examine RowLayout and FillLayout.

## Grid Layout

Within Eclipse, GridLayout is the most extensively used layout manager. Until the introduction of FormLayout, discussed next, GridLayout was the only way to construct even a modestly complex dialog.

A grid layout, as the name suggests, defines a grid of cells that will contain your controls. The number of columns in the grid defines the size of the grid. This is defined by the numColumns attribute. As controls are added, they fill in the grid from left to right, flowing to the next row when all the columns are filled. The complementary class, GridData, as we learned with RowData, allows for specification of layout data for each participating widget. There are several attributes, which we will examine, to define how a specific widget will appear in the layout.

The code for a trivial layout involving two columns looks like this.

```
GridLayout gridLayout = new GridLayout();
gridLayout.numColumns = 2;
parent.setLayout(gridLayout);
```

GridLayout has a number of other configuration attributes to define the layout: makeColumnsEqualWidth, marginHeight, marginWidth, horizontalSpacing, and verticalSpacing. The top and bottom margin in pixels is set using marginHeight. The left and right margin is set using marginWidth. Spacing between grid cells is defined using horizontalSpacing and verticalSpacing.

For GridData there are nine configuration attributes of interest (see Table 14.1). SWT requires that each control that uses GridData should have its own instance of this object. In other words, GridData objects should not be shared between controls. Like RowData, a GridData object is assigned to its control using the setLayoutData method. Recall that these attributes define the layout configuration of a specific control in its cell of the grid. Static values are defined in the GridData class. Centering a control in its grid cell would be specified as GridData.CENTER.

There are two ways to define GridData. One involves assigning values to each GridData configuration field, as seen in the following code.

```
Button b1 = new Button (shell, SWT.PUSH);
b1.setText = ("B1");
GridData b1GridData = new GridData();
b1GridData.horizontalAlignment = GridData.FILL;
b1GridData.grabExcessHorizontalSpace = true;
b1.setLayoutData(b1GridData);
```

**Table 14.1**   GridData Fields

| Grid Field Name | Description |
| --- | --- |
| grabExcessHorizontalSpace | Allows a control to fill the available space in the horizontal dimension of the grid, meaning the cell will be made wide enough to use the remaining horizontal space. This is not to be confused with the FILL value specification for horizontalAlignment and verticalAlignment, which applies to the cell and not the grid. |
| grabExcessVerticalSpace | Allows a control to fill the available space in the vertical dimension of the grid; the vertical equivalent of grabExcessHorizontalSpace. |
| heightHint | Specifies a minimum height in pixels for the widget. This affects the height of the row. |
| horizontalAlignment | Defines the horizontal alignment in the cell. Values of BEGINNING, CENTER, and END assign justification. Use FILL to use all the cell space. It won't use more space than assigned by the control's width attribute. |
| horizontalIndent | Defines the number of pixels assigned to the left of the control in its cell. |
| horizontalSpan | Specifies the number of columns a control will occupy. This allows a control to span more cells and can be very useful. Otherwise, all grid layouts would look like simple tables. |
| verticalAlignment | Works just like horizontalAlignment but relates to vertical positioning. |
| verticalSpan | Specifies the number of rows a control will occupy; the vertical equivalent of horizontalSpan. |
| widthHint | Specifies a minimum width in pixels for the widget. This affects the width of the column. |

A more common approach specifies the style bits in the GridData constructor. You may find this style more convenient and readable. Moreover, since GridData objects should not be reused, this technique guarantees that.

```
Button b1 = new Button (shell, SWT.PUSH);
b1.setText = ("B1");
b1.setLayoutData(
  new GridData(
    GridData.HORIZONTAL_ALIGN_FILL | GridData.GRAB_HORIZONTAL));
```

Figure 14.12 shows an example of a three-column grid layout that was generated using the SWT Layouts example plug-in. It uses the control classes Label, Text, Table, and Button. The layout uses 10-pixel margins and 5-pixel spacing between controls. The text spans two columns horizontally and the table spans all three columns. Button 5 has been centered inside its cell.

PART III

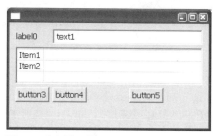

**Figure 14.12**   Three-Column Grid Layout

The following is the standalone SWT code for the layout shown in Figure 14.12. The layout code is set in bold.

```
public class MyLayout {
  public static void main (String [] args) {
    Display display = new Display ();
    Shell shell = new Shell (display);
    GridLayout gridLayout = new GridLayout ();
    gridLayout.numColumns = 3;
    gridLayout.marginHeight = 10;
    gridLayout.marginWidth = 10;
    shell.setLayout (gridLayout);
    Label label0 = new Label (shell, SWT.NONE);
    label0.setText ("label0");
    Text text1 = new Text (shell, SWT.BORDER);
    text1.setText ("text1");
    GridData data = new GridData ();
    data.horizontalAlignment = GridData.FILL;
    data.horizontalSpan = 2;
    data.grabExcessHorizontalSpace = true;
    text1.setLayoutData (data);
    Table table2 = new Table (shell, SWT.BORDER);
    table2.setLinesVisible (true);
    TableItem tableItem1 = new TableItem (table2, SWT.NONE);
    tableItem1.setText ("Item1");
    TableItem tableItem2 = new TableItem (table2, SWT.NONE);
    tableItem2.setText ("Item2");
    data = new GridData ();
    data.horizontalAlignment = GridData.FILL;
    data.horizontalSpan = 3;
    table2.setLayoutData (data);
    Button button3 = new Button (shell, SWT.PUSH);
    button3.setText ("button3");
    Button button4 = new Button (shell, SWT.PUSH);
    button4.setText ("button4");
    Button button5 = new Button (shell, SWT.PUSH);
    button5.setText ("button5");
```

```
          data = new GridData ();
          data.horizontalAlignment = GridData.CENTER;
          button5.setLayoutData (data);
        shell.pack ();
        shell.open ();
        while (!shell.isDisposed ()) {
          if (!display.readAndDispatch ())
            display.sleep ();
          }
          display.dispose ();
        }
    }
```

Between the GridLayout and GridData classes, you have many configuration parameters to play with. To use them for a complex layout, you need to lay out your intended dialog or window and then figure out what layout mechanisms will effectively do what you want. An important design consideration is to carefully decide how many columns a grid layout should contain. If you have to change it, all the widgets in the grid are affected. A convenient way to learn and explore GridLayout is to play with the SWT Layouts example or explore the Eclipse Visual Editor project.

## Form Layout

FormLayout allows for very precise positioning of each control. The previous layouts involve an underlying layout template (fill, row, or grid) to automatically place and position your controls. A form layout allows you to position your controls relative to a parent or sibling control. You can specify offsets in pixels such that you might position a button to be eight pixels to the right of an adjacent button. The position of each edge of the control—top, bottom, left, and right—can be positioned relative to another control. If you are familiar with the UNIX Motif layout XmForm or the IBM VisualAge Smalltalk layout class CwForm, you will be right at home with FormLayout.

This layout technique introduces three new classes: FormLayout, FormData, and FormAttachment. As you have seen before, methods in FormLayout apply to the configuration of the entire layout. FormData configures an individual control. A FormAttachment object is associated with a FormData object and specifies the position of one of the edges of the control. Since you can position all four edges, you could have up to four FormAttachment objects associated with a control's FormData object. Normally, because a control is being positioned on a two-dimensional surface, specifying two adjacent edges is sufficient in many cases. (The top and left edges will suffice, but the left and right edges will not.)

Before we discuss the details, let's look at an example. Figure 14.13 shows positioning of the last name in a name and address layout. Examining the code, you can see that a `FormLayout` has been specified. A text field for the last name is defined. The `FormData` object created is named `data`. In order to locate the text field where it's wanted, the top, left, and right edges are specified using the `FormAttachment` class. Recall that we said that two edges were sufficient. In this example, the right edge was specified to be very near the right edge of the parent control. This resulted in the text field spanning all the available space up to the right edge of its container. For each edge that is defined, a new `FormAttachment` object specifies that edge's position relative to the parent control or a peer control. The details of the information defined in the `FormAttachment` constructor are discussed below. Finally, the `FormData` object and its three `FormAttachment` objects are associated with the `lastName` field using the `setLayoutData` method.

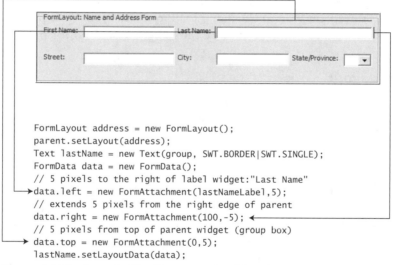

```
FormLayout address = new FormLayout();
parent.setLayout(address);
Text lastName = new Text(group, SWT.BORDER|SWT.SINGLE);
FormData data = new FormData();
// 5 pixels to the right of label widget:"Last Name"
data.left = new FormAttachment(lastNameLabel,5);
// extends 5 pixels from the right edge of parent
data.right = new FormAttachment(100,-5);
// 5 pixels from top of parent widget (group box)
data.top = new FormAttachment(0,5);
lastName.setLayoutData(data);
```

**Figure 14.13**    Example Edge Placement of an SWT Control in a Form Layout

The `FormLayout` class has two configuration attributes: `marginWidth` and `marginHeight`.

The `FormData` class has, as we have seen, four edge positioning attributes, `top`, `bottom`, `left`, and `right`, to which you associate a `FormAttachment` object. It also has `width` and `height` attributes to specify the control dimensions in pixels.

The FormAttachment class is coupled with the FormData class. It specifies the position of a particular edge of the control relative to another control. The control being used as the reference can be the parent control. As we stated, a FormAttachment object may be defined for each of the four edges of a control, but two are enough. Usually, all the edge placement information can be specified in the constructor of the FormAttachment object. There are a variety of constructors to suit various requirements. Let's examine two.

- FormAttachment(int parentPosition, int offset)

  This positions a control's edge relative to the parent control. The parentPosition value specifies a position relative to the width of the parent, as a percentage. A value of 50 would be centered, 0 is far left, and 100 is far right. The second parameter is an offset in pixels relative to the first parameter. Positioning a control in the center plus 20 pixels would be specified as (50, 20). In Figure 14.13 you can see that the top and right edges of the lastName field were specified this way.

- FormAttachment(Control siblingControl, int offset)

  This positions a control relative to a peer control. For example, you might position a text field to the right of its label. An offset in pixels is specified relative to the sibling. In Figure 14.13, you can see that the left edge of the lastName field is positioned five pixels to the right of its label.

Aligning controls vertically, as was done for the firstName and street text fields in Figure 14.13, is easy. The left edge of the firstName text field is positioned relative to its label control. For the street text field you simply align its left edge relative to the firstName label control.

In summary, you can see that FormLayout gives you very precise positioning of a layout because you can control the layout down to the pixel level. Moreover, the layout adapts nicely when the parent control resizes, retaining a pleasing presentation. Again, a convenient way to learn and explore form layouts is to play with the SWT Layouts example.

## Stack Layout

This is a very easy layout manager to understand. All the widgets in the stack will occupy the same location and will be the same size. It is common to use an array or some sort of collection object as the container for all the widgets in the stack. To reveal a particular widget, you simply set the value of the Stack-Layout field topControl to the widget you want to make visible. In the example in Figrue 14.10, all the layout examples are contained in an array of Composite objects. The selection from the list of example layouts determines which example is assigned as the `topControl`. The complete implementation is in the SWT Layouts example (project `com.ibm.jdg2e.swt.layouts` example plug-in); see the `LayoutView.setStackLayout` method. The Javadoc for the `StackLayout` class offers a more simplistic example involving a stack of buttons.

### Summary of Layout Managers

That's the story on layout managers. They are rich enough to satisfy nearly all your layout requirements. It is also possible to define a custom layout manager for special purposes (see the SWT Help topic "Custom Layouts" in the *Platform Plug-in Developer Guide* in the online help). For complex layouts you can use multiple layout managers by nesting one inside another. In this situation our friend the `Composite` widget can be helpful. The outer layout could contain a `Composite` and another layout manager could be assigned to it. Widgets created with this `Composite` as their parent will be laid out according to the assigned layout manager.

## Error Handling

Interestingly, there are only three types of exceptions in SWT: `IllegalArgument-Exception`, `SWTException`, and `SWTError`. These are unchecked exceptions, often representing rare situations (e.g., lack of memory). You don't want to be constantly checking for these. Most of the time you will not be writing exception-handling code when you use SWT, so we are not going to dwell on it. Searching the entire Eclipse source code yields only a modest number of classes containing methods with `catch` clauses for these exceptions. The best advice is to examine the documentation for any SWT method you are using, determine what exceptions are thrown, and decide how you want to handle them. The more robust your plug-in requirements, the more diligent you will need to be. For example, the JDT, which is robust, has its own `Exception-Handler` class, which is called for a variety of error situations (not just SWT errors). This class displays error dialogs and writes to the error log.

SWT is consistent across platforms with respect to exception handling. Here is a brief description of the three exception classes.

- `IllegalArgumentException`

  SWT validates arguments for the proper state and range prior to execution and throws this exception if required. Your code probably won't explicitly look for this exception, but obviously you should test your code sufficiently to satisfy yourself that it won't occur.

- SWTException

  This is thrown when a recoverable SWT error occurs. SWT is in a stable state and can continue. A string message is available for you to retrieve via the exception's getMessage method. For example, calling SWT outside the UI thread would throw this exception. Failure to access or load external resources, like fonts and images, would also throw this exception.

- SWTError

  This exception is thrown when an unrecoverable error occurs. There is little you can do. It is likely that the Workbench cannot continue. If you have high reliability requirements or some sort of special recovery needs, you want to be sensitive to this exception.

## Widgets Have Special Disposal Requirements

In Java applications, explicitly freeing resources is generally not an issue that concerns you. Java's garbage collection handles all of that. With SWT, you have some of that responsibility again. Recall that an SWT resource is a Java wrapper for a real operating system resource that allocates and consumes memory. It needs to be freed up when it is no longer needed.

SWT has two rules related to widget disposal.

1. If you created it, you must dispose of it.
2. Disposing of a parent disposes of its children.

So what does this mean? Which rule applies for any particular circumstance? Let's look at rule 2 first. It states that a parent control will dispose of its children. A Shell or any Composite object will dispose of its children. Most SWT controls require that you specify the parent in the control's constructor. This means that, in most cases, you don't have to explicitly dispose of your widgets. When you populate a wizard page, a preference page, or any dialog with SWT controls, you don't have to worry about disposal because you have a reference to a parent control, typically a Composite object.

So when does rule 1 apply? It applies to SWT objects that are created without a parent widget in their constructor. Some examples are Font, Image, and Color. They can be shared, and a parent does not exist; therefore disposal *is* required. The Shell class has a dispose method, as do the various dialog page classes. IWorkbenchPart, which is a superclass to views and editors, also has a dispose method. Use these methods to dispose of your widget.

The following example involves a font used on a wizard page. It has assigned a Font to a StyledText control. This control can have rich text attributes, like a Font. We have not discussed wizards yet, but this code snippet should be straightforward. When the wizard's dispose method is executed, it disposes of the font object. That will result in freeing any host operating system resources required by the Font object.

```
public class MyWizardPage extends WizardPage {
   ... Code not shown ...
   private Font font;
   public void createControl(Composite parent) {
      ... Create page contents ...
      myText = new StyledText(parent, SWT.SINGLE|SWT.BORDER);
      font =
        new Font(myText.getDisplay(),
          new FontData ("Courier", 16, SWT.BOLD));
      myText.setFont(font);
       ... Finish page creation ...
   }
    public void dispose() {
      super.dispose();
      font.dispose();
    }
}
```

If you want to be notified of a widget's disposal, you can do that through the addDisposeListener method, which is available to all SWT widgets. You pass this method an object that implements the DisposeListener interface. The interface has a widgetDisposed method, which is called during widget disposal. You might use this if you have a widget requiring disposal that is associated with another widget whose disposal is handled automatically. In the following example, a button has an image assigned. When the button is disposed of, its image is too.

```
fButton.setImage(fImage);
fButton.addDisposeListener(new DisposeListener() {
   public void widgetDisposed(DisposeEvent event) {
      if (fImage != null)  {
        fImage.dispose();
        fImage = null;
      }
   }
});
```

If you must manage several fonts or images, consider using the classes FontRegistry or ImageRegistry in the package org.eclipse.jface.resource. These classes maintain registries of fonts or images and automatically handle the disposal for you. In fact, you should never dispose of anything managed by these registries. The article on eclipse.org titled "Using Images in the Eclipse UI" discusses this topic in detail.

## Using Threads to Separate UI and Non-UI Activities

All native windowing systems use a queuing model for dispatching events. These events are responses to user actions and must be processed in a timely fashion (on the order of 1/10 second). Nontrivial operations are deferred to another thread so the user interface can remain responsive. The second thread will convey its completion to the user later, using one of the user interface's synchronization methods to display a message, update a status field, or increment a progress dialog. Plug-ins often divide the processing of their computational functions and user interactions into separate threads. Eclipse does not preclude the use of the Java threading model to handle long-running operations involving computational intensity or remote operations. Actually, it is a good practice. Your Workbench plug-in, that is, a plug-in loaded by Eclipse, runs in the main Workbench thread, the same thread in which all SWT processing occurs. Eclipse offers a variety of concurrency mechanisms that support an infrastructure for managing work outside the main Workbench thread. You should examine concurrency support (see Chapter 29, Implementing Responsiveness and Concurrency Using Jobs) before deciding whether or not you want to do your own threading. For synchronized operations, the platform concurrency support is recommended because it has stronger deadlock detection and other useful features.

If you spawn a separate thread and need to engage the Eclipse user interface, you must satisfy some special requirements. There are two situations where you may want to engage the user interface from your non-UI thread.

1. You need a response from the user before proceeding.

   Suppose you are running a database query in a separate database access thread, but the results are excessive and the query is not complete. You may want to ask the user to decide whether the query should continue or not.

2. You want to convey information to the user but don't wish to interrupt your processing.

   In this same query, you want to inform the user of progress but you don't need to interrupt any query processing.

SWT operations must run in the thread that the `Display` object was defined in. SWT runs in the main or primary thread of Eclipse. You must be careful not to do UI operations outside the thread that Eclipse is running in. Otherwise, an SWTException will be thrown. To help you, the SWT Display class has two methods, syncExec and asyncExec, to handle thread synchronization. As the method names imply, these two methods are used, respectively, when synchronous or asynchronous processing is required. Both methods pass a Runnable instance, which should be a familiar Java threading object. The current thread invokes the Runnable object at the next reasonable opportunity. In the Runnable object, you can invoke your UI code.

In the database query example, the excessive results situation is handled by the syncExec method. This allows you to display a message dialog to the user and wait until a response is received to continue the query or end it. The database access thread would be suspended until the user response is handled. In the following code snippet, a message is displayed using the Message-Dialog class. The Display.getCurrent static method is a convenient way to get the Display object of the current UI thread.

```
final Display display = Display.getCurrent();
new Thread() {  // Database query thread.
  public void run() {
    ... Query processing ...
    display.syncExec(new Runnable() {
      public void run() {
        if (MessageDialog.openQuestion
            (null, "Query","Continue query?") != true)
          {... Terminate query ...};
      }
    }
  });
    ... Continue query ...
}.start();  }
```

In the second case of the database query, you simply want to display a progress bar to the user and keep going. Here the asyncExec method comes to the rescue. The Runnable object in this method could update a progress bar in the UI thread without interrupting the query operation in the database access thread. In the following code snippet, an SWT ProgressBar is updated.

```
final Display display = Display.getCurrent();
final ProgressBar queryProgressBar =
  new ProgressBar(shell, SWT.SMOOTH);
queryProgressBar.setBounds(10, 10, 200, 32);
int progressValue;
new Thread() {  // Database query thread.
  public void run() {
    ... Query processing ...
    display.asyncExec(new Runnable() {
```

```
                    public void run() {
                      queryProgressBar.setSelection(progressValue);
                      ...
                    }
                });
                ... Continue query ...
            }
        }.start();
```

Another interesting method in the `Display` class, called `timerExec`, also takes a `Runnable` object. The `Runnable` object is executed in the UI thread after a specified number of milliseconds have elapsed. In the database query example involving long-running queries, it might be useful to inform the user after a minute of the amount of time that has elapsed since the query started. (Eclipse concurrency support has a delay feature also; see Chapter 29.)

When using threads, always observe good practices relative to thread safety to avoid deadlocks and unexpected interference between concurrent threads. The `syncExec` method, in particular, can be the source of deadlocks by holding locks that block other code from proceeding. Again, Eclipse concurrency support may be a more attractive alternative.

## An Overview of SWT Packages

You have been exposed to the essential elements you must understand to do plug-in development. You will use SWT in subsequent chapters and exercises.

Table 14.2 summarizes all the SWT packages and their primary functions. More information is available in the API reference in the *Platform Plug-in Developer Guide* that is available in the online help.

**Table 14.2**  SWT Packages

| Package | Description |
| --- | --- |
| org.eclipse.swt | SWT constants and error-handling support. |
| org.eclipse.swt.accessibility | Accessibility support. |
| org.eclipse.swt.awt | The `SWT_AWT` Swing interoperability class (see Chapter 33). |
| org.eclipse.swt.browser | The SWT `Browser` widget class |
| org.eclipse.swt.custom | Support for Eclipse custom widgets. |
| org.eclipse.swt.dnd | Drag-and-drop support. |
| org.eclipse.swt.events | Event handling for typed listeners like `MouseListener`. |

*continues*

**Table 14.2**    SWT Packages (*continued*)

| Package | Description |
| --- | --- |
| org.eclipse.swt.graphics | Support for SWT graphics. To get a feel for SWT graphics run the SWT Paint example plug-in that is available as a view when the example plug-ins are installed. See also the Graphical Editing Framework (GEF) Project under the Eclipse Tools Project. |
| org.eclipse.swt.layout | Support for layout managers. |
| org.eclipse.swt.ole.win32 | Support for OLE and ActiveX. This is available only on Windows platforms (see Chapter 34). |
| org.eclipse.swt.printing | Support for printing. |
| org.eclipse.swt.program | The class Program, which links an application associated with a specific file extension. |
| org.eclipse.swt.widgets | The public APIs for the various SWT widgets. |

## SWT Support for Swing

Since version 3.0, Eclipse supports hosting Swing controls within SWT (for specific operating systems only). This hosting is done using the SWT_AWT class (see Chapter 33, Swing Interoperability).

## Eclipse Forms

We have stated in this chapter that SWT widgets are typically used in some form of dialog. You see SWT widgets in preference pages, property pages, and wizard pages. Certainly, you have noticed that the Plug-in Manifest Editor has an entirely different look than dialogs (see Figure14.14). It has what is sometimes referred to as the "flat look" instead of the gray background "dialog look." The appearance or look that you see in the PDE editor was originally private to the platform. It has been exposed as a public API and is referred to as Eclipse Forms. Eclipse Forms can be used in views, editors, and wizards—wherever you require a form-based user interface. It contains its own set of widgets, which are extensions of SWT widgets. Table 14.3 lists the four packages that make up Eclipse Forms. After you have gained experience with SWT and creating Workbench parts like views and editors, consider where Eclipse Forms might be useful for your needs.

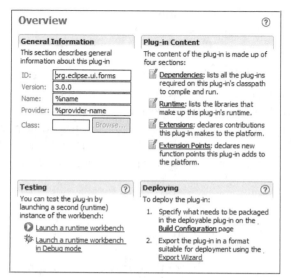

**Figure 14.14**  Plug-in Manifest Editor

**Table 14.3**  Eclipse Forms Packages

| Package | Description |
| --- | --- |
| org.eclipse.ui.forms | Form-based controls for use in views, editors, and wizards |
| org.eclipse.ui.forms.editor | Support for form-based multipage editors |
| org.eclipse.ui.forms.events | Events and listeners for form-based parts |
| org.eclipse.ui.forms.widgets | Custom widgets and controls for form-based parts |

## Example Summary

The CD-ROM accompanying this book contains example SWT widget and SWT layout code. The following examples are provided.

- The SWT Controls example in project com.ibm.jdg2e.swt provides some basic examples of SWT widgets and includes event handling, thread synchronization, and widget disposal.
- The SWT Layouts example exposes you to all the layouts discussed in this chapter. See project com.ibm.jdg2e.swt.layouts.
- Project com.jdg2e.swt.snippets provides nearly 150 small examples of SWT. These examples have been repackaged in convenient form

from the SWT developer resource page on eclipse.org. The companion project `com.ibm.jdg2e.swt.snippetLauncher` provides a launcher for the snippets.

The SWT Controls and SWT Layouts examples referenced earlier in this chapter (see Figures 14.2, 14.3, and 14.11) are available from the eclipsc.org downloads page. Download the file `eclipse-examples-3.0-win32.zip` for Windows and the file `eclipse-examples-3.0.zip` for other platforms. When installed, the documentation for the examples is located in folder `<install directory>/eclipse/plugins/org.eclipse.examples_3.0.0/doc-html`.

## Chapter Summary

In this chapter, we provided an introduction to SWT so you can begin to use it in your plug-in applications.

SWT is an efficient GUI library that provides robust, native platform performance and behavior. It is the foundation for the Eclipse user interface, and it is critical to Eclipse's ability to be a robust and responsive Java client application. This chapter covered the essential elements of SWT you are likely to encounter when developing plug-ins. For many plug-ins, you will use SWT to populate the contents of various dialogs like wizards, property pages, and preference pages.

In the face of alternate technologies, SWT was a controversial decision during the initial design of Eclipse. That controversy continued after Eclipse was released. Nonetheless, SWT serves its purpose admirably and has developed a significant following among the Eclipse community.

## References

Arthorne, John, and Chris Laffra. 2004. *Official Eclipse 3.0 FAQs*. Boston, MA: Addison-Wesley. http://eclipsefaq.org. (See Chapter 7 and FAQ 154.)

Northover, Steve, and Mike Wilson. 2004. *SWT: The Standard Widget Toolkit, Volume 1*. Boston, MA: Addison-Wesley.

See the Eclipse Forms Programming Guide (draft) under the Reference topic in the online help for this book.

SWT Developer Resource page on eclipse.org. From http://www.eclipse.org, navigate to Projects, the Eclipse Project, Platform, SWT, developers page.

There are many very good SWT articles on eclipse.org. All of them can be found in the SWT category on the articles page at http://www.eclipse.org/articles.

# CHAPTER 15

## JFace Viewers

When you contribute user interface components to Eclipse, you have several options you can use, and sometimes mingle, to create the user interface. These options include the use of SWT widgets, JFace viewers, or even Swing widgets.

The SWT option was just reviewed in Chapter 14, and the role of Swing for Eclipse user interface development is discussed in Chapter 33, Swing Interoperability. This chapter discusses JFace viewers. Common questions about viewers are addressed, the classes involved in the framework are reviewed, and the process of defining a working viewer is detailed. Additional information on how you can integrate viewers with the Workbench is also covered.

## Viewer Basics

There is much to learn about JFace viewers. A few basic questions about viewers are addressed in this section to start this learning process. The terms you need to master are introduced here; you can find the gory details in the sections that follow.

### What Is a Viewer?

JFace viewers are adapters on SWT widgets. Like widgets, a viewer can be created on any SWT Composite. The JFace viewer framework allows you to map your high-level model content onto the more primitive data types that

SWT list, table, and tree widgets expect and keep the values displayed in the user interface synchronized with the model.

The different viewer types build on each other; the `Viewer` class is extended by `ContentViewer`, which is extended by `StructuredViewer`. Each layer in this hierarchy adds to the structure and function of the JFace viewer framework. In other words, a viewer is a general-purpose framework for displaying arbitrary objects.

## What Do Viewers Look Like?

You use viewers to build the user interface, so we look first at the visual layer. As an Eclipse user, you have been using JFace viewers all the time; you just may not have realized this before. As shown in Figure 15.1, almost everything you see inside Eclipse views, editors, general-purpose dialogs, and even several preference and wizard pages include user interface content defined using JFace viewers.

The tree and table viewers are discussed in this chapter; the text viewer is discussed in Chapter 26, Building a Custom Text Editor with JFace Text.

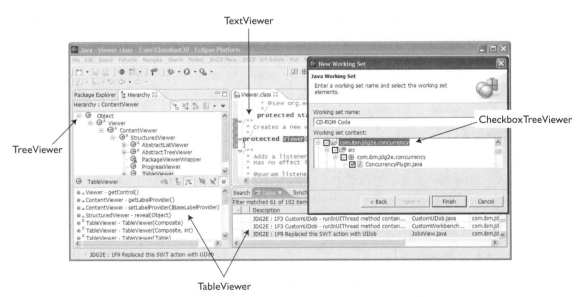

**Figure 15.1**    Examples of Viewer Types Used in the Eclipse User Interface

### What Types of Viewers Exist?

The JFace viewer hierarchy shown in Figure 15.2 displays the available viewer types. The hierarchy also indicates the layers of function that correspond to the Viewer, ContentViewer, and StructuredViewer types.

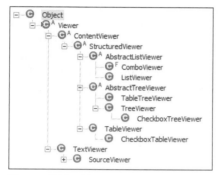

**Figure 15.2**   Viewer Hierarchy

Almost all viewers are both content viewers and structured viewers; these are the focus of this chapter. The TextViewer and SourceViewer classes define a document-based model. These are covered in Chapter 26, Building a Custom Text Editor with JFace Text.

The viewer type name indicates the widget type used; an SWT List, Table, or Tree. Check box viewers also include a selection toggle as shown in Figure 15.1.

### How Do I Use a Viewer?

To build a user interface using JFace viewers, you start by selecting the appropriate type of content viewer, such as a tree or table viewer. Next you associate the viewer with a content provider to access your data and a label provider to help it display appropriate content. Lastly you identify an input to the viewer, for example, the workspace itself. The input is typically a reference to your model, although static data could also be shown in a viewer.

The content provider knows how to access the input. It can adapt the model to the expected viewer content. This content is a set of objects; these objects have a parent/child relationship if you are using a tree viewer. A label provider can produce the specific names and icons needed to display the content in the viewer.

Filtering and sorting are also supported by a structured viewer. This optional layer of the API allows you to add filters and a sorter to control the display of content in the viewer. Filters can be used to determine what content should actually be shown in the viewer; sorters determine the order of that display.

### Why Should Viewers Be Used?

When creating views, editors, or dialogs, you will usually include both JFace viewers and SWT widgets. There are two key reasons to choose JFace viewers: viewers make you much more productive, and they are compatible with the Workbench selection processing and action contribution framework. Selection processing is discussed further in this chapter; action contributions are discussed in Chapter 21.

User interface development is easier when you use the JFace viewer framework. Viewers understand the concept of a model and can be layered with function to provide the richness of content and control required. You use the viewer's higher-level model-based API to help you display your data in the underlying SWT widgets; you can also choose to use viewers even if you don't have a corresponding model.

JFace viewers are valuable because they implement the interfaces required to participate in the Eclipse selection framework. This lets you just point to your viewer when you want your Workbench part (view or editor) to share its selection with the rest of the Workbench (see Sharing the Viewer Selection in Your View in Chapter 18, Views).

The support for the integration of Workbench action contributions is based on the viewer providing access to the model content corresponding to the user's selection. Once registered with the Workbench, a viewer's objects are easily accessible (see Registering Context Menus with the Workbench in Chapter 18).

Simply put, the viewer framework is ready to support the implementation of the coordinated set of behaviors found in the Workbench. Once you understand how to use viewers they will likely become your favorite technique for displaying list, tree, and table content in an Eclipse-based dialog, wizard, view, or editor.

## Viewer Framework

The JFace viewer framework is based on a layered implementation of function. We start with the Viewer class as the root but focus only on content and structured viewers in this chapter. This section reviews the structure, function, and relationship between the framework participants.

## Class Structure

The framework is defined by a set of classes and interfaces with a common inheritance structure. The function provided by viewers is layered in that hierarchy. The interfaces for content providers, label providers, and the other participants provide the specialized support required for different viewers. This structure is shown in Figure 15.3.

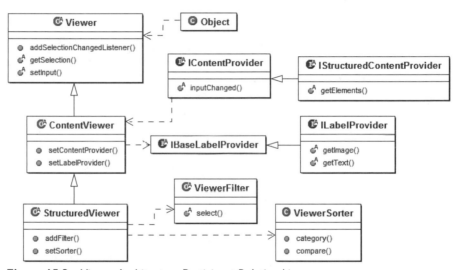

**Figure 15.3** Viewer Architecture Participant Relationships

Figure 15.3 shows only the key classes and methods necessary to understand the framework.

### Viewer

The Viewer class is the SWT widget adapter and supports selection processing by implementing the IInputSelectionProvider interface. A viewer understands the widget it contains, maps the content of the widget to the Workbench selection framework, and can pass scroll requests to the adapted widget. The Viewer class also defines the concept of an input, which is passed on to other participants in the framework.

### Content Viewer, Content Provider, and Label Provider

The set and get methods in the ContentViewer define the relationships between a viewer, content provider, and label provider. This is a classic example of the value of separating your model from your displayed user interface. The content provider adapts the model content to the structure displayed in the viewer, while the label provider maps the individual objects to the text and image content displayed in the viewer.

The IContentProvider isolates the viewer from model- or data-specific issues. The content provider is responsible for obtaining the objects that should be shown in the viewer from the input model. To do this the content viewers in Eclipse call methods defined in the corresponding content provider interface.

The content provider is also required to listen for model changes and tell the viewer to update or refresh its content as may be required. Each viewer collaborates with one content provider, although the viewer's content provider can be changed at runtime.

The ILabelProvider gives the viewer something to show on the screen for each object returned by the content provider. Each viewer collaborates with one label provider, although the viewer's label provider can be changed at runtime.

This is discussed further in the upcoming section Creating the Basic Content Viewer Arrangement.

### Structured Viewer, Filters, and Sorters

The StructuredViewer adds support for viewer helpers such as filters and sorters. These helpers are used to further customize the displayed content by applying filter logic to determine which objects are displayed and sort the content based on the appropriate object attributes. See Controlling the Content Displayed in a Structured Viewer later in this chapter.

## Content Provider–Content Viewer–Label Provider Relationships

There are some basic structural requirements when using viewers. The viewer type chosen forces certain capabilities in the content provider and label provider. Table 15.1 summarizes these relationships.

### Content Provider Structure

The content provider must reflect the structure of the widget; the requirements are different for list, table, and tree viewers. When a tree structure is involved, the content provider must support parent/child relationships.

**Table 15.1**   Viewer–Provider Relationships

| Content Provider | Content Viewer | Label Provider |
|---|---|---|
| IStructuredContentProvider | ComboViewer | ILabelProvider |
| | ListViewer | |
| | TableViewer | ITableLabelProvider |
| | CheckboxTableViewer | |
| ITreeContentProvider | TableTreeViewer | |
| | TreeViewer | ILabelProvider |
| | CheckboxTreeViewer | |

All viewers get their objects from a content provider using a method named getElements. Tree viewers use additional method calls to resolve the parent/child relationships. So to work with table and list viewers, your content provider must implement the IStructuredContentProvider interface. To work with tree viewers, the ITreeContentProvider interface must be implemented. This interface extends IStructuredContentProvider.

### Label Provider Structure

The label provider must be prepared to respond with an image and/or text value for an object. You can support this by creating a label provider that implements the ILabelProvider interface. The ILabelProvider interface defines two methods that must be implemented: getImage and getText.

If a table viewer is used, the label provider must be prepared to respond to requests for individual table columns. To support a table viewer, you must implement the ITableLabelProvider interface with the associated getColumnText and getColumnImage methods. The ITableLabelProvider interface extends IBaseLabelProvider.

## Creating the Basic Content Viewer Arrangement

The process of defining a working viewer, content provider, and label provider structure is a series of repeatable steps. You can just read along and create the basic content viewer arrangement at the same time, or review the examples on the CD-ROM. These are the steps that will be described.

1. Identify the input.
2. Create the viewer.

3. Create a content provider.
4. Create a label provider.
5. Connect the viewer with the content and label providers.
6. Define an input (model) to the viewer.
7. Implement model–viewer synchronization.

## Identifying the Input

You do not tell the viewer about it until later, but it is best to identify the input model first. The model you use could even be from Eclipse. The workspace is a common input for many views, such as the Navigator, Problems, and Tasks views. A simple model will be used as the input for this walkthrough.

The model will be obtained from a plug-in and be preloaded with some content. A set of ILocation objects can be accessed from the model. Each ILocation has three attributes (name, activity, and politicalUnit). This model can be obtained from a plug-in class and is loaded with an initial set of data. The following code gets the model reference and an array of ILocation objects; the result of printing the name to the console is also shown.

```
ILocation[] locs = LocationsPlugin.getRoadTrip().getLocations();
  for (int i = 0; i < locs.length; i++) {
    ILocation location = locs[i];
    System.out.println("\t" + location.getName());
}

    Dallas
    Brazil
    Cork
    Alaska
    England
```

The implementation discussion that follows is based on a working viewer example. This simple example and more complex ones are included on the CD-ROM. See Example Summary at the end of this chapter for details.

## Creating the Viewer

When you add a viewer to a Composite you are actually adding the widget that the viewer wraps to the user interface. Here is an example of creating a simple TableViewer on an instance of a Composite.

```
TableViewer viewer = new TableViewer(composite);
```

This type of logic might be found in the createContents method for a preference or property page, the createControl method for a wizard page or other form of dialog page, the createDialogArea method for a general-purpose dialog, or the `createPartControl` method for a view or editor Workbench part. Each of these methods gives you a `Composite` you can use to define your user interface content.

That is all it takes for many types of viewers. The viewer implementation creates the required widget in the passed `Composite`. You have the option of creating the widget yourself and passing it to the viewer as part of the constructor. This option allows you to create the widget with specific SWT styles. You can also define the number of columns required in a table. See Using Alternative Viewer Types later in this chapter for details on viewer customization.

## Creating the Content Provider

Here is an example of creating a `LocationsContentProvider` with the methods required by the `IStructuredContentProvider` interface for use with a `ListViewer`. The implementation reflects the type of input expected in this example, an `IRoadTrip`.

```
public class LocationsContentProvider
        implements IStructuredContentProvider {

  public Object[] getElements(Object inputElement) {
    return ((IRoadTrip) inputElement).getLocations();
  }

  public void dispose() {
  }

  public void inputChanged(
    Viewer viewer, Object oldInput, Object newInput) {
  }
}
```

A content provider implementation will always be specific to the type of input object expected. The `getElements` implementation returns an array of objects, in this case `ILocation` objects, for use by the viewer.

An `inputChanged` implementation is not provided at this time. This works fine when the identified input is constant (you do not assign a new input to the viewer).

When the input can change, the `inputChanged` method will do more work. Details on reacting to model changes and method timing are discussed in the upcoming subsection Implementing Model–Viewer Synchronization.

Eclipse provides a `WorkbenchContentProvider` that works for adaptable objects. This content provider also listens automatically to workspace changes and refreshes the viewer when required.

### Creating the Label Provider

To implement your own label provider, start by extending the LabelProvider
implementation provided by Eclipse. As the viewer being used is a List-
Viewer, the label provider only has to extend LabelProvider and override
the getText method. The LabelProvider class could have been used directly
if your objects had toString methods that returned appropriate values. The
LabelProvider implementation of getText is a simple toString call on the
object.

The following implementation of a LocationsLabelProvider supports
the ILocation element passed from the viewer. It overrides the getText
method to return the name of the location as the text value. The getImage
and dispose methods are also overridden to add image support, even though
they will not be used just yet (getImage is not called for a ListViewer).

```
public class LocationsLabelProvider extends LabelProvider {
   Image image = null;

   public String getText(Object element, int columnIndex) {
      return ((ILocation) element).getName();
   }

   public Image getImage(Object element) {
      URL url = SimpleViewPlugin.getDefault().find(
         new Path("icons/sample.gif"));
      ImageDescriptor id = ImageDescriptor.createFromURL(url);
      image = id.createImage();
      return image;
   }

   public void dispose() {
      super.dispose();
      if (image != null)
         image.dispose();
   }
}
```

This code probably does not seem to do very much work. Some function
is inherited, and things get more interesting if the viewer needs an image (you
have to dispose your images too). But this simple bit of code works just fine
for a ListViewer or even a TreeViewer.

If a TableViewer were used, your label provider would have to support
column-specific values by implementing the ITableLabelProvider interface
with the associated getColumnText and getColumnImage methods (see
Figure 15.1 earlier in this chapter).

---

**NOTE** A viewer is associated with only one label provider. However, a viewer may be displaying a heterogeneous model. For example, a tree viewer may have nodes that contain different types of objects. For a tree viewer, your label provider's getText method would need to query for the type of object that has been passed and return the appropriate text. The methods called to get a String value might be different for each layer in the tree.

---

Eclipse also provides WorkbenchLabelProvider, a more sophisticated and reusable label provider that works well for adaptable objects, such as when your model input to the viewer is the workspace.

### Connecting the Viewer with the Content and Label Providers

Once you have defined a content provider to supply the objects and a label provider to implement how they will be displayed, you need to associate these providers with your viewer. This is the standard setup required to use any viewer. You create an instance of the appropriate viewer, content provider, and label provider, and then wire them together using the appropriate set methods.

```
ListViewer viewer = new ListViewer(parent);
viewer.setContentProvider(new LocationsContentProvider());
viewer.setLabelProvider(new LocationsLabelProvider());
```

You must use unique instances of a content and label provider for each viewer. This requirement keeps the structure simple and makes sense as you will see soon; the content provider has to know which viewer to notify when changes occur.

### Defining an Input to the Viewer

The next step is to link the viewer and the input model. This step actually starts up the viewer framework. As you will see, identifying an input to the viewer triggers quite a bit of processing.

Your model may be global, such as the Eclipse workspace, which is the input to the tree viewer in the Navigator view. Or an object in your model may be the input, such that the active input to the viewer could change over time as your focus moves between object instances. This means that you may be able to define the input to your viewer only once or need to change the input as a reaction to some user selection.

Let's describe an example to lock the idea in your mind. When you open the Java Hierarchy view you actually see two viewers: a tree viewer and a table viewer. The selection in the tree viewer is detected and used as the input to the table viewer. So as you change the class selected in the hierarchy tree, the table shows you the appropriate list of class members.

As identified in the first step, an `IRoadTrip` object will be used as the input for this example. Telling the viewer about the input is simple; all it takes is one line of code.

```
viewer.setInput(LocationsPlugin.getRoadTrip());
```

The interesting part is what happens in response to this one line of code. The viewer shares the input with the content provider and then asks the content provider for objects from this input using the `inputChanged` and `get-Elements` methods. The viewer then continues and asks the label provider to get text and image values for each of the objects returned by the content provider. This is done with calls to the `getText` and `getImage` methods. (The `ListViewer` we have used does not need an image, but the framework will call `getImage` for other viewer types.) This processing is shown in Figure 15.4.

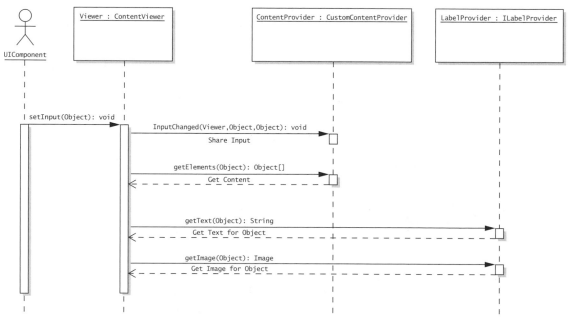

**Figure 15.4**   Viewer Input Definition and Related Model Access Processing Used in the Viewer Framework

Every time you set the viewer input, it will pass the new input to the content provider using the `inputChanged` method and rerun this processing. If the model input to the viewer does not change, the `inputChanged` method does not have to do much at all. This is how the code in the example is currently defined.

We now have completed the construction of a working viewer–content provider–label provider structure. This structure will work fine when the model is static. This results in a working view as shown in Figure 15.5.

**Figure 15.5**    Viewer in a View with Input Model Content

If new locations are added, the current implementation does not react. New locations are not shown unless the view is closed and opened, forcing the viewer content to be recreated. In a more realistic scenario, the input model content changes and the viewer must be informed. This is the focus of the next subsection.

### Implementing Model–Viewer Synchronization

The end user expects real-time changes in the model to be promptly reflected in the user interface. The viewer needs to react to these model events and update itself accordingly. This is the responsibility of the content provider.

When the model changes, it informs others about the change. If your model were written using the JavaBean architecture, the objects may have bound properties on your JavaBean such that when they change they signal a property change event. The content provider can subscribe to these events to keep the viewer synchronized.

There is at least one Eclipse-based alternative to the JavaBean architecture. The `org.eclipse.jface.util` package contains event management code that can be used to track changes on an observed model. The model can implement `addPropertyChangeListener` and `removePropertyChangeListener` methods to register listeners that need to be informed of model updates. The `ListenerList` class can be used to track these observers. They must implement the `IProperty-ChangeListener` interface. A `PropertyChangeEvent` is created when model changes occur, and a PropertyChangeEvent is sent to all observers using a firePropertyChange method. The supplied IRoadTrip model uses this technique to implement support for change notification.

In a scenario where the model content can change, the content provider uses the inputChanged method to register itself as a listener on the new input and to remove the listener from the old input, as may be appropriate. Both the new and old inputs are passed as parameters to the inputChanged method, and each can be null. The first time the inputChanged method is called, the old input is null. The new input is null when inputChanged is called when the viewer is being disposed.

To implement listener support, the content provider has to implement the IPropertyChangeListener interface, add and remove itself as a model change listener, and be prepared to talk to the viewer when events are triggered.

This is the basic logic structure required in the inputChanged method to keep a reference to the viewer in a field and register the need to be informed of changes in the input model. The field is defined as StructuredViewer viewer = null;.

This logic supports changes in the input model defined for the viewer.

```
public void inputChanged(
    Viewer viewer, Object oldInput, Object newInput) {

  this.viewer = (StructuredViewer) viewer;

  // If not the same input
  if (oldInput != newInput) {

  // Remove listener from old -- fires even if new is null.
    if (oldInput != null) {
      ((IRoadTrip) oldInput).removePropertyChangeListener(this);
    }
    // Add listener to new -- fires even if old is null.
    if (newInput != null) {
      ((IRoadTrip) newInput).addPropertyChangeListener(this);
    }
  }
}
```

Figure 15.6 shows the process of a content provider adding and removing listeners as part of the inputChanged method, which is triggered after any setInput call.

When the content provider receives an event that the model has changed, the content provider tells the viewer how to react. The content provider may invoke two methods on the viewer: refresh and update. The update method

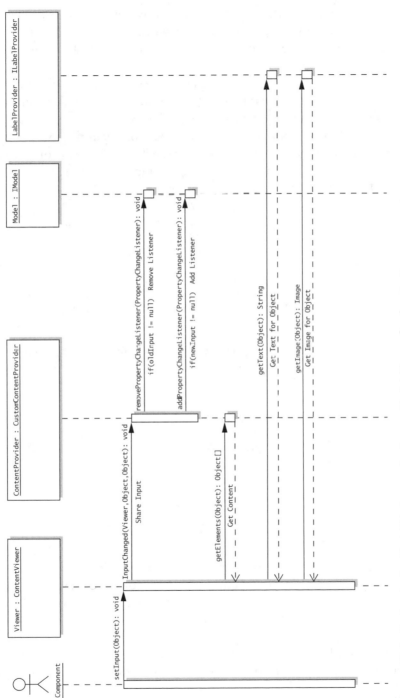

**Figure 15.6** Registering for Model Updates to Implement Model–Viewer Synchronization

381

assumes that the structure is unchanged, while refresh uses the content provider to reread the input. Use update when possible, as it performs best by limiting the number of objects processed. Use refresh if there are content or structure changes.

Figure 15.7 shows the complete process of setting up the viewer with an input model and requesting synchronization after a model change event using both the refresh and update methods.

The IRoadTrip model change notification identifies the type of change. Structure changes require a call to refresh; ILocation property changes require a call to update. With the following code, changes to the underlying model are now reflected in the viewer.

```
public void propertyChange(final PropertyChangeEvent event) {
  // Make sure control exists.
  Control ctrl = viewer.getControl();

  if (ctrl != null && !ctrl.isDisposed()) {
    // Use an asyncExec to run this code on UI thread.
    ctrl.getDisplay().asyncExec(new Runnable() {
      public void run() {

        if (event.getProperty() == IRoadTrip.LISTADD
            | event.getProperty() == IRoadTrip.LISTREMOVE)
          viewer.refresh();

        else {
          String[] propChange =
            new String[] { event.getProperty() };
          viewer.update(event.getNewValue(), propChange);
        }
      }
    });
  }
}
```

We have now completed the construction of a working viewer–content provider–label provider structure, with synchronization between the model and viewer. This basic structure will work for most viewer scenarios. The implementation must be expanded to support alternative viewer structures, such as a table with multiple columns or a tree.

A set of viewer examples is provided on the CD-ROM. In addition, the com.ibm.jdg2e.view.simplemodel project provides the LocationsView class. This uses model event processing, a multicolumn table, and both the refresh and update methods for synchronization.

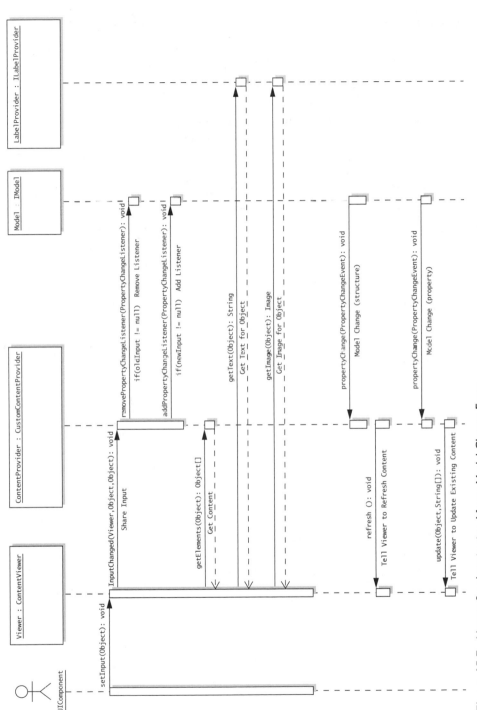

**Figure 15.7** Viewer Synchronization After a Model Change Event

383

## Controlling the Content Displayed in a Structured Viewer

Structured viewers have the ability to filter and sort objects displayed in the viewer. Most of the viewers shown in the hierarchy in Figure 15.2 earlier in this chapter are structured viewers. This simply means that they support the addition and removal of one or more filters and the use of a single sorter to control the display of the objects returned by the content provider. This is controlled using the `addFilter`/`removeFilter` and `setSorter` methods on a viewer. You can add as many filters as you want, but you can use only one sorter at a time.

Label decorators are another technique you can use to alter the displayed content in a viewer. Adding support for label decorators is discussed in Adding Label Decorations on Objects in a Viewer near the end of this chapter.

### Filtering the Viewer Content

To make it easier for users to use the data in a view, you can create and add filters to your viewer to allow users to control what they actually see. A good example of how this works is found in the Outline view content contribution made by the Java editor. Many of the actions on the Outline view toolbar add filters to the viewer. If you look at the action icons from left to right, they filter the viewer content in the following ways: **Hide fields**, **Hide static members**, **Hide non-public members**, and **Hide local types**. So as a user of filters you can see how useful they can be.

You can create a filter by writing a class that extends `ViewerFilter` and overriding the `select` method and optionally the `isFilterProperty` method. The `select` method returns a `boolean` to indicate whether the given element should be displayed.

The `isFilterProperty` method is passed property information from `update` processing requests sent to the viewer and returns `false` by default. When an input model change occurs, the content provider has the option of using the `update` method to pass the modified element(s) and property changes to the viewer. If you use the `update` method, your filter implementation should override the `isFilterProperty` method to return `true` when the filter logic is impacted by a change to the property. This will force a reprocessing of the filter logic when required.

The following implementation is from the `LocationsView` example. This logic will filter out `ILocations` that are not greater than a specified value. And if the attribute involved in the `select` logic is modified, the `isFilterProperty` method will return `true`.

```
public class PoliticalFilter extends ViewerFilter {

  /**
   * Return true if the political unit is county or smaller.
   */
  public boolean select(Viewer viewer, Object parentElement,
      Object element) {
    if (element instanceof ILocation
        && ((ILocation) element)
          .getPoliticalUnit() <= ILocation.COUNTY)
      return false;
    else
      return true;
  }
  /**
   * If the political unit changed, then say yes so the filter
   * is reprocessed.
   */
  public boolean
    isFilterProperty(Object element, String property) {
    // Say yes to political unit.
    return (property == ILocation.POLITICAL_CHANGED);
  }
}
```

The filter can be added or removed from the viewer as needed. A common location for add/remove filter requests is a toggle button in the user interface. This logic can be placed in an action to add the filter when required and remove it later if requested.

```
if (isChecked()) {
  if (filter == null)
    filter = new PoliticalFilter();
  viewer.addFilter(filter);
} else {
  viewer.removeFilter(filter);
}
```

The creation of a view action to support this type of function is discussed in Chapter 18, Views. An action of this type, with the associated filter logic, is included in the `LocationsView` example on the CD-ROM.

## Sorting the Viewer Content

To create a custom sorter, you define a class that extends `ViewerSorter`. The `ViewerSorter` has default behavior defined in the inherited `compare` method. It sorts the data first into categories as specified in the `category` method. The `category` method returns an integer representing a grouping of a set of objects; the default implementation is to return 0, that is, to treat all objects as belonging to the same category. The sort for a given category performed by the compare method uses a case-insensitive comparison based on the string returned by the getText method for the viewer's label provider. Both the category and compare methods in the ViewerSorter may be overridden in your sorter subclass to provide a different comparison.

Given the default implementation of the compare and category methods, the ViewerSorter can be used as is, to get an alphabetical sort on your objects based on the getText value returned by your label provider. This in fact is the default implementation used in the LocationsView example—the sorter is assigned to the viewer using the setSorter method. A viewer can have only one active sorter.

```
// Use the default ViewerSorter behavior in the viewer.
viewer.setSorter(new ViewerSorter());
```

Your sorter should also consider overriding the isSorterProperty method, which returns true if a sorter is affected by a property change. If true, the sort process will be run again; false will prevent unnecessary sort processing. This method is called after a call to the viewer's update method. A viewer update method call includes the properties that have changed. The active sorter will be asked if any of the changed properties impact the sort order.

You can create an alternative sorter that uses a customized version of the category method but still uses the default compare logic. However, now the compare logic is applied using the new categorization scheme. This allows you to create a sort within types where the types are defined by the category associated with the elements in the viewer.

The LocationsView example uses two sorters. The default is an instance of ViewerSorter, and the alternative is a customized implementation with an alternate category method. This function is wired into the view's user interface to allow the alternate sorter to be toggled in and out.

The following implementation of a simple custom sorter shows an alternative category method and code to react to property changes.

```
class PoliticalSorter extends ViewerSorter {
    /**
     * Categorizes the ILocation objects using their political
     * unit value. This is simple to do as this value is already
     * an int value, which is what must be returned.
     */
    public int category(Object element) {
        //
        return ((ILocation)element).getPoliticalUnit();
    }
    public boolean
```

```
            isSorterProperty(Object element, String property) {
            // Say yes to name.
            return ((property == ILocation.NAME_CHANGED) |
              (property == ILocation.POLITICAL_CHANGED));
        }
    }
```

When this code is run, the new sorter replaces any previously defined sorter.

```
// Change to the location within political unit sorter.
viewer.setSorter(new PoliticalSorter());
```

The end result is that when the alternative sorter is used, the locations are sorted by political unit and then name. This is noticeable only when the political unit type attribute is included in the viewer. The image used for each row in Figure 15.8 shows how the content has been sorted by political unit. The code for this viewer is part of the examples on the CD-ROM.

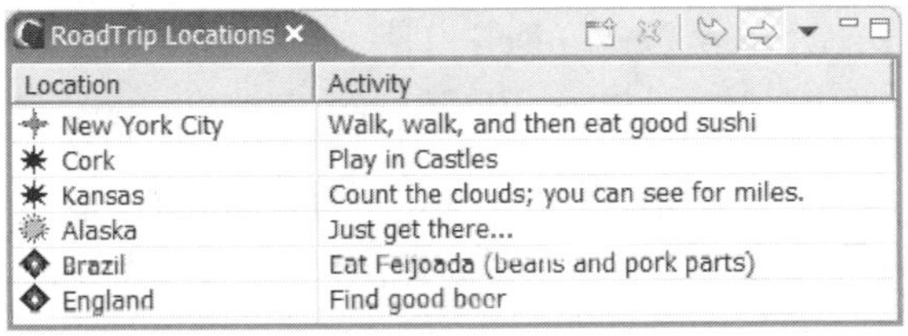

**Figure 15.8**   Viewer Sorting Content by Attribute within Category

Your sorter requirements may be more complex, but the basic process is the same.

**NOTE**   You may be interested in alternative sorting routines implemented as part of the Eclipse framework. Eclipse includes a class called `WorkbenchViewerSorter` that sorts elements with registered Workbench adapters by their text property.

## Interacting with Viewer Objects

All viewers are capable of both reporting and sharing the current selection. Listeners to selection changes are sent a `SelectionChangedEvent`, which provides access to the current `ISelection`. This same `ISelection` can be obtained directly from the viewer. Figure 15.9 shows how this is derived from the viewer's implementation of the `IInputSelectionProvider` interface, which extends `ISelectionProvider`.

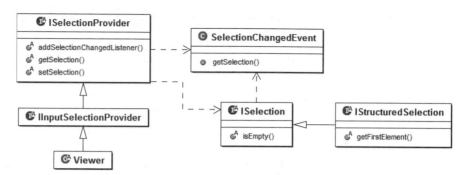

**Figure 15.9**   Viewer Support for Selection Processing

It is the `ISelectionProvider` interface that defines how you can interact with a viewer object. You can listen for the selection, get the current selection, and set the selection as required. The object interchanged on the get/set methods is an `ISelection`. This is the unit of exchange in the selection processing framework.

Having this selection support built into the viewer allows it to directly participate in the Workbench selection processing framework. Any Workbench part can choose to listen to and/or share selections with other Workbench parts. The viewer can be referenced in the method calls that share selection and register the viewer to support action contributions. The importance of this selection processing capability, with respect to views, editors, and sharing selection with other Workbench parts, is discussed further in Sharing and Listening for Workbench Part Selection in Chapter 18, Views.

## Handling User Selection of Viewer Objects

The `ISelectionProvider` interface specifies the methods `getSelection` and `setSelection` for a viewer. For a get request, an `ISelection` object is returned. For most viewers you can safely cast this to an `IStructuredSelection`, which can contain zero or more of the objects that were selected in the viewer. You can query the number of elements selected, iterate through selections, or just get the first selection.

When you retrieve an element from the `IStructuredSelection`, you will cast it to the type you expect. For some viewer implementations this will be easy because you have only one type of object; for others you may need to test the element's type. You can get just the first selection and cast it to your target object if you know what type to expect.

```
ISelection selection = viewer.getSelection();
ILocation location
  ((IStructuredSelection) selection).getFirstElement();
```

You may even need to process the full set of selected elements.

```
IStructuredSelection sSel =
    (IStructuredSelection) viewer.getSelection();

for (Iterator iter = sSel.iterator(); iter.hasNext();) {
    // Cast to an object that is appropriate for your viewer.
    ILocation loc = (ILocation) iter.next();
    // Do some processing here.
}
```

To react to changes in the user selection of viewer elements, you can implement the ISelectionChangedListener interface, possibly in your view. You would then use the viewer's addSelectionChangedListener method to add the view as an observer. Changes in selection will be sent to your selectionChanged method, where you react as appropriate.

Here is an implementation of the ISelectionChangedListener interface to adjust the enabled state of an action. The action involved is defined as part of the view where the viewer has been used. Actions themselves are discussed next.

```
public void selectionChanged(SelectionChangedEvent event) {
    if (event.getSelection().isEmpty()) {
        deleteAction.setEnabled(false);
        renameAction.setEnabled(false);
    } else {
        deleteAction.setEnabled(true);
        renameAction.setEnabled(true);
    }
}
```

### Options for Creating Viewer Pop-up Menu Actions

An aside on the ways you can create pop-up menu actions in Eclipse is in order. This topic is not specific to viewers, but it does intersect quite a bit. The full scope of action creation involves viewers, views, editors, and a series of extension points used to create action contributions.

If you did Exercise 6, Developing Your First Plug-in (see Chapter 9, Getting Started: Plug-in Development), you have created your own action that was added to the menu bar for the Workbench. Using a similar approach, you can add actions to views and editors. You can even go further and add actions to the pop-up menu for a viewer in a Workbench part if the viewer has been registered by the owning view or editor. The creator of the view or editor decides whether and how to register a viewer's context menu.

In the next subsection you will learn how you can directly add actions to a viewer's pop-up menu. This means you have two choices when adding pop-up menu actions to a viewer: you can add them by writing code or by creating action contributions for registered viewers in your plugin.xml file. This is important because there are implications to both design and implementation that are relevant as we discuss viewer actions. Just because actions can be added to a viewer in your code does not mean that all actions are or should be created that way. Nor should all viewer pop-up menu actions be defined as extensions. That said, the value of extensions is that they can target the object involved, in any viewer anywhere, both those that exist now and those you might add later.

> **NOTE**   The creation of actions in a view and the associated viewer registration process are discussed in the Adding View Actions and Registering Context Menus with the Workbench topics, respectively, in Chapter 18, Views. The Adding View Actions topic also includes a design considerations discussion on the use of action contributions versus locally defined actions. See Chapter 21, Action Contributions: The Integration Fast Track, for details on how to create these extensions and Chapter 30, Using Capabilities to Manage Too Much of a Good Thing, to understand why using contributions can provide additional flexibility.

### Adding Viewer Actions

Actions can be created and added to a viewer's pop-up or context menu. We will first focus on how to define the action, then on how to create a context menu for a viewer, and then on options for adding actions to the menu.

Creating actions is fairly straightforward. Fields for your action can be added to your user interface class so you can easily reference the action when adding it to a given viewer. A simple action definition includes the code required in the run method and the attributes required to describe the action appropriately in the user interface.

```
private Action deleteAction;
deleteAction = new Action() {
  public void run() {
    IStructuredSelection ssel = (IStructuredSelection) viewer
       .getSelection();
    SimpleModelViewPlugin.getModel().removeLocationElement(
        (ILocation) ssel.getFirstElement());
  }
```

```
};
deleteAction.setEnabled(true);
deleteAction.setText("Delete Location Element");
deleteAction.setToolTipText("Delete location from model");
deleteAction.setImageDescriptor(PlatformUI.getWorkbench()
    .getSharedImages().getImageDescriptor(
        ISharedImages.IMG_TOOL_DELETE));
```

You have to first create the context menu before you can add actions. A viewer can have a single active context menu; this menu either contains a static set of menu actions or can be dynamically loaded with the appropriate menu actions.

Creating a static context menu for a viewer that has two actions with a separator between them is pretty easy.

```
private void createMyContextMenuActions() {
    MenuManager manager = new MenuManager();
    Menu menu = manager.createContextMenu(viewer.getControl());
    viewer.getControl().setMenu(menu);
    manager.add(addAction);
    manager.add(new Separator());
    manager.add(deleteAction);
}
```

To create a context menu with dynamically determined action entries, you start by creating the same basic structure required for a static menu. To make the menu dynamic, mark it as such using the setRemoveAllWhenShown method and add a listener that adds the appropriate actions prior to the actual display of the menu.

```
private void createMyDynamicContextMenuActions() {
    MenuManager manager = new MenuManager();
    Menu menu = manager.createContextMenu(viewer.getControl());
    viewer.getControl().setMenu(menu);

    manager.setRemoveAllWhenShown(true);
    manager.addMenuListener(new IMenuListener() {

      public void menuAboutToShow(IMenuManager manager) {
        manager.add(addAction);
        manager.add(new Separator());

        IStructuredSelection selection =
          (IStructuredSelection) viewer.getSelection();
        if (selection.size() == 1) {
          propertyDialogAction.selectionChanged(selection);
          manager.add(deleteAction);
        }
      }
    });
}
```

Using dynamic menus allows your logic to determine what actions are appropriate based on the currently selected object, its state, and even the number of selected objects.

The use of actions and the creation of menus is discussed further in Supporting Action Contributions in Chapter 18, Views.

Since an action is an abstraction of menu choices, a single action definition can be used in many places. For example, the same action could be added to a context menu, a view toolbar, and a view pull-down menu.

We have now covered all the fundamentals for using JFace viewers. At this point you should spend some time reviewing the JFace viewer examples and trying to create your own working viewer-based user interface. Once you are comfortable, you can review the rest of this chapter. It discusses additional techniques for adding function to viewers and the unique aspects of the different types of JFace viewers.

## Using Alternative Viewer Types

In the discussion of building a working JFace viewer user interface, we stuck with simple viewers. A ListViewer is easy to use as it is a flat structure with only support for text content. A TableViewer can also be used as a simple list (one column), but it has support for both an image and text for each column in a row. While the basics for all viewers are the same, if you need to create more complex tables or use other types of viewers, you should understand some special considerations.

### Table Viewers

You can create a TableViewer directly, just like any viewer, given a Composite on which to create the viewer. When you do this the viewer creates the SWT Table widget that it will adapt to the viewer structure. You can use an alternate constructor that lets you also pass SWT style bits to the table that will be created, but either way the end result is a table with a single column.

If you want to create a multicolumn table, you need to create the SWT Table first and then pass the Table widget to the TableViewer when constructing the viewer. In this way you are identifying the widget you want the viewer to adapt to the viewer–content provider–label provider structure. This example shows the process of creating a TableViewer with a two-column Table.

```
Table table = new Table(parent, SWT.H_SCROLL | SWT.V_SCROLL
  | SWT.MULTI | SWT.FULL_SELECTION);

TableLayout layout = new TableLayout();
table.setLayout(layout);

table.setLinesVisible(true);
table.setHeaderVisible(true);
String[] STD_HEADINGS = { "Location", "Activity" };

layout.addColumnData(new ColumnWeightData(5, 40, true));
TableColumn tc0 = new TableColumn(table, SWT.NONE);
tc0.setText(STD_HEADINGS[0]);
tc0.setAlignment(SWT.LEFT);
tc0.setResizable(true);

layout.addColumnData(new ColumnWeightData(10, true));
TableColumn tc1 = new TableColumn(table, SWT.NONE);
tc1.setText(STD_HEADINGS[1]);
tc1.setAlignment(SWT.LEFT);
tc1.setResizable(true);

TableViewer viewer = new TableViewer(table);
```

When using a TableViewer, you need to have a label provider that can support the column-based structure. A TableViewer will ask its label provider for text and image content for each column. To support these requests, the label provider for a table must implement the ITableLabelProvider interface, which defines the getColumnText and getColumnImage methods. These methods receive the element and a column index that lets them return the appropriate content for each table column. The following implementation returns only an image in the first column and only text in the second.

```
class CustomLabelProvider extends LabelProvider
  implements ITableLabelProvider {

  URL url = ViewersPlugin.getDefault()
    .find(new Path("icons/sample.gif"));
  ImageDescriptor id = ImageDescriptor.createFromURL(url);
  Image image = id.createImage();

  public Image getImage(Object element) {
    return image;
  }

  public void dispose() {
    super.dispose();
    image.dispose();
  }
```

```
        public Image getColumnImage(Object element, int columnIndex) {
          if (columnIndex == 0)
            return getImage(element);
          else
            return null;
        }

        public String getColumnText(Object element, int columnIndex) {
          if (columnIndex == 1)
            return getText(element);
          else
            return "";
        }
      }
```

The `com.ibm.jdg2e.view.simplemodel` example on the CD-ROM implements a multicolumn table.

## Tree Viewers

The special considerations for tree viewers reflect the hierarchy of objects that can be displayed. The content provider required for a tree viewer must implement the `ITreeContentProvider` interface. This adds the `getChildren` and `getParent` methods to those required by `IStructuredContentProvider`.

These tree navigation methods have to follow the paths in the model you are presenting by placing your content in a tree structure. The children you want to display for the objects returned by the `getElements` method are obtained from your model when the `getChildren` method is called on your `ITreeContentProvider`.

You can generate a working example of the `TreeViewer` and the associated `ITreeContentProvider` implementation using the PDE.

## Table Tree Viewers

The `TableTreeViewer` combines the table and tree structures. You will need a label provider that implements `ITableLabelProvider` for the column structure and a content provider that implements `ITreeContentProvider` for the parent/child relationship.

This type of viewer is appropriate in certain circumstances; the Error Log view in Eclipse uses a `TableTreeViewer` to display errors that have been logged by plug-ins.

### Check Box Viewers

There are two types of check box viewers, CheckboxTreeViewer and CheckboxTableViewer. These viewers combine the standard widget with a check box on each node.

These viewers implement the IChecked interface. They also add methods such as getCheckedElements, getGrayed, setCheckedElements, and so on to help define and manage the selection state. Your code determines whether node selection carries down the tree and whether you want that gray box up the tree to visually clue the partial selection that may have been made.

## Advanced Workbench Integration Options

Viewers allow for other Workbench integration opportunities. For example, the Properties dialog can be opened for an object in your viewer and your plug-in, as well as others, can contribute to property pages for display in this dialog. Label decorators can also be used to adjust the appearance of objects displayed by your viewers.

Additional Workbench integration opportunities apply to viewers. As a viewer exposes objects, you have the option of adding function that targets these objects directly.

Both the properties page and label decorator extension points identify a target object using the objectClass attribute. This identifies the type of object that should be processed by the contributed extension. This section discusses how to support these types of contributions in your viewer.

### Adding Properties Dialog Support

A viewer's objects can support a common Properties dialog. If supported, property page extensions can be defined for the object and will be included in the Properties dialog once opened for that object instance.

The first step is to add the **Properties** action to the viewer's context menu.

- Create an instance of the PropertyDialogAction.
- Add the PropertyDialogAction to the viewer's context menu.
- Register the **Properties** action to the global action handler (optional).
- Have the objects displayed in the viewer implement or adapt to the IWorkbenchAdapter interface.

PART III

**NOTE**   The common Eclipse techniques for implementing or adapting to an interface are discussed in Providing Content in the Properties View in Chapter 18, Views.

The following code snippet outlines the process of setting up the **Properties** action for a viewer in a view (this in the code below represents a view class reference).

```
protected PropertyDialogAction propertyDialogAction;

Shell shell = this.getSite().getShell();
actionProp = new Action() {
  public void run() {
    propertyDialogAction.
      selectionChanged(viewer.getSelection());
    propertyDialogAction.run();
  }
};

actionProp.setText("Properties");
propertyDialogAction = new PropertyDialogAction(shell, viewer);

// Register global action -- Edit > Delete.
getViewSite().getActionBars().setGlobalActionHandler(
  ActionFactory.PROPERTIES.getId(), propertyDialogAction);
```

You can add this action to the pop-up menu for the viewer, and when run it will attempt to open the Properties dialog using the viewer's IStructured-Selection as input. At least one element must be selected, but only the first element in the selection is used. Typically the **Properties** action is not even displayed if more than one element has been selected. If at least one property page has been contributed in a plugin.xml file for the selected object, the Properties dialog is opened. Otherwise the Properties dialog responds with a "No property pages" message.

The title of the Properties dialog will be incomplete if the selected object does not implement or adapt to the IWorkbenchAdapter interface. The Properties dialog calls the getLabel method to obtain the value to use in the title of the Properties dialog.

The CD-ROM includes a working example of using the Properties dialog on the ILocation object used in the viewer examples.

## Adding Label Decorations on Objects in a Viewer

**Label decorations** are visual augmentations on objects in a viewer. They allow you to modify the icon text for objects displayed in a viewer. They can add information for user display not designed into the original viewer. Decoration examples in Eclipse include **CVS** and **Linked Resources** (see the **Workbench > Label Decorations** preference page).

You can do two things in the area of label decorations: contribute your own and support them in your viewer. These are covered quickly here. Adding label decorations is well documented. Providing support is not directly documented, but it is easy to implement because all you do is ask Eclipse to process decorations on your behalf.

## Adding Label Decorations

The extension point `org.eclipse.ui.decorators` allows you to contribute decorators to objects of interest. You identify the object you want to decorate using the `objectClass` attribute. Your decoration can appear in any view that displays that object and has a viewer that supports decoration. You must specify a `label`, which identifies your decorator on the preference page. Optionally, you can also include a `description`, which describes your decoration. This description is visible in the preference page. You must specify a `class` that implements your decorator class. The class identified must implement either the `ILabelDecorator` or `ILightweightLabelDecorator` interface. The lightweight decorator is the more appropriate approach because it offers improved performance and simplicity.

The following code defines an `IResource` label decorator that identifies resources ignored by CVS. (See Chapter 23 for a discussion of the workspace resource model.)

```
<extension point="org.eclipse.ui.decorators">
  <decorator
    lightweight="true"
    objectClass="org.eclipse.core.resources.IResource"
    label="CVS Ignore Decorator"
    class="com.ibm.jdg2e.resources.CVSIgnoredResourceDecorator"
    state="false"
    id="com.ibm.jdg2e.resources.programming.decorator">
    <description>
      Adds brackets around resources that are identified
      by name or type in the .cvsignore file. Entries
      using regular expression syntax in the .cvsignore
      file are not supported.
    </description>
  </decorator>
</extension>
```

The code involved has to determine whether the resource involved is actually mentioned by name or type in the `.cvsignore` file. This decorator, as described above, identifies resources that will be ignored by CVS. Only the decorate method for the class implementing ILightweightLabelDecorator is shown; you can find the findInCVSFile method on the CD-ROM.

```java
public void decorate(Object element, IDecoration decoration) {
  if (element instanceof IResource) {
    IResource res = (IResource) element;
    if (findInCVSFile(res)) {
      decoration.addPrefix("[ ");
      decoration.addSuffix(" ]");
    }
  }
}
```

Figure 15.10 shows the end result when several folders and files have been added to .cvsignore files and the decorator is active.

**Figure 15.10**   CVS Ignore Label Decorator in Action

Label decorators are typically disabled at first. Eclipse prefers to load plug-ins on demand. Moreover, label decorations may have performance implications if they must react to state changes on objects or represent information on a server like a repository. Unless the user explicitly enables a decorator type, the label decorations and the plug-ins that produce them are disabled. (A plug-in could set the initial state to enabled, but that should be avoided.)

For additional details on the implementation of label decorations, see the *Platform Plug-in Developer Guide* in the Eclipse Help system and the eclipse.org article referenced at the end of this chapter.

### Supporting Label Decorations in Your Viewer

Label decoration does not occur by magic in your own viewers. You must enable it as part of how you implement your label decorator. The process of implementing the label decorator need not change; you enable decoration by wrapping your label provider in a `DecoratingLabelProvider` supplied by the Workbench.

```
viewer.setLabelProvider(new DecoratingLabelProvider(
    new LocationsLabelProvider(),
        PlatformUI.getWorkbench().getDecoratorManager()
        .getLabelDecorator()));
```

By integrating the decorator manager and your viewer's label decorator, any label decorations defined for your objects are detected and processed as required.

**NOTE** Label decoration works well for tree viewers and single-column tables. The decoration interfaces do not support the column calls implemented as part of the `ITableLabelProvider` interface, so if you add label decoration support to a table viewer with multiple columns, the first column is decorated while the others are completely empty.

## Example Summary

You can find a complete demonstration of the use of a multicolumn table viewer with sorter and filtering capability in the `com.ibm.jdg2e.view.simplemodel` project on the CD-ROM. This example includes access to a simple model as provided in the `com.ibm.jdg2e.simplemodel` project, model event processing, and the use of both the `refresh` and `update` implementation options for synchronization. These projects also include support for the Properties view and the ability to open the common Properties dialog for the selected viewer object. Action contributions that target both the viewer and the object, using enablement and visibility rules, are also provided.

You can find additional viewer examples in the `com.ibm.jdg2e.jface.viewers` and `com.ibm.jdg2e.view.files` projects. Each project includes documentation to help you find the code sections that interest you.

## Chapter Summary

JFace viewers are the primary technique for user interface development in Eclipse. It should now be obvious that they can provide you with a productive approach to the development of high function and consistent user interfaces in your views, editors, and dialogs.

The value of a JFace viewer is how it makes your programming tasks easier to complete. The viewers themselves adapt to the SWT widgets, thereby allowing you to avoid low-level widget programming. And as you now know, viewers do not work alone; they use content providers and label providers to get data and determine what should be visible on the screen. The content provider is custom code you write. It adapts to your model, which was identified as input to the viewer. Label providers are also typically custom code. Your label provider adapts to the objects from your model that were returned for display in the viewer by the content provider.

Now that we have explored the workings of the JFace viewer architecture and the roles of each component, along with the basic steps required to use these components to build a viewer-based user interface, you are pretty much ready to go. Just create one of each of the three basic parts: instantiate the right viewer, create a custom content provider, and either use the `LabelProvider` as is or extend it to add additional display function. That is all it takes.

Feel free to hack at the examples we have provided, or use the **New > Plug-in Project** wizard or **New Extension** wizard to generate sample view code with the associated JFace viewer implementation. Once you are comfortable with using the framework, you will be a more productive developer, and your user interfaces will behave consistently across all the components you define.

## References

Arthorne, John, and Chris Laffra. 2004. *Official Eclipse 3.0 FAQs*. Boston, MA: Addison-Wesley. http://eclipsefaq.org. (See FAQs 146–149, 152, 177, 180.)

Krish-Sampath, Balaji. January 16, 2003. Understanding decorators in Eclipse. http://www.eclipse.org.

See the Table of Registered Context Menus under References in the online help for this book.

# CHAPTER 16

## *Dialogs and Wizards*

This chapter discusses the various types of dialogs and wizards available in Eclipse and how you can use and extend them as you develop your plug-in. This includes both general-purpose dialogs and the Preferences, Properties, and Wizard dialogs that you contribute to by defining an extension. General-purpose dialogs can be used as is or be the base for your own custom dialogs. Using an extension, you can define preference page, property page, and wizards that become part of the Eclipse user interface.

By reusing the dialogs provided as part of the Eclipse Platform, you can improve the overall function and level of user interface integration for your plug-in while helping your user perform the required tasks in a consistent fashion. Of course, this reuse also improves your development productivity.

## Dialogs—The User Interface Beyond Workbench Parts

Dialogs are the third user interface element in Eclipse. The two types of Workbench parts, views and editors, get most of the credit, but dialogs fulfill the requirement for a controlled interaction with the user while using a consistent user interface.

Dialogs exist throughout Eclipse. While many are internal to the features included in Eclipse, others are available for reuse during your plug-in development activity.

To better understand how to approach code reuse of the dialogs provided as part of Eclipse, you need to understand their role in the user interface framework and the techniques available for implementing dialogs as part of a plug-in you develop.

There are two basic techniques for adding dialogs to Eclipse as part of your plug-in:

- Defining an extension and implementing the requisite code for the contribution
- Defining and opening a dialog in your plug-in logic

An extension allows you to participate in one of the reusable dialog frameworks included in the Eclipse Platform, namely, Preferences, Properties, and Resource wizards. These types of extensions are easy to add and do not require that you implement much code at all. In fact, you can get a custom New File wizard added in five simple steps: add an extension, generate a class, add fields, add a method, and add as little as six lines of code. A preference page using the field editor approach can be implemented in four steps, which includes adding one additional method and writing four lines of code! Read on to learn how, and then explore the code examples for dialogs provided on the CD-ROM.

### Point of Reference—The User Interface Framework

Dialogs and their specialized implementation as task wizards are one of the major components of the user interface framework.

There are many types of dialogs, such as selection, find and replace, error display, task wizards, preferences, and properties. Many of these dialogs are directly reused or subclassed in your code to perform specific tasks such as displaying an error message, finding a folder or file, or prompting for selection from a list. In addition, preferences, properties, and wizard extensions can be defined to allow you to directly contribute to the standard dialog elements of the Eclipse user interface. Table 16.1 identifies the packages for the dialogs and wizard framework.

Inheritance relationships exist between many of the classes in the `org.eclipse.ui.*` and `org.eclipse.jface.*` packages. Classes in the `org.eclipse.ui.*` package extend the JFace dialog support by providing the implementation of the Workbench-specific dialogs and wizard framework included as part of Eclipse.

### Workbench Extension Points for Dialogs and Wizards

Table 16.2 lists the dialog and wizard framework extension points you will use.

When you use these extension points, your dialog page and wizard additions are tightly integrated into the Eclipse user interface.

**Table 16.1**  Packages in the Dialog and Wizard Framework

| Package Name | Description |
| --- | --- |
| org.eclipse.jface.dialogs | Core of the dialog framework that provides the base `Dialog` class. This includes layers that support messages and a progress monitor to provide user feedback. |
| org.eclipse.jface.wizard | Framework implementation for task wizards. This includes the definition of a wizard and the wizard page. |
| org.eclipse.ui.dialogs | Base implementation for wizards, property pages, and preference pages as used in Eclipse. This also includes other standard dialogs such as the Save As dialog, List Selection dialog, and a workspace File Selection dialog. |
| org.eclipse.ui.wizards.datatransfer | Specialized support for import and export wizards. |
| org.eclipse.ui.wizards.newresource | Specialized wizard pages to assist in the creation of resources. |
| org.eclipse.swt.widgets | Dialogs implemented as part of the SWT plug-in, including the `Dialog`, `FileDialog`, and `DirectoryDialog` classes. These are built on widgets from the operating system. |

**Table 16.2**  Dialog and Wizard Framework Extension Points

| Dialog/Wizard | Extension Points |
| --- | --- |
| Preference page | org.eclipse.ui.preferencePages |
| Property page | org.eclipse.ui.propertyPages |
| New wizard | org.eclipse.ui.newWizards |
| Import wizard | org.eclipse.ui.importWizards |
| Export wizard | org.eclipse.ui.exportWizards |

## Preference and Property Page Extensions

The Eclipse user interface includes two integrated dialogs, Preferences and Properties, which support common user interaction requirements. Figure 16.1 depicts the basic structure and capabilities of these Workbench dialogs. Your plug-ins add pages to each of these dialogs by contributing the appropriate extension.

The structure of the Preferences and Properties dialogs is the same, as shown in Figure 16.1. Note that while a Properties dialog can access resource properties, it is not required to do so. A Properties dialog can be used to support other types of data associated with an individual resource or other object for which the Properties dialog has been opened.

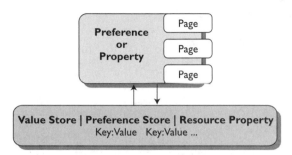

**Figure 16.1**    Structure of the Preferences and Properties Dialogs

All plug-ins may contribute to the single Preferences dialog that exists as part of the Workbench user interface. This integrates all available preference pages as part of one dialog. It also provides for navigation between pages and lazy activation of the target page. Each contributed preference page provides a plug-in-specific user interface and the opportunity to store preference values in a plug-in-specific preference store. This integrated approach allows multiple plug-ins to work as one with respect to the user's view of Eclipse. The user uses one Preferences dialog for all global settings in the environment. Not all plug-in control values are defined using a preference page; view-specific settings are typically defined as actions local to the view's specific user interface. These view-specific values can still be stored in the preference store.

The property page extension follows that same design; the common Properties dialog for Eclipse displays the contributed properties pages for the target object. Any view can choose to open the Properties dialog. The typical properties page extension adds pages to the Properties dialog opened from Navigator view and/or Package Explorer view. In this scenario the property page logic often uses the workspace API to define and store properties (see Resource Properties in Chapter 23, Workspace Resource Programming). There are alternatives for how resource specific values are stored; you could decide to use an approach based on user settings (see Scoped Value Management with User Settings in Chapter 17, Dialog Settings, Preferences, and User Settings).

You can even open the Properties dialog for an object that you have displayed in a viewer (see Adding Properties Dialog Support in Chapter 15, JFace Viewers). When the Properties dialog is opened for a given object, both you and other plug-in providers can define property page extensions that target the objects displayed in your view. These pages are then included in the Properties dialog that you open.

A design relationship you may want to follow is to use a preference value to define the default and allow properties to provide an alternative value that is resource-specific. This allows your plug-in to provide customized behavior by resource.

See Contributing to the Preferences Dialog and Contributing to the Properties Dialog later in this chapter for more detail on these types of extensions.

## Wizard Extensions

Wizards support a task-based interaction with the user. The task could require one or more wizard pages, each representing a step in the overall process leading to completion. Figure 16.2 depicts the basic structure of a wizard.

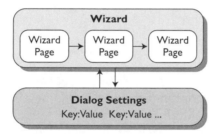

**Figure 16.2**   Structure of a Wizard

The wizard is the controller for the wizard pages; the pages contain the user interface, but the wizard implements page navigation and processing requests. When you implement a wizard, the pages that will be managed can be identified either up front or dynamically. You can also customize the image and title for a wizard and each page in the wizard.

Extension definitions can be used to add wizards to the user interface in three predefined places:

- In the **File > New** menu tree to create new types of resources
- In the **File > Import...** menu tree to import resources into Eclipse
- In the **File > Export...** menu tree to export resources outside Eclipse

Wizards are much more powerful and open-ended than a property or preference page. Wizards can be added to the Workbench by extension, but you also have the option of creating and opening a wizard dialog to add support for task-oriented processing as part of the custom function implemented by your plug-in. It may be appropriate to open a wizard when the input required, as part of an editor or a view, can be complex to define.

The wizard framework allows you to construct a wizard, wrap the wizard in a wizard dialog, and process the task to completion. For example, in the **Extensions** page of the Plug-in Manifest Editor, the **Add** button opens a wizard that allows you to create a new extension.

Wizards, and for that matter any dialog, can use plug-in-specific dialog settings to store values related to wizard or dialog interaction. These might be the values previously entered by the user or a list of recent choices; this allows the user interface to anticipate the users' needs. An example of this is an Import wizard that remembers the last import location, or a New Resource wizard that remembers the creation settings entered the last time the wizard was used. See Dialog Settings in Chapter 17 for more detail.

The process of defining and implementing a wizard is described in Contributing Wizards later in this chapter.

## Common Reusable Dialogs

Eclipse includes support for many types of dialogs that you can reuse as part of your plug-in. These dialogs are implemented using the SWT, JFace, and Workbench layers of the user interface.

The `org.eclipse.swt.widgets` package provides two dialogs that support commonly used functions.

- `DirectoryDialog` allows the user to navigate the file system and select a directory.
- `FileDialog` allows the user to navigate the file system and select or enter a file.

These dialogs are themselves SWT widgets, which means that their internal implementation may differ on different runtime platforms. This provides the platform look and feel for your plug-in, while you only have to write to the API of the reusable framework.

Table 16.3 lists several dialogs that the `org.eclipse.jface.dialogs` package provides to support user interaction in your plug-in.

The `org.eclipse.ui.dialogs` package also provides dialogs that can be used to support user interaction in your plug-in.

- `ListDialog` prompts for one element out of a list of elements. It requires that a content provider and label provider be used to control the available elements in the list.
- `ListSelectionDialog` is used to ask the user to select one or more entries from a list. A content provider and label provider are also used to control the elements.

**Table 16.3** Dialogs Provided in the `org.eclipse.jface.dialogs` Package

| Package Name | Description |
|---|---|
| `MessageDialog` | Displays a message. This can be opened with an appropriate image. The image options are `none`, `error`, `information`, `question`, and `warning`. |
| `InputDialog` | Allows the user to enter a `String` value. |
| `ProgressMonitorDialog` | Used when you are performing a long-running task that needs to provide feedback to the user. Your use determines whether the process should be run on a separate thread and whether the user is allowed to cancel the processing. The dialog is passed a runnable task to perform. This supports the monitoring process (the right to cancel the task currently processing) and can allow all resource changes to be reported as part of a single event. |
| `ErrorDialog` | Displays one or more errors to the user. Details on the error(s) can be opened if provided. |

- `ResourceSelectionDialog` is used to ask the user to select from a list of resources. The resource to use as the root for the list and a text message is passed to the dialog.
- `ResourceListSelectionDialog` is used to display a list of resources to the user with a text entry field that allows the list of resources to be filtered.
- `ElementTreeSelectionDialog` is used to select elements from a tree structure. You identify the input for the tree and can define a validator and filter to further refine the selection process.
- `SaveAsDialog` is used to solicit a resource path from the user for use in a save operation. The path returned may not yet exist.

We have only covered the dialogs that you should find readily reusable. Before you build your own specialized dialogs, you should review the identified packages to determine whether your specialized needs might be partially satisfied by existing code. If you do implement your own dialogs, you should consider beginning your implementation by extending one of these existing classes.

- `org.eclipse.jface.dialogs.Dialog`
- `org.eclipse.jface.dialogs.TitleAreaDialog`
- `org.eclipse.ui.dialogs.SelectionDialog`

You should try to reuse the SWT dialogs when possible to get the Eclipse platform look and feel in your plug-in. For instance, you shouldn't implement your own `FileDialog`.

## Contributing to the Preferences Dialog

Preference pages allow you to define settings that the user can use to control plug-in behavior. These settings are stored as data associated to your plug-in for either the current workspace or, if desired, the current installation.

---

**NOTE**  The options for where you store preference settings are discussed in Chapter 17, Dialog Settings, Preferences, and User Settings. In this discussion we will focus on the use of the `PreferenceStore` and `Preferences` APIs for saving values. These interfaces are discussed in the upcoming subsection Adding Preference Value Logic to a Preference Page.

---

Figure 16.3 depicts the structure of a preference page as it exists in the common Preferences dialog and how the preference page interacts with the preference store.

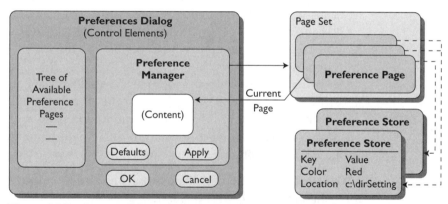

**Figure 16.3**   Structural View of a Preference Page in the Preferences Dialog

In Figure 16.3 the Preferences dialog presents the available preference pages to the user; the preference manager manages the available pages. Each preference page is built with a single `Composite` that can gain focus when selected in the tree of available pages. A `Composite` is an SWT widget to which you add other widgets as you develop your preference page user interface. (See Chapter 14, The Standard Widget Toolkit: A Lean, Mean Widget Machine, for more information on SWT.) The active page uses its plug-in class to find the associated preference store. The preference store is used to access the saved values associated with the plug-in that can be exposed to the user in a preference page.

The plug-in class manages the preference store. Preferences values are not related to individual resources but typically to the active workspace. They are stored unique to your plug-in in the state directory for the org.eclipse .core.runtime plug-in; they are not sent to a repository. Default preference key values can be defined and property change listeners can be used to notify interested parties when the value of a preference setting changes. Preference values can also be exported and imported, so you can share them outside the current workspace.

The user interface framework does most of the work; all you have to do is provide the dynamic content. The following steps are required to create a preference page.

1. Define a preference page extension.
2. Generate a preference page class.
3. Define the preference page user interface.
4. Establish default preference setting values.
5. Add preference value logic to the preference page.

The following sections describe these steps.

### Defining a Preference Page Extension

You add a preference page by adding an org.eclipse.ui.preferencePages extension definition to your plug-in manifest. Just state the name of your page, give it an id, and identify your class that implements a preference page. You can also identify a category attribute, which organizes the page with others in a tree. The following example contains two preference page extensions; one is defined under the other in the tree of preference pages.

```
<extension point="org.eclipse.ui.preferencePages">
  <page
    name="Primary Options"
    class="qrs.tool.preferences.PrimaryPreferencePage"
    id="qrs.tool.preferences.primary">
  </page>
  <page
    name="Specialized Options"
    category="qrs.tool.preferences.primary"
    class="qrs.tool.preferences.SpecializedPreferencePage"
    id="qrs.tool.preferences.specialized">
  </page>
</extension>
```

PART III

The extension above creates two pages in the Preferences dialog. The `category` attribute organizes the Specialized Options page under the Primary Options page.

Once the preference pages have been defined in an extension, they are visible in the Preferences dialog selection tree even if the implementation class referenced in the extension does not yet exist. The preference page tree shown in the Preferences dialog is constructed using the attribute values specified in the extension definition. Only when the user selects the page does Eclipse attempt to instantiate and then activate the implementation class.

### Implementing a Preference Page

You build a preference page by creating a class that extends `PreferencePage` and implements the `IWorkbenchPreferencePage` interface. This is how the initial implementation of a preference page, as generated by the PDE, would look in your project.

```
public class PrimaryPreferencePage extends PreferencePage
    implements IWorkbenchPreferencePage {
  public PrimaryPreferencePage() {
    super();
  }
  public PrimaryPreferencePage(String title) {
    super(title);
  }
  public PrimaryPreferencePage(String title,
    ImageDescriptor image) {
    super(title, image);
  }
  protected Control createContents(Composite parent) {
    return null;
  }
  public void init(IWorkbench workbench) {
  }
}
```

All you have to do is add the required user interface and custom preference store interaction logic; the rest of the implementation is inherited.

To implement the user interface, you customize the `createContents` method to create the appropriate widget controls required for the page. You can use the `init` method for any initialization processing you need to perform; this method is triggered when your page is first accessed with the Preferences dialog. The `init` method will be run again only if you close and then open the Preferences dialog and select your page.

To implement support for modifying the preferences displayed, you override the appropriate method for any displayed buttons.

- **OK**—performOk
- **Apply**—performApply
- **Restore Defaults**—performDefaults
- **Cancel**—performCancel

The performOk method will need to be customized to save preference values. This method is called when the user presses either the **Apply** or **OK** button. The **Restore Defaults** button can be used to obtain the defaults defined for the preferences. Defaults are defined as part of the plug-in management of a preference store; this is discussed in Storing Preference Values for a Plug-in in Chapter 17, Dialog Settings, Preferences, and User Settings. You do not typically need to override any of the other push button methods.

The **Restore Defaults** and **Apply** buttons are normally included in the user interface of a preference page. If you do not want to include them, call the noDefaultAndApplyButton method.

Now that you have an extension and a base class for implementing a preference page, you are ready to define the user interface definition and add logic to process the preference store values.

### Defining a Preference Page User Interface

You will need to customize the createContents method to add the widgets required in your user interface. These widgets use the control passed to the method as their parent. This is basic SWT programming as discussed in Chapter 14, The Standard Widget Toolkit: A Lean, Mean Widget Machine. The method shown below adds a label and a combo box to the preference page.

```
protected Control createContents(Composite parent) {
  Composite composite = new Composite(parent, SWT.NONE);
  RowLayout rowLayout = new RowLayout();
  rowLayout.justify = true;
  rowLayout.marginLeft = 5;
  rowLayout.marginRight = 5;
  rowLayout.spacing = 5;
  composite.setLayout(rowLayout);

  Label label = new Label (composite, SWT.NONE);
  label.setText("Pick one, any one, but just one:");
  Combo combo = new Combo (composite, SWT.NONE);
  combo.setItems(new String []
    {"Apple", "Pear", "Blueberry"});
  combo.setText("Fruits...");
  return composite;
}
```

PART III

The framework uses the control returned by the createContents method to calculate the size and layout of the preference page content in the Preferences dialog. The user interface created by the createContents method is visible when the preference page is selected in the Preferences dialog (see Figure 16.4).

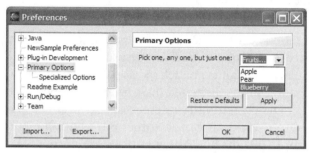

**Figure 16.4**    Preference Page with Customized User Interface Content

## Adding Preference Value Logic to a Preference Page

There are several steps required to add the preference value logic to your preference page. You have to obtain the object you will use to store the values, optionally associate it with your preference page and obtain values for display in your user interface, and store values when requested by the user. You may also need to set preference defaults. This process is described in the following subsections.

**NOTE**   This section describes the established APIs for plug-in managed preference values. The default and instance scopes of the user settings framework are used to implement the PreferenceStore and Preferences APIs. You may want to consider using the user settings API if you think your user would like the preference values maintained for the installation instead of just the workspace. See Chapter 17, Dialog Settings, Preferences, and User Settings.

### Finding the PreferenceStore or Preferences Object for Your Plug-in

You can get a handle for the object used to store preferences from your plug-in by using either of these methods.

```
IPreferenceStore ps =
  DialogsPlugin.getDefault().getPreferenceStore();
Preferences prefs =
  DialogsPlugin.getDefault().getPluginPreferences();
```

Once you have access to the stored preferences you can add the required logic to your preference page. The `get` and `set` API for preference settings is the same for the two different object types returned from these methods.

As a plug-in developer you have the option to use either object type to access preference values within a given plug-in or across plug-ins, except for the process used to define default values. If your plug-in class extends `Plugin` instead of `AbstractUIPlugin`, you only have access to the `getPluginPreferences` implementation. You can even have pages that use different approaches in the same plug-in. This is important in that the `FieldEditorPreferencePage` approach discussed later can only use a `PreferenceStore` object type.

### Obtaining Preference Values

You need to show the current preference setting values in your preference page user interface so that the user can review them for possible modification. The `get` methods for a preference setting are type-specific: if your saved value is a `String`, you use `getString`, and if the saved value is a `boolean`, you use `getBoolean`. The logic to get a `String` value for an identified preference setting for use in a user interface control is shown here.

```
// PreferenceStore approach
combo.setText(ToolPlugin.getDefault()
  .getPreferenceStore().getString("pref_key"));
```

```
// Preferences approach
combo.setText(ToolPlugin.getDefault()
  .getPluginPreferences().getString("pref_key"));
```

You should need to get the values only once, as the user interface is created. If you were to place the same preference setting on multiple preference pages, you would have to refresh the value as the user changed pages. This is not a good user interface decision, but if you had to implement support for refresh processing, you could override the `setVisible` method for the preference page.

### Getting Default Values

The **Restore Defaults** button in the preference page allows the user to request that the settings be returned to their default values. If you defined defaults in the plug-in, you can use this logic to obtain those defaults for display in the user interface.

```
// PreferenceStore approach
combo.setText(combo.setText(ToolPlugin.getDefault()
  getPreferenceStore().getDefaultString("combo_field_key"));
```

```
// Preferences approach
combo.setText(ToolPlugin.getDefault()
    .getPluginPreferences().getDefaultString("combo_field_key"));
```

### Saving Modified Preference Setting Values

If the user selects the **Apply** or **OK** button, you obtain the current preference values from the user interface and modify the associated preference settings. You add this support by overriding the performOk method. This method is triggered in response to selection of either the **Apply** or **OK** button.

There is one set method, setValue, which takes parameters of the preference setting and the value to be set. The method has several signatures (key, data type), which allow for the different data types that can be saved in a preference store (boolean, double, float, int, String, and long). An example of this logic is shown here.

```
// PreferenceStore approach
ToolPlugin.getDefault().getPreferenceStore()
    .setValue("combo_field_key", combo.getText());

// Preferences approach
  ToolPlugin.getDefault().getPluginPreferences()
    .setValue("combo_field_key", combo.getText());
```

The setValue method does not save the values to disk. The preference store obtained from the plug-in is automatically saved during Eclipse shutdown by the shutdown method when your plug-in class inherits from AbstractUIPlugin. However, you can use the savePluginPreferences method to save the preference setting changes. This is required when your plug-in inherits from Plugin and is a best practice you should follow.

You can also use the performApply method to include additional logic that would not be required as part of an **OK** request. But remember, the **Apply** button will still trigger the performOk method.

### *Building a Field Editor Preference Page*

When you build a preference page by extending the PreferencePage class, you must implement the user interface, retrieve preference settings, and override the appropriate methods to store settings and retrieve default values. There is another approach: You can choose to build a field editor preference page instead. When you build a field editor preference page, you must do the following.

- Add a preference page extension.
- Implement a class that extends FieldEditorPreferencePage and implements IWorkbenchPreferencePage to build on the field editor processing approach.

- Implement a null constructor. You use the constructor to define the layout for the field editors by passing a style to the superclass constructor. The style options are GRID and FLAT.
- Associate a preference store with the preference page (field editor pages must be passed a PreferenceStore object).
- Implement the createFieldEditors method to create and add specialized field editors that define the user interface for the page.

Once you have done this, the field editor preference page framework provides the required processing to manage retrieval, default processing, and storage of preference settings. The user interface is easier to build because each FieldEditor you add to the page does the work of adding the user interface components and interacting with the preference store.

The implementation of a field editor preference page with a style choice and the assignment of the active PreferenceStore object are shown as part of the null constructor below.

```
public class MyFieldEditorPrefPage
  extends FieldEditorPreferencePage
    implements IWorkbenchPreferencePage {
  public MyFieldEditorPrefPage() {
    super(GRID);
    setDescription("My Field Editor Preference Page \n");
    IPreferenceStore store = ToolPlugin.getDefault()
      .getPreferenceStore();
    setPreferenceStore(store);
  }
  // rest not shown
}
```

The field editors you add to the page provide a key part of the processing support offered by the field editor preference page framework. The field editors create the user interface, load the current setting from the associated preference store, and react as required to restore defaults and save settings requests. These requests are triggered by the processing logic implemented in the FieldEditorPreferencePage superclass.

Figure 16.5 shows the types of field editors that you can use to define the user interface and store preference settings; their roles are fairly evident from the class names.

Here is an example of how the createFieldEditors method can be used to add field editors.

```
protected void createFieldEditors() {
  // Note: The first String value is the key used in
  // the preference store and the second String value
  // is the label displayed in front of the editor on the page.
```

PART III

```
ColorFieldEditor colorField =  new ColorFieldEditor(
  "COLOR_KEY", "COLOR_KEY_Label", getFieldEditorParent());

BooleanFieldEditor choiceField = new BooleanFieldEditor(
  "BOOLEAN_KEY", "BOOLEAN_KEY_Label",
   org.eclipse.swt.SWT.NONE,
   getFieldEditorParent());

FileFieldEditor fileField = new FileFieldEditor(
  "FILE_KEY", "FILE_KEY_Label",
   true, getFieldEditorParent());
   fileField.setFileExtensions(
     new String[] { "*.jar", "*.txt", "*.zip" });

addField(colorField);
addField(choiceField);
addField(fileField);
}
```

This code implements the user interface shown in Figure 16.6. (The field editor preference page is contained within the Preferences dialog, which is not shown.)

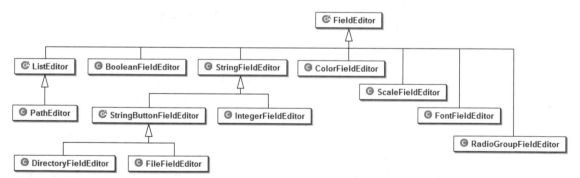

**Figure 16.5**    Field Editors Provided as Part of the Framework

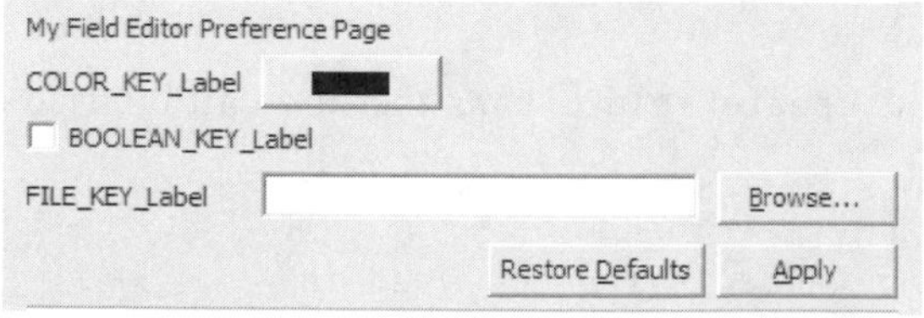

**Figure 16.6**    User Interface Implemented Using Field Editors

## Contributing to the Properties Dialog

If you have built preference pages, learning how to build a property page
will be easy. Property pages actually inherit from the preference page
implementation.

The role of a property page is to allow the user to see and modify values
associated with a specific object that supports the Properties dialog in Eclipse.
Several views, such as the Navigator, Package Explorer, and Error Log views,
will open a Properties dialog for the selected object. While you can contribute a
property page to any standard Properties dialog implementation, property
pages are most often associated with workspace resources or objects that adapt
to a resource type. This means you will typically define extensions for pages
that will be added to the Properties dialog opened from the Navigator or Package Explorer views. The capability to attach properties to individual resources
can allow your users to customize plug-in processing: They can set values, and
your plug-in can adjust by checking resource properties as part of your plug-in
logic. Figure 16.7 depicts the structure of a property page within a Properties
dialog. This includes how the property page interacts with the resource that
was selected when the Properties dialog was opened.

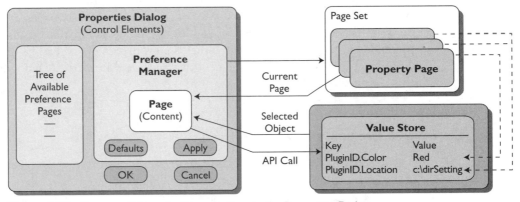

**Figure 16.7**   Structural View of a Property Page in the Properties Dialog

As shown in Figure 16.7, the Properties dialog presents the properties to
the user, while the property manager manages a collection of property pages.
Each property page implements a single panel that can gain focus when
selected in the tree of available pages. The selected resource (or other object)
is available to the property page.

If the selected object is a resource, keyed access to data associated with the resource can be obtained using the workspace API. Persistent property values are stored in a property store, which is internally maintained by Eclipse. Properties are not sent to a repository, so they cannot be shared outside the current workspace.

If you need to use a property page to maintain values about a resource but want these values to be shared between users via a repository or other file transfer technique, you should consider using the user settings API discussed in Chapter 17, Dialog Settings, Preferences, and User Settings.

The other components shown in Figure 16.7 are part of the framework that you build on by extension. The framework does most of the work. These steps are required to create a property page.

- Define a property page extension.
- Implement a property page.
- Define the property page user interface.
- Add resource property access logic.

The following subsections describe these steps.

**NOTE** The Navigator and Package Explorer views open the Properties dialog for objects contained in their viewer. We can contribute property pages by targeting an object type that either exists or can be adapted to by the objects displayed by these views. You should also know that the Properties dialog can be opened on any object in a viewer. See Implementing Your Own Properties Dialog later in this chapter for additional information.

## Defining a Property Page Extension

To add a property page, you create an `org.eclipse.ui.propertyPages` extension definition in your plug-in manifest. This needs to:

- State the name of your page and give it an id
- Identify the object type for which your page should be available
- Identify your property page class
- Optionally identify an icon that will be displayed as part of the page
- Optionally define a name filter to further refine the rules for when your page should be included in the Properties dialog for a given resource type

This definition adds your property page to any properties dialog opened for the object type identified in your extension. The object type is identified by the objectClass attribute. This value identifies the class or interface type with which your page should be associated. By using IFile, IFolder, or IProject, you can control when your page should be opened.

This extension defines a property page that will be available when the selected object is a file resource with a file type of .java. The class JavaPropertyPage implements the property page. This property page will be included in the Properties dialog when a file with a type of .java is selected in Navigator view, but not when the file is selected in the Package Explorer view, because this view shows Java elements instead of resource elements.

```
<extension point="org.eclipse.ui.propertyPages">
  <page
    objectClass="org.eclipse.core.resources.IFile"
    name="Java File Properties"
    nameFilter="*.java"
    class="qrs.tool.properties.JavaPropertyPage"
    id="qrs.tool.properties.qrsfile">
  </page>
</extension>
```

If your page will be available for .java files, you can also choose to have it included in the Properties dialog opened for a Java program (compilation unit) when selected in Package Explorer view. To do this, you identify that your page should be included when the selected object is *adaptable* to the resource model object type defined. Adding adaptable="true" to your code makes the property page available in both the Navigator and Package Explorer views.

```
<extension
  point="org.eclipse.ui.propertyPages">
  <page
    objectClass="org.eclipse.core.resources.IFile"
    adaptable="true"
    name="Java Resource Properties"
    nameFilter="*.java"
    class="qrs.tool.properties.JavaPropertyPage"
    id="qrs.tool.properties.qrsfile">
  </page>
</extension>
```

The Package Explorer view does not display files but displays objects (IJavaElement) as defined in the JDT's Java model. For example, what appears to be simply a .java file (an instance of IFile) in the Package Explorer view is actually part of the JDT model, an instance of ICompilationUnit. When opened from the Package Explorer view, the selected resource can still be adapted to an IResource.

PART III

If you only wanted your page to be added to the Properties dialog opened from the Package Explorer view, the objectClass attribute would identify org.eclipse.jdt.core.ICompilationUnit.

You can also use filters in the extension definition to further control your contribution. A <filter name="" value=""> entry added as part of the <page> entry will restrict your page contribution so that it participates only when the filter definition is true. Table 16.4 shows a partial list of the available filter values.

**Table 16.4**    Filter Options for Property Page Extensions

| Object Type | Filter Names | Values |
|---|---|---|
| Resources | extension | File extension name, as in txt or java |
| | name | resource name |
| | path | Path to resource (may include *) |
| | projectNature | The id of nature extension |
| | readOnly | Enter a value of true or false |
| Projects | nature | nature id |
| | Open | true or false |

For additional detail on filters, see Creating Elaborate Filters Using Action Expressions in Chapter 21, Action Contributions: The Integration Fast Track.

## Implementing a Property Page

You build a property page by creating a class that extends PropertyPage and implements the IWorkbenchPropertyPage interface. This is how the initial implementation of a property page, as generated by the PDE, would look in your project.

```
public class JavaPropertyPage extends PropertyPage
    implements IWorkbenchPropertyPage {
  public JavaPropertyPage() {
    super();
  }
  protected Control createContents(Composite parent) {
    return null;
  }
}
```

By inheriting the framework-provided implementation, you can focus on just creating the user interface controls and adding any processing logic required in your property page.

All you need to do to implement an information-only property page is define the user interface by implementing the `createContents` method. You add your user interface controls, populated with any required content, to the parent control passed in the `createContents` method. This makes your property page an information page; you share information about the selected resource. If this is the appropriate role of your page, you should also override the `noDefaultAndApplyButton` method and return `false` to hide the **Restore Defaults** and **Apply** buttons normally included in the user interface of a property page. The property page framework provides the required **OK** and **Cancel** button logic (which just shuts the Properties dialog).

If your property page is required to support both display and modification of data associated with the selected resource, you need to further customize your property page. The user will select push buttons included in the Properties dialog to direct processing. Table 16.5 lists the methods you need to override to implement support for the push buttons.

**Table 16.5**   Methods to Override to Customize Push Button Logic for Property Pages

| Push Button Name | Method |
| --- | --- |
| **OK** | `performOk()` |
| **Apply** | `performApply()` |
| **Restore Defaults** | `performDefaults()` |
| **Cancel** | `performCancel()` |

Now that you have an extension and base class for implementing a property page, let's discuss the user interface definition and addition of logic to process the property values.

### Defining the Property Page User Interface

You customize the `createContents` method to add the controls required in the user interface. For example, the following method adds a label and two check boxes to the property page.

```
protected Control createContents(Composite parent) {
    Composite composite = new Composite(parent, SWT.NONE);
    GridLayout gridLayout = new GridLayout();
    composite.setLayout(gridLayout);

    Label label = new Label(composite, SWT.NONE);
    label.setText("Choose state for selected resource.");
    Button regenB = new Button(composite, SWT.CHECK);
```

```
regenB.setText("Regeneration Supported");
regenB.setSelection(getRegenPropertyState());
Button managedB = new Button(composite, SWT.CHECK);
managedB.setText("Managed Entity");
managedB.setSelection(getManagedPropertyState());
return composite;
}
```

The current state of the check boxes is obtained from the saved resource property. The result of the customized `createContents` method is visible when the property page is selected in the Properties dialog (see Figure 16.8).

**Figure 16.8**    Property Page with Customized User Interface Content

### Adding Resource Property Access Logic

The workspace API (see Chapter 23, Workspace Resource Programming) provides support for getting and setting values for a specific resource. The `IResource` interface methods shown here support getting and setting both temporary (session) and permanent (persistent) values for any workspace resource.

```
setSessionProperty(QualifiedName key, Object value)
getSessionProperty(QualifiedName key)
setPersistentProperty(QualifiedName key, String value)
getPersistentProperty(QualifiedName key)
```

A `QualifiedName` is a multipart name, which consists of a qualifier and a local name. By convention, the plug-in id is used as the qualifier. Session properties exist only in memory, while persistent properties are saved and therefore available during subsequent invocations of Eclipse using the same workspace. A session property can be any type of object, but only `String` values can be saved as persistent properties.

You would use the get logic above to define the initial state of the property page user interface.

```
private static QualifiedName REGEN_PROPERTY_KEY =
  new QualifiedName("qrs.toolPlugin", "regen");
  ...
private boolean getRegenPropertyState() {
  IResource resource = (IResource) getElement();
  try {
    String propValue =
      resource.getPersistentProperty(REGEN_PROPERTY_KEY);
    if ((propValue != null) && propValue.equals("True"))
      return true;
    else
      return false;
  } catch (CoreException e) {
  // Deal with exception.
  }
  return false;
}
```

The set logic would translate the property to a String value and be integrated as part of the performOk method implementation included in your property page.

```
public boolean performOk() {
  setRegenPropertyState(regenB.getSelection());
  return super.performOk();
}

private void setRegenPropertyState(boolean value) {
  IResource resource = (IResource) getElement();
  try {
    if (value) {
      resource.setPersistentProperty(
        REGEN_PROPERTY_KEY, "True");
    } else {
      resource.setPersistentProperty(
        REGEN_PROPERTY_KEY, "False");
      }
  } catch (CoreException e) {}
}
```

The performOk method is invoked when the user selects the **OK** button. The performOk method is called by default by the performApply method. Typically you will just put the logic to save the property values in one location, the performOk method.

### Saving Resource Type-Specific Properties

A common approach for persistence of data exposed on a property page is to use the workspace API to save and retrieve property values for the selected resource. But if your plug-in wanted to define a generic value for what was appropriate for all resources of a given type, you could choose to implement the user interface as part of a property page while storing the value using a single keyed entry in a preference store. The property page implementation provided by the dialog framework inherits from the preference page definition, so implementing this approach is easy. Your property page implementation can reuse the inherited approach to preference store management.

If you use this approach, validate that this is the appropriate user interface design for the function being provided. You should ask this question: Is it more effective to have this control value available from a resource's property page, or should this value just be defined as a preference value and added to a plug-in-specific preference page?

You want to be sure that this is the appropriate user interface design for the plug-in function you are implementing. This means that the user of your plug-in will intuitively think to go to the resource's property page to establish this type of control. If not, it might be best to implement the function as part of a preference page contribution.

To save values that can actually be persisted in a repository, you should consider the user settings API. See Scoped Value Management with User Settings in Chapter 17, Dialog Settings, Preferences, and User Settings.

### Implementing Your Own Properties Dialog

We have covered how to extend the Properties dialog opened by the Navigator view and discussed how you can get your page in the Properties dialog opened from the Package Explorer view when your extension targets an `IFile` resource with a `.java` name filter and includes the `adaptable=true` attribute.

You can add pages to any Properties dialog that exists in Eclipse if you know what type of object is displayed in the view that offers an option to open a Properties dialog.

The Properties dialog can also be associated with other types of objects that are adaptable. A view that offers a **Properties** context menu option contains objects that are **adaptable**, that is, they implement the `IAdaptable` interface, which allows for the reuse of the logic to open a Properties dialog. The objects also need to either implement or adapt to the `IWorkbenchAdapter` interface so that the Properties dialog can call the associated `getLabel` method to complete the Properties dialog title. See Adding Properties Dialog Support in Chapter 15, JFace Viewers, for details on opening the Properties dialog from a viewer's context menu. An example of this is also included in the view examples on the CD-ROM.

## Contributing Wizards

Using the wizard framework, you can easily integrate wizards to create new resources or to import and export resources by defining an extension. Figure 16.9 depicts the structure of a wizard and the associated wizard pages as they relate to the `WizardDialog`.

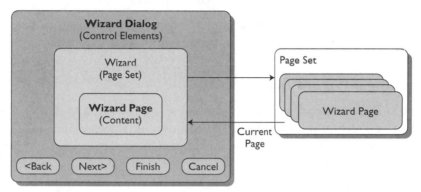

**Figure 16.9**    Structural View of a Wizard Dialog and the Associated Wizard Pages

A wizard represents the task, and your implementation of a wizard is identified in the extension definition. Each wizard page represents a step in the task. Pages are added to the wizard, and the page state determines whether the page is complete. When a page is complete, the user can move on to the next page in the wizard; when all pages known to the wizard are complete, the processing implemented by the wizard's `performFinish` method can be invoked.

Wizards defined by extension are automatically wrapped in a wizard dialog when opened by the Workbench. The wizard dialog manages the page set and includes user interface controls that support page navigation and task invocation. Techniques for opening a wizard yourself are discussed in Directly Opening a Wizard Dialog for Your Wizard near the end of this chapter.

The wizard itself acts as a controller, determining which wizard page, from a list of associated pages, is displayed in response to user interaction. If there are multiple wizard pages, **Next** and **Back** buttons are enabled to support forward and backward navigation. The push buttons are enabled when required, based on the number of wizard pages and the completion status of each page. As you define wizard extensions and then add pages to the `Wizard`

PART III

class defined for each extension, you are building on this core wizard processing logic. These steps are required to create a functioning wizard.

- Define a wizard extension.
- Implement a wizard.
- Implement a wizard page.
- Define the wizard page user interface.
- Add the appropriate wizard processing logic.

These steps, and additional wizard customization and control topics, are discussed in the subsections that follow.

### Defining a Wizard Extension

Three extension points allow you to add wizards to the Workbench. These extension points support the addition of entries to the set of resource creation, import processing, and export processing wizards integrated into the Workbench user interface.

```
org.eclipse.ui.newWizards
org.eclipse.ui.importWizards
org.eclipse.ui.exportWizards
```

This is an example of an import extension definition.

```
<extension
  id="qrs.tool.wizards.import"
  point="org.eclipse.ui.importWizards">
  <wizard
    name="QRS File Import"
    class="qrs.tool.wizards.ImportWizard"
    id="qrs.tool.wizards.import.file">
  </wizard>
</extension>
```

By using these extension points, you can add entries that are accessible from the matching points in the common Workbench menu tree.

- org.eclipse.ui.newWizards are added to one or both of the **File > New > Projects...** and **File > New > Other...** menu trees.
- org.eclipse.ui.importWizards are added to the **File > Import...** menu tree.
- org.eclipse.ui.exportWizards are added to the **File > Export...** menu tree.

Each of these menu options open up a dialog that lets you select from a list of wizards that have extended the matching extension point. The

**Projects...** menu option only displays newWizards extensions defined with the project="true" attribute. Categories can also be defined as part of the extension to organize the wizard selection dialog entries.

```
<extension
    id="qrs.tool.wizards.new"
    name="qrs new wizards"
    point="org.eclipse.ui.newWizards">
    <category
      name="Cool Wizard Category"
      id="qrs.tool.wizards.category">
    </category>
    <wizard
      name="A New Wizard Entry"
      category="qrs.tool.wizards.category"
      class="qrs.tool.wizards.QRSNewWizard"
      id="qrs.tool.wizards.new.entry">
      <description>
A wizard in the cool category. Select and enter the
processing implemented by my available pages.
      </description>
    </wizard>
</extension>
```

Figure 16.10 shows the dialog that includes the category and associated entry (with description) for this resource creation wizard extension definition.

**Figure 16.10** New Wizard for Resource Creation

The selection dialog is itself a wizard in that it supports forward (and backward) paging through a set of wizard pages. The selection dialog lets you select and launch your wizard, which then configures and manages access to the appropriate page content as part of your implementation of the task to be performed.

## Implementing a Wizard

You build a wizard by creating a class that extends the Wizard class and implements the appropriate interface (specific to the extension point). Table 16.6 lists the extension points and interface names.

**Table 16.6**   Extension Points for Adding a Wizard to the User Interface

| Extension Point | Interface |
| --- | --- |
| org.eclipse.ui.newWizards | INewWizard |
| org.eclipse.ui.importWizards | IImportWizard |
| org.eclipse.ui.exportWizards | IExportWizard |

The PDE knows what to generate for each extension option; for example, the code shown in the following example would be generated by the PDE for the QRSNewWizard wizard page identified in the extension definition shown in the previous subsection.

```
public class QRSNewWizard extends Wizard implements INewWizard {
  public QRSNewWizard() {
    super();
  }

  public boolean performFinish() {
    return false;
  }

  public void init(
    IWorkbench workbench, IStructuredSelection selection) {

  }
}
```

All you have to do is define and add the wizard pages required in the user interface and implement the appropriate processing logic as part of the performFinish method. Note that the performFinish method must return true when processing has successfully completed, otherwise the wizard dialog will not close.

### Implementing a Wizard Page

Implementing your own wizard page is as simple as creating a class that extends the WizardPage class and overriding the createControl method to define the appropriate user interface.

```
public void createControl(Composite parent) {
  Composite composite = new Composite(parent, SWT.NONE);
  RowLayout rowLayout = new RowLayout();
  rowLayout.justify = true;
  rowLayout.marginLeft = 5;
  rowLayout.marginRight = 5;
  rowLayout.spacing = 5;
  composite.setLayout(rowLayout);

  Label label = new Label(composite, SWT.NONE);
  label.setText("Select a processing option:");
  Combo combo = new Combo(composite, SWT.NONE);
  combo.setItems(
    new String[] { "Automatic", "Manual", "Hybrid" });
  setControl(composite);
  return;
}
```

In this code, the setControl method is used to identify the parent control for the user interface content defined in the createControl method. This approach is slightly different from that used in preference or property pages, which return the control as part of their createContents method. If you do not use the setControl method to define the control, your wizard page will be empty.

You can populate the wizard with your pages by overriding the addPages method. The following example adds SimpleWizardPage to the QRSNewWizard and customizes the wizard page.

```
public void addPages() {
  SimpleWizardPage testPage =
    new SimpleWizardPage("simplePage");
  testPage.setTitle("Title for first wizard page");
  testPage.setDescription(
    "Description for the first wizard page");
  addPage(testPage);
}
```

PART III

**NOTE** You can also add wizard pages that were provided as part of Eclipse (see Reusable Specialized Wizard Pages later in this chapter).

Once a wizard and wizard page have been defined and the required page(s) have been added to the wizard, you can select and open the wizard in the selection dialog (see Figure 16.11).

**Figure 16.11**　Basic Implementation of a Wizard and Wizard Page

The title and description values set for the wizard page are visible in Figure 16.11. If your logic were to display an error message, the description would no longer be shown. The same text widget is used to display these values.

## Customizing a Wizard

The next thing you have to do is customize the wizard to support the task you want the user to perform.

You can customize the wizard by adjusting the visual display (the title, icon, and use of a progress monitor) and implementing support for retrieval of values saved in a dialog settings object (if required).

You can customize the user interface of a wizard by adding to the `init` method. The `setWindowTitle` method defines the text that will be seen in the active wizard header. The `setDefaultPageImageDescriptor` method defines the image that will be shown in the wizard dialog for each wizard page (unless the page provides an alternate image using the `WizardPage` `.setImageDescriptor` method).

Here is an example of how you might customize a wizard.

```
public void init(
  IWorkbench workbench, IStructuredSelection selection) {

  setWindowTitle("Customized Wizard Title");
  setDefaultPageImageDescriptor(
    getImageDescriptor("eclipse.jpg"));
  setNeedsProgressMonitor(true);
}
```

The getImageDescriptor method provides an example of how an image can be obtained from the plug-in's icons directory.

```
private ImageDescriptor getImageDescriptor(
  String relativePath) {

  String iconPath = "icons/";
  try {
    ToolPlugin plugin = ToolPlugin.getDefault();
    URL installURL = plugin.getBundle().getEntry("/");
    URL url = new URL(installURL, iconPath + relativePath);
    return ImageDescriptor.createFromURL(url);
  } catch (MalformedURLException e) {
    // Should not happen.
    return null;
  }
}
```

The customization logic changes the user interface for the wizard by adding a title to the dialog and a graphic to the dialog header (see Figure 16.12).

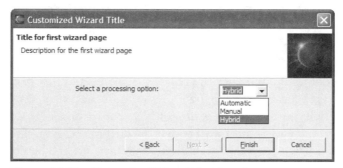

**Figure 16.12** Customized Wizard User Interface

## Controlling Wizard Page Progression

When more than one page is added to a wizard, the inherited control logic determines whether the **Next** button should be enabled. The logic to enable paging forward is integrated into the wizard processing framework. Your user can step into the next page or return to the previous page in the order the pages were added to the wizard; the Controlling the Next Page topic discusses how you can control page access and progression. You also have the option of refining this logic by managing the page status (setPageComplete method). If a page is not complete, the user is not able to move forward. The goals here are to ensure that your set of wizard pages collect the required information and that the information is correct.

If your customized addPages logic added multiple pages, the following would happen.

- Progression through the pages would be supported using the **Next** button.
- The **Next** button would be enabled as long as there were more pages and the current page status was complete.
- The **Finish** button would be enabled as long as all pages had a page status of complete.

### Forward Progress

If an entry field is mandatory or a choice must be made, do not set the page status to complete (isPageComplete is true) until the appropriate input has been provided. If the data entered can be validated, do so before allowing the user to continue on to the next page. You only want users to return to a page when they decide to change a value, not when your wizard logic tells them several pages later that the value provided is not appropriate. This requires that you coordinate the design of both page content and page flow.

### Finish Processing

When pages are added to a wizard, the associated isPageComplete status is used to determine whether the page must be visited before the task can be finished (processed by your logic). By default the isPageComplete status is true, which means that users do not have to traverse each page—they could just press the **Finish** button to trigger wizard processing. The **Finish** button is enabled when the canFinish method returns true. The default implementation of the canFinish method returns true if all pages indicate that they are complete.

If the **Finish** button is enabled, selecting it will invoke the performFinish method in the wizard. The performFinish method must perform your required processing and return true if the processing was successful (which will close the wizard). A return value of false leaves the wizard open.

**NOTE**  A wizard can be configured to use a progress monitor. This may be appropriate if your finish processing is not trivial.

### Controlling the Next Page

If you create a wizard with all the pages known up front, this could be called a defined-page wizard. The next page for any given page is the one added after it in the wizard's addPages method. The getNextPage method in a wizard page just forwards the request to the getNextPage method in the wizard; the wizard looks at the pages added previously and selects the next one in sequence.

If some user interaction or decision determines that another page, or an alternative next page, is required to support the ongoing wizard task, your implementation can override the getNextPage method in a wizard page or wizard to dynamically determine the next wizard page in the sequence.

You could take this further and add only one page to a wizard in the addPages method. Then that wizard page could have a customized getNext-Page method that detects whether another page is required and which type of page that might be, then adds it dynamically to the wizard. This type of logic is demonstrated in the wizard example on the CD-ROM that compares defined-page wizards and dynamic page wizards.

The getNextPage method returns the next page, but the page returned must also have been added to the wizard itself. Since there is no method that will remove a page from the wizard, if you change your mind about which page is next, things get interesting. The wizard uses the page returned by the getNextPage method, if other pages have been added to the wizard, but not returned at the point when next page navigation actually takes place—these pages are known to the wizard but never shown to the user.

The CD-ROM includes a demonstration of wizard programming that shows both dynamic management of the next page and dynamic page content, which is the next topic to discuss.

### *Delaying Creation of a Wizard Page User Interface*

The wizard framework creates the user interface for all wizard pages known to the wizard through addPage calls in the addPages method before it displays the first page. You can easily take control of this process by overriding the createPageControls method in your class that extends Wizard. This process is easier than it seems. The Java source editor generates an initial version of the overridden method.

To take control of creating a wizard page user interface, all you have to do is remove the call to the super implementation.

By telling the wizard framework to do nothing, it waits until each wizard page is about to be shown for the first time before calling the wizard page's createControl method to create the user interface. This delay allows your createControl logic to react to user input from a previous page.

This is not required for dynamically added pages. Once the first wizard page is shown, if you decide to add more pages to the wizard, the user interface for these pages is not constructed until the page is about to be entered.

**NOTE** The wizard example on the CD-ROM includes a scripted test cycle that demonstrates the use of page complete processing, the differences between defined-page and dynamic-page wizards, and the use of the createPageControls method to delay creation of a wizard page user interface.

### Reusable Specialized Wizard Pages

The pages used to support the creation of basic resource types (projects, folders, and files) can be integrated into your wizard and can even be customized, if required.

Looking at the classes that extend WizardPage can help you quickly find the reusable pages that exist as part of Eclipse itself. The following is a sample of the pages you may find useful in your own wizard (the names are self-explanatory).

```
WizardExternalProjectImportPage
WizardNewFileCreationPage
WizardNewFolderMainPage
WizardNewProjectCreationPage
WizardNewProjectReferencePage
```

In addition, you may consider extending the following pages for import, export, or selection.

```
WizardExportPage
WizardExportResourcesPage
WizardImportPage
WizardResourceImportPage
WizardSelectionPage
```

Additional wizard page classes are also available for reuse if your plug-in needs to create Java programming resources. The following pages are provided by the JDT and can be directly used in your wizards.

```
JavaCapabilityConfigurationPage
NewPackageWizardPage
NewClassWizardPage
NewInterfaceWizardPage
```

**NOTE** As described in the Javadoc, using `JavaCapabilityConfigurationPage` is preferred over the `NewJavaProjectWizardPage` alternative.

These two pages can be extended as part of a custom implementation.

```
NewContainerWizardPage
NewTypeWizardPage
```

From the set of wizard pages listed here, you can select pages that can be directly added to your wizard or create subclasses to support customization of their implementation (some of these pages allow you to do either).

For instance, if you wanted to create a file as part of your wizard, you could add the `WizardNewFileCreationPage` to your wizard. This requires that you save the selection parameter when the wizard is initialized so that it can be given to the New File wizard page. The relevant code sections are shown here.

```
...
private IStructuredSelection selection;
private WizardNewFileCreationPage myFilePage;
...
public void init(
  IWorkbench workbench, IStructuredSelection selection) {
  ...
  this.selection = selection;
}
...
public void addPages() {
  myFilePage =
    new WizardNewFileCreationPage("filePage", selection);
  addPage(myFilePage);
}
```

This would result in a wizard page in your wizard that supports selection of a container and creation of a file. All you need to do is override the wizard

PART III

`performFinish` method to trigger the required wizard page processing when a user presses the **Finish** button.

```
public boolean performFinish() {
  myFilePage.createNewFile();
  return true;
}
```

You can also enhance the New File wizard page by adding to the user interface and creating customized file creation logic. To add to the user interface, you extend the `WizardNewFileCreationPage` class and then override the inherited method.

```
public class MyNewFileWizardPage
  extends WizardNewFileCreationPage {
...
  public void createControl(Composite parent) {
    super.createControl(parent);
    Composite composite = (Composite)getControl();
    Label label = new Label(composite, SWT.NONE);
    label.setText("Choose state for selected resource.");
    Button button2 = new Button(composite, SWT.CHECK);
    button2.setText("Working copy");
  }
```

Figure 16.13 shows the customized user interface portion of the new creation wizard page.

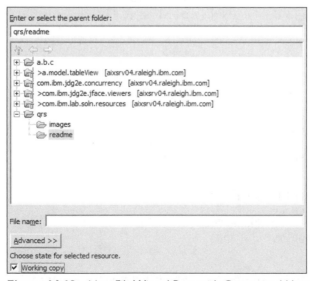

**Figure 16.13**   New File Wizard Page with Customized User Interface

## Directly Opening a Wizard Dialog for Your Wizard

Wizards can also be used in other places in your plug-in. The wizard and wizard page definition process is the same, but instead of using an extension to integrate the wizard with the user interface, you need to wrap the wizard in a WizardDialog and open the dialog yourself.

The following example shows how to open a wizard in a dialog as part of an action. A reference to the selected resource is also provided.

```
ToolWizard wizard = new ToolWizard();
wizard.init(getWorkbench(), mySelection);

WizardDialog dialog =
  new WizardDialog(
    getWorkbench()
      .getActiveWorkbenchWindow().getShell(), wizard);
dialog.open();
```

As an example of how often you may be using wizards without realizing it, Figure 16.14 shows a wizard that is opened by the PDE.

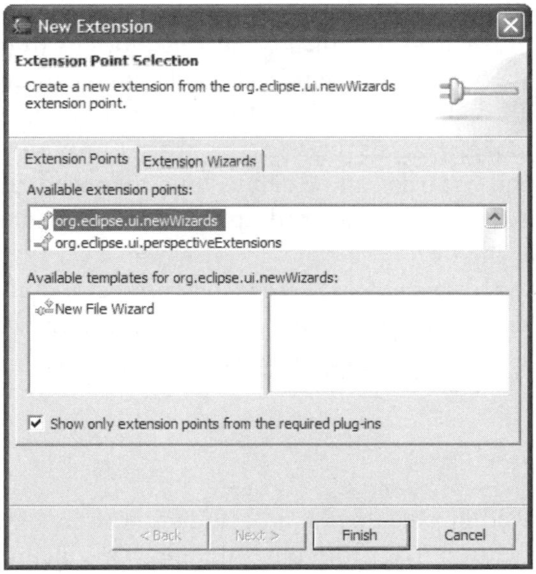

**Figure 16.14**   New Extension Wizard

When you select the **Add...** button on the Extensions page of the plug-in manifest editor, you start this wizard. Its title may not shout wizard, but the code involved extends the Wizard class. One giveaway is the user interface;

when you see **Finish** and **Cancel** buttons, chances are good you're working with a wizard.

## Example Summary

This chapter discussed the various kinds of dialogs that are part of the Eclipse Platform. This includes the general-purpose dialogs that can be used where required in your plug-in logic and the Preferences and Properties dialogs that are contributed to by extension. The wizard framework supports both techniuqes. You can define extensions for wizards that are integrated into predefined points of the Workbench or direcly invoked to run custom wizards.

You can now explore the various preference page, property page, and wizard examples found on the CD-ROM. The general-purpose nature of these dialogs accounts for the number of available examples.

The `com.ibm.jdg2e.view.simplemodel` project includes examples of both wizard programming and property page creation. This includes the ability to open the common Properties dialog for a specific object in a viewer.

The `com.ibm.jdg2e.usersettings` project includes examples of both preference and property page implementation. These pages also demonstrate the user settings API, including the initialization of preference values.

The `com.ibm.jdg2e.wizards.newwizards` project provides a detailed look at how multiple page wizards can be defined and managed. This includes an example of a wizard with pages defined up front and a wizard that dynamically adds pages on the fly.

The `com.ibm.jdg2e.resources.extensions` project includes an example of a new project creation wizard, while a new file creation wizard example can be found in the `com.ibm.jdg2e.msseditor.ide` project.

## Chapter Summary

This chapter reviewed how dialogs can be added, both by extension and through direct invocation in custom plug-in logic. This included the preference and property page contributions, as well as the specialized wizards for resource creation and import or export processing. Information on how to define and implement these reusable dialogs was provided. In addition, this chapter reviewed the techniques available for adding custom wizards and making use of the general-purpose dialogs included as part of the Eclipse code base.

This knowledge will help you integrate your pages with the common preferences and properties dialogs that are part of Eclipse, add wizards to support any customized resource processing you may need, and add other dialogs to your plug-in as required.

## References

Arthorne, John, and Chris Laffra. 2004. *Official Eclipse 3.0 FAQs*. Boston, MA: Addison-Wesley. http://eclipsefaq.org. (See FAQs 155, 156, 159, 161, 162, 178.)

Cooper, Ryan. August 21, 2002. Simplifying preference pages with field editors. http://www.eclipse.org.

Daum, Berthold. Mutatis mutandis—using preference pages as property pages. http://www.eclipse.org.

PART III

# CHAPTER 17

*Dialog Settings, Preferences, and User Settings*

This chapter discusses the various techniques available as part of Eclipse for storing plug-in-specific data as part of the Eclipse Platform. The techniques discussed are dialog settings, preference values, and user settings. Dialog settings support customizing the user interface. Preference values allow users to control plug-in behavior. User settings are more open-ended; they allow you to store values with an association to an installation, a workspace, or even a project. The goal of this chapter is twofold: to help you understand the classic scenarios for storing data and the opportunities provided by the available APIs.

## Overview of the Options

This section provides you with information about the available options for storing plug-in-specific data in Eclipse. This is data that you keep to help the user interact with and control your plug-in. This includes recently used values from a dialog, preferences values from a preference page, or any other user settings you wish to maintain. After reading this overview section, you may decide not to read any further if you are just getting started with plug-in development. Instead, you can return to this chapter later when you identify a need to store values as part of your plug-in.

441

## Dialog Settings

Users like to have the fields in their dialogs filled in before they are opened. Plug-ins that contribute to the user interface can use dialog settings to store various data types that are useful in this process. These discrete values and lists of values, which can be organized in sections and identified by key, are saved as part of the private data kept in your plug-in's state directory in the current workspace.

The classic role of a dialog setting is implied by the name: store values used in a dialog. An example would be the list of export targets found in an export wizard. Potential scenarios for the use of dialog settings are discussed in Chapter 16, Dialogs and Wizards, but the API details are discussed in this chapter in the upcoming section Storing Values in Dialog Settings.

## Preference Values

Preference values are typically provided by you to allow the user to control the behavior of your plug-in. Your plug-in class can provide you with an appropriate object that can be used to get and set keyed preference values. This API also allows you to define default preference values for your plug-in. These preference values are stored as metadata for your plug-in in the same place as instance values saved using the user settings API; in fact the APIs are compatible.

As you would expect, this is what you typically use to store values collected on a preference page, but view-specific settings can also be stored as a preference value; for example, the **Go Into Top Level Type** option in the Outline view for a Java editor is saved as a preference value. The techniques available for storing preference values are mentioned in Adding Preference Value Logic to a Preference Page in Chapter 16. The APIs available through your plug-in class are detailed in Storing Preference Values for a Plug-in later in the current chapter.

## User Settings

The user settings API is a general-purpose API. It allows you to define and store values by key and identify defaults for these values. You also have the ability to define where these values are stored. They can be stored with an association or scope of the Eclipse installation, the active workspace, or a specific project. These different storage points not only manage the scope of the value but also keep the keys used unique to your plug-in by storing values in a plug-in-specific container or node. You can even link these nodes in a hierarchy. For example, a project-level user setting could override a workspace-level user setting for the same key.

The opportunities for using the user settings API in preference pages and properties pages are discussed in Chapter 16. Information about the API and support for node-specific values and cascading values is detailed in Scoped Value Management with User Settings later in the current chapter.

## Storing Values in Dialog Settings

You get an `IDialogSettings` from your plug-in class. The `getDialogSettings` method is defined in `AbstractUIPlugin`, a common supertype for a plug-in class. Many types of values can be stored in an `IDialogSettings`. These values are saved in a file named `dialog_settings.xml` in your plug-in's state directory.

Storing values entered by the user in a dialog, like the last import or export location as done by Eclipse, is the classic dialog settings use case. While you could decide to use dialog settings for other purposes, you should first consider the other choices discussed in this chapter. You will want to evaluate the differences in behavior; for example, a dialog setting does not have a change notification mechanism.

### Dialog Settings Management

The `IDialogSettings` interface defines methods to store and retrieve the data types you can preserve. The data is saved in your plug-in's state directory by the plug-in class when the Eclipse Platform is shut down. The following code stores the data types supported by the API.

```
IDialogSettings dset =
  GamesPlugin.getDefault().getDialogSettings();

String[] sList = {"a", "b", "c"};

IDialogSettings dSection =
  dset.addNewSection("TestDialogSection");

dSection.put("int", 1);
dSection.put("double", 2000000000);
dSection.put("long", 300000000);
dSection.put("float", 400000000);
dSection.put("trueFalse", false);
dSection.put("string", "myValue");
dSection.put("stringArray", sList);
```

The following XML snippet is the stored result of this code as found in the `dialog_setting.xml` file saved in the plug-in's state directory.

```xml
<?xml version="1.0" encoding="UTF-8"?>
  <section name="Workbench">
    <section name="TestDialogSection">
      <item key="double" value="2000000000"/>
      <item key="string" value="myValue"/>
      <item key="trueFalse" value="false"/>
      <item key="float" value="400000000"/>
      <item key="int" value="1"/>
      <item key="long" value="300000000"/>
      <list key="stringArray">
        <item value="a"/>
        <item value="b"/>
        <item value="c"/>
      </list>
    </section>
</section>
```

## Usage Considerations

To avoid conflict, each of your dialogs should use the `addNewSection` method to create its own section; the section name could be the class name or display name of the dialog. This gives each dialog the freedom to choose key names without conflict.

A set of recently used values is straightforward to store and retrieve. The following example loads a drop-down list with recently used values. The first portion of the code stores values; the second retrieves them and loads a combo box.

```java
// Store values
IDialogSettings dialogSettings =
    GamesPlugin.getDefault().getDialogSettings();
IDialogSettings newDialogSection =
    dialogSettings.addNewSection("TestDialogSection");
String[] valueList =
    {"recent value", "another value", "hard-to-remember value"};
newDialogSection.put("stringArray", valueList);

// Get values
IDialogSettings dialogSection = GamesPlugin.getDefault()
    .getDialogSettings().getSection("TestDialogSection");
String[] lastUsed = dialogSection.getArray("stringArray");
Combo combo = new Combo(composite, SWT.NONE);
combo.setItems(lastUsed);
combo.setText("Recently Used Values");
```

This saves the user time and provides a reminder of previously used values.

## Storing Preference Values for a Plug-in

The classic use of the preference value API is to save the entries provided by the user on a preference page (see Contributing to the Preferences Dialog in Chapter 16, Dialogs and Wizards). You can also choose to store other values, from view settings to values that a user never sees.

Your plug-in class can inherit from `AbstractUIPlugin` or `Plugin`; each supertype provides support for storing preference values. The two implementations have differences in class and method names, but they function the same. Each inherited implementation allows you to get the object used to manage preference values.

Preference values are stored on behalf of your plug-in in the state directory for the `org.eclipse.core.runtime` plug-in. The file used, and therefore the keys you define, are unique to your plug-in. The preference values for a plug-in id of `a.b.c` would be found in this directory and file:

```
workspace\.metadata\.plugins\org.eclipse.core.runtime
    \.settings\a.b.c.prefs
```

The file is saved as part of the workspace so the values defined are known only to one workspace. The only way to share these values is to use the export/import processing available in the Preferences dialog (see Coordinating Preferences in Chapter 6, Managing Your Eclipse Environment). If you do not want to store values local to the workspace but instead want to manage them across workspaces, you need to skip ahead to Scoped Value Management with User Settings later in the current chapter.

When the file is actually saved depends on the supertype for the plug-in and the use of direct calls to the appropriate save method in the plug-in class. These details are described below. Note that when the preference values are written to disk, any key whose current value is the default value is not actually stored.

The provided preference value support is more than a get and set API. A change listener can detect when modifications are made. This is useful when portions of your tool need to react to the change made by the user in the Preferences dialog. You see this in action when you change the font used by the Java editor. As soon as you save the new font value by using the **OK** or **Apply** button, the font used in any open editors changes. The editors change because they are listening for preference changes made as part of that plug-in.

### Preference Value Management

Storing preference values is straightforward. You get the object used to store preference values from your plug-in. This object is used when you need to store values obtained from a preference page or some other area of your plug-in tool. You should also make sure the contents of the object are saved to disk when Eclipse shuts down.

Eclipse provides two options for storing preference values.

- `PreferenceStore` API: This option is available using the `getPreference-Store` method if your plug-in class inherits from the `AbstractUIPlugin` class.
- `Preferences` API: This option is available using the `getPlugin-Preferences` method if your plug-in class inherits from the `Plugin` class.

Each of these options provides the same basic function. You can save and retrieve keyed values. The values that can be stored are simple data types (`boolean`, `double`, `float`, `int`, `String`, and `long`). You can add a property change listener to support notification when preference values change.

Most plug-ins use the general-purpose implementation provided by the `AbstractUIPlugin`. A plug-in that did not contribute to the user interface would use the `Plugin` class implementation. Since the `Plugin` class is the superclass for `AbstractUIPlugin`, both APIs may be accessible. If you have multiple plug-ins, you could choose to manage all preference values using a single plug-in class that is shared by the other plug-ins.

### Establishing Default Preference Values

Defaults for preference values can be defined by your plug-in using the `set-Default` method. The method signature matches the data type you want to store. When a keyed value has not been saved, you get the default value. If a default has not been set, the default-default value is returned instead. This is either an empty `String` or a zero value, depending on the data type.

You can set a preference key to its default value using the `setToDefault` method. The defined default preference value can also be obtained using a `getDefault`*Type* method, where *Type* is the data type.

The preference value framework allows you to define defaults as part of the initialization process. You contribute your default initialization routine using the `org.eclipse.core.runtime.preferences` extension point. It identifies an initialization routine for default preference values.

```
<extension
    point="org.eclipse.core.runtime.preferences">
  <initializer class="com.ibm.jdg2e.preferences.ValueDefaults"/>
</extension>
```

The implementation of a default initialization routine is straightforward. You can use either the `getPreferenceStore` or `getPluginPreferences` method to get the preference value object. The choice available depends on the inheritance hierarchy for your plug-in class.

```
public class ValueDefaults
  extends AbstractPreferenceInitializer {
    public void initializeDefaultPreferences() {
      GamesPlugin.getDefault().getPreferenceStore()
        .setDefault("pref_key","myDefaultValue");
    }
}
```

## Reacting to Preference Value Changes

If you need to know when a preference value changes, you can add a property change listener to inform you. You add the property change listener to the `PreferenceStore` or `Preferences` object. The approach used to implement a property change listener depends on the type of preference object used. Your listener will be sent an event when any change is made; your code will have to query the event to determine whether the preference value that changed is of interest. The following example code uses an inner class to print the preference value identifier.

```
// PreferenceStore approach
ToolPlugin
  .getDefault()
  .getPreferenceStore()
  .addPropertyChangeListener(new IPropertyChangeListener() {
    public void propertyChange(PropertyChangeEvent event) {
      System.out.println("a preference value changed");
      System.out.println(event.getProperty());
    };
  });

// Preferences approach
ToolPlugin
  .getDefault()
  .getPluginPreferences()
  .addPropertyChangeListener(
    new Preferences
    .IPropertyChangeListener() {
      public void propertyChange(
        Preferences.PropertyChangeEvent event) {
        System.out.println("a preference value changed");
        System.out.println(event.getProperty());
      };
    });
```

## Scoped Value Management with User Settings

The dialog settings and stored preference value options provide a reasonable set of function, but there are problems as well. If a stored value should apply to all workspaces or needs to be unique to a single project, a dialog setting or stored preference value is not going to help much.

The user settings API addresses this problem by letting you use a storage mechanism called a **scope**. The scope used determines the visibility of your value. Eclipse provides scopes that are associated to the entire installation, a single workspace, or a specific project. A default scope is also available. You can even define extensions to add your own scopes.

### Scopes, Nodes, and Stored Values

The notion of a scope is related to the access and awareness of a keyed value. A scope that covers the Eclipse installation is termed a **configuration scope**. Values that are unique across a workspace are stored in an **instance scope**, while project-specific values are stored in a **project scope**. The nice thing about a project scope is that it can be shared with others on a team using a repository. The default scope allows you to have a source for defined defaults that you can reference while using any of these predefined scopes.

These are the class names for the scopes defined by Eclipse: `DefaultScope`, `ConfigurationScope`, `InstanceScope`, and `ProjectScope`. The function provided by these scopes can be described as follows.

- `DefaultScope`: defaults for keyed values identified by an initialization routine for a given plug-in.
- `ConfigurationScope`: values stored by key for a given plug-in as part of the installed Eclipse or Eclipse-based product.
- `InstanceScope`: values stored by key for a given plug-in that are associated with the active workspace.
- `ProjectScope`: values stored by key for a given plug-in that are associated with a specific project. This scope is contributed by the `org.eclipse.core.resources` plug-in.

Within each scope you can have nodes that represent the ownership or domain for the stored values. Equate scopes with layers in a pyramid and nodes with plug-ins that want to store values in each layer. These layers, and the class names used in the Eclipse implementation of the user settings API, are shown in Figure 17.1.

A plug-in can choose to have content in any or all of these nodes. The `DefaultNode` is typically populated with keyed value content using an initial-

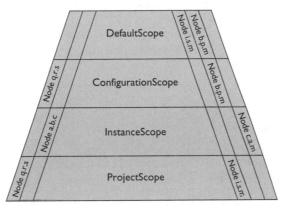

**Figure 17.1**    Scopes and Nodes for Stored Value Management

ization process. The `org.eclipse.core.runtime.preferences` extension point for defining this process was discussed earlier in the subsection Establishing Default Preference Values. Preference values and user settings coexist just fine. In fact, preference values are actually stored in the `InstanceScope` with a node value equal to the plug-in id. Preference value keys and instance keys use the same storage mechanism.

There are obvious hierarchies of nodes where access to values goes through a search of specific and then more generally scoped content. An implicit order of instance, configuration, and default is supported by the user settings API. Alternative search sequences can be defined, and direct access to any of the nodes in a specific scope is also supported.

## Scope Hierarchy

The scopes that implement this layered storage strategy are available as part of the Eclipse implementation. The built-in scopes provided by the `org.eclipse.core.runtime` and `org.eclipse.core.resources` plug-ins are visible in the implementation hierarchy shown in Figure 17.2.

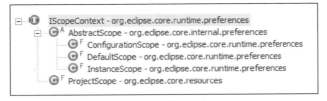

**Figure 17.2**    `IScopeContext` Hierarchy

You can define additional scopes if required. Use the `org.eclipse.core.runtime.preferences` extension point to identify new scope names and the associated implementation.

```
<extension
  point="org.eclipse.core.runtime.preferences">
  <scope
    class="com.ibm.jdg2e.preferences.CustomScope"
    name="customscope"/>
</extension>
```

The class you define must implement `IEclipsePreferences`. You might study other scopes defined in Eclipse for implementation guidance, but these are not part of the user settings API. The `IEclipsePreferences` API implemented by a scope includes support for change listeners. This is discussed in Change Notification later in this chapter.

## Accessing User Settings

You can use two strategies to access user settings: direct access to a specific node in a defined scope or access to a node as found in a cascaded sequence of scopes.

### Accessing Keyed Values in a Scope

To get or set a stored value that is global to the installed Eclipse environment, use the `ConfigurationScope` class. The following code gets a keyed value for a specific node in the `ConfigurationScope` while using a hard-coded default value for when the key is not found.

```
private String getMyConfigValue() {
  IScopeContext configContext = new ConfigurationScope();
  IEclipsePreferences configNode =
    configContext.getNode("id.of.plugin");

  String value = null;
  if (configNode != null)
    value = configNode.get("key_value", "default_value");

  return value;
}
```

In the preceding code, instead of hard-coding the default value on the get method, you could use a call to the default node. The following code sets a keyed value for that same scope/node combination and returns `true` if the save request succeeds.

```
private boolean setMyConfigValue(String value) {
  IScopeContext configContext = new ConfigurationScope();
  IEclipsePreferences configNode =
    configContext.getNode("id.of.plugin");
  if (configNode != null) {
    if (value.equals("default_value")) {
      // Value is same as default so no need to store it.
      configNode.remove("key_value");
    } else {
      // Set a configuration-specific value.
      configNode.put("key_value", value);
    }
    return saveNode(configNode);
  }
  return false;
}
```

This code also makes sure the default value is not actually saved in the node. Unlike the preference value API, this is not an automatic feature of the user settings implementation. You have to decide whether you want to save default values or not. The stored preference value API will not save default values.

The user settings calls shown are for the configuration scope. The example on the CD-ROM demonstrates different approaches using different scopes.

### Using the `IPreferencesService` to Access a Cascading Sequence of Scopes

While accessing a single scope/node combination to get a keyed value works just fine, you may want to do more. What if you need to override the value at a different level or scope in your domain? You can decide to override a scope by storing the keyed value at a lower level. To get this ordered access, you have to use the `IPreferencesService` API as provided by Eclipse. Using this API you can either define your own scope lookup order or use the order implemented by `IPreferencesService`.

The following logic shows how you can access a set of scopes in a specific order to find the most specific instance of a keyed value. The order of scope access defined is project-specific, configuration, and then default.

```
private String getMyCascadedValue(String key, IProject project)
{
  IPreferencesService service = Platform.getPreferencesService();
  String[] lookupOrder = new String[]{ProjectScope.SCOPE,
    ConfigurationScope.SCOPE, DefaultScope.SCOPE};
  service.setDefaultLookupOrder(
    "id.of.plugin", key, lookupOrder);
```

```
IScopeContext[] scope =
  new IScopeContext[]{new ProjectScope(project)};

return service.getString("id.of.plugin", key,
  "default_value", scope);
}
```

If you have not used setDefaultLookupOrder to define your own lookup sequence, IPreferencesService calls to get the keyed value will use the hard-coded sequence of instance, configuration, and then default.

### Change Notification

To receive a notification when a node changes, add a preference change listener to a node using the addPreferenceChangeListener method.

```
projectNode.addPreferenceChangeListener(
  new IEclipsePreferences.IPreferenceChangeListener() {
    public void preferenceChange(PreferenceChangeEvent event) {
      System.out.println("Node " + event.getNode()
        + " Preference " + event.getKey()
        + " was " + event.getOldValue()
        + " is " + event.getNewValue());
    }
});
```

This implementation just writes the changes to the console log.

```
Node /project/abc/com.ibm.jdg2e.usersettings Preference
  key value was null is a_new_value
```

## Example Summary

The CD-ROM provides multiple examples of using stored value support. The com.ibm.jdg2e.usersettings project demonstrates the implementation of preference and property pages and multiple techniques for interacting with the user settings API. The associated Javadoc walks you through a testing process that demonstrates the behavior of the API and where values are actually stored on disk.

## Chapter Summary

This chapter discussed the variety of techniques available for storing values as part of your plug-in's state data. While different options each have classic use scenarios, such as last-used dialog values in a dialog settings, they should be thought of as a generalized technique for storing information for your plug-in.

It should be clear now that a dialog setting is a simple store and retrieve API that can be used to segment stored values by section and use these values to populate a dialog user interface. Using this function allows you to make your user interface more pleasing to the user.

Preference values support is provided by two very similar APIs, which are implemented by the supertype of your plug-in class. The preference value support introduces the concept of a default value. These defaults are defined as part of the plug-in, but they can also be overridden by the active Eclipse-based product. This override technique is discussed in Chapter 13, Defining Features and Products.

User settings support is more flexible than preference values because of the support for both nodes and defaults, even if you have to implement the logic to not store default values in the node. The implementation of scopes provided by Eclipse allows values to be defined at the installation, workspace, and project layers, all with support for predefined defaults. You also have the option of creating your own lookup sequences and additional nodes for storing user settings. This provides you with the opportunity to manage the consistency of values for an installation or workspace, while allowing for the flexibility of localized overrides.

## Reference

Arthorne, John, and Chris Laffra. 2004. *Official Eclipse 3.0 FAQs*. Boston, MA: Addison-Wesley. http://eclipsefaq.org. (See FAQs 123–125, 166, 204.)

PART III

# CHAPTER 18

## Views

The fundamental user interface building blocks of Eclipse consist of views and editors. The extensibility of Eclipse not only allows you to add function to existing views and editors but also allows you to contribute your own. Your view might be an alternative navigator for workspace contents or a window into a portion of a domain-specific model. Your Eclipse plug-in development activity may require you to create more views than any other type of user interface component.

Eclipse provides a solid framework for the creation of views. This framework reduces the development cost and ensures that your view's behavior is consistent with the Workbench. You simply define the extension, add a little bit of user interface content, and it works. You still have a bit of work to do to complete a fully integrated and polished view, of course. Your first big decision is how to define the user interface for the view. You will probably use JFace viewers, so make sure you have read Chapter 15, JFace Viewers. We will use viewers in the code examples that follow.

This chapter covers the basics of creating a view, including how to define its contents and configure the view's own menu bar and toolbar. Information about the possible reuse of the Properties view in Eclipse is also presented, as the Properties view might be able to support the views you create. You should also remember that Eclipse itself has numerous views that can act as a guide to the kinds of function you can implement, so consider looking at how Eclipse has implemented a specific view if you see an implementation approach you want to better understand.

# Views: The General-Purpose Workbench Part

Views are one of the two types of Workbench parts, editors being the other. In contrast to editors, which have a predefined open/save life cycle, views are what you make them.

You may need a view to navigate and display objects in your domain model, or you could create a set of views that work together to support a modeling process. Only your imagination limits you to the variety of views you can create.

The basic capabilities of a view are defined by its behavior. Creating your own requires that you understand its architecture and also its role in the Workbench. This section covers these considerations. If you want to jump right in and get started, skip ahead to the View Implementation section. Once you have a working view you might want to return here to learn how it works.

## *Behavior*

Views are fairly self-contained units of function. Views typically exist in a Workbench window, but they can also be dragged outside the Workbench window. Either way, views have a specific set of behaviors that you want to be sure you understand as you build your own view. The following statements all apply to views.

- They can be closed from their local title bar.
- They can be opened programmatically.
- They can be opened by the user using the Workbench menu action **Window > Show View.**
- They can be resized, moved within a perspective, and placed on the shortcut bar as a fast view, minimized, or dragged outside the Workbench window.
- They can be maximized and minimized by double-clicking in the title area.
- They have their own menu and toolbar.

Unlike editors, views do not typically have their own open/save life cycle. Any change a user makes within a view is immediately applied. For example, a change made in a Properties view is automatically applied once the field loses the input focus. Of course, when a view is coupled to an editor, the changes made using the view are saved immediately, but the content involved would be part of the editor's open/save life cycle.

---

**NOTE** Views can choose to implement the `ISaveablePart` interface if they want to add open/save life-cycle support and be able to respond to global actions such as the **File > Save All** request available on the Workbench menu bar.

---

By default, only one instance of a view is available in the Workbench user interface at any one time. But, as described later in this chapter in Opening a Second Instance of a View, you can open multiple views; in this scenario each should have a unique input.

This is just a sample of some of the more prominent view characteristics. *The Eclipse User Interface Guidelines*, available in the "Articles" section of eclipse.org, describes many more. It is worth the time to familiarize yourself with these guidelines so your view appears and behaves similar to other Eclipse views. Fortunately, your view will inherit many of these behaviors automatically as part of the framework.

## Architecture

A view is a Workbench part that typically displays some identified input in the view's user interface. A view's user interface can contain SWT widgets, a viewer, multiple viewers, or a mix of widgets and viewers. But while this is permitted, you should consider making your view as simple as possible. Instead of overloading the user interface for one view, consider using two views that are linked to provide additional flexibility.

The input to a view could be a tool-specific domain model or a specific model object and its related content. The input could be fixed, as in the Navigator view, whose input is the workspace. The input could be identified by specific request, as in the **Open Type Hierarchy** request that identifies the input to the Hierarchy view. Or the input could be dynamic, possibly controlled by user selection, which is how the Outline and Properties views work.

We say a view "typically displays some identified input" because this is the common implementation. But you are not prevented from defining a view whose input is less precise, or a view that looks more like a dialog. This may be exactly what you need, but consider these alternatives carefully; your overriding goal should be a view that supports its designed task well and is easy to use.

The idea that a view has an input maps well to the JFace viewer architecture. The input is the model. This is identified as the viewer's input. The viewer uses an input-model-specific content provider and label provider to get the appropriate content and prepare it for display in the viewer. Views, through the use of the JFace viewer framework, interact with the input model and may display a single type of object or, when tree viewers are used, many different types of objects.

Many of the Workbench APIs assume that your view uses JFace viewers; this is especially true for the selection handling methods. You can use SWT widgets directly if you choose, but we will use JFace viewers in most of our examples. The use of viewers allows a view to match the standard appearance and user interface behavior found in the rest of the Workbench, and it supports the contribution of additional function as described in Chapter 21, Action Contributions: The Integration Fast Track.

The role and responsibilities of the JFace viewer components were covered in Chapter 15, JFace Viewers, so we will discuss only view-specific issues in this chapter.

## Function

You have to identify the function your view will provide. You can make a view do just about anything you want, but given that views typically have an input, they can be described as having one of a number of possible roles in the user interface.

The views provided as part of Eclipse are examples of how a view might be defined to provide a clean implementation of the designated function. Here is a short list of roles that a view might play, some of which actually overlap.

- **Alternative workspace navigator**: Eclipse comes with a workspace navigator, the Navigator view. But there is also the JDT's Package Explorer view; it could be considered as an alternative navigator in that it uses the same input but sees this input with Java-colored glasses. Note that while the use of views as customized navigators is common, there is an established requirement for a general-purpose navigator framework in Eclipse.
- **Domain model navigation or exploration**: If you have your own model, you may want to allow others to navigate or explore it. In this scenario your view would use your model as input and use viewers to expose the structure as appropriate. There are multiple examples of this in Eclipse: Navigator view, Plug-ins view, and Plug-in Registry view, to name a few. The Outline view navigates a model; the model just happens to be the content in the active editor. The Package Explorer view, another example of this type of view, presents content based on the Java model in the JDT.

- **Submodel explorer or details**: If your view listens to another view's selection, you may have a view that reacts to this selection by diving a bit deeper into that model object. This type of view is playing the role of a details view. The Properties view plays this role in a reusable fashion by exposing the selected object details. You have to decide whether you need a custom view or can reuse the Properties view.

These roles are representative of the function that a view can provide, but they are not a definitive list. You still have plenty of room to be creative and think of new roles. You can probably describe a fundamental type of view not listed here. The most valuable feature of a view is that its function depends only on the availability of its input model. Views that will expose things like remote database content, work queues, or outbound/inbound communication requests can work fine as part of the full Eclipse Platform or a Rich Client Platform application. What does not change are the fundamentals; each view has an input and inherits the standard behavior provided by Eclipse.

## View Implementation

Now that you understand the structure and behavior of a view, let's review the implementation process. Before you begin, you should have completed a bit of design to define the required user interface and function.

Given a basic design, all you need to do is add a view extension and create the appropriate class in which you will define the user interface. Get that much done and you can start testing.

From a working user interface, you can start adding menu and toolbar actions and share the context menu for any viewers you included in the user interface. As a final bit of polish, you can add logic to support saving the state of an open view.

### Designing the View

The first step is to design the user interface for your view, which depends on the role the view will play in your domain.

You can start by describing the role and then just sketch the shape of the user interface content that the view will provide. This will give you a sense of what JFace viewers you might use and what other, if any, user interface elements may be required.

One fundamental decision is how you identify the input to the view. The view may be a type of navigator if the input is predefined; the input could also be the one instance of your domain model. Or the view's input may be based on the object selected in another view.

The expected user interactions with the content of the view and the need for the view to either obtain information about user selections in other parts of the Workbench or provide that same type of selection information must also be identified.

You might want to start with a prototype and get some feedback through testing. This will generate some additional ideas for your design.

Just remember to keep your view focused on the task it is to perform. If your view is an overwhelming combination of user interface controls and content, you may be disabling some of the flexibility provided by how the Workbench manages the set of active Workbench parts. Try not to overload a view with function such that it conflicts with the flexibility in organizing the user interface that the Workbench provides to the user.

Let's assume you need to be able to navigate model content and interact with selected object details. To satisfy this requirement, you implement one view containing two viewers. You define a tree viewer on the left to navigate the model and a table viewer on the right to interact with details. You have thus limited the user's options for changing how the user interface works without changing your code. If you were to use two views that worked together, the user could control the relative size of each and their position with respect to each other. The user could also choose to minimize a view or make it a fast view. If you had overloaded one view with all the functions, either this flexibility would have disappeared or you would have had to replicate the function within one view. By keeping a view simple and using more than one when appropriate, you let the dynamics of the Workbench user interface provide limitless flexibility to your user.

**NOTE**  This does not mean a view with two viewers is forbidden, just that you should consider the user interface dynamic carefully first. Eclipse itself includes a Hierarchy view as part of the JDT. This view has both a tree viewer and a table viewer, but the role of each viewer is tightly coupled, and they provide support for which viewers are visible and how they will be arranged.

### Declaring the View Extension

To contribute a view, you need to add an extension to the Workbench extension point `org.eclipse.ui.views`. The extension definition includes the name of the view, an id, and the name of the implementation class. A view extension definition can also create a category and associate it with the view. Here is an example of a complete view contribution.

```
<extension
  point="org.eclipse.ui.views">
  <category
    name="JDG2E"
    id="com.ibm.jdg2e.views">
  </category>
  <view
    name="Locations"
    icon="icons/sample.gif"
    id="com.ibm.jdg2e.view.basic"
    category="com.ibm.jdg2e.views"
    class="com.ibm.jdg2e.view.basic.BasicViewPart">
  </view>
</extension>
```

The name of the view should be descriptive; it is visible in the view's title bar and the Show View dialog. The icon specified appears to the left of the view's title.

The id used for the view must be unique; the best option is to follow the Java package naming conventions. The class will extend `ViewPart` and include the user interface implementation.

The category controls the view's placement in the Show View dialog opened using the **Window > Show View > Other...** menu action. You can also add your view to an existing category if appropriate; all you need to find is the id. Here is a hint: Just search for `plugin.xml` files that contain `<category`.

If you are creating a collection of views in a single category, they can be defined in the same extension using a separate view entry for each view definition.

**NOTE** If required, you can redundantly define the category in multiple plug-ins. Just be sure to use the same id and, to avoid confusion, the same name. Eclipse will conveniently ignore the duplicates, choose one, and show all the views under a single instance of the same category. This technique also works for wizard categories and action sets. Using this technique allows plug-ins that may or may not be installed together still to be integrated into the same structure.

### Creating the View Class

The implementation of any view begins by extending the `ViewPart` class. This class has abstract methods that your view must implement. These methods

have you create and control the initial state of the user interface. The
`ViewPart` class extends `WorkbenchPart` and implements the `IViewPart` interface. Together, the `WorkbenchPart` and `ViewPart` classes provide much of
the standard behavior for your view.

What is left for you to provide is what is unique about your view; the
required methods are simply those that create the user interface and set
the focus when your view gets control. Empty implementations of these
abstract methods are automatically added when you create a class that
extends `ViewPart`.

```
public class BasicViewPart extends ViewPart {

    public void createPartControl(Composite parent)  {
    }

    public void setFocus()  {
    }
}
```

These required methods are what must be customized to define the user
interface for the view; then it can be tested.

## Defining the User Interface

A view's user interface is defined in one place, the `createPartControl`
method. The method is passed a parent SWT `Composite` object as a container
for any number of SWT widgets or JFace viewers. In Designing the View we
gave you some suggestions about what constitutes a good view, but what you
decide to include in your user interface is completely up to you. To keep
things simple, we are going to add a single viewer to the user interface. The
viewer is defined as a field so we can reference it later.

```
// Viewer for user interface
    private TableViewer tableViewer;
```

Here is a sample `createPartControl` method that uses a simple `TableViewer`
that has a simple model as its input. The model just returns an array of
objects that have `get` and `set` value methods (as seen in Chapter 15, JFace
Viewers). The `setFocus` method logic places focus on the `TableViewer`.

```
public void createPartControl(Composite parent) {
    Composite composite = new Composite(parent, SWT.NONE);
    FillLayout fillLayout = new FillLayout();
    composite.setLayout(fillLayout);

    // Add a TableViewer
    tableViewer = new TableViewer(composite);
```

```
tableViewer.setContentProvider(
  new LocationsContentProvider());
tableViewer.setLabelProvider(
  new LocationsTableLabelProvider());
tableViewer.setInput(LocationsPlugin.getRoadTrip();
}

public void setFocus() {
  tableViewer.getControl().setFocus();
}
```

Figure 18.1 shows the end result.

**Figure 18.1**   Simple View with `TableViewer` Content

The menu and toolbar actions that may be required still need to be defined. There are also other `ViewPart` methods that you may chose to override. Some of these will be discussed in Saving and Restoring View State.

## Adding View Actions

As discussed during the description of a view's behavior, actions can be added to the view's menu bar and toolbar. When a menu bar or toolbar choice is selected, the associated action is performed. Actions can even be shared between menu and toolbar choices. Actions can be defined internally to the view or contributed externally as part of an extension definition.

---

**NOTE**  Actions are used in many places and are similar in structure regardless of where they are used. For instance, all have a run method. Actions are discussed in multiple places in this book; see the appropriate section for the type of action involved. In Exercise 6, Developing Your First Plug-in, you are guided through the process of adding actions to the Workbench menu bar and toolbar. The creation and use of actions as part of a viewer's context menu is discussed in Adding Viewer Actions in Chapter 15, JFace Viewers. Finally, the creation of external action contributions is discussed in Chapter 21, Action Contributions: The Integration Fast Track. In the current section, we discuss the creation of internal actions for a view's menu bar and toolbar. Preparing for external action contributions that can be made to a view or viewer is discussed later in this chapter in Supporting Action Contributions.

Given the options of defining an internal action or contributing an action through extension, the best choice is not always that obvious. It would seem that you have total control when defining actions internally, and you do. But you lose some flexibility.

Actions defined through contributions can target the view's menu bar or toolbar, the viewer in the view, or the object in the viewer. By targeting an object type, an action contribution will exist anywhere the object can be found when the context menu involved has been registered. The process of registration is covered later in Registering Context Menus with the Workbench.

By using action contributions, you also have the option of including them in your tool when required; you might choose to include only some actions in an advanced version. Action contributions can also be filtered using the techniques discussed in Chapter 30, Using Capabilities to Manage Too Much of a Good Thing.

For now let's just discuss the creation of internal actions. To create an action, implement a class that extends `Action` and implements the `run` method. The code involved is not that different from the code used when actions are contributed by extension to the Eclipse menu bar and toolbar. However, in this scenario, the action is created locally and will operate only on the view's content.

Actions have many attributes that you can set. For example, an action can be enabled or disabled, given hover help text, and assigned an image for use in the user interface.

You can use multiple constructors when creating an action; one gives you the option of passing in style bits to create alternative action types. The following style bits are supported:

```
AS_UNSPECIFIED
AS_PUSH_BUTTON
AS_CHECK_BOX
AS_DROP_DOWN_MENU
AS_RADIO_BUTTON
```

When using an alternate constructor, you define the action text and the button type at the same time. This approach allows you to create different types of actions that work well in either a menu bar or a toolbar.

The Workbench framework provides the basic structure for your views (and editors); you focus on creating the content, and it handles the details of managing the layout, along with the local menu bar and toolbar. You just need to ask your view for the component and add actions as required.

As part of your `createPartControl` method, you can create actions and then get the view's `MenuManager` or `ToolBarManager` using the `getViewSite` method. From there you can add actions to the view.

```
public void createPartControl(Composite parent) {
  // Code not shown . . .
  getViewSite().getActionBars()
   .getToolBarManager().add(filterAction);
  // Code continues . . .
  getViewSite().getActionBars()
   .getMenuManager().add(sortAction);
  // Code continues . . .
}
```

Detailed illustrations of action creation and integration with a view can be found in the CD-ROM examples.

The `getViewSite` method returns the `IViewSite` for the view. The `IViewSite` not only contains the action bars but also extends `IWorkbench-PartSite`, which gives you access to the rest of the platform. We will discuss the services provided by the `IWorkbenchPartSite` in two upcoming sections: Registering Context Menus with the Workbench and Sharing and Listening for Workbench Part Selection.

**NOTE**  To be consistent with the rest of the Eclipse views, your sorting and filtering actions, which vary the presentation of objects within a view but not the objects themselves, should be available on the view's toolbar or pull-down menu. Actions that modify the objects exposed in a view's viewer should appear on context menus. The proper use of actions is described in *The Eclipse User Interface Guidelines* on eclipse.org.

## Saving and Restoring View State

You are not required to save and restore the state of your view, but if you want a polished final product, you should at least determine whether this is helpful. Saved state could be the current selection in the view, the state of toggle actions added to your view by your logic, the state of any sort request, and so on.

The `ViewPart` class has methods it calls as part of its processing framework. For example, the `init` methods are called when the view opens, and the `saveState` method is called if your view is open when the Workbench is shut down. You can use these methods to save and restore state. Override these methods from the `ViewPart` class if you want to participate in the state management process for a view.

```
public void init(IViewSite site) throws PartInitException {
  super.init(site);
}
public void init(IViewSite site, IMemento memento)
    throws PartInitException {
  super.init(site, memento);
}
public void saveState(IMemento memento) {
  super.saveState(memento);
}
```

The `IMemento` object allows you to store different types of information, from strings to integers to floats, or even other mementos. The `FileView` example on the CD-ROM has a simple implementation of memento processing you can review.

### Opening a Second Instance of a View

Typically, once a view is open, that is it; the view is not opened again in that perspective (`IWorkbenchPage`). This is common when a view has one input or if the input varies based on the active selection. But if you have a view whose purpose makes it appropriate to have more than one open instance, you can do so using the `showView` method.

To open another instance of a view, you need to provide it with an alternate id and most likely an alternate input unless you want to see the same thing twice. The following code is a snippet of logic from a pop-up menu action that can open a view multiple times, but only once for each possible selection known to the action. The current `selection` is known to this code, the field definition is not shown, and its value is set in the action's `selection-Changed` method. The method used to alter the part name is also shown below.

```
public void run(IAction action) {
  IContainer container = (IContainer)
    ((IStructuredSelection) selection).getFirstElement();
  String altViewID = container.getFullPath().toString();
  try {
    IViewPart view = PlatformUI.getWorkbench()
        .getActiveWorkbenchWindow().getActivePage()
        .showView("com.ibm.jdg2e.view.files.ui.FileView",
            altViewID, IWorkbenchPage.VIEW_ACTIVATE);
    ((FileView) view).setCustomPartName(altViewID);
  } catch (PartInitException e) {
  }
}
```

```
public void setCustomPartName(String partName) {
  if (nameSelectionAction.isChecked())
    setPartName(partName);
}
```

The use of an alternate view id based on the selected object ensures that an existing view for the same selection is used when it has already been opened. If the alternate view id is already in use, the existing view is activated.

### Supporting the *Show In* Request

Editors and views can support a navigation action called **Show In**. This action is found on the Workbench menu under **Navigate**.

Views can be targets in this framework by implementing the show method required by the IShowInTarget interface. The show method responds by selecting the appropriate content for the passed context and making it visible if possible, or possibly reusing this navigation to control when the input to a viewer is changed. This code uses an IContainer selection as the new input, but if the selection is an IFile, it is just selected in the viewer.

```
public boolean show(ShowInContext context) {
  if (context.getSelection()
    instanceof IStructuredSelection) {
    IStructuredSelection ss =
      (IStructuredSelection) context.getSelection();
    if (ss.getFirstElement() instanceof IContainer) {
      viewer.setInput(ss.getFirstElement());
      return true;
    } else if (ss.getFirstElement() instanceof IFile)
        viewer..setSelection(context.getSelection());
    return true;
  }
  return false;
}
```

It is not sufficient to support the IShowInTarget interface; to be included in the Navigate menu, you have to declare the view as a target. The following perspective extension adds a view to the list of show-in targets for the Resource perspective.

```
<extension
  point="org.eclipse.ui.perspectiveExtensions">
  <perspectiveExtension
    targetID="org.eclipse.ui.resourcePerspective">
      <showInPart
        id="com.tool.viewpart.id">
      </showInPart>
  </perspectiveExtension>
</extension>
```

If you want to send a show-in request to others, your view part must implement the getShowInContext method defined in the IShowInSource interface. The following example just creates the ShowInContext object using the input and selection for the viewer.

```
public ShowInContext getShowInContext() {
  return new ShowInContext(jcomp.getViewer().getInput(),
    jcomp.getViewer().getSelection());

}
```

See Navigating Between Editors and Views in Chapter 19 for additional details, and the FileView implementation on the CD-ROM for an example.

### Implementation Review

We have now reviewed the full process of creating a view in Eclipse. All you need to do is define the extension, implement the view by extending ViewPart, add viewers and/or SWT controls to the user interface, define any required actions, and optionally save your state. You should consider trying to create a view before you read on, or save the rest of this chapter for when you need more detail on view development.

Views seldom work in isolation. Your view's function may be extended by others, or you may need to interact with other Workbench parts. These objectives are discussed in the sections that follow.

## Supporting Action Contributions

You can support action contributions in your view in two ways.

- Create target areas in the menu bar and toolbar.
- Register a viewer and its context menu with the Workbench.

By creating target areas you can position contributions in specific locations. The registration process allows your viewer's context menu to support contributions that target either the viewer or the object types that the viewer might contain. The creation of action contributions is discussed in Chapter 21.

### Creating Contribution Target Menu Placeholders

Action contributions defined using the org.eclipse.ui.viewActions extension point can always be added to your view's menu bar and toolbar. They will be placed at the end unless you create a place for them instead; of course, the contribution must also know and use the placeholder name.

There is an Eclipse best practice you should follow when defining a target location for action contributions to your view's pull-down menu. Define an insertion point labeled `additions`. By using this common insertion point you are saving others time. The guidance for contributions made by others is to use the `additions` value in the path attribute of any menu bar or toolbar contributions they define. You can create these insertion point placeholders using the following constant.

```
// Eclipse constant for the standard insertion point "additions"
IWorkbenchActionConstants.MB.ADDITIONS
```

You can also define insertion points of your own. If you want to contribute actions to your own view, you could use an alternate insertion point. So, if you had a few actions defined by the view and placeholders for your own contributions as well as those made by others, you might define the following logic.

```
IMenuManager manager =
    getViewSite().getActionBars().getMenuManager();
manager.add(firstAction);
manager.add(addAction);

manager.add(new GroupMarker("privateTarget"));
manager.add(new Separator());
manager.add(middleToggle);

manager.add(
    new Separator(IWorkbenchActionConstants.MB_ADDITIONS));
manager.add(new Separator());

manager.add(deleteAction);
manager.add(lastAction);
```

If the `org.eclipse.ui.popupMenus` extension point is used to make `viewerContribution` action contributions, with target definitions of `menubarPath="privateTarget"` and `menubarPath="additions"`, actions will exist in these two placeholder locations. By using a `GroupMarker` in the logic above you can provide a simple placeholder; using a `Separator` gives a visual break in the menu if someone uses the target. If you add the insertion separator set and nobody uses it, it is invisible. Figure 18.2 shows the end result, with **Private Action** and **Additions Target** as the labels for the contributed actions.

You can do the same when adding actions to the toolbar. It is a good practice to prepare for contributions to the menu bar or toolbar. Others may attempt to use the standard insertion point, `additions`, so you should use that name as well.

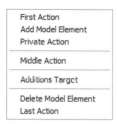

**Figure 18.2**　Pull-Down Menu for a View After Internal and External Contributions

## Registering Context Menus with the Workbench

You have control over access to the context menus that might exist for the viewers used in your view. You can make two types of registration calls to tell the Workbench about your viewer. The first only registers the viewer; it does not name it. The second gives the viewer a name. When registered, an `objectContribution` can be added using the `org.eclipse.ui.popupMenus` extension point. These actions target the object type that might be in the viewer. A `viewerContribution` can also be made if the viewer has been registered with a name.

You can never fully anticipate the potential need for a contribution from another plug-in; you should always register the context menu for your viewer unless you can convince yourself you have some special reason to disallow it. Both viewer and object contributions are discussed in Chapter 21, Action Contributions: The Integration Fast Track.

If you decide to share your context menu you must not only register it with the Workbench but also prepare an `additions` target location just as was done for the menu bar and toolbar. You have the same options for the use of `Separator` or `GroupMarker` elements in the menu bar.

Given a viewer and a context menu manager for the viewer, you can make the following call to register the menu with the Workbench for object contributions.

```
// Register viewer and context menu manager with Workbench
// Supports objectContribution actions
getSite().registerContextMenu(manager, viewer);
```

Given a viewer and a context menu manager for the viewer, you can make the following call to register the menu with the Workbench for both object and viewer contributions.

```
// Register viewer and context menu manager with Workbench
// Supports objectContribution and viewerContribution actions
getSite().registerContextMenu("your.view.contribution.id",
  manager, viewer);
```

The string value passed to register is the value used as `targetid` in the `viewerContribution`. If you had more than one viewer in your view and the need to register more than one context menu, a method call with parameter values such as these would be more appropriate.

```
// Register viewer and context menu manager with Workbench
// Supports external object and viewer contributions
getSite().registerContextMenu(
"#ViewerName_your.view.contribution.id", manager, viewer);
```

Eclipse itself uses a mix of values; for example, the `targetid` used when extending the text editor in Eclipse is `#TextEditorContext`. Yes, editors contain viewers too, so much of this registration process is the same.

When you register a context menu to support a `viewerContribution`, you are in a sense publishing one or more ids that can be used as the target value in a `plugin.xml` file. These ids should be documented somewhere if you are going to encourage others to extend your view.

---

**NOTE**   If you do not include the expected `additions` placeholder in the context menu being registered, the Workbench will actually shout out that it is missing. A message is written to the console every time the menu is opened. The message identifies the values used to name the context menu and the id for the part as defined in the `plugin.xml` file.

```
Context menu missing standard group
'org.eclipse.ui.IWorkbenchActionConstants.MB_ADDITIONS'.
(menu id = #ILocation_PopupMenu)
part id = com.ibm.jdg2e.view.simplemodel.core.model.ModelView)
```

---

## Interacting with Other Workbench Components

You can further enhance your view to improve its usability and allow it to integrate with other Eclipse-based processing. These integration options include reacting to selection changes in other views, notifying others of changes in your own selection, extending global actions, and providing support for the Properties view.

### Sharing and Listening for Workbench Part Selection

The Workbench attempts to track selection within the Workbench part that has focus. This is part of what makes Eclipse work so well. The value of this support makes more sense if you try it. Go to Eclipse, make sure you can see both the Navigator view and Properties view, and then select any one resource in the Navigator view while watching the Properties view. See it? The Navigator view's selection was shared with the Properties view, and the Properties view used that selection to find and display properties. You just witnessed both the sharing of selection and the listening for selection; any Workbench part can do one or both of these things.

Any Workbench part can use the active user selection in the Workbench. The selection may change the focus within the part and be used as the input to a view and therefore any of the viewers in the view. To use this selection, a Workbench part must ask to be a selection listener. The selection in any Workbench part that shares selection will then be sent to anyone who listens.

Even if your view will not be a selection listener, you should consider sharing your own selection. Sharing the selection is not only a prerequisite step for supporting the Properties view, it will also be useful if others add Workbench parts that extend the processing within your current view. If you share selection, they can listen and therefore react to what the user has selected in your view. So, the rule is, play nice and share.

### Sharing the Viewer Selection in Your View

It is easy to share the selection in your view if you have used a viewer in your user interface. The current selection is shared by a selection provider; a selection provider must implement the ISelectionProvider interface. All JFace viewers implement this interface. So to share the selection in your view, you must call the Workbench site and use either of the following methods to identify a viewer in your user interface.

```
// Either method works; IViewSite is a subclass of IPartSite
getViewSite().setSelectionProvider(viewer);
getSite().setSelectionProvider(viewer);
```

If needed, you can always create your own object that implements the ISelectionProvider interface and pass that on the setSelectionProvider method call.

### Listening to Selections in Other Workbench Parts

Anyone can listen to the current Workbench part selection. Selection events from any part that shares selection are sent to all known listeners. By implementing the ISelectionListener interface in your view it can become a listener. Quite often your view part class will implement this interface and have the required selectionChanged method. When you choose to listen, you can request to be sent selections from any Workbench part or from a specific Workbench part.

To be informed of the selection in any Workbench part, you would issue this method call with a reference to your listener, which in this example is the view part that wants to listen.

```
// Listen to all shared selections
getSite().getPage().addSelectionListener(thisView);
```

If you want to listen for selections from just one part, or a selected set of Workbench parts, you can request to be sent selections from a specific part using this method call.

```
// Listen only to selections in the Navigator
getSite().getPage().addSelectionListener(
    "org.eclipse.ui.views.ResourceNavigator", thisView);
```

The `String` parameter in this method call represents the id of the Workbench part, as defined as part of that part's `plugin.xml` extension definition.

## Implementing the `ISelectionListener` Interface

With either approach you need to have a class, often the view itself, which has the `selectionChanged` method required by the `ISelectionListener` interface. The complexity of the `selectionChanged` method depends on the number of Workbench parts that could send you selection notification.

If you are listening to selections from only one part, you will probably have a pretty good idea of what you might be sent. This might allow your `selectionChanged` method to just check a few things before getting down to more serious processing. This example starts by assuming that the selection sent is an instance of `IStructuredSelection`, which is always `true` for many views, including the Navigator view. Given the `IStructuredSelection`, the following logic just checks to make sure the selection is an `IContainer`, a type of object in the resource model. This implementation makes sense when only the Navigator view selection is being processed, as requested earlier.

```
public void selectionChanged(
    IWorkbenchPart part, ISelection selection) {
    IStructuredSelection ssel = (IStructuredSelection) selection;
    if (ssel.getFirstElement() instanceof IContainer)
        viewer.setInput((IContainer) ssel.getFirstElement());
    else
        viewer.setInput(ViewPlugin.getWorkspace()
            .getRoot());
}
```

If you have requested that all selections be sent to your implementation of the `selectionChanged` method, you may have to be a bit more defensive. You need to filter out unwanted selections. This can include selections sent by your own view along with selections of the wrong type, such as a text selection. The following code shows logic that refuses to respond to selections that are not in its own view part and that are not of the type IStructured-Selection.

```
public void selectionChanged(
  IWorkbenchPart part, ISelection selection) {
  if ((part != this) &&
    (selection instanceof IStructuredSelection )) {
  IStructuredSelection ssel =
    (IStructuredSelection) selection;
  if (ssel.getFirstElement() instanceof IContainer)
    viewer.setInput((IContainer) ssel.getFirstElement());
  else
    viewer.setInput(ViewPlugin.getWorkspace().getRoot());
  }
}
```

This implementation rejects selection messages from itself. It also rejects selections that are not the right type. The selection sent could be an instance of ITextSelection, IMarkSelection, or IStructuredSelection, the subtypes of ISelection. You want to process what you are interested in and understand.

### Removing the Listener

The last thing you need to do is remove your listener when it is no longer required. This can be done anytime, but it is often done in the dispose method for the view.

```
public void dispose() {
  getViewSite().getWorkbenchWindow().getSelectionService().
    removeSelectionListener(this);
  super.dispose();
}
```

This is similar to the requirement for a content provider to release its model listener in the content provider's dispose method, as mentioned in Chapter 15, JFace Viewers.

## *Providing Content in the Properties View*

Views often play a supporting role in the Eclipse user interface. Shared views such as the Properties view complement the active editor or view by providing quick user access to supplemental information. This is an example of how multiple Workbench parts can work together to effectively inform the user. Now that we have discussed building a view, we will explore how to add support for the Properties view. Read on if you think you need to provide support for the Properties view in your plug-in.

**NOTE** The Properties view is not the same thing as the Properties dialog; the Properties view only shows a two-column table of attributes and their values. If you have many complex items to edit and validate, you should contribute a property page to the appropriate Properties dialog. Adding property pages to a Properties dialog is covered in Chapter 16, Dialogs and Wizards. Adding Properties dialog support to your objects (as exposed in a viewer) is discussed in the Adding Properties Dialog Support section of Chapter 15, JFace Viewers.

## Properties View Basics

The Properties view provided by Eclipse is simply a shell. It exists only to display, and possibly edit, attributes or properties of an object that chooses to participate. For example, if the Properties view is open, the selection of a resource in the Navigator view will trigger the display of the resource properties in the Properties view. All the Navigator view did was share its viewer's selection. The Properties view listens for Workbench part selection and asks the selected object if it cares to contribute content to the Properties view shell. All resources, through the `IResource` object, are prepared to contribute content to the Properties view.

You should consider how the objects shown in views you provide could interact with the Properties view. By allowing the Properties view to implement part of your user interface, you get both more reusable code and more screen real estate.

The Properties view is not directly aware of every object that might be selected. The Properties view actually has little to do with what you see inside; it simply listens for the active Workbench part selection and asks the object involved if it implements or can adapt to the `IPropertySource` interface. The default behavior of the Properties view is implemented by a class named `PropertySheetPage`. The standard implementation of the `PropertySheetPage` is a table of property names and values, which the page can construct using anything that supports the `IPropertySource` interface.

So the basic requirements for implementing support for the Properties view support are the following.

- Share the selection of a viewer in your view with the Workbench.
- Add `IPropertySource` support to the object types that might be selected.

We just covered sharing selection in the previous section, so all we need to discuss now is what it takes to add `IPropertySource` support to an object you share through your viewer. Note that we did not say "implement," as that is not the only option.

## Providing `IPropertySource` Support

The `IPropertySource` interface defines the methods that provide property descriptors and get and set the property values. Property descriptors provide the descriptive name for the property; this name is shown in the **Property** column of the Properties view.

To show content in the Properties view, the object whose selection is shared by a registered viewer can do one of two things.

- Directly implement the `IPropertySource` interface.
- Implement the `IAdaptable` interface and return an appropriate `IPropertySource` object.

If you do not want to implement the `IPropertySource` interface directly, your object can take a simple approach and implement the `IAdaptable` interface and provide a `getAdapter` method that returns a class that can contribute property content for the object.

```
public Object getAdapter(Class adapter) {
    // Implementing IWorkbenchAdapter allows the getLabel() method
    // to be used for the Properties dialog title
    if (adapter == IWorkbenchAdapter.class)
      return this;

    // Returning an implementation of IPropertySource allows the
    // selected Location to share data in the Properties view
    else if (adapter == IPropertySource.class)
      return new Location_PropertySource(this);

    return null;
}
```

The `Location_PropertySource` class is passed a reference to the current model object, which allows the `IPropertySource` implementation to get and set property values when required. The code shown here works; the CD-ROM simple model example uses a different technique based on an `IAdapterFactory`. This allows the objects in the Locations view example to include support for the `IPropertySource` interface required by the Properties view.

---

**NOTE**   The Eclipse Platform provides support for an adapter architecture that allows you to define and register adapters for different types of objects. You may wish to investigate that approach further and use those techniques instead of that shown here. If available, the method shown in this section would continue on to ask the platform's adapter manager if an adapter was available for the current type, instead of returning null.

```
return Platform.getAdapterManager().getAdapter(this, adapter);
```

This involves the implementation of an IAdapterFactory, which can be defined and added to the Platform's adapter manager using a call to the register-Adapters method. The extension point org.eclipse.core.runtime.adapters provides an alternative approach; this technique is demonstrated on the CD-ROM.

## Create Property Descriptors

The first job of the IPropertySource implementation is to create a property descriptor for each entry that will be shown in the Properties view. The property descriptor defines String values for id and displayName and can also allow for categorization of descriptor entries. The PropertySheetPage will use the getPropertyDescriptors method to ask the IPropertySource for the description of what content will be displayed and whether specialized support will be provided to display the content. Specialized property descriptors, such as ComboBoxPropertyDescriptor and ColorPropertyDescriptor, are available. The ComboBoxPropertyDescriptor is interesting because it lets you display a combo box widget in the cell of the Properties view.

Properties are listed in alphabetical order; you cannot specify an alternative sort method. You have the option of using categories to organize the content. The default display of the Properties view hides any assigned categories. But if you select the Properties view **Show Categories** action toggle, the table is replaced by a table tree viewer that organizes the content by category. This works when categories have been defined; otherwise there is no change in the user interface. The Properties view content shown in Figure 18.3 includes the use of categories.

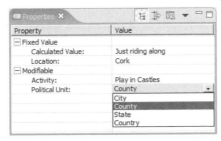

**Figure 18.3**   Property Descriptors Rendered in the Properties View

If the user will need help understanding the specific property, a string representing a help context id can be specified in the property descriptor using the setHelpContexts method. Even though the name of the method is plural, you can specify only one context id. You can also specify a label provider by using the setLabelProvider method.

The following code snippet from the example shows how an IProperty-Source implementation might provide descriptor content in two categories, with support for a drop-down list for one of the descriptors, which includes the use of a custom label provider.

```
static final protected IPropertyDescriptor[]
propertyDescriptors = new IPropertyDescriptor[4];

{
    //Location attribute
    propDescriptor = new
        PropertyDescriptor(PROP_ID_NAME, PROP_DISPLAY_NAME);
    propDescriptor.setCategory("Fixed Value");
    propertyDescriptors[0] = propDescriptor;

    //Activity attribute
    textDescriptor = new
        TextPropertyDescriptor(
            PROP_ID_ACTIVITY, PROP_DISPLAY_ACTIVITY);
    textDescriptor.setCategory("Modifiable");
    propertyDescriptors[1] = textDescriptor;

    //Political attribute
    comboDescriptor = new
        ComboBoxPropertyDescriptor(PROP_ID_POLITICAL,
            PROP_DISPLAY_POLITICAL, ILocation.POLITICAL_UNITS);
    comboDescriptor.setLabelProvider(new LabelProvider() {
        public String getText(Object obj) {
            Integer index = (Integer) obj;
            return ILocation.POLITICAL_UNITS[index.intValue()];
        }
    });
    comboDescriptor.setCategory("Modifiable");
    propertyDescriptors[2] = comboDescriptor;

    //Not an attribute, dynamically created value
    propDescriptor = new
        PropertyDescriptor(PROP_ID_NOTHING, PROP_DISPLAY_NOTHING);
    propDescriptor.setCategory("Fixed Value");
    propertyDescriptors[3] = propDescriptor;
}
```

Property descriptors based on PropertyDescriptor are read-only unless you override the createPropertyEditor method. If you use a TextProperty-

Descriptor, you get text editing support automatically. The use of a ComboBox-PropertyDescriptor allows you to create drop-down list editing support, but you need a custom label provider to define the content of the drop-down list.

The descriptor set above implements the Properties view structure shown in Figure 18.3.

### Add Property Getter and Setter Methods

The getPropertyValue and setPropertyValue methods in an IProperty-Source implementation are used to interact with the attributes of the model object. The getPropertyValue method returns the value based on the property descriptor id passed as the argument. The property descriptor id is used as the key. Any data conversions are done within the getPropertyValue and setPropertyValue methods. The following code is for the IPropertySource implementation found in the CD-ROM example.

```java
public Object getPropertyValue(Object id) {
    if (id.equals(PROP_ID_NAME))
        return location.getName();
    if (id.equals(PROP_ID_ACTIVITY))
        return location.getActivity();
    if (id.equals(PROP_ID_POLITICAL))
        return new Integer(location.getPoliticalUnit());
    if (id.equals(PROP_ID_NOTHING))
        return new String("Just riding along");
    return "";
}

public void setPropertyValue(Object id, Object value) {
    if (id.equals(PROP_ID_ACTIVITY))
        location.setActivity((String) value);
    else if (id.equals(PROP_ID_POLITICAL)) {
        Integer choice = (Integer) value;
        location.setPoliticalUnit(choice.intValue());
    }
}
```

Changes made in the Properties view should be shared with others; that is, when the model is changed, it should notify any listeners. This is not the direct responsibility of the Properties view, but the model object API used should send notifications as appropriate.

### Beyond IPropertySource

You can add more capabilities to the Properties view if you do more than support the IPropertySource interface. The Properties view allows you to contribute alternative implementations of the IPropertySheetPage interface.

PropertySheetPage, the default implementation of this interface, drives the standard Properties view behavior just discussed.

### Supporting Global Actions

Eclipse has a set of global actions that can be reused by different tools. Their official name is **retargetable actions**. For the Workbench, they are defined in ActionFactory and include **Undo**, **Redo**, **Cut**, **Copy**, **Paste**, **Delete**, **Find**, **Select All**, and **Add Bookmark**.

It is fairly simple to use one of these actions. You need an Action implementation, but that is probably already in your code. You must register a global action handler using the IActionBars.setGlobalActionHandler(String actionID, IAction handler) method. From a view, you can use getViewSite().getActionBars(). In a view, you might add the following code to your createPartControl method.

```
getViewSite().getActionBars().setGlobalActionHandler(
    ActionFactory.DELETE.getId(), deleteAction);
```

That is all there is to it. Your action, deleteAction, is registered with the **Edit > Delete** menu item.

## Examples Summary

The basics of creating a view have been described using simple code snippets to identify the fundamentals. As you might expect, real views are both more interesting and a bit more complex. So instead of flooding the chapter text with long code extracts, we have provided you with several working view examples on the CD-ROM.

The com.ibm.jdg2e.simplemodel project implements a model that can be accessed by other plug-ins. This model includes the definition of an adapter factory that supports the IPropertySource and IWorkbenchAdapter interfaces. This model is accessed by two views. The first, in the com.ibm.jdg2e.view.basic project, provides a simple view implementation. Some of this code was shown in this chapter. The com.ibm.jdg2e.view.simplemodel project contains the JDG2E: Locations view, a more complete example of a view that is fully configured and integrated with other Workbench components. This includes support for populating the Properties view, action contributions, and even support for opening the common Properties dialog for the object in the viewer.

The com.ibm.jdg2e.view.marker project provides a view that displays markers. And finally, the com.ibm.jdg2e.view.files project provides a view that is included in the CD-ROM tools feature. The File Resources view displays all files in the workspace for a selected IContainer (project or folder). This includes support for common resource actions.

The hope is that you find these view examples useful as demonstrations of both what is possible and what you should consider when developing your own views. You might even find you like the File Resources view; it can be helpful when exploring a busy workspace.

## Chapter Summary

Views are the fundamental user interface components in the Eclipse Workbench, and as we have shown, views are easy to create.

All views share a common look and feel, as well as a level of function within the Workbench user interface. All of this function is provided to your view through inheritance. You create a customized user interface and then add actions and support for restoring the previous state of the view as required.

The real value of a view lies in how it can declare its support for communication with other Workbench parts. Through this communication, customized content can be provided in the Properties view, and action contributions can be defined to further extend the views function. Make sure you consider the value of providing support for this level of integration as you implement your own views.

If you have not done so already, read Chapter 15, JFace Viewers. Most views use viewers to create their user interface content. You should also read Chapter 21, Action Contributions: The Integration Fast Track. Editors, the other type of Workbench part, are discussed next in Chapter 19.

## References

Arthorne, John, and Chris Laffra. 2004. *Official Eclipse 3.0 FAQs*. Boston, MA: Addison-Wesley. http://eclipsefaq.org. (See FAQs 126, 169, 177, 195, 197, 203, 213, 231.)

See the page titled "Table of Registered Context Menus" under the Reference topic in the book's online help.

# CHAPTER 19

## *Editors*

The fundamental user interface building blocks of the Eclipse Workbench consist of views, editors, and perspectives. Eclipse provides a number of editors and views and allows you to extend them in several ways, such as by adding new actions. However, there will be cases where you'll want to create your own editors, which is the focus of this chapter.

**NOTE** This chapter addresses the creation of editors in general, not just text editors. Chapter 26, Building a Custom Text Editor with JFace Text, explains how to create text editors with input-specific presentation and behavior.

Eclipse makes building editors easier by providing an editor framework. You concentrate on the unique behavior for your editor and the framework handles the common behavior. Remember, the Eclipse user interface is a wonderful resource of sample code for learning. So don't hesitate to look at how Eclipse has implemented a specific editor.

This chapter starts with the basics of creating an editor. Many of the implementation steps are similar to those described in Chapter 18, Views. While the roles that views and editors fulfill for the user are quite different, you'll find that they are very similar from an implementation standpoint. The chapter closes with an exploration of the interactions between editors and views.

## Editor Behavior and Architecture

Typically, one thinks of editors as solely a window in which to enter text. The important distinction, however, is the task that editors address and how they are presented to the user. Editors, simply stated, are generally used to modify some kind of logical input, and this task has a long duration. Subsequently, Eclipse reserves an editor area for all active editors. The input being edited could be a file, a group of logically related files, a database entry, or similar information whose presentation and modification fits well into a traditional open/edit/save sequence of user interaction.

As you have seen, text editors are common in the Eclipse user interface. However, editors are not limited to them. In fact, Eclipse does not impose a particular appearance within the editors themselves, just a common location in the open perspective and a standard frame in the Workbench user interface (of course, modeling the behavior of existing editors is recommended). Eclipse includes editors, other than simple text editors, that you may find worth emulating. For example, some editors have several pages to better structure the presentation of a complex text-based file. You've seen this presentation in the PDE, and you can reuse its "form-based" editors as part of the org.eclipse.ui.forms plug-in. These sorts of editors often include a page, typically labeled something like "Source" or the name of the underlying file, which allows unfiltered access to the document. However, in keeping with the idea of "one data source, many views of it," modifications made in one page are immediately communicated to all others, permitting users to choose how they visualize and modify their data.

At this point, the majority of your experience with Eclipse editors is probably the Java editor, and perhaps the multipage Plug-in Manifest Editor. The common appearance and behavior of editors is reflected in the user interface and implementation considerations. Before we look at the implementation of an editor, let's first review their appearance and behavior.

- Editors are generally opened by finding the desired input and selecting its **Open** action.
- Editors always appear within the main editor area, which all open editors share. An editor cannot be moved outside this area, but editors can be tiled within it.
- Each editor has a tab showing the name of its input. An editor can be maximized and restored by double-clicking in the editor's tab or clicking its maximize icon.
- Editors share the main menu bar and a common toolbar.
- Any change a user makes within an editor is not immediately saved; the user must explicitly request it.

This is just a sample of some of the more prominent editor characteristics. Some of these differences between editors and views are reflected in the implementation as well. This chapter will explore these differences.

## Basic Implementation Steps

The steps here include many of the same steps already covered for views, especially since they share a common superclass, `WorkbenchPart`. Since you have already learned about views, let's concentrate only on those steps that are new or notably different.

As with views, you specify an extension in your plug-in manifest to define an editor, using the extension point `org.eclipse.ui.editors`. You also write the Java code that defines the look and behavior of the editor, including the interactions with its model. The following steps outline how to create an editor.

1. Design the look of the editor.
2. Create a New Wizard for the editor input (optional).
3. Declare the editor extension.
4. Create the editor class.
5. Instantiate the model using the editor input.
6. Define the user interface.
7. Handle user modifications of the editor input.
8. Handle the saving of the editor input.
9. Associate the viewer and the model.
10. Synchronize the model and the editor.
11. Handle user selections.
12. Define editor actions.

Many of these steps are pretty short, several are the same as those you've learned earlier in Chapters 15 and 18, and others are optional, so don't be worried by the length of this list. The following sections describe these steps.

### Designing the Look of the Editor

This step is similar to that for designing a view, with of course the practical implications of the differences in view and editor appearance and behavior. You should look to your data model for hints of what portions of it would best be manipulated using an editor. Once you have a basic idea of what editors you'll need, decide how to present the data, what actions it should offer,

PART III

and with which views it might work. Figure 19.1 shows the user interface for the sample "mini-spreadsheet" editor that we use to demonstrate how to create an editor.

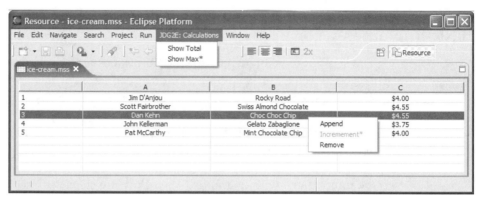

**Figure 19.1**   Sample Mini-Spreadsheet Editor

The mini-spreadsheet editor defines its own toolbar button (⊠ in Figure 19.1), main menu bar pull-down labeled "Calculations," and context menu. It will also allow others to extend it with their own actions; for example, the toolbar button **2x** in Figure 19.1 is contributed by another plug-in.

### Creating a New Wizard for the Editor Input (Optional)

Eclipse doesn't prescribe where views get their data. Some views get the data they display from a "well-known" source. The Navigator view, for example, displays the contents of the workspace. Other views display data derived from the current selection, like the Properties view. From the users' perspective, they open a view and it either explicitly (in Navigator view) or implicitly (in Properties view) determines its own data source.

The situation is different for editors. Users typically select the object they want to modify, such a file from the Navigator view, and open it with an editor. So in order to give them something to work with, you'll have to decide how instances of your editor's input come into being. A New wizard, from the **File > New** menu choice, is a natural fit. This way you can guide users through the necessary steps to create an initial valid input. Chapter 16 covers the necessary steps to create a wizard.

PART III

## Declaring the Editor Extension

To define an editor you specify an extension in your plug-in manifest. For example, look at the following extension declaration.

```
<extension point="org.eclipse.ui.editors">
  <editor
    name="JDG2E: Mini-Spreadsheet"
    icon="icons/spreadsheet.gif"
    id="com.ibm.jdg2e.msseditor"
    class=
      "com.ibm.jdg2e.msseditor.ui.MiniSSResourceEditor"
    extensions="mss"
    contributorClass=
      "com.ibm.jdg2e.msseditor.ui.actions     //(one line)
      .MiniSSEditorActionBarContributor">
  </editor>
</extension>
```

For file-based editors, the `extensions` attribute is a comma-separated list of extensions specifying the types of files this editor accepts. The value of the name attribute will be shown in the **Open With** menu choices. For example, when the user selects the open choice corresponding to your editor in the Navigator, Eclipse creates an instance of your class, an implementer of `IEditorPart`, and calls its `init` method to pass it the input.

---

**NOTE** This chapter only addresses the creation of internal editors, that is, editors that are contained in the Workbench window. If you want to add menu choices to the **Open With** cascade that will launch external editors (i.e., program executables independent of the Workbench), specify the `command` or `launcher` attributes of the `<editor>` tag. See the `org.eclipse.ui.editors` extension point in the online *Platform Plug-in Developer Guide* for more details.

---

While less common, some editors only manipulate specifically named files. The Plug-in Manifest Editor is one example, as it only works with files named `plugin.xml`, `fragment.xml`, and `manifest.mf`. You can specify such an editor's preference with the `files` attribute, where the value lists one or more comma-separated file names.

There are also editors that don't edit files at all. If you can define an input, you can define an editor for it. Of course, how your editor will be opened is for you to decide. Since the Workbench IDE works with files, most editors defined in it will be opened using a file as a starting point. Other editors may be opened by selecting menu choices, much in the same manner that the user opens a view. You may have cases where an editor is appropriate for your application's nonfile data (e.g., an "editor" for a remote server configuration, where the input is its IP address). The choice is yours, but you should consult *The Eclipse User Interface Guidelines* for design advice.

## Creating the Editor Class

The `EditorPart` class extends `WorkbenchPart` and implements the `IEditorPart` interface. Together, the `WorkbenchPart` and `EditorPart` classes provide a lot of standard behavior that your new editor will need. Of course, you are responsible for defining what your editor actually displays in its content area. To create your own editor, you create a class that extends `EditorPart` and implements the `createPartControl` method to describe the visual contents of the editor, just as with views. Also like views, the editor parts are designed to be based on a model. Such models are typically based on the contents of an input, but again you are free to decide what input makes sense for your application.

The following methods must be implemented as part of your editor implementation.

- `createPartControl(Composite)`
- `doSave(IProgressMonitor)`
- `doSaveAs()`
- `init(IEditorSite, IEditorInput)`
- `isDirty()`
- `isSaveAsAllowed()`
- `setFocus()`

Their use and implementation are discussed in the sections that follow.

## Instantiating the Model Using the Editor Input

Before you create your editor's widgets (or viewers) in the `createPartControl` method, the Workbench will provide the editor with its input by calling its `init` method. The editor decides in this method whether it will accept the proposed input, as shown in the example below.

```
public void init(IEditorSite site, IEditorInput editorInput)
    throws PartInitException {
  if (!(editorInput instanceof IStorageEditorInput))
    throw new PartInitException("Invalid Input");
  try {
    // Insert code to create model based on editorInput
    // (assume it will throw CoreException if an error occurs).
```

```
        setSite(site);
        setInput(editorInput);
        setPartName(editorInput.getName());
    }
    catch (CoreException e) {
      throw new PartInitException(e.getMessage());
    }
}
```

If the input is unacceptable, the editor must throw `PartInitException`. By checking the type of the input, the code above defends against what would probably be a programming error, that is, someone reusing your editor for unexpected input. The editor could also reject the input if an I/O error occurs or it finds that the input is corrupt or invalid. This stops all processing, and the Workbench informs the user with an error dialog showing the message of the `PartInitException` that was thrown.

The `IEditorInput` interface is a lightweight descriptor of editor input. You could think of it as a file name, but more abstract. It is not a model; it is a description of the model source for an `IEditorPart`.

If you are extending the Eclipse IDE, your file-oriented editors should accept two subtypes of `IEditorInput` in particular: `IStorageEditorInput` and its subtype `IFileEditorInput`. The latter is self-evident; it describes a file accessible from the workspace, an instance of `IFile`. Its parent class, `IStorageEditorInput`, describes an input stream. Accepting it means that your editor could be used in cases where a file isn't available locally, but the contents are available elsewhere as an input stream (e.g., from a socket). There is no hard requirement that your editor support this input—you could only accept files—but that might limit reuse by other Eclipse developers that you hadn't foreseen. That is, accepting `IStorageEditorInput` simplifies the reuse of your editor, since a caller whose data is not file-based does not need to create a temporary file only to satisfy your editor.

If you are not extending the Eclipse IDE, you will not be getting your data from a file referenced from the local `workspace` directory using an IDE-specific class like `FileEditorInput`. Instead, you must implement your own editor input class to represent Eclipse's reference to your editor's data, an implementer of the `IEditorInput` interface. This interface has only a few methods; the most interesting are

- `exists`, which determines if this is still a valid destination of the "last edit position" indicator (✱⇨).
- `getName`, which displays text in the editor's tab.
- `getPersistable`, which is the instance responsible for saving the state of this editor input.

PART III

The last method, getPersistable, returns the instance implementing the IPersistableElement interface. It handles recording the state of the editor input. Before shutting down, Eclipse invokes this method for all open editors and asks the returned instance (often implemented by the editor input class itself) to record the editor input state so it can be restored later during startup. Similarly, Eclipse needs your assistance during startup to restore your editors' inputs, so your editor implementation will also declare an IElementFactory in the plug-in manifest using the org.eclipse.ui .elementFactories extension point. Your class implementing the IElement-Factory interface only has one method to define: createElement. It accepts the state your IPersistableElement implementation recorded as key/value pairs of simple types like String and Integer during shutdown and returns a newly restored instance of the editor input.

The sample code associated with this chapter includes two implementations of the mini-spreadsheet editor. The first implementation is based on the Workbench IDE; the editor saves its data as an instance of org.eclipse.core .resources.IFile. The second implementation is based on the Rich Client Platform; the editor saves its data as an instance of java.io.File. For the rest of this example, let's assume that we're implementing an extension to the Workbench IDE and that both IFileEditorInput and its supertype, IStorageInput, are acceptable. The code below retrieves the editor's input.

```
IStorage storage = (IStorageInput) editorInput.getStorage();
InputStream stream = storage.getStorage().getContents();
```

This will return a stream instance for both cases. That is, whether the editor input is an instance of IFileEditorInput or IStorageEditorInput, you'll have a stream ready for reading.

### Defining the User Interface

This step is the same as that described for views in Chapter 18.

### Handling User Modifications of the Editor Input

Your editor's superclass, EditorPart, defines the isDirty method that you must override to indicate if your model has been modified. At the moment that your model is modified, you must call firePropertyChange(PROP_DIRTY) to update the modified indicator (an asterisk on your editor's tab) and enable the **Save** option.

### Handling the Saving of the Editor Input

If your editor returns `true` to `isDirty`, your editor's `doSave` method will be called when the user selects one of the save options. Your `doSave` method override should save the editor input, set the editor's dirty flag to `false`, and then call `firePropertyChange(PROP_DIRTY)` to update the modified indicator on your editor's tab and the save option(s).

Assuming that your editor is workspace-based, its `doSave` method would look something like this.

```
public void doSave(IProgressMonitor monitor) {
  IFile file;
  if (getEditorInput() instanceof IFileEditorInput) {
    // Input is an IFileEditorInput, save to the same location.
    file = ((IFileEditorInput) getEditorInput()).getFile();
  } else {
    // Input is an IStorageEditorInput.
    // Offer users the chance to save the input to a file.
    // If they accept, create an IFile and continue;
    // otherwise return without saving.
  }

  // Insert code to call your model's persistence method,
  // giving it an output (in this example, a string buffer).
  StringBuffer sb = new StringBuffer();
  ...

  // Set the file contents, specifying that local
  // history should be preserved.
  file.setContents(
      new ByteArrayInputStream(sb.toString().getBytes()),
      IResource.KEEP_HISTORY, null);

  // Update boolean field variable returned by isDirty().
  myIsDirtyFlag = false;
  firePropertyChange(PROP_DIRTY);
}
```

If you want to allow users to save in another output other than the original source, your editor should override the `isSaveAsAllowed` method to return `true`, and then override the `doSaveAs` method. In the `doSaveAs` method, you editor presents a Save As dialog, followed by the same processing as your `doSave` method. If the save is successful and the desired result is that your editor changes its input to the last saved location, your editor should create a new editor input referencing the new location and call `setEditorInput`, followed by `firePropertyChange(PROP_INPUT)`. If appropriate, you should also update your editor's tab text with `setPartName`.

PART III

### Associating the Viewer and the Model

This step is the same as that described for views in the section Connecting the Viewer with the Content and Label Providers in Chapter 15, JFace Viewers.

### Synchronizing the Model and the Editor

This step is basically the same as that described for views in the section Implement Model-Viewer Synchronization in Chapter 15. There are, however, other considerations that you should be aware of if your model is based on a resource (projects, folders, and files in the workspace).

As you will learn in Chapter 23, Workspace Resource Programming, Eclipse includes a means of detecting changes to workspace resources, called **resource change listeners**. We'll return to the details of this mechanism in Chapter 23, but for now just be aware that this notification strategy is inherent to the nature of the Eclipse user interface, since it allows—and even encourages—multiple views of the same input. Your editor, if it is based on a resource, must react to the possibility that your model's underlying resource could be modified or deleted by means outside your editor's control, bypassing your model's change events. The following are a sample of those actions that might result in a change in the resource underlying your editor's model.

- The content of the resource is replaced when a user selects the **Replace With > Local History** menu choice.
- The resource is deleted from the Navigator view while your editor is displaying its content.
- The resource is modified by an external editor, or deleted outside Eclipse, and then the user selects **Refresh**.

A robust editor implementation must address these possibilities. The most common technique that you will employ to detect these situations is explained in Chapter 23. This approach is what you'll see in the example associated with this chapter. The default implementation of a text editor, covered in Chapter 26, Building a Custom Text Editor with JFace Text, handles these cases for you.

### Handling User Selections

This step is the same as that described for viewers in the section Handling User Selection of Viewer Objects in Chapter 15.

### Defining Editor Actions

The most notable difference between editors and views, from an implementation perspective, is how they handle actions. Recall that these differences are also reflected in the user interface.

- Views have their own toolbar; editors share a common toolbar.
- Views have their own pull-down menus; editors share the main menu bar.
- Only one view of a given type is allowed in a perspective; there is no limit on the number of editors of a given type.

To simplify the management of a common toolbar and menu, editors include an **editor action bar contributor** as part of their definition. This class is specified in the `contributorClass` attribute of the `<editor>` tag and must implement `IEditorActionBarContributor`. The Workbench will create a single instance of this class when an editor of a given type is first opened, and it will remain until the last one is closed. That is, it will be shared among all editor instances having the same id. The class specified on the `contributorClass` attribute is responsible for contributing to shared areas like the editor's actions shown in the toolbar and main menu bar when the editor is activated. Eclipse informs the action contributor to add its actions by calling its `init` method. The standard implementation of the `IEditorActionContributor` interface, `EditorActionBarContributor`, implements an `init` method that calls the following convenience methods, which your subclass may override.

- `contributeToMenu(IMenuManager)`
- `contributeToToolBar(IToolBarManager)`
- `contributeToCoolBar(ICoolBarManager)`
- `contributeToStatusLine(IStatusLineManager)`

The code for instantiating and adding actions to the menu or toolbar is the same as for views. The difference is that these actions are shared, and therefore they will likely need a reference to the active editor to know to which editor the action should be applied. Subsequently, besides instantiating and adding actions, your action contributor has the additional responsibility of informing the actions it created of changes in the active editor. For this, `IEditorActionBarContributor` defines the `setActiveEditor` method. Most implementations simply forward the notification to the actions they created, but you could do whatever is necessary to support your actions' needs. For example, some actions may need to know the current selection of your editor's selection provider, which was registered with `IEditorSite.setSelectionProvider`. If this is a common need, it is easier to have the action bar contributor register as a selection listener, and then forward the selection (an ISelection) to interested actions, rather than having individual actions register as selection listeners.

The following is a skeletal example of a simple editor action contributor and its action. It will contribute a **Clear All** button to the toolbar in the contributeToToolBar method.

```
public class MiniSSEditorActionBarContributor
    extends EditorActionBarContributor {

  IEditorPart editor;
  IAction clearAllAction;

  public void contributeToToolBar(IToolBarManager tbm) {
    clearAllAction = new ClearAllAction();
    clearAllAction.setToolTipText("Clear All");
    clearAllAction.setId("#ClearAll");
    clearAllAction.setImageDescriptor(...);

    tbm.add(clearAllAction);
  }

  public void setActiveEditor(IEditorPart targetEditor) {
    editor = targetEditor;
    clearAllAction.setActiveEditor(targetEditor);
  }
}
```

Notice that the action contributor forwards its notification of the active editor to its new action in setActiveEditor. The action can then query the target editor for its model or any editor-specific state it might need. The skeletal code of the action is below.

```
public class ClearAllAction extends Action {
  IEditorPart editor;

  public void run() {
    if (MessageDialog.openConfirm
      (editor.getSite().getShell(),
      "Clear All",
      "About to clear the entire table. Continue?")) {
      editor.getMiniSpreadsheet().clearAll();
    }
  }

  public void setActiveEditor(IEditorPart targetEditor) {
    editor = targetEditor;
  }
}
```

Don't confuse the setActiveEditor method above with the method of the same name defined in IEditorActionDelegate, which we'll cover in Chapter 21, Action Contributions: The Integration Fast Track. The example uses the same method signature, but the ClearAllAction is not contributed via the org.eclipse.ui.editorActions extension point and isn't an action delegate. That is, the setActiveEditor method above isn't a method defined in the action's superclass, Action; we defined it in the ClearAllAction class to facilitate communication between the action and its editor's action bar contributor.

Now assume that the action bar contributor adds a new action that is dependent on the current editor selection, **Clear Selection**. In a similar fashion, the action bar contributor comes to the aid of the action, registering itself as a selection listener of the editor's selection provider.

```java
public class MiniSSEditorActionBarContributor
    extends EditorActionBarContributor
    implements ISelectionChangedListener {

  IEditorPart editor;
  IAction clearAllAction;
  IAction clearSelectionAction;

  // contributeToToolBar(...) not shown.

  public void setActiveEditor(IEditorPart targetEditor) {
    if (editor != null)
      editor.getSite().getSelectionProvider().
        removeSelectionChangedListener(this);
    editor = targetEditor;
    if (editor != null)
      editor.getSite().getSelectionProvider().
        addSelectionChangedListener(this);
    clearAllAction.setActiveEditor(editor);
    clearSelectionAction.setActiveEditor(editor);
  }

  public void selectionChanged(SelectionChangedEvent event) {
    clearSelectionAction.selectionChanged(event);
  }

  public void dispose() {
    if (editor != null)
      editor.getSite().getSelectionProvider().
        removeSelectionChangedListener(this);
  }
}
```

When all the editors that this contributor serves are closed, its dispose method is called, giving it the opportunity to remove itself as a listener, free unneeded images, and so on. Contributing to the main menu bar is similar.

```
public void contributeToMenu(IMenuManager menuManager) {
    MenuManager submenuManager =
      new MenuManager("JDG2E: &Calculations",
        "com.ibm.jdg2e.msseditor.calculations");
    menuManager.insertAfter(
        IWorkbenchActionConstants.MB_ADDITIONS, submenuManager);
    submenuManager.add(showTotalAction);
    submenuManager.add(
        new GroupMarker(IWorkbenchActionConstants.MB_ADDITIONS));
}
```

This will add a pull-down menu, **JDG2E: Calculations**, in the standard contribution point, IWorkbenchActionConstants.MB_ADDITIONS. The id of the menu, com.ibm.jdg2e.msseditor.calculations, is optional, but allows others to contribute to your editor's menu if you define one or more insertion points. The above example uses a GroupMarker instead of a Separator. Unlike a separator, a group marker is never shown and only serves as an insertion point.

Finally, editors can have their own pop-up menus too, just as views can. The steps to create and register them are the same as for views. This is described near the end of the section Adding View Actions in Chapter 18.

## Beyond the Basic Implementation Steps

The prior sections described the steps that are common to the implementation of all editors. The following sections will elaborate on the base functionality that you may want to take advantage of and optional steps to better integrate your editor with other Workbench components.

### Reusing Specialized Editors of the Rich Client Platform and IDE Workbench

Our sample mini-spreadsheet editor relied only on the editor base abstract class, EditorPart. However, the Eclipse Platform defines other editor classes that you may want to reuse as part of your implementation if their functionality is close to what you wish to accomplish. One of the most distinguishing features between these groups of editor classes, besides their appearance, is the source of their data. Table 19.1 summarizes the editor classes. The first column is the editor class, the second column is the plug-in and layer of the Eclipse architecture in which it resides, the third column is its expected input, and the last column provides a short description.

**Table 19.1**  The Editor Classes

| Class | Plug-in (Layer) | Data Source | Description |
|---|---|---|---|
| `EditorPart` | `org.eclipse.ui` (RCP base) | `IEditorInput` (determined entirely by subclass) | The abstract superclass of all editors. |
| `Multi PageEditorPart` | `org.eclipse.ui` (RCP base) | `IEditorInput` (determined entirely by subclass) | An abstract editor composed of tabbed pages. Each page represents an editor implementing the `IEditorPart` interface or an arbitrary SWT control. |
| `FormEditor` | `org.eclipse.ui.forms` (RCP optional) | `IEditorInput` (determined entirely by subclass) | An abstract editor composed of tabbed pages. Each page is a subclass of the `FormEditorPage`. A forms-based editor is used extensively in the PDE, such as the Plug-in Manifest Editor. This plug-in includes specialized UI parts that provide a distinctive "flat" appearance for SWT widgets as well as specialized layout and wrapping. |
| `Abstract TextEditor` and `AbstractDecorated TextEditor` | `org.eclipse.ui. workbench.texteditor` (RCP optional) | `IDocument` (based on the editor's `IEditorInput`; the edited document is returned by the editor's implementation of the `ITextEditor .getDocumentProvider` method) | Two abstract editors for manipulating the textual representation of `IDocument` instances. See Chapter 26, Building a Custom Text Editor with JFace Text, for more details. |
| `TextEditor` | `org.eclipse.ui.editors` (IDE) | `IFileEditorInput` | The standard text editor for workspace file resources. |

PART III

Some editors are IDE-centric, and therefore assume files are organized in projects and folders residing within a workspace. Other editors belonging to the RCP base and optional plug-ins are more abstract and allow their subclasses to decide the origin of the data they manipulate (see Figure 10.3 for a summary of these plug-ins and their relationship to one another).

## Linking an Editor and the Outline View

As you have likely noticed in the Java perspective, the Outline view works to complement the active Java editor. As methods and fields are created in a class, the Outline view is updated immediately to show the new structure of the class. There is a tight link between the Java editor and the Outline view. Another example is the Readme editor that is included with the Eclipse sample plug-ins. When the user saves the file, the doSave method of the ReadmeEditor class is invoked.

```
public class ReadmeEditor extends TextEditor {
  protected ReadmeContentOutlinePage page;
  ...
  public void doSave(IProgressMonitor monitor) {
    super.doSave(monitor);
    if (page != null)
      page.update();
  }
  ...
}
```

As shown above, the outline page associated with the editor and shown in the Outline view is notified to update by the editor's doSave method. In the particular case of the ReadmeEditor class, an update instructs it to parse the readme file to populate the associated Outline view page.

Let's explore the link between an editor and the Outline view in more detail. When the end user opens an Outline view, this creates an instance of the ContentOutline class. It in turn asks the active editor if it supports the content outline by invoking its getAdapter(IContentOutlinePage.class) method. If the editor supports an Outline view, then it creates and returns an instance of a ContentOutlinePage in its override of the getAdapter method, similar to the following.

```
public Object getAdapter(Class required) {
  if (IContentOutlinePage.class.equals(required)) {
    if (myOutlinePage == null)
      myOutlinePage = new MyEditorContentOutlinePage(this);
    return myOutlinePage;
  }
  return super.getAdapter(required);
}
```

(Alternatively, your editor can create the declarative equivalent of the above getAdapter method by defining an extension of the org.eclipse.core.runtime.adapters extension point; for more details, see the "Extension Points Reference" section of Eclipse's online *Platform Plug-in Developer Guide* and this chapter's example on the CD-ROM.)

The page is added to the Outline view, that is, the instance of `Content-Outline`. If another editor is activated, the currently displayed Outline view page is hidden and the Outline view page of the newly activated editor is shown again. If the editor does not support an Outline view, then the standard "An outline is not available" message displays.

To provide a content outline page, create a class that implements `IContentOutlinePage`. In the method `createControl`, you should

- Create the viewer within the outline page and a listener to notify the editor of changes in the viewer's selection.
- Create the content provider.
- Create the label provider.
- Create a context menu.
- Set the input to the model (the input typically being the editor and/or its input).

If your outline is based on a tree viewer, you can reuse the abstract class `ContentOutlinePage`. Then override the method `createControl` to configure the tree viewer created in the superclass with a proper content provider, label provider, and input element.

Note that these steps are similar to building a view as discussed in Chapter 18. Based on *The Eclipse User Interface Guidelines*, if the data within an editor is too extensive to see on a single screen and will yield a structured outline, the editor should provide an outline for the Outline view. Based on this guideline, you will frequently want to provide an Outline view.

*The Eclipse User Interface Guidelines* specify that if the editor supports errors and warnings, this must be communicated in the Outline view. For example, a syntax error in a method will show in that method's iconic representation in the Outline view. This is accomplished by using a label decoration. A simple editor like the Readme editor does not have this capability, but editors for most programming languages will need to support this guideline. In addition to showing an error indicator (▨) in your outline, you may also want to consider adding a problem marker to the Problems view and your editor's annotation area, just as the Java editor does.

## Navigating Between Editors and Views

Eclipse provides a general means of navigating between Workbench parts via the **Navigate > Show In** menu choice. You've probably used this many times to navigate between a Java source file that you're editing and the Package Explorer view, either using the Java editor's own **Show in Package Explorer** context menu choice or the general **Navigate > Show In > Package Explorer** menu bar choice. These choices are particularly handy when the target view isn't visible (Package Explorer in this case) or it's difficult to locate the source (`.java` file corresponding to the contents of the open editor in this case) in the target view.

To take advantage of the general navigation implementation, your editor implements two additional interfaces. The first, `IShowInTargetList`, declares the method returning what target(s) you want listed in the **Navigate > Show In** menu cascade, similar to the code below.

```
public String[] getShowInTargetIds() {
   return new String[] { IPageLayout.ID_RES_NAV };
}
```

Your editor returns an array of view identifiers of what it considers valid targets, that is, targets for which the editor can provide inputs the receiving target will recognize either directly or by adapting the input via the `getAdapter` method. In the code shown above, it returns the identifier of the Resource navigator, `IPageLayout.ID_RES_NAV`. The second interface, `IShowInSource`, provides the input and/or selection as an instance of `ShowInContext`, as shown in the following method excerpt from the mini-spreadsheet's implementation.

```
public ShowInContext getShowInContext() {
   FileEditorInput fei =
      (FileEditorInput) getEditorInput();
   return new ShowInContext(fei.getFile(), null);
}
```

The returned instance of `ShowInContext` is passed to the target so the target can locate your editor's input within the target's display area. In the case of our mini-spreadsheet editor, the context instance specifies an input that the Navigator will recognize, the instance of `IFile` associated with the editor's input.

To briefly summarize this, Eclipse will check if the active part implements the `IShowInTargetList` interface (or provides a `getAdapter` method capable of returning an implementer) when building the **Navigate > Show In > Navigator** menu cascade. If the user selects this menu choice, Eclipse similarly checks if the active part implements the `IShowInSource` interface to retrieve the context as an instance of `ShowInContext`, which it then passes to the target.

Workbench parts that want to declare themselves as targets for the **Show In** choice can either implement `IShowInTarget` or adapt to this interface by overriding the `getAdapter` method. Like the Navigator, targets should handle the presentation of the desired input in whatever manner makes sense, typically by scrolling the input into view and selecting it. See the section entitled Supporting the Show In Request in Chapter 18 for more details.

## Example Summary

You are now ready to explore the mini-spreadsheet editor provided on the CD-ROM. This sample code is defined in several related projects to demonstrate an IDE-centric editor and an RCP-oriented editor.

- `com.ibm.jdg2e.msseditor.common` contains the base code to the IDE- and RCP-based editor implementation of the mini-spreadsheet editor.
- `com.ibm.jdg2e.msseditor.extras` demonstrates how to make an editor extensible by contributing actions to the editor's menu, toolbar, and pop-up menu.
- `com.ibm.jdg2e.msseditor.ide` contains the IDE implementation; its input is an instance of `org.eclipse.core.resources.IFile`. It also defines a New wizard to create the initial editor input.
- `com.ibm.jdg2e.msseditor.miniwp` contains the RCP implementation; its input is an instance of `java.io.File`. This plug-in contributes actions to the Mini-Workplace (`com.ibm.jdg2e.miniwp`) that you saw earlier in Figure 10.7, which creates and opens existing mini-spreadsheet files.

The example is a simple but functionally complete editor. You will find more documentation and instructions on how to install and launch the editor on the book's CD-ROM.

## Chapter Summary

Building a customized editor can be a time-consuming task. The Eclipse user interface frameworks make it easier by providing the common editor behavior. This chapter explored the steps to build an editor, including contributing editor actions to the Workbench menu bar and toolbar, and closed with an overview of how to implement an outline page for the standard Outline view.

If you haven't done so already, now would be a good point to review the code and documentation for the Mini-Workplace associated with Chapter 10. It demonstrates how you can reuse views like its Calculator and Web browser, and editors like the mini-spreadsheet editor that we presented in this chapter.

PART III

## References

Arthorne, John, and Chris Laffra. 2004. *Official Eclipse 3.0 FAQs*. Boston, MA: Addison-Wesley. http://www.eclipsefaq.org. (See FAQs 126, 207, 212, 213, 217.)

See the Eclipse Forms Programming Guide (draft) under the Reference topic in the online help for this book.

Springgay, Dave, Jin Li, Julian Jones, and Greg Adams. May 2, 2002. *The Eclipse User Interface Guidelines*. http://www.eclipse.org.

PART III

# CHAPTER 20

## *Perspectives*

Is the glass half full or half empty? Well, it all depends on your perspective. During your workday, you play several roles. The extensibility of Eclipse allows you to combine the appropriate views and editors you require to create a new customized perspective. This ability is available to Eclipse users, as well as to the plug-in developers. As a tool provider, you can use Eclipse to create a standard set of perspectives. In the previous chapters you learned how to create views and editors. This chapter focuses on the development of a perspective by the plug-in provider. You can create a perspective using elements provided by Eclipse or elements you have developed.

A best practice tip, though, is to be judicious when creating new perspectives. Users have been confused by too many perspectives. Therefore, first see if you can contribute to an existing perspective. Another point of potential confusion for less experienced users is when they accidentally close or hide a perspective or a view; they probably will not know how to open the view or perspective. In that case it's best to implement a fixed view in a perspective. A fixed view is not closeable, nor can it be dragged and dropped from its fixed position. The initial layout of a fixed perspective cannot be changed.

## Creating a Perspective

As discussed in Chapter 2, a **perspective** is a collection of views and actions, as well as an optional editor area, that are useful for a specific user task or role. As a plug-in developer, you can extend Eclipse to create additional perspectives or augment existing ones. Suppose you are a tool supplier integrating tools for a specific market segment. You can tailor the supplied perspectives to make it easier for your users to visualize how they might want to organize the product's views, editors, and access key actions. When defining a perspective, you specify the initial set of views, their layout, and the initial visible actions. For example, in Figure 20.1 you can specify a set of views in a folder layout. If there are other perspectives that you anticipate your users will want quick access to from your perspective, you can add them to the perspective shortcuts.

There are two steps to create your own perspective.

1. Declare the perspective extension in the plugin.xml file.
2. Describe the layout of the perspective by creating a Java class that implements IPerspectiveFactory.

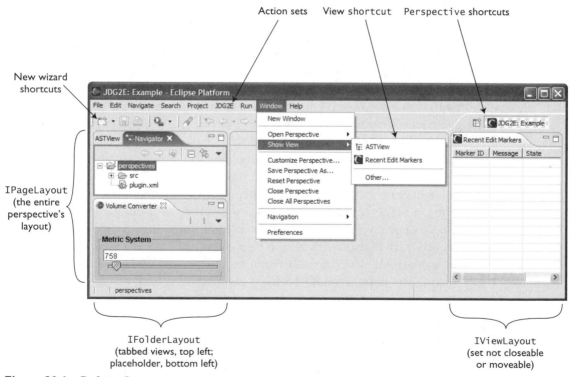

**Figure 20.1**   Defining Perspectives

To extend Eclipse to include a new perspective, you have to specify the extension point `org.eclipse.ui.perspectives` in the `plugin.xml` file. In addition, you must specify the class name that will implement the `IPerspectiveFactory` interface.

```xml
<extension
    point="org.eclipse.ui.perspectives">
  <perspective
      name="JDG2E: Example"
      icon="icons/J2Moon1616.gif"
      class="com.ibm.jdg2e.perspective.JDG2EPerspectiveFactory"
      id="com.ibm.jdg2e.example.perspective">
  </perspective>
</extension>
```

The `IPerspectiveFactory` interface contains the method `createInitialLayout` passing an instance of `IPageLayout`. You use this method to describe the initial layout of the views and editors. `IPageLayout` defines the initial layout for a page in an Eclipse window. You can add a view to a page layout. For example, you can add a view to the bottom of a perspective, just below the editor area. You use the page layout to specify the location of the added view. The following example adds the view referred to by `ID_JDG2E_MARKER_VIEW`, which is the view extension id, into the layout. Notice that the marker view layout is configured in a way that the view is not closeable or moveable. The result is that there is no **Close** or **Fast View** on its system menu and it's not moveable. Controlling the layout in this way is a good practice if you want to prevent a less experienced user from accidentally closing a view. Moreover, it's possible to make a fixed perspective, preventing its parts from being moved or zoomed and its initial set of views from being closed. This support for fixed layouts also applies to the `perspectiveExtensions` extension point, which is discussed later in this chapter.

In addition to views, you can add wizard shortcuts, perspective shortcuts, and actions. The following code snippet also illustrates how to create a perspective layout.

```java
public void createInitialLayout(IPageLayout layout) {
    // Add our marker view
    layout.addView(ID_JDG2E_MARKER_VIEW, IPageLayout.RIGHT,
        0.66f, IPageLayout.ID_EDITOR_AREA);
    layout.getViewLayout(ID_JDG2E_MARKER_VIEW).setCloseable(false);
    layout.getViewLayout(ID_JDG2E_MARKER_VIEW).setMoveable(false);
    // Add new wizard shortcut
    layout.addNewWizardShortcut(ID_JDG2E_NEW_WIZARDS);
    // Add our actions
    layout.addActionSet(ID_JDG2E_COMMON_ACTIONS);
    layout.addActionSet(ID_JDG2E_JDT_ACTIONS);
    ...
}
```

IFolderLayout adds a set of views to a perspective that are located in the same area, and each view has a tab similar to a notebook tab. You navigate to the particular view by selecting the tab. The folder layout's position is specified with respect to the editor area. For example, the following code will create a folder layout to the left of the editor area.

```
IFolderLayout topLeft =
    layout.createFolder("topLeft", IPageLayout.LEFT, 0.50f,
        IPageLayout.ID_EDITOR_AREA);
```

## Using the `perspectiveExtensions` Extension Point

To contribute views, wizard shortcuts, perspective shortcuts, and action sets to a perspective defined by another plug-in, use the `perspective extensions` extension point in your `plugin.xml` file. For example, the following XML code contributes wizards, views, view shortcuts, and perspective shortcuts from the plug-in examples in this book to the Eclipse Resource perspective.

```
<extension
  point="org.eclipse.ui.perspectiveExtensions">
  <perspectiveExtension
    targetID="org.eclipse.ui.resourcePerspective">
    <newWizardShortcut
        id="com.ibm.jdg2e.wizards.newwizards.definedpages"/>
    <viewShortcut id="org.eclipse.jdt.astview.views.ASTView"/>
    <perspectiveShortcut
      id="com.ibm.jdg2e.example.perspective"/>
    <actionSet id="com.ibm.jdg2e.common.actionSet"/>
    <view
      relationship="stack"
      relative="org.eclipse.ui.views.ResourceNavigator"
      closeable="false"
      moveable ="false"
      id="com.ibm.jdg2e.jdt.javametricsview"/>
  </perspectiveExtension>
</extension>
```

## Example Summary

An example of creating a new perspective in the project named `com.ibm.jdg2e.perspective`, shown in Figure 20.2, is included on the CD-ROM. This perspective uses the Recent Edit Markers view, a plug-in sample project contained on the CD-ROM (see Chapter 25, Resource Tagging Using Markers). The perspective initially will also contain the Navigator view, but no editor.

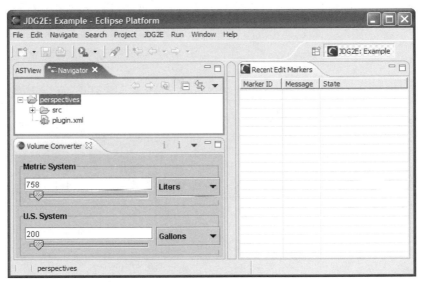

**Figure 20.2**   New Perspective Called JDG2E Example

The Java class `JDG2EPerspectiveFactory` created this new perspective using the page layout and folder layout. They are created in the `create-InitialLayout` method (see the second code snippet in this chapter).

## Chapter Summary

This chapter discussed how to build custom perspectives and to contribute to existing perspectives. As the developer of a perspective, you only describe the initial layout. The end user has the ability to further customize the perspective. Creating your own perspective is a very easy way to extend the Eclipse user interface.

## Reference

Arthorne, John, and Chris Laffra. 2004. *Official Eclipse 3.0 FAQs*. Boston, MA: Addison-Wesley. http://www.eclipsefaq.org. (See FAQs 192–194, 240, 345.)

PART III

# CHAPTER 21

## Action Contributions: The Integration Fast Track

In this chapter we are going to tackle a portion of the Eclipse user interface framework known as **action contributions**. What are action contributions? Briefly, they represent actions available to the user in menus and toolbars. However, they are not confined to the main Workbench menu or toolbar—they can appear in views and editors as well. They can appear as context menus and on selected objects in either an editor or a view. Most importantly, you can define actions that appear in Workbench parts authored by others (hence the term action contribution). In other words, you are free to enhance their work, and thanks to the extensibility of Eclipse, you are encouraged to do so. As you will learn, you can add context menu actions to objects in Workbench parts that have not been written yet or even imagined! As you can see in Figure 21.1, Eclipse provides plenty of opportunities to make your plug-in's presence known by using action contributions.

Some of the topics in this chapter require some understanding of information from previous chapters. In case you have arrived here before reading prerequisite material, references to relevant chapters are called out along the way. Implementations of examples in the projects com.ibm.jdg2e .actions and com.ibm.jdg2e.actions.ide on the CD-ROM are discussed in this chapter.

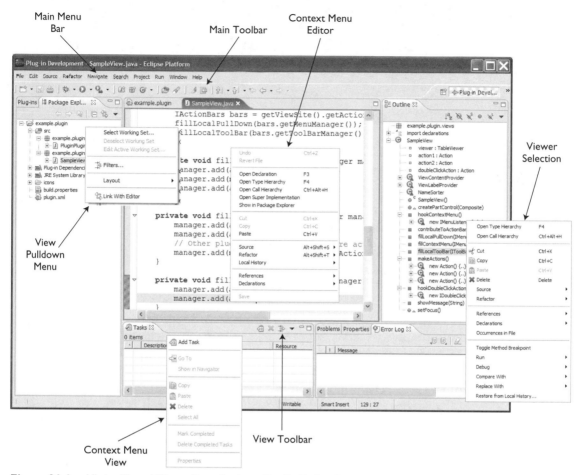

**Figure 21.1**    All the Places Where Contributions Can Be Defined

## Action Contribution Extension Points

As with almost everything related to extending Eclipse, creating action contributions starts with extension points. Eclipse provides a variety of extension points that permit you to contribute actions to the Workbench in the following places.

- In the Workbench menu bar and toolbar
- In the view menu bar and toolbar
- In context menus in views and editors
- In context menus on selected objects in views and editors

There are five extension points available to define action contributions. Table 21.1 lists the various types of contributions, where they may appear, and the applicable extension point. We will learn how to use all of them in this chapter. Another concept involves the use of **commands**, which have a close relationship to actions. Among other things, they provide a framework for assigning accelerator keys to actions (also known as key bindings). We will discuss commands after we have covered actions in some detail.

**Table 21.1**   Contribution Extension Points

| Contribution Location | Location | Extension Point |
|---|---|---|
| Menus and toolbars | Workbench window | `org.eclipse.ui.actionSets` |
| | Views | `org.eclipse.ui.viewActions` |
| | Editors | `org.eclipse.ui.editorActions` |
| | Views and editors | `org.eclipse.ui.actionSetPartAssociations` |
| Context menus | Editors, views, and viewer objects | `org.eclipse.ui.popupMenus` |

## The Fundamentals of Action Contributions

No matter which extension point you choose to use, the implementation mechanics for each are similar. You define an action extension in your plug-in manifest file. This defines where and when the action appears and how it looks to the user. In Java code you define what to do when the user selects your action. That's all there is to it. Contributing actions is one of the easier plug-in extensions to define and code.

Before we examine each of the plug-in extension points shown in Table 21.1, let's look at the common features that apply to most of these extension points. One common area is the definition of your action in your plug-in manifest file (`plugin.xml`). There are several common filtering mechanisms to determine where and whether an action is available. Finally, the extension point APIs are all derived from a single interface class, `IAction-elegate`. Let's start by discussing the API. Later, we will move on to each extension point and discuss examples.

### The Action Contribution API

The label of your menu item that the user sees is defined in an action extension in your plug-in manifest file. This allows your action to appear in the

PART III

Workbench even though your plug-in may not be loaded yet. Recall that plug-ins are loaded lazily, which means that a plug-in is not loaded until there is a need for it. In the case of your action, your plug-in's code will not be loaded until the user requests to run it (unless the plug-in is already active). If your plug-in has not been loaded, a proxy action stands in for your action. This proxy represents your action in the Workbench in terms of appearance, but it has no ability to perform the action. The proxy delegates to your action when the user selects it, and your action is executed. Since many Eclipse plug-ins define actions, if this were not the case, all these plug-ins would have to be loaded at startup just to show the menu contents. What a mess that would be!

As a delegate, the action extension must implement `IActionDelegate` or an appropriate subinterface. Figure 21.2 shows the relationship between various action contributions and their corresponding interface classes (in addition, you may extend the abstract class `ActionDelegate` and override the methods you need). Each contribution type uses an interface that derives from `IActionDelegate`. All actions include the `run` and `selectionChanged` methods defined in this interface. When the user chooses your action, the `run` method is called to execute the action. The `run` method passes an `IAction` object representing the instantiated action. Looking at the Javadoc for `IAction`, you will see that there are a number of convenient methods to get and set some of the action's attributes like id, tooltip text, and image. The `IAction.getId` method can be helpful in situations where you want to create a single action class and use the action's identifier to provide a context. Perhaps you offer several filters for a view, each specified as separate toolbar actions but implemented in a single action delegate class. The `getId` method can identify which action represented the filter chosen by the user.

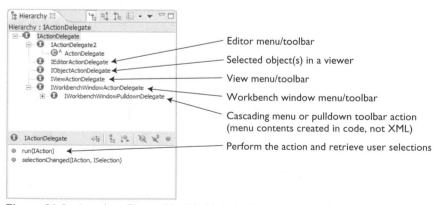

**Figure 21.2**  Interface Classes Used by Various Contribution Actions

If your action depends on a selection by the user, the selectionChanged method provides the object or objects selected as an ISelection object. An ISelection object is a generic object. You need to cast it to what the user has selected. The selectionChanged method is called for every selection, whether or not the user chooses your action (and only after your plug-in has been loaded!). Typically, you save a reference to the selected object, and when the run method is called, you interpret what was selected.

The following example illustrates the use of the run and selection-Changed methods. The run method lists all the selected projects and displays their names on the console. The action defined in the following code appears in the tree structure of the Navigator view, so selection was cast to an IStructuredSelection, which extends ISelection. You need some knowledge of the context in which your action appears to properly interpret the selection. An IStructuredSelection is used in structured viewers like trees and lists where the selection is easily identifiable.

```java
public class ListSelectedProjectsAction
    implements IActionDelegate {
    IStructuredSelection selection;
    public void selectionChanged
        (IAction action, ISelection selection) {
      if (selection instanceof IStructuredSelection) {
        this.selection = (IStructuredSelection) selection;
      }
    }
    public void run(IAction action) {
      if (!selection.isEmpty()) {
        Iterator iter = selection.iterator();
        while (iter.hasNext()) {
          Object obj = (Object) iter.next();
          if (obj instanceof IProject) {
            System.out.println(
              "Project name: " + ((IProject) obj).getName());
          }
        }
      }
    }
}
```

**NOTE**   As you might have concluded by now, the focus in this chapter is on actions defined as plug-in extensions. Actions created entirely programmatically as extensions of SWT widgets like menus and menu items are supported in the package org.eclipse.jface.action. For actions you might implement specifically in a view or editor, see the discussion in Chapter 18, Views, and Chapter 19, Editors. Additionally, the package org.eclipse.ui.actions contains extendable action classes for many common Workbench operations. This package name exists in both the Workbench and Workbench IDE plug-ins `org.eclipse.ui.workbench` and `org.eclipse.ui.ide`, respectively.

### Specifying Contributions in the Plug-in Manifest File

Table 21.1 listed five extension points that are available for contributing actions in various contexts. The XML schema definitions of these extension points have a number of common attributes defined, such as when and where the action appears in the Workbench as well as its visual appearance. We will cover some of the most frequently used attributes now rather than repeat this information for each extension point.

Table 21.2 lists a set of common attributes used in many of the action contribution extension points. This is by no means a complete set. For a description of each extension point, see the "Extension Points Reference" section in the *Platform Plug-in Developer Guide* in the Eclipse online help.

**Table 21.2**   Some Common Attributes Used by Action Contribution Extension Points

| Attribute Name | Description |
| --- | --- |
| class | Specifies the fully qualified name of the class that implements `IActionDelegate` or the appropriate subinterface (see Figure 21.2). Required. |
| disabledIcon | Defines an optional icon (and its relative path) that appears when an action is disabled. If not defined, the icon specified in the icon attribute appears grayed out. |
| enablement | Defines the conditions under which this action is enabled. See Creating Elaborate Filters Using Action Expressions later in this chapter. |
| enablesFor | Defines the enablement rule for single or multiple user selections. The implementer's action class can override this setting in its `selectionChanged` method after it is loaded. The following values are allowed. |
|  | !    No items selected. |
|  | ?    None or one item selected. |
|  | +    One or more items selected. |
|  | n+   n or more items must be selected, e.g., 2+ indicates two or more items are selected. |
|  | n    A precise number of items is selected. |
|  | *    Any number of items is selected. |
| helpContextID | Defines the help dialog displayed when the menu is selected and the **F1** key is pressed. |
| hooverIcon | Defines an optional icon (and its relative path) used to visually represent the action in its context when the mouse pointer is positioned over the action. |

PART III

**Table 21.2**  Some Common Attributes Used by Action Contribution Extension Points (*continued*)

| Attribute Name | Description |
| --- | --- |
| `icon` | Defines the icon file name and relative path within the plug-in's directory. It is conventional to include an explicit `icons` directory for plug-in icons. |
| `menubarPath` `toolbarPath` | Define the location of an action in a menu bar or toolbar. |
| `state` | Specifies the action's initial state (either true or false). Optional; it is used only when the `style` attribute has the value `radio` or `toggle`. |
| `style` | Defines the user interface style type for the action. If omitted, it is `push` by default. The following values are supported. |

| | | |
| --- | --- | --- |
| | `push` | appears as a regular menu item or tool item. |
| | `radio` | appears as a radio style menu item or tool item. This is coupled with the `state` attribute. |
| | `toggle` | appears as a checked style menu item or as a toggle toolbar item. This is coupled with the `state` attribute. |
| | `pulldown` | appears as a cascading style menu or as a drop-down menu beside a toolbar item. The `pulldown` attribute applies only to the Workbench menu or toolbars, and you must implement the `IWorkbenchWindowPulldownDelegate` interface. |

| Attribute Name | Description |
| --- | --- |
| `toolTip` | Describes in text the action in a toolbar when the mouse hovers over the action's icon. |

PART III

Let's look at an example of the XML that defines an action using some of these attributes.

```
<action id="com.mycompany.ourtoolaction"
  label="&amp;Run Our Super-Duper Tool"
  menubarPath="ourToolMenu/groupA"
  toolbarPath="ourToolMenu"
  icon="icons/ourtoolaction.gif"
  tooltip="Run Our Super-Duper Tool"
  helpContextId="com.mycompany.run_action_context"
  class="com.mycompany.tools.actions.OurToolAction"
  enablesFor="1">
</action>
```

This rather nonsensical example (don't worry, better examples are coming when specific extension points are discussed) defines an action that will appear in both a menu and the toolbar, but it does not specify the Workbench part that hosts it. It could be located in a specific view, editor, or the Workbench window, depending on the extension point we are using (see Table 21.1). How you define the `menubarPath` and `toolbarPath` will be covered shortly. The action displays in a menu item with the label **Run Our**

**Super-Duper Tool** and appears in the toolbar with its own icon. The &amp in the label specifies that the following character should be used to allow navigation using a keyboard instead of the mouse. Using `tooltip`, a short description displays when the mouse hovers over the icon. If the toolbar icon or the menu is selected and the **F1** key is pressed, a Help dialog appears (see Chapter 22, Providing Help). This example specifies a class called `OurToolAction` that implements, depending on the extension point, some subinterface of `IAction-Delegate`. Finally, the `enablesFor` attribute states that this action is enabled only when the user selects a single item. When your delegate class is loaded, you can modify the enablement conditions in the `selectionChanged` method.

It is important to understand that the attribute values specified in your action extension are *static* attributes that allow your action to appear in a menu before your plug-in is loaded. When your action class is loaded, there's no further need for the Workbench to refer to the values statically defined in your action's extension because it can query your action instance directly. You have the opportunity to dynamically change some of these attributes. The `run` and `selectionChanged` methods of `IActionDelegate` pass your action as an `IAction` object, which has getter and setter methods for a variety of action attributes.

### Specifying Actions in Menus and Toolbars

The attributes `menubarPath` and `toolbarPath` deserve a little more explanation. The previous example referenced an existing menu definition with the following statement.

```
menubarPath="ourToolMenu/groupA"
```

This references an existing menu definition defined using the `menu` attribute. Here is how our menu was defined.

```
<menu
  id="ourToolMenu"
  label="Our Company Menu">
  <separator name="separator1"/>
  <groupMarker name="groupA"/>
  <groupMarker name="groupB"/>
</menu>
```

Our action's `menubarPath` attribute identified the menu by its identifier of `ourToolMenu` using a menu-positioning marker specified as `groupA`. The attribute `groupMarker` is a placeholder that allows you to manage the placement of actions within the menu without any visual representation, unlike the separator element. A `separator` is another type of placeholder that is delineated in the user interface with a horizontal separator line. Normally, action contributions appear in a menu in the reverse order they are defined. (This is an Eclipse legacy that, if changed, would impact all existing menu items.) If a menu is shared by multiple plug-ins, actions might not appear in the sequence you wish. A groupMarker allows for more careful placement of actions so they appear where you want the user to see them. In the example, groupA and groupB are defined as groupMarker attributes. An action could be assigned to groupA, another action to groupB, or you could define multiple actions to a single groupMarker. The placement of the groupMarker attribute in the menu definition can help determine the order in which actions assigned to it will appear. If the groupMarker labeled groupA was specified before the separator labeled separator1, then an action assigned to it would appear above the separator. Finally, you can define a menu in your plug-in's extension definition or reference a menu in another plug-in's manifest.

The path attribute references something known as an **insertion point**. This specifies where in the menu bar your menu will appear. If the owner of a menu bar (Workbench or view) wishes to allow others to define extensions, the owner will define one or more insertion points (see Chapter 18, Views). Actually, the path usually maps to a predefined menu and group marker. The Workbench menu bar has defined an insertion point, named additions, which is located somewhere to the left of the **Window** pull-down menu. The value additions is a standard Workbench convention for the default insertion point for the Workbench and view menus. It is defined as the value in IWorkbenchActionConstants.MB_ADDITIONS. If the path attribute is omitted, a value of additions is assumed. Figure 21.3 illustrates how you define the linkage between a menu and an action. There may be additional insertion points defined, each with its own attribute name.

You could define your menu as a submenu. If you wanted to contribute to the **Window** menu, your menu path and action menubarPath values would look like this next example. The menu identifier window is also published in the Javadoc for IWorkbenchActionConstants (also see IIDEActionConstants, ITextEditorActionConstants, and IJavaEditorActionConstants). These are the places to look to specify actions that appear within any of the standard Workbench menus like **File**, **Edit**, and so on. The value additions is an insertion point in its menu list. Our menubarPath is specified like this:

```
<action
  ...
  menubarPath="window/additions"
  ...
</action>
```

PART III

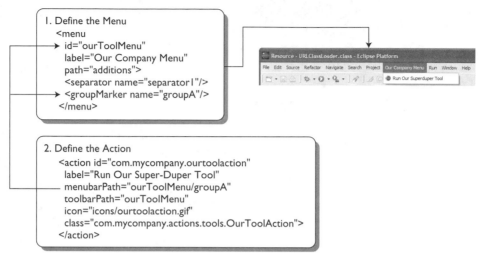

**Figure 21.3**    Relationship between a Menu Definition and Its Reference by an Action

The Workbench IDE defines a main toolbar and some insertion points within it. If your action contributes to the toolbar and it doesn't specify any of these predefined insertion points, it is automatically added to the end of the toolbar in its own group called a **coolbar**. A coolbar is a special kind of toolbar that appears on the main toolbar within horizontal separators that slide sideways. You can drag a coolbar around and reposition its contents. Similar to menus, you can define your own `toolbarPath` or reference another. Again, see `IWorkbenchActionConstants` for toolbar paths predefined by the Workbench.

Later in the chapter, we will discuss pop-up or context menus that can appear in viewers (see Chapter 15, JFace Viewers). Viewers are never defined in a plug-in manifest, only in code, so context menus for viewers have to also be defined in code. We will come back to that when we discuss the extension point `org.eclipse.ui.popupMenus`.

See also the topic "Menu and Toolbar Paths" in the *Platform Plug-in Developer Guide* in the online help.

### Using Filters to Refine Where Your Actions Appear

There are several ways you can define where, or even whether, actions are available. You don't want them to appear all the time unless they are truly global in nature. Your action may apply only to certain specific user selections, or you may want to control when the action is enabled or visible. In your extension definition, you can use a variety of filtering mechanisms to control the visibility and/or enablement of your actions. This can be summarized as follows.

- Selection filtering

  The enablement of an action is based on the type of object selected using the `selection` attribute.

- Action filtering

  This further refinement of the availability of an action is based on the value of one or more properties of the selected object. It uses the `filter` attribute.

- Action expressions

  The enablement and/or visibility of an action is based on a set of logical conditions using the operators and, or, and not that operate on a set of comparison elements. The conditions are specified within the `enablement` and `visibility` attributes.

We'll examine each of these filtering mechanisms in the following sections.

## The Class Selection Filter

The `selection` filter attribute defines an action's enablement based on the type of object selected and, optionally, its name (applicable to IDE workspace `IResource` objects). The following is an example of this extension attribute. As you can see, it is straightforward. In this instance, the action is enabled for Java file resources. Note that you can specify a wild card pattern in the name. This could be used to determine what actions might appear on selected resources in the Navigator view.

```
<selection class="org.eclipse.core.resources.IFile"
    name="*.xml"/>
```

## Creating Elaborate Filters Using Action Expressions

Action expressions allow you to define a more complex filter by specifying a set of logically connected conditions that determine the enablement and, for context menus, the visibility of an action. The operators and, or, and not can be applied against each condition. The comparison elements, listed in Table 21.3, are available for you to use in the condition.

**Table 21.3**  Comparison Elements Used in Action Expressions

| Comparison Element | Description |
|---|---|
| objectClass | This element tests whether an object selection is a member of a specified class or interface. |
| | Example: |
| | `<objectClass name="org.eclipse.core.resources.IProject"/>` |
| objectState | This is a name/value pair as defined by an object's implementation of IActionFilter (see text discussion). |
| | Example: |
| | `<objectState name="readOnly", value="false"/>` |
| systemProperty | This applies only to objects that can be evaluated against some system property. The value of the system property is determined by invoking the method System.getProperty. |
| | Example: |
| | `<systemProperty name="user.language" value="en" />` |
| pluginState | For the given identifier of a plug-in, you can test whether its state is installed or activated. The value installed means that the plug-in is known to Eclipse, although it may not be loaded. The value activated means that the plug-in's code has been loaded. In this example your action is not enabled unless the debug user interface plug-in is loaded. |
| | Example: |
| | `<pluginState id="org.eclipse.jdt.debug.ui" value="activated" />` |

When you define an action expression, you are specifying the condition by which the action is enabled using the `enablement` attribute. Any action defined using any of the available extension points may define an enablement condition. Here is an example in which the action is enabled only for XML files that are writable.

```
<action
    ... Action specification details omitted ...
    <enablement>
      <and>
        <objectClass
              name="org.eclipse.core.resources.IFile"/>
        <objectState name="readOnly" value="false"/>
        <objectState name="name" value="*.xml"/>
      </and>
    </enablement>
</action>
```

If you don't need the power of a conditional expression, the simpler `filter` attribute is available to specify the filters applicable to your object contribution. The filter contains a name/value pair for one or more action filters.

```
<filter name="readonly" value="true" />
```

If you wish to provide filters for your objects so they can be used in action expressions, the class supporting those objects must implement the `IActionFilter` interface (or provide an adapter using the `IAdaptable` mechanism). This interface requires you to implement the `testAttribute` method.

```
boolean testAttribute(Object target, String name, String value)
```

This method is straightforward. It will be called with the name/value pair from the `filter` attribute when your objects are selected in a viewer. All you need to do is evaluate the name and value against the object and return the correct Boolean value based on your test. Only the class that defines the object can do this. In other words, additional filters cannot be added to an object except by the class that implements the `IActionFilter` interface (or a registered adapter).

An example of an action filter is available in CD-ROM project `com.ibm.jdg2e.msseditor.common` and implemented in class `MiniSSRowActionFilter`. This implementation uses an adapter pattern design and incorporates the extension point `org.eclipse.core.runtime.adapters`.

## Built-in Action Filters for Resources and Markers

In Eclipse, workspace objects of type `IResource`, `IProject`, and `IMarker` support action filters (represented by the interfaces `IResourceActionFilter`, `IProjectActionFilter`, and `IMarkerActionFilter`) that you can use in your own action definition. (See Chapter 23, Workspace Resource Programming, if this is unfamiliar.) An `IResource` is a project, folder, or file. An `IProject` represents a project, of course. An `IMarker` is metadata on a workspace resource (see Chapter 25, Resource Tagging Using Markers). Compilation errors, bookmarks, and breakpoints are examples of markers. These filters, which are listed in Table 21.4, can determine the visibility or enablement of an action defined for one of these object types. See Additional Enablement Filtering for Object Contributions later in this chapter for some additional filtering capability information.

We have finished examining the common properties of action contributions. As you can see, there are several areas of commonality. There are powerful filtering capabilities to define when and whether your action is available to the user. Next, we examine each of the extension points listed in Table 21.1 and describe how to use them to contribute to the Workbench.

PART III

**Table 21.4**   Resource Action Filters

| Object Type | Filter Names | Values |
| --- | --- | --- |
| Resources | extension | File extension names like .txt or .java. |
| | name | A resource name. |
| | path | A file path (may include an asterisk (*) as a wild card character). |
| | persistentProperty | A string. Equivalent to IResource.getPersistentProperty. |
| | projectPersistentProperty | A string. Equivalent to IResource.getproject().getPersistentProperty. |
| | projectNature | A project nature identifier. |
| | readOnly | true or false. |
| | sessionProperty | A string. Equivalent to IResource.getSessionProperty. |
| | xmlDTDName | Applies to XML files. The DTD definition for this XML file is the value supplied with this attribute. |
| | xmlFirstTag | Applies to XML files. The first XML attribute (or top-level attribute) must have the value specified. |
| Projects | nature | A nature identifier. |
| | open | true or false. |
| Markers | done | true or false. |
| | message | A message string (may include an asterisk (*) as a wild card character). |
| | priority | 0 = low, 1 = normal, 2 = high. |
| | severity | 0 = information, 1 = warning, 2 = error. |
| | superType | Identifier of another marker. |
| | type | Identifier of another marker. |

It is important to understand that if your action's enablement can be determined only at runtime, you have some special issues to deal with. Recall that until this point, we've only discussed conditional actions using extension attributes in your plug-in manifest file. What do you do if your action is dependent on runtime information that you can't specify statically or that isn't part of an action filter definition?

For example, if you wish to enable or disable your action based on some Workbench state information, you must do this in your action's selection-Changed method. However, therein lies the problem: Your action may appear in a menu before your plug-in is loaded.

If your action depends on some inspection of the state of the system, this will require that your plug-in be loaded, so your code is available when the object is selected. In these situations, you can specify that your plug-in be loaded during Eclipse startup using the extension point `org.eclipse.ui` `.startup`. Use this feature judiciously because this adds time to the startup of Eclipse. Split your plug-in into more than one so that only the required code is loaded at startup. Note that the user can disable the automatic startup of your plug-in in the **Preferences > Workbench > Startup** dialog. You should be prepared for that possibility. The following code will return a non-negative integer if startup for your plug-in has been disabled by the user.

```
PlatformUI.getWorkbench().
  getPreferenceStore().
  getString(
    IPreferenceConstants.PLUGINS_NOT_ACTIVATED_ON_STARTUP).
    indexOf("your plug-in id");
```

## Contributing to the Workbench Menu Bar and Toolbar

We have been indirectly discussing contributions to the Workbench menu bar and toolbar; now let's get into it. The extension point is `org.eclipse.ui` `.actionSets`. As its name implies, you use this extension point to define a set of actions covering the requirements of a specific tool that would appear on the Workbench menu bar or the toolbar. Action set members operate on user selections in other Workbench parts or may ignore the user selection. An action set participates in the Workbench in three ways.

- It can be defined as a participant in a perspective. The action set is always available in that perspective. This is the most common application of action sets (see Chapter 20, Perspectives).
- The set of actions can be added to a perspective by the user with the **Window > Customize Perspective** menu choice. In the dialog your action set will be listed in the Available Command Groups column within the **Command** page of the dialog (command group is the end-user term for an action set). An action set may be made visible in all perspectives. You should do that only if your tool needs to be globally accessible.
- As you will learn later, the extension point `actionPartSetAssociations` allows you to link an action set to any perspective that incorporates one or more of the specified views or editors defined in its extension definition.

PART III

Normally, the classes in your action set will implement IWorkbench-WindowActionDelegate. As we have discussed, the run method is called to execute your action.

If your action participates in a toolbar pull-down menu (e.g., the action ☼ ▼, **Debug IDE test**), by specifying the extension attribute style=pulldown, your class must implement IWorkbenchWindowPulldownDelegate, a subinterface of IWorkbenchWindowActionDelegate. This interface includes a getMenu method that is used to construct the pull-down menu contents. In the case of a toolbar pull-down menu, you must create the contents dynamically. If not previously active, your plug-in will be loaded when the user displays the pull-down contents. An example of this is discussed below.

A behavior you might not expect, but should be aware of, is that actions defined in an action set appear in their menu in the *reverse order* that they were defined. However, as we discussed earlier, you can control this using the separator and groupMarker attributes.

Here is an example of the use of this extension point from the example project com.ibm.jdge2.actions.

```
<extension
    point="org.eclipse.ui.actionSets">
  <actionSet
    label="JDG2E: Actions Example"
    visible="true"
    id="com.ibm.jdg2e.actions.actionSet1">
    <menu
      label="JDG2E"
      id="com.ibm.jdg2e">
      <separator
        name="actionGroup">
      </separator>
    </menu>
    <action
      label="Show Perspectives"
      style="pulldown"
      icon="icons/jdg2e_perspectives.gif"
      tooltip="JDG2E: Open a perspective"
      class="com.ibm.jdg2e.actions.ShowPerspectivesAction"
      toolbarPath="com.ibm.jdg2e"
      id="com.ibm.jdg2e.actions.showperspectives">
    </action>
    <action
      definitionId=
      "com.ibm.jdg2e.actions.commands.samplecommand"
      label="&amp;Hello Action"
      icon="icons/jdg2eProd.gif"
      tooltip="JDG2E: Demonstrate accelerator key Shift+F11"
      class="com.ibm.jdg2e.actions.HelloAction"
```

```
            menubarPath="com.ibm.jdg2e/actionGroup"
            toolbarPath="com.ibm.jdg2e"
            id="com.ibm.jdg2e.actions.HelloAction">
      </action>
    </actionSet>
  </extension>
```

This example defines a menu and a set of two actions. One is a trivial version of Hello World, and the other adds a toolbar pull-down action that shows all available perspectives (providing a fast path to a similar platform action **Window > Open Perspective > Other...**). In all fairness, the Hello action is not quite so trivial because we defined an accelerator key for it. The link to the key is in the `definitionId` attribute. We will visit the topic of accelerator keys in more detail later in this chapter in Assigning Accelerator Keys to Your Actions.

The action set specifies the attribute `visible="true"`, meaning that the actions are visible in all perspectives. Unless that was your true intention, you would specify a value of `false`. We have defined our own menu with an id value of `com.ibm.jdg2e`, and the Hello action references it. We defined a `toolbarPath="com.ibm.jdg2e"`, and both actions reference it. They appear together in their own coolbar on the Workbench window toolbar (see Figure 21.4).

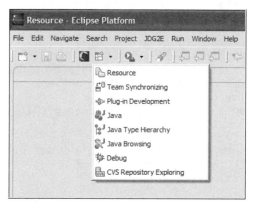

**Figure 21.4**  Show Perspectives Action Example

Examining our show perspectives action in more detail, you can see it is defined as a pull-down menu using the `style` attribute. The class `Show-PerspectivesAction` implements the `IWorkbenchWindowPulldownDelegate` interface, a subinterface of `IWorkbenchWindowActionDelegate`. Let's examine the implementation.

From the `IWorkbenchWindowActionDelegate` interface we implement the `init` method and use it to save an instance of Workbench window (`IWorkbenchWindow`). This allows us to get a reference to the Workbench (`IWorkbench`), which we will need later to retrieve the available perspectives.

```
public void init(IWorkbenchWindow window)  {
  this.window = window;
  workbench = window.getWorkbench();
}
```

We are not interested in the user selection (only the menu selection), so we ignore the `selectionChanged` method. Nor will we use the `run` method because we will perform our action in the pull-down menu selection (though your `run` method could act on the previous pull-down selection, if there is one). We will dynamically create our pull-down menu in the `getMenu` method and respond to user menu selections within it (in most other actions you will use the `run` method). The `getMenu` method implementation looks like this.

```
public Menu getMenu(Control parent) {
  IPerspectiveDescriptor[] perspectives =
    workbench.getPerspectiveRegistry().getPerspectives();
  if (menu != null)
    menu.dispose();
  menu = new Menu(parent);
  for (int j = 0; j < perspectives.length; j++) {
    MenuItem menuitem = new MenuItem(menu, SWT.NONE);
    menuitem.setText(perspectives[j].getLabel());
    menuitem.setImage(perspectives[j].
      getImageDescriptor().createImage());
    menuitem.setData(perspectives[j]);
    menuitem.addSelectionListener(new SelectionAdapter() {
      public void widgetSelected(SelectionEvent e) {
        perspective =
          (IPerspectiveDescriptor)e.widget.getData();
        try {
          workbench.
                showPerspective(perspective.getId(), window);
        } catch (WorkbenchException e1) {
          e1.printStackTrace();
        }
      }
    });
  }
  return menu;
}
```

First, we get an array of all the perspectives as `IPerspectiveDescriptor` objects by using the Workbench to get the perspectives registry. We now have a handle to all the perspectives. Note that we might have done this in the init method, but it's called only once. What if a perspective went away because the plug-in that owned the perspective was dynamically unloaded? This is a good time to mention that a handle to the Workbench as an IWorkbench object is quite useful. It gives you an anchor to all of the Workbench user interface. It can also be retrieved at any time from the static method PlatformUI.getWorkbench(). Next, we create the pull-down menu content by creating a Menu and adding to it a MenuItem for each perspective. As we create each menu item, we also add a selection listener for it.

We now have done enough to present the menu to the user, as shown in Figure 21.4. In the listener's widgetSelected method, we display the selected perspective with a single line of code, which requires us to provide the selected perspective, the Workbench, and the Workbench window:

```
workbench.showPerspective(perspective.getId(),window);
```

We are done! We have a handy little action extension with just a few lines of code.

Let's look at one more example. No doubt at times you have a dozen or maybe dozens of files open as a result of code exploring. Many are just open for examination. Let's explore the **File > JDG2E: Close Unmodified Files** action available on the CD-ROM in the project com.ibm.jdg2e.actions.ide. This action will close all files except those that have been updated and not yet saved. This time let's add the action to an existing menu, the Workbench **File** menu, and position it among the other **Close** actions by specifying this menubarPath.

```
menubarPath="file/close.ext"
```

We discovered this menu path in our friend IWorkbenchActionConstants. The purpose of the action is to close all open editors that contain unmodified content. Here is the code. Take a peek, and then let's review it.

```
public void init(IWorkbenchWindow window) {
  this.window = window;
}
public void run(IAction action) {
  execute(window);
}
public static void execute(IWorkbenchWindow window) {
  IWorkbenchPage[] pages = window.getPages();
  for (int i = 0; i < pages.length; i++) {
    IEditorReference[] editors =
      pages[i].getEditorReferences();
    for (int j = 0; j < editors.length; j++) {
      if (!editors[j].getEditor(true).isDirty()) {
        pages[i].closeEditor(editors[j].getEditor(true),
          false);
```

```
            }
          }
        }
      }
```

In the init method, we save a reference to the Workbench window, which is our path to the list of open editors. In the run method, we simply pass our reference to the Workbench window to a separate execute method that does all the work of retrieving all the open editors and closing any that are unmodified. You might be asking, "Why not do all the processing in the run method?" The reason is that we want to make this action available as a context menu in another Workbench part (read on!). Our action class really extends another abstract class that contains the execute method, which allows us to make the **JDG2E: Close Unmodified Files** action available elsewhere in the Workbench.

That's enough about action sets. Let's move on to another extension point.

### Defining Menu and Toolbar Actions Independent of Perspectives

There is a related extension point that is worth discussing briefly. The extension point org.eclipse.ui.actionSetPartAssociations is specialized, but very convenient when required. It allows you to define an action set that should appear if one or more views or editors are open in *any* perspective. Let's explain this with a Workbench example. The Java tools have a set of actions defining search functions that need to be available in several different views and the Java editor. This extension point does this for you. In the following extension definition, the action set is specified by using the targetID attribute. It is followed by the views and editor that this action set should be visible in.

```xml
<extension point="org.eclipse.ui.actionSetPartAssociations">
  <actionSetPartAssociation
    targetID="org.eclipse.jdt.ui.SearchActionSet">
    <part id="org.eclipse.jdt.ui.PackageExplorer" />
    <part id="org.eclipse.jdt.ui.TypeHierarchy" />
    <part id="org.eclipse.jdt.ui.CompilationUnitEditor" />
    <part id="org.eclipse.jdt.ui.ClassFileEditor" />
    <part id="org.eclipse.jdt.ui.ProjectsView" />
    <part id="org.eclipse.jdt.ui.PackagesView" />
    <part id="org.eclipse.jdt.ui.TypesView" />
    <part id="org.eclipse.jdt.ui.MembersView" />
    <part id="org.eclipse.search.SearchResultView" />
  </actionSetPartAssociation>
</extension>
```

If a user were to create or customize a perspective and include any of these views or the Java editor, the actions in `SearchActionSet` would appear.

## Contributing to the View's Menu and Toolbar

The extension point `org.eclipse.ui.viewActions` allows you to contribute actions to a view's menu and toolbar (see Chapter 18, Views). It is very similar to contributing to the Workbench menu and toolbar. In this extension point, you specify the view you are contributing to by using the `targetID` attribute. Your action class must implement the `IViewActionDelegate` interface. This interface adds an `init` method that provides a reference to the view as an `IViewPart` object.

We illustrate this with an example that defines a menu and a toolbar action that will appear in the Navigator view. The purpose of this action is to apply a filter to the view's tree viewer that displays only modified workspace resources and their parents. This allows you to easily see only what has been added or updated in the workspace since the filter was activated. The filter can be toggled on and off. Examining Figure 21.5, you can see the action is active because there is a check mark next to it in the menu. Our view shows only the new or modified projects in an otherwise busy workspace. As you can imagine, this can be a very handy action, especially if you are not using a repository like CVS to keep track of your updates. This example is on the CD-ROM in the project `com.ibm.jdg2e.actions.ide`. Here is our extension definition.

```
<extension
  id="com.ibm.jdg2e.actions.ide"
  name="JDG2E: View Actions"
  point="org.eclipse.ui.viewActions">
  <viewContribution
    targetID="org.eclipse.ui.views.ResourceNavigator"
    id="com.ibm.jdg2e.actions.ide.viewContribution1">
    <action
      state="false"
      style="toggle"
      id="com.ibm.jdg2e.actions.ide.action1"
      toolbarPath="additions"
      class="com.ibm.jdg2e.actions.ide.ShowModifiedAction"
      icon="icons/modified.gif"
      label="JDG2E: Show Modified"
      menubarPath="additions"
      tooltip="JDG2E: Show only modified resources">
    </action>
  </viewContribution>
</extension>
```

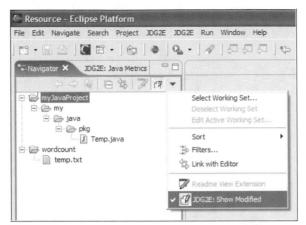

**Figure 21.5**   The Activated Show Modified Action in the Navigator View

Looking at our extension definition, you can see that our action is applied to the Navigator view as specified in the `targetID` attribute. The action itself is defined just like our earlier examples. It will appear in the view's pull-down menu and the toolbar. In this case, we have specified `style="toggle"` so the action toggles between active and inactive each time it is selected. We specify an initial state of inactive by using the `state="false"` attribute. The Navigator view permits other extensions to contribute actions to the menu and toolbar with the conventional path value of `additions`.

Frequently, the authors of a view will define their own menu and toolbar actions. If you contribute to the view, your actions are appended to existing ones but in the reverse order that they are defined in your extension definition.

This extension point does not provide direct access to the view's contents. For this extension point to be useful, the view must supply some sort of public API to the view's contents or its model. (We are in luck because this view offers the public method `ResourceNavigator.getTreeViewer`, permitting us access to the viewer and its contents.) If the view's author did not have contributions in mind, your choices are limited.

This extension point requires that we define an action class that extends `ActionDelegate` (offering us a `dispose` method we require) and implements `IViewActionDelegate`. We defined a class named `ShowModifiedAction` that extended the platform `ActionDelegate` class and specified it in our plug-in's extension. Consider extending this abstract class yourself. Our motivation for using it was the need for a `dispose` method, which this class provides. We also need a viewer filter, which requires us to extend `ViewerFilter` (see

Chapter 15, JFace Viewers). Our ShowModifiedFilter class takes care of that. Our action will add or remove the filter as the user toggles the action on and off in the Navigator view. The Navigator view responds to workspace additions and deletions but doesn't pay attention to resource updates. For updates to appear, we also need to include a resource change listener in our action so we can force a refiltering and refresh of the view's contents as files are modified and become candidates for our filter. (For more information on resource change listeners, see Chapter 23, Workspace Resource Programming).

Examining our action delegate, of the ShowModifiedAction class, we first implemented the init method, which in this interface supplies us with the view as a ViewPart object. All the setup is done here. As you can see in the upcoming code, we get access to the viewer, which our viewer filter needs. We obtain the current time, which we will pass on to our filter so we can compare it to the time stamp on workspace resources. You could enhance this to examine changes in the last day, week, or whatever. To do this you would probably want your own filter dialog. This implementation checks only for changes since the Navigator view was opened, which is normally when the Workbench is started. We create our filter and define a resource change listener, which requires our class to implement IResourceChangeListener and implement a resourceChanged method.

```
public void init(IViewPart view) {
  viewer = ((ResourceNavigator) view).getViewer();
  currentTime = System.currentTimeMillis();
  filter = new ShowModifiedFilter(currentTime);
   ResourcesPlugin.getWorkspace().
    addResourceChangeListener(this);
}
```

The run method toggles the filter on and off by adding or removing it from the viewer. Note that we expand the viewer's contents when the filter is on so all the modified resources are visible to the user.

```
public void run(IAction action) {
  if (filterOn) {
    filterOn = false;
    viewer.removeFilter(filter);
    viewer.collapseAll();
  } else {
    filterOn = true;
    viewer.addFilter(filter);
    viewer.expandAll();
  }
}
```

PART III

Lastly, our `resourceChanged` method responds to workspace changes. We want the view contents updated as files are updated (modifying and saving a file you are editing will pop that file into view). Refreshing the view when a resource change occurs will cause our filter to reevaluate what should be presented (the class's `dispose` method will remove this listener when it is no longer required).

```
public void resourceChanged(IResourceChangeEvent event) {
  if (filterOn) {
    viewer.refresh();
    viewer.expandAll();
  }
}
```

We won't examine the filter implementation (the `ShowModifiedFilter` class) because that is more relevant to JFace viewers, but you are welcome to examine it yourself.

## Contributing to an Editor's Menu and Toolbar

The extension point `org.eclipse.ui.editorActions` allows you to add editor actions to the menu bar and the toolbar. These contributions appear only if the target editor is active. The extension definition is nearly the same as `org.eclipse.ui.viewActions`. In this case, the `targetID` attribute specifies the identifier of the editor you are contributing to. Your extension's action class will implement `IEditorActionDelegate`. This interface adds the `setActiveEditor` method, which passes a reference to the editor that the action applies to.

Here is an example of a contribution to the Eclipse text editor that counts the number of words in some selected text. This toolbar action is enabled only when text has been selected (see Figure 21.6). The implementation is on the CD-ROM in project `com.ibm.jdg2e.actions.ide`. Let's look at the extension definition.

```
<extension
    point="org.eclipse.ui.editorActions">
  <editorContribution
    targetID="org.eclipse.ui.DefaultTextEditor"
    id="com.ibm.jdg2e.editorContribution.DefaultTextEditor">
    <action
      label="JDG2E: Word Count"
      icon="icons/sample.gif"
      tooltip="JDG2E: Show word count of selected text"
      class=
        "com.ibm.jdg2e.actions.ide.TextEditorWordCountAction"
```

```
            toolbarPath="additions"
            enablesFor="+"
            id="com.ibm.jdg2e.ec.TextEditorWordCount">
            <selection
              class="org.eclipse.jface.text.ITextSelection">
            </selection>
        </action>
      </editorContribution>
    </extension>
```

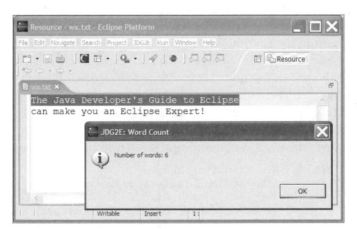

**Figure 21.6**    Example of the Word Count Text Editor Action

We specified the platform text editor by using the targetID attribute. The enablesFor attribute is defined and set to a plus (+) sign. As shown earlier in Table 21.2, this means our action is enabled for one or more selected items. Because this applies to a text editor, an item is a text character. If you try this, you will see that the action does not even enable on the toolbar until at least one character is selected. It does not appear at all when another type of editor is active. Observe that the extension uses the selection attribute to confine the contribution to a text selection, more specifically, an ITextSelection object. This means that the toolbar icon is disabled unless the user has selected some text in the default text editor. Let's examine the implementation.

The action class TextEditorWordCountAction implements IEditorAction-Delegate. Editor actions are shared by other instances of the same type of editor. If, for example, three default text editors are open, they are all using the same editor action instances on the toolbar. This sharing simplifies the Workbench code because it doesn't have to worry about duplicate entries. When the user activates (or reactivates) an editor, the Workbench invokes the `IEditorActionDelegate.setActiveEditor` method to tell the action which open editor the user is working in. The action saves the editor as a `TextEditor` so it can refer back to it in the `run` method if the user selects the action.

```
public void setActiveEditor
    (IAction action, IEditorPart targetEditor) {
  textEditor = (TextEditor) targetEditor;
}
```

The `selectionChanged` method shown next reports various states of the user selection on the system console. Why is this of any interest? Test the plug-in in the runtime Workbench by opening a file using the default text editor. Select some text. You should not see anything written to the host Workbench console by the `selectionChanged` method. Why is that? Your plug-in is not loaded! Eclipse has exposed your contribution based entirely on the XML in your plug-in manifest. Select some text again and then run the **JDG2E: Word Count** action; the console should light up with messages because the plug-in containing your action delegate is now loaded.

```
public void selectionChanged
    (IAction action, ISelection selection) {
  if (selection != null &&
    selection instanceof ITextSelection) {
    ITextSelection ts = (ITextSelection) selection;
    if (ts.getLength() == 0) {
      System.out.println("TextEditorWordCountAction disabled");
      action.setEnabled(false);
    } else {
      System.out.println("TextEditorWordCountAction enabled");
      action.setEnabled(true);
    }
  } else {
    System.out.println("TextEditorWordCountAction disabled");
    action.setEnabled(false);
  }
}
```

Finally, the work is done in the `run` method. Don't worry about the details of the text editor methods shown in the following code; we'll return to them in Chapter 26, Building a Custom Text Editor with JFace Text.

```
public void run(IAction action) {
  IDocument document =
  textEditor.getDocumentProvider().getDocument
    (textEditor.getEditorInput());
  ITextSelection ts =
    (ITextSelection) textEditor.
      getSelectionProvider().getSelection();
```

```
int tokenCount;
try {
  String text = document.get(ts.getOffset(), ts.getLength());
  tokenCount =
    new StringTokenizer(text, WORD_DELIMITERS).countTokens();
} catch (BadLocationException e) {
  tokenCount = 0;
}
MessageDialog.openInformation(
  null,
  "JDG2E: Word Count",
  "Number of words: " + tokenCount);
}
```

This example needs access to the document available from the text-
Editor that was saved in the setActiveEditor method. From the text-
Editor you obtain the document and get the text that the user selected as an
ITextSelection, which is a range of characters. (Yes, you also get the user
selection in the selectionChanged method. This is an alternative means of
retrieving the selection value.) Obtain a text string from ITextSelection
and use the Java StringTokenizer utility class to get a word count that is
reported by using a MessageDialog.

## Contributing Context Menus to Views and Editors

You contribute context or pop-up menus by using the org.eclipse.ui
.popupMenus extension point. It is very powerful and offers some unique
integration opportunities. You can contribute to the context menu of a view
or an editor by using the viewerContribution extension attribute.

You can also contribute to the context menu of a specific object type by
using the objectContribution attribute. When you contribute to an object
type, your action appears in the context menu of any and all view or editor
parts where that object is available. For example, if you defined an object
contribution for IResource objects (projects, files, and folders), your action
would be available on selections in the Navigator view *or any other view that
presents* IResource *objects*. In this way, you are assured that your action
appears in any current or future views that present objects you are interested
in. Pretty cool, huh?

You can apply all the filtering capabilities you learned earlier in this
chapter to ensure that your context menu action is enabled only where it
makes sense to do so. For context menu actions, you can also define visibility
conditions by using the visibility attribute. Visibility and enablement are
separate specifications in your plug-in manifest. You might define an action

that appears only on file objects that match your naming pattern. On the other hand, you might contribute an action that applies only to Java projects. A visibility condition applies to *all* the actions defined in your popup extension. The `visibility` attribute is specified as a child of the `viewerContribution` attribute and the `objectContribution` attribute.

You can only contribute to viewers in Workbench parts in which the author has permitted you to do so. Generally, it is a good practice to allow others to contribute to your views and editors. You must define context menus in code because they can't be defined in a plug-in extension. See Registering Context Menus with the Workbench in Chapter 18, Views, to see how to do this. Also, see the page titled "Table of Registered Context Menus" under the Reference topic in the online help for this book.

Let's examine in detail each of the three types of context menus you can define.

### Contributing a Context Menu to a View

When you contribute to the context menu of a view, you are contributing your actions to the context menu of its viewer. Recall from Chapter 8, Overview of the Eclipse Architecture, that the contents of a view or editor are normally seen by the user through its viewer. This is defined as a `viewerContribution`, which is specified in your extension definition. You specify the view's context menu identifier in your plug-in manifest file by using the `targetID` attribute followed by the actions you are contributing. The view's context menu identifier is, by convention, the identifier of the view, but it need not be. Your action must implement `IViewActionDelegate`, which includes an `init` method providing a reference to the view as an `IViewPart` object.

Here is an example. Recall that earlier we wanted to reuse our **JDG2E: Close Unmodified Files** action elsewhere. We decided to also make it a context menu action in the Navigator view, just for convenience. So anywhere in the view, no matter what is selected, this action will appear. The extension is straightforward.

```
<extension
    point="org.eclipse.ui.popupMenus">
  <viewerContribution
    targetID="org.eclipse.ui.views.ResourceNavigator"
    id="com.ibm.jdg2e.actions.ide.view.navigatorClose">
    <action
      label="JDG2E: Close Unmodified Files"
      class=
        "com.ibm.jdg2e.actions.ide.CloseUnmodifiedViewAction"
```

```
            menubarPath="additions"
            id="com.ibm.jdg2e.actions.ide.view.navigator">
        </action>
    </viewerContribution>
</extension>
```

The implementation follows a pattern similar to the one when we added this action to the Workbench **File** menu. In the run method, we took a different approach to retrieving a reference to the Workbench window and then simply delegated the work to the method named execute in our super class just as before. This way the real work of our action was reusable in another action extension.

```
public void run(IAction action) {
    this.window=
        PlatformUI.getWorkbench().getActiveWorkbenchWindow();
    execute(window);
}
```

## Contributing a Context Menu to an Editor

When you contribute to an editor's context menu, you are contributing to the editor's viewer. The next example defines the extension using viewer-Contribution in exactly the same way as previously in a view, with one exception: The action class will implement the same IEditorActionDelegate interface as when you contribute to the editor's menu or toolbar. This allows you to use the same action class in an editor's context menu, toolbar, or menu bar. Of course, to do this, you must specify this class in two different extension points: org.eclipse.ui.popupMenus and org.eclipse.ui.editorActions.

You specify the editor's context menu identifier in your plug-in manifest file by using the targetID attribute followed by the actions you are contributing. The identifier of the Workbench text editor is #TextEditorContext. The Java editor's context menu identifier is #CompilationUnitEditorContext.

Here is an example of a context menu contribution to the default text editor that is enabled when you have selected some text in your editor. It probably looks familiar. The editor action discussed earlier has been repackaged as a context menu. Selecting text in a text editor enables a context menu with the name **JDG2E:Word Count**.

```
<extension
    point="org.eclipse.ui.popupMenus">
  <viewerContribution
    targetID="#TextEditorContext"
    id="com.ibm.jdg2e.actions.ide.TextEditorContext">
    <action
      label="JDG2E: Word Count"
```

```
            class=
              "com.ibm.jdg2e.actions.ide.TextEditorWordCountAction"
            menubarPath="additions"
            enablesFor="+"
            id="com.ibm.jdg2e.pm.TextEditorWordCount">
            <selection
              class="org.eclipse.jface.text.ITextSelection">
            </selection>
          </action>
        </viewerContribution>
      </extension>
```

## Contributing a Context Menu to Selected Objects in a View or Editor

Object contribution is the most common use of this extension point because you can specify an action once and it will appear in all views or editors, present and future, in which the selected object(s) appears. This has tremendous integration value. Your action class will implement IObjectAction-Delegate. This interface adds the setActivePart method and provides a reference to the action and Workbench part. Using the extension's objectClass attribute, you can specify in what class of objects your context menu should appear. The action can be filtered to a set of object instances that interest you. The nameFilter attribute allows you to filter by name (if applicable). An action expression, as discussed earlier, allows you to do much finer filtering and is a powerful tool when applied to an object contribution.

Actually, we covered this extension point in some detail in Chapter 7, Extending Eclipse for Fun and Profit, which introduced Eclipse extensibility. Recall that this was the example where we added context menus to a member of a Java class that allowed you to adjust its visibility (named **JDG2E: Modifiers**). This was our first lesson in Eclipse extensibility. If want to brush up on that example, go back to Chapter 7 and read How to Extend Objects Like Those Shown in the Outline View.

Our final example, the **Run Ant** action, comes from Eclipse itself. The visibility attribute is interesting and has been set in bold in the following code. The nameFilter attribute tells us that the action appears on XML files. The use of the visibility and objectState attributes specifies that the action is visible only if the first XML attribute in the file has a value of project, which distinguishes it as an Ant script.

```
      <objectContribution
        adaptable="true"
        objectClass="org.eclipse.core.resources.IFile"
        nameFilter="*.xml"
        id="org.eclipse.ant.ui.RunAnt">
```

```
<visibility>
  <objectState
    name="xmlFirstTag"
    value="project">
  </objectState>
</visibility>
<action
  label="%PopupMenu.runAnt"
  class=
    "org.eclipse. ... .AntRunActionDelegate"
  tooltip="%PopupMenu.runAntTip"
  menubarPath="additions"
  enablesFor="1"
  id="org.eclipse.ant.ui.RunAntAction">
</action>
</objectContribution>
```

In this example, the extension attribute named `adaptable` is worth noting. It handles a special situation. When you specify `adaptable="true"` in your action extension, it means that the object is adaptable to a workspace object (`IResource`; see Chapter 23, Workspace Resource Programming). Generally, the `adaptable` attribute is used to allow actions to appear in the Navigator view and the Package Explorer view for the same resource. You avoid having to implement the action twice, once for each object type.

This attribute can have a value of `true` or `false`. It is applicable only when an object contribution applies to an `IResource` or its subclasses. When the attribute is `true`, it means that your action will apply to the specified `IResource` object *and* any object that is adaptable to an `IResource` object. Why is this interesting? Let's consider an example to better appreciate this attribute.

In the Java and PDE perspectives, the Package Explorer view lists projects, packages, Java classes, and other files. In this view, Java classes look like files, and you can edit them like files, but they are not files. They are actually instances of `ICompilationUnit`, a member of the model that the JDT uses to represent Java classes (see Chapter 27, Extending the Java Development Tools). An `ICompilationUnit` is derived from a file and can, when requested by using the `IAdaptable` protocol, return its underlying file. In other words, it is adaptable to an `IFile` object, a subclass of `IResource`.

Because `adaptable="true"` is specified in this example, when your action processes the selected objects, you will have to convert these "adaptable" objects to an `IResource` object or one of its subclasses. The `selectionChanged` method contains the code that handles this. The relevant code is highlighted in the following snippet.

```
public void selectionChanged(IAction action,
    ISelection selection) {
  ArrayList newFiles = new ArrayList();
```

```
IFile file = null;
if (selection != null &&
   selection instanceof IStructuredSelection) {
  IStructuredSelection ss = (IStructuredSelection) selection;
  for (Iterator iter = ss.iterator(); iter.hasNext();) {
    Object obj = iter.next();
    if (obj instanceof IFile) {
      file = (IFile) obj;
    } else if (obj instanceof IAdaptable) {
      IAdaptable a = (IAdaptable) obj;
      IResource res =
        (IResource) a.getAdapter(IResource.class);
      if (res instanceof IFile)
        file = (IFile) res;
    }
    if (file != null
      && !file.isSynchronized(IResource.DEPTH_ZERO)) {
      newFiles.add(file);
    }
  }
}
if (newFiles.isEmpty()) {
  selectedFiles = null;
  action.setEnabled(false);
} else {
  selectedFiles =
    (IFile[]) newFiles.toArray(new IFile[newFiles.size()]);
  action.setEnabled(true);
}
}
```

## Additional Enablement Filtering for Object Contributions

Additional functionality in the pop-up menus extension point allows you to create more sophisticated enablement conditions for actions defined as object contributions. In addition to the attributes objectClass, objectState, plugin-State, and systemProperty, there are instanceof, test, systemTest, equals, count, with, resolve, adapt, and iterate attributes. For example, the test attribute allows you to test the property state of the selected object. A property is defined in the extension point org.eclipse.core.expressons.property-Testers. In this extension point, you can define some property for an object. When the property tester is called, it returns a Boolean. This is similar to action filters (IActionFilter interface) except that you can define a property for objects you don't own, which is not true for action filters.

For example, you could define a property on a workspace file (IFile). Perhaps you want to define a "refresh required" property, meaning that your extension will return false if a workspace file is not in sync with the file system. An action could include this property test as an enablement condition.

This extension point could easily help you avoid the issue of preloading your plug-in just to enable your actions correctly.

For a complete description of these additional elements, examine the extension point documentation for pop-up menus and property testers.

## Assigning Accelerator Keys to Your Actions

Power users are accustomed to having accelerator keys available for frequently used actions. Moreover, they want to be able to assign their own key combinations. This is discussed in Chapter 2, Getting Started with Eclipse. Eclipse has evolved support for accelerator keys with each version. Initially, they were hard-coded in the actions. This had many disadvantages, such as duplicate key assignments and lack of user control. The current support is quite flexible for both the user and plug-in extensions. In this section, we cover the basic concepts of accelerator keys and show a simple example. If you want to pursue this subject, you should also read the "Workbench key Bindings" topic in the *Platform Plug-in Developer Guide* in the Eclipse online help.

An accelerator key or key binding is not defined in an action contribution extension. It is defined by using a command, which is a separate extension point named `org.eclipse.ui.commands`. A command defines a semantic action like **File > Open** or **File > Close**. You and other developers can associate your actions with an existing command, or you can create your own. Platform commands are defined in the `org.eclipse.ui` plug-in. Figure 21.7 shows a sampling of predefined commands.

A particular key binding is defined in a command extension, and you associate your action with that command. Key bindings can be grouped together into configuration sets, which are also defined in the commands extension. Eclipse defines two configurations named Default and Emacs. The latter offers Emacs users a set of familiar accelerator keys. In addition, key assignments can be context-sensitive, which means that the key binding might apply only in the situation or context in which a user is operating. Yet another extension point named `org.eclipse.ui.contexts` is used for this purpose. The platform predefines several contexts such as **In Dialogs**, **In Windows**, **In Dialogs and Windows**, **Editing Text**, **Editing Java Source**. One context might extend another. The debug component adds other contexts such as **Debugging** and **Debugging Java Source**.

Let's get back to our original objective of assigning an accelerator key to an action. Earlier in this chapter, we reviewed a Workbench menu action

**Figure 21.7**   Some of the Many Commands Defined by the Platform

extension named **JDG2E: Close Unmodified Files**. Wouldn't it be nice to define a key sequence for this action that matches up nicely with the existing **Close** and **Close All** menu actions? These actions are assigned the **Ctrl+F4** and **Ctrl+Shift+F4** key sequences, respectively. Through a little trial and error we determined that the key sequence **Shift+F4** is not assigned to the default key binding configuration. We will define a command that contains our key binding specification and associate our action with the command. Here is how it would look in our plug-in manifest. The relevant XML is highlighted in bold. Some XML is irrelevant and has been omitted.

```
<extension
   point="org.eclipse.ui.actionSets">
  <actionSet
    <action
      definitionId=
        "com.ibm.jdg2e.actions.ide.commands.close"
      label="JDG2E: Close Unmodified Files"
      class=
        "com. … .CloseUnmodifiedWorkbenchAction"
```

```
            tooltip="JDG2E: Close all unmodified files"
            menubarPath="file/close.ext"
            id="com.ibm.jdg2e.actions.ide.action1">
        </action>
      </actionSet>
    </extension>
    <extension
        point="org.eclipse.ui.commands">
      <category
        name="JDG2E: IDE Commands and Keybindings"
        id="com.ibm.jdg2e.actions.ide.commands.category">
      </category>
      <command
        name="JDG2E: Close Unmodified Files"
        categoryId=
          "com.ibm.jdg2e.actions.ide.commands.category"
        id="com.ibm.jdg2e.actions.ide.commands.close">
      </command>
      <keyBinding
        commandId="com.ibm.jdg2e.actions.ide.commands.close"
        contextId="org.eclipse.ui.contexts.dialogAndWindow"
        keySequence="Shift+F4"
        keyConfigurationId=
          "org.eclipse.ui.defaultAcceleratorConfiguration">
      </keyBinding>
    </extension>
```

The link from the action to our command is specified in the `definitionId` attribute in our action extension. That points to our command extension. In the command extension, we define our command, and our key binding is specified by using the `command` and `keybinding` attributes. Observe that our key assignment has been defined by using the `keySequence` attribute. We have defined our key assignment to be global in scope by associating it with the `contextId` named `org.eclipse.ui.contexts.dialogAndWindow` and associating it with the default key assignment configuration defined by the platform. Figure 21.8 displays our key assignment in the Preferences dialog.

Only the `actionSets` extension point allows linking of an action to its command in your plug-in manifest. For other actions, you will need to do this in code. It is a two-step process. First, you associate the action with the command extension by using the method `IAction.setActionDefinitionId(String id)`. Second, you register the action with the platform. This registration is done through platform key binding service available to views and editors. From a view or editor, use the following code.

```
getSite().getKeyBindingService.registerAction(yourAction);
```

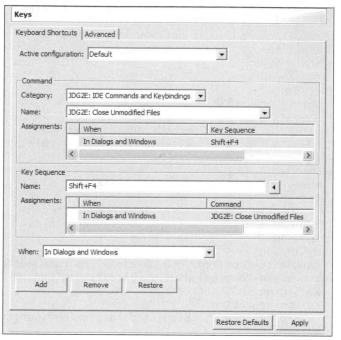

**Figure 21.8**    Key Assignment for **JDG2E: Close Unmodified** Action

## Example Summary

The examples have been thoroughly discussed in this chapter. The projects of interest are named com.ibm.jdg2e.actions and com.ibm.jdg2e.actions.ide. The project com.ibm.jdg2e.action.ide contains actions that require the Eclipse IDE Workbench.

## Chapter Summary

The action contributions framework distinguishes itself by allowing you to contribute to the work of others. This is a very effective integration and extensibility feature of Eclipse. You can contribute to the menu bars, toolbars, and context menus in the Workbench, its views, and editors. Object contributions allow you to add context menus to objects of interest in any view or editor that presents those objects. You have seen a rich variety of filtering mechanisms that allow you to refine when and whether your action is available. The API is reasonably consistent across all of the extension points we discussed that use some form of IActionDelegate. Your action contributions present themselves in the user interface without loading your code until the user chooses to run your action.

At this point, you should understand how easy it is to define action contributions. They will be a cornerstone of your integration activities with Eclipse.

## References

Arthorne, John, and Chris Laffra. 2004. *Official Eclipse 3.0 FAQs*. Boston, MA: Addison-Wesley. http://eclipsefaq.org. (See Chapter 12 FAQs 218–236 and FAQs 126, 191, 202, 213, 246, 309.)

See the page titled "Table of Registered Context Menus" under the Reference topic in the book's online help.

# CHAPTER 22

## Providing Help

At some point when using an application you realize you have to swallow your pride and request help by looking for some online assistance. Let's face it—every application needs to have online documentation. It is a required task of any tool development effort. Yet it is often relegated to the role of the forgotten child of the software development process. Eclipse puts the Help system on equal footing by including it in its integration architecture. In fact, integrating help documentation is an easy first step towards Eclipse integration because all you need to provide, in addition to the help content, is some simple XML for your plug-in. Your help content can be a set of HTML files or a PDF file. The Eclipse frameworks supports the following kinds of help.

- Integrated help documentation

  The online help documentation you provide for your tool integrates with online documentation from other providers, including Eclipse. By selecting **Help > Help Contents**, an Eclipse user sees all the books integrated together on one online bookshelf in the help window. You also get to take advantage of the search engine without any additional work because all integrated help documents are included in the search. The Advanced Search dialog includes your books, should your users want to customize their search to just your product-specific books. You do not have to code any special indexing tags.

- Context-sensitive help

  This is the type of help that appears when the user presses **F1** in Eclipse. You integrate context-sensitive help with Eclipse in a plug-in. The end user invokes context-sensitive help by pressing **F1**. This displays an **infopop**, a small pop-up window that contains information specific to the context that has focus. The content of the infopop contains links to the online doc.

  In Eclipse, you can run the help in a standalone mode. That is, you can leverage the Help system to display your help content outside of Eclipse without any changes to your help content files. In fact, you'll find that the online documentation for Eclipse at http://eclipse.org uses this capability, giving you the exact same help interface across the Web that you have locally.

- Translation of help content into multiple national languages

  You can provide translation packs for multiple languages. See Chapter 31, Internationalization and Accessibility.

- Search

  Eclipse uses the Jakarta Lucene search engine. Lucene is an open source project that has produced a full-featured search engine that indexes documents for fast retrieval (see http://jakarta.apache.org/lucene). It is designed for use in a variety of different applications across many platforms; therefore, it is ideal for Eclipse. This engine is used to index the set of integrated help documents. Lucene uses text analyzers that result in case-insensitive searches. The Help system includes analyzers for English (locale en) and German (locale de).

- A standalone Help system

  Allows users to access the Help system over the Internet or an intranet.

- Active help

  Active help looks like a hyperlink in the online documentation. However, the link invokes code in a plug-in. Use Active help as an alternative to guiding the user to a toolbar or menu action selection.

- Dynamic help

  The `org.eclispe.help.contentProducer` is an extension point used to generate help documentation at runtime. The plug-in contributing to dynamic help must include a Java class that implements the `IHelpContentProducer` interface. The Help system will call the method `getInputStream` for each document referenced by this plug-in. The content producer is also called when the Help system is building the search index, making the dynamic help content-searchable.

## Integrating Your Online Documentation

As mentioned, when you integrate your online documentation with Eclipse, users can easily find your documentation by selecting **Help > Help Contents**. For example, the help solution code on the CD-ROM produces the Help Table of Contents shown in Figure 22.1.

**Figure 22.1** Help Contents with Integrated Online Help

As you can see, the new entry **JDG2E: Help Example TOC** was added to the overall Help Table of Contents provided by Eclipse. The online documentation created in the solution is integrated with the other Eclipse books, such as the *Workbench User Guide*.

Follow the steps below to define your own documentation plug-in to integrate your online documentation with Eclipse.

1. Create the help content as HTML files and store them in your plug-in directory (a subdirectory of the plugins directory). The Eclipse naming convention is to use doc in the name of the plug-in and the plug-in directory. For example, the plug-in named org.eclipse.pde.doc.user contains the user documentation for the PDE. If there are many files, we recommend creating a ZIP file named doc.zip. This ZIP file must be in your documentation plug-in directory. Eclipse will first look for a doc.zip file and then the plug-in subdirectory for the appropriate HTML files.

2. Declare the Help Table of Contents in your plug-in using the `org.eclipse.help.toc` extension point and specify the table of contents files.

3. Create the table of contents files by linking the topics together.

The following sections describe these steps.

### Creating Help Content as HTML Content

If you are integrating your tool with Eclipse, you may already have the HTML files written that comprise the online documentation. If so, you just need to write the files that describe the table of contents, and then form the navigational links by writing a series of XML files. If you currently use JavaHelp, the XML file format is different from Eclipse and JavaHelp and you will need another set of XML files. However, you do not have to modify the HTML help content files; simply place them in your help plug-in directory or in `doc.zip`.

### Declaring the Help Extension

The second step is to tell Eclipse that you have online documentation to contribute. The extension point named `org.eclipse.help.toc` is used to list the XML files that contain table of contents information. Create a `plugin.xml` file that uses this extension point, as shown in the following example. The Eclipse standard practice is to create documentation-only plug-ins. Given this convention, the `plugin.xml` file only deals with the help documentation. The configuration markup for the following XML can be found in the online documentation *Platform Plug-in Developer Guide*.

Using the `toc` tag, specify each table of contents file required. The order of the files doesn't matter. These entries only declare the table of contents files; you will define the structure and order later. In the following example, you can see that the table of contents is based on the files `DialogTOC.xml`, `ViewTOC.xml`, `MoreTOC.xml`, and `TestToc.xml`.

```
<extension point="org.eclipse.help.toc">
    <toc file="DialogTOC.xml"/>
    <toc file="ViewTOC.xml"/>
    <toc file="MoreTOC.xml"/>
    <toc
        file="TestToc.xml"
        primary="true"
        extradir="lab">
    </toc>
</extension>
```

When describing the table of contents, you can use one or more XML table of contents files. For instance, suppose you have a team of writers who each have an area of expertise. You can assign writers ownership of their own table of contents and include them all together in a higher level or primary table of contents using the `primary` attribute. In the example, `TestToc.xml` is the primary table of contents file. The primary file describes the structure and order of the other files by linking them together. The label **JDG2E: Help Example TOC** is displayed to the user as the table of contents label because of the attribute `primary`. Figure 22.2 shows the contents of `TestToc.xml` file.

```xml
<?xml version="1.0" encoding="UTF-8"?>
<?NLS TYPE="org.eclipse.help.toc"?>
<toc label="JGD2E: Help Example TOC">
  <link toc="DialogTOC.xml"/>
  <link toc="ViewTOC.xml"/>
  <anchor id="moreLabs"/>
</toc>
```

**TestToc.xml**

**MoreToc.xml**

```xml
<?xml version="1.0" encoding="UTF-8"?>
<?NLS TYPE="org.eclipse.help.toc"?>
<toc link_to="TestToc.xml#moreLabs"
  label="More interesting labs>
  <topic label="JDT Main Topic" href="html/maintopic.html">
<topic label="JDT Sub Topic" href="html/subtopic.html"/>
  </topic>
  <topic label="Extra Topic" href="lab/doc1/info1.html">
<topic label="Using the extradir attrib"
href="lab/doc2/info2.html">
  </topic>
</toc>
```

**Figure 22.2** Anchor Tags and `link` Attributes

There is an `extradir` attribute that can be specified in the `toc` element that tells Eclipse to also use another directory for finding help-related files. You can only use one `extradir` attribute per table of contents entry and you can only specify one directory, but the help search also accesses and indexes its subdirectories. In the example above, the `extradir` attribute is used to indicate that the `lab` directory and its subdirectories contain help content to display and index.

PART III

### Creating Table of Contents Files

In addition to the `plugin.xml` file, you need to create the table of contents files. These files list the strings or labels that the user will see in the online documentation.

The table of contents files also associate these strings with the applicable HTML files that contain the help pages. For example, the contents of the `DialogTOC.xml` file, as shown below, list the topic label **Dialog Main Topic**, and this label is displayed in the Help window. When the end user selects the label, the HTML file named `maintopic.html` appears in the Contents pane. Similarly, when the user selects the label **Dialog Sub Topic**, the content in the `subtopic.html` file is displayed. The `href` attribute can also be used to reference help content in a PDF file. The label **Dialog Table of Contents** is not shown to the user because `DialogTOC.xml` was not labeled as the primary table of contents file.

```
<?xml version="1.0" encoding="UTF-8"?>
<?NLS TYPE="org.eclipse.help.toc"?>

<toc label="Dialog Table of Contents" topic="html/toc.html">
  <topic label="Dialog Main Topic"  href="html/maintopic.html">
    <topic label="Dialog Sub Topic" href="html/subtopic.html"/>
  </topic>
  <topic label="Main Topic 2"/>
</toc>
```

The `link` attribute, shown in Figure 22.2, is used to bring in or link together the table of contents entries specified in the XML files. The primary table of contents file, `TestToc.xml`, links the `DialogTOC.xml` and `ViewTOC.xml` files.

Another way to specify table of contents entries is with the `anchor` tag. The anchor serves as a symbolic placeholder. An author uses this symbolic name in an XML file to indicate where to insert the entries. For example, in Figure 22.2, the file `TestToc.xml` contains an anchor called `moreLabs` that allows additional lab-related table of contents entries to be inserted. In the file `MoreToc.xml`, the `link_to` attribute uses that anchor to add more labels. Therefore, the anchor and the `link_to` attributes work together.

You can reference files in other subdirectories under the `plugins` directory by using path notation and the plug-in id in the `href` tag, for example, `href="../other.plugin.id/docs/aFile.html" />`. This assumes that your plug-in id and directory names are the same.

While developing your online help content, it is likely that you will also be updating your XML files. Note that the Help system caches the index created by the search engine in the metadata directory. *Hint:* When you begin a new test of your online help, remember to delete the cached index to verify the modifications to your XML file. Otherwise, you will test your Help system and searches will fail because they will not include your new files. The cached index is located in the appropriate language subdirectory under \eclipse\configuration\org.eclipse.help.base\index\en_US. When your development is complete and you are ready to ship the updated help plug-in, remember to change the version number on the plug-in to regenerate the index.

As you create the XML files, it is a good idea to establish your naming conventions and a strategy up front for how the files link together, since there isn't a graphical view available that can show all the links and symbolic anchor points. It is common practice to store programming source code in a change management system, and it is equally advisable to store your help content under change control as well. This practice will help ensure that the XML and HTML file modifications are coordinated as a set.

When you have completed development of your help plug-in, you will have a collection of files as shown in Figure 22.3. It is probable that you will have many HTML files for your help content. We recommend that you create an archive file to easily distribute the help content. For example, compress the files into a doc.zip file. In this case, your plug-in directory will contain the HTML help content files in an archive file, the plugin.xml file specifying the use of the help extension point, and one or more XML files that specify the table of contents.

### Eclipse Online Documentation

The online documentation included with Eclipse also uses the help extension. The primary table of contents file in each case is called toc.xml. The HTML files are distributed in a doc.zip file. By convention, the plug-in subdirectory name and the plug-in id contain doc in the name. The Eclipse documentation plug-ins are

- org.eclipse.jdt.doc.isv
- org.eclipse.jdt.doc.user
- org.eclipse.pde.doc.user
- org.eclipse.platform.doc.isv
- org.eclipse.platform.doc.user

PART III

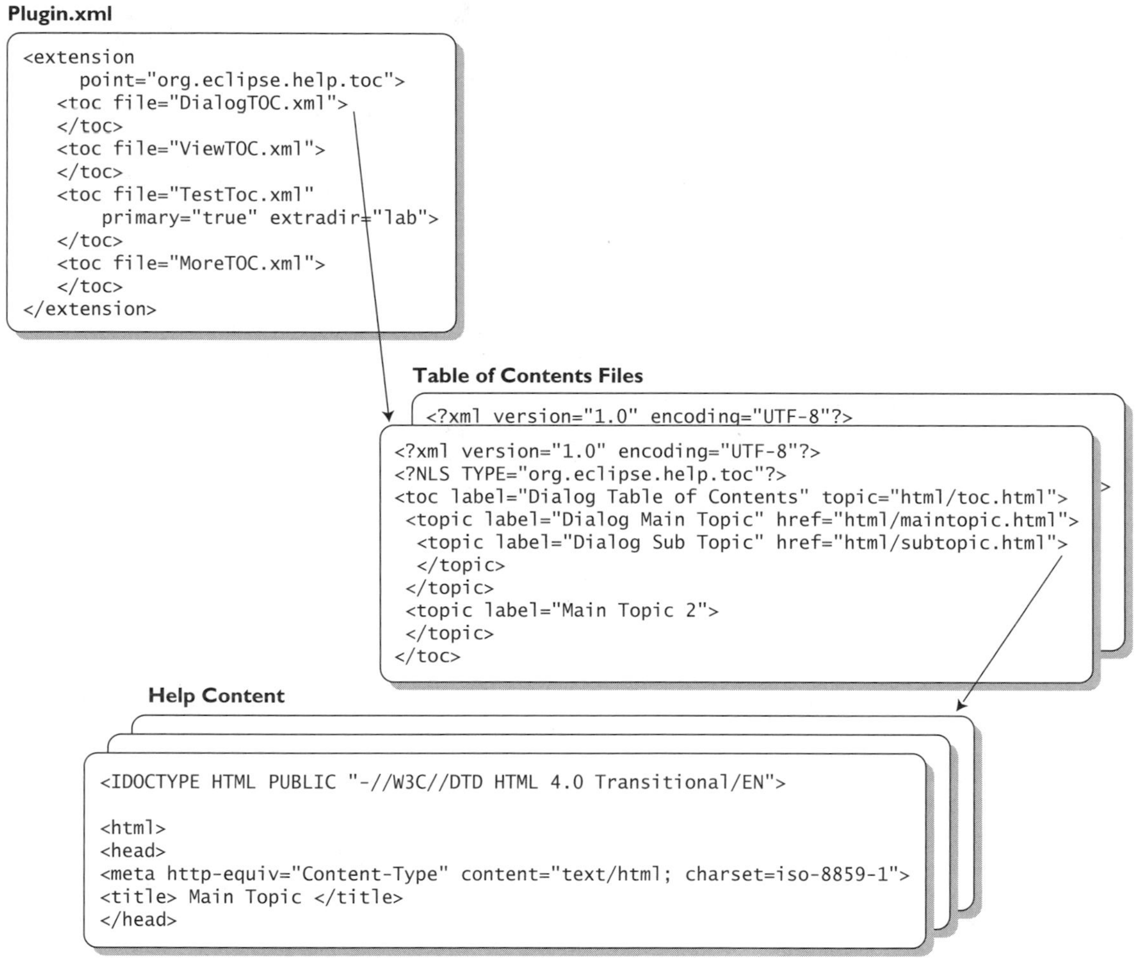

**Plugin.xml**

```
<extension
    point="org.eclipse.help.toc">
  <toc file="DialogTOC.xml">
  </toc>
  <toc file="ViewTOC.xml">
  </toc>
  <toc file="TestToc.xml"
      primary="true" extradir="lab">
  </toc>
  <toc file="MoreTOC.xml">
  </toc>
</extension>
```

**Table of Contents Files**

```
<?xml version="1.0" encoding="UTF-8"?>
```

```
<?xml version="1.0" encoding="UTF-8"?>
<?NLS TYPE="org.eclipse.help.toc"?>
<toc label="Dialog Table of Contents" topic="html/toc.html">
 <topic label="Dialog Main Topic" href="html/maintopic.html">
  <topic label="Dialog Sub Topic" href="html/subtopic.html">
  </topic>
 </topic>
 <topic label="Main Topic 2">
 </topic>
</toc>
```

**Help Content**

```
<IDOCTYPE HTML PUBLIC "-//W3C//DTD HTML 4.0 Transitional/EN">

<html>
<head>
<meta http-equiv="Content-Type" content="text/html; charset=iso-8859-1">
<title> Main Topic </title>
</head>
```

**Figure 22.3**    Structure of Help Files

## Creating Context-Sensitive Help

You can add context-sensitive help to your user interface. To invoke context-sensitive help, the user sets the focus to a JFace or SWT widget and presses **F1**. An infopop with textual information and reference links is displayed (see Figure 22.4).

There are three steps to create context help.

1. Declare the help context extension.
2. Define the contents of the infopop by creating a contexts.xml file.
3. Associate the infopop with the UI context.

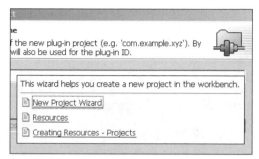

**Figure 22.4**   Sample Infopop

The following sections describe these steps.

### Declaring the Help Context Extension

You must specify your own context help by using the `org.eclipse.help`
`.contexts` extension point in your `plugin.xml` file. The sample plugin.xml
below specifies that context help and the context ids will be provided in a file
called `HelpContexts.xml`.

```
<extension point="org.eclipse.help.contexts">
  <contexts
    name-"HelpContexts.xml">
  </contexts>
</extension>
```

### Defining the Contents of the Infopop

For each unique infopop, you will need to define a unique context id. The
context id is how you reference the infopop in your Java code. When defining
the infopop, you also specify the text and any reference links you may want to
provide. For example, the XML below specifies the context id `viewContextId`.
The infopop will contain descriptive text and three reference links to other
HTML files. The HTML files only contain the help content; they do not contain any Eclipse-specific information.

```
<?xml version="1.0" encoding="UTF-8"?>
<contexts>
  <context id="viewContextId" >
    <description>Demonstrate Context Help </description>
    <topic href="contexts/RelatedContext3.html"
      label="Lab Help Related Topic 3"/>
    <topic href="contexts/RelatedContext4.html"
      label="Lab Help Related Topic 4"/>
```

```
      <topic href="../com.ibm.jdg2e.help/html/subtopic.html"
        label="Ref other plug-in"/>
    </context>
  </contexts>
```

## Associating the Infopop with the UI Context

The third step requires associating the context id with the applicable user interface context. Let's look at how to apply context-sensitive help to three examples: a text field within a dialog page, a view, and an action. First, let's add context help to a dialog page. Start with the dialog page class by defining a static string to represent the context id. Create a string that concatenates the plug-in id with the context id specified in the contexts.xml file. Using the plug-in id in the context id string is a recommended practice to improve maintainability.

```
public class MyBasicWizardPage1 extends WizardPage {
private static final String CONTEXT_HELP_ID =
  "com.ibm.lab.help.viewContextId";
}
```

In the dialog's createControl method, use the WorkbenchHelp.setHelp static method to assign help to the control. For example, in the createControl code, a text field named fileText is added to the wizard page. Using the WorkbenchHelp class, the fileText text field is assigned the context-sensitive help associated to the CONTEXT_HELP_ID string.

```
public void createControl(
  org.eclipse.swt.widgets.Composite parent)
{
    …
    fileText = new Text(container, SWT.BORDER | SWT.SINGLE);
    WorkbenchHelp.setHelp(fileText,CONTEXT_HELP_ID);
}
```

When the focus is on the fileText text field, pressing **F1** will display the context help.

Creating context help for a view is very similar. The plugin.xml and contexts.xml files are the same. In the view, you modify the createPartControl method to set the help using the WorkbenchHelp.setHelp method, just like the createControl method for the dialog page.

Creating context help for a contributed action is actually a little easier. Actions have a property for the context id. Edit the plug-in's action extension and set the helpContextId attribute to a string concatenating the plug-in id and the context id.

If the action is written programmatically by extending `Action`, associate a help listener to the action by using the `setHelpListener` method. A help listener receives a help event when **F1** is pressed. To handle the event, implement the `helpRequested` method and display the contextual help.

```
addAction.setHelpListener(new HelpListener() {
  public void helpRequested(HelpEvent event) {
    System.out.println("Help requested on add action");
    WorkbenchHelp.displayHelp(contextId);
  }
});
```

You can assign a context id to a widget that does not accept focus, but contains other widgets, such as a group or other type of container. This allows you to define reference links once, and all the widgets contained in that group or container inherit them. In other words, when the user presses **F1** on any widget within that group or container, context help is displayed.

For a very complex application, you may have a large number of context ids. To manage the complexity better, define all of the static context id strings in one Java interface, just as is done for many other constants. For more useful names, we recommend that the string help identify the context itself. When defining your context ids, make sure they contain the plug-in id. In the following example, compa refers to component A of a large project. In the example, the context id COMPA_NEW_WIZARD_ADDBUTTON indicates that it applies to the **Add** button. The following is a sample interface file.

```
public interface SampleContextIds {
  public static final String COMPA_PLUGIN_ID = "com.ibm.compa";
  public static final String COMPA_NEW_WIZARD =
    COMPA_PLUGIN_ID + ".NEWWIZ";
  public static final String
    COMPA_NEW_WIZARD_NAME = COMPA_PLUGIN_ID + ".WIZARDNAME";
  public static final String
    COMPA_NEW_WIZARD_ADDBUTTON =
      COMPA_PLUGIN_ID + ".WIZARDADDBUTTON";
}
```

You may have noticed that Eclipse does not have help push buttons in its wizards or dialogs. The Eclipse usability philosophy is that wizards and dialogs should be designed so they are intuitive enough not to need help. That is, there is a fundamental design flaw if you need a help button to describe how to use a wizard, because the whole point of the wizard is to handhold a user through a task. However, if users need help on a focused item in the wizard, they can press **F1** to see context-sensitive help in the form of an infopop. In the case of views, the same argument applies. For editors, the addition of functional add-ons such as context assist is much more helpful than including online help. In general, the expectation is that you would have a limited set of infopops and not necessarily provide one for every widget. However, Eclipse is flexible enough to handle the gamut of documentation standards.

## Running the Standalone Help Infocenter

You can invoke the Eclipse Help system from any Java program independent from Eclipse. This is called "standalone" mode. There aren't any changes to the help content; it remains implemented as a series of plug-ins. To run the Help system standalone, you simply use the Platform Runtime Binary version of Eclipse as opposed to the SDK (which is available on eclipse.org) and invoke the main method in the class org.eclipse.help.internal.standalone .StandaloneHelp. This invokes help as a separate nonintegrated Java application. You must pass the location of the plugins directory, which includes the online content, as a parameter. Additional information on running standalone help can be found in the Eclipse online documentation.

## Customizing Your Help System

Eclipse includes a default Help system plug-in, org.eclipse.help. In this plug-in directory, there are help preference settings saved in the preferences.ini file. You can customize these settings to suit your taste, your product, or company branding needs. For example, you may want to specify your own banner (the graphic banner displayed at the top of the Help view). The default banner displays the word "Eclipse" and its logo. You can also customize the initial page that Eclipse shows when help is requested and the order of the books on the bookshelf. To do this, you need to override the defaults in the help plug-in. This can be done as part of a product configuration, which can define a customization file. The name plugin_customization.ini is often used as the file name. So, if you have a custom product banner in mybanner.html that you want to use in the help system user interface, add the following lines to the active plugin_customization.ini file. For more information about packaging, see Chapter 13, Defining Features and Products.

```
org.eclipse.help.base/banner=
   /com.ibm.jdg2e.rcp.simple.exercisebanner.html
org.eclipse.help/banner_height=40
```

Another worthwhile class to be aware of is HelpSystem. This class has a set of static methods that provide direct access to help content that was defined in the extension points org.eclipse.help.toc and org.eclipse .help.contexts.

- IContext getContext(String contextID) computes and returns context information.
- InputStream getHelpContent (String href) returns an open stream on the contents of the specified help resource.
- IToc[] getTocs() returns a list all tables of contents that are available.

You can change the Eclipse search behavior by providing your own analyzer and defining it to Eclipse by using the extension point org.eclipse.help base.luceneAnalyzer. Text analyzers are unique for each language; therefore, when using this extension point you must specify the locale and the name of the Java class for the analyzer. The Java class must subclass org.apache .lucene.analysis.Analyzer.

## Example Summary

As illustrated in Figure 22.1, your own online documentation integrates easily with the Eclipse documentation. The sample code provided on the CD-ROM in project com.ibm.jdg2e.help includes sample help HTML files, the Table of Contents files, and the plug-in definition. Take a moment and browse through these files to reinforce the concepts of the chapter, or feel free to use them as a starting point for developing your own integrated help. The online help for this book is in project com.ibm.jdg2e.infocenter_3.0.0.

## Chapter Summary

When you are developing your product using Eclipse, it is nice to know that you have one place to search all the online documentation, no matter who supplied it. You gain this benefit because help is one of many integration points available in Eclipse. The same applies to context-sensitive help. All integrated tools can take advantage of context-sensitive help support, so **F1** works consistently across all tools. Though the user sees a consistent experience invoking and searching help, as a help content writer, you have a great deal of freedom to customize the content and visual appearance. Integrating help content into Eclipse leverages the plug-in architecture and is an easy integration entry point.

## References

Adams, Greg, and Dorian Birsan. August 9, 2002. Help—part 1: Contributing a little help. http://www.eclipse.org.

Arthorne, John, and Chris Laffra. 2004. *Official Eclipse 3.0 FAQs*. Boston, MA: Addison-Wesley. http://www.eclipsefaq.org. (See FAQs 274–277.)

PART III

# PART IV

*Extending the Eclipse IDE*

Part IV covers Eclipse extensibility that is specific to the classic Eclipse IDE and focuses on workspace programming. This is the configuration when using the standard Eclipse SDK and forms the base for the integration of development tools.

- Chapter 23, Workspace Resource Programming, is a core topic for anyone extending the Eclipse IDE. You will learn how to access and manipulate the workspace and its content.
- Chapter 24, Managing Resources with Natures and Builders, and Chapter 25, Resource Tagging Using Markers, cover the extension points of the resource component. Here you learn about natures, builders, and markers. These are commonly used extensions when building an IDE.
- Chapter 26, Building a Custom Text Editor with JFace Text, explains how to construct custom text editors. You will learn some of the same techinques that are used in the Java editor.
- Chapter 27, Extending the Java Development Tools, reveals the inner workings of the JDT and shows you how to create your own useful additions.

The CD-ROM that accompanies this book contains working examples that demonstrate the concepts presented in Part IV. These examples are well documented with both Javadoc and inline comments. The CD-ROM also includes documentation for the examples and exercises, both of which are integrated with the Eclipse Help system. See the `readme.html` file for installation instructions.

PART IV

# CHAPTER 23

## *Workspace Resource Programming*

This chapter discusses the resource framework, which is comprised of the programming interfaces and extension points related to the workspace, and is implemented by the org.eclipse.core.resources plug-in. The resources plug-in implements a model that provides support for the resources you can see in the Navigator view, resource event processing, and resource properties.

By understanding the structure of the resource model, you can effectively use the workspace API to create and manage resources and dynamically react to changes.

## Resource Concepts

If you have been using Eclipse to create Java programs or develop your own plug-in, you have been defining resources in a workspace and using tools that interact with the resource model. Tools use the workspace API to interact with both the visible resources and the underlying capabilities of the resource model. We start by looking at the physical implementation and then a logical view of the resource model.

First, let's define a few terms so we can use them in the discussion that follows.

- The **workspace** is the logical container of resources that can be accessed by plug-ins.
- The **resource model** is the logical representation of the content accessible in the workspace.

- A **project** is a management construct in the workspace; it is similar to, but not the same as, a folder.
- A **nature** is an approach used to associate behavior and function with a project. Tools can add extensions to define their own natures.
- A **builder** is a mechanism used by the workspace that allows tool-specific logic to process changed files at specific times. Typically, builders are used to implement processing that transforms resources from one form to another. Tools can add extensions to define their own builders.
- A **marker** is an abstract entity that can be associated with another resource. Several reusable marker types have already been defined as part of Eclipse itself; tools can use these or add extensions to define additional marker types.

## Physical View

The workspace exists in the file system as a directory, and only one workspace is active when using Eclipse. The resources plug-in is responsible for keeping track of resources added to the workspace and allowing tools to store private data separately from the resources visible to the user.

Three resource types are visible in the Navigator view.

- A **project** is a collection of files and folders. Projects exist as part of a workspace, but projects are not required to be physically contained in the workspace directory.
- A **folder** is a container of files; it is used for organization and namespace management. Folders are contained in a project or another folder.
- A **file** is a stream of bytes used to save the persistent state of a resource. Files are always contained in a folder or a project.

The workspace directory can physically contain projects and track references to projects that exist in a different location in the file system. This support for alternate project locations does not change any of the processing rules, so it will be ignored for the rest of the chapter.

The following example shows the directory structure of a workspace that has one project (a_project), one folder (a_folder), and two files (a.file1, a.file2).

```
D:\workspace\.metadata
D:\workspace\.metadata\.plugins\org.eclipse.core.resources
D:\workspace\.metadata\.plugins\org.eclipse.ui
D:\workspace\.metadata\.plugins\org.eclipse.team.core
D:\workspace\a_project
D:\workspace\a_project\.project
```

```
D:\workspace\a_project\a.file1
D:\workspace\a_project\a_folder
D:\workspace\a_project\a_folder\a.file2
```

The .project file was not added to the a_project directory by the user but was created by the org.eclipse.core.resources plug-in to store information about the project itself. The contents of the .project file can be read in a text editor but should not be directly modified. The .project file is discussed further in Project Descriptions later in this chapter.

A workspace contains a .metadata directory that is used to store private data. The .metadata directory includes a .plugins directory for state data for each plug-in. The .metadata entries shown in the directory example do not include the files in the plug-in state directories. The actual number of .metadata\.plugins state directories and files you would see depends on the plugins loaded and the Eclipse function exercised.

A plug-in uses the Plugin.getStateLocation method to get a reference to its state directory. A directory with the same id as the plug-in is created in the .metadata\.plugins directory when a plug-in stores state data. Plug-in-specific resources can be found in this directory.

The contents of the .metadata directory are not meant to be directly modified. However, there are times when you can find useful information through exploration or by searching the directory tree. For instance, the dialog_settings.xml files in the state directories store content for dialogs as saved by a given plug-in.

### Logical View

The resource model is more than what you can see on disk. A hierarchy of classes is defined as part of the workspace API; these classes represent the core of the model, the resources you can touch and see in the Navigator view. If you restrict your view to these resources, you can visualize how the resource model maps to the file system using the logical diagram and the hierarchy of interfaces as defined as part of the workspace API. This is illustrated in Figure 23.1.

The workspace API has interfaces for each element in the resource model, but Figure 23.1 shows only those represented directly in the file system. These interfaces allow you to work with the resources that your user can actually see in the Navigator view.

- IResource is the generalized interface for all workspace resources. Basic resource processing, including support for other services that exist as part of the workspace API, is provided by the IResource interface.

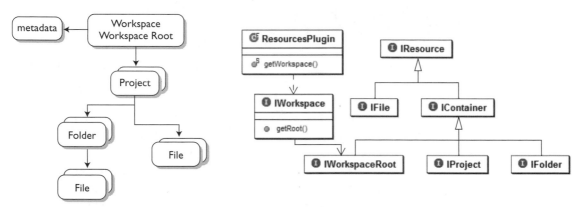

**Figure 23.1**    Resource Model: Logical View and Interface Hierarchy

- The IContainer interface is implemented by resource model objects that can contain other objects. As shown in the hierarchy, this includes the workspace root, projects, and folders. The IContainer interface allows you to work with the members of that container.
- The IFile interface provides support for the creation, deletion, and movement of a file. Access and modification of the file content are also supported.
- The IFolder interface provides support for folder-specific processing of get, create, delete, and move requests.
- The IProject interface provides support for project-specific processing. This includes basic create, delete, and move support as well as the additional capabilities available in a project (description, natures, builders, and references to other projects).
- IWorkspaceRoot provides an entry point to the contents of the workspace. Using the IWorkspaceRoot interface, you can get to projects and their resources. You get the workspace root from the workspace.

The workspace API contains Java interfaces for each resource type.

### Resource Model and File System Interaction

You may have noticed that the term **workspace** seems to have two meanings as it applies to Eclipse. The first is simply the directory in the local file system containing the projects, folders, and files you see in the Navigator view. The second is the in-memory representation of the *contents* of the workspace. As an Eclipse developer, you should understand the model so you can use the

APIs for common file system behavior, such as copying, moving, creating, and modifying file system entities, and Eclipse-specific capabilities, such as persistent properties and event notification for resource changes.

The in-memory model is loaded from a saved state when the workspace is activated during the startup of Eclipse. Figure 23.2 shows this mapping between the resource model and the file system using a lightly populated workspace.

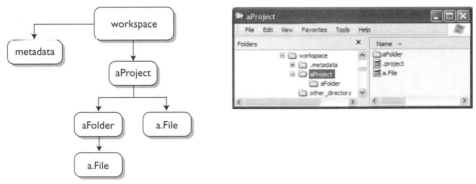

**Figure 23.2**   Resource Model and File System

All changes made through the workspace API, such as the addition of folders or files to a project, are immediately reflected in the in-memory work-space resource model. When a resource is created in the workspace, it also exists in the file system. Changes made directly to the file system, such as copying folders or files to a project using a command line or operating system user interface, are not known to the workspace until a refresh action is performed by the user or through the workspace API (`IResource.refreshLocal`). This refresh action can be automated, if desired, by the user. The **Refresh workspace automatically** preference found on the **Workbench** preference page can be used to request that the workspace listen for file system changes and react as required to keep the workspace and file system synchronized.

PART IV

**NOTE**  You should not rely on this preference being set; it must stay under user control. A common practice is to refresh the workspace, or better yet a specific resource or resource tree, after you have directly modified the file system. Doing this when the user had asked the workspace to maintain synchronization will not hurt, but you can find out whether you need to request a `refreshLocal` first. Logic such as the following will help you determine the current state and act accordingly.

```
if (!ResourcesPlugin.getPlugin().getPluginPreferences()
    .getBoolean(ResourcesPlugin.PREF_AUTO_REFRESH))
    try {
      project.refreshLocal(IResource.DEPTH_INFINITE, null);
    } catch (CoreException e) {
      e.printStackTrace();
    }
```

If you save the refresh setting locally, be sure to listen for changes. For details, see Reacting to Preference Value Changes in Chapter 17, Dialog Settings, Preferences, and User Settings.

Refreshing the workspace does not add projects; they must be created using the workspace API in order to become part of the workspace. For example, in Figure 23.2 there is a folder named other_directory in the file system that is not in the diagram of the resource model.

Changes could also have been made to the file system while Eclipse was shut down. The default processing is that these changes are not reflected in the workspace when Eclipse is started. You can use the **Refresh workspace at startup** setting to force resynchronization at startup.

This relationship between the resource model and the file system requires that you use certain patterns when using the workspace API. You can get a resource, but you need to be sure it exists before you attempt a modification, or be sure it does not already exist before you create the resource. These types of interactions and programming patterns are reviewed in the next section.

### Resource Visibility in the Navigator View

By default, resources in the workspace are visible in the Eclipse Platform's Navigator view. This is the general-purpose view for resource access and interaction. Tools often create their own views, some of which are alternatives to the Navigator view (e.g., the JDT's Package Explorer view). See Chapter 18 for details on view creation.

Your tool may create resources in the workspace as your user interacts with your tool and a project or other resource. You may want to consider hiding these resources from the user. Given they are in the workspace, the user has the right to see them, and they will go to a repository if the project is shared. But you may want to avoid confusion and clutter by either hiding these resources initially or at least allowing the user to hide them in the Navigator view. You can do this by creating a resource filter extension point to filter the resources actually displayed in the Navigator view. The filter mechanism is controlled by the Navigator Filters dialog shown in Figure 23.3.

**Figure 23.3** Navigator Filters Dialog

You can add a filter using the `org.eclipse.ui.ide.resourceFilters` extension point. Add the extension to your plug-in and specify the file name pattern to usc as the filter. In the following example, files with the extension `.private` will be filtered out of the view. Since the attribute `selected` has a value of `false`, this filter will not be enabled by default.

```
<extension
  point="org.eclipse.ui.ide.resourceFilters">
  <filter
    selected="false"
    pattern="*.private"/>
</extension>
```

This adds a file-filtering pattern to the Navigator Filters dialog; Figure 23.3 shows the result.

## Workspace API

This section focuses on key portions of the workspace API and the programming patterns that are useful when working with resources.

A full description of the workspace API is located in the Javadoc for the `org.eclipse.core.resources` package in the *Platform Plug-in Developer Guide* in the Eclipse Help system. In addition, there is also a resource programming example on the CD-ROM.

PART IV

## Workspace and Workspace Root

When you start Eclipse, you are accessing a single workspace. To access the workspace in your plug-in code, you need to get a reference to the currently available workspace. You can do this by accessing the plug-in class of the org.eclipse.core.resources plug-in and asking it for the following workspace.

```
IWorkspace myWorkspace =
    org.eclipse.core.resources.ResourcesPlugin.getWorkspace();
```

Once you have a reference to the workspace, you can add resource change listeners, add save participants, and navigate from there to the IWorkspaceRoot.

```
myWorkspace.getRoot();
```

The following is a list of the more interesting IWorkspace API methods.

- getDescription returns the workspace description. The description can be used to retrieve or change workspace-wide settings, such as the order in which the projects in the workspace will be built and whether the builds will be performed automatically on resource modification. Many of these settings correspond to the choices available on the **Workbench** page of the Preferences dialog.
- validateName(name,type) returns an IStatus that identifies whether the name passed is acceptable for the resource type identified.
- addResourceChangeListener(...) is used to add general-purpose or specific change event listeners to the workspace.
- addSaveParticipant(...) registers a class that will process workspace save events for an identified plug-in.

For more information on adding event listeners see the section Processing Workspace Resource Change Events later in this chapter; for adding save participants, see Using Workspace Save Events to Save Critical Data.

Validation provided by the validateName method performs the required tests to determine whether the name is valid for the resource type. Name validation also occurs when a resource is created, but not when you get a handle. Use the validateName method if you want to be sure that the name is acceptable before you actually create the resource.

Often you simply get the workspace and then use the getRoot method to get the workspace root; from there you can move to other areas of the resource model, such as finding a specific project, adding/modifying resources, and finding tool-specific content in the resource tree.

The workspace root is the container of projects and therefore all resources. The workspace root implements the IContainer interface, which also applies to projects and folders. However, the workspace root can contain only projects. Projects and folders can contain folders and files. This container is not shown in the Navigator view, but if you ask a project for its parent (getParent), you get the workspace root. Obviously, the workspace root itself returns null for getParent.

You could argue that the default workspace directory name could have been workspaceroot. There is an interface for the workspace itself (IWorkspace), but this interface does not extend IResource. Do not get confused by the structural differences and roles of the IWorkspace and IWorkspaceRoot interfaces; just remember that everything is in the workspace and that your code should always use the workspace API to create, access, and modify resources. If you are writing directly to the file system and then refreshing the workspace to synchronize with file system contents, you are weakening the power of the workspace API. Any resource change listeners or builders would not be notified until you remember to synchronize. You also lose the option of making changes to the resource with tracking of the changes in local history. The local history support built into the workspace API must be requested when making modifications to a workspace file; direct file system modification cannot be captured in the local history.

---

**NOTE** A workspace directory still exists for a Rich Client Platform application. The workspace directory, regardless of the name defined with the –data invocation option, has two roles. It acts as the parent for the .metadata directory and as the default location for projects. The workspace can contain projects only when the org.eclipse.core.resources plug-in is included in the configuration and appropriately started by the Workbench. This is automatic for an IDE configuration based on the org.eclipse.ui.ide.workbench application.

---

## *Resource Containers*

Once you have the workspace root, you can find other resources. Each resource type provides methods that can be used to navigate the resource tree, get handles to resources that may or may not exist, or find specific resource instances.

The IContainer interface is a general programming interface for resource constructs that have children. The containers are workspace root, project, and folder. Table 23.1 identifies resource model interfaces and their methods that can be used to navigate between resources, all the way down to the contents of a file.

**Table 23.1**   Resource Model Navigation

| Starting Point | Method | Description |
| --- | --- | --- |
| IWorkspaceRoot | getProjects() | Gets an array of projects, open or closed, in the workspace. |
|  | getProject("project_name") | Gets the handle for a specific project, which might not yet exist. |
| IProject | getReferencedProjects() | Gets an array of projects referenced by this project. References are set using the project description. |
|  | getReferencingProjects() | Gets an array of open projects that reference the current project. |
|  | getFolder("folder_name") | Returns a handle to the identified folder. This folder might not yet exist. |
|  | getFile("file_name") | Returns a handle to the identified file. This file might not yet exist. |
| IFolder | getFile("file_name") | Returns a handle to the identified file. This file might not yet exist. |
| IFile | getContents() | Gets an input stream for the file's content. Multiple method signatures exist. |
|  | setContents(InputStream, ...) | Uses the passed input stream to set the contents of the file. Multiple method signatures exist. |
| IResource | getParent() | Gets a resource that is the parent of the current resource and that returns null for the workspace root. |
|  | getProject() | Returns the project that manages this resource. |
|  | getWorkspace() | Returns the workspace. |
|  | findMarkers() | Returns all markers of a specified type for the resource and, if requested, the children of the resource. |
| IContainer | members() | Returns an array of resources with the same parent. The array can contain only projects when the referenced object is the workspace root. |
|  | getFolder("folder_name") | Returns a handle to the identified folder. This folder might not yet exist. |
|  | getFile("file_name") | Returns a handle to the identified file. This file might not yet exist. |
|  | findMember("member_name") findMember(IPath) | Returns the identified member, or null if the member does not exist. |

Many of the methods in Table 23.1 return resource handles; others indicate by a null value that the requested resource was not found in the workspace. You should access resources using only the workspace API. However, as you write your custom resource logic, you need to account for the fact that although the workspace is built on the file system, the file system may not match the workspace.

### Workspace Resource Handles

Workspace containers provide numerous getter methods to request a resource by name. These are handle methods in that they return a workspace resource handle, but there is no guarantee that a resource by that name exists in the workspace. You can request a handle to get a resource that might exist, or you can do this as the first step in the process required to create a new resource.

The findXxxx methods are capable of indicating whether the resource actually exists in the workspace; they return null when the workspace is not aware of the resource. That still does not tell you whether the resource is in the file system but not (yet) known to the workspace.

You need to be aware of the two tiers for resources: workspace and file system. You can get handles for workspace resources and test whether they are in the workspace, but the file system state is independent. Resources known to the file system could be missing in the workspace; resources known to the workspace might not be on the file system. To avoid collisions, you can ask whether the resource is synchronized with the file system, or check the file system status yourself. Many workspace API methods also ask you for guidance on how to handle synchronization issues—you can choose to let processing terminate or force the processing to continue.

You can ask a resource, its members, and all its children for synchronization information using the isSynchronized method. The following is an example of asking a folder whether it and its members are synchronized.

```
boolean inSync =
    folder.isSynchronized(IResource.DEPTH_ONE);
```

Other depth options that you can use on calls such as isSynchronized and refreshLocal are DEPTH_ZERO and DEPTH_INFINITE.

### Projects

Creating a project requires that you get a handle for the project from the workspace root, create a project description with a path to identify the file system location, and then create and open the project. The logic shown in the

next example creates a project named `new_Project` in a directory named
`d:\workspacehome\new_Project`.

```
private void createProject() {
  IWorkspace workspace = ResourcesPlugin.getWorkspace();
  IWorkspaceRoot root = workspace.getRoot();
  IProject newProjectHandle = root.getProject("new_Project");
  // Get a project descriptor.
  IPath targetPath = new Path("d:/workspacehome/"
    + newProjectHandle.getName());
  final IProjectDescription description =
    workspace.newProjectDescription(newProjectHandle.getName());
  description.setLocation(targetPath);
  try {
    newProjectHandle.create(description, null);
    newProjectHandle.open(null);
  } catch (CoreException e) {
    // Deal with exception.
  }
}
```

A `null` value for the location in the project description places the
project in the default location (the workspace directory). Projects are typically created with a New Resource wizard; the resource programming solution on the CD-ROM includes a New Project wizard that creates a project
with a specific nature.

The following are the key methods in the `IProject` interface that allow
you to work with a project.

- `isOpen` returns `true` if the project is open; you need to check this state
  as all projects still exist in the workspace, even when closed.
- `getDescription` returns the `IProjectDescription` for the project.
- `getNature(...)` returns the specified project nature for this project or
  `null` if the project nature has not been added to this project.
- `hasNature(...)` identifies whether the project nature specified by the
  given nature extension id has been added to this project.
- `isNatureEnabled(...)` returns `true` if the project nature specified by
  the given nature extension id is enabled for this project. There may be
  conflicts with the nature definition that force the nature to be disabled.

Some of these are convenience methods; much of the processing actually
involves the project description.

The workspace also supports the creation of a project-specific state directory. Unlike the state directory that can be obtained for a plug-in, the project
state directory is related directly to the project and the identified plug-in
requesting this support. You can use a `getWorkingLocation` call to obtain a

path value for a project state directory for the identified plug-in id. The following code shows an example of that call and the path value returned.

```
IPath path =
  project.getWorkingLocation("plugin.id");
E:/workspace/.metadata/.plugins/
  org.eclipse.core.resources/.projects/q.r.s/plugin.id
```

## Project Descriptions

Projects, which are represented by a folder in the file system, have Eclipse-specific behavior in the resource model that represents their abilities. To manage this information projects have descriptions; by using the project description, a project can be associated with one or more natures and builders and maintain references to other projects (see Figure 23.4).

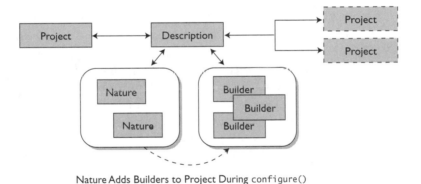

Nature Adds Builders to Project During `configure()`

**Figure 23.4**   Project Description: Management of Natures, Builders, and Project References

A project description is used to keep track of information important to the project. The API to the project description is defined by the `IProject-Description` interface. The description itself is maintained in a file in the workspace; a `.project` file exists for each project and is managed by the resources plug-in. The following example shows the contents of the `.project` file for a plug-in development project.

```xml
<?xml version="1.0" encoding="UTF-8"?>
<projectDescription>
  <name>com.ibm.tool.resources</name>
  <comment> </comment>
  <projects> </projects>
```

PART IV

```
<buildSpec>
  <buildCommand>
    <name>org.eclipse.jdt.core.javabuilder</name>
    <arguments> </arguments>
  </buildCommand>
  <buildCommand>
    <name>org.eclipse.pde.ManifestBuilder</name>
    <arguments> </arguments>
  </buildCommand>
  <buildCommand>
    <name>org.eclipse.pde.SchemaBuilder</name>
    <arguments> </arguments>
  </buildCommand>
</buildSpec>
<natures>
  <nature>org.eclipse.pde.PluginNature</nature>
  <nature>org.eclipse.jdt.core.javanature</nature>
</natures>
</projectDescription>
```

By placing this information in a file in the project folder, it can be stored in a repository. If this type of information were stored as resource properties, it would be kept in the `.metadata` directory for the current workspace, and `.metadata` files cannot be saved in a repository. If your tool requires that information about a project be shared by team members, you should consider a similar approach, or you could use the user settings API (see Chapter 17).

You can associate natures and builders with projects by adding them to the project description. To get a list of natures for a project, use the following method.

```
String[] natures = project.getDescription().getNatureIds();
```

Build commands are defined for a project, and each command knows the name of the builder. You can get the commands (`description.get-BuildSpec`) and then get the builder name from each command (`command.getBuilderName`).

The process of adding a nature to the project description for a project and using a nature to add a builder is discussed in Chapter 24, Managing Resources with Natures and Builders.

---

**NOTE** Although the builder and natures for a project are stored in a file, you should not edit the file to adjust this information. Adding a nature directly to the file will not trigger the processing to configure the nature. Natures and builders should only be added or removed as part of your tool function.

You can make references to other projects in two ways: by using the project property page in the user interface or by using the `IProjectDescription` API. When you use the user interface, you create simple project references. The `IProjectDescription` API allows you to create these same simple project references and also store a dynamically calculated set of project references.

Only simple project references are stored in the `.project` file. Here is an example of the project references section of the `.project` file with stored project references.

```
<projects>
  <project>com.ibm.tool.core</project>
  <project>com.ibm.tool.common</project>
</projects>
```

From a project you can find both projects it references and projects that reference it by using these API calls.

```
project.getReferencedProjects();
project.getReferencingProjects();
```

Projects that reference the current project are not stored in the `.project` file but are determined by accessing the workspace resource model.

The `IProjectDescription` API also supports the creation and access of a set of dynamically referenced projects. These projects are defined at runtime; the definition is saved not in the `.project` file but in the workspace metadata instead. Unlike a simple project reference, a dynamic reference is not displayed in the user interface; the only record of the reference is what is kept in the workspace metadata. Given that these references are not visible to the user and they are unable to modify them directly, you could call a dynamic project reference a sticky reference. Since these references are not sent to a repository, they also need to be recalculated after a project is checked out.

The following code snippets detail how you might define and get a set of dynamically referenced projects by interacting with `IProjectDescription`.

```
// Calculate project array and define as dynamic
// project references.
IProject[] projects =
  calculateToolSpecificProjectSet();
project.getDescription().setDynamicReferences(projects);

// Get a project array of dynamically referenced projects.
project.getDescription().getDynamicReferences();
```

You use these different project referencing capabilities as you see fit. Tools such as the JDT and PDE use them for their own purposes; the references created are managed as part of the workspace and/or stored in the

.project file but are not otherwise used in the Eclipse Platform. An example of using a project reference is included in the example builder implementation on the CD-ROM. See Defining and Implementing an Incremental Project Builder in Chapter 24, Managing Resources with Natures and Builders, for additional information.

## Resources

As the root of the resource model, the IResource interface is implemented by all the core resource objects except the workspace. The workspace is not in the inheritance hierarchy, but it is included in the logical representation of the resource model (as shown earlier in Figure 23.1). The IResource interface provides the fundamental function available in all resources. Using this level of the API, you may do things such as the following.

- Copy, move, or delete the resource (copy, move, or delete).
- Determine where the resource exists within the workspace (getParent, getProject, or getFullPath).
- Determine whether the resource exists in the workspace (exists or isAccessible).
- Identify resource-specific attributes, such as derived and read-only, or the state, such as synchronized (which indicates that the resource and its descendants to a specified depth match the file system).

**NOTE** The API for creating resources is type-specific; this function is not found as part of the general IResource API.

Resources can also be refreshed from the file system. This refresh process was introduced earlier in this chapter in Resource Model and File System Interaction. The IResource.refreshLocal method can be passed a depth value to indicate whether just the resource, the resource and its members, or all descendants should be refreshed. Performing a refresh before a create attempt could make your logic simpler (see Folders and Files later in this chapter), but it may not be appropriate to force a refresh on your users. They may be keeping files and folders in their project that are not meant to be included in the workspace. Externally launched editors can also create temporary files in the project resource tree. It would disrupt a user's ability to manage workspace content if your logic suddenly added these resources to the workspace.

Resources can be identified as derived. A tool—not a user—creates derived resources, and they can be recreated by processing another resource. When marked as derived, tools can choose to implement special processing, such as not sending the resource to a repository or deleting all derived resources as part of a cleanup action. For example, the Java `.class` files produced when the Java source files are compiled are marked as derived.

If resources are marked as read-only, changes to these resources are not permitted using the workspace API (but folders marked as read-only can still have files added to them). Editors should not allow you to modify a file marked as read-only, or at least they should warn you when you attempt such an action. An exception is thrown if you try to modify a file that has been marked as read-only. If the file system setting for read-only is modified, the `isReadOnly` method immediately reflects the new setting without a refresh of the workspace.

## Paths

In the workspace API, paths are used as parameters and return values. Paths are string values segmented by a standard separator character (/). A leading and/or trailing separator can be included. A device id prefix, such as `D:` or `Cork/Data:`, is optional. Path values can be relative or contain a reference to the absolute location for the resource.

Table 23.2 compares the different types of path values you can obtain for a resource such as `aFold`, a folder in a project named `a.proj`.

**Table 23.2**   Path Values

| Path Type | Method | Value |
|---|---|---|
| Relative to the workspace position | `IResource.getFullPath()` | `/a.proj/aFold` |
| Relative to the project | `IResource.getProjectRelativePath()` | `aFold` |
| Physical location in the file system | `IResource.getLocation()` | `e:/eclipse/workspace/a.proj/aFold` |
| Raw physical location in the file system | `IResource.getRawLocation()` | `e:/eclipse/workspace/a.proj/aFold` |

**NOTE** The difference between getLocation and getRawLocation is very subtle. As described in the Javadoc:

> If this resource is an existing project, the returned path will be equal to the location path in the project description. If this resource is a linked resource in an open project, the returned path will be equal to the location path supplied when the linked resource was created. In all other cases, this method returns the same value as getLocation.

The only noticeable difference is that for a project in the default location (in the workspace directory) the getRawLocation method returns a null.

You will use paths to define the location of the resource when making references or creating resource handles, such as with the getFile(IPath path) or getFolder(IPath path) methods. Paths are passed as parameters when copying or moving resources and returned when you query values such as the location of a resource, workspace root, or platform location.

The workspace API includes the IPath interface, but to create a new path you use the Path constructor.

```
IPath myPath = new Path("my/Path/");
IPath myPathLocation = new Path("D:\", "my/Path/");
```

The constructor for Path takes one String value for the path, or two String values, the first for the device and the second for the path. The path String value is valid if each segment (as defined by the / separator) is valid. Segments are valid if they are String values that are not empty and do not contain a colon (:) or begin or end with a space. If you include a backslash (\), it is converted to a forward slash (/).

The IPath interface provides methods that allow you to manipulate path values. Review the Javadoc or source for details on the available methods.

**NOTE** The resource programming example found on the CD-ROM includes some path manipulation logic as part of a Navigator view action. The action displays many of the path representations for the resource selected in the Navigator view.

### Folders and Files

Folder and file creation uses an identical pattern: You get a handle to the resource, and then if it does not exist, you can create the resource. You can get a folder or file handle from a folder or a project. If the request was for a resource that already exists, you have a real resource to use as needed. If it does not exist, you will need to create the resource before it exists in the file system. The parent of the resource must also be accessible.

The following logic gets a named folder for a project and then attempts to create the folder if it does not exist in the workspace.

```
private void createFolderInProject(
  IProject project, String folderName) {

  IFolder newFolder = project.getFolder(folderName);
  if (!newFolder.exists()) {
    try {
      newFolder.create(true, true, null);
    } catch (CoreException e) {
      // Deal with exception.
    }
  }
}
```

The file system could have already had a folder with the same name used during the get and create, or the name identified might have been invalid. As discussed earlier in the section Workspace Resource Handles, you must determine your own strategy for resource creation. In this example, you check whether the project was synchronized with the file system, but that only warns you of possible trouble.

Your creation logic needs to either catch or prevent creation errors when the file system has resources not known to the workspace. The Workbench New Folder wizard uses a mixed approach: The folder name is checked for validity before a create request can be processed, but the create attempt can fail if the folder already exists in the file system.

Files can be created and their contents defined using the workspace API. The `IFile` API supports the use of input streams to get, set, and append contents to a file through these methods.

- `getContents` obtains an input stream for the file contents.
- `setContents` uses a passed input stream or `IFileState` to set file contents.
- `appendContents` appends an input stream to the current contents of a file.

The following logic creates a file in the folder passed to the method. If the file exists, its content is replaced. The `getInitialContents` method is used to supply the content used for the new file or to replace the contents of the existing file.

```
private void createFileInFolder2(IFolder folder) {
  IFile newFile = folder.getFile("new_File.txt");
  try {
    if (newFile.exists())
      newFile.setContents(
        getInitialContents(),
        true, false, null);
    else {
      java.io.File systemFile =
        newFile.getLocation().toFile();

      if (systemFile.exists()) {
        // Skip create -- in file system.
        // Could refreshLocal on parent at this point.
      } else {
        newFile.create(getInitialContents(), false, null);
      }
    }
  } catch (CoreException ce) {
    // Failed.
  }
}
// Return input stream used to create initial file contents.
private InputStream getInitialContents() {
  StringBuffer sb = new StringBuffer();
  sb.append("My New File Contents");
  return new ByteArrayInputStream(sb.toString().getBytes());
}
```

This logic goes beyond the workspace API to ensure the file can be created. The file system is checked to see if the file already exists. If the file is in the file system but not in the workspace, the create and set contents process is skipped.

## Linked Resources

Resources do not always have to be physically inside a project's file system tree. In the root of a project you can create linked resources. A **linked resource** is a reference to a folder or file that is physically outside the project. Linked resources can be created by using the New Folder or New File wizards or by using the workspace API.

The following logic will create a linked folder and a linked file in a project.

```
IPath path = new Path("E:/SharedResources/This");

IFolder folder = project.getFolder("aFolder");
```

```
if (!folder.exists())
  try {
    folder.createLink(path,IResource.NONE,null);
  } catch (CoreException e) {
    e.printStackTrace();
  }


path = new Path("E:/SharedResources/That.txt");
IFile file = project.getFile("aFile.txt");
if (!file.exists())
  try {
    file.createLink(path,IResource.ALLOW_MISSING_LOCAL,null);
  } catch (CoreException e) {
    e.printStackTrace();
  }
```

The createLink call includes ALLOW_MISSING_LOCAL as a parameter. This allows the file create process to succeed even if the target resource does not exist. This option works for folders too.

If you are working with linked resources, you may need to consider some special processing options. If you request a copy or move operation, you can use the IResource.SHALLOW parameter to request that links are copied instead of ending up with another copy of the resource. You can also ask a resource whether it is a linked resource using the isLinked method.

If you have a folder or file that you think is linked somewhere in the workspace, you can ask the IWorkspaceRoot to find references. You need an absolute path location (e:\folderName or e:\folder\fileName.txt) as the IPath parameter to either findContainersForLocation or findFilesForLocation. Pass an IPath for a folder to the findContainersForLocation method to return an array of containers in which the folder is linked. Pass an IPath for a file to this same method to return an array of containers in which the file is linked. These methods work just as well for nonlinked resources, but the results are not as interesting; they are the equivalent of a getParent call.

### Visiting Resources in a Resource Tree

When you need to find all resources in a project, folder, or even the full workspace, you can use the IResourceVisitor or IResourceProxyVisitor provided as part of the workspace API. Using these visitors you can process a node in the resource tree and visit all the children of that node.

To process all elements of a given node in the resource tree, define a class that implements either the IResourceVisitor or IResourceProxyVisitor interface. These interfaces both define only one method, visit, which will be invoked for each element and subelement of the resource tree you want to process.

The difference between these two interfaces is simple: The IResource-Visitor is given a real IResource instance to process, while the IResource-ProxyVisitor is given an IResourceProxy. The IResourceProxy allows you to check attributes such as name and type but is much less expensive to create than a real IResource instance. This can reduce the overhead of processing a resource tree. The attributes available from an IResourceProxy instance can help you determine whether you can move on to the next proxy or need the real IResource instance. If you need the resource, just call IResourceProxy .requestResource.

You process the resource tree by calling IResource.accept with either an IResourceVisitor or IResourceProxyVisitor instance on the resource node of interest. There are multiple signatures to the accept method; in addition to the visitor, other parameters can be used to direct how the visitor will be processed.

A simple IResourceVisitor implementation is shown here. It is nearly identical in structure to the implementation of an IResourceProxyVisitor; the only difference is the parameter type passed to the visit method.

```
private void visitResourceTree(IResource resource) {

    IResourceVisitor visitor = new IResourceVisitor() {
        public boolean visit(IResource res) {
            // Process the resource.

            // ... Your logic here ...

             // By returning true, you are saying you want
             // to process the children.
            return true;
        };
    };
    try {
        resource.accept(visitor);
    } catch (CoreException e) {
        // Problem during visit processing.
    }
}
```

You implement an IResourceVisitor or IResourceProxyVisitor when you want to process all, or a portion of, the contents of the workspace. The visitor essentially allows you to *walk* the workspace resource tree. The boolean return value for the visit method instructs the visitor framework to continue to the children of the current resource.

**NOTE** The workspace API also includes an `IResourceDeltaVisitor` interface; this supports processing the resource tree provided as part of an `IResourceDelta`. For details on this approach, see the section Processing Workspace Resource Change Events later in this chapter and the section Defining and Implementing an Incremental Project Builder in Chapter 24.

## Resource Properties

Resources are more than just a collection of files and folders. The native capabilities of folders and files are supported as entities in the resource model, but the workspace API also includes support for specialized services that further enrich the resource model. The workspace API allows properties to be defined for any object that implements the `IResource` interface. Properties are keyed values associated with a resource. Two types of properties are supported: session and persistent.

### Session Properties

**Session properties** are used by plug-ins as a caching mechanism for resource-specific objects. Session properties are kept in memory until the resource is deleted, the containing project is closed, or Eclipse is shut down.

This is a powerful capability; as additional tools are integrated with Eclipse, each tool can add what amounts to a private instance variable to any resource in the workspace. Tool-specific behavior becomes easier to implement with this simple but powerful approach to extending the tool-specific content available as part of any resource.

The following methods support the definition and retrieval of session properties.

```
resource.setSessionProperty(QualifiedName key, Object value)
resource.getSessionProperty(QualifiedName key)
```

The `QualifiedName` parameter is a two-part identifier composed of string values for a qualifier and a local name. The common pattern is to use the plug-in id as the qualifier and a meaningful tool-specific local name. In the next example, the `QualifiedName` is created from a plug-in identifier and a local key. An object is then associated with the current resource.

```
public static final String TOOL_PLUGIN = "qrs.toolPlugin";
...
public static final QualifiedName PROP_VALUE = new
    QualifiedName(ResourcesPlugin.TOOL_PLUGIN, "Tool_Setting");
...
```

```
Object setit = getSomeObject();
...
try {
   resource.setSessionProperty(PROP_VALUE, setit);
} catch (CoreException e) {
// Deal with exception.
}
```

Once you've made that association, you can use the getSessionProperty method to retrieve the session value as long as the resource exists, its project stays open, and Eclipse is active.

## Persistent Properties

**Persistent properties** are keyed string values and are used by plug-ins to locally store resource-specific information as part of the workspace. Eclipse manages the storage and retrieval of persistent properties independently for each plug-in, and each plug-in has its own properties namespace. Properties are not sent to the repository and can be accessed only by using the workspace API. Once saved, the data is available for as long as the resource exists in the workspace. If you copy the resource, the properties are also copied; if you move the resource, they move as well.

The following methods support the definition and retrieval of persistent properties.

```
resource.setPersistentProperty(QualifiedName key, String value)
resource.getPersistentProperty(QualifiedName key)
```

This next example creates a String and saves it as part of the current resource.

```
public static final String TOOL_PLUGIN = "qrs.toolPlugin";
...
public static final QualifiedName PROP_VALUE = new
   QualifiedName(ResourcesPlugin.TOOL_PLUGIN, "Tool_Setting");
...
String setit = getSomeStringValue();
...
try {
   resource.setPersistentProperty(PROP_VALUE, setit);
} catch (CoreException e) {
// Deal with exception.
}
```

Once the string has been associated with the resource, you can use the getPersistentProperty method to get the associated String value when required.

If Eclipse is shut down and then restarted, the persistent property will still be available. However, if you delete the resource, the persistent property is destroyed. Even if you select the container for the deleted resource and use the context menu option **Restore From Local History...** to bring back the deleted resource, the persistent property is not restored. In the same fashion, if you restore alternate versions of the file, you do not get alternate versions of a persistent property.

---

**NOTE**  The persistent property workspace API is often used to set and retrieve values shown in the Properties dialog, as discussed in Chapter 16, Dialogs and Wizards. You could consider user settings as an alternative to the resource property API. User settings can be used to store project- or even resource-specific information in an Eclipse Platform managed file that is part of the project in the workspace. User settings and other methods of storing data in the Eclipse Platform are discussed in Chapter 17, Dialog Settings, Preferences, and User Settings.

---

## Processing Workspace Resource Change Events

The workspace API allows tools to register their interest in being notified of specific resource change events. You can use resource change listeners to be responsive and proactive and even to automate certain tasks. For example, a resource change listener is used to manage the items in the Bookmarks view. Adding or removing bookmark markers from a resource will trigger a resource change event; the Bookmarks view listens for events and determines whether it needs to react to the changes that might have occurred. Not all events require a change in the Bookmarks view, but the resource change listener used by the Bookmarks view can quickly determine whether any bookmark markers have changed and react as required. The user sees an instantaneous reaction to changes. (To try this, open the Bookmarks view and then add a bookmark or two to a file.)

### Tracking Changes Using the Workspace API

You use the `IWorkspace.addResourceChangeListener(...)` method to add your resource change listener to the workspace. This method allows your listener to be informed of changes like these.

- A file is added, modified, moved, or deleted.
- A project is opened or closed.
- Markers are added or removed.
- A builder event is about to start or has completed.

PART IV

The interfaces listed in Table 23.3 are used to implement support for resource change listeners. This includes support for creating a resource change listener, processing the events received, and visiting the resource deltas associated with an event. The listener is a class that implements the IResource-ChangeListener interface and defines a resourceChanged method. This method can query the event type using the passed IResourceChangeEvent. When appropriate, the listener can get an IResourceDelta, which contains details about the resources affected by the change event.

Some event types include an IResourceDelta, which contains information about the change(s) being reported in the event.

**Table 23.3**   Resource Change Event Interfaces

| Event Processing Interface | Description |
|---|---|
| IResourceChangeListener | You must implement this interface if you want to be sent messages when a resource change event has occurred. A resource change listener is notified of changes to resources in the workspace. |
| IResourceChangeEvent | Resource change events describe changes to resources. A resource change event is passed to you, as required, once you have registered to listen for resource changes. |
| IResourceDelta | A resource delta represents changes in the state of a resource tree between two discrete points in time. A resource change event contains a resource delta, which can be processed using the visitor pattern. |
| IResourceDeltaVisitor | To be a visitor of a resource delta, your class must implement this interface. The visitor pattern allows you to process each entry in the delta. |

A resource change listener can be added during plug-in startup processing, but this will provide visibility to resource change events only from that point forward. Figure 23.5 shows a set of changes (A, B, C, D, and E) as part of an Eclipse startup and shutdown life cycle.

A plug-in is typically not started until required by some user action. As the plug-in gets started, it can add the resource change listener to the workspace. The plug-in is notified of only the resource change events that occur after the listener has been added, so, as shown in Figure 23.5, the resource change listener is notified about only resource change events D and E.

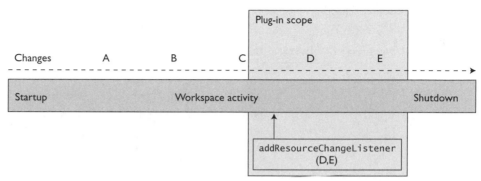

**Figure 23.5**   Event Processing with a Resource Change Listener

By default, every change made to the resource, excluding resource properties, is identified as an event that can be sent to an interested resource change listener. As you might imagine, if there were lots of changes and multiple resource change listeners, the processing of events could become a performance issue. The reduction of events is the responsibility of the code making the changes. The technique for reducing the number of events using an IWorkspaceRunnable is discussed later in this chapter in the section Resource Modification Event Management.

## Adding Resource Change Listeners

You can use either of the following two methods to add a resource change listener to the workspace so that you will be notified of the required resource change events.

```
addResourceChangeListener(
   IResourceChangeListener listener)
addResourceChangeListener(
   IResourceChangeListener listener, int eventMask)
```

The first method adds a basic listener that will be informed of all nonbuild resource change events that occur (close, delete, and change). The second method shows that you can use an event mask parameter when adding a listener to select the types of resource change events sent to your listener. This will filter out any events you know that you will not need to process. Table 23.4 lists the types of resource change events you can send to a listener.

PART IV

**Table 23.4**   Resource Change Event Types

| Change Event | Workspace | Has Delta? | Description |
|---|---|---|---|
| PRE_CLOSE | Locked | No | Notifies listeners that an identified project is about to be closed. Also triggered during workspace shutdown for each open project. |
| PRE_DELETE | Locked | No | Notifies listeners that an identified project is about to be deleted. |
| PRE_BUILD | Not locked | Yes | Notifies listeners before an auto-build. Always broadcast when Eclipse detects that an auto-build needs to occur, regardless of whether auto-building is actually enabled. |
| POST_BUILD | Not locked | Yes | Notifies listeners after an auto-build. Always broadcast after Eclipse would have performed an auto-build, regardless of whether auto-building is actually enabled. |
| POST_CHANGE | Locked | Yes | Notifies listeners of a resource change. Broadcast after any POST_BUILD notification is complete. Resource delta includes any changes made by builders that ran during auto-build processing. |

The PRE_CLOSE and PRE_DELETE events are just concerned with project state, not event history. These types of events are useful for triggering cleanup, such as removing in-memory or state directory representations of project resources. Only the PRE_BUILD and POST_BUILD events allow your listener to create or modify resources during the notification cycle. This allows all POST_CHANGE listeners, as defined by different tools, to get a chance to react to the same resource delta.

The following code shows an example of how a change event can be queried for information and the resource delta obtained for further processing.

```
public void resourceChanged(IResourceChangeEvent event) {
  switch (event.getType()) {
    case IResourceChangeEvent.PRE_CLOSE :
      System.out.println(
        "Closing: " + event.getResource().getFullPath());
      break;
    case IResourceChangeEvent.PRE_DELETE :
      System.out.println(
        "Deleting : " + event.getResource().getFullPath());
      break;
    case IResourceChangeEvent.PRE_AUTO_BUILD :
      System.out.println(" -> Auto build about to run.");
      break;
    case IResourceChangeEvent.POST_AUTO_BUILD :
      System.out.println(
        " -> Auto build complete, visiting the delta...");
```

```
        try {
          event.getDelta().accept(
            new SimpleResourceDeltaVisitor());
        } catch (CoreException e) {
          System.out.println(e);
        }
        break;
      case IResourceChangeEvent.POST_CHANGE :
        System.out.println(
          " -> Resource(s) changed, visiting the delta...");
        try {
          event.getDelta().accept(
            new SimpleResourceDeltaVisitor());
        } catch (CoreException e) {
          System.out.println(e);
        }
    }
  }
}
```

This code also shows how the resource delta is obtained from the event passed to the resource change listener, when one is provided (POST_ events only). As shown above, the event.getDelta method is used to get an IResourceDelta; a visitor is required to explore the changes identified in the delta.

You can also directly access the resource delta to determine whether resources you are interested in have been modified. This method allows you to query the delta based on a path:

```
event.getDelta().findMember(IPath);
```

This approach can be more efficient than visiting the entire resource delta tree, but you must have a specific file or folder that you are interested in tracking.

### Timing of Resource Change Events

Resource change events are triggered when resources have been changed in some fashion and as part of a build event cycle. You cannot guarantee the order of delivery between the two types of events (change and build).

When a resource is changed, be it an add, modify, delete, or move operation or a change to a marker for that resource, a resource change event is triggered. Likewise, a change in the state of a project (close or delete) can trigger a resource change event. These events are delivered in one notification pass. When resources are modified, build events are also triggered and then delivered on a different notification pass.

An example helps clarify this. Assume you have three resource change listeners; one is listening for only POST_CHANGE events, one for PRE_BUILD events, and one for both types of events. Call these listeners A, B, and C. If you were to delete a resource, listeners A and C would be called as part of the change notification cycle; listeners B and C would then be called as part of the build notification cycle. Simple enough, but let's go further.

Let's say five unique resource changes have been made in one action invocation. As these events are triggered rapidly, the workspace delivers all five of the change events to A and C in turn (A, C, A, C, and so on). Then after these events have been sent, the build events are sent to B and C; these resource change listeners are called only once, but they have information about all five resource changes in the resource delta.

Now these are the results of testing: If your logic takes its time making resource changes, you may see build events sneak in between change events. You can find additional detail on the delivery of resource change events on the project pages of the Eclipse Platform project on eclipse.org and in the Eclipse Help system.

### Visiting the Resource Delta

The listener can process the delta provided in a change event by using the visitor pattern. The visitor must implement the IResourceDeltaVisitor interface, which allows it to process the resource delta. The visitor can navigate to each change and implement any processing that might be required (see Figure 23.6).

To create a visitor, have your class implement the IResourceDeltaVisitor interface, which requires that you have a visit method. To get the delta and

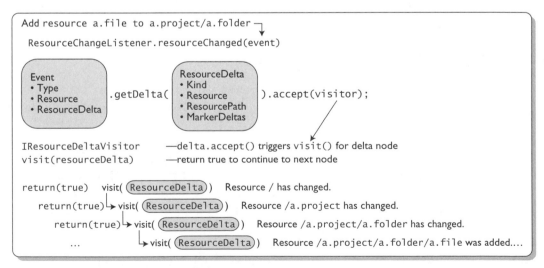

**Figure 23.6**   Visiting the Resource Delta

process it with the visitor, you would use this logic in your resource change listener.

```
event.getDelta().accept(new SimpleResourceDeltaVisitor());
```

The following is a simple example of the visit method in a resource delta visitor.

```
public boolean visit(IResourceDelta delta)
  throws CoreException {
  IResource res = delta.getResource();
  switch (delta.getKind()) {
    case IResourceDelta.ADDED :
      System.out.println(
        "Resource " + res.getFullPath() + " was added.");
      break;
    case IResourceDelta.REMOVED :
      System.out.println(
        "Resource " + res.getFullPath() + " was removed.");
      break;
    case IResourceDelta.CHANGED :
      System.out.println(
        "Resource " + res.getFullPath() + " has changed.");
      break;
  }
  return true; // Continue the visit process.
}
```

This example queries the resource delta to identify the type of resource modification. The resource delta will also have additional information about changes. For PRE_BUILD, POST_BUILD, and POST_CHANGE resource change events, this includes changes made to markers.

Here is an example of how a delta can be queried for additional detail about the change.

```
int eventFlag = delta.getFlags();

if ((eventFlag & IResourceDelta.CONTENT) != 0)
  traceMsg("--> Content Changed");

if ((eventFlag & IResourceDelta.REPLACED) != 0)
  traceMsg("--> Content Replaced");

if ((eventFlag & IResourceDelta.REMOVED) != 0)
  traceMsg("--> Removed");

if ((eventFlag & IResourceDelta.MARKERS) != 0)
  traceMsg("-------------------> Marker Changed");
```

Many types of flags are defined as constants in the IResourceDelta class. These have been summarized in Table 23.5, which was published as part of the "How you've changed!" article on eclipse.org.

PART IV

**Table 23.5**    Resource Change Event Flags

| Constant (in IResourceDelta) | Applicable Resources | Description |
| --- | --- | --- |
| CONTENT | IFile, IFolder | The file system modification time stamp has changed since the last notification. IResource.touch() will also trigger a content change notification, even though the content may not have changed in the file system. |
| MOVED_FROM | IFile, IFolder, IProject | The resource was moved from another location. You can find the path it came from by calling IResourceDelta.get-MovedFromPath. |
| MOVED_TO | IFile, IFolder, IProject | The resource was moved to another location. IResource-Delta.getMovedToPath indicates the location it was moved to. |
| OPEN | IProject | The project has either been opened or closed. If the project is now open, then it was previously closed, and vice versa. |
| TYPE | IFile, IFolder | The resource has changed type. If the resource was previously a file, then it is now a folder, and vice versa. |
| MARKERS | Applicable to all resource types | The resource's markers have changed. Markers are annotations to resources such as breakpoints, bookmarks, to-do items, etc. The method IResourceDelta.getMarker-Deltas() is used to find out which markers have changed. |
| ADDED | IFile, IFolder, IProject | The resource has been added to its parent. |
| REPLACED | IFile, IFolder, IProject | The resource has been replaced by a different resource at the same location (i.e., the resource had been deleted and then added again). |
| DESCRIPTION | IProject | The project description has changed. |
| SYNC | All | The resource's synchronization information has changed. Sync info is used to determine whether a resource is in sync with some remote server and is not typically of interest to local tools. See the API interface ISynchronizer for more details. |

To find out about the marker changes that are being reported you can use this next approach.

```
IMarkerDelta[] markers = delta.getMarkerDeltas();

for (int i = 0; i < markers.length; i++) {
    IMarkerDelta markerDelta = markers[i];
    int kind = markerDelta.getKind();
    System.out.print("\t Marker delta kind: " + kind);
    IMarker marker = markerDelta.getMarker();
```

```
            System.out.println("\t Marker itself: "
              + marker + marker.getType());
            System.out.println("\t Marker content: "
              + marker.getAttributes());
            System.out.println("<-------------------");
        }
```

Marker definition and implementation are covered in the section Creating Markers for Customized Resource Tagging in Chapter 25.

### Resource Delta Content

The delta may contain information on more than one change. For example, if you add a file (a.file) to a folder (aFolder) in a project (a.project), you get these entries in the delta.

```
/ changed (workspace root)
/a.project changed
/a.project/aFolder changed
/a.project/aFolder/a.file added
```

Some changes to the resource model can trigger multiple events. For example, if you close a project, the PRE_CLOSE event is triggered to identify the close action. Closing the project removes the resources contained in the project from the workspace, so the PRE_BUILD, POST_BUILD, and POST_CHANGE resource change events are also triggered. If you close the project where we just added a.file, the following entries would be in the resource delta.

```
/ changed (workspace root)
/a.project changed
/a.project/aFolder removed
/a.project/aFolder/a.file removed
```

Projects that are closed are not removed from the resource model; they exist as closed projects. If a project was deleted, the PRE_DELETE, PRE_BUILD, POST_BUILD, and POST_CHANGE resource change events are triggered. PRE_DELETE is told about the project, and the other resource change events include a delta with the following content.

```
/ changed (workspace root)
/a.project removed
/a.project/aFolder removed
/a.project/aFolder/a.file removed
```

## Resource Modification Event Management

The workspace.addChangeListener method allows tools to add change listeners to the workspace that can react to any resource changes that occur. If a tool, or the user, makes ten resource changes, each change listener is notified ten times. User-directed changes are usually simple, but tools might generate multiple changes as part of a single action. If each change triggers an event, there is a high cost for the change notification and reaction process.

There are two main options for how you can control the number of resource change events that might be triggered when performing resource processing. First, you can use the workspace API run method to request that the workspace batch changes up into a single event. Second, a WorkspaceJob can be created and scheduled to both package the resource processing to reduce resource events and run the processing asynchronously.

Note that this second approach represents an attempt to limit the number of resource change events that occur; it is not a guarantee that only one event will be triggered for the duration of the request. Other active workspace processing may require that a change event be triggered. This would mean that notification of some of your batched changes could occur earlier than others. These two approaches are discussed next; in addition, the CD-ROM has numerous examples for how a set of resource changes can be implemented and a view to track resource change events.

### Using IWorkspaceRunnable

You can create an IWorkspaceRunnable instance or implement the interface in your code. The run method defined in the interface is used to package your resource processing code. The code in an IWorkspaceRunnable can be invoked using the workspace API. The following code shows how an IWorkspaceRunnable can be used to create two folders in a project and trigger only one event when the work is performed.

```
IWorkspaceRunnable workspaceRunnable =
  new IWorkspaceRunnable() {
    public void run(IProgressMonitor monitor)
      throws CoreException {

      IFolder folder =
        project.getFolder("IWorkspaceRunnable_one");
      folder.create(true, true, null);
      folder = project.getFolder("IWorkspaceRunnable_one");
      folder.create(true, true, null);
    }
};

try {
  ResourcesPlugin.getWorkspace().run(workspaceRunnable, null);
} catch (CoreException e) {
}
```

An alternative signature for the run method allows you to process an IWorkspaceRunnable while adding support for a scheduling rule. A **scheduling rule** is a job processing control element that governs when jobs can be run. When a scheduling rule conflicts with a rule associated to an active job, the new work is delayed until there is no conflict. See the section Using a Scheduling Rule in Chapter 29, Implementing Responsiveness and Concurrency Using Jobs, for additional detail.

This code shows how the IWorkspaceRunnable shown above could be invoked using a scheduling rule and a request that resource change events not be triggered.

```
try {
  ResourcesPlugin.getWorkspace().run(
    workspaceRunnable,project,IWorkspace.AVOID_UPDATE,null);
} catch (CoreException e) {
  e.printStackTrace();
}
```

In this code the scheduling rule is the project parameter. Any workspace resource can be used as a scheduling rule; the IResource interface extends ISchedulingRule. The AVOID_UPDATE parameter is used to request that the workspace try to not trigger resource change events until change is complete.

---

**NOTE** You may also want to review these alternative techniques that build on the use of an IWorkspaceRunnable.

- IRunnableContext and IRunnableWithProgress implement an alternative technique for managing resource events when your activity needs to be represented by a progress indicator and must support a cancel request.
- The WorkspaceModifyOperation approach builds on the technique provided by IRunnableWithProgress.

---

## Using *WorkspaceJob*

As you would expect given the class name, a WorkspaceJob is a kind of Job. Jobs are discussed in Chapter 29, Implementing Responsiveness and Concurrency Using Jobs. A WorkspaceJob is designed to support the modification of the workspace as a scheduled job. In addition, the job is processed such that the workspace changes made are not reported as a change event until the job is complete.

The following code shows how a WorkspaceJob can be used to create two folders in a project and trigger only one event when the work is done.

```
WorkspaceJob workspaceJob = new WorkspaceJob("createFolder") {
    public IStatus runInWorkspace(IProgressMonitor monitor)
            throws CoreException {

        IFolder folder = project.getFolder("WorkspaceJob_one");
        folder.create(true, true, null);
        folder = project.getFolder("WorkspaceJob_two");
        folder.create(true, true, null);

        return new Status(IStatus.OK,
            "plugin.id", IStatus.OK, "worked", null);
    }
};
workspaceJob.schedule();
```

**NOTE**   A WorkspaceJob implements the required processing in the runInWorkspace method; a Job implements the processing required in a run method. WorkspaceJob extends InternalWorkspaceJob; the superclass implements the processing required to perform the runInWorkspace method while delaying the reporting of resource change events.

## Using the Workspace Scheduling Rule Factory

You may need a scheduling rule as part of using the run method just discussed, or when using a Job to perform some asynchronous processing. As you will learn in Chapter 29, Implementing Responsiveness and Concurrency Using Jobs, a scheduling rule can be used by any type of job. For the purposes of this discussion, just think of a scheduling rule as a gatekeeper that determines when your processing request can proceed. Using a scheduling rule with resources can prevent conflicting access.

Any IResource instance can be directly used as a scheduling rule, but using a single resource may not identify the scope of the change you want to make. To fix this, you can use the getRuleFactory method on the workspace to get an IResourceRuleFactory. This factory has methods such as create-Rule, deleteRule, and markerRule that return a scheduling rule that fits the need as defined by the method name and the IResource passed as a parameter. The rules returned by these methods are more appropriate than direct use of a given workspace resource. For instance, the deleteRule method knows that the scheduling rule to be used to delete a resource is not the resource itself but the parent of that resource.

By using the `IResourceRuleFactory`, you are allowing the architectural relationships of the workspace to be applied on your behalf to the creation of the right scheduling rule. The `IResourceRuleFactory` is used by resource programming APIs such as `IResource.move` to implement controlled processing of the move request.

See Using a Scheduling Rule in Chapter 29 for additional detail on scheduling rules.

## Using Workspace Save Events to Save Critical Data

When a plug-in has specific requirements for retaining information about resources, or private model data, the plug-in should participate in workspace save events to save data in a persistent store, such as a file in its state directory.

### Save Events—What and When

The workspace will trigger the following save events.

- `SNAPSHOT` is triggered as required, for example, when a project is added to the workspace.
- `PROJECT_SAVE` is triggered when a project is closed.
- `FULL_SAVE` is triggered when the workspace is about to be shut down.

By becoming a save participant, your plug-in gains two distinct capabilities.

- Once your plug-in has added a save participant to the workspace, you are given a chance to save data in your plug-in's state directory when workspace save events are triggered.
- At startup, once you have saved data, you can retrieve the data saved during a previous session.

Your plug-in's save participant is not called when the workspace is started. Startup participation is based on your plug-in being started and your startup logic adding a save participant.

### Save Participant API

You use the `IWorkspace.addSaveParticipant(plugin, saveParticipant)` method to become a save participant. The save participant API also allows you to request that a resource delta be provided to your plug-in. This gives you the opportunity to appropriately process any resource changes, other than marker changes, that may have occurred while your plug-in was inactive.

PART IV

You can use the interfaces shown in Table 23.6 when you want to implement save participant processing as part of the workspace life cycle.

**Table 23.6**   Workspace Save Event Interfaces

| Event Processing Interface | Description |
| --- | --- |
| ISaveParticipant | You implement this interface to participate in saving the workspace. |
| ISaveContext | The save operation context is used to control save participant processing options. |
| ISavedState | A data structure is returned when adding a save participant to the workspace. The returned object is null when adding a participant the first time. This contains a save number and an optional resource delta. |

The framework returns the previous saved state when you register as a save participant.

```
ISaveParticipant saveParticipant =
  new WorkSpaceSaveParticipant();
ISavedState lastState = ResourcesPlugin.getWorkspace()
  .addSaveParticipant(plugin, saveParticipant);
```

The saved state is null if the plug-in had not previously requested to be a save participant. Once requested, the save participant is called as part of Eclipse shutdown. The structure of a class that implements the ISaveParticipant interface is shown here.

```
public class SimpleSaveParticipant
  implements ISaveParticipant {

  public void doneSaving(ISaveContext context) {
  // Called when the save state process is complete (clean up).
  }

  public void prepareToSave(ISaveContext context)
    throws CoreException {
  // Called as a prelude to the task of
  // saving state information.
  }

  public void rollback(ISaveContext context) {
  // Called when a save has to be undone.
  }
```

```
public void saving(ISaveContext context)
  throws CoreException {
// Called when it is time to save state information.
  context.needDelta();
// needDelta() means that the next time you ask to add a
// save participant, you will be given a saved state that
// includes a delta.
}
}
```

Figure 23.7 provides a complete overview of the save participant process. The following steps are shown in Figure 23.7.

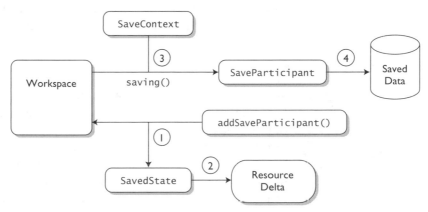

**Figure 23.7**  Save Participant Processing Overview

1. Add the save participant for the plug-in to the workspace. If this is not the first time, a saved state is returned. The saved state has information about any previous save, such as the save number.
2. If during a previous shutdown the save participant requested a resource change delta, then the resource change delta will contain all changes that have occurred to the workspace between the point where the state was saved and the point where the save participant was added again. This could span multiple launches and shutdowns of Eclipse. The API may not always have the delta. This may occur if it is too old or the saved state is invalid.
3. During a save event, all save participants are sent the message saving with a save context. The workspace can trigger save processing as part of a snapshot, a project save, or a full save event. Save participants implement the processing that is appropriate for their role for

each type of save event. The save context allows each save participant to set save context options for items like save number counters and whether a resource delta is required when the save participant is added again.

4. The save participant can save data in its plug-ins state directory as required. The save number, which can be obtained from the save context, can be used to determine the saved file name to avoid conflicts.

By participating in the workspace save event process, you will be given the opportunity to save information you may be tracking about projects at appropriate times. For example, the JDT implements a save participant (`JavaModelManager`) that saves project information during a PROJECT_SAVE and build state information used by the Java builder during a FULL_SAVE.

## Examples Summary

The use of the workspace API to create and interact with resources has been discussed. You can now explore the resource programming solution located in the `com.ibm.jdg2e.resources.programming` project on the CD-ROM.

The resource programming solution includes multiple pop-up menu actions that demonstrate resource programming techniques, a view that displays resource change events as they occur, and a decorator that identifies resources that are referenced in a `.cvsignore` file (see Chapter 5 for information on the use of a `.cvsignore` file). The actions demonstrate multiple approaches to how you can create new resource structures. The actions show different approaches for how resource creation calls can be packaged and resource change events managed.

In addition, the `com.ibm.jdg2e.resources.programming` plug-in class can be modified to add a workspace save event participant. The save participant implementation already exists, but is not added as part of the plug-in startup unless you modify the plug-in source. The save participant logic provided writes messages to the console to identify when save events occur.

## Chapter Summary

This chapter described using the workspace API to interact with resources. The resource model, its physical relationship with the file system, and its logical presentation to a tool were also discussed. The need to get a handle, validate that the resource was in the workspace, and possibly check whether the resource could also be in the file system but unknown to the resource was described.

Details on how to use the workspace API to add resource change listeners and save participants, which allow for very detailed tool reactions to changes in the workspace, were also discussed.

## References

Arthorne, John. August 23, 2002. How you've changed! Responding to resource changes in the Eclipse workspace. http://www.eclipse.org.

Arthorne, John, and Chris Laffra. 2004. *Official Eclipse 3.0 FAQs*. Boston, MA: Addison-Wesley. http://eclipsefaq.org. (See FAQs 284, 285, 289, 293, 296, 297, 311.)

PART IV

# CHAPTER 24

## *Managing Resources with Natures and Builders*

PART IV

This chapter discusses the role of natures and builders in the resource framework. It also describes their capabilities and the process of implementing them as part of your tool. This capability is available to tools that extend the IDE configuration of the Eclipse Platform or when the `org.eclipse.core.resources` plug-in is included in a Rich Client Platform configuration.

## Customizing Project Processing

If you have been using Eclipse to create Java programs or develop your own plug-in, you have created projects that have specialized capabilities. These capabilities have been added to a project using natures and builders.

A **nature** is used to associate behavior and function with a project. A **builder** is a mechanism used by the workspace that allows tool-specific logic to process changed files at specific times. Tools can add extensions to define new natures and builders.

Using the extensible resource framework, you can customize project behavior with natures and add builders to support incremental development.

### *How Natures and Builders Can Be Used*

A Java project has a Java nature and builder. A plug-in project not only has a Java nature and builder but also has a plug-in nature, a manifest builder, and a schema builder. These natures and builders provide specialized processing for the resources added to these types of projects. For example, when you add a .java file to a source folder in a Java project, the file is automatically compiled and a .class file is created in the build output folder for the project. A .java file in a simple project will not be compiled.

You can add this type of project customization as part of your tool by defining and implementing natures and builders.

### Extending the Workspace Resource Processing Framework

The process for adding nature and builder extensions to the workspace processing framework is similar to the steps you would follow for any other type of extension.

1. You contribute an extension as part of your plug-in for the desired extension point.
2. You define the class identified in the extension, extending a class or implementing an interface, as required for the specific extension point.

What is a bit different for workspace extensions is that it is not enough to just define and implement the extension. If you contribute a view, user interface action, or dialog, the contribution is immediately available in the user interface. When you contribute a workspace extension, you have just enabled the possibility of using the extension, but more work remains. For example, for a **nature extension**, the nature must be added to a project before it can configure additional function for the project. The class that implements the nature extension provides this customization. For a **builder extension**, the builder must be added to a project, which should be done as part of a nature configuration, so that the builder can start processing resources during a build event.

Once defined, these extensions can be associated with any number of projects and resources to support the functional goals of your tool.

## Defining and Implementing a Nature

There are two extension points you can use when creating a new nature to customize project capabilities:

- org.eclipse.core.resources.natures for natures
- org.eclipse.ui.ide.projectNatureImages for nature images

Natures add additional capabilities and processing to a project. Once they are defined, they can be installed on a per-project basis. They are configured automatically when added to a project and deconfigured when removed. A project can have more than one nature. A nature is often used to support the association of a builder to a project; a nature and builder can actually be linked as part of their definition.

The nature image extension point identifies an image that can be overlaid on the project icon to show that the nature is active. Only one image can be shown—the first nature found in a project that has an image is used.

You should create natures and add them to projects when your tool needs to customize the behavior of a project as the technique for delivery of function. If your tool function enhances the capabilities of other tools or is used to offer alternatives to existing editors, you may not need a nature (or a builder). If you are creating new resource types and need to tightly manage them as part of your domain, a nature might be the right approach. See the section Determining When Builders Are Required later in this chapter for additional considerations for builders.

### Creating Natures to Support Project Configuration

The `org.eclipse.core.resources.natures` extension point, like the other resource extension points, requires you to specify a unique id and provide a symbolic name. The id is used later to find and configure the nature. The run attribute specifies the name of the class that will provide the behavior for the nature.

```
<extension
  id="customnature"
  name="Custom Nature"
  point="org.eclipse.core.resources.natures">
    <runtime>
      <run
        class="com.ibm.tool.resources.CustomNature">
      </run>
    </runtime>
</extension>
```

The nature extension can also identify other natures that are prerequisites with this type of entry.

```
<requires-nature id="another.nature.id"/>
```

If multiple natures are defined but cannot coexist as part of the same project, they should identify themselves as part of a mutually exclusive set using an entry like the following one in each nature extension.

```
<one-of-nature id="com.ibm.limited.to.one.nature"/>
```

The class identified in the extension to provide runtime processing for the nature must implement the `IProjectNature` interface. The default implementation of a class that implements this interface is shown here.

```
public class CustomNature implements IProjectNature {

    public void configure() throws CoreException {
    // Do work here like adding builders.
    }
    public void deconfigure() throws CoreException {
    // Do work here like removing private resources.
    }
    public IProject getProject() {
      return null;
    }
    public void setProject(IProject project) {
    }
}
```

To customize the structure just shown, you must do the following.

- Add a project variable (`IProject`) to your class definition.
- Modify `getProject` and `setProject` to return/set the project field value.
- Modify `configure` and `deconfigure` to perform any required processing.

You need to keep a reference to the project in your nature to support the configure/deconfigure customization process.

Natures are installed on a per-project basis, and a project can have more than one nature. The `setProject` method is invoked when a nature is added to the project, followed by the `configure` method. The `deconfigure` method is run when a nature is removed.

## Adding a Nature to a Project

Once you have implemented your nature, you then need to determine when and how it will be added to projects. If you create your own projects, you can use the wizard framework and take advantage of the `WizardNewProject-CreationPage` class. This class can be used in your wizard to help create a project and associate your nature to the project in the process. The following logic will add a nature to the project description for a project.

```
public static final String NATURE_ID:
  "com.ibm.tool.customnature";
public void addCustomNature(IProject project)
  throws CoreException {
```

```
      if (!project.hasNature(IResourceIDs.NATURE_ID)) {
        try {
          IProjectDescription description =
            project.getDescription();
          String[] natures = description.getNatureIds();
          String[] newNatures = new String[natures.length + 1];
          System.arraycopy(
            natures, 0, newNatures, 0, natures.length);
          newNatures[natures.length] = IResourceIDs.NATURE_ID;
          description.setNatureIds(newNatures);
          project.setDescription(description, null);
          // Confirm nature add.
          resultInformation(
            "Soln: Resource -- Add CustomNature Request",
            "CustomNature added to the "
              + project.getName()
              + " project.");
        } catch (CoreException e) {
          // Problem with builder add.
          resultError(
            "Soln: Resource -- Add CustomNature Request",
            "Error adding the CustomNature to the "
            + project.getName() + " project ");
        }
      } else {
        resultError(
          "Soln: Resource -- Add CustomNature Request",
          "The CustomNature is already associated with the "
          + project.getName() + " project.");
      }
    }
```

The call to `setDescription` updates the project and adds the nature. The nature added will then be configured (or a removed nature deconfigured) unless the call includes the `IResource.AVOID_NATURE_CONFIG` parameter. This parameter tells the workspace to not configure or deconfigure any natures that were added or removed from the project.

The implementation of a wizard that reuses the `WizardNewProject-CreationPage` class and adds a nature to the project is included in the resource extensions solution on the CD-ROM.

See the Projects and Project Descriptions sections in Chapter 23, Workspace Resource Programming, for more information on the project API.

If you need to add your nature to an existing project, you could use a contributed action or a wizard. Using a wizard that requires the user to select the target project is the preferred approach. The PDE implements a wizard that uses this approach (see the **File > New > Other...** menu option and then the **Plug-in Development / Convert Projects to Plug-in Projects** entry).

PART IV

## Managing Nature–Builder Relationships

A nature can be mapped to one or more builders. This allows for a formalized relationship that implements rules for when a builder can be added to a project and automated removal of a builder when the nature is removed.

The nature configuration process is the recommended place to manage the process of adding and removing builders for a project. The following logic adds a builder to the project when the nature is configured.

```java
public static final String BUILDER_ID =
  "com.ibm.tool.custombuilder";
...
public void configure() throws CoreException {
  IProjectDescription desc = project.getDescription();
  ICommand[] commands = desc.getBuildSpec();
  boolean found = false;
  for (int i = 0; i < commands.length; ++i) {
    if (commands[i].getBuilderName().equals(BUILDER_ID)) {
      found = true;
      break;
    }
  }
  if (!found) { // Add builder to project.
    ICommand command = desc.newCommand();
    command.setBuilderName(BUILDER_ID);
    ICommand[] newCommands =
      new ICommand[commands.length + 1];
    // Add it before other builders.
    System.arraycopy(
      commands, 0, newCommands, 1, commands.length);
    newCommands[0] = command;
    desc.setBuildSpec(newCommands);
    project.setDescription(desc, null);
  }
}
```

> **NOTE** The builder id is a concatenation of the plug-in id and the id used in the builder extension entry. Therefore, if the plug-in id is `a.b` and the extension id is `c`, then `a.b.c` is the builder id. This same concatenated reference is used to identify a nature.

The nature can be formally connected with the builder if the entry `<builder id="a.linked.builder.id"/>` is included in the nature extension definition.

To enable the automated removal of a builder when the associated nature is removed, the builder must also include the `hasNature="true"` attribute on the `<builder>` entry. If the referenced builder includes a `hasNature="true"` entry, the builder cannot be added unless the nature is also present.

The nature `configure` method should still be used to add the builder. A builder is not automatically added because you may need to specify arguments as part of the builder command.

### Using a Custom Image to Identify Your Project Nature

You can help the user know your nature is involved in the project by adding a nature image. The extension point allows you to define an image that will be overlaid on the project image in the Navigator view. The following definition adds an image for the `customnature` nature defined earlier.

```
<extension
    point="org.eclipse.ui.ide.projectNatureImages">
  <image
      icon="images/CustomNature.gif"
      natureId="com.ibm.lab.soln.resources.customnature"
      id="com.ibm.lab.soln.resoures.natureimage">
  </image>
</extension>
```

Figure 24.1 shows the result of this definition in the Navigator view.

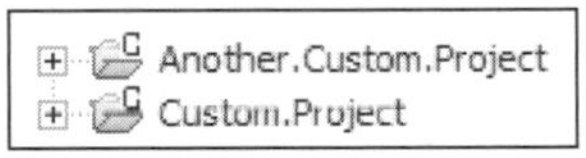

⊞ 🗁 Another.Custom.Project
⊞ 🗁 Custom.Project

**Figure 24.1**   Nature Image Overlaid on Project Image

# Defining and Implementing an Incremental Project Builder

The workspace provides an extension point that allows tools to define an incremental project builder (often just called a **builder**). Builders are defined and then added to a project when required. To define a builder you use the `org.eclipse.core.resources.builders` extension point.

By creating a builder, you can implement targeted **resource transformations**, the ability to react to individual resource changes and perform any tool-specific processing that may be required. This processing could be resource validation or incremental compilation. This type of processing can be implemented using builders. You define builder extensions to implement the resource transformation processing required in your tool. A builder is then associated with a project for which it needs to perform this task. Note that a project can have more than one builder.

## Builder Basics

Builders are associated to projects and invoked periodically to perform their designed processing. Figure 24.2 provides an overview of how build processing is invoked for builders that have been associated with a project.

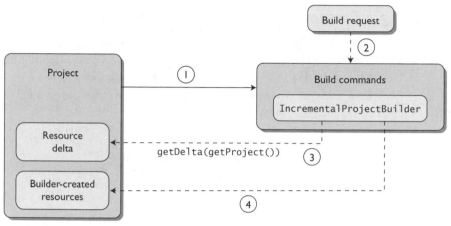

**Figure 24.2**    Build Processing Overview

The following steps describe the process illustrated in Figure 24.2.

1. Builders are associated with projects as build commands. Each project can have any number of build commands.
2. Each build command is invoked when build processing is triggered.
3. Projects have a resource delta that identifies all the changes that have occurred in the project since the last build. A builder can get this resource delta to guide the incremental build process. The delta is not available during a full build request.
4. Builder logic identifies what changed resources must be built and creates additional resources as required.

Custom builder logic determines which resources will be processed and whether any transformation is required. The builder framework does not automate any resource selection on behalf of the builder; each builder has access to the same input (an IResourceDelta), which identifies all resource changes for the project.

The resources produced by a builder should be marked as derived (review the IResource interface) so that other tools treat them appropriately.

For example, derived resources might be skipped during repository processing or considered as read-only by associated editors.

## Builder Invocation

Builders are invoked directly by Eclipse (when the Workbench preference **Build automatically** setting is selected) or by the user (using the build options on the **Project** menu). The builder is aware of what kind of build was requested. There are four types of builds as defined by fields in `Incremental-ProjectBuilder`.

- `INCREMENTAL_BUILD` is triggered by request when auto-build is off.
- `AUTO_BUILD` is automatically triggered by Eclipse based on the preference setting.
- `FULL_BUILD` is triggered by request to force a fresh build of all resources.
- `CLEAN_BUILD` is triggered by request for either the full workspace or a selected set of projects. The request clears all build state information and is followed by a `FULL_BUILD` request.

Incremental builds are invoked automatically when the **Build automatically** preference is selected. If a resource changes in a project with a builder, that builder will be invoked and have access to a resource delta for the project.

An incremental build can still be started when automatic builds are not requested. You can start an incremental build for a single project by using the **Build Project** menu option available on the context menu for the project or the Workbench's **Project** menu when a project is selected. An incremental build for all projects can be started using the **Project > Build All** menu option.

When an incremental build is started, the builder has access to a resource delta for its project. The builder then processes, or builds if you like, only the modified resources. The builder is given information about the resource changes that occurred since the last build and the opportunity to use this information to identify which resources it should select for processing. In fact, your builder can be as smart as you like and thereby improve the build processing efficiency.

The user can also manually request that all build information be disposed; this clean request can be made for a specific project or all projects by using the **Project > Clean...** menu option. The clean request asks builders to forget their last build state. Builders for projects that have been cleaned will be invoked in `FULL_BUILD` mode the next time a build request is sent;

INCREMENTAL_BUILD build requests for prerequisite projects of a cleaned project will also be sent at the same time. This ensures that there are no inconsistencies in the environment after the clean request; a project cannot be expected to build if its dependent projects are out of date.

### Determining When Builders Are Required

Both builders and resource event listeners can react to resource changes. Determining when automatic reactions are required and choosing between a builder and a resource change listener is an important consideration. Ask these questions to help you frame your options.

- Do I need to be aware of changes made to a specific project that my tool creates or customizes, or changes to a resource type regardless of the project?

  Builders are added to individual projects. You can process a change with a builder only if you have customized the project (using a nature, of course). A resource change listener is informed of changes to any resource in the workspace.

- Is the reaction to change a process of transforming a resource from format a to format b or tracking information about resources?

  Builders are designed to transform resources. Consider the Java builder as an example. Java source files are compiled by the builder to create .class files. If a Java source file is removed or renamed, the corresponding .class file is removed, and a new .class file is created if required.

- Would the time required to perform the resource transformation interrupt the tool users' thought processes?

  Do not assume your previous use of the term *builder* matches how it is used in Eclipse. In traditional development shops, a "build" is often viewed as a long-running task that involves a large number of resources; one "builds a product" or "builds a version of a product." In contrast, Eclipse builders often run immediately following a resource change (such as saving a Java program). They should be viewed as very fast processes that will not disrupt the flow of active development.

  If the task you need to perform is long-running, you should consider options other than a builder-based implementation. Think of it this way: If you could use the term "generate" or "deploy" to describe the task, it is probably something that should not be implemented as a builder or a resource change listener.

• Should the user be able to disable the processing being performed?

All build processing can be disabled by changing a Workbench preference setting. Builders can react to all pending changes once the build processing is restarted or specifically requested by the user. If other tool functions would be impacted while builds are disabled, the right choice might be a resource change listener.

You should create a builder when required, but at the same time be sure that the builder is fast so it does not delay the thought process of the user. As such, builders should scale with respect to the volume of changes rather than the number of resources in the project. This typically implies that builders can implement an approach to tracking the current build status in a build state and incrementally update the build state during build processing.

### Builder Definition and Implementation

Table 24.1 lists the classes and interfaces you use to implement an incremental project builder.

**Table 24.1**  Incremental Project Builder Classes and Interfaces

| Class/Interface | Description |
| --- | --- |
| IncrementalProjectBuilder | This class must be subclassed by all builders. It provides the framework for implementation of a custom builder. |
| IResourceDelta | A resource delta represents changes in the state of a resource tree between two discrete points in time. A resource change event contains a resource delta, which can be processed by using the visitor pattern. |
| IResourceDeltaVisitor | Your class must implement this interface to be a visitor of a resource delta. The visitor pattern will then be used to allow you to process each entry in the delta. |

To define and then use a builder, follow these steps.

1. Contribute a builder extension in your plug-in.
2. Implement a builder by creating a class that subclasses `Incremental-ProjectBuilder`.
3. Associate the builder with a project (best done as part of nature processing).

PART IV

After you associate the builder with a project, Eclipse sends build requests—either automatic or manual—to the appropriate projects, which then invoke the associated build commands.

To define a builder, extend the `org.eclipse.core.resources.builders` extension point.

```
<extension
     id="custombuilder"
     name="Custom Builder"
     point="org.eclipse.core.resources.builders">
   <builder hasNature="false">
     <run class="com.ibm.tool.resources.CustomBuilder">
        <parameter name="validate" value="true">
        </parameter>
        <parameter name="output" value="build_dir">
        </parameter>
     </run>
   </builder>
</extension>
```

The `hasNature` attribute, which defines that the builder is being managed by a nature, was discussed in the section Managing Nature–Builder Relationships earlier in this chapter.

The builder can access the `<parameter ... >` entries in the builder extension definition when invoked. You can use these parameters to provide build processing input. You can also customize the builder for a specific project. When you add the builder as a build command (`ICommand`), you can use the `setArguments` method to define runtime arguments. When the builder is invoked, a `Map` with the arguments is passed to the `build` method.

The class identified in the extension must inherit from `Incremental-ProjectBuilder`. You define your custom build logic in your implementation of the `build` method. Your custom build logic should implement the following.

- Identify any passed parameters (if defined in the extension).
- Determine what type of build has been started.
- Implement the appropriate build strategy.

If `<parameter ...>` entries were defined in the builder extension, the builder can read them. The `setInitializationData` method will be invoked before the `build` method, which allows the builder to perform any configuration based on the parameter settings. If you want to get the parameter in your builder, you need to override the `setInitializationData` method. The following logic shows how the parameters in the extension definition can be found at runtime.

```
public void setInitializationData(
   IConfigurationElement config,
   String propertyName,
   Object data)
   throws CoreException {

   super.setInitializationData(config, propertyName, data);
   IConfigurationElement[] run = config.getChildren();
   IConfigurationElement[] parms = run[0].getChildren();
   for (int i = 0; i < parms.length; i++) {
      System.out.println(
         parms[i].getAttribute("name") + " = "
            + parms[i].getAttribute("value"));
   }
}
```

This logic finds two attributes based on the builder extension previously shown.

The following `build` method performs the appropriate build based on the build type, obtaining an `IResourceDelta` when appropriate (using the inherited `getDelta` method), and using an `IResourceDeltaVisitor` (`CustomVisitor` in this example) to process the delta.

```
protected IProject[] build(
   int kind, Map args, IProgressMonitor monitor)
   throws CoreException {
   if (kind == IncrementalProjectBuilder.FULL_BUILD) {
      // Full build.
      // Use a ResourceVisitor to process the
      // project resource tree.
      performFullBuild();
   } else {
      // Build with a delta (Auto/Incremental).
      IResourceDelta delta = getDelta(getProject());
      if (delta == null) {
         performFullBuild();
      } else {
         delta.accept(new CustomVisitor());
      }
      // Custom visitor visit method will process changes.
   }
   return null;
}
```

The `build` method can return `null` or a list of projects for which the builder may want to request resource deltas in the next invocation. One option might be to return the projects referenced by the current project. This would allow your builder to respond to other projects as identified by your tool or the user. (The resource extensions example on the CD-ROM explores this capability.) If you wanted to avoid having the user control this relationship and the subsequent return value for the build method, you could calculate and use the dynamic project references supported by the `IProjectDescription` API. See the Project Descriptions section in Chapter 23, Workspace Resource Programming, for details.

For an incremental build or auto-build, the `getDelta` method returns an `IResourceDelta` for the project. The delta is processed by implementing a `ResourceDeltaVisitor`, which can visit the resource delta. The `Resource-DeltaVisitor` invokes the appropriate build processing when supported resources are found in the `IResourceDelta`. Your builder is not given an `IResourceDelta` when the build type is `FULL_BUILD` because all resources are to be rebuilt, not just those that changed. In this case your builder logic should use an `IResourceVisitor` (not `IResourceDeltaVisitor`) to process all the project's members. Be aware that the delta can be `null`, depending on the state of the project and decisions made by Eclipse (e.g., Eclipse can choose to delete the delta to save space; your builder would then have to process the build request as a full build). See the Javadoc for the `IncrementalProject-Builder` method `getDelta` for additional details.

Your implementation of the `visit` method in your `IResourceDeltaVisitor` can process the resource delta to determine what changes have occurred and implement any required processing. As an example, the following logic structure for the `visit` method filters through the resource delta to find a resource type of interest and then processes it based on the type of change.

```java
public boolean visit(IResourceDelta delta)
    throws CoreException {
    IResource resource = delta.getResource();
    int type = resource.getType();
    if (type == IResource.FILE) {
        if (resource.getFileExtension().equals("myFileType")) {
            switch (delta.getKind()) {
                case IResourceDelta.ADDED :
                    // Add custom logic here.
                    break;
                case IResourceDelta.CHANGED :
                    // Add custom logic here.
                    break;
                case IResourceDelta.REMOVED :
                    // Add custom logic here.
                    break;
```

```
            }
        }
    }
    return true; // Carry on.
}
```

This visitor logic processes the complete resource delta tree. If there were numerous changes but none of interest to your builder, you would be spending visitor cycles processing delta nodes that were not interesting to your builder. One way to improve your builder's focus is to find the content in the resource delta that you are interested in processing. You can get a specific portion of the delta using the `IResourceDelta.findMember(IPath)` method. The `IPath` value can identify the portion of the delta changes you are interested in processing. The method returns a resource delta you can process further, or `null` if no changes exist for your `IPath` value. This logic allows the builder solution to request the portion of the delta that contains changes to the project's `readme` folder.

```
// Path for where readme files will be found.
public final IPath README_FOLDER = new Path("readme");

// Use defined path to get portion of resource delta
// that is of interest.
IResourceDelta focusDelta =
    delta.findMember(IResourceIDs.README_FOLDER);
```

The resource delta returned by `findMember` can then be processed by a visitor. No time will be wasted processing changes in the full resource delta for the entire project.

Once the basic components (extension and builder) are in place, you can add the builder to a project. Use the `IProjectDescription` to get and set an array of build commands for the project. This logic was described earlier in the section Managing Nature–Builder Relationships.

## Example Summary

This chapter discussed the creation of natures and builders and their use to customize a project. You can now explore the nature and builder solution located on the CD-ROM in the `com.ibm.jdg2e.resources.extensions` project.

The plug-in defines a new nature (`customnature`) and an incremental project builder (`readmebuilder`). A New Project wizard is defined to create a project with the nature. Pop-up menu actions in the Navigator view can also be used to add and remove the nature from a project selected in that view. The nature includes a custom project image and adds the builder to the project as part of the `configure` logic.

The builder definition requires that the nature be associated to the project (`hasNature="true"`), but if you modify the builder definition in the `plugin.xml` file, you can directly add and remove the builder from a selected project using the provided actions. These actions will fail if the builder and nature relationship exists.

The builder will create a `.html` file for a `.readme` file that exists in the `readme` folder for the project. The `.html` file wraps the `.readme` file content in a little bit of HTML; this mimics the kind of transformation that a builder might perform on a given resource.

## Chapter Summary

This chapter described using the nature and builder workspace extension points to add additional capabilities to projects. Natures can be added to provide additional capability for a project and are the standard for how and when builders should be added to a project. Builders are typically defined to implement any resource-specific transformation processing required by your tool. Beyond that, the builder life cycle can be used when you want to relate a specific set of processing to a project. The preference and user interface controls available let the user of your tool fine-tune when and how this processing is invoked.

## References

Arthorne, John. August 23, 2002. How you've changed! Responding to resource changes in the Eclipse workspace. http://www.eclipse.org.

Arthorne, John. January 27, 2003. Project natures and builders. http://www.eclipse.org.

Arthorne, John, and Chris Laffra. 2004. *Official Eclipse 3.0 FAQs*. Boston, MA: Addison-Wesley. http://eclipsefaq.org. (See FAQs 291, 292, 318, 328, 329, 344.)

# CHAPTER 25

## *Resource Tagging Using Markers*

This chapter discusses the use of markers to tag a resource to identify areas of interest, problems, and even problem resolutions. The support for the creation of new marker types is also discussed.

By adding markers to a specific file, folder, or project, or even to the workspace root itself (which qualifies as a resource), you can add data that allows you to identify problems, share information, and track changes. New marker types can be added; these can be independent of all other marker types or build on the capabilities provided by the markers defined as part of Eclipse.

By understanding the capabilities of markers, you can effectively use them to implement your custom tool function. A common technique is to use a marker to identify problems and support direct user navigation to the source of the problem in a file. That is, the user can double-click on a problem marker and the tagged file will be opened and the file positioned at the appropriate place in the editor. This same support exists for task markers and bookmark markers.

### Using Markers

**Markers** are objects that can be associated with other resources, but they are not saved as part of the associated resource. They are managed and saved as part of the workspace by the `org.eclipse.core.resources` plug-in. Markers allow you to tag a resource, or even a specific location in the resource, to identify a problem or area of interest. Attributes can be used to store additional information in the marker. Markers are like Post-it notes; you can put them just about anywhere (with respect to resources) and use them for almost anything. The Workbench uses markers for many things.

- Tasks—for a common to-do list. Users can create them, but tools can also generate them to identify actions that are pending. For example, the JDT creates Task markers that correspond to the comments with a TODO phrase (these are called **task tags**). Task markers are displayed in the Tasks view.
- Bookmarks—for a list of places you want to remember and find fast. Bookmark markers are displayed in the Bookmarks view.
- Problems—to identify a place where a correction is needed. Problem markers are dynamically created by tools to mark files or specific locations in files. Problem markers are displayed in the Problems view.
- Text—to mark specific areas of text. Text markers can be used to identify precise areas of text in an editor.

Markers represent a way to associate additional data with resources. By using markers, you get an API to access the attribute data and additional function as well. Once markers are created for a specific resource, you can set and get values for named attributes; the attributes can be used to store String, integer, or boolean data.

The org.eclipse.core.resources plug-in defines the marker types shown in Table 25.1.

You can use the marker types that already exist or contribute extensions to define new marker types as might be required in your tool. Marker extensions identify the type, supertypes for the marker, and attribute information.

The marker types and attributes defined in the marker extensions that are part of the Eclipse Platform are detailed in the IMarker interface (see Table 25.1). You can use references to these fields in your marker logic.

The IMarker interface also includes methods to set and access attributes for the marker. The name of the attribute and the value to be set are passed to the marker for processing by the platform implementation of the IMarker interface.

The existence of a marker for a resource can be used to control the appearance of other tool contributions. You can define a pop-up menu so that it appears only when the resource has a marker of a specific type or supertype. This filter can be sensitive to the content of the message, priority, or severity attributes. See the section Built-in Action Filters for Resources and Markers in Chapter 21, Action Contributions: The Integration Fast Track, for more information on how you can refine action contribution enablement using marker details.

**Table 25.1** Marker Types Defined in the Resources Plug-in

| Type/Identifiers | Attributes | Usage Notes |
|---|---|---|
| Marker<br>org.eclipse.core.resources.marker<br>IMarker.MARKER | Transient:<br>IMarker.TRANSIENT | Common supertype for all markers. |
| Problemmarker<br>org.eclipse.core.resources.problemmarker<br>IMarker.PROBLEM | Severity:<br>IMarker.SEVERITY<br>Message:<br>IMarker.MESSAGE<br>Location:<br>IMarker.LOCATION | Shown in Problems view. Includes Quick Fix support. |
| TaskMarker<br>org.eclipse.core.resources.taskmarker<br>IMarker.TASK | Priority:<br>IMarker.PRIORITY<br>Message:<br>IMarker.MESSAGE<br>Done:<br>IMarker.DONE | Shown in Tasks view. Message values can be modified by user. |
| Bookmark<br>org.eclipse.core.resources.bookmark<br>IMarker.BOOKMARK | Message:<br>IMarker.MESSAGE<br>Location:<br>IMarker.LOCATION | Shown in Bookmarks view. Typically created by the user. |
| Textmarker<br>org.eclipse.core.resources.textmarker<br>IMarker.TEXT | Character start:<br>IMarker.CHAR_START<br>Character end:<br>IMarker.CHAR_END<br>Line number:<br>IMarker.LINE_NUMBER | Often combined with other markers to integrate marker with editor framework. |

PART IV

## Creating Markers for Customized Resource Tagging

The simplest approach to using markers in your tool is to use the markers already defined as part of Eclipse. If you have a handle to a resource, you can add a marker. For example, the following code adds a task marker with a normal priority to a resource.

```
IMarker marker = res.createMarker(IMarker.TASK);
marker.setAttribute(IMarker.PRIORITY, IMarker.PRIORITY_NORMAL);
marker.setAttribute(IMarker.MESSAGE, "Task marker added");
```

You can obtain a marker handle when you know the marker id by using the method `Resource.findMarker(id)`. The id is a numeric value for the marker that is generated when the marker was created. If you do not know the marker id, you can ask the resource for all known markers. You specify the marker type you want to find, whether subtypes of that type should be returned, and whether you want those for the identified resource or whether the children of the resource should be included as part of the find markers request. The syntax of this request is

```
IMarker[] findMarkers(String type, boolean includeSubtypes,
    int depth)
```

The depth parameter can be one of the following.

```
IResource.DEPTH_ZERO
IResource.DEPTH_ONE
IResource.DEPTH_INFINITE
```

These allow you to gather markers for a given resource, that resource and its members, or all resources in the resource tree below the given resource, respectively.

---

**NOTE** You can use the workspace root as the resource used to create a marker if the marker does not need to be associated with a specific file, folder, or project resource. By using the workspace root, you are essentially hiding the marker in the workspace .metadata. Even if all projects were deleted from the workspace, markers associated to the workspace root would still exist. You might find that this flexibility and permanence is useful to your tool development needs.

---

The following logic would return all task markers known to the identified resource and all the children of that resource.

```
IMarker[] tasks = null;
try {
  tasks = resource.findMarkers(IMarker.TASK,
    true, IResource.DEPTH_INFINITE);
  }
} catch (CoreException e) {
  // Something went wrong.
}
```

When you add or modify a marker, a resource change event is triggered. You can use the following statement to find changes to markers in a resource change event.

```
IMarkerDelta[] mdeltas = event.getDelta().getMarkerDeltas();
```

See the section Processing Workspace Resource Change Events in Chapter 23, for more details on resource change listeners.

### Setting Marker Attributes

A marker extension definition includes the attributes that should be well known to users of that marker type. But do not assume that these are the only attributes that can be defined for marker instances of that type; you can create attribute name/value pairs as you go. There is no limit enforced by the marker framework or extension definition. For example, the problem marker has attributes of severity, message, and location. You could add an attribute named your.plugin.id or anything else you might dream up.

The only reason to define attributes in a marker extension is to identify expectations for users of that marker type. The implicit assumption might be that if these well-known attributes are not set in a marker instance, places where that marker is used or displayed might show incomplete information. Imagine a problem marker without a value for the IMarker.MESSAGE attribute; the Problems view would have no value to place in the Description column.

### Limiting Resource Change Events during Marker Creation and Update

Each call made to the IMarker.setAttribute method can trigger a resource change event. A performance goal in Eclipse is to limit the number of change events that your code might trigger because each event can be sent to many listeners. The techniques for limiting events as discussed in the section Resource Modification Event Management in Chapter 23 are valid, but for markers you also have another approach available.

You can create a Map with the marker attribute keys and values and use the IMarker.setAttributes method to assign them all at once. This triggers one resource change event.

```
Map attributes = new HashMap(5);
attributes.put(IMarker.CHAR_START, new Integer(77));
attributes.put(IMarker.CHAR_END, new Integer(81));
attributes.put("reditKey", "Red");
attributes.put(IMarker.MESSAGE, "Message Text");
attributes.put(IMarker.USER_EDITABLE, new Boolean(true));
marker.setAttributes(attributes);
```

## Adding New Marker Types

The types of markers already known to Eclipse have been defined as an extension in org.eclipse.core.resources and other plug-ins. Marker extension definitions identify any supertypes, named attributes, and a persistency setting.

PART IV

## Defining Marker Supertypes

Markers can define one or more supertypes to combine attributes and default processing that exists for other markers as part of the new marker type. Note that this is not a complete match to "supertypes" in the Java language sense; this refers to a collection of attributes and function associated with a given marker type.

Table 25.1 lists the types of markers defined as part of the Eclipse Platform; the Eclipse JDT defines another marker, which we will discuss in a moment.

More than one supertype can be defined for a new marker extension. Sometimes choosing two supertypes is appropriate. Once a new marker is defined and used, you can use the API for markers to find all markers of a given type, with subtypes. This allows you to search for just your marker or for markers that are subtypes of a more generic kind of marker. If your marker were a subtype, it would be included in that typed set. The following technique is used in the JDT to define the Java problem marker.

```
<extension point="org.eclipse.core.resources.markers"
    id="problem" name="%javaProblemName">
  <super type="org.eclipse.core.resources.problemmarker"/>
  <super type="org.eclipse.core.resources.textmarker"/>
  <persistent value="true"/>
  <attribute name="id"/>
  <attribute name="flags"/>
  <attribute name="arguments"/>
</extension>
```

Java problem markers (org.eclipse.jdt.core.problem) are used to identify problems in the source that were found during the compile. These markers are displayed in the Problems view. The existence of these markers is also identified using label decorators to alter the resource icon in the Java editor and in the Package Explorer and Outline views.

The Java problem marker combines the attributes of problemmarker and textmarker and then adds several other attributes. The result is a marker with the following attributes:

- severity, message, and location from problemmarker
- charStart, charEnd, and lineNumber from textmarker
- id, flags, and arguments added as part of the Java problem marker

Some of these values are visible when looking at Java problem markers in the Problems view. Others are used to support direct navigation to the problem. Just double-click on the marker in the Problems view and the Java program with an error is opened, the line made visible in the editor, and the problem area in the source selected.

You can choose to define new markers so they are not automatically shown in existing views and instead create new views to display your new markers. Markers can be created, but they are not visible until some user interface component finds them and gives them a place in the user interface. Different views and editors already process, or consume, certain types of markers. The Bookmarks view displays all bookmark markers that have been defined; the Tasks and Problems views show all task and problem markers, respectively. The Tasks and Problems views also support filtering by resource or marker subtype.

You can add marker extensions by extending other markers. For example, you can define the following marker extension.

```
<extension id="custommarker" name="Custom Marker"
  point="org.eclipse.core.resources.markers">
  <super type="org.eclipse.core.resources.taskmarker" />
  <super type="org.eclipse.core.resources.bookmark" />
  <persistent value="true" />
  <attribute name="flags" />
  <attribute name="arguments" />
</extension>
```

After defining this, you can add the marker to a resource.

```
IMarker marker_Fi2 =
  res.createMarker("com.ibm.tool.resources.custommarker");
marker_Fi2.setAttribute(IMarker.SEVERITY, 0);
marker_Fi2.setAttribute(IMarker.CHAR_START, 20);
marker_Fi2.setAttribute(IMarker.CHAR_END, 70);
marker_Fi2.setAttribute(IMarker.LOCATION, "someplace close");
marker_Fi2.setAttribute(IMarker.MESSAGE,"Custommarker added");
```

The new marker type `custommarker` is consumed by both the Bookmarks view and Tasks view (see Figure 25.1). The new marker has inherited the platform implementation for problem and task markers.

**Figure 25.1** Marker Supertype Definition Forcing Display in Two Different Views

**NOTE** If you define a marker and keep adjusting the supertypes to see which behavior you want to extend, you may need to reset the test environment on occasion. During our test cycles we were able to confuse the workspace that was reused for every test; the workspace seemed to keep older marker type definitions in the .metadata cache. The same code would work differently in an older workspace and a fresh workspace; the fresh workspace had the expected behavior. So, if you see an AssertionFailedException in your console or error log, or other odd behavior, you might want to clear the workspace before continuing with your testing.

## Reusing Supertype Attributes

Attributes identify additional data that can be kept with the marker; these attributes can also be referenced when adding action contributions.

Your markers will be visible in existing views if they define appropriate supertypes. A marker extension with org.eclipse.core.resources.bookmark as a supertype will be visible in the Bookmarks view; if a marker has a supertype of org.eclipse.core.resources.taskmarker, marker instances will be in the Tasks view; and the same is true for the problem marker and the Problems view. When you define these markers as a supertype, you need to be prepared for this default processing by loading the supertype attributes with the values you want to see in these views. You can still have other attributes defined, but you should either use those defined by the supertype or not reference the supertype.

## Controlling Marker Persistency

The persistent setting for a marker extension determines whether the marker will be saved as part of the workspace .metadata. This decision can be changed from yes to no for a given marker by modifying the IMarker-TRANSIENT attribute.

```
marker.setAttribute(IMarker.TRANSIENT, true);
```

A marker defined as temporary (<persistent value="false"/>) cannot be changed to persistent using a call to set the IMarker.TRANSIENT attribute to false.

## Adding a Custom Image to a Text Marker

Text markers (IMarker.TEXT) are one of the predefined types of markers in the Eclipse Platform. When created, either directly or by having a marker that uses the text marker as a supertype, they are rendered in the user interface for an editor built using the JFace Text framework. If the marker involved is a subtype of both the text marker and either a problem, task, or bookmark, the image used in the prefix of a JFace Text-based editor is determined by the type of marker and, for problem markers, the severity of the marker.

If you build your own markers that use the text marker as a supertype, you need to provide an image if you want one to be visible in a JFace Text-based editor. This is done using the `org.eclipse.ui.ide.markerImage-Providers` extension point. A contribution to this extension point can either use the `icon` attribute to identify an image in the `plugin.xml` content or a class that will identify the image at runtime.

If a class is used, the class implements the `IMarkerImageProvider` interface; the `getImagePath` method returns a reference to an image in that plug-in's directory. Here is an example of the extension with both an image and a class reference.

```
<extension
  point="org.eclipse.ui.ide.markerImageProviders">
  <imageprovider
    markertype="com.ibm.jdg2e.resources.recentEdits"
    icon="images/getstart_b.GIF"
    class="com.ibm.jdg2e.resources.markers.ReditImageProvider"
    id="com.ibm.jdg2e.resources.imageprovider"/>
</extension>
```

If both options are included in the definition, the class takes control; the icon reference will not be used, even if you return a `null`.

There are other considerations when using a text marker for display in a JFace Text editor; the `IMarker.CHAR_START`, `IMarker.CHAR_END`, and `CharEnd` attributes are for the full file, not the line involved. The `AbstractTextEditor` framework shows the appropriate image, moves the marker as text is inserted or removed, and opens the editor and navigates to the marker's position when the editor's `goToMarker` method is called. This is done automatically for markers in the Problems or Tasks views.

## Extending Markers with Generators for Resolution and Help Support

The following two extension points add additional capabilities to markers.

- `org.eclipse.ui.ide.markerresolution`
- `org.eclipse.ui.ide.markerhelp`

A marker resolution extension allows you to implement a generator that determines whether quick fix support is available for a selected marker. The extension identifies a marker id and a marker resolution generator class that will be used to propose resolution options. The resolutions are available on the **Quick Fix** pop-up menu available when a marker is selected in the Problems view.

A marker help extension allows you to implement a generator that identifies an appropriate help context id, which could be unique to that marker instance, so that contextual help can be associated to the marker.

### Adding Marker Resolution

The Problems view provides support for processing marker resolutions; all markers shown in the Problems view are candidates for resolution. The Problems view includes a pop-up menu option named **Quick Fix**, which is enabled when the selected marker has resolutions available. If available, the resolutions can be shown in the Quick Fix dialog (see Figure 25.2).

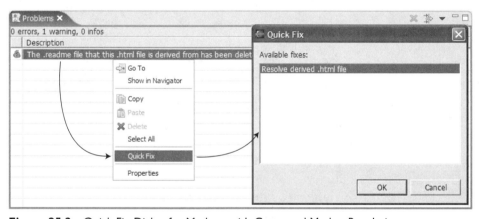

**Figure 25.2**    Quick Fix Dialog for Markers with Generated Marker Resolutions

To add support for marker resolution, you need to be able to target the marker that identifies the situation you want to help fix. This requires that you have an identifier for the marker type and an attribute name/value pair you can use to control when your resolution should apply. The identifiers for marker types defined as part of the resources plug-in are listed in Table 25.1.

When you select a marker, the quick fix logic determines whether there are any resolution generators defined for that marker type that pass the attribute name/value filter as may be defined in the extension. If possible, you should identify more than just a marker type in the marker resolution extension. Without a name/value pair, the resolution generator you provide would be called for every possible marker of that type that might be selected; your tool will perform better if you filter out as much as possible in the extension contribution.

The following example of a marker resolution generator contribution targets a problem marker with a specific keyed attribute.

```
<extension
  point="org.eclipse.ui.ide.markerResolution">
  <markerResolutionGenerator
   class=
     "com.ibm.jdg2e.resources.markers.ReadmeResolutionGenerator"
   markerType="org.eclipse.core.resources.problemmarker">
   <attribute
     value="derived"
     name="readme"/>
  </markerResolutionGenerator>
</extension>
```

The class identified as part of a resolution generator contribution must implement one of the two available interfaces; the IResolutionGenerator interface is extended by IResolutionGenerator2. Both of these interfaces require a getResolutions method; the second requires a hasResolutions method. The difference between the two is when the methods are called. The goal is to make a quick decision on the availability of a MarkerResolution for a given marker instance without triggering extensive processing. The problem is that the availability question is posed when the marker is selected, but the user may not be looking to use the **Quick Fix** option; he or she may simply be trying to get the full marker message in the status bar.

The next step is to determine whether any of these resolution generators are able to return a marker resolution instance when asked.

This user interaction scenario will help you understand the different call patterns.

- Select a marker in the Problems view.
- Request the pop-up menu.
- Choose the **Quick Fix** option.

For an IResolutionGenerator implementation in the user interaction scenario, the getResolutions method will be called three times; compare this with an IResolutionGenerator2 implementation where the hasResolutions method is called twice and then the getResolutions method is called only after the **Quick Fix** option has been chosen.

This pattern provides you with the opportunity to optimize your contribution. The hasResolutions method is useful when your resolution generators can rapidly determine whether a resolution can be offered, but you may need to do more work to actually create an IMarkerResolution instance. By implementing the IResolutionGenerator2 interface, you can delay the call to a more expensive getResolutions method.

A resolution generator returns an IMarkerResolution instance. This is a fairly straightforward implementation of two methods: getLabel to return the text used in the Quick Fix dialog and run to perform the processing required on the passed IMarker instance.

### Adding Marker Help

You can associate specific help content with a marker. This allows a marker to be selected and to respond to an **F1** Help request. All you need is help content, a marker help extension, and a marker of the appropriate type that includes the attributes defined in the marker help extension.

The help is defined as context help, which is described in Chapter 22, Providing Help. Context help can include text that will be seen immediately and pointers to other content that will be displayed using the Eclipse Help system.

```
<contexts>
  <context  id="readmeTEXT" >
    <description>The source <b>.readme</b> file was deleted,
      you can delete the generated <b>.html</b> file or the
      marker using the Quick Fix pop-up menu option.
    </description>
    <topic href="contexts/ Readme_HTML_Link.html"
      label="Details on Readme/HTML file relationship"/>
  </context>
</contexts>
```

The marker help extension links a type of marker with a specific attribute to a specific help context id.

```
<extension
    point="org.eclipse.ui.ide.markerHelp">
  <markerHelp
      helpContextId="com.ibm.jdg2e.resources.extensions.readmeTEXT"
      markerType="org.eclipse.core.resources.problemmarker">
    <attribute
        value="missing"
        name="readme"/>
  </markerHelp>
  <markerHelp
      helpContextId="com.ibm.jdg2e.resources.extensions.reditTEXT"
      markerType="com.ibm.jdg2e.resources.extensions.recentEdits">
  </markerHelp>
</extension>
```

Once you create a marker of the required type that has the target attribute value as defined in the marker help extension, it all just works. Find and select the marker in a view such as Problems, then press **FI** to see the available marker help content (see Figure 25.3).

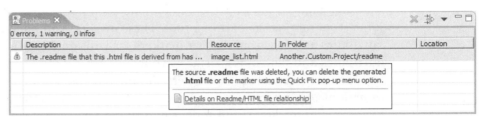

**Figure 25.3** Marker Help Displayed for a Specific Marker Type

## Example Summary

This chapter discussed the creation of resource markers and the ability to create marker extensions for new types of markers. The related extensions for marker images and both resolution and help generators were also discussed.

You can now explore the marker examples located on the CD-ROM. The com.ibm.jdg2e.resources.programming project includes an action named **JDG2E: Setup Project Structure**. This resource action adds a bookmark to one of the files that is created. The com.ibm.jdg2e.resources.extensions project implements a new marker type (recent edits) and a resource change listener that is added as part of the start logic in the ResourceExtensions plug-in class. The resource change listener creates a recent edit marker every time a file is modified. The recent edit custom marker builds on both the task and bookmark markers defined by Eclipse. This means these recent edit markers are visible in the Bookmarks and Tasks views and can be used to open the recently edited file.

By default, only five markers are kept, and only for resources that are not derived. You can customize the marker logic using preference and property pages that are included as part of this example. A preference page setting can be used to adjust the limit for the number of markers that will be created, and a property page setting for a file can be used to disable recent edit support for that resource.

The use of marker resolution generators is also included in the com.ibm .jdg2e.resources.extensions project. The readme file builder detects when a .readme file has been deleted, leaving a .html file derived from the builder. A problem marker that identifies this inconsistency is created; a marker resolution generator will create a marker resolution, which can be used to clean up the problem by either deleting the leftover file or removing the marker.

## Chapter Summary

This chapter illustrated how resource markers can be used for dynamic resource tagging and how the marker extension point supports the addition of custom markers as part of a tool. These markers can build on the attributes and function of other markers, or you can create new ones with attributes and functions specific to your tool.

The abstract nature of markers and the freedom to add attributes and functions in your tool domain make markers a powerful option as you develop and integrate your tool as part of the Eclipse Platform.

## References

Arthorne, John, and Chris Laffra. 2004. *Official Eclipse 3.0 FAQs*. Boston, MA: Addison-Wesley. http://eclipsefaq.org. (See FAQs 288, 304, 338, 339.)

Glozic, Dejan, and Jeff McAffer. April 1, 2001. Mark my words. http://www.eclipse.org.

# CHAPTER 26

## *Building a Custom Text Editor with JFace Text*

PART IV

As you know by now, Eclipse has focused on identifying patterns that reoccur in most IDEs. Editing is one of those patterns, as editors are one of the basic elements of any IDE. In Eclipse, an editor is a key Workbench part and has its own extension point that permits you to implement your own custom editor. Eclipse recognizes that text editing is an important form of editing in any IDE and provides a built-in text editor framework, JFace Text. Through JFace Text, Eclipse offers an extensible and reusable text editor framework that can satisfy the text editing needs of most tools and offers the user a consistent editing experience.

JFace Text provides a framework for creating, displaying, and editing text documents. Standard reusable text editing behaviors are implemented in the base abstract classes of JFace Text. The framework is domain-independent and extensible. You can build all types of text editors in JFace, but the foundation is especially rich with support for building editors of syntax-oriented text, such as programming language source, XML, HTML, and SQL. It is not surprising, then, that Eclipse's default text editor and Java editor are built using this framework.

The framework dictates the overall structure and defines where the key responsibilities and relationships lie. The advantage is that you are free to concentrate on design decisions pertaining to your editor domain. Building a domain-specific editor then becomes an exercise in customization. You create

635

application-specific subclasses of the abstract classes provided by the framework, accruing a wealth of function through reuse. There is still plenty of work you will need to do. Writing the code that the framework requires and implementing custom editor semantics is nontrivial. To help you get started, this chapter will focus on text editor customization using the JFace Text framework. Since this can be a complex topic, much of your learning will be through examination of a real-life example, an SQL editor. The solution for the SQL editor is included on the CD-ROM.

You should be familiar with Eclipse editors in general, as discussed in Chapter 19, before proceeding.

## Standard Text Editor Functions

When you look at text editors like Notepad, vi, and Emacs, you begin to recognize that without all the bells and whistles, they all boil down to the same basic set of text editing functions. The default text editor framework in Eclipse, JFace Text, doesn't have a lot of bells and whistles—it just provides basic text editing functions like cut, copy, paste, undo, and redo. We will get to customization and fancy editor functions later in this chapter, but first let's look at the basic features that come "for free" in JFace Text.

### Text Editing and Viewing

The Eclipse JFace Text editor framework handles the representation and manipulation of a text-based document. It controls the visual representation and assembles SWT widgets, such as StyledText, and the JFace TextViewer to control an editable viewer.

The SWT StyledText widget underpins the framework by providing the display and edits on the text. The StyledText widget supports changing the text foreground color, background color, text font style (i.e., normal or bold), and line background color. Text attributes are referred to as **styles**. While the Eclipse default text editor doesn't handle styles or colors, this function is necessary for syntax color highlighting. In addition, the StyledText widget provides standard navigation and editing keyboard behavior, and allows user-defined key bindings. See the article "Getting Your Feet Wet with the SWT StyledText Widget" on eclipse.org for more information.

The JFace TextViewer controls the raw StyledText widget by handling all scrolling events. Standard text editing operations like selection, copy, cut, paste, and save are applied to the text input and the visual representation is updated.

In addition, default behavior like double-click selection and automatic indentation are provided. The default double-click selection behavior automatically selects an entire word under the mouse pointer. The default automatic indentation strategy starts a new line with the same tab indentation used in the preceding line.

## Standard Menus and Toolbar Items

Tight integration between the Workbench window and the editor part involves sharing the common Workbench menu and toolbar. Menu bar and toolbar context menus react to user actions, and their enabled/disabled states are managed accordingly.

The Workbench defines retargetable (also called **global**) actions that can be handled by any view or editor, such as copy and paste. When a view or editor is active, its handler runs when the user chooses the action from the Workbench menu or toolbar. This allows views and editors to share Workbench menu space for semantically similar actions. The org.eclipse.ui .actions.ActionFactory implements static fields and methods to access standard actions that are preregistered with the Workbench. The TextEditor class uses ActionFactory to add the standard global actions. Here is a code snippet that enables the standard editor add task action.

```
ResourceAction ra = new AddTaskAction(bundle, "AddTask.", this);
ra.setHelpContextId(ITextEditorHelpContextIds.ADD_TASK_ACTION);
ra.setActionDefinitionId(ITextEditorActionDefinitionIds.ADD_TASK);
setAction(IDEActionFactory.ADD_TASK.getId(), ra);
```

The standard Eclipse editor menus are preloaded with a number of common actions such as **Content Assist**, **Content Tip**, and **Content Format**. The active JFace Text-based editor is expected to provide the custom implementation for these common actions. The editor framework manages all editor action contributions so that editor extensions can also contribute new custom actions to the Workbench menu. These actions only appear when the editor is active and are under the editor's control.

## Standard Marker Representation

JFace Text provides support for annotations (resource markers). The visual representation of resource markers appears adjacent to the text editing area in a widget called a **vertical ruler** (see Figure 26.1). Markers are attached to positions in the text, and the resource marker positions automatically update as the user edits text. Because the basic text editor supports markers, and the Search component uses markers to denote its results, search result markers automatically appear in the basic editor. Similarly, the editor supports bookmarks and tasks. Because these markers are persistent, this requires some custom configuration with connections to a document object. We will discuss documents and customization in more detail later in this chapter.

What makes this interesting is the ability to extend this vanilla editor into something particularly useful for a specific type of text file. Let's go there next.

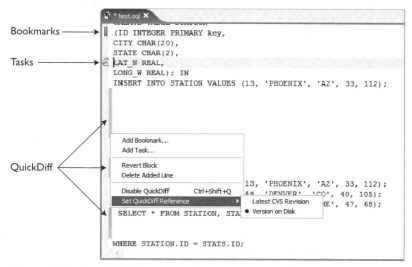

**Figure 26.1**    Vertical Ruler Annotations and Context Menu

## Editor Configuration: Customization Points

Up to now we have not discussed any editor domain-specific features. Let's look at the customization points in the JFace Text editor. These customization points are called **add-ons**.

The flexibility and extensibility in the JFace Text editor framework is achieved through configuration. The basic text editor is configurable in a number of ways (see Figure 26.2), but you must configure the editor and implement the specific add-ons needed in your editor domain. The add-ons consist of the **content assistant** (commonly shortened to **content assist**), syntax highlighting, and formatting. Content assist computes proposed text insertions. The intent is that the editor extension makes a best guess of what the user might want to insert into the document next. The JDT uses this to supply code assistance in the Java editor. **Content formatting** is used to "pretty up" or "beautify" the format based on some formatting strategy. **Syntax highlighting** is used to apply text attributes to text in the document based on a set of customization rules. The Java editor uses this to add color to language keywords.

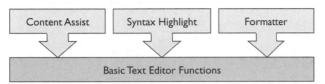

**Figure 26.2**   Basic Editor "Add-on"

## What Is Content Assist?

The content assist customization involves presenting completion proposal strings to the user. The user can request content assist by invoking the command from the menu or keyboard. The keyboard accelerator used by convention for content assist in Eclipse is **Ctrl+Space**. A pop-up menu opens with a list of possible syntax completions. The content assist item is inserted into the document after the user selects the item. Figure 26.3 illustrates a completion proposal list presented to a user editing a select statement in an SQL file.

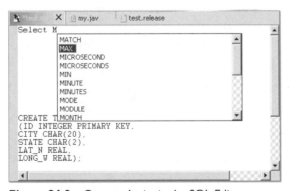

**Figure 26.3**   Content Assist in the SQL Editor

Content assist also provides context information. In the SQL editor example in Figure 26.4, context information appears just beneath the inserted proposal text. In this example, the context information describes the SQL keyword. In other cases, it could call out the parameters that a certain function expects next.

PART IV

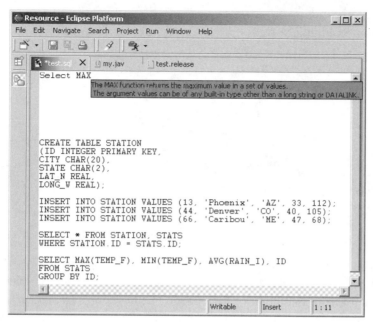

**Figure 26.4**    Content Assist Pop-up Tip

## What Is Syntax Highlighting?

Syntax highlighting is often associated with source editor keyword highlighting. Particular segments of text are highlighted within a text viewer. For example, Figure 26.5 shows Java programming language keywords highlighted.

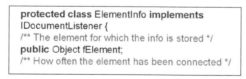

**Figure 26.5**    Java Editor Syntax Highlighting

## What Is Content Formatting?

Content formatting is responsible for formatting text ranges within documents. Suppose you have a document with a title section (as seen in Figure 26.6), and you want the title in all uppercase. A trivial use of content formatting action in your editor could be to apply the correct case to the text in the title section. The source code formatter in the Java editor is one example of content formatting that applies the text content format operation.

This is my release notes title
Content formatting reconciles to upper
THIS IS MY RELEASE NOTES TITLE

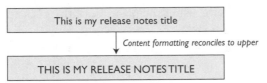

**Figure 26.6** Content Formatting Example

## *Miscellaneous Customizations*

There are a couple of other interesting customizations that you do not want to overlook when building your custom text editor.

### Automatic Indentation

The default automatic indentation on new lines of text copies the indention of the previous line. If you have unique requirements for automatic indentation, you can supply your own strategy. For example, in many programming languages the formatting following opening and closing braces follows a convention. Editors in that domain can provide an indentation strategy by subclassing the `DefaultAutoIndentStrategy` class and overriding the `customizeDocumentCommand` method to have their strategy used instead.

### Double-Click Behavior

Consider the selection behavior in the Java editor when clicking after a brace. When double-clicking just after the opening brace, all the text up to the corresponding closing brace is selected (see Figure 26.7).



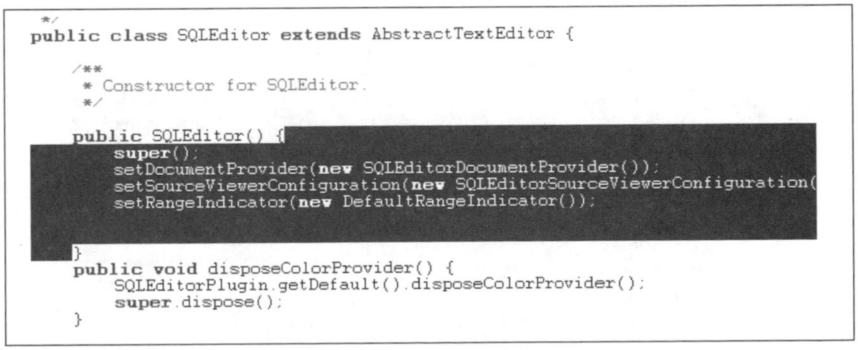

*/
public class SQLEditor extends AbstractTextEditor {
/**
* Constructor for SQLEditor.
*/
public SQLEditor() {
super();
setDocumentProvider(new SQLEditorDocumentProvider());
setSourceViewerConfiguration(new SQLEditorSourceViewerConfiguration(
setRangeIndicator(new DefaultRangeIndicator());
}
public void disposeColorProvider() {
SQLEditorPlugin.getDefault().disposeColorProvider();
super.dispose();
}

**Figure 26.7** The Java Editor Implements a Double-Click Strategy

Use the `ITextDoubleClickStrategy` interface in the framework to implement this strategy. You can override the `doubleClicked` method and implement the desired selection behavior using the position of the click to obtain the context with the surrounding text.

Now let's look at the implementation details of these text editor add-ons.

## Under the Covers of the Text Editor

Before you can customize the basic text editor, you need to understand how Eclipse defines editors as a Workbench part. This is covered in Chapter 19, Editors. You should review that chapter before proceeding.

With this foundation we can discuss the text editor as an `EditorPart`. We will start with a look at the `AbstractDecoratedTextEditor` class and its related classes.

### Choosing a Starting Point for Your Editor

The `AbstractDecoratedTextEditor` class extends `EditorPart` and implements the `ITextEditor` interface. This is the base class of the default text editor. We chose `AbstractDecoratedTextEditor` as our base for the SQL editor in the example that accompanies this chapter (see Figure 26.8).

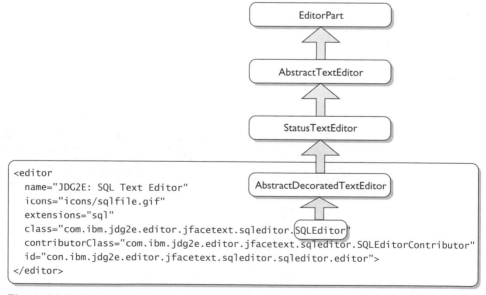

**Figure 26.8**   Defining an Editor

The `AbstractDecoratedTextEditor` class is a model-based part. This editor works on content that resides in a document model. The controller for this relationship resides with a document provider (we will discuss the classes associated with this architecture shortly). The implementation also handles that annoying problem of having multiple editors that are open on the same document. You have probably noticed in the Workbench that you never get multiple editors open on the same document, even across perspectives. Thank the framework for handling that headache for you.

Let's turn our attention to the framework's classes that "bolt on" to the `AbstractDecoratedTextEditor` class to enable editor customization. To do that, we will take a step back from the hierarchy and examine the relationships surrounding `AbstractDecoratedTextEditor`.

## *TextViewer* **Class**

The `TextViewer` class implements the `ITextViewer` interface. It is the `TextViewer` that turns SWT's `StyledText` class into a document-based text widget. The `setDocument` method sets the given document as the text viewer's model and updates the presentation accordingly.

A text viewer provides text-editing operations like selection handling and find and replace operations. Some text operations are configurable. The configurable operations at this hierarchy level include undo management, double-click behavior, automatic indentation, and hover text.

The `SourceViewer` class extends the `TextViewer` class and implements the `ISourceViewer` interface. `ISourceViewer` augments the document-based capability, picking up the standard annotations, bookmarks, and task markers. There are methods to support the customization "add-on" capabilities, content assist, content formatting, and syntax highlighting.

### About Annotations

A source viewer uses an `IVerticalRuler` as its annotation presentation (view) area for resource markers. The vertical ruler (see Figure 26.1) is a small strip shown to the left of the viewer's text widget. The information presented in visual annotations can be changed dynamically. You can set the hover text over an annotation using `setAnnotationHover`. The range over which an annotation pertains to is referred to as a **range indication**. The method `setRangeIndicator` is used to set the annotation range. The `showAnnotations` method controls the visibility of annotations. To learn more about annotation persistency, read about markers in Chapter 25, Resource Tagging Using Markers.

PART IV

## About Configuration

The `SourceViewer` class manages text viewer add-ons through configuration management. The `configure` method is used to set the configuration. It takes a `SourceViewerConfiguration` object parameter. It is through the customized `SourceViewerConfiguration` methods that your editor can define its custom text editor operations (add-ons). We'll discuss the `SourceViewerConfiguration` class at length later in this chapter.

Next we'll look at the framework pieces that "bolt on" to the `Abstract-TextEditor` class to enable editor customization and examine the relationships surrounding it.

## *AbstractDecoratedTextEditor* Class Relationships

Each class and interface referenced by the `AbstractDecoratedTextEditor` class has a specific role or responsibility. The following is a list of classes and interfaces referenced by `AbstractTextEditor`. This is just an introduction with a set of definitions to get you familiar with the individual roles and responsibilities. We will step through all the details in sections to come.

- `SourceViewerConfiguration` is used to describe what customizations this editor is adding on.
- `SourceViewer`  provides the text editor with a text viewer and allows explicit configuration.
- `IDocument` is the text model representation of the document. It provides listener support and gets line and position information.
- `IDocumentProvider` is the editor's interface to the data or model object. In this way it's possible to have concurrent editors open on the same document.
- `IDocumentPartitioner` is used to divide a document into sections so the text can be treated or manipulated in different ways, depending on what section of the document the changes are happening in.

The key classes and their relationships with the `AbstractTextEditor` class are shown in Figure 26.9. The solid lines indicate the "has a" relationships and the dotted lines indicate type hierarchy relationships. Cardinalities are indicated with 1 - 1 or 1 - *.

## *Where Do Documents Come From?*

Each editor is connected to its document input through a document provider, and the document provider is shared between editors. In other words, multiple editors can share one document provider on an open document.

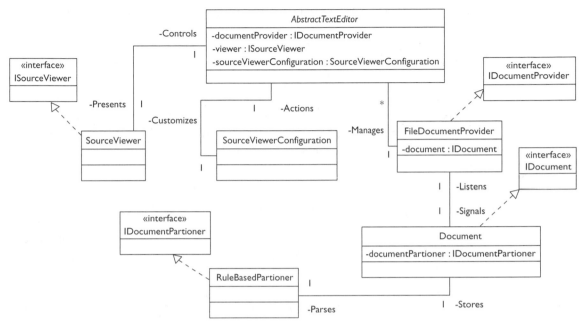

**Figure 26.9** Text Editor Class

## Document Class

The Document class extends the AbstractDocument class and implements the IDocument interface. IDocument defines the text model and provides text content manipulation, position management, document partition management, searching, and change notification.

## DocumentProvider Class

The DocumentProvider class, which implements the IDocumentProvider interface, creates and manages the document content. It notifies the editors about changes applied to the document model. The document provider also creates an annotation model on a document; these annotations are displayed in the vertical bar to the left of the text window. Bookmarks and breakpoints are examples of annotations. The provider also delivers the document input element's IAnnotationModel, the model that represents resource markers. The annotation model is used to control the editor's vertical ruler.

In addition to mapping the annotation model, the document provider tracks and communicates changes on the editor input to the change listeners (IElementChangeListener). The document provider also manages the dirty state (document has changed), modification stamps, and file encoding.

PART IV

If you don't create a document provider in Java code or specify one in the Plug-in Manifest Editor, the JFace Text framework will create a `TextFile-DocumentProvider` for you. A document is an abstraction; that is, it is not limited to representing text files. Document providers are specialized based on the type of editor input (`IEditorTnput`).

The framework provides a couple of document provider specializations. The `StorageDocumentProvider` is specialized on `IStorageEditorInput`. The `TextFileDocumentProvider` is specialized on `IFileEditorInput`. Specifically, the `TextFileDocumentProvider` class connects to resource-based (`IFile`) documents.

Because the `TextFileDocumentProvider` is aware that it operates on `IFile` resources, it prevents users from typing into what may be a read-only document based on the response when the class calls `Workspace.validate-Edit`. If you do not subclass `FileDocumentProvider` and you edit workspace resources, you must invoke `Workspace.validateEdit` and make the user aware of the file state.

Documents are shareable and a document provider can serve concurrent active editors. Eclipse manages shareable document providers through a document provider registry. The interface to the provider registry is implemented in the `DocumentProviderRegistry` class. To share a document provider, you must declare an extension to `org.eclipse.ui.documentProviders` in your plug-in manifest file. The following extension causes the text editor framework to create a shareable document provider object when opening files with the `.release` file extension.

```
<extension
    point="org.eclipse.ui.documentProviders">
  <provider
      extensions="release"
      class="com.ibm.labs.soln.ReleaseDocumentProvider"
      id="com.ibm.labs.soln.ReleaseDocumentProvider">
  </provider>
</extension>
```

Providers created in Java code and not defined as extensions to `org.eclispe.ui.documentProviders` are not added to the provider registry. Use this technique when you don't want to share interactive changes on the input element with other active editors. The `class` attribute must specify a class that extends `DocumentProvider` or one of its subclasses.

## Model–View–Controller Relationship

The main role of the document provider is to map between the input document and the editor (see Figure 26.10). The same document provider is nor-

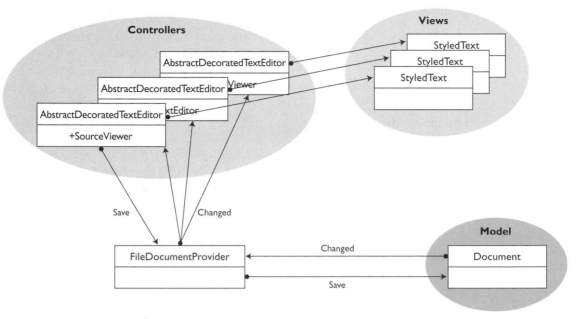

**Figure 26.10**   Model and View Relationship in JFace Text

mally shared between editors with the same input document. This is what gives you automatic update of the other editors when one changes.

The provider always has a document or "model part." The Document-Provider controls the "model" object. Overriding the changed method is the way that the provider propagates change notifications to each of the active editors. A document provider delivers a textual presentation (IDocument) of the editor's input element to the editor view part. The editor in turn manipulates the document and forwards all input element-related calls, such as save, to the document provider.

While one editor is changing the underlying text model, the other editors using the same input/document provider are kept informed of the changes, keeping their visual representations up to date.

### Partitioning a Document

**Partitioning** a document gives the text in your document some semantic meaning. Each partition has a content type. This allows an editor to customize the viewer behavior based on the content type. Specifically, the syntax highlighting and formatting can be applied differently based on the portion type.

### `IDocumentParticipant` Interface

The document creation and setup is managed by the file buffer manager. Text editors define custom document partitions by contributing to the `org.eclipse.core.filebuffers.documentSetup` extension point. In this way, you can identify a specific implementation of a document partitioner for a given file type. The class that you use to set up the document partitions must implement the `IDocumentParticipant` interface.

```
<extension
    id="SQLDocumentSetupParticipant"
    name="JDG2E: SQL Document Setup Participant"
    point="org.eclipse.core.filebuffers.documentSetup">
    <participant
        extensions="sql"
        class="com.ibm..........SQLDocumentParticipant">
    </participant>
</extension>
```

### `DocumentPartitioner` Class

A document consists of a sequence of nonoverlapping partitions. Partitions divide a document into sections so the text can be treated or manipulated in different ways depending on the partition. For example, you can apply a different set of content assist proposals in different partitions. Similarly, you can apply partition-specific syntax highlighting and formatting.

Each partition has a content type, offset, and length. The document partitioner is connected to one document and is informed about all changes in the document before any of the document's listeners. A document partitioner updates the partitions upon receipt of a document change event. Partitioners are expected to implement the `IDocumentPartitioner` interface.

Document partitions are computed dynamically as events signal that the document has changed. It's not surprising, then, that the framework includes a ready-made rule-based partitioner, the `RuleBasedPartitionScanner` class. The `RuleBasedPartitionScanner` class, an implementer of `IDocumentPartitioner`, partitions a document based on tokens that are relevant to the syntax of the document. Programming languages like XML and HTML are all document types that lend themselves to rule-based partition computation. For example, a C++ editor would define rules to scan for multiline and single-line comments. The scanner in turn returns tokens that represent multiline and single-line partitions within the C++ source document.

While a rule-based partition scanner computes partitions based on the text content such as HTML or C++, it is difficult to partition documents based on rules if your document is free-form and not self-described with tags or keywords. For instance, an "untagged" document might be partitioned based on line positions within the file and not the text content itself. Documents that can't be partitioned based on rules should compute partitions in a custom class that implements `IDocumentPartitioner`.

### SourceViewerConfiguration Class

The `SourceViewerConfiguration` class defines which editor add-ons you are enabling. It is the front door to any editor customization you are providing. You will subclass `SourceViewerConfiguration` and override the methods to enable content assist, content formatting, syntax highlighting, automatic indentation strategy, double-click strategy, or undo management based on what your editor needs.

So there you have it. These are the pieces that you connect to the `AbstractDecoratedTextEditor` viewer to make it into a full-fledged source editor. Well, not quite; we haven't discussed how you actually implement the domain-specific content assist, formatting, or syntax highlighting. The good news is that we have covered enough territory to learn the implementation details of a basic source editor that is enabled for further customizations.

## Example Summary

You are now ready to explore the sample code provided on the CD-ROM. The project `com.ibm.jdg2e.editor.jfacetext.sql` contains a sample source editor that implements all the features discussed in this chapter. The example also includes some advanced features such as folding code blocks. As the project name suggests, this example of a JFace text editor is designed for SQL statements and is the default editor for files with an `.sql` extension.

## Chapter Summary

This chapter described the JFace Text editing framework and its available customizations. JFace Text fills Eclipse's editing needs by providing an extensible text editor that allows you to build robust and dynamic source editors. Eclipse provides a default text editor and the framework classes for building more sophisticated editors like those used in programming languages. This is a very powerful framework; of course, its capabilities make it nontrivial. This is where examples can be helpful. In addition to the SQL editor, you may also want to look at the sample Java editor supplied in the project `org.eclipse.ui.examples.javaeditor`.

## References

Arthorne, John, and Chris Laffra. 2004. *Official Eclipse 3.0 FAQs*. Boston, MA: Addison-Wesley. http://www.eclipsefaq.org. (See FAQs 262–266, 268, 269, 273, 337.)

Kues, Lynne, and Knut Radloff. September 18, 2002. Getting your feet wet with the SWT StyledText widget. http://www.eclipse.org.

# CHAPTER 27

## *Extending the Java Development Tools*

The Java Development Tools (JDT) provided as part of the Eclipse SDK already impresses many of today's Java IDE aficionados. The fact that it is free is certainly welcome news too. That's great for Java developers, since they will get better and less expensive tools. However, the JDT story doesn't end there. Everyone knows that no Java IDE, however rich in functionality it may be, will have every productivity aid for which one could hope. Perhaps larger corporate software development organizations can afford a department or two dedicated to enhancing the productivity of their commercially available toolset, because the downstream productivity gains will offset the investment. But what about small development shops that cannot afford this luxury?

It is in just this situation where the elegant, open architecture of Eclipse shines by allowing easy customization, perhaps most notably of its Java development tools. Moreover, the JDT offers the exploitation of its infrastructure. For example, the JDT has already shelled (and roasted) one of the hardest nuts in programming to crack: source code analysis. All of this—source code included—is ready for your reuse.

This chapter first covers how the JDT works and how it builds upon the foundation of the Eclipse Platform. Later it describes how you can reuse the JDT framework and extend its user interface with your specific productivity enhancements. Finally, the example associated with this chapter presents several practical tools that demonstrate how you can implement such extensions.

## What Is the JDT and What Does It Do?

It is sometimes easy to forget that Eclipse is not simply a Java IDE. In fact, as stated in the Eclipse whitepaper, one of its goals is to provide a sort of "universal" IDE on which tool developers can build. The Java development environment was created in the early days of Eclipse as a case study to prove that it is a viable platform for this purpose. Subsequently, the JDT uses the same techniques and mechanisms to deliver its functionality as would any other plug-in; it avoids the use of internal interfaces and instead relies on plug-in extensions to integrate itself into the Workbench. The JDT demonstrates that the Eclipse architecture is robust and that it provides a productive development environment.

At its core, the JDT revolves around its model of the Java elements and the Eclipse-specific workspace artifacts. The Java elements will surely be familiar: They are the packages, classes, methods, fields, and so on that are defined in the Java language specification. The Eclipse-specific Java projects are implicitly familiar, since they are represented as an integral part of the JDT user interface, along with their associated attributes like the classpath/ Java build path and dependent projects. Many of the classes defined by the JDT model are characteristically similar to those defined in the Resources plug-in that you learned about in Chapter 23, Workspace Resource Programming; that is, they are in-memory representations of workspace files. This chapter will cover how the JDT provides specialized behavior for workspace resources like .java, .jar, and .class files to add Java model-specific behaviors.

Architecturally, the JDT is divided into two domains: the model and the user interface. The model is a nonvisual representation of the Java elements; the user interface is a set of views, actions, and Java-aware editors that work together. The classes defining the Java programming elements enable tool developers to create custom Java views and editors. These views and editors are based on a common model that is capable of notifying the user interface about changes in the model; this produces a user interface having a consistent and coherent presentation.

A plug-in developer can extend the JDT user interface using standard Workbench techniques, that is, by extending

- Perspectives
- View menu bars
- Editor menu bars
- Object, editor, and view pop-up menus

In addition, to support a sophisticated Java source code editor, the JDT also provides JFace Text enhancements to enable content assistance, syntax highlighting, annotations, and source code formatting.

The JDT includes a framework that addresses one of the more burdensome tasks for those wishing to provide enhanced development tools: syntactical analysis of Java source code. You will see how this support enables you to add sophisticated extensions to the Java source code editor with little programming effort. For instance, this chapter's example, located on the CD-ROM that accompanies this book, demonstrates how to extend the Java editor by adding a new toolbar button (🐞), as was shown earlier in Figure 8.1.

This new button adds debug statements to each method including method parameters. The **Source > JDGE2: Add Trace Statement** method pop-up menu choice works similarly for the selected method(s) in a view like the Outline or Package Explorer. The example also demonstrates how to create a new view that displays Java code metrics using the source code analysis capabilities of the JDT, as shown by the Java Metrics view in Figure 8.1.

If you look carefully, you'll also notice the "smart expand all" button (⊞) contributed to the Package Explorer's toolbar. We'll return to it in the section entitled Extending the JDT User Interface. However, before getting into the details of how to extend the JDT, we first must cover some JDT fundamentals, starting with the Java model.

## Java Model

The Java model itself is composed of high-level classes representing the objects in the workspace, like project directories and .java, .class, and .jar files. The Java model also includes classes that represent the syntactic content of these files, like types, fields, and members. These elements are not directly modified when programming to the JDT, but instead are kept synchronized with the help of a compiler and the syntax analysis framework (we'll return to this point later in the section Analyzing Java Source Code).

Thus for all practical purposes, the elements of the Java model are read-only for the typical developer wanting to extend the JDT. Instead, the JDT core provides APIs that update the Java model and synchronize interested parties with those changes. The editor and all the views of the Java perspective use this common model to implement the Java development environment. This means you are already familiar with the visual representation of quite a few of these classes, as was shown earlier in Figure 7.7.

As is often the case in Eclipse, the JDT API is defined via interfaces, with internal packages containing their default implementation. For this reason,

Figure 7.7 only shows the interface names that are public, and not the internal classes that implement the corresponding interface.

There are a few public "root" classes: `JavaCore`, `JavaUI`, `ToolFactory`, `SearchEngine`, `AST` (Abstract Syntax Tree), and `ASTParser`. These classes give you a means of creating and accessing instances via an API, where the result is typed to the corresponding interface. For example, `JavaCore` `.createCompilationUnitFrom(IFile)` returns an instance of `ICompilation-Unit`; there is no need to reference the `CompilationUnit` class directly, which is in an internal (implementation) package.

Most developers wanting to extend the JDT will find the Java model easier to navigate and manipulate than directly acting against their underlying resources. The Java model classes are defined in the plug-in having the id `org.eclipse.jdt.core` and the package of the same name. These elements are aware of their underlying resource and have a notification scheme much like the `IResourceChangeListener` mechanism, accessible from `JavaCode` `.addElementChangedListener`.

The JDT collectively refers to the individual model classes in Figure 7.7 as **Java elements**. Table 27.1 lists and describes these classes.

**Table 27.1**   Java Elements

| Java Element Interface | Definition |
| --- | --- |
| `IPackageFragmentRoot` | Package fragment roots corresponding to a project's source folders, ZIP files, and JAR libraries. |
| `IPackageFragment` | Package fragments corresponding to specific packages within a package fragment root. |
| `ICompilationUnit`, `IClassFile` | Compilation units and binary classes corresponding to individual Java source (`.java`) and binary class (`.class`) files. |
| `IPackageDeclaration`, `IImportContainer`, `IType`, `IMethod` `IField`, `IInitializer` | Various types of Java declarations that appear within a compilation unit or class file (package declarations, import declarations, class and interface declarations, method and constructor declarations, field declarations, and initializer declarations). |

The Java elements are kept in a cache once opened. You can use the `exists` method to determine whether the element is still present in the Java model. You will see comments in the JDT Javadoc saying, "This is a handle method." That means that the element is associated with a resource and will be added to or removed from the cache by the internal class, `JavaModel-Manager`, as necessary.

For example, consider the case where the user deletes a method but your code still has a dangling reference to the corresponding in-memory Java element. The `exists` method returns `false` since the object you're referencing has been deleted ("cut off" from the Java model). In effect, it alerts you to the fact that you're referring to a part of a stale cache. In addition to the in-memory cache, the JDT manages an index of summary information about compilation units in order to perform code searches more efficiently; the JDT's `SearchEngine` class is the public interface to this cache.

## Accessing Reusable JDT Functionality

Now that you have a firm grasp of the Java model, let's turn our attention to several noteworthy classes of the JDT that provide access to its central functionality: `JavaCore`, `JavaUI`, `ToolFactory`, and `SearchEngine`.

### *JavaCore Class*

`JavaCore` is the non-UI "root" access to common JDT functionality via static methods. It has quite a few of them, but they can be grouped into a reasonably small number of categories.

#### Java Element Creation

The `JavaCore.create(...)` methods create the top-level Java elements corresponding to a workspace resource (e.g., `IFile`, `IFolder`, `IProject`, and so on). This in-memory representation of Java elements serves much the same purpose as the `IResource` subclasses do for the workspace. It provides the programmer an easily navigable interface to the Java model, base functionality like model-view synchronization, and the common elements that are displayed in the user interface.

The code below creates an in-memory representation of the underlying workspace resource.

```
// Note: Input types are all subtypes of IResource.
//        Exceptions are not shown.
IProject myProject =
  ResourcesPlugin.getWorkspace().
      getRoot().getProject("myJavaProject");
IFolder myFolder = myProject.getFolder("mypackage");
IFile myFile = myFolder.getFile("MyClass.java");
```

```
// Get a Java project; you can request project content from
// it, i.e., package fragments, compilation units,
// class files, etc.
if (!myProject.hasNature("org.eclipse.jdt.core.javanature")) {
  // The project is not configured for Java (no Java nature).
  return;
IJavaProject myJavaProject = JavaCore.create(myProject);
...

// Get a IPackageFragment or IPackageFragmentRoot.
IJavaElement myPackageFragment = JavaCore.create(myFolder);
...

// Get a .java (ICompilationUnit),
// .class (IClassFile, like ICompilationUnit but read-only),
// or .jar (IPackageFragmentRoot).
IJavaElement myJavaFile = JavaCore.create(myFile);
```

A similarly named method, `JavaCore.create(String handle)`, also returns a Java element instance. But where the previous `create` methods started from an `IResource` to get the corresponding Java element, this method expects a handle identifier (from the Java element's `getHandleIdentifier` method) to retrieve a previously created Java element. This is a persistent reference used to retrieve a Java element between Workbench sessions without having to record precisely the resource upon which the element is based.

Note that in many cases it is unnecessary to use these `create` methods, since the Java element is already available to you. For example, when the selection changes within the Package Explorer view, registered implementers of `ISelectionChangedListener` of the active Workbench window are passed the actual Java element (see Listening to Selections in Other Workbench Parts in Chapter 18, Views, for more details). So the code above is only necessary when you are starting from an `IResource` such as a selection within the Navigator view or your own custom navigator.

## Java Element Change Notification

Figure 27.1 shows the flow of Java element change notifications. The Java model has no UI dependencies, but it does support a notification scheme so user interfaces can synchronize with changes in the model. This is what the Outline view, Hierarchy view, and other views use to keep up-to-date. The notifications can occur frequently. Creating a new project or package, deleting a Java source file, renaming a class, and deleting a method are just a few examples of what events might trigger such a notification. Your code can monitor these changes by registering interest with `JavaCore.addElement-`

ChangedListener. Once you have registered, the elementChanged method of your IElementChangedListener will be called when Java elements are added, removed, updated, or opened.

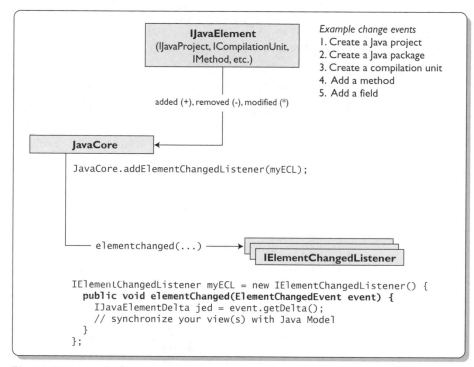

**Figure 27.1** Responding to IJavaElement Changes

The notification scheme is quite similar to the resource change listeners that you learned about in Chapter 23. In fact, some resource change events are mapped directly into Java element change notifications (e.g., events such as ICompilationUnit moved, deleted, and renamed). Source code modification events like adding an IField, renaming an IMethod, modifying a method, and so on also pass through this same mechanism. Along with the event type, the resulting delta is provided as an instance of IJavaElement-Delta. IJavaElementDelta, like IResourceDelta, is hierarchical. However, there isn't a visitor defined for IJavaElementDelta as there is for IResource-Delta. You will see that the example processes its changed elements similar to resource change listeners, using methods like ElementChangedEvent .getDelta, IJavaElementDelta.getAffectedChildren, and IJavaElement .getAncestor(int ancestorType).

To get a better idea of how the interaction shown in Figure 27.1 works, let's look at a small example. The code below shows an element change listener that prints the structure of the IJavaElementDelta.

```
IElementChangedListener myECL = new IElementChangedListener() {
  public void elementChanged(ElementChangedEvent event) {
    IJavaElementDelta jed = event.getDelta();
    System.out.println(jed);
  }
};
JavaCore.addElementChangedListener(myECL);
```

The following are the notification messages from the call to System .out.println(jed) above that occur as a result of a user creating and editing in the JDT. In the examples below, [+] stands for added, [-] for removed, [*] for modified, and {} indicates notification-specific flags.

1. Create a Java project called MyProject.

```
Java Model[*]: {CHILDREN}
  MyProject[+]: {} }
```

2. Create a Java package called com.ibm.jdg2e.jdt.demo.

```
Java Model[*]: {CHILDREN}
  MyProject[*]: {CHILDREN}
    <project root>[*]: {CHILDREN}
      com[+]: {}
      com.ibm[+]: {}
      com.ibm.jdg2e[+]: {}
      com.ibm.jdg2e.jdt[+]: {}
      com.ibm.jdg2e.jdt.demo[+]: {}
```

3. Create a compilation unit called HelloWorld.java.

```
Java Model[*]: {CHILDREN}
  MyProject[*]: {CHILDREN}
    <project root>[*]: {CHILDREN}
      com.ibm.jdg2e.jdt.demo[*]: {CHILDREN}
        HelloWorld.java[+]: {}
```

4. Open for edit.

```
Java Model[*]: {CHILDREN}
  MyProject[*]: {CHILDREN}
    <project root>[*]: {CHILDREN}
      com.ibm.jdg2e.jdt.demo[*]: {CHILDREN}
        [Working copy] HelloWorld.java[*] {...}
```

Notice this is a "working copy" of the compilation unit HelloWorld .java. We'll return to what this means and why this element is a working copy very shortly in the section Extending the JDT User Interface.

5. Add the field useCount.

```
[Working copy] HelloWorld.java[*]:
    {CHILDREN | FINE GRAINED}
  HelloWorld[*]: {CHILDREN | FINE GRAINED}
    useCount[+]: {}
```

The snippet of example code shown above demonstrates how to add a change element listener. If you wish to learn more about the workings of the JDT, enable one of the JDT tracing options. Output similar to the above can be generated by setting the option org.eclipse.jdt.core/debug/javadelta to true, as shown in Figure 27.2. See Chapter 28, Serviceability, for more information on tracing.

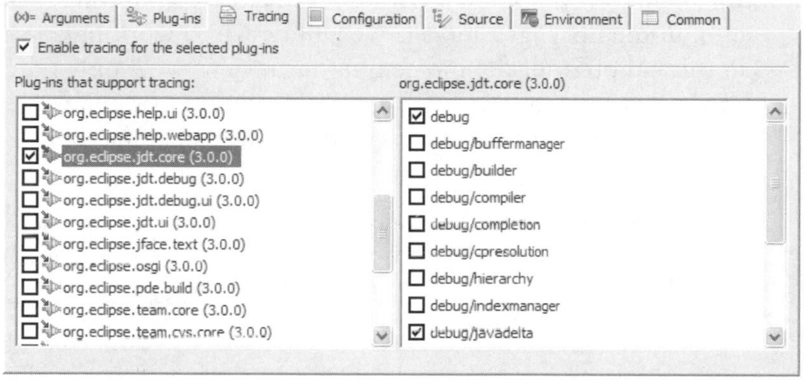

**Figure 27.2**  JDT Trace Options

The IJavaElementDelta.getElement method returns the element that was directly affected, that is, the method that was added, modified, or deleted. Your Java element change listener code may need to traverse the IJavaElementDelta structure to detect changes that affect your views beyond the immediately affected element, using its methods like getAddedChildren and getAffectedChildren. Note that there is some filtering available from JavaCore.addElementChanged-Listener based on the event type, but like the resource change listener interface, your code must expect to receive change notifications for all the affected Java elements, not just those affecting your view(s).

## Changing the Java Environment

The setClasspathVariable, getClasspathVariable, addClasspathVariable, and removeClasspathVariable methods in the JavaCore class correspond to the **Preferences > Java > Build Path > Classpath Variables** page. The set-Options, getDefaultOptions, and getOptions methods correspond to the majority of the remaining choices available from the **Preferences > Java** pages.

## JavaUI Class

The static methods in the JavaUI class provide access to function that is used to implement the JDT user interface. It includes methods to invoke common Java element selection dialogs, open an editor on a Java compilation unit (CU), and access the manager of CU working copies. These methods can be reused as you extend the JDT in your plug-in.

Java elements have the notion of a "working copy" that allows you to stage modifications in a separate area before committing them to the common in-memory Java model. We will return to working copies in detail later in this chapter; for the moment in our review, we'll only note that they are used extensively as part of the implementation of the Java editor.

Table 27.2 describes some of the JavaUI static methods.

**Table 27.2**   Static JavaUI Methods

| Method | Description |
| --- | --- |
| create<*topLevelElement*>Dialog | Creates a common Java element selection dialog. |
| getWorkingCopyManager() | Retrieves a manager of a working copy of Java elements. |
| openInEditor | Displays the desired Java element in the Java editor. |
| revealInEditor | Scrolls the desired Java element into view within the Java editor. |

The JavaUI class also defines interesting constants like JavaUI.ID_PACKAGES, which can be passed to methods like IWorkbenchPage.findView to redisplay the Package Explorer view. You will need reference constants like JavaUI.ID_CU_EDITOR when you want to extend a JDT editor. Unfortunately, there is no way to embed a Java constant in plugin.xml, so you have to look up the actual id, org.eclipse.jdt.ui.CompilationUnitEditor, in order to enter it into your plug-in manifest. Later in this chapter, the section entitled Contributing to Specific View or Editor Context Menus describes how you can use these constants to contribute your own actions.

## *ToolFactory Class*

The `ToolFactory` class creates various instances of tools, such as scanners, parsers, and class file handlers. There are only a handful of methods, and they fall into three categories: source code formatting, class file handling, and source tokenizing.

- Source code formatting

      ```
      public static ICodeFormatter createCodeFormatter();
      ```

  This returns an `ICodeFormatter`, which is either an instance of the default formatter or one contributed with the `org.eclipse.jdt.core.code‑Formatter` extension point.

      ```
      public static ICodeFormatter createDefaultCodeFormatter
        (Map options);
      ```

  This returns an instance of the default `ICodeFormatter` initialized to the values specified on the **Preferences > Java > Code Style > Code Formatter** page.

- Class file handling

      ```
      public static IClassFileDisassembler
          createDefaultClassFileDisassembler();
      ```

  This returns a class file disassembler capable of generating output similar to the `javap` utility.

      ```
      public static IClassFileReader createDefaultClassFileReader(…);
      ```

  There are several variants of this method with different input possibilities (e.g., fully qualified file name, class name within a ZIP file name, and so on). This returns a file reader capable of interpreting a `.class` file following the JVM specification.

- Source tokenizing

      ```
      public static IScanner createScanner
          (boolean tokenizeComments,
           boolean tokenizeWhiteSpace,
           boolean assertMode,
           boolean recordLineSeparator);
      ```

  This returns a Java source code scanner (tokenizer).

We'll cover the usage of this scanner in detail in the section Finer-Grain Parsing of Java Source Code as part of our review of the JDT's source code analysis capabilities.

### SearchEngine Class

The Java model is intended to be populated lazily. Consequently, if you wished to search for all references to a certain class, searching the Java model using a visitor pattern would force the loading of all Java elements into memory. Instead you should use the JDT's `SearchEngine` class. This class defines public methods like `searchAllTypeNames`, `searchDeclarationsOfReferenced-Types`, and `searchDeclarationsOfSentMessages` that you can use in your own extensions to Eclipse's Java development environment. See Using the Java Search Engine in Eclipse's online *JDT Plug-in Developer Guide* for more information.

## Compiling Java Source Code

It might seem odd at first that there is no direct API to the JDT's Java compiler. However, this is because the compiler is invoked by a builder that is registered with the `org.eclipse.core.resources.builders` extension point and installed as a builder for Java projects. When you save your Java source file, the JDT's `JavaBuilder` class is notified, depending on the setting of the Workbench's **Build automatically** preference setting. The builder, in turn, invokes the compiler as required.

## Analyzing Java Source Code

The JDT provides several levels of source code analysis that you can reuse. The most powerful is called the Abstract Syntax Tree (AST) framework. The refactoring code uses the AST to analyze source code as a tree of nodes, where each node represents a part of the source code (for example, `Case-Statement`, `DoStatement`, `IfStatement`, `Literal`, `TryStatement`, `Single-VariableDeclaration`, and so on). The AST framework defines over 60 `ASTNode` subclasses representing the different elements of the Java language. The AST analysis also tolerates incomplete or incorrect source, that is, it continues parsing at the next identifier should it find an error.

Don't confuse the term "JDOM" with the term "JDT DOM" you might see elsewhere. The former is "a complete, Java-based solution for accessing, manipulating, and outputting XML data from Java code" (http://www.jdom.org). Just keep in mind that the JDT's Java DOM is in the deprecated `org.eclipse.jdt.core.jdom` package and the AST is the `org.eclipse.jdt.core.dom` package. Admittedly, the package names are similar, but here's an easy way to remember this: The deprecated DOM classes that are prefixed with "IDOM" (e.g., `IDOMCompilationUnit` corresponds to the resource-aware `ICompilationUnit`) originate from the Eclipse version 1.0 code base.

As you'll see later in the section Finer-Grain Parsing of Java Source Code, the JDT has more than the AST to help you with syntactic analysis. It also includes interfaces that help retrieve precise source information beyond what is indicated by the AST node source pointers. Simply put, the AST relieves you from the nitty-gritty details of parsing Java source code. The example associated with this chapter on the CD-ROM demonstrates how you can navigate the AST's structure, from parent to child, as part of your source analysis.

## JDT Abstract Syntax Tree

You create an AST with its companion class, `ASTParser`:

```
StringWriter sw = new StringWriter();
PrintWriter pw = new PrintWriter(sw);
pw.println("package example;");
pw.println("public class HelloWorld {");
pw.println("public static void main(String[] args) {");
pw.println("\t\tSystem.out.println(\"Hello World!\");");
pw.println("\t}");
pw.println("}");
ASTParser parser = ASTParser.newParser(AST.JLS2)
parser.setSource(sw.toString().toCharArray());
CompilationUnit cu = ASTParser.createAST(null);
```

This returns the root node, `CompilationUnit`, a subclass of `ASTNode`. Don't confuse this class with a similarly named interface that is part of the Java model, `ICompilationUnit` in the `org.eclipse.jdt.core` package.

We have been circling around the particulars of the AST and its nodes. Let's look at a concrete example. The ASTView shown on the left of Figure 27.3 is one of the JDT tools you can download from eclipse.org or install from the book's CD-ROM. It shows the AST that corresponds to the snippet of "HelloWorld" Java source shown in the editor on the right.

Figure 27.3 shows the basic structure of a simple AST, including the names of the classes and their key fields in bold. The AST nodes are shown in mixed case and their attributes in uppercase.

The AST includes binding resolutions by calling `setResolveBindings(true)`. This name resolution is for cases where you want to be able to map names to nodes, for example, to find the node that declared a particular identifier. If you create the AST with `resolveBinding` set to `true`, then those AST nodes implementing `resolveBinding` will return a subtype of `IBinding`, representing the named entity in the Java language (i.e., named entities like packages, types, fields, methods, constructors, and local variables). You can use this to

PART IV

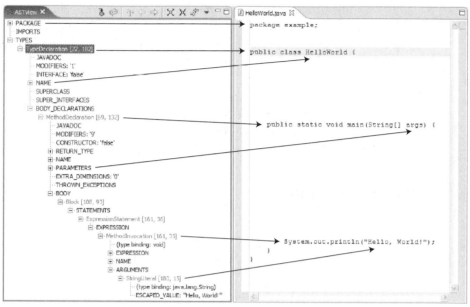

**Figure 27.3**   "Hello, World!" AST

answer sticky refactoring questions like, "Will adding this variable cause a duplicate definition error, or hide a declaration in an enclosing block?" or to retrieve a specific node in the AST referenced by name in another node. There is considerable overhead to creating the name bindings, so only specify true if it is genuinely needed. Otherwise, if the AST is created with resolveBindings set to false, the nodes' resolveBinding methods will return null.

This gives you a general idea of the structure of the AST. We'll examine several examples of how you might process an AST with an ASTVisitor in the next section. There are also other instructional examples within the JDT's refactoring code that you may want to study. For example, Access-Analyzer is a visitor that determines if an assignment affects a particular variable using the ASTNode subclass Assignment. Since Assignment knows the left and right sides of the assignment, it is relatively straightforward to sort the assignments into read and write accesses. StatementAnalyzer uses the start/end source code positions to find the ASTNodes within the bounds of a selection. This is helpful for refactoring that operates against the selection, such as when inserting a catch/try block for all potential exceptions within the current selection, or performing a structured selection (**Edit > Expand Selection To**).

## Creating and Traversing an AST

Here's an outline of the steps for working with the AST.

1. Create an instance of `ASTParser`, set its source, and then create an AST root by invoking the `createAST` method for parsing the source string or compilation unit.
2. Since the `AST` uses a visitor to define an operation that processes nodes in a natural order, define a subclass of `ASTVisitor`.
3. Override one or more `visit(nodeType)` methods (the boolean return value determines if children are visited).

Generally, you'll visit higher-level nodes and process subelements directly by calling the node's access methods (e.g., `MethodDeclaration` declares the access methods `getName`, `getReturnType`, and `getArguments`). However, you may find it helpful to create another visitor to do a "visit within a visit." This is perfectly reasonable and often simplifies the otherwise complex code of a single `visit` method.

A typical scenario would be to create a visitor that overrides a particular `ASTNode` type. For example, to get all type declarations, create a subclass of `ASTVisitor` and override `visit(TypeDeclaration)`. This method will be called for each node that is type "TypeDeclaration." Again, you could further refine this by visiting within a visit. For example, if you wanted to search for string literals within methods but not in field declarations, a visitor within a visitor would be easier than concentrating all the code into the `visit(MethodDeclaration)` method of a single visitor subclass. You will often find that you can get the information that you need directly from the node's fields; it depends on the complexity of the desired analysis. The `ASTVisitor` class also includes `preVisit/postVisit` methods for visiting all nodes independent of type.

The principal reason an API exists for the AST is to enable you to develop with a common framework, since parsing Java source code is not easy. Keep in mind that the AST is only a syntax parse, that is, no code is compiled. Thus it can work with Java source strings before they are actually compiled—this comes in handy when refactoring, since potential errors can be detected in advance. That is, the node's `getFlags` method will include `AstNode.MALFORMED` if a syntax error was detected. As you'll see later, ASTs can also be modified and then asked for the resulting source code; this capability is used to implement the JDT's before/after refactoring confirmation dialog.

PART IV

## Other Examples of AST Java Source Code Analysis

Table 27.3 shows the same "Hello World" Java source code example as in Figure 27.3 and is expanded to show how you might use an AST visitor to analyze the AST.

This table shows a HelloWorld source in the middle, the resulting AST tree on the left, and skeletal sample visitor code on the right that a tool builder might write to process the AST. In most cases, the visitor is interested

**Table 27.3**　Sample Uses of an AST for Code Analysis

| AST | Source Fragment | Sample Visitor Code |
|---|---|---|
| CompilationUnit | | **visit**(CompilationUnit cu) |
| PackageDeclaration<br>　SimpleName("example") | "package example;" | **visit**(PackageDeclaration pd)<br>　pd.getName() |
| TypeDeclaration<br>　SimpleName("HelloWorld") | "public class HelloWorld" | **visit**(TypeDeclaration td)<br>　td.getName() |
| MethodDeclaration<br>　PrimitiveType("void")<br>　SimpleName("main"); | "public void main(...)" | **visit**(MethodDeclaration md)<br>　md.getReturnType()<br>　md.getName() |
| 　SingleVariableDeclaration<br>　　ArrayType("[]")<br>　　　SimpleType<br>　　　　SimpleName("String")<br>　　　SimpleName("args") | "String args[]" | md.parameters() |
| 　Block<br>　　ExpressionStatement | "{" | bl = md.getBody()<br>stmts = bl.statements() |
| 　　MethodInvocation<br><br>　　　QualifiedName<br>　　　　SimpleName("System")<br>　　　　SimpleName("out")<br>　　　SimpleName("println")<br>　　　StringLiteral<br>　　　　('Hello World!') | "System.out.println<br>　　('Hello World!')" | mi = stmts.toArray()[0]<br><br>mi.getExpression()<br><br><br>mi.getName()<br><br>mi.getArguments() |

in higher-level elements like `CompilationUnit`, `PackageDeclaration`, `Method-Declaration`, and so on. The lower-level elements like `SimpleName`, `Qualified-Name`, `SingleVariableDeclaration`, and `StringLiteral` are generally referenced as part of the higher-level visitor's `visit` method.

The code on the right shows several examples of what you might do in your `visitor` method (in bold).

- What do you do if you don't have compiled code yet, but you want to know the name of the package? Code a `visit(PackageDeclaration)` and get its name as an instance of `SimpleName` or `QualifiedName`.
- Do you want to get the list of types referenced in a compilation unit? Code a `visit(TypeDeclaration)` and get their names as instances of `SimpleName` or `QualifiedName`.
- Do you want to extract signature information from all methods? Code a `visit(MethodDeclaration)` and get name, return type, parameters, and exceptions.
- Do you want to find all literal strings referenced only within methods (and not fields)? Code a visit as in the previous bullet item, and then a "sub" `visit(StringLiteral)`.

In general, the AST visitor code tends to come in two flavors: transformations and derivations. A **transformation** takes some nodes and transforms them more or less one-for-one into a more palatable form. For example, a visitor that takes a `MethodDeclaration` generates a refactored method signature. A **derivation** collects information and stores results along the way, producing a result derived from the AST. The example that generates code metrics as shown back in Figure 8.1 is one such instance.

PART IV

### *Finer-Grain Parsing of Java Source Code*

Each AST node includes source pointers that you can use to extract the corresponding source string. But what if you want to examine the Java source code at a finer grain than defined by a particular `ASTNode` subclass? This is where the Java code scanner in the `org.eclipse.jdt.core.compiler` package comes in handy for parsing a Java source string and categorizing its tokens.

The `ToolFactory.createScanner` method returns an instance of `IScanner`. After setting the Java source string with `IScanner.setSource`, invocations of `IScanner.getNextToken` return the current token type. The token types are defined as integer constants of the `ITerminalSymbols` interface. This interface has a unique integer constant for each terminal symbol in the Java grammar.

Table 27.4 shows a sample of the Java syntax elements and their corresponding constants.

**Table 27.4**   Sample `ITerminalSymbol` Constants Returned by `IScanner.getNextToken()`

| Java Grammar | ITerminalSymbol **Constant** |
| --- | --- |
| abstract | TokenNameabstract |
| assert | TokenNameassert* |
| && | TokenNameAND_AND |
| // This is a comment line | TokenNameCOMMENT_LINE* |
| /**<br> * This is a Javadoc comment<br> */ | TokenNameCOMMENT_JAVADOC* |
| whitespace | TokenNameWHITESPACE* |
| int x;    // 'x' is an identifier | TokenNameIdentifier |
| , . ; | TokenNameCOMMA, TokenNameDOT, TokenNameSemicolon |
| "this is a string literal" | TokenNameStringLiteral |
| { } | TokenNameLBRACE, TokenNameRBRACE |
| throws | TokenNamethrows |

Those constants shown in Table 27.4 followed by an asterisk will be treated differently depending on the `ToolFactory.createScanner` invocation parameters.

- `tokenizeComments` ignores or returns tokens for comments.
- `tokenizeWhiteSpace` ignores or returns tokens for whitespace.
- `assertMode` treats the assert keyword, which was introduced in Java 1.4, as an identifier instead of a keyword. That is, `IScanner.getNextToken` will return `TokenNameIdentifier` instead of `TokenNameassert`. A second `createScanner` method introduced in Eclipse version 3.0 maps this to a more general `sourceLevel` parameter.
- `recordLineSeparator` records line separators so the scanner can map between character positions and line number start/stop positions.

Here is a sample instantiation of an `IScanner`, with typical values for the constructor.

```
IScanner scanner =
    ToolFactory.createScanner(
```

```
false,   // Do not include comments among returned tokens
         //   (i.e., no TokenNameCOMMENT_LINE
         //    or TokenNameCOMMENT_JAVADOC).
false,   // Do not include whitespace among returned tokens
         //   (i.e., no TokenNameWHITESPACE).
false,   // Treat 'assert' as an identifier
         //   (i.e., return TokenNameIdentifier not
         //    TokenNameassert).
false);  // Do not record line separators
         //   (IScanner.getLineStart(int) and
         //    IScanner.getLineEnd(int) will return -1).
```

The scanner is appropriate for tokenizing relatively small chunks of Java source code when the context is well known and limited. As an example of its use, recall the example that you were first introduced to in Chapter 7, Figure 7.1. It includes an action contribution to the Java model's IMember of menu choices for changing some of its modifiers. This object contribution allows the developer to change the modifiers of the selected method(s) or field(s) without typing. They simply open the source in an editor; select the members they want to change in the Outline, Package Explorer, or Hierarchy view; and select one of the newly contributed menu choices.

Of course, somebody has to do the work of finding the precise location of the associated keyword (public, private, final, and so on) and making the appropriate changes within the editor. This is easily accomplished using IScanner to parse the member declaration.

We could use the AST to parse the entire Java source, for example, to locate the beginning of a method, and then use an IScanner to do fine-grain parsing of the method signature. However, in this example there is no need to use an AST, because source-dependent Java elements already know their defining source. More precisely, those Java elements implementing the ISourceReference interface have getSource and getSourceRange methods to retrieve the corresponding source of their defining .java file.

Therefore, the IMember selected in the outline in Figure 7.1, being an implementer of ISourceReference, can return its defining source ready to be parsed with an IScanner. This same approach for extracting finer-grain source details can be applied to the following ISourceReference implementers as well.

- IClassFile
- ICompilationUnit
- IField
- IImportContainer
- IImportDeclaration
- IInitializer

- IMethod
- IPackageDeclaration
- IType

To put it another way, when your code is working with the above Java model objects, you can rely on them to retrieve the portion of the compilation unit source code that defined them. If you are working directly against Java source code that has yet to be compiled, then the AST and its nodes can be used to calculate the necessary source start and end offsets, followed by fine-grain parsing with an IScanner instance.

Thus you can use these different frameworks to approach your source code analysis at the desired level of granularity: the Java model (via ISource-Reference) for the first level of granularity, AST for the next level of granularity, and IScanner for the finest level of granularity.

Analysis at the finest level of granularity can perhaps be shown best with a simple example. Let's assume that you'll extract your snippet of Java source code using one of the aforementioned techniques. The code below is an example of how source for the first method in the first class appearing in an existing MyClass.java compilation unit might be retrieved.

```
IProject myProject =
  ResourcesPlugin.getWorkspace().
    getRoot().getProject("myJavaProject");
IFolder myFolder = myProject.getFolder("mypackage");
IFile myFile = myFolder.getFile("MyClass.java");
ICompilationUnit myCU = (ICompilationUnit)
  JavaCore.create(myFile);
IMethod myMethod = myCU.getTypes()[0].getMethods()[0];
String source = myMethod.getSource();
```

Let's assume that myMethod.getSource() above returns the "public void reset(float delta) { x = (float) 2.1 + delta; }" string. Your scanning logic will have the following general form.

```
IScanner scanner =
    ToolFactory.createScanner(false, false, false, false);
scanner.setSource(source.toCharArray());
try {
  int token = scanner.getNextToken();
  while (token != ITerminalSymbols.TokenNameEOF) {
    if ("add test for desired token here")
      break;
    token = scanner.getNextToken();
  }
} catch (InvalidInputException e) {}
```

Figure 27.4 shows which integer tokens will be returned by IScanner.getNextToken().

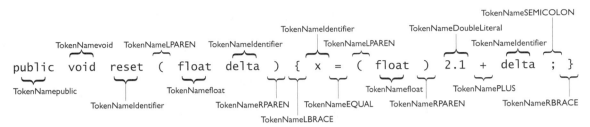

**Figure 27.4**  Tokens Returned by IScanner

All you have to do is write the conditions as an `if` or `switch` statement to test for the desired type of integer token. Once found, use `IScanner` methods like `getCurrentTokenStartPosition`, `getCurrentTokenStartPosition`, and `getCurrentTokenSource` to extract more information about the token. The `IScanner` instance returned by `ToolFactory.createScanner` can save you the tedium of writing parsing code that recognizes the basic Java terminal symbols.

Hint: When debugging your parsing code, select the `IScanner` instance in the Variables view and show the Detail pane as depicted in Figure 27.5. The Detail pane will show the scanner source string and the position of the current token as its `toString` output.

**Figure 27.5**  `IScanner` `toString` Output

## Manipulating Java Source Code

More times than not, you're analyzing Java source code not simply to collect information; you want to modify it in some fashion. This section presents a simple approach for minor modifications and more involved approaches for complex modifications.

## Simple Source Code Manipulations using *ISourceManipulation*

If your source code modifications are limited to copying, moving, renaming, or deleting Java elements from the compilation unit to the field level, consider the ISourceManipulation interface. It defines a common protocol that supports these simple source code manipulations. The following interfaces extend the ISourceManipulation interface.

- ICompilationUnit corresponds to a Java source file.
- IImportDeclaration corresponds to a Java import statement.
- IMember and its subinterfaces IField, IInitializer, IMethod, and IType correspond to the similarly named Java source statements.
- IPackageFragment corresponds to elements having the same package name.

If you want your extension to manipulate source code in a fashion similar to the **Refactor** menu choices, you'll need to learn a bit more about the Java source code editor, known within the JDT as the **compilation unit editor.**

## Modest Source Code Manipulations Using *IBuffer*

The example associated with this chapter demonstrates how you can perform complex source code manipulations. However, to appreciate fully what is going on, it helps if you understand the sequence of events when the user opens and updates a source file with the Java editor. What follows is a high-level overview to ground our discussion of source code manipulation in a more concrete context.

The working copy is a staging area for modifications that is maintained transparently by the Java element ICompilationUnit. A working copy allows editor or refactoring code to modify its client's source code without firing notifications (or committing changes) until desired. Figure 27.6 shows the sequence of events that occurs when a user opens, modifies, and saves a Java file.

1. The user opens a .java file. The editor gets a working copy of the Java element's containing compilation unit, an implementer of ICompilationUnit:

```
IWorkingCopyManager mgr =
    JavaUI.getWorkingCopyManager
        (compilationUnitEditor.getEditorInput());
ICompilationUnit cu =
    mgr.getWorkingCopy
        (compilationUnitEditor.getEditorInput());
```

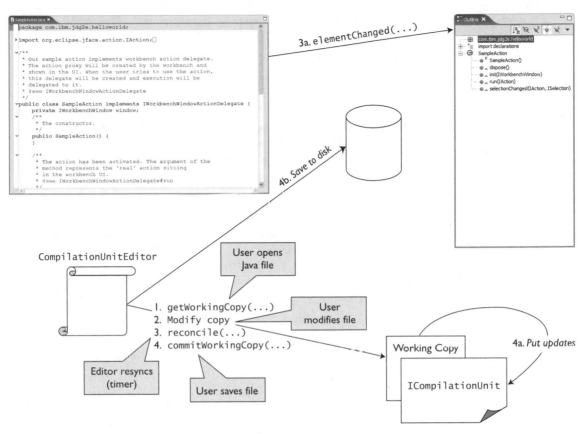

**Figure 27.6**    Sequence of Events Following Modification

Note that the working copy manager requires the editor input. This is to ensure that the same editor is returned the same working copy.

2. The user makes the desired modifications in the editor. The editor uses a `SourceViewer` instance, a specialization of the `TextViewer` class, as its part control. The source viewer has a built-in delay as part of its reconciliation processing to avoid signaling an excessive number of notifications. The working copy has not yet been modified and therefore no Java element change listeners are notified at this point.

3. The reconciler background timer expires and the `SourceViewer`'s widget, `StyledText`, is queried to synchronize the contents of its text buffer with what's displayed. The editor receives this notification and recognizes that it is time to inform the Java element change listeners about

the modifications. It calls `reconcile` against the working copy. That triggers an `elementChanged` event, as shown in 3a in Figure 27.6. It is actually handled by the internal class `JavaModelManager`, but is conceptually shown as originating from the editor. Note that the delta is based on the original copied contents as captured by the working copy and those changes that have occurred since its inception. In other words, the delta is based on the working copy and not its original source. This is because the changed contents have not yet been committed to the model. Thus, the receivers of the element change notifications will be given access to the working copy. This is the explanation for the appearance of `[Working copy]` in Step 4 in the section entitled Java Element Change Notification earlier in this chapter (and repeated here).

```
IJavaElement delta <[Working copy] HelloWorld.java[*]: {CHILDREN}
  HelloWorld[*]: {CHILDREN}
    sayHello[+]: {}>
```

That is, receivers of Java element change notifications can receive notifications originating from working copies if they have registered with `ElementChangedEvent.POST_RECONCILE`. They represent uncommitted changes to the Java model.

4. The user saves the modifications. During the save processing, the editor calls the compilation unit's `commitWorkingCopy` method to put its changed contents to the underlying Java element (see 4a in Figure 27.6) and save the code to disk (see 4b in Figure 27.6).

Now that you have a better understanding of the classes involved in the compilation unit editor's source code manipulations, let's turn to how you can introduce your own. Below are two key points to remember during this discussion.

- A working copy is indistinguishable from its Java element.
- Java elements implementing `IOpenable` have a `getBuffer` method, returning an instance of `IBuffer`. This instance has an API similar to the `StringBuffer` class. Modifying it has the effect of updating the associated Java element(s).

Modifications to this buffer, which are effectively the source of the compilation unit, are interpreted by the compiler and the affected Java elements applied to the working copy. These changes are stored in the working copy until they are explicitly committed.

In most cases, you won't be concerned about the inner workings between the Java element, its working copy, and the working copy's buffer. Instead, you will focus on sequences like the pseudocode below. The JDT's own refactoring framework ultimately follows this same pattern, albeit with the help of a sophisticated modification framework.

```
// Get working copy of compilation unit.
IWorkingCopyManager manager = JavaUI.getWorkingCopyManager();
IEditorInput editorInput = cuEditor.getEditorInput();
manager.connect(editorInput);
ICompilationUnit cu = manager.getWorkingCopy(editorInput);

// Get and modify CU buffer (no notifications
// until reconcile() is called).
IBuffer buffer = cu.getBuffer();
buffer.append(...);  buffer.replace(...);

// Notify others of change (if listener registered
// with ElementChangedEvent.POST_RECONCILE).
cu.reconcile(...);

// Before exiting.
cu.commitWorkingCopy(...);
cu.discardWorkingCopy(...);
manager.disconnect(editorInput);
```

In summary, all that you need to do to update a Java element is to transform a compilation unit into a working copy, modify its buffer, and then call the compilation unit's `reconcile` method to fire off notifications (so changes are reflected in the Outline view, for example). The actual changes are not written to the underlying resource; that is done by sending `commitWorking-Copy` to the compilation unit during the editor's save processing.

## Complex Source Code Manipulations Using AST Rewriting

You have read how ASTs can help you analyze Java source code and how to apply source code changes using the compilation unit's `IBuffer` interface. This approach works well for straightforward modifications but becomes unwieldy for complex changes. In these cases, you can employ an **AST rewriter** to describe the changes you wish to make to an AST node and let it calculate the necessary source code modifications. The AST itself is not modified; instead, the AST rewriter maintains a list of text edit updates representing the proposed code additions, deletions, and modifications of the target AST. The JDT Refactoring Confirmation dialog uses this ability to present the "before" and "after" source to the developer that you saw in Figure Ex2.15 in Exercise 2, where the left pane contains the original source and the right pane contains the source after the rewriter has applied its text edits. If the developer accepts the proposed changes, the resultant source is then applied to the compilation unit's IBuffer similar to the examples in the previous section.

To make this point clearer, recall the "Add Trace Statements" toolbar button shown earlier in Figure 8.1 (🔲). This action inserts a System.out.println statement at the beginning of each method that outputs the method name and parameters. Let's consider two ways of implementing this action.

The first approach begins by parsing the source using ASTParser.createAST. This method returns a tree of AST nodes rooted at an instance of Compilation-Unit (a subclass of ASTNode; don't confuse this with the similarly named class that is part of the Java model, an implementer of ICompilationUnit). The AST describes the structure of the source code, including methods, represented by the ASTNode subclasses MethodDeclaration and its method body, Block. Our first implementation of the code that processes the AST might simply look for all instances of MethodDeclaration, enumerate their parameters, and insert the System.out.println statements immediately following the opening brace of the method body, similar to the simplified code extract below.

```
Block block = methodDeclaration.getBody();
int i = block.getStartPosition();   // Insert after opening brace
buffer.replace(i+1, 0,              // using replace(...)
  "\n\tSystem.out.println(\""
  + methodDeclaration.getName() +
  "\"); // debug");
```

This works just fine for most methods, for example:

```
public void setStartTime(long ms) {
  System.out.println("setStartTime"); // debug
  starttime = ms;
}
```

What if this modification is applied to a constructor method, as shown below?

```
public Checkpoint(long ms) {
  System.out.println("Checkpoint");   // Syntax error!
  super();
  this.startTime = ms;
}
```

Blindly inserting the trace statement immediately after the opening of the method body works in most cases, but as we see here, there are syntactical exceptions. To correct our implementation, we could add checks in the trace statement insertion code to look for the appearance of the token super to handle this specific case. However, this code will get unnecessarily complicated when other possibilities need to be considered, such as parameters on the call to super, intervening comments, empty method bodies, and so on. The AST rewriting infrastructure addresses this problem by allowing you to introduce code updates in the form of new or modified AST nodes and then letting the rewriter figure out the corresponding source code modification.

The JDT defines two rewriters. The first, ASTRewrite, handles moving and copying AST nodes within an existing tree, deleting and replacing nodes, and modifying node properties using the ASTRewrite.set method. This method relies on the declared properties that most nodes define in their propertyDescriptors method, indicating to AST rewriters what aspects of them can be modified in a generic fashion. For example, the AST node representing the declaration private int i; is the class Single-VariableDeclaration, and it has among its properties MODIFIER_PROPERTY (a declaration modifier refers to keywords like public, private, protected, final, and static). The code below would record in the rewriter the change of this statement's modifier to public.

```
public void makePublic
    (SingleVariableDeclaration svd, ASTRewrite astRewriter) {
  int modFlags = svd.getModifiers();
  modFlags &= ~(Modifier.PRIVATE|Modifer.PROTECTED);
  modFlags |= Modifier.PUBLIC;
  astRewrite.set(svd,
      SingleVariableDeclaration.MODIFIERS_PROPERTY,
      new Integer(modFlags),
      null);
}
```

In this case, the property was a simple value, an integer. Some properties are lists of nodes. For example, a Block node has one or more Statement instances as a list property. Another rewriter, ListRewrite, handles manipulating such lists.

Let's return to our trace statement code that processes each AST method declaration node and see if we can improve our first implementation by taking advantage of AST rewriters. The method below is from the AddTraceStatementsAction class in the com.ibm.jdg2e.jdt project on the book's CD-ROM, simplified slightly for readability. This class handles the two cases that concerned us earlier, that is, the difference in syntax required for inserting a statement in a constructor versus a nonconstructor.

```
void private addTraceStatement
    (MethodDeclaration md, ASTRewrite rewriter) {

  Block block = md.getBody();
  Statement[] statements =
    new Statement[block.statements().size];
  block.statements().toArray(statements);
```

PART IV

```
ListRewrite listRewrite = rewriter.getListRewrite
  (block, Block.STATEMENTS_PROPERTY);
// Calculation of trace source string not shown
String traceSource = "System.out.println...";
ASTNode newNode =
    rewrite.createStringPlaceholder(traceSource,
      false,
      ASTNode.EXPRESSION_STATEMENT);
if (statements.size == 0) { // Empty method body
  listRewrite.insertFirst(newNode, null);
} else {
  if (statements[0].getNodeType() ==
      ASTNode.CONSTRUCTOR_INVOCATION ||
      statements[0].getNodeType() ==
      ASTNode.SUPER_CONSTRUCTOR_INVOCATION)
    listRewrite.insertAfter(newNode, statement[0], null);
  else
    listRewrite.insertBefore(newNode, statement[0], null);
}
}
```

When the recorded changes of the rewriter are played back, it will include the new trace statement inserted at the proper location relative to other statements. Note that the sample code above creates a **string placeholder** node instead of creating a more specific node instance like `MethodInvocation` using the method `AST.newMethodInvocation`. A string placeholder allows you to insert arbitrary strings into the appropriate source location, but since it isn't interpreted, the formatting rules that can be applied to it will be limited to indentation, as opposed to the automatic formatting rules that can be applied when inserting typed AST nodes.

## Where the JDT Extends Eclipse

The prior sections have focused on the base functionality of the JDT, Java source code analysis, the Java model, and the basics of working with the compilation unit editor. The only thing missing is how you introduce your new user interface extensions to the JDT user interface. This will be the focus of the final part of this chapter.

However, first let's look at some of the extensions that the JDT uses to define its user interface and support infrastructure. This will give you an appreciation of how the Eclipse Java development environment is defined; it may also prove helpful when you need to find examples similar to what you want to do.

The plug-in `org.eclipse.jdt.core` uses the following extension points.

- Java nature: `org.eclipse.core.resource.natures`
- Java builder: `org.eclipse.core.resource.builders`
- JDT markers: `org.eclipse.core.resource.markers`

The plug-in `org.eclipse.jdt.ui` uses the extension points shown in Table 27.5.

**Table 27.5** Extension Points Used by the `org.eclipse.jdt.ui` Plug-in

| Where in the JDT User Interface | Defined Using This Extension Point |
| --- | --- |
| Java and Java Browsing perspectives | `org.eclipse.ui.perspectives` |
| Package Explorer, Hierarchy view, Projects, and so on | `org.eclipse.ui.views` |
| Editors for `.java`, `.class`, and `.properties` files | `org.eclipse.ui.editors` |
| Project and Java elements creation wizards | `org.eclipse.ui.newWizards` |
| JAR and Javadoc export wizards | `org.eclipse.ui.exportWizards` |
| Project and JAR file property pages | `org.eclipse.ui.propertyPages` |
| Preference pages | `org.eclipse.ui.preferencePages` |
| Action sets, menu extensions, and perspective extensions | `org.eclipse.ui.actionSets,`<br>`org.eclipse.ui.editorActions,`<br>`org.eclipse.ui.viewActions,`<br>`org.eclipse.ui.popupMenus,`<br>`org.eclipse.ui.perspectiveExtensions` |

The JDT also defines some new extension points. For example, the plug-in `org.eclipse.jdt.ui` defines the extension points `javaEditorTextHovers` and `javaElementFilters`. The key observation is that the JDT uses the standard extension points to do its work, and you can extend the JDT using these same techniques with the help of the JDT frameworks.

## Extending the JDT User Interface

The JDT user interface is implemented as a set of Eclipse extensions. Now let's consider how the JDT extensions (views, editors, perspectives, and so on) can be used as targets for your own extensions and how to use the JDT framework when defining your own contributions. As noted at the beginning of this chapter, the JDT is ore than a nice Java development environment—its implementation is a model of how you extend Eclipse.

### Contributing View Actions

Perhaps the easiest way to contribute to the JDT user interface is by adding menu actions to its existing views or editors. The techniques were covered in general terms in Chapter 21, Action Contributions: The Integration Fast Track. Now let's consider these techniques as they apply to the JDT. The Package Explorer view with the view id `org.eclipse.jdt.ui.PackageExplorer` is just one potential contribution candidate. The example associated with this chapter, plug-in `com.ibm.jdg2e.jdt`, includes a "smart expand all" button contribution to the Package Explorer, as demonstrated in Figure 27.7.

This button is the converse of the standard collapse all (▣) button; that is, it shows you more about a Java project by expanding all its contained packages (a mere three mouse clicks versus nine in the example shown in Figure 27.7). This comes in handy when you're learning a project and want to see the "big picture" of what classes are found where in the project. Selecting one or more projects and then the plus sign in the Package Explorer will expand all the source directories representing packages, skipping over JAR files. You can expand JAR files too by selecting them and then the "smart" plus sign. Of course, it can get out of hand—watch out if you expand a large JAR file like the JRE with its dozens of packages!

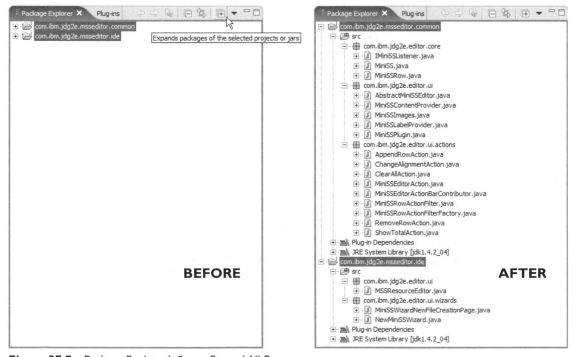

**Figure 27.7**    Package Explorer's Smart Expand All Button

At this point in your studies of Eclipse, contributing actions to views is nothing new, so let's focus principally on what's different, that is, handling the JDT-specific capabilities. We begin with defining an action for the Package Explorer toolbar and menu pull-down, as shown in the plug-in excerpt below.

```
<extension point="org.eclipse.ui.viewActions">
  <viewContribution
      targetID="org.eclipse.jdt.ui.PackageExplorer"
      id="com.ibm.jdg2e.jdt.viewcontribution.packageexplorer">
    <action
        label="JDG2E: Expand Packages"
        icon="icons\expand-e.gif"
        disabledIcon="icons\expand-d.gif"
        tooltip=
          "Expands packages of the selected projects or jars"
        class="com.ibm.jdg2e.jdt.              // one line
          extras.SmartPackageExplorerExpandAction"
        menubarPath="additions"
        toolbarPath="additions"
        enablesFor="+"
        id="com.ibm.jdg2e.jdt.extras.expand">
      <enablement>
        <or>
          <objectClass name="org.eclipse.jdt.core.IJavaProject"/>
          <objectClass
            name="org.eclipse.jdt.core.IPackageFragment"/>
          <objectClass
            name="org.eclipse.jdt.core.IPackageFragmentRoot"/>
        </or>
      </enablement>
    </action>
  </viewContribution>
</extension>
```

As you may recall, the class attribute of this extension point specifies an implementer of IViewActionDelegate. This interface includes the init(IView-Part) method that the action can use to establish the context of the action request. In this particular case, the class SmartPackageExplorerExpandAction handles expanding the nodes when its run method is invoked, working directly with its view part, an implementer of IPackagesViewPart. This interface defines the method getTreeViewer to return the view part's viewer needed to control the Package Explorer's presentation.

Whew! That's a lot of detail for adding just a single action. However, this short example demonstrates that defining an extension is only the beginning. An extension introduces your code into the user interface, but it is up to your action's implementation and the underlying framework to accomplish something useful. When adding view action extensions, you need to familiarize yourself with the *public* capabilities of the corresponding view part class and especially its underlying model.

The simple "smart expand all" action shows the importance of knowing what is public and what is not. If the author of the view part that you're interested in didn't provide public interfaces or any access to its viewer, the possibilities for extensions may be diminished. This may be intentional, especially if the author's views are based upon a public and functionally rich model. In such a case, you may act directly against the view's selection (in our earlier example, instances of `IJavaElement` belonging to the Java model), knowing that the other views will be notified and will synchronize themselves appropriately. The Package Explorer and Hierarchy views especially lend themselves to action contributions acting against the view's selection, since the JDT defines a public interface class to which you can cast the generic `IViewPart` parameter of your action's `init(IViewPart)` method, namely `IPackagesViewPart` and `IType-HierarchyViewPart`, respectively. In addition, those views found together as part of the Java Browsing perspective and its Projects, Packages, Types, and Members views are good candidates. Their view identifiers are publicly declared as constants of the `JavaUI` class (having values `org.eclipse.jdt.ui .ProjectsView`, `org.eclipse.jdt.ui.PackagesView`, `org.eclipse.jdt.ui .TypesView`, and `org.eclipse.jdt.ui.MembersView`). Your contributed actions can perform an operation on their selected objects (in this case, instances of `IJavaProject`, `IPackageFragment`, `IType`, and `IMethod`, respectively), as was discussed in Chapter 21, Action Contributions: The Integration Fast Track.

You should always look to a public interface first when extending the JDT. If none is available that performs the functionality you want, you might consider those public methods in classes contained in internal packages, with the caveat that your implementation may be broken by a subsequent version of Eclipse. Should you choose to do so, it is wise to ask on the Eclipse tools newsgroup (news://www.eclipse.org/eclipse.tools) if you may have overlooked another possibility, or open an enhancement request (https://bugs.eclipse.org/bugs/) describing how the JDT might better address your plug-in's requirements.

## Contributing Editor Actions

Contributing to the JDT editors' common toolbar via `org.eclipse.ui .editorActions` is a bit more complicated than view actions for a couple of reasons. First, the class implementing the `IEditorActionDelegate` interface is slightly more involved because it must recognize that it can be shared among editors of the same type. Common editor types share a single common toolbar, unlike views, where each has its own toolbar. The `IEditorAction-Delegate` is notified of a change in editor instances when its `setActiveEditor` method is invoked.

This point is only a gentle reminder, since we've already covered this detail in Chapter 21. The next issue, however, brings us back to the JDT: Once you have defined your editor action, you then have to interact with the editor's underlying framework. There is little doubt that the JDT provides a rich Java source code editor; thus, its framework has a more complex model than the default text editor does, as was discussed earlier in the section Complex Source Code Manipulations Using AST Rewriting.

In our prior discussion, we took it for granted that from the user's point of view, there is a single compilation unit editor. However, there are actually two editor classes—`CompilationUnitEditor` and `ClassFileEditor`—which have a common superclass, `JavaEditor`. There is little visual difference between these two editors; the basic distinction is that the class file editor is a read-only version of the standard Java source code editor. This enables you to target your editor actions specifically, that is, separate your actions into those that apply in the context of editing a Java source file (e.g., code refactoring) versus browsing the read-only source code associated with a Java class file (e.g., pretty printing).

## Contributing to Java Element Context Menus

Contributing to Java element context menus is independent of its context, that is, the choices are available in whatever view the targeted object is displayed. You specify the target class to which you want to add a menu choice and include the action, an implementer of `IObjectActionDelegate`, which will handle the action's implementation. Again, you are provided the context of the action invocation, in this case by the `setActivePart` method.

All object context menu contributions have a similar form; the key attributes are shown below.

```
<extension point="org.eclipse.ui.popupmenus">
  <objectContribution
    objectClass="org.eclipse.jdt.core.IMember"
    id="com.ibm.jdg2e.jdt.extras.objectcontribution.imember">
    <action
      label=
      class=
      ...
    </action>
  </objectContribution>
</extension>
```

This approach was used to contribute the field modifiers shown in Figure 7.1.

### Contributing to Specific View or Editor Context Menus

The menu extension point ids for views and editors are defined in their plugin .xml file. It is less obvious for pop-up menus, since there aren't any corresponding declarative entries in a plug-in manifest file. In most cases, a given view or editor only has one pop-up menu, and thereby the convention is that the pop-up menu id is the same as its associated view or editor id. However, there are cases where a view or editor has more than one registered context menu. The Javadoc for the target class should define its context menu id(s). To save you the trouble of looking in the Javadoc or source code, the table entitled Registered Context Menus in the book's infocenter shows the context menu ids associated with the JDT views and editors; you'll find it in the Reference section on the CD-ROM.

You can use this table along with the contribution techniques described in Chapter 21 to extend the JDT user interface. The example associated with this chapter also demonstrates how to create action contributions to the Java source code editor toolbar and context menu.

### Contributing to Global Actions

The JDT has a set of global actions, defined in JdtActionConstants, which can be reused by different plug-ins. You'll be familiar with most of these actions from your experience with the JDT: **Navigate > Go To > Type…**, **Edit > Show Tooltip Description**, **Source > Add Import**, **Refactor > Rename…**, and **Search > References > Workspace**, to name only a few. You can define your own implementation of these global actions using the techniques described in the section Supporting Global Actions in Chapter 18, Views. This allows you to provide new views and editors for the JDT while retaining the JDT's common menu structure.

### Displaying JDT Elements in Your Own Views

If you are writing your own extension to the JDT, you may need to present a dialog or wizard that presents elements of the Java model. To make this easier, the JDT provides an implementation of the ITreeContentProvider, StandardJavaElementContentProvider, LabelProvider, and JavaElement-LabelProvider, with which you can specialize JFace-structured viewers such as `ListViewer`, `TreeViewer`, and `TableTreeViewer`. For more details, refer to Chapter 15, JFace Viewers, and the section entitled Presenting Java Elements in a JFace Viewer of the *JDT Plug-in Developer Guide*.

### Reusing Common JDT Selection Dialogs

Before ending this chapter, let's briefly mention what the JDT provides as reusable dialogs. These are accessible from the `JavaUI` class.

- `JavaUI.createPackageDialog`

  Selects a package from a Java project; same as the **Navigate > Go To > Package...** dialog.

- `JavaUI.createTypeDialog`

  Selects a type; same as the **Navigate > Open Type** dialog.

- `JavaUI.createMainTypeDialog`

  Selects "launchable" classes, that is, those having a `public static main` method. The selection can be scoped as desired, using the same criteria as for searches.

Reusing these dialogs in your user interface, rather than creating your own, will help your extensions appear more like seamless additions to the JDT user interface.

## Examples Summary

Figure 8.1 shows the addition of the Add Trace Statements toolbar button to the editor and the Java Metrics view. The source code is located in the `com.ibm.jdg2e.jdt` project on the CD-ROM, in the `com.ibm.jdg2e.jdt` package. In addition, the `com.ibm.jdg2e.jdt.extras` package in the same project includes an object extension of the Java model's `IMember` that adds menu choices for changing some of its modifiers, as was shown in Figure 7.1, and the Package Explorer "smart expand all" button shown in Figure 27.7. This package also includes sample usage of the `AST` and `ASTRewriter` classes and the `IScanner` interface.

## Chapter Summary

The JDT was the case study that proved the viability of the Eclipse Platform, and it represents a realistic and useful demonstration of Eclipse's capabilities.

PART IV

The workspace and Java elements are modeled and include a user interface framework, freeing you to concentrate on the Eclipse extension techniques to add value. In addition, since the JDT uses standard Eclipse extension techniques, all of the extension techniques that you have learned apply. Finally, the JDT provides in the AST a solution to one of a Java tool builder's most difficult problems: Java source code analysis.

## References

Arthorne, John, and Chris Laffra. 2004. *Official Eclipse 3.0 FAQs*. Boston, MA: Addison-Wesley. http://www.eclipsefaq.org. (See FAQs 354, 357, 360, and 361.)

Part II of the Eclipse Platform technical overview (Eclipse whitepaper). February 2003. http://eclipse.org/whitepapers/eclipse-overview.pdf.

# PART V

## *Extensibility Special Topics*

Congratulations! To get here you have made a big personal investment in understanding Eclipse and are ready to take on more. The topics in Part V are either advanced topics or specialty topics. Chapter 28, Serviceability, is required reading for every developer creating plug-ins for public use. After that, pick and choose among the other chapters that interest you.

- Chapter 28, Serviceability, tops our list of chapters in Part V. It is essential to diagnosing problems in your plug-ins after they have been deployed.
- Chapter 29, Implementing Responsiveness and Concurrency Using Jobs, shows you how Eclipse provides a responsive user interface through background processing and how you can do the same.
- Chapter 30, Using Capabilities to Manage Too Much of a Good Thing, applies to Eclipse products that offer rich functionality. Capabilities will help you reduce the complexity of your user interface.
- Chapter 31, Internationalization and Accessibility, as the name suggests, helps you reach the global marketplace and users with special needs.
- Chapter 32, Performance Tuning, is a chapter we highly recommend after you have gained some proficiency with plug-in development. It will help you avoid some of the common plug-in development pitfalls.

- Chapter 33, Swing Interoperability, shows you how to integrate your legacy Swing applications with Eclipse and SWT.
- Chapter 34, OLE and ActiveX Interoperability, applicable only to the Windows platform, explains how you can reuse your OLE and ActiveX components in Eclipse.

Remember that this book comes with a CD-ROM containing working examples that demonstrate the concepts presented in each chapter. Many chapters will refer to them as part of their explanations, extracting bits of code to reinforce your understanding. These examples are well documented with both Javadoc and inline comments. The CD-ROM also includes documentation for the examples and exercises, both of which are integrated with the Eclipse Help system. See the `readme.html` file for installation instructions.

# CHAPTER 28

## *Serviceability*

The term **serviceability** refers to the ability to isolate, determine, and apply fixes to problems. This chapter describes how to implement and run the serviceability features in Eclipse.

Eclipse extensions are not launched separately but are integrated alongside other extensions. From the application user's perspective, it's sometimes difficult to see the seams between the extensions. After all, it is Eclipsc's aim to provide a platform for seamless extensions integration. Seamless integration is normally viewed as a positive; it lowers the learning curve and yields higher productivity than when switching between separate extensions. However, seamless integration can be a liability if something goes wrong, like when a plug-in fails and you are unable to isolate the failure to a specific plug-in and provider.

Consider the problem of determining which plug-in a particular message originates from. The point is that there may not be any way to tell which tool produced the message. It should be apparent that extension providers need to implement serviceability features to assist their users or customers in problem isolation.

Service-friendly plug-ins characteristically use error dialogs with **Details** buttons to make problem determination and isolation easier. Figure 28.1 shows a typical error dialog with problem-solving information.

Eclipse has three major serviceability features.

- **Error dialogs,** which are simple message dialogs with the addition of a **Details** button. The Details section of the dialog provides space for plug-in and service-specific information.

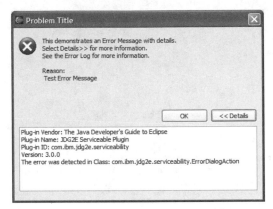

**Figure 28.1**   Error Dialog with Details Button

- **Runtime tracing,** which provides product service representatives with mechanisms to collect runtime debug information from installations out in the field.
- **Error logging,** which captures data on the first failure and writes it to a log file on the disk. The trace and error log facilities are used together for determining and isolating problems.

## Plug-in Diagnostics: System and Configuration Information

Capturing plug-in diagnostic failure information is an important characteristic of serviceable plug-ins. Diagnostic information needs to include vital plug-in identification including the provider name, plug-in name, plug-in id, and version.

Capturing the plug-in state (configuration information) is especially useful in diagnostics. Open database connections and open socket ports are examples of state information that could be extremely useful in problem determination. Plug-in identification and state information should be provided in the event of an error.

## Eclipse Status Objects: A Status Collector

The Eclipse SDK provides a `Status` class used as a container for details that you may collect about exceptions. `Status` objects are used in error log entries and in error dialogs. A `Status` object contains the following information.

- Plug-in identifier (required)
- Severity (required)

- Status code (required)
- Message (required)—localized to current locale
- Exception (optional)—for problems stemming from a failure at a lower level

Getting to the root of a problem sometimes requires "walking back" through a sequence of errors that led up to the failure. In those cases, a chain of Status objects is built using a MultiStatus object. A MultiStatus object is derived from Status and contains a list of child Status objects.

## MultiStatus Example

In the following example, a MultiStatus object contains vital plug-in information. The collection of the information is performed in a helper method implemented by the Plugin class. The Plugin class represents the entire plug-in rather than any particular extension. It is typical for the Plugin class to provide helper methods. Therefore, it makes sense that plug-ins provide diagnostic data capture also.

The simple example discussed here collects some static information, information vital to the problem isolation process. In practice, this method should probe deeper, collecting dynamic runtime information painting a detailed picture of the plug-in state.

Having the convenience of the generalized data-capture method, exception handlers from anywhere within the plug-in can call for the creation of Status objects and then open error dialogs or create Eclipse error log entries.

In the following example, the vitalInfoStatus method creates Status objects for each attribute of the general information that describes the plug-in. The messages in each Status object are set to provider name, plug-in name, plug-in id, and version. The plug-in description attributes are collected at runtime from the plug-in Bundle. The bundle object equates to a plug-in descriptor. The plug-in id or unique identifier is accessed using the getSymbolicName() method. The remainder of the plug-in data comes from the values from the main section of the plug-in manifest file. The bundle headers are accessed using a dictionary object, returned by the getHeaders()method. Having collected the plug-in information elements and set the messages in each Status object, the Status objects are added to the MultiStatus object.

```
Bundle bundle = getBundle();
String symbolicName = bundle.getSymbolicName();
String bundleName = bundle.getHeaders().get("Bundle-Name")
    .toString();
String bundleVendor = bundle.getHeaders().get(
    "Bundle-Vendor").toString();
```

PART V

```
String bundleVersion = bundle.getHeaders().get(
    "Bundle-Version").toString();
MultiStatus vitalInfoStatus = new MultiStatus(symbolicName,
    exception.getStatus().getSeverity(), exception
        .getMessage(), exception);
// Put the information into their own status containers to
// force new lines in the Details section of the ErrorDialog

// Vendor name
vitalInfoStatus.add(createStatus(exception.getStatus()
    .getSeverity(), "Plug-in Vendor: " + bundleVendor));
// Plug-in name (user-friendly name)
vitalInfoStatus.add(createStatus(exception.getStatus()
    .getSeverity(), "Plug-in Name: " + bundleName));
// Plug-in ID
vitalInfoStatus.add(createStatus(exception.getStatus()
    .getSeverity(), "Plug-in ID: " + symbolicName));
// Version
vitalInfoStatus.add(createStatus(exception.getStatus()
    .getSeverity(), "Version: " + bundleVersion));
```

## Exception Handling: Error Detection

Serviceable plug-ins characteristically implement error detection with exception handling. A CoreException represents a failure in the Eclipse. A CoreException contains a Status object that describes the failure. Furthermore, Status objects are input to error dialogs and the Eclipse error log, which we'll discuss shortly.

## Error Dialogs: Providing Detailed Status in Error Messages

Plug-in providers should implement an ErrorDialog for internal programming error messages. It is essential to provide enough information in the dialog so whoever is trying to pinpoint the problem can quickly isolate the error to a specific plug-in and extension provider. Assuming that extension providers are implementing error message conventions, we do not propose replacing a provider's conventions with something new. What we are recommending is that tool providers consider including enough information to identify which tool the error is coming from.

Error dialogs can display one error or an entire sequence of errors. The user can display or hide error details by pressing the **Details** button in an error dialog. However, a **Details** button only appears in the dialog when the error dialog is opened on a MultiStatus object that contains children.

It is the child Status object message text that appears in the **Details** section of the error dialog. In this way the user-friendly error message is separated from the potentially messy details that problem-solvers require for determining and isolating the problem. In Figure 28.1, the error dialog is opened on a `MultiStatus` object that contains five `Status` children. Each status object is displayed on a separate line.

## Error Dialog Example

This example shows an exception handler implemented inside a `catch` block. The error handler accesses the plug-in through the static `getDefault()` method. Through access to the plug-in's implementation of the `Plugin` class, the handler calls the `getServiceInfo()` helper method to get some detailed plug-in diagnostic information. The helper method returns a `MultiStatus` object that is used to create an error dialog.

The `ErrorDialog` constructor has a parameter that controls how child items are displayed; for example, to hide warning messages, you set the display mask to `IStatus.ERROR`. Notice the example doesn't use the constructor, but uses `openError` because it is not filtering the error details. Here's the syntax of the `ErrorDialog` constructor, followed by a description of the parameters.

```
public ErrorDialog(Shell parentShell,
                   String dialogTitle,
                   String message,
                   IStatus status,
                   int displayMask)
```

- `parentShell` is the shell under which this dialog is created.
- `dialogTitle` is the title to use for this dialog, or else you can specify `null` to indicate that the default title should be used.
- `message` is the message to show in this dialog, or specify `null` to indicate that the error message should be shown as the primary message.
- `status` is the error to show to the user.
- `displayMask` is the mask to use to filter the display of child items, according to the `Status.matches` method.

The following sample code opens the error dialog shown in Figure 28.1.

```
public void run(IAction action) {
  try {
    throwIt();
  } catch (ServiceException exception) {

    MultiStatus errorStatus = ServiceablePlugin.getDefault()
      .getServiceInfo(exception);

    // Add error-specific info
    String className = this.getClass().getName();
```

```
errorStatus.add(new Status(IStatus.ERROR,
    ServiceablePlugin.getDefault().getBundle()
        .getSymbolicName(), IStatus.ERROR,
    "The error was detected in Class: " + className,
    exception));

// Write to the error log
ServiceablePlugin.getDefault().getLog().log(errorStatus);
// Show an error dialog

ErrorDialog
    .openError(workbenchWindow.getShell(),
        "Problem Title",
        "This demonstrates an Error Message with details."
            + "\n"
            + "Select Details>> for more information."
            + "\n"
            + "See the Error Log for more information.",
        errorStatus);
    }
}
```

## Runtime Tracing: A Runtime Diagnostic Tool

It is typical for programmers to put trace points in code during development
and to remove them before deploying the application to a production environment. After all, your user doesn't want to see a console polluted with
trace-debug statements coming from every plug-in in the system! The good
news is that Eclipse provides a trace facility with which your users can turn
tracing on and off with a fine level of filtering. In this way, the plug-in providers can write to the trace facility during development and deploy the plug-in
without removing the trace statements.

We recommend that you implement runtime tracing with fine-level filter
options to enable collection of runtime debug information from Eclipse
installations in the field. Consider tracing high-level operations like plug-in
startup, which might generate trace messages such as the following.

- `"Plugin started"`
- `"Opening socket to database server"`
- `"Socket open, attempting login on port 2345"`
- `"Login successful"`
- `"Sending database query 'select * where...' "`
- `"Query response valid: data='354z4zyzr4gg'"`

You specify the default trace options with flags defined in a file named
`.options` using the following syntax.

```
<plug-in Id>/debug = true/false   (master switch)
<plug-in Id>/<tracing flag> = <value>
```

The first entry represents a master switch for tracing your plug-in. For example, if you call the method isDebugging in your plug-in class, it will return true if the value of this tracing variable is true. You can also define additional tracing flags. Their values can be obtained programmatically by using Platform.getDebugOption(optionName), where optionName is the fully qualified name in the format <plug-in Id>/<tracing flag>.

At development time (before deployment), trace options are configured using the Launch Configurations wizard, which is shown in Figure 28.2. The developer interacts with the wizard to set up parameters for different types of launch instances. In this way, you can create different launch configurations and give them different names, each having different trace parameters.

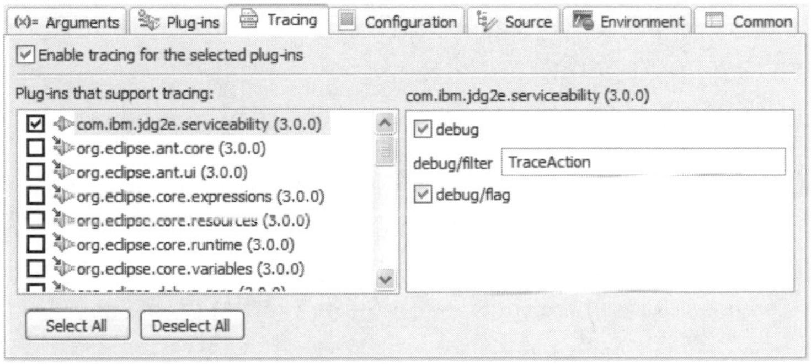

**Figure 28.2**   Setting Trace Options for a Plug-in

Most of the Eclipse plug-ins define tracing flags, particularly the platform core. Plug-in loading is a common problem that new plug-in developers face. Therefore, for a new plug-in developer, an interesting set of trace flags are those related to class loading, because they follow tracing of plug-in loading problems. If you have problems—for example, it seems that your plug-in is not loading—run with tracing on and look for load trace messages. We recommend that you add plug-in flags to define fine-grain control of specific trace points.

## *Tracing Example*

You can define trace points by defining various flags. The flag values filter which trace points are fired. For instance, in the code example below, the trace point will trigger only when the `filter` trace option is set to Trace-Action. See the trace/filter properties and value associated with the plug-in `com.ibm.jdg2e.serviceability` in Figure 28.2.

The `.options` file, located in the root directory of the plug-in project, defines the following flags.

```
com.ibm.jdg2e.serviceability/debug = true
com.ibm.jdg2e.serviceability/debug/flag = true
com.ibm.jdg2e.serviceability/debug/filter = TraceAction
```

This example demonstrates displaying information tracing an execution path inside a class named `TraceAction`. This kind of trace point is typical of a footprint (that is, execution path walk) type trace. Other trace strategies you should consider are adding to trace points to include plug-in startup, plug-in shutdown, TCP/IP socket operations, and database operations.

This example writes trace output only when tracing and the filter are set to `TraceAction` or when the filter is set to `"*"`, meaning that it is an all-inclusive footprint.

```
public void run(IAction arg0) {
  traceFilter = Platform
    .getDebugOption("com.ibm.jdg2e.serviceability/debug/filter");
  if ((traceFilter != null)
      && (traceFilter.equals(allCases) ||
      traceFilter.equals(thisClassName))) {
    System.out.println("----------> TraceAction.run()");
  }
  if (ServiceablePlugin.getDefault().isDebugging())
    org.eclipse.jface.dialogs.MessageDialog
      .openInformation(
        (Shell) null,
        "Serviceability Example",
        "Trace message was sent: ----------> "
        + "TraceAction.run() See console or trace messages.");
  else
    org.eclipse.jface.dialogs.MessageDialog
      .openInformation(
        (Shell) null,
        "Serviceability Example",
        "Trace message was NOT sent. Must run under trace/debug mode.");
}
```

Now, when you run this plug-in in Eclipse with runtime tracing, you will see the trace result in the Console view.

Adding trace points should not degrade the readability or maintainability of your plug-in. Consider implementing a trace(String aFilter, String aMessage) method in a helper class to hide the messy details behind your filter logic. Your extension code simply invokes the `trace` method. This snippet demonstrates just how clean and readable trace points can be.

```
doSomeDBStuff();
MyTrace.trace("DBSubSys", "Successfully did some database stuff");
doSomeCommStuff();
MyTrace.trace("CommunicationsSubSys",
    "Communication stuff was ok");
```

## Using Tracing in a Production Environment

Distributing an `.options` file along with your plug-in enables tracing after your plug-in is deployed in a production environment. Tracing your plug-in in the field requires that the tool user, that is, the customer, start Eclipse in debug mode while pointing at your `.options` file. To invoke your plug-in under trace, instruct your users to perform the following steps.

1. Copy the plug-in `.options` template file from `<installLocation>/ plugins/<your plug-in>/.options` to the `<installLocation>`, in the same folder as the `eclipse.exe` file.
2. Edit the `.options` file, and set the trace flag values according to the type of trace that you want to run.
3. Start Eclipse in debug mode using the `-debug` option, and mirror the Console view output to the command line console using the `-consolelog` option. When you run the trace, the output is written to the system console.

## Diagnostics: A Comprehensive Error Log

So far, we have discussed how you can write more serviceable plug-ins. Now let's look at the Eclipse plug-ins. Eclipse diagnostics are available in the form of a report that is created and opened in an editor. To check the system diagnostics, look at the About Eclipse Platform dialog by choosing **Help > About Eclipse Platform**. Selecting the **Configuration Details** button opens a dialog with the following contents.

- Date stamp
- System properties (about the Java and OS environments)
- Plug-in registry (plug-ins and fragments—ids, versions, and names)
- Update Manager log
- Current error log contents

Users can copy/paste this information to a file of their choice; that file can then be sent to a tool provider for analysis. The developer's role, writing to the error log, is described next.

PART V

## Error Logging: Writing to the Workbench Error Log

You should use the error logging facility to capture data that will assist in problem determination and isolation, but avoid using the error log as a general-purpose event log. Be advised that since Eclipse version 3.0 there is no maximum limit on the log file size. If you do write to the error log, monitor that usage.

To use and manage the log file in your development environment, use the PDE's Error Log view. To do this, select **Window >Show View Other….** From the Show View dialog, open the **PDE Runtime** folder, and select the **Error Log view** (see Figure 28.3).

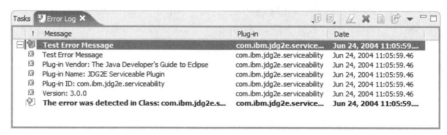

**Figure 28.3**   Plug-in Development Environment Error Log View

For IDE tools, and RCP plug-ins using the Eclipse resource workspace, you can find the log, a text file, stored at <installLocation>\eclipse\workspace\.metadata\.log. For RCP applications not using a workspace, the log file is found in the <installLocation>\configuration folder. The log file in this case is in the form of 1087857696338.log.

### Adding Error Logging

To obtain a handle to the error log, use the org.eclipse.runtime.Plugin .getLog() method. To write to the log, use the log(IStatus status) method. It is simple to write to the error log, because the log facility takes care of the entry header and line formatting. The following code illustrates writing to the error log.

```
try {
    throwIt();
} catch (ServiceException exception) {

    MultiStatus errorStatus = ServiceablePlugin.getDefault()
        .getServiceInfo(exception);
```

```
                    // Add error specific info
                    String className = this.getClass().getName();
                    errorStatus.add(new Status(IStatus.ERROR,
                        ServiceablePlugin.getDefault().getBundle()
                            .getSymbolicName(), IStatus.ERROR,
                        "The error was detected in Class: " + className,
                        exception));

                    // Write to the error log
                    ServiceablePlugin.getDefault().getLog().log(errorStatus);
```

## Example Summary

You are now ready to explore the solution code provided on the CD-ROM. In this example code, defined in the project com.ibm.jdg2e.serviceability, you will see the resulting implementation of all the serviceability features discussed in this chapter.

## Chapter Summary

The Eclipse serviceability features are useful both when developing your plug-in and after your plug-in is deployed to the field. It is a good practice to include serviceability features when you begin development of your plug-in. A good rule of thumb is to use error dialogs and error logs whenever you trap an error that could result in a call for service. Be sure to leave information that helps problem-solvers quickly isolate the problem back to the failing plug-in. Collect information that would be helpful to the problem-solver. Use the Eclipse tracing facility, conditionally writing to the system console rather than removing debug statements before deployment to production.

## Reference

Arthorne, John, and Chris Laffra. 2004. *Official Eclipse 3.0 FAQs*. Boston, MA: Addison-Wesley. http://www.eclipsefaq.org. (See FAQs 27, 34, 121, 163, 164, 173.)

# CHAPTER 29

## *Implementing Responsiveness and Concurrency Using Jobs*

Responsiveness should be one of the key goals of any user interface, with the same importance as ease of use and other classic usability requirements. The Eclipse Platform is a well-designed user interface. Its use of perspectives to support specific roles and the assignment of responsibilities to the view and editor Workbench parts make it a very effective user interface.

What may not be as apparent is the dynamic nature of the Eclipse user interface; therein lies a good portion of its magic. When using Eclipse, few tasks actually make you wait for their completion. Trigger a build, be it automatic or full, and it runs to completion in the background. Check out a project from CVS, and you can actually open files in the project before the checkout has completed. The worst-case scenario is a progress dialog; even this can be dismissed by selecting **Run in Background**. The **Always run in background** Workbench preference setting automates this decision.

This architected support for concurrent execution is implemented using Eclipse jobs; you create and run a job to get your plug-in's work done while letting your user continue working too. In short, jobs can completely change the way your plug-in performs work and interacts with the user. The responsiveness of the Eclipse user interface sets the standard; the platform provides the opportunity. All you need to do is understand and implement these same techniques in your plug-in.

## Concurrency Framework

In Eclipse, **jobs** are a unit of work. The **job manager,** surprisingly enough, manages the environment. And you, the **job creator,** choose to use jobs in the implementation of a plug-in. So to help you better understand the concurrency framework, let's discuss the following:

- The basic participant and role structure of the concurrency framework
- The types of jobs that can be created
- The participant interactions for job creators, jobs, and the job manager
- How jobs are visible in the user interface
- The techniques available for controlling conflict during job processing

This discussion includes pointers to sections that follow, where the details of defining and running jobs are covered. Keep in mind as you read that the goal in this section is a general introduction of all the key concepts, a big-picture view of the key players and key classes. This first, and then you can delve into the details.

### Who Does What in the Framework?

You can create jobs in your plug-in. Once you have created a job, you can request that the job be run; this process involves the job manager. You can directly interact with a job or use the job manager to process job requests. All the while, the job manager is processing jobs to completion. In addition, a Progress view and other techniques allow the user to see some of the jobs being processed in the Eclipse user interface.

So your plug-in will interact with jobs, the job manager, and the Eclipse user interface; that's a lot of activity. Let's start with a short introduction to the key players (see Figure 29.1).

### Jobs Do the Work

A job is a unit of work that is defined and then scheduled for execution by the platform. Using jobs, your plug-in can run multiple background operations concurrently or schedule work that is queued to run on the user interface thread.

Jobs have a stated priority and a user or system role. The job priority influences the job manager's scheduling logic. The user or system role defined by `setSystem` determines the level of visibility in the user interface.

Jobs have a life cycle and support a listener interface to report job events. Jobs can also belong to one or more families. A **family** is a set of related jobs

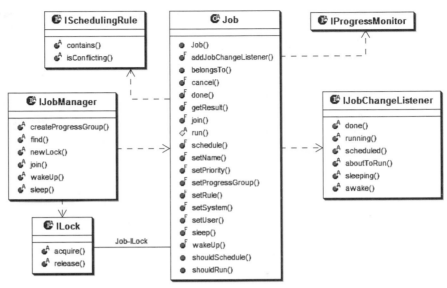

**Figure 29.1** Overview of the Job Concurrency Framework

that can be managed together. Jobs also support contention management through the use of locks and scheduling rules. Additional detail is provided in Job Fundamentals.

## The Job Manager Schedules Work and Coordinates Shared Resources

The job manager processes jobs from the schedule request to completion. The job manager also provides services for processing families of jobs and obtaining locks that may be required to help control conflicts between running jobs.

In addition, the job manager coordinates the scheduling of jobs that use scheduling rules to avoid conflicts over shared resources. This includes the dynamic use of scheduling rules by an active job. See Scheduling Rules for further details.

## The User Interface Keeps the User Informed of Progress

Job processing is not hidden from the user. The existence and progress of the active jobs in the Eclipse Platform is visible if you know where to look.

In the Eclipse user interface shown in Figure 29.2, you can see an active full build, a CVS synchronize, and two views that are preparing to update their user interfaces; all this is occurring while the user prepares to launch a test.

PART V

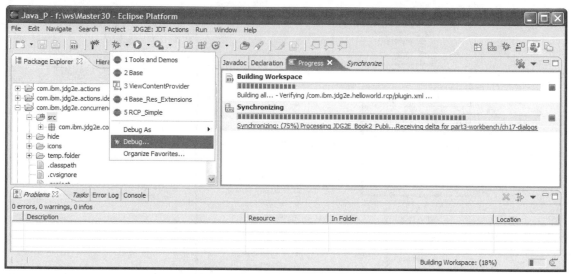

**Figure 29.2**    Responsive User Interface on a Busy Platform

Jobs have several ways to tell the user when jobs are active, or you can choose to run jobs quietly. The available support for user interaction is discussed further in User Interaction Options.

## Job Fundamentals

A job is a package of work that can be managed to completion by the platform. A job is implemented using a `Job` class. The `run` method contains the logic for the job. A job can be instantiated and placed on the job manager's queue using the `schedule` method. In addition, there are two strategies you can use to avoid inter-job conflict: locks and scheduling rules.

**NOTE**  Since jobs run on separate threads, all the issues that apply to multiprocessing using Java's `Thread` class apply equally well when using jobs. To learn the essentials, see the "Threads: Doing Two or More Tasks At Once" trail of The Java Tutorial.

### Starting a Job, Doing Work, and Reporting Progress

To get things started, you have to first create a `Job` instance. You can get by with as little as an inner class with a `run` method. Once you have created an instance, you can schedule a job to run; the job manager takes over then and will run the job as soon as possible. This basic process is demonstrated in Creating a Simple Job.

Jobs can report progress. A job has access to an `IProgressMonitor` that can be used to report progression through the defined unit of execution. Eclipse incorporates this progress information into the Workbench user interface.

As the job progresses through the life cycle, it goes through specific states. A job can have no state or a state of `scheduled`, `waiting`, `running`, or `sleeping`. The transitions in job state are more interesting. You can detect these state changes by adding an `IJobChangeListener` to an individual job or to the job manager to listen to all jobs. See Listening for Job Change Events for more detail.

## Creating a Simple Job

Let's define a very simple job to bring these ideas together. All it takes to use a job is the implementation and a schedule request. The implementation of an inline job is straightforward; create a `Job` instance and provide a `run` method. The job name is defined in the constructor, and it can also be modified using the `setName` method. We have captured a few extra bits of information about the job in the console to show some job details.

```
System.out.println("Create InlineJob");

Job customJob = new Job("InlineJob") {

  protected IStatus run(IProgressMonitor monitor) {

    System.out.println(this.getName() + " Priority: "
        + this.getPriority()
        + " State: " + this.getState() + " Thread: "
        + this.getThread());

    return new Status(IStatus.OK,
        "com.ibm.jdg2e.concurrency", IStatus.OK,
        "Job Completed Fine", null);
  }
};
```

You don't directly run a job; instead, you *schedule* a job by using a `schedule` request. As shown below, this request is sent to the job but is actually processed by the job manager.

```
System.out.println("Schedule InlineJob");
customJob.schedule();
System.out.println("Schedule Done.");
```

The job will run at some point after the `schedule` request. Our simple job implementation has not defined any rules or a job priority, so there is very little for the job manager to consider beyond the defaults and its own ability to create the thread and start the job. Here is the output from our earlier example, which illustrates a typical job execution sequence.

```
Create InlineJob
Schedule InlineJob
InlineJob Priority: 30 State: 4 Thread: Thread[Worker-20,5,main]
InlineJob Done.
Schedule Done.
```

As shown, a job can start before the `schedule` request has returned. A `schedule` request is essentially an instruction to start when ready. This is the essence of the framework; jobs are units of concurrent processing that run when the platform is ready, and you just schedule them and get out of the way. If the job had real work to do, the `Schedule Done` message would have shown up before the `InlineJob Done` message. Of course, if the platform were busy, none of the job messages would have shown up until a bit later. And as you can see from the console message, this is not only like how threads work in Java, but the jobs actually run on threads created by the job manager.

### Grouping Jobs into Families

Jobs can be grouped by family, and the job manager can help you find and interact with all jobs that are part of a given job family. This allows you to do things like cancel or wake up a family of jobs all at once.

A job family is simply a set of jobs that recognizes an object. Jobs are associated with a job family by overriding the `belongsTo` method. By returning `true` when this method is called for a given object instance, the job declares itself as part of that family. A job can be part of more than one family; it just needs to recognize the passed object.

Jobs are asked about family relationships when one of the job manager methods for processing sets of jobs is called. The job manager's family-oriented methods are passed an object that will be used to determine whether a given job is a member of that family. See Job Manager for additional detail on families.

### Types of Jobs

The Eclipse Platform defines multiple types of jobs; some are general purpose, while others are specialized. They differ in the method that contains the work to be performed, whether they run on a background or user interface thread, and whether they link their execution with the state of the Workbench. The org.eclipse.core.resources plug-in even contributes a job for use during resource processing. Figure 29.3 shows the Job class hierarchy.

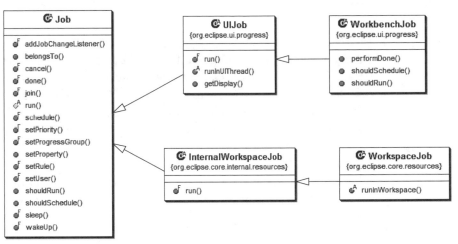

**Figure 29.3** Job Class Hierarchy

## Job

You use a Job when you need to perform some processing on a background thread but you still want the ability to determine when the processing is complete, avoid contention over shared resources, balance the processing request with other platform demands on the system, and possibly display the results to the user in a nonintrusive fashion.

## UIJob

A UIJob is a specialized Job that runs on the user interface thread for the Workbench. The processing to be run is defined in the runInUIThread method. When scheduled, the job manager queues the UIJob until it can be executed on the Workbench's user interface thread. Only one UIJob can run at a time; this makes sense because it blocks the user interface thread while it is running.

You use a UIJob when you need to run a set of nontrivial processing on the user interface thread and are willing to let the job manager balance your requests with others that also need access. By using the job manager to access the user interface thread, you also have the ability to use scheduling rules and other elements of the job API to control and manage the processing. You have to use a UIJob wisely to avoid locking the user interface.

---

**NOTE** Trivial user interface thread requests may be best performed using the `asyncExec` approach discussed in Chapter 14, The Standard Widget Toolkit: A Lean, Mean Widget Machine.

---

### WorkbenchJob

A `WorkbenchJob` is a specialized `UIJob`. The `runInUIThread` method still defines the processing. There are two main differences: A `WorkbenchJob` checks whether the Workbench is running before allowing the job to be scheduled or run, and a job change listener is used to ensure that the `performDone` method included in a `WorkbenchJob` is also called when the job has completed successfully.

You can consider a `WorkbenchJob` a convenience class because it is a safer version of a `UIJob`. The `WorkbenchJob` saves you from having to check whether the Workbench is running and forces the termination of user interface updates when the Workbench is shutting down. Use a `UIJob` when you need to interact with the user interface even if the platform is shutting down.

You use a `WorkbenchJob` when you want to be closely tied to the Workbench platform itself. If the job starts, you can be sure it has access to the display from the Workbench, and if the Workbench is not running when the job completes, your `performDone` method will not be called.

### WorkspaceJob

The `org.eclipse.core.resources` plug-in contributes the `WorkspaceJob`, a specialized type of `Job` designed to make controlled resource modifications. The processing to perform is defined in the `runInWorkspace` method.

A `WorkspaceJob` is similar in concept to an `IWorkspaceRunnable`, which is discussed in Chapter 23, Workspace Resource Programming. Just like an `IWorkspaceRunnable`, a `WorkspaceJob` controls when resource change events are triggered. The difference is that the execution of a job is performed on an alternate thread.

You use a `WorkspaceJob` when you want to access and potentially modify workspace resources while allowing the job manager to coordinate when the `WorkspaceJob` should be run. See Using `WorkspaceJob` in Chapter 23 for additional details.

## Job Manager

All jobs are known to the job manager once they have been scheduled. The job manager processes job schedule requests, queues jobs until they can be started, and runs them when appropriate. The job manager API is defined by the IJobManager interface.

The job manager also provides support for processing job family requests, grouping job processing user feedback, and creating locks. You may not need to directly interact with the job manager for simple jobs. But some provided services may require you to interact with the job manager. You get the job manager from the platform.

```
IJobManager jobManager = Platform.getJobManager();
```

### Job Families

The job manager can help you find and interact with all jobs that are part of a single job family. The job manager API methods such as cancel, find, join, sleep, and wakeup accept a family object as a parameter and can perform the request on all jobs that identify themselves as part of the family. This support allows you to create and manage a related set of jobs and cancel all jobs related to a specific task.

### Progress Groups

You can coordinate progress reporting across multiple jobs. The job manager's createProgressGroup method allows you to create a single progress monitor with a set amount of work that can then be shared by multiple jobs. This allows the jobs to report overall progress in a coordinated fashion.

```
Job jobOne = new CustomJob("JobOne");
Job jobTwo = new CustomJob("JobTwo");

IProgressMonitor pm =
  Platform.getJobManager().createProgressGroup();
pm.beginTask("Work",100);

jobOne.setProgressGroup(pm, 50);
jobOne.schedule();

jobTwo.setProgressGroup(pm, 50);
jobTwo.schedule();
```

### *Job Visibility in the User Interface*

Eclipse informs the user of running jobs in the status bar as your plug-in defines and runs jobs. The user can request additional detail by double-clicking the progress indicator in the status bar; this displays the Progress view. Call the job's setSystem method to suppress the display of the job's activity. These forms of user feedback are discussed in this section. Later in the chapter, the

PART V

User Interaction Options section offers additional detail on how your job can add further user interaction and job completion feedback.

## Workbench Job Activity

The Workbench status bar has feedback mechanisms for running jobs. Job feedback is visible on the right side of the Workbench status bar, showing one job at a time. This activity is not visible if the job is very short or does not provide feedback using the monitor provided as part of the run method; no feedback will be visible. The availability of an action for a completed job is also shown (see Figure 29.4). Job actions are discussed in Providing Job Completion Feedback.

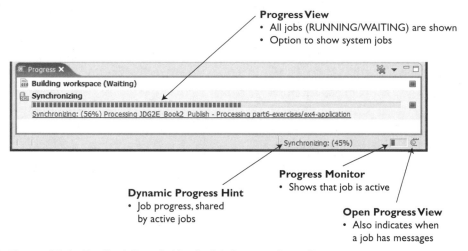

**Figure 29.4**    Feedback Provided by the Job Progress Status Bar

Double-clicking on the job progress display in the status bar, or selecting the active job icon, opens the Progress view. This and more details are discussed in Job Visibility in the User Interface.

## Progress View

Additional details on running jobs can be found in the Progress view, a window into the active jobs. Figure 29.4 shows the Progress view with two jobs: one waiting and one active.

A mix of active jobs and jobs that have completed their processing can also be seen in the Progress view, depending on the work being performed.

UIJob and WorkbenchJob instances are not shown; they lock the user interface during execution anyway, so progress updates would not be posted. You can use the **Verbose** toggle on the Progress view's pull-down menu to show system jobs.

Jobs can control what is displayed in this view by returning the appropriate status at job completion. You can find a description of the job completion options for reporting status in Providing Job Completion Feedback.

## Conflict Management

You may need to coordinate your job processing if there is a potential for conflict. This conflict could be between your own jobs or between your jobs and others that are running and attempting to manipulate the same objects. An example of this is workspace resources.

The concurrency framework provides two techniques for conflict management: locks and scheduling rules. Choose the one that best meets your needs.

### Locks

A **lock** is an object obtained from the job manager using the newLock method. You can use a lock to coordinate access to some logical resource. The meaning of a given lock is up to you. The concurrency framework provides the basic lock mechanism; you give it meaning in your plug-in.

The job manager is aware of all locks that it supplies, and this knowledge is used to identify and resolve any deadlocks that might occur. This allows multiple jobs to use a given lock to manage access to shared assets, as long as they have a reference to the same ILock instance. The job could then put sensitive code in a structure that acquires and releases the lock. Locks are discussed further in Using Job Manager Locks.

### Scheduling Rules

**Scheduling rules** are a mechanism for determining when a job can be scheduled or proceed. A scheduling rule implements the contains and isConflicting methods defined by the ISchedulingRule interface. You can use the setRule method to associate a job with a scheduling rule prior to a schedule request. When a job has an associated scheduling rule, the job manager will interrogate the rule to determine when a scheduled job can actually be started.

Jobs can also use a scheduling rule to protect certain sections of code by calling the job manager beginRule and endRule methods. The beginRule method blocks the job until the job manager has determined that the scheduling rule is clear to proceed.

The `org.eclipse.core.resources` plug-in has implemented scheduling rule support for all workspace resources. Any workspace object that implements IResource also implements ISchedulingRule.

Scheduling rules are discussed further in Using a Scheduling Rule and Workspace Resource Support for Scheduling Rules.

### Framework Review

We have now defined the basics of the concurrency framework. Jobs are code that can be scheduled for execution, job conflict can be avoided using locks and scheduling rules, and the overall process is governed by the job manager. If you choose to run jobs, you can have them interact with the Eclipse user interface to involve the user in the job execution process.

The rest of this chapter reviews these concepts in greater detail. You can read on or return when you choose to start using jobs in your plug-in. You may also want to load the jobs example from the CD-ROM, which includes a scripted demonstration of the jobs API that will let you better understand job processing mechanics and the user interaction options.

## Using Jobs

The process of creating, running, and managing a job to completion is covered in greater detail this section. It includes how to provide processing feedback, the use of advanced job management options, tracking job state changes, and implementing support for cancel requests. Additional examples of using jobs are provided in the examples on the CD-ROM.

**NOTE**    Much of this discussion focuses on the use of the Job class as opposed to UIJob or other job types. Most of the considerations are the same beyond the method used to implement the job processing (run versus runInUIThread). Major differences are identified in the discussion.

### Creating a Job

You can create a job any time one is required to perform a set of processing that can be run in another thread. You have to identify these opportunities. Once you have found them, you have two choices: create the job as an inner class, or define your own class that extends the Job class. Here is an example of an inner class implementation of a simple Hello Job World job. It includes monitor setup for the units of processing to be performed, updates to the monitor to show progress, and calls to a few methods that perform some processing. Yes, the job does not appear to do any interesting work, but the goal is to understand the behavior, not get lost in implementation details.

```java
Job customJob = new Job("InlineJob") {

    protected IStatus run(IProgressMonitor monitor) {

        monitor.beginTask("Hello Job World", 200);
        System.out.println(this.getName() + " Starting...");

        doSomeWork();
        monitor.worked(100);

        System.out.println(this.getName() + " Working...");

        doSomeWork();
        monitor.worked(100);

        System.out.println(this.getName() + " Done.");
        monitor.done();

        return new Status(IStatus.OK, "com.ibm.jdg2e.concurrency",
            IStatus.OK, "Job Completed Fine", null);
    }
};
```

Be sure to close out your monitor with a call to the done method, which is required to free up the monitor and its associated memory.

The run method must return an IStatus that describes the result of the job when it ends. The Hello Job World example is a simple creation of a Status that identifies normal job completion. The status codes you can return are defined in the IStatus interface: OK, INFO, WARNING, ERROR, and CANCEL. You can find additional information on the use of IStatus in Chapter 28, Serviceability.

If the job completes with an ERROR status, a dialog with information about the job is automatically shown. When a job completes with an ERROR or WARNING status, an entry is automatically written to the Workbench log. You can get the completion status of a job by using the getResult method. The getResult method returns a null until after a job has completed.

There are additional techniques you can use to provide feedback at the end of a job. These range from messages left in the Progress view to actions associated to a job that has finished. You can find information on these techniques in Providing Job Completion Feedback. For now, we will just have the job return an OK status.

## Defining Job Attributes

Job attributes are used to control the runtime behavior, user interaction, and job manager scheduling logic. Some must be set before the job is scheduled; others can change as the job runs.

The following methods define attributes that must be set before the job is scheduled.

- `setPriority`: This provides an integer value for the importance of the job.
- `setSystem`: A value of `true` hides the job from the user.
- `setUser`: A value of `true` forces a dialog to show job activity to the user.
- `setRule`: This identifies the scheduling rule to use to validate that the job can start.
- `setProgressGroup`: This associates the job with a given progress group.

The `Job` class defines the priority values, such as `INTERACTIVE`, `SHORT`, and `BUILD`, that can be used in the `setPriority` method. The default priority is `LONG`. The `setUser` method is similar to another API for scheduling jobs discussed in Running the Job with Active Progress Reporting. The job's `setRule` method is discussed in Using a Scheduling Rule. The progress group association lasts for only one execution cycle.

You can use the `setName` method to change the job name (displayed in the Workbench status bar and Progress view) while the job is running.

Property values that are specific to the job can also be defined using the `setProperty` method. You can use this to set plug-in-specific properties as required. Several predefined properties (`IProgressConstants`) actually influence the job's behavior in the user interface. These are discussed further in Providing Job Completion Feedback.

## Scheduling the Job

Once you have an instance of a `Job` set up the way you want, you have to decide how you want to schedule the job. There are two method signatures for the `schedule` request.

```
// Schedule job to run as soon as possible.
job.schedule();

// Schedule job to run after a specified delay (milliseconds).
job.schedule(1500);
```

A schedule request sends the job to the job manager. The job manager will consider the job priority, any scheduling rule that may have been defined, and the availability of system resources as part of deciding when to start the job. Quite often the job starts immediately, but it may be delayed if not enough threads are available.

You can schedule the same job instance repeatedly. If the job is active, it will be rescheduled once complete if one or more schedule requests are received. You cannot queue multiple schedule requests. A job can even schedule itself to repeat the processing immediately or schedule itself with a delay to become a recurring job.

### Pausing a Job by Using a Sleep Request

Jobs can be put in a waiting state by telling the job to sleep. A job will accept a request to sleep only if it has not yet started running.

The time frame in which you can issue a `sleep` request is often very short. If you schedule the job with a delay or have a scheduling rule that has kept the job from starting, you have a chance to issue a `sleep` request. A job sleeps until sent a `wakeUp` request.

### Waiting for a Job to Complete

After you schedule a job, how will you find out when the job has finished? Your code can either wait on the job by using the `join` method or ask to be informed by using a job event change listener. The use of the `join` method is discussed here. The job event change listener is described in the next section, Listening for Job Change Events.

The `join` method can be issued against an individual job or for a job family using the job manager interface. A `join` request says you would like to wait until the job or job family completes. This code will both schedule a job and, using a `join` request, wait until the job completes.

```
customJob.schedule();
try {
   System.out.println("Going to wait on the job...");
   customJob.join();
   System.out.println("Job Done -- Can continue now");
} catch (InterruptedException e) {
}
```

The output on the following page is written to the console log as a result of running this code, which includes the logic defined in the job's run method as shown earlier in Creating a Job.

```
InlineJob Starting...
Going to wait on the job...
InlineJob Working...
InlineJob Done.
Job Done -- Can continue now
```

The caller of the join request will be waiting until the "joined" job has finished. If the caller happens to be running on the user interface thread, the user interface is locked for the duration.

**Warning:** Avoid using a join request to wait on a job when your code is running on the user interface thread. If your code is running on a user interface thread and you use a join request to wait on a UIJob, the system may deadlock. A common scenario for using the join method is to wait on a cancel request. This is discussed in Asking a Job to Cancel.

### Listening for Job Change Events

A listener can be added to either a specific job or the job manager if you need to listen to all jobs; in either case, the addJobChangeListener method is called.

Your listener must implement the IJobChangeListener interface. The listener is informed of state changes and is given information about the job in the event object passed to the listener. This information includes the IStatus returned at the end of the job for the done method. Listening for state change events is more reliable than using getState for a job because the state can change quickly.

You also have the option of using the JobChangeAdapter. This lets you implement only the methods for the events you want to track. Here is an example of using an adapter to respond to only the done event.

```
customJob.schedule();
customJob.addJobChangeListener(new JobChangeAdapter() {
  public void done(IJobChangeEvent event) {
    System.out.println(event.getJob().getName()
      + " has finished.");
    System.out.println("  Job result: \n\t"
      + event.getJob().getResult());
  }
});
```

The result of running this code to schedule the job and listen for the completion event and associated result writes the following output to the console log.

```
InlineJob Starting...
InlineJob Working...
InlineJob Done.
```

```
InlineJob has finished.
  Job result:
  Status OK com.ibm.jdg2e.concurrency code=0
    Job Completed Fine null
```

Table 29.1 shows the sequence of state changes and methods that would be called in a listener, as part of the life cycle of a job.

**Table 29.1**  Job State Changes and the `IJobChangeListener` Methods They Trigger

| Job Action | Job State | Job Change Listener Method |
|---|---|---|
| Job is created | NONE | |
| Job is scheduled | NONE > WAITING | scheduled |
| Job manager is ready to start job | WAITING > RUNNING | aboutToRun |
| Job starts | RUNNING | running |
| Job ends | NONE | done |
| Job is put in sleep state | SLEEPING | sleeping |
| Job is wakened | WAITING | awake |

### Asking a Job to Cancel

You have the right to ask a job to stop by issuing a `cancel` request; however, the job may not honor it. A `cancel` request is simple to send, given a handle to the job instance.

```
customjob.cancel();
```

What happens depends on the job state. If the job has not yet started, it is removed from the queue and `cancel` returns `true`. If the job has started, the `cancel` request is implemented not by terminating the job but by informing the job's monitor that it has been canceled. If the job does not check, it will just continue. This is the logic that would need to be added to the Hello Job World example (presented earlier in Creating a Job) to support processing a cancel request.

```
if (monitor.isCanceled())
  return new Status(IStatus.CANCEL, "com.ibm.jdg2e.concurrency",
    IStatus.CANCEL, "Job was canceled", null);
```

It is a job's responsibility to query the monitor on occasion to determine whether a cancel request has been made. It might not make sense to check for cancellation when the bulk of the job processing is already complete; you have to decide whether and where to support a cancellation attempt. When a cancel request is detected, the job should perform any required cleanup and return an IStatus with a Status.CANCEL code. A canceled job still exists, meaning that it could be rescheduled.

Processing required to support a cancel request is specific to your design and how the job processing was structured. Some jobs might be able to terminate immediately; others might need to roll back previous processing. The IStatus result returned as part of the job cancellation may reflect the state of the job and what may need to occur next.

You might want to use the join method to wait on the job after a cancel request.

```
if (!customJob.cancel())
  try {
    customJob.join();
  } catch (InterruptedException e) {
  } finally {
    if (customJob != null)
      if (customJob.getResult().getCode() == Status.CANCEL)
        System.out.println(customJob.getName()
          + "was canceled");
      else
        System.out.println(customJob.getName()
          + "ran to completion");
  }
else
  System.out.println(customJob.getName() + "was canceled");
```

Using this approach, you can determine whether the job ran to completion or accepted the cancel request.

## User Interaction Options

Your users may not be directly aware of how jobs are used in your plug-in. Still, there may be times when they need to be involved, for example, when jobs are running in the background and they need to know the result of the job processing. This section discusses the techniques for informing the user that a job is running and providing feedback after the job completes.

### Using a Job-Specific Image

One technique for user interaction is to make your job recognizable to the user in the Progress view by providing your own image descriptor for use when the job is running. You can do this by setting the appropriate job property.

```
ImageDescriptor id = ImageDescriptor.createFromURL(url);
setProperty(IProgressConstants.ICON_PROPERTY, id);
```

You can also define an image for a job family by calling the IProgress-Service to register an image descriptor.

```
PlatformUI.getWorkbench().getProgressService()
    .registerIconForFamily(id, getYourFamilyObject());
```

### Running the Job with Active Progress Reporting

By default, a job will run in the background with only small clues to the user that it is active. When you start a job, you can choose to have it initially displayed to the user in a dialog. The dialog shows progress and allows the user to ask that the work continue in the background, issue a cancel request, or see the details as the job runs.

This dialog can be displayed using either of two techniques. One choice is to use the IWorkbenchSiteProgressService object that can be obtained from a Workbench part. The following code obtains and uses an IWorkbenchSite-ProgressService instance to display a dialog when the job starts.

```
IWorkbenchSiteProgressService siteps =
  (IWorkbenchSiteProgressService) getSite()
    .getAdapter(IWorkbenchSiteProgressService.class);
siteps.showInDialog(getSite().getShell(), job);
job.schedule();
```

Figure 29.5 shows the editing dialog displayed for the job.

**Figure 29.5**  Foreground Progress Reporting for an Active Job

The other much simpler option is to define the job as a user job by using job.setUser(true); this must be issued before the job is scheduled. The setUser approach is simpler than the first one described. The user can set the Workbench preference setting **Always run in background** to force all jobs started with a dialog to be run in the background automatically.

## Workbench Part Support for Job Processing

Jobs could be started as the result of some user interaction with a view or editor. If the user requests an action that requires a bit of time-consuming processing, it is good to show the user that your view is busy processing the last request. Workbench parts (views and editors) can change their look to reflect that jobs scheduled on their behalf are active. Figure 29.6 shows a before-and-after view of how a view's tab changes the view name font to italic when a job is active. In addition, a half-busy cursor is displayed when the mouse is over the Workbench part

**Figure 29.6**    Workbench Part Indication of an Active Job

To support this dynamic activity clue, the WorkbenchPart hierarchy has added support for job processing to the inherited API for views and editors. A default progress hint is provided if the job is scheduled from a view or editor using the available IWorkbenchSiteProgressService.

```
IWorkbenchSiteProgressService ps =
    (IWorkbenchSiteProgressService)
    getSite().getAdapter(IWorkbenchSiteProgressService.class);
```

With the IWorkbenchSiteProgressService you can schedule a job with or without a start delay or ask that a half-busy cursor be displayed when the cursor is above the Workbench part.

```
ps.schedule(job);
ps.schedule(job, delayTime);
ps.schedule(job, delayTime, true);
```

Another approach is a bit more robust. The showBusyForFamily method found in the IWorkbenchSiteProgressService allows you to identify a family object. If this family is used for all jobs scheduled by a given Workbench part, all instances of the Workbench part will show busy when any job in the family is active.

Another option for integrating dynamic feedback as part of the user interface is provided by the DeferredTreeContentManager. This class can be used with JFace tree viewers to support delayed delivery of content with user feedback during the process. If you have used the CVS support provided by Eclipse, you have seen this approach in action. Expand requests for a tree result in the display of **Pending...** while a job runs to obtain the required content.

### Providing Job Completion Feedback

There are several built-in behaviors you can use when your job reaches normal termination. Some are straightforward; others build on the job result as defined by the IStatus returned by the run method. The job can also throw an exception and force a dialog to draw the user's attention as well.

#### Keeping the Job in the Progress View to Show the Result

You can use the job name itself as a form of feedback. The name can be changed dynamically, so at the end of the job you can set the name to a short result message and just ask that the job stay in the Progress view after completion. The user can remove it when desired. Enable this functioning by setting the appropriate job property.

```
job.setProperty(IProgressConstants.KEEP_PROPERTY, Boolean.TRUE);
```

#### Adding an Action to the Job to Perform Postcompletion Processing

An action (IAction) can be associated with a job, and the user can run this action once the job completes. To allow this, set the appropriate job property.

```
IAction jobAction = new Action() { ... };
job.setProperty(IProgressConstants.ACTION_PROPERTY, jobAction);
```

The action might open a dialog or perform some other processing as required to inform the user about the job results. The user sees this action as either an exclamation point (**!**) or an error (**x**) in the progress icon in the status bar (visible in Figure 29.7).

#### Returning an Appropriate Status for Normal Termination

When your job reaches the end of the run method, you return an IStatus indicating the state of the job request. The status options were discussed earlier in Creating a Job. The processing that results and what the user sees are discussed here.

The basic options are to return an IStatus with the appropriate status code and to attach an IAction as a job property to interact with the user when required. The status code alone triggers Workbench user interface processing for specific codes. Attaching an action gives the user a visual clue that there is something to see about some recent processing. How this clue is presented depends on how the job has been run, with or without a progress group. This is reviewed in Table 29.2.

Figure 29.7 shows the Progress view, the status bar, and the Errors Running Operations dialog that can be triggered depending on how the IStatus returned by the run method is defined.

**Table 29.2**    Normal Job Termination Feedback Options

| Presentation | | Job Status Code | | | |
| --- | --- | --- | --- | --- | --- |
| | | OK | INFO | WARNING | ERROR |
| Job detail remains in Progress view | | No | No | No | Yes |
| Visual clue in status bar | No action | No | No | No | Yes |
| | Action property set | Yes | Yes | Yes | Yes |
| Job detail hyperlink added in Progress view | No progress group | No | No | No | No |
| | Progress group | Yes | Yes | Yes | Yes |
| Display Errors Running Operations dialog | | No | No | No | Yes |

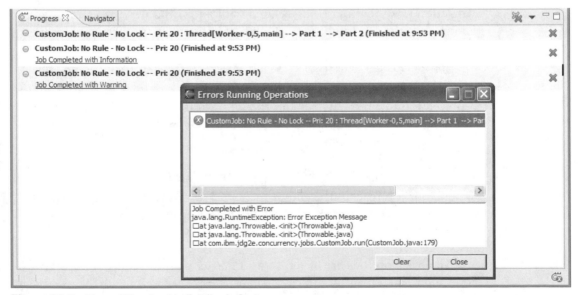

**Figure 29.7**    Normal Termination Feedback Options

### Identifying Failure by Throwing an Exception

A job has the right to throw an exception if the job processing triggers a situation where a severe error needs to be identified. We say "severe" because the use of an appropriate status at normal termination may be more effective when there is a situation where you need to get the user involved. Any exception that extends `RuntimeException` can be thrown when you have no other option. When the exception is thrown, it is caught by the job management framework; the framework opens an Errors Running Operations dialog. The dialog and the available error details are similar to what Figure 29.7 shows.

## Job Contention Management Options

If you decide to use jobs, you may need to worry about collisions. That is, the processing being performed in one job may negatively influence the processing in another job. If there are reasons for isolating the processing involved in different jobs, you have two main options to consider. You can use locks to force other jobs to wait until the lock is available. Alternatively, you can use a scheduling rule to control when a job is started and what other jobs can be running at the same time.

Both locks and scheduling rules are discussed in this section, including the implementation of a scheduling rule. Scheduling rule support provided by workspace resources is also discussed.

### *Using Job Manager Locks*

Locks can be used by jobs to restrict access to a common asset. It does not matter whether the asset is an API that can't be called by more than one task or part of a model that needs managed access. Locks provide a simple enqueue/dequeue structure known to the job manager.

All locks are obtained from the job manager. Here is the call required to get a new instance of a lock.

```
ILock lockOne = Platform.getJobManager().newLock();
```

The lock instance is not specific to one job but must be accessed by any job that wishes to enqueue on a shared asset. All jobs that wish to use locks to restrict access to a shared asset must have access to the same lock instance. Once the lock is available to the job, the following logic is required to protect more than one job from interacting with a critical asset.

```
// Acquire lock prior to start of critical processing.
accessLock.acquire();
```

```
// Do processing.
. . .
// Release lock to allow others to access critical asset.
accessLock.release();
```

Just remember to release the lock; releasing it twice will not hurt. A wise man once said, "It is better to give it up when you do not have it than to hold it by accident."

The simplicity of a lock and the fact that a lock is used only when the job is running distinguish a lock from a scheduling rule. A scheduling rule typically prevents the job from starting until the rule is satisfied. However, as you'll see in the next section, you can dynamically use a scheduling rule such that it behaves as a more sophisticated lock.

## Using a Scheduling Rule

You can use a scheduling rule to control when a job begins. The scheduling rule logic is used to determine whether the rules of the currently unscheduled job conflicts with rules of the active jobs. This does not affect the scheduling of the first job because no other rules are active. However, if one job is running with a scheduling rule and another is scheduled, the scheduling rule will not let the second job start running until the scheduling rule determines that there is no conflict or that the other job has finished and has removed the conflict. This gives you the opportunity to craft scheduling rules that reflect the potential for conflict in your domain. These rules could implement exclusive access, enforce a job processing sequence, or allow jobs to run simultaneously when there are no conflicts based on the intent of the job. All you have to do is implement a scheduling rule with your custom logic; the concurrency framework does the rest.

The `org.eclipse.core.resources` plug-in provides an example of the implementation of a custom scheduling rule framework. The `IResource` interface now extends `ISchedulingRule`. That is, any workspace resource can now be used as a scheduling rule. This is discussed further in Workspace Resource Support for Scheduling Rules.

If you use only one scheduling rule in your jobs, the rule can act much like a lock. The difference is that when you use a lock, jobs will start and then attempt to acquire the lock; when you use a scheduling rule, the job will wait until the scheduling rule processing determines that the job can actually start. This scenario is well documented in the *Platform Plug-in Developer Guide*. When there are multiple scheduling rules, their logic determines whether one rule conflicts with any that are associated to an already scheduled or running job.

It is easy to associate a scheduling rule with a job. The job manager does the rest once you schedule the job.

```
ISchedulingRule rule = customDomain.getSchedulingRule();
job.setRule(rule);
```

That is all it takes to associate a job and scheduling rule; the real work is the design and implementation of a custom set of rules.

A fine-grained approach to using scheduling rules is also available. Instead of associating a scheduling rule with the start of a job, you can make calls to the job manager to associate specific sections of logic with a specific scheduling rule.

```
ISchedulingRule rule = customDomain.getSchedulingRule();
JobManager.getInstance().beginRule(rule, monitor);
// Do processing.
  . . .
JobManager.getInstance().endRule(rule);
```

This `getSchedulingRule` method does not exist. You have to either use an existing implementation of the `ISchedulingRule` interface or implement a scheduling rule yourself. The scheduling rule support implemented as part of the workspace is discussed next.

### Workspace Resource Support for Scheduling Rules

All `IResource` types implement `ISchedulingRule`. This means you can use an `IResource` reference anywhere the method signature requires an `ISchedulingRule` (`setRule`, `beginRule`, and `endRule`). The following code shows the use of the workspace root as the rule, essentially blocking all other workspace access.

```
ISchedulingRule rule = ResourcesPlugin.getWorkspace().getRoot();
customJob.setRule(rule);
customJob.schedule();
```

The `ISchedulingRule` implementation for `IResource` objects is basically a hierarchical rule. This means that if you have a running job using the workspace root as its rule, you are using the parent of all other resources. Any other job that is scheduled using any other `IResource`, the workspace root included, will be blocked. It follows that if a project is used as the rule, any folder or file contained in that project would represent a blocking rule. Two different resources, where one was not contained in the other, could be used as a scheduling rule, and each job could run at the same time.

There is another approach you may want to use as well. The workspace provides an `IResourceRuleFactory` implementation that allows you to request a scheduling rule that fits your needs. Given an `IResourceRuleFactory` and

IResource instance, you can request a scheduling rule using one of these methods: copyRule, createRule, deleteRule, markerRule, modifyRule, moveRule, refreshRule, and validateEditRule. The following logic obtains the appropriate rule for making a modification to a specific file and assigns it to a job.

```
IResourceRuleFactory ruleFactory = workspace.getRuleFactory();
customJob.setRule(ruleFactory.modifyRule(file));
```

What is important about this list of methods is that they represent the actions you typically need to perform on a given IResource. The value of these methods is that they return an accurate scheduling rule that reflects the scope of the modification. For example, the scheduling rule for a move is not the current parent folder or the target parent folder; it is the combination of both. This is shown by the implementation of the moveRule method.

```
public ISchedulingRule
   moveRule(IResource source, IResource destination) {
      // move needs the parent of both source and destination.
      return
         MultiRule.combine(parent(source), parent(destination));
}
```

You can actually use the MultiRule yourself to combine the scheduling rules that represent the true scope of your work. The following invocation produces a rule that supports the creation and modification of a file.

```
IResourceRuleFactory ruleFactory = workspace.getRuleFactory();
ISchedulingRule rule =
   MultiRule.combine(ruleFactory.createRule(file),
      ruleFactory.modifyRule(file));
customJob.setRule(rule);
```

**NOTE** There is one interesting side effect when using an IResource as a scheduling rule. If a shutdown request is sent to the Eclipse Platform, it will shut down, and any in-flight jobs are terminated immediately. But if an IResource instance is used as the scheduling rule for a job, the platform will delay its shutdown until the scheduled job is complete.

The com.ibm.jdg2e.concurrency plug-in jobs example on the CD-ROM includes the use of an IResource as the scheduling rule.

### Defining a Scheduling Rule

Defining your own set of scheduling rules is not that hard. You need a set of rules because one rule will not add much value; any given rule typically conflicts with itself.

You also need a set of associations that either do or do not cause conflict. These are represented by scheduling rules. The decisions on conflict are then implemented in the methods required by the ISchedulingRule interface.

```
public boolean contains(ISchedulingRule rule);
public boolean isConflicting(ISchedulingRule rule);
```

When one rule contains another, they are compatible and can run together. If rules conflict, they are not permitted to run at the same time.

## Example Summary

The com.ibm.jdg2e.concurrency project on the CD-ROM demonstrates many of the functions provided by the job processing API. A view is used to select job processing options and invoke jobs. An ISchedulingRule implementation is also included and used in the demonstration. The example does not do any real work, but it does include a guided script to demonstrate the use of the API.

You can review the code and run the demonstration. This will provide you with a solid understanding of the behavior of jobs and what you can accomplish with the API.

## Chapter Summary

The job processing framework is a valuable addition to the Eclipse runtime platform. Jobs provide a first-class concurrency framework, with support for running concurrent asynchronous tasks and multiple levels of user interaction. These capabilities allow you to implement function that maintains a highly responsive user interface and improves overall use of the processing platform.

## References

Arthorne, John, and Chris Laffra. 2004. *Official Eclipse 3.0 FAQs*. Boston, MA: Addison-Wesley. http://eclipsefaq.org. (See FAQs 127–132, 185, 186, 290.)

The Java Tutorial. Threads: Doing Two or More Tasks at Once. http://java.sun.com/docs/books/tutorial/essential/threads/.

# CHAPTER 30

## Using Capabilities to Manage Too Much of a Good Thing

We have all had the experience at one time or another of using a software product that we found simply overwhelming. It could be an IDE, a word processor, or even a game. It contains such an abundance of function that you hardly know where to begin. Unless you use it every day, you never quite feel comfortable with it. The user interface may resemble the cockpit of a jumbo jet airplane with menus a mile deep, multiple toolbars, palettes floating everywhere, and an options or preferences dialog that rivals your tax forms in complexity and detail. There is no argument that functionally rich applications can be marvelous. They help us complete complex or tedious assignments with relative ease. But if we aren't a power user, wouldn't it be nice if a user interface with the complexity of a jet cockpit could adapt *on demand* to the relative simplicity of an automobile dashboard?

Some Eclipse-based products have over one thousand plug-ins and user interfaces that expose over one hundred fifty views and hundreds of preference pages. These products offer the function that their customers desire and the marketplace demands, but for an individual user who may be inexperienced or require only a subset of functionality, the user interface is far too cluttered. Finding what you need to get your job done can be challenging and sometimes exasperating.

Eclipse has mechanisms to help with this issue. Perspectives help reduce what you see on the menu bar and toolbar and show only views that are relevant to the task. The Preferences and Properties dialogs organize pages into categories. Working sets help you focus on a portion of your workspace. But this is not enough for some large, functionally rich applications. It would be better if only the functionality that the user needed, based on the type of work he or she was doing, showed through in the user interface.

You know that Eclipse has built-in support for Java, plug-in development, and CVS team programming. Now if you were not a plug-in developer, or didn't use CVS, wouldn't it be nice if you saw no references to PDE or CVS functionality unless you used them? Certainly the user interface would be less cluttered. Or imagine that you were a Java developer and used CVS but did not create plug-ins. Then one day you checked out a plug-in project. Perhaps you were asked to help a colleague who developed plug-ins and needed your help with some coding issue. Wouldn't it be nice if the creation of the plug-in project in your workspace automatically revealed the PDE user interface so you could continue helping your colleague? Eclipse addresses this issue through **capabilities**.

Capabilities filter what functionality is visible to the user and help address the problem of overwhelming user interfaces. Capabilities can also automatically enable the visibility of hidden functionality based on certain user actions. By the way, you may hear capabilities referred to as activities. That original term for capabilities still exists in the API.

Let's learn more about capabilities and see how they can address some of the issues we have been discussing.

## Introducing Capabilities

Eclipse-based products have the option of organizing their user interface contributions into capabilities. A capability is a grouping of functionality. Capabilities can be enabled or disabled (by the user or programmatically), providing a functionality filter. This allows you to easily expose only the function that the user needs and avoid some of the problems described earlier. Capabilities can be enabled explicitly through a user interface or implicitly by trigger points. A **trigger point** enables one or more capabilities based on an operation the user performs (recall the example of checking out a plug-in project for the first time). This way functionality is exposed only if the user needs or desires to use it. Eclipse calls this controlled revelation of functionality **progressive disclosure**. Note that capabilities are not designed to be a secure mechanism for limiting functionality. Later in the chapter we discuss how you might create trigger points to enable function for your users.

What kinds of user interface contributions can be filtered by capabilities? What defines a capability? What are the built-in trigger points that enable a capability? Who defines them? How are capabilities affected by dynamic plug-ins? These are all good questions. Let's answer them one at a time.

Capabilities can filter the visibility of the following user interface contributions.

- Views.
- Editors.
- Perspectives.

  The Select Perspective dialog has a **Show All** check box, which reveals all disabled perspectives. Selecting a disabled perspective causes a prompt to enable the capability that the perspective is associated with (progressive disclosure in action).

- Toolbar contributions.
- Menu contributions.
- Preference pages.
- Property pages.
- New wizards.

  If disabled wizards exist, they will display if the user explicitly requests them by checking **Show All Wizards** in the New dialog or the New Project dialog (see Figure 30.5 later in this chapter). Selecting the wizard results in a prompt to enable the capability shown later in Figure 30.3.

Through the use of capabilities, an extensive list of preference pages can be managed down to a size that is appropriate for the user. The Show Views dialog and Select Perspective dialog show only those items that are members of enabled capabilities. Figures 30.1 and 30.2 show the differences in the Preferences dialog when no capabilities are enabled and when all capabilities are enabled, respectively.

If the intent is to filter the user interface elements just listed, how might such a filter be defined? You know by now that user interface contributions defined in a plug-in manifest always have a unique identifier defined by their id attribute. These identifiers usually follow well-defined naming conventions like org.eclipse.core.*<some unique pattern>* or org.eclispe.ui.*<some unique pattern>*. This turns out to be the solution to the problem. The identifiers for user interface contributions are matched against some set of string patterns defined in your capabilities filter that allows sets of user interface function to be visible or not. All that is needed is some formal way to define this filter. (Hint: An extension point might serve our purposes; we will get to that later.)

PART V

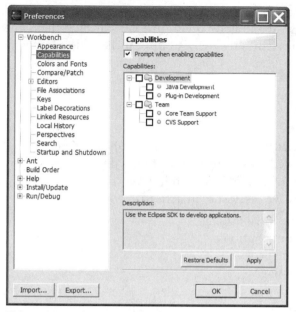

**Figure 30.1**    Eclipse SDK Preferences Dialog with All Capabilities Disabled

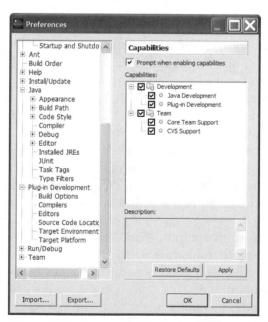

**Figure 30.2**    Eclipse SDK Preferences Dialog with All Capabilities Enabled

The formal definition of a capability is a set of identifiers. As we just mentioned, these identifiers come from the `id` attributes assigned to user interface contributions defined in a plug-in. When a capability is active, the user interface contributions are enabled if their identifiers match those defined by the capability. Since an identifier (say, the `id` of a view) could conceivably be specified in more than one capability, Eclipse enables that user interface contribution if its identifier matches any one of the enabled capabilities it participates in. (Formally, it is enabled if and only if it is a member of the union of all the sets of identifiers for all enabled capabilities.) In the case of the view, it is enabled if its identifier matches any enabled capability. Finally, if a contribution's identifier is not a member of any capability, the contribution is always enabled.

To summarize, let's look at a simple example. It turns out that user interface contributions in the PDE plug-ins have a common identifier prefix named `org.eclipse.pde`. If we want to enable or disable the entire PDE, specifying some identifier string-matching pattern like `org.eclipse.pde.*` should be sufficient to ensure that all PDE actions, views, perspectives, menus, editors, and preference and property pages could be collectively enabled or disabled. (The actual matching pattern looks a little different, as you will soon learn.) That is the essence of how capabilities work. We will cover the details later.

Recall that capabilities can be enabled or disabled by the user or by trigger points. For the user to do this, there must be a user interface. Eclipse offers a preference page that displays what capabilities are defined and which of them are enabled. The user can change the capability state between enabled and disabled, as shown in Figures 30.1 and 30.2. On the **Workbench > Capabilities** preference page, the Eclipse SDK defines two categories of capabilities, **Development** and **Team**. **Development** consists of **Java Development** and **Plug-In Development**. **Team** consists of **Core Team Support** and **CVS Support**. By default, they are all enabled.

Capabilities can also be enabled automatically by using trigger points. A trigger point results in the automatic enablement of a capability based on some action by the user (the user is prompted to accept the enablement of the capability). Eclipse has defined several trigger points. The most common triggers are based on the New, Import, and Export wizards. For example, using a wizard to create a new Java project enables the Java Development capability. (You might ask why that wizard was visible if the Java Development capbability was disabled. As you will learn later, it is possible to make a wizard visible even when the capability it participates in is disabled.) A project's nature(s) can also trigger enablement of an activity (see Chapter 24, Managing Resources with

Natures and Builders, to learn more about project natures). Another trigger enables the Core Team Support capability and the repository provider capability if there are any projects in the workspace managed by that provider. Recall our earlier example where a plug-in project checked out from CVS caused the PDE to be enabled. Sharing a project with CVS would trigger the CVS capability. You can start to see the possibilities. Some examples of possible use cases for your own triggers are described in Defining Your Own Triggers later in this chapter.

When a trigger must enable capability, the user is prompted with the dialog shown in Figure 30.3. This would occur, for example, if you tried to create a plug-in project when the Plug-in Development capability was disabled.

**Figure 30.3**   Confirmation Request Displayed Before a Trigger Enables a Capability

The expectation is that a product manager or systems integrator, who best understands his or her users, will define the capabilities for a product or product extension. However, there are no specific technical limitations on which plug-ins can define capabilities. Capabilities are defined using an extension point (described next). All of the information about a capability is defined in the plug-in extension through XML. With this no-code implementation, the capabilities for a product or product extension can be defined and refined very late in the product development cycle.

If a dynamic plug-in is added or unloaded, a capability associated with that plug-in is automatically reconfigured to recognize the change.

Let's summarize before we get into the details of defining a capability.

- A capability represents a set of user functions that can be enabled or disabled.
- A particular Workbench user interface element is included in a capability if its `id` attribute in the plug-in extension that defined it matches the id pattern defined in a capability.
- Capabilities can be enabled or disabled by the user in the **Workbench > Capabilities** preference page.

- Capabilities can be enabled programmatically through a trigger point, a situation that necessitates disclosure of additional function.
- A person who understands the product's customers and their usage patterns is well qualified to define capabilities.

## The Capabilities Extension Point

As we mentioned earlier, capabilities are defined by using an extension point, `org.eclipse.ui.activities`. ("What?" you may be thinking. "You just used the term activities." Recall that, originally, capabilities were called activities. We now have this legacy term that exists in the extension point and Java APIs. Capabilities and activities are synonymous in this context.) This extension point is not difficult to understand, and there is no code associated with it. This means that you can define (or redefine) a set of capabilities very late in the development effort, perhaps based on early customer feedback and without having to change any code. The six primary extension attributes of this extension point are covered next. Refer to Figure 30.4 (shown on the following page) as you read this.

- `activity`

  This attribute defines a capability and its external name like Development, Administration, Testing, or Modeling. A capability represents a logical set of identifiers (representing user interface contributions) that can be enabled or disabled.

- `activityPatternBinding`

  This is the most important attribute because it defines what functionality will be visible to the user when the capability is enabled. The pattern we are discussing here is a **string** pattern (specified in the `pattern` child attribute), which is defined as a regular string expression representing a collection of user interface contributions defined by their identifier attribute in their respective plug-in extension definitions. When the capability associated with this pattern binding is disabled, all user interface contributions with extension identifiers that match the pattern string are not visible in the user interface (unless an identifier is also a member of another capability that is enabled). If it is not possible to define an activity in a single string pattern, more than one `activity-PatternBinding` attribute can be defined for an activity. This string pattern must conform to the requirements of the `java.util.regex.Pattern` class. For example, the string pattern `org\.eclipse\.jdt\..*` would

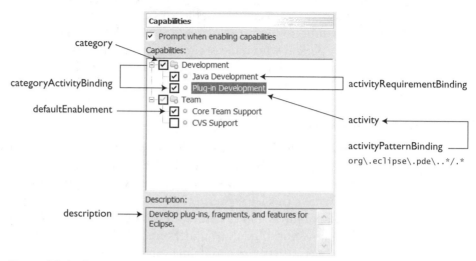

**Figure 30.4**   Primary Attributes of the Activities Extension Point

apply to all identifiers in the JDT that contain the string prefix
`org.eclipse.jdt` (see note that follows). Since the JDT has a consistent
pattern for defining identifiers, this pattern could represent the entire JDT.

- `category`

  This attribute allows groupings of capabilities and is simply for organizational purposes in the **Workbench > Capabilities** preference page.

- `categoryActivityBinding`

  This attribute associates a capability to a category.

- `activityRequirementBinding`

  This attribute permits you to associate a capability with a dependent
  capability. For example, if Plug-in Development and Java Development
  are two associated capabilities, the Java Development capability must
  be enabled when the Plug-in Development capability is enabled. You
  can specify that requirement with the `activityRequirementBinding`
  attribute.

- `defaultEnablement`

  The specified capability is enabled by default the first time the Workbench starts. This allows you to define which capabilities should be initially enabled.

**NOTE** The conventions used when defining a pattern string require a little explanation. In the pattern `org\.eclipse\.jdt\..*` shown in the `activityPatternBinding` description, the backslash is an escape character and `\.` is a way to define a period in your string; otherwise a period is interpreted as "any character" in an expression. The `.*` at the end means zero or more instances of any character. Any string of characters following `.jdt.` are permitted. Here is a snippet of code you can use to easily verify that a string matches a given pattern.

```
public class PatternTest {
  public static void main(String[] args) {
  if (Pattern.matches
    ("org\\.eclipse\\.jdt\\..*", "org.eclipse.jdt.ui.debug"))
      System.out.println("Match");
    else
      System.out.println("No match");
  }
}
```

To understand these attributes better, let's examine some portions of the activities extension defined for the Eclipse SDK. You can view this extension from the Plug-ins view by opening the `plugin.xml` file in the `org.eclipse.sdk` plug-in. Our example exposes the use of the activities extension point in discrete pieces. First, of course, we need to define our extension to the `org.eclipse.ui.activities` extension point.

```
<extension
    point="org.eclipse.ui.activities">
```

Next, the capabilities and their external names are defined by using the activity attribute. There isn't anything special about this. A `description` attribute is optional. The name and description appear in the **Workbench > Capabilities** preference page.

```
<activity
  name="%activity.java"
  description="%activity.java.desc"
  id="org.eclipse.javaDevelopment">
</activity>
<activity
  name="%activity.plugin"
  description="%activity.plugin.desc"
  id="org.eclipse.plugInDevelopment">
</activity>
```

Next, let's look at the `activityPatternBinding` attribute, which is more interesting. Specifically, let's look at the two activity patterns defined for the Plug-in Development capability.

```
<activityPatternBinding
   activityTd="org.eclipse.plugInDevelopment"
   pattern="org\.eclipse\.pde\..*/.*">
</activityPatternBinding>
<activityPatternBinding
   activityId="org.eclipse.plugInDevelopment"
   pattern="org\.eclipse\.pde/PluginNature">
</activityPatternBinding>
```

The `activityId` attribute associates a pattern binding to an activity by specifying the identifier of the `activity` attribute. The `pattern` attribute specifies a string pattern (as a regular expression), which denotes the set of user interface identifiers that will be associated with a particular capability (activity!). Here the pattern `org\.eclipse\.pde\..*/.*` specifies that all PDE plug-ins and their contents belong to the Plug-in Development capability. You can see that having a well-defined convention for defining identifiers for your plug-in extensions can make capability pattern definitions much easier. The second pattern `org\.eclipse\.pde/PluginNature` means that any project created in the workspace with a plug-in nature will enable the Plug-in Development capability. (If you are unfamiliar with natures, see Chapter 24, Managing Resources with Natures and Builders. Simply put, a nature is a way to specify a type of project.) Creating a plug-in project, importing a plug-in project, or checking out a plug-in project from a team repository will trigger enablement of the Plug-in Development capability. If you examine the SDK capabilities, you will see a similar activity pattern defined for Java projects. Because this specification applies to any project nature, you can use this for project natures you have defined. To make a more general statement, if you define your own triggers using the activities API discussed later in the chapter, you are free to specify your own activity pattern. It need not conform to the protocol we have discussed so far.

The `activityPatternBinding` attribute is important to understand. Take a few minutes and look at the XML snippet just shown and the other patterns defined in the Eclipse SDK extension point.

It gets easier now. Next are categories, which organize the user's choices in the **Workbench > Capabilities** preference page (see Figure 30.1 earlier in the chapter). One or more capabilities can be associated with a category. When we discuss the activities API later in this chapter, you will learn that only capabilities are enabled or disabled, not capability categories. Here is the specification of the Development category.

```
<category
  name="%activity.cat.development"
  description="%activity.cat.development.desc"
  id="org.eclipse.categories.developmentCategory">
</category>
```

The next attribute, `categoryActivityBinding`, simply associates capabilities to categories.

```
<categoryActivityBinding
  activityId="org.eclipse.javaDevelopment"
  categoryId="org.eclipse.categories.developmentCategory">
</categoryActivityBinding>
<categoryActivityBinding
  activityId="org.eclipse.plugInDevelopment"
  categoryId="org.eclipse.categories.developmentCategory">
</categoryActivityBinding>
```

To specify a capability's dependence on another capability, use the `activity-RequirementBinding` attribute. As you know, the PDE has a dependency on the JDT so when the Plug-in Development capability is enabled, the Java Development capability must also be enabled. This is how you define that dependency.

```
<activityRequirementBinding
  activityId="org.eclipse.plugInDevelopment"
  requiredActivityId="org.eclipse.javaDevelopment">
</activityRequirementBinding>
```

To complete our review, let's examine how to specify which capabilities are enabled by default, by using the `defaultEnablement` attribute. The Eclipse SDK has chosen to enable all defined capabilities by default.

```
<defaultEnablement
  id="org.eclipse.javaDevelopment">
</defaultEnablement>
<defaultEnablement
  id="org.eclipse.plugInDevelopment">
</defaultEnablement>
<defaultEnablement
  id="org.eclipse.team">
</defaultEnablement>
<defaultEnablement
  id="org.eclipse.team.cvs">
</defaultEnablement>
```

That completes our review of the activities extension point. As you can see, all filtering is based on the identifier of the user interface contribution defined in a plug-in extension. This means user interface contributions created directly through the Java API and not through an extension point are not filtered. For example, this applies to wizards and actions defined directly in code. To maintain flexibility and allow maximum use of capability filtering, we recommend that you define your user interface contributions as much as possible through extension points and follow standard naming conventions for all identifiers in your plug-ins. In particular, use the various action contribution extension points defined in Chapter 21, Action Contributions: The Integration Fast Track, to define actions you want to appear on the Workbench menu, toolbar, views, and editors.

## Defining Primary Wizards

When your capability is disabled, it will also filter from the user any wizards belonging to that capability. As a product manager, you might want to maintain visibility of wizards that provide an entry point to key product functions while keeping the capability encompassing those functions disabled. This is the easy way to lighten up your user interface. If the user selects such a wizard, Eclipse's wizard trigger will prompt the user to enable the capability that the wizard participates in. For example, the Eclipse SDK chose to make sure that the new Java Project wizard and the new Plug-in Project wizard (as well as a few others) are always visible in the New dialog and the New Project dialog. The `org.eclipse.ui.newwizards` extension point (see Chapter 16, Dialogs and Wizards) allows you to define primary wizards. A primary wizard is visible in the New wizard dialog even if the capability it belongs to is disabled. All you need to provide is the identifier of the wizard from the plug-in it was defined in. Eclipse defined the primary wizards in the same plug-in as the activities extension, which is a good practice because this is essentially another portion of the overall capabilities specification.

```
<extension
    point="org.eclipse.ui.newWizards">
  <primaryWizard
    id="org.eclipse.jdt.ui.wizards.JavaProjectWizard">
  </primaryWizard>
  <primaryWizard
    id="org.eclipse.pde.ui.NewProjectWizard">
  </primaryWizard>
  ... Some other primary wizards were omitted for clarity ...
</extension>
```

This results in the Plug-in Project and Java Project wizards appearing as shown in Figure 30.5, even when their capabilities are disabled. Attempting to create a Java project will produce the capability enablement prompt dialog shown earlier in Figure 30.3.

This completes the discussion on how to specify capabilities. Using capabilities isn't difficult, but they don't apply to every product situation. We recommend that you isolate your capabilities extension in its own plug-in so that

**Figure 30.5**   Primary Wizards Always Appear Regardless of Their Enablement Status

it can be managed independently of other plug-ins (as Eclipse did in plug-in `org.eclipse.sdk`). If you are developing a product, place this extension in the same plug-in that contains your runtime product extension (see Chapter 13, Defining Features and Products, for information about features). Isolating the capabilities extension is still recommended if your product is an extension of another product. As a product extension, if your capabilities are dependent on another product's capabilities, consider defining them in a plug-in fragment associated with the plug-in that defines the product capabilities.

## The Activities API

You have learned that capabilities are defined entirely inside your plug-in manifest and require no code to do so. If you want to access capabilities at runtime, you need to use the available APIs. The **Workbench > Capabilities** preference page shown in Figure 30.1 is intended for experienced users (that page is hidden well enough that a new user might not locate it right away). The expectation is that a user will be prompted to enable capabilities in appropriate situations and never really need to enable them manually. Eclipse has given you some help by enabling capabilities automatically when wizards are used or projects are created through trigger points that it has created. If that is not sufficient and you need to enable capabilities based on other criteria, a rich API is available, defined in the package `org.eclipse.ui.activities`. (Remember, the term capabilities is synonymous with activities.) The API allows you to programmatically do the following.

- Enable or disable capabilities (e.g., those used by triggers).
- Access activities extension specifications.
- Listen to state changes (e.g., if you need to be informed that a capability changed state due to a user action or another plug-in).
- Determine what capability filtering is currently active.
- Determine whether a user interface contribution is subject to filtering, whether it is a member of an enabled capability, and what capabilities it participates in.

In this section we give you a general overview of the API. It would be helpful to have the Javadoc accessible as you read. You can access capabilities through the Workbench root object `IWorkbench`, which you can obtain from the static method `PlatformUI.getWorkbench`. The root of all capability support is `IWorkbenchActivitySupport`, available from the method `IWorkbench .getActivitySupport`. Two methods, `getActivityManager` and `setEnabledActivitiesIds`, are available in `IWorkbenchActivitySupport`. The method `getActivityManager` returns an `IActivityManager` object, which provides access to all defined categories, capabilities, and the set of enabled capabilities. `IActivityManager` has a number of useful getter methods. In particular, `getDefinedActivityIds` and `getEnabledActivitiyIds` each return a Java `Set` of `IActivity` objects. You can retrieve everything about a capability from an `IActivity` object. To enable capabilities, use the method `setEnabledActivitiesIds`. You must pass it a Java `Set` object containing a set of `IActivity` objects. When you enable or disable a capability through the API, you may modify the `Set` returned from the `getDefinedActivitiyIds` method and pass it to the `setEnabledActivitiesIds` method. You are responsible for not disturbing capabilities in the set that you are not involved with.

The following snippet of code enables all defined capabilities.

```
// Obtain a reference to capability support
IWorkbenchActivitySupport activitySupport =
  PlatformUI.getWorkbench().getActivitySupport();
Set activitySet = new HashSet();
activitySet.addAll(
  activitySupport.
  getActivityManager().
  getDefinedActivityIds() );
// Enable the capability set
activitySupport.setEnabledActivityIds(activitySet);
```

These are the essential elements of the API. What follows is an overview of the rest of the API. You might find it helpful to examine the Eclipse internal class `ActivityEnabler`, which enables or disables Eclipse capabilities based on what the user specifies in the **Workbench > Capabilities** preference page. This class contains several examples of how to use the API we have been discussing.

As we stated earlier, categories exist for organizational purposes only. The capabilities associated with them, not the categories, are enabled or disabled. If you need to retrieve the capabilities associated with a particular category, use the `ICategory` method `getCategoryActivityBindings`.

All the key objects we have discussed offer event listeners. For example, an `IActivity` has the methods `addActivityListener` and `removeActivity-Listener`. You can listen to events like changes in enablement state of the capability, or you can find out whether the capability is no longer defined because the plug-in that defined it has been dynamically removed.

A particular user interface contribution that participates in a capability is defined as an `IIdentifier` object. You can retrieve it by its identification string using the method `IActivityManager.getIdentifier`. An `IIdentifer` has useful methods to determine what capabilities it participates in and whether it is enabled.

The `WorkbenchActivityHelper` class has useful methods to determine whether any capability filtering has been defined for the Workbench, whether a particular user interface contribution is being filtered or not, and whether use of a particular user interface contribution is allowed based on the enablement state of the capability it participates in.

## Defining Your Own Triggers

Earlier we stated that Eclipse defined a trigger point that enables a capability if a project is created in the workspace and contains a project nature associated with a defined capability. In the Eclipse SDK, a Java nature and a plug-in nature for a project are each associated with their respective capability by using an `activityPatternBinding`. You learned in the previous discussion of the activities API that you can also programmatically enable capabilities. This gives you the opportunity to create custom triggers of your own that will enable a capability based on the requirements of your trigger.

Here are a couple of possible use cases to stimulate your thinking about developing custom triggers. Imagine that you offered extensive support for end users to query the contents of relational databases. Perhaps you only want to make that support visible to the user when they have a database connection. Otherwise, it just clutters the user interface to make this function visible. The plug-in that performs the database connection could enable your query facility when the database connection is successfully completed. Or perhaps your application has the notion of different users who specialize in certain tasks. These roles might be administrator, information modeler, user interface designer, tester, and so on. Depending on the role of the user, you could enable the appropriate capabilities that best serve their needs. Note that you should not use capabilities to hide a function that handles sensitive information or must be secure (e.g., changing employee salaries). An informed user can easily access your capability definitions and modify the default enablement.

## Example Summary

A very basic example in the plug-in project named com.ibm.jdg2e.activities is available on the CD-ROM. It defines a capability category named **The Java Developer's Guide to Eclipse**. The objective is to allow you to enable or disable the plug-ins you installed from the CD-ROM.

## Chapter Summary

Capabilities offer a great way to make a function-rich product more approachable for inexperienced users. As we said at the beginning, a user interface that resembles a jet cockpit can be trimmed back to resemble an automobile dashboard without much effort at all. When users are ready to fly, they can crawl into their jet cockpit and take off! Capabilities don't apply to every product, but for large products, and those extending large products, they can be quite helpful. The activities extension point allows for programmatic specification of capabilities and the function associated with them. By defining wizards as primary wizards, they become visible even when the capability they participate in is disabled. All of this is specified without a single line of Java code. This means you can define and refine capabilities late in the product development cycle based on the latest understanding of your customer's needs. If you want to create triggers to automatically enable capabilities, the activities API puts you in the driver's seat.

# References

Additional user interface filtering is available by using contexts, which determine which Workbench commands are available in a given situation. For more information, see the extension point documentation for `org.eclipse.ui.contexts`.

Arthorne, John, and Chris Laffra. 2004. *Official Eclipse 3.0 FAQs*. Boston, MA: Addison-Wesley. http://eclipsefaq.org. (See FAQs 237–240.)

In the online help, see the *Platform Plug-in Developer Guide* topic "Filtering Large User Interfaces."

# CHAPTER 31

## *Internationalization and Accessibility*

Providing a software product solely in English is no longer acceptable from a usability, quality, marketing, and in some cases, legal standpoint. Enabling your product for the global market simply makes economic sense. And the Eclipse internationalization enablement process is relatively straightforward, as this chapter will demonstrate.

A few notes before we begin. Because the Eclipse Platform adopts the internationalization implementation provided with Java, it's helpful to read the *Java Tutorial: Internationalization Trail* before continuing (see http:// java.sun.com/docs/books/tutorial/i18n/). The tutorial presents a fine overview of the issues and steps involved in the process. We will assume that you've already read the tutorial so we can underscore the key points, surface other noteworthy items, and cover Eclipse-specific issues and steps in this chapter.

## What Does Internationalization Affect in Your Plug-in?

Plug-in text that requires externalization for translations include text messages, labels in the graphical user interface, and online documentation.

### *Text Message and Labels on GUI Components*

Resource bundles nicely handle language-dependent texts. The strategy is either to load all strings at once into a `ResourceBundle` subclass or to retrieve them individually. The Eclipse Java Development Tools (JDT) provides wizards to support the detection of translatable strings. We'll return to them shortly in the internationalization steps.

Loading translated strings into memory is only the first step. The next step is to pass them to the appropriate controls for display (such as a label, text field, and menu choice). The UI designer and programmer must work together to ensure that the chosen layout allows for appropriate resizing and reflowing of the dialog. The layout support in the Standard Widget Toolkit (SWT) library relies heavily on the programmer to "do the right thing" by specifying layout descriptions that react appropriately to changes in field sizes. Chapter 14, The Standard Widget Toolkit: A Lean, Mean, Widget Machine, covers the implementation issues in detail.

This is particularly important because text length often increases during translation. English phrases are often shorter than their equivalent translations, usually on the order of 40%. Font sizes also may need to be modified to accommodate the local language.

Online help (`*.html`) and plug-in manifest files (`plugin.xml`) are more involved than simple key/value-oriented properties files, so the steps to their externalization are slightly more complex.

The manifest file is coupled with a similarly named property file, `plugin.properties`, which contains only the externalized text. Special care must be taken with manifest files like `plugin.xml` and `fragment.xml`, since the attributes of the tags can contain both translated and untranslated text. Consider this benign example:

```
<plugin
   id="com.ibm.jdg2e.nls.example.helloworld"
   name=" Helloworld Plug-in"
   version="3.0.0"
   provider-name="The Java Developer&apos;s Guide to Eclipse"
   class="com.ibm.jdg2e.nls.example.helloworld.HelloworldPlugin">
```

Here we see a mix of translatable text, untranslatable text, and "gray area" translatable text, all as tag attributes. Clearly the `id` and `class` attributes are not translatable, since they represent programming identifiers. It is equally certain that the `name` attribute should be translated.

You might be tempted to consider the `version` attribute (because of the locale-dependent decimal separator) or `provider-name` attribute (because of the locale-dependent legal attribution "Corporation") as candidates for translation, since they will be displayed to the end user. However, version numbers are generally left untranslated for two reasons: end users attribute little meaning to their numeric value, and programmers sometimes write code that expects version numbers to be composed string-like: `3.5.4`. It is arguably a better design decision that the version information be stored as separate numbers—like major, minor, and service update—to avoid needing to parse a version string, but that discussion is beyond the scope of this book.

The `provider-name` attribute may be left untranslated as well, since "Corporation" has a legal meaning that can defy accurate translation. After identifying what text needs to be externalized, our example now looks like this:

```
<plugin
  id="com.ibm.jdg2e.nls.example.helloworld"
  name="%name"
  version="3.0.0"
  provider name="The Java Developer&apos;s Guide to Eclipse"
  class="com.ibm.jdg2e.nls.example.helloworld.HelloworldPlugin">
```

where `plugin.properties` contains the externalized string "Helloworld Plug-in" associated with the key `plugin.name`.

This simple example demonstrates that translating isn't simply providing equivalent words or phrases for your text; it also involves an understanding of the local cultural considerations and potential legal impacts. We suggest involving a translation professional, as well as planning for translation verification testing.

## Internationalization Steps

Now let's turn to the actual steps for internationalizing your Eclipse plug-in.

1. Move translatable strings into `*.properties` files.
2. Separate presentation-dependent parameters.
3. Use proper locale-sensitive data formatting and substitution APIs.
4. Test in your domestic language.
5. Create one or more initial translated plug-in fragments.
6. Prepare and send domestic language materials for translation.
7. Repackage translated plug-in fragments (as described in step 5) and validate translated materials.
8. Deploy fragments.

The following sections discuss steps 1 through 5. For more information on how to validate your Eclipse plug-in translations, see "How to Test Your Internationalized Eclipse Plug-in" on eclipse.org. To learn more about deployment, see Chapter 13, Defining Features and Products.

## Move Translatable Strings into *.properties Files

Fortunately, Eclipse's JDT provides considerable help to properly separate translatable strings. Chapter 3, Using Java Development Tools, describes how to use the tools for finding and externalizing strings using the Externalize Strings wizard. This wizard will lead you through the steps to locate hardcoded strings in your code, classify them as translatable or not, and then modify the code to use a resource bundle where appropriate. You might want to go back to that chapter and refresh your memory before continuing with this chapter.

You can create a resource bundle accessor class that contains code to load the properties file and a static method to fetch strings from the file. The wizard will generate this class, or you can specify your own existing alternative implementation. In the latter case, you may want to specify an alternative code pattern for retrieving externalized strings. If the accessor class is outside of the package (for example, a centralized resource bundle accessor class), you can optionally specify that you want to add an import declaration to the underlying source.

After you finish running the wizard, the wizard performs the source code modifications, creates the resource bundle accessor class Messages, and generates the initial properties file. Here is the code for the standard resource bundle accessor class:

```
package com.ibm.jdg2e.nls.example.helloworld;
import java.util.MissingResourceException;
import java.util.ResourceBundle;
public class Messages {
  private static final String BUNDLE_NAME =
"com.ibm.jdg2e.nls.example.helloworld.messages";//$NON-NLS-1$

  private static final ResourceBundle RESOURCE_BUNDLE =
      ResourceBundle.getBundle(BUNDLE_NAME);
  private Messages() {
  }
  public static String getString(String key) {
    try {
      return RESOURCE_BUNDLE.getString(key);
    } catch (MissingResourceException e) {
      return '!' + key + '!';
    }
  }
}
```

The only variation in this generated code is the value assigned to the static final, BUNDLE_NAME.

### Separate Presentation-Dependent Parameters

Not all externalized text is simply words and phrases that will be translated to a target language. Some are more specifically related to your plug-in's implementation, such as properties, preferences, and default dialog settings. Here are a few items you might consider putting in a properties file.

- Size or layout constraints, for example, the appropriate width of a nonresizable table column.
- Default fonts that are dependent on the language or operating system. A good default font for Latin-1 languages is an invalid choice for Double Byte Character Set (DBCS) languages.

### Use Proper Locale-Sensitive Data Formatting and Substitutions APIs

For information on this, refer to the detailed coverage in the *Java Tutorial: Internationalization Trail* at http://java.sun.com/docs/books/tutorial/i18n/.

### Test in Your Domestic Language

Testing the readiness of a product for translation is nontrivial and requires careful planning. The article "How to Test Your Internationalized Eclipse Plug-in" on eclipse.org presents strategies for validating the national language-sensitive aspects of your product.

### Create Initial Translated Plug-in Fragments

At this point, we could simply copy our domestic language property files to similarly named files with locale-specific suffixes (for example, `messages_xx` `.properties`, where xx is the locale), and move to the next step. In this case, the product is delivered with its code and whatever languages it supports as a single install.

However, this approach has a few drawbacks. First, the code and its national language resources are intermingled in the same directory's /JAR file (the plug-in binary code). If the translation lags behind the code delivery, the plug-in JAR file must be updated, despite the fact that the underlying code is unchanged. Second, files other than property files are not inherently locale-sensitive, so they must be segregated to separate directories for each language (for example, HTML, XML, and images).

To address these issues, the Eclipse Platform introduces the notion of another reusable component that complements plug-ins, called a **plug-in**

**fragment.** A plug-in fragment provides additional functionality to its target plug-in. At runtime, a plug-in is merged with all its dependent fragments. These fragments can contain code contributions and contributions of resources associated with a plug-in, like property and HTML files. In other words, the plug-in has access to the fragment's contents via the plug-in's classloader. See Chapter 12, Advanced Plug-in Development.

A plug-in fragment is an ideal way to distribute translated information including HTML, XML, INI, and bitmap files in Eclipse. Fragments let you deliver translations in a nonintrusive way; translations are packaged in fragment JAR files and are added to existing Eclipse installations without changing or modifying any of the original runtime elements.

Eclipse merges fragments with their target plug-ins so that the runtime elements in the fragment augment the target plug-in. The target plug-in is not moved, removed, or modified in any way. Since the fragment's resources are located by the classloader, the plug-in developer has no need to know whether resources are loaded from the plug-in's JAR file or one of its fragments' JAR files.

### Eclipse Language Pack JAR

The Java language supports the notion of a language pack with the `ResourceBundle` facility. Java resource bundles do not require modifying application code to support another language. The `*.properties` file avoids collisions through the naming convention `basename_lang_region_variant`. At runtime, the `ResourceBundle` facility finds the appropriate properties file for the current locale.

The approach to deploying files such as HTML and XML files in fragments is slightly different than Java resource bundles—the Eclipse fragment uses a directory structure to sort out the different language versions.

### Sample Fragment Contents

Plug-ins and the plug-in fragments reside in separate subdirectories found immediately under the `eclipse` subdirectory. For example, Figure 31.1 shows the plug-in `com.ibm.jdg2e.nls.example.helloworld` after deployment. This plug-in (which is included on your CD-ROM) has the following files.

- `plugin.xml`
- `plugin.properties`
- `helloworld.jar` (containing `com.ibm.jdg2e.nls.example.helloworld.messages.properties`)

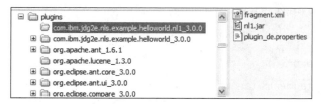

**Figure 31.1** Fragment Structure

However, looking at our sample fragment after deployment, you see the files `fragment.xml`, `nl1.jar`, and `plugin_de.properties`.

So, in general, the corresponding `nl` fragment must be structured as follows.

- `fragment.xml`
- `plugin_fr.properties`
- `plugin_pt_BR.properties`
- `nl1.jar` (`<package name>xxxx_fr.properties,<package name>xxxx.pt_BR.properties`)

Typically, translated `*.properties` files are suffixed according to the resource bundle rules and deployed in JAR files.

### Fragment Manifest Files

Each plug-in folder can optionally contain a fragment manifest file, `fragment.xml`. The manifest file describes the plug-in fragment, and is almost identical to the plug-in manifest file (`plugin.xml`), with the following two exceptions.

- The class attribute is gone, since fragments do not have a plug-in class (they just follow their target's specification).
- There are no dependencies, because the fragments have the same dependencies as their target plug-in.

Manifests used to describe a national language fragments are typically quite simple, specifying only the `<fragment>` and `<runtime>/<library>` tags. The following is a sample fragment manifest file in its entirety.

```
<?xml version="1.0" encoding="UTF-8"?>
<?eclipse version="3.0"?>
<fragment
    id="com.ibm.jdg2e.nls.example.helloworld.nl1"
    name="Nl1 Fragment"
    version="3.0.0"
    provider-name="The Java Developer&apos;s Guide to Eclipse"
    plugin-id="com.ibm.jdg2e.nls.example.helloworld"
```

```
            plugin-version="3.0.0">
            <runtime>
               <library name="nl1.jar"/>
            </runtime>
</fragment>
```

The `<fragment>` tag attributes are:

- `name`—the user-displayable name for the extension.
- `id`—the identifier for this fragment configuration, which uniquely identifies this fragment instance.
- `plugin-id`—the reference to the target plug-in. This plug-in fragment merges with this target extension.
- `version` and `plugin-version`—the version of the fragment and the plug-in which it depends on.
- `type`—the default is `code`. Specifying `resource` indicates the library includes resource files and no code. This improves overall performance significantly because resource-only libraries are skipped when loading code.

The `<runtime>` section contains a definition of one or more libraries that make up the plug-in fragment runtime. The Platform Runtime treats the fragment's referenced libraries as if they were part of the plug-in's own `<runtime>` declaration. The `name` attribute accepts a library name (`nl1.jar` above) or a directory containing resources. A directory reference must contain a trailing path separator. Optionally, the specification may include a substitution variable. For example, when the library includes a variable substitution, `$nl$`, the locale is used to reference a language/region specific folder to the library search path (e.g., a locale of `it` for Italy, `fr` for France, or `de` for Germany would add the corresponding plug-in subdirectory—`it/`, `fr/`, or `de/`—to the list of searched paths). The `nl` substitution variable is used in those cases where it is not possible or practical to suffix files with the locale name.

The value of the `nl`, `os`, `ws`, and `arch` substitution variables can be displayed and modified on the **Window > Preferences > Plug-in Development > Target Environment** page. Keep this in mind, since you can change the `nl` value to test your fragment without actually switching the locale on your local system. The other alternative is to start Eclipse using the `-nl` parameter.

## Accessibility

In addition to enabling internationalization, Eclipse supports accessibility features that help people with physical disabilities, such as restricted mobility and limited vision, use it. Eclipse complies with the U.S. Federal Government Section 508 Regulations. The major accessibility features in Eclipse are:

- Support for screen readers

    Eclipse uses Microsoft Active Accessibility (MSAA) APIs to render user interface elements accessible to assistive technology, so on Windows systems you can use screen-reader software such as Freedom Scientifics' JAWS or the Window-Eyes digital speech synthesizer to hear what is displayed on the screen.

- Keyboard access instead of the mouse

    Every action implemented in a plug-in can be made accessible from the keyboard, and you can also move the focus between SWT widgets using the keyboard.

Keyboard accessibility is important to users with restricted mobility and, in general, those unable to use a mouse. To make your plug-in's user interface navigable using the keyboard requires that you assign mnemonics to menu and widget items. The mnemonics allow the user to navigate the menu and widget items by typing **Alt** and the underlined letter instead of using the mouse.

Mnemonics are specified using the ampersand (&) character in front of a selected character in the label text. In places where the ampersand is not allowed, such as the `plugin.xml` file, use the `&amp;` character entity. Be careful to come up with unique mnemonic letters to avoid "collisions."

Be aware that in cases where two or more actions are contributed to a menu or toolbar by a single extension, the actions will appear in the reverse order of how they are listed in the `plugin.xml` file.

A nice accessibility feature in Eclipse is getting help with multistroke keyboard shortcuts. Using the **Workbench > Keys** preferences page, the user can request that the help keyboard shortcuts appear. The setting shown in Figure 31.2 causes the keyboard mnemonics to appear 1,000 milliseconds after pressing the first key.

**Figure 31.2**  Multistroke Keyboard Help

## Example Summary

The CD-ROM accompanying this book contains an example of an Eclipse plug-in and fragment. The base plug-in example is contained in the project `com.ibm.jdg2e.nls.example.helloworld`. The plug-in fragment is contained in the project `com.ibm.jdg2e.nls.example.helloworld.nll`.

## Chapter Summary

Enabling your product for the world market simply makes economic sense, and this chapter shows that the process is relatively straightforward. Fortunately, developers with products based on Eclipse benefit from it already having ready translations.

Eclipse is enabled for persons with disabilities by supporting visual assistive technologies and keyboard access. Workbench Keys preferences can be used to show extra keyboard help. The accessibility of the Eclipse IDE is impressive because the Eclipse developers took full advantage of enabling technologies.

## References

Arthorne, John, and Chris Laffra. 2004. *Official Eclipse 3.0 FAQs*. Boston, MA: Addison-Wesley. http://www.eclipsefaq.org. (See FAQs 109, 257, 276.)

Creasy, Tod. May 20, 2003. Designing Accessible Plug-ins in Eclipse. http://www.eclipse.org.

IBM Accessibility Guidelines. http://www-3.ibm.com/able/guidelines/index.html.

Kehn, Dan. August 23, 2002. How to Test Your Internationalized Eclipse Plug-in. http://www.eclipse.org/articles/Article-TVT/how2TestI18n.html.

U.S. Federal Government Section 508 Regulations. http://www.section508.gov/.

# CHAPTER 32

## *Performance Tuning*

Almost every day we hear of new companies adopting Eclipse as their application development platform of choice. With all these companies' products (not to mention all the Eclipse board member companies' products) potentially converging on the same installation, the risk of memory bloat and performance degradation is high. Fortunately, the standard performance-tuning practices for improving Java code apply to Eclipse, and you can select from many titles on the subject. There are, however, optimization considerations that are unique to Eclipse; this chapter will cover some of the more noteworthy ones and introduce you to Eclipse-specific tools to help you optimize your plug-in's performance.

This chapter assumes that you are familiar with the basics of Java performance tuning. We'll begin with a short introduction of the problem at hand and then move on to a handy tool for analyzing your plug-ins' startup performance, the **Runtime Spy**. To give you a better appreciation of what it can do, we'll also step through a case study analysis of how we once used the Runtime Spy to improve the startup performance of IBM WebSphere Studio Application Developer version 5.1 (since renamed to IBM Rational Application Developer). Finally, the chapter will close with an introduction to the **Performance Monitor**. The Performance Monitor helps you avoid performance regressions by recording key performance metrics that you can compare build-to-build and release-to-release to detect if your product's CPU or memory usage has changed. This capability has proven invaluable to analyzing the IBM Eclipse-based product offerings.

## Why Eclipse Should Start Quickly

Eclipse's architecture is designed to enable the discovery of extensions to its environment at runtime. This architected extension capability allows many tools and applications to integrate seamlessly into Eclipse. The Eclipse architects recognized early in the project that these extensions could not be defined programmatically in client code, since the cumulative startup cost would become prohibitive as Eclipse integrated more and more extensions.

To avoid this startup cost while retaining flexibility, the plug-in manifest file defines enough information to enable the Eclipse Platform to postpone loading code while still recognizing the initial contributions of an extension. For example, the user interface extension points require enough information to render the initial user interface element (e.g., the icon and tooltip text of a contributed toolbar button), so the platform can defer loading the plug-in code until the user actually chooses a menu option, selects a toolbar button, opens a preferences page, or starts a creation wizard. This "pay as you go" approach enables Eclipse to act as an integration platform for literally thousands of plug-ins on a single installation. The initial cost of a plug-in is only the parsing of its manifest file. The XML format parses quickly, and the binary result is saved to disk for the next time, so startup is not significantly affected by the number of plug-ins and extensions that are defined. There are, however, means by which this benefit can be unwittingly defeated, thereby increasing startup time and memory consumption. Fortunately, you can use the Runtime Spy perspective to help track down these problems.

## Diagnosing Startup Problems Using the Runtime Spy

A quick startup is something users expect, and anything short of that expectation gets immediate attention, none of which is positive. Developers are therefore well advised to pay attention to this important metric and not inadvertently undo the deferred activation strategy that Eclipse has put in place. This section introduces the Core Tools plug-in and its Runtime Spy, which will show you what plug-ins are activated and, more importantly, why. Answering these questions will prove very helpful in ensuring your team avoids the all too common performance gaffe of provoking the premature (or even unnecessary) loading of a plug-in. Unlike an ordinary Java-based profiler, the Runtime Spy knows all about Eclipse's plug-in architecture, so its views present performance metrics grouped by plug-in, not just as classes, making your job of figuring out what plug-in is responsible for a slowdown easier. The next section will also offer some tidbits that demonstrate the Spy's utility beyond what is already covered in its readme file.

PART V

### Installing the Core Tools

The installation is simple:

1. Follow the instructions on the CD-ROM documentation for this chapter, or download the latest version from the Core Tools update site using the **Help > Software Update** menu option (see http://dev.eclipse.org/viewcvs/index.cgi/%7Echeckout%7E/ platform-core-home/updates).

2. Next decide whether you want to spy on your development/deployed Eclipse installation (use the -debug command line option when you start Eclipse) or whether you want to spy on your Runtime Workbench (use the **Tracing** page of its launch configuration). We'll return to this in the next section. For now, let's go with the first choice: spying on your development Eclipse installation.

   To begin, enable the common Spy options by creating a .options file in the <inst_dir>\eclipse directory with the following content:

   ```
   org.eclipse.osgi/monitor/activation=true
   org.eclipse.osgi/monitor/classes=true
   org.eclipse.osgi/trace/activation=true
   org.eclipse.osgi/trace/filename=runtime.traces
   org.eclipse.osgi/trace/filters=trace.properties
   ```

   This monitors plug-in activation with a stack trace and class loading. We'll come back to how you specify class stacc traces in the section Seeing What Classes of a Plug-in Were Loaded.

---

**NOTE** The versions of the Core Tools and Eclipse SDK on the book's CD-ROM are compatible. If you have a more recent version of Eclipse, check the Core Tools update site before continuing.

---

Now start Eclipse, and remember to specify the -debug command line option, which will read the .options file found in the <inst_dir>\eclipse directory. Alternatively, you can identify the location of the .options file as a parameter to the -debug option (for example, -debug file:d:\spy\.options).

### Spying on the Workbench Development

Let's assume you've installed the Core Tools files and restarted Eclipse. Since the -debug command line option is specified, you'll see some startup messages directed to the console. When in debug mode, these are displayed in a separate Command Prompt window.

Now that everything is up and running, let's take a quick tour of the Runtime Spy's views. Keep in mind that the Spy runs in the same Workbench as the "spied" plug-ins, so some plug-in activation may occur through the natural course of using the tool itself. Usually this isn't an issue, since it only uses base functionality that will probably already be loaded or would have been loaded soon enough anyway. In the unlikely case that it does matter, remember that its views are only refreshed on demand, so the first time the Runtime Spy perspective is opened, it will show only those plug-ins that were active *before* its own activation.

### Seeing What Plug-ins Were Activated

Selecting **Window > Open Perspective > Runtime Spy** opens four views, as shown in Figure 32.1.

If you forgot to specify the -debug option, you'll see the message "Plug-in monitoring is not enabled" displayed in the **Activated Plug-ins** view. Since the default is no class monitoring, the **Loaded Classes** view will contain the message "Class monitoring is not enabled." Capturing class loading stack traces slows Eclipse, so you must list which classes you're interested in by specifying the package(s) or plug-in(s) that contain them.

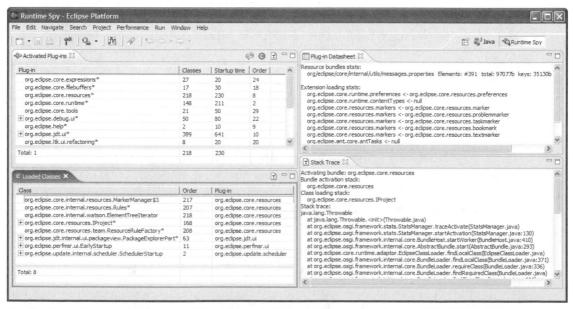

**Figure 32.1**    Runtime Spy (Activated Plug-ins, Loaded Classes, Plug-in Datasheet, and Stack Trace Views)

For now we're only interested in what plug-ins are loaded. Figure 32.2 shows the Runtime Spy's main view, **Activated Plug-ins**.

| Plug-in | Classes | Startup time | Order |
| --- | --- | --- | --- |
| org.eclipse.core.tools | 32 | 50 | 29 |
| org.eclipse.update.scheduler | 4 | 40 | 28 |
| org.eclipse.perfmsr.core | 10 | 20 | 27 |
| org.eclipse.perfmsr.ui | 11 | 110 | 26 |
| org.eclipse.ui.externaltools* | 2 | 30 | 25 |
| org.eclipse.core.expressions* | 27 | 20 | 24 |
| org.eclipse.debug.core* | 30 | 30 | 23 |
| org.eclipse.debug.ui* | 50 | 80 | 22 |
| org.eclipse.search* | 8 | 20 | 21 |
| org.eclipse.ltk.ui.refactoring* | 8 | 20 | 20 |
| org.eclipse.team.core* | 9 | 30 | 19 |
| org.eclipse.core.filebuffers* | 17 | 30 | 18 |
| org.eclipse.ltk.core.refactoring* | 31 | 20 | 17 |
| org.eclipse.ui.views* | 4 | 30 | 16 |
| org.eclipse.ui.editors* | 26 | 20 | 15 |
| org.eclipse.jface.text* | 38 | 20 | 14 |
| Total: 4 | 57 | 220 | |

**Figure 32.2**   The Runtime Spy's Activated Plug-ins View

Clicking the first column heading, **Plug-in**, changes the sort order to ascending, descending, and ascending with grouping. The plug-ins grouped under the **+** symbol are the required plug-ins that were loaded during the activation of the parent. When loaded plug-ins are grouped, the row's values are for the plug-in and all its child plug-ins. Use this ordering when you want to see the big consumers collectively.

The plug-in names followed by an asterisk are those that were loaded during startup. Despite what the name may suggest, the set of startup plug-ins marked with an asterisk in the Activated Plug-ins view will *not* include those that were loaded because of the Workbench processing its `org.eclipse.ui.startup` extension point. The Workbench processes these extension contributions after the initial startup, so you won't see them among the "asterisked" plug-ins.

Of particular interest is the **Order** column. Clicking the column heading sorts the list of plug-ins in activation order. If you want to quickly see what plug-ins are activated by a given action, select all the plug-ins beforehand (**Ctrl+A**), perform the action, return to the Activated Plug-ins view, and then select the Refresh button (⟳). The unselected plug-ins are those that were just activated. Alternatively, note the order value of the last plug-in that was activated before your action, and then afterward refresh to see those plug-ins that are ordered higher.

PART V

## Seeing What Classes of a Plug-in Were Loaded

Classes of a plug-in are loaded on demand. You can potentially save memory and startup time by deferring these references or reducing the reference set of classes. The **Loaded Classes** view will help you see what classes of the selected plug-in have been loaded so far. To update the Loaded Classes view, select one or more plug-ins from the Activated Plug-ins list, and then select the Classes button (C). The loaded classes for the `org.eclipse.jdt.core` plug-in are shown in Figure 32.3, sorted in load order.

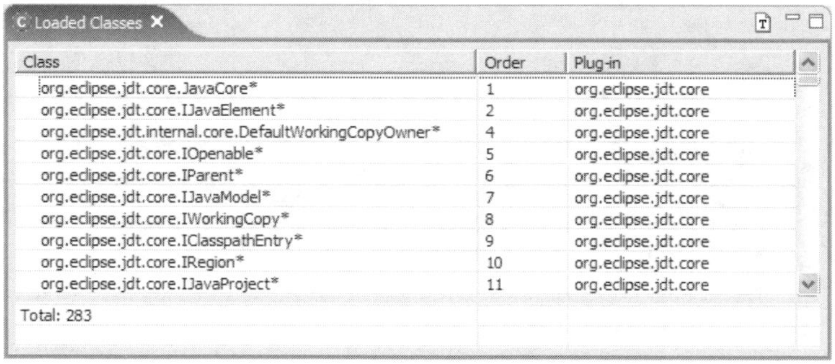


| Class | Order | Plug-in |
|---|---|---|
| org.eclipse.jdt.core.JavaCore* | 1 | org.eclipse.jdt.core |
| org.eclipse.jdt.core.IJavaElement* | 2 | org.eclipse.jdt.core |
| org.eclipse.jdt.internal.core.DefaultWorkingCopyOwner* | 4 | org.eclipse.jdt.core |
| org.eclipse.jdt.core.IOpenable* | 5 | org.eclipse.jdt.core |
| org.eclipse.jdt.core.IParent* | 6 | org.eclipse.jdt.core |
| org.eclipse.jdt.core.IJavaModel* | 7 | org.eclipse.jdt.core |
| org.eclipse.jdt.core.IWorkingCopy* | 8 | org.eclipse.jdt.core |
| org.eclipse.jdt.core.IClasspathEntry* | 9 | org.eclipse.jdt.core |
| org.eclipse.jdt.core.IRegion* | 10 | org.eclipse.jdt.core |
| org.eclipse.jdt.core.IJavaProject* | 11 | org.eclipse.jdt.core |
| Total: 283 | | |

**Figure 32.3** The Runtime Spy's Loaded Classes View

In addition to the plug-in activation order, this view is useful to get a "big picture" of what classes and sequences a given action initiates by sorting in order of reference by clicking the **Order** column. The plug-in startup code is included in this list and gives you a good idea of the cost of executing it. The moral of that story is often "too much is done at startup."

## Tracing Why a Class Was Loaded

To get a better idea of what led to the loading of a specific class within a plug-in, first enable the trace options for the plug-ins or packages of the classes that interest you. In this example, we created a `trace.properties` file in the startup directory containing the line `packages=org.eclipse.jface.text`. Then you:

1. Select the `org.eclipse.jface.text` plug-in in the list of Activated Plug-ins.
2. Update the Loaded Classes list by pressing the Classes (C) button.
3. Select the `org.eclipse.jface.text.ITextViewer` class.
4. Select the Trace (T) button to update the Stack Trace view.

PART V

This will display what code led to the classloader loading the class, and if it wasn't already done earlier, activated its containing plug-in, as shown in Figure 32.4.

**Figure 32.4**    The Runtime Spy Stack Trace View

The top of the stack generally isn't interesting, since that's tracing the classloader code itself. The useful information is about midway down. In this case, the stack trace shows the ITextViewer class was ultimately loaded because the Runtime Spy perspective was opened, as indicated near the bottom of the highlighted stack trace lines by the reference to WorkbenchPage, which represents a perspective.

The perspective opened its initial views, including the **Plug-in Datasheet** view, which uses the JFace Text class TextViewer to display its data. While verifying the class during loadClass, the JVM found it needed ITextViewer as well because TextViewer implements this interface. The JVM's runtime classloading can be nested quite deeply; for performance purposes you'll generally focus on the code leading up to the classloader calls, similar to the highlighted portion of the stack trace shown in Figure 32.4.

PART V

## Tracing Why a Plug-in Was Activated

The previous section showed why a specific class was loaded. You can also see why a given plug-in is loaded, but the reason for a plug-in being activated may not seem as obvious because the causes are indirect. Unlike a class that is typically loaded because it is referenced in another class' method (and has a corresponding `import` statement you can refer to), plug-ins are loaded because of some indirect reference. Recall that the goal is to avoid loading plug-ins until they are needed, so references to the plug-ins themselves are by:

- Explicitly stated identifiers, such as `<import plugin="org.eclipse.ui">` in the plug-in manifest file

  or

- Implied identifiers, such as the exported packages in the runtime JARs for that plug-in

Both of these examples are highlighted in the extract from the "Hello, Eclipse" plug-in manifest file, shown below (some tags and attributes are not shown for reasons of brevity).

```
<plugin ...>
  // ... lines omitted ...
    <runtime>
      <library name="helloworld.jar"/>
        <export name="*"/>
      </library>
    </runtime>
    <requires>
      <import plugin="org.eclipse.core.resources"/>
      <import plugin="org.eclipse.ui"/>
    </requires>
  // ... lines omitted ...
    <extension point="org.eclipse.ui.actionSets">
      <actionSet label="Sample Action Set" ...>
        <menu label="Sample &Menu" ...>
          <separator name="sampleGroup"/>
        </menu>
        <action
          label="&Sample Action"
          class="com.ibm.jdg2e.helloworld.SampleAction"
          menubarPath="sampleMenu/sampleGroup"
          toolbarPath="sampleGroup" ...>
        </action>
      </actionSet>
    </extension>
```

In Chapter 21, Action Contributions: The Integration Fast Track, you learned the details of how to contribute an action using the `org.eclipse.ui`

`.actionSets` extension point. This extension point's contribution implicitly depends on the defining plug-in, the Workbench UI plug-in (`org.eclipse.ui`). The Workbench plug-in will read the plug-in registry, which includes this contribution to its `org.eclipse.ui.actionSets` extension, and create the appropriate action sets. The `SampleAction` class will not be loaded at this point and therefore neither will its containing plug-in. Instead, the Workbench plug-in defines a delegate action to represent the choice in the user interface that waits until the user actually selects it before creating an instance of `SampleAction` to handle the response.

To create an instance of `SampleAction`, the action delegate calls the `createExecutableExtension` method of the plug-in registry instance `IConfigurationElement` that represents the `<action class="hello .actions.SampleAction"...>` tag specified in our example manifest file.

---

**TIP**    Need a reminder of how a plug-ins handles contributions to their extension points, or how you can enable others to contribute to your plug-in? See Chapter 11 for details.

---

That's fine, but sometimes it isn't obvious looking at the resulting stack trace. Let's take a closer look at a more difficult example than the selection of a "Hello, Eclipse" menu choice. Figure 32.5 shows a typical activation that resulted from the processing of an executable extension. Now let's use the Stack Trace view to determine what caused it, following the same steps as before.

In this case, as we see by the reference to `ResourceNavigator` near the bottom of the highlighted portion of the stack trace, the plug-in's activation all began with a double-click in the Navigator view. The default action handler responsible for handling the action requested the Workbench to open the Plug-in Manifest Editor, which subsequently activated the `org.eclipse.ui.editors` plug-in. The highlighted portion of the stack trace shows only the code of the extension point processor because its reference to the Workbench plug-in classes, `org.eclipse.ui`, is indirect. After working through half-a-dozen similar stack traces, you'll recognize the important parts are before and after the calls to `ConfigurationElement.createExecutableExtension` and quickly see who started it and what happened as a result. You can refresh the loaded classes by selecting the Classes button again and resort by load order to get a better idea of what happened after the plug-in's activation.

**Figure 32.5**　Stack Trace View Showing Executable Extension Activation

## Other Helpful Views

Finally, the Plug-in Datasheet view, shown earlier in Figure 32.1, summarizes some interesting statistics, such as how many resources and extensions the plug-in defines.

This tracks the Resource bundle data that has been loaded. This summary information takes advantage of the fact that the Eclipse Platform Runtime provides its own classloader, and classloaders handle resource bundles in the same fashion as classes, so keeping track of resource data statistics is straightforward. The "not loaded yet" message refers to the fact that the plug-in registry is written to disk, and referenced portions of it are reloaded only as needed.

### Spying on the Runtime Workbench

The previous sections covered spying on the base installation of Eclipse itself. During development, you'll more than likely want to spy on your test version of the Workbench, the **Runtime Workbench**. You can configure the instance of the Runtime Workbench you wish to launch by selecting **Run > Run As... > Run-time Workbench** and turning to the **Tracing** page, as was discussed in Chapter 28, Serviceability. The tracing options that the Spy relies on are specified by the `org.eclipse.osgi` and `org.eclipse.core.resources` plug-ins; the options of the former are shown in Figure 32.6.

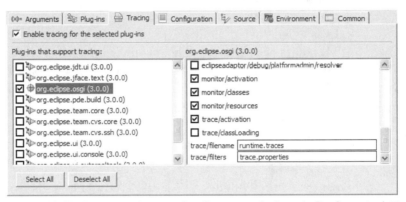

**Figure 32.6**  Setting the Runtime Spy Options in the Launch Configuration's **Tracing** Page

The debug options of the `org.eclipse.osgi` plug-in are populated with the `.options` file choices we discussed earlier. The settings below are those you'll more than likely want initially.

```
org.eclipse.osgi/monitor/activation=true
org.eclipse.osgi/monitor/classes=true
org.eclipse.osgi/trace/activation=true
```

However, if you want to take reasonably accurate performance measurements of elapsed time, you should minimize the number of active options, especially those that require taking a stack trace (that is, `trace/activation`, `trace/classLoading`, and so on). Setting `monitor/activation` to true and all others to false in the `.options` file introduces little performance overhead.

### Where to Go from Here

You can find a lot of information on Java performance tuning, but very little specific to Eclipse. The first part of this chapter introduced you to one of best tools for understanding and diagnosing startup performance problems

PART V

related to plug-in activation. Before continuing with our case study, it is worth noting some of the other useful diagnostic information that the Core Tools provide you that are not directly related to performance analysis.

- The **Plug-in Dependency** perspective shows information similar to that shown in the **Plug-in Registry** view (accessible from **Window > Show View > Other... > PDE Runtime > Plug-in Registry**), but with an exhaustive listing of the dependent and required plug-ins of the selected plug-in.
- Ever wonder what the workspace's .metadata directory contains? The **Metadata** perspective will help you walk its structure. It does, however, presume considerable understanding of the Workspace implementation.
- The **Resource Tools** category of views presents useful insights into the inner workings of resource change listeners and resource deltas, builders, and more. The **Resource, Delta,** and **Builder/Listener** views are especially interesting for those learning the Workspace API. Select **Window > Show View > Other... > Resource Tools** to access these views.

The next section will describe a case study of how the Runtime Spy was used to diagnose several startup problems in IBM WebSphere Studio Application Developer version 5.1. The subsequent improvements in startup performance varied from 11% to 37%, depending on the active views and perspectives, demonstrating that knowing when and why your plug-ins are activated can help deliver on Eclipse's promise of a quick startup.

## Case Study: Improving IBM WebSphere Studio's Startup

In the previous section, you got a general idea of how the Runtime Spy can help you locate startup trouble spots. Let's turn to some specific examples of how to use it to reduce your plug-in's startup time. To make it more interesting, we'll look at some problems that were corrected with the help of the Runtime Spy as part of the performance improvements of IBM WebSphere Studio Application Developer, a J2EE development tool composed of over six hundred plug-ins.

**NOTE**  This case study examines an earlier version of Eclipse and the Runtime Spy. Some of the figures will look slightly different from current versions of these tools.

### Helping Eclipse Start Quickly

The two general goals for improving the startup performance of an Eclipse-based application are:

- Defer plug-in activation until as late as possible
- Minimize the amount of work involved in activating your plug-in

A common tenet of both goals is **defer code execution whenever possible**. Here are some ways you can do this:

- Don't load your plug-in

  How? First and foremost, follow the lead of Eclipse's own plug in extensions. Recall that many of the Eclipse extension point definitions require the contributor to statically declare enough information so that loading code can be deferred until the requested action is needed. This idea is fundamental to the Eclipse architecture and embodied in the plug-in manifest file declarations. Your own extension point definitions should embrace this approach.

- Reduce class loading during plug-in initialization

  The most common culprits are references within the `Plugin.start` method. Many plug-ins override this method to perform their initialization. The ideal solution is often for your plug-in to defer its initialization until the user requests a specific action of your product. Otherwise, minimizing the number of referenced classes and plug-ins is the next best choice. In either case, the Runtime Spy can point to those that might be taking too much time or triggering the activation of too many other plug-ins.

- Reduce CPU usage during plug-in initialization

  Again, the most common cause points to code within the plug-in's `start` method or code called by it. Lazy initialization of memory structures will save CPU time and may defer the activation of other plug-ins. Another possibility is to start a separate job during startup to perform initialization when the system is idle, although this choice requires more care to handle synchronization. See Chapter 29, Implementing Responsiveness and Concurrency Using Jobs, for more details.

By deferring the activation of a plug-in, the user is given the impression of a zippier product. It may well be that the *cumulative* CPU usage is the same, but having it spread it out in small chunks over a long period is less noticeable than paying the brute cost upfront. A delay is especially objectionable if it occurs at the first invocation (that is, starting your product, or opening the first perspective, editor, or view), as this is the very moment the user is focused on getting work done and not feeling especially patient.

### Reintroducing the Runtime Spy

The Runtime Spy gives you the basic statistics for tracking several ways of speeding up startup, as was shown earlier in Figure 32.1. Minimizing the number of items in the Activated Plug-ins view is your number-one goal. Of those that do appear in this list, make it your number-two goal to minimize the number of items in the Loaded Classes view. The **Startup time** column in the Activated Plug-ins view will point you to the big hitters. Selecting the Trace 🔲 button from the Activated Plug-ins view will update the Stack Trace view to show you why a *plug-in* was loaded, and selecting the Trace button from the Loaded Classes view will show you why a *class* was loaded.

### Spying on WebSphere Studio

Let's begin with examples of how to use the Runtime Spy to diagnose and correct a startup coding error. As you'll see, the corrections will not "improve" performance in an absolute sense but rather defer startup costs, giving the user the perception of an overall faster product. This is something that the base Eclipse product does very well, staging its startup costs in little chunks as you use it.

To first survey the situation, let's start Studio with only the Runtime Spy perspective open. This should give a near-minimum load of plug-ins and the fastest startup, as shown in Figure 32.7.

| Plugin | Classes | Alloc | Used | Startup time | Order | ROM Alloc | ROM Used |
|---|---|---|---|---|---|---|---|
| org.apache.xerces* | 210 | 819200 | 730616 | 31 | 3 | 655360 | 569032 |
| org.eclipse.core.boot* | 426 | 1967016 | 1711376 | 0 | 1 | 1573800 | 1353512 |
| org.eclipse.core.resources* | 137 | 786432 | 708088 | 687 | 6 | 655360 | 584576 |
| org.eclipse.core.runtime* | 78 | 491520 | 331032 | 31 | 2 | 393216 | 264544 |
| org.eclipse.core.tools* | 35 | 163840 | 99320 | 110 | 9 | 131072 | 75072 |
| org.eclipse.jface.text* | 1 | 163840 | 792 | 15 | 11 | 131072 | 576 |
| org.eclipse.swt* | 254 | 1343488 | 1269032 | 15 | 7 | 1048576 | 988904 |
| org.eclipse.text* | 1 | 163840 | 4080 | 16 | 10 | 131072 | 3216 |
| org.eclipse.ui* | 1 | 163840 | 2272 | 31 | 8 | 131072 | 1616 |
| ⊞ org.eclipse.ui.workbench* | 467 | 1966080 | 1874552 | 78 | 4 | 1572864 | 1498632 |
| Total: 10 | 1610 | 8029096 | 6731160 | 3310 | | 6423464 | 5339680 |

**Figure 32.7**  Minimal Activated Plug-ins at Startup

Notice the trailing asterisks in the plug-in names. These are plug-ins that were loaded during the activation of the plug-in that is responsible for launching Eclipse, the plug-in known as the **application plug-in**. This plug-in contributes a class that implements the `IPlatformRunnable` interface to the `org.eclipse.core.runtime.applications` extension point. By default, the Workbench UI plug-in contributes an implementation of this interface that creates the Workbench window; collects action contributions to the main menu bar, toolbar, and so on; and generally prepares the Eclipse Workbench user interface for business.

The actual elapsed clock time will be greater than the sum of the **Startup time** column shown in the Activated Plug-ins view. This is because the Runtime Spy doesn't include JVM activity prior to the loading of the Platform Runtime, CPU activity outside of plug-in startup, or delays caused by initial I/O. In the case shown in Figure 32.7, the start time was actually around 13 seconds from the time the launch configuration started the instance of the Runtime Workbench. It also includes some overhead that the development-time launch configuration itself introduces for tasks like building the plug-in list.

Even with this overhead, the startup time looks pretty good, right? Not so, as we'll see when we refresh the Runtime Spy's views.

## Consequences of the Workbench's `startup` Extension Point

Let's update the list of active plug-ins by pressing the Refresh (⟳)button. Voilà! Our first surprise is shown in Figure 32.8.

| Plugin | Classes | Alloc | Used | Startup time | Order | ROM Alloc | ROM Used |
|---|---|---|---|---|---|---|---|
| com.ibm.etools.ctc.cheatsheet | 15 | 163840 | 62880 | 422 | 15 | 131072 | 51360 |
| ⊞ com.ibm.etools.internet | 2 | 163840 | 9856 | 1031 | 18 | 131072 | 7928 |
| com.ibm.etools.rad.codegen.preview | 1 | 163840 | 3792 | 47 | 22 | 131072 | 2984 |
| com.ibm.etools.rad.codegen.struts | 1 | 163840 | 3768 | 172 | 16 | 131072 | 2960 |
| com.rational.xtools.umlvisualizer.bootstrap | 3 | 163840 | 11752 | 15 | 17 | 131072 | 9464 |
| org.apache.xerces* | 211 | 851968 | 732688 | 15 | 3 | 655360 | 570480 |
| org.eclipse.core.boot* | 430 | 1999784 | 1739824 | 0 | 1 | 1573800 | 1375672 |
| org.eclipse.core.resources* | 151 | 819200 | 748856 | 3156 | 6 | 655360 | 616728 |
| org.eclipse.core.runtime* | 81 | 491520 | 335648 | 110 | 2 | 393216 | 267752 |
| org.eclipse.core.tools* | 39 | 163840 | 112960 | 125 | 9 | 131072 | 86128 |
| ⊞ org.eclipse.debug.ui* | 21 | 163840 | 93912 | 844 | 13 | 131072 | 76152 |
| org.eclipse.jface.text* | 29 | 163840 | 115792 | 16 | 11 | 131072 | 93240 |
| org.eclipse.swt* | 284 | 1343488 | 1286248 | 16 | 7 | 1048576 | 1000288 |
| org.eclipse.text* | 29 | 163840 | 70224 | 32 | 10 | 131072 | 53672 |
| org.eclipse.ui* | 1 | 163840 | 2272 | 109 | 8 | 131072 | 1616 |
| org.eclipse.ui.externaltools* | 4 | 163840 | 14160 | 62 | 12 | 131072 | 11304 |
| ⊞ org.eclipse.ui.workbench* | 502 | 1998848 | 1942920 | 265 | 4 | 1572864 | 1548736 |
| Total: 10 | 1757 | 8061864 | 6730256 | 3844 | | 6423464 | 5336592 |

**Figure 32.8**  Plug-ins Activated by the `org.eclipse.ui.startup` Extension Point

The selected plug-ins are those that were initially activated. What are these additional 11 plug-ins? Perhaps some were loaded because of the Runtime Spy perspective. More interestingly, there are several Studio plug-ins that look suspicious in Figure 32.8. Shown at the top of the list are "cheat sheet" and "internet." What are they and why are they loaded now? Going back to the user interface, we find choices related to the first plug-in under the **Help** pull-down menu, as shown in Figure 32.9.

**Figure 32.9**   Plug-in Activated by `org.eclipse.ui.startup` Extension Point

It is likely that only new users would choose the **Cheat Sheets** menu options, so why are we paying the cost of loading their associated plug-in at startup? The **Workbench > Startup** preference page reveals the answer, as shown in Figure 32.10.

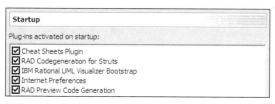

**Figure 32.10**   Plug-ins Contributing to the `org.eclipse.ui.startup` Extension Point

This extension point is a request to the Workbench UI to activate a plug-in once the Workbench window is opened, bypassing the deferred load strategy. There are legitimate uses of this API, but the length of this chapter doesn't allow for treatment of every item in this list. So let's consider the validity of a couple of the extenders shown in Figure 32.10.

- **Cheat Sheets.** The cheat sheet menu choices are built dynamically based on the installed features and reordered after each selection. There is no Workbench UI means to implement this dynamic behavior via extensions.

- **Internet Preferences.** This startup code initializes the **Window > Preferences > Internet** settings based on the system properties of the URL class. Since there is no way to know when this class will be referenced and since it has no explicit initialization methods, this appears legitimate. It may be prudent, however, to consider using a library extension. We'll return to why in a moment.

While these two cases turned out to be legitimate, it's still worth checking for potential misuse of this extension point. You may also be wondering why the Workbench defines a **Startup** preference page in the first place. Deselecting one of the listed plug-ins gives the user the choice of having a faster startup with reduced functionality. For example, experienced developers with no need of the hints provided by the **Cheat Sheets** cascade menu could choose to disable its contribution to the `org.eclipse.ui.startup` extension point, thus removing the **Help > Cheat Sheets** menu option but shaving almost half a second off the startup time. Keep this in mind if your own plug-in contributes to this extension point. That is, code your plug-in defensively under the assumption that the contributed class' `IStartup.earlyStartup` method may not have been called.

Returning to our example in Figure 32.8, consider the nonasterisked plug-in `com.ibm.etools.internet` in the list. Its stack trace confirms this plug-in was activated after the Workbench window opened, since it shows it originated in the line of code in the `Workbench.run` method that processes the `org.eclipse.ui.startup` extensions, as shown in Figure 32.11.

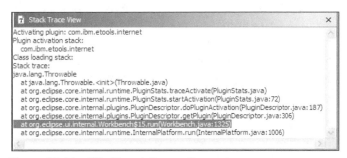

**Figure 32.11**    Workbench Startup Processing

The Workbench's `run` method is highlighted where the contributions to the `org.eclipse.ui.startup` extension point are processed. Subsequent plug-in activations at this point are all attributed to either the `startup` extension point or references thereof.

## Sorting Through Potential WebSphere Studio Hotspots

To see something Studio specific, let's open the J2EE perspective. (If you want to diagnose an easier scenario, open a single view, for example, **Window > Show View > DB Servers**, not its corresponding perspective; the list of activated plug-ins should be much shorter.) After opening the J2EE perspective, return to the Runtime Spy and select the Activated Plug-ins view's Refresh (🔄) button. *Wow!* The list jumps from 22 to 73 plug-ins, adding 20 seconds in plug-in activation (the units below are in milliseconds; prior total was just over 3 seconds). Figure 32.12 shows them sorted in plug-in activation order, with the most recently activated plug-in shown at the top.

| Plugin | Classes | Alloc | Used | Startup time | Order | ROM Alloc | ROM Used |
|--------|---------|-------|------|--------------|-------|-----------|----------|
| com.ibm.etools.sqlj | 3 | 163840 | 26384 | 141 | 73 | 131072 | 20736 |
| com.ibm.etools.subuilder | 64 | 861000 | 746392 | 1828 | 72 | 729928 | 627440 |
| com.ibm.etools.b2bgui | 4 | 163840 | 10152 | 93 | 71 | 131072 | 7952 |
| com.ibm.etools.viewbuilder | 9 | 163840 | 94400 | 234 | 70 | 131072 | 77368 |
| com.ibm.etools.b2butil | 2 | 163840 | 8552 | 78 | 69 | 131072 | 6600 |
| com.ibm.etools.sqlbuilder | 19 | 163840 | 80664 | 297 | 68 | 131072 | 61944 |
| com.ibm.etools.rdbexport.ui | 5 | 163840 | 26272 | 78 | 67 | 131072 | 21016 |
| com.ibm.etools.rdbschemagen.ui | 4 | 163840 | 22000 | 94 | 66 | 131072 | 17888 |
| com.ibm.etools.sqlparse | 3 | 163840 | 7928 | 78 | 65 | 131072 | 5984 |
| com.ibm.etools.rsc | 26 | 327680 | 193056 | 156 | 64 | 262144 | 157704 |
| com.ibm.sed.preferences | 2 | 163840 | 11368 | 125 | 63 | 131072 | 9240 |
| Total: 73 | 3886 | 24684272 | 16827080 | 23251 | | 19605232 | 13349016 |

**Figure 32.12**   Activated Plug-ins After Opening the J2EE Perspective

In all fairness, the Runtime Spy adds overhead, especially if stack traces are captured, so true uninstrumented elapsed time is closer to 37 seconds overall from a warm start. But let's see if anything beyond the startup plug-ins jumps out as potentially unnecessary. To save space, the list below isn't exhaustive, since we accept that base components like EMF, JDT, and J2EE UI are required. But what about these?

1. `com.ibm.etools.validation.*` (could be deferred or made optional?)
2. `com.ibm.etools.rsc.core.ui` (database)
3. `com.ibm.etools.rdblib` (database)
4. `com.ibm.etools.sqlmodel.*` (database)
5. `com.ibm.sed.preferences` (could be deferred until truly needed?)
6. `com.ibm.etools.rsc` (database)
7. `com.ibm.etools.sqlparse` (database)
8. `com.ibm.etools.rdbschemagen.ui` (database)
9. `com.ibm.etools.rdbexport.ui` (database)
10. `com.ibm.etools.sqlbuilder` (database)

11. `com.ibm.etools.subuilder` (database and takes 1,828ms to load!)
12. `com.ibm.etools.sqlj` (database)

No views or editors specifically related to databases have been opened yet. So why were the relational database schema center (6) and so many other database-related plug-ins activated? The parenthetical comment "could be deferred" denotes those capabilities for which Eclipse has architected solutions to avoid activation until needed, as is especially evident in the case of preferences. Nonetheless, even when considered collectively, most of these are small potatoes, so we'll only note them in our "to be investigated" list for the moment. There are, however, some plug-ins that consume a lot of startup time and, as we'll see, their costs are tied to plug-in activation during the processing of extension points. The next section explains this cost more fully as it explores how startup costs are initially incurred. Then we'll return to our analysis of the J2EE perspective startup.

### Understanding the Relationship Between Plug-in Activation and Extension Point Processing

Saving some startup time by avoiding the activation of the `subuilder` plug-in (named the *Stored Procedure and UDF Builder*, according to its plug-in manifest file) looks promising since it required almost 10% of the total time. Moreover, it is near the end of the activation sequence (72 of 73), so it may be easier to "trim off" than avoid the activation of an earlier plug-in. The stack trace of this plug-in's activation is shown in Figure 32.13.

**Figure 32.13**　Plug-in Activation Stack Trace for `com.ibm.etools.subuilder`

There is no need for Studio's source code to understand what's happening; the stack trace alone points to the cause. The Eclipse class PartPane manages tabbed views like those you see containing the J2EE Hierarchy, Package Explorer, and Navigator views. As shown in Figure 32.13 near the bottom of the text selection, the tabbed view PartPane is attempting to create an instance of the view associated with the **J2EE Hierarchy** tab, a class named J2EEView. Looking further up the stack, we see this class is in turn calling a helper that then calls the createExecutableExtension method.

The ConfigurationElement.createExecutableExtension method merits special attention. As you'll discover when debugging your own performance problems, this method instigates many of the plug-in activation cases that the Runtime Spy uncovers. To better understand what it does and how it affects plug-in activation, recall the simple extension point contribution of our canonical "Hello, Eclipse" example from earlier in the chapter (not repeated for reasons of brevity).

We're specifically interested in the processing of the class attribute of the <action> tag. This specifies the name of the class that will handle the menu choice selection, a class that must implement the IWorkbenchWindowAction-Delegate interface. This class isn't located in the same plug-in as the one that processes the org.eclipse.ui.actionSets extension point, the Workbench UI plug-in, or any of its prerequisite plug-ins. So how does the Workbench UI plug-in create an instance of this class when it doesn't appear to be on the plug-in's classpath?

It is the responsibility of a plug-in's classloader to resolve references to classes within its libraries. The classloader maps plug-in references to their corresponding JAR files containing the plug-in's classes, as in our example, SampleAction. Therefore, the Workbench UI plug-in doesn't have to "know" about the classes referenced by attributes like class of the <action> tag. Rather, it is the "Hello, Eclipse" plug-in defining a dependency on the Workbench UI plug-in that allows it to access the target plug-in and thereby have access to Hello Eclipse's classes via the target plug-in's classloader. To restate it more concisely, when Eclipse is unable to find a class, it asks the target plug-in's classloader to load the class; that's what the createExecutableExtension method does.

## Avoiding Premature Plug-in Activation Linked to Extension Point Processing

Returning to the stack trace shown in Figure 32.13, we recognize that the code near the middle of the text selection is processing extension contributions by calling createExecutableExtension—and bingo!—plug-ins start loading. We're especially interested because the list of activated plug-ins includes the slowest to load when opening the J2EE perspective, `com.ibm.etools` `.subuilder` (as was shown in the list of activated plug-ins in Figure 32.12). Our quest turns to answering the burning questions: Is it necessary at this point? Can it be deferred until later?

Practically all classes that provoke the activation of another plug-in can ultimately be traced back to an invocation of the `createExecutableExtension` method. The invocation parameters specified on these calls denote the name of the attribute (often "`class`") and its value, the fully qualified name of the class to be loaded. This leads back to the plug-in extension contribution responsible for the activation, in our case, the `subuilder` plug-in. An extract of its manifest is shown below.

```
<extension point="com.ibm.etools.rsc.sp">
  <sp
    id = "com.ibm.etools.subuilder.sp.NewSQLSPAction"
    name="%STR_NEWWIZARD_SQLSP"
    group ="SPFolderAction.New"
    view = "datadef"
    class=
      "com.ibm.etools.subuilder.actions.create.NewSQLSPAction"/>
</extension>
```

In terms of parameters, this extension contribution looks similar to the `org.eclipse.ui.popupmenu` extension point for defining menu choice contributions; that is, it defines a label (attribute "name"), placement (attribute "group"), target (attribute "view"), and most notably, a handler (attribute "class"). What differentiates the Eclipse extension and this particular implementation is that Eclipse's extension creates a delegate class to act as a proxy for the menu choice. It isn't until the menu choice is actually selected that the corresponding handler class is created, thereby deferring the activation of the plug-in containing the handler class. This same proxy strategy was applied to Studio's case above and the J2EE perspective opened almost seven seconds faster. The cost of creating the subuilder plug-ins' `NewSQLSPAction` instance and activating the plug-ins containing its referenced classes wasn't eliminated but rather changed to pay-as-you-go. Since the cost of loading this plug-in was closer to when the user expected a delay—when connecting to a database—the user's overall perception is that the product is more responsive.

## Avoiding Performance Regressions Using the Performance Monitor

Few things irritate a performance analyst more than discovering that hard-earned improvements were wiped out by newly introduced code or corrections

PART V

to existing code. Known simply as **regressions**, they are the bane of every software development project. In many projects, they are quietly accepted as natural, much like graying hair. Ironically, this analogy to growing older is apt, since regressions, like aging, happen day in and day out, without us really noticing until we look back and compare the present to the past.

Unlike the relentless advancement of time, performance regressions don't have to be accepted as unavoidable. The key to preventing performance regressions lies in detecting them as early as possible, and that's where the **Performance Monitor** plug-in helps.

The Performance Monitor plug-in is small and simple to use. It can record key metrics that allow you to compare your product's past performance to today's. The monitor introduces almost no overhead, so you can either instrument your code to capture data each time your product is run, or use its client user interface to capture ad hoc performance data. Its performance data is written to disk in a simple XML format. The Performance Monitor's user interface includes a Performance Snapshots view that displays the captured data and calculates basic statistics for its metrics like standard deviation, averages, and T values (a measure of the probability that the comparison of two sets of data represent a true deviation from a normal distribution).

Detecting regressions requires that you decide what in your project you will measure and how. You should define several scenarios that are representative of how your product will be used and where degradations or improvements in performance would be most noticeable to your users. There are two ways you can use the Performance Monitor to capture data:

- Code instrumentation

  Begin by defining locations in your code that you want to measure. These intervals should represent a natural starting and stopping point for your users, such as creating a project, completing a modification, or saving the result. These points are known as **steps**. You record the performance metrics of a step ("take a snapshot") by first adding `org.eclipse.perfmsr.core` to the list of plug-ins in your plug-in's `<requires>` definition, and then calling `PerfMsrCorePlugin.getPerformanceMonitor(true).snapshot(step#)` in your code. If you use JUnit to exercise your code, it is natural to instrument your testcases with calls to the Performance Monitor. See the section Configuring the Performance Monitor in the online documentation for details on how to set your product-specific data like the test number, driver name, or driver date via the Performance Monitor's `etools_perf_ctrl` environment variable.

- Ad hoc/manually

  The Performance Monitor adds a **Performance** pull-down menu choice to the Workbench where you can take a "snapshot" of its metrics. We call this method "ad hoc" because some measurements, such as elapsed process, won't be repeatable if it includes the varying time a user would take to make menu selections. This variation can be controlled using automated test tools like JUnit or a GUI testing tool like Abbot for SWT.

Once you have defined your user scenarios and decided on the best points to take measurements (steps), you are ready to begin. Each step is assigned a number of your choosing. Later in performance analysis, you may want to define **variations** too. Variations of a scenario are changes that you introduce that may produce different performance results, such as a different JRE, different operating system, or different version of Eclipse. Again, you decide what represents a significant enough change to the environment to merit creating a variation. You might also use variations for testing your performance improvement hypotheses.

Since a product will perform differently when it is launched for the first time ("cold start") versus subsequent launches ("warm start"), the Performance Monitor organizes steps into **runs**. A run begins when Eclipse launches and ends when Eclipse exits. In between, you can define one or more steps where you'll capture data. Thus, the Performance Monitor's data is organized by runs subdivided into steps. A variation is associated with the entire run (e.g., a variation denoting a particular JRE), so once you've recorded a step having a variation, the variations are fixed for the remainder of the run.

To summarize, the general process is to:

1. Define one or more scenarios (this is a one-time activity).
2. Run the scenarios, recording performance data at the prescribed steps.
3. Analyze the data using the Performance Snapshots view.

Next, we'll discuss the installation of the Performance Monitor, and then close with a brief example of its use.

## Installation

The Performance Monitor is on the book's CD-ROM in the `org.eclipse`
`.perfmsr.*` projects, or you can get it from eclipse.org as part of the "JUnit Plugin Tests and Automated Testing Framework" download. Eclipse uses the

monitor as part of the automated testing to detect performance regressions. There are quite a few plug-ins in this package; search for the plug-in subdirectories prefixed with `org.eclipse.perfmsr` to obtain only the Performance Monitor. Unzip them into the `<inst_dir>\eclipse` directory and restart Eclipse.

**NOTE**  The versions of the Performance Monitor and Eclipse SDK on the book's CD-ROM are compatible. If you have a more recent version of Eclipse, get the matching version of the Performance Monitor in the "JUnit Plugin Tests and Automated Testing Framework" package from the download page of eclipse.org before continuing.

To see the **Performance** pull-down menu, you may have to enable its action set, Performance Monitor Actions, from the **Commands** page of the **Window > Customize Perspective** dialog.

### Example Use

Before taking a snapshot, verify the configuration of the Performance Monitor using the **Window > Preferences > Performance Monitor** page. There you can specify the location of the data file `timer.xml`, from which the Performance Snapshots view will display the results. Your settings are confirmed in the **Snapshot** dialog, as shown in Figure 32.14.

You should repeat your scenario several times using the same steps to validate that the results are consistent. The consistency of a set of results for a number of runs can be seen in the standard deviation of the runs. These results become your baseline by which you compare future drivers of your product. Figure 32.14 also shows the Performance Snapshots view in the background; the two selected items are steps in the same scenario, comparing two drivers.

The idea is to capture key performance data for comparison with later evolutions of your product. If newly introduced code causes a performance regression, you will be able to easily find where it began. The Performance Monitor groups its metrics into:

- Machine

  Metrics applicable to the machine as a whole, such as total physical memory and committed swap space.

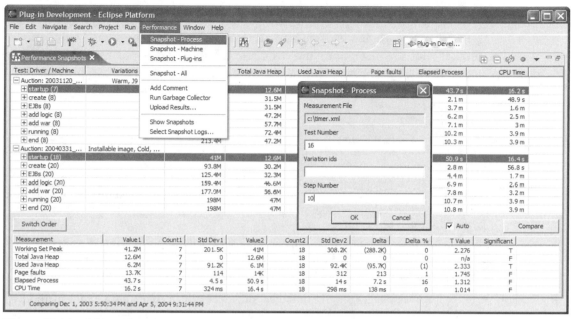

**Figure 32.14**   Taking a Snapshot and the Performance Snapshots View

- Process

  Metrics specific to the current process such as I/O read count and CPU usage.

- Plug-ins

  The list of active plug-ins similar to those shown in the Runtime Spy.

The Performance Snapshots view is capable of displaying most of the data captured in the Performance Monitor's `timer.xml` file, but not all since the data quickly become too copious for local analysis. For example, the Performance Snapshots view displays no plug-in data, such as the list of active plug-ins. If you wish to record the active plug-ins between two releases of your product at a given step, specify the `-debug` command line option and then select the **Performance > Snapshot - Plug-ins** menu choice. In our own analysis at IBM, we download the data the monitor records into databases to track each Eclipse-based product's performance during development. The Performance Monitor's online documentation includes the schema definition you can use if you wish to do so yourself.

## Common Solutions to Eclipse-Specific Performance Problems

Performance tuning is often a matter of searching for the same "silly" mistakes that are made over and over again. Table 32.1 is our list of the most common Eclipse performance gaffes you should check for first, plus some optimizations you might consider implementing.

**Table 32.1**   Common Performance Problems

| Area | Possible Solutions |
| --- | --- |
| Startup | • Check for extensions to `org.eclipse.ui.startup`; in general, avoid this extension point by using other techniques like static enablement and visibility rules for action contributions, action filters, etc.<br><br>• Avoid autoload bundles; look for `start` tag specified on the `osgi.bundles` key in `configuration/config.ini` (infrequently used).<br><br>• Package plug-in as a single JAR file (benefit depends on plug-in size and hardware). |
| Initialization | • Look for overly eager plug-in initialization, especially in `YourPlugin.start` method.<br><br>• Defer loading `ResourceBundle/` properties files, especially for infrequently used strings like error messages.<br><br>• Restructure to use delegates and extension points; adding this level of indirection avoids references to classes until actually needed to perform work. |
| Extension processing | • If your plug-in defines extension points, defer reading them since the Platform Runtime reads the registry lazily from disk; the internal class `RegistryReader` demonstrates one approach.<br><br>• Defer calling `IConfigurationElement.createExecutableExtension` until truly necessary; it can trigger a cascade of plug-in activations. Use delegates or proxies to represent the content contained in a configuration element, similar to the Workbench's `<action>` tag processing. |
| User response time | • Use Jobs to move low-priority tasks to the background.<br><br>• Look for excessive notifications to listeners, especially resource change listeners.<br><br>• Check for inefficiently or incorrectly coded incremental builders. |
| Notifications and update | • Batch together updates to the workspace with `IWorkspace.run(IWorkspaceRunnable, IProgressMonitor)`.<br><br>• Reduce the number of updates sent to listeners using filters, where available (for example, the `eventMask` parameter in `JavaCore.addElementChangedListener` allows the listener to specify the types of events they are interested in).<br><br>• Take advantage of visual elements that defer rendering (for example, `MultiPageEditor`, `PreferencePage`, dynamically created `WizardPage`, `Table` using the `SWT.Virtual` style).<br><br>• Reduce multiple redraws using `Widget.setRedraw`. |

## Chapter Summary

Improving performance is almost like winning at the infamous "shell game": It's all about managing the user's expectations and keeping their eyes away from what you hope they won't notice. In this chapter's case study, the startup is now faster but the user will pay the same CPU costs later if they activate the database tools. That's acceptable since it is in small chunks, and more importantly, it moves the delay closer to the associated action where the user expects to pay.

If you only remember one point about this chapter, this is it: Eclipse's goal is to *defer code execution where possible*, because not only may it result in a perceived improvement in performance, but also from your viewpoint, the easiest code to optimize for speed is code that never executes. Eclipse's plug-in architecture makes it straightforward for you to create extensions that accomplish this, the Runtime Spy helps you find those cases where your implementation could be improved, and the Performance Monitor helps you detect regressions before your users do.

## References

Abbot Java GUI Testing Framework. http://sourceforge.net/projects/abbot/.

Arthorne, John, and Chris Laffra. 2004. *Official Eclipse 3.0 FAQs*. Boston, MA: Addison-Wesley. http://www.eclipsefaq.org. (See FAQs 57, 101.)

IBM Development Package for Eclipse (this download includes the latest IBM runtime for the Java platform with J9 technology). http://www.ibm.com/developerworks/java/.

PART V

# CHAPTER 33

*Swing Interoperability*

This chapter is for those not quite ready to jump in and rewrite their Swing-based development tools or applications based on SWT (see Chapter 14). There are a various reasons for choosing an SWT–Swing hybrid approach: time-to-market considerations, for example, or the desire to create a proto-type that demonstrates the value of Eclipse integration. In either case, the goal is to add your existing function to the Eclipse Platform with minimal changes to your existing code base while at the same time providing some level of integration with Eclipse that affords a good end user experience.

There are a couple of ways to integrate SWT and Swing. Embedding AWT and Swing components in SWT is supported on Windows platforms. However, there is still more work to do to bridge these two technologies on other platforms. On Linux and UNIX platforms, that work requires the XEmbed technology, an AWT enhancement to the Java 2 SDK, V 1.5; this is not supported in Eclipse 3.0.

Note: At this writing, there are unsupported solutions for embedding Swing on the UNIX platforms; solutions on other platforms are not yet implemented.

There are two examples that complement this chapter: There is a Windows-specific example, a plug-in with a view that demonstrates how to embed an AWT/Swing application, and an example of a hybrid application that incor-porates a Swing editor in a launch-and-edit scenario, which keeps the Eclipse workspace synchronized with the file system changes made by the editor. The launch-and-edit example is provided as an alternative implementation for those platforms where embedding is not yet supported.

This chapter shows you where and how to get started. As you proceed to deeper levels of integration, you will need to change more and more of your existing Swing application and dig deeper into the Eclipse API. You will most certainly continue to reevaluate the benefits of proceeding on the Swing–SWT hybrid path versus jumping into a pure SWT implementation. Deciding when to convert to a pure SWT implementation is up to you.

## Embedding AWT and Swing in Views and Editors

It is possible to run Swing components inside an SWT `Composite`. That means you can embed Swing just about anywhere within the Workbench GUI, views, editors, dialogs, preference pages, wizards, and so on. The Swing and AWT bridge support is included in the SWT class `org.eclipse.swt` `.awt.SWT_AWT`. The bridge depends on SUN platform-specific extensions in the `sun.awt.<platform>` packages. SWT supports the use of AWT and Swing components on Win32 platforms in an embedded frame defined by the class `sun.awt.windows.WEmbeddedFrame`. We'll learn later in this chapter about the implications of using `WEmbeddedFrame` rather than the more commonly used `JFrame`.

### Embedding Swing/AWT in a View

While it is possible to embed Swing components just about anywhere in the Eclipse UI, dialogs, wizards, editors, and so on, let us look at how to embed an existing Swing application into a view (views are discussed in Chapter 18). This process does not require that you rewrite your Swing application; rather, with just a few minor adjustments you can run your application inside Eclipse. The major adjustment is to move the standalone Swing application user interface into a view contributed in an Eclipse plug-in by doing the following:

- Decouple the Swing application from its `main()` method
- Refactor inheritance from `JFrame` to `WEmbeddedFrame`
- Create the Swing GUI from within an Eclipse plug-in
- Set up listeners from the Swing GUI to Eclipse actions
- Set up listeners from an Eclipse plug-in on Swing component events

Let's get the ball rolling and take a look at what it takes to embed an existing Swing "Volume Converter" application in a Workbench view, as shown in Figure 33.1. See project `com.ibm.jdg2e.swt_swing.embed.converter` on the CD-ROM.

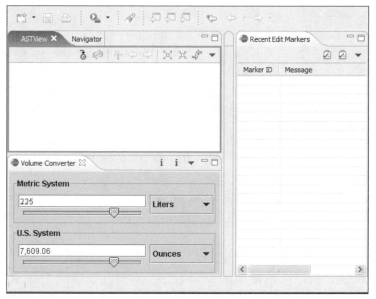

**Figure 33.1**    Swing Application Embedded in a Workbench View

## Let's Start with the `main()` Method

It may or may not be obvious, but your embedded Swing application does not require a `main` method when embedded in the Workbench. Typically it is in the `main` method where you create and run the UI. In a Workbench view, your chance to create the UI comes when the Workbench calls the `createPartControl` method. You will need to create a `Composite` object (a widget container) and fill it with your Swing components and/or AWT widgets. The `Composite` instance you create needs to be aware of embedded components because its size algorithm is specialized for embedded components. To make that distinction, use the `SWT.EMBEDDED` style when you create your composite. The following code example shows how you can start embedding the Swing application in the `createPartControl()` method for your view.

```
public void createPartControl(Composite parent) {
    // Create composite using the embedded style. The size method in
    // composite handles embedded Swing frames differently.
    converterComp = new Composite(parent, SWT.EMBEDDED);
    final java.awt.Frame converterFrame = SWT_AWT
        .new_Frame(converterComp);

...code omitted...

}
```

### WEmbeddedFrame Versus JFrame

The WEmbeddedFrame differs from the more familiar JFrame. Some methods found in JFrame don't apply when embedding a frame in a view or editor part, because some of the behavior that you need in a monolithic Swing application is not required of an embedded frame since the Workbench is in control. For example, your embedded frame is not responsible for exit and close, or for the frame's look and feel characteristics. Again, the Workbench is in control of these behaviors.

The following are some methods commonly used on a JFrame that are undefined in WEmbeddedFrame:

- JFrame("Window Title")
- setDefaultLookAndFeelDecorated()
- setContentPane()
- setDefaultCloseOperation()

The set methods are not required of an embedded frame. Rather than setting the title during construction of the frame, the title is defined as part of the view extension in your plug-in. Or, if required, you can set the title by calling the setPartName() method as part of your createPartControl() method definition.

## Thread Safety Between the SWT and Swing Toolkits

For thread safety, if you are using Java threads in your Swing code, it is wise to schedule a thread to run the Swing event-dispatching thread, creating and showing this Swing application's GUI. Otherwise, you will soon discover that your Swing components or AWT widgets are missing mouse clicks and/ or become unresponsive. This thread runs asynchronously on the AWT event-dispatching thread and will happen after all pending AWT events have been processed.

The GUI in our original Swing application is created in the createAndShowGUI() method of our VolConverter class. Here is a snippet of that code as implemented in the view's createPartContol() method.

```
javax.swing.SwingUtilities.invokeLater(new Runnable() {
    public void run() {
        VolConverter.createAndShowGUI(converterFrame);
        VolConverter.getConverter().getMetricVolPanel()
            .getVolUnitChooser().addActionListener(thisView);
        VolConverter.getConverter().getUsaVolPanel()
            .getVolUnitChooser().addActionListener(thisView);
    }
});
```

The call to the `createAndShowGUI()` method implemented in the `Converter` class of our original Swing application is safely tucked inside a `Runnable` in the `invokeLater()`method.

## Putting Focus on the Composite with an Embedded Frame

You should always set the focus within your view. In this case, putting the focus on the embedded composite window does the trick. Here is the implementation of the `setFocus()` method in the view class. The Workbench calls this method.

```
public void setFocus() {
    converterComp.setFocus();
}
```

## Sending Swing Component Messages

If you decide to move deeper into Workbench integration, you might decide to integrate some Workbench actions with Swing component actions. The intent is to wire Workbench JFace actions to Swing components for bidirectional interactivity. For example, you could affect the selections in a Swing `JComboBox` from a view menu or toolbar and at the same time listen to events on the Swing components from within your view. Implementing this messaging between the two toolkits is straightforward—you just need to add some access methods to get to your Swing components from the non-Swing portions of your view. Then in your implementation of the JFace actions, you can access the Swing components and send them messages. Here is a snippet that illustrates a JFace action handler that interacts with a Swing `JComboBox` component.

```
literAction = new Action() {
    public void run() {
      VolConverter.getConverter().getMetricVolPanel()
          .volUnitChooser
          .setSelectedIndex(VolConverter.LITERS);
    }
};
literAction.setText("Liters");
literAction.setToolTipText("Set Metric System to Liters");
literAction.setImageDescriptor(PlatformUI.getWorkbench()
    .getSharedImages().getImageDescriptor(
        ISharedImages.IMG_OBJS_INFO_TSK));
gallonsAction = new Action() {
  public void run() {
     VolConverter.getConverter().getUsaVolPanel().volUnitChooser
        .setSelectedIndex(VolConverter.GALLONS);
  }
};
```

The view relates to the Swing application as a singleton object implemented in the class `VolConverter`. The `getConverter()` static method is used whenever the view needs the instance of the Swing application. The `get-MetricVolPanel()` method is used to access the `JPanel`. The `unitChooser()` method is used to access the `JComboBox` component.

### Completing the Round Trip: Listening for AWT and Swing Component Events

To be a first-class Workbench Swing hybrid, you will need to make your view aware of Swing UI events and act accordingly. We already discussed changing the selection in a `JComboBox` from a `JFace` action. Now it is time to learn how to make a Workbench view listen for selection changes in a Swing component.

To listen for AWT action events, you will need to implement the `java.awt.event.ActionListener` interface in your view. This requires that you implement the `actionPerformed()` method. We will discuss that method in detail later, but first let's look at how and where to add the `JComboBox` listener. Refer back to the `invokeLater` method. This is the point in time where you create and run the Swing GUI: It is in this method that you will add your listeners. Here is the `invokeLater()` method, illustrating the addition of AWT event listeners.

```
javax.swing.SwingUtilities.invokeLater(new Runnable() {
  public void run() {
    VolConverter.createAndShowGUI(converterFrame);
    VolConverter.getConverter().getMetricVolPanel()
        .getVolUnitChooser().addActionListener(thisView);
    VolConverter.getConverter().getUsaVolPanel()
        .getVolUnitChooser().addActionListener(thisView);
  }
});
```

In this example, the view adds the `actionPerformed` method as required by the `ActionListener` interface to handle the selection changes in the `unitChooser` (`JComboBox`).

In the execution of the `actionPerformed()` method, you will learn what happened in the Swing component and respond with any changes required in the Workbench view. For example, you might need to enable or disable JFace actions based on the current selection. Here is an example of an `actionPerformed()` method that toggles the enablement of a Workbench view menu and toolbar actions.

```
public void actionPerformed(ActionEvent e) {
    String value = VolConverter.getConverter()
        .getMetricVolPanel().getVolUnitChooser()
        .getSelectedItem().toString();
```

```
      if (value == VolConverter.S_LITERS) {
        literAction.setEnabled(false);
      } else {
        literAction.setEnabled(true);
      }
      value = VolConverter.getConverter().getUsaVolPanel()
          .getVolUnitChooser().getSelectedItem().toString();
      if (value == VolConverter.S_GALLONS) {
        gallonsAction.setEnabled(false);
      } else {
        gallonsAction.setEnabled(true);
      }
    }
}
```

This concludes the example of a Swing embedded in-place solution. However, there are more general integration issues to consider, such as using workspace resources. We will discuss data integration and resource sychronization in the launch-and-edit integration scenario in the next section, a subject pertinent to embedded Swing as well. Moreover, we discuss the more general integration issues later in this chapter. Embedded Swing is a much better solution in terms of the end user experience than either a standalone or a launch-and-edit use case. Eclipse plans to support embedded Swing on other platforms in the future; however, until the embedded use case is supported, the launch-and-edit scenario described in the next section is the best alternative.

## Launch-and-Edit Integration

There are two other alternative integration approaches to consider when bringing your existing Swing applications to Eclipse: internal-launch and external-launch tools. If embedded Swing is not supported on your platform of choice, you must use these alternatives.

**Internal-launch Java tools** implemented in Java and using Swing or AWT can be implemented so they run in the same JVM and use the same class libraries as Eclipse. This mechanism allows Swing-in-process tools to be opened as separate windows (not in place). By definition, legacy tools are Eclipse-unaware and loosely coupled, and operate in much the same manner as external-launch tools.

An advantage to this alternative is the ability to launch a Swing application with other applications and achieve a single point of control for all project resources. You can also use Eclipse to manage team development and versioning. This level of integration usually requires users to manually refresh their local resources to update Eclipse metadata after a save. (Of course, users may have their Workbench preferences set to auto-refresh, but it is not safe to assume this.) This synchronizes the Eclipse resources and provides data integration with other tools.

As demonstrated in the Swing ABCEditor example later in this chapter, making the Swing-in-process tool Eclipse resource-aware is a simple matter of calling the Eclipse workspace to refresh the resource. In fact, the ABCEditor Swing–SWT hybrid is now coupled in a way so the user does not need to refresh from the local file system manually. However, sticking to the objective of making minimal changes to the ABCEditor, the integration is not so deep that the *.abc file changes are recorded in the Eclipse local file history. That would require replacing all `java.io` references in the ABCEditor with calls to the Eclipse resource API.

**External-launch tools** are tools invoked as external programs and may be implemented in any language. These tools open in a separate window and are not visually integrated into the Workbench. This is the simplest form of integration. The Eclipse Platform provides automatic launching of external editors based on file type associations provided by the user or obtained from the underlying operating system. At this level of integration, you get the same benefits of the internal-launch Java tool. However, making an external-launch tool Eclipse-aware requires implementing some form of inter-process communications between the components. Internal-launch Java tools are a simpler alternative for making Swing applications Eclipse-aware.

### Modes of Invocation

External editors are the fastest way of integrating existing code into Eclipse because fewer code changes are required. At the same time, external editors are the least integrated. Use external editors if time-to-market is the primary consideration. The extension point `org.eclipse.ui.editors` is used by plug-ins to integrate editors into Eclipse. Plug-ins that contribute an editor must register the editor extension in their `plugin.xml` file, along with configuration information for the editor.

An external editor opens its own window outside the Eclipse Workbench. Two modes of invocation are possible.

- In a separate JVM, which is known as **out-process invocation**.
- Inside the same JVM as Eclipse, known as **in-process invocation**.

In either case, making both Eclipse and the Swing applications aware of each other requires implementing a plug-in. There are a variety of ways to communicate context information between Eclipse and Swing components. Here are the differences.

- Out-process invocation requires some form of inter-process communication.
- In-process invocation uses intra-process components inside the same JVM as Eclipse. Both the Swing and Eclipse components communicate directly. The Swing-in-process tool has access to the entire Workbench since it shares the same JVM, for example, by using your plug-in class to gain access to other Eclipse components.

### Improving the End User Experience

Launching Swing components from Eclipse can lead to a less-than-desirable end user experience. External tools typically operate on files in the local file system and do not update the Eclipse workspace. When this happens, the workspace is no longer synchronized with the local file system.

With just a little work, you can make both Eclipse and Swing notify each other of changes and to a limited degree integrate with each other. Turning your existing Swing tool into an Eclipse-aware tool opens the possibility of improving the Workbench end user experience in a multitude of use cases.

### General Integration Issues

Here are just a few integration items that significantly improve the Eclipse end user experience.

- Resource synchronization
  When your Swing application changes Eclipse project resources, your application can call your Eclipse plug-in so that changes are reflected in the Eclipse workspace. This level of integration requires that you learn about the Eclipse resource framework (see Chapter 23, Workspace Resource Programming).
- Tool preferences
  Use the Eclipse preference page framework to control the attributes of the Swing application.
- Workbench contributions
  Contributions can be in the form of actions and decorators. The contributions framework (see Chapter 21) can be used to associate actions that launch Swing components.

PART V

# ABCEditor Example—In-Process Invocation

The ABCEditor, described in the next section, is a simple example of a Swing application that provides a text editor for .abc file types. The editor provides a **File** menu and a couple of toolbar buttons to perform simple actions. You will see in this example how Swing applications are integrated into Eclipse in the form of an in-process internal editor launch. The ABCEditor is launched in a separate window but runs in the same JVM as Eclipse. This allows the tool to integrate with the Eclipse core but not the Eclipse UI. This implementation enables API integration with tool models provided by other plug-ins.

To launch an editor that runs in a separate window but runs in the same JVM requires two steps.

1. Define an editor extension in the `plugin.xml` file.
2. Create a Java class that implements `org.eclipse.ui.IEditorLauncher`.

These steps are described in the following sections.

### Editor Extension for an External Editor

You define an editor extension in your `plugin.xml` file to associate the file type for your external editor with the class that implements the launcher. This use of the extension point `org.eclipse.ui.editors` registers your launcher for the identified files. Once registered, the launcher will appear as an **Open With** menu choice for those file types.

```
<extension point="org.eclipse.ui.editors">
  <editor
     name="JDG2E: Internal Launch ABC File Editor"
     icon="icons/abc.gif"
     extensions="abc"
     launcher=
        "com.ibm.jdg2e.swing.external.launch.ABCEditorLauncher"
     id="com.ibm.jdg2e.swing.external.launch.ABCEditor">
  </editor>
</extension>
```

The `launcher` attribute specifies the name of a class, which implements the interface `IEditorLauncher` and registers this launcher for use with .abc files. When the **ABCEditor** menu choice is selected, Eclipse will create an instance of the `launcher` class and invoke it, passing the selected file. That is, the editor launcher is given an `IPath` to use as its input.

In the in-process example on the CD-ROM, the class `ABCEditorLauncher` launches the ABCEditor. The example encapsulates the communications

between the Eclipse plug-in and the ABCEditor in a singleton utility class
`SwingEditorPlugin` (see Figure 33.2).

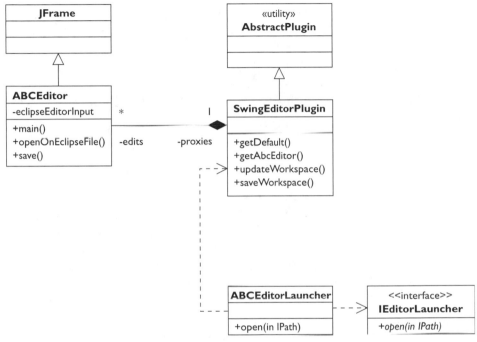

**Figure 33.2**  ABCEditor Design

The `ABCEditorLauncher` class overrides the open method of the `IEditor-Launcher` interface. The expression `SwingEditorPlugin.getDefault()`
`.getAbcEditor` resolves to an instance of the ABCEditor. The `ABCEditor`
`.openOnEclipseFile` method is called with an IPath instance that represents
this editor's input.

```
public void open(IPath) {
  System.out.println(
    "Launch Successful : file Location = "
      + file.toString());
  SwingEditorPlugin.getDefault()
    .getAbcEditor().
    openOnEclipseFile(file);
}
```

The ABCEditor saves the instance in a variable that is referenced later
when the ABCEditor communicates changes in the file to the editor's plug-in

class. The Eclipse workspace resource location is obtained using the IPath, file location object. The ABCEditor opens the file input.

```
public void openOnEclipseFile(IPath eclipseFileResource) {
    eclipseEditorInput = eclipseFileResource;
    runStandAlone = false;
    open(new File(eclipseFileResource.toString()));
    fileOpenAction.setEnabled(false);
}
```

## Adding Workbench Awareness—Resource Synchronization

Because the ABCEditor is a standard file-based tool and does not use the Eclipse resource API, the Eclipse plug-in is otherwise unaware of changes made to the file in the local file system. Let's look at adding a programmatic solution to the manual file refresh.

The ABCEditor is modified to inform the Eclipse workspace whenever it makes updates to the file system. In the following code example, a call is added to the Eclipse editor extension plug-in class from the ABCEditor-Launcher.save method. The class SwingEditorPlugin implements a static method, getDefault, which returns the singleton plug-in instance. The ABCEditor uses the singleton instance to call the method updateWorkSpace. The updateWorkSpace method requires an IPath input parameter. The workspace changes handled in this example are simple and are limited to file resource updates. A more complete solution might provide a generalized method to refresh all types of IResource.

```
public void save() {
    PrintWriter out = null;
    try {
        out = new PrintWriter(new FileWriter(input));
        out.write(contents.getText());
        SwingEditorPlugin.getDefault().
          updateWorkspace(eclipseEditorInput);
    } catch (Exception exc) {
        exc.printStackTrace();
    }
    if (out != null) {
        try {
            out.close();
        } catch (Exception exc) {
        }
    }
}
```

The Eclipse resource API allows you to manipulate the workspace resource tree. The resource API is defined in a series of interfaces in `org.eclipse.core.resources` (see Chapter 23, Workspace Resource Programming, for more information about this). Ignore for now that the ABC-Editor may affect other workspace resources, such as adding new files to folders, and instead concentrate on keeping the resources synchronized.

The `updateWorkspace` method invokes the `refreshLocal` method to synchronize the workspace with the file system. You can make the scope of the refresh as small or as large as you require. The scope of the refresh depends on the given resource and the depth parameter. While a refresh of the file resource instance is all that is actually required in this example, it illustrates walking the workspace resource tree back to the parent container, and then refreshing that container to the depth of one. By walking back to the parent, the contents of the parent container are refreshed. If the depth is set to one, the contents of any child containers are not refreshed. Use `DEPTH_INFINITE` to refresh the entire workspace tree starting with the parent. Setting `workSpaceChanged` to `true` sets an internal, dirty flag. The dirty flag is checked in the `saveWorkspace` method.

```
public void updateWorkspace(IPath eclipseEditorInput) {
    try {
        ResourcesPlugin.getWorkspace().getRoot().getFile(
            eclipseEditorInput).getParent().refreshLocal(
            IResource.DEPTH_ONE, null);
        workSpaceChanged = true;
    } catch (Exception e) { e.printStackTrace();
    }
}
```

### Adding Workbench Awareness—Tool Preferences

This level of integration requires that you know about preferences pages (refer to Chapter 16, Dialogs and Wizards, if necessary).

In resource synchronization, you saw how event messages flowed from the ABCEditor to Eclipse through a plug-in proxy (`SwingEditorPlugin`). Likewise, you should consider maintaining and synchronizing ABCEditor tool preferences with the Eclipse Workbench Preference store. This would require that event messages flow in the opposite direction, from Eclipse to the ABCEditor, when the user changes preferences on the ABCEditor through an Eclipse preference dialog.

To implement support for modifying the preferences displayed in Eclipse, you must supply the logic for any displayed push buttons: **Apply**, **OK**, **Cancel**, and **Defaults**. In that logic, call the plug-in proxy to communicate preference changes back to the ABCEditor. In addition, the ABCEditor then must provide public preference update methods to the plug-in proxy. The plug-in proxy then uses the association shown in Figure 33.2 to call the preference update methods in the ABCEditor.

### Handling System Exit

Most Swing applications call `System.exit` when they terminate. The result of calling `System.exit` from the ABCEditor is that it terminates all threads in the process, including Eclipse and any internal-launch tools running in the same JVM. To prevent closing Eclipse, change your Swing editor code so it does not call `System.exit`. Deleting the call to `System.exit` means you will have to write some clean-up code. For example, you should invoke `saveWorkspace` to save pending changes in the Eclipse workspace. This can be done from the `windowClosing()` method in the ABCEditor.

## Example Summary

You are now ready to explore the two Swing interoperability examples provided on the CD-ROM.

The embedded Swing example illustrates a former Swing-based application reengineered into a Workbench view. The example code is contained in the project `com.ibm.jdg2e.swt_swing.embed.converter`.

The ABCEditor is provided on the CD-ROM. This example code, defined in the project `com.ibm.jdg2e.swing.external.launch`, illustrates how to create an Eclipse–Swing hybrid editor. As the Swing part of the hybrid makes changes on the local file system, the hybrid programmatically synchronizes the Eclipse workspace.

## Chapter Summary

Swing interoperability provides a way to protect investments in existing tools by allowing them to participate in Eclipse without a rewrite. In-process invocation allows a Swing application to communicate with Eclipse in a way that it is possible to build a hybrid application. On some platforms Swing components and AWT are embeddable in an SWT `Composite`. This chapter shows only a preliminary level of integration and how to get started. On some platforms, you are off to the races using the embedded support. For other platforms, the chapter outlines an alternative launch-and-edit level of integration.

Now that you have the basics, you can further improve your hybrid application by implementing Workbench contributions and preferences, and participate in Eclipse local history by replacing your current `java.io` with calls to the Eclipse resource API. The decision when to jump to a pure SWT implementation is up to you.

## References

Arthorne, John. August 23, 2002. How you've changed! Responding to resource changes in the Eclipse workspace. http://www.eclipse.org.

Arthorne, John, and Chris Laffra. 2004. *Official Eclipse 3.0 FAQs*. Boston, MA: Addison-Wesley. http://www.eclipsefaq.org. (See FAQ 144.)

# CHAPTER 34

## *OLE and ActiveX Interoperability*

If you want to extend Eclipse and you have a considerable investment in existing Windows applications, you are probably searching for some alternative to "starting from scratch." This chapter discusses the legacy integration capabilities provided by the Eclipse Platform and how to incorporate existing tools into Eclipse quickly.

The SWT Object Linking and Embedding (OLE) integration capabilities in Eclipse offer a good compromise between "starting from scratch" and "100% code reuse." If you are willing to invest some effort learning about Eclipse's tool integration frameworks, you can integrate your legacy application into a proper Eclipse-aware user interface.

In the example code provided on the CD-ROM that complements this chapter, you see the Internet Explorer Web browser control integrated into an Eclipse multipage editor (see Figure 34.1). This Eclipse–ActiveX hybrid editor uses input from Eclipse resources and connects custom editor actions (for example, **Bold**, **Italic**, and **Underline**) to the Eclipse toolbar and menus.

## COM Support in Eclipse

Microsoft introduced Object Linking and Embedding (OLE 1.0), which was based on Dynamic Data Exchange (DDE), in the early 1990s. It started with the linking and embedding of different application source data into a single compound document, for example, inserting a Microsoft Excel spreadsheet into a Microsoft Word document, thereby linking the two documents

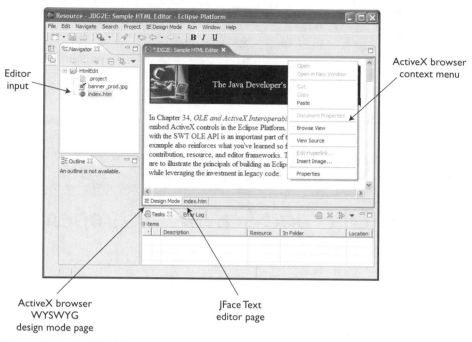

**Figure 34.1** HTML Editor Plug-in Using COM Support in SWT

together. This started a revolution and evolution of how software modules on Windows interacted. On Windows platforms, Eclipse provides the capability to embed ActiveX controls and OLE documents in SWT widgets, and JFace parts such as `EditorParts` and `ViewParts`.

SWT supports Component Object Model (COM) automation clients in that SWT implements the required interfaces of a COM container. If you normally program to COM server interfaces in C++, the SWT OLE support in Java should look familiar. However, the COM support provided is only what is required to support embedding and automating OLE documents and ActiveX controls; there are no methods to create other types of COM servers. In addition, implementing other types of COM clients and servers inside Eclipse is beyond the intended scope of the current SWT OLE framework.

So how does Java-based Eclipse integrate with COM-based applications and controls? The answer is that the package `org.eclipse.swt.ole.win32` provides lightweight Java wrappers, covering the in-proc COM automation servers. Specifically, this supports embedding and in-place activation of OLE documents and ActiveX controls.

### In-Place OLE Documents

This form of integration allows standard OLE-enabled tools that support in-place OLE documents (such as Microsoft Word and PowerPoint) to be invoked in Eclipse to edit documents of the corresponding type. Embedding an OLE document such as Word or PowerPoint is equivalent to embedding the entire application. The OLE document provides its own toolbar and menu bar for accessing its behavior. Built into Eclipse is a generic OLE document editor. In fact, this is how Eclipse runs Microsoft Office products like Word as an in-place editor. These tools are otherwise Eclipse-unaware, loosely integrated, and functionally they are the same as external-launch tools; that is, they open a document, edit it, and save it. Microsoft Word does not present Tools Options in places like Workbench properties or take advantage of the Resource API to create markers to display in the Task view. However, Eclipse provides support for accessing extended behaviors of in-place OLE documents, making way for a tightly integrated Eclipse-aware application.

### In-Place ActiveX Controls

Eclipse provides integration support for embedding and accessing the extended behavior of ActiveX controls. ActiveX controls such as a Web browser or calendar are a type of in-proc COM server that exposes its methods, properties, and events to Eclipse through the SWT COM container. It is this COM container support, which provides for the embedding and in-place activation, that makes possible deep Eclipse-aware integration, contributing Eclipse actions, properties, task views, and so on.

## COM Container Support

Embedding OLE documents and ActiveX controls in an SWT widget requires a COM container. Let's now look at some of the key COM interfaces that containers are required to implement, and then see how those interfaces relate to the SWT COM container implementation.

OLE containers are responsible for handling the interaction with the OLE objects they are hosting. OLE document containers provide storage for the document, listen to content object change notifications, and respond to mouse clicks.

OLE document containers implement the COM `IOleClientSite` interface to communicate with the document. OLE control containers handle the interaction with ActiveX controls. OLE control containers implement the

COM `IOleControlSite` interface to notify the container of activation changes and to inform it of the control of events.

Containers also manage the user interface by implementing the `IOleIn-PlaceSite` interface. It is through this interface that an OLE document can join a control site, take over the container's menus, and add toolbars.

Containing an embedded OLE object in an SWT widget requires two parts.

- An `OleFrame`
- An `OleClientSite` (for OLE documents) or `OleControlSite` (for ActiveX controls)

The "heart and soul" of the SWT OLE support lies in the `OleClientSite` and the `OleControlSite` objects. The "skeleton" of the SWT OLE support lies in the `OleFrame` object, which handles the menu management and window placement responsibilities.

### Creating an *OleFrame* Object

Embedded OLE objects require a frame to "hang" their user interface on. When integrating with the Eclipse user interface, you would typically create the frame in the `createPartControl` method of a `ViewPart` or an `EditorPart` object. Here is an example of creating an `OleFrame` object in a `createPart-Control` method.

```
public ActiveXWebBrowser createBrowserPartControl(Composite
                                                  parent) {
    displayArea = parent;
    FillLayout fillLayout = new FillLayout();
    displayArea.setLayout(fillLayout);
    webFrame = new OleFrame(displayArea, SWT.NONE);
    return createBrowserControl();
}
```

### Creating an *OleClientSite* Object

The next step is to create the `OleClientSite` object. There are two ways to create a client site.

- Create an `OleClientSite` object from a `ProgramID`. A `ProgramID` is a string that identifies the application. For example, the `ProgramID` for Word is `Word.Document` and the `ProgramID` for Excel is `Excel.Chart`. You can find the `ProgramID` for an application by looking in the Windows registry or by using the OLE/COM Object Viewer included in the Microsoft Platform SDK Tools (see Figure 34.2).

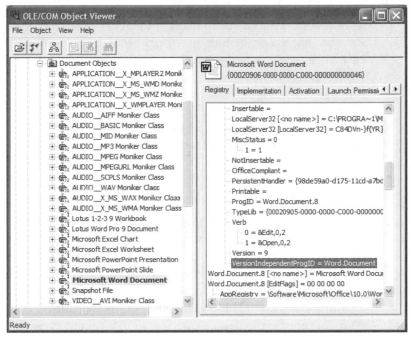

**Figure 34.2**  Finding the `ProgramID` Using the OLE/COM Object Viewer

To create a blank document, construct the `OleClientSite` object using the `ProgramID`.

```
-OleClientSite clientSite = new OleClientSite(frame,
SWT.NONE, "Word.Document");
```

- Create an `OleClientSite` object from an OLE storage file. For example, a .doc file created by Word is a storage file. The `OleClientSite` is typically created in the `createPartControl` method when embedded in a `WorkBenchPart`. Here is an example of how an `OleClientSite` is created on an OLE storage file.

```
File file = new File("C:\\OleDocumentation.doc");
OleClientSite clientSite = new OleClientSite(frame,
    SWT.NONE, file);
```

### Activating an OLE Object

The final step before an OLE document or ActiveX control becomes visible inside Eclipse is to activate the OLE object (often referred to as **in-place activation**). That is, the content object is edited in place without leaving the

PART V

Eclipse shell. You typically activate the client site immediately after creating the client site. To activate an object in place, invoke the object using one of the verbs that are predefined in the `org.eclipse.swt.ole.win32.OLE` class. You would typically find the following code for in-place activation of an OLE document. Invoking the `OLE.OLEIVERB_SHOW` verb makes the document's client site visible and active inside Eclipse.

```
if (!oleActivated) {
  clientSite.doVerb(OLE.OLEIVERB_SHOW);
  oleActivated = true;
}
```

### Deactivating an OLE Object

When embedding several OLE documents or ActiveX controls in Eclipse at the same time, you may want only one control active at a given time. Deactivated OLE objects are in a "Running" state. That means that the OLE object document contents are visible but removed from the toolbar and menu bar. The document is still running but does not respond to mouse or keyboard actions.

To deactivate an OLE document or ActiveX control, call `deactivate-InPlaceClient` on the `OleClientSite` or `OleControlSite` object.

```
currentSite.deactivateInPlaceClient();
```

It is not good to leave the `OleFrame` object for the parent to dispose of. When you are done with the embedded control/document, specifically call the `dispose` method. In addition, remember that `OleFrame`, `OleClientSite`, and `OleControlSite` are SWT widgets and that you must follow the SWT disposal rule: if you create a widget, then you must take care of disposing the widget. Typically you would dispose of the `OleFrame` object, and this would cause `OleClientSite` or `OleControlSite` to be disposed of too. Disposal of the site deactivates the embedded control/document, so a direct call to the `deactivateInPlaceClient` method is unnecessary.

In this example, the class `ActiveXBrowserView` creates the `OleFrame` object, so it is in the `dispose` method of that class that the `OleFrame` (see `web-Frame.dispose` ) is disposed of. Here is that `dispose` method.

```
public void dispose() {
  webFrame.dispose();
}
```

### Eclipse OLE Editor Support

When you create or use OLE documents within Eclipse, the file is the editor input to an instance of the class `OleEditor` in the package

org.eclipse.ui.internal.editorsupport.win32. The OLE editor does the
work of embedding the OLE document. The Workbench automatically
opens the OLE document editor in place and integrates its pull-down menu
options into the menu bar. If you require deeper integration, you should
consider implementing your own OLE editor. You might implement all that
is in the OleEditor class and then add in things like participating in the
Workbench preferences. The OleEditor then provides a good example to
start with.

An operation in the OleEditor class (an EditorPart) worth examining is
how the editor gains access to the java.io.File object in preparation to
open an OLE storage file. Recall from the editor framework discussions (in
Chapter 19, Editors) that the editor input is based on Eclipse resources.
Looking at the createPartControl method you will see that the editor gets
its IFileEditorInput as an IFile resource object.

```
// Set the input file.
    IEditorInput input = getEditorInput();
    if (input instanceof IFileEditorInput) {
      setResource(((IFileEditorInput) input).getFile());
      resource.getWorkspace().
        addResourceChangeListener(resourceListener);
    }
```

The next step then is to call the getLocation() method to get the location used to construct the java.io.File.

```
    protected void setResource(IFile file) {
      resource = file;
      source = new File(file.getLocation().toOSString());
    }
```

The OleEditor class has the right parameters to create the OleClientSite.
The following is the code that creates the OleClientSite.

```
    //If there was an OLE error or nothing has been created yet.
    if (clientFrame == null || clientFrame.isDisposed())
      return;
    // Create an OLE client site.
    clientSite = new OleClientSite(clientFrame, SWT.NONE, source);
    clientSite.setBackground(
      JFaceColors.getBannerBackground(clientFrame.getDisplay()));
    }
```

## Creating an *OleControlSite* Object

You create an OleControlSite object from the ProgramID of the ActiveX control. The Internet Explorer Web browser control shown below is one example

of an ActiveX control that you might consider using. The `ProgramID` for the Internet Explorer Web browser equals `Shell.Explorer`.

```
try {
  // Create Site and Automation obj(methods, properties & events).
  webControlSite =
    new OleControlSite(webFrame, SWT.NONE, "Shell.Explorer");
  OleAutomation oleAutomation = new OleAutomation(webControlSite);
  webBrowser = new ActiveXWebBrowser(oleAutomation, webControlSite);
} catch (SWTException ex) {
  // Creation may have failed because control is not installed on machine.
  Label label = new Label(webFrame, SWT.BORDER);
  InteropeditPlugin.logError("Could Not Create Browser Control", ex);
  label.setText("Could Not Create Browser Control");
  return null;
}
```

Here is an example that demonstrates embedding the Internet Explorer Web browser control inside a multipage editor.

```
// Create an Automation object for access to extended capabilities
webControlSite =
  new OleControlSite(webFrame, SWT.NONE, "Shell.Explorer");
OleAutomation oleAutomation = new OleAutomation(webControlSite);
webBrowser = new ActiveXWebBrowser(oleAutomation, webControlSite);
```

### Activating the *OleControlSite* Object

The `OLE.OLEIVERB_INPLACEACTIVATE` verb opens the OLE control for editing in place.

```
// In-place activate the ActiveX control.
activated =
  (webControlSite.doVerb(OLE.OLEIVERB_INPLACEACTIVATE) == OLE.S_OK);
```

## OLE Automation—Accessing Extended Behavior

OLE automation is a way that a COM server exposes its properties, methods, and events to a COM client. Automation is a richer interface than the predefined commands available for the `exec` command. In this way, an application can make all sorts of operations available to automation. For example, Microsoft Word defines many OLE automation classes. Using the Object Browser (see Figure 34.3) in the Microsoft SDK, you will find classes like the `Paragraph` class and its members. The members listed on the right side of Figure 34.3 provide you the opportunity to access the extended behavior. The `Paragraph` class exposes both properties, such as `Alignment`, and methods, such as `Indent`.

**Figure 34.3** Word Automations, Properties, and Methods

The COM interfaces that we have discussed up until now—IOleControl-Site, IOleClientSite, and IOleFrame—all use early binding. That is, the interfaces to the COM objects are known at compile time. Automation requires a runtime, late binding. It is the IDispatch interface in OLE that makes automation possible. The OLE document or ActiveX control must support the IDispatch interface in order to provide OleAutomation support.

## OLE exec Command

The exec command is a generic but limited way of sending a predefined set of commands to either an OLE document or an ActiveX control. It is implemented as a method in OleClientSite:

```
int OleClientSite.exec(int cmdID, int options, Variant in,
Variant out)
```

The OLE object may or may not implement the command you send. You can ask an OLE object if it recognizes the command using OleClientSite.queryStatus(int cmdID).

Here is an example of how the exec method is used in the OleEditor class to invoke the print function in Word.

```
public void doPrint() {
  if (clientSite == null)
    return;
  BusyIndicator.showWhile(clientSite.getDisplay(), new Runnable() {
    public void run() {
      clientSite.exec(
        OLE.OLECMDID_PRINT,
        OLE.OLECMDEXECOPT_PROMPTUSER,
        null,
        null);
      // Note: to check for success: above == SWTOLE.S_OK
    }
  });
}
```

## IDispatch Interface

The SWT OleAutomation object implements the IDispatch interface. In the following example, the automation object is created on the Internet Explorer Web browser control.

```
OleControlSite controlSite =
  new OleControlSite(frame, SWT.NONE, "Shell.Explorer");
OleAutomation automation = new OleAutomation(controlSite);
```

With an automation object that has a reference to the object's IDispatch interface, you can begin to automate the object, that is, listen for events, invoke methods, and get and set properties. In the case of Internet Explorer, that means you can call a method that will navigate to a URL and load a Web page. To find the appropriate method, look at the typelib (interface definition). You can use the OLE/COM Object Viewer that comes with the tools in the Microsoft Platform SDK (see Figure 34.4) to view the typelib. The Interface Definition Language (IDL) describes the OLE automation interfaces. In the right pane of Figure 34.4 you can see the IDL that pertains to the `Navigate` method. You can then browse the automation members, properties, methods, named arguments, and so on. In addition, this is where you will find the member's dispatch ID. The `Navigate` method's dispatch id is 0x00000068 hex or 104 in decimal.

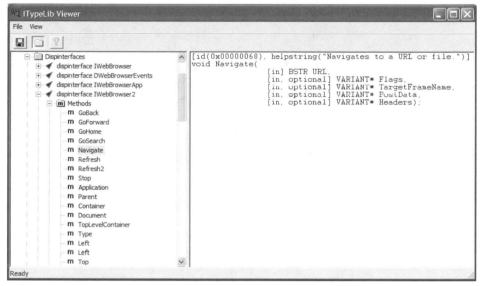

**Figure 34.4** `typelib` View of `IDispatch` Interface of Internet Explorer

The `OleAutomation` class implements the `getIDsOfNames` method, which, given a list of strings, makes a call into the OLE automation object to retrieve their ids. Therefore, given the method name string and the named parameter, the method returns the dispatch ids necessary to automate the navigation of the Internet Explorer Web browser control.

```
int[] rgdispid =
  oleAutomation.getIDsOfNames(new String[] { "Navigate", "URL" });
int dispIdMember = rgdispid[0];
```

## Methods

There are three ways to invoke methods on an automation object.

- Invoke without parameters.
- Pass multiple parameters.
- Because some of these parameters may be optional, you must pass an identifier for the parameter as well as the value of the parameter.

PART V

Here are the variations on invoking methods. We will examine each in detail.

- `Variant invoke(int dispIdMember)`
  This method doesn't take any parameters.
- `Variant invoke(int dispIdMember, Variant[] rgvarg)`
  All parameters are mandatory but none are named.
- `Variant invoke(int dispIdMember, Variant[] rgvarg, int[] rgdispidNamedArgs)`

Some parameters are optional, so all the parameters are named.

### Invocation Without Parameters

The Refresh method in the Web browser object doesn't take any parameters. Here is the IDL that corresponds to the Refresh method. Notice that there are no mandatory or optional parameters for this method and that it doesn't return anything. The typical method returns a type as specified in the IDL like int, long, IDispatch *, BSTR, VARIANT_BOOL, or VARIANT_*.

```
[id(0xfffffdda), helpstring("Refresh the currently viewed page.")]
void Refresh();
```

Here is the Eclipse code that demonstrates invoking the Refresh method without specifying any parameters.

```
public void Refresh() {
// dispid= 4294966746, type=METHOD, name="Refresh"
int[] rgdispid =
  oleAutomation.getIDsOfNames(new String[] { "Refresh" });
int dispIdMember = rgdispid[0];
oleAutomation.invoke(dispIdMember);
}
```

### Variant Types

Invocation that involves passing parameters requires a discussion about Variant types. A **Variant** is a generic OLE mechanism for passing data of different types via a common interface. Uses of OLE automation objects require Variants for getting properties, setting properties, or invoking methods on an OLE control or OLE document. Figure 34.5 shows the methods of the Variant types.

To invoke the Navigate methods on the Web browser controls, you need to wrapper the Java type into a Variant object before it can be passed to the

**Figure 34.5**   Variant Class Constructors and Methods

automation object. The SWT OLE Variant class supports many but not all COM Variant types.

The following is an example that uses the www.eclipse.org Java String constant to convert to a Variant type using the Variant(String) constructor.

```
public int Navigate(String url) {
  // dispid=104, type-METHOD, name-"Navigate"
  int[] rgdispid =
    oleAutomation.getIDsOfNames(new String[] { "Navigate", "URL" });
  int dispIdMember = rgdispid[0];
  Variant[] rgvarg = new Variant[1];
  rgvarg[0] = new Variant("www.eclipse.org");
```

## Invocation with Parameters

The Navigate method of the Web browser takes several arguments, but there is only one mandatory parameter: the URL. This is illustrated in the following IDL that defines the parameters of the Navigate method.

```
[id(0x00000068), helpstring("Navigates to a URL or file.")]
void Navigate(
              [in] BSTR URL,
              [in, optional] VARIANT* Flags,
              [in, optional] VARIANT* TargetFrameName,
              [in, optional] VARIANT* PostData,
              [in, optional] VARIANT* Headers);
```

PART V

This example sets only the mandatory parameter, not any of the optional arguments. It is the call on the `invoke` method on the OLE automation object that actually completes the navigation behavior.

```
public int Navigate() {
  // dispid=104, type=METHOD, name="Navigate"
  int[] rgdispid =
    oleAutomation.getIDsOfNames(new String[] { "Navigate", "URL" });
  int dispIdMember = rgdispid[0];

  Variant[] rgvarg = new Variant[1];
  rgvarg[0] = new Variant("www.eclipse.org");
  int[] rgdispidNamedArgs = new int[1];
  rgdispidNamedArgs[0] = rgdispid[1]; // identifier of argument
  Variant pVarResult =
    oleAutomation.invoke(dispIdMember, rgvarg, rgdispidNamedArgs);

  if (pVarResult == null)
    return 0;
  return pVarResult.getInt();
}
```

## Properties

The COM `typelib` controls properties. What is interesting is that not only can you set and get properties, but you can also listen to when those properties are changed, such as when a set property has been called.

### Getting Properties

To get a property from an automation object, use the `OleAutomation` method `getProperty`, as shown in the following example.

```
/**
 * Returns the current state of the control.
 *
 * @return the current state of the control, one of:
 *         READYSTATE_UNINITIALIZED;
 *         READYSTATE_LOADING;
 *         READYSTATE_LOADED;
 *         READYSTATE_INTERACTIVE;
 *         READYSTATE_COMPLETE.
 */
public int getReadyState() {
  // dispid=4294966771, type=PROPGET, name="ReadyState"
  int[] rgdispid =
    oleAutomation.getIDsOfNames(new String[] { "ReadyState" });
  int dispIdMember = rgdispid[0];
```

```
    Variant pVarResult = oleAutomation.getProperty(dispIdMember);
    if (pVarResult == null)
      return -1;
    return pVarResult.getInt();
  }
```

## Setting Properties

Setting a property is very similar to getting a property. In this case the method is `boolean OleAutomation.setProperty(int dispIdMember, Variant rgvarg)`.

The `designmode` property in the HTML document object indicates when the control is in rich HTML edit mode. Here is the IDL that defines that property.

```
[id(0x000003f6), propget, hidden]
BSTR designMode();
```

The following code, taken from the example that accompanies this chapter, turns the browser into a rich HTML editor by setting the `designmode` property to "On."

```
public boolean setDesignModeProperty(String flag) {
  OleAutomation document = getDocumentAutomation();
  // Call Getter method.
  int[] rgdispid = document.getIDsOfNames(new String[]
    { "designMode" });
  int dispIdMember = rgdispid[0];
  Variant[] rgvarg = new Variant[1];
  rgvarg[0] = new Variant(flag);
  boolean rc = document.setProperty(dispIdMember, rgvarg);
  return rc;
}
```

## *Events and Property Listeners*

The `addEventListener` method of the `OleControlSite` object is used to set up an `OleListener` to receive events fired by the ActiveX Control.

### Event Listeners

Here is the method to call to add an event listener.

```
public void addEventListener(int eventID, OleListener listener)
```

The `eventID` is the dispatch id associated with the control event. The `OleListener` is an interface that defines the method `handleEvent(OleEvent event)`.

```
public void addEventListener(OleAutomation automation,
  int eventID, OleListener listener)
```

As shown in this example, to listen for progress change events in the Web browser control you look into the IDL for the dispatch id (0x0000006c hex or 108 decimal) that corresponds to the `ProgressChange` event.

```
[id(0x0000006c), helpstring("Fired when download progress
  is updated.")]
void ProgressChange(
                [in] long Progress,
                [in] long ProgressMax);
```

The OLE client adds the listener implementing the `handleEvent` in an anonymous class. Using the `OleEvent`, the handler interrogates the event object for event context information and reacts to what it finds there.

```
// Respond to ProgressChange events by updating the Progress bar.
  webControlSite.addEventListener(108, new OleListener() {
    //0x6C from the type library.
    public void handleEvent(OleEvent event) {
      Variant progress = event.arguments[0];
      Variant maxProgress = event.arguments[1];
      if (progress == null || maxProgress == null)
        return;
      webProgress.setMaximum(maxProgress.getInt());
      webProgress.setSelection(progress.getInt());
    }
  });
```

## Property Listeners

The `OLEAutomation.addPropertyListener`, similar to the event listener, adds the listener to receive notifications when the property changes.

```
public void addPropertyListener(int propertyID,
                               OleListener listener)
```

The parameter `propertyID` identifies the property.

This example is listening to changes to the Web browser control Ready-State. Here is the IDL that defines the `ReadyState` property.

```
[id(0xfffffdf3), propget, bindable]
tagREADYSTATE ReadyState();
```

The `addPropertyListener` is added to the Web browser control on the dispatch id `-525`, which corresponds to the `ReadyStateProperty`. Like event listeners, the `OleEvent` listener is required to implement the `handleEvent` method inside an anonymous class.

```
// Listen for changes to the ready state and print out the
// current state.
  controlSite.addPropertyListener(-525, new OleListener() {
    public void handleEvent(OleEvent event) {
      if (event.detail == OLE.PROPERTY_CHANGING) {
```

```
                    // Print out the old state.
                    Variant state = automation.getProperty(READYSTATE);
                    System.out.println("Web State changing from " +
                      state.getInt());
                    event.doit = true; // Allow property change to happen.

                }
```

## Example Summary

You are now ready to explore the example provided on the CD-ROM. In this example, defined in the project com.ibm.jdg2e.activex.editor, you will see how to integrate the Internet Explorer Web browser control deeply into an Eclipse multipage editor. This Eclipse–ActiveX hybrid editor demonstrates how to use the input from Eclipse resources and connects custom editor actions to the Eclipse toolbar and menus.

## Chapter Summary

SWT allows OLE tools to open in place in Eclipse and contribute views or editors into the Workbench perspectives, thereby avoiding a major rewrite on Windows platforms. Because OLE document applications are monolithic in nature, it is more difficult to hide the seams between the OLE document and Eclipse. Therefore, the best option for seamless integration of legacy tools written for the Windows platform in C++ is by embedding ActiveX controls.

## Reference

Irvine, Veronika. March 22, 2001. ActiveX support in SWT. http://www.eclipse.org.

# PART VI

## *Exercises*

Concepts and examples are great, but there is no substitute for digging in and getting your hands dirty. This is especially true in those cases where the journey (learning Eclipse) is more important than the destination (creating some code).

This final part of the book includes nine highly structured exercises to ensure that your initial Eclipse experience proceeds smoothly.

- Exercise 1, Using Eclipse, gives you a hands-on tour of Eclipse to reinforce the concepts covered in Chapter 2, Getting Started with Eclipse.
- Exercise 2, Using Java Development Tools, provides sample code and step-by-step exercises to illustrate the use of the JDT as covered in Chapter 3, Using Java Development Tools.
- Exercise 3, Running and Debugging Java, continues Exercise 2 and takes you through debugging Java programs, as covered in Chapter 4, Running and Debugging Java.
- Exercise 4, Developing a Simple Web Commerce Application with Eclipse, pulls together what you learned in Chapters 3 and 4 by showing you how to create a simple Web commerce application based on a

Java servlet. The servlet is developed under Eclipse and deployed on an Apache Tomcat server.

- Exercise 5, Working as a Team with CVS, builds on Chapter 5, Teaming Up with Eclipse, by providing hands-on experience similar to everyday use of CVS.
- Exercise 6, Developing Your First Plug-in, shows how to create your first plug-in, building on what you learned in Chapter 8, Overview of the Eclipse Architecture, and Chapter 9, Getting Started: Plug-in Development.
- Exercise 7, Developing Your First Rich Client Application, shows you all the steps required to create a basic rich client application running inside Eclipse. It builds on what was covered in Chapter 10, Creating Applications Using the Rich Client Platform.
- Exercise 8, Developing a Rich Client Application with Dynamically Added Plug-ins, continues your understanding of rich client application programming and focuses on creating and installing dynamic plug-ins.
- Exercise 9, Deploying Your Product Using Features, complements Chapter 13, Defining Features and Products, by allowing you to experience the complete process of feature creation, packaging, and several deployment options.

In addition, the CD-ROM accompanying this book is packed with well-documented working examples that you're free to adapt to your needs. You'll find detailed instructions about how to install them and the code that you'll need for the exercises in the `readme.html` file on the CD-ROM. The CD-ROM also includes documentation for the examples and exercises, both of which are integrated with the Eclipse Help system.

# EXERCISE 1

## *Using Eclipse*

The objective of this exercise is to provide you with a hands-on introduction to using Eclipse, including creating and using resources, manipulating the user interface, and accessing online documentation. This exercise assumes you are relatively new to IDEs in general. If not, it may be enough for you to skim this exercise and go on to the next.

This exercise is designed to reinforce what we presented in Chapter 2, Getting Started with Eclipse. To get the most out of the exercise, you should read the chapter first because much of the explanation for why you are doing something in an exercise step is presented there. The exercise is divided into logical sections, each building on the previous one.

At the end of this exercise you should be able to do the following.

- Understand the basic structure of Eclipse.
- Navigate the Eclipse user interface.
- Move and resize views.
- Compare and replace projects and editions of resources.
- Recover deleted files and projects.
- Customize a perspective.
- Open multiple Eclipse windows.
- Access the online documentation.

## Section 1: Your First Eclipse Project

Let's get started. In this section you'll explore the Eclipse user interface and create and import projects, files, and folders. There is no setup for these exercises, nor any sample code or files. You just need to have Eclipse installed. You'll create what you need as you go.

1. In your Eclipse installation directory, invoke `eclipse.exe`. You will see the Workspace Launcher dialog asking you which workspace you want to work with. Select **OK** to accept the default. We'll get to this again a little later. When you bring up Eclipse for the first time, you see an introductory view with an overview of information about Eclipse. Click around on some of the links if you want to explore this information. Try **What's New** and then **New and Noteworthy** to see the new stuff in the latest Eclipse release. Use ⇨ and ⇦ as your browser **Forward** and **Back** actions; ⌂ returns you to the initial home page. When you're through, click on **Go to the workbench** 🐾. This puts you in the Resource perspective, as shown in Figure Ex1.1. The Eclipse user interface is presented as an adjustable multipaned window comprising a menu bar and menu items, a toolbar, editors, views,

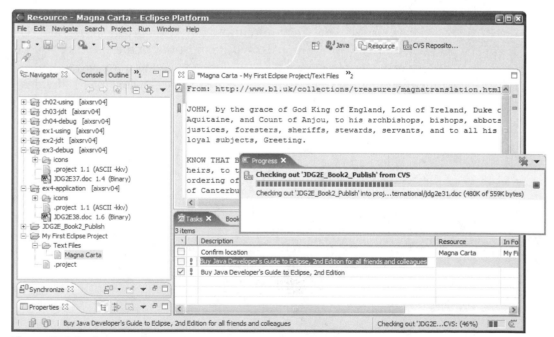

**Figure Ex1.1**　Resource Perspective

message and status areas, and a fast view bar for views. For an overview of these visual elements, refer to Chapter 2.

2. Create a project by selecting **File > New > Project....** You can also
   select **New** 🗂. This opens the New Project wizard (see Figure Ex1.2).

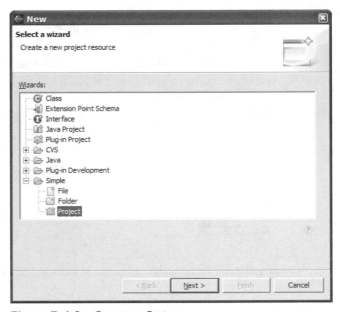

**Figure Ex1.2**   Creating a Project

3. Select **Project** under **Simple**, and then select **Next**. You'll go to the
   next page of the wizard, where you'll be prompted to enter the name
   of the project.

4. Enter My First Project as the project name, leave the other defaults,
   and select **Finish**. Your new project appears in the Navigator view. If
   you expand the project (by clicking on the **+** symbol to the left of the
   project), you'll see that Eclipse has added the file .project. This is a
   file Eclipse maintains to keep information about your project. Don't
   worry about this file; it's for Eclipse's use only.

5. Next you'll create a folder to hold your files. Select **File > New > Folder**,
   or select the **New** pull-down menu 🗂 ▼ from the toolbar and then
   select **Folder....** Enter Text Files as the folder name, and select **Finish**.
   In the Navigator view, you'll see the folder added to your project.

6. In the Navigator view, select the folder you just created. From the
   Navigator menu bar or the toolbar, use the **New** pull-down menu

again to create a new file. Enter My First File as the file name, and select **Finish**. In the Navigator view, you'll see that the file has been added to your project. The file will also be opened in its associated editor. In this case, there's no file extension, so Eclipse opens the file in the default text editor.

7. In the editor, add some text to the file. As soon as you start typing, an asterisk (*) is added as a prefix to the file name on the editor tab. This indicates that you have changed the contents of the file.

8. Create a second text file in the same folder and name it My Second File. Add some text to this file as well. Create a second simple project called My Second Project.

     The Navigator view should now appear as shown in Figure Ex1.3.

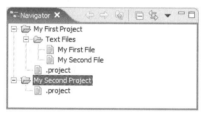

**Figure Ex1.3**    Project Organization in the Navigator View

9. You've created files; now let's add some existing files to one of your projects. You're going to do this by importing files you have on your file system. Select **My Second Project** in the Navigator view and select **Import...** from the context menu (use a right-click). In the Import wizard, select to import from the **File system**, and then select **Next**.

10. Select **Browse...** to browse your file system for a folder with some files to import (it really doesn't matter which files). In the Import from Directory dialog, select a folder and then select **OK**.

11. In the Import wizard, expand the folder in the left pane to see its files and any subfolders it has (see Figure Ex1.4). If you check a folder in the left pane, you will import the folder and all the folders and files it contains. If you expand the folder, you can select from the subfolders and the files in each subfolder. If you select a folder in the left pane, you can individually select its files in the right pane. Select a set of folders and/or files, and select **Finish** to import the folders and/or files you selected.

     You'll see the files you selected to import in the Navigator view.

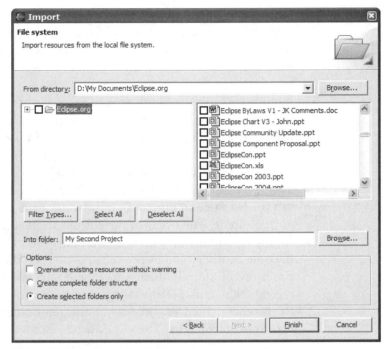

**Figure Ex1.4**  Importing Resources

Here's a tip: You can also drag and drop files to add them to a project. For example, open Windows Explorer, drag a file from it, and drop it on **My Second Project**.

You have just created your first Eclipse project and populated it with files and folders.

## Section 2: Editors and Views

Let's take a look now at using editors and views. You'll learn how to edit files, manipulate views and editors, and use tasks and bookmarks. You're going to start where you left the previous section. You should be in the Resource perspective with two editors open.

1. Close **My Second File** by clicking on the **X** on the editor's tab. You can also do this by selecting **Close** from the context menu on the editor tab or by using the menu option **File > Close** (**Ctrl+F4**). You can even close all open editors at once by using **File > Close All** (**Ctrl+Shift+F4**).

2. Reopen **My Second File** by double-clicking on it in the Navigator view. You can also select the file and select **Open** or **Open With** from the Navigator context menu. When you use **Open With**, the **System Editor** option refers to the program registered with the operating system for files of this type.

3. Double-click on the blank area to the right of the editor tabs or on one of the file names on the tabs. You'll see that the editor expands to fill the entire window. This is useful for serious editing when you need more screen real estate. Double-click again to restore the editor to its original size. You can also use ⬜ and ⬓ in the editor tab area.

4. You can change the order of the editors in the editor pane. Select the tab for **My Second File**, drag it in front of the tab for **My First File**, and release it. The order of the editor tabs is updated.

5. If you have many editors open on many files, the number of tabs can become cumbersome as the tabs become smaller and smaller, sometimes revealing only the first few characters of the editors' labels. To remedy this, collapse the editor tabs to one by selecting **Window > Preferences**, then **Workbench**, and then **Editors**. Deselect **Show multiple editor tabs**. There is now one editor tab with an annotation, **>>**, and a subscript indicating the number of other editors. Click on this annotation to see a list of open editors. Begin typing to narrow the list to select the editor you want displayed (see Figure Ex1.5). You can see the same pop-up editor list by pressing **Ctrl+E**.

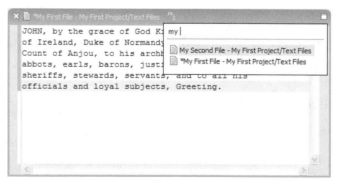

**Figure Ex1.5**   Selecting an Editor Session

6. Resize the area the editors occupy by selecting and dragging the bottom or left border of the editor pane. You can also do this by selecting

**Size** from the editor tab's context menu, choosing a side to move (e.g., **Size > Left**), and using the arrow keys.

7. Open editors are stacked one in front of another. You can change this organization by tiling one or more of the editors within the editor area. Create another file called **My Third File**. Select the tab of **My Third File** and drag it to the left border of the editor pane. When the cursor changes to a left arrow, drop the editor. Select the tab of **My Second File**, drag it to the bottom border of the editor pane below **My Third File**, and drop it. Figure Ex1.6 shows the result.

**Figure Ex1.6**   Reorganizing Editors

8. Of course, you can also restack the editors. Select the tab of **My First File** and drag it on top of the tab of **My Second File** or to the area to the right of it. Select the tab of **My Third File** and drag it on top of the other two tabs or to the area to the right of them. The editors should be stacked again. The order of the tabs may have changed from what it was before, depending on where exactly you dropped the editors.

9. Click anywhere in the Tasks view, which is below the editor, and then press **F12**. The editor for the resource you were most recently editing is now active. This is a quick way to get back to your most recent active editor. If you want to get back to the last change you made in an open editor, select **Last Edit Location** ⤺.

10. Press **Ctrl+F6** to see a pop-up with a list of all open editors. Continue to press **F6** to cycle through the editors in the pop-up. The editor selected when you release **Ctrl** will be made the active editor. When you have a lot of editors open, this is more efficient than working your way through the editor tabs.

11. You've opened, closed, moved, and resized the editors. You can do the same with views. Click on the **X** on the top right of the Tasks view to close the view. You can also select **Close** from the Tasks view menu. Reopen the view by selecting **Window > Show View > Tasks**. Not all views are listed in this short list; you may have to select **Other...**, a category, and then the view you actually want to open.

12. Like editors, views can be reorganized in the window. Select the title bar of the Navigator view and drag it onto the title bar of the Outline view. These views are now stacked (see Figure Ex1.7). You can navigate between them with the tabs or in the same way that you selected from multiple editors by clicking on the **>>** annotation.

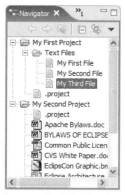

**Figure Ex1.7**    Stacked Views

13. Grab a view by its title bar and try dragging it around. Observe how the cursor changes. A folder icon 🗗 indicates that the view will be stacked. An arrow icon ◀ indicates that the view will be placed to that side of the view or editor it's over. You can do this with a single view by dragging its tab and with a group of stacked views by dragging the whole tab area.

14. You can also take a view and condense it to an icon on the fast view bar. By default, this is the wide border on the bottom of the window, to the left of the message area. This is a handy way to free up screen real estate. Select **Window > Show View > Bookmarks** to open the Bookmarks view. Right-click on the view's tab and select **Fast View**. You will now see an icon for the view on the fast view bar. You can also grab the view by its title bar, drag it to the fast view bar, and drop it there.

15. Select the icon for the Bookmarks view you just placed in the fast view bar. Watch as it slides out to become visible (see Figure Ex1.8).

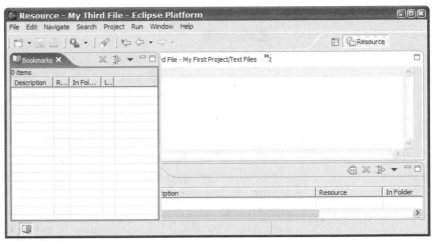

**Figure Ex1.8**    Displaying a Fast View

16. Select the same icon again to see it slide back to become hidden. If you resize the view while it is being displayed, it will return to that size each time you reshow it as a fast view. You can restore the view to its original state by right-clicking on the fast view icon and deselecting **Fast View** or by simply dragging it from the fast view bar back onto the main window.

17. In addition to stacking views and reducing them to fast views, you can drag a view out of the main window, or "tear it off," and have it appear as its own window. Try this by grabbing the Bookmarks view by its title bar, dragging it outside of the main window, and dropping it there. To redock it, simply drag it back.

18. At this point, you're probably wondering how to clean up the mess you've created of your user interface. Select **Window > Reset Perspective** to do so. The user interface returns to its original configuration.

19. As with the editors, you also have keyboard shortcuts for switching between views or the set of editors. The set of open editors is treated as a view for purposes of navigation, denoted simply as **Editor** in the list of views. Press **Ctrl+F7** to switch to the next view and **Ctrl+Shift+F7** to go back to the previous one (see Figure Ex1.9). The list of views

remains visible as long as you hold down the keys. Pressing **F7** repeatedly while holding **Ctrl** or **Ctrl+Shift** moves the view selection.

**Figure Ex1.9**   Views List

20. Use bookmarks for marking files or specific locations in a file. Open
    the Bookmarks view again and drag it to stack it on top of the Tasks
    view. Select the open editor for **My First File**. In the marker area of the
    editor (the left margin), display the context menu and select **Add
    Bookmark....** Name the bookmark Start here tomorrow and select
    **OK**. You'll see the bookmark added in both the marker area of the
    editor and the Bookmarks view (see Figure Ex1.10).

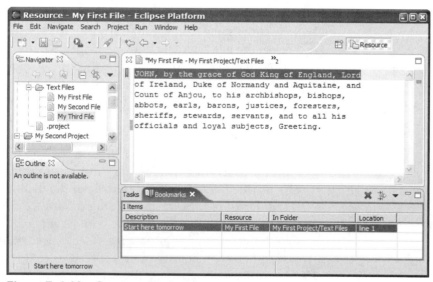

**Figure Ex1.10**   Creating a Bookmark

21. Close **My First File** and then double-click on the bookmark you just
    added. The file associated with the bookmark is opened and the line it

refers to is selected. You can delete a bookmark by using the context menu of the Bookmarks view or by selecting **Remove Bookmark** from the context menu of the bookmark in the editor marker area.

22. Tasks are for tracking specific work items or just creating reminders for yourself. Like bookmarks, tasks can be associated with a resource and location in the resource, although they don't have to be. Unlike bookmarks, tasks have state and priority information. You create tasks in the same way you create bookmarks. Select the editor on **My Second File**. In the marker area, bring up the context menu and select **Add Task....**. Enter text for the task, select a priority, and then select **OK** to create the task (see Figure Ex1.11).

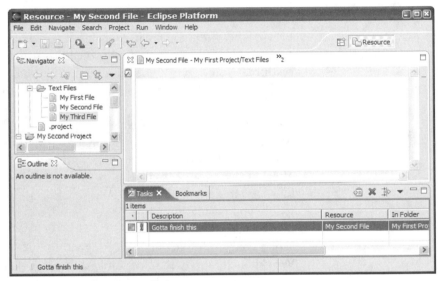

**Figure Ex1.11**    Creating a Task

23. Close **My Second File** and double-click on the task you just created. As with bookmarks, an editor is opened on the file associated with the task, and the line the task references is selected.

    To create a task associated with no file, select **Add Task** 🗒 in the Tasks view.

24. Finally, let's take a look at the toolbars. You can reorganize a group of icons on the toolbar to reorder them or to put them on another toolbar line. Select one of the dividers between the groups of toolbar buttons and try moving the group on the same line or to another line.

The divider between the toolbar icons and the perspective icons can be moved by clicking and dragging. Select **Window > Preferences** and then **Appearance** under **Workbench**. Deselect **Show text on the perspective bar**. This allows more of your open perspective icons to be visible.

Now you've seen how to manipulate views, editors, the toolbar, and the perspective bar. You've also created tasks and bookmarks on files.

## Section 3: Working with Resources

In this section you're going to look in a bit more detail at projects. You'll also see how to compare and replace resources with earlier revisions and recover resources you've deleted.

1. Previously, when you created projects, you accepted the default values provided by Eclipse, including project location. By default, the resources you define are located in a folder named workspace in your main Eclipse folder. Browse this folder to view its contents. You'll see a folder structure that pretty much mirrors the project structure you see in your workspace. Next we're going to explore two ways in which you reference resources outside the default workspace location, first with linked resources, and second with a project defined at an alternate location. This flexibility gives you all the features of projects, files, and folders managed by Eclipse while allowing you to store them where you prefer. For those of you familiar with Linux, this is similar to an alias.

2. Open your preferences by selecting **Window > Preferences**. Expand **Workbench**, and then select **Linked Resources**. Ensure **Enable Linked Resources** is checked. Select **OK** to close the Preferences dialog.

3. Right-click on **My First Project** in the Navigator view and select **New > File** from the context menu. Select a name for the folder. Select **Advanced** to make visible the specifications for linked resources. Check **Link to file in the file system**. Select **Browse...** to browse your file system for a file. Select a file, provide a name for the linked file, and then select **Finish** to define the linked file. You'll see a new linked file included as part of the project. Notice that it doesn't have to have the same name as the file to which it is linked.

   Now, right-click on **My First Project** and select **New > Folder**. Perform the same steps to create a linked folder in **My First Project**. The Navigator view should now look something like Figure Ex1.12.

**NOTE** Take care when you clean up your work. You can delete the linked file or folder and only the link is deleted. The folder and files they point to are not deleted. However, if you open a linked folder and delete files or folders it contains, you are deleting them from the file system.

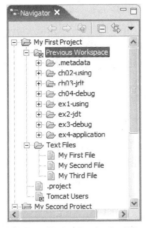

**Figure Ex1.12** Linked Resources

4. When you create a project, you can create it in an alternate location, which is not the default location in the folder workspace. Open the wizard to create a new project (see Figure Ex1.13). Call it My Alternate Project. Deselect **Use default** for **Project contents** and select **Browse...**

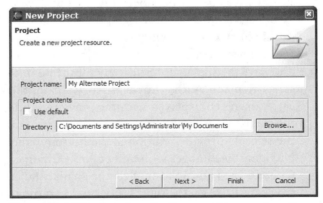

**Figure Ex1.13** Creating a Project at an Alternate Location

to select a location for your project. Choose a folder in your file system with a few files and subfolders. Select **Finish** to create the project.

In the Navigator view, you'll see the new project. You'll also see that the files and folders at the location you specified are automatically part of the project. A `.project` file is added to the file system to identify the target folder as an Eclipse project.

**NOTE**  You created a project referring to the files and folders at the location you specified, *but you did not copy the files and folders*. They still exist only in their original location. This means that if you delete the project and you select to have it contents deleted, you will also delete the files and folders at the alternate location. If this is the only copy of these resources, they will be lost. Take care when deleting projects at alternate locations, especially when you mapped the project to an existing folder and file tree with content. Choosing **Do not delete contents** from the Confirm Project Delete dialog will remove the project from your workspace but preserve the files and folders it referenced.

5. Copying and moving files and folders between projects and other folders is easy. Select a file or folder in the Navigator view, and then select **Copy** from the context menu. Select another project or folder, and then select **Paste** from the context menu. Your first selection is copied to the second project or folder.

To move a file or folder, simply drag it and drop it on another folder or project. You can also copy a file with drag and drop. If you want to copy the file to another folder, press **Ctrl**, and then drag and drop the file to the target folder. Not only does this work within Eclipse, it also works between Eclipse and Windows Explorer.

6. Now let's replace a file with a previous edition of it. Open an editor on **My First File** or switch to this editor if it is already open. Make a few changes to your text and save the file. Make some more changes and save the file again. Select **My First File** in the Navigator view and select **Replace With > Local History...** from the context menu.

A dialog is displayed with the previous editions of **My First File** in the top pane and a side-by-side comparison of the current contents with the selected previous edition in the bottom pane (see Figure Ex1.14).

7. Navigate the changes with **Select Next Change** ⇩ and **Select Previous Change** ⇧. You can also select the change indicators (rectangles) in the overview ruler on the right border. Select a previous edition of **My First File** and then select **Replace** to replace its contents in the editor.

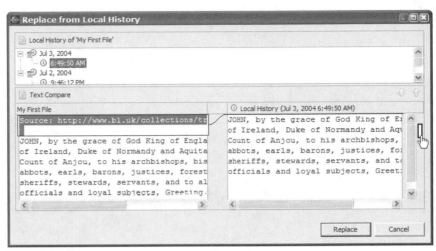

**Figure Ex1.14**  Replacing a File from Local History

Selecting **Compare With > Local History...** is similar to **Replace With**, except that **Compare With** only shows the differences. It does not allow you to modify the file.

8. You can also compare two projects. In the Navigator view, select **My First Project** and **My Second Project**. Then select **Compare With > Each Other** from the context menu.

   A compare editor is displayed showing the files and folders that are different between the two projects. The small plus (**+**) indicates the resource exists in the first project but not the second, and the minus (**-**) indicates the resource exists in the second project but not the first. The file .project has no label decoration because it exists in both projects. Double-click on the .project file. The differences are shown in the bottom pane (see Figure Ex1.15). Close the Compare Editor by clicking on the **X** on the tab of the editor. You can perform the same kind of comparison between two folders and two files.

9. Now you'll see how to recover files you've deleted. From the Navigator view, delete **My First File** and **My Second File** from **My First Project**. Select **My First Project** and then select **Restore From Local History...** from the context menu. A list of files you have deleted from the project is displayed.

10. Select a file to see the editions of the file Eclipse is maintaining. Select an edition to see its contents in the bottom pane (see Figure Ex1.16). To restore a file, select the file in the upper left pane, select

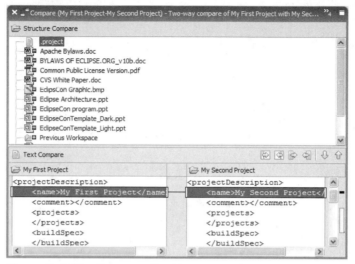

**Figure Ex1.15**   Comparing Two Projects

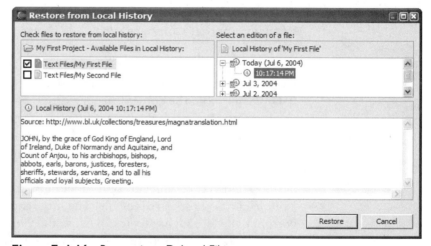

**Figure Ex1.16**   Recovering a Deleted File

an edition, and then select **Restore**. Restore the files you deleted from **My First Project**.

11. You can also recover projects you delete, if you do not delete their contents. Select **My First Project** in the Navigator view and then select **Delete** from the context menu. At the prompt, do *not* select to delete its contents. From the Navigator view, select **Import...** from the context menu. Select **Existing Project into Workspace** and then select

**Next**. Select **Browse...** Browse your file system to go to folder workspace in your main Eclipse folder. In this folder, you'll see the folder **My First Project**. This is the contents of the project left when you deleted the definition of the project. Select this folder and then select **OK**. If this folder is recognized as a project (by the presence of the file .project), **Finish** is enabled. Select **Finish** to recover the project. Verify this in the Navigator view.

You've now seen a bit more detail on creating projects and how to use local history information to compare resources and recover ones you've deleted.

## Section 4: Perspectives

Let's work a little more with perspectives. In this section, you'll customize your own perspective.

1. At this point, if you have followed these procedures, you have modified the default layout of the Resource perspective by adding the Bookmarks view. Close the Resource perspective by selecting **Close** from the context menu of the Resource perspective icon (to the right of the toolbar icons). Select **Window > Open Perspective > Other...** and then select the **Resource** perspective. The Resource perspective opens again, but without the layout changes you had made.

2. Change the Resource perspective by reorganizing the views and adding or deleting views. Select **Window > Save Perspective As...**, name the new perspective My First Perspective (no pun intended), and select **OK** to create your customized perspective.

    Observe the change to the perspective icon text. It now reflects that this is your perspective. Select **Window > Open Perspective > Other...** You'll see that your customized perspective is added to this list. Select **Cancel** to close the dialog.

3. Select **Window > Customize Perspective...** You'll see a dialog listing the menu actions that can be included in your perspective (see Figures Ex1.17 and Ex1.18). On the **Shortcuts** page, you select entries to appear in the menus for your perspective. The entries you select here will appear under **File > New**, **Window > Open Perspective**, and **Window > Show View** in your customized perspective. The other items will be available but are selected through the **Other...** menu button first and then selecting the item from a list. On the

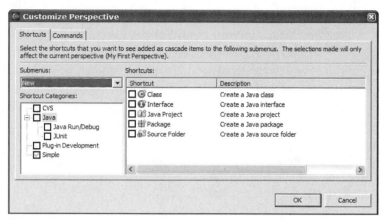

**Figure Ex1.17**   Shortcuts to Add to a Customized Perspective

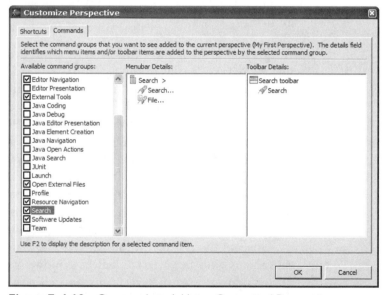

**Figure Ex1.18**   Commands to Add to a Customized Perspective

**Commands** page, you select the groups of commands that are shown on your customized perspective's menu bar and toolbar. Try customizing **My First Perspective** by adding some items. Select **OK**. Verify the changes to your perspective.

4. To make these changes permanent, you need to save your perspective again with **Window > Save Perspective As...**. Select **My First Perspec-**

**tive** to replace it with your changes. Or restore your perspective to its previously saved state by selecting **Window > Reset Perspective**.

5. When you create a new project, by default, you will be asked whether or not you want to switch to the perspective associated with the kind of project you are creating or want to use the default perspective instead. You can change the setting for the default perspective or what happens when a new project is created. Open your **Workbench > Perspectives** preferences, select a perspective, and then **Make Default**.

6. At this point, you probably realize you've been to the Preferences dialog many times to make changes to your preference settings. Well, instead of selecting **Window > Preferences** each time to open the Preferences dialog, let's define a keyboard shortcut to get there quickly.

   Select **Window > Preferences** and the **Keys** category under **Workbench**. Under **Command**, select **Window** for **Category** and **Preferences** for **Name**. Tab to the **Name** field under **Key Sequence**. Press a key sequence, such as **Alt+Shift+P**. Your key sequence will display as you press the keys. Leave **In Windows** as the value for **When**. Select **Add** to define the keyboard shortcut. Finally, select **OK** to set the preference change. Try it now. Press the key sequence you defined (e.g., **Alt+Shift+P)**, and the Preferences dialog will display.

In this section you customized a perspective and saw how to change your default perspective.

## Section 5: Using Multiple Eclipse Windows and Workspaces

We've been working with one Eclipse window. You can have multiple windows open at the same time on the same resources or different sets of resources in one workspace. These windows are kept in sync. You can also have multiple instances of Eclipse running at the same time on different workspaces.

1. Select **Window > New Window**. Another window opens in the same workspace. You see the same projects, files, and folders in the Navigator view.

2. In one window, add a file or folder to one of your projects. You'll see the new file or folder reflected in both windows. Open an editor on the same file in both windows. Make changes to the file in one window. Watch as changes appear simultaneously in the other window.

3. A common use of this is to have different projects or sets of resources appear in each of the windows. This makes it easier to manage the

PART VI

projects and their resources. You can do this for a specific project or folder when you open the new window. Select a project or folder in the Navigator view and choose the context menu option **Open in New Window.**

4. As an alternative, you can filter which projects appear in the Navigator view. From the Navigator view pull-down menu, select **Select Working Set....** You are going to define a working set to filter what is shown in the Navigator view. A working set is simply a predefined set of resources.

5. In the Select Working Set dialog, select **New....** This displays the New Working Set wizard. In the New Working Set wizard, select **Resource** for **Working Set Type** and then select **Next.** Name the working set My First Project and select **My First Project** to add it to the working set (see Figure Ex1.19). Select **Finish** to create the working set.

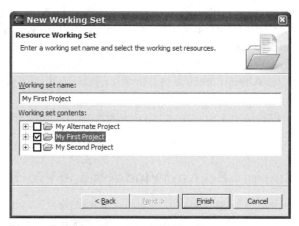

**Figure Ex1.19**   Creating a Working Set

6. In the Select Working Set dialog, select the working set **My First Project** and then select **OK.** You see in the Navigator view that only **My First Project** appears.

7. Switch to the other window and repeat steps 4 through 6 to define a working set in that window to show only **My Second Project.** You now have two windows open, each showing only one project.

8. To remove the working set specification, select **Deselect Working Set** from the Navigator view pull-down menu.

9. You can also choose to open a new window when you open a perspective. To do this, select **Window > Preferences** and then select **Perspec-**

**tives** under **Workbench**. Under **Open a new perspective**, select **In a new window**.

10. Up to this point in this exercise, you've been using multiple windows open on the same workspace. That is, the windows are managing the same set of resources that exist (by default) in the folder workspace. You can also run multiple Eclipse instances on different workspaces. Start another instance of Eclipse by executing eclipse.exe. This time at the Workspace Launcher prompt, select **Browse...** to see the Select Workspace Directory dialog. Select your Eclipse installation folder and then **Make New Folder**. Name the folder workspaceNew. Select **OK**. Select **OK** at the Workspace Launcher prompt to select this new workspace. You're now running a second instance of Eclipse on another workspace. You'll note that it's not obvious which Eclipse instance is working on which workspace. Let's look at how to fix this with a command line parameter.

11. The -showlocation parameter causes the location of the workspace to appear in the window title. The -showlocation parameter is case-sensitive. Open a command prompt and navigate to your main Eclipse folder, the one with the program eclipse.exe. Execute the following command:

```
eclipse -data workspaceAnother -showlocation
```

The -data parameter is another way to specify a different workspace. Given that the default workspace location is the folder workspace, if you prefix all your workspace names with workspace, the folders will be listed together in the Eclipse installation folder. This makes them easier to keep track of.

12. Eclipse starts with a new workspace. Because you used the -data parameter, the Workspace Launcher dialog did not display. Finally, note the workspace location information on the window title bar.

In this section you learned how to simultaneously run multiple Eclipse windows, both on the same workspace and on different workspaces.

## Section 6: Getting Assistance

In this section you'll see how to get help, including viewing and searching online content, and how to get help from the Eclipse user interface.

1. Select **Help > Help Contents** from the menu bar. The online documentation opens in a separate window (see Figure Ex1.20).

PART VI

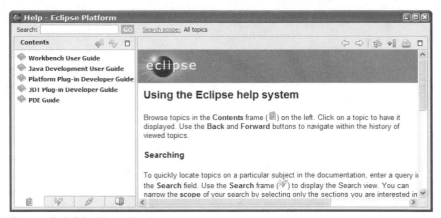

**Figure Ex1.20**　　Help Window

2. On the left is the Navigation pane; on the right is the Contents pane. The Navigation pane has four pages: The Contents *page* (not to be confused with the Contents *pane*) is on top, and behind it are the Search Results, Links, and Bookmarks pages. You'll see these in a moment. On the Contents page you'll see links for the online books that Eclipse provides: *Workbench User Guide, Java Development User Guide*, and others. Click on **Workbench User Guide** to see its contents. Expand **Getting Started** and browse its contents by selecting different topics.

3. After you have viewed several topics, try the **Forward** ⇨ and **Back** ⇦ buttons. The Contents pane contains an embedded browser. These buttons execute the **Forward** and **Back** commands in the browser.

4. In the **Search** field, enter using help and click on **Go**. If this is the first time you have used help, you may see information about indexing. This is a one-time task for an Eclipse installation. On the Search Results page, you'll see a list of topics whose contents contain the word "using" and the word "help" (see Figure Ex1.21). Select one or more of the topics to see the related information.

5. You can see that a number of the topics are related to adding help capability and content to Eclipse versus using help. Let's restrict the search a little. In the **Search** field, enter using help not plug not org and click on **Go**. This looks for content with the words "using" and "help" and without the words "plug" and "org." This eliminates most of the content about adding help, something you may wish to learn about later (see Chapter 22, Providing Help).

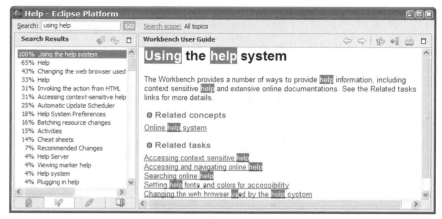

**Figure Ex1.21**   Searching Help

6. Now let's see how to restrict a search to certain sections. Click on **Search Scope** to open the search scope dialog. Select **New…** to create a new search scope definition. You'll see the search scope definition dialog as shown in Figure Ex1.22. Enter Concepts search for the **List name**. Select to search only the **Concepts** sections of the **Workbench User Guide** and the **Java Development User Guide**, and then select **OK** to define the search scope.

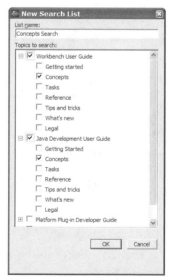

**Figure Ex1.22**   Advanced Help Search

Select **Concepts Search** and then **OK** on the search scope dialog to change the search scope. You'll see the search scope changed as shown in Figure Ex1.23.

**Figure Ex1.23**   Changing Search Scope

7. Click again on **Go** to execute the same search but with a more restrictive scope. You see a list of topics limited to the "Concepts" sections of the *Workbench User Guide* and *Java Development User Guide* that match the search expression. Select one of the matches in the Search Results pane and then select **Synchronize Navigation** ⚙. In the Navigation page, the topic is selected in the help table of contents (see Figure Ex1.24)

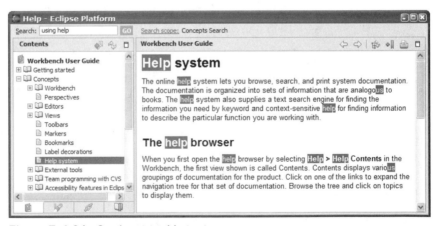

**Figure Ex1.24**   Synchronizing Navigation

8. Now let's look at searching from the main Eclipse window. Switch to the main Eclipse window, select **Search** 🔍, and then select the **Help Search** page (see Figure Ex1.25). Enter using help for the **Search expression** and then select **Search**.

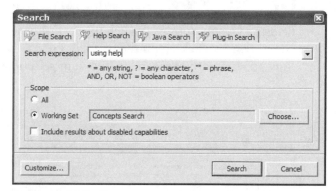

**Figure Ex1.25**   Searching Help from the Eclipse Window

9. The search results are shown in the Search view (see Figure Ex1.26).
   Double-click on one of these matches to see the related information in
   the Help window.

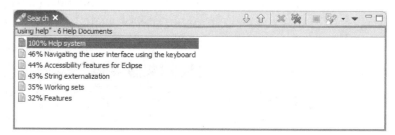

**Figure Ex1.26**   Search View

10. Select **Search** again from the main Eclipse indow and try a couple
    more searches. If you execute a search from this window, your search
    results are saved in the Search view. If you select the **Search History**
    drop-down menu 📖 ▼ on the right of the Search view title bar, you
    see a list of previous search results. Select one of these to see the previ-
    ous results.

11. In one of your sets of search results in the Search view, select some
    entries that you're not interested in. Select **Remove Selected
    Matches** ✖. In this way, you can customize your search results to
    a list of matches that are of interest.

12. Help is available for individual user interface items, for example, entry fields and menu options. Switch to the Tasks view and make it the active view by clicking on the title bar. Press **F1**. A small infopop window appears with topics related to your selection (see Figure Ex1.27).

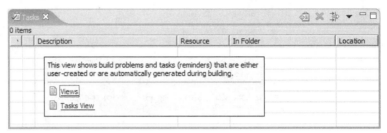

**Figure Ex1.27**    Infopop Help

13. Select **Tasks View**. The related information is shown in the Help window. You'll see that the entries that appeared in the infopop appear on the Links page in the Navigation pane (see Figure Ex1.28). This is so you don't have to press **F1** again to go to another topic.

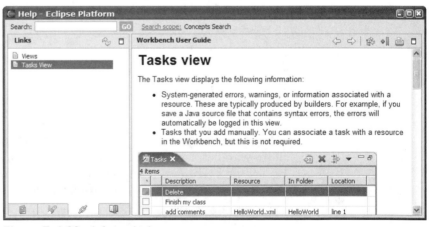

**Figure Ex1.28**    Infopop Links

In this final section, you used the Help system and search capabilities to access online content.

## Exercise Activity Review

This exercise introduced you to the fundamental use of Eclipse as a general-purpose IDE. Topics covered included creating and managing resources, using local history, comparing and recovering work, setting preferences, customizing your Eclipse installation, and running multiple Eclipse windows. At this point, you should have a solid foundation on which to build additional expertise. Nice work!

## Reference

Arthorne, John, and Chris Laffra. 2004. *Official Eclipse 3.0 FAQs*. Boston, MA: Addison-Wesley. http://eclipsefaq.org. (See FAQs 40– 43, 297, 298.)

# EXERCISE 2

## *Using Java Development Tools*

The objective of this exercise is to provide a hands-on demonstration of using Eclipse's JDT to edit and run Java programs. We'll start with a basic "Hello World" program and then get into more detail on various JDT capabilities. This exercise is designed to reinforce what we presented in Chapter 3, Using Java Development Tools. To get the most out of these exercises, you should read the chapter first because much of the explanation for why you are doing something in an exercise step is presented there.

At the end of this exercise you should be able to do the following.

- Write and run a simple "Hello World" program.
- Use the Java editor to more quickly and efficiently write Java code, including quick fix, code assist, code generation, and refactoring.

### Section 1: Hello World

Let's start with the basics: the minimum required to create a class that you can execute, and two ways you can run the class.

1. Start Eclipse. Select **Window > Open Perspective > Java** to open the Java perspective.
2. Select **New Java Project** ![icon]. Name the project com.ibm.jdg2e .usingjdt.helloworld. Leave the other values as the defaults and select **Finish** to create the project.
3. Ensure your project is selected in the Package Explorer view and select **New Java Class** ![icon]. Name the class HelloWorld. Select only the option to generate method stubs for the main method.

At the top of the New Java Class wizard, you'll see a warning about using the default package. We're going to tolerate this for now to keep things simple. Select **Finish** to generate the class.

4. A default package is created for the class `HelloWorld` and the file `HelloWorld.java`. You should have two tasks ☑ showing up in the marker bar of the editor. These are created by task tags included in the default templates used to generate this code. We'll update these shortly.

5. Edit the `main` method as shown in Figure Ex2.1 and save your changes to `HelloWorld.java` by selecting **Save** from the context menu or by pressing **Ctrl+S**.

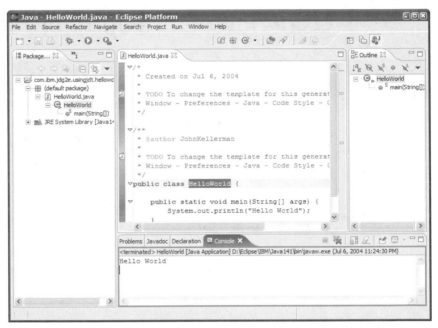

**Figure Ex2.1**   `HelloWorld` Class

6. Expand `HelloWorld.java` in the Package Explorer view. The decoration 🐾 on the class icon indicates that the class contains a `main` method and can be executed. Right-click on the file `HelloWorld.java` in the Package Explorer view and then select **Run > Java Application** from the context menu. The `main` method in the class `HelloWorld` runs, and its output is shown in the Console view (see Figure Ex2.1).

7. Now let's see another way to run a Java program. Ensure your project is selected in the Package Explorer view and press **Ctrl+N**. In the New

wizard, expand the **Java** category, expand **Java Run/Debug**, select **Scrapbook Page**, and select **Next**. Call the page HelloWorldSnippets. The file HelloWorldSnippets.jpage is added to your project. Scrapbook pages are another way to execute Java code. In addition to running your program, you can use them to try out snippets of Java code. Enter the following Java expression in the scrapbook page.

```
String[] array = {};
HelloWorld.main(array);
```

8. Select the entire expression (both lines) and then select **Display** [J] from the context menu. The expression is evaluated, which causes the main method of the HelloWorld class to execute. The return value displays in the scrapbook page (in this case, there is no return value), and its output is shown in the Console view.

9. Since the output of these two executions is the same, it may not be immediately apparent that the second execution was successful. To verify, in the Console view select **Display Selected Console** 🖥 ▼ to see a list of console sessions. Note that if you simply evaluate the same code snippet multiple times or run the same program multiple times, each execution will happen in the same console. You will see multiple consoles when you perform multiple different executions, as you did in steps 6 and 8.

10. Finally, recall those task tags? That was a gentle reminder from JDT that you may want to customize those templates. Let's do this now. Select **Window > Preferences** to open the Preferences dialog. Then select **Java > Code Style > Code Templates**. Edit both the **Types** template under **Comments** and the **New Java files** template under **Code** by selecting the template and then **Edit...** to something more of your liking. For example, you could enter a copyright statement in the **Code > New Java files** template. We recommend at least removing the task tag line, the one starting with ${todo}. Select **OK** in the Edit Template dialog to save your changes. Now try your changes by creating a new Java class.

You just created and ran your first Java program! Well, most likely it was your first in Eclipse. You also updated a couple common code generation templates.

## Section 2: Quick Fix

In this section you'll see how to navigate and fix errors in Java code. You'll also be introduced to some typing assistance JDT provides and to the quick diff facility. On the CD-ROM we've provided the project com.ibm.jdg2e .usingjdt, which contains several packages. Be sure you have this in your workspace. If you do not, refer to the instructions on the CD-ROM. Each package contains code for one part of this exercise, as indicated by the name of the package. The sample code represents several iterations of a program to generate numbers, prime numbers at first. While the code is relatively simple and at times may appear a bit contrived, the example allows you to focus on using JDT with a minimal amount of code.

The same class is defined in multiple packages. We've done this to provide one set of programs that will carry through the different parts of the exercise. The packages hold different versions of the same classes, so you don't have to do Sections 1 through 3 if you're only interested in Section 4. In this part of the exercise, you'll be working with the package com.ibm.jdg2e .usingjdt.quickfix. You should see a number of errors in the package quickfix. They are what you are going to navigate and fix.

1. First, we need to point out some useful preferences. The annotations that appear on the editor marker bar on the left and on the overview ruler on the right are customizable. These are your **Window > Preferences > Workbench > Editors > Annotations** preferences. Your **Workbench > Editors > Quick Diff** preferences specify how quick diff flags changes. Quick diff provides a simple real time view in the editor of your most recent changes.

2. Let's simplify what is shown in the Package Explorer view. The package names are often too long and you really don't need to see the JRE entries. Switch to your **Java > Appearances** preferences. Select **Compress package name segments** and enter 0 as the **Compression pattern**. Select **OK** to set the preference. This will cause only the final segment in each package name to display.

3. To hide the JRE entries, select **Filters...** from the Package Explorer pull-down menu. In the Java Elements Filters dialog (see Figure Ex2.2), select to exclude **Referenced libraries** and then select **OK**.

4. Now preferences are set and the Package Explorer view is tidied up, so let's get on to using quick fix to remedy these errors. In the quick-fix package, open the PrimeNumberGenerator class. JDT indicates errors in a number of ways (see Figure Ex2.3).
   • Error annotations (small red rectangles) in the overview ruler in the right margin of the editor
   • Red underlining on text in the editor

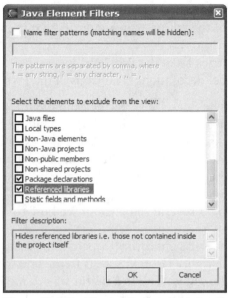

**Figure Ex2.2**   Filtering Package Explorer Contents

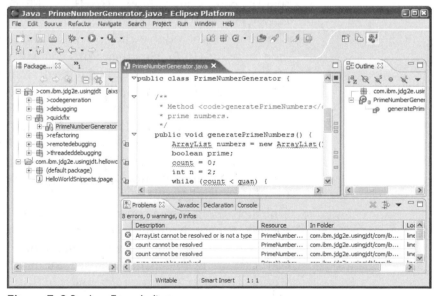

**Figure Ex2.3**   Java Error Indicators

- Quick fix 🔧 and error ⓧ annotations on the marker bar in the left margin of the editor, which indicate that there are suggestions to fix the error
- Error entries ⓧ in the Problems view
- Error label decorations ⊠ on icons in the Java views and editor tab(s)

Error markings are a specific kind of annotation. Eclipse uses annotations for a number of things, including breakpoints, search results, tasks, and bookmarks. You can customize how these annotations show up in the editor with your **Workbench > Editor > Annotations** preferences. You just took a look at these at the beginning of this exercise.

In the next several steps you'll see how to navigate errors and get information about them.

5. Click on an error indicator (the small red rectangles) in the overview ruler on the right. The text scrolls to the line with the error, and the error is highlighted. This is a useful way to navigate to errors without having to manually scroll the file. Now click on **Next Annotation** ⬇. The next error is selected. We saw previously that you could customize how annotations appear in the editor. You can also customize annotation navigation. Select the next annotation pull-down menu ⬇ ▼. You'll see a list of annotation types. The checked types are the ones that the **Next Annotation** ⬇ **(Ctrl+.)** and **Previous Annotation** ⬆ **(Ctrl+,)** navigation buttons seek.

6. Close the file and double-click on one of the errors in the Problems view or select **Go To** from the error's context menu. The file with the error is opened and the error highlighted. If an error message in the Problems view is truncated, you can hover over it in the Problems view to see the full message or select it to see it in the message area.

7. Hover over text underlined in red in the editor and you'll see a description of the error, or position the cursor in the error text and observe the error message in the message area. Hover over one of the error or quick fix indicators on the marker bar or the overview ruler to see the error message.

8. One more thing before you start fixing the errors we so graciously left for your benefit. Note the ruler just inside the marker bar with the triangle annotations. The triangles pointing down indicate sections of code that can be folded, or collapsed, for more efficient viewing of the whole file. Hover over the ruler, and you'll see a vertical line that marks the extent of the code in this section that would be folded. Triangles pointing to the right indicate sections of code that are folded

(see Figure Ex2.4). Fold a section of code. Now hover over the triangle, and you'll see a hover listing the code that is folded.

**Figure Ex2.4** Folding Code

9. To use quick fix to fix these errors, click on the first quick fix icon, the one for the `ArrayList` reference. You will see a list of possible solutions (see Figure Ex2.5). Scroll through some of the proposed solutions, and you'll see the code that would be generated or a description of the fix. In this case, an `import` statement is missing. Select **import 'ArrayList' (java.util)** and press **Enter**. A grayed error annotation remains on the marker bar. This will remain there until you save the

**Figure Ex2.5** Quick Fix Proposed Solution

PART VI

file. Save the file by pressing **Ctrl+S**; the error annotation disappears. On to the rest of the errors.

10. Go to the next problem by selecting **Next Annotation** 🔁. The error message is displayed in the message area at the bottom of the window. In this case, there is a problem with local variable count. This time, instead of clicking on the quick fix icon, press **Ctrl+1** to activate quick fix. In this case, the definition of a local variable was omitted. Select **Create local variable 'count'** to see the code that would be generated, including the original initialization, and press **Enter** to make the change.

Note the lines and shading around the code change (see Figure Ex2.6). Try successively pressing the **Tab** key. You'll cycle through three positions. The first two, shown by rectangles enclosing strings, are strings you may want to alter. The third, shown by a vertical bar at the end of the line, is the presumed place for you to continue entering text. At any point, press **Enter** to get to the end of the line, or **Tab** there, and then press **Enter** to continue on a new line after this one. The goal here is to enable you to make these changes and to alter what JDT adds or generates with the minimum keystrokes, as efficiently as possible.

**Figure Ex2.6**    Modifying Quick Fix Suggestions

11. Notice the coloring in the quick diff ruler (on the left margin of the editor, just to the right of the marker bar) opposite the line of code you just changed. This is a visual cue designed to enable you to quickly see the lines you changed. Hover over the shading to see how the lines changed (see Figure Ex2.7). Right-click on the shading, and you'll see two choices on the context menu that allow you to undo these changes, **Revert Line** and **Revert Block**. If you try this, be sure to repeat the previous step to declare local variable count.

**Figure Ex2.7**  Quick Diff Changes

12. Press **Ctrl+.** to go to the next error, an unresolved reference to quan. The number of prime numbers to generate, quan, was not defined. Activate quick fix and you'll see several options. Let's make quan a field on PrimeNumberGenerator. Select this option and press **Enter.** By default, the new field is private. Change this to a public field. Initially, you're going to access this field directly outside the class for simplicity, but you'll change this later.

13. Go to the next error, a simple misspelling. The JDT can detect and fix these too. Click on the quick fix icon, select **Change to 'prime'**, and press **Enter.**

14. On to the final error: a missing definition for results. In this case, define results as a field of PrimeNumberGenerator. Click on the quick fix icon, select **Create field 'results'**, and press **Enter.** Change the definition of this field from private to public. Do this by pressing **Tab** to quickly navigate to the field definition you just added. All of the quick fix icons should be gone. Save the file; all errors should be resolved.

15. Great! You're finished with the first version of the code. The code should look like this, minus the generated comments. Note that, after this, in order to save trees, we're not going to list the whole solution or large parts of the solutions in the exercise. We'll refer you to the CD-ROM.

```
package com.ibm.lab.jdg2e.usingjdt.quickfix;
import java.util.ArrayList;

public class PrimeNumberGenerator {
  public int quan;
  public Object[] results;
  public void generatePrimeNumbers() {
    ArrayList numbers = new ArrayList();
    boolean prime;
    int count = 0;
```

```
      int n = 2;
      while (count < quan) {
        prime = true;
        int factor = 2;
        while (factor <= n / factor && prime) {
          if (n % factor == 0) {
            prime = false;
          } else {
            factor++;
          }
        }
        if (prime) {
          numbers.add(new Integer(n));
          count++;
        }
        n++;
      }
      numbers.trimToSize();
      results = numbers.toArray();
    }
  }
```

16. Let's test the code. You're going to do this with a Java scrapbook page. Select the package `quickfix` in the Package Explorer view and press **Ctrl+N**. Select **Java > Java Run/Debug > Scrapbook Page**. On the next page of the wizard, name it `QuickFix` and select **Finish**. Enter the following expression in the scrapbook page to test your code.

```
PrimeNumberGenerator p = new PrimeNumberGenerator();
p.quan = 10;
p.generatePrimeNumbers();
p.results
```

Select this text and then select **Display Result of Evaluating Selected Text** [J]. This leads to an error because there are multiple definitions of the `PrimeNumberGenerator` class. This is a common error when using scrapbook pages. Let's see how to fix it.

17. You need to set an `import` statement in the scrapbook page so `Prime-NumberGenerator` can be uniquely resolved. From the scrapbook page editor context menu, select **Set Imports....** Select **Add Type...**, and the Add Type as Import dialog displays (see Figure Ex2.8). Select `Prime-NumberGenerator` for **Matching types** and `com.ibm.jdg2e.usingjdt .quickfix` for **Qualifier**. Select **OK** and then **OK** again to set the `import`.

18. In the scrapbook page, again select the entire expression and then select **Display** from the context menu. The `generatePrimeNumbers` method runs and the output displays in the scrapbook page (see Figure Ex2.9). If you get an error, check your `import` statement for the scrapbook page and ensure you declared the `results` field as `public`.

**Figure Ex2.8** Setting Imports for a Scrapbook Page

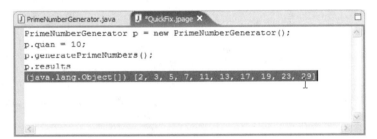

**Figure Ex2.9** `PrimeNumberGenerator` Results

In this section you used quick fix to remedy a variety of errors we planted in a Java program for you. When you're through, close the editors open on `PrimeNumberGenerator.java` and `QuickFix.jpage`.

## Section 3: Code Generation

In this section we're going to take a closer look at how you can generate code with code assist, including completing statements, generating code from templates, and generating anonymous inner classes. You're going to enhance the `PrimeNumberGenerator` class with methods to output and to sort its results, the prime numbers.

Unless otherwise specified, references to a class or some other Java element or resource refer to the element or resource in the `com.ibm.jdg2e.usingjdt` `.codegeneration` package. The code in this package is the same as the code in the `quickfix` package now, if you did Section 2.

1. First, you're going to code the method to output the prime numbers. In the `codegeneration` package, open the `PrimeNumberGenerator` class. Just after the `generatePrimeNumbers` method, enter a new line, begin typing pub, and with the insertion cursor just after the b press **Ctrl+Space** to activate code assist and see a list of suggestions (see Figure Ex2.10).

**Figure Ex2.10**    Code Assist Suggestions

2. Select **public_method – public method**. This is a code template for defining `public` methods. Press **Enter**, but don't type any more keystrokes (see Figure Ex2.11).

**Figure Ex2.11**    `public` Method Template

You now have a stub for the new method. Because the method is incomplete (and incorrect), you'll see the quick fix icon. You could use quick fix at this point, but there is an easier way.

3. The placeholder for the return type of the method is selected. Overtype return_type with void for the method return type. Press **Tab** and name is selected. This is the next placeholder you can modify. Overtype this with outputResults. Press **Tab** again and the cursor is between the parentheses where you would define the method's parameters. In this case, we have none. Press **Tab** one more time and the cursor is placed in the body of the method for you to begin coding. Neat-o!

4. On to the rest of the method. Enter Date d = new Date(); for the first statement of the method. You'll see an error with this statement. Hover over the text that's underlined in red and you'll see that Date cannot be resolved—it needs the import statement. You saw previously how you could use quick fix here. You can also use code generation to fix this. Select one of the Date references and then select **Source > Add Import** from the context menu. You have two choices in the Add Import dialog. Select **java.util.Date** and then **OK** to generate the import statement. The error is resolved.

5. Create a new line after Date d = new Date();. On the new line type System. and then press **Ctrl+Space**. You'll see a list of valid expressions that can be used after what you had just typed, System. Select the field **out** and press **Enter**. Type a period and then press **Ctrl+Space** again. Select **println(String x)** and then press **Enter**. The statement is completed, the cursor is positioned between the parentheses, and a prompt appears indicating the parameter type (see Figure Ex2.12). Note that when you have many choices in the code assist prompt, you can continue typing to narrow the choices.

**Figure Ex2.12** Parameter Hint

Type d. and press **Ctrl+Space**. Select **toString()** and press **Enter**. Tab to get to the end of the line and add a semicolon to complete the statement, which should appear as follows.

```
System.out.println(d.toString());
```

6. Code assist helps here, but even so, this is a bit of typing for something you will type a lot, at least if you're anything like us. We can make this even easier with a template. Select **Window > Preferences** to open your preferences, and then go to your **Java > Editor > Templates** preferences. Select **New...** to create a new template. Name it sop and define its **Pattern** as follows.

```
System.out.println(${cursor});
```

The variable ${cursor} indicates where the cursor will be placed when the template is inserted. Be sure the **Context** is set to **Java**. Select **OK** to create the template and **OK** again to close the Preferences dialog. Now you have a template to make entering this statement quicker. We'll use it in the next step.

7. Create a new line after the System.out.println(d.toString()); statement, begin typing for, and press **Ctrl+Space**. Select the template **for – iterate over array** in the list and press **Enter** to add a block of code for the for statement. Press **Tab** to go to array, delete this, and press **Ctrl+Space**. Select to add the results field. Press **Tab** to go to the new line in the body of the for statement. Now we want another println statement. This time, you're going to use the template you just created. Type sop and press **Ctrl+Space**. The println statement is inserted with the cursor positioned between the parentheses. Complete the statement as follows.

```
System.out.println(results[i]);
```

8. You have finished coding the method. To add a Javadoc comment, position the insertion cursor in the code in the method and select **Source > Add Javadoc comment** from the context menu. Create a new line in the comment and press **Ctrl+Space**. Code assist also allows you to add content to Javadoc comments, for example, a @version tag.

9. Save the file. Your code for outputResults should look like this.

```java
public void outputResults() {
  Date d = new Date();
  System.out.println(d.toString());
  for (int i = 0; i < results.length; i++) {
    System.out.println(results[i]);
  }
}
```

Wow! This gives you an idea of the power of code assist and code generation. Save your changes. Now test the code.

10. In the Package Explorer view, create a new scrapbook page in the package codegeneration and call it CodeGeneration. Select **Set Imports** from the context menu of the scrapbook page editor and add an import statement for the package codegeneration. Enter the following expression. Code assist works in scrapbook pages; try it.

```
PrimeNumberGenerator p = new PrimeNumberGenerator();
p.quan = 10;
p.generatePrimeNumbers();
p.outputResults();
```

Select the entire expression and then select **Evaluate** ![icon] from the context menu. The results appear in the Console view.

11. Let's look at a more involved example of code assist in which you'll define an anonymous inner class and override a method. To do this, you're going to create a method to sort the results. Since the results are already in order because of the way you generated them, your sort routine will sort in reverse order. Granted, this is a bit contrived, but it will illustrate this feature with a minimal amount of code.

   In the editor for PrimeNumberGenerator, add import statements for java.util.Arrays and java.util.Comparator. Remember that after typing just three or four letters, you can use **Ctrl+Space** to help finish. Don't worry about the warnings; they indicate the import statements are not used. We'll use them here shortly.

12. Below the outputResults method, use code assist to create a new public method named sortResults, return type void, with no parameters. Did you know you can match up opening and closing braces and parentheses? Position the insertion cursor just after a brace or parenthesis, and the corresponding opening or closing one will be indicated with an enclosing rectangle (see Figure Ex2.13).

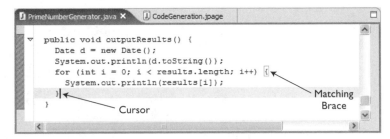

**Figure Ex2.13** Matching Braces and Parentheses

13. Position the cursor in the body of the method, type `Arrays.`, and press **Ctrl+Space**. Select **sort(Object[] a, Comparator c)** and press **Enter**. Enter `"results,"` for the first parameter. Once you type the comma, watch as the highlighting on the parameter prompt changes to indicate you need to enter the `Comparator` for the second argument.

14. For the second argument, press **Enter** to start a new line. Begin typing `new Com` and press **Ctrl+Space**. Select **Comparator** from `java.util` and press **Enter**. Add `() { }` (a pair of parentheses and curly braces) to create the body of the class. Here you're defining an anonymous inner class to be used to sort your `results` array. Position the cursor in the body of the class definition, that is, between the curly braces— `{` and `}`—and press **Ctrl+Space**. Select **compare** and press **Enter**. Code assist knows which methods you can override.

15. Replace the `return 0` line to complete the invocation of `sort` as follows. Recall how to match parentheses and braces; that technique comes in handy here. When you're done, save the file.

```
public void sortResults() {
  Arrays.sort(results,
    new Comparator() {
    public int compare(Object o1, Object o2) {
      if (((Integer) o1).intValue()
        < ((Integer) o2).intValue()) {
          return 1;
      } else {
        return -1;
      }
    }}
  );
}
```

16. Test `sortResults` with the following code in the `CodeGeneration` scrapbook page.

```
PrimeNumberGenerator p = new PrimeNumberGenerator();
p.quan = 20;
p.generatePrimeNumbers();
p.sortResults();
p.outputResults();
```

In this section you completed code expressions and generated code from templates using code assist. When you're through, don't forget to close the editors you opened on `PrimeNumberGenerator.java` and `CodeGeneration.jpage`.

# Section 4: Refactoring

In this section you're going to look at refactoring Java. You're going to use JDT quick assist and refactoring capabilities to clean up the `PrimeNumber-Generator` class, reorganize it, and add a new class to generate the prime factorials.

Unless otherwise specified, references to a class or some other Java element or resource refer to the element or resource in package `com.ibm.jdg2e .usingjdt.refactoring`. The code in this package is the same as the code in the `codegeneration` package now, if you did Section 3.

1. First, we need to clean up references to the two fields, `results` and `quan`. Open the `PrimeNumberGenerator` class in the `refactoring` package. To start with, let's give quan a more appropriate name, `quantity`. Select quan in the editor and press **Ctrl+I**. This activates quick assist. Quick assist presents suggestions for assistance based on the current state of your editing. In this case, we want to select **Rename in File**. All references to quan in the file are marked by enclosing rectangles (see Figure Ex2.14).

**Figure Ex2.14**  Quick Assist Local Rename

Press **Tab** to navigate between them. Change one instance of quan to quantity and they all change. Make this local rename from quan to quantity.

2. Now let's clean up the references to the `quantity` and `results` fields. Select the `quantity` field in the Package Explorer view, the Outline view, or the editor, and then select **Refactor > Encapsulate Field...** from the context menu. If you have editors open with unsaved changes, you will be prompted to save them; do so. Leave the selections on the

Refactoring wizard as they are and select **Preview.** You will see the proposed changes, as shown in Figure Ex2.15. On this page of the Refactoring wizard, you can select which code changes you want to keep. Expand the list in the top pane to see the list of fields and methods that will be changed. Select entries in the list to see their respective changes in the bottom panes. You can also select a rectangle on the overview ruler to the right of the source panes to go directly to the respective change. Leave all of the proposed code changes selected, and then select **OK** to complete the refactoring.

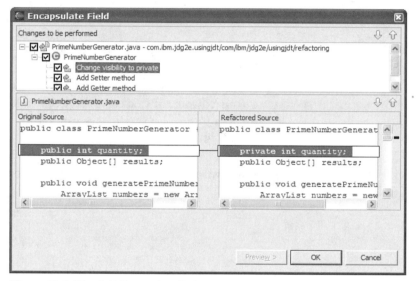

**Figure Ex2.15**   Self-Encapsulate Refactoring

3. Repeat the same operation on the results field.
4. The name results is not very descriptive; change it to generated-Numbers. Select the results field (in a view or in the editor), and then select **Refactor > Rename...** from the context menu. In the Rename Field dialog (see Figure Ex2.16), enter generatedNumbers for the name. Select to update the getter and setter methods.
5. Select **Preview** to review the proposed code changes, then select **OK** to make the changes to the file.
6. Select the local variable n in the editor, and then select **Refactor > Rename...** or press **Ctrl+1** to use quick assist to do a local rename. Rename n to something more descriptive, like candidate. Save the file.

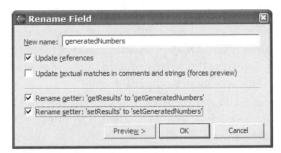

**Figure Ex2.16**   Rename Refactoring

7. One final bit of cleanup. Change the line that sets generatedNumbers from

```
generatedNumbers = numbers.toArray();
```

to the following to use the setter method.

```
setGeneratedNumbers(numbers.toArray());
```

Save the file. Your code should look like the following.

```
package com.ibm.jdg2e.usingjdt.refactoring;
// import statements omitted

public class PrimeNumberGenerator {

  private int quantity;
private Object[] generatedNumbers;

  public void generatePrimeNumbers() {
    ArrayList numbers = new ArrayList();
    boolean prime;
    int count = 0;
    int candidate = 2;
    while (count < getQuantity()) {
    // code omitted - no change
    }
    numbers.trimToSize();
    setGeneratedNumbers(numbers.toArray());
  }
  public void outputResults() {
  // method body omitted
}

  public void sortResults() {
  // method body omitted
}

// getter and setters for getQuantity and
// generatedNumbers omitted
}
```

PART VI

8. You've cleaned up the code a bit. Now you're going to add the class to generate prime factorials, `PrimeFactorialGenerator`. To do this, you're going to create a superclass for `PrimeNumberGenerator` and `PrimeFactorialGenerator` called `NumberGenerator` and move methods and fields to this new superclass.

    Select the `refactoring` package in the Package Explorer view and create the `NumberGenerator` class. Do not select to have any method stubs generated.

9. In the superclass, you need a method the subclasses will override to generate numbers. Create the following method in `NumberGenerator` (try generating it from a template).

    ```
    public void generateNumbers() { }
    ```

10. Now you need to fix `PrimeNumberGenerator` to override this method. In the `PrimeNumberGenerator` class, select the `generatePrimeNumbers` method and then select **Refactor > Rename...** to rename it to generate-Numbers. If you did not save the changes to `NumberGenerator.java`, you will be prompted to do so.

11. `PrimeNumberGenerator` should be a subclass of `NumberGenerator`, so change the class `PrimeNumberGenerator` to extend `NumberGenerator` by editing its definition as follows.

    ```
    public class PrimeNumberGenerator extends NumberGenerator {
    ```

    Verify this change quickly and simply by opening a type hierarchy pop-up. In the editor, select type `PrimeNumberGenerator` or `Number-Generator` and then press **Ctrl+T**. You'll see a pop-up with the hierarchy of these classes (see Figure Ex2.17). Press **Esc** to dismiss the pop-up.

**Figure Ex2.17**   Type Hierarchy Pop-up

12. Because `PrimeNumberGenerator` and the class you will create to generate prime factorials will inherit from `NumberGenerator`, the `quantity` and `generatedNumbers` fields and their getter and setter methods really belong in `NumberGenerator`, as do the `outputResults` and `sortResults` methods. Select the editor of the `PrimeNumberGenerator` class. In the

Outline view, select the generatedNumbers and quantity fields, and then select **Refactor > Pull Up...** from the context menu. Confirm NumberGenerator as the destination class. Also select to pull up all the methods except for generateNumbers (see Figure Ex2.18). This ends up being a substantial change. Preview the changes by pressing **Next** twice. Review the code changes and select **Finish**.

You may have noticed that these changes span multiple files. In fact, when you perform a refactoring operation, the refactoring analysis includes all open projects in your workspace. To undo refactoring operations (including ones that span multiple files), use **Refactor > Undo**, instead of **Edit > Undo**. The former works across multiple files, the latter does not.

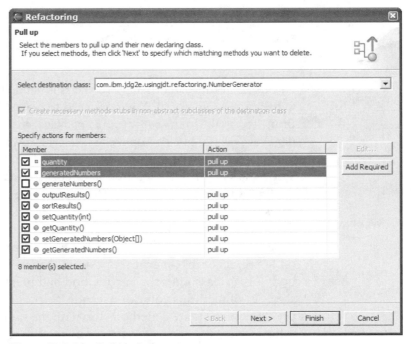

**Figure Ex2.18** Pull Up Refactoring

13. The following import statements are no longer required in Prime-NumberGenerator. Use **Ctrl+Shift+O** to remove them.

```
import java.util.Date;
import java.util.Arrays;
import java.util.Comparator;
```

14. The organization of the `NumberGenerator` and `PrimeNumberGenerator` classes should look like Figure Ex2.19.

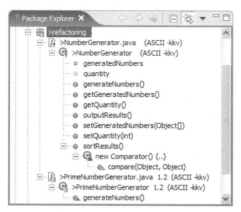

**Figure Ex2.19**   Code Organization After Refactoring

15. At this point the `NumberGenerator` class is defined and `PrimeNumber-Generator` is refactored. You now need to create the class to generate prime factorials. In the `refactoring` package, create the `PrimeFactorial-Generator` class. For its **Superclass**, select **Browse...** and then enter `NumberGenerator`. In the Superclass Selection dialog, for **Qualifier** be sure to specify the package `com.ibm.jdg2e.usingjdt.refactoring`. Select **OK** to set the superclass. Do not generate any of the method stubs. Select **Finish** to generate the class.

16. To generate the numbers, `PrimeNumberGenerator` needs to override `generateNumbers`, which is defined in `NumberGenerator`. In the editor on `PrimeFactorialGenerator`, position the insertion cursor in the body of the class after the last method and press **Ctrl+Space**. You'll see a list of methods you can override. Select `generateNumbers` and press **Enter** to create a method stub with the same signature. Enter the following for the `generateNumbers` method in the `PrimeFactorial-Generator` class.

```
public void generateNumbers() {
  PrimeNumberGenerator primes = new PrimeNumberGenerator();
  primes.setQuantity(getQuantity());
  primes.generateNumbers();
  Object[] numbers = new
    Object[primes.getGeneratedNumbers().length];
  int factorial = 1;
```

```
    for (int i = 0; i < primes.getGeneratedNumbers().length; i++) {
      factorial = factorial
        * ((Integer) primes.getGeneratedNumbers()[i]).intValue();
      numbers[i] = new Integer(factorial);
    }
    setGeneratedNumbers(numbers);
  }
```

17. Congratulations, you're done! Save your changes to the three files you're editing. You code should look as shown in project `com.ibm.jdg2e` `.soln.usingjdt`, package `com.ibm.lab.jdg2e.usingjdt.refactoring`.

18. Give the new and refactored code a try by executing the following in a scrapbook page (remember to set an `import` statement).

```
PrimeFactorialGenerator f = new PrimeFactorialGenerator();
f.setQuantity(5);
f.generateNumbers();
f.sortResults();
f.outputResults();

PrimeNumberGenerator n = new PrimeNumberGenerator();
n.setQuantity(5);
n.generateNumbers();
n.outputResults();
```

When you're through, don't forget to close any editors open on `.java` and `.jpage` files.

In this section you used some of JDT's refactoring capabilities to clean up and enhance your program.

## Exercise Activity Review

In this exercise you got an in-depth look at a large subset of the JDT's capabilities. We focused on using the Java editor to code, solve errors, and refactor Java code efficiently and productively. The JDT provides a wealth of capability for your Java development needs. We hope you've come out of this exercise with a good overview and understanding of this and a motivation to learn even more!

## Reference

Arthorne, John, and Chris Laffra. 2004. *Official Eclipse 3.0 FAQs*. Boston, MA: Addison-Wesley. http://eclipsefaq.org. (See Chapter 3 and FAQs 313, 315–318.)

# EXERCISE 3

## *Running and Debugging Java*

The objective of this exercise is to provide a hands-on demonstration of running and debugging Java using Eclipse's JDT, including debugging threads and remote programs. The goal here is not to develop or refine code but to take you through several debugging sessions, teaching you how to perform specific debugging tasks with the JDT.

This exercise is designed to reinforce what we presented in Chapter 4, Running and Debugging Java. To get the most out of these exercises, you should read the chapter first because much of the explanation for why you are doing something in an exercise step is presented there.

At the end of this exercise, you should be able to do the following.

- Create a launch configuration to run a Java program and manage its execution environment.
- Launch a debug session.
- Set different kinds of breakpoints, including conditional ones.
- Control execution of a program in the debugger.
- Examine the state of a program's execution.
- Debug multithreaded programs.
- Debug a remote program.

## Section 1: Launch Configurations

In this section, you're going to run Java programs by using launch configurations, including passing program arguments, passing JVM parameters, and referring to classes in a runtime library (JAR file). To illustrate these points, we've provided the `TestLaunchConfiguration` class on the CD-ROM.

Ensure that you have the project `com.ibm.jdg2e.usingjdt.launch-configurations` in your workspace. If you do not, refer to the instructions on the CD-ROM. Don't worry about the errors—you'll be fixing them. You're also going to need the code you completed at the end of Exercise 2, Using Java Development Tools. If you didn't do this, you can get the solution from project `com.ibm.jdg2e.soln.usingjdt`.

1. Open the `TestLaunchConfiguration` class. There is an unresolved reference to `PrimeFactorialGenerator`. We'll get to this in a moment. The `main` method outputs the value of a Java system property, `myName`. You'll define this with a JVM parameter. The `main` method takes an input parameter you'll pass to it in the launch configuration to set the number of prime factorials to generate.

```
package com.ibm.jdg2e.usingjdt.launchconfigurations;
public class TestLaunchConfiguration {

public static void main(String[] args) {
  System.out.println("Java System property \"myName\": " +
    System.getProperty("myName"));
  PrimeFactorialGenerator p = new PrimeFactorialGenerator();
  p.setQuantity(new Integer(args[0]).intValue());
  p.generateNumbers();
  p.sortResults();
  p.outputResults();
}
```

To fix the unresolved reference to `PrimeFactorialGenerator`, you need to add a declaration to it to the build path of the project. One way to do this is to add the project `com.ibm.jdg2e.usingjdt` to the build path of `com.ibm.jdg2e.usingjdt.launchconfigurations`. Instead, you are going to learn how to do this by referencing an external JAR file (i.e., one outside your workspace).

2. If you did Section 4 from Exercise 2, you can use your results of this. From the Package Explorer view, select the `refactoring` package in the `com.ibm.jdg2e.usingjdt` project. Otherwise, select the same package in `com.ibm.jdg2e.soln.usingjdt`. Select **Export...** from the context menu. Select to export a JAR file and then select **Next**. On the **JAR Package Specification** page, expand the project with the `refactoring` package (see Figure Ex3.1). In the right pane, select (check) the files `NumberGenerator.java`, `PrimeFactorialGenerator.java`, and `PrimeNumberGenerator.java`. Ensure **Export generated class files and resources** is selected, choose a location on your file system, and name

the JAR file `NumberGeneratorBinaries.jar`. Select **Finish** to create the JAR file. Remember its location.

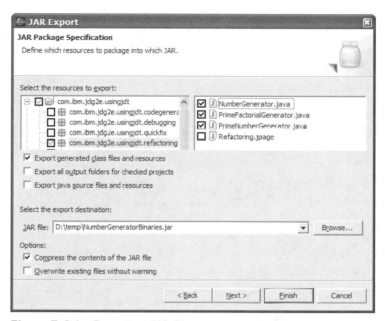

**Figure Ex3.1**    Exporting a JAR File

3. The JAR file you just created contained only the class files. Let's create another JAR file with the corresponding source. Repeat what you did in the previous step. This time, instead of selecting **Export generated class files and resources**, select only **Export java source files and resources**. Name the file `NumberGeneratorSource.jar`. We're separating these two JAR files because you'll see later how to debug binary class files, step into a method in a binary class file, and then attach source code to continue debugging.

4. You have the declarations of `NumberGenerator` and its subclasses in a JAR file. You now need to update the build path of the project containing `TestLaunchConfiguration` so you can refer to the JAR. One way to do this is to define this JAR as an external JAR file. The limitation of this approach is that if the JAR file's location changes and you reference it in multiple projects, you'll have to change the build paths of these multiple projects. A more flexible way to do this is to define a user library with the JAR file and then add the user library to the

PART VI

project's build path. This way you update only the library when the JAR location changes, not the projects referring to it.

Open your **Java > Build Path > User Libraries** preferences. Select **New…** to define a new user library. Enter `NumberGeneratorLibrary` for the name and select **OK**. Now select **Add Jars…**. In the Jar Selection dialog, find `NumberGeneratorBinaries.jar` and add it to the user library. Do not add Javadoc or source attachments. Your library should like what Figure Ex3.2 shows. Select **OK** to close the Preferences dialog.

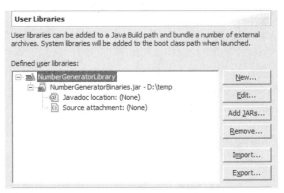

**Figure Ex3.2**   Defining a User Library

5. Now you need to update the build path of the project. Select the project `com.ibm.jdg2e.usingjdt.launchconfigurations` in the Package Explorer view, and then select **Properties** from the context menu. Select **Java Build Path**, and then select the **Libraries** page. Select **Add Library…**. Select to add a **User Library**, and then select **Next**. Select **NumberGeneratorLibrary**, then **Finish** to add the library, and **OK** to close the Properties dialog.

6. Now the JAR file with a declaration for `PrimeFactorialGenerator` is in the project's build path. Go to the editor on the `TestLaunchConfiguration` class, and then press **Ctrl+Shift+O** (**Organize Imports** on the editor's context menu). This adds an `import` statement to correct the unresolved reference. Save the file. The errors are eliminated.

7. In the editor, select the `PrimeFactorialGenerator` class and press **F3** to open its declaration. The editor will show "source not found" because we included only the binaries when we defined the library. We

did not include the corresponding source. Let's fix this. Select **Attach Source...** in the editor. In the Source Attachment Configuration dialog, select **External File...**. Browse the file system for the Number-eneratorSource.jar file you created. Select **OK** to attach the source. You will see the source for the class in the editor. Note that while you associated the source from the editor, the definition of this user library was updated as well.

8. On to the launch configuration. Select **Run > Run...** to display the Run launch configurations dialog. You may see several launch configurations listed. Some are from the sample code you imported to use with this exercise, and you may have others if you have run other Java programs. Eclipse creates default launch configurations for you when you run Java programs.

    Select **Java Application** as the type of launch configuration and then select **New** to create a new one. Name the launch configuration TestLaunchConfiguration. Depending on what is currently selected in the Package Explorer, **Project** and **Main class** may or may not have entries. Ensure that these entries are com.ibm.jdg2e.usingjdt.launchconfigurations and com.ibm.jdg2e.usingjdt.launchconfigurations.TestLaunchConfiguration, respectively. Note that selecting **Search...** initiates a search for classes with main methods (see Figure Ex3.3).

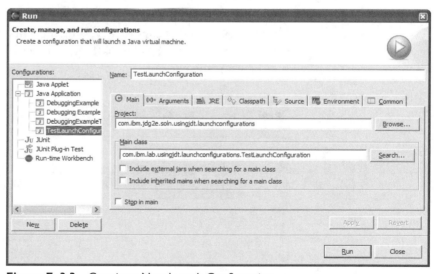

**Figure Ex3.3**   Creating a New Launch Configuration

9. Switch to the **Arguments** page (see Figure Ex3.4). Enter 5 for **Program arguments**. This is the number of prime factorials you want to generate. Enter the following for **VM arguments**.

   `-showversion -DmyName="D'Anjou et al"`

   This defines a system property called myName. The name of this property is case sensitive.

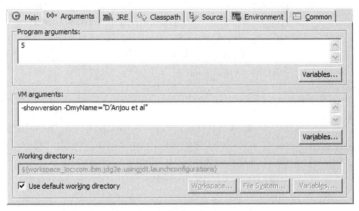

**Figure Ex3.4**   Specifying Launch Configuration Arguments

10. Select the **Classpath** page (see Figure Ex3.5). Observe that the user library NumberGeneratorLibrary, which points to NumberGenerator-Binaries.jar, is on the classpath. This is set based on the project's build path information.

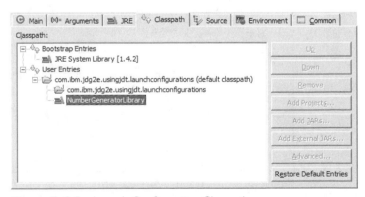

**Figure Ex3.5**   Launch Configuration Classpath

11. Select the **Common** page (see Figure Ex3.6). You're going to change the settings here to save the launch configuration as a file with the project. This way you can easily share it with your colleagues and track changes to it in a code repository. Select **Shared** and then select **Browse....** Select **com.ibm.jdg2e.usingjdt.launchconfigurations** in the Folder Selection dialog and then select **OK**. For **Display in favorites menu**, select **Run**. This will cause this launch configuration entry to appear as a favorite under **Run** on the toolbar the first time it is run. Leave **Launch in background** selected. In the Package Explorer view, you should see a new file called TestLaunchConfiguration.launch in the com.ibm.jdg2e.usingjdt.launchconfigurations project; it contains the launch configuration settings you just configured in XML.

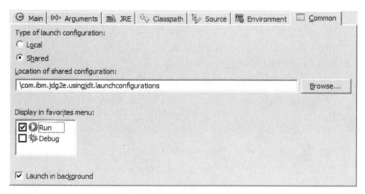

**Figure Ex3.6** Sharing a Launch Configuration

12. Rather than having to select your new launch configuration before it appears on the favorites under **Run**, did you know you can directly edit your favorites? Select the **Run** pull-down menu ▶ ▼ and then **Organize Favorites....** Select **Add...**, select **TestLaunchConfiguration**, and then select **OK** and **OK** again to add this launch configuration as a favorite.

13. Let's test the code. First, because we elected to run this in the background, open up the Progress view to watch it run. Select **Window > Show View > Other....** Expand the **Basic** category and select the **Progress** view. From the **Run** pull-down menu select **TestLaunch-Configuration**. TestLaunchConfiguration runs with the program and JVM arguments you defined in the launch configuration. You'll briefly see processing displayed in the Progress view (there's not a lot of code

executing) and output displayed in the Console view. You'll see the output for the system property you defined with the JVM arguments. Once you've run a program, in addition to any favorites you have defined, you have a run history available from **Run > Run History**. You can also select **Run** ● to rerun the last program you ran.

If you got an error, the most common mistake is forgetting the input parameters in the launch configuration. Review these.

In this section, you used launch configurations to specify more information about a program's execution, including input and JVM parameters and its classpath. You also defined a launch configuration so that it could be shared. When you're through, don't forget to close any open editors.

## Section 2: Debugging

In this section, you're going to debug Java programs, use breakpoints, examine program execution, and see how to control program execution. To help illustrate this exercise, on the CD-ROM we've provided the project com.ibm .jdg2e.usingjdt, which contains several packages. This code represents several iterations of a program to generate numbers. It is the same code used in Exercise 2, Using Java Development Tools. Be sure you have this project in your workspace. If you do not, refer to the instructions on the CD-ROM.

If you haven't completed Exercise 2, you may see errors in some of the packages. Don't worry about the errors—they're intentional. We put them there so you could fix them in Exercise 2. In any case, you can ignore them for this exercise. The packages you'll be using do not have errors.

The same class is defined in multiple packages. Unless otherwise specified, references to a class or some other Java element or resource are to the element or resource in the package com.ibm.jdg2e.usingjdt.debugging. We've also added the DebuggingExample class with a simple main method to drive the code and a launch configuration, DebuggingExample.launch.

1. From within one of the Java perspectives, edit the DebuggingExample class in the debugging package and set a breakpoint on the first statement in the method by double-clicking on the marker bar of the editor next to the line.
2. From the **Debug** pull-down menu 🐞 ▾, select **Debug As > Java Application**. If you are asked whether you want to switch to the Debug perspective, answer **Yes**. The main method in the Debugging-Example class executes and execution suspends before the line on which you defined the breakpoint, as shown in Figure Ex3.7.

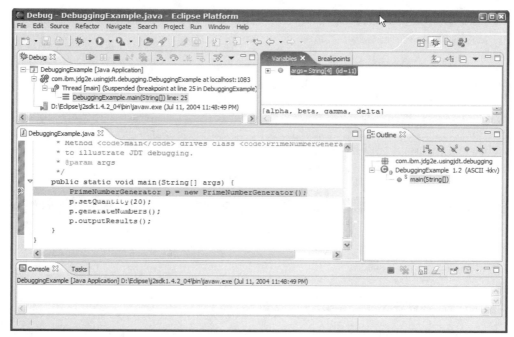

**Figure Ex3.7** Debug Perspective

3. The breakpoint icon is decorated with a check mark. This indicates that the class has been loaded by the JVM running in this debug session. Note that the breakpoint marker may be obscured if the instruction pointer ➡ is on top of it.

4. In the Debug view, select debug target 🦴 com.ibm.jdg2e.usingjdt .debugging.DebuggingExample, and then select **Properties...** from the context menu. You see information on how the debug session was started, including the input parameters you defined in the launch configuration (see Figure Ex3.8). Select **OK** to close this dialog.

5. In the next several steps you'll use debugging commands to control program execution. Select the current stack frame ≡ in the Debug view, and then select **Step Over** 🦴 or press **F6**. One line executes and execution suspends on the next line. The variable p appears in the Variables view (see Figure Ex3.9).

6. Select **Step Into** 🦴 or press **F5**. A new stack frame is created for the method invocation setQuantity, the editor opens on NumberGenerator .java, and execution suspends on the first statement in the method (see Figure Ex3.10).

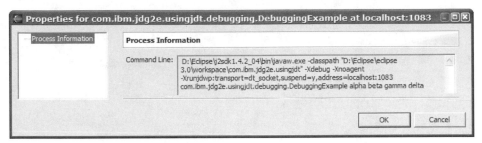

**Figure Ex3.8**   Debug Target Properties

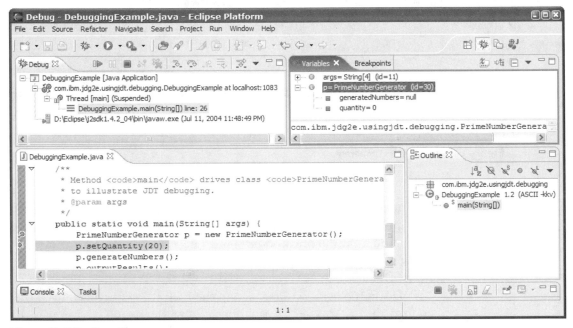

**Figure Ex3.9**   Step Over

7. **Step Over** this line and the next one to exit the method. The top stack frame is discarded and execution suspends on the statement following the one you just stepped into. **Step Into** p.generateNumbers(). Select **Step Return** _◻ or press **F7**. Execution resumes to the end of the method in the current stack frame, returns from the method execution, and suspends on p.outputResults(), the statement following the method invocation.

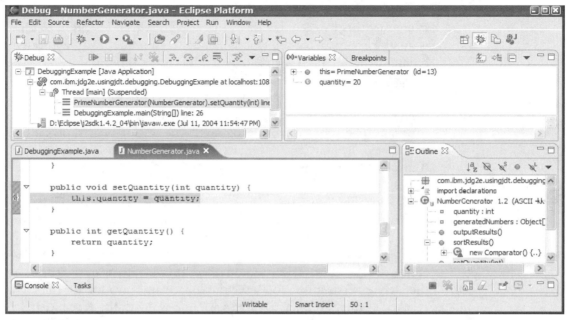

**Figure Ex3.10**  Step Into

8. **Step Into** p.outputResults(). Set a breakpoint on the line with the for statement and select **Step Return**. Execution suspends at the breakpoint rather than after the method returns because the breakpoint is encountered first.

9. **Step Over** the for statement. Hover the cursor over the variable i. The value of the variable is displayed, as shown in Figure Ex3.11.

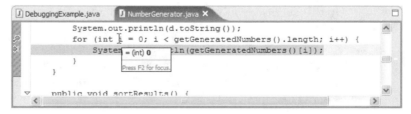

**Figure Ex3.11**  Hovering to View a Variable Value

10. Select **Run to Line** from the context menu or press **Ctrl+R**. Execution resumes and then suspends on the line that was selected, after an

iteration of the loop. You did not have to define a breakpoint. You can verify this by the increase in the value of variable i. **Run to Line** is an efficient way to step through code in an ad hoc way without having to define (and then remove) a lot of breakpoints.

11. Select **Step Return** to complete the outputResults method. The output appears in the Console view. Select **Terminate** ■ to stop execution, or select **Resume** ◫▶ to continue execution to the end of the program. The status of your program in the Debug view shows it has terminated. Remove the terminated entries in the Debug view with **Remove All Terminated** ✖.

12. Finally, given that the Debug perspective includes the Java editor, its navigational aids and other assists are available. Select **Debug** ✿ to restart the debug session. You have a breakpoint defined on the first line of the main method, so execution will suspend there. Select **Window > Show View > Other...** and then select to show the **Java Declaration** and **Javadoc** views. As you select Java elements in the editor in the Debug perspective, you'll see the source and Javadoc for the selected element. Press **Ctrl+T** to see a pop-up with the type hierarchy of the current type. Press **Ctrl+O** to see a pop-up with an Outline view. Press **Esc** to dismiss these pop-ups. These are very useful techniques to quickly get information about the code you're debugging from within your debug session.

In this section, you got a quick introduction into debugging with JDT. You used the primary commands for controlling program execution.

## Section 3: Debugging II

In this section, you're going to pick up where the previous exercise ended and see more kinds of breakpoints, view and change variable values, and refer to classes in a runtime library. This exercise uses project com.ibm.jdg2e.usingjdt, which contains several packages. This code represents several iterations of a program to generate numbers. It is the same code used in Exercise 2, Using Java Development Tools.

Ensure you have the project com.ibm.jdg2e.usingjdt in your workspace. If you do not, refer to the instructions on the CD-ROM. The same class is defined in multiple packages. Unless otherwise specified, references to a class or some other Java element or resource are to the element or resource in the package com.ibm.jdg2e.usingjdt.debugging.

1. Now you'll see how to view and change variable values. Continue your current debug session, or start a new one, on the Debugging-Example program. **Step Over** 🔁 the first line and then **Step Into** 🔁 p.setQuantity(20).

2. Switch to the Variables view. Successively select the variables and watch as the values display in the Detail pane in the bottom of the view. These are the values of the variables' toString methods. To change what appears here, you have two choices. First, of course, you can override the toString method for the class. Second, if you don't want to do this, you can define a detail formatter for the class in your **Java > Debug > Detail Formatters** preferences. This allows you to customize what shows up for values in the Detail panes without overriding toString. You can also select a nonprimitive variable in the Variables view and then **New Detail Formatter...** from the context menu.

3. Double-click on the quantity variable and enter a new value (see Figure Ex3.12). You can also double-click on a value to change it. Enter a new value in the pop-up window and then select **OK**. You can also change a variable's value by editing it in the Detail pane of the Variables view. Select **Assign Value** from the context menu or press **Ctrl+S** to save your changes.

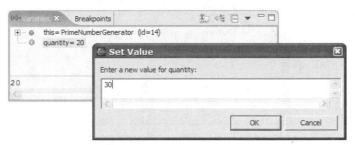

**Figure Ex3.12**  Changing a Variable's Value

Select **Step Return** 🔁, then **Step Into** the line p.generate-Numbers() to go into this method. In the Variables view, expand this and verify that the quantity field has the changed value.

4. With the Variables view visible, **Step Over** lines to continue through an iteration of the while loop. The colors of the entries in the Variables view change as the values change.

5. Breakpoints can have hit counts. To see this, set a breakpoint on the second line of the outer while loop, prime = true;. From the context

PART VI

menu on the breakpoint on the marker bar, select **Breakpoint Properties...**. In the Properties dialog, select **Hit Count** and set its value to 5 (see Figure Ex3.13). Select **OK**. This will cause execution to suspend the fifth time the breakpoint is encountered.

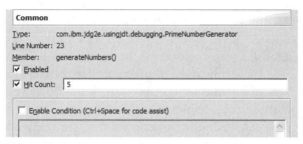

**Figure Ex3.13**   Setting a Breakpoint Hit Count

6. Hover over the breakpoint icon to verify its hit count (see Figure Ex3.14). Hover over the `candidate` variable in the editor and remember its current value.

```
┌─ DebuggingExample.java  ─┬─ PrimeNumberGenerator.java ✕ ──────────────────┐
│        public void generateNumbers() {                                    │
│            ArrayList numbers = new ArrayList();                            │
│            boolean prime;                                                  │
│            int count = 0;                                                  │
│                                                                           │
│            int candidate = 2;                                             │
│            while (count < getQuantity()) {                                │
│  ┌─ Line breakpoint: PrimeNumberGenerator [line: 23] [hit count: 5] - generateNumbers() │
│                int factor = 2;                                            │
└───────────────────────────────────────────────────────────────────────┘
```

**Figure Ex3.14**   Viewing a Breakpoint Hit Count

7. Select **Resume** ▯▶. Execution resumes and then suspends on the breakpoint after five iterations of the `while` loop. Hover again over the `candidate` variable to verify this; its value should be incremented by five (or four, depending on where you were in the loop). The breakpoint shows as disabled (a white dot appears in the left margin instead of blue). Enable it for five more iterations by selecting **Enable Breakpoint** from the marker bar context menu. Select **Resume** again. Execution suspends on the same line after another five iterations. Hover over the `candidate` variable to verify this.

8. Close the editor on the `PrimeNumberGenerator` class and go to the Breakpoints view. You can quickly get back to the source where you've set breakpoints by double-clicking on one in the Breakpoints view. This opens the associated source file and selects the line containing the breakpoint. Do this for the disabled breakpoint. Select the current (top) stack frame in the Debug view to see where execution is currently suspended (see Figure Ex3.15).

**Figure Ex3.15**   Selecting a Stack Frame

9. Let's change this breakpoint to suspend execution when a condition (Java expression) evaluates to `true`. In the Breakpoints view, select the disabled breakpoint in the `generateNumbers` method and then select **Properties...** from the context menu. In the Properties dialog, select **Enabled** to enable the breakpoint. Then deselect **Hit Count** and select **Enable Condition** to make this a conditional breakpoint (see Figure Ex3.16). Enter a condition like `candidate == 10`. Obviously the value should be more than the current value of `candidate`. Select **OK**.

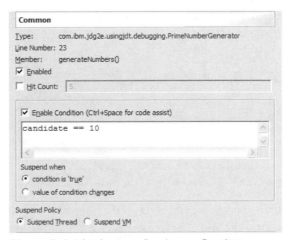

**Figure Ex3.16**   Setting a Breakpoint Condition

PART VI

In the editor, the question-mark label decoration on the breakpoint indicates it is a conditional one.

10. Select **Resume**. Execution resumes and then suspends. Hover over the count variable in the editor to verify that its value is 10, or the value you used.

11. Finally, let's look at evaluating expressions. In this step, we're going to use the Display view, so open it now. Select **Window > Show View > Display**. **Step Over** lines until you are inside the inner `while` loop on the line `if (candidate % factor == 0) {`. In the editor, select the `candidate % factor == 0` expression. From the context menu, select **Display** or press **Ctrl+Shift+D** to evaluate the expression and show the results in a small pop-up window. You can press **Esc** to dismiss the pop-up or press **Ctrl+Shift+D** to save the results in the Display view. Do the latter to save the results of the expression evaluation in the Display view.

12. You can evaluate expressions in the Display view, including the use of code assist. This evaluation, as well as the one we did in the previous step, is done in the context of the current stack frame. You're going to be using the Expressions view, so open it now. In the Display view, enter `numbers.` (note the period). Press **Ctrl+Space** to activate code assist, and then select **toArray()**. Select this expression and then select **Inspect** from the context menu or press **Ctrl+Shift+I**. The results are shown in a small pop-up. Press **Ctrl+Shift+I** to save the results in the Expressions view.

13. Finally, you can evaluate expressions in the Detail pane areas. In the Detail pane of the Expressions view, enter `numbers.get(1)`, select it, and then select **Inspect** from the context menu. Press **Ctrl+Shift+I**, and another entry is added to the Expressions view with the result (see Figure Ex3.17).

**Figure Ex3.17**   Evaluating an Expression in the Detail Pane

14. Expand the **numbers.toArray()** entry in the Expressions view and modify the value of the first entry to a number that is obviously not

prime, like 100. The result of evaluating `numbers.toArray()` returned an array of `Integers`, or more precisely, an array of references to the `Integers` of the variable `numbers`. In the Expressions view, when you change a value to a referenced object, you change the value in the current stack frame. The point here is that with object references, you are not just changing a value in the Expressions view. While you make the change there, you are actually changing the value of an object in your executing program and (potentially) altering its behavior.

15. Select **Resume** to continue execution to the end of the program. Verify that the value you changed in local variable `numbers` is reflected in the output in the Console view.

When you're through, don't forget to close all open editors, terminate and remove existing debugging sessions, and remove your existing breakpoints. Use **Remove All** ✖ in the Debug and Breakpoints views to do this.

In this section, you took a tour through the main line debugging capabilities of JDT. You set breakpoints, examined and changed variable values, and controlled program execution.

## Section 4: Debugging Threads

In this section, you're going to look at an example of debugging a program that uses multiple threads. In multithreaded programs, threads run in parallel, and the order in which individual threads execute and suspend can be nondeterministic. You'll see how to separately control individual threads in a program to make this order deterministic. You're also going to see field watchpoints and method breakpoints, including a method breakpoint on a class in a runtime library (JAR file). You're going to use a version of `Number-Generator`; its subclasses have been modified to create threads and output their results with thread names so you can tell which output is coming from which thread. The `DebuggingExampleThreaded` class drives this code. It takes one input parameter that specifies the number of threads to create. On the CD-ROM, we provide a launch configuration, `DebuggingExampleThreaded`, to start the debugging session and pass the input parameter. We've set this parameter to 2 to create two threads.

Ensure you have the project `com.ibm.jdg2e.usingjdt` in your workspace. If you do not, refer to the instructions on the CD-ROM. The same class is defined in multiple packages. Unless otherwise specified, references to a class or some other Java element or resource are to the element or resource in the package com.ibm.jdg2e.usingjdt.threadeddebugging.

1. Select **Run > Debug...** to see your launch configurations. Select the **DebuggingExampleThreaded** launch configuration. Select **Stop in Main** and then select **Debug**. This will start a debugging session, and execution will suspend on the first statement in the main method. If you are prompted to switch to the Debug perspective, respond **Yes**.

2. When execution suspends, open PrimeNumberGenerator by selecting the class name in the editor and then pressing **F3** or selecting **Open Declaration** from the context menu. From the editor, set a breakpoint on the first line of the generateNumbers method (see Figure Ex3.18). Select the stack frame ≡ in the Debug view to activate the editor for the DebuggingExampleThreaded class.

**Figure Ex3.18**   PrimeNumberGenerator Breakpoint

3. Now you'll step through the execution of the program and watch as it creates additional threads. **Step Over** lines through one iteration of the for loop. As you **Step Over** p.start(), a new thread is created in the Debug view. The source for the method executing on this new thread, generateNumbers(), is shown in the editor. Switch back to the original thread by selecting its stack frame ≡ **DebuggingExample-Threaded.main(String[]) line: 26**. Continue to **Step Over** ⟳ another iteration of the for loop to create a second new thread in the Debug view (see Figure Ex3.19).

   The initial thread executing the main method is Thread [main]. The other two threads the main method created are Thread [Thread-0] and Thread [Thread-1]. Depending on the JRE you're running, these thread names may differ slightly from what we show here. If so, in the following steps, modify the instructions based on your thread names. Select the top stack frame for each of the threads to see the state of its execution, that is, where its execution has suspended.

**Figure Ex3.19**   Debug View with Multiple Threads

Thread-0 and Thread-1 have suspended on the breakpoint you set
in generateNumbers.

You have multiple threads running. In the next several steps,
you're going to set three breakpoints: one restricted to Thread-0,
another restricted to Thread-1, and a third common to all threads.

4. On Thread-0, you're going to set a watchpoint. Watchpoints are useful when you want to observe how a field is accessed. It's often easier to use a watchpoint on a field than it is to try to set breakpoints
on all the lines that might access the field. In the editor, showing the
generateNumbers method, press **Ctrl+T** to display a hierarchy pop-
up of types implementing generateNumbers. Select **NumberGenerator** and press **Enter** to open an editor on this class. In the Outline
view for **NumberGenerator**, select the quantity field and then select
**Toggle Watchpoint** from the context menu. The watchpoint icon
will appear in the editor marker bar on the quantity field. You will
also see a new entry in the Breakpoints view. Right-click on the
watchpoint in the marker bar and select **Breakpoint Properties...**
from the context menu. Select **Filtering**. Expand the list of threads in
the bottom pane and select (check) Thread-0 (see Figure Ex3.20).
Select **OK**. This watchpoint will suspend execution when the quantity field is accessed or modified from Thread-0.

5. On Thread-1, you're going to define a method breakpoint on a class in
a JAR file. Being able to set breakpoints on classes in JAR files allows
you to do so in code outside your workspace and in code for which
you do not have the source. This exercise assumes you do not have
source for your JRE. If you do, this will still work, but it may be a bit
less compelling. In the editor on the PrimeNumberGenerator class,
select type ArrayList in the generateNumbers method and then press
**F4** or select **Open Type Hierarchy** from the context menu to display a

PART VI

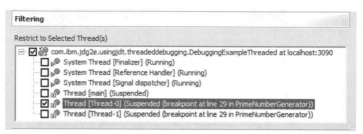

**Figure Ex3.20**   Restricting a Watchpoint to a Thread

Hierarchy view of `ArrayList`. The editor will show no source. Be sure the Breakpoints view is visible so you can see as the breakpoint is created. In the bottom pane of the Hierarchy view (or the right pane, depending on how you have it organized), select the method `add(Object)` and then select **Toggle Method Breakpoint**. In the Breakpoints view, edit the properties of the method breakpoint you just created. Restrict this breakpoint to `Thread-1`. This breakpoint will suspend execution on entry into the `add(Object)` method of the `ArrayList` class (in the JRE) in `Thread-1`.

6. You need one more breakpoint, on the `NumberGenerator` class. Switch to the editor on the `NumberGenerator` class. Add a breakpoint on the `println` method invocation in the `for` loop of `outputResults` (see Figure Ex3.21). Do not restrict the threads for this breakpoint.

```
DebuggingExampleThreaded.java      PrimeNumberGenerator.java      NumberGenerator.java ✕

        public void outputResults(String threadName) {
            Date d = new Date();
            String prefix = "";
            if (threadName != "") {
                prefix = threadName + ": ";
            }
            System.out.println(prefix + d.toString());
            for (int i = 0; i < getResults().length; i++) {
                System.out.println(prefix + getResults()[i]);
            }
        }
```

**Figure Ex3.21**   Breakpoint in `outputResults`

7. You should have the breakpoints defined as shown in Figure Ex3.22.
8. Let's see how these breakpoints work. In the Debug view, select the top stack frame in `Thread-0`. Recall that the watchpoint on the quantity field is restricted to `Thread-0`. Select **Step Return** ⏎. Execution proceeds and then suspends in the `getQuantity` method on the access

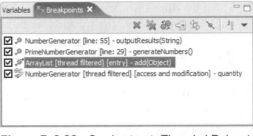

**Figure Ex3.22**    Breakpoints in Threaded Debugging Example

to the quantity field. Select **Resume** ▯▶. Execution suspends on the next access to quantity. In the Breakpoints view, select the watchpoint and then select **Disable** from the context menu. Note the change in the icon's color when you do this. Select **Resume** again. Execution proceeds and then suspends on the breakpoint in the outputResults method, which was not restricted to a specific thread. Execution on this thread (Thread-0) did not suspend on the method breakpoint because it is restricted to Thread-1. Leave Thread-0 in its current state. Go back and reenable the watchpoint.

9. In the Debug view, select the top stack frame in Thread-1. Recall that the method breakpoint you defined is restricted to this thread. Select **Resume**. Execution proceeds and then suspends on entry into the add(Object) method. Even though the editor displays no source, you can tell where the method breakpoint suspended execution by noticing the selected breakpoint in the Breakpoints view, the title on the editor tab, Arraylist.class, and the selected method in the Outline view, add(Object). Select the previous stack frame on Thread-1 in the Debug view to see that add(Object) was invoked from the numbers.add() statement in the generateNumbers method. **Step Over** this stack frame to return to the line that invoked add(Object).

10. In the Breakpoints view, disable this method breakpoint (on the method add(Object)). In the Debug view, ensure that you have the top stack frame in Thread-1 selected. Select **Resume**. Execution proceeds and then suspends on the breakpoint in outputResults(String). Execution in this thread, Thread-1, did not suspend on the watchpoint because it is restricted to Thread-0. Watch as the first two lines of output appear in the Console view, prefixed with the threads' names.

11. Both threads are now suspended at the same line in output-Results(String). Select the top stack frame for Thread-0 in the Debug view and **Step Over** a few lines. Select the top stack frame for

Thread-1 and do the same. Watch as output appears in the Console view. Without intervention, the threads would run in parallel, and the order of the sequence of lines executed by the threads would be non-deterministic. Using this technique, you can make the order of these statements deterministic. Finally, allow the program to run to completion, or terminate the debugging session.

When you're through, don't forget to close all open editors, remove terminated debugging sessions from the Debug view, and remove your existing breakpoints.

In this section, you debugged a multithreaded program and independently controlled the different threads of execution in the program.

## Section 5: Remote Debugging

In this section, you'll debug a remote program, that is, a Java program launched outside of Eclipse. To do this, we've prepared a JAR file, Remote-Example.jar, with the class NumberGenerator and its subclasses, and the class RemoteDebuggingExample to drive the class PrimeNumberGenerator. We've also provided the remote.bat file to invoke the main method of the class Remote-DebuggingExample outside of Eclipse, and a Remote Java Application launch configuration, RemoteDebuggingExample, to start the remote debugging session.

Ensure that you have the project com.ibm.jdg2e.usingjdt in your workspace. If you do not, refer to the instructions on the CD-ROM. The same class is defined in multiple packages. Unless otherwise specified, references to a class or some other Java element or resource refer to the element or resource in the package com.ibm.jdg2e.usingjdt.remotedebugging.

1. Edit the file remote.bat in the remotedebugging package by selecting **Open With > Text Editor**. Double-clicking on it will cause it to execute. The code is shown below, with line breaks added to improve readability. Note the JVM parameters required for Eclipse to be able to connect to the remote Java program and initiate a debugging session. You are going to use port 8000. You are passing the main method of Remote-DebuggingExample input parameter 20. For a short explanation of the debug parameters, refer to the Remote Debugging section in Chapter 4, or refer to your JVM documentation for a more complete treatment.

```
rem set path=
java
   -classpath RemoteExample.jar
   -Xdebug
```

```
-Xnoagent
-Xrunjdwp:transport=dt_socket,server=y,suspend=y,address=8000
-Djava.compiler=NONE
com.ibm.jdg2e.usingjdt.remotedebugging.RemoteDebuggingExample
20
```

In some cases, you may need to set the `path` variable. We'll get to this in a moment.

2. Open a command prompt. Go to your Eclipse workspace folder, `workspace` by default, under your main Eclipse folder. Go into the folder `com.ibm.jdg2e.usingjdt` and then down through the subfolders to get to the folder `remotedebugging`. If you installed Eclipse on `c:\eclipse3.0`, the full path would be (on one line):

```
c:\eclipse3.0\eclipse\workspace\com.ibm.jdg2e.usingjdt
   \com\ibm\jdg2e\usingjdt\remotedebugging
```

Alternatively, and here's a neat trick, open the properties for package `com.ibm.jdg2e.usingjdt.remotedebugging`. Select the **Location** value and press **Ctrl+C** to copy it. Now you can quickly paste this into a command prompt.

Run `remote.bat`. The JVM will start and then wait for a connection.

If you receive an error message and the JVM terminates, one possible cause may be that the JVM can't find the dynamic link libraries (DLLs)—`jdwp.dll` and `dt_socket.dll`—it needs to do remote debugging, or it may be finding ones that don't match the JVM. If this is the case, you'll need to define the `path` variable in `remote.bat` to point the JVM to the correct DLLs.

3. Switch to Eclipse and open the `RemoteDebuggingExample` class in the `remotedebugging` package. Set a breakpoint on the first line of the `main` method.

Select **Debug > Debug…** and then **RemoteDebuggingExample** under **Remote Java Application** to review the settings for the launch configuration. You are going to be running the "remote" Java program on the same machine as Eclipse, `localhost`, but outside of Eclipse. Eclipse is going to use port 8000 to communicate with the JVM running the remote program, as specified in the command line parameters in `remote.bat`, and corresponding to the connection properties of the launch configuration (see Figure Ex3.23).

4. Select **Debug** in the Debug launch configurations dialog. A debugging session starts, connects to the JVM running `RemoteDebugging-Example`, and displays the source for `RemoteDebuggingExample`, with the line with your breakpoint selected. The entries in the Debug view indicate a remote debug target and its location (see Figure Ex3.24).

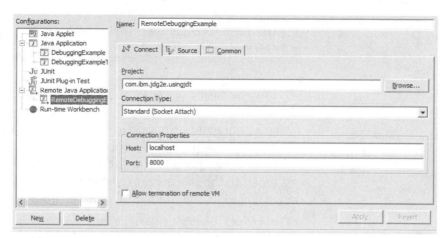

**Figure Ex3.23**   Remote Java Application Launch Configuration

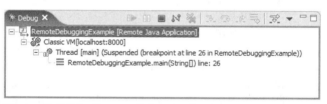

**Figure Ex3.24**   Remote Debugging Session

At this point, you can run your debugging session as you would a local Java program.

5. Now let's see how debugging a remote program is just like debugging one running in Eclipse. In the `main` method, **Step Over** 🔁 statements until you get to `outputResults`. **Step Into** 🔽 this method. In the Variables view, expand **this** and then expand its **generatedNumbers** field. Double-click on the value of the first element of the array and change its value from 2 to something obviously nonprime, like 100. Select **OK** to save the value and verify, in the Variables view, that the value is changed.

6. **Step Over** lines in the `outputResults` method until you see the output of the result you changed. Note that the output will not appear in the Console view because the execution of the Java program you're debugging is happening outside Eclipse. Rather, the program's output will appear in the command prompt window.

7. Now let's take a look at hot code replace. At this point, the current stack frame is on the `outputResults` method. Let's edit this method. Add a line, inside the `for` loop and before the `println()` statement: a simple `print()` statement, like `System.out.print("Number " + i + ": " );`. Save your changes. Execution will reset to the beginning of the method. Now start stepping over statements. You'll see your changes to the `outputResults` method reflected in the output in the command prompt window.

8. Select **Resume**. The remote program completes execution, and its output is displayed in the command prompt window.

   When you're through, don't forget to close all open editors and remove terminated debugging sessions from the Debug view.

In this section, you debugged a program running outside of Eclipse. You used JDT to set breakpoints, examine and change variable values, and control program execution just as if the program had been running within Eclipse.

## Exercise Activity Review

This concludes this exercise, in which you saw how you can run and debug your Java programs from Eclipse. The debugging included detailed steps for debugging multithreaded programs and debugging remote programs outside of Eclipse. These last two techniques are especially important as they form the basic building blocks for debugging server-side applications, such as Web applications running under a Web application server. In fact, this is the purpose of Exercise 4, to use many of the concepts you learned in Exercises 1 through 3 and to expand on them to build a simple Web commerce site. Good stuff! We'll see you in Exercise 4.

## Reference

Arthorne, John, and Chris Laffra. 2004. *Official Eclipse 3.0 FAQs.* Boston, MA: Addison-Wesley. http://eclipsefaq.org. (See Chapter 3 and FAQs 313, 317, 318.)

PART VI

# EXERCISE 4

## *Developing a Simple Web Commerce Application with Eclipse*

In the first several chapters of this book, we introduced Eclipse and provided a general overview of its use. We looked specifically at writing, running, and debugging Java and managing team development in Eclipse using CVS. In this exercise, we're going to put much of this together in a robust example. Our goal is to put together many of the individual things you saw in Part I into a more comprehensive application of Eclipse to a programming problem, to illustrate a realistic example similar to what you might do every day with Eclipse as part of your work.

This chapter will walk you through the steps of developing and deploying a small e-commerce Web site (see Figure Ex4.1), from code creation to application deployment. The Web site will be implemented with a servlet application that displays some book titles and allows you to select one or more for purchase. If you are unfamiliar with servlets, there are a number of books and tutorials on the topic, including several free online.

We'll start by installing and configuring Tomcat, your runtime environment. Next, you'll introduce the servlet application and deploy it in Tomcat to verify the example and the Tomcat configuration. Once you've verified the servlet application, you'll see how to configure your development environment to effectively manage development and deployment between Eclipse and Tomcat. You'll bring Ant, an open source make utility, into the picture to perform this build and deploy between Eclipse and Tomcat. Finally, you'll

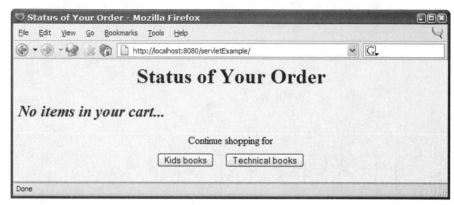

**Figure Ex4.1**    Web Commerce Site Example

also see remote debugging from Eclipse into Tomcat. The instructions we provide are for Windows. You may need to adapt the steps for other platforms, mostly around installing and configuring Tomcat.

## Exercise Setup

This exercise uses code from a variety of sources. As a convenience, we've included everything you'll need on the CD-ROM in project `com.ibm.jdg2e` `.servletApp.input`. You can work this exercise by getting the required input code from the various sources, or you can load this project into your workspace. You can find the end result of going through all the sections of this exercise in project `com.ibm.jdg2e.soln.servletApp`. We implemented this example using a version 1.4.2 JRE. If you are on a different level of JRE, you may see slightly different results.

## Section 1: Setting up the Runtime Environment

Tomcat is a servlet container from the Apache Jakarta project. It can run standalone or in conjunction with an HTTP server, such as the Apache HTTP server. You'll be using Tomcat standalone. You're going to begin by installing Tomcat and getting its management console up and running. Once that is finished, you'll then install the example to double-check that everything is working before returning to Eclipse's development environment. If you already have Tomcat installed and running, you can skip to the next section, provided you have configured management console access. If you've done this, note the URL of the console, and your user id and password.

1. You can download the Tomcat binaries from the Jakarta project binary download page, http://jakarta.apache.org/site/binindex.cgi. The file you want is `jakarta-tomcat-5.0.19.zip`. This exercise was created using this release. Download the file or get it from project `com.ibm.jdg2e.servletApp.input` and unzip it in a convenient location. You're going to run Tomcat on the same computer as Eclipse and access it through hostname `localhost`.

   As we mentioned earlier, we'll be focusing here on the Windows operating system. For information about installing Tomcat on non-Windows systems, please refer to http://jakarta.apache.org/tomcat/tomcat-5.0-doc/setup.html.

2. Next you need to verify that hostname `localhost` is defined on your computer. The simplest way to do this is to "ping" the hostname. Enter the following at a command prompt.

   ```
   ping localhost
   ```

   If `localhost` is defined, you'll see a response like this:

   ```
   Pinging Roma [127.0.0.1] with 32 bytes of data:

   Reply from 127.0.0.1: bytes=32 time<1ms TTL=128
   Reply from 127.0.0.1: bytes=32 time<1ms TTL=128
   Reply from 127.0.0.1: bytes=32 time<1ms TTL=128
   Reply from 127.0.0.1: bytes=32 time<1ms TTL=128

   Ping statistics for 127.0.0.1:
       Packets: Sent = 4, Received = 4, Lost = 0 (0% loss),
   Approximate round trip times in milli-seconds:
       Minimum = 0ms, Maximum = 0ms, Average = 0ms
   ```

   If it is not defined, consult your TCP/IP documentation for how to define it.

3. Tomcat will need access to an installed JRE. It gets this from the `JAVA_HOME` environment variable. If you've installed a JRE, this is most likely set. You can find out, for example, by executing the following command at a command prompt. Do this now.

   ```
   Echo %JAVA_HOME%
   ```

   If it's set, you'll see a response like:

   ```
   D:\Eclipse\j2sdk1.4.2_03
   ```

   If `JAVA_HOME` is not set, you need to set it. One possibility is to set it in the script that starts Tomcat. On Windows, this is `startup.bat`. It's important that the JRE Tomcat is using is the same JRE you use in Eclipse to develop your Java code. At the risk of stating the obvious,

PART VI

we want to ensure the development environment matches, as closely as possible, the test/production environment. This is all there is to setting up Tomcat on Windows.

4. The easiest way to start Tomcat is through `startup.bat` in the `bin` folder under the Tomcat installation folder. If `JAVA_HOME` is defined, `startup.bat` usually works with no modifications. You know Tomcat has started successfully when you see a message like the following in the command prompt window, usually after a bunch of other log messages detailing the startup process.

```
INFO: Server startup in 7641 ms
```

For future reference, to stop Tomcat, use `shutdown.bat` located in the same folder as `startup.bat`.

Finally, try the installation. Open a browser on http://localhost:8080/, which is Tomcat's home page. The home page should look like Figure Ex4.2. If you have problems with Tomcat's installation and configuration, consult the Tomcat resources at Apache's site, http://jakarta.apache.org/ tomcat/index.html.

Once we see the Tomcat home page, we know that Tomcat is running. Now, on to the management console.

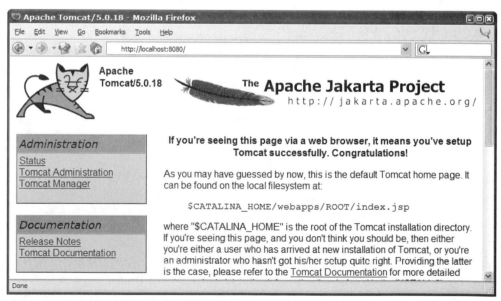

**Figure Ex4.2**    Tomcat Home Page

5. The Tomcat management console is a means by which you deploy, start, stop, and list Web applications running under Tomcat. This is the **Tomcat Manager** link on the Tomcat home page. The URL for it is http://localhost:8080/manager/html. If you try this, you'll discover you are prompted for a user id and password. For security reasons, Tomcat does not come preconfigured with a default user id and password. To define your user id and password, edit file tomcat-users.xml in the Tomcat conf subdirectory. Add a line like the following (set in **bold** in the following snippet) to define a user with manager-level access.

```
<?xml version='1.0' encoding='utf-8'?>
<tomcat-users>
  <role rolename="tomcat"/>
  <role rolename="role1"/>
  <role rolename="manager"/>
  <user username="Kellerman" password="xyzzy" roles="manager"/>
  <user username="role1" password="tomcat" roles="role1"/>
  <user username="both" password="tomcat" roles="tomcat,role1"/>
</tomcat-users>
```

You'll need to stop and start Tomcat for this definition to take effect. Do this now. Use shutdown.bat and startup.bat in the bin folder of the Tomcat installation folder. Try the **Tomcat Manager** link on the Tomcat home page. When prompted, enter the user id and password you defined. You should see the Tomcat Manager interface as shown in Figure Ex4.3.

6. The interface is pretty much self-explanatory. Experiment a bit, for example with the servlet or JSP examples. Try stopping, starting, and reloading them. We'll see later in this exercise how to programmatically execute these same actions through Ant tasks.

Now that you have verified Tomcat is installed, configured, and running and you can access the Tomcat Manager functions through the Manager console, let's take a look at the example, install and configure it, and verify its operation.

## Section 2: Creating a Project for the Example

As shown earlier in Figure Ex4.1, the example we'll be using is a servlet program, a simple Web commerce application, written by Marty Hall and illustrated in his book, *Core Servlets and JavaServer Pages*, and later adapted by Professor George Corliss at Marquette University.

**Figure Ex4.3**    Tomcat Manager Console

We chose a servlet application rather than a standalone Java program because it provides a more interesting deploy and debug exercise.

1. You'll need the following files. We have included them on the CD-ROM in project `com.ibm.jdg2e.servletApp.input`.
   - `Catalog.java`
   - `CatalogPage.java`
   - `Item.java`
   - `ItemOrder.java`
   - `KidsBooksPage.java`
   - `OrderPage.java`
   - `ServletUtilities.java`
   - `ShoppingCart.java`
   - `TechBooksPage.java`
   - `Checkout.html`

2. Now that you have the example code, you're going to configure a project so you can manage development of the servlet application. Create a Java project called com.ibm.jdg2e.servletApp. Make sure you specify that the project should have separate source and output folders. You can name these as you choose. In this example, we're going to use the Eclipse defaults, src for source and bin for output. Select **Finish** to create the project. Respond **Yes** if asked if you want to switch to the Java perspective.

3. You also need to set the target JRE you use to develop Java code in this project to match what Tomcat is using. Recall that the JRE that Tomcat is using is the one indicated in the JAVA_HOME environment variable. Check your **Java > Installed JREs** preferences by selecting **Window > Preferences** to see the Preferences dialog. If the JRE that Tomcat is using is not listed, select **Add...** to add it. Otherwise, go on to the next step.

    When you add this JRE, do not make it the default. The default JRE is indicated on the **Installed JREs** preference page with a check box. We don't want this JRE to be the default JRE for all your Java projects, only this one project.

4. If Tomcat is already using the Eclipse default JRE, it means your target JRE for this project (and all other Eclipse projects) matches what Tomcat is using. You can skip to the next step.

    Otherwise, you need to make this JRE you just installed the target only for project com.ibm.jdg2e.servletApp. Open the project's properties by selecting the project in the Package Explorer view and then selecting **Properties** from the context menu. Select **Java Build Path** properties and then select the **Libraries** page. Select the existing JRE and then select **Remove**. Select **Add Library...**. In the Add Library wizard, select to add a **JRE System Library**. Finally, in the Add Library dialog, select the JRE Tomcat is using (see Figure Ex4.4). Now the target JRE for this project matches the JRE Tomcat is using.

5. Now let's import the source. In the source folder, src, create a package called coreservlets. Use the Import wizard or drag and drop the nine Java files into the coreservlets package. Your project should now look like what Figure Ex4.5 shows.

6. You'll notice several errors. These are due to unresolved references to various Java servlet declarations. You need to add these declarations to the build path of the project. They are contained in a Tomcat file, servlet-api.jar. You're going to do this with a user library. Go back to the **Libraries** page of the **Java Build Path** properties of the project.

PART VI

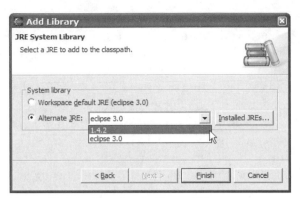

**Figure Ex4.4** Changing the Target JRE

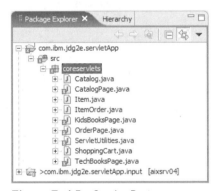

**Figure Ex4.5** Servlet Project

Select **Add Library...**. This time select to add a **User Library** and press **Next**. On the **User Library** page of the Add Library wizard, select **User Libraries...**. This will display your User Library preferences. Select **New...** to define a new user library, name it Servlet, and press **OK**. Now that you have defined the library, you need to add files to it. Select **Add Jars...**. Open folder /common/lib in the main Tomcat folder and select file servlet-api.jar. Your library should appear as in Figure Ex4.6.

Select **OK** and then **Finish** to exit out of these dialogs, and you'll see you have user library Servlet added on the **Libraries** page of your **Java Build Path** properties. Select **OK** here to save the properties. You'll see the unresolved references errors are fixed. Some warnings will remain. Let's sort these out next.

**Figure Ex4.6**  Defining a User Library

7. The warnings left are for use of deprecated methods, unused `import` statements, and an incorrect access to a static field. Strictly speaking, we don't need to fix these. The example will work as is. However, by going through the work to fix these, we can show you some cool stuff. Skip to the next step if you don't want to try this.

From the Problems view, double-click the first warning about an unused `import` statement. The file with the warning opens in the editor. Press **Ctrl+Shift+O** for **Source > Organize Imports**. This resolves that unused `import` statement. Repeat for the remaining unused `import` statement warnings. To have the warnings removed from the Problems view, save the changes in the file you are editing.

You should have three warnings remaining. Double-click the warning for an incorrect static field access to open the file. Press **Ctrl+I** for content assist. Select the entry for changing access to use `HttpServletResponse`. Save these changes.

What's left now are two warnings about the use of deprecated methods, `getValue` and `putValue`. To determine the correct method to use, you'll need to refer to the Javadoc. These methods are defined in `servlet-api.jar`. Tomcat 5.0.18 implements the Java Servlet 2.4 specification, which is part of J2EE 1.4. Javadoc for this is available at http://java.sun.com/j2ee/1.4/docs/api/. You need to associate this Javadoc with `servlet-api.jar` in the user library you defined. To do this, open the properties on the project and select the **Libraries** page of the **Java Build Path** properties. Expand the entries under the **Servlet** user library and edit the Javadoc location to define it to be the aforementioned URL (see Figure Ex4.7). Select **OK** to save these properties changes.

PART VI

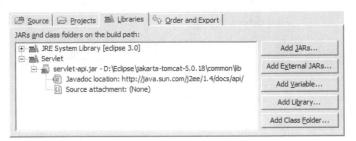

**Figure Ex4.7**   Associating Javadoc

Now you're ready to fix these remaining two warnings. Position the insertion cursor in the `getValue` method invocation and press **Shift+F2**. Javadoc for this method is displayed. The Javadoc indicates the correct method is `getAttribute`. Make this change. Repeat for the `putValue` method invocation. You'll see that this should be changed to `setAttribute`. Make this change. Save the file. You should now have no errors or warnings.

8. You need an HTML file for the checkout page, `Checkout.html`. Create a nonsource folder, named web, in the project. You're going to use this later for other, non-Java content for the example application. Copy `Checkout.html` from `com.ibm.jdg2e.servletApp.input` into this folder.

9. Finally, we need to create one more file to complete the example, a file called `web.xml`. This is the Web application deployment descriptor and describes to Tomcat how the application is installed and configured. Tomcat looks for this file in a specific place, a `WEB-INF` folder in the application's root folder. You're going to create a similar folder structure in your application project to make it easier to deploy later. Create a folder called `WEB-INF` in the web folder and create file `web.xml` in the `WEB-INF` folder. Edit the contents of `web.xml` to match the version of the file we have included in `com.ibm.jdg2e.servletApp.input`.

    Basically, here you're defining references to servlet classes and then mapping these definitions to URL patterns that will be used to reference them. We do this for the three pages that comprise the application, the order page, the kids books page, and the tech books page.

10. There's one final thing to add to the project. Recall that in Section 1 of this exercise you modified a configuration file, `tomcat-users.xml`, to define a `user id` and password so that you could access the manager console. Let's manage this file as part of the project, so you don't lose track of it. You'll do this by means of a linked file. Linked files are pointers in your projects to files (or folders) elsewhere on the file sys-

tem. Select the project and then select to create a new file. Name it TomcatUsers and then select **Advanced** and check **Link to file in the file system**. Select **Variables...** to define a new path variable and point it to tomcat-users.xml in the Tomcat conf folder. Use this variable as the link to the file (see Figure Ex4.8).

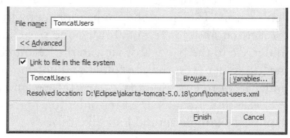

**Figure Ex4.8** Defining a Linked File

You may be wondering why we're using a variable—this is one file and we're accessing it only in this one project. We're using a variable mainly because in the future you may find a need to reference it from other projects. Doing so through a variable makes it easier to change should its location change, for example, if you changed Tomcat installations. Beyond that, this is simply good practice.

Your project organization should look like what Figure Ex4.9 shows.

**Figure Ex4.9** Organization of the Servlet Example Project

PART VI

11. As Sergio would say, "Bravissimo!" Tomcat's set up and running, and we have the example code configured in a project in Eclipse. Now, let's make sure the example works. To test the example, you need to deploy it to Tomcat. As we'll see shortly, there are some pretty slick ways to do this within Eclipse. However, this first time, you're going to do it manually because a manual deploy is a useful exercise to gain a better understanding of the correct organization of a runtime deployment. To deploy the application, copy the web folder from project `com.ibm.jdg2e.servletApp` and paste it in Tomcat's webapps folder. Go to the Navigator view in the Resource perspective and copy the `bin` folder (yes, the `bin` folder and not the `coreservlets` folder under it) from `com.ibm.jdg2e.servletApp` and paste it in `webapps/web/WEB-INF`. Rename the `bin` folder to `classes`. The structure of the deployed example should look like this.

```
/Jakarta-tomcat-5.0.18
  ...
  /webapps
    ...
    /web
      Checkout.html
      /WEB-INF
        web.xml
        /classes
          /coreservlets
            Catalog.class
            CatalogPage.class
            Item.class
            ItemOrder.class
            KidsBooksPage.class
            OrderPage.class
            ServletUtilities.class
            ShoppingCart.class
            TechBooksPage.class
```

12. Normally, at this point you would use the manager console to deploy this application. However, you're going to taking a shortcut. Tomcat automatically deploys an application when you copy it into Tomcat's webapps folder. Give it a try. Open a browser on http://localhost:8080/web/orderpage. You should see an order with no entries, as shown earlier in Figure Ex4.1.

If this didn't work, check whether the application got deployed. When you copy files into Tomcat's webapps folder, Tomcat normally detects this and deploys the application automatically. If you started Tomcat from a command prompt, you can check the session for a message like the following

```
INFO: Installing web application at context path /web
from URL file:D:\Eclipse\jakarta-tomcat-5.0.18\webapps\web
```

If Tomcat didn't install the application correctly, most likely there is a mismatch between your web.xml file, the organization of your files in the application folder, (web), and the URLs you used to access the application.

If the application was installed correctly, first try reloading the application from the Tomcat manager console. If this doesn't work, try stopping and starting Tomcat.

13. Poke around the example application a bit. Try adding items to your shopping cart. You'll soon discover an error when you attempt to check out. The error is because the URL specified in the code is incorrect for our example. It results in an HTTP 404 error. You'll fix this in the next section.

Excellent—you have now defined a project for the example Web application and the application is deployed and running under Tomcat. Let's get on to debugging it.

## Section 3: Debugging the Example

In this section, you're going to set up Eclipse so you can start and stop Tomcat and debug from Eclipse your servlet application running in Tomcat.

1. During servlet development, you'll discover you end up starting and stopping Tomcat a lot. Let's configure Eclipse so you can do it from within the development environment. You're going to do this by means of external tool definitions that reference the scripts that start and stop Tomcat, startup.bat and shutdown.bat. You're going to make this reference through a variable so that if the location of the scripts changes later, it will be easier to adapt. Select **External Tools...** from the **External Tools** pull-down menu ▶ ▼. Under **Configurations**, select **Program**, and then select **New** to create a new external tool definition. Name the external tool Start Tomcat. Under **Location**, select **Variables....** On the Select Variable dialog, select **Edit Variables....** Define a variable called Tomcat Home and set its location to the root Tomcat installation directory. Back on the Select Variable dialog, select the variable you just defined, **Tomcat Home**, and then select **OK**. On the External Tools dialog, add \bin\startup.bat to complete the location of the external tool. Using the same variable, set

the **Working Directory.** Your external tool should look as shown in Figure Ex4.10.

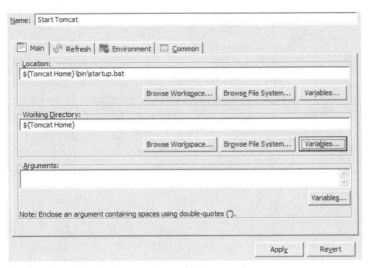

**Figure Ex4.10**    Defining an External Tool

Switch to the **Common** page. Select to share the external tool. Set **Location of shared configuration** to be project \com.ibm.jdg2e .servletApp. Complete the settings as shown in Figure Ex4.11. Select **Apply** to save your changes.

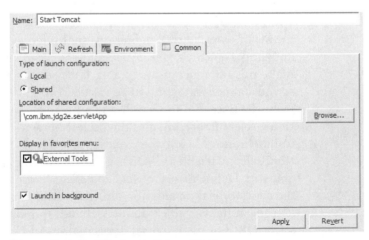

**Figure Ex4.11**    Sharing an External Tool

2. Repeat the process you went through in the previous step to create another external tool, this time one that points to shutdown.bat. Call this one Stop Tomcat. The only things different will be the **Name** and the **Location** on the **Main** page. Apply these changes and select **Close** to close the External Tools dialog. Select **Organize Favorites...** from the **External Tools** pull-down menu and add the two external tool definitions you just created to the favorites menu.

3. Try starting and stopping Tomcat through these external tools definitions. You'll select **Start Tomcat** or **Stop Tomcat** from the **External Tools** pull-down menu.

4. Now, let's start debugging. To debug a servlet running in Tomcat, you need to start Tomcat with a specific set of parameters. See Remote Debugging in Chapter 4, Running and Debugging Java, for an explanation of these parameters. They are as follows (enter them all on one line, although they're shown here on separate lines because of printed line length limitations).

```
-Xdebug -Xnoagent
-Xrunjdwp:transport=dt_socket,server=y,suspend=n,address=8000
-Djava.compiler=NONE
```

Tomcat expects to get parameters like these in environment variable CATALINA_OPTS. Fortunately, external tools definitions provide a convenient way to do this.

You're going to create a third external tool definition, this one to start Tomcat in debug mode. Select **External Tools...** from the **External Tools** pull-down menu and create a new external tool definition called Start Tomcat in Debug. Repeat what you did in step 1 to create the **Start Tomcat** external tool definition. Now, switch to the **Environment** page, create a new environment variable called CATALINA_OPTS, and set its value to be the parameters listed in the previous code lines (see Figure Ex4.12). Select **Apply** to save your changes and then **Close**. Add it to your favorites as you did with the two previous definitions. Don't stop and restart Tomcat just yet—one more step first.

5. You've configured your Tomcat startup so you can start Tomcat and debug into it. Now you need to set up the JDT to connect to Tomcat to enable a debugging session. You do this through a Remote Java Application launch configuration. Select **Debug...** from the **Debug** pull-down menu 🐞 ▼. Select **Remote Java Application** and then select **New** to create a new Remote Java Application launch configuration. Name it Web Commerce Example and set its values as shown in Figure Ex4.13.

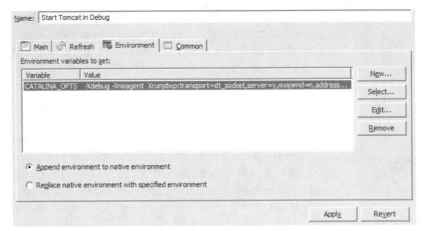

**Figure Ex4.12**　Defining an Environment Variable

**Figure Ex4.13**　Defining a Remote Java Application Launch Configuration

As you did for the external tools definitions you created, switch to the **Common** page and share this as part of your project, com.ibm .jdg2e.servletApp, and select to have it appear in the **Debug** favorites menu.

6. Let's move on to debugging. If Tomcat is running, select **Stop Tomcat** from the **External Tools** pull-down menu. Start Tomcat in debug mode with **Start Tomcat in Debug**, again under the **External Tools** pull-down menu (*not* the **Debug** pull-down). Once Tomcat has

started, you're going to start a remote debug session and connect to Tomcat. Do this by selecting your Remote Java Application launch configuration, **Web Commerce Example**, from the **Debug** pull-down menu. JDT will connect to the JVM running under Tomcat and start a debugging session. Because you have not yet defined any breakpoints, you won't see a switch to the Debug perspective.

7. To verify that you have successfully connected to Tomcat, open the Debug perspective by selecting **Window > Open Perspective > Debug**. You should see at least two entries in the Debug view, as shown in Figure Ex4.14. The second is your remote debug session.

**Figure Ex4.14**   Remote Debug Session

8. So let's give it a try. Set a breakpoint on the first line of the doGet method in the OrderPage class. Open a browser on http://localhost:8080/web/orderpage. Switch to Eclipse and you will see that JDT is starting a debug session. Switch to the Debug perspective. You'll see execution has suspended on your breakpoint. Try stepping through some of the code. When you're done, be sure to select **Resume** in the Debug view to permit the request to complete. Back in the browser, once you select **Resume**, you'll see the request complete in the browser and the order page display.

9. Now let's fix the problem with the incorrect URL for the checkout page. You're going to do this using hot code replace. That is, you're going to fix the code while it is executing in Tomcat. Note that this requires a JVM that supports hot code replace. If your JVM supports this feature, JDT detects it and enables a **Drop to Frame** button on the Debug view toolbar. If you do not see this button, skip ahead to step 11.

In the Breakpoints view, disable your breakpoint. Add an item or two to your shopping cart. Go back to the Breakpoints view and reenable the breakpoint. From your browser on the order page, refresh it, and execution will again suspend on the breakpoint you set. Look down to where the String variable checkoutURL is intialized in the `OrderPage.java` file. Change this line in `OrderPage.java` to be the following.

```
String checkoutURL = "Checkout.html";
```

Save your changes. In the Debug view, you'll see the current stack frame reset and execution suspend on the first statement in the `doGet` method. Select **Resume** again to complete the request to refresh the order page. In your browser, select the **Proceed to Checkout** button. Now you'll see the checkout page. Neat-o!

10. In this example, the user can access the checkout page not only from the order page but also from the kids books and tech books pages. This means that to eliminate all the HTTP 404 errors, you also need to fix the URL for these pages. Fortunately, they are both subclasses of the `CatalogPage` class. Back in JDT, disable your first breakpoint. Set another breakpoint on the first line in the `doGet` method of `Catalog-Page`. In the browser, on the checkout page, select the **Kids Books** button. Execution will suspend on your breakpoint in the `CatalogPage` class. As you did in the previous step, change the value of `checkout-URL` to `"Checkout.html"`. Save your changes, disable all breakpoints, and resume execution to complete the request. In your browser, when the kids books page displays, select the **Proceed to Checkout** button. You'll see this now works. Go to the tech books page and try it from there. It works too.

    One final comment here. You fixed the URL references in the two Java files in your workspace. Using hot code replace, you loaded these changed classes into the running JVM while you were debugging the application. What you did not do, however, was actually deploy this changed code to Tomcat. For example, if you were to stop and start the application in Tomcat, your changes in Tomcat would be gone. We'll see how to automate a process for this in the next section.

    The next step shows a way to fix these problems without using hot code replace. If you were able to complete step 10, skip the next step and go to step 12. Don't forget to remove or disable your breakpoint.

11. If you cannot perform a hot code replace, select **Search** 🔍 to open the Search dialog and switch to the **File Search** page. Search all files in your current project for occurrences of the `checkoutURL` string. Examine these and change the declarations to `"Checkout.html"`. You should find two references, in `OrderPage.java` and `CatalogPage.java`. Save your changes.

12. Now you need to "redeploy" these changes. Switch to the Resource perspective and copy the class files from the `bin` folder for these two

classes you changed to the /web/WEB-INF/classes/coreservlets folder. Open the Tomcat Manager interface and start and stop the example. Now try the example again and go to the checkout page. The problem is resolved.

Superb. You've defined external tools to start and stop Tomcat, including starting Tomcat in debug mode. You debugged the example while it was running under Tomcat. The example application, for our purposes here, is complete. Let's look now at how to automate the deployment of the application to Tomcat.

## Section 4: Deploying the Example

You have set up your project with the servlet application. You've done a manual deploy from Eclipse to Tomcat and verified that the application works. Now let's set up Eclipse to make deployment a little less tedious. We're going to use Ant to automate deployment actions between Eclipse and Tomcat. We presented a brief overview of Ant in the Eclipse Ant Integration section of Chapter 3, Using Java Development Tools. If you haven't read this, you might want to take a moment now to do so before following the steps in this section of the exercise.

1. Create a new file in project com.ibm.jdg2e.servletApp called build.xml. This is thc dcfault name for an Ant build file. When deploying servlets with Ant, a good place to start for the contents of build.xml is the example Ant script that Tomcat delivers, which you can find at http://jakarta.apache.org/tomcat/tomcat-5.0-doc/appdev/build.xml.txt. We've also included this with the project input files on the CD-ROM for your information. This Ant script from Tomcat defines a series of Ant tasks for use in deploying and managing servlets in Tomcat. These Ant tasks are implemented in a JAR file that comes with Tomcat. Copy the contents of the build.xml file from the project input files to the build.xml file you just created. You'll see several warnings because the JAR file defining these Ant tasks is not yet included in your Ant classpath. Let's fix this.

2. The Tomcat JAR file that defines the Ant tasks is Catalina-ant.jar in Tomcat's \server\lib folder. You're going to add this file to your Ant classpath through a classpath variable by first defining the variable and then using it. This can be a bit tedious; hang in there, it's worth it.
   Open your **Ant > Runtime** preferences and select the **Classpath** page. Select **Ant Home Entries** and then select **Add Variable....** Recall

that in step 1 of the previous section, you defined a variable, Tomcat Home, to point to the main Tomcat folder. You're going to use this variable again here. In the Add Variable Classpath Entry dialog, select **Variables....** In the Select Variable dialog, scroll down, select **Tomcat Home,** and select **OK**. In the Add Variable Classpath Entry dialog, edit the value to match Figure Ex4.15 and select **OK** to add the entry to the Ant classpath.

**Figure Ex4.15**   Adding a Variable to the Ant Classpath

Finally, select **OK** to save your Ant preferences changes. The warnings in your build.xml file should now be resolved. We'll get to customizing this file in a moment.

3. If you look at the initial contents of build.xml, you'll see that a number of properties need to be defined. Certainly, you could define these in the build.xml file. However, several of these properties are global and will not change from project to project and file to file. It makes more sense to define these once for your Eclipse workspace and be done with it. The global properties we need to define are the URL of the Tomcat Manager console, a user id and password for access, and the home directory of the Tomcat binaries. As you might expect, Eclipse has preferences for these global Ant properties. Go to the **Properties** page of your **Ant > Runtime** preferences and select **Add Property...** to define the following properties.

| | |
|---|---|
| manager.url | http://localhost:8080/manager |
| manager.username | [as specified in tomcat-users.xml] |
| manager.password | [as specified in tomcat-users.xml] |
| catalina.home | [top-level Tomcat folder] |

We suggest you use a variable for catalina.home. Your properties should be as shown in Figure Ex4.16, with your values.

4. Now it's time to customize build.xml to define the steps, or Ant targets, that will deploy, start, and stop our servlet example in Tomcat.

**Figure Ex4.16** Defining Ant Properties Preferences

Copy the build.xml file from the solution project on the CD-ROM, or, using the build.xml file from the solution project as a guide, try the Ant editor to modify this build.xml to match what's in the solution. For lengthy or complex Ant scripts, you might find the Outline view provides an efficient way to get a view into the file's contents and structure.

The Properties section contains simple property definitions used throughout the rest of the script. Custom Ant Task Definitions are the Ant tasks provided by Tomcat and implemented in Catalina-ant.jar. Targets are the unit of execution Eclipse works with. Table Ex4.1 describes the targets.

**Table Ex4.1** Ant Targets

| Target | Description |
|---|---|
| deploy | Executes the Tomcat manager task to deploy the servlet example. It depends on targets prepare and copyfiles. |
| prepare | Sets up in your workspace the directory structure Tomcat expects for an application. This is the same directory structure you used when you first tested the example. The root of this structure is specified by the ${deploy.home} property. |
| copyfiles | Copies files into the directory structure set up by the prepare target; class files and the files in the /web folder. The net result of executing the deploy target is that, because it depends on prepare and copyfiles, these targets will be executed first and then the deploy target will run to deploy the example application to Tomcat. |
| reload | Uses the Tomcat reload task to instruct Tomcat to reload the specified application. It depends only on the copyfiles target. |
| remove | Does the opposite of deploy. |
| clean | Removes the folders the other targets create. |
| all | Removes the application and does a deployment starting from scratch. |
| Dist | Provides an example of how you can create a WAR file to distribute the example. |
| javadoc | Generates Javadoc for the example. |

PART VI

5. You've created your Ant script. Now you need to define the Ant tasks to Eclipse so you can invoke them. The simplest way to do this is to use the Ant view. Open the Ant view and then drag your Ant script, build.xml, from the Package Explorer view onto the Ant view. You can also use **Add Buildfiles** ⊹⊱. The targets defined in the Ant script will show up as individual entries in the Ant view (see Figure Ex4.17).

**Figure Ex4.17**   Ant View

6. Now let's give it a try. Double-click on the **list** target. In the Console view, you should see a list of the applications currently deployed to Tomcat. If you get an error, the error message will also show up in the Console view. Parts of the output in the Console view are enabled as links. For example, you can click on an error and see the failing statement in your Ant script. The most common error here is one defining or using the properties to access the Tomcat Manager console, user id, password, and URL. It may be something as simple as spelling or capitalization. If you have trouble debugging your Ant script, try inserting statements to output diagnostic data, like the following:

```
<echo message="${manager.url}"/>
```

7. Finally, let's deploy the example using the Ant targets. First, you need to undeploy what you had previously deployed. Open the Tomcat manager at URL http://localhost:8080/manager/html in your browser. Your application is the one with a display name of **Web Commerce Example**. Select **Undeploy**. Now, back in Eclipse, go to the Ant view and double-click on the **deploy** target. The application deploys in Tomcat, this time under a new path, /catalog, because

you set this in the Ant script in property `app.path`. Console output is shown in Figure Ex4.18.

**Figure Ex4.18** Deploy Target Output

Go to the Ant view and double-click on the **list** target. You should see the application listed in the console view. Finally, try the application again in your browser. Open URL http://localhost:8080/catalog/orderpage. Congratulations!

8. This is pretty slick, but you can do even better. Wouldn't it be nice if you could redeploy the example every time you made a change? You can do this by adding an Ant builder to your project, `com.ibm.jdg2e.servletApp`. Open the project's **Builders** properties. Select to create a new builder, and make it an **Ant Build**. Name the builder `redeploy`. On the **Main** page of the New Builder wizard, for the location of the Ant script, select **Browse Workspace...** and select `build.xml` in project `com.ibm.jdg2e.servletApp`. On the **Refresh** page, select to refresh resources on completion and specify to refresh the project containing the selected resource. On the **Targets** page, select the `reload` target. On the **Build Options** page, select only **Auto builds**. Auto build means Eclipse automatically executes a build because one or more resources changed. Now when you change a file in your project, Ant target **redeploy** will run, redeploying the application. Select **OK** and then **OK** again to define the builder.

9. Let's try it. Make a change to one of the application's classes. For example, tweak the HTML text generated in the `CatalogPage` class. Save your changes. The Output view will display the results of the redeploy target. It should appear as shown in Figure Ex4.19.

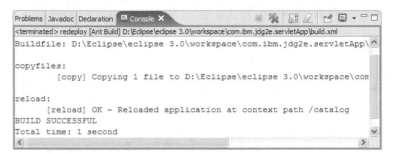

**Figure Ex4.19**    Redeploy Target Output

Congratulations! You're done. You now have defined your servlet application in Eclipse and configured it for efficient development and deployment in Tomcat.

## Exercise Activity Review

In this exercise, you used a good cross-section of the capabilities Eclipse provides to solve a nontrivial, modestly real-world programming problem. We hope you've found these sections and steps useful and illustrative of how you can use various Eclipse capabilities to solve nontrivial programming problems. Nice work!

## References

Arthorne, John, and Chris Laffra. 2004. *Official Eclipse 3.0 FAQs.* Boston, MA: Addison-Wesley. http://eclipsefaq.org. (See Chapter 3 and FAQs 64, 313, 315–318.)

Hall, Marty. 2000. *Core Servlets and Java Server Pages.* Upper Saddle River, NJ: Prentice Hall, 2000.

Tutorial from Sun Microsystems on servlets at http://java.sun.com/j2ee/tutorial/1_3-fcs/doc/Servlets.html.

# EXERCISE 5

## *Working as a Team with CVS*

In this exercise you will examine a series of progressively more sophisticated scenarios to learn how you might use Eclipse and CVS in everyday situations. If you follow this chapter carefully, you will become much more confident and comfortable using Eclipse with CVS.

We assume that you have already read Chapter 5, Teaming Up with Eclipse. This exercise is defined such that you may simply read it without actually doing anything in Eclipse or CVS. If you have access to a CVS repository, you will gain experience with the most common uses of CVS with Eclipse.

At the end of this exercise, you should be able to do the following.

- Use the CVS user interface in Eclipse.
- Connect to a CVS repository.
- Place a project under CVS control.
- Version your project.
- Commit changes to CVS.
- Synchronize your workspace project with the CVS repository and identify differences between them.
- Using CVS Watch/Edit to identify and resolve conflicts caused by more than one person updating the same file.
- Perform CVS branching and merging.

### Exercise Setup

Unless you are simply reading this exercise, you will need access to a CVS repository with authority to commit changes. This exercise was verified on

923

CVS servers running on Linux and Windows. However, CVSNT on Windows is not officially supported by Eclipse, and some portions of the exercise may not work as expected.

The projects in your workspace that you'll manage in CVS will be generated by Eclipse using sample Eclipse plug-in projects. A plug-in is used to extend Eclipse functionality. Even though you may not be familiar with Eclipse plug-ins, this should not be a problem. The changes you will make to the code are trivial and require no special understanding of Eclipse plug-ins.

Let's start by creating an Eclipse plug-in project that you will put under CVS control.

1. Verify that the necessary platform capabilities are enabled. Open the **Workbench > Capabilities** preference page. All capabilities under **Development** and **Team** should be checked. Under normal circumstances, if you had not done this, you would have been prompted to enable CVS when you attempted to share your project with CVS. For the purposes of this exercise, the **CVS Support** capability should be enabled now (see Figure Ex5.1).

**Figure Ex5.1**   Capabilities Preference Page

2. Create a project by selecting **File > New > Project...**. In the New Project wizard, select **Plug-in Project**. Select **Next**. On the next page,

name the project org.button.helloworld. Select **Next** two times to go to the page titled **Templates**. Check the box labeled **Create a plug-in using one of the templates**. Select the **Hello, World** project (see Figure Ex5.2). Accept all the default values on the subsequent wizard pages and press **Finish**. You may be asked if you want to switch to the Plug-in Development perspective. Reply **Yes**. Your workspace should have a project in it that looks like Figure Ex5.3. If everything went well, the Problems view in this perspective should not show any problems with this project (you can ignore any deprecation messages that might be present).

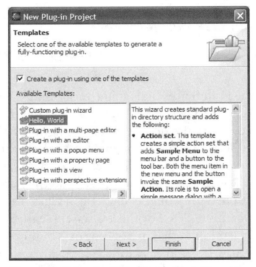

**Figure Ex5.2**   Available Plug-in Code Templates

**Figure Ex5.3**   Eclipse-Generated Project That Will Be Managed in CVS

Setup is now complete. You are ready to proceed with the exercise.

## Section 1: Getting Started

In this section you will connect to a CVS repository and store your `org.button`
`.helloworld` project there. This involves the following major steps:

- Setting your team and CVS preferences
- Defining a CVS repository location
- Storing the project contents in CVS
- Versioning the project

Let's get started!

### Setting Your Team and CVS Preferences

Before you store your project in CVS, you need to define some useful preference settings.

1. Open the Preferences dialog and verify that CVS decorators are enabled. Select **CVS** in the **Workbench > Label Decorations** page. CVS decorators provide visual clues about the CVS state of workspace projects and their contents for projects under CVS control.

2. While you are looking at the preference pages, go to the **Team > Ignored Resources** page. You could add the pattern `*.class` using the **Add** button. This would exclude Java class files in your project from being stored in CVS. For this exercise, please don't make this change.

    In general, files that are output of a build process are not stored in a repository. It is too easy for the repository to become out of sync between the runtime files and the source files that created them. It also takes up unnecessary space. In this case, it is not required due to an Eclipse property called **derived resources**. The project's class files produced from the compilation process have this property. Eclipse automatically excludes derived resources from being stored in CVS. Other tools that create runtime resources may or may not set this property. There is no harm in adding an Ignore Pattern to the **Ignored Resources** page, even if it is superfluous.

3. In the **Workbench > Compare/Patch** preference page, select the preference **Show additional compare information in the status line**. This provides a quick summary that can be very helpful during repository synchronization when there are conflicts or differences. Select the

preference **Ignore white space**. This ensures that only the real differences are shown when comparing two files.

4. Select **OK** to set the preferences and close the dialog.

## Defining a CVS Repository Location

Next, you need to define a CVS repository location using the CVS Repositories view in the CVS Repository Exploring perspective.

1. Open the perspective by selecting **Window > Open Perspective > Other...**, select **CVS Repository Exploring**, and press **OK**.

2. From the CVS Repositories view context menu, select **New > Repository Location....** A toolbar button 🗄 for this operation is also available.

   The Add CVS Repository dialog is displayed. In Figure Ex5.4, the dialog has been completed with sample values for repository hostname, repository path, user, and password. The repository path (here,

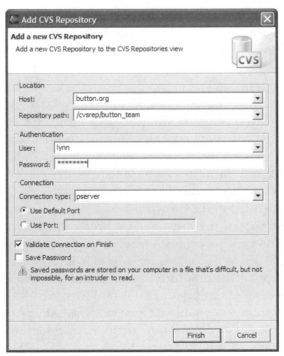

**Figure Ex5.4**    Defining a New CVS Repository Location in Your Workspace

/cvsrep/button_team) is the directory name on the CVS server where your team's work is maintained. Here we are using the default connection method of pserver. Fill in the correct information for your CVS repository, which your repository administrator can supply. (If your repository requires a different CVS connection method, you may have to specify additional information in the appropriate CVS connection method preference page.) Select **Finish**. Your CVS repository location should appear in the CVS Repositories view. Your CVS repository is now ready to use.

3. With your connection complete, expand your repository location in the view to see the contents under **Branches**, **HEAD**, and **Versions** (see Figure Ex5.10 later in this exercise). You will be adding your org.button.helloworld project to **HEAD**, the main line of development.

## *Storing the Project Contents in CVS*

Now you will let CVS know that you want it to manage your org.button .helloworld project and its contents.

1. Switch to the Plug-in Development perspective. In the Package Explorer view, select your project and then select **Team > Share Project...** from the context menu. This will start a wizard to complete the task (see Figure Ex5.5). Select the CVS location you just defined. If there were additional CVS repository locations or non-CVS repositories available, they would also be listed on this page. Note that you could have defined your repository connection in the wizard instead of the CVS Repositories view as you did in the previous section. As you will learn, this wizard incorporates all the tasks necessary to put your project under CVS management.

2. Proceed through the wizard until you see the page titled **Share Project Resources**. If you expand the project, you can see from the icons that all the project contents are about to be committed to your repository.

3. The bin folder, which includes our Java .class files, will always be empty in the repository because these derived resources are not stored in CVS. Let's exclude the bin folder too by selecting it and displaying the context menu (see Figure Ex5.6). Select **Add to .cvsignore...** and press **OK** in the resulting dialog. The folder was removed from the Changes list and another file named .cvsignore was added. This is a special CVS file that identifies resources to be excluded from the repository. Don't press **Finish** yet.

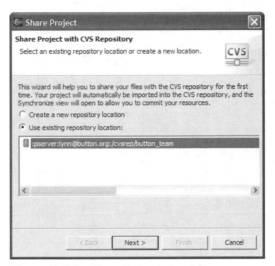

**Figure Ex5.5**   Share Project Wizard Page

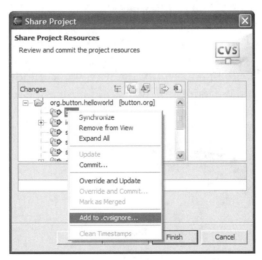

**Figure Ex5.6**   Identifying Resources to Be Ignored by CVS

4. Select the project and in the context menu select **Commit...** (or use the **Commit All Changes...** button on the toolbar). The dialog titled Add to CVS Version Control, shown in Figure Ex5.7, will ask if you want to add the project resources to CVS control (the **Details** button shows all resources that will be placed under CVS supervision). Since we do want to do this, respond **Yes**. Committing new

PART VI

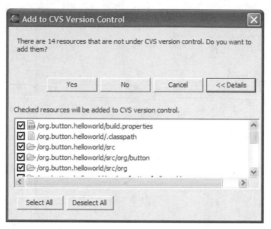

**Figure Ex5.7**    Add to CVS Version Control Dialog

resources to the repository is a two-step process: defining them to CVS and then checking them in.

5. You are now presented with the Commit dialog shown in Figure Ex5.8. Enter a comment and press **OK**. The project contents on the wizard page should disappear. Press **Finish** to close the wizard and complete the process. (By the way, you could have pressed **Finish** earlier and these same dialogs would have appeared, but we wanted you to spend a little time to fully understand the process.)

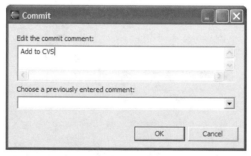

**Figure Ex5.8**    Commit Dialog and Associated Comment

Your project has been updated in the Resource Navigator and Package Explorer views, reflecting the fact that this project is under CVS management. Looking at Figure Ex5.9, you can see that all the project resources icons have been decorated with a small repository decorator, the name of the

CVS repository is listed next to the project, and a revision number of 1.1 is associated with each file.

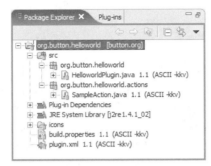

**Figure Ex5.9**   Appearance of the Hello, World Project After Committing It to CVS

Returning to the CVS Repository Exploring perspective, you can see your project in the CVS Repositories view (see Figure Ex5.10). You may have to refresh the view contents using the **Refresh** toolbar button. From this view, expand your project, expand the src folder and subfolders, and select the HelloworldPlugin.java file. Select **Show in Resource History** from its context menu; in the CVS Resource History view, you will see that it has a revision number of 1.1 as expected.

**Figure Ex5.10**   Hello, World Project in CVS

PART VI

Conveniently, we can accomplish everything using the CVS Sharing wizard. Another variation is to use the wizard to share your project and defer committing. When you are ready to commit, select the **Team > Commit...** dialog from the context menu.

## Versioning the Project

Finally, let's identify an easily recallable copy of your project by versioning it. This is not going to make any special archival copies of the project or place it in a space in the repository reserved for versions (in CVS there is no such thing!). Rather, all the resources in the project, at their current revision level, will simply be tagged with a name of your choosing. This tag represents a version name, or a point of reference, should you want to refer to the project or its contents at this point in time.

1. Return to the Plug-in Development perspective, select the project from the Package Explorer view (or the CVS Repositories view), and select **Team > Tag as Version...** from the context menu. This operation can also be done from a selected project in the CVS Repositories view. You can even create version-specific files in a project if you need to.

2. Complete the Tag Resources dialog with the version string V1_0_0 (tags cannot contain periods and must start with an alphabetic character). Selecting **Details** allows you to view or find any known tags. Select **OK** to close the dialog. Now the version and its contents are listed under the **Versions** tree in the CVS Repository view, as shown in Figure Ex5.11.

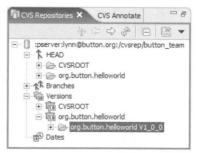

**Figure Ex5.11**   Your Project with Its Version Tag in CVS

If you want to go back to this version, it is available for checkout or simply viewing. You can also compare it with other versions, or compare it with your workspace project. We recommend you version after key milestones or after making important changes. If you do not version, you can still go back to earlier instances of your code, but it is more difficult. You would need to identify the revision number of every resource of interest. Your commit comments in the CVS Resource History view might help, as they represent a kind of identifier. Note that all repository projects are listed in the **Versions** tree, even those that do not contain any versions.

You're done! The project is under CVS repository management, and you have a version that you can go back to or make available to others. Now you can safely make local changes knowing that the last good copy is in CVS.

## Section 2: Updating, Committing, and Resolving Conflicts

This section of the exercise covers normal day-to-day operations like making local changes and committing those changes in CVS. You will encounter the situation where your changes are in conflict with changes committed by someone else. Conflicts are usually infrequent; however, because CVS does not "lock" resources when they are checked out, the potential for updates to the same file does exist. The CVS architecture works on the assumption that conflicts are relatively rare and team members are capable of resolving them. CVS and Eclipse provide assistance when conflicts do occur. To see how to minimize conflicts, in this section we will also explore the CVS Watch/Edit function, in which CVS keeps track of who is updating a resource. The major steps are the following:

- Modifying the code in your project
- Storing your changes in CVS
- Making additional changes in your project
- Resolving conflicts with CVS
- Minimizing conflicts by using CVS Watch/Edit

### *Modifying the Code in Your Project*

You will make a few changes in your project in preparation for committing them to CVS. This project adds a simple action to the Eclipse menu bar, which displays "Hello, Eclipse world" in a message dialog. You will update the menu action title and the message it displays. This is a simple change that doesn't require you to understand the details of the modification at this time.

It requires changing two files, `plugin.xml` and `SampleAction.java`. The `plugin.xml` file is a special file needed to extend Eclipse functionality. Don't worry about trying to understand its contents now.

1. If you're not in the Plug-in Development perspective, switch to it now.
2. Next you will change the name of the menu action. If not already open, open the file `plugin.xml`, select the **plugin.xml** tab, and change the line `label="&amp;Sample Action"` to `label="Eclipse Greeting"` and save your changes (if you want you can make a similar change to the `tooltip` value).
3. Now you will change the message text. Open the file `SampleAction.java` and examine the `run` method. Change the line `"Hello, Eclipse world"` to `"Hello, welcome to Eclipse"` and save your changes.
4. Notice that the files you changed and their parent folders have been prefixed with a greater-than character (>) in the Package Explorer view (see Figure Ex5.12). This indicates that these files have been updated and are *outgoing* changes, meaning that they supercede what was in the CVS repository since the last time they were updated in this workspace.

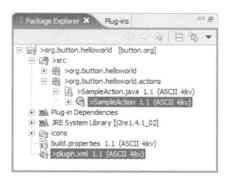

**Figure Ex5.12**   Local Updates Prefixed with a > Symbol to Identify Outgoing Changes

5. Let's assume that you tested your changes and they look good. You are now ready to commit your changes to CVS. If you would like to test your changes, continue with step 6; otherwise, you can proceed to Storing Your Changes in CVS.
6. If you are not familiar with plug-ins and how to test them, see Chapter 9, Getting Started: Plug-in Development. From the Plug-in Development perspective, select the project, and then select **Run > Run As > Run-time Workbench** from the Workbench menu bar. A test instance

of Eclipse will start. In this test instance, select the **Sample Menu > Eclipse Greeting** from the Workbench menu bar. You will see the dialog shown in Figure Ex5.13. That completes the test. Close this test instance of Eclipse. (If the **Sample Menu > Eclipse Greeting** menu does not display, perform this check. From the test instance of Eclipse, select **Window > Reset Perspective**, select **OK** in the resulting dialog, and **Sample Menu** should appear.)

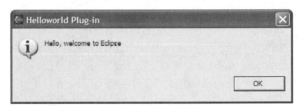

**Figure Ex5.13**   Result from Testing Your Code Changes

## Storing Your Changes in CVS

The changes you just completed will now be committed to CVS. Before you store your changes, you want to obtain any updates in the CVS repository that may have occurred since you checked out the project. You can choose **Team > Update** or **Team > Synchronize with Repository…** from the project's context menu. The **Team > Update** action will not allow you to see any changes because the operation of merging from the repository is automatic. Choosing **Synchronize with Repository…** allows you to examine all differences between your workspace and the repository.

1. Select the project in the Package Explorer view and then select **Team > Synchronize with Repository…** from the context menu. You will be prompted to switch to the Team Synchronizing perspective. Select **Remember my decision** in the prompt dialog. In the perspective, examine the Synchronize view. You may be prompted with a message to switch the view to Outgoing Mode. Do so by selecting the message or use the Outgoing Mode toolbar button ➡️. The Outgoing Mode view lists the two files you updated (see Figure Ex5.14). We will return to this in a moment after you check for other possible differences between your workspace and the CVS repository.

   The view's toolbar has icons for filtering the contents by incoming changes, outgoing changes, incoming and outgoing changes, or conflicts. Try them!

**Figure Ex5.14**    Result from Testing Your Code Changes

2. Let's complete the repository update. In the Synchronize view, select the project and then select **Commit...** from the context menu (or use the toolbar button ![icon]). In the Commit dialog, enter a comment to describe your changes and press **OK**. After the operation completes, the view contents should display a message indicating that there are no remaining changes. In the Package Explorer view, the two files you committed should now display a revision number of 1.2 (see Figure Ex5.15). If you think you might want to reference these changes in the future, you can version your project now by selecting **Team > Tag as Version...** from the project's context menu.

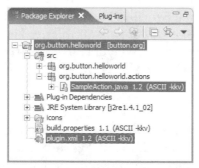

**Figure Ex5.15**    Project View Showing Updated Files and Their Updated Revision Number

### Making Additional Changes in Your Project

You will continue to update your project, but this time it will be more interesting: When you commit your changes, there will be conflicts to resolve. Someone else has also been working on your project!

1. Your change will involve printing some diagnostic information to the console. Add the following code to the run method of the `Sample-Action.java` class. Save the changes.

```
// Display IAction information.
System.out.println("1. ID: " + action.getId());
System.out.println("2. Description: " +
  action.getDescription());
System.out.println("3. Tooltip text: " +
  action.getToolTipText());
```

   If you want to test this change, from the Plug-in Development perspective, select the project, and then select **Run > Run As > Run-time Workbench**. In the test instance of Eclipse, select the menu labeled **Sample Menu > Eclipse Greeting**. The console output will appear in the Console view of the development instance of Eclipse (where your project resides).

2. Meanwhile, a colleague has been working in parallel on this same project, externalizing strings for internationalization purposes. An e-mail notification was sent, but you were away and missed the message.

3. To reproduce what your colleague did, that is, a parallel change by another user, launch Eclipse in a separate workspace using the Workspace Launcher dialog at startup (see Figure Ex5.16). You may also want to confirm that CVS label decorations are set in the **Workbench > Label Decorations** preference page.

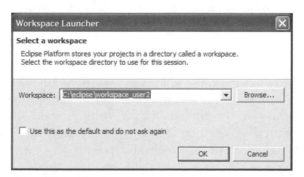

**Figure Ex5.16**   Specifying Another Workspace at Startup

4. In your other instance of Eclipse, open the CVS Repository Exploring perspective. As you did in Section 1, connect to CVS using **New > Repository Location...** from the CVS Repositories view, and check

out the `org.button.helloworld` project in **HEAD** to your workspace using the **Check Out** action.

5. Open the Plug-in Development perspective and select the `Sample-Action.java` file. Externalize the strings by selecting **Source > Externalize Strings...** from the context menu. A wizard will appear. (For more information, see the Externalizing Strings section in Chapter 3, Using Java Development Tools.) Accept all the other wizard defaults and select **Finish**. This will update `SampleAction.java` and create a `messages.properties` file and a `Messages.java` file in your project.

6. Commit your changes to CVS by selecting the project and then selecting **Team > Commit...** from the context menu. Respond with **Yes** when asked to add the new files to version control. Supply the comment "`Externalize strings`" in the Commit dialog and press **OK**. This will force a conflict in `SampleAction.java` in your other Eclipse workspace.

7. Close this instance of Eclipse and return to the original exercise workspace.

### Resolving Conflicts with CVS

Next you will learn how to resolve conflicts due to concurrent changes to the same file. You should be using your original workspace now.

1. You are ready to commit your simple update to the run method of the `SampleAction.java` class. You could use **Team > Commit**, but you would be ignoring changes that may have been put in CVS since you checked out your copy. You could use **Team > Update** to get any CVS changes that might exist, but you can't control what changes are made to your local project. Instead, select the project in the Package Explorer view and then select **Team > Synchronize with Repository**.

2. Eclipse switched to the Team Synchronizing perspective. (If you were prompted for this perspective, you can make this switch happen automatically by setting this in Preferences dialog available in the pull-down menu of the Synchronize view.) This time the project's decorator has a red bidirectional arrow ◆ indicating a conflict. What has been happening? Make sure the view is in Incoming/Outgoing mode; use the toolbar button 🖳. Look at the fully expanded Synchronize view shown in Figure Ex5.17 (for now only the Synchronize view is relevant in that figure). A lot has been going on in your project! There are two new files, `messages.properties` and `Messages.java`, and a folder named `.settings` (for Eclipse internal use). Each is indicated by an

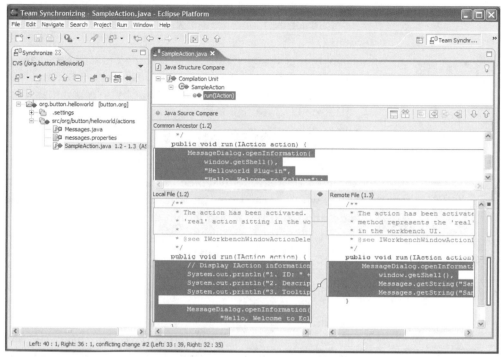

**Figure Ex5.17**  Synchronize View Showing Incoming Changes and a Three-Way Compare of the Conflicting File

icon with a left arrow with an imbedded plus sign 📄▪ 📄▪. Sample-Action.java, the file you wanted to commit, is in conflict with the repository, as indicated by the two-way arrow ◆. At this point, you need to check with your teammates to find out what is going on.

3. After catching up with the rest of the team, you conclude that you must resolve the conflicts detected by CVS. Double-click on the file SampleAction.java to see a side-by-side comparison of the local file with the CVS version. Select **Show Ancestor Pane** ⊞ in the Java Source Compare view toolbar. In this example, you have gone a step further and done a three-way compare. The middle pane shows the common ancestor to your change and the latest revision in CVS. This is revision 1.2 in CVS.

4. The lower left pane is your updated but uncommitted change to revision 1.2, and the lower right pane shows revision 1.3, the latest in the repository, which, in this case, was committed by your colleague. You can navigate through your file and visually examine the differences.

PART VI

Since this is a Java file, you have an outline view of your file titled Java Structure Compare showing you that the conflict is in the run method.

5. Now that you understand what's going on, let's take care of the easy work first. Add the new files, `messages.properties` and `Messages.java`, and folder `.settings` to your project by selecting the files and then selecting **Update** from the context menu. They should disappear from the Synchronize view.

6. Select the `SampleAction.java` file again to see the conflicts. This file will require a little more work. The **Override and Update** action from the file's context menu would replace your local file with the latest in CVS, which is revision 1.3, and destroy your own changes. The **Override and Commit** action would destroy your teammate's changes. You don't want to do either, so you must manually merge the CVS changes into your local file. The toolbar of the Java Source Compare view allows you to copy selected conflicts from the repository to your local copy. In this situation you may have to manually select the code for the `MessageDialog.open` statement from the repository file and paste it to your local file. See what works best for you.

7. When you are through merging, save the file using the **Save** action on the context menu of the local file editor pane (lower left pane). Select the file `SampleAction.java` in the Synchronize view and then select **Mark as Merged** from the context menu. By doing this, the merged file in your workspace is marked as an outgoing change. It has not yet been committed to CVS; all you have done so far is catch up with the repository changes. If there are no compilation errors, you are now ready to commit your update.

8. From the Synchronize view, commit `SampleAction.java` to CVS by selecting it and then selecting **Commit...** from the context menu and completing the Commit dialog. The Synchronize view is now empty. Returning to the Package Explorer view, note that the revision is 1.4, as expected.

You now have gained experience with using CVS in a team environment and learned how to properly handle situations that involve conflicting changes to CVS managed resources. We intentionally created a situation that was avoidable, but genuine conflicts are not uncommon. The lesson here is that you would have avoided this if you had synchronized with CVS *before* making your changes!

## Minimizing Conflicts by Using CVS Watch/Edit

CVS Watch/Edit support is integrated into Eclipse's CVS support. It allows you to know who else is editing the same file so accidental conflicts can be avoided. In this portion of the exercise you will learn how to use this function. It might be a good time to refresh yourself on this subject by reviewing the section Avoiding Concurrent Updates to the Same File by Using CVS Watch/Edit in Chapter 5, Teaming Up with Eclipse.

To practice using Watch/Edit support, you will have to pretend to be two different users who need to update the same file. As we did earlier, the easiest way to simulate this is to access the same file from two different workspaces. The only difficulty is that CVS will always report that you are the editor of the file regardless of which workspace it is edited from.

1. Make sure you have two instances of Eclipse running with each of the two workspaces you used earlier. Also make sure they are both current with the repository contents. (Hint: Use **Team > Synchronize with Repository....**)

2. In both workspaces, enable CVS Watch/Edit on the CVS page of the project's properties dialog as shown in Figure Ex5.18 (open from the project context menu labeled **Properties**). Note that the CVS Watch/Edit preference page allows you to enable Watch/Edit automatically on all projects during checkout.

3. From the first workspace, select the `SampleAction` class and from its context menu run the action **Team > Show Editors**. The CVS Editors view will open and should be empty. Now run the action **Team > Edit** followed by the action **Team > Show Editors**. Your user id should be listed in the view as shown in Figure Ex5.19. In the Navigator or Package Explorer view, your file receives a small blue decorator ⬚ in the lower right corner indicating that you are the current editor. CVS recognizes you as the editor of this file and, until you commit your changes, Eclipse will warn others who have Watch/Edit enabled for this project when they attempt to edit it.

4. Let's repeat this sequence from the other workspace. Select the `SampleAction` class and from its context menu run the action **Team > Show Editors**. The CVS Editors view should show that the "other" you is editing this file. Now run the action **Team > Edit**. This time you will receive a warning that says the file is already being edited and displays who is editing it. Selecting **OK** will add you to the users concurrently editing the file. The two users will have to resolve their conflicts during commit. Let's avoid that by selecting **Cancel**. If you skip the

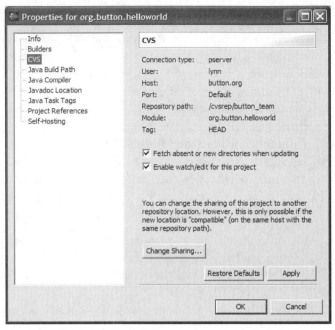

**Figure Ex5.18**   CVS Watch/Edit Support Enabled on the Project's CVS Properties Page

**Figure Ex5.19**   CVS Editors View

formal **Team > Edit** operation and simply open the file in the Java editor, it opens fine, but the first time you type in the editor, you receive the same editor warning. This occurs because Eclipse detects that the file is read-only, which is the state of all files in a Watch/Edit project until you explicitly request to edit a file.

5. Return to the previous workspace where you have the file reserved for editing. Open it in the Java editor, enter a comment somewhere, and save the file. Check the file into CVS using the **Team > Commit** action. When this is completed, you will no longer be listed in the CVS Editors view. (It does not automatically refresh itself; you will need to run **Team > Show Editors**.)

This is not a foolproof way to protect you and your teammates from conflicts, but it can help avoid unintentional conflicts.

# Section 3: Branching and Merging

This final section shows you how to work in CVS independent of your colleagues and perhaps avoid some of the issues you encountered in the previous section. To do this, you'll create a branch in CVS. By creating a branch, you create a fork in a project's development. You can independently make changes and commit them to CVS under the name of the branch, without concern for changes that might be occurring in the same files elsewhere. Eventually, you may want to merge your changes back to the point where you started the branch. We will cover both branching and merging. In this exercise we will take you through all the necessary steps. However, if you do this infrequently, it can be difficult to recall the process. Fortunately, Eclipse provides a branch and merge cheat sheet under **Help > Cheat Sheets... > CVS Tasks** that will help you recall the appropriate steps.

This part of the exercise involves your overworked org.button.helloworld plug-in project. You will work on it independently of any activity in the main line of development in **HEAD**. If this project had interdependencies with other projects, you might do this to avoid breaking the application while you spend sufficient time coding and testing your changes. In this section, you'll be performing a branch and merge on the org.button.helloworld project. First, we'll review the branch and merge process. Then we'll walk through the major steps as follows.

- Updating your project and storing the changes in a CVS branch
- Merging your project changes from the branch back to CVS **HEAD**

## *Review of the Branch and Merge Process Using Eclipse and CVS*

Before you start, let's review the process from the perspective of Eclipse and CVS. (For more details, see Branching and Merging: Support for Parallel Development in Chapter 5, Teaming Up with Eclipse.)

- After checking out the project of interest, you perform a **Team > Branch...** action. This allows you to create a named branch. Your project will be versioned at this point. The version marks the point of development where the branch occurred and becomes the point of reference when you later merge.

- You can now work independently on your project and commit changes to CVS. The revision numbers will indicate the branch. A file at revision 1.4 before the branch will become 1.4.2.1 after the branch is created.
- When you want to merge your changes, you perform the action **Team > Merge…**. You must have a copy of the project in your workspace that is the target of the merge. You will be prompted for the version name at the time the branch started and the name of the branch that contains your work. The merge will complete if there are no conflicts.
- To complete the operation, you commit your workspace project containing the merged changes back to CVS. The changes will be committed in the branch of development you targeted, either **HEAD** or another branch.

## Updating Your Project and Storing the Changes in a CVS Branch

Start with the org.button.helloworld project in its state at the end of Section 2. The changes in the branch will be easy to make, although it will result in several resource additions to the project. You will create Javadoc for the org.button.helloworld project.

1. If you do not have project org.button.helloworld checked out from **HEAD** in CVS, do so now. If you already have the project in your workspace, select it and then select **Team > Synchronize with Repository…** to ensure you have the latest copy. If your workspace copy is current, you will see an informational message indicating that no changes were found. If there are any new changes in the repository, you should run the **Update** action in the Synchronize view's context menu.

2. Let's create a branch in which you will make your changes. From the Package Explorer view, select the project and then select **Team > Branch…** from the context menu. The dialog shown in Figure Ex5.20 displays. Set the **Branch Name** to be AddJavadoc and use the default **Version Name** of Root_AddJavadoc. Also, accept the default option **Start working in the branch**, so that your subsequent changes will be maintained in this branch. The **Details** button allows you to see what branch and version tags exist, so you can avoid duplicates. The version you will create provides a reference point, identifying the state of your project at the start of the branch. Remember the version name; it will be required later when you do the merge. Complete the branch operation using the **OK** button.

**NOTE** If you had decided to branch off a previous version, that version's name would appear in the dialog. You might want to do this because a specific version represents a stable code base to work from. However, you won't be able to merge your changes back. Recall that a version is a static instance of the project; it can't be modified, so a merge is disallowed.

**Figure Ex5.20**    Defining a New Branch

3. The branch name, **AddJavadoc**, appears as a string decorator next to the project name in your workspace. In the CVS Repositories view, the branch is listed when you expand the Branches element of the view (see Figure Ex5.21).

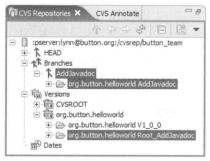

**Figure Ex5.21**    Repository View with New Branch and Root Version Defined

4. Now let's make your changes by adding the Javadoc. From the Package Explorer view, select the project. Then select **Export...** from the context

menu, select **Javadoc** in the dialog, and start the Export wizard. Define the location of the Javadoc command by using the **Configure...** button. You must also specify the path for the javadoc executable provided by your supplier of Java (in Windows, this is commonly the javadoc.exe file in the bin directory where Java has been installed). For more information on creating Javadoc, refer to the Generating Javadoc section in Chapter 3, Using Java Development Tools.

5. On the first page of the wizard, make sure your project is selected. Accept all the default choices and select **Finish**. When prompted, respond **Yes** to the dialog titled **Update Javadoc Location**. The wizard will create a doc folder in the project containing the generated Javadoc, as seen in Figure Ex5.22.

**Figure Ex5.22**   Project After Creating Javadoc

6. Let's make one more change, to update the messages.properties file and replace the last line.

   Replace this line:

   ```
   SampleAction.1=Hello, welcome to Eclipse
   ```

   with this line:

   ```
   SampleAction.1=Hello, using Eclipse is fun and efficient!
   ```

   Then save the file.

7. Your changes are complete, so it's time to commit them to CVS. Select the project and then select **Team > Synchronize with Repository...** from the context menu.

8. You have several new files and folders that are not yet under version control, as you can see in the Synchronize view shown in Figure Ex5.23. You are confident that you are the only one working in the branch, so this time you will go ahead and commit the changes. Select the project in the top pane of the Synchronize view and then select **Commit...** from the context menu. Respond **Yes** to the dialog prompt that asks you to add the new files to version control and enter a comment in the Commit dialog and press **OK**. Return to the Plug-in Development perspective.

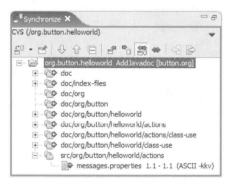

**Figure Ex5.23**    Getting Ready to Commit the New Javadoc Resources

Observe that your new and modified files in your workspace project have a revision number that reflects the revision in the branch (see Figure Ex5.24). The updated files have a revision number of 1.1.2.1. The revision ordinal of 2 reflects the branch off revision 1.1. The last ordinal of 1 indicates this is the first revision in the branch.

If you were to examine one of the new Javadoc files in the CVS Resource History view, you would notice two entries with revision numbers, 1.1 and 1.1.2.1. CVS has created a base revision of 1.1 and followed it with a branch revision of 1.1.2.1. Notice that you cannot open revision 1.1. It is grayed out. CVS views it as a deletion and has done some magic to ensure that even a new file in a branch has an initial revision number of 1.1.

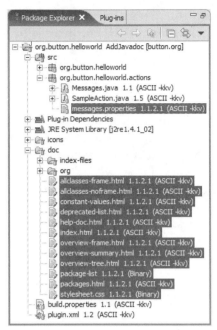

**Figure Ex5.24**   Workspace Project After Changes Are Committed to the CVS Branch

## Merging Your Project Changes from the Branch Back to CVS HEAD

Your task is complete and it is time to merge your changes back into the **HEAD** development branch. You need to replace your workspace project containing the branch changes with the instance in CVS under **HEAD**, as this will be the target of your merge. You could delete the project from your workspace and then check it out again from the **HEAD** branch. However, there's an easier way.

1. Select the project, and then select **Replace With > Another Branch or Version...** from the context menu. When prompted, confirm to overwrite local changes. In the Replace with Branch or Version dialog, select **HEAD** and then select **OK**.

    Had you originally branched off an existing branch, you would need the project from your parent branch in your workspace.

2. Ensure that the project is selected in the Package Explorer view and then select **Team > Merge...** from the context menu. The Merge wizard displays.

3. On the first page, select the version created when you branched off **HEAD**. In your case, it is **Root_AddJavadoc** (see Figure Ex5.25). Select **Next**.

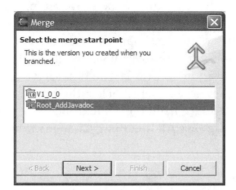

**Figure Ex5.25**    First Page of the Merge Wizard

4. On the next page, select the name of the branch containing your changes, which in this case is **AddJavadoc** under **Branches** (see Figure Ex5.26). Select **Finish**.

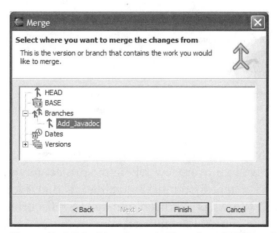

**Figure Ex5.26**    Identifying the Branch to Be Merged

5. When the Merge wizard completes, the Synchronize view appears showing all the changes from the work in the branch (adds, updates,

and conflicts, if any). You should see lots of additions (all the Java-doc) and one update (`messages.properties`) to process. Now you can merge the changes from the **AddJavadoc** branch in the repository to the target project in your workspace that was checked out from **HEAD**. You should examine the proposed merge changes carefully. You are mostly adding new resources, but there could be conflicts if other people committed changes to the project in **HEAD** while you were working in the branch. When conflicts occur, you must resolve them as you did in Section 2. You don't have that situation here, so you can complete the merge. Select the project in the top pane and then select **Update** from the context menu (see Figure Ex5.27) or use the toolbar **Update All Incoming Changes...** button.

**Figure Ex5.27**   Completing the Merge

6. The Synchronize view should now be empty, so you return to the Package Explorer view where the project in your workspace now has all the changes from the branch merged in. However, the project in CVS **HEAD** has not been updated to reflect the merge operation. Previously, you had committed your changes to the **AddJavadoc** branch only. To complete the merge you need to add the new files to version control and commit the changes to CVS. You'll do this as you did before. Select the project in your workspace and then select **Team > Synchronize with Repository...**. From the Synchronize view, select the project and then select **Commit...** from the context menu and

complete the commit operation. You will add the new files to version control and check them in as one operation. After the commit to CVS is complete, the latest instance of your project in **HEAD** contains all the updates from your branch (see the CVS Repositories view in Figure Ex5.28). Your branch and merge is complete! It might be a good idea to version the project at this time.

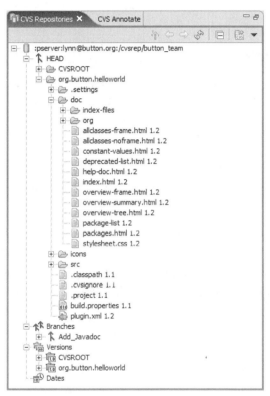

**Figure Ex5.28**    CVS Repositories View After Merge to HEAD Is Completed

Note that with the merge complete, the file revision numbers reflect revisions to **HEAD** and not the revision numbers used in the **AddJavadoc** branch. Examine the CVS Resource History view in Figure Ex5.29. Also note that your branch and the resources in it still exist in the repository. It is possible to continue working in the branch and perform another merge to **HEAD**, but any changes made in the branch will appear as conflicts. A better approach is to create another branch.

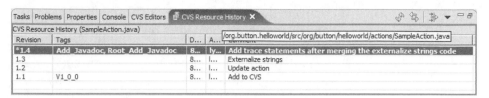

**Figure Ex5.29**   CVS Resource History View After Merge Is Completed

## Exercise Activity Review

In this exercise, you used all the major CVS features supported by Eclipse. Recall that you started out by sharing a new project in CVS and versioning it. Next, you took on the task of committing new changes to the repository, followed by the more complicated task of resolving conflicts in a file that had been updated in parallel by another person. You learned about the value using CVS Watch/Edit for projects when lots of folks have a hand in it. Finally, in the last section you completed the most advanced CVS feature, branching and merging. Congratulations!

## Reference

Arthorne, John, and Chris Laffra. 2004. *Official Eclipse 3.0 FAQs.* Boston, MA: Addison-Wesley. http://eclipsefaq.org. (See FAQs 65, 67, 79, 299, 310, 312.)

# EXERCISE 6

## *Developing Your First Plug-in*

Chapters 7 through 9 introduced you to the terms and concepts behind Eclipse, and briefly discussed the steps of creating your first plug-in. However, sometimes the best way to learn is by doing it yourself. In this exercise you will implement a Workbench action extension to contribute a menu item to the window menu bar that displays the message box "Hello, Eclipse world." While admittedly the final result is anticlimactic, it is definitely worth doing for the experience. You'll have a chance to see how the different parts of the Plug-in Development Environment (PDE) work and will also verify that your environment is correctly set up for your future plug-in development projects.

At the end of this exercise you should be able to

- Create an XML manifest file for a plug-in using the Plug-in Manifest Editor
- Write the Java code to be executed for the extension
- Test and debug your plug-in in the runtime Workbench

In case you skipped some (or all) of Chapters 7 through 9 to get right to coding, here's an ultra mini-review.

- A plug-in is an extension of the Eclipse Platform. It is a set of related files that implement some function and a manifest file, called plugin.xml, which describes the content of the plug-in and its configuration.
- A plug-in can contribute to the Workbench user interface by declaring an extension of an existing Workbench extension point. The manifest

file describes this contribution. A plug-in can also declare new extension points that other plug-ins may use. This will be covered in Chapter 11, Creating Extension Points: How Others Can Extend Your Plug-ins.

## Exercise Setup

First verify that all external plug-ins are visible, which is the Eclipse default setting. Access the PDE's **Target Platform** preferences page using **Window > Preferences**. Expand **Plug-In Development** and select **Target Platform**. Select **Not In Workspace** to make all plug-ins visible, as shown in Figure Ex6.1. Select **OK** to close the dialog.

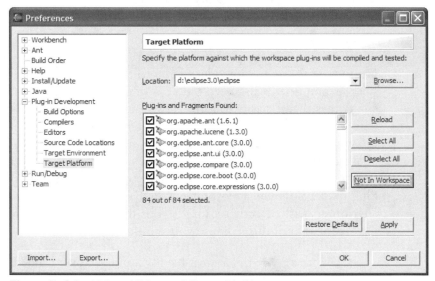

**Figure Ex6.1**    Making All External Plug-ins Visible

You have a choice of how to complete this exercise.

- The first approach uses the PDE's New Plug-in Project wizard to generate all the necessary code and the plug-in manifest details for an action extension. This option is presented in Section 1.
- The second approach will proceed step-by-step, showing all the dialogs and editors that you need to use when creating a plug-in with the PDE. This offers you the chance to use the PDE when the example is quite simple, so you can concentrate on using the tool, not the details of the

coding at hand. The steps are similar to those presented by the Eclipse SDK's **Help > Cheat Sheets > Other > Create an Eclipse plug-in using PDE** choice, except this exercise provides additional hints and details along the way. If you prefer this second approach, turn to Section 2.

**REMINDER** Unlike some of the earlier exercises, this exercise has no template associated with it. Once you have installed the Eclipse SDK and configured it as described above, you can start immediately. Also, remember that if you have trouble during this exercise, look to Section 8, Correcting Common Problems, for possible solutions.

## Section 1: "Hello, World" in Five Minutes or Less

Eclipse should already be installed and open; you should have already completed the steps described in the Exercise Setup section.

1. Begin by creating a plug-in project using the New Plug-in Project wizard. Select **File > New > Project**. In the New Project dialog, select **Plug-in Development** and **Plug-in Project** in the list of wizards, and then select **Next**. Name the project com.ibm.jdg2e.helloworld. Accept the default workspace location and project settings and select **Next**. The PDE will create a plug-in id based on this name, so it must be unique in the system (by convention, the project name and the plug-in id are the same). Accept the default plug-in content by selecting **Next**. Select the **Create a plug-in using one of the templates** check box and the **Hello, World** option, as shown in Figure Ex6.2, and then select **Next**.

2. The next page, shown in Figure Ex6.3, is where you can specify parameters that are unique to the "Hello, World" example, such as the message that will be displayed. To simplify the resulting code, change the target package name for the action from com.ibm.jdg2e .helloworld.actions to com.ibm.jdg2e.helloworld, the same package as that of the plug-in class. While you might choose to have a separate package for grouping related classes in a real-world plug-in, in this case there will only be two classes (the plug-in class and the action), so let's put them together in the same package.

3. Select **Finish** and continue with Section 3, Testing with the Runtime Workbench. If this is the first time you've created a plug-in project, a message dialog will offer to switch directly to the Plug-in Development perspective. Accept the suggestion, clicking **Remember my decision** if you prefer.

PART VI

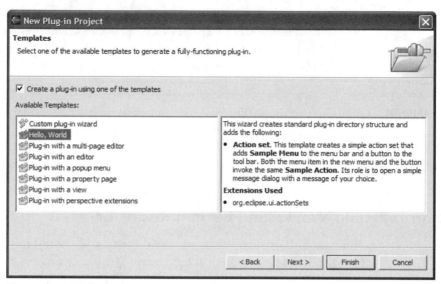

**Figure Ex6.2**   Hello, World Plug-in Template

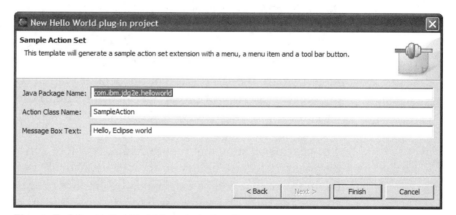

**Figure Ex6.3**   Hello, World Sample Action Set

## Section 2: "Hello, World" with Detailed Step-by-Step Instructions

Instead of using Eclipse's plug-in templates as shown in Section 1, this section focuses on how to use the PDE to create your first plug-in in a step-by-step fashion. It sometimes omits the explanation of minor implementation details, but rest assured that the chapters in Part II will cover them.

Eclipse should already be installed and open; you should have already completed the steps described in the Exercise Setup section.

1. Begin by creating a plug-in project using the New Plug-in Project wizard. Select **File > New > Project**. In the New Project dialog, select **Plug-in Development** and **Plug-in Project** in the list of wizards, and then select **Next**. Name the project com.ibm.jdg2e.helloworld. Accept the default workspace location and project settings and select **Next**. The PDE will create a plug-in id based on this name, so it must be unique in the system (by convention, the project name and the plug-in id are the same).

2. The proposed plug-in name and plug-in class name are based on the last word of the plug-in project, com.ibm.jdg2e.helloworld. This example doesn't need a plug-in class, so you could uncheck the **Generate the Java class that controls the plug-in's lifecycle (recommended)** option, but most of the time you'll want one, so leave it checked and select **Finish**. If this is the first time you've created a plug-in project, a message dialog will offer to switch directly to the Plug-in Development perspective. Accept the suggestion, clicking **Remember my decision**, if you prefer.

   The Plug-in Manifest Editor displays the generated plugin.xml in the PDE perspective, as shown Figure Ex6.4.

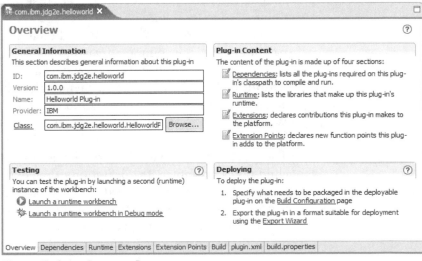

**Figure Ex6.4**   Overview Page

3. Select the **plugin.xml** page. Verify that the generated `plugin.xml` content is as follows.

```
<?xml version="1.0" encoding="UTF-8"?>
<?eclipse version="3.0"?>
<plugin
    id="com.ibm.jdg2e.helloworld"
    name="Helloworld Plug-in"
    version="1.0.0"
    provider-name="IBM"
    class="com.ibm.jdg2e.helloworld.HelloworldPlugin">

    <runtime>
        <library name="helloworld.jar">
            <export name="*"/>
        </library>
    </runtime>

    <requires>
        <import plugin="org.eclipse.ui"/>
        <import plugin="org.eclipse.core.runtime"/>
    </requires>

</plugin>
```

Note that the `<requires>` section states that the basic user interface and core services must be present for this plug-in to load successfully.

4. Select the **Extensions** page and select **Add...** to open the New Extension dialog, and then select the `org.eclipse.ui.actionSets` extension point (see Figure Ex6.5).

This extension point is used to add menus, menu items, and toolbar buttons to the common areas in the Workbench window. These contributions are collectively known as an **action set** and appear within the Workbench window menu or toolbar. Select **Finish** to create the new extension (you could cheat and select the "Hello, World" action set template, but remember, we're going the long way).

5. There are very few extension points that do not require one or more child tags to complete the definition of the extension. In this particular case, the `<actionSet>` child tag must be added. Right-click on the `org.eclipse.ui.actionSets` extension in the **All Extensions** list and select **New > actionSet** to create an `<actionSet>` child tag.

6. Select the extension's `actionSet` child tag and set the `id` and `label` property values as shown in Figure Ex6.6.

**Figure Ex6.5**   New Extension Wizard

**Figure Ex6.6**   Adding An Action Set

If you turn to the **plugin.xml** page, you will see the XML that you've created.

```
<extension
  point="org.eclipse.ui.actionSets">
    <actionSet
      label="Sample Action Set"
      id="com.ibm.jdg2e.helloworld.actionSet">
    </actionSet>
</extension>
```

The id is a required unique identifier that can be used as a reference to this action set. The visible attribute (not shown in this code) indicates whether the action set should be initially visible in all perspectives. The XML code will create an action set called "Sample Action Set."

7. Now create a top-level menu. Right-click on the action set element and select **New > menu**. Update the menu's id and label, as shown in Figure Ex6.7. The ampersand (&) in the value for the label indicates the next character, M, is a menu accelerator.

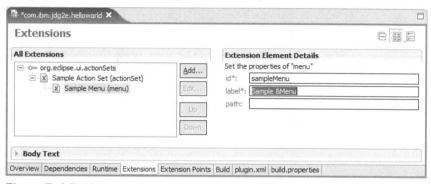

**Figure Ex6.7**    Adding a Menu

When you turn to the **plugin.xml** page, this value is shown as &amp;, since the plug-in manifest is specified in XML, and that is the proper representation of an ampersand in XML. If you had entered it directly in the **plugin.xml** page as &, the Manifest Editor would detect an XML error when you attempted to save it.

8. Now add a menu separator by right-clicking on the top-level menu and selecting **New > separator**.

Actions are generally inserted into a menu relative to another item. Follow this convention by adding a separator that provides a placeholder for your action and for other plug-in developers who might want to contribute menu items. Contributors would do so by specifying the separator's id in their action's menubarPath or toolbarPath attribute. Change the separator's name attribute to sampleGroup in its Extension Element Details pane.

9. Now add a new action. Do this by selecting **Sample Action Set (actionSet)** in the **All Extensions** list and then selecting **New > action**.

In the Extension Element Details pane, set the action's tooltip property value to Hello, Eclipse world, the id to com.ibm.jdg2e

.helloworld.SampleAction, and the label to &Sample Action. Then set menubarPath to sampleMenu/sampleGroup and toolbarPath to sampleGroup, as shown in Figure Ex6.8. These attributes are slash-delimited paths that are used to specify the location of the action in the menu. Also note that while it is more typical to add an action to either the window menu or the main toolbar, you can add them to both at the same time in a single <action> tag by specifying both the menubarPath and toolbarPath attributes.

**NOTE** The "Hello, World" plug-in project wizard used in Section 1 copies a toolbar icon, sample.gif (⬤), into the icons subdirectory of the plug-in project. If the toolbar button doesn't have an image specified in the icon attribute for its <action> tag, the Workbench displays the label instead, as you'll see when you test your plug-in.

**Figure Ex6.8**   Adding an Action

The <action> tag declares an action that will be available from the window menu and/or the main toolbar. When the user clicks on the action, the class referenced in the class attribute will be instantiated and its run method called.

If you prefer, you can enter these parameters directly in XML syntax by switching to the **plugin.xml** page. When you turn back to the **Extensions** page, notice that the updates you made are shown in the Extension Element Details pane. The Plug-in Manifest Editor keeps page modifications synchronized, wherever they are entered. This comes in handy when you want to make a minor change. For example, you can modify an attribute directly in the **plugin.xml** page instead of selecting the associated extension in the **Extensions** page list and then modifying the attribute in its Extension Element pane.

10. Next you'll code a simple action class that will display a message dialog. To create the action class, click the `class` attribute in the action's details pane (that is, the hyperlink label `class`) to display in the Java Attribute Editor dialog, as shown in Figure Ex6.9. Enter the `com.ibm.jdg2e.helloworld` package name (or use the **Browse** button) and the class name `SampleAction` and then select **Finish**.

**Figure Ex6.9**   Creating a Sample Action

The following XML will be added to the manifest file, along with XML for the other entries you just created.

```
<action
   label="&amp;Sample Action"
   class="com.ibm.jdg2e.helloworld.SampleAction"
   tooltip="Hello, Eclipse world"
   menubarPath="sampleMenu/sampleGroup"
   toolbarPath="sampleGroup"
   id="com.ibm.jdg2e.helloworld.SampleAction">
```

Then the class generator opens an editor on the source it created and adds a reminder to the Tasks view to implement your action (see Figure Ex6.10).

| | Description | Resource | In Folder | Location |
|---|---|---|---|---|
| | TODO Auto-generated method stub | SampleAction.java | com.ibm.jdg2e.helloworld/src/com/ibm/jdg2e/helloworld | line 26 |
| | TODO Auto-generated method stub | SampleAction.java | com.ibm.jdg2e.helloworld/src/com/ibm/jdg2e/helloworld | line 34 |
| | TODO Auto-generated method stub | SampleAction.java | com.ibm.jdg2e.helloworld/src/com/ibm/jdg2e/helloworld | line 42 |
| | TODO Auto-generated method stub | SampleAction.java | com.ibm.jdg2e.helloworld/src/com/ibm/jdg2e/helloworld | line 50 |
| | TODO To change the template for this generated file go to | SampleAction.java | com.ibm.jdg2e.helloworld/src/com/ibm/jdg2e/helloworld | line 4 |
| | TODO To change the template for this generated type comment go to | SampleAction.java | com.ibm.jdg2e.helloworld/src/com/ibm/jdg2e/helloworld | line 17 |

**Figure Ex6.10**   Reminders in Tasks View

11. Verify the plugin.xml in the **plugin.xml** page. It should look like this.

```
<?xml version="1.0" encoding="UTF-8"?>
<?eclipse version="3.0"?>
<plugin
    id="com.ibm.jdg2e.helloworld"
    name="Helloworld Plug-in"
    version="1.0.0"
    provider-name="IBM"
    class="com.ibm.jdg2e.helloworld.HelloworldPlugin">

   <runtime>
     <library name="helloworld.jar"/>
       <export name="*"/>
     </library>
   </runtime>

   <requires>
      <import plugin="org.eclipse.ui"/>
      <import plugin="org.eclipse.core.runtime"/>
   </requires>

   <extension
        point="org.eclipse.ui.actionSets">
```

```
<actionSet
    label="Sample Action Set"
    id="com.ibm.jdg2e.helloworld.actionSet">
  <menu
      label="Sample &amp;Menu"
      id="sampleMenu">
    <separator name="sampleGroup"/>
  </menu>
  <action
      label="&amp;Sample Action"
      class="com.ibm.jdg2e.helloworld.SampleAction"
      tooltip="Hello, Eclipse world"
      menubarPath="sampleMenu/sampleGroup"
      toolbarPath="sampleGroup"
      id="com.ibm.jdg2e.helloworld.SampleAction">
  </action>
</actionSet>
</extension>

</plugin>
```

The plug-in manifest is complete.

12. Save the `plugin.xml` file.
13. Finish the implementation of the action logic in the `SampleAction` class. Add the instance variable declaration, `private IWorkbench-Window window;`. Before an action's run method is invoked, the Workbench first calls its `init` method, providing the current Workbench window. Some actions need to know the context in which they are invoked, so adding `this.window = window;` to the `init` method will save that context for later reference in the `run` method. Finally, display your "Hello, Eclipse world" message. Add the code below to the action's run method.

```
public void run(IAction action) {
  MessageDialog.openInformation(
    window.getShell(),
    "Helloworld Plug-in",
    "Hello, Eclipse world");
}
```

Notice that the editor indicates that a quick fix is available to correct the "undefined" `MessageDialog` class (see Figure Ex6.11).

Clicking the light bulb in the left margin next to the error marker will propose several possible solutions. Choose to import the missing class reference, and then save your modifications to `SampleAction.java`.

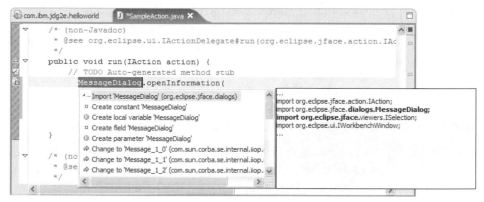

**Figure Ex6.11**   Quick Fix

You have just completed coding your first plug-in, equivalent to the one that you can create with the PDE's Plug-in Code Generator. Continue with the next section to test it.

## Section 3: Testing with the Runtime Workbench

You should have already completed Section 1, "Hello, World" in Five Minutes or Less, or Section 2, "Hello, World" with Detailed Step-by-Step Instructions. Whether you got here by taking the shortcut or the long way, you're ready to test your plug-in!

1. Test your com.ibm.jdg2e.helloworld plug-in by selecting the **Run > Run As > Run-time Workbench** menu choice (if you don't see this menu choice, verify that you're in the Plug-in Development perspective and the com.ibm.jdg2e.helloworld project is selected). After a few seconds, a second instance of the Workbench will open. If you don't see it, select the **Window > Customize Perspective...** menu choice and look for your **Sample Action Set** in the list on the **Commands** page. Select your action set to add it and then **OK**. You should see your addition in the Workbench menu bar. Selecting **Window > Reset Perspective** will also show all action sets having the visible attribute set to true.

2. Select **Sample Menu > Sample Action** to display the message box. Be sure to close the second instance of the Workbench before continuing.

Congratulations, you have just created and tested your first plug-in for Eclipse! Now you are ready to try your hand at debugging a plug-in in the next section. If your plug-in didn't work as expected, see Section 8, Correcting Common Problems, for help.

## Section 4: Debugging with the Runtime Workbench

This section explores the tools the PDE has to help debug your plug-ins. You already have coded and tested your "Hello, World" example, so how about intentionally introducing some bugs to see how they manifest themselves? The short debug session that follows is an example of how to find plug-in errors. Begin by verifying that you've closed the runtime Workbench from the prior section, and then return to the Plug-in Development perspective of your Eclipse development environment. Next, open your plug-in's manifest file `plugin.xml`.

1. Turn to the **plugin.xml** page and introduce an error in the `class` attribute of the `<action>` tag.

```
<action
  label="&amp;Sample Action"
  class="com.ibm.jdg2e.hello.SampleAction"
      <!- error, was "helloworld" ->
  tooltip="Hello, Eclipse world"
  menubarPath="sampleMenu/sampleGroup"
  toolbarPath="sampleGroup"
  id="com.ibm.jdg2e.helloworld.SampleAction">
</action>
```

When you launch the runtime Workbench and select **Sample Action**, a dialog is displayed that indicates that the chosen operation is not currently available, and a message is displayed in the Console of your development Workbench, as shown in Figure Ex6.12.

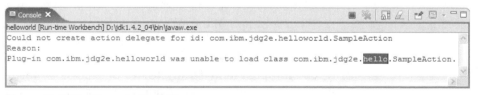

**Figure Ex6.12**   Console Error Message

That is, messages in the runtime instance of System.out and System.err are redirected to the Console in the development Workbench. Before closing the runtime instance, open the Plug-in Registry view (**Window > Show View > Other... > PDE Runtime > Plug-in Registry**) and select your plug-in, as shown in Figure Ex6.13.

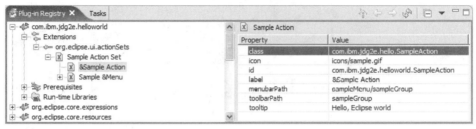

**Figure Ex6.13**   Plug-in Registry

From here you can see precisely what was parsed from your plugin.xml file, similar to the Outline view of the plug-in manifest, but available at runtime. Close the runtime Workbench.

2. Correct the error from the prior step (e.g., by selecting plugin.xml and then **Replace With > Previous from Local History**).

3. Now let's introduce a more serious error. Comment out the code below from SampleAction.

```
public void init(IWorkbenchWindow window) {
//      this.window = window;
}
```

This change will provoke a null pointer exception in the run method. Save the change and relaunch the runtime Workbench, again using the **Run > Debug As > Run-time Workbench** menu choice.

4. Select the **Sample Action** menu choice. Nothing appears to happen. No message from the runtime instance, so look in the Console of the *development* Workbench. As expected, the message Unhandled event loop exception Reason: java.lang.NullPointerException is displayed. To get more details, go back to the runtime instance of the Workbench and open the plug-in Error Log (**Window > Show View > Other... PDE Runtime > Error Log**). Indeed, there are two new entries. Double-click the java.lang.NullPointerException message to see the **Event Details**, as shown in Figure Ex6.14.

(If the Error Log entry says "An exception stack trace could not be found," look in the .log file of your runtime Workbench's workspace,

PART VI

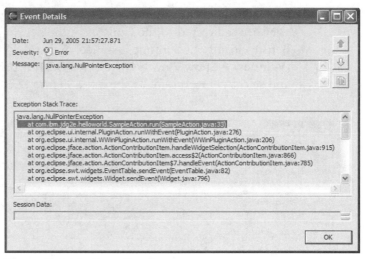

**Figure Ex6.14**   Event Details

specifically `runtime-workbench-workspace\.metadata\.log`). At this
point in a real development session you might consider relaunching
the debugger and setting an exception breakpoint for `NullPointer-
Exception` from the **J!** button on the **Breakpoints** page to further diag-
nose the problem. However, don't set such an exception breakpoint
before launching the Workbench; it will stop in a lot of places that
have nothing to do with your problem. Instead, set and then disable
the exception you want to debug before starting the Workbench, then
enable it when you're ready to reproduce the problem.

5. Correct the error from the prior step (e.g., by selecting `SampleAction`
   `.java` and then **Replace With > Previous from Local History**).
6. Close the runtime instance before continuing.

This short debug session gives you a flavor of debugging plug-ins. As you
create your own plug-ins, you may find more difficult problems than this
one. When that happens, refer to Section 8, Correcting Common Problems.

## Section 5: Defining a Feature to Support the Plug-in

A plug-in is not enough. Before you can deploy a plug-in so that it can be
supported by the configuration management function built into Eclipse, you
need to define a **feature**. Plug-ins without features are called **unmanaged
plug-ins** because Eclipse does not recognize such plug-ins for management by

the user. You can create a plug-in manifest and its JAR file and even copy them into an Eclipse configuration, but it will not be something that can be managed by Eclipse. What this means is that you can't use the Eclipse configuration management dialogs to enable/disable the code or service the code; these capabilities only work for features.

We will begin by defining a feature. We will then step through the process of deploying the feature.

1. First create a feature project. Plug-ins are defined in a plug-in project, and features are defined in a feature project. Press **Ctrl+N** to open the New wizard selection dialog, select **Plug-in Development > Feature Project**, and then **Next**.

2. Enter com.ibm.jdg2e.exercises.feature as the project name and select **Next**. Make the Feature id com.ibm.jdg2e.exercises and then enter any value you want for the Feature Name and Feature Provider fields, maybe even your name. We will use a Feature Name of JDG2E Exercises and a Feature Provider of IBM.

   Select **Finish** to create the feature project. The Feature Manifest Editor opens automatically.

3. Identify the plug-in(s) you want to include in the feature by selecting the **Content** tab in the Feature Manifest Editor to show the **Plug-ins and Fragments** page. Use the **Add...** button to find plug-ins and fragments that you could add to the feature. You should see the com.ibm .jdg2e.helloworld plug-in listed that you just created; select it and then **Finish**. Once the plug-in has been defined select the **Compute** button. This defines the dependencies for the feature based on the dependencies for the plug-ins referenced by the feature. You now have a feature that references your plug-in.

4. If you review the multipage Feature Manifest Editor, you will see areas on the **Information** page where you can add description, copyright, and license content. Enter some text for at least one of these areas and then save the file.

5. Change to the **feature.xml** page and review the XML for the feature definition. As you can see, the structure is somewhat similar to a plug-in definition. The <requires> syntax is similar, but in a feature you can define a requirement for both plug-ins and other features.

You've now created a feature and it's ready to be deployed. This was only a brief introduction to features. Chapter 13, Defining Features and Products, and Exercise 9, Deploying Your Product Using Features, cover this topic in considerable detail.

PART VI

## Section 6: Deploying a Feature and Its Associated Plug-ins

To complete the full life cycle of plug-in development, we will now deploy your feature and the "Hello, World" plug-in you have written using the export utilities.

**NOTE** The PDE can generate Ant scripts to prepare features and plug-ins for deployment. These scripts can perform build and packaging tasks that are similar to the export utilities. Their use is not covered here, but the required `build.properties` file definitions are the same. Ant scripts are used in Exercise 9, Deploying Your Product Using Features.

A plug-in project's `build.properties` file controls what will be included when it is packaged for deployment. The file identifies the JAR file that should contain the code and which additional files and directories the plug-in requires in the runtime environment. If the files are not identified, they will not be included in the plug-in directory created for runtime deployment.

The `build.properties` file for your "Hello, World" plug-in should already have been created by the wizard used to create the plug-in project.

1. Double-click the plug-in project's `build.properties` file to open it or turn to the **Build** page of the Plug-in Manifest Editor. You can review the source by turning to the **build.properties** page. It should contain the following:

```
source.helloworld.jar = src/
output.helloworld.jar = bin/
bin.includes = plugin.xml,\
               helloworld.jar
```

If you had a folder with images (`icons/`), then it would also have to be in the `bin.includes` list. This is the definition of what content should be in the runtime plug-in directory. Test this if you wish by adding a folder or file to your plug-in project and then adding these directly to the `build.properties` definition. Alternatively, use the **Build Configuration** page of the editor to select from the list of files those that should be included in a binary build; this in turn updates the source of the `build.properties` definition. Remember to save your changes with **Ctrl+S**.

2. Verify the `build.properties` file for the feature project. There should already be a `build.properties` definition in the project containing the following:

```
bin.includes = feature.xml
```

3. Use the Export wizard to create the runtime code for your feature and associated plug-in. Select **File > Export...** and then **Deployable Features** from the list of available export wizards. Select **Next** and then the feature you defined, `com.ibm.jdg2e.exercises`.

4. Select the option **a directory structure** for **Deploy as:**, then type in or select **Browse...** to fill in the destination directory. You should probably create a new directory; do not export directly into your Eclipse installation directory. Select **Finish** to complete the export.

5. Find the destination directory of your exported feature and browse the contents. You should find both `features` and `plugins` directories with subdirectories for the feature and its associated plug-ins. (If you only find a `plugins` subdirectory, you may have inadvertently selected **Export > Deployable plug-ins and fragments** instead of **Deployable Features** in the previous step.)

6. We are not ready to get into the details of Update Manager until Exercise 9, so for this exercise we'll manually add your code to the current Eclipse installation. Copy the subdirectories of your newly exported `features\com.ibm.jdg2e.exercises_1.0.0` and `plugin\com.ibm.jdg2e.helloworld_1.0.0` directories into the respective `eclipse\features` and `eclipse\plugins` directories of your current Eclipse installation.

7. Exit and then restart Eclipse.

8. Check that Eclipse is aware of the new contribution by selecting **Help > Software Updates > Manage Configuration...** to open the **Product Configuration** dialog. Find the feature you exported in the tree on the left of the dialog that opens; if you don't see it, you may have to select the **Show Disabled Features** button (🔲) and explicitly enable it. If all is well it should report that it is enabled. Close the dialog.

**NOTE** If you find that the feature is not available when you start Eclipse, try the following: Shut down Eclipse, and for one invocation specify the `-clean` command line parameter to `eclipse.exe`. This rebuilds the runtime configuration (content of the `eclipse\configuration` directory). If this doesn't work, see Section 8, Correcting Common Problems, for other possible solutions.

9. Try out the sample action that was added. Does it work?

Note that while the PDE can manage having the same plug-in in the workspace and installed in the `plugins` directory (an "external plug-in"), it is a more accurate test of what your users will do if you export to a second copy of an Eclipse installation.

Optionally, you can disable the new feature. You can do this by opening the Product Configuration dialog using the **Help > Software Updates > Manage Configuration...** menu option. Find and select your feature in the tree on the left of the dialog. On the right side there should be an option to disable the feature. Select it, and when prompted agree to stop/start the Workbench. Your code is now ignored, but if you want, you can use the dialog to bring it back later. Just make sure you choose the toolbar option of the Product Configuration dialog to display disabled features (⬚).

You have just completed the simplified process of packaging and installing a plug-in. As you do the remaining exercises in this book, you can add your new plug-ins to the current feature definition and perform the export/copy again.

## Section 7: Exploring (and Sometimes Correcting) the Eclipse Platform Code

One of the benefits of an open source project is the fact that the source is yours to study, and if necessary, correct. Let's see how the PDE helps you to learn and modify Eclipse code.

You have already been introduced to the notion of "external" versus "workspace" plug-ins; the **Target Platform** preference page, shown back in Figure Ex6.1, allows you to add external plug-ins to the list of those available in the test environment and your plug-in's build path. But what if you want to modify the code found in an external plug-in to help you debug or to correct a bug in the Eclipse code? The PDE includes options in the Plug-in view that makes it easy, as shown in Figure Ex6.15.

To get a better idea of how this works, let's import one of the Eclipse plug-ins and add some debug code.

1. If you haven't closed the runtime instance of Eclipse, do so now. Then turn to the Plug-ins view as shown in Figure Ex6.15, select the `org.eclipse.core.resources` plug-in, and then select **Import > As Source Project**. This will copy the plug-in from the `plugins` directory to your workspace, including its source, and recompile it.

2. Repeat step 1 for the `org.eclipse.core.runtime` plug-in, but this time select **Import > As Binary Project** instead. Look at both projects in the Package Explorer view. Notice that the source importation results in Java source files available in the `src-resources` folder, and Java class files in the `runtime.jar` file, as shown in Figure Ex6.16.

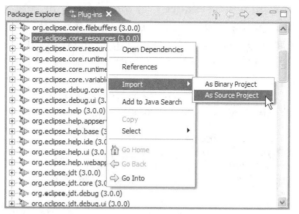

**Figure Ex6.15**   Import External Plug-ins as Source Project

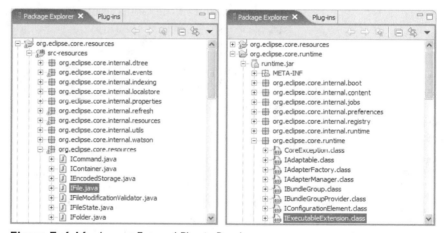

**Figure Ex6.16**   Import External Plug-in Results

Both projects are now in your workspace and included on the search path, but the `org.eclipse.core.resources` plug-in can be modified. If you turn back to the Plug-ins view, note that the project icon has changed from an external plug-in (⚙) to a folder, indicating that it is now in your workspace.

3. To see an example of how you might use this to help your debugging, let's assume that you want to know more about what resources (projects, files, and folders) are created and when. Begin by opening the class that represents them, `Resource`, in the package `org.eclipse` `.core.internal.resources` by selecting **Navigate > Open Type...** or

PART VI

pressing **Ctrl+Shift+T** (if more than one matching package is shown in the Open Type dialog, choose the one located at /org.eclipse .core.resources/<u>src-resources</u>). Add a debug System.out.println statement in the constructor, as shown below.

```
protected Resource(IPath path, Workspace workspace) {
  this.path = path.removeTrailingSeparator();
  this.workspace = workspace;

  // Debug code.
 System.out.println
    ("Created resource " + path
    + " in workspace " + workspace);
}
```

This will generate output to the Console whenever a new resource is created.

Launch the runtime Workbench. Verify that your debug code shows its output in the Console by creating a new project, folder, and file.

This short example demonstrates how you can add debug code, and how you could also apply your own fixes to Eclipse Platform code, should the need present itself.

## Section 8: Correcting Common Problems

Table Ex6.1 includes problems that are not very likely for your "Hello, World" exercise, but they may prove helpful should you decide to experiment beyond the instructions in this exercise. (Don't be intimidated by the number of entries in this table!)

**Table Ex6.1**   Common Errors and Possible Resolutions

| Symptom | Source | Possible Resolution |
|---|---|---|
| Your plug-in isn't recognized, or error log contains "Bundle 'xxx' version 'm.n.s' has already been installed from: yyy." | Runtime Workbench | Select the **Clear the configuration area before launching** choice on the **Configuration** page of the launch configuration (test environment). Verify your launch configuration includes your plug-in's required plug-ins. |

**Table Ex6.1**   Common Errors and Possible Resolutions (*continued*)

| Symptom | Source | Possible Resolution |
|---|---|---|
| "The project was not built since it is involved in a cycle or has classpath problems," or one of several errors similar to "Missing required Java project: org.eclipse.xxx." | Tasks view | Verify that the manifest file includes the required plug-ins in the `<import>` statements of the `<runtime>` tag. Verify that required plug-ins are either imported into workspace or available from the **Preferences > Plug-In Development> Target Platform** list. Then select **PDE Tools > Update Classpath...** for the affected project.<br><br>If the problem is still not corrected, try the following: Use the Plug-in Manifest Editor's **Dependencies** page to add another plug-in to the set of required plug-ins and save the `plugin.xml` file. Immediately delete the plug-in reference and save the file again. This can often "reboot" the PDE's automatic classpath configuration. |
| "This compilation unit indirectly references the missing type java.lang.object (typically some required class file is referencing a type outside the classpath)" or "This plug-in contains unresolved and/or cyclical references to other plug-ins." | Tasks view and **Overview** page of Plug-in Manifest Editor | Project build path is incorrect. The PDE should automatically update the build path of plug-ins when the `<requires>` tag is modified. Try **PDE Tools > Update Classpath...** for the affected project. If this doesn't correct the errors, manually add the required plug-ins from the project's **Properties > Java Build Path > Library > Add Library** dialog. |
| Contributed action is not present. | Runtime Workbench | Verify the `id` attributes of your actions—there may be a duplicate. The actions are stored in a keyed table, so duplicate entries are lost. |
| Contributed action is not present. | Runtime Workbench | Verify the action set (commands) is active by selecting **Window > Customize Perspective > Commands** and selecting your action set. **Window > Reset Perspective** will also activate all commands whose action set `visible` attribute is not set to `false`. |
| Contributed action is not present. | Console | Verify the `menubarPath` attribute. Look in the Console for the message "Invalid Menu Extension (Path is invalid)." |
| Contributed action is not present. | Console | Check the spelling, especially if the word "separator" is in the menu path. Many programmers misspell this word. Consider using "groupXXX." |

*continues*

**Table Ex6.1**    Common Errors and Possible Resolutions (*continued*)

| Symptom | Source | Possible Resolution |
|---|---|---|
| Your plug-in doesn't appear to be recognized by the Platform Runtime. | Deployed Workbench | By default, the Runtime Platform does not check for new plug-ins for an existing installation. Specify the -clean command line option to force the platform to recalculate the installation configuration. This is not necessary in the PDE since it includes the -dev option for the Runtime Workbench instances it launches.<br><br>If the -clean command line option doesn't correct the problem, delete the subdirectories in the eclipse\configuration directory (just leave the config.ini file). If your plug-in is part of a deployable feature, select the **Show Disabled Features** toolbar button (🔧) in the Product Configuration dialog; if your feature is in the list, check its status by selecting the **Show Properties** hyperlink in your feature's summary page. |
| "The chosen operation is not currently available" is displayed after selecting a contributed action. | Runtime Workbench | There are several possibilities.<br><br>• Check the Console. If it contains the error message, "Could not create action. Reason: Plug-in xxx was unable to load class yyy," where "xxx" is your plug-in and "yyy" is your action class, verify that your specification of the action's class attribute is correct, the code compiled correctly, there are no exceptions in the workspace's .log file, and there are no build path errors associated with your plug-in.<br>• Check the enablement specification of your action; it may be inconsistent with the enablement logic of your action's selectionChanged method. For example, your action's XML specifies the action is available only if the selection is an IFile with extension .java, but the action's selectionChanged method checks for an IFile with the extension .class. The static enablement logic of your action and its dynamic logic must be consistent. |

If none of the entries in Table Ex6.1 match your problem, consult the hints in *Official Eclipse 3.0 FAQs* by John Arthorne and Chris Laffra (Addison-Wesley, 2004, http://www.eclipsefaq.org), FAQs 27, 29, 73, and 74, or consider posing a question in the Eclipse tools newsgroup (news://www.eclipse.org/eclipse.tools).

## Exercise Activity Review

In this exercise you used the PDE to create, test, and debug a plug-in and deploy it as a feature. You now know the basics of plug-in development. Return to Part II where you left off—it will lead you further in your study of the Eclipse extension points and frameworks that you can employ to enhance the Workbench's capabilities.

# EXERCISE 7

## *Developing Your First Rich Client Application*

Chapter 10, Creating Applications Using the Rich Client Platform, is a sign-post chapter that guides you towards a Generic Workbench extension or an IDE-specific extension. This exercise starts by building a bare-bones extension on the Generic Workbench base. Figure Ex7.1 illustrates the most general of Eclipse components. Missing from the diagram are some components that are also useful but considered optional and which depend most on your application requirements. In any case, the base and optional components are not IDE-centric. To round out the getting started experience with the RCP components, the exercise winds up with adding the optional Help component (see Figure Ex7.15 later in the exercise).

The objective of this exercise is to show you how to construct extensions on the Generic Workbench and deploy a minimal Workbench configuration supporting a standalone client application. This exercise illustrates the inherent extensibility mechanisms of Eclipse in context with an RCP application. The exercise briefly discusses a few of the UI constructs such as actions and perspectives.

To get the most benefit from this exercise, you will need to have mastered the plug-in concepts presented in Chapter 10 and have practical experience using the Plug-in Development Environment (PDE), presented in Exercise 6. In case you skipped some or all of Chapter 9 to get right to the

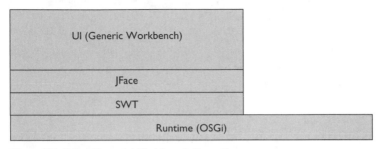

**Figure Ex7.1**    Generic Workbench Base Components

coding, here is a brief overview of what is involved in the construction of a rich client extension.

- Create a runnable extension to the Eclipse core runtime; in other words, a main program that creates the Workbench window and runs the user interface loop.
- Configure the appearance of the application by defining a perspective, showing the menu bar, adding standard menu options, and showing a toolbar.

Chapter 21, Action Contributions: The Integration Fast Track, and Chapter 20, Perspectives, provide the comprehensive description of the UI frameworks used in this exercise. However, it's not mandatory to read those chapters before beginning this exercise.

At the end of the exercise you should be able to

- Define the correct dependencies for a rich client application
- Define an application extension and implement the requisite runtime interface
- Create a perspective
- Customize the Workbench window containing a menu bar and toolbar
- Handle menu and toolbar actions
- Test and debug a rich client application
- Deploy the Generic Workbench that includes your rich client extension
- Add an optional RCP component (Help)

## Exercise Setup

Before starting the exercise, import the project com.ibm.jdg2e.rcp.simple .exercise. The import process is described fully in the readme.html file on the CD-ROM. This project contains the initial `plugin.xml` as well as `jpage` files containing text that you copy and paste into your code as you work through this exercise. See the `JPages` folder in the project `com.ibm.jdg2e` `.rcp.simple.exercise`.

## Getting Started

Before you get started, look at the structure of the minimal client application that you are building (see Figure Ex7.2). The line through the diagram separates the Eclipse framework on top from the client implementation on the bottom. In this exercise you will implement the classes in the diagram depicted below the line and name them:

- `SimplePerspectiveFactory`
- `SimpleApplicationRunnable`
- `SimpleWorkbenchAdvisor`

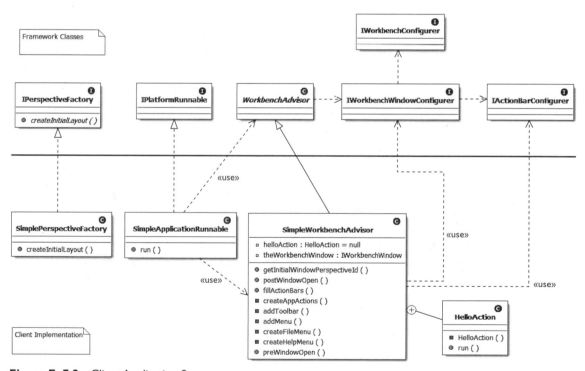

**Figure Ex7.2**   Client Application Structure

The objective of the first sections of this exercise is to create a minimal RCP application (see Figure Ex7.3). Sections 1 through 4 guide you through the mechanics of wiring up your application to the RCP framework. In Section 2 you lay the foundation for the user interface customization coming in Section 3. In Section 4 you will complete the wiring, establishing the relationship between your components to the RCP framework.

In Section 4 you will develop a main application class (see `Simple-ApplicationRunnable` in Figure Ex7.4). It is in this class that you will implement your application's `main` method.

The RCP framework requires that every application define and implement a perspective—your default perspective. Perspectives are a way of organizing views, editors, actions sets, and other contributions around some user tasks. In Section 2 you will tackle the creation of a perspective extension. It is referred to as the **default perspective** because it is the perspective users see when they start your application for the first time. The default perspective typically includes a Welcome view that presents some information about getting started using the RCP application. The perspective also often includes other views, actions, or wizards that users will most likely need to get started. For example, in the Eclipse IDE the default is the Resource perspective.

Chapter 20 discusses the details behind creating the contents and controlling the layout of perspectives. We want to focus on getting the RCP application going, so we'll start with the easiest kind of perspective to create: an empty one (see the class `SimplePerspectiveFactory` in Figure Ex7.5).

In Section 3 you will enable customization of the Workbench window by implementing the `SimpleWorkbenchAdvisor` class, a subclass of the `Workbench-Advisor`, shown in Figure Ex7.6.

In Section 4 you will wire your application into the RCP framework by implementing the `run` method of your `SimpleApplicationRunnable` class. You'll instantiate your `SimpleWorkbenchAdvisor`, and then you will create and run the Workbench window in your advisor.

With an application, perspective, and advisor classes implemented, in Section 5 you will validate that you have a runnable application. You will set up a run-and-debug launch configuration in a way that runs your RCP extension on the Generic Workbench (see Figure Ex7.3).

Creating the minimal Workbench is a huge step, but it is a very uninteresting application from the user's perspective. In Sections 6 and 7 you will begin to add some character to your application by adding menus and toolbar actions.

In Section 8 you will package the application and deploy it outside of the Eclipse development test environment.

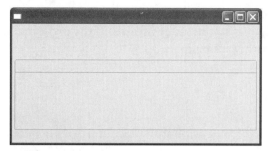

**Figure Ex7.3**   Minimal Workbench

Growing your application beyond the components in the RCP SDK and using components from the Eclipse SDK is covered in Section 9. You will add the Eclipse Help system to your RCP application.

## Section 1: Creating an Application Extension

In this part you will

- Define your client's plug-in dependencies in the plug-in manifest
- Create a main application class that implements `IPlatformRunnable`

### Adding Plug-in Dependencies

The minimal rich client application requires just two platform plug-ins:

- `org.eclipse.core.runtime`
- `org.eclipse.ui`

1. Open the `plugin.xml` file in the Plug-in Manifest Editor.

    Use the Dependencies page in the editor to add these plug-ins; this identifies that you need both basic runtime and user interface support:

    - `org.eclipse.core.runtime`
    - `org.eclipse.ui`

    This should be what you now see in the `plugin.xml` page of the Plug-in Manifest Editor.

    ```
    <requires>
      <import plugin="org.eclipse.core.runtime"/>
      <import plugin="org.eclipse.ui"/>
    </requires>
    ```

2. Save the manifest file. Remember that you can avoid typing the code in by hand. Refer to the JPages folder in the project, and use copy and paste to your heart's delight.

## Creating an Application

A rich client application extension in Eclipse starts with a contribution to the extension point org.eclipse.core.runtime.applications. The application extension serves as the main program and is identified in the class attribute. The class defined here must implement the IPlatformRunnable interface, as depicted in Figure Ex7.4.

1. Open the plugin.xml file in the Plug-in Manifest Editor and turn to the source page. Add the following application runtime extension to the manifest file.

```
<extension
  id="SimpleApplicationRunnable"
  name="JDG2E RCP Exercise"
  point="org.eclipse.core.runtime.applications">
  <application>
  <run
    class=
    "com.ibm.jdg2e.rcp.simple.exercise.SimpleApplicationRunnable">
  </run>
  </application>
</extension>
```

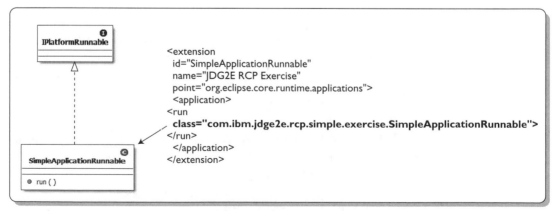

**Figure Ex7.4**   Application Declaration and Definition

2. Create an application (main program) class. Expand the `src-RCPexercise` folder, and select the package `com.ibm.jdg2e.rcp.simple.exercise`.

3. Add a class named `SimpleApplicationRunnable` that implements the interface `org.eclipse.core.runtime.IPlatformRunnable`. Keep the **Inherited abstract methods** choice selected.

## Section 2: Creating a Perspective Extension

The RCP framework requires the definition and the creation of a perspective. The perspective extensions are declared in the plug-in manifest file by contributing to the extension point `org.eclipse.ui.perspectives` (see Figure Ex7.5).

### Declaring a Perspective

1. Declare a perspective extension in the plug-in manifest file.

```
<extension
point="org.eclipse.ui.perspectives">
  <perspective
    name="JDG2E RCP Exercise"
      class=
      "com.ibm.jdg2e.rcp.simple.exercise.SimplePerspectiveFactory"
     id="com.ibm.jdg2e.rcp.simple.exercise.perspective">
  </perspective>
</extension>
```

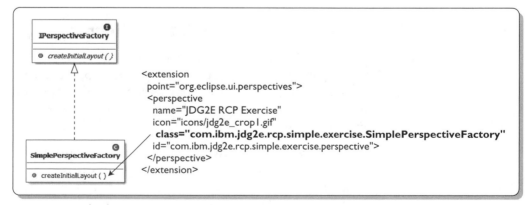

**Figure Ex7.5**  Perspective Declaration and Definition

### Implementing a Perspective Class

A perspective defines the views, editors, and their layout within the Workbench. Perspectives may also define the available action sets and wizard shortcuts. To keep this exercise simple, and until you learn more about perspectives, views, and editors, you will just create an empty perspective.

1. Select the package com.ibm.jdg2e.rcp.simple.exercise and create a perspective class named SimplePerspectiveFactory that implements IPerspectiveFactory interface. Make sure **Inherited abstract methods** is selected.

This is a very simple example, without views and editors, so there is nothing to do in the method createIntialLayout.

## Section 3: Creating a Workbench Advisor

Associate your initial (default) perspective to your implementation of the WorkBenchAdvisor, which you will name the SimpleWorkbenchAdvisor class.

1. Select the package com.ibm.jdg2e.rcp.simple.exercise and create a WorkbenchAdvisor. Name the class SimpleWorkbenchAdvisor and extend the WorkbenchAdvisor class. Leave the **Inherited abstract methods** selected.
2. Update the method getInitialWindowPerspectiveId(), and return the perspective identifier as declared in your plug-in manifest.

```
public String getInitialWindowPerspectiveId() {
   return "com.ibm.jdg2e.rcp.simple.exercise.perspective";
}
```

## Section 4: Implementing the Application's Main Program

In this section you will implement your application's main program by completing the implementation of the run method in the SimpleApplicationRunnable class. In the run method, you will create an instance of a SimpleWorkbenchAdvisor, derived from the WorkbenchAdvisor class. You'll also need to create the GUI, in other words, create the Display object.

1. Add the following code to the run method and then organize the imports.

```
int returnCode = 0;
WorkbenchAdvisor workbenchAdvisor = new
   SimpleWorkbenchAdvisor();
Display display = PlatformUI.createDisplay();
```

```
                    try {
                      returnCode = PlatformUI.createAndRunWorkbench(display,
                          workbenchAdvisor);
                      if (returnCode == PlatformUI.RETURN_RESTART) {
                        return IPlatformRunnable.EXIT_RESTART;
                      } else {
                        return IPlatformRunnable.EXIT_OK;
                      }
                    }
                    finally {
                      if (display != null)
                        display.dispose();
                    }
```

## Section 5: Running and Testing Your RCP Application

In this section you will work with the Launch Configuration wizard to define your application launch point and include plug-in dependencies.

1. To edit the launch configuration, select **Run > Debug > Debug...**, then select **Run-time Workbench** and select **New**.
2. Change the name of the launch configuration to `Hello_RCP`. In the drop-down box next to **Application Name:** select `com.ibm.jdg2e.rcp` `.simple.exercise.SimpleApplicationRunnable` and then select **Apply**.
3. Now turn to the **Plug-ins** tab. Select **Choose plug-ins and fragments to launch from list**. Deselect both **Workspace Plug-ins** and **External Plug-ins**.
4. Select the Workspace Plug-in entry `com.ibm.jdg2e.rcp.simple.exer-cise`, select **Add Required Plug-ins**, select **Apply**, and then select **Debug**. When you run the configuration, you should see a minimal Workbench (see Figure Ex7.3).

Now you have mastered the mechanics involved in producing a minimal RCP application. The fun begins in the next sections, where you add the user interface and function to your application.

## Section 6: Configuring Workbench Window User Interface Elements

Your RCP application will interact with the Workbench window through the RCP framework's `WorkbenchAdvisor` methods. These methods are orchestrated around the RCP application life cycle. Your `SimpleWorkbenchAdvisor` implementation participates in the life cycle by overriding the `Workbench-Advisor` methods.

The WorkbenchAdvisor uses an IWorkbenchConfigurer reference to manipulate the Workbench window (see Figure Ex7.6). The IWorkbenchConfigurer instance is passed in as a parameter in the initialize method and other methods where configuration might be required. From the IWorkbenchConfigurer you can get the IWorkbenchWindowConfigurer instance. This has methods to show the menu bar, coolbar (a container for one or more toolbars), a status line, and so on.

Table Ex7.1 suggests what to do when with regard to the life cycle methods. This is your guide on where and when to perform application customizations. The methods listed in column one are where you can implement the customizations. The Suggested Usage column points out some possible customizations, and the When Called column provides the context within the application life cycle when the methods listed in column one are called.

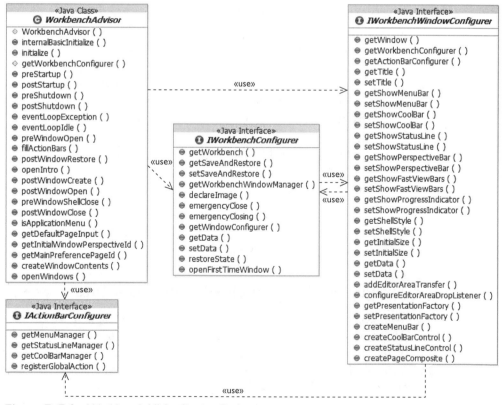

**Figure Ex7.6**   Workbench UI Application Package

**Table Ex7.1**   WorkbenchAdvisor Life Cycle Methods

| Method | When Called | Suggested Usage |
|---|---|---|
| `initialize` | First | Keep a reference to `configurer` for future use. Handle any application command line arguments and create any common application images. |
| `preStartup` | Called after initialization but before the first window is opened | May be used to set options affecting which editors and views are initially opened. |
| `openWindows` | Called when the Workbench opens windows on startup | Good time to restore Workbench state. |
| `preWindowOpen` | Called in the constructor of the Workbench window | Set options such as whether the window will have a menu bar, coolbar, or status line.<br><br>Warning: None of the window's widgets have been created yet, so they can't be referenced in this method (see `postWindowOpen`). |
| `fillActionBars` | Called before the Workbench window is opened | Create menu bar actions; create toolbar and toolbar actions and then add to coolbar. |
| `getInitialWindowPerspectiveId` | Called after the action bars and status line are added | Return the initial (default perspective) id. This is the perspective that is opened the first time the RCP application is opened. |
| `postWindowOpen` | Called right after the Workbench window (shell) is opened | Set the shell title or image, or change its size. |
| `postStartup` | Called after all windows have been opened or restored, but before the event loop starts | Use to start automatic processes, open tips, or open other windows. |
| `eventLoopIdle` | Called when the event loop has nothing to do | Initiate tasks that are required, not initiated by a user event. |
| `preWindowShellClose` | Called before the shell is closed | Last chance for user to initiate a task, e.g., save a file or cancel the shutdown. |
| `postShutdown` | Called after all windows have closed in the shutdown process | This can be used to save the current application state, clean up anything created by initialize, and dispose of images. |

### *Setting the Title and Image of the Workbench Window*

In this part of the exercise you will augment the shell window with a title and image in the implementation of the `postWindowOpen` life cycle method. You will override the life cycle method `postWindowOpen` and customize the Workbench window by adding your title and an image. For convenience (and the assumption that you have not worked with SWT images before), you will use a predefined Workbench image.

1. Open the `SimpleWorkbenchAdvisor` class. Using the pop-up menu, select **Source > Override/Implement Methods...** and override the `postWindowOpen` method. In this method you will set the title text and specify a shell window image. (You'll learn more about creating and disposing of SWT resources such as images in Chapter 14, The Standard Widget Toolkit: A Lean, Mean, Widget Machine. For now, just reuse one of the Workbench's reusable images.) Use the existing image `IMG_TOOL_FORWARD` for the shell's image.

   ```
   public void postWindowOpen(IWorkbenchWindowConfigurer configurer) {
       configurer.setTitle("JDG2E: Hello RCP World");

   configurer.getWindow().getShell().setImage(configurer.getWindow().
       getWorkbench().getSharedImages().
       getImage(ISharedImages.IMG_TOOL_FORWARD));
   }
   ```

2. Now run the application. You will see the image and title in the window title bar (see Figure Ex7.7).

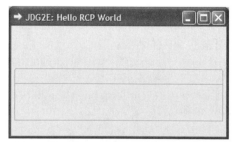

**Figure Ex7.7**   Application with Image and Title

## Section 7: Adding Menu and Toolbar Actions

The Workbench plug-in provides some standard top-level menus that you can use as insertion points for your actions. Alternatively, you can define new top-level menus. The standard top-level menus and insertion points are defined in the `IWorkbenchActionConstants` class (see Table Ex7.2).

**Table Ex7.2** Standard Menu Constant Identifiers

| Menu Label | IWorkbenchActionConstants |
|------------|---------------------------|
| File       | M_FILE                    |
| Edit       | M_EDIT                    |
| Window     | M_WINDOW                  |
| Help       | M_HELP                    |

The RCP framework also makes standard actions accessible, such as **File > New, File > Exit, Edit > Copy, Edit > Cut, Edit > Paste**, and so on.

Standard action functionality is also reusable. Access to the standard actions is provided by the `ActionFactory` class, and the functionality is provided by static methods and fields. The following example demonstrates typical usage.

```
MenuManager newMenu =
    new MenuManager("&New", ActionFactory.NEW.getId());
newMenu.add(new Separator(ActionFactory.NEW.getId()));
newMenu.add(new Separator(IWorkbenchActionConstants.MB_ADDITIONS));
newMenu.add(ActionFactory.NEW.create(window));
menu.add(newMenu);
```

In this example, `ActionFactory.NEW.create(window)` adds the **File > New** action.

### Adding the Menu Bar

To add a menu and toolbar, override the `fillActionBar` method of the `WorkbenchAdvisor`. Because this method is called multiple times during the Workbench life cycle, the method call sets a flag bit to identify when you are supposed to add your menu bar and toolbar actions.

1. You don't want to add an action handler each time the `fillAction-Bars` is called, so we will create a field to store the action handler in a field in the `SimpleWorkbenchAdvisor` class. You will need a reference to the Workbench window in the action handler, so store that reference in a field in the `SimpleWorkbenchAdvisor` class.

   ```
   private HelloAction helloAction;
   private IWorkbenchWindow theWorkbenchWindow;
   ```

2. Notice that after adding the code in the previous step that the compiler is complaining that the `HelloAction` class is undefined, so go and fix that now by implementing this as an inner class of the class `SimpleWorkbenchAdvisor`. The `HelloAction` class extends the `Action` class. The most important method in the `Action` class is the run method. The action is a reusable class that you will use to handle both your menu bar and toolbar actions. You will associate the action to a menu item and toolbar item in subsequent steps of this exercise. The action setup involves setting the label, tooltip text, and images (both the enabled and disabled versions). Here is that inner class implementation.

```
private class HelloAction extends Action {
    private HelloAction() {
     setText("JDG2E: Hello");
     setToolTipText("JDG2E: Push to activate Hello RCP World.");
     ISharedImages sharedImages = theWorkbenchWindow
        .getWorkbench().getSharedImages();
     setImageDescriptor(sharedImages
        .getImageDescriptor(ISharedImages.IMG_TOOL_FORWARD));
     setDisabledImageDescriptor(sharedImages
        .getImageDescriptor(ISharedImages.IMG_TOOL_FORWARD));
    }
    public void run() {
     if (theWorkbenchWindow != null)
       MessageDialog.openInformation(theWorkbenchWindow
         .getShell(), "JDG2E: Hello RCP Plug-in",
         "Hello RCP World");
    }
}
```

3. Using the pop-up menu, select **Source > Override/Implement Methods...** to override the advisor's `fillActionBars` method.

4. The `fillActionBars` method is called multiple times during the Workbench life cycle. You need to examine the flag to determine when it's time to add menu or toolbar items. Call the (not yet implemented) helper methods `createAppActions`, `addMenu`, and `addToolbar`. Use the quick fix to add the unimplemented method stubs.

```
public void fillActionBars(IWorkbenchWindow window,
                           IActionBarConfigurer configurer,
                           int flags) {
  theWorkbenchWindow = window;
  if (helloAction == null) {
    createAppActions();
  }
  if ((flags & FILL_MENU_BAR) != 0) {
   addMenu(window, configurer);
  }
```

```
      if ((flags & FILL_COOL_BAR) != 0) {
        addToolbar(configurer);
      }
    }
```

5. Create your application actions in the `createAppActions` method.

```
private void createAppActions() {
  helloAction = new HelloAction();
}
```

6. Complete the implementation of the `addMenu` helper method in the class `SimpleWorkbenchAdvisor`. First, get the menu manager from the Workbench action bar configurer. Use the menu manager to create the top-level menu, then add the menu action item. After adding your custom top-level menu, add a call to create the standard file menu structure.

```
private void addMenu(IWorkbenchWindow window,
                     IActionBarConfigurer configurer) {
  IMenuManager menuBar = configurer.getMenuManager();
  // Call my helper method that adds File>Exit
  menuBar.add(createFileMenu(window));
  MenuManager menu = new MenuManager("&JDG2E",
    IWorkbenchActionConstants.MB_ADDITIONS);
  menu.add(helloAction);
  menuBar.add(menu);
}
```

7. Implement the helper method `createFileMenu` that creates the **File** menu structure and adds an **Exit** action.

```
private MenuManager createFileMenu(IWorkbenchWindow window) {
    MenuManager menu = new MenuManager("&File",
        IWorkbenchActionConstants.M_FILE);
    menu.add(new
        GroupMarker(IWorkbenchActionConstants.FILE_START));
    menu.add(new
        GroupMarker(IWorkbenchActionConstants.MB_ADDITIONS));
    menu.add(ActionFactory.QUIT.create(window));
    menu.add(new
        GroupMarker(IWorkbenchActionConstants.FILE_END));
    return menu;
}
```

8. Now configure the Workbench to show the menu bar and the toolbar. Using the pop-up menu, select **Source > Override/Implement Methods...** to override the `preWindowOpen` method.

```
public void preWindowOpen(IWorkbenchWindowConfigurer
                          configurer) {
  super.preWindowOpen(configurer);
  configurer.setShowMenuBar(true);
  configurer.setShowCoolBar(true);
}
```

9. Run the RCP application to test it. Your application should now look like the application shown in Figure Ex7.8.

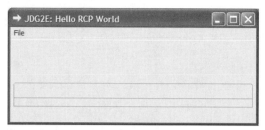

**Figure Ex7.8**   RCP with Menu Bar

## Implementing the Toolbar

Adding toolbar actions are a lot like adding a menu bar actions: You get the coolbar from the configurer, create a toolbar manager and a group of application actions, add your action to the toolbar manager, and then add your toolbar manager to the coolbar (see Figure Ex7.9).

1. Complete the implementation for addToolbar now.

```
private void addToolbar(IActionBarConfigurer configurer) {
    ICoolBarManager cbManager = configurer.getCoolBarManager();
    cbManager.add(new
        GroupMarker(IWorkbenchActionConstants.GROUP_APP));
    // Application Created Group
    IToolBarManager appToolBar = new
        ToolBarManager(cbManager.getStyle());
    appToolBar.add(new
        Separator(IWorkbenchActionConstants.NEW_GROUP));
    appToolBar.add(helloAction);
    // Add to the coolbar manager
    cbManager.add(new ToolBarContributionItem(appToolBar,
        IWorkbenchActionConstants.TOOLBAR_FILE));
}
```

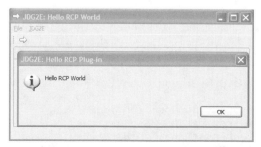

**Figure Ex7.9**   Complete, though Trivial, Client Application

---

**NOTE** Take care when adding imports because there are multiple Separator classes in the class libraries. Select the `org.eclipse.jface.action.Separator` class.

---

2. Run the RCP application to test it.

# Section 8: Deploying Your Application

For the purpose of this exercise, we'll look at the essential packaging requirements involved in the distribution of this minimal rich client application. Comprehensive explanations of product branding, feature development, and Workbench configurations are in Chapter 6, Managing Your Eclipse Environment, and Chapter 13, Defining Features and Products.

While there is not an **Export > Deployable Rich Client Application** wizard in Eclipse 3.0, there are numerous manual techniques that you can use. In this section we use the technique where you discover your plug-in dependencies using the `launch` configuration. Having found the required plug-ins, you will copy those plug-ins to your deployment folder.

The steps outlined in this section involve picking out the parts of the Eclipse SDK that you need from those parts that you don't need in your client application. The RCP has its own download packages. The RCP SDK contains the same plug-ins, source, and documentation, but you will not be able to build RCP applications with the RCP SDK alone. It is useful to set up your **Target Platform Location** to point to the RCP SDK. The **Target Platform Location** is described in Chapter 9, Getting Started with Plug-in Development. In that way you will be compiling and testing with just the RCP plug-ins. The RCP binary may be helpful in deployment because you can send just your plug-ins and tell the customer to download the RCP binary to get the required plug-ins.

## Verifying That the Build Configuration Is Correct

Before you get started with the deployment process, verify that your build configuration is correct. This is easy to do using the Build Properties Editor.

1. Find the `build.properties` file in the root of your project and open the file.
2. Look at the **Binary Build** configuration (see Figure Ex7.10). This allows you to configure what you want included in the binary build. The `JPages` folder was included as a convenience for the exercise and is not required in the deployable binary build, so make sure that folder is not selected.

**Figure Ex7.10**   Configuring the Binary Build

## Deploying an Application

The deployment process starts with creating a simplified Eclipse distribut-able, an Eclipse-like install directory structure that the core plug-in loader expects. To get started you will export the plug-in project.

1. Right-click on the plug-in project com.ibm.jdg2e.rcp.simple.exercise. Select **Export... > Deployable plug-ins and fragments** and then select **Next**.
2. Select the plug-in project com.ibm.jdg2e.rcp.simple.exercise.
3. Your intent is to build an executable binary directory structure, so in the field labeled **Deploy as:** select the option **a directory structure**.
4. In the destination, enter a directory name (jdg2e_rcp, for example, on Windows c:\jdg2e_rcp). Select **Finish**.

   Your plug-in folder structure now looks like Figure Ex7.11.

**Figure Ex7.11**   Initial Distribution Structure

5. Next, determine the dependent plug-ins that are required in your dis-tribution. The list includes not only the plug-in dependencies listed in the <requires> section of the plug-in manifest file, but also those

plug-ins required by the plug-ins that you reference. To find your dependencies, open your launch configuration using **Run…**, and then select the **Hello_RCP** configuration. On the **Plug-ins** page, look at the external plug-ins. All external plug-ins required by your plug-in are checked (see Figure Ex7.12).

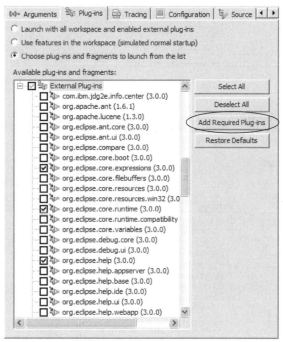

**Figure Ex7.12**   Launch Configuration Plug-ins—Add Required Plug-ins

6. Review the required plug-ins to find the set of dependencies. You find that your plug-in requires

```
org.eclipse.core.expressions
org.eclipse.core.runtime
org.eclipse.help
org.eclipse.jface
org.eclipse.osgi
org.eclipse.swt.win32 (differs by platform)
org.eclipse.swt
org.eclipse.ui.workbench
org.eclipse.ui
```

7. Copy all dependent plug-ins into the plugins folder.

8. In addition, copy org.eclipse.update.configurator to the plugins folder.

   While org.eclipse.update.configurator does not turn up on the required plug-ins list, we will include that plug-in to discover and install the plug-ins. You will learn in the next section how to remove the update configurator from your distribution package and hard-code the list of plug-ins to install in a config.ini file.

9. Copy the startup.jar file from the Eclipse SDK <install loc>\ eclipse folder into the folder jdg2e_rcp.

   The source tree should look like Figure Ex7.13 now. There should be 11 plug-ins in the plugins folder.

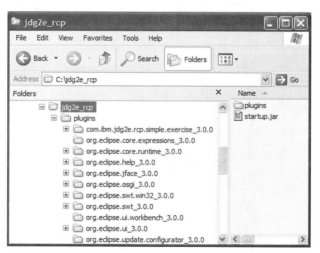

**Figure Ex7.13**   The Plug-in Folder Structure

10. You are all set to test a command line execution of your Eclipse client application. Open a command prompt and change to the folder containing the startup.jar file (on Windows, C:\jdg2e_rcp). To run the application use this command (on one line):

```
javaw -cp startup.jar org.eclipse.core.launcher.Main
-consoleLog -application
com.ibm.jdg2e.rcp.simple.exercise.SimpleApplicationRunnable
```

11. For troubleshooting, see the configuration folder for the `.log` file for errors. It has a name in the form of `1082150558915.log`.
    - Make sure that the spelling of the application class name specified in the extension `org.eclipse.core.runtime.applications` matches that in the application parameter.
    - The following message may indicate that the loader was unable to resolve all of the plug-in dependencies:

    "`!MESSAGE Unable to locate application extension: com.ibm.jdg2e.rcp.simple.SimpleApplicationRunnable`"

**NOTE** If you make changes to the plugin.xml file you may need to delete the configuration directory, otherwise these changes will not be read (they are in the registry already).

### Running Without Assistance of the Update Configurator

You really haven't accomplished what you set out to do—to run a minimal RCP application—until you run your application without the convenience of using the Eclipse Update Manager. The role that the `org.eclipse.update .configurator` plays is that it discovers the plug-ins in your deployment and calls the runtime to install them. So you cheated and used what turns out to be an optional component from the Eclipse (IDE) SDK (that is, the `org.eclipse .update.configurator` plug-in configurator that comes in the Eclipse SDK and not in the Eclipse RCP binary). There are certainly some nice advantages in using a dynamic configurator with continued plug-in discovery and extensibility, but in fact all that is required is a hard comma-separated list of bundles to install. You might want to try running without the `org.eclipse.update .configurator` plug-in.

1. Delete the `org.eclipse.update.configurator` plug-in from the runtime directory.
2. Delete the contents of the configuration folder that was generated in the previous section.
3. Add the configuration list in the form of a `config.ini` file. You will find a sample `config.ini` file in the root directory of the template project. The `config.ini` file instructs the runtime about which Eclipse plug-ins to install. Each entry in the list is of the form:

   `<url to bundle>[@<start-level>]`

PART VI

For example, here are the contents of the `configuration\config.ini` file.

```
#Eclipse Runtime Configuration File
osgi.install.area=file:c:/jdg2e_rcp
osgi.bundles = org.eclipse.core.runtime@2:start, \
org.eclipse.core.expressions, org.eclipse.help, \
org.eclipse.jface,org.eclipse.osgi, org.eclipse.swt, \
org.eclipse.swt.win32, org.eclipse.ui.workbench, \
org.eclipse.ui,com.ibm.jdg2e.rcp.simple.exercise
eclipse.application=SimpleApplicationRunnable
eof=eof
```

4. Open a new command prompt and launch the RCP application using the same command you used in the previous section.

## Section 9: Adding "Optional" Components

Up to this point you have worked within the confines of the Generic Workbench, using the Platform Runtime, SWT (widgets), JFace (actions), and the standard Workbench menus and actions. There are additional components in the Eclipse SDK that are applicable to a variety of rich client applications. The following are a few of the notable optional components (see Figure Ex7.14).

- Help—Use if you need a well-integrated and extensible Eclipse help format. This is considered an optional component because some applications will use something other than Eclipse help.
- Update—Use when your application requires a lightweight configuration and Update Manager. For instance, the Update Manager can be used to distribute corrective service updates to your application. It is considered optional component because:
  - Some application configurations are more or less static and don't require user configuration.
  - User configurations are updated and managed using some other facilities, such as an enterprise desktop management system.
- Text—Use when your application requires a text editor and document model.
- Resources—Use if your application needs a workspace. This is considered an optional component because the notion of a workspace is more commonly found in IDEs, not applications.

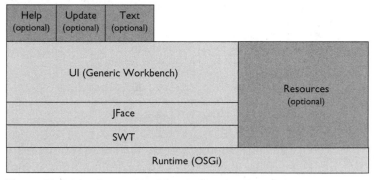

**Figure Ex7.14** Generic Workbench Optional Components

### Adding the Standard Help Menu and Help Action

The following steps will guide you through adding the optional help component. You will add the standard help menu and help action. Rather than implement your own help plug-in at this time, you will import the help example that accompanies Chapter 22.

1. Import the `com.ibm.jdg2e.help` help example project from the CD-ROM.

2. Implement the `createHelpMenu` method in your `SimpleWorkbench-Advisor` class. This creates the standard help menu and action.

```
private MenuManager createHelpMenu(IWorkbenchWindow window) {
    MenuManager menu = new MenuManager("&Help",
    IWorkbenchActionConstants.M_HELP);
    menu.add(new
      GroupMarker(IWorkbenchActionConstants.HELP_START));
    menu.add(ActionFactory.HELP_CONTENTS.create(window));
    menu.add(new
      GroupMarker(IWorkbenchActionConstants.HELP_END));
    menu.add(new
      GroupMarker(IWorkbenchActionConstants.MB_ADDITIONS));
    return menu;
  }
```

3. Add the standard help menu to the menu bar by inserting this line of code at the end of the `addMenu` method.

```
menuBar.add(createHelpMenu(window));
```

4. Update the `<requires>` section of your plug-in manifest file to include these required plug-ins.

```
<import plugin="org.apache.ant"/>
<import plugin="org.apache.lucene"/>
<import plugin="org.eclipse.help.appserver"/>
<import plugin="org.eclipse.help.base"/>
<import plugin="org.eclipse.help.ui"/>
<import plugin="org.eclipse.help.webapp"/>
<import plugin="org.eclipse.tomcat"/>
```

5. To test this new function, open the launch configuration dialog and make sure that the com.ibm.jdg2e.help plug-in is included in the list of plug-ins. To add the required help-related plug-ins to your dependencies, select the com.ibm.jdg2e.help plug-in and then select the **Add Required Plug-ins** button. Now select **Run** or **Debug** to start the application.

6. When the application starts you will see the help menu. Select **Help > Help Contents**. You should see the JDG2E help example in the table of contents (see Figure Ex7.15).

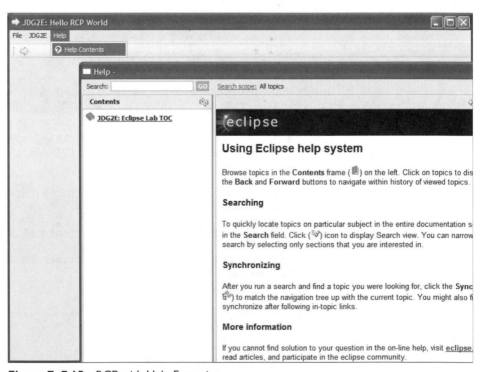

**Figure Ex7.15**   RCP with Help Extension

**NOTE** If you want to go back and try to deploy the help outside of the PDE, you need to copy the following plug-ins to the `plugins` folder:

- `org.apache.ant`
- `org.apache.lucene`
- `org.eclipse.help.appserver`
- `org.eclipse.help.base`
- `org.eclipse.help.ui`
- `org.eclipse.help.webapp`
- `org.eclipse.tomcat`
- `com.ibm.jdg2e.help`

## Exercise Activity Review

In this exercise you used the PDE to create, test, and debug a client application extension on the Generic Workbench. Taking a step into the category of optional components, you added the help example that comes with this book to your RCP application.

You now have the basics of developing, testing, debugging, and deploying an extension to the Generic Workbench. Return to Part II where you left off—it will lead you further in your study of the Eclipse extension points and frameworks that you can employ to enhance the Workbench's capabilities. You'll be learning more about perspectives, contributions, views, and editors as you dive deeper into the book. The CD-ROM contains an advanced example that demonstrates many more of the Workbench capabilities in context with a mini-workplace, an extensible desktop client platform application base (see the project `com.ibm.jdg2e.miniwp`). Also see Exercise 8, Developing a Rich Client Application with Dynamically Added Plug-ins.

PART VI

# EXERCISE 8

## *Developing a Rich Client Application with Dynamically Added Plug-ins*

In this exercise you will learn how to add plug-ins dynamically to your RCP applications using the installation and configuration components of the Eclipse framework.

The term **"dynamic plug-ins"** simply describes the ability to add plug-ins to the Eclipse IDE or RCP application without restarting Eclipse. The advantage for users is that they can expand the function on their desktops on demand. Because the plug-ins are built on the common Eclipse user interface frameworks, that new function will integrate seamlessly with the existing plug-ins in their applications. The whole process requires little user intervention; the discovery of new plug-ins and the subsequent installation and configuration can be automated to a large degree.

The Eclipse runtime architecture is built on the Open Services Gateway Initiative (OSGi) framework. The Eclipse runtime install and configurator is extensible in a way that enables software distribution, installation, and configuration management agents to deliver managed plug-ins to the Eclipse platform. For convenience, we will refer to these installation and configuration plug-ins to Eclipse as **configurators**. For example, the Update Manager component in the Eclipse SDK supplies a configurator. The Eclipse runtime architecture also opens up to the world of service-oriented application providers. A common scenario is the configurator working as a plug-in service provider, using directory and security services to find the logged-on user's role in an organization. With that information, it then delivers just the right plug-ins and installs them dynamically (this assumes, of course, that the user's subscription is paid up).

Examples of Eclipse configurators specifically designed for the on-demand world of desktops and devices include the Lotus Workplace platform and the Tivoli Device Manager.

At the very minimum, a configurator is responsible for:

- Discovery and acquisition of deployable plug-ins from local or remote systems.
- Installation of new plug-ins into the application.
- Uninstall of plug-ins from the application.

Let's start with a simple configuration manager that will implement a simple discovery mechanism, a "mini configurator." This configurator is simplistic compared to configurators previously mentioned, but you need to start somewhere. Consider this exercise the "Hello, world" example for configurators.

Here is an overview of the parts in this exercise.

- Exercise setup

    You are provided a template with a basic RCP application, a perspective, and a couple of familiar-looking tools. You don't need to complete Exercise 7; rather, all parts of the base RCP application are provided to you in template form. Your job is to build an Eclipse configurator that allows the user to find a "Bonus pack" plug-in and add that new function to the existing base application in a dynamic and seamless way. You don't need to implement anything in the Bonus pack plug-in; it is also provided along with the setup materials.

- Set up the launch configuration

    You will set up the development environment launch configuration. This section exposes you to tools useful when working with the OSGi platform runtime.

    You will learn about the OSGi runtime loader and how it handles resolving dependencies. You will also learn about the OSGi plug-in state transitions and the plug-in life cycle methods.

- Explore the OSGi plug-in development model.

    The Bonus pack plug-in, as provided to you, is built according to the Eclipse 3.0 OSGi plug-in development model. You'll take a quick tour of OSGi bundle development and look at the implementation inside the Bonus pack plug-in.

- Implement a plug-in configurator.

    Given a plug-in location, you will make calls to OSGi to install and resolve the plug-in's dependencies.

- Mock up a simple discovery mechanism.

  Present to the user a folder dialog; you'll direct the user to browse to the CD-ROM where the Bonus pack plug-in is saved in its deployable form.

- You will launch the mini-configurator to test that you can dynamically install the Bonus pack plug-in. The result of adding the Bonus pack is a much cooler application than what the user started with (see Figure Ex8.10).

## Exercise Setup

Before starting the exercise, import the project `com.ibm.jdg2e.mini` `.configurator.exercise`. The import process is described fully in the `readme.html` file on the CD-ROM. This project contains the initial `plugin.xml`, a rich client application with a browser view and a calculator, with application functions similar to those illustrated in the `com.ibm.jdg2e.miniwp` example. In addition, the template includes scrapbook pages, that is, `.jpages`, containing text that you copy and paste into your code as you work through implementing your very own application configurator. See the `JPages` folder in the project. Have the CD-ROM handy or the contents thereof because you will test your application configurator loading a plug-in named `com.ibm.jdg2e.miniwp.bonus_pack`.

## Section 1: Create Your RCP Application Launch Configuration

Before you start the main implementation of your mini-configurator, you need to establish an RCP application launch configuration. The launch configuration is configured in a way that is most useful when working with the OSGi framework and the Platform Runtime.

It's helpful to understand the division of responsibilities in the Platform Runtime. The Eclipse runtime is split into two pieces: the OSGi part is responsible for class loading and prerequisite management, and it defines APIs that are part of the cradle-to-grave application life cycle; the other part handles plug-in extensions and extension points. Together they provide the capability for dynamic plug-in installation, updating, uninstall, and configuration.

1. Create a new runtime Workbench configuration. **Select Run > Run...**, select **Run-time Workbench**, and press the **New** button. Optionally define a configuration name if you don't like the default name. On the **Arguments** page select **Run an application** and select this class: `com.ibm.jdg2e.configuratorEx.JDGEDynamicApplicationEx` (see

Figure Ex8.1). For **Program Arguments**, add -console to the end. This requests that an OSGi console opens at runtime.

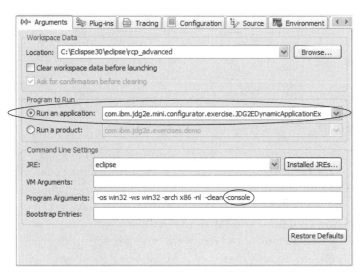

**Figure Ex8.1**    Workbench Runtime Launch Arguments Page

2. On the **Plug-ins** page, select **Choose plug-ins and fragments to launch from list** and press the **Deselect All** button. Next, select the com.ibm.jdg2e.mini.configurator.exercise plug-in and then click on the **Add Required Plug-ins** button (see Figure Ex8.2).
3. Turn to the **Configuration** page, select **Clear the configuration area before launching**, and then select **Apply and Close** (see Figure Ex8.3).

This setting clears any previous configuration state information that org.eclipse.osgi keeps in its configuration cache. The platform remembers the configuration state, including the location of all the previously installed plug-ins. This means that if you want to experience the glee of installing and loading your Bonus pack plug-in dynamically the next time you run the application, you need to clear it.

The act of installing and resolving the Bonus pack plug-in sets off a broadcast. The OSGi plug-in resolve event unfolds a sequence of processing in the runtime framework. The extension and extension point management parses the new plugin.xml and updates the Eclipse extension registry. In a ripple effect, the interested components, such as plug-ins that provide the extension points to the Bonus pack, are notified of the addition of the new Bonus pack extensions. These new

**Figure Ex8.2**   Plug-in Launch Configuration

**Figure Ex8.3**   OSGi Runtime Console

contributions are rendered in the UI with the appearance of a new perspective, actions, view, and preference page, and all without restarting the application.

You will use the console illustrated in Figure Ex8.4 shown below, so let's take a few minutes to become familiar with OSGi and the console facility before proceeding.

You will find that the console is a useful tool for determining what is going on in the OSGi runtime environment. The console **ss** command shows the state of every plug-in in the system. You can see which plug-ins are installed but not yet resolved (meaning that their dependencies are not yet resolved), and which plug-ins are active. If after installing your plug-in it remains in an installed state, this may indicate that you missed a call to OSGi service to resolve the plug-in, or that the service failed to resolve all plug-ins. With more experience, you'll begin to appreciate the feeling of success when you see your plug-in move to the resolved state (see Figure Ex8.4). Otherwise, that means that the original product distribution did not include required plug-ins. The alternative is to include required plug-ins in your distribution.

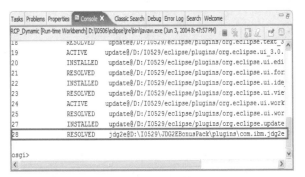

**Figure Ex8.4**    Plug-in States and State Transitions

For more information on resolving plug-in dependencies, see the Eclipse Java documentation for the `org.osgi.service.packageadmin` `.PackageAdmin.refreshPackages(Bundle[] bundles)` method.

Another interesting phenomenon that you will witness using the OSGi console is Eclipse's lazy loading in action. When you observe plug-ins in the resolved state, that means they have not been loaded; however, you will see the user interface elements, views, actions, and so on in the application while the plug-in is in the resolved state

because the plug-in's list of extensions have been processed by the
Platform Runtime. Dynamically aware plug-ins like the Workbench
react by adding contributed views, editors, menus, and actions. The
OSGi framework broadcasts events such as install, resolve, start, stop,
and uninstall. These bundle state transitions are illustrated in Figure
Ex8.5. In OSGi terms, the plug-in moves to an Active state after the
bundle is loaded. The arrows with dashed lines indicate state transitions that are not possible or require a platform shutdown and restart.

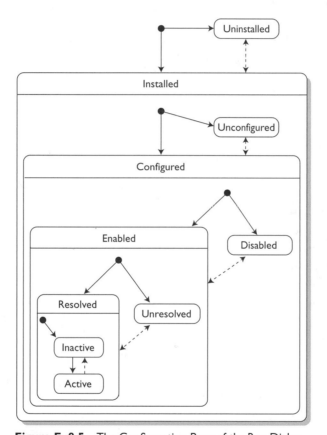

**Figure Ex8.5**   The Configuration Page of the Run Dialog

## Section 2: Implement Your Plug-in Life Cycle start() Method

Now it's time to get down to the business of writing code to the OSGi framework services. Before continuing, let's briefly discuss some key OSGi framework terms before writing to the Eclipse OSGi frameworks.

PART VI

The term **bundle** comes from the OSGi world. It's a manifest file that describes a unit of function. Perhaps it's a bit oversimplistic, but for our purposes a bundle and a plug-in are synonymous, and from now on we will use the terms interchangeably.

The contents of the bundle manifest file, `manifest.mf`, equate to the plug-in's descriptor, runtime, and requires sections in the `plugin.xml`. What's missing is the extension and extension point description. The Platform Runtime looks for `manifest.mf` first, and if it can't find the file, it generates one based on the contents of the descriptor, runtime, and requires sections of the plug-in's `plugin.xml` file.

Just for the fun of learning about OSGi and plug-in development, the Bonus pack plug-in provided to you for this exercise, `com.ibm.jdg2e.miniwp .bonus_pack,` is built on the OSGi development model. It contains a `manifest.mf` file that specifies the information required for class loading and prerequisite management, and a `plugin.xml` file where Eclipse-specific declarations, namely the definitions of extensions and extension points, are specified (see Figure Ex8.6). There is absolutely no need to develop this Bonus pack plug-in in this fashion, and nothing in the Bonus pack exploits any features in OSGi. It's presented here in the interest of demonstrating the two sides of the Eclipse runtime: the OSGi side and the extensibility mechanism of Eclipse application frameworks.

The attribute `Bundle-Activator` in the bundle manifest is a class that extends the `Plugin` class. If you recall, it defines two plug-in life cycle methods, `start` and `stop`. The framework calls the plug-in's `start` method when the state of the plug-in turns to active. The platform plug-in activator passes a `BundleContext` in a parameter on the `start` method. This is how the framework gives individual bundles access to functions in the OSGi frameworks. For example, the plug-in class can call the `BundleContext.getBundles()` method to discover all the bundles in the system.

1. Go to into the class `com.ibm.jdg2e.mini.configurator.Configurator-Plugin` and define a field to store the `BundleContext` parameter of the start method. Remember the trick to organize imports as you add references to external packages using the **Ctrl-Shift-O** key combination.

   ```
   BundleContext pluginContext;
   ```

2. Set the field value in the `start` method.

   ```
   public void start(BundleContext context) throws Exception {
     super.start(context);
     pluginContext = context;
   }
   ```

```
Manifest-Version: 1.0
Bundle-Name: Bonus_pack Plug-in
Bundle-SymbolicName: com.ibm.jdg2e.miniwp.bonus_pack; singleton=true
Bundle-Version: 3.0.0
Bundle-ClassPath: bonus_pack.jar
Bundle-Activator: com.ibm.jdg2e.miniwp.bonus_pack.Bonus_packPlugin
Bundle-Vendor: The Java Developer's Guide to Eclipse
Bundle-Localization: plugin
Require-Bundle: org.eclipse.ui,
   org.eclipse.core.runtime
Eclipse-Autostart: true
```

```xml
<?xml version="1.0" encoding="UTF-8"?>
<?eclipse version="3.0"?>
<plugin>
  <extension
    id="com.ibm.jdg2e.common.actions"
    name="JDE2E"
    point="org.eclipse.ui.actionSets">
  <actionSet
     label="JDG2E Bonus Action Set"
     description="JDG2E Bonus Pack"
     visible="true"
     id="com.ibm.jdg2e.miniwp.bonus_pack.actionSet">
          o
          o
          o
```

**Figure Ex8.6**  `manifest.mf` and `plugin.xml` Buddies

3. Add a public getter method on the bundle context. You'll use the bundle context to install plug-ins later.

```
public BundleContext getPluginContext() {
  return pluginContext;
}
```

## Section 3: Implement Your Configurator

In this section you will use the OSGi framework to install the Bonus pack plug-in into the system, request the system to resolve the dependencies, and then you are ready for business. Some user action will force the plug-in activation. You will be working from these key OSGi packages:

- `org.osgi.framework.Bundle`
- `org.osgi.framework.FrameworkEvent`
- `org.osgi.framework.FrameworkListener`
- `org.osgi.framework.ServiceReference`
- `org.osgi.service.packageadmin.PackageAdmin`

You might want to browse the Eclipse documentation to learn more about these packages before proceeding, or you can do it at your leisure sometime later—there is sufficient information here to get you through.

Because there may be more than one configurator in an OSGi context at any one time, it's a good practice to mark any bundles that you are installing with an eye-catcher. You'll notice when looking into the OSGi console later in this exercise that the Update Manager marks its installed bundles with an at-sign (@) update eye-catcher.

1. Open the class `com.ibm.jdg2e.mini.configurator`
   `.JDG2EConfigurationActivator` and add the following:

   ```
   public static final String JDG2E_PREFIX = "jdg2e@";
   ```

2. Add the `installBundle()` method. The purpose of this method is quite simple; it:
   – Installs the bundle.
   – Gets all the bundles that are not yet resolved.
   – Calls the framework services, specifically the package administrator service, to compute the dependency graph and resolve all unresolved plug-ins. The reason for resolving previously unresolved bundles is the chance that installing the new bundle into the system might resolve dependencies in the existing installed bundles in the system.

   From here on you will be using the bundle context heavily. Remember that your plug-in has the context object tucked away for safekeeping. You'll see the following code pattern used to access the bundle context repeatedly in the code: `ConfiguratorPlugin.get-Default().getPluginContext()`

   It looks impressive, but it's just calling a getter method in your plug-in class for the bundle context.

   Note that text marked in bold in the following code snippet are methods not yet implemented; you will get there in the next step. In addition, the reference to `List` is a reference to `java.util.List`.

```
public boolean installBundle(String dir) {
    boolean rc = true;
    List toRefresh = getUnresolvedBundles(); //Get all unresolved
    Bundle target;
    try {
      URL bundleURL = new URL("reference:file:" + dir);
      target = ConfiguratorPlugin.getDefault()
          .getPluginContext().installBundle(JDG2E_PREFIX + dir,
              bundleURL.openStream());
      toRefresh.add(target);
// any new bundle should be refreshed too
      refreshPackages((Bundle[]) toRefresh
      .toArray(new Bundle[toRefresh.size()]));
//refresh all bundles specified and their dependents
if (target.getState() != Bundle.RESOLVED) {
        return false;
      }
    } catch (Exception e) {
      e.printStackTrace();
      rc = false;
    }
    return rc;
}
```

3. Add the private method getUnresolvedBundles that gets all unresolved plug-ins in your context. You will need to import the ArrayList from the java.util package.

```
private List getUnresolvedBundles() {
  Bundle[] allBundles = ConfiguratorPlugin.getDefault()
      .getPluginContext().getBundles();
  List unresolved = new ArrayList();
  for (int i = 0; i < allBundles.length; i++)
    if (allBundles[i].getState() == Bundle.INSTALLED)
      unresolved.add(allBundles[i]);
  return unresolved;
}
```

4. Add the refreshPackages method, which simply makes the calls to the package administrator to resolve the dependencies, then waits and listens for the result.

```
private void refreshPackages(Bundle[] bundles) {
  if (bundles.length == 0)
    return;
  ServiceReference packageAdminRef = ConfiguratorPlugin
      .getDefault().getPluginContext().getServiceReference(
          PackageAdmin.class.getName());
  if (packageAdminRef == null) return;
```

```
        PackageAdmin packageAdmin =
           (PackageAdmin) ConfiguratorPlugin
           .getDefault().getPluginContext().getService(
           packageAdminRef);
      if (packageAdmin == null)
        return;
    }
    final boolean[] flag = new boolean[]{false};
    FrameworkListener listener = new FrameworkListener() {
       public void frameworkEvent(FrameworkEvent event) {
         if (event.getType() ==
                          FrameworkEvent.PACKAGES_REFRESHED)
           synchronized (flag) {
             flag[0] = true;
             flag.notifyAll();
           }
       }
    };
    ConfiguratorPlugin.getDefault().getPluginContext()
       .addFrameworkListener(listener);
    packageAdmin.refreshPackages(bundles);
    synchronized (flag) {
      while (!flag[0]) {
        try {
          flag.wait();
        } catch (InterruptedException e) {
        }
      }
    }
    ConfiguratorPlugin.getDefault().getPluginContext()
       .removeFrameworkListener(listener);
    ConfiguratorPlugin.getDefault().getPluginContext()
       .ungetService(packageAdminRef);
  }
```

## Section 4: Develop a Simple Plug-in Discovery Mechanism

An elaborate look-up and discovery mechanism—such as accessing some directory service, finding the role of a logged-on user in an organization, and provisioning functions to that user—is a very interesting and compelling configurator use case. However, that scenario is a bit more involved and deals with technologies well beyond the scope of this exercise. Let's cheat a little and not use such a sophisticated discovery mechanism. Let's imitate the plug-in discovery using a DirectoryDialog. The user will initiate the discovery using a menu or toolbar items. The action implementation is found in the class com.ibm.jdg2e.mini.configurator.actions.AddBundleAction.

1. Next you will set up a DirectoryDialog with the message to browse to the folder com.ibm.jdg2e.miniwp.bonus_pack_3.0.0. In your case, that target folder would be on the CD-ROM (see Figure Ex8.7).

**Figure Ex8.7** Dialog for Locating the Bonus Pack Plug-in

The more robust configurators, such as the Eclipse update configurator, simply uses the plug-ins in the plugins folder to resolve the dependencies. All plug-in dependencies in the Bonus pack were carefully considered in advance, and the Bonus pack dependencies are already conveniently included in the mini-configurator RCP application. This is probably not the case in a real-life scenario; you should plan on dealing with the situation that the plug-in to be installed does not resolve on the current mini-configuration. Make an allowance in the way you choose to package and/or discover dependent plug-ins.

2. Complete the action's run method by inserting the following code.

```
DirectoryDialog dlg = new DirectoryDialog(window.getShell());
dlg.setMessage
  ("Browse to com.ibm.jdg2e.miniwp.bonus_pack_3.0.0");
dlg.open();
String dir = dlg.open();
if (dir == null) {
  notFoundMessage();
  return;
}
dir.trim();
if (dir.length() == 0){
  notFoundMessage();
return;
}
JDG2EConfigurationActivator activator = new
    JDG2EConfigurationActivator();
if (activator.installBundle(dir)) {
  MessageDialog.openInformation(window.getShell(),
  "JDG2E Mini Configurator Plug-in", "Bonus pack bundle was
    added");
  action.setEnabled(false);
} else {
  notFoundMessage();
}
```

## Section 5: Installing the Bonus Pack Dynamically

In this section you will launch your RCP application using the launch configuration that you set up in Section 1 of this exercise. However, after launching the application and before pressing the Install button in the application, take some time to play with the OSGi console.

1. Run the configuration that you defined in Section 1 by selecting **Run > Run...**, select your configuration name, and press the dialog's **Run** button. Find the Console view in the development environment and look for the **osgi>** prompt (see Figure Ex8.8).

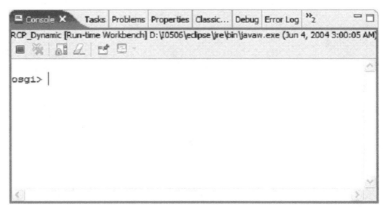

**Figure Ex8.8**    The OSGi Prompt

2. Enter **help** at the **osgi** command prompt. Observe what happens. Now enter the **ss** command to display the bundle status. Notice that the mini-configurator plug-in, `com.ibm.jdg2e.mini.configurator .exercise`, is active, but that there is no evidence of the Bonus pack plug-in

3. Press the Add Bonus Pack button on the toolbar (currently the one and only button on the toolbar). Use the file directory dialog to browse to the location on the CD-ROM (or wherever you installed the CD-ROM contents) containing the folder:

```
plug-in_development
\exercises\plugins
\com.ibm.jdg2e.miniwp.bonus_pack_3.0.0.
```

4. Select it and click on **OK** two times. Now you should see that the Eclipse framework detected the new extension addition and that continuing will affect changes to your current perspective (see Figure Ex8.9).

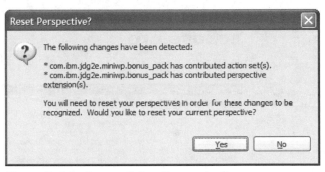

**Figure Ex8.9**   Prompt Before Perspective Reset

5. Select **YES** in the Reset Perspective dialog. Go back to the **osgi** prompt and enter the **ss** command again. You now should see that the Bonus pack state is **resolved** as shown earlier in Figure Ex8.4. This means that the plug-in has been successfully installed. You might be thinking that there would be a state change to **active**. However, remember the lazy loading rule. You just installed—but more importantly, resolved—the plug-in dependencies. Fortunately for you, the base RCP application already included all the plug-ins that your plug-in was dependent on.

6. Do not touch anything in the user interface yet, but notice that a view labeled JDG2E Sample View has been added behind the Calculator view, and that a new icon has been added to the toolbar with the tooltip "JDG2E: Hello, Dynamic Eclipse world" (see Figure Ex8.10).

7. Select the **JDG2E Sample View** tab in the view or press the **JDG2E > JDG2E Bonus Sample Action** menu item, and reenter the **ss** command at the **osgi** prompt. Now you should see that the state is **Active**, the plug-in is loaded, and the plug-in life cycle has begun. If you continue to examine the application you will see that the bonus pack also includes a second perspective and a preference page (as defined in the extensions in the bonus plug-in manifest file).

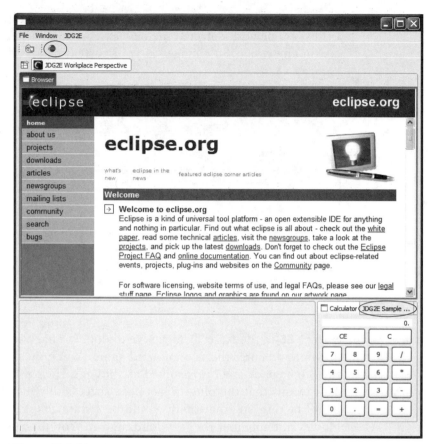

**Figure Ex8.10**    Application with Bonus Pack Installed

## Exercise Activity Review

In this exercise you constructed a very trivial Eclipse plug-in configurator. You
became familiar with a few rudimentary concepts and terms used around
OSGi framework. You set up the PDE launch configuration in a way that
allowed running, testing, and debugging your plug-in on top of the OSGi
framework. You learned how to use the OSGi console and watched the plug-
in state transitions. You witnessed that plug-ins lay dormant in a resolved
state until some user action causes the runtime to load and transition the plug-
in to an active state. You watched, through the OSGi console, the Eclipse
framework respond to the runtime state transitions, to resolved state with the
parsing the plugin.xml, and the subsequent announcement of new extensions
and pending changes to the default perspective. You experienced "dynamic
plug-ins" in action.

# EXERCISE 9

## *Deploying Your Product Using Features*

In Chapter 13, Defining Features and Products, the role of features in an Eclipse installation was discussed. This exercise takes you through the process of developing a feature and then deploying that feature for installation using three different approaches. This exercise is designed to help you understand how features are created and how you can use the PDE to assist in the packaging steps required for plug-ins and features. Once the feature has been packaged, you configure your feature for use as an extension to an existing Eclipse installation and then as the active product. Once all these steps are complete, an invocation of Eclipse will result in a product launch with your branding content.

The Update Manager provides the user with built-in support for installing and managing features. It falls on you, the plug-in developer, to define features that organize your plug-ins so your users can integrate your function as part of an Eclipse-based product. The feature definition also allows you to supply feature branding for the function you want to add.

Once you have packaged a feature, it can be added to an existing product as an extension or be included on an update site so that it can be installed using the Eclipse Update Manager.

Features and their associated plug-in content can be packaged with Eclipse to create a branded product. To do this, you define a product extension in one of your plug-ins; this product is then configured as the active product for the Eclipse launch point.

This exercise looks at the definition and use of features, with you playing one of four roles.

- In Section 1, you will play the role of a *feature developer*, a plug-in developer who wants to deliver your plug-ins by way of features. In this section, you'll learn how to define and package features and plug-ins so that they can be used to add function to Eclipse through an install process. If you performed Exercise 1 you will have already performed most of the processing required for Section 1 of this exercise.
- In Section 2, your role will be as an end user, or *feature consumer.* You will add a new install site to an existing Eclipse installation.
- In Section 3, you'll go through the exercise as a *product developer.* You will bundle one or more features and their associated plug-ins as part of a branded Eclipse-based product.
- In Section 4, as a *member of a product service team*, you will update the plug-ins and features and place them on an update site for distribution to consumers.
- In Section 5, you will encore as an end user. You will find and install new versions of features found on an update site.

The steps defined in each section are continuous. That is, they must be done in sequence; you cannot jump straight to a later portion of the exercise. Feel free to stop at any time when you have learned enough for your role. Not everybody on a team is involved in package features for runtime, branding, and service delivery.

The installation process discussed in Section 2 may actually be automated by a formal install routine. That is beyond the scope of this exercise, but the process is the same.

## Exercise Setup

The following setup tasks are required before you can begin this exercise.

1. Install a second copy of Eclipse.

   *This task is actually optional.* You may wish to work with an alternate Eclipse installation if you are not comfortable with manipulating your primary one. If you do not keep backup copies of the files that you will be modifying, you might find it difficult to return to your original configuration.

   If you do not use a second copy of Eclipse, you will need to reverse the final product configuration steps in Section 3 because these steps will change the configuration of your original Eclipse installation.

2. Import the `com.ibm.jdg2e.exercises` plug-in project to your workspace.

    Import this project from the `plug-in_development\exercises` directory on the CD-ROM using the **External plug-ins and fragments** import wizard. On the **Import Plug-ins and Fragments** page, of the plug-in import wizard, follow these steps.

    – Deselect **The target platform**.
    – In the **Plug-in Location** field, browse to the appropriate directory location on the CD-ROM.

        `\plug-in_development\exercises\`

    – For **Import As**, select **Projects with source folders**.

    On the **Selection** page of the plug-in import wizard, choose the `com.ibm.jdg2e.exercises` plug-in and use the **Add ->** button to move this project to the import column. Once done, select **Finish**.

3. Choose the plug-ins that will be packaged as part of your feature.

    You may choose the Hello World plug-ins from the first exercise or your own plug-ins that you wish to deliver as features for this install/update packaging exercise. You don't need to use all your plug-ins just now; try to limit the number so you can focus on the process instead of the processing required for each plug-in. These plug-ins must be in your workspace and must compile without errors.

## Section 1: Tasks of a Feature Developer

In Section 1, you will define a feature and package it with the references plug-ins so it is ready to be used as part of a runtime configuration.

### Step 1: Define a Feature to Support the Plug-in

We will begin by defining a feature. We will then step through the process of deploying the feature.

---

**NOTE**  Step 1 should not be necessary if you completed Sections 5 and 6 of the first plug-in development exercise (Exercise 6, Developing Your First Plug-in). If you already have a `com.ibm.jdg2e.exercises.feature` project in your workspace, you should skip to Step 2: Prepare the Feature for Packaging.

---

1. Create a feature project. Plug-ins are defined in a plug-in project; features need their own project.

   Use the **Ctrl+N** option to open the New wizard selection dialog. Choose **Feature Project** in the **Plug-in Development** category.

   Enter com.ibm.jdg2e.exercises.feature as the project name and select **Next**. Change the **Feature id** to be com.ibm.jdg2e.exercises, enter 3.0.0 as the **Feature Version**, and then enter any value you want for the **Feature Name** and **Feature Provider** fields, maybe even your name. We will use JDG2E Exercises and IBM.

   Select **Next** to get to the **Referenced Plug-ins and Fragments** page. Here you should see all the plug-ins you have defined so far in your workspace. Select at least one plug-in and then select **Finish**.

   You now have a feature that references your plug-in.

   If you do not have plug-in projects in your workspace, you will not be able to get to the **Referenced Plug-ins and Fragments** page. If that is the case, just select **Finish**. You can add plug-ins later using the editor.

2. Change to the **feature.xml** page and review the XML source for the feature definition.

   As you can see, the structure is somewhat similar to a plug-in definition. The <requires> syntax is about the same, but in a feature you can actually define both plug-ins and features. We will not customize this further. Branding and other feature content will be discussed later in the exercise.

---

**NOTE** It is very important that the version reference in a feature.xml file match the version defined in the target plug-in's plugin.xml file. If these do not match, the feature manifest editor will identify on the **Content** page that there is a mismatch; errors will also occur when you attempt to package the feature-install JAR. When you initially add the plug-in to the feature, all is fine. But later, when you update the plug-in but not the feature to match, things can get out of sync.

---

If you select a plug-in entry on the **Content** page of the feature manifest editor, you can use the **Synchronize Versions...** context menu option to open the Feature Versions dialog. The Feature Versions dialog allows you to synchronize plug-in versions as specified in the feature manifest file (feature.xml) with the plug-in versions defined in the respective plug-in manifest files (plugin.xml).

## Step 2: Prepare the Feature for Packaging

1. Enter some additional content to customize the feature definition.

   If you review the feature manifest editor, you will see areas on the **Information** page where you can add description, copyright, and license content. Choose the **License Agreement** tab and enter some text for the license, then save the file.

---

**NOTE**   If you do not have any text in your license, the install button will not be visible when the feature is processed by the Update Manager. Some form of license text is required.

---

When an HTML version of the license is identified in the `feature.xml` file, it can be opened from the About [product] Features dialog (**Help > About [product] > Feature Details > More Info**).

2. The PDE automatically creates a `build.properties` file for the feature. You can see this content in the feature manifest editor by switching to the **build.properties** page. The `bin.includes` entry identifies the files that should be included in the runtime distribution for the feature. The PDE-created `build.properties` file contains this entry:

   ```
   bin.includes = feature.xml
   ```

   If your feature includes a `feature.properties` file, an HTML version of the license, or a banner graphic, these must also be included in the `bin.includes` entry. This process is not automatic by design; you have to decide what portion of your project should actually be included in the runtime distribution.

   Now it's time to test the feature packaging process.

3. Select the `feature.xml` file in the Package Explorer view and choose the context menu option **PDE Tools > Create Ant Build File**.

   The **Create Ant Build File** action will generate the `build.xml` file based on the current `feature.xml` and `build.properties` definition. The processing will also create `build.xml` files required for each plug-in referenced by the feature. You must regenerate the `build.xml` file after each modification of the `feature.xml` or associated `build.properties` files. The same holds true for the referenced plug-ins' `build.xml` files.

4. Select the `build.xml` file and choose the **Run > Ant Build...** context menu option.

The **Run > Ant Build...** option opens the Ant launcher (the **Run > Ant Build** option starts the last Ant invocation without the dialog).

Only the `build.update.jar` target is selected in the **Targets** page by default. You may have to scroll to see this, or select **Hide internal targets** to see only the targets designed to be run by you. If required, adjust the selections until only the `build.update.jar` target is selected.

You can deselect/select the available targets in the Ant launcher dialog to choose which targets will be processed and to control the order. The order in which they will be invoked is displayed as part of the dialog. The targets chosen will first run their dependent targets. You may want to experiment with alternative target selection later. For the duration of this exercise, to ensure you get the expected results, stick with the target selection guidance provided.

5. Select **Run** to invoke Ant for only the `build.update.jar` target. The build starts, and output appears in the Console Log view. Building target `build.update.jar` causes the following to happen.

   – The `build.xml` for each plug-in referenced in the feature is processed to do the following.

   • Generate the runtime JAR(s) for the plug-in.
   • Generate the plug-in-install JAR.

   – The feature-install JAR for the feature project is created.

When the build completes, you should see a BUILD SUCCESSFUL message in the Console Log view. The output in the Console Log view is enabled for navigation. Select one of the task links to see the source in the Ant script file. If there are errors, you can select the error link to navigate to the failing task.

Be aware that you may need to refresh the plug-in and feature projects before you can see the JAR files that were created. Do this by selecting the project(s) and then **Refresh** from the context menu. You can also select the Ant refresh target before invoking the build to automate this process.

The following JAR files would be created for the `com.ibm.jdg2e.helloworld` plug-in project, assuming it was included in your feature:

– `helloworld.jar`
– `com.ibm.jdg2e.helloworld_1.0.0.jar`

The first file, `helloworld.jar`, is the plug-in runtime JAR file. If the feature is composed of more than one plug-in, runtime JAR files are created for each plug-in included in the feature. The second JAR file is the plug-in-install JAR file; it incorporates the version id in the file name.

The file `com.ibm.jdg2e.exercises_3.0.0.jar` is created in the `com.ibm.jdg2e.exercises.feature` project. This is the feature-install JAR.

The plug-in-install JAR and feature-install JAR file names are based on the respective plug-in or feature id, not the project name. During an install, the Update Manager will read the `feature.xml` file from the feature-install JAR and, using the plug-in id references, find the plug-in-install JAR files that should be processed when an installation is requested.

You may choose other target options in the Ant launcher dialog, but be sure you understand the overall processing flow before you add to the list of targets to be processed. The different target options in the `build.xml` file sometimes include `depends="…"` definitions along with directed activity. The `depends="…"` definitions are targets that are performed before the directed activity. The tasks or other targets in the directed activity are then invoked. You do not need to select targets that will be run anyway; you may want to review the `build.xml` source to become familiar with the processing for each target.

The `build.update.jar` target triggers processing that includes the following targets:

- `init` processing—a dependency for the `build.update.jar` target.
- `all.children`—a directed target that runs the `build.xml` script for each plug-in in the feature.
- `gather.bin.parts`—a directed target customized from the `bin.includes` entry in the `build.properties` file. This target gathers all the files required in the feature-install JAR into a temporary directory.

This is followed by `jar` processing to create the feature-install JAR file from the contents of the temporary directory. This processing flow is visible (key sections are in bold) when you review the Ant `build.update.jar` target definition from the feature `build.xml` file.

```
<target name="build.update.jar" depends="init"
  description="Build the feature jar of: com.ibm.jdg2e.exercises
    for an update site.">
  <antcall target="all.children">
    <param name="target" value="build.update.jar"/>
  </antcall>
  <property name="feature.base" value="${feature.temp.folder}"/>
```

```
<delete dir="${feature.temp.folder}"/>
<mkdir dir="${feature.temp.folder}"/>
<antcall target="gather.bin.parts" inheritAll="false">
  <param name="arch" value="*"/>
  <param name="ws" value="*"/>
  <param name="nl" value="*"/>
  <param name="os" value="*"/>
  <param name="feature.base" value="${feature.temp.folder}"/>
</antcall>
<jar
  jarfile=
    "${feature.destination}/
      com.ibm.jdg2e.exercises_3.0.0.jar"
  basedir=
    "${feature.temp.folder}/
      features/com.ibm.jdg2e.exercises_3.0.0"/>
<delete dir="${feature.temp.folder}"/>
</target>
```

6. In the Package Explorer view, delete the JAR files you just created. This will include the feature and each plug-in referenced by the feature.

7. Select the build.xml file and open the Ant launcher dialog again using the **Run > Ant Build...** context menu. Leave build.update.jar selected and select the refresh target as the second target to be processed. You may have to resize the dialog to see all of the user interface controls.

   Select **Run** to start the Ant processing. This time the build will proceed and the plug-in and feature projects will be refreshed so that you can see the JAR files created during the Ant build.

   Remember, if you change the feature definition or build.properties file, you need to regenerate the build.xml file.

## Step 3: Add Product and Feature Branding to the Feature

Features support the definition of branding information, in the form of graphics, descriptive text, and license content. This allows the feature to uniquely identify itself in the Workbench through entries in the About [product] Features dialog.

By default, almost all of the branding content is kept in a plug-in that has the same id as the feature; the feature only provides the license information that can be seen in the Product Configuration dialog. The feature license can also be seen when you select the **More Info** button (**Help > About [product] > Feature Details > More Info**). In this step, you will add a plug-in that will supply branding content for the feature you just defined.

1. Create a plug-in to provide branding content for your feature.

   A plug-in with the required branding content has been provided for your use. If required, import the plug-in `com.ibm.jdg2e.exercises` into your workspace from the exercise template location.

   Because the plug-in and feature ids are the same, this plug-in will automatically be used to supply branding content for the feature. The feature attribute `plugin="some.other.plugin.id"` can be defined as part of the `<feature>` element in the `feature.xml` file if you want to use a plug-in that has a different id to supply branding content. This can also be defined using the **Overview** page of the feature manifest editor to identify `some.other.plugin.id` as the id for the branding plug-in.

2. Add the `com.ibm.jdg2e.exercises` plug-in to the `feature.xml` definition.

   Use the feature plug-ins and fragments **Add...** button on the **Content** page of the `feature.xml` manifest editor to select the `com.ibm.jdg2e.exercises` plug-in. Save the `feature.xml` file when done by pressing **Ctrl+S**.

3. Recreate the `build.xml` file for the feature by selecting the `feature.xml` file and using the **PDE Tools > Create Ant Build File** pop-up menu option.

## Step 4: Package the Feature for Use at Runtime

Multiple techniques are available when you want to prepare a runtime distribution. You can create either of the following using the feature build process.

- Distribution ZIP file with a directory structure for the feature, its plug-ins, and their files.
- Feature-install JAR for the feature and a plug-in-install JAR for each plug-in included in the feature. These JARs are added to an update site and can then be used to install function by using the Update Manager.

In this exercise step, you will create both distribution formats. This could be done using export utilities, but we will use the Ant processing provided by the `build.xml` files generated by the PDE.

1. Package the feature by selecting its `build.xml` file and choosing the **Run > Ant Build...** context menu option to open the Ant launcher dialog.

2. In the Ant launcher dialog, make sure you have selected the three targets with the **Target execution order** shown in Figure Ex9.1.

   To get the target invocation order correct you can deselect/select the targets or use the **Order...** button. Select **Hide internal targets** to filter out targets.

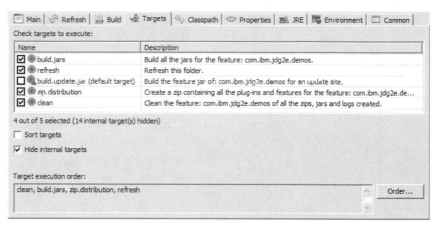

**Figure Ex9.1**    Target Selection for Feature Packaging

3. Select **Run** in the dialog to generate runtime JAR files, install JAR files for the plug-ins contained in the feature, and then a feature-install JAR file for the feature itself. A distribution ZIP file of the feature and plug-ins is also created. The content of both the packaged JAR files and the ZIP file is determined by the bin.includes setting in the appropriate build.properties file for each plug-in and feature project.

   The distribution ZIP file can be used to support installing the feature by either unzipping the contents into an existing Eclipse installation or unzipping the contents to a new location and adding this content to an existing Eclipse Platform installation as an extension. You will use the packaged JAR files to implement an update site in Section 4. The distribution ZIP file will be used in Section 2. You should now have a set of projects with a runtime JAR and plug-in-install JAR for each plug-in and a feature-install JAR and distribution ZIP file for the feature project.

## Section 2: Tasks of an Eclipse User

In Section 2, you will play the role of an Eclipse user and add function to the current Eclipse installation. There are two options for how a new feature can be installed as part of an Eclipse installation.

- Install a new feature as an extension to an existing Eclipse installation.
- Add a feature to an existing Eclipse configuration by using the Update Manager.

The result of these two techniques is the same; the feature is added to the current configuration. In this section of the exercise we will create a new install site and add this site to the existing Eclipse configuration.

## Step 5: Installing Features in an Install Site as Part of an Existing Installation

Using the ZIP file created in Section 1, you can integrate its contents with an existing Eclipse installation. Unzipping the feature and plug-in content to a specific directory tree emulates how a tool provider would use a product installation routine to allow others, like you, to install and use the tool (or packaged feature in this case).

Tool providers may decide to use installer technology, such as InstallShield, to extend an existing Eclipse Platform installation. The installer would add features and plug-ins to the file system and then modify the Eclipse configuration to identify the new install site. The new site would be processed during the next startup of Eclipse, which would add the features and plug-ins to the existing Eclipse installation.

1. Remove the feature and plug-in you may have installed as part of the first plug-in exercise.

   In Exercise 6, we asked you to create a feature to support your plug-in and then export this feature/plug-in set. The result was then copied into your current \features and \plugins directories. This code must be removed before we can continue with this portion of the current exercise.

   So, if you completed Sections 5 and 6 of the first plug-in development exercise (Exercise 6, Developing Your First Plug-in), you need to shut down Eclipse and then delete the following directories from your Eclipse installation:

   ```
   \features\com.ibm.jdg2e.exercises
   \plugins\com.ibm.jdg2e.helloworld
   ```

   Once done, restart Eclipse; you should no longer see your **Hello-world** menu action as part of the Resource perspective.

2. Unzip the feature and plug-ins distribution file created earlier to a new location on your file system and add the required .eclipseextension marker file.

   First create a directory tree (e.g., d:\toolSite\eclipse) to use as a target, and then unzip the com.ibm.jdg2e.exercises_3.0.0.bin .dist.zip file into this directory. Extensions added to Eclipse must be

PART VI

found in an `eclipse\features` and `eclipse\plugins` directory structure. You need to create this structure because the ZIP file contains only `\features` and `\plugins` directory trees.

Next, copy the `.eclipseextension` marker file found in the `com.ibm.jdg2e.exercises` plug-in project to the `eclipse` directory for your extension (`d:\toolSite\eclipse`). Eclipse checks for this file before allowing you to add the directory contents as an extension.

3. Add the extension to the Eclipse configuration.

This can be done in one of two ways.

– Use the Eclipse Product Configuration dialog to find and add the extension (Choice A).
– Invoke Eclipse with a special application and command options that directly manipulate the active configuration (Choice B).

Choose *one* of these approaches and follow the appropriate steps.

**Choice A:** Use the Product Configuration dialog (*recommended approach*).

- Open the dialog using the **Help > Software Updates > Manage Configuration...** menu option.
- Select the **Add an Extension Location** hyperlink on the right side of the dialog.
- Locate and select the directory where you unzipped the extension (`d:\toolSite\eclipse`), and then select **OK**.
- You will be prompted to choose between shutting down and restarting Eclipse or attempting to add the extension dynamically. Choose the dynamic option by selecting **Apply Changes**. If prompted, say **Yes** to the perspective reset request.
- Review the configuration in the dialog; you should now see that the extension is referenced.
- Close the Product Configuration dialog.

**Choice B:** Use the command option to add the extension.

- Shut down Eclipse.
- Open up a command prompt and change to the directory for the instance of Eclipse you want to modify. Once there, enter this command to add the extension:

```
java -cp startup.jar org.eclipse.core.launcher.Main
   -application  org.eclipse.update.core.standaloneUpdate
    -data tempWorkspace
      -command addSite -from D:\toolSite\eclipse
```

- Restart Eclipse.

4. Validate that the extension is now available.

If you included the plug-in from Exercise 6 in the feature, your **Helloworld** menu action should be in the menu bar (you may need to reset the perspective if not done for you). Search for any additional function you added to prove it has been configured and works.

The new extension site and feature should also be visible in the Product Configuration dialog. The feature will also be visible in the About [product] dialog that can be opened using the **Help > About [product]** menu option. A small image for the feature should be visible. This came from the feature-branding content provided in the branding plug-in. You can find additional feature details if you select the **Features Details** option and select the feature you added.

This content was defined as part of the about.ini and about .properties files included in the branding plug-in. Review this content in the plug-in project. The about.mappings file is used to implement substitution of values (see the {0} string in the about.properties file, which is replaced by the matching mapping value at runtime).

## Section 3: Tasks of a Product Developer

In Section 3 you will create your own branded version of the Eclipse Platform. In the previous step, you added the new feature as part of an extension to Eclipse. Hidden inside the plug-in was product branding as well. We are now going to alter the configuration so that Eclipse starts using this branding and you can create a fully branded Eclipse-based product.

### Step 6: Implement a Branded Product

A product definition was provided in the com.ibm.jdg2e.exercises plug-in. You will identify this product as the active product, which will allow it to then contribute product-branding information and graphics to the Eclipse startup and user interface.

1. Shut down Eclipse.
2. Modify the config.ini file in the eclipse\configuration directory.

The config.ini file controls the Eclipse configuration by identifying things like the active product and splash image location. These values are processed by Eclipse during startup.

PART VI

Edit the config.ini file and change the following settings to these new values (you can place a #, which denotes a comment, before the current definitions to keep them around).

```
osgi.splashPath =
  file:/D:/toolSite/eclipse/plugins/com.ibm.jdg2e.exercises
```

```
eclipse.product = com.ibm.jdg2e.exercises.demo
```

The splashPath entry is a pointer to where a splash.bmp file can be found. The eclipse.product entry identifies your product-branding content.

3. Review the product-branding content (shown here) provided for you in the com.ibm.jdg2e.exercises plug-in.

```
<extension id="demo" point="org.eclipse.core.runtime.products">
  <product name="%productName"
    application="org.eclipse.ui.ide.workbench"
    description="%productBlurb">
  <property name="windowImages"
      value="icons/jdg2eProd.gif,icons/jdg2eFeat.gif"/>
  <property name="aboutImage" value="icons/jdg2eAbout.gif"/>
  <property name="aboutText" value="%productBlurb"/>
  <property name="appName" value="JDG2E"/>
  <property name="preferenceCustomization"
      value="plugin_customization.ini"/>
  </product>
</extension>
```

The extension id maps to the eclipse.product entry in the config.ini control file; plugidID.extensionID is the value used.

The property names are described in IProductConstants, the product definition interface. Go ahead and review that definition. The values shown here identify what content to use when applying product branding. The preferenceCustomization entry identifies the product file used to override plug-in-defined defaults.

## Step 7: Launch and Review a Branded Product Installation

This step will allow you to see how the product definition has added branding content to the Eclipse user interface.

1. Start Eclipse.

   You should see a new splash screen during startup processing.
2. Review the product-branding information by selecting **Help > About [product]** or **Help > Software Updates > Manage Configuration….**

There are many indicators of the active product in use by Eclipse. The identified product extension controls the Eclipse product branding. Content from the product definition in the plug-in is used to modify the system icon, default Welcome page, About [product] dialog, configuration shown in the Product Configuration dialog, and window title.

Many of these changes are visible in the Workbench image shown in Figure Ex9.2.

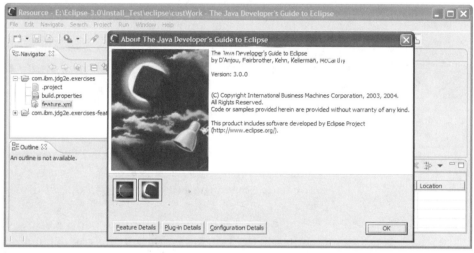

**Figure Ex9.2**    Workbench with Customized Product Branding

## Section 4: Tasks for a Product Service Team—Implementing an Update Site

In Section 4, you'll adjust the feature to include additional plug-in content, then package the new version of the feature as part of an update site. We want to simulate applying service to a feature that has already been installed.

### Step 8: Add Plug-ins to the Existing Feature Definition

To service the installed feature, you need to first change its definition. This includes content but most importantly a change in the feature version. The Update Manager will install only newer versions of the installed features.

1. Add a plug-in to the feature definition.

    You will need at least one more plug-in to make this work, or you can change an existing plug-in in a way that is detectable at runtime. If you do not add another plug-in, change the one you have (such as the text displayed by an action), and then change the plug-in version id.

Open the feature definition (feature.xml) in the feature manifest editor and adjust the content, on the **Content** page, to add at least one plug-in that was not referenced before, or update the existing reference to the modified plug-in's new version id.

2. On the **Overview** page, modify the feature's version id. It should currently be 3.0.0; change it to be 3.0.1. Any change is fine as long as you increase only the value in the last position.

3. Save the feature definition.

### Step 9: Use an Update Site Project to Define and Build the Update Site Content

The PDE supports the creation of an update site that can also be used to build the referenced features.

1. Use the New Project wizard to create a PDE update site project. Name the project com.ibm.jdg2e.delivery and select **Finish**. The site manifest editor on the site.xml file will open for the new update site definition.

2. Use the **Add...** button in the editor to add a feature. Choose com.ibm.jdg2e.exercises, the feature you defined earlier.

3. Use the **New Category...** button to add a category; it will be used to organize the features that you will publish. Enter jdg2e.service as the **name**, JDG2E Service as the **label**, and then select **OK**.

4. From inside the editor, drag the feature you added and drop it on the publishing category you just created. Once done, save the site definition by pressing **Ctrl+S**.

5. Build the update site by selecting the **Build All** button in the site.xml editor. Distribution JARs for the feature and referenced plug-ins will be added to the site project. You can see this in the Navigator view.

6. Export the update site content by selecting the project and then **File > Export**. Select the **File system** export option and then **Next**. Expand the com.ibm.jdg2e.delivery entry in the wizard. All you need to export is the site.xml file and the \features and \plugins directories. Use the **Browse** button to find an export target. Create a directory named UpdateSite somewhere on your file system. Select that directory, choose the **Create only selected directories** option, and then select **Finish**.

7. Review the content on the file system. If you are able, open one or more of the JAR files using a ZIP file utility. You will see that they contain the files you would need in a runtime feature or plug-in.

## Section 5: Tasks of an Eclipse User—Redux

In Section 5, you will use the update site created in Section 4 to service the installed feature.

### Step 10: Add a Feature to an Existing Product Configuration from an Update Site

At this point you should have a working Eclipse instance with your branding; this is supported by the feature and plug-ins that were previously configured as part of the Eclipse Platform. You should also have an update site with a newer version of the feature and associated plug-ins. Now it's time to service the previously installed feature. If necessary, start the installed instance of Eclipse that includes your branded feature and plug-in content; this might be the one you are using, and that is fine.

1. Find the feature updates available on the update site.

   Use the **Help > Software Update > Find and Install...** menu option to open the Install/Update dialog.

   Choose the **Search for new features to install** option, and select **Next**.

   If the installed feature was defined appropriately, you could use the **Search for update of the currently installed features** option to let Eclipse look at the update sites defined in the feature for new code. However, the earlier steps for this exercise did not include an update site URL, so you need to do this manually.

2. Select the **New Local Site...** button, navigate to the UpdateSite directory you created earlier, and select **OK**. Then select your update site node in the **Sites to include in search:** list.

   Select **Next** to move on to the list of available features.

3. You should see version 3.0.1 of your feature listed; choose that feature, select **Next**, and then accept the license. If you can't get this far, it might be because you forgot to enter the license text when the feature was initially created in Section 1. (Don't ask why it must be there; it's a lawyer thing.)

PART VI

4. Select **Next** to leave the license accept page. You should now see that the feature is listed along with the site where the feature will be written. It should already have chosen the site you created in Section 2. In other words, it knows to update this site. Select **Finish** to start the actual install.

5. The install process will warn you that you are using an unsigned JAR. Just select **Install**. The code will be obtained from the update site and written to the install site.

   Note that the JARs created during the site build could be processed further using Java JAR signing utilities if you want to have either a self-signed or formally authenticated JAR. We are not doing that now, so you'll see a dialog asking whether you want to install an unsigned feature. Select **Install** to proceed.

6. When prompted, agree to the restart of the Workbench. Once it restarts, validate that the new version of your feature is available. If you can't remember what you added, just open the Product Configuration dialog (**Help > Software Update > Manage Configuration...**) and check that you have a new version of the feature loaded.

**NOTE** This approach had you, the user, finding the feature updates manually. The installed feature could have been defined with an update site URL that identified where feature updates would be found when available. This lets the Update Manager search for updates as opposed to making the user find them. This process of identifying a URL and placing the updates on an HTTP server is the classic way of delivering service when using Eclipse and the Update Manager. The update site created here would work when placed on an HTTP server; all that would be required is the appropriate update site URL entry in the 3.0.0 version of the `feature.xml` file.

## Exercise Activity Review

Here's what you did in this exercise:

- Learned how to use the PDE and Ant processing to automate the creation of runtime JAR files for a plug-in
- Identified the content required in a `build.properties` file to instruct the Ant processing on what should be included in a runtime JAR, plug-in-install JAR, and feature-install JAR

- Defined features to organize plug-ins and provide feature and product branding
- Packaged the feature and plug-ins to create runtime JAR files and plug-in-install JAR files for each plug-in and a feature-install JAR for the feature project
- Learned how to install a feature using a variety of techniques (extension using a link file, installation using the Update Manager to pull code into the Workbench configuration)
- Configured a branded product by adding an alternative product definition to an Eclipse Platform installation
- Applied service to an installed feature

# Index

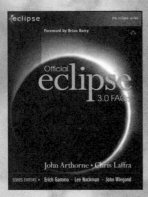

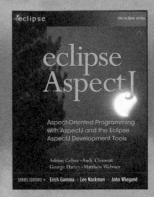

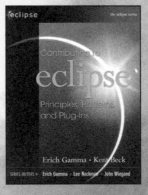

# Register
## Your Book

at www.awprofessional.com/register

You may be eligible to receive:

- Advance notice of forthcoming editions of the book
- Related book recommendations
- Chapter excerpts and supplements of forthcoming titles
- Information about special contests and promotions throughout the year
- Notices and reminders about author appearances, tradeshows, and online chats with special guests

## Contact us

If you are interested in writing a book or reviewing manuscripts prior to publication, please write to us at:

Editorial Department
Addison-Wesley Professional
75 Arlington Street, Suite 300
Boston, MA 02116 USA
Email: AWPro@aw.com

Visit us on the Web: http://www.awprofessional.com

## CD-ROM Warranty

Addison-Wesley warrants the enclosed CD-ROM to be free of defects in materials and faulty workmanship under normal use for a period of ninety days after purchase (when purchased new). If a defect is discovered in the CD-ROM during this warranty period, a replacement CD-ROM can be obtained at no charge by sending the defective CD-ROM, postage prepaid, with proof of purchase to:

Disc Exchange
Addison-Wesley Professional
Pearson Technology Group
75 Arlington Street, Suite 300
Boston, MA 02116
Email: AWPro@aw.com

Addison-Wesley makes no warranty or representation, either expressed or implied, with respect to this software, its quality, performance, merchantability, or fitness for a particular purpose. In no event will Addison-Wesley, its distributors, or dealers be liable for direct, indirect, special, incidental, or consequential damages arising out of the use or inability to use the software. The exclusion of implied warranties is not permitted in some states. Therefore, the above exclusion may not apply to you. This warranty provides you with specific legal rights. There may be other rights that you may have that vary from state to state. The contents of this CD-ROM are intended for personal use only.

More information and updates are available at: www.awprofessional.com/

# Common Public License—v 1.0

THE ACCOMPANYING PROGRAM IS PROVIDED UNDER THE TERMS OF THIS COMMON PUB-
LIC LICENSE ("AGREEMENT"). ANY USE, REPRODUCTION OR DISTRIBUTION OF THE PRO-
GRAM CONSTITUTES RECIPIENT'S ACCEPTANCE OF THIS AGREEMENT.

## 1. DEFINITIONS
"Contribution" means:
a) in the case of the initial Contributor, the initial code and documentation distributed under this Agreement, and
b) in the case of each subsequent Contributor:
i) changes to the Program, and
ii) additions to the Program;
   where such changes and/or additions to the Program originate from and are distributed by that particular
   Contributor. A Contribution 'originates' from a Contributor if it was added to the Program by such Contributor itself or anyone acting on such Contributor's behalf. Contributions do not include additions to
   the Program which: (i) are separate modules of software distributed in conjunction with the Program
   under their own license agreement, and (ii) are not derivative works of the Program.
   "Contributor" means any person or entity that distributes the Program.
   "Licensed Patents " mean patent claims licensable by a Contributor which are necessarily infringed by
   the use or sale of its Contribution alone or when combined with the Program.
   "Program" means the Contributions distributed in accordance with this Agreement.
   "Recipient" means anyone who receives the Program under this Agreement, including all
   Contributors.

## 2. GRANT OF RIGHTS
a) Subject to the terms of this Agreement, each Contributor hereby grants Recipient a non-exclusive, worldwide, royalty-free copyright license to reproduce, prepare derivative works of, publicly display, publicly
   perform, distribute and sublicense the Contribution of such Contributor, if any, and such derivative
   works, in source code and object code form.
b) Subject to the terms of this Agreement, each Contributor hereby grants Recipient a non-exclusive, worldwide, royalty-free patent license under Licensed Patents to make, use, sell, offer to sell, import and otherwise transfer the Contribution of such Contributor, if any, in source code and object code form. This
   patent license shall apply to the combination of the Contribution and the Program if, at the time the Contribution is added by the Contributor, such addition of the Contribution causes such combination to be
   covered by the Licensed Patents. The patent license shall not apply to any other combinations which
   include the Contribution. No hardware per se is licensed hereunder.
c) Recipient understands that although each Contributor grants the licenses to its Contributions set forth
   herein, no assurances are provided by any Contributor that the Program does not infringe the patent or
   other intellectual property rights of any other entity. Each Contributor disclaims any liability to Recipient
   for claims brought by any other entity based on infringement of intellectual property rights or otherwise.
   As a condition to exercising the rights and licenses granted hereunder, each Recipient hereby assumes sole
   responsibility to secure any other intellectual property rights needed, if any. For example, if a third party
   patent license is required to allow Recipient to distribute the Program, it is Recipient's responsibility to
   acquire that license before distributing the Program.
d) Each Contributor represents that to its knowledge it has sufficient copyright rights in its Contribution, if
   any, to grant the copyright license set forth in this Agreement.

## 3. REQUIREMENTS

A Contributor may choose to distribute the Program in object code form under its own license agreement, provided that:

a) it complies with the terms and conditions of this Agreement; and

b) its license agreement:

   i) effectively disclaims on behalf of all Contributors all warranties and conditions, express and implied, including warranties or conditions of title and non-infringement, and implied warranties or conditions of merchantability and fitness for a particular purpose;

   ii) effectively excludes on behalf of all Contributors all liability for damages, including direct, indirect, special, incidental and consequential damages, such as lost profits;

   iii) states that any provisions which differ from this Agreement are offered by that Contributor alone and not by any other party; and

   iv) states that source code for the Program is available from such Contributor, and informs licensees how to obtain it in a reasonable manner on or through a medium customarily used for software exchange.

When the Program is made available in source code form:

a) it must be made available under this Agreement; and

b) a copy of this Agreement must be included with each copy of the Program.

Contributors may not remove or alter any copyright notices contained within the Program.

Each Contributor must identify itself as the originator of its Contribution, if any, in a manner that reasonably allows subsequent Recipients to identify the originator of the Contribution.

## 4. COMMERCIAL DISTRIBUTION

Commercial distributors of software may accept certain responsibilities with respect to end users, business partners and the like. While this license is intended to facilitate the commercial use of the Program, the Contributor who includes the Program in a commercial product offering should do so in a manner which does not create potential liability for other Contributors. Therefore, if a Contributor includes the Program in a commercial product offering, such Contributor ("Commercial Contributor") hereby agrees to defend and indemnify every other Contributor ("Indemnified Contributor") against any losses, damages and costs (collectively "Losses") arising from claims, lawsuits and other legal actions brought by a third party against the Indemnified Contributor to the extent caused by the acts or omissions of such Commercial Contributor in connection with its distribution of the Program in a commercial product offering. The obligations in this section do not apply to any claims or Losses relating to any actual or alleged intellectual property infringement. In order to qualify, an Indemnified Contributor must: a) promptly notify the Commercial Contributor in writing of such claim, and b) allow the Commercial Contributor to control, and cooperate with the Commercial Contributor in, the defense and any related settlement negotiations. The Indemnified Contributor may participate in any such claim at its own expense.

For example, a Contributor might include the Program in a commercial product offering, Product X. That Contributor is then a Commercial Contributor. If that Commercial Contributor then makes performance claims, or offers warranties related to Product X, those performance claims and warranties are such Commercial Contributor's responsibility alone. Under this section, the Commercial Contributor would have to defend claims against the other Contributors related to those performance claims and warranties, and if a court requires any other Contributor to pay any damages as a result, the Commercial Contributor must pay those damages.

## 5. NO WARRANTY

EXCEPT AS EXPRESSLY SET FORTH IN THIS AGREEMENT, THE PROGRAM IS PROVIDED ON AN "AS IS" BASIS, WITHOUT WARRANTIES OR CONDITIONS OF ANY KIND, EITHER EXPRESS OR IMPLIED INCLUDING, WITHOUT LIMITATION, ANY WARRANTIES OR CONDITIONS OF TITLE,

NON-INFRINGEMENT, MERCHANTABILITY OR FITNESS FOR A PARTICULAR PURPOSE. Each Recipient is solely responsible for determining the appropriateness of using and distributing the Program and assumes all risks associated with its exercise of rights under this Agreement, including but not limited to the risks and costs of program errors, compliance with applicable laws, damage to or loss of data, programs or equipment, and unavailability or interruption of operations.

## 6. DISCLAIMER OF LIABILITY

EXCEPT AS EXPRESSLY SET FORTH IN THIS AGREEMENT, NEITHER RECIPIENT NOR ANY CONTRIBUTORS SHALL HAVE ANY LIABILITY FOR ANY DIRECT, INDIRECT, INCIDENTAL, SPECIAL, EXEMPLARY, OR CONSEQUENTIAL DAMAGES (INCLUDING WITHOUT LIMITATION LOST PROFITS), HOWEVER CAUSED AND ON ANY THEORY OF LIABILITY, WHETHER IN CONTRACT, STRICT LIABILITY, OR TORT (INCLUDING NEGLIGENCE OR OTHERWISE) ARISING IN ANY WAY OUT OF THE USE OR DISTRIBUTION OF THE PROGRAM OR THE EXERCISE OF ANY RIGHTS GRANTED HEREUNDER, EVEN IF ADVISED OF THE POSSIBILITY OF SUCH DAMAGES.

## 7. GENERAL

If any provision of this Agreement is invalid or unenforceable under applicable law, it shall not affect the validity or enforceability of the remainder of the terms of this Agreement, and without further action by the parties hereto, such provision shall be reformed to the minimum extent necessary to make such provision valid and enforceable.

If Recipient institutes patent litigation against a Contributor with respect to a patent applicable to software (including a cross-claim or counterclaim in a lawsuit), then any patent licenses granted by that Contributor to such Recipient under this Agreement shall terminate as of the date such litigation is filed. In addition, if Recipient institutes patent litigation against any entity (including a cross-claim or counterclaim in a lawsuit) alleging that the Program itself (excluding combinations of the Program with other software or hardware) infringes such Recipient's patent(s), then such Recipient's rights granted under Section 2(b) shall terminate as of the date such litigation is filed.

All Recipient's rights under this Agreement shall terminate if it fails to comply with any of the material terms or conditions of this Agreement and does not cure such failure in a reasonable period of time after becoming aware of such noncompliance. If all Recipient's rights under this Agreement terminate, Recipient agrees to cease use and distribution of the Program as soon as reasonably practicable. However, Recipient's obligations under this Agreement and any licenses granted by Recipient relating to the Program shall continue and survive.

Everyone is permitted to copy and distribute copies of this Agreement, but in order to avoid inconsistency the Agreement is copyrighted and may only be modified in the following manner. The Agreement Steward reserves the right to publish new versions (including revisions) of this Agreement from time to time. No one other than the Agreement Steward has the right to modify this Agreement. IBM is the initial Agreement Steward. IBM may assign the responsibility to serve as the Agreement Steward to a suitable separate entity. Each new version of the Agreement will be given a distinguishing version number. The Program (including Contributions) may always be distributed subject to the version of the Agreement under which it was received. In addition, after a new version of the Agreement is published, Contributor may elect to distribute the Program (including its Contributions) under the new version. Except as expressly stated in Sections 2(a) and 2(b) above, Recipient receives no rights or licenses to the intellectual property of any Contributor under this Agreement, whether expressly, by implication, estoppel or otherwise. All rights in the Program not expressly granted under this Agreement are reserved.

This Agreement is governed by the laws of the State of New York and the intellectual property laws of the United States of America. No party to this Agreement will bring a legal action under this Agreement more than one year after the cause of action arose. Each party waives its rights to a jury trial in any resulting litigation.